JIMMY SWAGGART
BIBLE
COMMENTARY

Hebrews

JIMMY SWAGGART BIBLE COMMENTARY

- Genesis (639 pages) (11-201)
- Exodus (639 pages) (11-202)
- Leviticus (435 pages) (11-203)
- Numbers
  Deuteronomy (493 pages) (11-204)
- Joshua
  Judges
  Ruth (329 pages) (11-205)
- I Samuel
  II Samuel (528 pages) (11-206)
- I Kings
  II Kings (560 pages) (11-207)
- I Chronicles
  II Chronicles (528 pages) (11-226)
- Ezra
  Nehemiah
  Esther (288 pages) (11-208)
- Job (320 pages) (11-225)
- Psalms (688 pages) (11-216)
- Proverbs (320 pages) (11-227)
- Ecclesiastes
  Song Of Solomon (245 pages) (11-228)
- Isaiah (688 pages) (11-220)
- Jeremiah
  Lamentations (688 pages) (11-070)
- Ezekiel (508 pages) (11-223)
- Daniel (403 pages) (11-224)
- Hosea
  Joel
  Amos (496 pages) (11-229)
- Obadiah
  Jonah
  Micah
  Naham
  Habakkuk
  Zephaniah *(will be ready Spring 2013)* (11-230)
- Matthew (625 pages) (11-073)
- Mark (606 pages) (11-074)
- Luke (626 pages) (11-075)
- John (532 pages) (11-076)
- Acts (697 pages) (11-077)
- Romans (536 pages) (11-078)
- I Corinthians (632 pages) (11-079)
- II Corinthians (589 pages) (11-080)
- Galatians (478 pages) (11-081)
- Ephesians (550 pages) (11-082)
- Philippians (476 pages) (11-083)

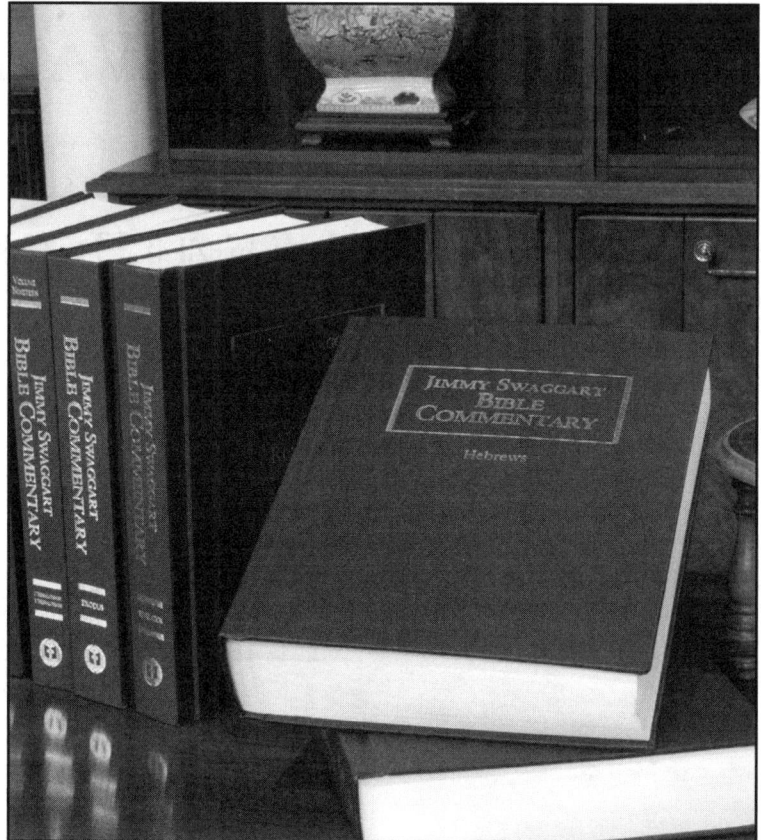

- Colossians (374 pages) (11-084)
- I Thessalonians
  II Thessalonians (498 pages) (11-085)
- I Timothy
  II Timothy
  Titus
  Philemon (687 pages) (11-086)
- Hebrews (831 pages) (11-087)
- James
  I Peter
  II Peter (730 pages) (11-088)
- I John
  II John
  III John
  Jude (377 pages) (11-089)
- Revelation (602 pages) (11-090)

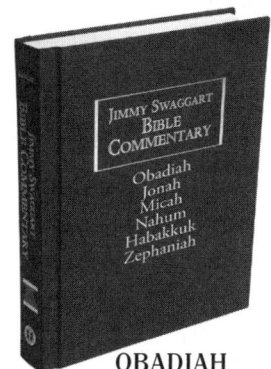

OBADIAH
JONAH
MICAH
NAHAM
HABAKKUK
ZEPHANIAH

For prices and information please call: 1-800-288-8350
Baton Rouge residents please call: (225) 768-7000
Website: www.jsm.org • Email: info@jsm.org

Jimmy Swaggart Bible Commentary

Hebrews

WORLD EVANGELISM PRESS

ISBN 978-1-934655-18-4
11-087 • COPYRIGHT © 2001 World Evangelism Press®
P.O. Box 262550 • Baton Rouge, Louisiana 70826-2550
Website: www.jsm.org • Email: info@jsm.org • (225) 768-8300
13 14 15 16 17 18 19 20 21 22 23 24 25 26 27 28 / RRD / 19 18 17 16 15 14 13 12 11 10 9 8 7 6 5 4

TABLE OF CONTENTS

∎

INTRODUCTION

THE INTRODUCTION OF THE EPISTLE OF PAUL THE APOSTLE TO THE HEBREWS

It is Monday, April 17, 2000, as I begin the Commentary on Paul's great Epistle to the Hebrews. As possibly no other Book or Epistle in the New Testament, Hebrews deals with the Finished Work of Christ, as it regards the Crucifixion, Resurrection, and Exaltation of our Lord. Paul correlates in this Epistle as in no other, this great Finished Work with Old Testament typology.

Consequently, this Book is unlike any other in the New Testament. In subject matter it is distinctive, and its picture of Jesus as our great High Priest is its own.

Some have claimed that this work was meant for a restricted circle of Readers, and not the general public or even the general Christian public. I beg to disagree.

If every Believer knew and understood this which Paul gives us in this great Book, much false doctrine would be cleared up. The Church stumbles about attempting to find the answer to a victorious, overcoming, Christian life, introducing one fad after the other, when if this Epistle were properly understood, the great question of Christian victory would be answered.

In 1997 the Lord, in answer to several years of heart searching prayer, began to give me a Revelation of the Cross which has gloriously and wondrously changed my life. In fact, that Revelation continues unto this hour, and I pray shall continue until the Lord comes or else He calls me home. That for which I had so long sought was now found, and it has produced a *"joy unspeakable and full of glory!"*

Even though it is very involved, and will hopefully be detailed minutely in this Commentary, the following will reduce it to a very simplistic form.

THE VICTORY OF THE CROSS

The Lord related to me the following:

1. He told me that every single answer for which I sought is found in the Cross of Christ. This means every Blessing, every Grace, in fact every single thing we receive from the Lord, comes unequivocally and totally, through and by the Cross of our Lord and Saviour, Jesus Christ.

2. Inasmuch as everything comes through the Cross of Christ, the Cross must ever be the object of our Faith. This is so very, very important. Every Christian has Faith, but the major problem is, the object of our Faith many times is wrong, which closes the door to the results for which we seek. The object of our Faith must always, and without exception, be the Cross of Christ.

3. Once our Faith is in the Cross of Christ, and remains in the Cross of Christ, the Holy Spirit will then perform His great Office work of Sanctification within our hearts and lives. He functions totally and completely by, of, and through the Cross of Christ. In other words, His parameters are the great Finished Work of Christ. He only demands that we have Faith in the Cross, which in reality is to have Faith in what Christ did there. When we resort to law, in order to bring about victory, which means any type of effort outside of the Cross, the Holy Spirit will not help us, and we're left on our own, which spells guaranteed defeat. Conversely, victory is guaranteed for every Saint of God over the world, the flesh, and the Devil, providing our Faith is properly placed in the Cross, which guarantees the help of the Holy Spirit (Rom. 8:1-2, 11, 13).

THE AUTHORSHIP OF THE EPISTLE

Even though the authorship of Hebrews has been and is greatly debated, it is my contention that Paul is the author of this great work. In fact, I do not see how it could be anyone else.

First of all, anyone who would have written this Book would have had to have been a Scholar of unparalleled proportions of the Old Testament. It would have otherwise been impossible. I realize that some may claim that the Lord can inspire anyone to do anything. That is not exactly correct.

If one closely studies the Scriptures one sees that as far as instruction is concerned, the Holy Spirit does not go beyond the intelligence of the writer. While tremendous predictions were given by the Prophets concerning things they did not know or understand, this was not the case as it regards instruction. Regarding instruction, the Holy Spirit definitely inspired the writers, but did so only up to the limit of their understanding.

No one knew the Old Testament as Paul. Admittedly, it had to be rethought after his conversion, but the Holy Spirit grandly carried out this instruction in Paul's understanding. If that is correct, and I know that it is, then Paul is the only one who could have written this Book.

THE MESSAGE OF THE CROSS

As well as knowing and understanding the Old Testament, as Paul obviously did, the most telling factor of the authorship of the Book of Hebrews is that the writer understood the Message of the Cross, actually, as no one else. In fact, it was to Paul that this great Revelation was given (Gal., Chpt. 1). So, to have written the Book of Hebrews, which, in effect, is an explanation of the Message of the Cross from Old Testament principles, and especially from the perspective of the Tabernacle and the Sacrifices, Paul alone knew this subject in this capacity. As stated, it was to this man that the understanding of the Message of the Cross was given, which, in effect, is an explanation of the New Covenant.

While we could address ourselves to the various councils of the ancient past, such as the Council of Laodicea (A.D. 363), the Syrian Churches (A.D. 370), the Council of Carthage (A.D. 397), and how they accepted the authorship of Paul, and that Paul was named as the author in the Alexandrian Manuscript in A.D. 500, still, it is obvious that the writer of Hebrews had to be extremely knowledgeable as it regards the Message of the Cross. Only Paul could fit this bill, so to speak.

When it came to theology, at least as it regards other New Testament Epistles, all of their writers, even though inspired by the Holy Spirit, in essence, learned what they wrote from the Apostle Paul. In some cases, what Paul taught would be enlarged upon, even as the Holy Spirit is wont to do, still, it was Paul alone who understood the meaning of the New Covenant, at least at the beginning, with the explanation having been given to him by Christ (Gal. 1:11-12). A perfect example of Paul's teaching being enlarged upon was given by Peter in his First Epistle, Verses 18 through 20.

So, to argue the authorship of Paul, as it regards the Epistle to the Hebrews, simply means that the individuals who disclaim Paul as the author little understand the Cross themselves. If they understood the Cross as they ought to understand the Cross, they would instantly know that Paul wrote Hebrews.

THE PURPOSE OF THE BOOK

The argument of this Epistle is that the First Covenant was indeed Divine but was only a shadow of the promised Second Covenant; and that being so, if the shadow was Divine how much more must the substance be!

So here the Holy Spirit teaches that all the Divinely given Shadows, Types, Symbols, and Figures are satisfied in Christ Who is their substance, and He leaves nothing before the heart of the worshipper but the glorious form of the Great High Priest Who is passed into the Heavens.

In Him the worshipper finds his Priest, his Altar, his Sacrifice, his Baptism, his Pascal Supper, his Circumcision and his place of worship. The Epistle to the Romans, someone has said, is a Court of Justice. The Epistle to the Hebrews is a Temple of Worship.

CONTRAST

Contrast rather than comparison is prominent in this Epistle. It is addressed to the many thousands of Jews who believed that Jesus was the Messiah, and who were all zealous in keeping the Law and in not forsaking Circumcision or the customs (Acts 21:20). To understand the purpose and teaching of the Epistle this fact must be clearly grasped. Consequently, the interpretation belongs to them; however, the application belongs to all Christians, both Jews and Gentiles.

This Letter primarily aimed at leading the Hebrews who believed in Jesus as the Messiah to recognize that He fulfilled, and consequently abrogated, all the Types and Shadows of the Law; and that in the true Messianic fellowship and worship, all material and visible elements were put aside and only that which was spiritual and unseen enjoyed. This is very important, not only as being the Mind of God, but also because the Temple and its Sacramental worship were about to be destroyed by God at the hands of the Romans (Heb. 8:13). This Letter prepared these Hebrew Believers for that event, and taught them that worship was not destroyed, for in Christ they would find a Temple and a spiritual worship that nothing could destroy — Christ was the substance; the former only the Shadow.

However, let not the Gentile think that this great Book holds but little meaning for him. In fact, it is one of the most important Books in the entirety of the Bible, that is if we dare highlight one over the other. As we've said many times, if the Christian doesn't understand the Old Testament, he can little understand the New.

Paul goes into detail as to what the Old Testament Types and Shadows actually mean as it refers to Christ. Consequently, Christ becomes more and more real, as the Epistle to the Hebrews is more and more understood. And anything that makes Christ more real, presents itself as the grandest thing anyone could ever learn.

BETTER

The Camp of old had its glory, but this Epistle invites the Hebrew Believers, and all Believers, for that matter, to go on to better glories. In fact, one might even say that the word *"better,"* as used of Christ in this Epistle, constitutes the theme-word of Hebrews.

The idea is that whatever the Old Testament presented, which was only meant to point to a better way, was totally and completely fulfilled in Christ (Heb. 7:19, 22; 8:6; 9:23; 10:34; 11:35, 40).

The Holy Spirit is mentioned seven times. His Personality (2:4); His Inspiration (3:7); His Impartation (6:4); His Teaching (9:8); His Deity (9:14); His Testimony (10:15); and His Grace (10:29) (Williams).

JESUS

Paul sees, or rather the Holy Spirit through him sees, the entirety of the Old Testament pointing to Jesus. What the ancient Writings say is fulfilled in Him. This means more than that specific Prophecies are fulfilled in Jesus. Rather the thrust of the whole Old Testament is such that it leads inescapably to Him.

Paul writes of Bible Christianity as the final thrust, actually the Everlasting Covenant, not because he regards the Faith of the Old Testament as mistaken, but because he sees it as God's Way of pointing men to Jesus (Heb. 13:20).

Judaism is not so much abrogated by Christianity as brought to its climax. In other words, the fuller meaning of the Old Testament is to be seen in the Person and Work of Jesus. The Old Testament and the New are rightly seen only when they are recognized as parts of one whole. And it is Jesus Who enables us to discern that whole and its meaning.

THE TIME WHEN WRITTEN

Of course, there is no way that one can know the exact time, for this information is not given, which is true about most all the Books in the Bible. Dates are given anywhere from A.D. 61 to early 68, with the latter probably closer to the actual time.

We do know it was written while the Temple was still standing, and before Jerusalem was destroyed, which took place in A.D. 70. It is my opinion that Paul was executed in early 68, so the Epistle had to be written before that time.

It is almost positive that it was written in Italy. Thus, in Hebrews 13:24, Paul says, *"They of Italy salute you."* This would be the natural form of salutation, on the supposition that it was written there. He mentions none by name, as he does in his other Epistles, for it is probable that none of those who were at Rome with him would be known by name in Israel. So this would have been a general salutation, showing the interest which those in Rome had regarding the Christians in Judea, and expressive of regard for their welfare.

THE GREAT DOCTRINE OF HEBREWS

This Book was written to prove that a certain proposition is true. Paul states the proposition in the following words:

"He (Christ) is the Mediator of a Better Covenant, which was established upon Better Promises" (8:6). *"By so much was Jesus made a surety of a Better Testament"* (7:22). *"For if that First Covenant had been faultless, then should no place have been sought for the Second. For finding fault with them, He saith, Behold, the days come, saith the Lord, when I will make a New Covenant with the house of Israel and with the house of Judah"* (8:7-8). *"He taketh away the First (Covenant), that He may establish the Second"* (10:9). The proposition is, therefore: *"The New Testament in Jesus' Blood is superior to and supplants the First Testament which consisted only of animal blood."*

We must be careful to note that the Book is not an argument to prove that Christianity is superior to and takes the place of Judaism, to which we have already alluded. The New Testament is the reality of which the First Testament was the type. The type consisted of the blood sacrifice of an animal, which symbolically gave the offerer Salvation, while in reality his Salvation came from the New Testament which necessarily is a Sacrifice, even the Lord Jesus at Calvary. Christianity is neither a Sacrifice nor a means of Salvation. Christianity is a result of what happened at the Cross, namely, the Christian Church made up of all Believers from Pentecost to the Rapture, together with the Doctrines and Duties of the members of this Church.

Furthermore, the New Testament is also a Covenant made with the Jewish nation.

ISRAEL

The Jewish nation must be distinguished from the Church. It is not a matter of a choice between Judaism and Christianity with which Paul is dealing, but between the type and the reality, between the Levitical Sacrifices and the Substitutionary Atonement of the Lord Jesus.

Since the argument of the Book has to do with the abrogation of the Levitical system of Sacrifices at the Cross, called in this Book, *the "First Testament"* (9:18), and the supplanting of the same by the Sacrifice of our Lord, called in this Book the *"New Testament"* (9:15), the concern of Paul must, therefore, be with reference to the Jews who had accepted Christ, but because of discouragement or persecution from unsaved Jews, were wavering in their Faith as it regards Christ. The Jew had to put his Faith totally in Christ as the High Priest, making it necessary to forsake any dependence he may have had upon the typical sacrifices, recognizing the Lord Jesus as the fulfillment of all these things.

In addition to proving that the New Testament in Jesus' Blood is superior to and takes the place of the First Testament in animal blood, the writer warns those of the believing Jews who had made a profession of Christ, against the act of renouncing their profession and returning to the Temple sacrifices which they had left, and urges them to go on to Faith totally and completely in Christ.

He warns them against letting the New Testament Truth slip away (2:1-4), against hardening the heart against the Holy Spirit (3:7-19), against falling away (5:11-6:12), against committing the willful sin of treading underfoot the Son of God, counting His Blood as common Blood, and doing insult to the Holy Spirit (10:26-29), all this being involved in the act of renouncing professed Faith in Christ and returning to the Levitical sacrifices. These are not separate and distinct sins, but one sin described in various ways, the sin of the believing Jews at that particular time, renouncing their professed Faith in Christ as High Priest and of returning to the abrogated sacrifices of the First Testament.

GENTILES

The warning that was given to the believing Jews of old holds true for believing Gentiles presently. In effect, the Church presently is facing the same problem as the Jews of old. As they were tempted to turn back to the animal sacrifices, the Church today is tempted to turn to things other than the Cross. I speak of humanistic psychology, and actually, I speak of anything other than total Faith in the Finished Work of Christ.

Forsaking Christ is the great problem, not so much that for which He is forsaken. Irrespective of the direction taken, whether back to the animal sacrifices of old, or to humanistic psychology presently, the results are the same. It is what Christ did at the Cross on our behalf, or it is nothing!

"Lord, with glowing heart I'd praise Thee for the bliss Thy love bestows,
"For the pard'ning Grace that saved me, and the Peace that from it flows:
"Help, O God, my weak endeavor; this dull soul to rapture raise:
"Thou must light the flame, or never can my love be warmed to praise."

"Praise, my soul, the God that sought thee, wretched wand'rer far astray;
"Found thee lost, and kindly brought thee from the paths of death away:
"Praise, with love's devoutest feeling, Him Who saw thy guilt-born fear,
"And, the light of hope revealing, bade the bloodstain'd Cross appear."

"Praise thy Saviour God that drew thee to that Cross, new life to give,
"Held a blood-sealed pardon to thee, bade thee look to Him and live:
"Praise the Grace whose threats alarm thee, roused thee from thy fatal ease,
"Praise the Grace whose promise warm'd thee, praise the Grace that whispered peace."

"Lord, this bosom's ardent feeling vainly would my lips express:
"Low before Thy footstool kneeling, deign Thy suppliant's pray'r to bless:
"Let Thy love, my soul's chief treasure, love's pure flame within me raise;
"And, since words can never measure, let my life show forth Thy praise."

THE
BOOK OF HEBREWS

———■———

(1) "GOD, WHO AT SUNDRY TIMES AND IN DIVERS MANNERS SPAKE IN TIME PAST UNTO THE FATHERS BY THE PROPHETS,"

The exposition is:

1. Revelation is given by God.

2. The manner in which the Revelation was given.

3. To whom it was given, the Prophets!

THE REVELATION OF GOD

"*God*" in the English text is placed first, but in the Greek Text His Words are placed at the beginning of the sentence for emphasis. Therefore, the main idea in the writer's mind here is not that God spoke, but rather the manner in which He spoke (Wuest).

As we begin our study of this sublime Epistle, we are brought face-to-face with God Himself, ever yearning for the love and confidence of the race created in His Own Image and after His Own Likeness, but which in the person of its first head (Adam) was scarcely placed in a position of authority before departing from the Creator, obedience to Whomever means Blessing; and disobedience, misery and remorse.

Sin had no sooner come into the world than God came in Grace seeking the sinner, and so from the first question, "*Adam, where art thou?*" on to the Incarnation, God has been speaking to man.

So here at the beginning, let us bow our whole being at this word, "*God.*" God has spoken! An old Puritan Preacher used to say there were just two things he desired to know: "*First, does God speak (concerning any matter)? Second, what does God say?*"

Atheists — fools, deny God's Being. Deists deny that He has revealed Himself — that

He has spoken. The great multitude of humanity ignore Him, and live in their little selfish Earth-lives, to hear at last the fearful words, "*Depart from Me.*"

"*Hear, and your soul shall live*" is the constant Message of Scripture. Nor is God named in this Verse as "*The God and Father of our Lord Jesus Christ,*" as in Paul's Epistles to the Church as such. For the subject immediately taken up in Hebrews Chapter 1 is not our Salvation or Blessing, but the Person and place of God's Son! (Newell).

The Genesis account begins with "*in the beginning — God,*" whereas the Hebrews account simply begins with "*God,*" taking it for granted that the Reader has made his way past the beginning.

The idea is, that from the very beginning God set in motion the Redemption Plan to save sinners, a plan incidentally, that was formulated from before the foundation of the world (I Pet. 1:18-21). And if one desires to know what God is like, one only need look at the Life and Ministry of Christ. Philip said, "*Lord, show us the Father . . . and Jesus said unto him, 'Have I been so long with you, and yet hast thou not known Me, Philip? He that hath seen Me hath seen the Father'*" (Jn. 14:8-9).

THE MANNER OF THE REVELATION

The phrase, "*Who at sundry times and in divers manners,*" refers to the many and varied ways.

In the giving of Old Testament Truth, God did not speak once for all, but in separate Revelations, each of which set forth only a part of His Will. One would be given a Revelation, and then later another would be given added

Revelation, which fleshed out the first and so forth. God spoke in different ways.

This does not refer to different ways in which He imparted His Revelations to the writers, but to the difference of the various Revelations in contents and form. He spoke to Israel in one way through Moses, and another, through Isaiah, etc. At the beginning of the Revelation, the presentation was elementary. Later it appealed to a more developed spiritual sense. Again, the Revelation differed according to the faithfulness or the unfaithfulness of Israel.

First of all, the Old Testament Revelation was progressive. This means that all could not be revealed at once, and because all could not be understood at once. Thus, the Revelation was given in many parts. In addition to this, it was given in different modes. It was given in the form of Law, Prophecy, History, Psalm, Sign, Type, and Parable. Someone has said, *"The people of Israel were like men listening to a clock striking the hour, always getting nearer the Truth but obliged to wait till the whole is heard"* (Wuest).

DIRECTION

Irrespective of the manner in which the Revelation was given by God, and to whom it was given, in effect, it was always one Revelation, with more light given each time, the Redemption of humanity through the Lord Jesus Christ, i.e., *"Jesus Christ and Him Crucified"* (I Cor. 2:2).

The first Revelation was in Genesis 3:15, concerning the *"Seed of the woman,"* Who is Christ, and Satan bruising His heel, which speaks of the Crucifixion. It continued thereafter, with the entirety of the Old Testament serving as that Revelation in one way or the other.

From all the ways that God spoke, we get a perfect harmony, as in musical sounds made up of different parts. And yet, despite all the means and ways by which He spoke, there is only one Plan of God for man. All the Prophets gave perfect and harmonious Testimony that Jesus Christ was and is the Son of God and Saviour of the world (Acts 10:43).

TO WHOM HE SPOKE, THE PROPHETS

The phrase, *"Spake in time past unto the Fathers by the Prophets,"* refers to Old Testament times.

The first Divine activity commented on in this Passage is that God has spoken in a variety of ways. He spoke to Moses in the Burning Bush (Ex. 3:2), to Elijah in a still, small voice (I Ki. 19:12), to Isaiah in a Vision in the Temple (Isa. 6:1), to Hosea in his family circumstances (Hos. 1:2), and to Amos in a basket of summer fruit (Amos 8:1). God might convey His Message through Visions and Dreams, through Angels, through the Urim and Thummim, through symbols, natural events, ecstasy, a pillar of fire, smoke, or other means. He could appear in Ur of the Chaldees, in Haran, in Canaan, in Egypt, in Babylon. There is no lack of variety, for Revelation is not a monotonous activity that must always take place in the same way. God used variety, as is obvious!

PROPHETS

Even though the Office of the Prophet began with Samuel, still, there were others before Samuel who were used in a prophetic manner. Abraham is an example (Gen. 20:7). In fact, I think the prophetic voice went all the way back to Abel. The Scripture says concerning this man, *"By Faith Abel offered unto God a more excellent Sacrifice than Cain, by which he obtained witness that he was righteous, God testifying of his gifts: and by it he being dead yet speaketh"* (Heb. 11:4).

As is here obvious, in Old Testament times, it was through the Prophets that the Lord guided His Work. While the Lord certainly used others, the course was always charted in one way or the other by the Prophets. This is at least one of the reasons that Israel was at such a loss during the some 400 years between the Prophet Malachi and John the Baptist. In fact, this was the first time they had been without the voice of a Prophet since their origination as a nation.

While the Office of the Prophet is still valid presently (Eph. 4:11), it is through Apostles that the course of the Church regarding Doctrine and emphasis is now charted.

The prophetic thrust of Old Testament times, in one way or the other, always had to do with the coming Christ. Those predictions now fulfilled in Christ, the Office of the Prophet is now relegated to a lesser role.

The manner in which Paul speaks here, proclaims the fact that while the Old Testament

Revelation was not to be cast aside, yet it was time for a new one to be given, one that would be God's final word, one that would complete and round out the first one.

Prophets were the mouthpieces of God.

John the Baptist said, *"I am a voice of One who is crying out in the wilderness"* (Jn. 1:23). John did not use the definite article *"the"* before the word *"voice."* Consequently, it should not have been used in the King James Translation. He was merely one among many voices which God used in the Old Testament dispensation. But note: The One crying out, giving the Message, was God. John was His articulate voice, a mere instrument in His Hands (Wuest).

(2) "HATH IN THESE LAST DAYS SPOKEN UNTO US BY HIS SON, WHOM HE HATH APPOINTED HEIR OF ALL THINGS, BY WHOM ALSO HE MADE THE WORLDS;"

The exposition of this Verse is as follows:

1. The last days referred to here, concern the time from Christ unto now, presently about 2,000 years.

2. The manner in which He has spoken to us, which is by His Son, the Lord Jesus Christ, which speaks of the Incarnation.

3. By the use of the word *"Son,"* we see the Cross, which is the Message delivered, and as well, the last Message.

4. Christ is the heir of all things by virtue of His great Redemptive Work, i.e., *"the Cross."*

5. The last phrase of this Verse proclaims the fact that the *"Son"* is *"God,"* and in a more particular sense, *"God the Creator!"*

LAST DAYS

The phrase, *"Hath in these last days,"* speaks of the final dispensation before the coming Kingdom Age. It is in this dispensation under which the affairs of the world will be wound up.

Phrases similar to this occur frequently in the Scriptures. They do not imply that the world is soon coming to an end, but that this is the last dispensation, the last period of this era. There has been the Patriarchal period, then the period under the Law, and *"this"* and we speak of this Dispensation of Grace, which is the *"last days"* of which Paul

speaks here. As stated, it will precede the coming Kingdom Age.

It should be very interesting to the Reader to understand that these *"last days"* of which Paul spoke, are fastly coming to an end. In other words, we are down to the very last days of the *"last days."* That should give us pause for thought!

THE SON

The phrase, *"Spoken unto us by His Son,"* speaks of the Incarnation. Now, at the very termination of the times in which He is speaking to man, He speaks, not through the Prophets, but as the Greek says, *"in Son!"*

The definite article in the Greek appears before *"Prophets,"* actually saying *"the Prophets,"* and sets these individuals off by themselves as a class. The fact that the article is absent before the word *"Son,"* in the original Greek, emphasizes character and nature. It speaks of the Son-relationship of the Messiah to God the Father. It speaks of the distinction that exists between the Prophets as God's creatures used as instruments in His Hands and the Son Who by nature is Deity. The Son belongs to a different category. The idea is, God spoke through One Who is in character a Son (Wuest).

The Revelation God gave in His Son, consisted not merely in what was said, as in the case of the Prophets, but in What the Son was and is, not merely in what He (the Son) said. In other words, it was neither primarily nor finally a Revelation given through words, but through a Personality. It was a Revelation made by One Who in all that He is and all that He does and says, reveals the Father. He is the *"Logos,"* the total concept of Deity, Deity told out, the Word of God, not in the sense of a spoken or a written word, but in the sense of a Person Who in Himself expresses all that God the Father is.

John said, *"In the beginning was the 'Logos'* (the Word), *and the Word* (Logos) *was in fellowship with God* (the Father), *and the 'Logos' was as to His nature Deity"* (Jn. 1:1). This is the Person in Whom God gave His final Revelation to the human race.

Under the Old Testament there were many parts, ways, and persons used in speaking to men, but in the New Testament all was done through the Son Who fulfilled the Law and the Prophets and made the New Covenant (Mat. 26:28; Acts 1:2).

SUPERIORITY

The argument of Paul is to prove just one proposition to be true; *"The New Testament is superior to and takes the place of the Old Testament."*

His first major argument shows that the Founder of the New Testament is superior to the founders of the Old Testament, which makes the New Testament superior to the Old.

The first class of individuals he selects among the founders of the Old Testament are the Prophets. He has now shown that the Founder of the New Testament (New Covenant) is superior to the Prophets in that they were merely created beings used as instruments by God, whereas the former is the Son, God the Son, thus Very God of Very God.

But not only is the Son superior in His Being, but the mode of revealing God's Word to the human race was superior in His case. When the Prophets spoke, it was merely as mouthpieces. When the Son spoke, it was God Himself Who spoke. Thus, by two counts already, has Paul shown that the One Who gave the Truth of the New Covenant to man is superior to those who gave the Truth of the Old Covenant.

In the Son, God made a full Revelation of Himself to man. Prior to His Advent He spoke partially through the Hebrew prophets, but now perfectly in Christ. A king speaks by, not in, his Ambassador, but God speaks in the Son, for He is the last and highest manifestation of Deity — the fullness of the Godhead bodily (Col. 2:9).

HEIR

The phrase, *"Whom He hath appointed Heir of all things,"* seems to be a contradiction of the last phrase of this Verse. If He made the worlds, and He definitely did, then how can He become the *"Heir"* of all these things, when in reality they already belong to Him?

The idea is found in the word *"Son,"* which speaks of the Incarnation, which speaks of Christ as Saviour.

When God originally created man, and we speak of the original Adam, He gave him

dominion over all things (Gen. 1:28; Ps. 8). The Reader must understand that this dominion was complete, which takes in all of God's creation, which refers to even more than this present world. It refers to everything that God has created, even including the Angelic Hosts, etc.

When Adam fell in the Garden of Eden, which refers to falling from his total God-consciousness, down to the far lower level of self-consciousness, he lost his life-support, which is God (Jn. 1:4; 3:15-16, 36; 4:14; 5:24, 26, 29, 40). Because God had given Adam the dominion, he had the right to do with this dominion what he liked. Due to his weakened state, he now becomes a captive of Satan, which means that his dominion is forfeited to the Evil One. What happened to Adam was far beyond his original comprehension.

He now has become a pawn in the great rebellion instituted originally by Lucifer, the mightiest Angel ever created by God, who had led a revolution against God sometime in eternity past. This revolution was so severe, that it actually drew away a third of the angelic hosts, who threw in their lot with Satan. So now, this revolution includes God's choice creation, man.

THE MANNER OF CREATION

The manner in which God created man, seems to have been different than any of His other creations. For instance, when He created the Angels, it seems they were all created at the same time, and fully mature. In other words, there's never been such a thing as a baby Angel. While they hold different ranks and different powers, they are all the same age.

But when God created man, He gave man the power of procreation, which means the ability to bring offspring into the world. In fact, Adam and Eve were originally intended to bring sons and daughters of God into the world, with the race continuing in this manner. But when Adam fell, for the seed of the Fall was in Adam and not Eve, ceasing to be a son and daughter of God, they could now only bring sons and daughters into the world after the likeness of Adam (Gen. 5:3), which refers to all the attendant sin nature, which is the cause of all the heartache, war, trouble, sickness, death, and dying in the world.

As well, the Fall of man was of far greater dimension than anyone could ever begin to realize. At the Fall, man ceased to have the nature of God, which speaks of total Goodness, Mercy, Grace, Love, and Compassion, and now has the nature of Satan, which speaks of transgression, iniquity, sin, and failure, which translates into pain, suffering, poverty, heartache, ignorance, sickness, etc. In essence, God was no longer the Father of humanity, except in creation, which means the life force of God no longer abides within man. In essence, Satan is now the father of humanity with all its attendant problems. That's why Jesus told the Pharisees, *"Ye are of your father the Devil, and the lusts of your father ye will do. He was a murderer from the beginning, and abode not in the Truth, because there is no Truth in him. When he speaketh a lie, he speaketh of his own: for he is a liar, and the father of it"* (Jn. 8:44).

There in brief, you have just read the cause of all problems in the world, *"lusts, murder, and the lie."* That is the realm in which unredeemed man resides.

JESUS

Everything that God has created, He has done so by a system of laws. In other words, the dominion given to Adam was a legal thing, i.e., *"the law."* Now that Satan has this dominion, it is actually his in a legal sense, even though he gained it through *"a lie."* Consequently, he has a legal right before God to place unredeemed man into captivity, and even because of the very Laws of God. For instance, God had made a law which states, *"the wages of sin is death"* (Rom. 6:23). By the law of dominion, and the law of sin and death (Rom. 8:2), both laws originally made by God, Satan has a legal right to hold man in captivity. In other words, Satan's legal right is brought about by sin and iniquity.

Some people have asked as to why God doesn't do thus and so as it regards the Devil? In other words, why doesn't God just simply do away with the Devil, for He certainly has the power to do so?

While He definitely does have that power, and while He is definitely doing away with

him, which will ultimately come to pass, it all has to be done legally, or else the very Nature and Righteousness of God will be violated. And it is for certain, that God cannot violate His Own Nature, which means to violate His Own laws, which He has originated Himself. If He were to do that, all of Heaven would instantly become a hell. God made all of these Laws, and God abides by His Laws.

To abide by these Laws, God will have to become man, which He did, in the form of the Lord Jesus Christ. God had originally given dominion to a man, and it would have to be a man who would restore this dominion. In effect, the Creator would have to become a created being, which is absolutely beyond our comprehension.

For this to be done, this man would have to come into the world as all other men, but at the same time not as all other men. In other words, He would have to be born as a baby, but He could not be conceived as all other babies. To have been conceived in the manner as all others, He would have been born in original sin as all others, and would, therefore, be unable to redeem humanity. In fact, had He been born in that manner, He would have needed a Redeemer Himself!

So He would be born without the benefit of an earthly father, actually conceived by decree, brought about by the Holy Spirit (Lk. 1:26-35). But yet this did not destroy the original type, simply because the original Adam was made by God and not by procreation.

THE LAST ADAM

Paul refers to Christ as the *"Last Adam,"* meaning that He would undo what the original Adam did (the Fall), and do what the original Adam failed to do (render a perfect obedience to God) (I Cor. 15:45-50).

After the Fall, man's condition was so deplorable, so evil, so wicked, that the Scripture says that God *"repented . . . that He had made man on the Earth, and it grieved Him at His heart."*

The reason being, *"that the wickedness was great in the Earth, and that every imagination of the thoughts of his heart was only evil continually"* (Gen. 6:5-6).

Due to this depraved condition, with man having the nature of Satan, which means that Satan now had total dominion over this part of God's creation, it took many centuries before the Plan of Redemption could be instigated.

In fact, the situation was so bad, that God was forced to drown the Earth in water, saving only Noah and his family, plus specimens of the animal creation, etc. (Gen. 6:7-22). Noah and his family found Grace in the sight of God, simply because Noah continued to believe God concerning a coming Redeemer, which the Lord had promised to send as early as the Fall (Gen. 3:15). Incidentally, Noah lived about 1,600 years after creation.

After the horror of the flood, the entirety of the human race, in effect started over, having as its fathers the sons of Noah, *"Shem, Ham, and Japheth"* (Gen. 10:1). However, the results of the Fall still were in Noah and his family, just as it had been in the entirety of mankind. Noah was spared only because he had Faith in God, and His Promise to send a Redeemer into the world. In fact, it has always been Faith, but more particularly, Faith in the Lord Jesus Christ, and what He would do at the Cross to redeem humanity.

Some 400 years after Noah, God spoke to Abraham, then called Abram (Gen. 12:1). He gave to Abraham the meaning of the Law of Justification, which would be by the Law of Faith so to speak (Rom. 3:27). The *"Law of Faith"* refers totally to belief in Christ and what He would do at the Cross. That's why it's also called *"One Lord* (Christ Jesus), *one Faith* (Faith in the Cross of Christ), *one Baptism* (the Baptism of the believing sinner into the Crucifixion of Christ, which is brought about in the Mind of God, when the sinner exhibits Faith in Christ, and what He did at the Cross on our behalf)" (Eph. 4:5). Referring to Noah and Abraham, and others, we are now going back to the previous Verse of our study, which speaks of the manner in which God dealt with the human race in Old Testament times.

THE CROSS

The Last Adam, the Lord Jesus Christ, would have to do two things in order to redeem fallen humanity.

About 400 years after Abraham, the Lord would call a man by the name of Moses, and

in the process of the manner in which He dealt with Him, would give him the Law, referred to often as the *"Law of Moses."* This was God's Standard of Righteousness which He demanded of fallen man, but which of course fallen man could not keep or do. Nevertheless, this was the Standard which God demanded, and in fact, which He must demand, that is if His Nature is not to be violated.

Jesus would have to keep this Law in perfection, not failing even one time, which He did. Consequently, as our Representative Man He accomplished this great task, which means that He did this totally and completely on our behalf. We must not forget this! Every single thing that Christ did, He did as our Representative Man or as our Substitute, all on our behalf, which means that we could not do it for ourselves. But Him doing these things, was reckoned by God as our doing them, at least if we evidence Faith in Christ. It has always been Faith, and it still is Faith; however, we must remember, if it is to be Faith that God will recognize, it must always be Faith in the proper object, which is *"Jesus Christ and Him Crucified"* (I Cor. 2:2).

As the Last Adam, our Lord kept the Law perfectly and as stated, all on our behalf, but then He had to deal with the sin question.

The wages of sin being death, and remembering that God originally made this Law, and considering that He cannot violate His Own Law, its penalty will have to be satisfied in full.

In actuality, man dying eternally lost, which means to be banned from the Presence of God forever and forever, actually in Hell itself, satisfies the terms and penalty of the broken Law; however, as would be obvious, for this to happen with all men, would exterminate the race, thereby destroying all of God's choice creation, which means, in that case, that Satan would win as it regards his revolution (Isa. 14:12-20; Ezek. 28:11-19).

The only way to solve this problem, which means to redeem mankind, at least those who will believe, is for Jesus to also be our Substitute, which means that He took the penalty of death which we should have taken. However, there is a vast difference in Him taking this penalty and us. The difference at least in part, is according to the following:

In order to pay for every single sin, even the worst sins and transgressions that one could ever think, Jesus would have to die the most awful death, in this case, death by Crucifixion. In fact, if Christ was to suffer the curse of the broken Law, He would have to be crucified, which means that He could not be stoned to death or thrust through with a spear, etc. It had to be by Crucifixion.

In the ancient Law of Moses, God had stated that if an individual committed a particular, heinous crime, he was to be stoned to death, and then his body was to be hung on a tree as a spectacle to all, that he had died under the curse of God (Deut. 21:22-23).

The Reader must understand, that sin is so awful, so destructive, that it has literally killed every single human being who has ever lived upon this Earth, which means that all alive presently are actually dying. It has filled the Earth with violence, murder, poverty, sickness, and sorrow, which means it is far worse than man could ever begin to think or realize. This is what makes it so absolutely ridiculous for the Church to think that humanistic psychology, which has been birthed entirely by unredeemed man, can in any manner assuage this terrible condition. If it could, why did Jesus have to come down here and die on a Cross?

So, when Jesus died, He would have to die in the most awful way, which was the Cross, and because He had to pay the price for all sin (Jn. 1:29).

However, when Jesus hung on that Cross, several things must be understood. They are as follows:

THE MEANING OF THE CROSS

1. In order for the terrible sin debt to be paid, God demanded a perfect sacrifice, which of course man could not furnish. Jesus was that Perfect Sacrifice, with Paul saying of Him, *"For such an High Priest became us, Who is holy, harmless, undefiled, separate from sinners, and made higher than the Heavens"* (Heb. 7:26).

This means that the abominable teaching that Jesus took upon Himself the terrible, depraved, sin nature of Satan, while on the Cross, thereby dying as a sinner and going to the burning side of Hell when He died, is blasphemy! Those who promote such a doctrine

may be doing so in ignorance, but it is blasphemy just the same!

Those who teach this doctrine, discount the Cross as though it had no validity, placing the Salvation of humanity in the cock-and-bull story (for that's what it is), of Jesus being born again in Hell. In other words, they state that Jesus had to die like every sinner, go to Hell, and be born again in Hell, thereby effecting our Redemption. There's not a shred of such stupidity found in the Bible, and stupidity it is!

Jesus didn't redeem us by dying as a sinner, but by offering up Himself as a Perfect Sacrifice before God, which satisfied the demands of the broken Law. The Scripture plainly says that Christ was *"made a curse for us,"* which means that He died in our place. He did not have the curse upon Himself, and neither was He cursed by God, but rather only *"smitten"* (Isa. 53:4). He had to be *"made a curse,"* because He was not a curse, which actually means, that He suffered the penalty or curse of the broken Law, which was death. He did not take upon Himself our sin, but rather the penalty for our sin.

It's impossible for one to be a sinner without at first sinning, and Jesus never sinned.

As our Substitute He took our penalty, and did so by dying.

2. His Death was totally unlike any other death that ever was. He did not die as all other human beings die, which refers to the physical body shutting down, etc. And to be sure, had He become a sinner on the Cross as some teach, He would have died, as one might say, of natural causes. But Jesus did not die in the sense of His heart quitting, or from the suffering of the Cross, etc. In fact, He said of Himself, and concerning death, *"No man taketh it* (My life) *from Me, but I lay it down of Myself. I have power to lay it down, and I have power to take it again. This Commandment have I received of My Father"* (Jn. 10:18). So what am I saying?

He literally breathed out His Life, purposely giving it up, in order that the terrible sin debt might be paid, i.e., *"satisfying the curse of the broken law."*

The difference in Him voluntarily giving up His Own Life, which means He could not have died had He not done this, is vastly different from dying, as we have stated, of natural causes. The latter would have meant that He was a sinner, while the former means that there was no sin in Him, therefore, death could not claim Him as it does all others.

When He died, He not only satisfied the curse of the broken Law, but He also atoned for all sin, in that His death and dying were a Perfect Sacrifice. Consequently, inasmuch as all sin has now been atoned, Satan has lost his legal claim on the human race, at least for all who will believe (Jn. 3:16).

HEIR OF ALL THINGS

So, as a result of being the Last Adam, which means that He purchased back with the shedding of His Own Blood, the dominion that Adam originally lost, He as the Second Man (I Cor. 15:47), is now the *"Heir of all things."* He gained this by what He did at the Cross, and did it all on our behalf, and not at all for Himself. This is a point that must be clearly understood.

All of this was for us, and none at all for Himself. And for us to attempt to comprehend such love is actually and literally beyond our understanding.

The Creator literally stepped down from His Judgment Throne, in order to become the Saviour, which He had to do, if man was to be redeemed.

No wonder that God has highly exalted Him, and given Him a Name that is above every name, with that Name being *"Lord"* (Phil. 2:6-11).

But once again, let us understand, that Christ did all of this through the Cross. If we fail to understand the Cross, then we fail to understand Christ, and we fail to understand Redemption. And that's the major problem of the modern Church:

There has been so little preaching and teaching on the Cross in the last several decades, that this generation of Christians has little understanding of the Cross of Christ. Consequently, it by and large walks in defeat instead of victory, because all victory is found in the Cross, and our Faith in that Finished Work (Rom. 6:3-5, 11, 14; 8:1-2, 11, 13).

THE CREATOR

The phrase, *"By Whom also He made the worlds,"* proclaims His Deity, as the previous

NOTES

phrase of Him being the *"Heir of all things"* proclaims His humanity. As stated, Jesus was and is *"Very God and Very Man."*

"Worlds" in the Greek is *"aion,"* and means, *"God's Revelation of Himself in a sphere whose conditions are time and space, and so all things existing under these conditions, plus these conditions themselves which exist not independently of the Creator, but are His Work, His appointed conditions of all created existence, so that the universe, as well in its great primeval conditions, — the reaches of Space, and the ages of Time, as in all material objects and all successive events, which furnish out and people Space and Time, God made by Christ Who is God."*

The idea in the Greek word *"aion"* is not merely that of vastness and magnificence of the physical universe, but the thought of the times and ages through which the Purpose and Plan of God are gradually unfolding. Thus, the Son is the Divine Agent not only in the original creation of the physical universe, but also in the operation and management of that universe and all its creatures all down the ages of time. And that makes Him of course, much better than the Prophets.

To say it in a brief way, it means that Christ was the agent in planning the ages and making God's Plan for man. In this sense He is the Everlasting Father (Isa. 9:6). He not only planned the ages, but all creations (Jn. 1:3; Eph. 3:9; Col. 1:15-18).

THE JEWS AND THE SON

The Old Testament Scriptures were very plain as it regarded the coming of the Messiah. First of all, it said that He would come through the lineage of Abraham and Sarah (Gen. 12:3; 17:8, 19, 21).

This nation which would come from the loins of Abraham and the womb of Sarah, would be called Israelites, and would consist of 13 Tribes. Jacob prophesied at the end of his life that it would be through the Tribe of Judah that the Messiah would come, i.e., *"the Redeemer not only of Israel, but also of the entirety of the world"* (Gen. 49:10). Then the Lord related to David, who was of the Tribe of Judah, that it would be through his family that the Redeemer would come (II Sam., Chpt. 7).

Then the Lord through Isaiah told how this *"One"* would be born. He said, *"Therefore the Lord Himself shall give you a sign; Behold, a virgin shall conceive, and bear a Son, and shall call His Name Immanuel"* (Isa. 7:14).

The Name *"Immanuel"* means *"God with us."* So from this, Israel should have known that the Messiah would be God manifested in the flesh.

Isaiah also foretold as to how the Messiah would die, thereby redeeming humanity (Isa., Chpt. 53). My point is this:

Even though the Bible was crystal clear as it regarded Who and What the Messiah would be, which means that Israel should have known, instead they had fixated their own version of the Messiah, which had no relationship whatsoever to that introduced in the Word of God.

They wouldn't accept the idea that God would have a Son. And the reason they wouldn't accept that is because they didn't understand the Incarnation, or their need for Redemption. While they admitted that the world needed Redemption, they not at all admitted that they fell into the same category. So, in their minds, this Messiah was going to restore Israel to her place of supremacy, making her the greatest nation in the world, and all other nations subservient to her. That was the role they had planned out for the Messiah, which is actually the role He will play, in the coming Kingdom Age.

In fact, Jesus plainly offered the Kingdom to Israel when He came (Mat. 4:17). But to receive that Kingdom, they would have to receive the King, Who was and is the Lord Jesus, which necessitated their repentance, which they did not agree that they needed. So they rejected the Kingdom, which submitted them to destruction as a nation, which happened in A.D. 70.

Inasmuch as they had a totally wrong conception of Who and What the Messiah would be, they did not understand Him as God's Son. They in fact thought that He would be a very charismatic individual, or even a reincarnation of one of the Prophets of old, but not God manifest in the flesh.

Had they understood their need for Redemption, they would have understood

NOTES

Christ as the Son of God, and the necessity of such in order that He might become flesh and die on a Cross (Jn. 1:1, 14, 29).

So, this is the reason that Paul is establishing the fact of the Messiah being the Son of God, and the reason for Him being such — the Redemption of mankind, which would be brought about by the giving of Himself on the Cross.

(3) "WHO BEING THE BRIGHTNESS OF HIS GLORY, AND THE EXPRESS IMAGE OF HIS PERSON, AND UPHOLDING ALL THINGS BY THE WORD OF HIS POWER, WHEN HE HAD BY HIMSELF PURGED OUR SINS, SAT DOWN ON THE RIGHT HAND OF THE MAJESTY ON HIGH;"

The breakdown of this Verse is as follows:

1. Jesus Christ is God!

2. Jesus Christ is the exact replica or reproduction of the Father!

3. The universe and all creation for that matter, are sustained by the Word of the Son.

4. The Cross of Christ is the means by which Redemption was brought about.

5. This great Work is a Finished Work, meaning that nothing else will ever have to be done or added, and is signified by Jesus being seated on the Right Hand of God.

GLORY

The phrase, *"Who being the brightness of His Glory,"* presents Christ as being *"the radiance of God's Glory."*

It is of all importance that we grasp this tremendous fact. The Son is One with the Father and with the Spirit. All are coequal and coeternal. When the Son became incarnate, He was the same Person that He had been from eternity, but by His Incarnation He took humanity into union with Deity and so became the Son in a new sense as man born of a virgin.

Having no human father, God Alone was the Father of His humanity as truly as of His Deity. I admit the awkwardness of the last expression, but this is a mystery almost unlawful for man to utter, and of necessity our poor language is a most imperfect vehicle to convey to the mind such sublime Truths. Yet there can be no question as to the Truths themselves, for one who accepts the Testimony of the Word of God (Ironside).

The Son is superior to the Prophets as should be obvious, because He is the brightness of God's Glory.

"Brightness" in the Greek is "apaugasma," and means "a radiance, or effulgence." It is used of light beaming from a luminous body.

The word, Expositors say, seems to mean, not rays of light streaming from a body in their connection with that body or as part of it, still less the reflection of these rays caused by their falling upon another body, but rather rays of light coming out from the original body and forming a similar light-body themselves.

That may not be easy to understand, and in fact cannot literally be understood, but that's the best that expositors can come up with as it regards the translation of the Greek words.

Maybe one could say, "Even though Christ draws from the Father, it is not necessary that He do so, in that He is Deity Himself, but does so not in order to become Deity, but because He, in fact, is Deity."

Alford says that "The Son of God is, in this His essential majesty, the expression and the sole expression of Divine Light, not as in His Incarnation, its reflection."

"Glory" spoken of here refers to the expression of the Divine attributes collectively. It is the unfolded fullness of the Divine perfections.

The "Glory" of the Son was not rightly seen on Earth except for the small moment of the Transfiguration (Mat. 17:1-5).

In the glorified form of the Son of God, John saw Him as He records the incident. He described "His countenance as the Sun shineth in his strength."

In fact, the Glory of Christ at that time was of such magnificence, that John said, "And when I saw Him, I fell at His feet as dead. And He laid His right hand upon me, saying unto me, 'Fear not; I am the first and the last:

"'I am He that liveth, and was dead; and, behold, I am alive for evermore, Amen; and have the keys of Hell and of death'" (Rev. 1:16-18).

IMAGE

The phrase, "And the express image of His person," refers to a distinctive mark or a token impressed on a person or thing, by which it is known from others, a characteristic, the character of. It refers here to an exact reproduction.

NOTES

Vincent says, "Here the essential Being of God is conceived as setting its distinctive stamp upon Christ, coming into definite and characteristic expression in His Person, so that the Son bears the exact impress of the Divine Nature and Character." Jesus is absolute Deity because He is the exact reproduction of the essence of God. Incidentally, the words "express image" as used here occur nowhere else in the New Testament.

And yet the word "Person," proclaims His humanity, in the fact that He has a spirit, soul, and body. Among other things, this phrase tells us the following:

1. In His original mode of Being, or before the Incarnation, He had a "glory with the Father before the world was" (Jn. 17:5). He was "in the beginning with God, and was God" (Jn. 1:1). He was in intimate union with the Father, and was one with Him in certain respects; though in certain other respects, there was a distinction.

Even though Jesus has always been God, and in that mode had no beginning, was not formed or made or begotten and is, therefore, uncaused; however, knowing that He has always been God, the question must be asked, "Was He always the Son of God?"

The Nicene Creed says that He is, "God of God, Light of Light, Very God of Very God, begotten, not made"; however, the word "begotten" implies that He had a beginning, which in fact as God is not correct.

Every Scriptural evidence is, that Jesus Christ has always been God, is God, and ever will be God, unformed, uncaused, and unmade, had no beginning and in fact has always been; however, the word "Son" or "Son of God," all pertain to the Incarnation, and refers to something that happened at a point in time. In other words, God literally became the Son of God, which refers to taking upon Himself the form of human flesh, in order that He might redeem humanity by the way of the Cross. God cannot die, so He would have to become man in order to carry out this part of the Redemption process. As well, and as we've already stated, in order to redeem mankind, God would literally have to become a "Last Adam," which demanded that He become human (I Cor. 15:45-50).

2. And yet, even though He became the *"Son of God"* in order to become human, He still was the brightness of the Divine Glory, and the express image of God's Person. It was by Him, eminently, that God was made known to men — as it is by the beams of the Sun that that orb is made known.

He bore an exact resemblance to God. He was just such a Being as we should suppose God to be, were He to become Incarnate, and to act as a man. He was the embodied human representation of the Deity. He was pure — like God, and because He was and is God!

JESUS CHRIST

Uninspired men could never have drawn such a character as that of Jesus Christ, unless that character had actually existed.

The attempt has often been made to describe God, or to show how He would speak and act if He came down to Earth. Thus, the Hindus speak of the incarnations of Vishnu; and thus Homer, Virgil, and most of the ancient poets, speak of the appearance of the gods, and describe them as they imagined them to be. But how different from the character of the Lord Jesus! These false gods made up by men, are full of passion, lusts, anger, contention, and strife; they come to mingle in battles, and to take part with contending armies, but yet they evince the same spirit as men, and are merely men of greater power, and more gigantic passions, at least in the imagination of their creators.

But Christ is God in human nature. The form is that of man; the Spirit is that of God. He walks, eats, and sleeps as a man; He thinks, speaks, and acts like God. He was born as a man — but the Angels adored Him as God. As a man He ate; yet, by a word, He created food for thousands, as if He were God, and because in fact, He is God.

Like a man He slept on a pillow, while the vessel was tossed by the waves; like God He rose, and rebuked the winds, and they were stilled. As a man He went, with affectionate interest, to the house of Martha and Mary. As a man He sympathized with them in their affliction, and wept at the grave of their brother; like God, He spoke, and the dead came forth back to the land of the living.

As a man He prayed in the Garden of Gethsemane; He bore His Cross to Calvary; He was nailed to the tree; yet then the Heavens grew dark, and the Earth shook, and the dead arose — as if He were God. As a man He slept in the cold tomb; like God He rose, and brought life and immortality to light. He lived on Earth as a man — He ascended to Heaven like God.

And in all the life of the Redeemer, and in all the variety of trying situations in which He was placed, there was not a word or action which was inconsistent with the supposition that He was the Incarnate God. There was no failure of any effort to heal the sick or to raise the dead; no look, no word, no deed, that is not perfectly consistent with this supposition; but, on the contrary, His life is full of events which can be explained on no other supposition than that He was the appropriate shining forth of the Divine Glory, and the exact resemblance of the Essence of God.

And yet, even though the Father and the Son are two distinct Persons, there are not two Gods, but only One. In fact, there are Three personalities, *"God the Father, God the Son, and God the Holy Spirit"*; but these Three are One!

This doesn't mean that they are One in number, but rather One is Essence.

THE RELIGIONS OF THE WORLD

Most, if not all, the religions of the world, in some manner, some way, attempt to elevate man either to the position of God, or else a Godlike position. In fact, this was the Devil's lie at the beginning, *"Ye shall be as Elohim,"* and is the foundation principle of all false religious systems. In Christianity alone do we learn that God became Man, and this for our Redemption.

Jesus was not a Godlike Man, striving after holiness and piety. He was God Himself come down to Earth in flesh, reconciling the world unto Himself. As stated, nothing like this is known in any human religious system. It is unique because it is Divine, and Divine because it is unique (Ironside).

POWER

The phrase, *"And upholding all things by the Word of His Power,"* carries the meaning of Jesus not only sustaining the weight of the universe, but also with maintaining its coherence and carrying on its development. Paul in essence said the same thing in Colossians 1:17 where he says, *"By Him all things consist."* That is, all things maintain their coherence in Him. The Lord Jesus holds all things together and in their proper relationship to each other by His Own Power (Wuest).

The idea is not that Christ is continuing to create the universe, but that during its original creation, He by the Word of His Power originated the laws that cause the universe to function correctly, and to continue to function correctly. In other words, these laws are perpetual, unless suspended by the Lord Himself.

All of this was done, as stated, *"by the Word of His Power,"* which means, that the universe was called into being by the Word of God (Heb. 11:3), and is sustained by that same Word. God willed it. His Power brought into being that which He willed.

THE WORD OF HIS POWER

The phrase *"Word of His Power"* is a Hebraism, and means His efficient command. There could not be a more distinct ascription of Divinity to the Son of God than this. He upholds and sustains all things. How can He do this Who is not God? That a simple command should do this is beyond our comprehension, but that's exactly what happened!

The Psalmist said, *"By the Word of the Lord were the Heavens made; and all the host of them by the breath of His mouth . . . For He spake, and it was done; He commanded, and it stood fast"* (Ps. 33:6-9).

The simple fact of creation, that is if creation could be referred to as simple, demands a Creator. That is the law of all things made; consequently, the foolish idea that the Earth and all of the universe came into being as a result of blind chance, is so utterly ridiculous that it defies the explanation of stupidity.

When God created the Heavens and the Earth, we aren't told. The Scripture just says, *"in the beginning,"* and gives us no clue as to when that beginning actually was (Gen. 1:1). However, we do know that according to the Bible, man was created approximately 6,000 years ago.

The argument concerning the *"old Earth"* and *"young Earth,"* creation has raged for centuries; however, it really doesn't matter, in that God created it whenever the time.

THE PURGING OF OUR SINS

The phrase, *"When He had by Himself purged our sins,"* presents the greatest miracle of all, even greater than the miracle of creation and the sustaining of the universe. The actual Greek says, *"Having made purification of sins."*

It should be noted that the Greek Text does not read *"purification from sins,"* but *"purification of sins."* There is a difference!

"Purification from" in effect says that the sins committed have been dealt with. *"Purification of"* says that the problem of sin itself is dealt with, which is altogether different.

The idea is, when God saves a sinner, He breaks the power of the indwelling sin nature at the moment that particular sinner places his Faith in the Lord Jesus (Rom., Chpt. 6). At that moment, God removes the guilt, in effect declaring the believing sinner *"not guilty,"* which is *"Justification by Faith."* The penalty of sin is also removed, which gives the Believer a righteous standing before God. The Son of God made all of this possible when He died on the Cross.

The Cross of Christ was a once-for-all act, with continuing results, which in fact, will never be discontinued.

THE SIN QUESTION

With the statement about Jesus having effected purification of sins, Paul comes to what is for him the heart of the matter. His whole Epistle shows that the thing that had gripped him was that the very Son of God had come to deal with the problem of man's sin. He sees Him as a Priest and the essence of His priestly work as the offering of the Sacrifice that really put sin away. The Apostle has an unusual number of ways of referring to what Christ has done for man. He says:

The Saviour made a propitiation (an atoning Sacrifice) for sins (Heb. 2:17). He put sins away so that God remembers them no more (Heb. 8:12; 10:17). He bore sin (Heb. 9:28), He offered a Sacrifice for sins (Heb. 10:12), He made an offering for sin (Heb.

10:18), and brought about remission of sin (Heb. 10:18). He annulled sin by His Sacrifice (Heb. 9:26). He brought about Redemption from transgressions (Heb. 9:15).

In other Passages Paul speaks of a variety of things the former Covenant could not do with respect to sin, the implication in each case being that Christ has now done it (Heb. 10:2, 4, 6, 11). It is clear from all this that Paul sees Christ as having accomplished a total and complete Salvation, in other words, a many-sided Salvation. Whatever had to be done about sin He has done.

The word *"purification"* as Paul uses it here, refers to the removal of all sin. It also points to the defiling aspect of sin stains. Christ has effected a complete cleansing.

THE CROSS

All of this was done at the Cross. Sin is so awful, so killing, so destructive, so powerful, that only the Cross could handle the problem.

Sin appears as the power that deceives men and leads them to destruction, which influence and activity can be ended only by Sacrifice. But the usual Sacrifices could not remove sin, and as the Holy Spirit says through the Apostle, and in many and varied ways, it took *"Jesus Christ and Him Crucified"* to remove it. In Him and Him Alone are sin and sins really dealt with.

This is the reason that the Cross of Christ is the centrality of the Gospel. Before the Cross, everything streamed *toward* that Finished Work. Since the Cross, everything streams *from* that Finished Work. It is the central core of all things that pertains to God's dealings with man. If the Believer doesn't understand that, then he doesn't rightly understand Redemption, and neither does he rightly understand the Word of God. In fact, the understanding of anything as it pertains to the Lord, at least to understand it properly, requires a proper understanding of the Cross of Christ. Otherwise, everything is somewhat skewed, and to the degree that the understanding is lacking.

A FINISHED WORK

The phrase, *"Sat down on the Right Hand of the Majesty on high,"* speaks of the Finished Work of Christ. The work of the Priests

NOTES

in Old Testament times was never completed; therefore, as it regards their work, there was no chair in the Tabernacle or Temple. Sacrifices were continually offered, and because the blood of bulls and goats could not actually take away sin, only cover it. In other words, the animal sacrifices which were woefully insufficient, served only as a stopgap measure until the actual Sacrifice of the Son of God.

When Jesus finished His great Work at the Cross, it was total and complete, with Paul even referring to this Sacrifice as *"The Everlasting Covenant"* (Heb. 13:20). This means it will never have to be amended, taken from, or added to in any respect. Jesus, sitting down at the Right Hand of the Father, illustrates perfectly the completed work of the great Sacrifice carried out at Calvary.

THE HOLY SPIRIT

The Spirit hastens over the Glories of Christ as Heir of all things, even as Maker of all worlds, even as upholder of all things, even as the Revealer of all Deity in order to emphasize the Highest Glory of Christ as the Sin-purger seated on the Throne of God; consequently, the argument is: that purification of sin must have been effectual and perfect in contrast with the imperfection of the Levitical purification, for how could the Sin-purger take His seat on that Throne if sin is still attached to Him in any fashion?

Therefore, the sin penalty of death which He took on the tree, absolutely purged away all sin; therefore, He could now be seated on the Throne. This great Truth fills the heart of the Believer with a peace that nothing can overthrow.

Backup to the previous phrase, the words *"our sins,"* refer to the fact that one must express Faith in Christ and what He has done at the Cross, in order for sins to be purged. God requires that man believe (Jn. 3:16).

DIGNITY AND AUTHORITY

The words *"sat down"* denote a solemn, formal act. It speaks of the assumption of a position of dignity and authority.

The reference is to the Son's glorification and ascension. In His exalted state He is still bearing on all things toward their destined consummation, and is still dealing with sin as the Great High Priest, saving believing sinners in His Precious Blood and cleansing Saints from the defilement of sin that at times enters our lives.

But yet, His intercessory work functions totally and completely on the Finished Work of the Cross. It is not really something that He has to do, but in effect, something that He has already done, i.e., *"His Sacrifice of Himself."*

SEVEN SUPERIORITIES

With this, the inspired writer closes his argument to the effect that the Son of God is superior to the Old Testament Prophets. He has enumerated seven superiorities:

1. The Son is superior to the Old Testament Prophets in that, whereas they were the mouthpieces of God, He was God Himself speaking on Earth.

2. The Son inherits all things, the Prophets being part of that inheritance.

3. The Son created all things and is the One Who operates and manages the universe and all its creatures, all down the successive ages of time.

4. The Son is very God of very God, possessing in Himself life and light. This means that He is not merely the outshining of God's Glory, but the outshining of that Glory which in itself becomes a center from which the Glory of God actually resides.

5. The Son is the exact impression of the Person and the Character of Deity, thus its exact expression.

6. The Son carries the weight of the universe, maintains its coherence and carries on its development.

7. He has by the shedding of His Own Blood on the Cross, put away sin, which is the greatest miracle of all!

Is He better than the Prophets? Yes, infinitely so! Not one of these superiorities could be ascribed to the Old Testament Prophets, or for that matter, to any so-called ancient or modern Prophet of any religious system.

In view of the Son's superiorities over God's Prophets, what audacity it is for Modernism to place Socrates, or anyone else for that matter, alongside of the Son of God. What sacrilege to say that He was only a human being.

NOTES

The Jesus of the Gospels is the Jesus of the Epistle to the Hebrews (Heb. 2:9). Again, what a low-estimate that Israel had of its Messiah, as shown by the fact that the writer needed to demonstrate that He was superior to its Prophets. But of course, they crucified Him, so we know what they thought of Him!

(We are indebted to Kenneth Wuest for the material on the superiorities of Christ.)

(4) "BEING MADE SO MUCH BETTER THAN THE ANGELS, AS HE HATH BY INHERITANCE OBTAINED A MORE EXCELLENT NAME THAN THEY."

The exegesis of this Scripture is:

1. As Christ is so much better than the Prophets, He is also much better than the Angels.

2. The Name by which the Son has obtained through inheritance is, *"Lord"* (Phil. 2:9-11).

3. The inheritance of which here is spoken, pertains to what Christ did at the Cross, all on our behalf, that mankind might be redeemed.

BETTER THAN THE ANGELS

The phrase, *"Being made so much better than the Angels,"* proclaims the fact that the Apostle was addressing Jews, who were familiar with the important part the Angels played in the Old Testament, particularly in the giving of the Law.

The word *"made"* in the Greek is *"ginomai,"* and means *"to become."* It is in contrast to the Greek word *"poieo"* which means *"to make,"* referring *"to constructing or fashioning something out of existing materials."*

This means that the Son became better than the Angels, inferring that at one time He was lower than the Angels, which of course speaks of His Incarnation, *"God becoming man."* When the Son of God was in the stage of humanity, and we speak of the time before His glorification, He of necessity was lower than the Angels.

After He had passed through the experience of His humanity (before glorification) described in Philippians 2:6-8, He sat down on the Right Hand of the Divine Majesty as Messianic Sovereign, and thus became and was proved to be that which in reality He always was, superior to the Angels.

The superiority mentioned here, is not that of moral excellence, even though that is certainly included, but of dignity and power. He became superior to the Angels when He resumed His preincarnate dignity at His Resurrection. So, Paul is here telling us, that for a little time, i.e., *"during His Incarnation previous to His glorification, He was made lower than the Angels"* (Wuest).

THE CROSS AN ABSOLUTE NECESSITY

Everything we are reading here proclaims what Jesus did at the Cross on our behalf. This means that the Cross was an absolute necessity. In fact, the Cross was actually the destination of Christ, even planned by God from before the foundation of the world (I Pet. 1:18-20). Understanding that, we surely should recognize the absolute significance of the Cross, which of course is an understatement.

I believe I can say without any fear of exaggeration, that all false doctrine in some manner, in some way, has its beginnings in an improper understanding of the Sacrifice, or a registering of unbelief in that great Finished Work. In fact, I know that is the Truth. If one has a proper understanding of the Cross, one will have a proper understanding of everything else in the Word of God, which means that the Cross is the foundation of all Doctrine, with all Doctrine based on that Finished Work. That's the reason we have said many times, that the Cross is not a Doctrine, but is actually the foundation of all that we know, understand, and believe, at least if we properly understand Christianity.

As an example, the so-called Faith Ministry completely ignores the Cross, claiming that it was the greatest defeat in human history. They teach that Jesus Christ purchased man's Redemption, not by shedding His Precious Blood on the Cross of Calvary, in effect giving Himself, but rather by going to the burning side of Hell as a sinner, and then being born again in Hell. In fact, one of their bright lights claims that the Lord told him, that any Born-Again man could die on a Cross, and that their doing so would have the same effect as that which was done by Christ.

That is more than error. Actually, it is blasphemy!

Of course, the question must be asked, as to how anyone who calls themselves a Preacher of the Gospel, could come up with such a ridiculous interpretation. The following constitutes the reason for this:

THE FAITH MINISTRY

This particular ministry which has swept the world, had its beginnings one might say, in the 1960's. Actually, I had a part in its beginnings.

In the early 1970's airing our daily Radio Program, *"The Campmeeting Hour,"* over some 600 Stations, I began to teach this particular subject. At this time, having the greatest means of spreading this Message, our part was significant to say the least.

I taught this particular message I suppose for about two years, and then the Lord began to speak to my heart as to the error of this teaching. In fact, I actually stated over my Program that the Lord had been dealing with me about this, and that some things I had been teaching I now believed to be wrong, and felt it was my duty to proclaim that fact, which I did. I didn't know if I would lose the entirety of my audience or not, but I did know that the Lord had instructed me to take this stand, and obeying Him was what I must do. To my surprise, my audience doubled!

Among many other reasons as to why this Message is unscriptural, the greatest problem is that the Faith being taught is not Faith in the Cross of Christ, but something else altogether. It's Faith in self, Faith in Faith, or as its proponents love to claim, *"Faith in the Word!"* However, I must remind the Reader, the *"Word"* of which they speak, is a perverted word. In other words, it is the Word of God taken completely out of context, endeavoring to force it into the wishes of this great so-called Faith person. It's the age-old effort of Satan to turn Faith toward self instead of Christ. While of course, the Name of Christ is constantly used, I must remind the Reader that it's *"another Jesus"* which is being promoted, and not the Christ of the Cross (II Cor. 11:4). And let me say that again:

If it's not *"Jesus Christ and Him Crucified"* that's being promoted, then it's not the right Jesus. To separate Jesus from the Cross, is to preach *"another gospel,"* which Paul said is *"not another,"* meaning that there is no True Gospel other than *"Jesus Christ and Him Crucified"* (Gal. 1:6-7).

In fact, Paul said, *"But though we, or an Angel from Heaven, preach any other gospel unto you than that which we have preached unto you, let him be accursed"* (Gal. 1:8).

We only have to look to where the faith message has degenerated, in other words, what the fruits have been, in order to see what it is. As I've said several times previously, many tried to make this message work as it regards Divine Healing. In other words, if a person could get their Faith level up to a certain degree, then they could do away with all sickness, etc. That didn't work, and because it's unscriptural.

It has now degenerated to what I refer to as the *"greed gospel."* Everything now is centered on money. That's their message, their belief system, their Faith, in other words the *"through all"* and *"end all"* of all things — is money. They completely ignore the words of Paul where he said, *"Perverse disputings of men of corrupt minds, and destitute of the Truth, supposing that gain is Godliness: from such withdraw thyself."*

He then went on to say, *"For the love of money is the root of all evil . . . But thou, O man of God, flee these things; and follow after Righteousness, Godliness, Faith, Love, Patience, Meekness"* (I Tim. 6:5-11).

The faith message as a whole, and simply because it's not true Bible Faith, has probably done more damage to the Work of God in the last half of the Twentieth Century, than any other error. I personally think that statement is indisputable.

The problem is, despite all this teaching on Faith, erroneous I might quickly add, the Church is presently left with almost no Faith at all.

TRUE FAITH

When the Lord began to open up to me the Revelation of the Cross, at the same time He opened up to my heart the great rudiments of Faith. The central core of this which He showed me is, that our Faith, that is if it is to be true Faith which God will recognize and honor, is to always be anchored in the Cross of Christ. The Cross of Christ,

which is the Finished Work of Christ, is to always be the object of our Faith. If that is not the case, then it's not Faith that God will honor (Rom. 6:3-5, 11, 14; 8:1-2, 11, 13; 10:17).

Faith properly placed, and I speak of Faith in Jesus Christ and Him Crucified, places it where it belongs. Our Saviour is the One Who paid the price for lost humanity. Everything is in Christ; our Salvation, the mighty Baptism with the Holy Spirit, Divine Healing, prosperity of all types, and actually victory in every capacity. Consequently, if any teaching or doctrine draws us away from the centrality of Christ, and more particularly, what Christ did at the Cross, then it is obviously false.

For one to place one's Faith totally and completely in the Cross of Christ, is the same thing as placing one's Faith in the Word of God (Rom. 10:17). In fact, over and over again Paul uses the term *"the Faith,"* which speaks of the Greek definite article, specifying a particular Faith, and in this case, Faith in what Christ did at the Cross. This Faith incorporates the entire body of teaching as it concerns Christianity, and in effect, the entirety of the Bible.

The story of the Bible, with the exception of the first three Chapters in Genesis, is the story of man's Redemption. And what is the story of man's Redemption?

It is all centered up in the Cross. All the Prophets pointed toward Jesus. All of the Old Testament ceremonies, Sabbaths, Feast Days, along with the Tabernacle and the Temple, which even includes all of the sacred vessels, all and without exception, in one way or the other, pointed to Christ. And more particularly, all of these things pointed to what Jesus would do as it regards Redemption, which refers to the Cross. Therefore, when one puts one's Faith totally and completely in the Cross of Christ, one is giving proper glory to Christ for what He has done. So, when we speak of Faith, we must always correlate it with *"Jesus Christ and Him Crucified"* (I Cor. 2:2). That is the only hope of humanity. In fact, the only thing standing in-between man and eternal hell is the Cross of Christ. As well, when we speak of the Cross, we are at the same time, speaking of the Resurrection of Christ, and even His Exaltation (Rom. 6:3-14; Eph. 2:6).

OTHER ERRORS CONCERNING FAITH

In the modern Faith teaching, which we've already stated is grotesquely wrong, the emphasis is never on the object of Faith, but always in the degree of Faith. As stated, it is taught that if one can increase one's Faith, then one can get anything from God, etc. In effect, if this teaching is followed to its ultimate conclusion, man becomes a god unto himself, which is the sin of all sins.

These so-called Faith teachers hold themselves up as great examples of great Faith, etc. One sometime back, at one of their seminars where hundreds of Preachers were brought in, took these Preachers over to a hanger and showed them his jet airplane. This was the example of his great Faith, with the idea being, that if you climb up to my level, this is what you can have also.

I should remind the Reader, that in this genre there is no mention of Salvation of souls, of Believers being Baptized with the Holy Spirit, of the sick truly being healed, and of lives truly being changed. It's all centered, as said, on money.

So, these gurus hold themselves up on a pedestal, with the fawning masses encouraged to look up to their heroes, hoping that someday they might have at least a part of this great Faith, which will bring to them all type of good things.

The Truth is, Faith is not difficult. And by that I mean, true Faith in God is available to all, and not just a few.

In fact, Faith is very simple, actually meaning to simply believe. If one believes the Lord and His Word, one is exercising Faith. Actually, one doesn't even have to understand every single thing about the great Promises of God in order to exercise Faith. To be truthful, no one understands everything about these great Promises, considering that they are given by God. But Faith even though definitely demanding some knowledge, does not demand total knowledge. If it did, none of us would qualify.

All the Believer has to do is just simply believe the Lord, which means to believe His Word, and that is Faith. Anyone can have

NOTES

that. So it's really not the great amount of Faith that one has, but rather the object of our Faith which is really the important thing. That of course must be the Finished Work of Christ, i.e., *"the Cross of Christ."*

THE HOLY SPIRIT

As I've already said many times in other Commentaries, and will no doubt say it many more times even in this Commentary, the Holy Spirit works exclusively within the parameters of the great Sacrifice of Christ. Before the Cross, the Holy Spirit could not come in to abide permanently within the hearts and lives of Believers (Jn. 14:17). While He definitely helped Believers, and in every capacity, He could only do so by being *"with"* Believers, instead of being *"in"* Believers (Jn. 14:17).

The reason that the Holy Spirit could not come in to permanently abide, was because the terrible sin debt hanging over man, even the great champions of the Faith of the Old Testament, had not yet been paid. The blood of bulls and goats, which we will later study in detail in this very Epistle, could not take away sin, but only cover it after a fashion. The sin debt remained! As a result, whenever Believers in Old Testament times died, they could not be taken to Heaven, but were actually taken captive by Satan down into Paradise. Even though they were not in the burning side of Hell, they were still captives of Satan. That's the reason that Paul said concerning the Crucifixion and Resurrection of Christ, *"Now that He ascended* (back to Heaven after the Resurrection), *what is it but that He also descended first into the lower parts of the Earth?"* (Eph. 4:9). And what did He do there?

Paul also said, *"He led captivity captive, and gave gifts unto men"* (Eph. 4:8).

This means that all the Old Testament Saints which had literally been held captive by Satan in Paradise, were now set free from that captivity, actually now being made captives of Christ. He could do this, simply because the legal debt had now been legally paid. Now the Holy Spirit is free to come into the hearts and lives of Believers and to permanently abide.

This is all because of Jesus Christ and what He did at the Cross. In the eyes of God, every

Believer is perfect in every way, and because of our Faith in the Cross of Christ, we are *"in Christ,"* which means that we also have His perfection. As stated, everything is in Christ! (Rom. 6:3-5).

Jesus said of the Holy Spirit, *"Howbeit when He, the Spirit of Truth is come, He will guide you into all Truth: for He shall not speak of Himself . . . He shall glorify Me: for He shall receive of Mine, and shall show it unto you"* (Jn. 16:13-14).

Christ is speaking here totally and solely of what He did at the Cross, and how the Holy Spirit will make all its benefits real to the Believer, that is, if proper Faith is evidenced.

Inasmuch as the Holy Spirit works exclusively within the Finished Work of Christ, that means that He will not work outside of that Sacrifice. So, if we place Faith in anything, and I mean anything, other than the Cross of Christ, we have just closed the door to the Holy Spirit. While He definitely continues to abide within our hearts and lives, He cannot function in the capacity of error, so He withdraws. So, if one wants His help, and to be sure, anything and everything done for us by the Lord always comes through the Person and Ministry of the Holy Spirit, we then must evidence Faith in the Finished Work of Christ (Rom. 8:1-2, 11, 13).

THE ETERNAL SONSHIP OF CHRIST?

The Bible, I think, does not teach the eternal Sonship of Christ. While it definitely does teach the eternal Godhead of Christ, it does not teach eternal Sonship.

In fact, *"Sonship"* pertains to the Incarnation and, therefore, the Redemption of mankind. At a point in time, God became *"the Son,"* in order to give Himself in the form of humanity on the Cross, to bring about Redemption (Phil. 2:5-11).

This Sonship is referred to by Paul in the Old Testament, where the Messiah, then future, was spoken of as *"Son."* Paul, in support of this fact of Sonship, then gives us an abundance of evidence in these particular Passages before us in this First Chapter, actually citing several Scriptures. In the Fifth Verse, Paul actually cites the Scripture which tells us that One of the Persons of the Trinity, became the Son, and did so at a certain

NOTES

time, of which we will have more to say momentarily.

WHY THE COMPARISON BETWEEN THE SON AND ANGELS?

The answer is as follows:

The entire Old Testament Dispensation is related to the New Testament Dispensation as the Angels are related to the Son. In the former Dispensation, mankind and God are separated by sin. The Angels in a sense, stand as mediators between God and man. At that time, there was a chain of two links, Moses, and the Angel of the Lord.

In this capacity, and I continue to speak of Old Testament times, we have a mere man (Moses) raised above his fellows by being given a commission to lead Israel, and to thereby bring them nearer to God. But sadly so, he is a sinner like his Brethren. So, in a sense, we see God in Old Testament times, revealing Himself in angelic form, one might say to Israel, but without becoming Man. Consequently, there was no real union of the Godhead and Manhood.

THE NEW TESTAMENT DISPENSATION

How different it is in the New Testament Dispensation. God and Man become Personally One in the Son Incarnate. God no longer accommodates Himself to the capacities of man in Angel form or manifestations of Himself in other ways, but has revealed Himself in the Son become Incarnate.

Paul's thought throughout this Epistle is that the New Testament is better than the Old Testament. If he can show that the One Mediator between God and man of the New Testament is superior to the mediators of the First, who were in a sense the Angels and Moses, then he has shown that the New Testament takes the place of the First. And this he proceeds to do (Wuest).

The whole idea here is that Christ has put away sins by His Death on the Cross, and is now sat down on the Throne in the place of highest honor, and it is in this aspect that He is seen as greater than any Angel. Naturally, Christ has always been greater than any Angel, in fact, infinitely greater. He is the Creator, while they are mere creatures, actually created by His Hand.

But Paul is bringing out here the great Redemption process of Christ, with God becoming man, and in this capacity, of which the Apostle is actually speaking, He is seen as greater than any Angel. Angels could not redeem humanity, but He could and did!

INHERITANCE

The phrase, *"As He hath by inheritance obtained a more excellent Name than they,"* refers to what Christ did at the Cross, with the present result that the inheritance is in His permanent possession. Paul is speaking of a past completed action, and of the present abiding results, results in fact, which will never end.

As we've said over and over, the Cross is a past completed action, which has continued results, and in fact, results which will never be discontinued.

The idea is, that the title *"The Son of God"* is to be given to Him Alone. It has been conferred on no others. Though the Angels, and though Saints in general are called *"sons of God,"* yet the title *"The Son of God"* has been given to Him only.

However, let it be understood, that this *"inheritance"* of *"a more excellent Name than the Angels,"* did not come to Him because of the fact of His Deity, for that has always been, but rather because of what He did at the Cross. Actually, everything said here pertains to the Cross in some manner.

THE ERROR AGAINST WHICH PAUL CONTENDED

Whereas the fundamentalist sector of the modern Church has no problem with the Deity of Christ, but rather with the Cross, the Jews of course, had great problems with Christ in any capacity. In fact, this unbelief rubbed off on believing Jews, which occasioned this Epistle to the Hebrews.

This tells us that the most dangerous and persistent error against which Paul and other Apostles had to contend, was the doctrine of emanations. This doctrine sprang from Gnosticism, which teaches that a Holy God could not have brought an evil universe into existence. Otherwise, one is driven, they claim, to the inescapable conclusion that God created evil, which is impossible, since He is altogether Holy.

So they explain all of this by claiming that God created the world and all that therein is, by a series of emanations. In other words, there was a germination from God, and this first germination evolved a second, and then a third, and so the process went on. The more numerous the emanations, the farther away from Deity they became, until finally the furthest emanation was far enough away, that the work of creation could be carried out through him without it affecting God. Thus, the gap between a Holy Creator God and matter which, according to the Gnostic is evil, is bridged by these emanations.

Believing that all matter is evil, they taught that Jesus fell into the same category because He was made up of flesh, which is matter, and, therefore, evil. Therefore, He couldn't be the Son of God.

In this way, the Gnostic brushes aside the Lord Jesus as Creator, and as well, the fact that God put a curse upon the perfect creation because of sin (Rom. 8:20). Paul says in the Romans Text that the creation was made subject to futility (vanity). That is, as a result of the Fall, God rendered it relatively futile so far as glorifying Him was concerned (Wuest).

The persistence of this error as it regards Christianity, lay in the contrast between the Christian conception of mediation between God and men, Who is Jesus Christ, and another mediation altogether, which in fact is no other (Gal. 1:6-7). Its danger sprang from its complete inconsistency with the Christian idea of the Person and Work of the Mediator. In fact, the Hebrew conception of God, as the *"I Am,"* tended more and more in the lapse of ages to sever Him from all immediate contact with created beings.

It would be the natural boast of the Jews that Jehovah dwelt in unapproachable light. They would point to the contrast between Him and the human gods of the Greeks, in effect, putting Jesus in the same categories of these false deities, which fabrication they hold to unto this present hour.

Consequently, in view of the fact that the Jews had come to the place of an entirely, erroneous view of God, this at least in part fueled their rejection of Christ. They could not, or perhaps it would be better to say, they would not accept the fact that God became flesh and dwelt among men (Jn. 1:14). So they somewhat bought into this Gnostic error of Angels being mediators, carrying it over from the Old Testament. Of course, there was much more to their rejection of Christ than this particular problem, but it definitely did enter into their thinking. Consequently, Paul here in the Text of our study, addresses the Angels in relationship to *"The Son."*

(5) "FOR UNTO WHICH OF THE ANGELS SAID HE AT ANY TIME, THOU ART MY SON, THIS DAY HAVE I BEGOTTEN THEE? AND AGAIN, I WILL BE TO HIM A FATHER, AND HE SHALL BE TO ME A SON?"

The breakdown of this Passage is as follows:

1. The supremacy of Christ over Angels.
2. The begetting of the Son.
3. This begetting as it regarded the Incarnation did not lessen the relationship of Christ to the Father or His Deity.

ANGELS AND SONSHIP

The question, *"For unto which of the Angels said He at any time, Thou art My Son . . .?"*, refers to a denial of the fact that the Angels were ever given the name *"Son,"* and he follows that by bringing to the attention of his Jewish Readers several quotations from the Old Testament Scriptures. The answer to the questions in Verses 5 through 13 is, that God never spoke such words to an Angel, however exalted, but only to His Son the Messiah.

That the appellation *"sons of God"* may be used in an inferior sense, and thus that Angels may be so designated (Job 1:6; 38:7), does not affect this argument; for every Reader must perceive that in these Scriptural quotations given by Paul, *"Son"* is used of One, and in a sense that is unique.

THE BEGETTING OF CHRIST

The phrase, *"This day have I begotten Thee,"* is derived from Psalms 2:7. God never said such of Angels, only of His Son.

While Christ has always been God, and, as such, had no beginning, was not formed, created, or begotten, but, in fact, has always been (Jn. 1:1), the great question is, *"Has Christ always been the Son of God?"*

When the *"Sonship"* of Christ is addressed, it always refers to His humanity, and never to

His Deity. As stated, as God, our Lord had no beginning; however, as a Man, He most definitely did have a beginning (Isa. 7:14). In fact, when God became a Man, in essence, one might say that the Creator became a Creature, for Jesus definitely was the Creator (Jn. 1:1-3). This is beyond our comprehension. We might quickly add that God became a Man for the express purpose of going to the Cross, and for that purpose alone. It was in this manner that man was to be redeemed, and only in this manner. God, being Spirit, cannot die. So, in order to die, as stated, God would have to become Man, which He did.

When God became a Man, The Man Christ Jesus, He never for a moment lost the full potential and possession of His Deity; however, He most definitely did lose the expression of His Deity, and did so purposely. But losing the expression of His Deity in no way lessened the possession of His Deity. He was Very God while, at the same time, He was Very Man. This means that He wasn't half-God and half-Man, but rather, fully God and fully Man, The God-Man, Jesus Christ.

When Jesus was born into the world as a Man, He was then begotten, and was God's Son (Ps. 2:7, 12; Mat. 1:18-25; Lk. 1:35; Heb. 1:5-6). He is now the Son of God and, in fact, will remain the Son of God forever and forever. This was all done for us, God becoming Man, in order that we might be redeemed (Gal. 1:3-4).

FATHER AND SON

The phrase, *"And again, I will be to Him a Father, and He shall be to Me a Son,"* is derived from II Samuel 7:14. Again, the words *"I will be"* and *"He shall be"* refer to a future tense which was yet to come to pass at the time it was spoken, which was during the days of David. This means that at the particular time the prophecy was uttered, God was not known as *"Father"* or as *"Son,"* at least in the capacity of that which we speak here.

The entire Doctrine of *"Father"* and *"Son"* and *"Son of God,"* as well as *"Christ"* and *"Jesus,"* etc., has to do exclusively with the Redemption process. In order to redeem humanity, God would have to become man, would have to die on a Cross, and be raised from the dead, and then exalted at the Right Hand of God (Jn. 1:1, 14, 29; Rom. 6:3-5; Eph. 2:6). Consequently, when we think of the magnitude of such a thing, it humbles us to say the least!

As someone has well said, the Trinity, at least as we understand such, may well have to do totally with Redemption. We do know there is one God, but manifested in three Persons, *"God the Father, God the Son, and God the Holy Spirit."* Whether God was addressed in such terms before the Fall of man and the subsequent Redemption, we have no clue. But this we do know:

The designations by which we now know God, which we have just quoted, will remain forever. Paul plainly says that all of this is *"the Everlasting Covenant"* (Heb. 13:20).

(6) "AND AGAIN, WHEN HE BRINGETH IN THE FIRSTBEGOTTEN INTO THE WORLD, HE SAITH, AND LET ALL THE ANGELS OF GOD WORSHIP HIM."

The exposition of this Scripture is as follows:

1. *"Firstbegotten"* or *"firstborn"* describes in this case, the relationship between Messiah the Son, and God the Father.

2. This Passage as well, describes a particular time which this would be, which actually refers to the Birth of Christ.

3. Even though He took upon Himself at this time, the form of a servant, and was made in the likeness of men, which was lower than the Angels, still, the Angels of God worshiped Him no less, and because He, although now human, was also Deity. In other words, His Deity did not diminish at all. While He was *"Very Man,"* He was also *"Very God."*

THE FIRSTBEGOTTEN

The phrase, *"And again, when He bringeth in the firstbegotten into the world,"* refers to Jesus being born of the Virgin Mary, in other words, the time of His First Advent.

Some have attempted to claim that the words *"and again"* means that God is referring to the Second Coming of the Lord; however, that is incorrect. *"And again"* is used here exactly as it is in the previous Verse, simply meaning that Paul is quoting another Scripture referring to the predictions of the coming Christ as given in the Old Testament.

The word *"firstbegotten"* proclaims the

fact that God had never taken on this form before, which is the form of humanity, or any other form of similar nature (Phil. 2:5-11).

When one attempts to understand the great Redemption Plan, one is left aghast. First of all, that God would go to these lengths to save lost humanity is beyond comprehension, especially considering that we're speaking of humanity who in effect hates Him. However, two words can probably explain this great Redemption plan more so than anything else.

The first is *"Love,"* which means that Love created humanity, and Love had to redeem humanity.

The second word is the "Cross," which refers to the manner and way in which this great Redemption Plan was brought about. And in effect, the *"Cross"* is the greatest exhibition of *"Love"* that mankind has ever known, and will ever know. And as well, the Cross is of such moment, such significance, and carries such place with God, that Christ in eternity future, will ever be proclaimed as the *"Lamb"* signifying that momentous occasion (Rev. 21:9, 14, 22-23, 27; 22:1, 3). As well, Paul refers to the Cross as *"The Everlasting Covenant"* (Heb. 13:20). So, if the Word of God places the Cross in such a central position, should not we as Believers take the same position?

THE CHRISTIAN AND THE CROSS

As we've said over and over again, the Church has had almost no teaching on the Cross in the last several decades. Consequently, we now have a Church which really does not know where it is, where it's been, or where it's going. Understanding that the Cross of Christ is the Foundation of the Church, and that all Doctrine must be built upon that premise, which is actually the story of the Word of God, and knowing that the Church as a whole little understands this, it is easy to see the cause of the modern drift into apostasy. If the house is built upon the Rock, the house will stand. Otherwise, it will fall (Mat. 7:24-27). The *"Rock"* is Christ, and if the Believer doesn't understand Christ in the realm of the Cross, i.e., *"Jesus Christ and Him Crucified,"* then the Believer doesn't really understand Christ, but in reality is believing *"another Jesus"* (II Cor. 11:4).

The Believer must understand that every

single thing as it relates to God begins with the Sacrifice of Christ, i.e., *"the Cross"* (Rom. 6:3-5; 8:1-2; Gal. 6:14). In fact, after the Fall, the entirety of God's relationship with man, and man's relationship with God, are centered up in the Sacrifice. Genesis, Chapter 4 graphically proclaims this fact. Abel offered up an innocent victim, a slain lamb, as an offering to God, which was a type of the coming Christ, and actually the manner in which God had designed until Christ actually came. God accepted that Sacrifice, and because it predicted Christ.

The Lord would not accept the sacrifice of Cain, which constituted vegetables or whatever, i.e., *"the labor of his own hands."* Of course every Bible student knows that Cain then murdered Abel, which example of the entirety of this scenario sets the stage for which was to follow, and continues unto this hour.

God's solution to fallen humanity is *"Jesus Christ and Him Crucified,"* and that is the only solution. Satan has ever attempted to offer up other solutions, and to be sure, He does His best work within the Church.

The only thing that makes the Church a viable institution is the Cross of Christ. If it does not believe the Cross, preach the Cross, thereby proclaiming the Cross as the only answer to the ills of mankind, then the Church is of no worth. Paul said, *"But we preach Christ Crucified"* (I Cor. 1:23).

THE WORD OF THE CROSS

In I Corinthians 1:18, the Holy Spirit through Paul said, *"For the preaching of the Cross is to them that perish foolishness; but unto us which are saved it is the Power of God."*

The Greek word translated *"preaching"* is *"Logos."* It means *"Word"*; consequently, it should have been translated, *"For the Word of the Cross is to them that perish foolishness. . . ."*

The word *"preaching"* in I Corinthians 1:21, however, is a different Greek word, and is there correctly translated.

"The Word of the Cross" is a much more powerful statement than *"the preaching of the Cross."* The phrase *"Word of the Cross"* incorporates the entirety of all Christian Faith. It presents the foundation of all that we believe. And to the degree that the Believer

misunderstands this *"Word of the Cross,"* to that degree, the Believer will suffer harm and hurt in some way.

One might even say that the *"Word of the Cross"* is the Bible. It is for sure the story of the Bible, which is the story of man's Redemption.

To bring this about, God would have to become man, hence the terminology *"the Firstbegotten."*

THE WORLD

The phrase *"the world"* as Paul uses it here, refers to *"the inhabited Earth."*

Of all the creation of God, this world is the only part of that creation, at least as far as we know, which is out of harmony with Him.

Before Lucifer's rebellion against God, which took place sometime in eternity past, there is some thought as evidenced in Isaiah, Chapter 14, that he ruled under God, this planet called Earth (Isa. 14:12-15).

With his revolution everything was destroyed, which characterizes Genesis 1:2. The Lord then brought this destroyed world back into a habitable state, as proclaimed in Genesis, Chapter 1. Newly created man, actually created higher than the Angels, was given dominion of this Earth (Gen. 1:28; Ps., Chpt. 8). Satan immediately set about to take this dominion away from Adam, which he did by subterfuge, deception, and lies (Gen. 3:1-7). Consequently, Satan from then forward, controls this world's system, thereby the cause of all sickness, death, pain, suffering, sorrow, poverty, ignorance, war, etc.

So, when Adam and Eve fell, they actually entered into a rebellion against God that had long since begun under Lucifer. This rebellion was in fact so severe and so powerful, that it took the Cross of Christ to address the situation. Even then, the full import of what Jesus did at the Cross will not be realized, until the coming Resurrection of Life when *"this corruptible must (shall) put on incorruption, and this mortal must (shall) put on immortality."*

At that time, *"death will be swallowed up in victory"* (I Cor. 15:53-54).

The Cross was a necessity if man was to be cleansed from sin; however, sin is so powerful, that it has even corrupted the material substance of this planet. Consequently, God will one day cleanse the Heavens and the Earth with fire. Peter said:

"Nevertheless we, according to His Promise, look for new Heavens and a new Earth, wherein dwelleth Righteousness" (II Pet. 3:12-13).

In respect to that, John the Beloved on the Isle of Pathos said, as God gave him a preview of the future, *"And I saw a new Heaven and a new Earth: for the first Heaven and the first Earth were passed away; and there was no more Sea."*

John then said, *"And I . . . saw the holy city, New Jerusalem, coming down from God out of Heaven, prepared as a bride adorned for her husband"* (Rev. 21:1-2).

In effect, God is going to transfer His Headquarters from Heaven to Earth. As the song says:

"What a day that will be!"

John then said, *"And God shall wipe away all tears from their eyes; and there shall be no more death, neither sorrow, nor crying, neither shall there by any more pain: for the former things are passed away"* (Rev. 21:4).

It took and takes the Cross to bring all of this about; consequently, that's the reason that we say its potential will never be exhausted.

WORSHIP

The phrase, *"He saith, and let all the Angels of God worship Him,"* is quoted by Paul from Psalms 97:7: *"Confounded be all they that serve graven images, that boast themselves of idols: worship Him, all ye gods."* The word *"gods"* as it is used here, comes from the Hebrew word *"Elohim,"* and can be translated *"God"* or *"Angels."* In fact, two Jewish Rabbins of distinction — Raschi and Kimchi — affirm, that all the Psalms, from 93 to 101 are to be regarded as referring to the Messiah. In fact, the entirety of the Psalms refer to the Messiah!

The idea is, only Deity can be worshipped, and considering that the Angels worshipped Him and do worship Him, contains but another example of the many proofs of His Deity.

Concerning worship, Satan demands that all his followers worship him, which speaks of all of mankind which isn't redeemed. In some manner, all sin is a form of worship of Satan. Consequently, all sinners worship him, whether they realize such or not!

NOTES

As well, and of course, God demands worship, and because He is rightly due all worship. He as the Creator of all things must be paid such homage.

And to be sure, the worship with He demands is not the result of an inflated ego, as it is with Satan and men. In fact, all worship of God is for our good, and not His. Why would God need worship from us, when He already has at least a hundred trillion Angels worshipping Him? (Rev. 5:11-14).

Worship is what we are, while praise is what we do. Every single thing that the Believer does, whether it be spiritual, or that which we refer to as secular, or whatever, is to be in some way, worship of God. While all praise is worship, all worship is not necessarily praise. However, if a Believer sins, we all know that such is not worship of God, but actually of Satan. Understanding that, we begin to realize how bad and how awful that sin actually is.

To the true Believer, worship of Satan is abhorrent. And yet, let us all understand, that all sin is actually worship of Satan. So when the Christian sins, he is doing the same thing as his unredeemed counterparts in the world, worshipping Satan!

(7) "AND OF THE ANGELS HE SAITH, WHO MAKETH HIS ANGELS SPIRITS, AND HIS MINISTERS A FLAME OF FIRE."

The exegesis is:

1. Paul continues to address himself to Angels and their inferiority to the Son of God.

2. God made the Angels according to the needs of His service, and being such as they are, they are changeable, in marked contrast to the Son Who is their ruler, and, therefore, unchangeable.

3. Since the Messiah is the Creator and Master of Angels, He is superior to them, which fact makes the New Testament superior to the First which it displaces.

ANGELS

The phrase, *"And of the Angels He saith,"* presents the Apostle continuing in the vein of Angels, proving to the Jews that Christ is superior to such, and doing it from the Scriptures of the Old Testament which they professed to believe.

If one follows Paul's writings, one notices him constantly using the Old Testament

Scriptures. Of course, that is understandable, inasmuch as the Old Testament was the Bible in those days. But the point I wish to make is, everything we find in the New Testament, has its seedbed in the Old, which always points toward the New. So, if the Believer doesn't understand the Old Testament, then it is virtually impossible for him to understand the New.

Everything in the Old Testament shadows and types Christ in some manner. All the prophecies pointed toward Him, as did all the Ceremonies speak of Him, with the various items of the Tabernacle and the Temple, being shadows and types of Him. And more particularly, the entirety of the Old Testament refers to the Sacrifice of Christ. In fact, the Sacrificial System of the Old Testament was the central core of that means and ways, which of course typified Redemption.

SPIRITS

The phrase, *"Who maketh His Angels spirits,"* is taken from Psalms 104:4.

"Spirits" in the Greek is *"pneuma,"* and means *"wind, spirit, messenger."* Here the meaning is *"winds."* The emphasis is upon the variableness of the Angelic nature. They are what they are at any time by the decree of God, fitted by their character to any special service.

This means they can be sent in any form, function in any capacity, and perform any deed. They always do the bidding of the Lord, no more, no less!

MINISTERS

The phrase, *"And His Ministers a flame of fire,"* does not speak of Preachers of the Gospel as it has been suggested by some, but continues to address itself to Angels, even as the beginning of this Scripture proclaims. *"Ministers"* as used here, is the same as *"Angels."*

All of this means that Angels are prompt to do the Will of God — rapid, quick, obedient in His service; they are, in all respects, subordinate to Him, and occupy, as the winds and the lightenings do, the place of servants. They are never addressed in language like that which is applied to the Son of God, and they must all be far inferior to Him.

NOTES

(8) "BUT UNTO THE SON HE SAITH, THY THRONE, O GOD, IS FOR EVER AND EVER: A SCEPTRE OF RIGHTEOUSNESS IS THE SCEPTRE OF THY KINGDOM."

The breakdown is as follows:

1. The Holy Spirit now addresses the Son of God and His total superiority.

2. He is referred to as God, and occupies the Throne, which speaks of total dominion and rulership, which will be forever and ever.

3. His Sceptre represents the emblem of His Kingly Office and Power. His Kingdom is a Kingdom of Righteousness.

THE SON

The phrase, *"But unto the Son He saith,"* now refers to the Holy Spirit, as stated, speaking of the Son, as He had previously spoken of the Angels. He will now show the vast superiority of the Son, in fact, so vast, that it is beyond comprehension. We are speaking now of the Creator, whereas we were previously speaking of the creation.

Going back to Verse 5, the phrase *"Thou art My Son,"* appears to be the Divine formula for the Anointing of Christ as Prophet (Mat. 3:17), as Priest (Mat. 17:5), and as King (Ps. 2:7). His Glories in eternity as Son of God are set out in Verses 2 and 3, and His Glories as Son of God in time in Verses 3 through 13.

The Godhead of Jesus is declared by the Holy Spirit in Verses 3, 8, and 10; but the special beauty and wonder of this Truth is based here upon Psalms that contain the most complete expressions in Scripture of the consciousness which Jesus had of His weakness as man, of His dependence on Jehovah, and of the certitude that He was to be cut off in the midst of His days, which speaks of the Crucifixion.

THE THRONE OF GOD

The phrase, *"Thy Throne, O God, is for ever and ever,"* is taken from Psalms 45:6-7.

A Throne is the seat on which a Monarch sits, and is here the symbol of dominion, because kings, when acting as rulers, sit on thrones. Thus, a throne becomes the emblem of authority or empire. Here it means, that His rule or dominion would be perpetual — *"forever and ever"* — which assuredly could not be applied to any mortal.

By the use of the Name *"God"* as applied to the Messiah, it proves what the Apostle is aiming to prove — that He is above the Angels. The argument is that a Name is given to Him which is never given to them. They are not called God in any strict and proper sense. The idea is, Jesus Christ is God!

As well, the Throne mentioned here applies not only to Heaven but as well, to Earth. Concerning the earthly realm, it is taken from II Samuel 7:13, *"He shall build an house for My Name, and I will stablish the Throne of His Kingdom for ever."* As stated, Jesus Christ is *"Prophet, Priest, and King."* But all of these designations apply to His humanity as our Representative Man. As we've stated, Jesus had to become the *"Last Adam"* in order to undo what the original Adam did (I Cor. 15:45-50). Inasmuch as the original promises were made to Israel, and that these people were raised up for the very purpose of bringing the Redeemer into the world, it is in a sense through them that He will reign as *"Prophet, Priest, and King."* The Scripture actually says that *"the testimony of Jesus is the spirit of prophecy"* (Rev. 19:10). As well, Paul also said that Christ is the *"High Priest of our profession"* (Heb. 3:1; 4:14). The Priests of the old Jewish economy, were but types of Christ, and were meant to serve in that capacity.

As *"King,"* Jesus will reign over Israel, and thereby the world, in the coming Kingdom Age.

RIGHTEOUSNESS

The phrase, *"A Sceptre of Righteousness is the Sceptre of Thy Kingdom,"* speaks of the manner of His Kingdom. It is totally unlike any other Kingdom which has ever existed.

"Righteousness" as used in this Verse is from the Greek *"euthutetos"* and means *"rectitude, uprightness."*

"Sceptre" represents the emblem of His Power, and refers to the fact that this Throne is His by two means: A. The means of His Deity; and, B. The means of His inheritance (vs. 4). It refers to Heaven as to His Deity, and to Earth as it regards His humanity.

The idea is, Righteousness itself (so to speak, the very ideal of righteous Government) bears sway in His Kingdom. As stated, this

proclaims the fact that there has never been another kingdom such as this.

(9) "THOU HAST LOVED RIGHTEOUSNESS, AND HATED INIQUITY; THEREFORE GOD, EVEN THY GOD, HATH ANOINTED THEE WITH THE OIL OF GLADNESS ABOVE THY FELLOWS."

The exegesis is as follows:

1. The Holy Spirit continues to speak of Jesus as the Messiah. As a Man, The Man Christ Jesus, He portrayed a living Righteousness, in effect the Righteousness of God, which means that He gained the Righteousness of the Law, by keeping it perfectly. All of this was done as our Representative Man. As well, to the degree that He loved Righteousness, and in fact was Righteousness, to that degree He hated iniquity.

2. As a result of His perfection, the Holy Spirit occupied and controlled Him in a manner which can be said of no other. In the Ministry, Work, Operation, and Person of the Holy Spirit, He was *"above all His fellows,"* meaning that the Holy Spirit has never been able to work through anyone as He was able to work through Christ.

RIGHTEOUSNESS

The phrase, *"Thou hast loved Righteousness, and hated iniquity,"* proclaims the True Man, Christ Jesus. Christ was the True Israel, is the True Man, and is the True Church.

The word *"Righteousness"* in this Verse is the translation of the Greek *"dikaiosune,"* which means *"that which conforms to a standard or norm which is itself in keeping with what God is in His Holy Character"* (Wuest).

In essence, *"Righteousness"* is that which is right; however, it is that which God deems as *"right"* and not man. As well, if one truly loves Righteousness, one at the same time, will truly hate iniquity, which is the antithesis of Righteousness.

Deity is Righteousness and can be no other way. Actually, it is impossible for God to be anything but Righteous, i.e., *"Righteousness."* But when God became man, He had to be perfectly righteous in every respect, but not in the realm of Deity. As someone has well said, when God became man, He laid aside the expression of His Deity, while never losing the possession of His Deity.

And it must be understood, if He was to be the *"Last Adam,"* then the possibility of unrighteousness on His part had to be a factor. Otherwise, He could not have been the *"Last Adam!"* Many deny this claiming that it would have been impossible for Jesus to have sinned; however, had that been the case, Satan would not have wasted his time regarding the temptations of Christ (Mat., Chpt. 4).

No! Christ as the Representative Man, had to be subject to all temptations like as we are, but yet without sin (Heb. 4:15). In other words, He must not fail, meaning that it was possible for Him to fail; however, He did not fail!

The Law of God as given to Moses, was God's Standard of Righteousness for mankind, and in fact still is. Many people think that with the Day of Grace which we are now in, that this Law is no more. While it is certainly true that Jesus satisfied all its demands, both in His Life and Death, still, considering that the Law of Moses was a moral law, such cannot change. If it was wrong to steal 3,000 years ago, it's wrong presently!

The only people in the world on which the Law has no claim, are those who have trusted Christ. As it regards all others, they will answer to God at the great White Throne Judgment regarding its precepts, that is if they do not accept Christ.

There is a Righteousness in the Law, but for one to acquire that Righteousness, total and perfect obedience are demanded. No human being could ever do that, but Jesus did do that, meaning that He kept the Law perfectly, and did it all on our behalf. Simple Faith in Him, changes us from Lawbreakers to Law-keepers. In other words, our Faith in Him, causes God to look at us not only in the capacity of perfect Law-keepers presently, but actually as if we have never broken the Law.

PLEASING GOD

At the Baptism of Christ, the Scripture says, *"And lo a voice from Heaven saying, 'This is My Beloved Son, in Whom I am well pleased'"* (Mat. 3:17).

This means that Christ is the only human being of which God has made such a statement in this way. Consequently, the only way that God will be pleased with any individual,

irrespective as to what they might do, is for that person to be *"in Christ"* (Rom. 6:3-5). In fact, this is the upshot of the Gospel.

Individuals attempt to please God by other means than Christ, or else they attempt to force the issue, which of course, God will never accept. He is pleased only with His Son, and our Redeemer, the Lord Jesus Christ, and if we desire God to be pleased with us, we have to do it God's Way. That *"Way"* is to trust exclusively in what Christ has done at the Cross on our behalf, placing our Faith totally in that Finished Work. Then God is pleased, and only then!

THE OIL OF GLADNESS

The phrase, *"Therefore God, even Thy God, hath anointed Thee with the oil of gladness above Thy fellows,"* refers to the Holy Spirit.

"Anointed" is the translation of the Greek *"chrio"* which is always used in the New Testament of the Anointing with the Holy Spirit.

"Oil" in the Greek is *"aleipho,"* but here has a different meaning than usual. Here the oil of joy refers not to literal oil as usual with this particular Greek word, but to the Holy Spirit Who bestows joy, and thus the Greek word *"chrio,"* is used fittingly here.

Our Lord was anointed with the Holy Spirit for His threefold Office of Prophet, Priest, and King, at His Baptism in the River Jordan, which was at the time of His entrance into His Ministry.

The word *"fellows"* as it is used here, refers to the Angels as co-participants with the Messiah in His work of Salvation, and future sovereignty over the redeemed creation. The emphasis of the Passage is upon the fact that Messiah's future Kingdom is an eternal one, and that He as the Anointed King will rule in Righteousness. Isaiah, Chapter 11 speaks of His Millennial Reign and of the fact that He will be the King anointed with the Spirit. As such, the Angels will be associated with Him in that Reign, but He will be their sovereign Lord, they His servants. All of which again means that the Messiah is far better than the Angels (Wuest).

Some have claimed that the word *"fellows"* refers to other kings; however, I don't really think they are worthy of consideration as compared to the Messiah. I doubt very seriously that the Holy Spirit would go to the trouble of even recognizing earthly kings, as being worthy to be compared in any measure with the Son of God. No, as stated, I think the Holy Spirit through Paul, is referring to Angels when He uses the word *"fellows,"* which harks back to what He's been saying about that particular creation.

GLADNESS

"Gladness" in the Greek is *"agalliasis,"* and means *"exultation and exceeding joy."*

The idea as presented here, is not so much the gladness which He possesses, but rather the gladness which He dispenses. Finding Christ, knowing Christ and serving Christ, presents the greatest joy that one could ever begin to know.

Upon one's acceptance of Christ, the umbilical cord so to speak, between God and man is restored. One might say that the *"life-support system"* is once again in working order. Man was created by God, and can only be sustained by God.

While man may exist in a physical state without God, at least for a period of time, he can have no real life. As well, let it be understood, that the only way that man can reach God, can know God, can restore this life-support system so to speak, is through Jesus Christ. Anyone attempting to go in any other direction is classified by God as *"a thief and a robber"* (Jn. 10:1). Jesus plainly said, *"I am the Door: by Me if any man enter in, he shall be saved, and shall go in and out, and find pasture"* (Jn. 10:9).

As well, by Jesus using the symbolism of the *"Door,"* He was referring back to the blood that was applied to the doorposts upon the deliverance of Israel from Egypt (Ex. 12:13). The blood came from a slain lamb, which had been used in the Passover, and which represented the coming Redeemer Who would give His Life on the Cross, in order that man might be saved. The idea is this:

Jesus is the Door to the Father; however, it must be understood that it is *"Jesus Christ and Him Crucified"* (I Cor. 2:2).

While the *"Healing Jesus,"* or the *"Miracle Jesus,"* or the *"Blessing Jesus,"* are all well and good and very desirable; still, it is only

the *"Crucified Jesus"* which the Word of God presents. Let me say it another way:

The one who accepts the *"Crucified Jesus"* gets everything. The one who doesn't accept the *"Crucified Jesus,"* gets nothing!

This means that the Preachers who have rejected the *"Crucified Jesus,"* despite all their bluster and blow about miracles, are in fact receiving nothing. It is the *"bloody door"* or else it is a door that doesn't lead to God!

(10) "AND, THOU, LORD, IN THE BEGINNING HAST LAID THE FOUNDATION OF THE EARTH; AND THE HEAVENS ARE THE WORKS OF THINE HANDS:"

The exposition is as follows:

1. The word *"beginning"* corresponds with Genesis 1:1. It has to do with the creation of the Earth, and the universe. It has nothing to do with God, for God has no beginning.

2. This Verse proclaims that Jesus Christ as the Living Word is the Creator (Jn. 1:1-3).

3. The phrase, *"works of Thine hands,"* is not to be taken literally, only meaning that Christ is the Creator. Actually, the Lord spoke creation into existence (Heb. 11:3).

THE FOUNDATION OF THE EARTH

The phrase, *"And, Thou, Lord, in the beginning hast laid the foundation of the Earth,"* proclaims Jesus the Messiah, as the Creator as well! In fact, this is a quotation from Psalms 102:25-27.

The unchangeable and eternal power and majesty of the Son, spoken of in Verses 11-12, find their basis in the fact that He is the One Who laid the foundation of the Earth and fashioned the Heavens (Wuest).

The word *"and"* in this Verse links up with Verse 8, as presenting the second part of the contrast between Angels and the Son. As there, we read of a Divine sovereignty, so here, of the work of creation, the power to change all created things, the Divine attribute of changeless existence.

Some may think that Verse 10 is merely speaking of God as the Creator. If, however, Psalm 102 be examined, it will be found to contain the expression of hopes which in reality were inseparably united with the fulfillment of the Messianic Promise.

"The Lord shall appear to build up Zion": this is the Psalmist's theme, and it is to the

same Lord that he addresses the words which are quoted here. The Christian Jew, plus all other Believers as well, saw Christ as fulfilling all these Promises of God (Ellicott).

THE CROSS

Continuing in Psalm 102, which the Holy Spirit had Paul to use, in Verses 23 and 24, the Son is heard addressing the Father in view of the Cross. He cries:

"He weakened My strength in the way; he shortened My days. I said, O My God, take Me not away in the midst of My days: Thy years are throughout all generations."

The Verses that follow might seem at first glance to be a continuation of the plea of Christ, but with the light that this Divinely inspired commentary of Paul throws upon them, we see that they are the answer of the Father to the Son.

God replies to the Sufferer of Calvary: *"Of old hast Thou laid the foundation of the Earth: and the Heavens are the work of Thy hands. They shall perish but Thou shalt endure: yea, all of them shall wax old like a garment; as a vesture shalt Thou change them, and they shall be changed. But Thou art the same, and Thy years shall have no end"* (Ps. 102:25-27).

Thus, the Apostle has established the means of Redemption and as well, the full Deity of our Blessed Lord in contrast with Whom, Angels, however glorious, are but creatures, ministering spirits sent forth to minister for them who shall be heirs of Salvation, and who themselves worship the Son of God (Ironside).

THE WORKS OF THY HANDS

The phrase, *"And the Heavens are the works of Thine hands,"* presents the fact that only Deity could do such a thing. This must demonstrate the Lord Jesus to be Divine. He that made the vast Heavens must be God. No creature could perform a work like that; nor can we conceive that power to create the vast array of distant worlds could possibly be delegated. If in fact, that power could be delegated, there is not an attribute of Deity which may not be, and thus all our notions of what constitutes Divinity would be utterly confounded.

No, it is impossible for anyone to have created the Heavens and the Earth except Deity,

i.e., *"God."* And the Holy Spirit here ascribes this creation to Christ, corresponding with what the Spirit also said in John 1:1-3.

The word *"Heavens"* here speaks of all parts of the universe except the Earth, with the Earth of course being included in the previous phrase.

The idea is: This same One Who came down to the world and was born of the Virgin Mary, lived His Life as a peasant, and then for about three and one half years portrayed His glorious Ministry, actually fulfilling all the predictions of the Prophets, is in fact, the Creator of all things.

The religious leaders of Israel greatly opposed Christ; did they not know that this One Whom they were opposing, was God?

ISRAEL

It is true that the wise sages of the time of Christ were looking for the Messiah according to the Prophecies. In fact, Daniel had almost pinpointed the time when He would come (Dan. 9:25-26). So they knew this was the time of the appearance; however, they had a totally contrary view of the Messiah than what the Scriptures had actually promised.

As in Psalm 102 which Paul quoted, the Cross was predicted, so did many other Passages (Isa., Chpt. 53). So, there was no excuse for Israel not to know.

Do any Jews at this present time ever stop and think, that if Jesus wasn't the Messiah, even as they contend, then who was? No other Messiah appeared at that time, even though as stated, their wise sages knew that the Scriptures predicted His appearance at the time Jesus came.

So why did they reject Christ?

Why does most of the Church reject Christ presently?

There is a difference in the two! Israel rejected Him altogether, at least as a nation; the modern Church is different in its rejection, in that it replaces the True Jesus with *"another Jesus"* (II Cor. 11:4). But yet, the end result of both is, and will be the same — destruction! Even though the two are different, it is chilling to witness the obvious similarities.

Israel rejected the Christ of the Cross, but maybe would have accepted the Christ of the miracles.

Isn't this identical with the modern Church?

When we speak of rebellion against God, or the rejection of Christ in any capacity, when it all boils down, it is a rejection of the Cross, the same as Cain of old! If the viewpoint of the Cross is wrong, even as it is presently in most of the Church, then everything else will be wrong as well!

(11) "THEY SHALL PERISH; BUT THOU REMAINEST; AND THEY ALL SHALL WAX OLD AS DOTH A GARMENT;"

1. As stated, this is the answer of the Father to the Son as it regards the suffering of the Cross.

2. Jesus Christ did all of this as our Representative Man.

3. The creation may perish, but the Cross will not destroy Christ, and He will remain forever.

PERISH

The phrase, *"They shall perish,"* refers to the following:

"Perish" in the Greek is *"apollumi,"* and means *"to mar or ruin,"* but doesn't mean annihilation (Mat. 10:28). In fact, the Earth is eternal (Ps. 104:5; Eccl. 1:4), so *"perish"* here means to wax old as a garment.

As we have stated, these words were uttered by the Father to the Son, quite possibly even as He hung on the Cross. And yet, Psalm 102, from which Paul quotes, was written from 800 to 1,000 years before Christ.

This is not a statement given by God the Father as it refers to Christ, in order to give information about the Earth, even though what is said is absolutely correct, but rather to point out the absolute indestructibility of the Son of God, proving His Deity.

THOU REMAINEST

The phrase, *"But Thou remainest,"* tells us several things, but more particularly points to the Cross.

The entirety of the terminology as given here seems strange, that is if we do not properly understand what is actually happening.

1. First of all, Jesus was fully human. As such, this means that He only knew what all other human beings know, plus what the Heavenly Father desired to tell Him. When most people think of Christ, they think of

Deity, which means He knew everything. He didn't! As stated, He was fully human, even though He never ceased to be God; however, all the expressions of Deity were laid aside at this time, which included His all-knowing capacities.

Now the Reader is not to misunderstand what we are saying. Christ knew that He was going to rise from the dead (Mat. 16:21). Of course He also knew that He was to be a Sin-Offering, in other words, the fulfillment of all the Prophecies.

In no way do I desire to limit Him in this capacity, but at the same time I want to impress upon the Reader that Jesus didn't die as God, but as a man. God cannot die, which is the very reason, at least in part, for the Incarnation, i.e., *"God becoming man."*

2. The Cross was so horrible, so awful, that it literally defies description. And when I speak of these things, I'm not necessarily speaking of the physical pain, etc. I'm speaking of what Jesus actually had to do and be. To take the latter first, He had to be our Representative Man. That which He was to do, and in fact did do, was to be our Substitute, which refers to taking the terrible penalty of the broken Law upon Himself, actually being made a curse (Gal. 3:13).

THE MEANING OF THE CROSS

The Cross was not an accident or even an incident, and neither was it an execution, even though that's what the Jews and Romans thought. In fact, it was a planned destination, even from before the foundation of the world (I Pet. 1:18-20). For man to be redeemed, the Cross had to be. That's why the Cross is the central focus point of the entirety of the Redemption Plan. This is where the sin debt was addressed, and the penalty of the broken Law cured. All men were guilty, and so all men were doomed — that is, if Jesus had not gone to the Cross. In fact, the Cross is the only thing that stands between humanity and eternal Hell.

As well, the Cross was not carried out in order to appease Satan, or actually address Him in any manner. To be sure, it definitely did address Him, but that was not its purpose.

The Cross was carried out and demanded by God, in order to satisfy the Righteousness of a thrice Holy God. The debt that man owed, a debt incidentally brought on by sin, was owed directly to God. Man had offended God, and in fact, had offended Him terribly. Adam had taken the dominion given to him by God (Gen. 1:26), and had passed that dominion to Satan, the arch enemy of God, by forfeit. The results were, instead of Adam and all who would follow him being sons of God, in effect all were now sons of Satan (Jn. 8:44). Consequently, man now has the very nature of Satan, the evil of Satan, which is the cause of all the problems in the world.

The Cross of Christ dealt with that, but just how did it deal with it?

THE LAST ADAM AND THE SECOND MAN

Paul said, *"And so it is written, the first man Adam was made a living soul; the Last Adam was made a quickening Spirit."*

He then said, *"The first man is of the Earth, earthy: the Second Man is the Lord from Heaven"* (I Cor. 15:45-47).

Paul uses the term *"the Last Adam,"* simply because that's what Jesus would be. He would do what the first Adam failed to do, and undo what the first Adam actually did. As well, He would do all of this to such magnitude, that there would be no need for such to ever be repeated, hence Him being referred to as the *"Last Adam."*

First of all, in His earthly life, He kept the Law perfectly, which the first Adam did not do. As the Last Adam, He also paid the penalty for our sins, by dying on the Cross. This satisfied the demands of Heavenly Justice, as well as the demands of the broken Law (Ex., Chpt. 20).

In the doing of all of this, He atoned for all sin, past, present, and future, at least for those who will believe (Jn. 3:16).

In this Last Adam, every single Believer died which of course is demanded. That's why Paul also said, *"Know ye not, that so many of us as were baptized into Jesus Christ were baptized into His Death?"* (Rom. 6:3).

In His Death, we all died, at least all those who accept Christ, which is exactly the way He intended it to be. What do I mean by this?

The world is fond of using the word *"rehabilitation"*; however, such word is not found in the Bible. God does not seek to

rehabilitate anyone, but rather to make of them a total and complete new creation (II Cor. 5:17), actually making a *"new man"* (Eph. 2:15; 4:24). However, for this *"new man"* to be brought about, which in effect is the *"Second Man,"* the old man must die. This is what happened at the Cross, and why it is so very, very important. Again, this is what is meant by being Baptized into the death of Christ. Incidentally, Romans 6:3 is *not* speaking of Water Baptism as many believe, but rather the Crucifixion and resulting death of the Lord Jesus Christ.

His Death paid the terrible sin debt for us. And the manner and way in which we reap this benefit, is by evidencing Faith in what He did, which in the Mind of God puts us in the very place of Christ.

All the old residue of Adam, all the old ways of Adam, all the old manner and degree of what we once were, must die in totality. Not a vestige of it can be left, with us being brought forth as a *"new man."* That's what the Cross did, and that's why the Cross was so necessary.

THE SECOND MAN

That's why Paul referred to Christ as the *"Second Man"* (I Cor. 15:47).

Again, Christ was the Second Man, all on our behalf, in order that we might become as Paul would say, *"the new man"* (Eph. 2:15; 4:24).

The Resurrection of Christ is what accomplished the factor of the *"new man."* Paul said, *"Therefore we are buried with Him by baptism into death: that like as Christ was raised up from the dead by the glory of the Father, even so we also should walk in newness of life"* (Rom. 6:4). This *"newness of life"* is the *"new man."*

However, it must be emphatically, even dogmatically understood, that before we can have this great Resurrection life, we must first *"have been planted together in the likeness of His death"* (Rom. 6:5), meaning that we understand what the Cross is and what it means.

FAITH

The only thing that is required to have this glorious and wonderful life provided by the Lord is for us to have Faith in this which Christ has done. However, for the Believer to have proper Faith, he must at least have some understanding as to that which must be the object of his Faith. That's the reason some 14 times in Romans, Chapters 6, 7, and 8, Paul uses the word *"know,"* or *"knowing,"* or *"known."* It's difficult to have much Faith in something of which we know nothing. And the sad fact is, most Christians don't have the foggiest idea of the veracity of the Cross. While they certainly believe in the Cross, in which all had to do in order to be saved, most left the Cross at their initial Salvation experience. Consequently, it is impossible to live a life of victory in the Lord, unless we properly understand the Cross and how its benefits function within our hearts and lives on a daily basis. In fact, this is exactly why Jesus told us that we must *"deny ourselves and take up the Cross daily and follow Him"* (Lk. 9:23).

Paul plainly said, *"But God forbid that I should glory, save in the Cross of our Lord Jesus Christ, by Whom the world is crucified unto me, and I unto the world"* (Gal. 6:14).

Paul plainly says here, that the only way the Believer can overcome the world, which refers to all of its spirit of sin and darkness, is through our Faith in what Jesus did at the Cross on our behalf. To be frank, there are no exceptions to this.

Irrespective as to whom the individual might be, or how large the Church is which he pastors, or the size of the crowds that the Evangelist is attracting, if he doesn't understand the Cross, in his own personal life, without the shadow of a doubt, in some way, he will walk in defeat. God has one way of victory, and that is the Way of the Cross.

THE FUNCTIONING OF THE HOLY SPIRIT

Irrespective that we are now a *"new man,"* if we are to be what this new man should be, we must understand that it is only the Holy Spirit Who can do all of these things. As we've said over and over again, every single thing done in the heart and life of the Believer by the Lord, comes through the Office, Ministry, Work, Power, and Person of the Holy Spirit. However, His Work is never automatic, and what do we mean by that?

The Holy Spirit functions entirely within the Finished Work of Christ (Rom. 8:2). This means that what Jesus did at the Cross provides the boundaries in which the Holy Spirit works.

While He doesn't require that we understand all about this, He does require us to have Faith in that Finished Work. This gives Him the latitude to do all the great and glorious things which Alone He can do. This also means, if we make something else other than the Cross of Christ, as the object of our Faith, that we tie the hands of the Holy Spirit. He simply will not function on our behalf in that capacity. He only asks that we have Faith in the Cross, but He does demand that! (Rom. 8:11, 13). So, all of this can be summed up in three short lines:

1. Everything for the Believer comes through the Cross (Rom. 6:3-5).

2. Our Faith at all times must have the Cross as its object, referring to what Jesus there did (Rom. 6:11, 14).

3. Upon our being faithful in this respect, the Holy Spirit will then work mightily on our behalf (Rom. 8:1-2, 11, 13). This is the only way that one can walk in victory.

THE CREATION

The phrase, *"And they all shall wax old as doth a garment,"* proclaims the fact that there's going to have to be a change as it regards the creation, even as the next Verse proclaims.

Even though it is here unsaid, at least in so many words, I feel the Holy Spirit in shadow is bringing out the fact that it is sin that has caused the creation to diminish, in which it will have to ultimately be addressed. Chapters 21 and 22 of Revelation proclaim this.

Of course, the creation other than man hasn't sinned. But the idea is, that man's sin has caused the deterioration. In fact, it has affected every single thing made by God, and because of the original dominion given to Adam. Of course, Satan's rebellion greatly figures into this as well.

This is the reason that the Heavens and the Earth are ultimately going to have to be renovated by fire (II Pet. 3:7-13).

(12) "AND AS A VESTURE SHALT THOU FOLD THEM UP, AND THEY SHALL BE

CHANGED: BUT THOU ART THE SAME, AND THY YEARS SHALL NOT FAIL."

1. A change is coming for all of creation, with everything being cleansed by fire, and once again made new.

2. Despite the Cross, the Deity of Christ did not suffer, and in fact, if such a thing be possible, was enhanced (Phil. 2:8-11). As a result of the Cross, not only will all sin ultimately be removed from all of mankind, which of course refers to those who accept Christ, with the balance of mankind being consigned to Hell, but the damage that sin has done to the creation will be removed as well.

3. The supremacy of Christ will not fail, because it cannot fail. The idea is, there will never be another revolution or another rebellion against God. What Christ did ended it all. Admittedly, we do not have all the results of what He did as of yet, that awaiting the coming Resurrection, but come it shall! (Eph. 1:10).

CHANGED

The phrase, *"And as a vesture shalt Thou fold them up, and they shall be changed,"* refers to this coming time as stated, which Peter described in his Second Epistle. He said:

"Looking for and hasting unto the coming of the Day of God, wherein the Heavens being on fire shall be dissolved, and the elements shall melt with fervent heat?

"Nevertheless we, according to His Promise, look for new Heavens and a new Earth, wherein dwelleth Righteousness" (II Pet. 3:12-13).

CHRIST

The phrase, *"But Thou art the same, and Thy years shall not fail,"* refers to the superiority of the Creator over the creation.

In these statements we see that the Holy Spirit has placed Christ in the most elevated position, even as the unchangeable Creator of all things. Jesus Christ is God!

What could more clearly prove that He of Whom this is spoken is immutable? Yet it is indubitably spoken of the Messiah, and must demonstrate that He is Divine. These attributes cannot be conferred on a mere creature; therefore, nothing can be clearer, as it regards the mind of Paul respecting the Son

of God as Divine. So let the Reader understand the following:

If we do not believe Christ to be *"Very God"* even as He is *"Very Man,"* then we are proclaiming *"another Jesus"* (II Cor. 11:4).

(13) "BUT TO WHICH OF THE ANGELS SAID HE AT ANY TIME, SIT ON MY RIGHT HAND, UNTIL I MAKE THINE ENEMIES THY FOOTSTOOL?"

1. The supremacy of Christ over Angels.

2. The posture of Christ as it regards *"sitting"* portrays a Finished Work.

3. Even though the Work is finished, all the results of the Work have not yet accrued. A great part will come at the First Resurrection of Life. The balance will come at the conclusion of the Millennial Reign, when Satan will be then forever defeated and cast into the Lake of Fire, where he and all who followed him will remain forever and forever (Rev. 20:10-15). And then, the last two Chapters of Revelation, proclaim a restored Heavens and Earth, *"wherein dwelleth Righteousness,"* which means, that nothing dwells there but Righteousness (II Pet. 3:13).

THE INFERIORITY OF THE ANGELS

The beginning of the question, *"But to which of the Angels said He at any time . . .?"* is taken from Psalms 110:1. As mighty, wonderful, beautiful, gracious, and glorious, as the Angels might be, as the song says, *"Jesus will outshine them all!"*

The greatness of the position of Christ is proportionate to the excellency of the name of *"Son."* This name He has not obtained by favor nor attained by effort, but inherited because of what He did at the Cross. As we shall see, Angels do His bidding, and not He theirs!

THE POSTURE OF CHRIST

The phrase, *"Sit on My Right Hand,"* goes back up to Verse 3. Since the Angels stand before God (Dan. 7:10; Lk. 1:19; Rev. 8:2), it is a mark of superior dignity that the Son sits. But yet, this statement concerning the posture of Christ strikes a more startling note than this which we have mentioned, and pertains to Redemption, i.e., *"The Finished Work of Christ."*

The following is described by the one word *"sitting"*:

A. Christ is portrayed as sitting on the Throne which proclaims His superiority over all things.

B. He is seated at the Right Hand of the Father, showing the first position. The *"Right Hand"* signifies not only a position of honor, but as well of power — almighty power!

C. His posture proclaims the fact which is the greatest of all, that what He originally went to the Earth to do, has now been accomplished and in totality. That's why it is referred to as a *"Finished Work,"* meaning that it will never have to be repeated. Consequently, and as stated, Paul refers to this great Work as *"The Everlasting Covenant"* (Heb. 13:20).

Considering the place where He is seated, if there remained one iota of work to be accomplished, which means that He did not finish it all at the Cross, then He would be instantly exposed. However, He sits under the streaming light of altogether Righteousness, which would expose any flaw no matter how small, but upon the Son of God exposes nothing but purity and perfection.

This is what makes it so bad for any Believer to attempt to add something to the Finished Work of Christ. The tragedy is, all of us have done this at one time or the other and no doubt many times. Sadder still, most of us have done it through ignorance, but the damage was no less severe.

Now the question must be asked, *"Do we as Believers actually know and understand what the Finished Work of Christ actually is and actually means?"*

It is the work which we could not do for ourselves, but which Christ did for us in totality. Concerning spiritual things, man was and is totally helpless. The Fall cut the life source with God the Father, which left man with no spirituality whatsoever. This is what is meant by *"total depravity."*

Consequently, if man was to be saved, Christ would actually have to become as stated, the *"Last Adam,"* in which role He would serve as our Representative Man. Now the idea is:

Christ addressed every single thing at the Cross which was lost in the Fall. This means that nothing was left undone, unaddressed, and unrepaired one might say.

For the Believer to obtain all that Christ did, the Believer is required only to exhibit Faith in this Finished Work, which means at the same time that he will not try to do it himself.

Now the question may be asked as to what we are referring to as it regards *"doing it ourselves"*?

THE KEY TO VICTORY

There is no way the Believer can make himself holy or righteous. As well, there is no way that the Believer can walk in victory over the world, the flesh, and the Devil, as it regards the Believer's own ability, etc. Such a quest lies outside our capabilities. However, when we attempt to bring about Righteousness and Holiness through our own machinations, we are in effect insulting Christ, telling Him that what He did at the Cross is not enough, and that something must be added. I would hope that the Reader can see the awful insult to Christ of such action.

To walk in perpetual victory as the *"new man,"* which we addressed some pages back, all one has to do is to anchor his Faith in the Cross, understanding that the Cross provided not only Salvation for the lost, but as well, Victory for the Believer and on a daily basis.

The Believer is to keep his Faith anchored in the Cross, which will allow a daily, even a continuous flow of Grace. However, the moment we seek to insert works, i.e., *"the flesh,"* at that moment we frustrate the Grace of God, and we're doomed to failure in some way (Gal. 2:20-21). The secret is to always look to the Cross, which will keep the Grace flowing, and the Holy Spirit moving and working. In fact, it is the Holy Spirit Who adjusts the flow of Grace, and all predicated upon our Faith in the Finished Work of Christ (I Cor. 12:13; Eph. 2:18).

FOOTSTOOL

The phrase, *"Until I make Thine enemies Thy footstool,"* refers to God rendering all of Christ's enemies utterly powerless.

The phrase, *"To make an enemy a footstool,"* is borrowed from the custom of ancient warriors, who stood on the necks of vanquished kings, on the occasion of celebrating a triumph over them, as a token of their complete prostration and subjection.

The *"enemies"* here referred to are the foes of God and of God's Way; and the meaning is, that the Messiah will be exalted until all those foes are subdued. Then He will give up the Kingdom to the Father (I Cor. 15:24-28).

The exaltation of the Redeemer, to which the Apostle refers here, is to the *"Mediatorial Throne."* In this He is exalted far above the Angels. His foes are to be subdued by Him, but Angels to be employed as mere instruments in that great work.

(14) "ARE THEY NOT ALL MINISTERING SPIRITS, SENT FORTH TO MINISTER FOR THEM WHO SHALL BE HEIRS OF SALVATION?"

1. All Angels as here designated, have a role to play in this great Plan of God.

2. They are *"sent forth"* implying that they all have special missions.

3. They are sent by the Lord to help, aid, and abet, the *"heirs of Salvation,"* i.e., *"those who have accepted Christ."* Such help is not forthcoming to anyone else.

MINISTERING SPIRITS

The beginning of the question, *"Are they not all ministering spirits . . .?"* proclaims their function, and also the manner of their function.

These ministering spirits are not servants of men. The words properly mean . . . *"sent forth (that is, continually sent forth) to do service (to God), for the sake of them who are to inherit Salvation."* One might say, *"A ministering spirit is one who is employed to execute the Will of God."*

This means that Angels do not do our bidding, but rather the bidding of God. So, the idea as proclaimed by some, that Believers can order Angels to go do certain things, is facetious, to say the least! They respond only to the bidding of the Lord.

What type of ministering do they do?

First of all, they feel a deep interest in man. Thus, the Saviour says, *"There is joy in Heaven among the Angels of God over one sinner that repenteth"* (Lk. 15:10). Thus, He says when speaking of those who compose His Church, *"In Heaven their Angels do always*

behold the face of My Father which is in Heaven" (Mat. 18:10).

They also feel a special interest in all that relates to the Redemption of man. Thus Peter says of the things pertaining to Redemption, *"Which things the Angels desire to look into"* (I Pet. 1:12).

I believe we can also say that Angels are sent to give us strength to resist temptation. Aid was thus furnished to the Redeemer in the Garden of Gethsemane, when there *"appeared an Angel from Heaven strengthening Him"* (Lk. 22:43). In this aid, there is possibly more there than meets the eye, one might say!

Man was at first tempted by a fallen angel. No small part — if not all the temptations in the world — are under the direction now of fallen angels.

The Scripture also bears out that they attend dying Saints, and conduct them to Glory. Thus the Saviour says of Lazarus, that when he died he *"was carried by the Angels into Abraham's Bosom"* (Lk. 16:22).

HEIRS OF SALVATION

The phrase, *"Sent forth to minister for them who shall be heirs of Salvation,"* proclaims they attend only those who have made Christ their Saviour. While of course, God is free to send them wherever He likes, and to do whatever He desires done; still, the major work carried forth, is for those who are redeemed.

Considering the Angels who are contrasted with the Son, He sits in royal state; they, however, are no more than servants. *"All"* applies without distinction. Not only are they servants, but they are servants of saved men. *"Spirits"* preserves their place of dignity, but their function is service.

The word *"Salvation"* is used in Hebrews seven times, the most of any New Testament Book. His use of it here without explanation or qualification shows that it was already accepted by the Readers as a technical term for the Salvation Christ brought. And the Angels are the servants of those saved in this way, which of course, is the only way one can be saved.

*"Christ is our Cornerstone, on Him
    Alone we build;*

*"With His true Saints alone the courts
   of Heaven are filled:*
"On His great love our hopes we place
"Of present Grace and joys above."

*"O then with hymns of praise, these
   hallow'd courts shall ring;*
*"Our voices we will raise, the Three in
   One to sing;*
"And thus proclaim in joyful song,
*"Both loud and long that glorious
   Name."*

*"Hear, gracious God, do Thou, for
   evermore draw nigh;*
*"Accept each faithful vow, and mark
   each suppliant sigh,*
"In copious shower on all who pray,
"Each holy day Thy blessings pour!"

*"Here may we gain from Heaven, the
   Grace which we implore;*
*"And may that Grace, once given, be
   with us evermore,*
"Until that day when all the blest,
"To endless rest are called away!"

—■—

CHAPTER 2

(1) "THEREFORE WE OUGHT TO GIVE THE MORE EARNEST HEED TO THE THINGS WHICH WE HAVE HEARD, LEST AT ANY TIME WE SHOULD LET THEM SLIP."

1. Pay careful attention to the Word of God.

2. We should understand the great significance of the Word, realizing that it's the single most important thing in the world.

3. We should diligently study the Word, availing ourselves of every opportunity to learn more, and making certain that we do not forget what we have learned. We do that by putting the Word into practice.

THEREFORE

"Therefore" in the Greek means *"on account of this."*

It refers to the exalted dignity and rank of the Messiah, as stated in the previous Chapter. The sense is, *"Since Christ, the Author*

NOTES

of the new dispensation, is so far exalted above the Prophets, and even the Angels, we ought to give the more earnest attention to all that has been spoken."

Paul in addressing Jews, is in a sense reminding them that the entirety of the Old Testament, with all its glory, with all its power, with all its Revelation, with all its miracles, still, had but one purpose, and that was to point toward the coming Redeemer. Every miracle performed was for that purpose; every Revelation given was for that purpose; every move of God was for that purpose. Considering this, why was it so hard for Israel to accept Christ? In fact, only a few accepted Him, with the nation as a whole rejecting Him, and doing so with great antagonism, even murdering Him, murdering their own Messiah!

Because of their spiritual blindness they could not see His greatness. To be sure, the evidence was not only ample, it was overwhelming. He fulfilled every prophecy; exhibited every power in the realm of healing the sick, casting out demons, and even raising the dead. His miracles were so astounding as to defy all description, but yet they rejected Him.

The prophecies had been specific. The Redeemer, i.e., *"the Messiah,"* must come from the Tribe of Judah, and actually the house of David (Gen. 49:10; II Sam., Chpt. 7). To be sure, the Temple contained the genealogies of every family in Israel. One can be certain that they checked those genealogies.

They would have found that Joseph, the foster father of Christ was a direct descendent of David through Solomon. They would have found as well, that Mary His Mother, was also a direct descendant of David through another son, Nathan. So, the genealogy was perfect.

Had they looked at the prophecies of Isaiah, they would have found that His birth was to be supernatural, actually being conceived by a Virgin (Isa. 7:14). Had they bothered to question Mary, which possibly they did, they would have found that she indeed had been a virgin when Jesus was conceived.

Also, had they checked the Prophet Micah, they would have found that he had prophesied some 700 years before Christ, that the Messiah would be born in Bethlehem (Mic.

5:2). They would have found that he also prophesied that they would *"smite the judge of Israel with a rod upon the cheek"* (Mic. 5:1). This they did as well! Had they read Isaiah closely, they would have found that the Prophet predicted the healings, deliverances, and miracles of Christ, which Jesus gloriously fulfilled (Isa. 61:1).

Therefore, considering all of this, how could they be so blind? The very purpose for which they were raised up, the bringing of the Messiah into the world, they missed. For some 2,000 years they had been in preparation for this day, and when it came, they were blind to its appearance. Jesus said concerning this:

"If thou hadst known, even thou, at least in this thy day, the things which belong unto thy peace! But now they are hid from thine eyes.

"For the days shall come upon thee, that thine enemies shall cast a trench about thee, and compass thee round, and keep thee in on every side,

"And they shall lay thee even with the ground, and thy children within thee; and they shall not leave in thee one stone upon another; because thou knewest not the time of thy visitation" (Lk. 19:42-44).

He also said, *"I am come in My Father's Name, and ye receive Me not: if another shall come in his own name, him ye will receive"* (Jn. 5:43).

The *"another"* of which He here spoke, is the Antichrist, who will soon come, and who Israel will accept; however, they will find to their dismay, that the one they thought was the Messiah wasn't, and the One Who they thought wasn't the Messiah, the Lord Jesus Christ, actually was and is.

TO KNOW CHRIST

The basic problem with Israel of old, as it is with us presently, was pride. Self-will, pride, arrogance, self-determination, ego, haughtiness — all these things — keep us from receiving from the Lord. And religious pride and arrogance are the worst of all!

The world is too proud to admit their need for God, while the Church is so proud of its religiosity, that it cannot receive from God.

The Holy Spirit through the Prophet Isaiah said: *"But to this man will I look, even to him that is poor* (poverty of spirit)

and of a contrite spirit (broken spirit), *and trembleth at My Word"* (Isa. 66:2).

Jesus said: *"Blessed are the poor in spirit: for theirs is the Kingdom of Heaven"* (Mat. 5:3).

What do these terms mean, *"broken in spirit,"* or *"poor in spirit"*?

HUMILITY

Matthew 18:1-4 helps us see humility expressed in relationship with God. The Disciples asked Jesus who was greatest in the Kingdom of Heaven. The Text tells us that Jesus *"called a little child and had him stand among them."* Jesus then told them that unless they were to *"change and become like little children"* they would be unable to enter Heaven's Kingdom.

He explained, *"Whoever humbles himself like this child is the greatest in the Kingdom of Heaven."* Just before this, Jesus had presented Himself to Israel as God's Son and their promised Messiah.

Israel refused to respond. But what of the child? When he was called, he came immediately, responding to Jesus' Word.

Humility in our relationship with God is seen when we refuse to stand in judgment on His Word, but instead respond immediately, recognizing God as the ultimate authority in our lives. The dependence and responsiveness of the child is to mark our attitude and our personal relationship with the Lord.

The New Testament often exhorts humility in relationships with other Believers (Eph. 4:2). Paul gives the example of Jesus' humility (Phil. 2:5-8) to encourage compliance with his exhortation: *"In humility consider others better than yourselves. Each of you should look not only to your own interests, but also to the interests of others."*

This attitude is explored further in Romans 12:3-16. The introductory instruction goes like this:

"Do not think of yourself more highly than ye ought, but rather think of yourself with sober judgment, in accordance with the measure of Faith God has given you."

That Faith is to find expression within the Body of Christ, as each member of the Body uses his gifts to serve his Brothers and

Sisters in the Lord. Moved by sincere love, each is told:

"Honor one another above yourselves," and *"Do not be proud, but be willing to associate with people of low position. Do not be conceited."*

It is in seeing others as persons of great worth because they are loved by God and in seeing ourselves as servants that we find the fulfilling lifestyle of humility.

THE GREEK WORDS FOR HUMILITY

In Greek culture, the Greek word for humility *"tapeinos"* and its derivatives were words of contempt. In other words, the Greeks saw humility as weakness. The reason for this was as follows:

The Greeks saw man as the measure of all things. Thus, to be low on the social scale, to know poverty, or to be socially powerless was seen as shameful. Consequently, only seldom in classical Greek do these words for humility have a positive tone, commending an unassuming or obedient attitude.

In fact, the spirit of the world continues to function in the same fashion. The man with money, power, prestige, etc., is looked at as the great one. His opposite counterpart, is looked at with disdain!

Scripture, however, sees the universe as measurable not against man, but only against God. Compared to Him, human beings are rightly viewed as humble, and obviously so! Thus in Scripture the Greek word for humility (tapeinos) and its derivatives are nearly always used in a positive sense (exceptions are in II Cor. 10:1; Col. 2:18, 23).

Humility represents a person's proper estimate of himself in relation to God and to others. In this sense, Jesus Himself lived a humble life, depending completely on God and relating appropriately to all around Him (Mat. 11:29).

It is the humble, Jesus says, whom God will exalt in His good time (Lk. 14:11; 18:14).

THE CROSS

This is one of the many reasons that the Cross and one's proper attitude toward that Finished Work of Christ, is so very, very important. In fact, it is impossible for a Christian to have proper humility, without at

the same time having a proper viewpoint of the Cross.

The Cross within itself, is the greatest example of humility the world has ever known, and in fact, ever will know.

Concerning this, Paul said, *"Let nothing be done through strife or vainglory; but in lowliness of mind* (humility) *let each esteem other better than themselves"* (Phil. 2:3).

As an example of true humility, he portrayed to us Christ and the Cross. He said:

"Let this mind be in you, which was also Christ Jesus:

"Who, being in the form of God, thought it not robbery to be equal with God (was equal with the Father because He was God, but humbled Himself to do the following)*:*

"But made Himself of no reputation, and took upon Him the form of a servant, and was made in the likeness of men:

"And being found in fashion as a man, He humbled Himself, and became obedient unto death, even the death of the Cross" (Phil. 2:4-8).

Christ is our example, and the example He portrayed, was the Cross. So, what does that mean to the Believer?

WHAT THE CROSS OF CHRIST MEANS

When a Believer understands the Cross, which means he has a proper viewpoint of the Cross, this means several things:

1. It means that he properly understands himself. And what do I mean by that?

We come now to humility. Such an individual knows that he is unable within himself to do anything that God requires, and we mean anything. In fact, the very Faith which God demands that we have and exhibit toward Christ and His Finished Work, has to be given to us by the Holy Spirit, because we have none of our own (Rom. 12:3).

Whatever it is that God demands, and that means in any and every capacity, we cannot do. We must understand that, and understand it fully.

Consequently, this means that all of our good works, all of our good deeds, all of our efforts, all of our religiosity, anything that we may attempt to do, as noble and good as it might be in our own eyes, and even the eyes of others, we must understand, is of no consequence to God. So, true humility understands this, and places no dependence on self whatsoever.

2. True humility understands that whatever it is we must do, God must give us the means to do this thing, and that He does all of this through what Jesus did at the Cross. In other words, the Sacrifice of Christ is the means by which God can deal with hurting humanity. That being the case, we as Believers, must look always to the Sacrifice of Christ on our part as well. The Cross is ever the meeting point between God and man. There is no other!

When we have a proper viewpoint of the Cross, we understand that Christ did for us on that terrible day what we could not do for ourselves. As the *"Last Adam"* He undid the terrible evil which the first Adam did. As well, He gave up His Life, in order that the terrible sin debt which we rightly owed, could be paid, and in fact was paid.

As the *"Second Man"* one might say (I Cor. 15:45-47), He rose from the dead, in order that we might be a *"new man"* (Eph. 4:24; Col. 3:10).

As we have said in previous commentary, the *"old man"* had to die, which speaks of our before-conversion experience, which death took place with the Crucifixion of Christ, for He died in my place, which means that I died in Him, and then was raised in *"newness of life"* (Rom. 6:3-5).

The *"old man"* with its pride, arrogance, haughtiness, and self-will was buried (Rom. 6:4). The *"new man"* was raised in newness of life, and is supposed to walk in humility, understanding that all of this has come about because of what Christ did at the Cross, and only because of what Christ did at the Cross.

Again I emphasize, it is not possible for a Christian to have true humility without having a proper viewpoint of the Cross.

EARNEST HEED

The phrase, *"We ought to give the more earnest heed to the things which we have heard,"* actually refers to the New Testament Message. The nature of the sin of Adam was a careless, indifferent attitude towards the Commands of God. The particular word which is translated *"disobedience"* in Romans 5:19

means literally *"to hear alongside,"* thus, *"a failing to hear, a hearing amiss."* But this failure to hear is due to a carelessness in paying attention to what God had to say. In back of that carelessness is the desire to have our own will.

Under pressure of persecution, the Jews of Paul's day were discontinuing their attendance of the Church Services (Heb. 10:25), and thereby, giving less and less heed to New Testament Truth. The reason for this failure to attend earnestly upon the Truth was that these Hebrews were desirous of getting out from under the persecution to which they were being subjected from apostate Judaism. Entrenched and apostate ecclesiasticism was trying to take these Jews away from the visible Church and bring them back to the Temple. Thus does sin lead us to take the easy road, tempting us to sell our birthright for a mess of pottage (Heb. 12:16-17).

The words *"give the more earnest heed"* are literally *"to give heed more abundantly."*

Israel had given heed to the Old Testament Truth, or rather claimed to, which was ministered to it by the Prophets and the Angels. Now, because the Son is superior to these, the Testament He brought in is better than the one they introduced. They should, therefore, hold their minds the more earnestly to it (Wuest).

Both *"speak"* and *"hear"* are words which carry weighty emphasis in this Epistle (Heb. 1:1; 2:2; 3:5, 7; 4:2; 12:25, etc.).

Of course, anything of God is extremely important; however, considering that the New Testament is one might say, the very Words of Christ, as humanly possible as it might be, we must understand the significance of what is being said, and thereby take it to heart with all diligence.

The Son of God is the great subject of this Epistle; and His suitability to sit upon the Throne of God — having made purification for sin and satisfied all the demands of Heavenly Justice, which means that He has done away with all outward and visible symbols — He Alone, is the declared means of Salvation.

TRUE DILIGENCE TO THE WORD OF GOD

The phrase, *"Lest at any time we should let them slip,"* carries the idea of a ring slipping from the finger.

The Holy Spirit gave this admonition through Paul, simply because this is one of the greatest problems in the Church presently, and in fact, as here stated, has always been. That to which we give so much diligence, and I speak of temporal things, are fleeting, and that to which we give so little time, and I speak of the eternal, we seem not to understand its significance. Please allow me to make the following statement even at the risk of sounding self-serving.

I know that these Commentaries contain material, especially concerning the Cross, that is of extreme value to any Believer. And yet, most Believers little take advantage of that offered. With many it might be prejudice or bias; however, with many yet, it is just lack of interest in the things of God. The Truth is, most Christians I think, do not give the *"more earnest heed to the things of God"* as they should, and thereby, *"let them slip."* Consequently, we bring upon ourselves troubles and problems simply because we do not know the Word of God as we should.

As I've stated over and over again, in 1997 the Lord began to give me a Revelation on the Cross. (It actually began in 1996, but the greater thrust was in 1997 and following.) Knowing what this great Revelation has done for my life, I know what it will do as well for others. I also know that the Lord didn't give this to me solely for me, but actually for the entirety of the Church.

The Cross is the key to all Victory, all overcoming power, the key to the great *"rest"* in Christ. In fact, it is absolutely impossible for any Christian to walk in victory unless they understand the rudiments of the Cross. And sadly, most Christians, due to the paucity of teaching on this all-important subject, little know or understand this of which we speak.

And yet, it is so difficult to get Christians to see this of which we speak. Satan is a master at directing our attention elsewhere, or clouding our minds until we do not think properly. Consequently, and as stated, *"we let them slip!"*

Concerning spiritual things, Paul used the word *"sleep."* He said:

"Therefore let us not sleep, as do others; but let us watch and be sober.

"For they that sleep sleep in the night; and they that be drunken are drunken in the night" (I Thess. 5:6-7).

The type of *"sleep"* of which the Apostle here spoke, is similar to a stupor. In this case, there is a spirit behind the action.

To fall into this state, and we speak of this spiritual stupor, one simply has to do nothing. To keep from falling into this state, we have to set ourselves to have the things of God. In a sense, it has to be worked at. That doesn't mean that we earn these things, it just means that we stir ourselves to action.

The world is constantly bidding with new attractions every moment. They are alluring, titillating, and attractive. Never mind that it's all a façade, the damage has been done. We have frittered away our time that could have been put to better use learning the things of the Lord.

AN ILLUSTRATION

A wealthy man and his son loved to collect rare works of art. The father was quite wealthy and, therefore, had the means to do so. They had everything in their collection, from Picasso to Raphael. They would often sit together and admire the great works of art.

When the Vietnam conflict broke out, the son was drafted into service. He was very courageous and regrettably, died in battle while rescuing another soldier.

The father was notified and of course grieved deeply for his only son.

About a month later, just before Christmas, there was a knock at the door. A young man stood at the door with a large package in his hands.

He said, *"Sir, you don't know me, but I am the soldier for whom your son gave his life. He saved many lives that day, and he was carrying me to safety when a bullet struck him in the heart and he died instantly.*

"He often talked about you, and your love for art."

The young man held out his package. *"I know this isn't much. I'm not really a great artist, but I think your son would have wanted you to have this."*

The father opened the package. It was a portrait of his son, painted by the young man. He stared in awe at the way the soldier had captured the personality of his son in the painting. He thanked the young man and offered to pay him for the picture.

"Oh, no sir, I could never repay what your son did for me. It's a gift."

The father hung the portrait over his mantle. Every time visitors came to his home he took them to see the portrait before he showed them any of the other great works he had collected.

The man died a few months later. There was to be a great auction of his paintings. Many influential people gathered, excited over seeing the great paintings and having an opportunity to purchase one for their collection. On the platform sat the painting of the son as well!

The auctioneer pounded his gavel.

"We will start the bidding with this picture of the son. Who will bid for this picture?" There was silence.

Then a voice in the back of the room shouted, *"We want to see the famous paintings. Skip this one."* But the auctioneer persisted.

"Will someone bid for this painting? Who will start the biding? $100, $200?"

Another voice shouted angrily. *"We didn't come to see this painting. We came to see the Van Goghs, the Rembrandts. Get on with the real bids!"* But still the auctioneer continued. *"The son! The son! Who'll take the son?"* Finally a voice came from the very back of the room.

It was the longtime gardener of the man and his son.

"I'll give $10 for the painting." Being a poor man, it was all he could afford.

The auctioneer continued, *"We have $10, who will bid $20?"*

Somebody in the room shouted, *"Give it to him for $10, and let us see the Old Masters."*

The auctioneer continued, *"$10 is the bid, won't somebody bid $20?"*

The crowd was becoming angry. They didn't want the picture of the son. They wanted the more worthy investments for their collections.

The auctioneer pounded the gavel. *"Going once, twice, sold for $10!"*

A man sitting on the second row shouted. *"Now let's get on with the auction!"*

The auctioneer laid down his gavel. *"I'm sorry,"* he said, *"The auction is over."*

"What about the paintings?" the people shouted!

"I am sorry," the auctioneer said! *"When I was called to conduct this auction, I was told of a secret stipulation in the will. I was not allowed to reveal that stipulation until this time. Only the painting of the son would be auctioned."* He then paused and said:

"Whoever bought that painting inherits the entire estate, including all the Old Masters. The man who took the son gets everything!"

God gave His Son 2,000 years ago to die on a cruel Cross. Much like the auctioneer, His Message today is, *"The Son, The Son, who'll take the Son?"*

Because you see, whoever takes the Son gets everything.

(2) "FOR IF THE WORD SPOKEN BY ANGELS WAS STEDFAST, AND EVERY TRANSGRESSION AND DISOBEDIENCE RECEIVED A JUST RECOMPENCE OF REWARD;"

1. The *"Word"* spoken of here by Paul pertains to the Old Testament. It is the Word of God the same as the New.

2. When Jesus said to Satan: *"It is written, man shall not live by bread alone, but by every word that proceedeth out of the Mouth of God,"* He was speaking of the Old Testament (Mat. 4:4). So, Paul is by no means denigrating the Old Testament, but rather portraying the New as the finished product — in other words, that to which all the Old Testament pointed.

3. Man was held accountable for every single word given in the Old Testament, and if that was the case, and it definitely was, then how much more will man be held accountable for the new Revelation, which actually completes the Old!

4. The entirety of the world whether they believe the Word of God or not, will be accountable at the Judgment Bar of God for every single Statute and Commandment.

THE WORD SPOKE BY ANGELS

The phrase, *"For if the Word spoken by Angels was steadfast,"* actually refers to the Law of Moses, which had many Angels in attendance (Acts 7:53; Gal. 3:19). Angels were also used by God as messengers (Gen. 19:17-26; Judg. 13:5; 16:19-22, etc.).

To be sure, the Word given in the Old Testament was indeed given by Jehovah; but it was the common opinion of the Hebrews, that it was, at least at times, by the Ministry of Angels. As Paul was discoursing here of the superiority of the Redeemer by comparison to the Angels, it was to the point to refer to the fact, that the Law had also been given by the Ministry of Angels.

The word *"steadfast"* means that it was *"settled and established."* It was not vacillating and fluctuating. It determined what crime and sin were, and it as firm in its punishment. However, by no means does this claim that every violation was addressed, but that the Law so given could not be violated with impunity. In other words, it was not safe to violate it, as should be obvious.

TRANSGRESSION AND DISOBEDIENCE

The phrase, *"And every transgression and disobedience received a just recompense of reward,"* proclaims to us several things:

1. These are the Laws of God, which means every single human being on the face of the Earth comes under their jurisdiction. Only a few would believe that; however, that is of no consequence as far as the validity of the Law of God is concerned.

This means that many negative things happen to people, to cities, and even to entire nations, because of the Law of God being disregarded. It also means, that many good things happen to people because of obedience to the Word of God. Some may claim that in this age of Grace that the Judgment mentioned does not hold true. That is not the case, which we will address momentarily.

2. Transgression and disobedience being addressed doesn't mean that God is cruel or unjust. Actually, He would be cruel and unjust if He did not take stern measures. If in fact, the Laws of God are broken with impunity, with no corresponding action resulting, very soon the entirety of the planet would be destroyed. In other words, all of these Laws given by God, which are ensconced in His Word, are given for a Divine purpose and reason — all for our good.

That shouldn't be difficult to understand. Even the laws made up by men, providing they are just, are for the good of all concerned. If that be the case, and it is, then how much more are the Laws of God for our good!

3. This means, exactly as Paul has been saying, that the Word of God is the single most important thing in the world. In fact, the Word of God is the only Truth in the world, and in fact ever has been. While of course, many things are true, but that in no way speaks of *"Truth."* God's Word is Truth (Jn. 17:17).

Considering how important all of this is, we should make it our business to diligently study and learn the Word, asking the Lord to help us understand its contents, a prayer which He most definitely will answer. Nothing could be more important!

4. Some claim that inasmuch as we're now living in the Dispensation of Grace, that Judgment no longer holds true. In fact, it holds true now more than ever.

Paul said in his sermon to the Athenians: *"And the times of this ignorance* (Old Testament Times) *God winked at* (didn't call everything to account as much as He does now, due to the spiritual ignorance of the people); *but now* (this age of Grace) *commandeth all men everywhere to repent"* (Acts 17:30).

Under the New Testament Gospel, which has spread all over the entirety of the world, and has brought great, spiritual, light to the world, God now expects much more of mankind, and rightly so!

THE NEW COVENANT

The agency of Angels one might say, shows the limits of the Dispensation of Law. The setting aside of the First Testament, means the abolition of man's subordination to Angels. Such subordination is inconsistent with man's ultimate destiny to sovereignty over all creation.

Man lost this sovereignty at the Fall, but it was regained symbolically through Jesus Christ. At the Second Coming, man will once again come into his rightful place and position, as planned by God at the very beginning.

As we are studying *"transgression and disobedience"* and as it refers to the Word of God, it would be profitable for us to look at the words *"justice and injustice."*

JUSTICE AND INJUSTICE

In our culture, *"just"* and *"justice"* are often used as political code words. To some, justice means that there should be harsh punishment for criminals. For others, justice is a social issue: it demands a war on poverty and ridding the *"system"* of inequities. But in all the talk about justice, we must be careful to read the Bible so that it speaks with its own meanings. It is all too easy to let contemporary issues so color our notion of what justice is that we fail to develop a proper, Biblical perspective.

HEBREW WORDS FOR JUSTICE

Where the English versions read *"just"* or *"justice,"* one of two Hebrew terms is usually found.

The Hebrew *"mispat,"* which occurs over 400 times in the Old Testament, is usually found where the King James speaks of *"doing what is just"* or of justice. The root, *"sapat,"* encompasses all functions of government.

Among these functions are the judicial. Thus, *"mispat"* can be a case in litigation, a judicial decision, the execution of a judgment, and even a statement of the code against which actions are to be judged. In essence, then, justice has to do with one's rights and duties under law.

A number of words formed from the Hebrew root *"sadaq"* are also translated *"just"* and *"justice."* This family of words has in common the idea that moral and ethical norms exist and that actions in harmony with the norms are *"just,"* while actions not in harmony with the norm are unjust or constitute injustice. This important Old Testament root and its derivatives is also translated *"right"* and *"righteous."*

GOD AND JUSTICE

It is important when we read of justice and of just behavior in the Old Testament to remember that these are not abstract philosophical concepts. People today struggle to find an acceptable definition of what justice is. God's Old Testament people knew what it meant.

The writers of the Bible were convinced that the Lord Himself revealed the norms and

standards by which all human behavior can be judged. Justice, then, is doing what is in harmony with the Divinely revealed norms of interpersonal behavior. God has given *"regulations and laws that are just and right"* (Neh. 9:13), and it is these that define justice for mankind.

But the concept of justice has even deeper roots. Ultimately our understanding of justice has its source in the Person of the One Who gave mankind His Law. *"He is the Rock, His works are perfect, and all His ways are just. A faithful God Who does no wrong, upright and just is He"* (Deut. 32:4).

God's historic punishments of Israel for deviation from the revealed norms are also an aspect of justice. Again and again Israel was forced to admit, *"In all that has happened to us, You* (God) *have been just"* (Neh. 9:33; II Chron. 12:5-6).

Justice, then, is rooted in the very nature of God, and His Character is the true norm or standard. All His acts are just and right, even those we may not be able to understand. But in Scripture, God has given us norms that we can grasp. These Standards, expressed in the Old Testament in the Mosaic Law and in the Prophets, take justice from the realm of the abstract and make it a practical issue indeed.

DOING JUSTICE: AN OLD TESTAMENT PERSPECTIVE

Often the Prophets called Israel back to a just lifestyle. Their call is rich in illustration of the actions of a just individual and the just society. Listening to the Prophets, we can sense the perspective of the Old Testament:

"They ask Me for just decisions and seem eager for God to come near them.

"'Why have we fasted,' they say, 'and You have not seen it? Why have we humbled ourselves, and You have not noticed?' Yet on the day of your fasting, you do as you please and exploit all your workers.

"Your fasting ends in quarreling and strife, and in striking each other with wicked fists. You cannot fast as you do today and expect your voice to be heard on high.

"Is this the kind of fast I have chosen, only a day for a man to humble himself? Is it only

for bowing one's head like a reed and for lying on sackcloth and ashes? Is that what you call a fast, a day acceptable to the Lord?

"Is not this the kind of fasting I have chosen: to loose the chains of injustice and untie the cords of the yoke, to set the oppressed free and break every yoke?

"Is it not to share your food with the hungry and to provide the poor wanderer with shelter — when you see the naked, to clothe him, and not to turn away from your own flesh and blood?

"If you do away with the yoke of oppression, with the pointing finger and malicious talk, and if you spend yourselves in behalf of the hungry and satisfy the needs of the oppressed, then your light will rise in the darkness, and your night will become like the noonday" (Isa. 58:2-10).

Jeremiah picks up the same themes:

"This is what the Lord says: Do what is just and right. Rescue from the hand of his oppressor the one who has been robbed. Do no wrong or violence to the alien, the fatherless or the widow, and do not shed innocent blood in this place" (Jer. 22:3).

Jeremiah goes on to commend the Godly king, for *"he did what was right and just, so all went well with him. He defended the cause of the poor and needy, and so all went well.*

"Is that not what it means to know Me? declares the Lord. But your eyes and your heart are set only on dishonest gain, on shedding innocent blood and on oppression and extortion" (Jer. 22:15-17).

THE UNDERLYING PRINCIPLES OF BOTH OLD TESTAMENT LAW AND OF JUSTICE

Old Testament Law was a Divine Revelation of that which was good. It taught Israel how to love God and how to love their neighbors.

This loving way of living by the Law is doing justice. Justice is doing good to others and showing an active concern for the well-being of the weak. The just society and the just individual alike demonstrate this active concern to meet the needs of the powerless and to defend the oppressed.

It is important to note that justice and injustice have an impact on one's relationship with God. God is the One Who calls

humanity to do justice. He is also the Governor of the universe, Who must enter into judgment with evil doers.

For God to be just means that He will both act according to His Own standards in His treatment of human beings and exercise His responsibility to punish those who are unjust.

In summary, then, justice is an interpersonal concept in the Old Testament. Doing justice has to do with how human beings treat one another, individually and in society. The norm or standard that defines just behavior is a moral and ethical one. It is derived from God's Character and is expressed in those Commands of the Law and exhortations of the Prophets that reveal how God expects His people to relate lovingly to those around them.

Jumping to the New Testament for a moment, Jesus addressed this by saying, *"Judge not, that ye be not judged.*

"For with what judgment ye judge, ye shall be judged: and with what measure ye mete, it shall be measured to you again" (Mat. 7:1-2).

The idea is, if we expect God to be good to us, we must be good to others. And inasmuch as He has been good to us, we must reciprocate in kind to others.

INJUSTICE AND THE UNJUST

As we might expect, justice and injustice are mirror images of each other. Honesty in business practices is just; dishonest practices are unjust. Impartial courts are just; courts that show partiality to any individual or social group are unjust (Lev. 19:15; Hab. 1:4). Oppression of others is always injustice (I Chron. 17:9; Hab. 2:12).

In the Hebrew, *"unjust gain"* is *"tarbit"* (which occurs six times in the Old Testament), a profit made by violent or criminal acts (Prov. 28:8).

But where the English versions speak of injustice or the unjust, the Hebrew nearly always has a similar word. The underlying concept is also the mirror image of the concept underlying the idea of *"just."* A moral or ethical norm exists. Unjust acts or acts of injustice are those that violate the norm or deviate from it.

TEACHINGS ON LEGAL JUSTICE

One major emphasis on justice in the Old Testament finds focus in the legal system. The Mosaic Law established a system in which responsibility to deal with criminal matters was distributed throughout the society. Each community was to have its own panel of Elders who would serve as Judges in civil and criminal matters. The Old Testament emphatically enjoins the Judges to show no partiality and to accept no bribes (Deut. 16:18-20). Rules of evidence were established for serious cases (Deut. 17:1-7; 19:15) and a *"Supreme Court"* of Priests was established to inquire of the Lord in cases *"too difficult"* for the Judges.

Later, when the Monarchy was established, the King became the chief judicial officer. In Biblical times, all governing functions were considered to be located in the King as the head of the nation. But the King, like the lower courts, was to be subject to God. The Law established the standards according to which the ruler must judge.

HOW WERE CRIMINAL MATTERS DEALT WITH?

The Old Testament justice system, unlike our own, did not rely heavily on imprisonment to punish criminals. The Old Testament does report a number of cases of imprisonment — many of them under foreign jurisdiction (Gen. 39:20-22; 40:3, 5, 14; 42:16, 19; Judg. 16:21, 25; II Ki. 17:4; 25:27, 29; Jer. 52:11, 31, 33; Ezek. 19:9) and some under rulers in Israel in Judah (I Ki. 22:27; II Chron. 16:10; 18:26).

Confinement could involve simply restriction to one's residence or city (I Ki. 2:36), but in other instances it seems to have been in a room or pit in some official's residence (Jer. 20:2; 32:2; 37:4, 15, 18; 38:6).

RESTITUTION

The Old Testament justice system relied more on restitution than on imprisonment. A person who was responsible for another's loss was to reimburse the value of the property destroyed (Ex. 22:1-15). Property that was stolen or obtained illegally had to be returned, and a penalty of one to four times its value was added. Murder and accidental

homicide were special cases with a distinct code to govern how they were to be judged.

Other penalties were prescribed for various personal-injury and civil violations, including provisions for covering a person's loss of income if an injury prevented work.

With many such guiding principles provided in the Mosaic Law, local judging Elders were to call on witnesses within the community to establish the facts of a case and to supervise payment of the appropriate restitution or penalty.

The Old Testament justice system relied heavily on the existence of a community in which individuals were responsive to God and to His Laws. History shows that, with few exceptions, God's kind of justice was not administered during the Old Testament era.

TEACHINGS ON SOCIAL JUSTICE

Old Testament Law is not concerned only with individual justice. It is concerned with social justice also.

Thus a number of mechanisms were built into the Law that were designed to create a just moral community. Individuals were urged to have a generous concern for those less fortunate than they were. And the community was to maintain structures to meet needs as well. The spirit of justice continues to be that of concern for one's neighbor, and God shows His deep concern by designing a social system within which justice can be done.

NEW TESTAMENT JUSTICE AND INJUSTICE

The concept of New Testament justice is expressed by the Greek word *"dikaios,"* which means *"just," "upright," "righteous."*

Words in this family reflect the meanings of the Old Testament root *"sadaq."* At times the New Testament uses *"dikaios"* in a purely Old Testament sense to describe persons whose lives conform to the Divine norm expressed in Law. At times too the Greek *"adikos"* (*"unjust," "unrighteous"*) indicates one who deviates from the norm. Thus Joseph is spoken of as a *"dikaios* (righteous)" man (Mat. 1:19), and God is described as sending rain on the *"dikaios* (just)" and "adikos (unjust)" alike (Mat. 5:45).

However, the translators of the King James have chosen to use *"righteous"* and *"unrighteous"* in these as in almost all other cases where these Greek words are used of human beings. This may be because the New Testament concept of Righteousness is so dynamic and significant. It moves beyond evaluation of behavior, even by the Divine standard, and looks deeply into character, which is the wellspring of all actions.

GOD IS JUST

As stated, the translators of the King James invariably chose *"righteous"* rather than *"just"* to express the meaning of the Greek *"dikaios"* when it is applied to human beings. In three instances they used *"just"* when describing God's dealings with humankind. Thus, the New Testament affirms God as just, on the one hand justifying those who believe in Jesus (Rom. 3:26) and forgiving those who confess their sin (I Jn. 1:9), on the other hand punishing those who persist in unbelief (II Thess. 1:6).

Romans, Chapter 3 develops the first theme. Because all have sinned, human beings must be redeemed. Salvation is given freely, as a gift of Grace, through *"the Redemption that is in Christ Jesus."*

Paul explains that *"God presented Him (Christ) as a Sacrifice of Atonement, through Faith in His Blood. He did this to demonstrate His justice, because in His forbearance He had left the sins committed beforehand unpunished — He did it to demonstrate His justice at the present time, so as to be just and the One Who justifies those who have Faith in Jesus"* (Rom. 3:24-25).

THE SACRIFICE OF CHRIST

Paul's point is that God, as Governor of the universe, is morally bound to condemn the guilty. Since all have sinned, God might be criticized for failure to condemn Old Testament Saints. The Death of Christ has at least demonstrated that there is a basis on which God as Judge could validly leave sins unpunished. And Jesus' Self-Sacrifice provides a basis on which God can be just and offer Salvation to people today, and which addressed the sins of the Old Testament Times as well.

Because of the Cross, God can remain true to His Own moral commitment to what is right, and still freely acquit sinners, and because Jesus took the punishment on the Cross that we should have taken (I Jn. 1:9).

THE FAIRNESS OF GOD

The second theme is found in a number of New Testament Passages. God is not unfair in punishing sinners.

In II Thessalonians, Paul graphically portrays the destiny of those *"who do not know God and do not obey the Gospel of our Lord Jesus Christ"* (II Thess. 1:8). When Christ returns, they will be punished everlastingly.

Paul affirms, *"God is just: He will pay back those who trouble you and give relief to you who are troubled"* (II Thess. 1:6-7). The emphasis on just punishment is also seen elsewhere in the New Testament (Rom. 3:5-6; 9:14; Heb. 2:2; Rev., Chpts. 15-16).

GOD IS NEVER UNJUST

Considering the positive side of the subject, Paul in Hebrews 6:10 uses the fact of God's justice to encourage Believers. God is not unjust. So He will *"not forget your work and the love you have shown Him as you have helped His people and continue to help them."*

It is important to note that in these Passages the Bible is neither defending God nor trying to explain His actions. After all, God is the Standard of morality in the universe. Human beings may resist and challenge the *"humanity"* of God's decisions. But God is Himself the measure of Righteousness. Thus the Bible simply affirms that God is just.

In both Salvation and condemnation, God's actions are in full harmony with His righteous Character.

TO SUMMARIZE

God has communicated to human beings His Standards of behavior. Within the context of His Covenant relationship with Israel, God shared His norms for a people who would live in intimate relationship with Him. A nation and a person that was identified with the Lord must do justice and live in accordance with the Divine Standards of what is loving and right. Old Testament Law, which expresses these Standards, is an expression of God's Own Character as well as His explanation of how His Old Testament people were to live a life of love.

Justice in the Old Testament is both a personal and a societal issue. Law not only shows individuals how to act toward each other but also lays the foundation for a moral society. Thus Old Testament Law contains developed legal justice and social justice mechanisms.

Conversely, the New Testament says less about society. This is in part because the Church, unlike Israel, is not a nation. It is also in part because in the New Testament the emphasis shifts from just behavior (behavior and conformity to a standard or norm) to Righteousness. The New Testament emphasis on Righteousness focuses attention on the character, the inner person, from which behavior springs. And God shows us that His solution to injustice is not to be found in life regulated by law; rather, it is found through God's action in Christ to change human nature and character.

OLD TESTAMENT INSIGHTS INTO JUSTICE

Considering what we've just said about the New Testament definition of justice, what is the importance of studying the Old Testament for insights into justice?

For one thing, we are immediately confronted with the importance to God of the way we treat other persons. Justice is a concept that calls us to loving concern for those who are weak and oppressed, not simply to moral action in our interpersonal dealings. What is more, the social mechanisms that God established for Israel suggests positive ways that our society might presently act to correct inequities in both our legal and social justice systems.

While the New Testament deals particularly with individuals as it regards justice, and not so much with society as a whole as does the Old Testament, and of which I think we have given ample explanation; still, there is still much to be learned from the Old Testament. In the Old Testament God was dealing with community, which of course government has to deal with presently, and ever shall.

For instance, society might presently be better served, if the Old Testament method

of restitution was instituted. While this certainly would not work for all offenders, it definitely would work for some. Instead, all we seem to do presently is to build more and more prisons, which throws an intolerable tax load on the taxpayers.

When it comes to that which is *"just,"* and that which is *"justice,"* God's Ways are not only better, they are immeasurably better, which should be obvious. There is no unfairness or inequity in His Laws, whether the Old or the New Testaments. And when a nation seeks to guide its destiny according to the Word of God, that nation has just attached itself to the greatest fountain of blessing and prosperity that it could ever know.

(3) "HOW SHALL WE ESCAPE, IF WE NEGLECT SO GREAT SALVATION; WHICH AT THE FIRST BEGAN TO BE SPOKEN BY THE LORD, AND WAS CONFIRMED UNTO US BY THEM THAT HEARD HIM;"

The exegesis is as follows:

1. A great warning is given.

2. Humanity has been provided a great Salvation.

3. This Salvation is exclusively by Jesus Christ, and more particularly, *"by Jesus Christ and Him Crucified"* (I Cor. 2:2).

4. The Apostles and others faithfully recorded what He said and did, as given unto us in the Four Gospels.

THE WARNING

The phrase, *"How shall we escape,"* proclaims a warning of such proportions that it literally staggers the imagination.

All that man can do is to kill the body, but God can put the soul and the spirit into Hell (Mat. 10:28).

The way this statement is said in the original Greek actually tells us that there is no escape.

The words *"if we neglect"* have their primary reference to the Jews of the period in which Paul lived, who had accepted Christ, thereby outwardly leaving the Temple sacrifices, but who under stress of persecution from apostate Judaism, were neglecting attendance upon the means of Grace (Heb. 10:25), were allowing themselves to drift from New Testament Truth, were actually leaning back towards the Old Testament, and were seriously considering returning to the Temple sacrifices, an act that would constitute the sin known as apostasy, from which there could be no recovery, that is if they continued on that path. Paul is warning them of the terrible consequences of such an action.

SALVATION

The word *"Salvation"* refers to Salvation itself, not necessarily to the teaching concerning it as it is given here.

The idea is, *"Salvation which is of such a character"* as to have been spoken by the Lord. The Message of Salvation given by the Angels was typical in its method of presentation. It looked forward. It was not final in itself, since sin had not actually been dealt with. It was given in many parts and in many ways, but all looking forward to something which was to come.

But the Message of Salvation given by the Lord was in its character, final, and because it was that to which all the Old Testament Prophecies and Sacrifices pointed.

Christ was not only the Spokesman but the One Who brought into being and made available to believing sinners, the Salvation which He announced. In fact, our Lord announced the New Testament as taking the place of the First Testament, when He said, *"This is My Blood of the New Testament, which is shed for many for the remission of sins"* (Mat. 26:28).

These Jews who had in fact accepted Christ, even as we will see in Chapters 6 and 10, were convinced of the trustworthiness of the Old Testament; however, they were beginning to doubt the validity of the New Testament. The Law of Moses had proved its validity by punishing transgressors. But the certainty of the new Revelation was becoming doubtful to them. Therefore, Paul speaks of the New Testament as *"so great Salvation,"* and shows its trustworthiness by adducing the following three features:

1. It was originally proclaimed by the Lord.

2. It was confirmed by those who heard Him.

3. It was certified as from God by reason of the miracles that accompanied its announcement (Wuest).

THE GREATNESS OF OUR LORD

The phrase, *"Which at the first began to be spoken by the Lord,"* actually speaks of Jehovah. Jesus is God!

The word *"Lord,"* in the Greek is *"Kurios,"* and is used to translate the august title of the God of Israel, Jehovah. To the Jewish Readers of this Epistle, it meant just that.

The Old Testament (First Testament) was given by Angels, or rather they were used greatly during those times; the New Testament, was given by Jehovah Personally. And, being of such a nature as would be expected of Jehovah, the Jews were certainly obligated to give more earnest heed to this Word than the word given by Angels.

The idea of this must be looked at in two ways:

As the Salvation under Christ is much greater, the punishment for *"neglecting so great Salvation"* will be far greater also. One may ask as to how this could be?

Jesus Himself said:

"And that servant, which knew his Lord's will, and prepared not himself, neither did according to His will, shall be beaten with many stripes.

"But he that knew not, and did commit things worthy of stripes, shall be beaten with few stripes. For unto whomsoever much is given, of him shall be much required: and to whom men have committed much, of him they will ask the more" (Lk. 12:47-48).

"Stripes" are really not in question here, used only as a symbolism for degrees of punishment.

Even though all who reject Christ and for whatever reason, will be eternally lost, still, the degrees of punishment will be different for those who lived in Old Testament times, than those who have lived in New Testament times, and especially the present. The more Gospel that is presented in the world, the more Light is given; consequently, men become more responsible. So, the day of Grace cuts two ways.

THE GREAT PRICE PAID BY CHRIST

When we consider the price that has been paid by our Lord in order that men might be saved, and how that it is so freely given to all who will simply believe, if we understand it properly, we do not wonder that there is an eternal Hell awaiting those who have rejected the Grace of God. But yet we must ask ourselves the question, is it that simple?

It is that simple, if it's properly presented; however, when I say properly presented, I'm speaking of the Message of the Cross. If any other message is preached, which regrettably it usually is, the issue ceases to be clear at all. In reality, the entirety of the situation is very simple:

Men are lost. Jesus Christ has provided Himself as the Solution, and did so by dying on the Cross. If men will accept that, they can be eternally saved (Jn. 3:16).

However, the great problem is, and which Paul opposed constantly, Preachers who will not preach the Message of the Cross, but something else entirely.

I have no doubt, that the Jews whom Paul was addressing, had been greatly hindered and confused by false teaching from the Judaizers. These false teachers were claiming that the Law of Moses must be added in some way to the Grace of God. And if this Message sought to confuse Gentiles, how much more must it have been confusing to Christian Jews.

The Gentiles had no history of the Law, and in fact, knew nothing about the Law. They had been saved by strictly trusting Christ, even as Paul said (Gal. 3:1-2). But the Jews had been Law-keepers all their lives, and now it was very hard for them to give up the Law. And the false teachers coming in confused the issue even more, causing many of them to desert Christ, going back to the Temple sacrifices, which Paul is here addressing. I think the situation presently is no better.

THE MODERN GOSPEL

Any Message that's not the Message of the Cross, pure and simple is not the Message of Jesus Christ, but something else altogether. It might contain many things that's good, even as humanistic philosophy; however, if it's not the Cross, there is no Salvation, no Redemption, no victory! Understanding that, we must ask the question as to how much the Cross is being presently preached?

The sad fact is, almost none! As stated, a lot of good things are being preached, but of

which Satan is little alarmed. So, we must come to the conclusion, that many people presently are very confused, or else sadly deceived, because of the wrong message they are hearing, exactly as the Jews of old. Simply because this is so important, please allow me to state this again:

When one reads the Book of Hebrews, one is reading an entire Epistle that was written simply because of false doctrine that was being preached. It was causing souls to be eternally lost. It is doing no less presently.

We must ever understand, that God has but one Way of Salvation, and that is the Cross, and our Faith in that great Finished Work (Gal. 6:14).

As Satan fought the true Message of the Cross during Paul's day and time, he is doing no less presently. As stated, he's not too concerned with us preaching good things. It's the Cross which he fights and opposes with all of his power.

As well, he little opposes this Message from without, but rather from within. In other words, he uses other Preachers, or Churches, or entire Denominations for that matter. When he can turn a Denomination which is supposed to be Spirit-filled, thereby totally following the Lord, causing them to go in another direction entirely, even as he is doing presently, then the damage is catastrophic.

As I dictate these notes in April of 2000, the major fundamentalist Denominations have all but rejected the Holy Spirit. Consequently, they preach little more than a social gospel, and what little Gospel they do preach that might have some Truth, is devoid of all power. Therefore, little or nothing is actually done for the Lord in those circles.

As it regards the Pentecostal Denominations, most of these have opted for humanistic psychology, which is an open repudiation of the Cross. Irrespective as to what they may claim, one cannot have both. As our Lord said, *"One cannot serve two masters."*

When one adds to this list almost all Christian Television Stations and Networks along with Radio as well, one should be able to see how critical the present situation actually is. The Truth is, despite all the religious hullabaloo and fanfare, despite the greatest crowds in the history of the Church, and the greatest amount of money received, there is less Gospel being preached presently than possibly during the last 100 or so years.

There must be a revival of the preaching of the Cross, or untold millions will die eternally lost, and especially millions who think they are saved when they really aren't.

As I've stated over and over again, the Lord began to give me a Revelation of the Cross in 1997. I believe along with this He has told me two things:

1. First of all, this Revelation which is not something new, but rather that which has actually always been, is not for me alone, but for the entirety of the Church.

2. We are entering the last great apostasy, and the dividing line between the true Church and the apostate Church, is the Cross of Christ. In fact, it has always been the Cross of Christ, but is going to be such at the present time in a more pronounced way than ever.

I would ask you the Reader to help me disseminate this great Message, by praying for us and as well helping us financially with Television air time, and the construction of Radio Stations, which the Lord has pointedly told us to do. You who are the *"sender"* are just as important in the eyes of God, as the one *"sent"* (Rom. 10:13-15). I do pray that you can see how important all of this actually is. So I'll say by Faith, *"Thank you for your prayers and your support."*

CONFIRMATION

The phrase, *"And was confirmed unto us by them that heard Him,"* proclaims the great Salvation way ministered by the Lord, proved by Him as it regards healings and miracles, and attested to by those who were His chosen Disciples. An eyewitness presents the strongest testimony in any court of law as to the validity of what has been alleged.

One might say that this Great Salvation was announced by the Lord, confirmed by His Apostles, and accredited by the miracles of the Early Church. But Israel rejected all three testimonies; consequently, Israel became Lo-ammi and has continued to be so unto this day. But yet, the Messiah will come back in what is referred to as the Second Coming, when the Tabernacle of David which is fallen down, will then be restored (Acts 15:16).

(*"Lo-ammi"* was a son of the Prophet Hosea, born about 750 years before Christ. The Prophet was instructed by the Lord to give him this name, which means *"not My people."* It was to be a symbol of Israel, which meant that God would cut them off officially as a people, and during that time would refuse to be their God. This came to pass at the rejection of Christ, and has continued unto this hour. But as stated, Israel will be restored at the Second Coming.)

PROOF OF MINISTRY

Paul is appealing to the Jews who had heard the original Twelve, as many of them had, as to the validity of their Message. While those particular Apostles did not at that time understand the rudiments of the Cross, that later being given to Paul, still, they strongly preached Jesus, and in every capacity which they knew, with the Holy Spirit confirming their words with signs following. In other words, the Message they brought at that time, saw souls saved, Believers baptized with the Holy Spirit, and with the evidence of speaking with other Tongues, I might quickly add, the sick truly healed, and lives gloriously changed by the Power of God. In effect, He is actually saying, that any preaching to be genuine, even unto this particular hour (the year 2000) must agree with theirs. If it does not, then it will stand convicted of being an innovation instead of the genuine article. And let us hurriedly say:

Regrettably, most of the preaching presently, little resembles that of the Early Church. Consequently, very little happens, at least that can be substantiated. Let us say it again:

Preachers presently are to be called of God the same as the Apostles of old. We are to have the same Baptism with the Holy Spirit which they had. We are to proclaim the same Message by the power of the Spirit. And if we do this, preaching what they preached, which of course is Christ, and better yet, *"Christ and Him Crucified,"* we will see the same results now in one way or the other, that they saw then. If we don't, then that's a sure sign that we're not preaching the right Message.

The tragedy is, there is so little preaching today which coincides with that of the Early

Church. As I've said many, many times, if our Churches do not match up presently with the Churches of those early times, then what we are calling *"Church,"* is really not Church, that is, that which God will recognize as such. Every Preacher should ask himself the question as to what He is preaching? What kind of results is he seeing?

The modern Ministry too much and too often seeks to please man instead of God. Consequently, the Holy Spirit has little opportunity to get anything done, that is if He is present at all!

Considering that we're speaking here of the issues of life and death, which simply mean that it is the most important thing on the face of the Earth, the Preacher should carefully scrutinize what he is preaching, and the laity should carefully scrutinize what they are hearing.

(4) "GOD ALSO BEARING THEM WITNESS, BOTH WITH SIGNS AND WONDERS, AND WITH DIVERS MIRACLES, AND GIFTS OF THE HOLY SPIRIT, ACCORDING TO HIS OWN WILL?"

The exegesis is:

1. God is a witness to Jesus Christ, and there could be no greater Witness.

2. He proved His witness by giving power to the Apostles to perform miracles, etc.

3. The Holy Spirit was present, Who in fact, performed all these great things in the Ministries of these men, and was able to do so because of what Jesus had done at the Cross, making all of this possible.

4. This was all according to the Will of God, meaning that it is something that was planned long before, with that plan now carried out. Actually, Peter said that the Crucifixion of Christ on behalf of lost mankind was planned even before the foundation of the world (I Pet. 1:18-20).

GOD, THE ULTIMATE WITNESS

The phrase, *"God also bearing them witness,"* presents the highest evidence of all, actually that which is absolutely indisputable. This means, that no less a One than God has shared in this. In John's Gospel we have the bold thought that God has born witness to Christ (Jn. 5:37). Since anyone who bears witness commits himself by that very act,

God has gone on record, so to speak, that He too is a Witness to the great Salvation afforded by His Son.

The idea is, that God attested to the fact of Christ as to Who He was, and to what He had come to do. He was the Son of God; He came to deliver mankind, which He did at the Cross.

SIGNS, WONDERS, AND MIRACLES

The phrase, *"Both with signs and wonders, and with diverse miracles,"* proclaims that by the word *"with"* that the Preachers were not left to bear their witness alone.

Here, however, we have an even bolder thought: God has been pleased to commit Himself through the original Apostles. He gave the signs that attested their preaching. This means that the Gospel is not a human creation, and the early hearers were not left in doubt as to its origin. They actually saw the way God attested it. So Paul stresses the miraculous accompaniments of their preaching.

"Signs" is a word used often in John to designate miracles, and as well, puts emphasis on the meaning of the miracles. They were not pointless displays of power but, in the literal sense of the word, they were significant. The idea is, they pointed beyond themselves. The miracles were full of spiritual meaning and led those who heeded them to see that they were signs from God and conveyed His Message.

"Wonders" emphasize the marvelous aspect of the signs. They were such that no man could produce them and they were not explicable on merely human premises.

"Miracles" are properly *"mighty works"* and is the term usually employed in the Gospels. It brings out the Truth that in Christ's Miracles there is superhuman power. These mighty works prove something about the Gospel because they are not of human origin and thus show that the Gospel they attest is not human either. As well, one could say that there was no flat uniformity about the accompaniments of the preaching of the Gospel, but a mini-hewed attestation. In other words, the *"signs, wonders, and miracles"* were different, which means they did not necessarily follow a pattern.

SHOULD SIGNS, WONDERS, AND MIRACLES ACCOMPANY MODERN MINISTRY AS WELL?

Most definitely they should, for these are Gifts of the Spirit, as we will study in the next phrase; however, some things should be said about this.

These are Gifts of the Spirit (I Cor. 12:8-10), and actually should be sought and requested of the Lord by Believers (I Cor. 12:31).

Even though these *"Gifts"* have no time limit on them, which mean they are appropriate presently even as they were in the Early Church, some things should be noticed:

Using the Book of Acts and the Epistles as our criteria, which we are intended to do by the Holy Spirit, we find that these *"signs, wonders, and miracles"* were much more pronounced, even as Paul here brings out, at the very outset of the Early Church, than they were at any other time. In fact, the further we go into the Book of Acts, even though they continue, it seems they definitely do not continue with the same frequency. Does this mean that the original Twelve, or even Paul, had less Faith in the latter years of their Ministry than previous?

Quite the contrary, the more they learned of the Word of God, the greater was their Faith. So we must ask the question, as to why the frequency of the miracles did not continue, if in fact that is the case?

It seems that these *"signs, wonders, and miracles"* were used by God to verify the Ministry and Work of Christ, and as well to establish the Early Church. In fact, this happens quite often at present, whether in the United States or the foreign field. Once the Church is established, it seems that the frequency of such is not nearly as pronounced as previous.

FAITH

Some have contended that all of these great things are hinged totally and completely on the degree of one's Faith. While Faith definitely plays a part in all of this, it is not Biblically true, despite the claims of some, that if one could increase their Faith, one could automatically bring about *"signs, wonders, and miracles."* It simply doesn't work that way.

These *"Gifts of the Spirit"* are not given to men for them to use at their own whim and fancy, but rather according to the Will of God. Men cannot take Faith and force the Hand of God, and neither is God sitting up in Heaven looking down upon men, taunting them by measuring their Faith level, and if they can get their Faith level up, they can then perform great miracles, etc. To be sure, such foolishness has been suggested, but it's simply unbiblical.

Back in the 1950's, when I was just beginning to preach, God moved mightily all over the world as it regarded *"signs, wonders, and miracles."* The Lord called Preachers, giving them particular Gifts of the Spirit, which served to put the Pentecostal Message on the map so to speak. Massive crowds attended these Meetings, with God doing great and mighty things.

As a result, the Pentecostal Message which had been little noticed previously, now took on a brand-new aura, and then to go along with that, in the 1970's, the Lord began to pour out His Spirit even in greater ways all over the world. My own personal Ministry was very instrumental in that, along with seeing hundreds of thousands brought to a saving knowledge of Jesus Christ. But yet, the Lord did not actually give me Gifts of the Spirit as it regarded *"signs, wonders, and miracles,"* at least in the realm of Divine Healing, etc. While we definitely saw some miraculous healings, they were not to the degree of which the Scripture here portrays. And in fact, that was pretty well the case all over the world.

At the present time (2000) despite the wild claims of some, there are very few *"signs, wonders, and miracles,"* taking place which are actually Scriptural. In fact there are some things happening, but which cannot be proved Scripturally, and in fact are not Scriptural.

I speak of some of these so-called *"miracles"* which in reality are no miracles at all, and the phenomenon of Preachers blowing on individuals and them falling down, etc. One should notice the following:

When the *"signs, wonders, and miracles"* took place in the Early Church, it resulted in untold numbers of people being saved, along with being Baptized with the Holy Spirit. No such thing accompanies this modern phenomenon, which means that it's not real. So if it's not real, what is it?

APOSTASY

Paul said, *"Now the Spirit speaketh expressly, that in the latter times* (the times in which we now live) *some shall depart from the Faith* (this speaks of the Cross of Christ), *giving heed to seducing spirits, and doctrines of Devils* (I Tim. 4:1).

He also said, *"For the time will come when they will not endure sound doctrine* (that time has already arrived)*; but after their own lusts shall they* (Christians so-called) *heap to themselves teachers, having itching ears;*

"And they shall turn away their ears from the Truth, and shall be turned unto fables" (II Tim. 4:3-4).

The Apostle then spoke of the rise of the Antichrist which actually is just ahead, and said that *"his coming would be after the working of Satan with all power and signs and lying wonders"* (II Thess. 2:9).

To be sure, the *"power and signs and lying wonders,"* are not mere tricks, but the Greek bears it out, that these things will be real. They will be carried out with the intent to *"deceive,"* which they will do readily (II Thess. 2:10). The idea is this:

These things will not just suddenly happen when the Antichrist makes his debut, but will begin to take place years before he actually reveals himself. In fact, I personally believe that this time of apostasy which will lead up to the Antichrist has already begun. Such phenomenon can be produced in one of three ways:

1. The power of suggestion.
2. The power of Satan.
3. The power of God.

Many of the things which are taking place presently (2000), are too strong to be credited to the power of suggestion. So this rules out this particular means.

If what is being done is not similar to the Book of Acts and the Epistles, then we know it's not the Power of God, irrespective as to what might be happening. The criteria for everything done must always be the Word of God. And if it doesn't match the Word perfectly, then it should be refused and rejected.

If it's not the Power of God, then it must be the power of Satan. But this is what deceives many weak and shallow Christians.

Because *"power"* is definitely involved, and because the Name of Jesus is used repeatedly, then it's automatically passed off as being of God. To be sure, all types of miracles are claimed, with astounding healings being announced almost on a wholesale basis; however, whenever proof for such healings is sought, it's very difficult to be found. There's one other thing that must be said about such deception as well:

DECEPTION

Let it be understood, that the Preachers and the people who attend Meetings which are really not of God irrespective of the claims, will not leave as they came. If it is truly the powers of darkness which are at work, these spirits of darkness which are functioning in the so-called Preacher, will as well, attach themselves in some way to those who participate in such *"lying wonders."* Once again I emphasize, that just because actual power is being presented, doesn't mean that it's of God. In fact, the Ministries of such Preachers associating themselves with such, will be destroyed. And instead of the people being bettered spiritually by their involvement, the very opposite will be the result. There will be more sickness, more spiritual bondage, simply because that in which they have participated, is not of God, but actually of Satan.

Let the Reader understand, that Satan doesn't wave a red flag announcing himself as Satan. But he rather comes as *"an angel of light"* which deceives many.

Paul said, *"For such are false apostles, deceitful workers, transforming themselves into the Apostles of Christ.*

"And no marvel; for Satan himself is transformed into an angel of light.

"Therefore it is no great thing if his ministers (Satan's ministers) *also be transformed as the ministers of Righteousness; whose end shall be according to their works"* (II Cor. 11:13-15).

As someone has said, Satan as a wolf in sheep's clothing is very dangerous (Mat. 7:15). As a *"roaring lion"* he is even more dangerous (I Pet. 5:8). But as an *"angel of light"* he is the most dangerous of all!

That's the reason that Paul also said, that Believers should *"examine themselves, whether ye be in the Faith; prove your own selves. Know ye not your own selves, how that Jesus Christ is in you, except ye be reprobates?"* (II Cor. 13:5).

However, let the Reader understand, that despite the fake and the phony, the Lord is still healing the sick, performing miracles, and doing great and glorious things. We must not allow the false to drive us away from the real. But at the same time, we must be very careful that we do not accept that which is false. And let it be understood, that most accept the false and the phony, simply because they do not properly know the Word of God as they should. Once again we emphasize, that Believers should *"examine themselves!"*

GIFTS OF THE HOLY SPIRIT

The phrase, *"And Gifts of the Holy Spirit,"* have to do with those listed in I Corinthians 12:8-10, and which the Church desperately needs. Let the Reader understand, that these Gifts are meant just as much for the present time as they were during the time of the Early Church. The idea that all of this passed away with the original Apostles, or after the Canon of Scripture was completed at about A.D. 100 with the death of John the Beloved, is facetious indeed! As well, the following should be noted:

The Churches and Denominations which deny the Baptism with the Holy Spirit, with the evidence of speaking with other Tongues (Acts 2:4; 10:44-46; 19:1-7), to be sure, have absolutely nothing of the Spirit operating within their midst. This means that in these ranks, which cover about half of Christendom, absolutely nothing is done for the Lord. Anyone who knows their Bibles, knows that everything of God must be carried out by the Power, Work, Office, Ministry, and Person of the Holy Spirit. This means that all works of God supposed, which are born of man, instituted by man, and carried out by man, even though involving much religious machinery, get nothing done for Christ. The reason should be obvious: It's a work of man and not of God; therefore, it is something that

God cannot honor, cannot bless, and cannot sanction. To make it a little clearer, again note the following:

Understanding the magnitude of the Work of the Spirit in the Early Church, with the Book of Acts giving the account, and knowing that this is to be our criteria for Church and all the Work of God in general, I must come to the conclusion, that any Preacher, Church, or Denomination, which denies and rejects the Baptism with the Holy Spirit, with the evidence of speaking with other Tongues, are of no consequence as it regards the Work of God. I realize that's quite a statement, but I think the evidence is overwhelming.

The Lord cannot sanction anything that's not born of the Spirit. And when one denies the Baptism with the Holy Spirit according to Acts 2:4, one has just shut off the pipeline from God. It doesn't matter how educated these people might be, how big their Churches might be, how much religious machinery may be involved, if it's not of the Spirit, it's not of God!

WHAT ABOUT THE SPIRIT-FILLED CHURCHES?

Among these Preachers and these Churches, who claim the Baptism with the Holy Spirit, which as we've stated over and over again, is always accompanied by the speaking with other Tongues, there are many problems and much wrong direction, even as we have also hammered over and over again; however, whatever is being done for God in the world presently, comes from this Source. For in the midst of all the problems and difficulties, all the wrong direction, there are some Preachers and Churches who truly love God, are walking close to Him, and are seeing things done for the Lord.

Unfortunately, most of that which comes over so-called Christian Television paints a ludicrous picture, at least as it refers to the Pentecostal Message. Of course, that's exactly what Satan desires to do. He wants the balance of the Church world, and the world in general, to think that the presentation of which I have just mentioned is indicative of the Spirit-controlled life. Nothing could be further from the Truth! Most of the antics claimed to be of the Spirit, are actually of the flesh, with some even being the work of evil spirits (II Cor. 11:4, 12, 15). In fact, most of that which is labeled *"Christian Television,"* is controlled altogether by evil spirits. That means every dollar given by deceived Christians to such efforts are actually aiding and abetting the work of Satan.

But yet there is a genuine and real. In reality Satan wouldn't bother to develop counterfeits, if there were no genuine. But regrettably, most of the so-called Spirit-filled Church is in such sad condition, that they don't know the difference in the real and the false. But thank God for the few who do!

THE WILL OF GOD

The phrase, *"According to His Own Will,"* tells us several things:

1. It is the Will of God for *"signs, wonders, and miracles"* to be working and evident in the modern Church. In fact, according to the Scriptural indication, this has always been God's Will.

2. Dealing with particulars, all of these *"Gifts"* are carried out in the lives and Ministries of Believers, according to the Will of God and not the will of man. In other words, the *"Gifts"* cannot be operated on cue.

3. If the Lord is moving, working, and operating within one's life, in other words if He is truly there, there will be some manifestations of the nature given here.

4. All of these *"Gifts"* are in the domain of the Holy Spirit, which demands, as we've already stated, that Acts 1:4 be heeded in every Christian life.

(5) "FOR UNTO THE ANGELS HATH HE NOT PUT IN SUBJECTION THE WORLD TO COME, WHEREOF WE SPEAK."

The exposition is:

1. As powerful as Angels are, the Lord has given them no dominion.

2. The word *"Angels"* also includes Satan, for he is an angel; therefore, in this statement as given by the Holy Spirit through Paul, Satan is informed, that he and the angels who fell with him, will not have dominion of this Earth. The die was cast for his total defeat at the Cross of Calvary, which results and benefits will most definitely carry forth forever, therefore, meaning his total destruction (Rev. 20:10-15).

3. Jesus Christ, as the Representative Man, will rule and reign over the entirety of this Earth, and do so forever (Rev., Chpts. 21-22).

4. *"The world to come"* speaks of this coming glad day, when all of the forces of darkness will have been put down forever.

THE ANGELS

The phrase, *"For unto the Angels,"* refers in this case to righteous Angels. These are glorious Beings, created by God, and created one might say without number, but as glorious as they are, no dominion is promised to them.

The first mention of Angels is found in Genesis 16:7. The last mention is in Revelation 22:16. In-between as it regards the entirety of the Bible, some 104 appearances of Angels are recorded. Concerning their number, if we are to take Revelation 5:11 literally, there are at least 100 trillion of these beings, most of them employed in worship of God.

SUBJECTION

The phrase, *"Hath He not put in subjection,"* refers to dominion and rulership.

"Put in subjection" in the Greek is *"hupotasso,"* and refers to *"a military term used of arranging soldiers in order under the commanding General. The word speaks of an economy, a system of administration."*

The position and ministry of Angels interrupted at Hebrews 1:14 is now resumed in this Verse, but only to put them aside so as to present the Messiah as Man, for a time made lower than the Angels, in order to carry out the suffering of death on the Cross, thereby to redeem lost humanity, now crowned with glory and honor, and so satisfying the statements of Psalm 8. The purpose of the Spirit in Verses 5 through 18 of Hebrews, Chapter 2 is several things, but mostly to declare the actual humanity of Christ.

The pronoun *"He"* refers to God, meaning that He and not Satan has the final authority.

Paul proceeds with this discussion, showing that an honor has been conferred on the Lord Jesus which had never been bestowed on the Angels — to wit, *"the supremacy over this world."* This he does by proving, from the Old Testament, that such a dominion was given to *"man,"* and that this dominion was in fact exercised by the Lord Jesus, which we will see in the next three Verses.

At the same time, he meets an objection which a Jew would be likely to make. It is, that Jesus appeared to be far inferior to the Angels. He was a man of humble condition. He was poor and despised. He had none of the external honor which was shown to Moses — the founder of the Jewish economy; none of the apparent honor which belonged to Angelic beings, even which humility Isaiah predicted in his Fifty-third Chapter. This implied objection he removes, by showing the reason why He became so.

It was proper, since He came to redeem man, that He should be a man, and not take on Himself the nature of Angels; and, for the same reason, it was proper that He should be subjected to sufferings, and be made a man of sorrows, which Paul proclaims in Verses 10 through 17 of Hebrews, Chapter 2.

The remark of the Holy Spirit through the Apostle in this Verse before us is, that God had never put the world in subjection to the Angels. They had or have no jurisdiction over it; they were and are mere ministering spirits; the world has been put under the dominion of the Lord Jesus, which is fastly coming to a head as it regards total domination by Christ.

THE WORLD TO COME

The phrase, *"The world to come, whereof we speak,"* actually regards the coming Kingdom Age, of which the Old Testament amply proclaims.

This Kingdom will not be administered by Angels. An Angel once was the regent of God on the first perfect Earth, which Angel (Lucifer) with his associated Angels administered the affairs of a pre-Adamic race. His throne was on Earth. He was the anointed Cherub, the guardian so to speak, of the Holiness of God. He struck at God's Throne, and forfeited the regency of this Earth (Isa. 14:12-14; Ezek. 28:1-19).

As stated, that Angel was Lucifer. He is now Satan. The Earth over which he had ruled, was rendered a desolation and a waste, and he, with his angelic cohorts, were banished.

NOTES

After the restoration of the Earth as recorded in Genesis, Chapter 1, God placed man upon it (Gen., Chpts. 1-2), but man handed the scepter of power over to Satan (Gen., Chpt. 3), who now is the god of this world-system (II Cor. 4:4), and whose throne is again on Earth (Rev. 2:13).

But the Lord Jesus, through the Blood of His Cross, has regained for man the dominion over this Earth, and will in the coming Millennial Kingdom dethrone Satan, and rule as King of kings and Lord of lords. The saved of the human race in glorified bodies will be associated with Him in this Reign. Thus, the Angels will not administer the Millennial Earth, but man in the Person of the Son of Man and those of the human race saved by His Precious Blood (Wuest).

COMING EVENTS

The times in which we are now living are at the same time the most dangerous and the most rewarding. The Scripture proclaims an apostasy of the last days which will lead up to the Advent of the Antichrist. That apostasy has already begun (I Tim. 4:1). At the same time, the Lord has promised to pour out His Spirit upon all flesh, which actually began at the turn of the Twentieth Century, but will see even a greater manifestation in the near future (Acts 2:16-21).

All of this means that the Rapture of the Church is even at the door (I Thess. 4:13-18), after which the world will be plunged into great tribulation, brought about by the Judgment of God poured out upon this world and the rise of the Antichrist. This is referred to as *"Daniel's Seventieth Week,"* a time span of some seven years (Dan. 9:27). This seven year span of time will conclude with the Second Coming (Rev., Chpt. 19), which will commence the Kingdom Age, with Jesus ruling and reigning Personally upon this Earth (Ezek., Chpts. 40-48; Rev. 20:1-4).

Israel will then accept Christ, and be restored to her place of supremacy among the nations, as God originally intended (Zech., Chpts. 12-14).

(6) "BUT ONE IN A CERTAIN PLACE TESTIFIED, SAYING, WHAT IS MAN, THAT THOU ART MINDFUL OF HIM? OR THE SON OF MAN, THAT THOU VISITEST HIM?"

The exegesis is:

1. A quotation from Psalms 8:4-6 is introduced; however, Paul tells us neither the place where the words are found nor who said them. Consistently he regards all that is in the Bible as coming from God and puts no emphasis on the human author.

2. David, for David wrote this Psalm, is concerned with both the insignificance and the greatness of man.

3. The phrase *"son of man"* as given here by David, does not refer to Christ, even though He refers to Himself as such many times in the Gospels. It refers to mankind in general.

4. However, due to the Fall, all of this will be fulfilled in our Representative Man, the Lord Jesus Christ.

5. The visitation mentioned here concerns the entirety of the Plan of God for the human race, but more particularly, it concerns the Incarnation of Christ, *"God with man,"* and what Jesus did at the Cross on our behalf.

THE TESTIMONY

The phrase, *"But one in a certain place testified, saying,"* proclaims the Apostle using such terminology for a specific reason. In other words, the Holy Spirit wanted him to say this in this manner.

Of course, Paul knew exactly in the Psalms where this quotation was found. The idea is, as we've already stated, that irrespective as to who it was who wrote the words, or where it's found in the Bible, it is all the Word of God. In studying the Word now not too much short of 60 years, I have noticed some things.

First of all, the Believer makes a grand mistake when we think that some parts of the Bible are not relative to us. It is not relative, only because we do not understand what is being said.

Every single Book in the Bible, every single Epistle, has a special message for each and every individual. And if we fail to get that particular message, our Bible education is deplete in some manner. And that will play out in our lives to a loss in some way. That's why it is such a shame for Believers not to make the Bible a part of their daily study — yes, I said *"daily study!"* In fact, every Believer ought to read the Bible completely through at least once a year. And to be frank,

I cannot really understand how any Believer would not want to do that or even more.

As well, every Believer ought to take advantage of every Biblical aid that comes their way, such as these Commentaries, that will help them, hopefully, to understand the Word a little better. This much is obvious:

If a Believer truly hungers after the Word, truly desiring to understand its meaning, the Holy Spirit will see to it, that such hunger and thirst are satisfied (Mat. 4:4; 5:6).

MAN

The question, *"What is man, that Thou art mindful of him?"*, delves into the reason that God has given man so much notice.

When we consider that the entirety of the story of the Bible, with the exception of the first three Chapters, is the story of man's Redemption, and when we consider the most awful price that was paid in order for man to be redeemed, we surely should get the idea as to the validity of this question as asked by David so long ago.

Why has God conferred on him such signal honors? Why has He placed him over the works of His hands?

At first glance, man seems to be so insignificant; his life is so much like a vapor; he so soon disappears, that the question may well be asked why this extraordinary dominion is given him? He is so sinful, also, and so unworthy; so much unlike God, and so wicked and revengeful; he is so prone to abuse his dominion, that it may well be asked as to why God has given it to him?

In effect, David is saying, *"When I look at the Heavens, and survey their greatness and their glory, why is it that man has attracted so much notice, and that he has not been wholly overlooked in the vastness of the works of the Almighty? Why is it, that instead of this he has been exalted to so much dignity and honor?"*

THE PRESENT SITUATION

If one observes man in his present situation, his degradation, the wino on the street, the drug addict stealing whatever he can get his hands on in order to get another fix, the despots who control much of this world, and will kill anyone who gets in their way, one is quickly turned off. However, that is to look at man in his fallen state, and not as God originally intended, or as it shall be in the coming days.

Man was originally created to live forever, actually created in the very Image of God, with God-like powers and creative abilities, which absolutely defy description. It is sin that has brought man to this particular state; sin which has wrecked him; sin which has destroyed his capabilities and his powers; sin which has alienated him from God; sin which has cut him off from his life-support system so to speak; sin which has marred him, degraded him, degenerated him, and darkened him.

THE POWER OF SIN

Adam and Eve eating the forbidden fruit in the Garden (Gen. 2:15-17), constituted the beginning of this horror. When this disobedience took place, man in effect took himself away from God and placed himself in the domain of Satan. Consequently, instead of God-consciousness he now has self-consciousness, i.e., *"evil-consciousness,"* actually becoming the very personification of evil. In effect, God is no longer the Father of man except in creation, with Satan now becoming man's lord (Jn. 8:44). Consequently, man now has the nature of Satan, the spirit of Satan, which Jesus said can only *"steal, kill, and destroy"* (Jn. 10:10). That's the reason for all the problems, heartache, loneliness, war, sickness, hatred, and iniquity in the world today. It is the evil nature in man caused by the Fall.

Perhaps no one can fully understand the totality of what evil is all about, in other words, how awful and horrible it actually is, but we can at least get some idea.

When we consider that sin has killed every single person in this world who has ever lived, and that all alive now are dying, and all because of this monster, then we begin to get an idea of how bad this thing really is. When we consider that sin is the cause of all suffering, sickness, sorrow, poverty, and man's inhumanity to man, then again we begin to get the idea.

But above all, when we understand that sin is so awful that even God could not speak it out of existence, then we start to understand the magnitude of this evil. Think about it!

God could speak worlds into existence. In fact, He has created the entirety of this universe simply by the spoken word (Heb. 11:3), but yet He couldn't speak Redemption into existence.

To roll back this tide of evil, to assuage this death-dealing horror, to stop the encroachment of evil, for evil ever worsens, God would literally have to become man, die on a Cross, in order for man to be redeemed.

THE SECOND MAN

To fully understand man, we have to go beyond what man presently is, and look at the *"Second Man,"* the Lord Jesus Christ. If we try to figure man out in any other capacity, any other way, we will come to no satisfactory conclusion. We can only understand man, and his worth, as we look at the *"Second Man."*

Paul said, *"The first man (Adam) is of the Earth, earthy: the Second Man (Christ Jesus) is the Lord from Heaven"* (I Cor. 15:47).

Paul used this term *"Second Man"* for a particular reason.

The first man was destroyed, which means that all who followed after him were destroyed, and for the simple reason that in the loins of Adam was every single human being who would ever live, other than Jesus Christ. So, when the first Adam fell, due to his power of procreation, his fall included all who would follow thereafter. This is the manner in which God made man, giving him the power of procreation, which refers to the ability to bring offspring into the world.

As we have said previously, God originally intended that man and woman were to bring sons and daughters of God into the world, because Adam originally was a *"son of God"* (Lk. 3:38).

(The King James version has *"the son of God,"* but the two words *"the son"* are not in the original Text, having been erroneously added by the translators. While Adam was *"a son of God,"* he definitely was not *"the Son of God,"* that prerogative applying only to Christ.)

After the Fall, Adam and Eve could only bring offspring into the world after the likeness and image of Adam, which refers to his fallen condition (Gen. 5:3).

As we've mentioned previously, sin is of such power, actually becoming more and more evil as it goes along, that if it had not been for the Gospel, man would have destroyed himself a long time ago. Paul likened sin to *"leaven,"* which ultimately takes over everything (I Cor. 5:6). That's the reason the *"Blood of Jesus Christ cleanses from all sin"* (I Jn. 1:7), and that the Holy Spirit seeks strongly to remove every vestige of sin from the heart and life of the Believer after conversion (Rom. 8:1-2, 11, 13). God cannot abide sin in any form; consequently, the idea that Christians are to sin a little bit everyday, as some teach, is facetious indeed! The Lord does not save us in sin but rather from sin.

The Scripture is abundantly clear on this subject. All sin is of the Devil, and any Believer who sins, is functioning in the realm of Satan with all of its attendant destructive powers (I Jn. 3:8). In fact, the Scripture also plainly says, that *"Whosoever is born of God doth not commit* (practice) *sin; for his seed remaineth in him* (the seed of life in Christ Jesus)*: and he cannot sin* (cannot practice sin)*, because he is born of God"* (I Jn. 3:9).

John further said, *"In this the children of God are manifest, and the children of the Devil"* (I Jn. 3:10). In other words, if a person claims to be a Christian, and is continuing on in their old lifestyle of constant sinning, this plainly tells us that the man or woman is not saved. The moment a person comes to Christ, from that moment on sin is abhorrent to them. While there may be failure along the way, it will always grieve one terribly so, because the individual is now a new creation in Christ Jesus (II Cor. 5:17).

Christ as the *"Second Man"* had to come to this world in order to bring man back to the original Plan of God. In doing this, He became the *"Last Adam,"* which means He would do what the first Adam did not do (perfectly obey), and undo what the first Adam did do (do so by paying the penalty which was incurred, which could only be paid by dying, which He did on the Cross).

Whereas the *"Last Adam"* had to do with the things just mentioned, the *"Second Man"* had to do with the Resurrection of Christ, and all Believers being raised with Him in

"newness of life" (Rom. 6:5), and then becoming a *"new man,"* all in Christ Jesus.

Paul said, *"And that ye put on the new man, which after God is created in Righteousness and true Holiness"* (Eph. 4:24).

Jesus in the role of the *"Second Man,"* refers to what man ought to be, what God intended for man to be, and how man can be that only in Christ Jesus.

FAITH IN THE CROSS AND THE RESURRECTION

In the next few paragraphs I would like to briefly relate the manner of victory given to us by the Lord, enabling us to walk Righteously before the Lord. Every person who is truly saved, desires strongly to be what they ought to be in Christ, that sin not dominate them in any manner, and that they walk victoriously on a day-by-day basis, which in fact, the Lord has provided. The following, I think, will definitely be of some help.

THE LAST ADAM AND THE SECOND MAN

As Paul said in I Corinthians 15:45-50, Jesus Christ came to this world to serve as the *"Last Adam,"* and the *"Second Man."* As we've already stated, as the *"Last Adam,"* He kept the Law of God perfectly, obeying its every precept, thereby attaining its Righteousness, and all on our behalf. As well, He suffered the curse of the broken Law, even though He in fact, never sinned, again, all on our behalf.

As the *"Second Man,"* He rose from the dead and is presently sitting at the Right Hand of the Father in Heaven (Rom. 6:3-5; Eph. 2:6).

OUR SUBSTITUTE

As we've said over and over again, He did all of this on our behalf. Our Faith in Him, and what He did, which refers to the Cross and the Resurrection, obtains for us all the great Victory which He purchased with His Own Blood (Eph. 2:8-9).

Whenever the believing sinner exhibits Faith in this which Christ has done, in the Mind of God, we are literally placed in Christ, which means, that all that He did now becomes ours.

FAITH

Our Faith in Him takes us through the entirety of the process of Crucifixion, Burial, and Resurrection, even to the Exaltation of Christ (Rom. 6:3-5; Eph. 2:6).

BORN AGAIN

This which we have stated is the *"born again"* experience, which every person must have if they are to become a Child of God (Jn. 3:3). The Believer is now a *"new man"* in Christ Jesus, meaning that the *"old man"* has died, and been buried, and no longer exists. This is what Paul meant when he said that we are *"Baptized into the Death of Christ"* (Rom. 6:3). Please understand, that the Apostle is not speaking here of Water Baptism, but actually the death of Christ, and our being baptized into His Death, which is all done by Faith on our part. In other words, we simply believe the things that I've just related, and the work is carried out within our hearts and lives (Jn. 3:16).

THE NEW MAN

The old man actually having died in Christ, means that the Lord did not try to rehabilitate us, or patch us up so to speak, but actually did away with the old person, spiritually speaking, and now makes a brand-new creation (II Cor. 5:17).

This is the reason that the Church is a million miles off base, when it speaks of Christians being *"rehabilitated,"* or anyone for that matter. Such terminology comes from the world of psychology, and has absolutely no place whatsoever in the Gospel. As stated, the Lord doesn't rehabilitate anyone. He makes them brand-new, i.e., *"a new man,"* all in Christ Jesus (Eph. 2:12-16). He does all of this by what Christ did at the Cross, and our Faith in that (Eph. 2:16). The idea is, the *"Second Man,"* the Lord Jesus Christ, has made it possible through His Death and Resurrection, for us to be a *"new man."*

SATAN

After one is now a *"new man"* all in Christ Jesus, does that mean that Satan will no longer bother the individual?

No, not at all! Satan will continue to hinder and try to cause problems in every

respect. He will constantly probe for weaknesses in our armor, and will take advantage of every weakness he sees.

THE CROSS OF CHRIST

Now that the Believer is a *"new man,"* as everything has functioned on Faith, everything will continue to function on Faith. If there is failure, and I've never yet met a Christian where there hasn't been failure, it is always because of improper Faith. In other words, our Faith is not as strong as it ought to be, and Satan takes advantage of that.

I've had many Christians to hear this great Message of the Cross, embrace it, which they certainly should, and then experience failure. They would be somewhat confused, thinking that *"it just doesn't work!"* To be factual, it's the only thing that does work. God has no other method of victory other than the Cross of Christ, and our Faith in that Finished Work. The Believer must understand that, get it down into his spirit, that the Cross of Christ is the only victory there is, which of course, includes the Resurrection of Christ.

The following is what the Believer must now do:

ACCOUNT YOURSELF VICTORIOUS

The Believer should *"reckon ye also yourselves to be dead indeed unto sin, but alive unto God through Jesus Christ our Lord"* (Rom. 6:11).

If one is to notice, Paul did not say here that sin was dead, for it definitely isn't dead. But we are to be dead to sin. And in fact, the Apostle is actually speaking of *"the sin,"* or *"the sin nature."* Now being a *"new man in Christ Jesus,"* we are *"dead"* to all the things of the past. The Believer is to understand that. This is the great ingredient of one's Faith.

Now the Believer might quickly ask, how they could be dead to sin, or the sin nature, when they are having so much problem with sin, if in fact, that is the case? This is where Faith comes in.

The Believer is not to look to himself, his failure, his problems, his weaknesses, but rather to what Christ has done. If we continue to look at ourselves, we will never climb out of the failure side of the ledger over into the victory side. We must always understand that we are not only *"dead unto sin,"* but as well, we are *"alive unto God."*

This means that God is going to handle the situation, that victory will be ours, that the Holy Spirit will bring it all to pass, that is if we place our Faith in the Finished Work of Christ, and not in ourselves.

The Believer at all times, must put his Faith in the Cross of Christ, keep his Faith in the Cross of Christ, and never allow his Faith to be removed from the Cross of Christ. As stated, the Cross is the key to all victory.

To understand the word *"reckon,"* one must vision in his mind a tally of figures such as one did in grade school, with the Teacher telling us that we must add them up and come up with the answer. The answer of course is, the bottom line. That is the *"reckoning"* or the *"computing"* of this tally of figures.

The idea is, everything that Jesus did tallies up to the bottom line of total and complete victory for the Child of God.

However, *"reckon"* has its roots in the Greek word *"logos."* To make it easy to understand, this particular word means *"the Word of God."* In other words Paul is saying:

"The Word of God says that you are dead indeed unto sin, but alive unto God through Jesus Christ your Lord."

Now you can believe your own failures, or you can believe the Word. As stated, this is where Faith comes in. If we start looking at ourselves, we're going to find problems. And to be sure, Satan doesn't care how much you look at yourself, he just doesn't want you to look at the Word of God.

So, as a Believer, you are to reckon yourself to be dead to sin and all that it is, and above all, alive unto God, with all of this being given to you through what Jesus Christ did at the Cross and in His Resurrection.

YIELDING

Paul now has another word of instruction for the Believer. He says, *"Neither yield ye your members as instruments of unrighteousness unto sin: but yield yourselves unto God, as those who are alive from the dead, and your members* (body members) *as instruments of Righteousness unto God"* (Rom. 6:13).

So the great question is, as some Christians would ask, *"How do I yield to Righteousness and not to sin?"*

Most Christians fail in this, simply because they do not understand what *"yielding"* actually means. Of course it has to do first of all with the will. And this is where most Christians go wrong.

Most Believers think that after they are saved, they now have the power to say *"yes"* or *"no"* to whatever it is they so desire. That is incorrect! And that's how many Believers get in trouble. They are relying on their *"willpower"* instead of the Cross of Christ, which means their Faith is now misplaced.

The *"will"* of the individual is a very powerful factor; however, it is powerful only in one aspect.

God protects the will of every single person in the world, even the worst sinner on the face of the Earth, as it regards their acceptance or rejection of Him. In other words, the worst alcoholic on the face of the Earth, even though his willpower is definitely not strong enough to say *"no"* to drink, can definitely say *"yes"* to Jesus Christ if he will only do so. God protects the will in that fashion. But of course, if he can say *"yes"* to Christ, he can at the same time, if he so desires, say *"no,"* which regrettably, most do.

The same thing follows through with the Christian. After one comes to Christ, God continues to protect the will, in that the Believer can always place his Faith and Trust in what Christ did at the Cross, and there is nothing that Satan can do about that. However, the moment that the Christian moves his Faith from the Cross to something else, which at the same time means to move his will to something else, he is then at the mercy of Satan, and will always fail. So let's say it again:

Inasmuch as we're dealing now with Christians, we will address ourselves only to the Child of God.

When it comes to the willpower of the Believer, God protects the will of the individual in their *"yielding capacities,"* only as it regards the Finished Work of Christ. In other words, if you will place your Faith in the Cross of Christ, in effect obeying *"whosoever will,"* God will protect your will, and

Satan will never be able to overcome you. This is what *"yielding"* the members of your body to Christ, actually means.

However, if you pull your will, which means to pull your Faith, away from the Cross of Christ to other things, Satan will quickly override your will, and you'll find yourself being forced to do things you don't want to do. Paul said this in Romans 7:18.

"For to will is present with me; but how to perform that which is good I find not."

Romans, Chapter 7 proclaims the position of Paul immediately after his conversion experience on the road to Damascus. He was now saved and Baptized with the Holy Spirit, but not knowing the victory of the Cross, at least at that time, he found he couldn't live the righteous life, no matter how hard he tried. He had the will to do it, but not the power, so he failed. But then, thank the Lord, God showed him the great victory of the Cross, which actually in effect, is the meaning of the *"New Covenant,"* which the Apostle then gave to us in Romans, Chapters 6 and 8.

So, the Apostle plainly tells us here, that if the Believer doesn't know and understand the Cross of Christ, and what Jesus there did, and in effect, places his Faith in something else, Satan can definitely override a person's will.

No, this doesn't mean that they are no longer responsible. In fact, every Believer is definitely responsible and in every capacity. Every Believer has the willpower to trust what Christ did at the Cross on our behalf. That's the only place that his will is protected by God. If the Believer strays outside of that, in effect, as stated, placing his Faith in something else, such as the Church, himself, another Preacher, or whomever or whatever, he will quickly find his will being overridden by the powers of darkness. Let me emphasize it again:

My victory and your victory are found totally and completely in the Cross of Christ. It is impossible for any human being, no matter that they're saved and Baptized with the Holy Spirit, to live a holy life, without understanding this of which we have said. We must always, and without exception, understand, that every victory comes through the Cross. Consequently, our Faith must rest in the Cross. And when we do that, the Holy Spirit then does great and mighty things on our behalf (Rom. 8:1-2, 11, 13).

THE DOMINION OF SIN BROKEN

Once the Believer knows and understands this of which we have stated, thereby placing his Faith in the Finished Work of Christ, the Holy Spirit through Paul then said, *"For sin shall not have dominion over you: for ye are not under the Law, but under Grace"* (Rom. 6:14).

This Passage doesn't teach sinless perfection, for the Bible doesn't teach sinless perfection. But it does teach, that sin is not to dominate the Believer. And regrettably, that's where most Christians are presently, I think. Sin is dominating them in some way. In fact, if the Believer doesn't know and understand the Cross of Christ, then without a doubt, sin will definitely dominate them in some manner. It is impossible for it to be otherwise.

When we say *"sin,"* we're not necessarily meaning one of the vices, even though that definitely will be the case in the hearts and lives of many Believers. There is a greater sin than the vices, and that is the sin of *"resisting the Holy Spirit"* (Acts 7:51).

RESISTING THE HOLY SPIRIT

This sin is the worst sin of all. It means the following:

Any time we resist God's Plan of Salvation and Victory, which is the Cross of Christ, and if we do so in any manner, we are *"resisting the Holy Spirit."*

That means, if any person reads these things we have stated, and refuses to believe them, or anything else the Bible teaches about the Cross, especially understanding that it is the story of the Bible, then that person is *"resisting the Holy Spirit."* In fact, it cannot be any other way!

So, the Believer who resists the Cross of Christ, is being dominated by sin, i.e., *"the sin nature,"* in one way or the other, whether through the vices, i.e., *"works of the flesh"* (Gal. 5:19-21), or resisting the Holy Spirit.

LAW AND GRACE

What does Paul mean by the statement, *"For ye are not under the Law, but under Grace?"*

NOTES

We'll look at Grace first.

The Grace of God is the means by which the Goodness of God is extended to undeserving mankind. It all comes through the Cross of Christ.

Many Christians make the mistake of majoring in Grace and minoring in the Cross. They have it backwards, and will suffer consequences.

While the Grace of God is certainly to be paramount within our thinking, we are to always understand, that Grace is a product of the Cross, meaning that the Cross is the foundation of all things.

Whenever the Believer exhibits Faith in the Cross of Christ, understanding that it is from this Source that all Blessings flow, the Grace of God will automatically come to him in an uninterrupted flow. This means that the Holy Spirit will continue to work mightily within his life, making all the benefits of the Cross applicable.

However, if the Believer puts his Faith in anything else, and I mean anything else, other than the Cross of Christ, such action always frustrates the Grace of God, which places the Believer in *"Law,"* which guarantees failure (Gal. 2:20-21). The sad fact is most Christians are functioning under *"Law."*

Sadder still, most are functioning under Law and simply don't know they are, and because they've had no teaching whatsoever on the Cross. Or what little they have had is mostly in the realm of sentimentality, which is little better than nothing.

And then again, when many Christians read this particular Scripture, if they think about it at all, they think Paul is merely speaking about the Dispensation of Law versus the Dispensation of Grace, in which the latter Dispensation we now are. However, Paul is not speaking here of Dispensations, but rather the problem that faces every Christian and does so constantly. The facts are, every single Believer in the world is either functioning in Law or Grace, and as stated, the sadness is most don't know the difference.

However, it is guaranteed that one will know the difference as it regards victory or lack of it. In other words, if one is functioning in Grace, which means to function by having Faith in the Cross, victory will be the

lot of such a person. Otherwise, it will be failure. Everything is tied to the Cross of Christ.

THE GREAT VISIT

The question, *"Or the son of man, that Thou visitest him?"*, refers to looking upon in order to help or to benefit, to look after, or one for which to have care. This clearly indicates, as stated, that the *"son of man"* spoken of here is the human race and not Christ. God looks upon the human race in order to help or to benefit it. Thus, the picture in Verses 6 through 8 is that of the human race in Adam (Wuest).

Even though the word *"visitest"* covers a lot of territory, it can all be summed up in the Cross of Christ. Everything done by the Lord toward the human race, every Revelation, every advancement, have always and without fail, pointed toward the Cross, i.e., *"the great visitation."* So, when the Holy Spirit through the Apostle mentions this *"visitation,"* He is in actuality speaking of the Cross.

It was to the Cross that all the prophecies pointed; it was to the Cross that all the great Laws of Moses, with all of its Sacrifices, Ceremonies, and Feast Days, pointed. In fact, this great *"visit"* was in actual preparation some 4,000 years, counting from the time of Adam before Christ was born. And if we want to back further, for Peter tells us, that all of this was done in the Mind of God, even before the foundation of the Earth, then the time is beyond comprehension (I Pet. 1:18-20).

(7) "THOU MADEST HIM A LITTLE LOWER THAN THE ANGELS; THOU CROWNEDST HIM WITH GLORY AND HONOUR, AND DIDST SET HIM OVER THE WORKS OF THY HANDS:"

The exegesis is:

1. The Hebrew Text has *"a little less than God,"* and because the word translated *"Angels,"* is *"Elohim,"* and means *"God."*

2. This means that man was originally created higher than the Angels, but lost that great position due to the Fall.

3. Man lost this glory and honor at the Fall, and it will be gained back only in Christ.

4. Originally, God gave man total dominion over all His creation, but that was forfeited to Satan, and again, will only be brought back in Christ.

THE CREATION OF MAN

The phrase, *"Thou madest him a little lower than the Angels,"* should have been translated, and as stated, *"Thou madest him a little lower than God."* This is taken from Psalm 8. As we've already stated, it is difficult for one to look at man presently and understand his original creation. The only One the world has ever seen Who portrays that original creation is Christ. Consequently, it's impossible to find a perfect example otherwise. While it is certainly true that Christians should be that example, and in fact are to a certain extent; still, all of us fall short, as would be obvious. So, as the *"Representative Man,"* i.e., *"Second Man,"* Christ Jesus is the perfect example of what Adam was originally intended by God to be. All of this being lost at the Fall, man presently is a sorry example of what God originally intended.

But yet, we see the worth of man in the great price that God has agreed to pay, and in fact did pay, in order that man might be saved. Of course, the worth of something is always judged by the price that is paid. And to be sure, no higher price could have been paid than what was paid by our Lord and Saviour Jesus Christ in order that man might be saved.

CROWNED WITH GLORY AND HONOR

The phrase, *"Thou crownedst him with glory and honor,"* proclaimed that which was never said of Angels. This is a picture of Adam in the paradise of Eden, before he sinned. The distinctive word for *"crowned"* here is *"stephanos."* The *"diadema"* is the royal crown, the *"stephanos,"* the victor's crown, the crown given to a person because of his exalted rank or station. The word used here refers to the *"victor's crown."* The idea is as follows:

Even though man has suffered a terrible setback, through Jesus Christ everything lost will be regained and then some. The reason is obvious; *"Where sin did abound, Grace did much more abound"* (Rom. 5:20).

So, Jesus Christ has already been crowned with *"glory and honor,"* and whatever He has, and whatever He has done, have all been for mankind, and are given totally and completely

to mankind upon Faith (Jn. 3:16). Admittedly, we do not yet have all that He has given us, that awaiting the First Resurrection of Life; however, that coming time is nearer today than it ever has been before. In fact, according to the signs of the times, it could happen at any moment (I Thess. 4:13-18).

DOMINION

The phrase, *"And didst set him over the works of Thy hands,"* is taken from Psalms 8:7, and continues with the words, *"all sheep and oxen, yea, and the beasts of the field;*

"The fowl of the air, and the fish of the sea, and whatsoever passeth through the paths of the seas."

As well, it seems to include *"the moon and the stars, which Thou hast ordained"* (Ps. 8:3-8).

Some of that dominion is retained, despite the Fall; however, as would be obvious, much has been lost. But to be sure, it has all been regained in Christ, and will ultimately be realized in Christ.

(8) "THOU HAST PUT ALL THINGS IN SUBJECTION UNDER HIS FEET. FOR IN THAT HE PUT ALL IN SUBJECTION UNDER HIM, HE LEFT NOTHING THAT IS NOT PUT UNDER HIM. BUT NOW WE SEE NOT YET ALL THINGS PUT UNDER HIM."

The breakdown is as follows:

1. The all things in subjection under his feet, have to do with what Christ did at the Cross.

2. The *"subjection"* of which is here spoken, includes everything, for the Cross proclaims a total victory.

3. At the present time having only a down payment concerning all that the Atonement has provided, to be sure, it will all be ultimately realized.

SUBJECTION

The phrase, *"Thou hast put all things in subjection under his feet,"* speaks of Adam before the Fall, but more particularly, this Passage speaks of the Lord Jesus Christ and what He did at the Cross on our behalf.

Concerning Christ Paul also said, *"And what is the exceeding greatness of His power to us-ward who believe, according to the working of His mighty power,*

"Which He (God) *wrought in Christ, when He* (God) *raised Him* (Christ) *from the dead, and set Him at His Own Right Hand in the Heavenly Places,*

"Far above all principality, and power, and might, and dominion, and every name that is named, not only in this world, but also in that which is to come:

"And hath put all things under His feet (the feet of Christ, denoting total victory through the Cross), *and gave Him to be the Head over all things to the Church,*

"Which is His Body, the fullness of Him that filleth all in all" (Eph. 1:19-23).

As we have stated over and over again, Christ did all of this for us, and inasmuch as we are His Body, and we speak of the True Church, *"all things are in subjection under our feet."*

At this time, it speaks of victory over the world, the flesh, and the Devil. This means that every Believer, even as we've already brought out, should always think of himself as being *"dead indeed unto sin, but alive unto God through Jesus Christ our Lord"* (Rom. 6:11).

Actually, the word *"subjection"* will ultimately include the Lordship of the Earth under Christ; however, this regained dominion which Believers presently enjoy, accounts for victory over sin, with the other later to come. The problem now is not dominion over the Earth, but sin.

I realize that many Believers do not want to admit this fact; nevertheless, it is true. Satan attempts to overcome us, and his attempts are in the realm of causing us to fail God in some way. As we have already stated, sin comes in many forms. So, dominion must be totally won over sin before it can be taken over all other things. This is absolutely imperative!

Now we know that total dominion has already been won through Christ; however, in a practical sense this dominion must be played out in the hearts and lives of Believers. Regrettably, all Christians, although truly saved, will not gain the victory they ought to gain. While their Salvation is not affected by this, that is if they continue to trust Christ, failure can definitely bring about pain and suffering as well as great difficulties, and the loss of many things. So let not the Christian

NOTES

think that just because we are now redeemed, and thereby a Child of God, that we can sin with impunity. God forbid!

But victory over the world, the flesh, and the Devil, will definitely be realized in the hearts and lives of many Christians. As we've stated over and over again, such victory is always found in the Cross, and in fact, is only found in the Cross. If it is to be noticed in Romans 6:14, Paul said, *"For sin shall not have dominion over you."* That means we are to have dominion over it (Rom. 6:11-12). That is the dominion and the subjection to which the Believer must presently aspire, and which the Believer can have in Christ.

TOTAL SUBJECTION

The phrase, *"For in that He* (God) *put all in subjection under him, He* (God) *left nothing that is not put under him,"* once again speaks of the original Adam, but more than all, speaks of the *"Last Adam,"* the Lord Jesus Christ.

God put all things in subjection to Adam. Before the Fall, he was the head of the human race, the lord of the Earth. Even the animal kingdom was in subjection to him. And in fact, it seems as though all the works of God's hands fell into that category. So here we see two things:

1. When we think of all the creation of God, it is more than the mind could even begin to contemplate. And yet, it seems, that all of this was placed under Adam's care.

2. Understanding this, we must be made to realize that the original man was quite a creation. Understanding that he was made a little less than God, staggers the imagination. As great as the Angelic host is, such dominion it seems was never given to them.

THE FALL

The phrase, *"But now we see not yet all things put under him,"* refers to the Fall. All of this points to the fact that Adam through his fall into sin, lost the dominion he had before enjoyed. He was no longer master of himself. He had become a fallen creature, with a totally depraved nature. He was a slave to sin.

The animal kingdom was subservient to him not now through affection but fear, for the Fall affected them as well.

The ground, instead of yielding only good things, now produced also thorns, weeds, and other harmful things. Extremes of heat and cold, poisonous reptiles, earthquakes, typhoons, hurricanes, all conspired to make his life a constant battle to survive. He had lost the dominion over all these things (Wuest).

As we have previously stated, there is indeed now a general dominion by man over the Works of God, and over the inferior creation, but only in a limited way. The control is not universal.

In fact, man is seeking presently to find a way to control the weather, to conquer so-called outer space, because this instinct is in him. He was originally created to control all of these elements, and to do so with timely precision, thereby eliminating all the negatives which mankind now suffers. And this I might quickly add:

Man will not find supremacy over sickness and disease, over the elements, over outer space, and over so much else we could name, despite his efforts, despite all the hundreds of billions of dollars being spent, other than through Jesus Christ. To be sure, in the coming Kingdom Age, all of these things we have mentioned will be brought under control, under the control of Christ, and thereby under the control of all those who have believed Him and serve Him. In fact, this is soon to come.

Regenerated man will then know how to make the desert blossom as the rose, how to eliminate all sickness on the Earth, and how to control all the negative elements of weather. It is my belief as well, that interplanetary travel will then be common.

In fact, I think there is enough Biblical evidence to show that all the billions and even trillions of worlds in outer space were no doubt affected as well by the Fall. It left them a burned-out hulk, exactly as the Earth was in Genesis 1:2. When Jesus Christ comes to rule and to reign, and when Israel is finally once again in her place of responsibility and position, and the First Resurrection has now been brought about, all of these planets of outer space, will no doubt be brought to a successful conclusion as it regards their creation. I think that no sensible person can believe that out of all the billions, if not trillions,

of worlds in outer space, that it is only the Earth that God intended to be inhabited. I personally feel that His creation is much bigger than that. So what am I saying?

I am saying, that every Saint of God has a glorious eternity ahead, an eternity that will never end, which will be filled with the glorious creation of God, which is presently beyond our comprehension, but will definitely be placed within our grasp in that coming day *"when we shall all be changed"* (I Cor. 15:51-58).

And to be sure, all of this has been made possible, and will be made possible, because of what Jesus did at the Cross and in His Resurrection. To underestimate that Finished Work is a tragedy; to overestimate that Finished Work is impossible!

(9) "BUT WE SEE JESUS, WHO WAS MADE A LITTLE LOWER THAN THE ANGELS FOR THE SUFFERING OF DEATH, CROWNED WITH GLORY AND HONOUR; THAT HE BY THE GRACE OF GOD SHOULD TASTE DEATH FOR EVERY MAN."

The exposition is:

1. The Incarnation of Christ.

2. The Incarnation was brought about totally and solely for the purpose of the Cross.

3. Jesus, because of the Cross, is now crowned with glory and honor, which speaks of victory over all the powers of darkness, which addressed everything lost at the Fall.

4. It was the Grace of God which brought all of this about, which speaks of the Goodness of God, and not at all the goodness of man.

5. Jesus tasted death for every man; therefore, every man can be saved, if they will only believe (Jn. 3:16).

JESUS

The phrase, *"But we see Jesus, Who was made a little lower than the Angels,"* speaks of the Incarnation of Christ.

Now, in the midst of this dark picture of man's lost dominion, Paul calls our attention to a bright beam of light that pierces the surrounding gloom. It is *"Jesus!"*

When the Reader of the English translation comes to this Name here, at once there flashes into his mind the Jesus of the Gospels, the Jesus of Paul, the Saviour of lost sinners, and rightly so. And that is all good, so far as it goes. But to the Jewish Reader of the Greek Text of this Letter, the reaction would be somewhat different.

He would say to himself that the Name Jesus in the Greek Text is just the transliteration of the Hebrew name *"Jehoshua,"* the name of the God of Israel that points to His distinctive nature as the One Who saves. In other words, the idea of Deity would come to his mind (Wuest).

Paul now begins to close his argument. When he speaks of Jesus being made for a short time lower than the Angels, this would lead the Reader to the Person in the Gospels known as *"Jesus of Nazareth."* The idea is, the entirety of Jesus must be accepted, and not just part.

Paul has already stated that this One called *"the Son,"* and referring to the Son of God, is greater than the Prophets, and greater than the Angels. Now he will tell the real purpose for which he came. The Jews will read in no uncertain terms, that Jesus Christ is the Jehovah of the Old Testament and the Jesus of Nazareth of the New. In other words, they are One and the same!

The vision of Jesus which Paul wishes to bring to his Readers is that of the Son Incarnate, glorified, crowned with glory and honor, seated at the Right Hand of God, a position of glory and honor which the saved of the human race will share with Him in His future Millennial glory and Earth domain. That is the glorious ray of light which Paul brings into the dark picture of man's present estate (Wuest).

The Apostle is once again referring back to Philippians 2:5-11. It is called *"the self-emptying of Christ,"* referring to the Incarnation, i.e., *"God becoming man."*

THE SUFFERING OF DEATH

The phrase, *"For the suffering of death,"* unequivocally proclaims the fact that Jesus came to this world for one specific purpose, and that was to die upon a Cross, a work incidentally which was planned from even before the foundation of the world (I Pet. 1:18-20). The Holy Spirit through Paul is here plainly saying that this is the reason for which He came. This is why He was made lower than the Angels. They are immortal and cannot

die, just as God is immortal and cannot die (Mat. 22:30). It was necessary for Christ to be capable of death that He might taste death for every man.

This is the reason that the Believer must understand the Cross in the capacity of it being the foundation of all Faith. The Cross was not just one of the many incidents in the Life of Christ. It was the signal purpose for which He came. In fact, the Cross of Christ is not a Doctrine, but rather the foundation of the Church. It is that on which all Doctrine is built. And if any and all Doctrine doesn't have its roots totally and completely in the Cross of Christ, then in some way that Doctrine is unscriptural.

It is absolutely imperative that the Believer learn the significance of the Cross, the worth of the Cross, the power of the Cross, and in fact, the very idea that the benefits and potential of the Cross are absolutely inexhaustible.

Without at least some Faith in the Cross, the sinner cannot be saved (Jn. 3:16; Rom. 10:9-10, 13; Rev. 22:17).

As well and equally as important, and in one sense of the word even more important, the Believer must understand that all Victory, all prosperity, all Grace, all spiritual blessings and in their entirety, come totally and completely through what Jesus did at the Cross. This means that the Holy Spirit works exclusively according to the Finished Work of Christ. The tragedy is, millions of people are truly Spirit-filled, but do not know this Truth of which I have just spoken. Consequently, they expect the Holy Spirit to help them even though they are functioning in law. Never mind, that it may be in ignorance, and most likely is, the Holy Spirit still cannot work on their behalf. As a result, that Christian walks in defeat in one way or the other. And when I say *"that Christian"* I'm not speaking of only a few, but virtually all, and for the reason that most modern Christians know almost nothing about the Cross of Christ, except some sentimental thought. They know that Jesus died on the Cross, and they know that it was a horrible, excruciating death, but they have almost no knowledge whatsoever as to what it all means, especially as it concerns their everyday victory and walk before the Lord.

SO WHAT IS THE MODERN CHURCH DOING?

The modern Church is chasing fads, perverting the Gospel of Christ by trying to twist the Scripture into a means to get rich, when in reality, it's only the Preachers who are getting rich, and I speak of the Preachers who peddle this fallacious doctrine of the *"greed gospel."* Almost half the modern Church completely ignores the Holy Spirit, if not outright rejecting Him. Consequently, there is absolutely nothing happening in their ranks, at least for the Lord. Even those who claim to be Fundamentalists, which means to believe all the Bible, but who have rejected the Spirit, have denied themselves the Power of the Holy Spirit, which leaves them with nothing but man-instituted and man-operated religiosity, which to be frank, is worse than nothing at all! (II Tim. 3:1-5).

In the last half century there's been so little teaching on the Cross of Christ that the modern Church anymore little knows the veracity and the power of this of which Christ has done. This means that the *"Jesus"* that's being worshiped, is not the Jesus of the Bible. Pure and simple, it is *"another Jesus,"* prompted by *"another spirit,"* which fosters *"another gospel"* (II Cor. 11:4). Please allow me to say the following as boldly as I can:

If it's not the Jesus of the Cross, or as Paul said, *"Jesus Christ and Him Crucified,"* then it's not the Jesus of the Bible. It may be a philosophical Jesus, or a miracle Jesus, or a money Jesus, or even an intellectual Jesus, or a religious Jesus, or a Water Baptism Jesus, or possibly a Lord's Supper Jesus, or even a Preacher Jesus. And with millions, it's a Denomination Jesus, or a Faith Jesus. And with some it's a Grace Jesus. But let the Reader understand and unequivocally so, that if it's not *"Jesus Christ and Him Crucified,"* or rather the *"Cross Jesus"* one might say, then it's not the Bible Jesus. In fact, some of these things we have mentioned are very close to being right, but the reason I have named them, such as the *"Grace Jesus,"* is because even with many who believe in the great Doctrine of Grace, as all should, they

NOTES

make that the priority, instead of the Cross which makes Grace possible. We must always stick with the Word of God (I Cor. 2:2).

If one is to notice, Paul highlighted many things as it pertains to the benefits of the Cross; however, the Cross of Christ was ever the foundation of all that he taught, and as well, was a foundation which he portrayed constantly. No one had any doubt, at least if they want to be honest with the Bible, as to what the man preached and taught. To give Scriptural foundation for that which I have just said, all one has to do, is to name any one of Paul's 14 Epistles.

The Word of God is exactly like a schematic for a piece of equipment. If we want to know how it works, we go to that schematic. As should be obvious, if we deviate from the schematic, the piece of equipment will probably not function correctly.

The Bible is even more particular than that. While schematics are drawn up by men and at times could be incorrect, the Bible is error free, and because it is the Word of God. Consequently, the Lord said exactly what He meant, and meant exactly what He said. I have learned in serving Him all these many years, that if we deviate from he Word of God one iota, we will suffer at least some negative consequences. As well, I've also learned, that if we will ask the Lord to show us the meaning of the Word, and do so with a faithful and sincere heart, that He will definitely answer that prayer (Mat. 5:6).

Regrettably, many people are in unbelief and error, simply because that's where they want to be. They try to soothe their conscience, so they find a Church that will agree with them, whatever their error might be. And to be sure, there are Churches of every stripe on every corner, that makes that task very easy. In fact, it is a hundred times more difficult to find a Church where the True Gospel is truly preached, which means the True Spirit of God is truly operative, than to find the other kind.

If the Reader is to notice, I said *"True Church,"* and *"True moving of the Spirit."* There are all types of spirits operating nowadays, which aren't of God. They may look like God, sound like God, and even function in some manner like God, but they are merely "angels of light" masquerading as God (II Cor. 11:13-15).

Paul said, *"But I fear, lest by any means, as the serpent beguiled Eve through his subtilty, so your minds should be corrupted from the simplicity that is in Christ."*

And then he said, *"For if he that cometh preacheth another Jesus, whom we have not preached* (Paul preached the Jesus of the Cross), *or if you receive another spirit, which ye have not received* (it is not the Holy Spirit irrespective of the claims), *or another gospel, which ye have not accepted* (any gospel, that's not *'Jesus Christ and Him Crucified'*), *ye might well bear with him* (the false apostle)" (II Cor. 11:3-4). The tragedy is, the modern Church is bearing with many false apostles!

CROWNED

The phrase, *"Crowned with glory and honor,"* speaks of Christ seated at the Right Hand of God, a glorious position which the saved of the human race will share with Him in His future Millennial Glory and Earth dominion. This is the glorious ray of light which the writer brings into the dark picture of man's present estate.

But this path of glory and honor for the Son was through Incarnation and the Death of the Cross.

Paul frames his words in this manner, simply because the controversy centered around the claims of Jesus of Nazareth to the Messiahship. The unconverted Jews were hammering at these claims, which they continue to do even unto this day. To be sure, many Jews had in fact, accepted Christ in those particular times. But the moment they did, they came under a steady barrage from fellow Jews who had rejected Jesus; consequently, many Christian Jews were growing discouraged, with some of them even turning their backs on Christ, going back into the Law and Temple worship. It is to that difficulty and those particular individuals, which Paul writes.

The *"crown"* here mentioned by Paul as given to Christ, is the *"stephanos,"* which refers to *"the victor's crown."* It is the same crown mentioned in Verse 7, which is given to a person because of his exalted rank or

station, brought about through a tremendous victory.

The first Adam was given this crown, even though the great victory was not his but belonged exclusively to God. The Last Adam, however, did in fact, win a victory of unparalleled proportions, and did it because the victory had been lost. The first Adam's victory had not been lost, but was perpetual with God; however, when He gave this victory to the first Adam, it was a victory which Adam could lose or forfeit, which he did. Consequently, the Last Adam would have to regain this victory, which He did through and by the Cross. This victory is now held by the Last Adam, and can never be lost again. In fact, this is what makes the New Covenant absolutely unbreakable.

A Covenant has to be between two or more parties. Jesus Christ is God, and He is also the Representative Man. So the Covenant is in Him exclusively, as He serves in both capacities, which guarantees its veracity and its perpetuity. Hence Paul refers to it as *"The Everlasting Covenant"* (Heb. 13:20).

THE TASTING OF DEATH

The phrase, *"That He by the Grace of God should taste death for every man,"* proclaims the fact that He needed the Grace of God to accomplish this task, and because He was a man, *"the Man, Christ Jesus."*

The penalty of sin was paid by Him. He through the Blood of His Cross regained for man that which Adam through his Fall lost for man.

Man today may have Salvation from sin, plus its penalty and its power, by simply believing in what Jesus did at the Cross, thereby taking unto himself this great victory there won. The Earth itself, and the animal kingdom will shortly be relieved of the curse that was put upon it because of Adam's sin, and in the eternity to come, the saved of the human race will live on the Earth remade into a Paradise, with the Son as our Sovereign and Lord.

Thus, the Angels will neither rule over the Millennial Earth, nor will the Earth in its eternal state consequent upon its renovation, be under the administration of Angels. The saved of the human race and our glorious

Head, the Last Adam, will rule over the Earth Paradise of God. Thus, the Messiah is better than the Angels, since He will bear the rule and the Scepter, and they will be His servants.

Going back to the previous phrase, *"For the suffering of death"* is in the Greek Text associated with the words, *"crowned with glory and honor."* It was through our Lord's sufferings and because of them that He was crowned with glory and honor. His Exaltation and preeminence over the Angels were obtained through His humiliation. God manifested His Grace toward man in that He set forth His Son as the propitiation which would pay for sin. It was at the Cross that the Last Adam gained the victory through the Blood of His Cross over the Serpent under whose attack the first Adam had gone down in defeat, dragging down with him the entire human race of which he was the federal head. But the Last Adam, raising Himself out from under that awful thing called death, brings with Him from that sphere into which He vicariously (as our Substitute) descended, the Saints of all ages, to someday share His glory and honor on His Throne (Eph. 2:6) (Wuest).

THE GRACE OF GOD

Even though the Grace of God does pertain to Christ as stated, its actual meaning does not really direct itself to the Saviour, but to mankind in general. In other words, it was totally and completely *"the Grace of God"* which brought about the Salvation of man through the Death of Christ. It certainly wasn't any goodness on the part of man which brought this about, as should be obvious. In fact, man has no argument at all.

He may claim that he's not responsible for someone who did something thousands of years ago, whom he is not even sure actually existed. Of course, the argument in that capacity doesn't hold water.

While it is true that man is in the condition that he's in because of what Adam long ago did; still, there are two other factors which must be brought to bear as well. They are:

1. Unredeemed man will not stand before God someday to answer for what Adam did, but for what he personally has done. The idea is, the guilt of man is beyond question. So we're not speaking here of something that happened thousands of years ago, but something that's happening right now in the hearts and lives of unbelievers. They are rebelling against God, with Paul aptly describing them in Romans, Chapter 3. So, every person who doesn't know Christ will answer to God *"according to their works"* (Rev. 20:13).

2. It is true that man cannot help what Adam so long ago did, or the terrible dilemma in which this has placed man. However, God has provided a solution for man's dilemma, and that solution is *"Jesus Christ and Him Crucified"* (I Cor. 2:2).

In the final analysis, man will be lost because he rejects that Solution. The Lord Himself said, *"That the Holy Spirit has come to reprove the world of sin, and of Righteousness and of judgment."*

He then said, *"Of sin, because they believe not on Me,"* or as one might say, *"The Holy Spirit will convict men of the sin of not believing on Christ"* (Jn. 16:8-9).

Therefore, considering who man is (a child of Satan one might say), and what man is (totally depraved with no Righteousness whatsoever), we certainly can understand that it had to be the Grace of God extended to undeserving man, in order for this great Plan of Redemption to be brought about.

TASTE DEATH

The verb *"taste death"* means to taste with the mouth, from which the sense of *"come to know"* develops. It means here that Jesus died, with all that that entails.

He actually tasted death in a realistic consciousness proper only to Him, and for the purpose of redeeming man; and that Redemption was not motivated by the moral beauty of man, but by the Grace of God.

In fact, I think one could say that the death of Jesus was totally unlike any other death that's ever been. In the first place, He could not have died in the manner in which we think of death. In other words, no one could have killed Him, and because there was no sin in Him. The wages of sin is death, and inasmuch as He had never sinned, death had no claim on Him, as it does the entirety of the human race.

Every human being other than Christ is born in original sin, meaning that all are born with death in them, as is obvious. Jesus was not conceived by man, so was not born in original sin and, therefore, had no seed of death in Him. Concerning His Life He plainly said of Himself, *"No man taketh it from Me, but I lay it down of Myself. I have power to lay it down, and I have power to take it again* (Resurrection). *This Commandment have I received of My Father"* (Jn. 10:18).

Jesus had no sin. Sin separates man from God, which is spiritual death, which is the cause of physical death. God is the life-support system, and if that support system is broken, death is the inevitable result.

So Jesus had to literally give Himself into death, or as one might say, *"breathe out His life,"* which He did!

As well, because the life of Jesus had been literally perfect, and perfect in every respect, His Death could be a Perfect Sacrifice, which it was, which means it was a Sacrifice which God could accept, and in fact did accept, which the death of no other human being could do.

One bright light of the Faith movement claims that the Cross is fairly insignificant, in that *"any Born-Again man could die on a Cross thereby redeeming mankind,"* as he put it. And he claims that God told him this!

The Truth is he was given that word by an evil spirit. Such a statement is not merely ludicrous, it borders on blasphemy, if not that crucial sin.

In the first place, every Born-Again man in this world is totally and completely dependent upon Christ for all that he has, and even despite that, is constantly *"coming short of the Glory of God"* (Rom. 3:23). We are saved from this constant *"coming short"* simply because the *"Blood of Jesus Christ, God's Son* (constantly) *cleanseth us from all sin"* (I Jn. 1:7).

And then John turned around and said, *"If we say that we have no sin, we deceive ourselves, and the Truth is not in us"* (I Jn. 1:8).

So, the idea that a Born-Again man could hang on a Cross and redeem humanity, exactly as Christ did, is as stated, either gross ignorance or blasphemy. I trust it's the former, because if it's the latter, this man is in serious trouble indeed!

Jesus' Death was a Sacrifice, and more particularly, *"a Sacrifice for sin"* (Heb. 9:26;

10:12, 26). No other human being could serve in that capacity. Him tasting death for every man is the only way that the terrible sin debt could be settled. In other words, this was what God demanded.

This is why Peter said that *"we were not redeemed with corruptible things, as silver and gold . . . but with the Precious Blood of Christ, as of a Lamb without blemish and without spot"* (I Pet. 1:18-19).

WHY DID GOD DEMAND THE DEATH OF HIS ONLY SON?

There is a mystery to the demands of God as it regards this awful thing, which means that as a human being we can only go so far into the Atonement and what it actually meant. After a certain point is reached in our understanding, God pulls the veil, and no doubt for many reasons. Being but finite creatures, our understanding is naturally limited; however, that which we do actually understand, opens up to us the Love of God for lost humanity, as nothing else.

At the Fall in the Garden of Eden, life was forfeited. When God told Adam and Eve that they could partake of the fruit of any tree in the Garden, with the exception of *"the tree of the knowledge of good and evil,"* all of this was done for a reason (Gen. 2:17).

When He told them concerning this particular tree, *"For in the day that thou eatest thereof thou shalt surely die,"* He was speaking of spiritual death and not physical death. Spiritual death refers to total separation from God, Who is the Life Source of all things. Satan contains no life, only death (Jn. 10:10). Of course, spiritual death, would ultimately lead to physical death, which it did and has.

The medical profession doesn't quite understand why the physical organs of the human body age and after awhile cease to function. They claim that this should not be the case, and in fact, that these organs should function forever. They tell us that the human body somewhat rejuvenates itself every seven years. So, they are at a loss as to the why of the aging process.

To be sure, the aging process is not a physical problem, but rather a spiritual problem. It is as stated, that man has cut himself off from his life-support system, if one would be allowed to use such terminology, Which and Who is God. Thank God, through Jesus Christ that the life-support system has been restored, with its final installment coming at the Resurrection of Life, which will happen very soon!

Man's sin was disobedience, but it was far more than that. In effect, man changed masters. God had been his life and Lord, and now Satan would be his lord, but with no life. As well, and as previously stated, all the dominion given by God to Adam is now forfeited to Satan.

Inasmuch as life had been forfeited, it would take the sacrifice of a life, a perfect life, in order for this terrible problem to be addressed. However, there was a problem with this:

Man could not provide a perfect sacrifice in any capacity, considering that due to the Fall, he is totally, spiritually depraved.

Angels could not suffice because they were of another creation. So in the mind of Satan, he had pulled off the great coup, a victory so complete in his eyes, that even God could not assuage the situation. However, Satan in his terrible, fallen condition, even as wise as he had originally been and to a degree still was, couldn't think now as he once did. In other words, due to sin, his thinking had become warped and twisted. Due to his own fall, he could no longer think in terms of love, Which and Who God is. Love created mankind, and love must redeem mankind. And that means that God would go to any length in order that Redemption would be brought about, a length and degree incidentally, to which Satan could not relate.

God would become man, the *"Last Adam,"* and even at great price, the price of Himself on the Cross, in effect offering up Himself as a Sacrifice, which would pay the terrible sin debt owed by man. Life had been forfeited, and a perfect life would have to be offered up in Sacrifice in order that the original life could be regained. This God only could do! And this God only did! He tasted death for every man, thereby paying the price for the Redemption of lost humanity.

EVERY MAN

When Jesus died on the Cross, the great Sacrifice of Himself which He offered up, was

NOTES

definitely not just for a select few, but for the entirety of the human race, and for all time. That means the good moral man can be saved, and it also means the vilest can be saved. In fact, all are judged as to be lost (Ps. 14:2-3; 52:2-4; Eccl. 7:20; Rom. 3:10), then all may be saved (Jn. 3:16).

Through death the fulfillment of God's purpose might seem to be frustrated; through the death of Jesus on behalf of every man, however, (I Pet. 3:18) it is fulfilled.

Man's inheritance was forfeited through sin, and that only through the virtue of a death which made atonement for sin is the promise again made sure. All of this proclaims the Cross as the wellspring of all Blessings, and in every capacity, from God. In other words, anything that we receive from the Lord must without exception come through the Cross of Christ. It is through His great Sacrifice of Himself, that all things are made possible.

Man as a sinner could not be approached by God, and could not approach God. There had to be a go-between, a Mediator if you will. That Mediator is Jesus Christ and Jesus Christ Alone, and He is the Mediator by virtue of what He did at the Cross and in His Resurrection (I Tim. 2:5). Actually, we will have much more to say about this as we comment on Chapter 8 of this Epistle.

If we attempt to make anything else a Mediator, such as our Church, a Preacher, a Denomination, or the Pope for that matter, or even the Virgin Mary, we sin greatly. Actually, we blaspheme! Jesus is what He is *to* us, by virtue of what He did *for* us. And He did it *"for every man."* That's what makes it so useless, so horrendous, so unnecessary, for anyone to die lost. And yet, there are many, even great multitudes dying lost, simply because they do not know the Way of Salvation, because no one has bothered to explain it to them.

How much will the Church answer for in regard to not taking the Gospel to the world? And worse yet, great segments of the Church not only will not take the grand Message to lost humanity, but will regrettably, attempt to stop anyone who does. Being extremely familiar with world evangelism, and in just about every capacity, please believe me I know what I'm talking about.

The Church is both the best place in town, and the worst place in town. There are some few Churches which fall into the category of the former, with the far greater majority falling into the category of the latter. It is through the Church that Satan carries forth his greatest work.

The Message of the Church must ever be *"Jesus Christ and Him Crucified,"* or else it's not the Gospel, but something else entirely (I Cor. 2:2). To be sure, that which it espouses might be good, but if it's not the Cross, it will not set any captives free. Only what Jesus did at the Cross can accomplish that.

(10) "FOR IT BECAME HIM, FOR WHOM ARE ALL THINGS, AND BY WHOM ARE ALL THINGS, IN BRINGING MANY SONS UNTO GLORY, TO MAKE THE CAPTAIN OF THEIR SALVATION PERFECT THROUGH SUFFERINGS."

The exegesis is as follows:

1. Before the foundation of the world, the Godhead deemed it desirable that God would become Man and die on a Cross, in order that man might be saved (I Pet. 1:18-20).

2. *"By Whom"* refers to the fact that God is the final reason for all things.

3. *"By Whom"* is literally *"through Whose agency"* all things came into being.

4. The great Redemption Plan will see many sons brought from sin to Salvation.

5. It was *"through sufferings"* that this great Plan of Redemption was brought about by Christ, which refers to the Cross.

THE PLAN OF GOD

The phrase, *"For it became Him,"* refers to God's Way, as it concerns the Redemption of mankind.

Christ Crucified (I Cor. 1:23), was a stumbling block to the Jew. In fact, this may have been one of the factors which was influencing these Hebrews in their drift away from their profession of Christ as the Messiah, back to the Levitical sacrifices.

Paul seeks to justify his bold assertion of Verse 9. He senses the recoil which his Readers would have from the thought of a suffering Messiah, and he now shows that Jesus' suffering and death were according to the Divine fitness of things (Wuest).

"It became" in the Greek means that the Cross of Christ was not a logical necessity; it was not an obligation growing out of circumstances. The idea is, the fact that God the Father decreed that it must be through the Blood of Christ's Cross that the Captain of our Salvation would become the Saviour of sinners, did not find its origin in a Divine fiat, but in the very constitution of the nature of God.

A *Holy* God cannot look upon sin with any degree of allowance. A *Righteous* God cannot but require that the demands of the violated Law be satisfied. And a *Loving* God cannot but provide the very payment of the penalty which His Law demands. Thus, Paul shows the sweet reasonableness of the Cross. And because only God can satisfy the demands of God, so only the Messiah Who is One of the Persons of the Godhead, could in the great Plan of Salvation, provide the Sacrifice, which would be the Sacrifice of Himself.

One might well say that God the Father provides the Salvation, God the Son procures it, and God the Holy Spirit applies it (Wuest).

THE JEW

The Jewish religious leaders just might have accepted a grandiose, conquering, rich, powerful Messiah. But of course, such an attitude only showed the evil of their hearts. While they screamed to the highest heavens that all Gentiles were lost, they did not at all agree that they were in the same boat so to speak. This is why Paul addressed them in this manner so strongly in Romans, Chapters 2 and 3. In fact, he placed them in the same category as the Gentiles, greatly needing a Redeemer, in fact needing Him just as much as did the Gentiles. To be sure, the Jews did not agree with that at all!

They wanted a Messiah which would satisfy their lusts. They did not at all agree that they needed to be redeemed from those lusts. They equated all the dealings of God with them in the past as favor; they did not at all think of it as Grace and Mercy, which it was!

To be sure, the signs were everywhere as to God's displeasure with them, but they couldn't seem to see it. At this very moment, the Jews were ruled by Rome, which was a bitter sign and in glaring detail, of their estrangement from God. But they saw themselves as being right with God, strictly on the basis of being a Jew, thereby being in the natural lineage of Abraham. They wouldn't recognize their need, or realize their need. So they rejected the Lord of Glory, actually killing Him in the Name of the Lord, which was and is the greatest travesty of injustice the world has ever known.

But wonder of wonders, the Holy Spirit predicts that they ultimately will be brought back. To be sure, it will be only after tremendous suffering and pain, which in fact are just ahead of them in the form of the coming Great Tribulation. Jeremiah said it would be *"the time of Jacob's trouble"* (Jer. 30:7). But he also said, *"He shall be saved out of it."*

FOR WHOM

The phrase, *"For Whom are all things,"* refers to God the Father. *"For Whom"* is literally *"on account of Whom,"* that is, for Whose sake all things exist. God is the final reason for all things.

The idea of this statement is that the creation, and to whatever extent it might be, is *"for"* God, because it was created *"by"* God. This means that it is not for Satan, or even for man. Now here is the problem:

Satan using man as a tool, and I speak of unredeemed man, seeks to take over the creation of God. Actually he said, *"I will ascend into Heaven, I will exalt my throne above the stars of God: I will sit also upon the mount of the congregation, in the sides of the north:*

"I will ascend above the heights of the clouds; I will be like the Most High" (Isa. 14:13-14). In fact, that's what this great struggle is all about, *"dominion!"*

BY WHOM

The phrase, *"And by Whom are all things,"* literally means, *"through Whose agency"* all things came into being. The idea is, that God created all things, and He keeps all things running and operating on the Laws that He Himself has made; however, Satan has sought to circumvent those Laws by *"stealing, killing, and destroying"* (Jn. 10:10). He is attempting to usurp the order of creation, which in actuality is the cause of

NOTES

all inclement weather, such as earthquakes, storms, etc.

So we see in these two statements as given by Paul *"for Whom,"* and *"by Whom,"* a glimpse of the entirety of the struggle which is taking place.

The phrase, *"By Whom are all things,"* while pertaining to the work of creation as stated, leans more heavily, however, toward the Plan of Salvation, perfected by our Heavenly Father, and carried out by the Son. All of this means that it was not the work of fate or chance, but that the whole plan should bear the mark of the infinite wisdom of its Author.

Usually we do not speak of things as being *"fitting"* for God, but here the word is appropriate. The way of Salvation is not arbitrary but befitting the Character of the God we know, the God *"for Whom and by Whom everything exists."* In other words, He is the Goal and the Author of all that is, and of course we speak of Righteousness.

WHAT DOES *"ALL"* INCLUDE?

Does *"all"* include sin? Transgression? Failure?

Directly, no! Indirectly, yes! Let us explain:

God answers to no one, which means He is subject to no one. He is uncaused, unformed, unmade, had no beginning, will have no ending, and has always been, and always will be. Can the human mind grasp such statements, which mind demands a beginning and ending to everything? No, the human mind cannot grasp or understand such terminology. It is beyond our realm of conception.

But yet there are some things about the nature of God which we are taught in the Bible, that does tell us things about Him, which gives us a clue as to why certain things are done, or as one might say, permitted or allowed.

In the first place, God is not the Author of sin or iniquity in any fashion.

Through the Prophet Isaiah, God said of Himself, *"That they may know from the rising of the sun, and from the west, that there is none beside Me. I am the Lord, and there is none else.*

"I form the light, and create darkness: I make peace, and create evil: I the Lord do all these things" (Isa. 45:6-7).

The Hebrew word for *"evil"* is *"rah,"* and means *"adversity, sorrow, trouble,"* but does not refer to sin or iniquity.

The idea is, God has created everything by a system of Laws. And if those Laws are broken, which they were with the fall of Lucifer and the fall of man, trouble, sorrow, and problems will definitely occur. One might say that it's the law of *"sowing and reaping"* (Gal. 6:7). As an example one might use explosives. If used correctly, these things can help to build roads, move mountains, construct great works; however, if they are used incorrectly, they can destroy these great works they have built. Such are the Laws of God.

When God originally created the Angel Lucifer, He created him perfectly righteous, holy, and pure. But He also gave this Angel, as He did all other Angels, the ability to reason and the power of choice. To get what He wanted, this had to be done in this manner. However, to choose to do good, one at the same time has to have the ability to choose to do evil. In fact, God made man in the same fashion, even higher than the Angels, in effect creating man in the very Image of God.

The Laws of God, by which all creation is brought into being, are perfect in every way. But some of these Laws, although, altogether perfect, of necessity, fall out to a negative aspect. For instance, the Scripture says, *"For the wages of sin is death"* (Rom. 6:23). This is a Law made by God, and definitely has a negative aspect. So, if certain things are done, certain things will occur. But if those things are negative, this doesn't mean that God is the One Who has done them, but only that He made the laws of *"Sowing and reaping,"* and *"cause and effect."*

It's like a giant 747 airliner built by Boeing. If it's handled correctly, it will perform a great service for mankind; however, if handled incorrectly, it can kill many people. Now the question should be asked, if that giant airliner is handled incorrectly, and kills many people, is it the fault of Boeing?

The answer to that is obvious, no it isn't the fault of Boeing! It's the fault of the one operating the equipment, that is if it's handled incorrectly.

Now some may surmise that Boeing should build an airplane which would be

impossible to handle incorrectly. Of course, that is impossible! The very nature of law demands a cause and effect.

So, God is definitely responsible for making the laws, which are all perfect one might quickly add, but He is not responsible for the way that created beings address or handle these laws. Therefore, *"all things"* definitely mean all things, but only in the context of which we have attempted to explain.

God made all the Angels and all of mankind, giving them the ability to reason and the ability to make a free, moral choice; however, He cannot be held responsible for the choices made.

MANY SONS

The phrase, *"In bringing many sons unto Glory,"* speaks of the Divine Purpose. The word *"many"* pertains to the number ever how large it will be, taken from all centuries. It will be large; however, as it regards the overall population for all time, Jesus plainly said, *"Strait is the gate, and narrow is the way, which leadeth unto life, and few there be that find it"* (Mat. 7:14).

"Glory" refers to the Presence of God, the way of the Lord, into Christ, Eternal Life, i.e., *"Heaven."*

We become *"sons"* through the *"born again"* experience (Jn. 3:3). Legally we are adopted into the Family of God, which means that although we have all the rights and privileges of a son in this family, still, we will never be a son (or daughter) in the same way as is Christ (Rom. 8:15). As well, we come into this status *"by Grace through Faith,"* which places us *"in Christ"* (II Cor. 5:17; Eph. 2:8-9).

However, it should be understood, that even though this number has been comparatively small up to now regarding Salvation, in the coming Kingdom Age, untold hundreds of millions will be brought to a saving knowledge of Jesus Christ (Isa. 11:10).

SUFFERINGS

The phrase, *"To make the Captain of their Salvation perfect through sufferings,"* carries the idea that Christ had to suffer on the Cross in order for Redemption to be brought about for humanity. It doesn't mean that suffering within itself effects any Redemption. That's not the idea at all!

The words *"to make perfect"* are literally *"to carry to the goal or consummation."* This does not imply any moral imperfection in the Lord Jesus, but speaks of the consummation of the human experience of suffering the Death of the Cross, through which He must pass if He is to become the Captain of our Salvation.

The word *"Captain"* actually means *"one who goes first,"* or *"Leader."* The Son precedes the saved on the road to Heaven. That's why He said, *"I am the Way,"* i.e., *"road,"* *". . . No man cometh to the Father but by Me"* (Jn. 14:6).

Paul also said, *"Having therefore, Brethren, boldness to enter into the Holiest by the Blood of Jesus, by a new and living way"* (Heb. 10:19-20). This is a road one might say, which is sprinkled with the Blood of Jesus. Our blessed Lord is, therefore, not only the Leader on the road to God, but actually the Road itself, and that by reason of His Precious Blood (Wuest).

There was never any imperfection in Him as Man. He was always the Perfect One, but let it never be forgotten that the Perfect Life of Jesus would never have saved one poor sinner. In order to become the Captain of Salvation, that He might lead many sons to Glory, He must go by the Way of the Cross, where He was perfected by sufferings. Apart from His bitter passion, there could be no Redemption for lost men and women.

Redemption was not motivated by the moral beauty of man, but by the Grace of God. Such a descent, such a subjection beneath Angels, and such a death did not dishonor Christ but *"became Him"* — glorified Him *for* Whom all things exist and *by* Whom all things exist; for thus God perfected His Beloved Son, as the Captain, or File-Leader of the many sons to be surely brought by Him unto Glory.

As stated, moral imperfection is not here intended by the words *"make perfect,"* but rather the great price that He would pay. He undertook the cause of *"sons"* whom God purposed to bring to Glory, and it was, therefore, necessary that He should enter into the circumstances in which we were found,

suffer our penal consequences, and so deliver us. Such a subjection into man's nature honored God and *"became Him"*; so the Captain of Salvation was made perfect through sufferings, even the Death of the Cross. As the Sin-Offering He died (vs. 9), as the Meal-Offering He suffered (vs. 10).

Such an oblation being infinite, it is consequently suitable and sufficient for the Salvation of every man without distinction — not without exception — for its saving virtue only affects those who believe upon Him.

THE CROSS, THE FOUNDATION OF THE FAITH

The modern Church for the most part, needs to go back and rebuild its foundation. That foundation has to be the Cross of Christ. Through the Cross came and comes all Salvation; through the Cross comes the Baptism with the Holy Spirit; through the Cross comes all healing; through the Cross comes all Blessings; through the Cross comes all deliverance; through the Cross comes all victory; through the Cross comes all prosperity. As we've said many times, the Cross is not a Doctrine, actually the very foundation of the Faith, on which all Doctrine is built. If this is not the case, the doctrine is wrong.

When the Bible speaks of *"Faith"* or *"believing,"* it is without exception speaking of Faith in the Finished Work of Christ. When it speaks of *"Grace,"* or *"hope,"* or *"peace,"* or any such like terminology, always and without exception, these things come totally and completely through the Cross of Christ.

The entire sacrificial system of the Old Testament, which began at the very dawn of time (Gen., Chpt. 4), points totally and completely toward the coming Redeemer, Who would bring Salvation by the price paid at the Cross. Every prophecy streams toward the Cross, as every Blessing today streams from the Cross.

Concerning this, the great question is, *"Does the Church understand this?"*

Some small part of it does, but the far greater majority doesn't! The Truth is, if the Preacher is not preaching *"Jesus Christ and Him Crucified,"* he's really not preaching the Gospel (I Cor. 2:2). As well, if any doctrine is given preeminence over the foundation, which is the Cross, the priority then becomes wrong and the end results will never be good.

The only way that the sinner can be saved is to have Faith in Christ and what he did at the Cross on their behalf. That is the very heart of Redemption.

Likewise, the only way the Christian can live a victorious, overcoming life, is by having constant Faith in the Cross of Christ, which means that he looks to the Finished Work of Christ constantly for all things, understanding that Jesus paid it all.

The greatest problem of the Child of God is twofold:

The Christian tries to be holy and righteous, by trusting in his good works, instead of having Faith totally in what Christ did at the Cross. Such an attitude only breeds self-righteousness, which plagues the modern Church to a disastrous degree.

Second, the Christian sins, and then tries to overcome the problem, whatever it might be, through a serious of laws and rules, which in effect, only compounds the situation. In other words, instead of solving his problem, he only makes it worse, because of succumbing to law. He may not understand it as law, but that's exactly what it is. And of course, law has no power, only a penalty. So, in trying to keep the rules and laws, whatever they might be, by the effort of self-will, the problem only gets worse.

FAITH

The entirety of our union with Christ is predicated solely upon Faith. Most Christians understand that, but they pretty well draw a blank after that. Faith in what?

Well of course, the answer would automatically be, *"Faith in Christ!"*

That is correct, at least as far as it goes; however, one must understand, as we've already stated, that Faith must always have as its object the Cross of Christ. If it's anything else, it will not be Faith which God can recognize.

The Christian can only be holy and righteous, by trusting in the Righteousness of Christ, which is freely given upon Faith in the Finished Work of Christ. Likewise, if the Christian fails, he must understand that all victory over all failure comes about only by renewing our Faith in the Finished Work of Christ. This

is the Faith that the Holy Spirit recognizes, and the only type of Faith that the Holy Spirit will recognize (Rom. 8:1-2, 11, 13).

(11) "FOR BOTH HE THAT SANCTIFIETH AND THEY WHO ARE SANCTIFIED ARE ALL OF ONE: FOR WHICH CAUSE HE IS NOT ASHAMED TO CALL THEM BRETHREN,"

1. Christ is the Sanctifier.

2. Everyone who is sanctified is sanctified by Christ, or else they aren't sanctified.

3. All, the Sanctifier and the Sanctified, are all out of one Source, God the Father. Consequently, He is not ashamed to call us Brethren.

CHRIST THE SANCTIFIER

The phrase, *"For both He that sanctifieth and they who are sanctified,"* refers to Christ Who puts the Believer on the path to glory, and then through the Ministry of the Holy Spirit leads him on that road through the process of progressive Sanctification and finally through Glorification into the eternal conditions where all through the eternal ages will grow more and more like the Lord Jesus and approach toward His likeness; however, will not in the infinite years of eternity, ever become in an absolute sense just like Him, for finiteness (that which is limited) can only approach toward infinity (that which is unlimited, Who and Which is Christ), never equal it (Wuest).

SANCTIFICATION

The words *"sanctify,"* or *"Sanctification,"* or *"holy,"* or *"holiness,"* all come from the same Greek root *"hagiazo,"* or *"hagios."* It means *"to purify or consecrate, to set apart solely for God."*

The moment the believing sinner comes to Christ, at that moment he is instantly and totally sanctified (I Cor. 6:11). In fact, the believing sinner must be sanctified (made clean) before he can be justified (declared clean). All of this is a legal work which actually takes place in Heaven upon the believing sinner exhibiting Faith in Christ, and what Christ did at the Cross on his behalf. This is what we refer to as *"Positional Sanctification,"* meaning that this is one's position in Christ, and is gained totally by Faith.

However, there is also that which we refer to as *"Progressive Sanctification."* Paul said, *"And the very God of peace sanctify you wholly; and I pray God your whole spirit and soul and body be preserved blameless unto the coming of our Lord Jesus Christ"* (I Thess. 5:23).

The idea is, at the time of conversion, the actual, spiritual *"condition"* of the new convert, is not up to his actual, spiritual *"position,"* which is all in Christ. Consequently, the Holy Spirit sets about, to bring the *"condition"* up to the *"position."* Actually, it is a lifelong work, and that is the reason it is referred to as *"Progressive Sanctification."*

The actual position is that of total Christlikeness, which can only come by Faith in Christ. In Truth, Progressive Sanctification functions in the same manner — by Faith, which we will explain more fully momentarily. While it is impossible for the Believer to become 100 percent Christlike, and for all the obvious reasons, to be sure, the Holy Spirit definitely brings us as close as He can to this exalted position, which is His chief work in the heart and life of the Believer — to make one Christlike! In fact, the type of Sanctification of which Paul here speaks, is *"Progressive Sanctification."* It speaks of a process, which is actually carried forth as stated, all the days of our lives.

HOW DOES CHRIST CARRY FORTH THE SANCTIFICATION PROCESS?

This question is extremely important, and if it's not answered properly, which means it is understood improperly, the Believer can accrue to himself great spiritual difficulties, which will have a negative fallout in every other aspect of life as well.

In point of fact, it is the Holy Spirit Who actually performs the work in the heart and life of the Believer. So, the meaning is that Christ sanctifies the Believer through the Office and Person of the Holy Spirit. However, the Holy Spirit is able to carry forth this excellent work solely on the basis of what Christ did at the Cross on our behalf, hence it being said that it is Christ Who sanctifieth! Two things must be carried forth in order for the Holy Spirit to perfect this work within our lives. They are as follows:

NOTES

1. The Holy Spirit must have the cooperation of the Saint of God. To be sure, none of this is automatic, despite the fact that many Christians erroneously think it is. Self-will is the greatest hindrance. The Spirit of God cannot work and function in a climate of self-will, which always leads to works of the flesh, i.e., *"sin."* So, the will of the Believer must *"hunger and thirst for Righteousness."*

We must understand that the work of Sanctification can never be carried out by our own abilities or religiosity. All of the things which we do, which we think bring us merit with God, in fact, have no place at all. So, the Believer must understand that Sanctification is beyond his grasp, and can only be done by the Holy Spirit. Actually one might say, that Sanctification is not an activity but rather a position.

Understanding this, we come to the second point:

2. Realizing that we cannot sanctify ourselves, and that it can only be done by the Holy Spirit, we must come to understanding as to how the Holy Spirit works (Rom. 8:1-2, 11, 13).

The Holy Spirit only asks that we exhibit Faith in the Cross of Christ, understanding that it was there that all victory was won. That's why Paul here said that Christ is the Sanctifier. He is the One Who made all of this possible through His Death and Resurrection on the Cross. We are to understand that, believe that, and place our Faith in that.

With the Cross ever as our object of Faith, the Holy Spirit, Who works strictly within the parameters of the Finished Work of Christ, can then do mighty things in our hearts and lives. As stated, He only demands that we exhibit Faith in the Cross of Christ, and continue to do so, in fact, all the days of our lives.

So, the criteria is Faith, but it must ever be understood, that it's always Faith in *"Jesus Christ and Him Crucified"* (I Cor. 2:2).

THE CHRISTIAN AND THE CROSS

Most Christians have an understanding of the Cross as it pertains to the initial Salvation experience. In other words, in order to be saved, they place their Faith in Christ, understanding that He died for them on the Cross. But regrettably, most Christians park the Cross after the initial Salvation experience, attempting to go elsewhere with their Faith. Please let the following be clearly understood:

The Cross of Christ, i.e., *"the Finished Work of Christ,"* has just as much to do with your everyday walk before the Lord, with your everyday victory, with your everyday progress in the Lord, as it did your initial Salvation experience. Regrettably, most Christians don't know that!

And that's the reason we have Christians running all over the world chasing one fad after the other, attempting to find victory. They don't know anything about the application of the Cross within their lives on a daily basis; therefore, they walk in defeat.

One of my associates sometime back was in a particular meeting where God was moving. The Evangelist specialized in laying hands on people, with them being *"slain in the Spirit,"* etc. They asked my associate to help catch the people when they fell, etc.

He told me that many of them upon coming up to be prayed for, whispered in his ear, *"Please pray that the Lord will move mightily upon me, for I'm hooked on pornography,"* or whatever!

Not knowing the great Word of the Cross, which incidentally is the only source of victory, these individuals, whomever they may have been, were hoping that the Lord would use this particular Evangelist to lay hands on them, and they would be delivered.

While the *"laying on of hands,"* is certainly Scriptural, and definitely beneficial if it's carried forth Biblically, used in this manner, however, it is wrong, which means, that the individual will not find the victory for which he seeks.

In fact, at that particular time they might be mightily moved on by God. They may in fact be *"slain in the Spirit,"* or some such thing, but they still will not receive deliverance. But yet, that's where most Believers presently are. They're trying to get the Preacher to deliver them by the laying on of hands, or something of that nature.

DELIVERANCE

Jesus never really said anything about Preachers delivering people, at least in this

NOTES

manner. He did say that we are to *"preach deliverance to the captives"* (Lk. 4:18). What did He mean by that?

He meant that Preachers should do exactly what I'm doing right here, tell you the way of deliverance, which is the Cross of Christ, and that only I might quickly add!

When Jesus died on the Cross, He atoned for all sin by the giving of His life. He as well satisfied the curse of the broken Law, which in effect, hung over every human being. In the doing of this, He handled the claims of the Law against us (the Law of God, Ex., Chpt. 20). The Scripture plainly says, *"Blotting out the handwriting of ordinances that was against us, which was contrary to us, and took it out of the way, nailing it to His Cross"* (Col. 2:14).

However, when He did that, He also destroyed Satan's legal claim on humanity, which is sin. Having atoned for all sin, Satan now has no more claim, at least as it regards those who place their Faith in Christ and what He has done for us at the Cross.

In doing that, He *"spoiled principalities and powers* (all fallen angels and demon spirits), *and made a shew of them openly, triumphing over them in it"* (Col. 2:15).

This means that every single demon spirit and Satan himself for that matter, were totally defeated at the Cross. This also means that every individual in the world, at least if they will only believe, is already delivered. In fact, *"deliverance"* is the great Message of the Cross. It's the great hallmark of Christianity. Jesus sets men free (Jn. 8:32). However, for deliverance to be carried out in the heart and life of any individual, such comes, and in fact can only come, by one having Faith in what Christ did at the Cross. The moment we attempt to deliver people by laying hands on them, or something else of this nature, whether we realize it or not, we are trying to add to the Finished Work of Christ, which God can never honor, and in which the Holy Spirit can never function. In fact, such is an insult to Christ of the highest order, as should be obvious.

Due to its great significance, please allow me to say it again:

Every single person in this world has already been delivered, which was carried out at the Cross, which is effected within their hearts and lives by simple Faith in what Christ did there. When Faith is exhibited accordingly, the Holy Spirit then works mightily, guaranteeing to us all that Christ did there (Rom. 8:1-2).

Now it's not wrong to lay hands on Believers respecting deliverance, if the Believer and the Preacher understands what is taking place. In other words, I'm to understand that my performing this act will never set anyone free, that having already been done at the Cross; however, the laying on of hands can definitely be a blessing as it is intended to be, and can even help one's Faith, doing so as a point of contact. But if I believe that this particular action will set people free, then I've just made something else other than the Cross of Christ, the true object of my Faith, which God can never honor.

FAITH

In every single thing as it pertains to the Child of God, it is Faith! It really doesn't matter what we need from the Lord, it is all gained by Faith, and never by works. Now what do we mean by that?

Whether it's Salvation for the sinner, or the Baptism with the Holy Spirit for the Saint, whether it's healing for the Believer, prosperity, or Blessing, etc., it is all generated by Faith and exclusively by Faith. However, if we leave it there, we've really not said enough, which will leave the Believer hanging so to speak.

For Faith to be Faith, at least that which God will recognize, which is anchored solely and squarely in the Word of God, it must always be Faith in the Cross. Whenever Faith is mentioned, it is always in that capacity. It always has as its object, the Cross of Christ, for it is there that every victory was won by Christ.

So, just saying that we have Faith in God, or Faith in Christ, or Faith in the Word, is really not quite enough. We must understand what all of that means, and to make it brief, it means that we are having Faith in what Christ did at the Cross of Calvary on our behalf.

The Cross made possible every single thing that we possess from the Lord. Absolutely nothing has ever come to the Believer except

NOTES

it came through the great Sacrifice of Christ. In fact, the entirety of the Bible and in every capacity, points toward the Cross of Christ. The Cross is the centrality of the Gospel.

WILLPOWER

While the will of the Believer is definitely a factor (Rev. 22:17), it within itself cannot bring about the desired results. Unfortunately, that's where most Christians are.

I had a man say to me the other day, *"Now that I'm a Christian, I have the willpower to say 'yes' or 'no' to sin,"* etc.

The dear Brother is totally wrong!

The will of the Believer can only flow successfully in one channel, and what is that?

You as a Believer are to use your willpower in the sense of placing your Faith and Trust in Christ and what He did at the Cross on your behalf. That is where the will of man is to be. If you bring your will outside of the great Sacrifice of Christ, thereby attempting to bring about desired results outside of those parameters, which actually refers to your own strength, you will quickly find that your willpower is not able to bring about the desired results. In fact, in that capacity, which is the capacity outside of the Cross which God can never honor, Satan can literally override one's will. Now I realize that comes as a shock to most Christians, but it just happens to be true.

Paul said *"For to will is present with me; but how to perform that which is good I find not"* (Rom. 7:18).

Please understand, that this is not Paul's experience before conversion as some claim, but rather after he was saved and Baptized with the Holy Spirit. At that particular time, the time of Romans, Chapter 7, he did not know or understand the Message of the Cross; therefore, he attempted to bring about victory in his life by his own strength and willpower, which are impossible. But yet, that's where most modern Christians presently find themselves.

Thankfully, the Lord gave Paul the great answer to this dilemma, which is actually the meaning of the New Covenant. We find it in Romans, Chapters 6 and 8, which gives us the meaning of the Cross, and how the Holy Spirit functions according to our Faith in the Cross.

So, Paul plainly says that *"willpower"* within itself is not enough! And as stated, the Holy Spirit aids and abets our wills, and Satan respects our wills, only as that will is anchored firmly and totally in the Cross of Christ, understanding that the Cross is the means by which all Blessings come from God to the Believer.

YIELD

Paul said, *"Neither yield ye your members as instruments of unrighteousness unto sin: but yield yourselves unto God, as those that are alive from the dead, and your members as instruments of Righteousness unto God."*

He then said, *"For sin shall not have dominion over you: for ye are not under the Law, but under Grace"* (Rom. 6:13-14).

There are millions of Christians right now who read these words in the Bible, and try with all their might and strength to do what the Holy Spirit through the Apostle demands to be done, but are unable to do so. So, in their hearts the great question is, *"How do I yield the members of my body to Righteousness?"*

They try to do it with willpower, their own strength, their own ability, by making up rules, laws, and regulations, and find that not only do all of these things fail, but despite all the efforts, the situation is gradually getting worse. So, how does one yield one's members to Righteousness instead of unrighteousness?

Once again, we go back to the *"will"* of the individual.

Notice that Paul said, *"we are not under the Law but under Grace."* What did he mean by that?

Before we address ourselves again to the *"will,"* let's look at this *"Law/Grace"* issue!

When he said *"ye are not under the Law,"* he was speaking of the Law of Moses, or any type of law that we might make up, or that our Church might make up, or our Denomination, etc. In other words, as it regards the problem of sin, the Believer is not going to get out of this dilemma, and I speak of failing over and over again in some way, by subscribing to a set of rules and regulations, hoping that by keeping them, that victory will

NOTES

be his. It just doesn't work that way. That is law, and law never has any power.

Whenever the Believer attempts to find victory in this manner, the Holy Spirit will not help him, and he is left on his own. To be sure, his own strength and ability are not able to overcome sin. I don't care if you're saved, Baptized with the Holy Spirit, speak in Tongues everyday of your life, and have all nine Gifts of the Spirit. There is no way that you within your own ability, even though having all of these great things, can overcome sin. You have got to have the Power of the Holy Spirit to help you, and how does this come about?

When Paul said that you are *"under Grace,"* he is meaning that Christ has already done all of these things for us, and I speak of victory in every capacity. As stated over and over again, it was all done at the Cross.

When we place our Faith in that great Sacrifice of Christ, understanding that it is from this Source that all Blessings come, and we speak of victory in every capacity, then the goodness of God is extended to us, which is actually the Grace of God, and all guaranteed by the Holy Spirit. In other words, the Holy Spirit strictly on the merits of the Grace of God, brings about victory within our lives, making it possible for us to properly *"yield"* our members to Righteousness, instead of unrighteousness.

Grace means that it's not done by our works or abilities or efforts, but that it has already been done in Christ, and we receive it by simply believing in what He has already done.

In fact, if we attempt to add our own efforts to the Finished Work of Christ, we frustrate the Grace of God, which guarantees that we're going to fail (Gal. 2:20-21).

"Yield" in the Greek is *"paristemi,"* and means *"to stand beside, to exhibit, to present."* It does not appear as a struggle or battle. So, if the Believer is struggling and battling in this capacity, and I speak of trying to yield the members of his body to Righteousness, that shows that he's not doing it by the Grace of God, but rather by Law, which will guarantee his failure. He might succeed for awhile, but down the road, and without exception, he is going to fail. I've said it many, many times:

"If one is fighting and winning, after awhile one is going to fight and lose."

THE GOOD FIGHT OF FAITH

The only fight that we are called upon in which to engage ourselves, is *"the good fight of Faith"* (I Tim. 6:12). This is always the center of the struggle, whether we realize it or not.

And let us quickly state, that the Faith he mentions here is Faith exclusively in the Cross of Christ. The fight centers up on Satan trying to move our Faith from the Cross of Christ to some other object. In fact, he really doesn't too much care what the other object might be, just so it's not the Cross of Christ.

In other words, Satan is perfectly willing for you to spout Scripture all day long, providing that you have no understanding that all Scripture in one way or the other, points to the Cross of Christ (Jn. 3:16). So, one can say the following:

Whether the attack comes in the physical sense, material, financial, domestical, mental, or spiritual, it is all for but one purpose, and that is to destroy your Faith in Christ and His Finished Work, or at least, to seriously weaken your Faith in that capacity. That is the center and core of all the struggle!

In fact, Satan has been very successful in steering the Church away from Faith in the Cross of Christ to something else. In the last 50 or more years, the Church has had so little teaching on the Cross of Christ, that it little more knows its true foundation. In other words, in most Church circles, Satan has won this battle.

Actually, the Message of Paul is identical in all his Epistles, even though he approaches the subject in different ways. We actually have the Apostle saying the same thing over and over again, and I speak of the great Finished Work of Christ, but saying it in different ways in order that individuals may understand.

Likewise, I realize that I'm being very repetitive in my statements regarding the Cross; however, I have found out that Satan fights this more than anything else; consequently, we are forced as well to say the same thing

over and over again although in different ways, praying that this great Truth will ultimately get into your spirit.

The Message of the Cross of Christ, which in effect is the Gospel, is the simplest Message there is. Man is lost and Jesus Christ is the solution; however, due to the fact that the human being is a very complex creature, this Message is at the same time complex as well. The problem is, to understand the Message of the Cross we have to think spiritual, when our first nature is to think carnal.

If the Believer will understand, that he has to look to the Cross for everything, at least he will then have the foundation in order. Our problem is, oftentimes we think our Faith is in the Cross of Christ, and in reality, it's in something else. The flesh is so subtle, so tricky, so deceitful, that's where we have our problem.

OF ONE

The phrase, *"Are all of one,"* definitely has bearing in the fact that it is all of one Father; however, it as well means that Christ and the many sons are all a unity in human nature. In fact, this is the great argument of the entire Passage.

Most commentators, supporting themselves upon John 20:17, understand the words *"are all of one"* as meaning only that *"are all of one Father."* But did it mean this only? Christ could not possibly have been ashamed to call us Brethren. In fact, He could not do otherwise. But guided by the argument of the Chapter it appears more reasonable to believe that the greater focus of the unity intended is His association with humanity.

Such an association might well cause Him shame, for *"the many sons"* with whom He became One were by nature sinful — He Himself being sinless — and had been redeemed from the lowest depths of vice and shame. But still, He calls us *"Brethren,"* and because of His Cross, which addressed all the negative factors, and our Faith in that Finished Work.

The thought of all this is that Jesus is qualified to be our Priest and Saviour because He shares our nature, which means He is not some remote being, but is truly *"one of us."*

Since the entire universe, Angels, as well as men have their origin in God, it is merely a truism to say that we all come from Him. However, that gives no reason for Christ being qualified to save. The fact that He shares with us a descent from Adam does, one might say, enable Him to call us *"Brothers."*

BRETHREN

The phrase, *"For which cause He is not ashamed to call them Brethren,"* refers to the fact that He became one of us. However, He does not call every man His Brother, He is such only to the sanctified. He and we appear before God in the nature and position of men. He sanctifies us, and this means we are sanctified, and on this account He is not ashamed to call us Brothers.

However, this proclamation of union is brought about, due to the change effected in the hearts and lives of Believers — a change incidentally, which could only come about through Faith in what Christ did on the Cross, and the great price there paid. This exalted position did not come easily or cheaply. Consequently, the worth of something is derived from the price paid regarding the item in question.

Jesus has paid for us with His Own Blood, which refers to the Sacrifice of His Life. Our Faith in that has brought about the great change, making it possible for us to literally be a *"Child of God,"* i.e., *"Heir of God, and joint-heir with Christ"* (Rom. 8:17).

There is no shame on the part of the Son of God in referring to Believers coming into this exalted position; however, such is done only through His merits and not at all through the merits of man.

(12) "SAYING, I WILL DECLARE THY NAME UNTO MY BRETHREN, IN THE MIDST OF THE CHURCH WILL I SING PRAISE UNTO THEE."

The exposition is as follows:

1. Christ declares that this great work on the Cross will make it possible to address all Believers as *"Brethren."*

2. This statement is taken from Psalms 22:22, and due to the fact that this is the great Passion Psalm of Christ on the Cross, we are here told, that it is the great Sacrifice of Christ which made all of this possible.

3. Due to what Christ has done on the Cross, the Church is to praise Him forever.

THE DECLARATION OF PERSONAL SALVATION

The phrase, *"Saying, I will declare Thy Name unto My Brethren,"* presents this Passage, as stated, as being found in Psalms 22:22. These words, *"I will declare Thy Name unto My Brethren,"* were actually uttered on the Cross by the Lord Himself. While the Psalm has its background in David's own experience, yet the final and full application of its Truth is to the Son of God.

In Verses 19 through 21, He prays to be raised out from among the dead. In Verses 21 through 31, He gives thanks for answered prayer even before His prayer is actually answered. In view of the fact that God will raise Him from the dead, He will declare His name to His Brethren (Wuest).

In Psalm 22 we see Him hanging on the Cross, the forsaken One, drinking the wormwood and the gall, bearing the judgment due to our sins. In Verses 1 through 21 of that Psalm He is seen alone, suffering at the hands of God, what, in fact, our guilt deserved. Then from Verse 22 on He is no longer alone, but as the Risen One is surrounded by multitudes who owe their Salvation to His sufferings on the tree, and it is in Resurrection He exclaims:

"I will declare Thy Name unto My Brethren (meaning that Christ will declare the Name of God to all the Brethren, in effect owning them)*; in the midst of the congregation will I praise Thee* (meaning that Christ will praise God because of this great victory which has brought many sons into the Kingdom)."* This is the Passage that is quoted in the Verse of our study; but for *"congregation"* we have the word *"Church,"* a translation, as we know, of the Greek word *"ekklesia,"* which was the Septuagint rendering (Old Testament translated into Greek) for the Hebrew term translated *"congregation."*

It is the assembly of the redeemed, and in the midst of that assembly the Risen Christ takes His place as the Chief Chorister leading the praises of His people's hearts (Ironside).

THE CHURCH AND PRAISE TO GOD

The phrase, *"In the midst of the Church will I sing praise unto Thee,"* refers to Christ in the midst of this congregation of redeemed Saints, singing praise to God, as it regards the great victory won at the Cross.

The idea is, we are *"Brethren,"* which means *"Brothers of our Lord,"* only because of what was done at the Cross. This is borne out by the Holy Spirit having Paul use this particular quotation from Psalm 22, which is the great Crucifixion Psalm.

If Christ can praise God for this great thing, how can we, who have actually been the recipients of this Blessing of all Blessings, not do the same!

In the mind of God, every single Blood-washed Believer stands supreme with Christ in our midst, praising God for this great victory won, and if He does this, and He definitely does, then how can we as His Brethren, do less!

This Passage, among many others of similar nature, places the seal of approval by the Holy Spirit upon the worship of the Lord as it regards singing and music. In fact, the Book of Psalms, which is Earth's first songbook, is the largest Book in the Bible. This should tell us the priority which the Holy Spirit places on worship and praise.

In fact, let me hear the music of a Church, and I can pretty well tell what kind of Church it actually is. If it's stilted and formal, as it is with most Churches which have denied the Holy Spirit, this portrays the fact that He is not present.

If it's the contemporary flavor, which characterizes many modern Churches, this tells me that *"another spirit"* is actually being engaged, instead of the Holy Spirit (II Cor. 11:4).

If it's the true worship of God, it will be obviously evident in the music and the singing. It will glorify Christ and not man. It will be generated by the Holy Spirit and not *"another spirit."*

In fact, Churches, Radio Programs, and Television Programs, which claim to be Christian, which promote so-called Contemporary Christian Music are pure and simple operating in the realm of the powers of darkness. As stated, all of this is by *"another spirit."* Most Churches have no true worship at all, and because the Holy Spirit is not present. With many others, and I speak of those who function in the genre mentioned, they have a form of worship, but it's definitely not of God.

The idea that this style of music draws in young people to Christ is so facetious as to be absurd. In the first place, it is only the Holy Spirit Who can draw anyone to Christ. And to be sure, He does not use the ways of the world, and the word *"contemporary,"* at least in this capacity, speaks of music which is similar to or identical with that in the world. Music either glorifies God, or it glorifies self. And if it glorifies self, it is actually glorifying Satan! So, let me say it again:

One can gauge the spiritual barometer of a Church by the style of music it promotes. If that in fact is the case, and it definitely is, then *"the Church"* is in sad shape spiritually.

(13) "AND AGAIN, I WILL PUT MY TRUST IN HIM. AND AGAIN, BEHOLD I AND THE CHILDREN WHICH GOD HATH GIVEN ME."

The exegesis is:

1. The key to all life and victory is trust in the Lord.

2. More particularly, it is trust in what Christ did at the Cross, all on our behalf.

3. Because of what Jesus did at the Cross, there will be many brethren, i.e., *"Children of God."*

TRUST

The phrase, *"And again, I will put my trust in Him,"* is derived from II Samuel 22:3. This particular Chapter is the same as Psalm 18, with but little change in the wording.

"Trust" is the very theme of Psalms, actually being mentioned some 50 times in Earth's first songbook. The entirety of this Book is a portrayal of Christ in one way or the other, in His Mediatorial and Intercessory roles. The idea is His Incarnation, i.e., *"Humanity."*

Christ puts His trust totally in God, providing an example for us to follow, and of course, the greatest example of all! So human is He that, conscious of other weakness, He leans on God, as the feeblest of His Brethren. This fulfills Isaiah, Chapter 53 perfectly, *"A Man of sorrows, acquainted with grief. . . ."*

Proper trust in the Lord requires proper relationship. The Holy Spirit, Who abides within us, will lead us perfectly according to the Will of God, if we will only strive after that perfect Will. To have the type of relationship which can generate such trust, is the most wonderful life and living there could ever be. As stated, Christ was the greatest example of all concerning this.

Frances and I began in Evangelistic Work in 1956. Donnie was only two years old at the time. To be sure, it was not at all easy. Finances were in very short supply, along with what seemed to be about everything else as well.

It was 1958 if I remember correctly. My cousin Jerry Lee Lewis was vying with Elvis Presley for the number one spot in the nation regarding the new craze of rock-'n'-roll.

At this particular time, I was preaching a Meeting at my home Church in Ferriday, Louisiana. It was a Sunday, and we were having a dinner on the ground, which was quite common in those days, and which took place immediately after the morning Service.

The table was spread in the open space in back of the little Church. The Church was small, with the attendance that day probably being 25 or 30.

We were in the midst of this particular meal, when I looked up and saw my Uncle, Jerry Lee's dad driving up, in his brand-new Cadillac. He got out of the car, greeting everyone, and then came over to me, and with a twinkle in his eye, said, *"Jimmy I have great news for you!"*

He then continued, saying, *"Sam Phillips has sent for you. Sun Records is starting a Gospel line, and you will be the very first artist."*

Sam Phillips, the owner of Sun Records, had started Elvis Presley, Johnny Cash, Charlie Rich, Carl Perkins, along with Jerry Lee and a host of others. At that particular time, Sun Records, jumping on the rock-'n'-roll bandwagon, was fastly becoming one of the biggest record labels in the world.

I remember my Uncle looking around and finally spotting my car. I can still hear his voice.

"Jimmy in 30 days you can buy a new car. And to be sure," he continued, *"you sure need one!"*

He was certainly right about that!

I opened my mouth to say, *"I'll be ready to go immediately,"* when deep down inside me, the Spirit of God spoke to my heart, saying, *"You cannot do this!"*

I'm sure I must have looked somewhat startled, because my Uncle looked at me very closely, and said, *"Jimmy, did you hear what I just said?"*

"Yes," I answered, *"and I appreciate the offer so very, very much. I'm sorry,"* I continued, *"but I cannot accept."*

My Uncle looked at me very puzzled for a few moments and then said, *"But Jimmy, it's Gospel music!"*

"I know it," I answered, *"but I can't do it."*

My eyes filled with tears, because I didn't really understand myself. My Uncle looked at me for a few moments, and then put his arms around me and said, *"Jimmy I think you're making a mistake, but I'll accept your answer."*

My Uncle was a very tall, angular man, always friendly, always personable, a man whom everybody liked. He always had a smile, and he was still smiling as I saw him walk away, get in that new Cadillac and drive off.

I remember hearing one lady standing nearby, who obviously had overheard the short conversation, saying to another lady standing nearby, *"Did you hear what he just did?"* She continued, *"He turned down that offer!"*

There were a hundred questions in my mind, of which the Lord had provided no answers. As stated, our financial picture was very near desperate. We badly needed a new car, plus about everything else as well.

I wanted to be alone for a few moments, so I walked away from the crowd, going into the little Church. There was a small broom and mop closet in one corner, and I walked in it, shutting the door.

I stood there for a few moments and then through tears asked the Lord, *"Why couldn't I accept this offer? It's Gospel music. What's wrong with that?"*

The Spirit of the Lord came upon me, with the Lord saying one thing to me. He simply said, *"Trust Me!"*

That was all, no more, no less! *"Trust Me!"*

However, it was enough to ease my mind, and to know that I was in His direct Will, which was the only thing that really mattered.

To be sure, that story has not ended yet. Not long after that, I made my very first Recording. And from that time until now, and without the help of Record companies and such like, the Holy Spirit serving as my company, my distributor, and everything else for that matter, has helped me to sell some 15 million Albums. Had I taken the lure offered by Satan, I know in my heart that the Blessings that the Lord gave me, would not have been given.

As it regards Satan's lure, I do not in any way mean to implicate my Uncle in that. He was trying to help, for which I was very grateful. However, that particular direction, even though seemingly right to the natural eye, was not right, and would have turned out to great loss.

To be led by the Lord is the greatest thing there could ever be. And to be led by Him, one must learn to trust Him. Again I state, Jesus was the perfect example!

THAT WHICH GOD HAS GIVEN ME

The phrase, *"And again, behold I and the children which God hath given Me,"* is derived from Isaiah 8:18.

The idea of this statement from Isaiah is that Jesus Christ is the Messiah, and that He is such in order to go to the Cross where Redemption will be effected for all of mankind. As a result, many will be born into the Kingdom of God; consequently, the idea is:

Paul is addressing this to Jews who had accepted Christ as their Saviour, but now through discouragement, or for whatever reason, were contemplating going back into Temple worship, which would necessitate a denial of Christ as the Son of God. No doubt, some had already done this, with many others thinking of following suit.

He is in effect telling them, that the only way that one can be a Child of God is to accept Christ. And if He is rejected, God in totality is as well rejected. In other words, Israel could not have God if they rejected Jesus Christ. Rejecting Him, they in effect would be rejecting all things, even their history. Regrettably, that is exactly what happened.

(14) "FORASMUCH THEN AS THE CHILDREN ARE PARTAKERS OF FLESH AND BLOOD, HE ALSO HIMSELF LIKEWISE

NOTES

TOOK PART OF THE SAME; THAT THROUGH DEATH HE MIGHT DESTROY HIM THAT HAD THE POWER OF DEATH, THAT IS, THE DEVIL;"

1. This speaks of the Incarnation, God becoming man.

2. The Incarnation was necessary in order to redeem humanity. The great Plan of Redemption demanded death, and God cannot die; consequently, He would have to become man, thereby becoming the Last Adam, to carry out this great work.

3. His death on the Cross would destroy Satan and his powers.

FLESH AND BLOOD

The phrase, *"Forasmuch then as the children are partakers of flesh and blood,"* refers to the fact that this creation has a human and not an Angelic nature. Since we are men, He became a man. There was a fitness and propriety that He should partake of our nature, which He did!

"Partakers" in the Greek is *"koinoneo,"* and means, *"to have a share in common with someone else."* Thus, all of the human race have in common with one another, flesh and blood.

There is evidence in the coming Resurrection of Life, that the glorified bodies of all Saints, will be made up of flesh and bone, but no mention is made of blood (Lk. 24:39). The idea is this:

Whereas at the present time, the life of the flesh is in the blood, in the Resurrection, the life of the flesh will be the *"Spirit,"* i.e., *"the Holy Spirit!"*

THE INCARNATION

The phrase, *"He also Himself likewise took part of the same,"* speaks of the Incarnation of Christ, God becoming man.

"Likewise" would have been better translated *"in like manner."* It means that the Lord Jesus, in His Incarnation, took His place alongside and nearby the human race.

The words *"took part of"* are the translation of a different Greek word from that translated *"partakers."* It is *"metecho,"* and means, *"to hold with."* Thus, our Lord took hold of human nature without its sin in the Incarnation, and held it to Himself as an additional nature, thus associating Himself with the human race in its possession of flesh and blood. He took to Himself, something with which by nature He had nothing in common. Human beings possess human nature in common with one another. The Son of God united with Himself, something that was not natural to Him.

God, as to His nature, is Spirit, that is, incorporeal Being (Jn. 4:24) (Wuest).

Westcott says that the word *"partakers"* marks the characteristic sharing of the common fleshly nature as it pertains to the human race at large, whereas the words *"took part of"* speak of the unique fact of the Incarnation as a voluntary acceptance of humanity. This throws great light on the dual nature of our Lord as *"Very* (True) *God and Very* (True) *Man."*

DEATH

The phrase, *"That through death He might destroy him that had the power of death,"* refers to the Cross and what it did.

As the *"Last Adam"* (I Cor. 15:45), Christ had to come into this world similar to the first Adam, which refers to being without sin. Consequently, He was born of the Virgin Mary, thereby, not incurring original sin brought on by Adam's Fall.

As the *"Last Adam"* He also had to keep the law of God (Law of Moses) perfectly, thereby rendering a perfect obedience, which the first Adam did not do.

However, for all His perfection, and all His miracles and healings, even to the raising of the dead, not one soul was truly saved until He went to the Cross. While in fact there definitely were people saved before the Cross, still, they were saved by looking forward to that coming Redemption. There has never been but one Salvation, and it has always come by Faith, which pertains to Faith in the Cross (Gen., Chpt. 4).

THE POWER OF DEATH

Satan held the power of death over humanity by reason of man's failure, i.e., *"sin."* The legal claim upon humanity by the Evil One is sin and transgression. Inasmuch as the wages of sin is death (Rom. 6:23), this constituted Satan's power.

HOW DID THE DEATH OF CHRIST DESTROY THE DEVIL?

When Verse 14 says that Satan is destroyed, it doesn't mean that he is dead, but rather that his power is broken. In fact, Satan is an angel, albeit fallen, and cannot die.

When Adam and Eve fell in the Garden of Eden, which they did by disobedience to God and His Word (Gen. 2:15-17), at that time, they spiritually died, exactly as God said they would. Spiritual death means *"separation from God."* Man's life-support system was intended to be his Creator, and with man dead to God through disobedience, the life-support system was severed. Consequently, spiritual death ultimately led to physical death, and in fact, the death of all things. God had decreed that the *"wages of sin would be death,"* once again meaning separation from God, and so it was and so it is (Rom. 6:23).

When Adam and Eve did this, they in effect changed Lords. Where God had been their Lord, now Satan is their lord, which he is regarding all of mankind who doesn't know Christ Jesus (Jn. 8:44). As a result, the total God-consciousness which man had before the Fall was now lost, with man sinking down to the far lower level of self-consciousness, and beside that, being literally possessed by the evil nature, or as some call it, the *"sinful nature."* This means that man's every passion and attitude, instead of being turned toward God, is rather turned toward that which is evil, which is the cause of all the problems and difficulties in the world today.

Satan's legal claim upon mankind is sin and transgression. As a result of sin and in fact, all being born in sin, which is referred to as *"original sin,"* which actually stems from the first Adam, Satan literally holds man in captivity.

Concerning this captivity, that's what Jesus was speaking about when He said, *"How can one enter into a strong man's house, and spoil his goods, except he first bind the strongman? And then he will spoil his house"* (Mat. 12:29).

And that's exactly what Jesus did at the Cross! By being made a curse for sin (Gal. 3:13-14), which He did by dying, the terrible sin debt owed to God by man was then paid.

Consequently, Satan then lost his legal hold upon humanity, at least for those who will believe (Jn. 3:16). Satan's power of death is sin, because the wages of sin is death, and so decreed by God (Rom. 6:23). With sin removed, which it was at the Cross, as stated, Satan's legal claim upon humanity is lost, which means that the power of death is broken as well.

This power of death before the Cross, extended even to Hell itself. In other words, when the righteous died before the Cross, due to the blood of bulls and goats not being able to take away sin, even though these individuals were saved, and we speak of Old Testament Times, that sin debt was still hanging over their heads. Hence, Satan still had a claim upon them; consequently, when they died, and I speak also of the greats such as David, Abraham, Moses, etc., they were taken captive by Satan down into Paradise.

To be sure, this was not the burning side of the Pit, that being separated from them by a great gulf (Lk. 16:19-31); however, due to the sin problem not being yet settled, and because the Cross was yet in the future, they were still captives of Satan.

In fact, after Jesus died on the Cross, thereby settling the terrible sin debt, which destroyed the power of death held by Satan, He liberated these righteous souls from Paradise, which Paul addressed in Ephesians 4:8-10. Due to the sin debt being settled at the Cross, when a Saint of God now dies, their soul and spirit immediately go to Heaven to be with Christ (Phil. 1:23), which means the power of death is broken.

HOW WERE PEOPLE SAVED BEFORE THE CROSS?

They were saved in the same manner then as we are now, by Faith. Their Faith was centered in the Cross which was coming, and our Faith is centered in the Cross which has now been accomplished. They were saved by looking forward to a prophetic Jesus, while we are saved by looking backward to a historic Jesus. Both ways, however, centered up at the Cross.

As stated, the sacrificial system of Old Testament Times, which consisted of the deaths of certain types of animals such as lambs,

goats, rams, etc., was only a stopgap measure, until *"the Sacrifice"* could be offered, which would be God becoming man, and then offering up Himself (Isa. 7:14; Chpt. 53).

Even though the Old Testament Saints were definitely saved, and by Faith exactly as we are now, still, their system at that time was woefully inferior to the New Covenant, in that *"the blood of bulls and goats could not take away sins"* (Heb. 10:4). That's the reason that Paul in Hebrews, keeps stressing the fact that we now have a *"Better Covenant . . . established upon Better Promises"* (Heb. 8:6).

JESUS CHRIST AND HIS CROSS, THE SOURCE OF ALL VICTORY!

When Jesus died on the Cross, He atoned for all sin and for all time (I Jn. 1:7). So that means that theoretically, every single person who has been alive since the Cross, has been set free from all sin; however, to reap such benefits, God requires that the sinner place his Faith and confidence in Christ and what He did at the Cross on his behalf, which means to accept Christ as one's Lord and Saviour (Jn. 3:16). If Faith in Christ, and Christ only, is not enjoined, the individual retains his sins, and is thereby eternally lost (Jn. 16:8-9).

As we've said previously, God does not hold man nearly as accountable for his condition, a condition incidentally over which he had no control, as He does man's rejection of Christ, Who is God's Solution to man's dilemma.

Going back to before the Cross, even though the death of Christ atoned for all sin during that period of some 4,000 years, still, it could only apply to those who had placed their trust in Christ, or in other words, the One Who was to come. God honored their Faith in that coming Finished Work, even as He now honors our Faith in that completed Finished Work.

Death then (before the Cross) ended the opportunity to be saved, even as death now (after the Cross) ends all opportunity to be saved. In fact, all opportunities for Salvation are on this side of the grave, with there being no more opportunity after death. This means there is no such thing as purgatory, reincarnation, etc. The Scripture plainly says:

"It is appointed unto men once to die, but after this the Judgment" (Heb. 9:27).

CAN THE BELIEVER LIVE FREE FROM SIN?

The Bible doesn't teach sinless perfection, and for all the obvious reasons, but it definitely does teach victory over sin, in that *"sin shall not have dominion over you"* (Rom. 6:14). So, that means that no Believer should ever be bound by sin in any capacity, should ever be overcome by sin, should ever practice sin, but should live victorious, overcoming, Christian lives, which Jesus paid for at the Cross.

Now the great question should be asked, if such victory is actually the case?

To be sure, it definitely is with some few, but not many. The Truth is, most Christians are bound by sin in one way or the other.

Considering what Jesus did at the Cross on our behalf, why is this the case?

It is the case, because the Church for all practical purposes, has abandoned the Cross. Most of the Church world no longer even believes that what Jesus did at the Cross addressed the sin problem, so they recommend humanistic psychology, which is actually of Satan. Even the most elementary Sunday School child ought to know that if the terrible sin problem, with all of its perversions and aberrations, can in fact, be solved by the prattle of pitiful man, then Jesus needlessly came down here and died on a cruel Cross.

The great problem in the modern Church is unbelief and Scriptural ignorance. Let's deal with unbelief first.

UNBELIEF

We either believe that Jesus at the Cross addressed every sin, every perversion, every aberration, every nuance of which one could think, and in every manner, or else we don't believe. One cannot have it both ways.

If we claim to believe that He in fact did address all sin at the Cross, then we know instinctively that man has no solution to this problem. As stated, that's actually elementary! So, for Preachers to recommend humanistic psychology, must mean they have weighed the evidence, and they have come

to a conclusion of unbelief in their own minds, that Calvary did not answer it all. As stated, one cannot have it both ways. Either He did, or He didn't!

I happen to believe that He did, and I have proven in my own life that He did, and so have untold millions of others. In other words, the evidence is so overwhelming as to be undeniable. Every single heart and life that's been set free, has its freedom today, simply because of what Jesus did at the Cross.

On the other hand, the world of humanistic psychology, cannot show me one single individual anywhere, at any time, that they have set free. So, for Preachers to believe this *"wisdom of the world"* which is *"earthly, sensual, and devilish"* (James 3:15), simply says, that they do not believe the *"wisdom of God"* which is the Cross of Christ (I Cor. 1:21).

"Unbelief" is the most dangerous place and position of all, in that the bottom line is, that men simply do not believe that *"Jesus Christ is the propitiation for our sins: and not for ours only, but also for the sins of the whole world"* (I Jn. 2:2).

IGNORANCE

However, Scriptural ignorance is probably almost as big as unbelief. In fact, that's why Paul said over and over again, and to Believers, *"I would not have you to be ignorant"* (Rom. 1:13; 11:25; I Cor. 10:1; 12:1; II Cor. 1:8; I Thess. 4:13).

As we've also said over and over again, even to the point of being overly repetitive, the Church, at least for the most part, has had so little teaching on the Cross in the last 50 or more years, that this great foundational Truth has all but been lost. Let the Reader understand, that the Cross of Christ is not a Doctrine. It is in fact, the foundation on which all Doctrine is built. And if doctrine is not built on that foundation, then in some way it is spurious. And that's where the Church is presently!

While the foundational Truth of the Cross is possibly buried in its constitution and by-laws, as far as living out its practical applications, that regarding the Church has long since ceased to be. So, the Christian stumbles along in failure, not nearly living up to his or her potential in Christ.

SIN

Even though most in the Church, I think, are so lifted up with spiritual pride that they are loathe to admit it, the problem of the Church is sin, as the problem of the Church has always been sin! And when we say *"the Church,"* we're speaking of its individual members, namely you and me. The Truth is, the Church treats sin, at least for the most part, in one or two ways:

1. The part of the Church world which doesn't believe in the Baptism with the Holy Spirit with the evidence of speaking with other Tongues, mostly claim that we as Believers are merely *"sinners saved by Grace."* In other words, we were sinners before we got saved, and we continue to be sinners after we are saved, and are saved only because of our trust in Christ. In fact, they place very little confidence in victory over sin, claiming that Christians have to sin a little bit or a whole lot each day, etc.

Paul addressed this error by asking the question, *"Shall we continue in sin, that Grace may abound?"*

His answer was instant, *"God forbid. How shall we* (Believers), *who are dead to sin, live any longer therein?"* (Rom. 6:1-2).

2. The part of the Church world which claims to believe in the Baptism with the Holy Spirit with the evidence of speaking with other Tongues, for the most part, claims that sin is no problem. Claiming to be Spirit-filled, and, therefore, mighty men and women of Faith, the idea that they could be overcome by sin, or that sin is a problem, is for all practical purposes denied. In other words, they address the problem by claiming that it doesn't exist.

The Truth is, that's about like trying to ignore a 2,000 pound elephant that's sitting in one's living room. Due to having almost no knowledge of the Cross, most Pentecostals and Charismatics are living lives of spiritual failure, the same as their non-Pentecostal and non-Charismatic Brethren.

In fact, in much of the Charismatic world, they claim that Preachers should not even address the problem of sin. In other words,

it should not even be mentioned, because to do so, only creates a *"sin-consciousness,"* they say! That in effect is *"a spirit of denial,"* which of course is spurious. Denying reality doesn't change things.

This doctrine of the denial of sin is strange, especially considering that the Holy Spirit through Paul as well as the other writers, addressed this thing in every way and in every capacity. In fact, victory over sin in the heart and life of the Believer is the main topic of Paul's Epistles. The same would go for Peter and John as well!

But again, much of the Charismatic world completely denies the Cross of Christ, claiming that it was the worst defeat in human history; consequently, they say, the Cross, or the Blood, or the Crucifixion of Christ, or anything of that nature, should never be mentioned. Pure and simple, this is *"another gospel, fostered by another spirit, presenting another Jesus"* (II Cor. 11:4). Regrettably, this part of the Spirit-filled Church world, but not Spirit-led, must be placed in the ranks of unbelief, and not Scriptural ignorance.

Scriptural ignorance regarding the Cross, on the other hand, does not register unbelief, but rather a lack of knowledge on the subject. And that's where much of the Church world stands presently. It simply doesn't know what the Holy Spirit gave to Paul, as it regards the victory of the Cross. And let it be clearly understood:

A proper understanding of the Cross, and Faith in that Finished Work of Christ, are the only means of overcoming sin. There is no other sacrifice for sin! So, if the Believer doesn't know or understand, this all-important Truth, then irrespective as to how sincere the Believer might be, how dedicated the Believer might be, in one way or the other, that Believer is going to live a life of spiritual failure. While they definitely are saved, at the same time, they definitely aren't victorious.

TYPES OF SIN

There are sins of passion and there are sins of pride. Sins of passion, which are works of the flesh (Gal. 5:19-21), are very obvious, while sins of pride are not so very obvious. Sins of passion include all the vices, and of course, are very evil.

Sins of pride function in another category altogether. When Stephen addressed the religious leaders of Israel, just before they stoned him to death, he said to them, *"Ye stiffnecked and uncircumcised in heart and ears, ye do always resist the Holy Spirit"* (Acts 7:51).

Many of these men would not have dreamed of associating themselves with any of the vices; nevertheless, their evil hearts were filled with murder, in that they did crucify the Lord and stoned to death His servant.

Even though all sin is deadly and horrible, the sin of *"resisting the Holy Spirit,"* which many religious people, and especially religious leaders fall into, is the worst sin of all. It presents a face of piousness to the world, and most of the time has an excellent reputation; however, its character, which God Alone knows, is grossly evil.

WHAT DOES RESISTING THE HOLY SPIRIT ACTUALLY MEAN?

Even though much is said on the subject, to make it simple in order that we may fully understand, *"resisting the Holy Spirit"* is resisting the One to Whom the Holy Spirit always points as the Deliverer from all sin, the Lord Jesus Christ. It is resisting God's solution for dying humanity, the Cross of Christ.

Israel wanted Jesus the conqueror of Rome, but they didn't want Jesus the conqueror of sin. They were so lifted up in their own self-righteousness, that they couldn't admit that they were sinners and desperately needed a Redeemer. Their sin was in rejecting God's Solution for their dilemma, a dilemma incidentally which they refused to admit.

So, just because a Christian is not mixed up in one of the vices, doesn't mean they are living a life of victory over sin. In fact, there are millions of so-called Christians who the world thinks of as very moral, but in reality, are trusting in their own self-righteousness, instead of the Righteousness of Christ, which refers to Faith in what Christ did at the Cross. These people are obvious by their *"works religion,"* which they attempt to add to the Finished Work of Christ, of which the latter is all but ignored.

VICTORY!

Defeat is *"walking after the flesh,"* while victory is *"walking after the Spirit"* (Rom. 8:1).

To *"walk after the Spirit,"* simply means to trust in what Christ did at the Cross, in which parameters the Holy Spirit always works.

Paul said, *"For the Law* (an unbreakable Law) *of the Spirit* (the Holy Spirit) *of life* (this Law, which is the Law of the Cross, gives life) *in Christ Jesus* (refers to what Jesus did at the Cross and the Resurrection, all on our behalf) *hath made me free from the law of sin and death* (also a law, and impossible to overcome, other than by the Law of the Spirit)*"* (Rom. 8:2).

So, if one wants to have total victory in one's life, which in fact Jesus paid for at the Cross, one must abide by *"the Law of the Spirit."* And what is that Law? Paul tells us in the next Verse.

"For what the Law (Law of Moses, not the Law of the Spirit) *could not do, in that it was weak through the flesh* (the Law of Moses had no power to give man to help him to obey), *God sending His Own Son in the likeness of sinful flesh* (the Incarnation), *and for sin, condemned sin in the flesh"* (Rom. 8:3).

As an aside, if our Word of Faith friends are right, in that sin should never be mentioned, Paul is sure speaking of the subject an awful lot.

This Verse means that God became man, in order to die on a Cross that the terrible sin debt would be paid, and in so doing, overcame sin in the flesh, all on our behalf. In other words, everything that Jesus did, was done totally and completely for us, and not at all for Himself.

To be more specific, the Law of the Spirit which is in Christ Jesus means the following:

BAPTIZED INTO THE DEATH OF CHRIST

The Holy Spirit through Paul said, *"Know ye not* (and regrettably many Christians don't know), *that so many of us as were baptized into Jesus Christ were baptized into His death?"* (Rom. 6:3).

First of all, understand that Paul is not speaking here of Water Baptism, as many think. He is speaking of the death of Christ on the Cross. So, that being the case, how were we baptized into His death, when we were not even there?

Whenever the believing sinner exhibits Faith in Christ, in the Mind of God this legal work of the sinner being baptized into Christ at His Death, was carried out. Christ, as the *"Last Adam"* (I Cor. 15:45), did all of this as our Substitute, which means that we couldn't do such for ourselves.

The wages of sin being death, Christ had to die in order to pay this debt. If I had died upon a Cross, or if you had died upon a Cross, our hearts and lives being polluted by sin, such would have been a sacrifice which God could not accept. But His Son dying on the Cross, and doing so by offering to God a Perfect Body and a Perfect Life, was a Sacrifice which God could accept, and in fact, did accept. As stated, it was all done on our behalf. What we couldn't do for ourselves, He did for us.

To acquire the benefits of what He did, all we have to do is to register Faith in this great Finished Work (Eph. 2:8-9).

BURIED WITH HIM

We were not only crucified with Him, but as Paul also said, *"We are buried with Him by baptism into death"* (Rom. 6:4).

This means that our *"old man,"* as Paul refers to in Verse 6, which pertains to our old life before conversion, had to die. To be sure, that death was accomplished in the Crucifixion of Christ, which we gain by Faith.

So, the old Jimmy Swaggart was not only crucified with Christ, but was also buried with Him. This means all the old transgression, sin, iniquity, old ways, and old life, all and without exception, were buried with Him, which means, none of this can ever be held against you or me, anymore. It is dead and buried!

This also means, that the Lord doesn't attempt to rehabilitate the sinner, or to patch him up so to speak, but rather does away altogether with the *"old man,"* and then brings forth a *"new man."*

NEWNESS OF LIFE, THE NEW MAN

Paul said as well, *"That like as Christ was raised up from the dead by the Glory of the Father* (all on our behalf), *even so we also should walk in newness of life"* (Rom. 6:4). In other words, as we were crucified with Him, and buried with Him, we were also raised with Him in *"newness of life,"* i.e., *"the new man."* That's the reason that the Apostle said, *"Therefore if any man be in Christ, he*

is a new creature: old things are passed away; behold, all things are become new" (II Cor. 5:17).

He said as well, *"Having abolished in His flesh* (the Crucifixion) *the enmity, even the Law of Commandments contained in ordinances* (the Law of Moses which had condemned us); *for to make in Himself* (through what He did at the Cross and the Resurrection) *of twain* (by His death being our death) *one new man* (what we are in Christ), *so making peace"* (Eph. 2:15; 4:24).

So, every Believer is a *"new man"* in Christ Jesus, which means that the *"old man"* doesn't live there anymore (Rom. 6:6).

HOW DOES THE CHRISTIAN CONTINUE TO WALK AS THE NEW MAN?

Paul tells us how in Romans, Chapters 6 and 8.

First of all, and as stated, we must understand that when we were saved, in the mind of God, we were baptized into the death of Christ, we were buried with Him, which means that our *"old man"* died with Him and was buried, and that we were raised in newness of life (Rom. 6:3-4, 6). Understanding this, there are several things we must now continue to do as it regards Faith. If these things are done, we can stay free from every bondage of iniquity, or we can get free, whatever the case might be. These things are as follows:

RESURRECTION LIFE

Paul said, *"For if we have been planted together in the likeness of His death, we shall be also in the likeness of His Resurrection"* (Rom. 6:5).

The idea here is, that it is intended by God that we walk and live in Resurrection Life. Of course, that means victory over the world, the flesh, and the Devil. This is that for which Jesus died, and it is that which we can have, if we will only follow His prescribed order.

However, to have this *"Resurrection Life,"* we must ever understand the first part of this Verse, which refers to *"being planted together in the likeness of His Death."* In other words, our Faith must never leave the Cross. We must understand that we have this Resurrection Life, which gives us all things, because of what Jesus did at the Cross. Understanding and knowing this, the Cross of Christ must ever be the object of our Faith, understanding that this is the Source of all Blessings. Now this is very, very important!

Satan will do everything within his power to move your Faith to something else. He will probably do so by getting you to direct your attention to other things which are good. And because they are good, we are deceived. But please understand, Satan doesn't really care what you believe, just as long as it's not Faith in the Cross. So, you must not allow your Faith to be moved to anything else. And by that I mean the following:

The Church belongs to Christ, but the Church didn't die on the Cross for you. Consequently, millions of Christians have their Faith in the Church or some particular Denomination. That is Faith that God will not honor.

As well, other Christians have their Faith in other types of good works such as, fasting, praying, the giving of money, witnessing to souls, etc. All these things we have mentioned, plus many we haven't mentioned, are wonderful, great, and good, and should be the staple of all Believers; however, we must never put our Faith in these things, thinking that such will grant us favor with God, etc. It won't!

Again I emphasize, these things mentioned, should be practiced daily by every Child of God, but rather because of what Jesus has already done for us at the Cross, and not in order to get Him to do things for us. The Faith of the Child of God must ever be anchored in the Cross of Christ, not allowing it to be moved elsewhere, understanding that what Jesus did at the Cross provides us all things.

DEAD TO SIN

The Holy Spirit through Paul also said, *"Likewise reckon ye also yourselves to be dead indeed unto sin, but alive unto God through Jesus Christ our Lord"* (Rom. 6:11).

The word *"reckon"* means *"to account."* In other words, you are to conclude yourself as being what the Holy Spirit says you are. And what does He say?

He says that you are *"dead unto sin, and alive unto God through Jesus Christ your Lord."*

Remember? You died with Christ! So that means you died to all of Satan's wares, all sin, and everything held by the Evil One. It has no more hold on you. And please understand, when a person is dead to something, that means *"dead!"* Now please consider the following:

That doesn't mean that now you have the power to say *"no"* to sin, but rather that you have the power to say *"yes"* to God. While you are dead to sin, at the same time, you are alive unto God. What am I saying?

I'm saying that you don't hold conversations with something to which you are dead. As stated, dead means dead! So, it's not a question of me saying no to anything the Devil has, for the simple reason that I'm not even supposed to get that far with such a thing in my thinking. I'm alive unto God, and not unto Satan or anything he has.

As well, the word *"reckon"* in the Greek also has as its root, the word *"logos,"* which means *"Word,"* or *"Word of God."* In other words, you are to understand, that God says of you that you are dead to sin and alive unto Him. You are to believe that, understand that, act upon that, realizing, that God cannot lie.

BUT WHAT IF I HAVE DONE THIS AND FAILED ANYWAY?

When the Believer starts out on the road of victory, which is the road of the Cross (Lk. 9:23), this doesn't mean that Satan is going to fold up. To be sure, he will test your Faith in every way possible, making every attempt to get you to look to other than the Cross. Regrettably, he usually succeeds in some manner.

If you fail in some way, and irrespective as to what it is, ask the Lord to forgive you, which He has assured us that He shall (I Jn. 1:9). And then understand, that you have failed because your Faith failed in some manner. In other words, your Faith is not quite as strong as it ought to be. To be sure, the Cross cannot fail, and because Jesus cannot fail.

Now that you've asked the Lord to forgive you, ask the Lord also to help you as it regards your Faith being anchored in the Cross. Please understand that the Lord is not trying to find ways to wash us out, but rather to help us make it through. He has invested the Precious Blood of Jesus in our hearts and lives, in our very souls, and to be sure, if He loved us enough to die for us while we were yet sinners, think how much more He loves us now, in that we are serving Him (Rom. 5:8).

Now don't let the Devil lie to you, trying to tell you that due to your failure, that the Cross of Christ simply doesn't work. To be sure, the Cross works and works perfectly. But unfortunately, we as poor human beings are very prone to failure. In fact, the very purpose of the Cross is to address this weakness in our hearts and lives. The more we understand this, and I speak of our weaknesses, then we will begin to understand the Cross, and what Jesus did there.

No human being who has ever lived is able to live this life as one ought to live, at least by his own efforts and machinations. It simply cannot be done. That's the very reason that Jesus had to come down here and die on a Cross. He had to do for us what we could not do for ourselves, in order that in Him we might be able to live the life we ought to live. And as stated, it can only be done *"in Him"* (II Cor. 5:17).

So if you stumble, get up, understanding that the Lord will never let you down, zero your Faith once again in the Cross, understanding that you are now on the road to victory. So what am I saying?

I'm saying, that no matter your weaknesses, if you'll keep your Faith in the Cross of Christ, you are guaranteed of victory. The very word *"reckon"* which is the *"Word of God,"* guarantees this to be so. You will ultimately have victory and I speak of total victory, over the world, the flesh, and the Devil.

HOW TO YIELD

Paul said, *"Neither yield ye your members as instruments of unrighteousness unto sin: but yield yourselves unto God, as those that are alive from the dead, and your members as instruments of Righteousness unto God"* (Rom. 6:13).

Even as I dictate these words, there are millions of Christians at this very moment, who are attempting with all their strength and might to yield themselves to Righteousness, but are rather yielding themselves otherwise. In other words, in some manner, they are

bound by sin. And please understand, this doesn't refer only to new converts, but also to Pastors of some of the largest Churches in the world; also, to Evangelists who are drawing some of the largest crowds. The Truth is, if the Believer, whomever that Believer might be, doesn't understand the Cross of Christ, in some way, in some manner, that Believer is going to walk in defeat. It cannot be otherwise! Victory is found only in the Cross, and if the Believer doesn't understand that, which most don't, there can be no other outcome but failure.

Please understand, that for every one failure you hear about, there are probably a hundred or even a thousand, that you don't hear about. Irrespective, God knows the situation, and to be sure, the person involved knows the situation as well.

So, how does a Believer obey this admonition to yield ourselves unto Righteousness?

Even as we've explained some pages ago, yielding pertains to willpower. The Scripture plainly says, *"Whosoever will . . ."* (Rev. 22:17). However, it must be understood, and understood clearly, that the will of the Believer is not free to say *"no"* to sin, even to which we have just alluded. That is not the position in which the Believer ought to be.

Many Christians erroneously think that now that they belong to Christ, their willpower has been greatly strengthened, and they are free to say *"yes"* or *"no"* to anything they like. That's not true!

You as a Believer are free to say *"yes"* to the Lord. In other words, you are free to put your Faith in the Cross of Christ, which means to *"will"* your self in that direction. Satan cannot stop you from doing that, and God guarantees your freedom in this respect.

However, if you drift outside of the Cross of Christ, attempting to depend on something else other than the Cross, you as a Believer, despite the fact that you are saved and even Spirit-filled, will quickly find yourself being overcome by Satan. Let me say it again:

It comes as a shock to many Christians for them to realize, that Satan can actually override their wills. Think about that for a moment!

But it definitely is true. As long as you will to trust Christ, and by that I mean to trust in what He did at the Cross, all the powers of Hell cannot stop you, in fact, cannot even touch you. But if you drift outside the parameters of the Finished Work of Christ, depending on something else, and irrespective as to how good that something else might be, you will find Satan overriding your will. In fact, He's doing it right now to millions of Christians. They are doing things they don't want to do, and are trying with all their strength and might not to do these things, but despite all their efforts, they are failing anyway. And that's where some of you holding this Book in your hands are at this very moment.

But please understand that it doesn't have to be this way. You are failing, because your Faith is in something else other than the Cross of Christ, and when this happens, the Holy Spirit, Whose help you must have, simply will not function. He functions totally and completely within the parameters of what Christ did at the Cross. He only asks that we have Faith in the great Sacrifice of Christ, and then He will do His work (Rom. 8:1-2). In other words, He guarantees a free flow of Grace if our Faith is in the Cross. Otherwise, we frustrate the Grace of God, and we are guaranteed of defeat (Gal. 2:20-21).

When one anchors their Faith in the Cross of Christ, one then is guaranteed the help of the Holy Spirit, and one can then easily yield oneself unto Righteousness. But it can be done only in this manner.

DOMINION, LAW, AND GRACE

The Holy Spirit through Paul now says, *"For sin shall not have dominion over you: for ye are not under the Law, but under Grace"* (Rom. 6:14).

If it wasn't possible for *"sin"* or rather *"the sin nature"* to have dominion over a Believer, then Paul wouldn't have made this statement. The Truth is, the sin nature is dominating every single Believer in this world in some way, in some manner, who doesn't understand their victory in the Cross of Christ. And that's the shame of it all. Jesus died on the Cross, which of course speaks of such great price; consequently, it's a terrible shame for any Believer not to be able to enjoy the benefits for which He paid such a price. But if the

Christian doesn't understand the Cross, and precious few actually do, in some way sin will dominate that individual. What do we mean by that?

I'm speaking of Christians who cannot control their temper. I'm speaking of Christians who are eaten up with jealousy, or envy! I'm speaking of Christians who are drinking secretly, or taking drugs. I'm speaking of Christians who are involved in immorality in some manner. In fact, the list is very, very long!

The facts are, the far greater majority of these Christians aren't hypocrites. They love God. And as previously stated, they are trying with all their power to yield to Righteousness, but are not successful.

Many of these Christians have gone to their Pastor, confessing their problem. He has instructed them to *"try harder,"* or *"pray more,"* or *"get in the Altars!"* Or if he is the of the modernist type, he has referred them to a Psychologist, stating that they need *"professional help."*

Even though the former certainly pertains to good things, in fact, what every Christian ought to do; still, those things mentioned will not bring victory. And it is for certain, that the world of psychology has no answer whatsoever.

This is the reason that untold thousands of Christians are running all over the world, trying to find a Preacher who they think God is using, who can lay hands on them and solve their problem. While the *"laying on of hands"* is definitely Scriptural, and will definitely help and bless, still, there is no deliverance whatsoever in this method. Despite all the manifestations, and they definitely will be of help, that is if they are from the Lord, no victory will be assured whatsoever in this capacity. Think about it a moment:

If these things could give Believers victory over sin, and to be sure it is sin of which we speak, then Jesus would not have had to come down here and die on a Cross. He could have rather just trained Christians to confess properly, or Preachers to rebuke demon spirits, and the problem would be solved. However, we know that these things solve no problems whatsoever.

To be sure, a good confession is Scriptural and proper and will definitely help. As well, demon spirits definitely get involved in every failure. But the answer for that Believer, is not rebuking demons, but rather knowing the Truth.

THE TRUTH

Jesus said, *"And ye shall know the Truth, and the Truth shall make you free"* (Jn. 8:32).

And what is the Truth?

The Truth is, that man is in such a terrible dilemma that he cannot help himself. To address this terrible problem, God became man, and as the *"Last Adam"* (I Cor. 15:45), did for man what man could not do for himself. *"He gave Himself for our sins, that He might deliver us from this present evil world, according to the Will of God and our Father"* (Gal. 1:4).

That is the Truth, and the only Truth! Man only has to believe in what Christ did at the Cross, and that for which Jesus died will be gloriously his.

This is the Truth which we must tell the entirety of the world. This is the Truth which we must ever cling to as it regards our own personal lives and victory. As one of my associates said, *"The Church needs the Truth, a whole lot more than it needs a touch."* It could not be better said.

As long as the Church believes anything other than the Cross, the Church will continue to walk in defeat. And to be sure, and I say this sadly, the Church presently, knows little victory.

When the Lord gave me this Revelation of the Cross, beginning in 1997, to be sure, it wasn't something new. In fact, the Cross is the oldest Message known to man. It actually had its beginning in the Garden of Eden, and has been the only Source of life and victory from then until now.

In this Revelation given to me, which actually continues to expand unto this hour, the Holy Spirit has grandly informed me that this Message is not for me only, but for the entirety of the Church.

Paul said, *"But we preach Christ crucified"* (I Cor. 1:23).

He also said, *"For the preaching of the Cross is to them that perish foolishness; but unto us which are saved it is the power of God"* (I Cor. 1:18).

Actually, *"preaching"* should here have been translated *"Word,"* because in the Greek it is *"Logos."* Therefore, it should read, *"For the Word of the Cross. . . ."*

This gives it a much broader meaning, actually covering every aspect of Christianity. In fact, the *"Word of the Cross"* is the Gospel.

The Apostle also said, *"It pleased God by the foolishness of preaching* (the Cross) *to save them that believe"* (I Cor. 1:21).

So, the Church must live the Cross, preach the Cross, proclaim the Cross, ever hold up the Cross as the answer to dying humanity.

THE HOLY SPIRIT

It is the Holy Spirit Who makes real within our hearts and lives all the benefits of the Cross. In other words, the Spirit of God delivers to the Believer all the product of the Finished Work of Christ. To be sure, it is the Holy Spirit Alone Who can do these things. And as we've stated, He works 100 percent within the parameters of the great Sacrifice of Christ. He will not veer outside of those parameters, and if we go outside of them, which refers to having Faith in anything other than the Cross, we will find ourselves without the help of the Spirit, which means that we're on our own, which spells defeat.

Concerning this, Paul said, *"There is therefore now no condemnation to them which are in Christ Jesus, who walk not after the flesh, but after the Spirit"* (Rom. 8:1).

In this statement, the Holy Spirit through Paul plainly tells us, that it is quite possible for a Believer to *"walk after the flesh,"* and not *"after the Spirit."*

How can one know after which one he is walking?

If one is failing, then one is *"walking after the flesh."* If one is walking victoriously, one is then *"walking after the Spirit."*

"Walking after the flesh" simply refers to trusting in anything and everything, other than the Cross of Christ. This means that if you are trusting in your Church, you're walking after the flesh. It also means, if you're trusting in your prayer life to give you victory over sin, you are walking after the flesh.

That may seem strange to Believers, considering that prayer is the highest and holiest thing in which a Believer can engage; however, it's all a matter of Faith. Do you have your Faith in your prayer life, or do you have your Faith in what Christ did at the Cross.

No! We're not demeaning prayer by any means. In fact, we have two prayer meetings a day at the Ministry, and have done so since the Fall of 1991. In fact, the Lord told me to do this, which we have kept up unto this hour, and by the Grace of God will continue until Jesus comes.

But to be sure, it's not these prayer meetings that guarantee us victory of any nature. While they are of definite, immeasurable help, it is not prayer or my prayer life that defeated the powers of darkness, but rather what Jesus did at the Cross.

So, if I exhibit Faith in the Cross of Christ, and continue there with my Faith, I am then *"walking after the Spirit."* As we've said over and over again, the Spirit of God works exclusively within the parameters of the Finished Work of Christ, which we will see in the next Verse.

THE LAW OF THE SPIRIT

Paul said, *"For the Law* (an unbreakable Law) *of the Spirit* (Holy Spirit) *of life* (the only means of victory) *in Christ Jesus* (what Jesus did at the Cross and the Resurrection on my behalf) *hath made me free* (the only manner in which one can be made free) *from the law of sin and death* (another Law which is so strong that it cannot be overcome, without the power of the Spirit)*"* (Rom. 8:2).

Notice the two *"Laws"* mentioned here. The first one is *"the Law of the Spirit,"* while the latter is *"the law of sin and death."* The only thing that's going to overcome the latter, is the former.

Now understand, these things are *"laws,"* which means that first of all, they were designed that way by God, which means they cannot be broken. They are set in concrete, so to speak!

As a Believer, I want this great *"Law of the Spirit"* working within my heart and life. Especially considering, that I cannot have victory without this which the Holy Spirit Alone can do, it is imperative that I know here what is being said.

What is this *"Law of the Spirit"*?

Please notice, it is *"the Law of the Spirit of life in Christ Jesus."* This means, that this *"Law"* is wrapped up totally and completely in Christ Jesus, and more particularly, what He did at the Cross, and in His Resurrection, all on my behalf. In other words, what Jesus did there, makes it possible for the Holy Spirit to do great and mighty things with us and for us.

Paul plainly said, that *"Christ was made a curse for us . . . that the Blessing of Abraham* (Justification by Faith) *might come on the Gentiles through Jesus Christ."* And then he said:

"That we might receive the Promise of the Spirit through Faith" (Gal. 3:13-14).

In other words, it took what Christ did on the Cross to settle the terrible sin debt. When this was done, with the believing sinner exhibiting Faith in Christ and what He did for us at the Cross, the Holy Spirit could then come into our hearts and lives to abide forever (Jn. 14:16-17).

To say it a better way, before the Cross, the Holy Spirit could not come into the hearts and lives of Believers to abide. The terrible sin debt had not yet been settled, because the blood of bulls and goats could not take away sin. But due to what Jesus did at the Cross, all sin was removed, thereby making it possible for the Holy Spirit to come in and to abide forever.

Consequently, all that He does for us and with us are done exclusively according to what Jesus did at the Cross. As we have stated repeatedly, all He requires of us, is that we exhibit Faith in the Cross, and continue to do so, and then He will do great and mighty things for us and with us. This *"Law of the Spirit,"* is all in Christ Jesus, meaning that it functions totally according to what Christ did at the Cross, and our Faith in that.

Now let's see what this *"Law of the Spirit"* does!

MAKING ALIVE OUR MORTAL BODIES

The Apostle said, *"But if the Spirit of Him* (God the Father) *that raised up Jesus from the dead dwell in you, He that raised up Christ from the dead shall also quicken your mortal bodies by His Spirit that dwelleth in you"* (Rom. 8:11).

In this Verse, we are given a most amazing Truth. We're told, that the same Holy Spirit Who raised Jesus from the dead, which proclaims a power that is beyond our comprehension, also dwells within us. And also, we are told, that this same power that raised Jesus from the dead, can be used, and in fact, will be used, to *"quicken our mortal bodies,"* which means, to make our mortal bodies alive unto God.

The reason that the Holy Spirit quoted this in this manner is because the physical body is the weak link in the makeup of the Believer. We are created, *"spirit, soul, and body"* (I Thess. 5:23). Also, even though our souls and spirits have been redeemed, our physical body has not yet been redeemed (Rom. 8:23). That awaits the coming Resurrection of life, *"when we shall be changed"* (I Cor. 15:50-54). In other words, at that time, the physical body will be *"glorified,"* whereas now, it is only sanctified (I Cor. 6:11). In fact, the Sanctification process, as a continued progressive work, is carried on constantly by the Holy Spirit, as it concerns the entire man, which speaks of *"spirit, soul, and body."* Hence, Paul would pray that *"the very God of Peace sanctify you wholly; and I pray God your whole spirit and soul and body be preserved blameless unto the coming of our Lord Jesus Christ"* (I Thess. 5:23).

Actually, the word *"Redemption"* in Romans 8:23, doesn't refer to the fact that the physical body isn't saved, for it definitely is. It is merely speaking there of the coming Glorification. Salvation always includes the whole man, hence Paul's statement in I Thessalonians 5:23.

This means that there is no such thing as a part Salvation. We are saved *"spirit, soul, and body."* And as well, if a Believer sins, he also sins *"spirit, soul, and body."* One cannot be divorced from the other. In fact, the spirit and the soul cannot be separated from the body, until death. Even then, the separation will only last for a time, awaiting the Resurrection, when a glorified body will then be reunited with the soul and the spirit. As stated, the physical body is merely the weak link, through which Satan carries out his perfidious designs.

Even though temptation includes spirit, soul, and body, and even though sin begins in

the heart, and this refers to the seat of one's passions, and not the physical organ, that sin is carried out, as we know and understand, through the physical body, as it regards the five senses.

That's the reason that in the Middle Ages, many Monks, and others, tried to conquer sin, by torturing their physical bodies. This of course, was a fruitless task.

In fact, the physical body is actually neutral. That means it's not inherently evil, or inherently good. Paul used the word *"instruments,"* referring to the fact that our body members can be used for sin or Righteousness (Rom. 6:13).

The physical body is somewhat like for example, a gun. The gun can be used to kill poisonous serpents, or used in crimes against society. It's not really the gun that does the doing, but actually the man or woman holding the gun and willing that it do certain things. As the gun is an instrument, the physical body is also an instrument, hence Paul telling us that we should *"yield our members* (body members) *as instruments of Righteousness."* It is the spirit and the soul which puts the body into operation. And it is the Holy Spirit, Who will give us the power and strength to use the members of our bodies as *"instruments of Righteousness."* He has the power to do it, and He will readily expend that power on our behalf, and do so constantly, providing we place our Faith in the Cross of Christ, and do so totally and completely.

WHY MUST WE PLACE OUR FAITH IN THE CROSS OF CHRIST?

The facts are, all of the things which we need to do in order to be what we ought to be, we can not do. By that, I do not mean that it's difficult to do, or even impossible for some to do, but rather, that which God requires, is impossible for any human being to do, due to the Fall.

It's somewhat like a car that's supposed to run a race. It can little do such with three flat tires and only about three cylinders hitting.

And it must be quickly added, that what God demands, is the least which He can demand. A thrice holy God cannot tolerate imperfection or sin in any manner. Consequently,

He would totally and completely do for us, what we could not do for ourselves. And I might quickly add, He did it at a frightful price.

Consequently, one can hardly fault God for demanding what He did, considering that He paid the price. So, in all of this, all that God demands of us, is that we exhibit Faith in what He did in order to assuage this terrible situation. That's why we have to exhibit Faith in the Cross, and Faith in the Cross alone.

So, why wouldn't man want to do this, considering that God is asking so little?

The world hates the Cross, because it portrays in glaring detail the Love of God, and at the same time, the terrible depravity of man. For if man was so bad, that God would have to become man and die on a Cross in order to redeem fallen humanity, then man was bad indeed!

As stated, the world doesn't agree with that. While they admit that there is a problem, they claim that it is only slight, and can be adjusted with proper education or psychological therapy. Never mind that they never succeed! They keep trying!

There is only one answer for man's dilemma, and that is the Sacrifice of Christ.

When it comes to the Church not believing the Cross, that's another story entirely. In fact, Satan does his best work inside the Church.

Even though the problem of the Church is totally different than the world, and for that reason much worse; still, in many ways the problem is very similar.

As the problem is unbelief as it regards the world, it is unbelief, at least for the most part, as it regards the Church; however, with the world it is unbelief in the realm of darkness, while in the Church it is unbelief in the realm of light, which as stated, makes it much worse. It is one thing to not know and thereby, not believe. It is something else altogether, to be shown the light, which means that one knows, and then to reject that light with purpose and intent. That is unbelief of which Paul will address in Chapters 6 and 8 of this Epistle. Concerning the unbelief of the Church, the Holy Spirit through him said, *"It is a fearful thing to fall into the hands of the Living God"* (Heb. 10:31).

NOTES

THROUGH THE SPIRIT

The Apostle said, *"For if you live after the flesh, ye shall die: but if ye through the Spirit do mortify the deeds of the body, ye shall live"* (Rom. 8:13).

Paul plainly says here, that it's possible for a Christian to *"live after the flesh."* If this happens, and regrettably, it is happening in the far greater majority of Christians, the end result and without fail, is defeat. This happens because of looking elsewhere other than the Cross.

As well, and as we've been saying, the text here plainly tells us, that we can *"mortify the deeds of the body,"* which refers to evil deeds, only *"through the Spirit."* It cannot be done any other way.

This means that the powers of darkness are so strong, meaning that sin is so strong, that only the Spirit of God can bring that monster to bay. And again let us reiterate, that the Spirit of God functions in our hearts and lives only on the basis of what Christ did at the Cross, and our Faith in that Finished Work.

The problem is, many Christians think just because they are saved, and even Spirit-filled, that they can do whatever needs to be done. The Truth is, despite these things we've mentioned, the Christian cannot do anything within himself. He must have the leading, guidance, direction, anointing, and power of the Holy Spirit. He must understand that, and do so without fail!

And as well, in order for the Holy Spirit to work within our lives, we must understand, even as we have repeated over and over again, that the object of our Faith must ever be the Cross (Rom. 6:3-5, 11, 14).

THE DEVIL

The phrase, *"That is, the Devil,"* portrays this archenemy of God, this despot of darkness, this fallen angel, as being the head of the kingdom of darkness.

Most of the world denies the existence of the Devil, and regrettably, so does much of the Church. Nevertheless, Satan is a real person, an angel as stated, who in fact, was originally created by God.

However, let it be understood, that God did not create Lucifer originally in this manner, for that is his name (Isa. 14:12).

Sometime in eternity past, Lucifer led a revolution against God, which drew away a third of the angels with him (Rev. 12:4). Exactly why he did this we are not told, and exactly why a third of the angels followed him, of that we have no knowledge either.

Some may ask the question as to how Satan, being a mere creature while God is the Creator, turned evil and thought he might have a chance to succeed as it regards his revolution.

While not being all-knowing as God, still, Satan knew that God would work and function within a prescribed set of Laws — Laws incidentally, which God had Himself made. As well, sin, which incidentally Satan himself invented one might say, has a terrible power of deception connected with its precepts; consequently, Satan is very much deceived, even as are all his dupes.

Knowing that Satan can read the Bible, and knowing that the Word of God foretells his doom (Rev. 20:10-15), and considering that we're coming down to the very end, what must his thoughts be presently?

That question is easy to answer. Satan doesn't believe the Bible, the same as most of the world doesn't believe the Bible. He still thinks he will pull it off, with in fact, his greatest effort yet to come.

He has refused to admit the supremacy of Christ, at least in the overall picture. But the Second Coming, will handle this situation, and without a doubt. Jesus will come back as *"King of kings, and Lord of lords"* (Rev. 19:16). At His Coming, He will *"lay hold on the dragon, that old serpent, which is the Devil, and Satan, and will bind him a thousand years, casting him into the bottomless pit, shutting him up, and then setting a seal upon him"* (Rev. 20:2-3). There will be no doubt then as to Whom the Master actually is.

While Satan does recognize the Cross, he only does so if forced.

CHRIST

Incidentally, Verse 14, the Scripture of our study, overthrows the Gnostic and Christian Science doctrine that Christ had no physical human body, and that He never died in that body.

Concerning Christ Himself taking part of flesh and blood, we must understand, that even though He did this, the humanity of fallen men, was not His. Here there must be strict limitation. We must add, as the Apostle does afterwards with regard to His temptation, *"sin apart."* In other words, sin, and the consequences of sin, He could not take and did not take. Consequently, death could have no power over Him, except as He might submit Himself voluntarily to it, and this He did; but it was obedience to His Father's Will, and no necessity of His condition, as it is of ours.

And if it be remembered that sin is not inherent in human nature as such, but that it is a foreign thing brought in through the Fall, it can be readily understood how it could be said that our blessed Lord *"took part of the same"* without involving full participation in all that had come in through man's failure.

It must be ever understood, that He had to be the Unblemished One if He would make satisfaction for sins.

Having thus become Man, though sinless, our Lord became man's Champion and went forth as our David to destroy or annul the great Goliath who had terrorized the world ever since the Fall, *"him that had the power of death, that is, the Devil."*

The Cross was for Christ a Valley of Elah where He met our cruel foe and put an end to his authority over the souls of all who believe the Gospel, thus delivering us even now, who in times past through fear of death were held in bitter bondage all our lives.

Satan is a conquered foe and no Believer need now fear him, that is, if we maintain our Faith in the Cross of Christ which was brought about, in order that this great victory might be carried out.

(15) "AND DELIVER THEM WHO THROUGH FEAR OF DEATH WERE ALL THEIR LIFETIME SUBJECT TO BONDAGE."

1. Christ had to deliver mankind, for all of humanity due to the Fall was held captive by Satan.

2. As is here clearly portrayed, death is an aberration. In other words, it was never originally intended by God. Inasmuch as it is an aberration, there is a terrible fear as it regards this monster, and rightly so. However,

that fear was taken away, by what Christ did at the Cross. He conquered death!

3. The fear of death was and is a bondage, and perhaps, the greatest bondage of all, and a bondage incidentally, from which Christ Alone can deliver.

DELIVERANCE

The phrase, *"And deliver them,"* speaks of mankind held in captivity, and by Satan at that!

The word *"deliver"* proclaims the fact that these souls were taken captive by force, held by force, and then delivered by force, with the latter being of greater power. Once again we go back to what Jesus said about Him being stronger than the strong man (Satan), so much stronger in fact, that He would bind Satan, enter into his house, spoil his goods, and in fact, the entirety of this evil house, which Jesus did at the Cross (Mat. 12:29).

However, that which was done had to be done in a legal manner, which legality satisfied the Laws of God, which the Master did at the Cross. If we're speaking merely of strength, then we have no contest. God is almighty, and only has to speak the word and it is done. Satan being a creature, in fact, is at the Mercy of God. So, we're not speaking here of strength as one normally defines such. We're speaking of strength which comes about as a result of the Law of God being carried out in totality.

Jesus didn't go to the Cross because of Satan, but rather because of God. The Righteousness of God had been grossly insulted; consequently, the righteous demands of God had to be satisfied. By Jesus offering up Himself as a Perfect Sacrifice on behalf of lost humanity, which incidentally, mankind could not do, this Offering satisfied the demands of Heavenly Justice. In the giving of Himself, all sin was atoned, i.e., *"paid in full."* In the doing of this, Satan, even as we've already stated, lost his legal claim on humanity, and was, therefore, defeated. This is what Jesus meant by binding him, entering into his house, and destroying his goods.

As well, this deliverance is of such capacity, so final, so complete, that one of the Greek words used to define Redemption (lotroo), carries forth the meaning that such

a price was paid, that no created being in eternity future will ever be able to say that the price was insufficient. In other words, we definitely have a *"great Salvation."*

FEAR OF DEATH

The phrase, *"Who through fear of death,"* concerned itself with much more than the fact of dying. Is there life beyond the grave? What is there awaiting the departed soul on the other side? In fact, of what does the other side consist?

In the First Century this fear was very real. The Philosophers urged people to be calm in the face of death, and some of them managed to do so. But to most people this brought no relief. Fear was widespread, as the hopeless tone of the inscriptions on tombs clearly illustrates.

If this fear has been alleviated somewhat in modern times, and it definitely has, it is because of the power of the Gospel which has addressed this terrible question, and in fact, it is the Gospel of Jesus Christ alone which addresses this question.

It has been well said that the two terrors from which none but Christ can deliver men are guilt of sin and fear of death. The latter is the offspring of the former. When the conscience of sin is no more, meaning that Jesus has taken its penalty and washed away its stain, the dread of death yields to peace and joy.

BONDAGE

The phrase, *"Were all their lifetime subject to bondage,"* presents slaves of fear; and it must be remembered, that all slaves have a master. In this case, it is Satan himself! Such people have no freedom; no comfort; no peace. From this miserable state Christ comes to deliver man.

The unredeemed, having no spiritual perception whatsoever, cannot comprehend the glory and the beauty of Salvation in Christ. In fact it is impossible for one to know and understand such, until one makes Christ one's Saviour.

So, when the Holy Spirit convicts of sin, and of Righteousness and of Judgment, He never does so on the basis of what one will gain by accepting Christ. It is impossible for even the Holy Spirit to grant such knowledge to a person who is dead in trespasses and sins.

Men are saved, as the Holy Spirit convicts them of sin, referring to their terrible condition, with some of course much worse than others, and that Jesus is the only solution, of Righteousness which none have, and yet which God demands, which at the same time lays waste their own brand of righteousness (self-righteousness), and of Judgment, referring to the fact that all will one day answer to God. It is either accept Christ now as Saviour, or face Him tomorrow as Judge. One way or the other, men will face Christ!

When the Holy Spirit gets through with an individual, they are thoroughly undone. And if they accept Christ, thereby being Born-Again, then and then only, do they know and understand the tremendous life force they now have. To explain such beforehand, is impossible!

Satan is very successful at getting the unredeemed to believe that if they come to Christ, they will go into bondage. In other words, they'll never have anymore fun, never have another good time, and to be sure, in the unredeemed state, there's nothing in the world more boring than Church. They don't realize that after they come to Christ, they will be so changed, that old things will pass away and all things will become new (II Cor. 5:17). But once the sinner comes to Christ, a glorious new world opens up, a world of such staggering proportions and dimensions that it literally defies all description. Instead of the person going into bondage, they actually now are free, and for the first time in their lives. The *"bondage"* is always with Satan. In fact, all unredeemed individuals are slaves more or less; and of course, we speak of slaves of Satan.

"Subject to bondage," means that one is subject to all that the bondage implies, such as fear, doubt, unbelief, error of every description, wild fantasies and thoughts, all wrong, all in error, and all a fabrication of Satan. He is truly a hard taskmaster.

To know Christ, is to know life; it is to know freedom; it is for the first time, to know what the future brings, for only the Lord holds the future in His hands.

"All their lifetime," concerns the entirety of their existence. In fact, almost all the world, at least all who do not know Christ, live a life of fear, privation, and want, and we speak of these things in the spiritual. That's the reason that money and power can never satisfy the hunger and the thirst of the soul. Only God can do that, and He does it totally and completely, through Christ.

(16) "FOR VERILY HE TOOK NOT ON HIM THE NATURE OF ANGELS; BUT HE TOOK ON HIM THE SEED OF ABRAHAM."

The exegesis is:

1. Jesus Christ is God; consequently, anything else He would become, would have to be less than what He is.

2. He did not take upon Himself the nature of Angels, because it was not Angels that He was redeeming.

3. He took upon Himself the Seed of Abraham, which, of course, refers to humanity. It was necessary that this be done for many reasons; however, one of the greatest reasons of all was that He might be a *"merciful and faithful High Priest,"* Who would serve as a Mediator between God and Man (Heb. 7:24-28; I Tim. 2:5).

4. This was the only way that Redemption was possible.

5. The phrase *"Seed of Abraham,"* refers to the fact that in order for men to be saved, they have to come in under the order of the Abrahamic Covenant, which is *"by Faith"* (Gen. 15:6; Gal. 3:6).

6. This speaks of Faith exclusively in the Cross, i.e., *"that which Jesus did in the Atonement in the giving of Himself as a Perfect Sacrifice, in order to pay the terrible sin debt."*

JESUS IS GOD

The phrase, *"For verily He,"* refers to the fact that Jesus Christ was God, is God, and ever shall be God. While He definitely laid aside the expression of His Deity in order to become man, He never for a moment lost possession of His Deity. On this one fact hinges the argument of the world concerning Christ. Was He merely a good man? a great healer? a great miracle worker? even a great philosopher? some might muse.

The Jews, His Own people, have denied Him. Some few in the world, and by that I speak of the unredeemed, will admit that He was and is God, but the far greater majority deny that fact, or else they meet the question with a shrug of the shoulders.

After Napoleon was banished to the Island of St. Helena, the man incidentally who came very close to conquering the world, he was asked the following question by a reporter during a particular interview.

"Do you believe that Jesus Christ was the Son of God, and actually rose from the dead?" or words to that effect.

After the question was asked, Napoleon stood for a long while looking out over the waters of the ocean, so long in fact, that the reporter thought he was not going to answer.

But then he finally turned and looked at the questioner and said, *"Yes I believe that Jesus Christ was the Son of God, and that He really rose from the dead."* He then followed that statement by these remarks:

"You can go to the poorest of the poor anywhere in the world, and if they have heard that Name 'Jesus,' when it is mentioned, their eyes will light up. You can go to the crowned heads of Europe, and at the mention of that Name, it is instantly recognizable and they bow to Him." He paused for a moment, and then being the soldier he was, said:

"At His Name mighty armies march. For His Name millions have died."

And then with another pause, finally concluding, he said, *"Sir, no dead man could command that type of respect. I will soon be dead and mostly forgotten, and if He were dead, He would have long since been forgotten. And because He lives, He has not been forgotten, but is more revered today than ever."*

The word *"verily"* means *"truly"* or *"doubtless."* So we might say, *"Doubtless"* He was and is God, and became man, and did so for a specific purpose, that purpose being the Redemption of lost humanity, which He carried out by His atoning work at the Cross.

NOT OF ANGELS

The phrase, *"Took not on Him the nature of Angels,"* would have probably been better translated, and using the entirety of the phrase from the beginning of the Verse, *"For*

truly He taketh not hold of Angels, but of the Seed of Abraham He took hold."

That is, Christ did not come to be the Saviour of fallen angels. They are of another creation.

While it is true that one third of the angels threw in their lot with Lucifer at his revolution against God, carried out sometime in eternity past, but of any effort to redeem them, of that we aren't aware.

The general idea is that of seizing upon, or laying hold of anyone or anything — no matter what the object is — whether to aid, or to drag to punishment, or simply to conduct. Here it means to lay hold with the reference to *"aid"* or *"help"*; and the meaning is, that He did not seize the nature of Angels, or take it to Himself, with reference to rendering them aid, but He assumed the nature of man in order to aid *"him."* He undertook the work of human Redemption, and consequently it was necessary for Him to be a man.

The words in the Authorized Version *"Him the nature of,"* are in italics indicating that they are not in the original Greek Text, but are supplied by the translators in an effort to translate the Passage. They probably would have been better left off, for they in essence say too much.

The idea here is that the Lord Jesus, in His work on Calvary's Cross, did not provide for the Salvation of fallen angels but for the Salvation of fallen human beings. In Perfect Righteousness He passed by fallen angels, and in infinite mercy and condescension, stooped to provide Salvation for man. In man's fallen condition, now inferior to the angels, He passed by those superior beings in order to save inferior beings. Consequently, He gets more glory in taking an inferior being and raising him to an exalted position in Himself, i.e., *"in Christ Jesus,"* than in saving a superior being and raising him to those heights of blessedness, although *"glory"* was not at all His purpose.

As stated, there is no Biblical proof that attempts were made to redeem fallen angels. That is not to say that no attempt was made, but is meant to say that we have no information regarding such. However, there is the hint of the following in Paul's reference to angels.

THE SPIRIT WORLD

In the Fall, man dropped from such exalted heights, heights which included the image of God, even the very nature of God, in fact able to bring sons and daughters of God into the world, down to the far, far lower level of the very nature of Satan himself, so far lower in fact, that quite possibly it was wondered in the spirit world, if man was actually worth saving. Concerning the righteous Angels and man's Redemption, we are told, *"which things the Angels desire to look into"* (I Pet. 1:12). The idea is, Satan had so wrecked man, so destroyed him, had made him so worthless, so useless, even beyond that, so destructive even to himself and to all that which are righteous and holy, that the question may well be asked, as to why God would even desire to bother as it regarded his Redemption? However, as we have previously said, love created man, and love must redeem man. As well, in Satan's fallen condition, he can no longer understand such love.

Moved by a profound love for man, and by that motive alone, the Son of God — became the Son of Man — humbled Himself to all the circumstances of man in order to deliver him, and was fully equipped to redeem and bring to glory His Brothers, the many sons; and, as a Priest, having made propitiation, He presents them before God in all the beauty and perfection of His Own Person and Work (Williams).

THE SEED OF ABRAHAM

The phrase, *"But He took on Him the Seed of Abraham,"* refers to His humanity, which He became, and to the manner in which Redemption would be brought about.

Why is the name of Abraham used? What did he have to do with all of this?

The Salvation of all humanity comes in under the Abrahamic Covenant.

God promised a Redeemer immediately after the Fall, with the Promise being given to Satan through the serpent more so in the form of a threat than anything else. It spoke of the Seed of the woman bruising the head of the serpent (Gen. 3:15).

God immediately gave the sacrificial system to the first family, with Abel obeying in

the offering up of the proper sacrifice (Gen., Chpt. 4). Unfortunately, due to the anger of his brother Cain, who would not offer up the correct sacrifice, Abel lost his life; however, he didn't lose his soul.

The sacrificial system continued for the next 1,600 years, despite the terrible evil of mankind. We know this from the sacrifices offered by Noah immediately after the Flood (Gen. 8:20-21). It is certain that it was only a few who offered up these sacrifices during the intervening 1,600 years. And they were saved by having Faith in the Seed of the woman Who was to come, of which the Sacrifices were a symbol.

Abraham lived about 400 years after Noah, about 2,000 years after the Fall in the Garden of Eden. How God revealed Himself to Abraham, we aren't told; however, the entirety of this Revelation would necessitate him leaving his home country and his family, going to Canaan, the appointed place directed by God. The account of this Revelation began in Genesis, Chapter 12, and continued through Genesis 25:11. However, the core of what God gave him can be found in Genesis 15:6, *"And he believed in the Lord; and He* (God) *counted it to him for Righteousness."* It is what we refer to as the *"Blessing of Abraham"* (Gal. 3:14), or *"Justification by Faith"* (Rom. 5:1).

All of this simply meant, that Abraham believed that God was going to send a Redeemer into this world, and Faith in Him, and I might quickly add, Faith without works of any kind, would guarantee Salvation, and to anyone (Rom. 3:27).

A NATIONAL OR GENERATIONAL SALVATION?

Unfortunately, the Jews by the time of Christ had come to believe that by simply being a Jew, which referred to their natural descent from Abraham, that this meant they were saved. In response to that, John the Baptist said to them, *"And think not to say within yourselves, we have Abraham to our father: for I say unto you, that God is able of these stones to raise up children unto Abraham"* (Mat. 3:9).

This means that Salvation does not come by descent, by generation, by heritage, by nationality, by race, or by works of any nature, but rather by Faith, and more particularly, Faith in what Jesus did at the Cross and in His Resurrection, all on our behalf (Jn. 3:16).

So, the Holy Spirit here through Paul, speaks of Abraham for the following reasons:

1. It was to Abraham that the great word of Justification by Faith was given. In fact, Jesus said of this situation, *"Abraham rejoiced to see My day: and he saw it, and was glad"* (Jn. 8:56).

2. This makes Abraham the father of us all, both Jews and Gentiles, at least all who will believe (Gal. 3:6-9).

3. Salvation is entirely by Faith, and not at all by works (Eph. 2:8-9).

4. More particularly, it is Faith in what Christ did at the Cross and in His Resurrection. This was graphically portrayed to Abraham in the offering of Isaac (Gen. 22:1-14).

5. The *"Seed of Abraham,"* actually refers to Christ (Gal. 3:16). As well, it refers to all Believers, due to the fact of being *"in Christ"* (Rom. 8:1).

(17) "WHEREFORE IN ALL THINGS IT BEHOVED HIM TO BE MADE LIKE UNTO HIS BRETHREN, THAT HE MIGHT BE A MERCIFUL AND FAITHFUL HIGH PRIEST IN THINGS PERTAINING TO GOD, TO MAKE RECONCILIATION FOR THE SINS OF THE PEOPLE."

The exposition is:

1. God would have to become man, that is if man was to be saved. And this means fully man, in other words, *"very man,"* while at the same time, never ceasing to be *"very God."*

2. He was to be, and was a *"High Priest,"* Who would serve as a Mediator between God and the people. A Priest must always partake of the nature of the one for whom He officiates. Thus, the Incarnation was a necessity in the nature of this case.

3. He was to be a *"merciful"* High Priest, which speaks of the feeling of sympathy with the misery of another that leads one to act in his behalf to relieve that misery.

4. The word *"Faithful"* proclaims the fact that He would do whatever it was that was necessary, to carry forth Redemption. The word is linked to the phrase *"in things*

pertaining to God," which in effect refers to the satisfying of the Justice and Righteousness of God, which He Alone could do.

5. *"Reconciliation"* in the Greek is *"hilaskomai,"* and is translated in Romans 3:25, *"propitiation."* It refers to the act of our Lord offering Himself on the Cross to satisfy the righteous demands of God's justice so that His Government might be maintained, and that mercy might be shown on the basis of justice satisfied.

THE INCARNATION

The phrase, *"Wherefore in all things it behoved Him to be made like unto His Brethren,"* refers to the fact of our Lord laying hold of the human race for the purpose of saving those in it who would accept Salvation by Faith (Wuest).

"It behoved" or *"it behooved,"* are in the Greek Text *"opheilo."* It speaks of an obligation imposed upon one by reason of a certain consideration. Here the consideration is that of the position of our Lord assumed as the One Who would come to the aid of lost sinners. The obligation arising out of this position was that in order to provide a Salvation for the human race, He had to become like the human race, namely, Man, for a Priest must always, as stated, partake of the nature of the one for whom he officiates (Wuest). Thus, the Incarnation was a necessity.

He became *"like unto His Brethren."*

Vincent says regarding this connection: *"Likeness is asserted without qualification. There was a complete and real likeness to humanity, a likeness which was closest just where the traces of the curse of sin were most apparent — in poverty, temptation, and violent and unmerited death."*

In respect to His Body; His Soul; His rank and Character, there was a propriety that He should be like man, and should partake of man's nature. However, by that statement, we do not refer to the sinful nature, but rather human nature. The meaning is, that nothing should be wanting in Him in reference to the innocent propensities and sympathies of human nature.

Going back to the words *"it behooved Him,"* presents the sense of moral obligation. It actually could mean, *"He owed it."* The nature of the work Jesus came to accomplish demanded the Incarnation.

So, how can we say that He owed such a thing to the human race?

The question asked in that manner is not actually proper. In fact, God owed or owes nothing to the human race, or anyone or anything else for that matter. The idea is, that if He was going to redeem lost humanity, He would have to become man. The fact of Redemption, and the satisfying of the righteous demands of God's justice, demanded the Incarnation, that is if it was to be done right. Consequently, in that light, Christ *"owed"* to the human race, the best that Heaven could give. And naturally, God does things in no other way but the very right way.

By the use of the word *"Brethren,"* several things are said:

First of all, even though the seed of Abraham included the entirety of the human race, it especially pertained to the Jews, of whom Jesus would come, and of which Jesus would be.

Also, if He refers to them (the Jews) and us (the Gentiles) as Brethren, and He definitely does, then it was proper that He should show that He regarded them and us as such by assuming our nature.

HIGH PRIEST

The phrase, *"That He might be a merciful and faithful High Priest in things pertaining to God,"* presents the term *"High Priest"* as being unique to this Epistle. In fact, it is used 15 times in Hebrews (2:17; 3:1; 4:14-15; 5:1-10; 6:20; 7:1, 26-27; 8:1, 3; 9:11, 25; 10:21; 13:11).

With the Law of Moses, God had set up the Jewish Priesthood, headed up by the High Priest, who would serve as go-betweens or Mediators between God and the people. Aaron, the brother of Moses, was the very first High Priest of Israel, when actually the people were in the wilderness, instituted almost immediately after being delivered from Egyptian bondage. Consequently, all Jewish High Priests were the successors of Aaron, and stood at the head of the Levitical ceremonies.

When he came into this position, he was set apart with solemn ceremonies — clad in his sacred vestments — and anointed with

oil (Ex. 29:5-9; Lev. 8:2). He was by his office the general judge of all that pertained to the great Mosaic institution, and even, of the Judicial affairs of the Jewish nation (Deut. 17:8-12; 19:17; 21:5; 33:9-10).

He had the privilege of entering the Most Holy Place once a year, on the great Day of Atonement, to make Atonement for the sins of the whole people (Lev. 16:2).

He was as well the oracle of Truth — so that, when clothed in his proper vestments, which was the Ephod, which contained the Urim and Thummim, he made known the Will of God in regard to future events.

Somewhat in this capacity the Lord Jesus became, in the Christian dispensation, what the Jewish High Priest was in the old; and an important object of this Epistle is to show that He far surpassed the Jewish High Priest, and in what respects the Jewish High Priest was designed to typify the Redeemer. Paul, therefore, early introduces the subject, and shows that the Lord Jesus came to perform the functions of that sacred office, and that He was eminently endowed for it (Barnes).

IN THINGS PERTAINING TO GOD

Man was helpless to perform these tasks, so God would have to become man and do such for Him.

For Mercy and Grace to be properly shown to mankind, it could only be done on the basis of justice satisfied. There was no way, however, that man could satisfy this justice.

In Old Testament times, a picture of this was the offering up of sacrifice in order to make intercession for the people. In fact, of all the many duties of the Priesthood, this was the great purpose. But the difference in this High Priest and those under the Aaronic institution was, they offered up clean animals in sacrifice to God, but He would offer up Himself. In fact, all the old Jewish sacrifices, and down through the centuries they numbered into the untold millions, all and without exception, pointed to this one great Sacrifice which was coming. In fact, God based all Mercy and Grace, all forgiveness and cleansing from sin, at least as far as it could be done under the old economy, not on those animal sacrifices, but rather on what and more particularly, Who they represented. In fact, for those in Israel, which numbered the vast majority, who failed to see this, but trusted rather in the ceremony itself, they lost their way and couldn't be saved. Salvation has always been on what this great High Priest, the Lord Jesus Christ, would do on our behalf in the offering up of Himself in Sacrifice.

Actually, this staggers the imagination! It is of such moment, such consequence, of such power, such Grace, such glory, that the mind of man literally beggars its implications. That God would become man, in effect the Creator becoming a creature, and then even above that, taking upon Himself the punishment for our sins, punishment that we should have taken, literally boggles the mind. We dare not make less of this than it actually is, and it is impossible to make more of it than it is. In fact, this Sacrifice of Christ, this momentous work, this staggering implication, this greatest display of love and Grace that the world has ever known, is of such magnitude, that the Holy Spirit through Paul refers to it as *"The Everlasting Covenant"* (Heb. 13:20). It is so perfect, so fashioned, so without exception, so entire, so total, that it will never need an amendment, but will rather serve forever.

When the Lord began to open up to me this great Revelation of the Cross, I soon realized that I had only scratched the surface. In fact at the very beginning, I knew what was being given to me, incidentally in answer to over five years of seeking the Face of God, and quite possibly a lifetime, was far larger than I could even begin to know.

THAT WHICH THE LORD SHOWED ME

As someone has well said, desperation usually precedes Revelation. Perhaps all of us, at least in one way or the other, have to come to the end of ourselves before we can properly look to Christ as we should.

In the Fall of 1991, at a desperate, even crisis time in my life and in this Ministry, I began to cry to the Lord as I had never cried to Him before, as it regards the ways and means of living a victorious, overcoming, Christian life. In fact, the Lord instructed me to begin two prayer meetings a day, which we immediately set out to do, and continue unto this hour. In this, the Lord told me,

that I was not to seek Him so much for what He could do, but rather for Who He is. As stated, that began in the Fall of 1991.

Through the nearly next six years, the Lord would give me promise after promise, which of course, were of tremendous encouragement. But yet, I knew that the answer had not yet come. And then in 1996, it began to come, and I will never forget the beginning of that most momentous time.

The Lord took me to Romans, Chapter 6, with the Holy Spirit actually explaining it to me. However, it was really in 1997 that the full brunt of this Revelation began to take place, at least to the extent that I felt it was complete at least as far as the foundation was concerned. Of course, the Lord has built on that foundation from then until now.

The following three statements, although very brief, are what the Lord told me, and which I have built upon. They are as follows:

1. The answer to every question which I had sought, the solution to every problem for which I had asked, the Lord informed me, are all in the Cross (Rom. 6:3-6, 11, 14).

2. Understanding that, my Faith must ever be in the Cross of Christ. In other words, the Cross must ever be the object of my Faith, and not something else (Jn. 3:16).

3. With my Faith properly placed, the Holy Spirit is then able to do His great Office work within my heart and life, which He has beautifully done since, and continues to do (Rom. 8:1-2, 11).

Now that which I have just given is very brief, and requires much explanation, which we are attempting to give in these Commentaries. But this I know, if you the Reader will heed the Message of the Cross, which is the Message of the Bible, which in reality is Christ, you will find that which He has promised, which is glorious indeed (Rom. 6:3-5, 11, 14; 8:1-2, 11, 13).

MERCIFUL

The High priest was meant to be the representative of men to God; without such likeness He could be no true High Priest for man. The order of the Greek words throws an emphasis on *"compassionate"* which is in full harmony with what we have seen to be the pervading tone of the Chapter.

One who has not so understood the infirmities of his Brethren as to be *"compassionate,"* cannot be their *"faithful"* representative before God. The nature of the work Jesus came to accomplish demanded the Incarnation. This meant that this great thing was not aimless; it was for the specific purpose of Jesus' becoming a High Priest, another way of saying that it was to save men. *"Merciful"* receives emphasis from its position as being first.

By the time of Christ, the Jewish Priesthood had become cold and calloused, and in the words of Philo, a Jewish historian, *"men without pity."*

Not so our great High Priest. He is One Who is first and foremost merciful. He is this that He might know how to pity us in our infirmities and trials, by having a nature like our own.

FAITHFUL

The way the word *"faithful"* is used, it can refer to the Faith that relies on someone or something or that which on one can rely. Jesus is, of course, both. But here the emphasis is on His relationship to God the Father, and so the first meaning is more probable (Rev. 1:5; 3:14; 19:11).

Only in Hebrews, as we have stated, is the term *"High Priest"* applied to Jesus in the New Testament. In fact, this is the first example of its use, and Paul does not explain it. He may want us to see Jesus as superior to all other Priests. Or he may be using the term because He sees Jesus' saving work as fulfilling all that is signified by the ceremonies of the Day of Atonement, for which the High Priest's Ministry was indispensable. Sometimes in this Epistle Paul calls Jesus simply a *"Priest,"* but there seems to be no great difference in meaning.

By the time of Christ, the Office of the High Priest in Israel was bought and sold like so much merchandise. Consequently, there was not a shred of faithfulness left to the Word of God in this capacity. The people were poorly served to say the least, and God was not served at all!

So, Christ was faithful in totality, in the way that it was always meant to be, but of course to an even greater degree, because of Who He was.

RECONCILIATION

The phrase, *"To make reconciliation for the sins of the people,"* would have probably been better translated *"propitiation."* The word means, *"to make an Atoning Sacrifice in order to regain the favor and goodwill of God."* In effect, *"reconciliation"* is what *"propitiation"* actually does. With the Sacrifice offered and accepted, then God and man can be reconciled. Propitiation relates to putting away the Divine Wrath. When people sin, they arouse the Wrath of God (Rom. 1:18); they actually become and are, enemies of God (Rom. 5:10).

One aspect of Salvation deals with this wrath, and it is to this that Paul is directing attention at this point. Christ saves us in a way that takes account of the Divine Wrath against every evil thing, in effect removing the evil thing which is sin.

In order to do all of this, it was necessary that Christ should be made like unto His Brethren, as we have already seen, that thus having passed sinlessly through all human experiences, He might be a merciful and faithful High Priest in things pertaining to God, to make — not *"reconciliation,"* as in the Authorized Version text, but — Expiation or Atonement for the sins of the people, which would then reconcile believing mankind.

In this we see the fulfillment of the type of the Great Day of Atonement when the High Priest first offered the Sacrifice at the Altar and then presented the Blood in the Holy of Holies. So our Lord, at the close of His pilgrim path, on our behalf offered up Himself upon the Cross to make Expiation (to pay the penalty), Atonement (a satisfaction), or Propitiation (offer sacrifice), for our sins.

The original Greek Word is that used in the Greek Version of the Old Testament to translate the Hebrew word for Atonement. As we have stated, reconciliation is the result of all of this, but it is we who are reconciled to God, not He Who has to be reconciled to us. We are the ones who have sinned, and not Him.

SIN IS THE PROBLEM

The reason for the Cross is the problem of sin. It could only be handled in this way.

So that should tells us just how powerful and destructive that sin actually is.

The Church bounces from one extreme to the other as it regards sin. For the most part, the non-Pentecostal side of the Church, functions in the realm of a *"sinning Salvation,"* so to speak. In other words, they little teach that Salvation actually changes one's life. In the thinking of many of these teachers in this realm, the only difference between the saved and the unsaved is, that the saved trust Christ, while the unsaved don't! As far as lifestyle is concerned, there is no difference, they say!

Of course, this is ridiculous, inasmuch as the very foundation of the Gospel of Christ is that it changes our lives, and dramatically so. In fact, if the life of the proposed Christian is not changed, that simply says the person isn't saved.

No, that doesn't speak of sinless perfection, because the Bible doesn't teach such. But it definitely does teach victory over sin (Rom. 6:14).

The Truth is, many of these people aren't actually saved, and the few who actually are, are saddled with an erroneous doctrine that gives them little chance or opportunity for Spiritual Growth.

Regarding the Pentecostal and Charismatic worlds, the problem is the very opposite. Many in this realm deny sin, in fact claiming it is no problem, and if it is, it's only a problem with a minute few, and only now and then.

The so-called Faith Ministry has been more instrumental in this erroneous direction than probably any other group. The climate is such, that if anyone admits to any type of problem, they're automatically hailed as a person without Faith. Faith giants don't have problems with sin, etc., they say! So, the Truth is, untold millions lie about their situation, and for two reasons:

1. To admit sin or failure of any type, in this element, is admitting weakness, and to admit that is not to be in the privileged class, etc. So they lie!

2. To admit to any type of sin or failure, is a display of a lack of Faith, they say, and considering that the *"Faith level"* is the barometer of one's experience with God, to admit to

any type of problem, automatically puts one in the position of being inferior. So they claim victory over a problem they also claim doesn't exist. Cannot one see the ugliness of flesh in all of this? Self is supreme here, not Christ!

The Truth is, despite this segment of the Christian population claiming to be Spirit-filled, there is as much failure in these ranks as in the non-Pentecostal ranks. However, to be sure, the fault is not in the Holy Spirit, but rather in erroneous doctrine.

While problems abound on every side as it regards all of this of which we've mentioned, the core problem, in other words the worst and biggest problem of all is, that there is precious little understanding of the Cross of Christ.

A great part of the Church claims that the problem is a lack of Faith, with others claiming something else, but the real problem is *"sin!"*

WHAT IS SIN?

Whenever we think of sin, we almost always think of acts of sin. While of course those things definitely constitute sin, they are more the result of sin than the cause.

The cause of sin is the trusting in self instead of Christ. Man's only hope, is a total and complete trust in Christ, and what He did at the Cross on our behalf. If we venture away from that in any capacity, such an act constitutes rebellion against God and His Way, which is the highest form of sin there is. In other words, that's what sin is all about.

When this takes place, then acts of sin in every capacity are going to follow. But too often, the Church looks at the symptom instead of the cause itself. The cause is not trusting in what Christ has done at the Cross, but rather trusting in self. We may not understand it in that fashion, but that's what is happening.

However, it's very difficult for individuals to trust in the Cross, when they know very little about the Cross and because it's seldom preached and taught behind most modern pulpits. Consequently, the people perish for a lack of knowledge.

Everything hinges upon Christ, with Satan doing everything within his power to pull us away from that Source, to efforts or machinations of our own making. To be sure, Satan doesn't really care what direction we take, just as long as he can pull us from the Cross. And the tragedy is, most Christians have been away from the Cross almost from the moment they got saved, so the task of the Evil One is not too difficult. Unfortunately, most Christians have been led to believe that the Cross of Christ pertains to their initial Salvation experience, and has no further significance. Such thinking could not be more wrong, and, therefore, more destructive to our spiritual experience.

The Christian cannot live a victorious, overcoming life, unless he understands that his victory is totally and completely in the Cross of Christ. It is literally impossible to have victory otherwise. And considering that most Christians don't know this, and in fact look to other things, lets us know what state that the modern Church has actually come to.

So what are we doing?

The Church has mostly succumbed to the world of humanistic psychology. In other words, we treat symptoms instead of the real cause.

Having the erroneous idea that Christians fail simply because they make a decision to do so, we then summarize that this being the case, the Christian must be punished.

While some few Christians might want to do something wrong, the far greater majority don't. They fail not because they want to fail, but because they're trusting in something other than the Cross. Consequently, they do not have the help of the Holy Spirit, even though He resides within their hearts and lives. Considering that He will not function outside of the Finished Work of Christ, which demands that we have Faith in that Finished Work, the Christian in such a state, is left on his own, which automatically spells defeat.

No, most of Christendom is not failing because they want to fail, in fact, most are fighting with all their strength not to fail, but failing anyway, reliving Romans, Chapter 7 all over again. In fact, that's where most Christians actually are, Romans, Chapter 7!

Punishing such Christians is not the answer. And this goes for preachers who fail as well. Christ doesn't have two solutions, one

for the Laity and one for Preachers. Such thinking is silly!

People fail God, because they have left the secret place of the Most High, which is the Cross of Christ. It doesn't matter that most left it in ignorance, the results are the same. But something else is taking place at this present time, which is probably the most dangerous of all.

ENEMIES OF THE CROSS

Paul said, *"For many walk, of whom I have told you often, and now tell you even weeping, that they are the enemies of the Cross of Christ:*

"Whose end is destruction, whose God is their belly, and whose glory is in their shame, who mind earthly things" (Phil. 3:18-19).

First of all, of whom was Paul speaking, and second, what did he mean by *"enemies of the Cross"*?

As to whom these false teachers were, it would have included anyone who attempted to present any other type of Salvation other than that afforded by Christ and what He did at the Cross. More particularly, the Apostle was speaking of the Judaizers. These were individuals, who claimed to accept Christ as the Son of God and the Messiah of Israel, but who claimed that the Law of Moses had to be added to Faith in Christ, in order for one to be saved. Consequently, the Cross entered into their thinking not at all (Acts 15:1).

However, let it be understood, that irrespective as to the so-called Gospel being promoted, if the Cross is lessened or ignored, one can only conclude such teachers as being *"enemies of the Cross."* In other words, the Salvation they promote, is not of Faith in the Finished Work of Christ, i.e., *"the Sacrifice of Christ,"* but something else entirely. And again, it doesn't matter what else it might be, or even how much Truth it might contain in some ways, if it's not Salvation according to Faith in Christ and what He did for a lost world on the Cross, then it's not Salvation.

And let it be quickly understood, when we speak of *"Salvation,"* we are not speaking only of the initial Salvation experience, but the entirety of the Work of God as it relates to the individual Believer, which takes in the entirety of our walk before God.

Now where does that leave the modern Church?

The Gospel that Paul preached, which was the Gospel of the New Covenant, which is actually the meaning of the Cross, and which God gave to the Apostle (Gal. 1:11-12), is preached but little in the modern Church. In virtually all of the major religious Denominations, both Pentecostal and non-Pentecostal, humanistic psychology is held up as the answer to the sins and aberrations of mankind. The big word in the modern Church is, and has been for several decades, *"you need professional help!"* And let it be quickly understood, it is not possible to espouse the wisdom of this world, which is *"earthly, sensual, and Devilish,"* which is humanistic psychology, and at the same time, espouse the Cross. Psychology is actually the religion of Satan, and claims to hold the answer to the ills of mankind, while the Cross which is diametrically opposed to humanistic psychology, also claims to hold the only answer; therefore, it is impossible to hold up both as the solution to man's dilemma. So, that which espouses the wisdom of this world can be none other than an enemy of the Cross of Christ (James 3:13-15).

Many in the modern Faith Movement openly demean the Cross, claiming that it is *"past miseries."* Their followers, which number into the hundreds of thousands, if not millions, are told to leave the Cross, as it was the greatest defeat in human history.

Money being the driving force behind this popular teaching, Paul's description, *"whose end is destruction, whose God is their belly, and whose glory is in their shame, who mind earthly things,"* fits them exactly! These are open, blatant, avowed enemies of the Cross of Christ. What they preach and teach are pure and simple *"another Jesus,"* promoted by *"another spirit,"* which is *"another gospel"* (II Cor. 11:4).

Consequently, at least as it concerns those Preachers and Teachers who are full-bore into this error, no one is saved, no one is Baptized with the Holy Spirit, no one is healed, and no one is delivered. The reasons should be obvious, the Holy Spirit cannot bless or condone the gross error of a blatant denial of the Cross, which is the only means

whereby man is saved and whereby he receives from God.

There are untold numbers of Preachers, however, who do not preach the Cross as they should, but are not enemies of the Cross. They just simply don't have the proper light on the subject. However, let it be known that to what degree such light is lacking, to that degree they will suffer loss in some way. God is merciful and patient; however, if a road is going east, and we are on that road, when in reality we want to go north, even though we might sincerely think we're going right, our sincerity will not make up for the wrong direction. In other words, despite our sincerity, we will not come out at the right destination.

That's one of the reasons I plead with you the Reader to obtain some of these Commentaries for Preachers of your acquaintance. If they understand the light of the Cross, then they will be able to enlighten those who sit under their ministries.

HOW DEFICIENT IS THE CHURCH AS IT REGARDS THE SUBJECT OF THE CROSS?

Regrettably, the deficiency is so widespread and so deep, that it is almost total. As I've said any number of times, in the last half century or more, the Church has had so little teaching on the Cross of Christ, that anymore it little knows its true foundation.

While all true Christians know and understand that the Cross played an extremely important part in their initial Salvation experience, beyond that, with some few exceptions, they know almost nothing. Consequently, the Church walks in defeat.

It's a tragedy for a person to love God supremely, and even to be used of God which many are, and not know and understand God's prescribed order of victory, which is the Cross; consequently, despite the fact of that man or woman being used of God, and despite the fact that these particular individuals love God, not knowing God's Way, they will be deficient in their own everyday lives and living. In fact, it's impossible for it to be any other way.

I personally know what the Word of the Cross (I Cor. 1:18) can do in one's life. I know what it is to love God with all of one's heart, and to work for Him diligently, and be consecrated totally and completely, at least as far as is possible for one to do so without the light of the Cross, and because of that, not be able to walk victoriously. And regrettably, almost all of Christendom is in that particular situation at present. Naturally, there are exceptions, but not many!

God's prescribed order for a victorious, overcoming, Christian life, is the Cross of Christ. And what do we mean by that?

We mean that when Jesus died on the Cross, He died not only to save man from sin, but as well, to keep man from sin. This is found in Romans, Chapters 6 and 8, and in fact, in all of Paul's writings, for the simple reason, that it was to Paul that the answer to this great question was given. In fact, the New Covenant is pure and simple the meaning of the Cross, in other words what the Cross afforded.

Most Christians understand the initial Salvation part, but they do not understand the Cross as it regards keeping one from sin, in effect, in victory, and doing so on a perpetual basis. Not understanding that, Christians cast about for other means of help and support, and never really find it, simply because there is no help other than the Cross.

Once the Believer understands that all that he receives from God, and in every capacity, comes entirely through the Cross of Christ, which of course includes His Resurrection as well, they are then to make the Cross the object of their Faith. And this is the secret! Everything hinges on Faith, but it's always Faith in the Cross of Christ. If it's any other type of Faith, God simply will not honor the particular effort, and the Christian is left holding the bag, proverbially speaking.

FAITH

As we've already stated, everything hinges on Faith, but it has to be Faith in the proper object, and that object must ever be the Cross of Christ.

The Believer must understand and without fail, that the Cross is the Source of all blessings from God, and we mean *"all blessings!"* If the Believer doesn't understand that, then his Faith is deficient, and he will suffer negative consequences. Let me say it another way:

NOTES

If the Believer is divided in his Faith, which means that he somewhat believes what we are saying here, but as well tries to add something else, he is then double-minded, and as the Holy Spirit through James said, *"Let not that man think that he shall receive anything of the Lord"* (James 1:7-8).

Such Faith is called *"wavering Faith"* (James 1:6). And that's where the problem is with many Christians.

Since the Lord began to open up to me the Revelation of the Cross, which incidentally is not something new, but is rather the foundation of all that God gives us, I have had, and continue to have, a number of people who say, *"I've tried it, and it doesn't work,"* or words to that effect. That's *"wavering Faith."*

In the first place, one doesn't *"try the Cross!"* One must understand, that the Cross is the only way, the only road, there being no other. If the Believer is in doubt about that, then the admonition is plain and simple, he's not going to get anything from the Lord.

One doesn't try the Cross! One rather anchors his Faith there, understanding that what he seeks comes from no other source. While we may fail in our Faith, and that's always where the failure is, the Cross does not fail. So if we want to blame the Cross, instead of placing the blame where it rightly belongs, which is on ourselves, then we're in deep trouble.

When the Lord first began to open up to me this great Revelation, after a period of time, I asked him as to why there was apparent failure in hearts and lives, from those who claim to be placing their trust in the Finished Work of Christ?

This was early one morning, and if I remember correctly, sometime in early 1999. I was sitting behind my desk, writing Commentary on Ephesians. I was pondering this question, and had been actually seeking the Lord about the situation for some time.

Very distinctly the Lord spoke to my heart that morning, saying, *"It's the individual's Faith. Anytime there is failure, it's always a failure of Faith."*

And then He said, *"Your Faith is never as strong as you think it is."*

It was just that simple! But I knew the Lord had spoken to my heart, and of course, I knew this was right.

First of all, if the Believer's Faith is anchored in the right source, which is the Cross, and it's not a wavering Faith, meaning that it's divided with other things, even if there is failure of some sort, that particular Believer will not quit, but will get up, start back out, with his eye ever toward the goal of perpetual victory. In other words, true Faith won't quit!

The Believer is to then ask the Lord to show him as to where his Faith is deficient, and to be sure that prayer will be answered.

While the Lord definitely gives to every Believer *"a measure of Faith"* (Rom. 12:3), the development of that Faith is always a process. That's why the Holy Spirit through Peter said, *"But grow in Grace, and in the knowledge of our Lord and Saviour Jesus Christ"* (II Pet. 3:18).

This I can guarantee:

If the Believer will understand and believe that every Blessing comes through the Cross of Christ, and that his Faith must at all times be anchored in the Cross, which will then guarantee the help of the Holy Spirit (Rom. 8:1-2, 11, 13), and not allow his Faith to be moved from that source, total and complete victory over the world, the flesh, and the Devil, will be realized in one's life. It might take awhile for total victory to be brought about, but it is guaranteed that it will come.

THE PROMISE OF THE SPIRIT

If one is to notice, over and over again, the word *"promise"* is connected in some way to the Holy Spirit. In fact, Paul said, *"That the Blessing of Abraham* (Justification by Faith) *might come on the Gentiles through Jesus Christ* (through what Jesus did at the Cross and in His Resurrection)*; that we might receive the Promise of the Spirit through Faith* (meaning that it cannot be earned, but can only be received as a Gift from God)*"* (Gal. 3:14).

Now what does that phrase mean, *"the Promise of the Spirit"*?

"Promise" in the Greek is *"epaggelia,"* and means *"an announcement or pledge, to engage to do something, to assert."* Consequently, the meaning is twofold:

Before the Cross, the Promise was given by God, that all of this was coming (Gen. 15:6;

Isa. 28:9-11; Joel 2:28-29; Mat. 3:11; Jn. 1:31-34; Acts 1:4-8; 2:33-39; 11:14-18; 15:7-13).

When Jesus died on the Cross, due to the sin debt now being paid, the Holy Spirit could now come and dwell in the hearts and lives of Believers, in fact to abide forever (Jn. 14:16). However, the word *"Promise"* has another aspect:

All the things that Jesus did at the Cross, i.e., *"the Atonement,"* are promised by the Holy Spirit to the Believer, that is, those things which are now possible to have. Paul referred to this as a down payment, *"the earnest of the Spirit"* (II Cor. 1:22; 5:5). The balance will come at the Resurrection.

However, the Holy Spirit has promised us, that if we will properly place our Faith in the Cross of Christ, that He will do certain things within our lives. In fact, every single thing that the Believer receives from the Lord, is all and without exception, brought about, by the work, operation, and Person of the Holy Spirit. He is the only One Who can do these things, which means we cannot do them ourselves. Of us, Faith alone is required for Him to do this great work. And I said all of that to say this:

If you will anchor your Faith properly in the Cross of Christ, the Holy Spirit has promised that He will give you total and complete victory over the *"world, the flesh, and the Devil."* It doesn't matter who you are, how weak you may think you might be, how many failures you've had in the past, or how much in bondage at present you might be to a particular vice, the Holy Spirit can rid you of all of these problems. It may take a little time, and not because of Him, but because of us, but if we will keep our Faith anchored in the Cross of Christ, not allow it to waver, the Holy Spirit without fail, will perform His great work of victory within us.

No, that doesn't mean sinless perfection, for the Bible doesn't teach such; but it definitely does mean that sin will not have dominion over you in any shape, form, or fashion (Rom. 6:14).

THE WORK OF THE SPIRIT

Last night in Prayer Meeting (May 12, 2000), I asked the small group assembled, *"How does a person get closer to God?"*

The answers were many and varied, and right in their own way, but the problem was, the answers didn't go far enough.

Were that question to be asked to the entirety of the Body of Christ, most would instantly retort, *"We should pray more!"* Or *"We should study the Word more!"* Or *"We should be more faithful to Church!"* etc.

While those things mentioned and many we haven't mentioned, are very good, and to be sure, the closer one gets to the Lord, the more that these things will be obvious in one's life, still, that's not the way that one gets closer to the Lord, or does anything with the Lord for that matter. So what is the answer?

While those things are very good, if one places one's Faith in that, then these things are turned into works, which God cannot honor. All of this is so subtle that most of the time, it deceives us. Let's ask another question:

If there's a problem in your life as a Christian, and I'm speaking of sin, and it's something over which you seem to not be able to obtain the victory, how do you go about getting victory?

Most probably, most Christians would give the same answer to this as the folk in our Prayer Meeting gave regarding getting closer to the Lord. *"We must pray more,"* *"be more Faithful,"* etc. Listen to what Paul said:

"Was then that" (the Law of God) *which is good made death unto me? God forbid. But sin, that it might appear sin, working death in me by that which is good; that sin by the Commandment might become exceeding sinful"* (Rom. 7:13).

Now I want the Reader to zero in on the phrase, *"working death* (spiritual failure) *in me by that which is good."*

First of all, we could readily understand how that failure, which Paul refers to as *"death,"* can be brought about in us by that which is bad; however, it's very confusing to us to understand, that such can be brought about in us by that *"which is good."*

What does he mean by that statement?

First of all, he was dealing with the Law of Moses, and how that the advent of the Law, which incidentally was good and because it was given by God, had the effect, however, of the very opposite. In other words, even though the Law was definitely good, instead

of it bringing good out of people, it rather brought bad out of them. However, the fault wasn't the Law, but rather the people. It only showed up what was already there, in effect bringing it to the surface.

Because man was insufficient, and even the best of men at that, they simply couldn't keep the Law, that is within their own strength and power. Not one succeeded in doing so. In fact, their efforts in this respect, even brought on more failure, and because it showed how weak and ineffectual the flesh actually was.

Now that seems strange doesn't it! And I speak of a person in Old Testament Times, trying to keep the Law of God, and such efforts making the situation worse instead of better. The question may well be asked: Were they not supposed to try to keep the Law? Didn't God intend for them to do that?

Yes He did; however, He had to show them that they could not do it in this way, in other words, by their own efforts. Man, even the best of men, and by that I mean the Godliest, were simply unable to do so. So, *"death was worked in them by that which is good."* I'll give you the answer to that dilemma momentarily.

It is the same presently! We unfortunately have a very high opinion of ourselves, thinking that because we are now under the New Covenant, meaning that we have the Holy Spirit living within us, which Old Testament Saints did not have, that we in fact, can do these things. We boast about our power, our great Faith, calling ourselves *"new creation people,"* etc. However, we conveniently overlook the statement of Christ given to Paul, *"My Grace is sufficient for thee: for My strength is made perfect in weakness"* (II Cor. 12:9).

We too often ignore Paul's statement in respect to that when he said, *"For when I am weak, then am I strong"* (II Cor. 12:10).

What is meant by all of that?

BY HIS OWN EFFORTS THE BELIEVER CANNOT DRAW HIMSELF CLOSER TO GOD OR BRING ABOUT VICTORY WITHIN HIS LIFE

To be sure, the Believer can definitely draw closer to God, and can see victory brought about in his life, but if he tries to do so by the ways normally mentioned, even as we have related, he will find himself having the very opposite results. In other words, *"sin will work death in him by that which is good."* Let's say it in a clearer and plainer way:

About the holiest thing that a Believer can do, is to have a strong prayer life. In fact, such is absolutely imperative if one is to have a proper relationship with Christ; however, if the Believer tries to use prayer as a means or vehicle, in order to bring about nearness to God or victory over sin, he will find in such a case, that *"prayer"* which definitely is good, just as the Law of God was good in Old Testament Times, will bring about the opposite results. In other words, he definitely will not find victory, but will find the very opposite, which is most confusing!

In fact, there are millions of Christians at this very moment, who are perplexed and confused. Were you to ask them and were they to be honest with you, they would say, *"I'm doing everything I know to do! I'm trying my best to live as close to God as I know how to live, but I cannot get victory over this thing,"* whatever the thing might be. And in Truth they'll never get victory in that manner, because these good things they are doing, while definitely good in their own right, have been turned into *"works,"* even though the Believer may not understand such, but the results are the same whether understood or not — failure! And worse yet, continued failure, and even with the failure growing worse by the passing months. The sin is working death in them by that which is good.

That's the reason that untold thousands of Christians are running all over the world, trying to find some Preacher whom they think God is using, who can lay hands on them, which then they will hopefully have some type of manifestation, which will give them the victory for which they seek.

While the Preacher may or may not be of God, and while laying on of hands is definitely Scriptural, and will definitely bless and help in the individual, it won't bring about the victory sought.

So what is the answer?

THE ANSWER IS THE CROSS OF CHRIST

The Believer must understand that within himself, that he can really receive nothing

from God. In fact, all the Believer can do, which in fact has always been the case, is to *"furnish a willing mind and an obedient heart."* That's all the Believer can do, and that's all the Believer is asked to do.

The Holy Spirit through David, said to his son, Solomon, *"Know thou the God of thy father, and serve Him with a 'perfect heart and with a willing mind:' for the Lord searcheth all hearts, and understandeth all the imaginations of the thoughts: if thou seek Him, He will be found of thee; but if thou forsake Him, He will cast thee off forever"* (I Chron. 28:9).

The Believer must understand that all of his efforts, machinations, strength, ability, and religious works, even as good as those works might be, cannot effect him anything with the Lord. All of this deceives us, simply because these things we do are good, and we think that surely it ought to merit us something with God, or at least bring about some desired result. As stated, in doing these things, we have turned good things into works, which God can never honor.

Everything that we receive from the Lord, and everything that God gives us, and that means everything, is based 100 percent on Faith, and never on works (Rom. 4:1-5). However, at this juncture, allow me to make this statement:

"Works will never produce true Faith, but true Faith, and by that we speak of Faith in the Cross, will always produce good works."

The Believer is to understand that he cannot grow closer to God, or find victory in his life, by doing good things, or even engaging in very spiritual things. He can only find what he seeks, by understanding that everything we receive from the Lord comes totally and completely through the great Sacrifice of Christ. Consequently, we are to anchor our Faith in that, and then the Holy Spirit will perform the intended and desired work within our hearts and lives.

Does this mean that all works are out? They are definitely out, as far as using them to receive from God are concerned.

When the Believer places his Faith totally in the Finished Work of Christ, this shows that he understands that within himself he cannot bring about the intended and desired result, but that God has to do such, and He has done such through the great Sacrifice of Christ. There the sin debt was paid, with all sin atoned, which makes it possible for man to approach God, and God to approach man. But it can only be done by Faith, and by that we mean, Faith in that great, Finished Work of Christ. It is always the Cross! The Cross! The Cross!

ABRAHAM AND SARAH

The Lord spoke to my heart once and in a powerful way, saying, *"Before Isaac could be born, Abraham and Sarah had to deal with their sin."*

When He spoke those words to me, to be frank, the Spirit of God came greatly upon me, and I knew beyond the shadow of a doubt, that the Lord had ministered to me a great Truth; however, I actually didn't know what He meant.

What sin? Was He speaking of the sin with Hagar? But in my heart, I knew that wasn't the answer.

About a year after the Lord spoke these words to me, He then gave me the answer.

"The sin of Abraham and Sarah was in their attempt to bring about the Promise of God through their own efforts, instead of depending on the Spirit." To be sure, such efforts resulted in the sin of Hagar, which produced Ishmael, a work of the flesh. But in fact, that was not the real sin, but rather the result of the real sin, which was rebellion against God. Of course, Abraham at the time did not think of such as rebellion against God, and neither do we, but that's exactly what it is.

God has one way of victory, one way of fulfilling the Promise, and that is of Faith in Him, and more particularly, Faith in what Jesus did at the Cross.

Now some may quickly retort, claiming that Abraham could not have had Faith in the Cross, for such had not yet even come about; however, I remind all concerned, that the very foundation of the Abrahamic Covenant is in reality, the Cross of Christ (Gen. 15:6). In fact, that's what it was all about! That's why Jesus said to the Jews, *"Your father Abraham rejoiced to see My day: and he saw it, and was glad"* (Jn. 8:56).

As well, there came a day even after Isaac was born, that the Lord told Abraham, that Ishmael, along with his mother, Hagar, would have to be cast out of the family (Gal. 4:29-30).

This speaks of the flesh, or self-efforts in our own lives, which ultimately have to go. In other words, all dependence on the flesh must cease.

The effect of the birth of Isaac was to make manifest the character of Ishmael. Ishmael hated him, and so did his mother. Prompted by her he sought to murder Isaac (Gal. 4:29), and with his mother was justly expelled. Both merited the severer sentence of death. Thus, the birth of Isaac which filled Sarah's heart with mirth, filled Hagar's with murder.

Isaac and Ishmael symbolize the *"new"* and the *"old"* nature in the Believer. Sarah and Hagar typify the two Covenants of works and Grace, of bondage and liberty (Gal., Chpt. 4). The birth of the new nature demands the expulsion of the old. And let the Reader understand, that it is impossible to improve the old nature.

The Holy Spirit says in Romans, Chapter 8, that *"it is enmity against God, that it is not subject to the Law of God, neither indeed can be."*

If, therefore, it cannot be subject to the Law of God, how can it be improved? How foolish appears the doctrine of moral evolution! The Divine way of Holiness is to *"put off the old man"* just as Abraham *"put off"* Ishmael. Man's way of holiness is to improve the *"old man,"* that is, improve Ishmael, that is, to try to make the thing work by our own efforts. And to be sure, such efforts are both foolish and hopeless.

Of course the casting out of Ishmael was *"very grievous in Abraham's sight,"* because it always costs a struggle to cast out this element of bondage, that is, Salvation and/or victory by works. For legalism is dear to the heart. Ishmael was the fruit of such, and to Abraham the fair fruit of his own energy and planning.

The Epistle to the Galatians states that Hagar, the bondwoman, represents the Covenant of the Law, and that her son represents all who are of *"works of Law,"* that is, of all who seek Righteousness on the principle of works of Righteousness. But the bondwoman cannot bring forth a free man! The Son Alone makes free, and He makes free indeed (Jn. 8:32).

WHAT DO WE MEAN BY WORKS OF THE LAW?

It is ironical but yet sad, most all Christians, due to not knowing or understanding the Word of the Cross, while thinking they are functioning in Grace, are rather functioning in law. Consequently, they are living less than victorious lives, because such is the way of the flesh and not the Spirit. Let me explain.

Sometime back, several Preachers were on our morning, Radio Broadcast, which is 90 minutes in length, aired seven days a week. We were teaching on the Cross, which actually we have continued doing uninterrupted, since 1998. The Preachers were guests, but had very little knowledge of the Cross, which regrettably characterizes most Preachers.

We were discussing the overcoming of sin, etc. One of the Preachers spoke up and said, *"Whenever I have a problem, I fast three days, and that handles the situation."* He then went on to say, *"When it comes back, I fast three more days,"* etc.

He didn't say what the problem was, and actually it didn't really matter.

When he finished his statement, I very gently and kindly said to him, *"While fasting is very definitely Scriptural, and will definitely help the Believer, it is not the answer to sin or failure."*

I then went on to briefly explain how that the Cross is the only answer for sin, and our Faith in that Finished Work.

He grew somewhat irritated, and said very sharply as it concerned fasting, *"Well it works for me!"*

Well the Truth was, it wasn't working for him, or else he would not have to keep repeating it, even as he had admitted!

Why did he respond in that fashion?

Going back to Abraham and his love for Ishmael. This young man was the work of his flesh; consequently, he was very fond of that particular work. *"Fasting"* was the work of my dear Brother's flesh, and he was very fond of that work, as we all are of our own

particular works. That's the reason we don't give them up easily! It's also the reason why we're loathe to admit that they are not doing us any good. They are our works, our efforts, and we put a lot of time, trouble, and attention into these works, and it's very shattering to our pride for us to have to admit, that all of these things, as good as they might be in their own right, are useless when it comes to receiving things from God.

We have to forsake all of that, and by forsaking it, I'm meaning forsaking our dependence on such things. To be sure, the Christian must definitely have a prayer life, must fast as the Lord leads him to do so, and must engage himself in what we refer to as *"Christian disciplines"*; however, even as we've already stated, these things are to be the result of our Righteousness, not our Righteousness the result of those things. The latter can never come to pass.

The Believer must quit placing dependence in anything, no matter how good it might be, in order to find the victory for which he seeks. He must look totally and completely to the Cross of Christ, understanding that it was there that Jesus paid it all and did it all, and that He did these things for us, simply because we couldn't do it for ourselves. So we must have Faith in this which He has done, trusting in that alone, which will then bring about the Work of the Holy Spirit within our hearts and lives, Who Alone can bring about the desired results.

Why is that so hard?

It's hard because we like our own works. Once again I go back to Abraham and Ishmael. He loved this boy, because he was a product of his own efforts. So, he gave him up very reluctantly.

That's a picture, a shadow, a symbol, of our works of the flesh. Again I emphasize, we are speaking now of dependence. While prayer must never be forsaken, or such like things, it is the dependence on such or whatever, which must be transferred totally and completely to the Cross of Christ. This is alone, the Faith that God will honor (Rom. 8:1-2). Then the Holy Spirit can perform the work within our lives, which will definitely bring us closer to God, and give us victory in every capacity. Everything in the Believer's heart and life must always be according to the following:

1. Everything and totally comes through the Cross of Christ, and not at all from ourselves.

2. Our Faith must ever be in the Cross, and not at all in ourselves, etc.

3. When this is done, which the Holy Spirit demands, He will then perform His constant work of progressive Sanctification within our hearts and lives, but only then!

(18) "FOR IN THAT HE HIMSELF HATH SUFFERED BEING TEMPTED, HE IS ABLE TO SUCCOUR THEM THAT ARE TEMPTED."

The exegesis is:

1. Jesus suffered temptation, for as a man He had to suffer such!

2. Even though the temptation by Satan of Christ, concerned many things, its basic intent was for Christ to go around the Cross. In fact, that is the basis of all temptation by Satan of man presently, and always has been.

3. Considering that our temptation is the same as that which was His, with Him of course overcoming that temptation, He is able to show us the way of victory as well. That way, incidentally, is the Cross.

TEMPTATION

The phrase, *"For in that He Himself hath suffered being tempted,"* means that our Lord in His Incarnation as the Last Adam, was put to the test and was also solicited to do evil (Mat. 4:1-11).

Some claim that it would have been impossible for Christ to have failed; however, that is incorrect!

In the first place, He was the *"Last Adam"*; therefore, He had to have the same possibility of failure as the first Adam. Otherwise, it would have all been meaningless!

According to the Greek Scholars, Paul here has in view the testings and solicitations to do evil that were associated with His expiatory sufferings on the Cross. There are three examples of this:

1. In Matthew 4:8-9, Satan tempts our Lord to go around the Cross and accept from his hands (the hands of Satan) the world-dominion He is yet to have.

2. Peter, an unconscious tool of Satan dismisses as absurd the idea that Jesus as

Messiah should die at the hands of the leaders of Israel (Mat. 16:21-22).

3. In Gethsemane, He shrank back from the prospect of being made a Sin-Offering, which meant He would have to bear the sin penalty of all of mankind and for all time. To His perfectly, holy soul, this was more abhorrent than we could even begin to comprehend. Consequently, He prays, *"If it be possible, let this cup pass from Me,"* but of course, concluded by saying, *"Nevertheless not as I will, but as Thou wilt"* (Mat. 26:36-46).

As is obvious, all three temptations concern the Cross.

Bringing it all into a proper perspective, as it concerns ourselves personally, and our daily living, we are confronted with Satan telling us that the Cross is unnecessary, with the Apostate Church also telling us it's not the way, and with self-will demanding another direction. That is the heart of all temptation, and in which Satan is so successful. Let's look at it a little closer:

SATAN, SIN, AND SELF

As Satan solicited Jesus to obtain world-dominion other than by going to the Cross, likewise, Satan proposes dominion for us in the same manner. It's the world's way, and with Satan actually giving dominion for a short period of time; however, the end result is slavery to Satan instead of the other way around.

This is the attraction of the world, and it is in that which the world revels, and sadly and regrettably, to which many Christians have also succumbed.

That's the reason that the Holy Spirit through John the Beloved, said, *"Love not the world, neither the things that are in the world. If any man love the world, the love of the Father is not in him.*

"For all that is in the world, the lust of the flesh, the lust of the eyes, and the pride of life, is not of the Father, but is of the world."

He then said, *"And the world passeth away, and the lust thereof: but he that doeth the Will of God* (look to Christ and His Sacrifice) *abideth forever"* (I Jn. 2:15-17).

The only way to overcome the world with all its lusts and attractions is for the Believer to understand that all things which his heart seeks, are found only in the great Sacrifice of Christ. Through that means alone, can the human soul be satisfied. That must never be forgotten! But again I emphasize, that it all comes through the Cross.

Whereas I labeled this first approach as that of *"Satan,"* I've labeled the efforts of the Apostate Church as *"sin."* Of course, Satan is involved in all of this, but he does his doing in different ways.

When Peter began to rebuke Jesus, and because Christ had stated that He must go to Jerusalem and die on the Cross, Peter as stated, was being an unconscious tool of Satan. Peter saw many things, but the Cross definitely wasn't one of them.

This shows that at that particular time, the Apostle didn't really understand his true condition, and that the Cross of Christ was the only answer to that condition. He rather saw greatness, glory, and grandeur, with Jesus using His mighty miraculous powers to restore Israel again to a place of prominence. And of course, Peter would be one of His chief lieutenants.

In fact, all of the Apostles wanted the Kingdom, but they didn't want it by the way of the Cross. So they would then deny that part of the Life and Ministry of Christ, which were actually the very reason He came. Consequently, Jesus said to Peter:

"Get thee behind Me, Satan: thou art an offence unto Me: for thou savourest not the things that be of God, but those that be of men" (Mat. 16:23).

Peter, at that time, was a type of the Church, and apostate I might quickly add, which would deny the Cross. But let it ever be known, that all such denial of the Cross is of Satan, exactly as Jesus said here.

The modern Church wants a certain Jesus. They want a miracle Jesus, a Denominational Jesus, a Church Jesus, a Preacher Jesus, a healing Jesus, a money Jesus, an intellectual Jesus, etc. But that is *"another Jesus,"* in effect, a Jesus which doesn't really exist.

It is only *"Jesus Christ and Him Crucified,"* or else it's not Jesus (I Cor. 2:2).

Regrettably, most of the Church world denies the Cross. They either do so covertly, which refers to accepting humanistic psychology in His place, while all the time claiming

NOTES

Christ, or overtly, which refers to blatantly rejecting the Cross, as do many so-called Word of Faith people!

Then we have the problem of self, which is epitomized by Jesus being in the Garden. Of course, this happened hours before the Crucifixion.

Self shrank back from the hideous task that lay before Him. He met this temptation by denying self, and accepting the will of the Father.

In this triad of temptations, perhaps *"self"* just might be the most dangerous. This is where pride is fostered and nurtured! Self-will is the culprit of all our problems, in one way or the other.

As we've been teaching, it's very difficult for unredeemed self to abandon its own ways of Salvation, and it is equally difficult for Christian self to abandon its very, religious ways. Self loves these ways, and because they are a product of one's own ingenuity and abilities.

This means that we think that the *"old man"* can somehow be improved; consequently, we ever attempt to do so. What do we mean by the *"old man"*?

In fact, the *"old man"* was buried with Christ, and that speaks of His Crucifixion (Rom. 6:6). But even though he is dead and buried, which speaks of all of our old life, our past life, but more particularly, it speaks of our *"old self."* This speaks of dependence on any and all things other than Christ.

Unfortunately, the *"old man"* has means and ways of being resurrected. And then we find the *"old man"* struggling and doing battle with the *"new man"* (Eph. 2:15).

However, this *"old man"* can only be defeated by the *"new man,"* which means to put him back into the grave, and for him to there remain, by the Believer placing his Faith totally in the Cross of Christ. As someone has well said, Jesus died not only to save us from sin, but as well, from self.

Paul said, *"And that He might reconcile both unto God in one body by the Cross, having slain the enmity thereby"* (Eph. 2:16).

This plainly tells us, even as we've been teaching in paragraph after paragraph, that it is only through the Cross, that the *"old man"* can be defeated, and the *"new man"* reign supreme. The Believer cannot do it any other way.

The moment we attempt to get closer to God, or to bring about victory in any manner, except by trusting totally and completely in what Jesus did at the Cross, at that moment, the *"old man"* revives, and our problem exacerbates.

So, *"self"* can be conquered only by succumbing to the Will of the Father. And what is that Will?

The Will of the Father was for Jesus to go to the Cross. The Will of the Father is for us to go to the Cross, and in fact, to stay in the Cross. This is what the Psalmist was talking about when He said, *"He that dwelleth in the secret place of the Most High shall abide under the Shadow of the Almighty"* (Ps. 91:1).

When this is done, the following will happen. Even though this Psalm, which was probably written by Moses, refers directly to Christ, it also refers to the Believer, who is *"in Christ."*

The following are the results, of dwelling in the secret place of the Most High, which is the Cross of Christ, and abiding (thereby) under the Shadow of the Almighty:

"I will say of the Lord, He is my refuge and my fortress: my God; in Him will I trust.

"Surely He shall deliver thee from the snare of the fowler, and from the noisome pestilence.

"He shall cover thee with His feathers, and under His wings shalt thou trust: His Truth shall be thy shield and buckler.

"Thou shalt not be afraid for the terror by night; nor for the arrow that flieth by day;

"Nor for the pestilence that walketh in darkness; nor for the destruction that wasteth at noonday.

"A thousand shall fall at thy side, and ten thousand at thy right hand; but it shall not come nigh thee.

"Only with thine eyes shalt thou behold and see the reward of the wicked.

"Because thou hast made the Lord, which is my refuge, even the Most High, thy habitation;

"There shall no evil befall thee, neither shall any plague come nigh thy dwelling.

"For He shall give His Angels charge over thee, to keep thee in all thy ways.

"They shall bear thee up in their hands, lest thou dash thy foot against a stone.

"Thou shalt tread upon the lion and adder: the young lion and the dragon shalt thou trample under feet.

"Because he hath set his love upon Me, therefore will I deliver him: I will set him on high, because he hath known My Name.

"He shall call upon Me, and I will answer him: I will be with him in trouble; I will deliver him, and honor him.

"With long life will I satisfy him, and show him My Salvation" (Ps. 91:2-16).

HE IS ABLE

The phrase, *"He is able to succour them that are tempted,"* means, *"to run to the cry of those in danger and bring them aid."*

In this Scripture we see the great difference between Christ and ourselves. Here we read that Christ *"suffered being tempted."*

In commenting on this, Peter said, *"Forasmuch then as Christ hath suffered for us in the flesh, arm yourselves likewise with the same mind: for he that hath suffered in the flesh hath ceased from sin"* (I Pet. 4:1).

These two Passages bring out most vividly the difference between Christ's perfect humanity and our sinful natures. To us, the temptation to sin is attractive and alluring. In fact, that's what makes it a temptation. If it wasn't attractive and alluring, it simply would not be a temptation. And we suffer in the flesh when we resist it.

With Christ it was the very opposite. The very fact of temptation to Him caused the keenest suffering, in that it was not at all attractive and alluring. It was the presentation of that to His holy soul which He abhorred, and even to have to do with it, in any sense of temptation, caused Him pain and anguish.

When we come to that place, we are then becoming Christlike, to which place, to be sure, the Holy Spirit is working constantly to bring us, sin then has lost its attraction.

Paul also said that Christ can be *"touched with the feeling of our infirmities"* (Heb. 4:15). When Jesus touched the blind eyes, He felt the world of darkness. When He touched the deaf ear, He felt the world of silence. When He touched the leper, He felt what it was to be afflicted in body and to be outcast.

This is why He is a Merciful High Priest. Man may not understand. It may be impossible for man to relate completely to another's situation, but there is One Who realizes perfectly all of man's needs. He is the Merciful and Faithful High Priest, Jesus, our Saviour.

We are in the wilderness of this world which provides nothing to us spiritually. We rather live in a world that is actually opposed to everything of spirituality, Righteousness, and Godliness. Everyday we are called into the battle against sin, temptations, and tests. We are called upon to fight the good fight of Faith; for this we need the daily help of the Hand of the Intercessor. *"He is able"* implies that He has the power, the ability, and the willingness to help us.

VICTORY IN THE CROSS ALONE

He still says to us, *"Do you believe that I am able to do this? Do you believe that I am able to give you peace, assurance, deliverance — to supply and meet your need?"*

Remember all the experiences that He passed through, the trials He overcame, the temptations over which He was victorious. He is able!

He, too, suffered and was tempted. This is our glorious, precious High Priest, the Creator of the universe, Who became Man, lived among us, went to the Cross for us, and now ever lives as our High Priest! (Fjordbak).

But the question is, how does He do all of this for us?

We somehow think, erroneously I might add, that He extends His great power toward us, thereby driving away the Tempter and his allurements. Or perhaps we think that He tells the Holy Spirit what to do on our behalf, etc. None of this is correct!

There has never been a victory won by any Child of God outside of the Cross. Let the Reader think about those words very carefully and contemplate them at length. Every single victory that you have ever won over the powers of darkness has been won totally and completely through the Cross of Christ. There is no other way.

Sometimes, we might think that we have brought about victory through our great Faith, which in reality, at least as it is presently taught in most circles, is no Faith at

all; or through our ability to fling at Satan, the Name of Jesus. But have you noticed that many times we rebuke Satan, but as one Preacher said, *"He don't 'buke?'"*

No! Us stamping our feet and shouting loud, creates no problems for the Evil One. Likewise, when something good happens to us, get the thought out of your mind that it was your great Faith that did it. The Truth is, all these efforts we make in this capacity, center up on self and not Christ. Consequently, at first glance we should see the wrongness of such thinking.

The very reason that so many Christians are failing, or rather I should say, are living a life of spiritual failure, and despite the claims otherwise, that's exactly what's happening, is because they do not understand the Cross.

Ever since I've been a child, I have heard Preachers talk about the manner in which Jesus overcame Satan regarding the temptation in the wilderness. They speak of Him answering Satan's suggestions with the Word of God.

That is correct; however, what they don't understand is that all of these answers, in one way or the other, had to do with His obedience to the Father, as it regarded the coming Cross. As we've previously stated, Satan, irrespective of the manner of the temptation, was attempting to get Jesus to go around the Cross. He was trying to get Him to fall for the bait of gaining supremacy or dominion, other than by the Cross. Do it with His miraculous powers by turning the stones to bread; do it by public acclaim, as it concerned His throwing Himself from the pinnacle of the Temple; do it by worshipping Satan! Irrespective, it was all for but one purpose, and that was to gain what He came to do, other than by the Cross.

Consequently, Satan's temptation as it regards the Believer, is to get him to resist temptation other than by the means of the Cross. To be frank, he doesn't care how much we hurl the Word of God at him, if we don't really know what it means, he knows it will have but little effect.

THE TRUE DEFINITION
OF THE WORD OF GOD

What do I mean by Christians not knowing the true definition of the Word of God?

If the Believer doesn't understand that the Word of God in any and every instance centers up in the Cross, then the Believer doesn't properly understand the Word. He may have a surface knowledge of its surface meaning, but that will not suffice.

Hearing Preachers say that we must answer Satan with the Word, have you not noticed that your efforts in such direction have not brought much fruitful results?

Jesus answered Satan with the Word in the temptation, but of course, Jesus knew exactly what the Word of God meant, and by that I speak of it being anchored in the Cross.

The story of the Bible is the story of man's Redemption; consequently, every single nuance of that Word centers up in the Cross.

John the beloved opens his great Gospel with the words, *"In the beginning was the Word, and the Word was with God, and the Word was God"* (Jn. 1:1).

So we are told here, that the written Word is literally the expression of the Living Word, the Lord Jesus Christ.

John then said, *"And the Word was made flesh, and dwelt among us"* (Jn. 1:14).

Of course, we know that He was made flesh in order to be the last Adam, with the culminating effect of dying on the Cross. In other words, the Cross was the very reason for which He came.

John then said, *"Behold the Lamb of God, which taketh away the sin of the world"* (Jn. 1:29).

This Passage is obvious as to its meaning, regarding Jesus accomplishing this task, by going to the Cross.

So, if the Christian answers Satan by the Word, which he certainly should, he must at the same time know and understand what the Word means. If he doesn't understand that it is centered up in the Cross, then by and large, he is attempting to use the Word as some type of magic talisman, which of course, God can never honor. To be sure, Satan full well knows, what we are doing, and why we are doing what we are doing.

THE NAME OF JESUS

Other Believers have been taught to use the *"Name of Jesus"* against Satan; however, even though that is correct as well, if we don't

exactly know what the name means, then our use of such will have but little effect. Once again, most Christians in their attempt to use that mighty Name, do such only as some magic word. They seem to think by the mere use of such, that Satan is going to fold and run. He won't!

You as a Believer must know and understand that the very Name *"Jesus,"* means Saviour. And how did He and how does He save us? Of course, if we think a moment, we know that all of this was done at the Cross. He is Saviour only by virtue of His sacrificial, atoning Death, on the Cross of Calvary.

Understanding that, our use of the Name of Jesus will greatly change. Satan will know that you know what that name means, and that you are using it only on the basis of the great sacrificial work carried out at the Cross. To be sure, that causes Satan to tremble to no end.

He has no problem with the money Jesus, with the Denomination Jesus, or as I should say, a Baptist Jesus, an Assembly of God Jesus, a Church of God Jesus, a confession Jesus, a Jesus the Psychologist, a healing Jesus, a miracle Jesus, a Preacher Jesus, etc. The only Jesus Who causes him to tremble is *"the Crucified Jesus,"* hence, Paul saying, *"I determined not to know anything among you, save Jesus Christ, and Him Crucified"* (I Cor. 2:2).

Unfortunately, when most Christians use the *"name of Jesus,"* they are doing so from the foundation of how they understand Jesus, which is a *"money Jesus,"* or *"Church Jesus,"* etc. In short, all of these are *"another Jesus"* (II Cor. 11:4).

I'm sure that the Reader can now see, as to how Satan is put off not at all by the use of the name of *"another Jesus!"*

SO, HOW IS THE CHRISTIAN TO FACE THE EVERYDAY TEMPTATIONS OF THE POWERS OF DARKNESS?

1. The Christian is to understand that all of his help and strength comes totally and completely through what Christ did at the Cross on his behalf.

2. He must understand, that Satan totally and completely, was defeated at the Cross, and this applies not only to the Evil One himself, but as well to all of his fallen angels and

demon spirits. Concerning the Cross, Paul said, *"And having spoiled principalities and powers, He made a show of them openly, triumphing over them in it"* (Col. 2:14-15).

2. The Believer must place his Faith in the Cross, which in effect, says two things:

A. There was no way I could do this thing myself, as we speak of defeating the powers of darkness.

B. Jesus did it all on my behalf, and actually for me, and did it all at the Cross.

3. Understanding this, my Faith is not now in myself, but in Christ and what He has done on my behalf. Regrettably, the Faith of most Christians, is actually in themselves, whether they realize it or not. Consequently, God can never honor such!

4. With our Faith properly placed, the Holy Spirit, Who abides within us, will now work mightily on our behalf, which guarantees that Satan will honor the great victory won at the Cross. The key is the Cross, our Faith and the Holy Spirit.

The mere fact of understanding this, which means that you are not at all trusting in yourself, but rather Christ, and more particularly what He did for you at the Cross, guarantees your victory. Only in that manner can the Evil One be overcome. Then your use of the Word of God, and the Name of Jesus, will mean something.

So, Jesus definitely helps us in our temptations, but to know how that He helps us, which is through the Cross and our Faith in that Finished Work, guarantees that help. The Holy Spirit works on the premise of the Cross and that alone (Rom. 8:2). In fact, when Paul uses the phrase *"in Christ,"* or one of its derivatives such as *"in Him,"* which he does about 170 times in his 14 Epistles, without exception, he is always referring to what Jesus did at the Cross on our behalf and our acceptance of that (Rom. 6:3-5).

DOES A PROPER UNDERSTANDING OF THE CROSS STOP ALL TEMPTATION?

No, not at all!

Satan is going to probe and tempt all the days of our lives, or until the Trump sounds. And as we've already said, all of his temptations or solicitations, and in whatever manner, are for but one purpose, and that is to

destroy our Faith, or at least for it to be seriously weakened.

Satan doesn't want you to know about the Cross, hence him fighting this particular Message more so than anything else.

And if you understand this Message, he will try to get you to doubt it in some way. Or else he will attempt to get you to divide your Faith between the Cross and something else, which we referred to some pages back as *"wavering Faith"* (James 1:6-8).

The Bible doesn't teach sinless perfection, as should be obvious; however, it definitely does teach that sin will not have dominion over us (Rom. 6:14).

You as a Believer can live above sin, and I speak of sin dominating you. Unfortunately, living in a world filled with evil, and considering the fact that these bodies of flesh are not yet redeemed, there are many times that the best of Christians have to ask the Lord to forgive them of particular things done wrong, etc. But that is a far cry from sin dominating the Believer, which regrettably, it does, in many, if not most Christians.

A dear lady called our prayer line a short time back, commenting on this very subject. She stated that she had been controlled by a spirit of gossip, and had been unable to cease this activity, until she heard the great Message of the Cross. She was exuberant with joy in that her Faith now properly placed, had guaranteed her victory through what Jesus did at the Cross on her behalf.

Now most Christians wouldn't think very much about *"gossip,"* and would probably meet this statement with a smile; however, the Truth is, gossip is worse than alcohol, drugs, or nicotine, etc. We certainly don't think of such as being worse, but it definitely is.

These other things mentioned, plus a lot we haven't mentioned, hurt ourselves and our testimony, with most hurt confined to ourselves, but gossip, plus other similar type sins, greatly hurts others.

Whenever Paul used the words *"He is able,"* we need to understand the meaning of what is being said.

As God, we know that Christ is able to do anything. That's a foregone conclusion. So knowing that, why would the Apostle have used this statement in this fashion?

To answer before we explain, He is able to deliver us due to what he did for us on the Cross. Now let's look at the explanation:

WHAT DOES IT MEAN, HE IS ABLE?

As stated, we know that Paul is not speaking here of the great power of Christ. That's a foregone conclusion, such a conclusion in fact, that it really doesn't need to be said. Jesus is God, and as well, is the Creator, therefore, Almighty. Satan is but a creature, and literally trembles in the presence of Christ. So what does Paul mean?

Redemption is a legal work. Justification by Faith is a legal work. In fact, Satan's hold on humanity is a legal right. Man's sin gives Satan that right. In other words, he has a legal right to place man in captivity because of man's sin and transgression against God. As well, it was God Who made these rules, and not Satan!

When Jesus died on the Cross, he satisfied the terrible sin debt owed by man to God, by the giving of Himself, which was a legal work, which satisfied a legal claim. As well, He atoned for all sin, which was another legal work, which destroyed Satan's legal right regarding his hold on humanity, at least for those who will believe (Jn. 3:16).

Legally, Satan had a right to claim mankind, but with all sin removed, i.e., "atoned for," which was a legal work, Satan lost his legal rights. Therefore, upon that basis, and we speak of the Finished Work of Christ, Christ is able to deliver us. But He does it on that basis alone.

The idea is, and as we have previously stated, the Lord offered Himself on the Cross to satisfy the righteous demands of God's justice, so that His Government might be maintained, and that help, mercy, forgiveness, and Grace, might be shown on the basis of justice satisfied.

"Joyful, joyful, we adore Thee, God of
    Glory, Lord of love;
"Hearts unfold like flowers before
    Thee, opening to the Sun above.
"Melt the clouds of sin and sadness,
    drive the dark of doubts away;
"Giver of immortal gladness, fill us
    with the light of day."

NOTES

"All Thy works with joy surround Thee,
    Earth and Heaven reflect Thy rays,
"Stars and Angels sing around Thee,
    center of unbroken praise.
"Field and forest, vale and mountain,
    flowery meadow, flashing sea,
"Chanting bird and flowing fountain,
    call us to rejoice in Thee."

"Thou art giving and forgiving, ever
    blessing ever blest,
"Wellspring of the joy of living, ocean
    depth of happy rest!
"Thou our Father, Christ our Brother,
    all who live in love are Thine;
"Teach us how to love each other, lift
    us to the Joy Divine."

"Mortals, join the happy chorus which
    the morning stars began;
"Father love is reigning o'er us, Brother
    love binds man to man.
"Ever singing, march we onward,
    victors in the midst of strife,
"Joyful music leads us Son-ward in the
    triumph song of life."

CHAPTER 3

(1) "WHEREFORE, HOLY BRETHREN, PARTAKERS OF THE HEAVENLY CALLING, CONSIDER THE APOSTLE AND HIGH PRIEST OF OUR PROFESSION, CHRIST JESUS;"

The exposition is:

1. Paul refers to these Christian Jews as "holy brethren," which applies to all Believers, both Jew and Gentile. The word "holy" as here used, does not refer to conduct, but rather to position.

2. All who accept Christ are "partakers of the Heavenly Calling."

3. Christ was sent on a Mission, hence the word "Apostle" applying to Him. The word "Apostle" means, "one sent, furnished with credentials."

4. He was sent among other things, to serve as our "High Priest," which stands for "Mediator."

5. The word "profession" should have been translated "confession," and here means

the Believer agreeing with God as to the report He gives in the Bible of His Son. This is the Believer's confession.

6. Christ Jesus is the One Whom we confess, and do so on the basis of His Finished Work on the Cross.

WHEREFORE

By the use of the word *"wherefore,"* Paul harks back to the preceding argument, and draws a conclusion. Having shown that the Messiah, the Lord Jesus Christ, is better than the Prophets and the Angels, he now asks his Readers to consider Him in relation to Moses (Wuest).

Paul steadily develops his argument that Jesus is supremely great. He is greater than the Angels, the Author of a Great Salvation, and great enough to become man to accomplish it. Now Paul turns his attention to Moses, regarded by the Jews as the greatest of men.

They could even think of him as greater than Angels. Perhaps then he was superior to Jesus? In addressing this, Paul does nothing to belittle Moses. Nor does he criticize him. He accepts Moses' greatness but shows that as great as he was, Jesus was greater by far (Morris).

HOLY BRETHREN

Knowing that Paul is writing to Jews, but which serves as great instruction for all Believers, and understanding that some of these Jewish Believers were on the very edge of going back into Temple worship, which meant they would have to deny Christ, how could he refer to them as *"holy"*?

He does so on the basis of their position in Christ, and not on the basis of their actual condition. In fact, the Holy Spirit is actually the One Who inspired these words. All Believers are referred to in the same manner, and because it speaks of our position in Christ, and is, therefore, based totally on Christ, and what He did for us on the Cross, and not at all on ourselves. The only way that any Believer can be referred to as *"holy,"* is through, in, by, and of Christ. However, many tragically think of themselves as holy, because they keep certain rules and regulations, or do certain things, or don't do certain other things.

No! All that we have, all that we are, all that we hope to be, are bound up totally and completely in Christ, and His vicarious work on the Cross, and our Faith in that. God honors us only on that basis, and that basis alone! If we fail to understand that, and get our eyes on ourselves, which means they are no longer on Christ, then we will do the same thing that some of these Christian Jews were doing — resorting to works and not Grace, which spells doom for the Believer.

The broad foundation of Christianity has now been laid in the Person of the Son of God. In the following Chapters of this Epistle this doctrine is made to throw light on the mutual relations of the two Dispensations of the Old Covenant and the New.

The first deduction is that the Mosaic Dispensation was itself created by Christ; that the threats and Promises of the Old Testament live on into the New; that the central idea of the Jewish Faith, the idea of the Sabbath rest, is realized in its inmost meaning in Christ only. In other words, the entirety of the Old Testament points toward the New, and more particularly, toward Christ, and more particular yet, toward Christ and Him Crucified. Consequently, Paul will not be slow to expose the wide difference between the two Dispensations.

But it is equally true and not less important that the Old Covenant was the vesture of Truths which remain when the old garment has been changed to the new garment.

At the outset Paul's tone is influenced by this Doctrine. He addresses his Readers as Brethren, holy indeed, but not holy after the pattern of their former exclusiveness; for their holiness is inseparably linked with Christ and what He did on the Cross, regarding His great Sacrifice.

The emphasis throughout Hebrews is upon the manhood or humanity of Jesus. What He accomplished He did as a man, perfect, sinless, and undefiled, but as man. It is this Man, Christ Jesus, Whom Paul now compares with the man Moses, who held a unique position as one who had spoken to God *". . . face to face, as a man speaketh unto his friend . . ."* (Ex. 33:11).

Such a comparison between Jesus and Moses may have seemed needless. After all, if Jesus were superior to Angels, was it not evident that He was superior to mortal man?

To grasp the significance of this comparison, it is necessary to remember the great reverence the Jewish people had for Moses. There was no higher personage in all Jewish history, thinking, or theology than Moses. Angels may have been present at the communication of the Law, they may have even been instrumental in its giving, but Moses was the Lawgiver. The Divine Revelation of the Old Dispensation came through Moses.

COMPARISON

Paul realizes the sensitive ground upon which he stands. He is comparing God's Ambassador to Jesus Christ. In making this contrast and comparison, he points out more than Christ's superiority. The absolute finality of God's Revelation in Christ is the real object of his presentation.

Though Old Testament men, including Moses, spoke God's Message, yet the fullness of the Message and completion of the Revelation came through the Son. In other words, their Message and in totality, pointed to the One Who was to come, Who is the Lord Jesus Christ. Consequently, the only access that man has to God is through God's Son, the Lord Jesus Christ.

"For the Law was given by Moses, but Grace and Truth came by Jesus Christ" (Jn. 1:17) (Fjordbak).

PARTAKERS

The phrase, *"Partakers of the Heavenly Calling,"* pertains to all Saints, who are associated with one another in a Heavenly Calling. Paul speaks of the *"Calling from above,"* that effectual Call into Salvation which comes from Heaven and is to Heaven (Phil. 3:14).

This expression in Hebrews 3:1 speaks, therefore, of the Church. Israel has an earthly calling and an earthly destiny, and of course we speak of the nation as a whole.

The Church has a Heavenly Calling and a Heavenly destiny. Thus does Paul mark the Jews to whom he was writing, as belonging to the Church and as distinct from Israel as a nation.

So, all who have been saved from the very

NOTES

beginning, including all of those in Israel regarding the Old Testament, and of course including the Church as well, are partakers, partners, and fellows in the Heavenly Calling.

However, Israel as a nation had an earthly calling and continues to have an earthly calling, which will be completed during the coming Kingdom Age, i.e., *"Millennial Reign."*

This means that those Jews who are alive at the Second Coming, and who will accept Christ, and every indication is that most all Jews will do so at that particular time, will then enter an earthly program as a nation, of replenishing the earth forever.

All those who have been saved up unto the Resurrection of Life will have Glorified Bodies and will, therefore, help Christ administer the affairs of this Earth and over all Creation, and do so forever and forever (Rev. 1:5-6; 5:10; 22:4-5).

Our calling is Heavenly in that we will not be limited to an earthly program as all men would have been if man had not sinned (Gen. 1:27-31; Mat. 22:30; Lk. 20:34-35; Heb. 11:10-16; 12:22-23).

All who have been saved, both Jews and Gentiles, even from the time of the Garden of Eden, will have part in the First Resurrection, and will have glorified bodies, and will help Christ administer the affairs of all creation forever. And then as we've already stated, Israel will be the predominant nation in the Millennial Reign, with every evidence, that it will continue forever in that state. Also as stated, the nation will consist of Jews who are alive at the time of the Second Coming, and who will accept Christ.

Paul in addressing the Jews in this Book of Hebrews, appeals to them as *"Holy brethren, partakers of the Heavenly Calling,"* which distinguishes them from other members of the Jewish community. These were Hebrew Christians who had a personal experience with the Lord in the new birth. By the experience of the new birth they were no longer only Jews in the flesh, but, having been born of the Spirit, they were now spiritual Jews. In effect, Paul had said previously:

"For he is not a Jew, which is one outwardly; neither is that Circumcision, which is outward in the flesh: but he is a Jew, which

is one inwardly; and Circumcision is that of the heart, in the spirit, and not in the letter; whose praise is not of men, but of God" (Rom. 2:28-29).

ISRAEL

Israel had claimed its relationship with God on the basis of the call they had received through Moses. But Paul explains here in Hebrews, that a Heavenly Call has been issued through God's Son, Christ Jesus, to Whom Moses pointed. While the Hebrews had an earthly calling by right of their natural birth, they had now been transferred from an earthly to a Heavenly Calling. They now had a destiny entirely different from that which they had here upon Earth.

While the Jewish worship, ritual, tradition, Priesthood, Sacrifice, and the Temple, had been great and wonderful, and that which had been ordained by the Lord; still, all of that pointed to something greater, something which was coming, and more particularly, Someone Who was coming, namely, the Lord Jesus Christ; consequently, they, the Jews as well as the Gentiles, are now partakers of something far greater, a Heavenly Calling. As a result, they must not consider returning to Judaism.

Paul also said, *"giving thanks unto the Father, which hath made us meet to be partakers of the inheritance of the Saints in Light"* (Col. 1:12).

Peter said, *"Whereby are given unto us exceeding great and precious promises: that by these ye might be partakers of the Divine Nature, having escaped the corruption that is in the world through lust"* (II Pet. 1:4).

GENTILES

Due to what Christ did at the Cross, the Gentiles had now been brought into this great Calling. The great Call of God now includes all, Jews, Greeks, barbarians, bond and free, male and female, great and small. They all come under the same Calling, the same Covenant, which is actually the Abrahamic Covenant.

The idea is, those (Gentiles) who sometime were far off have been made nigh; the strangers and sojourners are henceforth fellow-citizen with the Saints and of the Household of God. In other words, the Gospel is now one Gospel, including the entirety of the human race.

However, many Jews had a great problem with this. They could not see themselves needing Christ as the Gentiles, with the Gentiles being brought into this great Covenant, all on the same basis. This was very difficult for them to grasp and to accept. They desired to think of themselves in a far greater posture than the Gentiles. They were reckoning on their history, and the dealings with them by God all through the centuries. What they failed to see was, that God doesn't give Salvation on the merit of race, nationality, or God's past dealings with the nation as a whole, but only on personal Faith, which is required of all, both Jews and Gentiles.

APOSTLE

The phrase, *"Consider the Apostle,"* presents the only time that Christ is referred to as an *"Apostle."*

"Consider" in the Greek is *"katanoeo,"* and means, *"to consider attentively, to fix one's eyes or mind upon."*

This word *"consider"* is used here by Paul in this fashion, because the Jews were allowing their attention to relax so far as the Messiah and the New Testament were concerned, with their gaze slowly turning back upon the Old Testament Sacrifices.

Consequently, this word bids the Reader or the hearer to fix their close attention on Jesus.

The purpose of this admonition is to prevent apostasy by urging the Reader to realize and perceive the incomparable glory and saving power of Christ. If God has spoken, and His final Message is in His Son, Jesus the Christ, *"the Apostle and High Priest of our profession,"* then we must not only consider Him, we must also hear Him. We must wholeheartedly consider Him, never once allowing our attention to turn back from the things of the Truth.

THE CROSS OF CHRIST

In fact, the entirety of this phrase as given by Paul, which includes Christ as the High Priest, without fail turns one to the Cross. Jesus Christ as an Apostle, was sent by God to redeem mankind, which could only be done by dying on the Cross. So the Cross was ever in view.

However, the modern Church has allowed its attention and its gaze to drift away from the Cross of Christ to other things, exactly as the Christian Jews of Paul's time were allowing their attention to drift in the same manner. Paul will address this very succinctly in Chapters 6 and 10; however, the great problem was, that the Doctrine of *"Jesus Christ and Him Crucified"* was being minimized, or ignored, or even denied, with these Jews going back into Temple worship. The same identical thing is happening presently, but without the Temple; however, the end result is the same. But yet there is a subtle difference.

Then, the Christian Jews were in the position of totally denying Christ. Now He is not so much denied, as *"another Jesus"* is substituted to take His place (II Cor. 11:4). As I've said over and over again, the modern Church, at least as a whole, is not worshiping and serving the Christ of the Cross, but another Jesus entirely. However, even though that is different than the problem that Paul is addressing here in Hebrews, the end results are the same. To reject the Jesus of the Cross is to reject Jesus.

Having said that, I must at the same time explain that many in the modern Church have not really rejected Jesus Christ and Him Crucified; in fact, they think this is the same Jesus they are serving. And in many cases it is. But the problem is, they have limited the Crucified Christ to the initial Salvation experience, not understanding the great part that the Cross plays in our continued living for God.

The Lord is in the process of remedying this situation. The Message of the Cross is going out from this Ministry all over the world. And as well, the Lord is beginning to deal with the hearts and lives of other Preachers of the Gospel, who are beginning to preach this Message of all messages. And to be sure, the Message of the Cross is not something new. It is actually the foundation of the Church. The sadness is, if something is not preached behind the pulpit, then it's not possible for Faith to be exhibited in that particular subject (Rom. 10:17).

NOTES

Worse yet, in the last several decades, psychology has taken the place of the Cross, with that particular humanistic drivel being promoted from pulpits instead of the True Gospel of Jesus Christ, which is the Cross. As a result, the Church has lost its way, for without the Message of the Cross, there is no way or direction (Rom. 10:17).

HIGH PRIEST

The phrase, *"And High Priest of our profession, Christ Jesus,"* is presented by Paul in this manner for a reason. Among the Jews the High Priest was also considered the Apostle of God. Consequently, the two Apostles are now compared. Consequently, realization of Christ may be said to be the gist of the whole Epistle to the Hebrews.

To be sure, this spiritual vision is not ecstasy. We realize Christ as Apostle and as High Priest. We behold Him when His Words are a Message to us from God, and when He carries our supplications to God. But above all, we observe Him in His Redemptive Work, which He carried out, by dying on the Cross, which paid the penalty for our sins, and by being resurrected on the third day.

None of this, Moses could do! But all of this, Christ was able to do, and did do, which effected Salvation for the entirety of the human race, at least for those who will believe, to which Moses could only point.

The word *"Apostle"* presents the basic idea as that of mission. Jesus was sent by the Father to accomplish His purpose.

"High Priest" brings before us the Sacrificial nature of that mission. In the Greek the Verse ends by naming Him simply *"Jesus,"* which of course, denotes *"Saviour,"* which could only be, according to what He did at the Cross.

Though He is the most glorious of Beings, this Name draws attention to His humanity, which was necessary as it regards the Cross. It is as man that His work as Apostle and High Priest is accomplished.

TITLES

The Holy Spirit through Paul seeks to portray Jesus from the Reader's consideration. Throughout the Epistle many exhortations and doctrines are given to draw the mind back to a determined choice to follow Jesus completely, even in the midst of persecution and threatened martyrdom. The Reader is brought face-to-face with the supremacy of Christ by many comparisons and contrasts. By the use of many names and titles the Lord Jesus is vividly described, so that the mind of the Reader may perceive the majesty and glory of the Crucified, Risen, Glorified, Exalted Lord. He is called:

1. Apostle: *"Wherefore, Holy Brethren, partakers of the Heavenly Calling, consider the Apostle and High Priest of our profession, Christ Jesus"* (Heb. 3:1).

2. Author and Finisher: *"Looking unto Jesus the Author and Finisher of our Faith; Who for the joy that was set before Him endured the Cross, despising the shame, and is set down at the Right Hand of the Throne of God"* (Heb. 12:2).

3. Captain: *"For it became Him, for Whom are all things, and by Whom are all things, in bringing many sons unto glory, to make the Captain of their Salvation perfect through sufferings"* (Heb. 2:10).

4. First Begotten: *"And again, when He bringeth in the Firstbegotten into the world, He saith, and let all the Angels of God worship Him"* (Heb. 1:6).

5. Forerunner: *"The Forerunner is for us entered* (within the Veil), *even Jesus, made an High Priest forever after the order of Melchisedec"* (Heb. 6:20).

6. God: *"But unto the Son He saith, Thy Throne, O God, is forever and ever: a Sceptre of Righteousness is the Sceptre of Thy Kingdom"* (Heb. 1:8).

7. High Priest: *"Wherefore in all things it behoved Him to be made like unto His Brethren, that He might be a merciful and faithful High Priest in things pertaining to God, to make reconciliation for the sins of the people"* (Heb. 2:17).

8. Jesus Christ: *"Jesus Christ the same yesterday, and today, and forever"* (Heb. 13:8).

9. Lord: *"How shall we escape, if we neglect so great Salvation; which at the first began to be spoken by the Lord, and was confirmed unto us by them that heard Him"* (Heb. 2:3).

10. Mediator: *"But now hath He obtained a more excellent Ministry, by how much also*

NOTES

He is the Mediator of a better Covenant, which was established upon better Promises" (Heb. 8:6).

11. Priest: *"He saith also in another place, Thou art a Priest forever after the order of Melchisedec"* (Heb. 5:6).

12. Shepherd: *"Now the God of Peace, that brought again from the dead our Lord Jesus, that great Shepherd of the sheep, through the Blood of the Everlasting Covenant"* (Heb. 13:20).

13. Son and Heir: *"Hath in these last days spoken unto us by His Son, Whom He hath appointed Heir of all things, by Whom also He made the worlds"* (Heb. 1:2).

14. Son of God: *"Seeing then that we have a great High Priest, that is passed into the Heavens, Jesus the Son of God, let us hold fast our profession"* (Heb. 4:14) (Fjordbak).

OFFICE OF THE HIGH PRIEST

One great object of this Epistle is, to compare the Lord Jesus with the High Priest of the Jews, and to show that He was in all respects superior. This was important, because the Office of High Priest was that which eminently distinguished the Jewish Faith, and because the Christian Faith, which should be an extension of the Jewish Faith, proposed to abolish that.

It became necessary, therefore, to show that all that was dignified and valuable, in other words, all that was right in the Jewish system, was to be found in the Christian system as well.

This was done by showing that in the Lord Jesus was found all the characteristics of a High Priest, and that all the functions which had been performed in the Jewish ritual were performed by Him, and that all which had been prefigured by the Jewish High Priest was fulfilled in Him.

The Apostle here merely alludes to Him, or names Him as the High Priest, and then postpones the consideration of His Character, in that respect, until after he has compared Him with Moses (Barnes).

In fact, the entirety of the Old Testament system, and we speak of that under Moses, was only meant to be a stopgap measure, which would serve its purpose until the coming of the One to Whom it pointed, which was Christ. It was an inferior system, and was never meant to be permanent. It would only serve until the permanent came, Who and What is Christ Jesus.

THE SACRIFICE

The whole Jewish system, as given by God, was built around the Sacrificial system. However, that system was meant to point only to the One Who was to come, Who in fact, would be the Sacrifice. In fact, the Sacrifices pointed to the Truth, that the Cross of Christ was ever in view. Of course, we know and understand, that the Cross within itself effected nothing. It was rather, Who was on that Cross; however, make no mistake about it, the Cross was an absolute necessity. This means that it was not an incident or an accident. It also means that Jesus was not executed. In fact, He literally gave up His Own Life, which was demanded if He was in fact, to be a legitimate Sacrifice.

A Sacrifice demands something that is given up voluntarily. While of course, the lambs and goats of old did not give themselves up voluntarily; however, they were given up by their owners. Jesus gave Himself as an Offering for sin, which was the only Sacrifice, which could actually atone for all sin, in effect, wiping it out forever (Jn. 1:29).

WHY DID THE JEWS HAVE A PROBLEM SEEING THIS?

The nation of Israel, plus its Religious Leadership, didn't see this, because they really did not know God. Despite all their talk of Him, and all their claims made upon Him, the Truth was, they didn't really know Him at all!

As a result, they were looking for a type of Messiah which the Bible had never promised. In other words, they read into the Text that which wasn't there, and they refused to read into it that which was actually there. In fact, millions do the Word of God the same way during these modern times.

For instance, they did not think of Christ as being the Son of God, but rather a great, charismatic figure, Who would have the wisdom of Solomon, and the war making ability of David. A Suffering Messiah, Who Isaiah predicted (Isa., Chpt. 53), was not in their thinking. So they made up their own

Messiah; consequently, when Jesus came, even though He fulfilled all the prophecies in totality, and as well His genealogy was perfect all the way back to David, and to Abraham, still, they would not accept Him. As stated, He didn't fit their mold, so they would have none of Him!

It is the same presently with much of the Church. They will not have the Salvation afforded by the Lord, and to be frank, and as already stated, they will little have the Christ portrayed in the Word of God. Consequently, they make up their own Salvation, and manufacture their own Jesus.

To be sure, these problems affected even the Christian Jews of Paul's day. Was Jesus really the Son of God? Was He really the Messiah? Was His death on the Cross really the answer to the problem of sin? Must they abandon the Temple and all of its sacrificial system? Is the Law completely fulfilled in Christ?

And then on top of all of these questions, which incidentally they should not have had, their fellow non-Christian Jews were bombarding them daily, even hourly, with accusations of every sort. By this time, the nation of Israel, which had crucified Christ, and of course, who refused to admit that He had come from the dead, had fabricated all types of stories about Him, some of them the most vile and most awful that one could begin to imagine. Therefore, in this atmosphere, many Christian Jews were becoming very discouraged, with some of them even denouncing Christ, and going back into Temple worship.

JAMES AND THE CHURCH AT JERUSALEM

It is my belief that Paul wrote this Epistle to the Hebrews. In fact, and as already stated, I cannot see how anyone else could have written the Epistle, for the simple reason, that whoever wrote this Book must be of tremendous knowledge concerning the Old Testament. To be sure, there was no one in Paul's day who knew the Old Testament as that Apostle. Also, it is my belief that he wrote this Epistle from Rome, at about the time he wrote II Timothy. That would have been in the latter part of A.D. 67 or the first part of 68.

Even though the Epistle was certainly intended for all Jews everywhere, it was more so, I think, directed toward the Christian Jews in Jerusalem.

Furthermore, it is my feeling that the refusal of James, the Senior Pastor of the Church in Jerusalem, to take a firm stand concerning the Law/Grace issue, served to bring about the problem that was causing some Jews to now defect.

As is recorded in Acts, Chapter 15, James made the right decision as it regarded the Law and the Gentiles, but he stopped short of including the Jews. The Jews, and we speak of Christian Jews, were to continue to keep the Law, which of course was wrong. Jesus fulfilled all of that, and Jews, or anyone for that matter, continuing to be faithful to that Old Covenant, served as an insult to Christ and all that He had done, to bring about Redemption for the human race. In fact, in A.D. 70, the Lord used the Romans to completely destroy the Temple, making continued worship there impossible.

As well, because of the Christian Jews in Jerusalem continuing to engage in Law-keeping, and which seemed to be sanctioned by James (Gal. 2:11-14), such practice caused Paul tremendous problems in the building of the Church. Those we refer to as Judaizers, were constantly coming from Jerusalem, going into the Churches built by Paul, attempting to claim that Law must be added to Grace if in fact, people were to truly be saved. In fact, much of Paul's writings contradict this fallacy. It was without a doubt, the major problem in the Early Church.

Once again, it is my opinion, that this problem could have been avoided, had James taken a strong stand at the outset. As well, it had now led to at least some Christian Jews, and possibly many, turning their backs upon Christ, going back into the old Levitical system, which Paul strongly denounced in this Epistle, and especially in Chapters 6 and 10.

To what degree we misinterpret the Word of God, or fail to obey the Word of God, to that degree we will suffer loss. And if I'm right in my summation, and I definitely believe that I am, then we must understand that the loss we suffer, is always far greater than at first we are led to believe. In other words, to miss the Word of God to any degree, is to miss God!

(2) "WHO WAS FAITHFUL TO HIM THAT APPOINTED HIM, AS ALSO MOSES WAS FAITHFUL IN ALL HIS HOUSE."

The exegesis is:

1. The pronoun "Who" refers to "Christ," and means "Messiah," or "The Anointed."

2. Jesus was faithful in all that He did, meaning that He did exactly what the Father sent Him to do.

3. Moses was faithful as well; however, the house in which he was faithful was actually built by Christ Jesus. And the builder of the house is always greater than the house.

FAITHFUL

The phrase, "Who was faithful to Him that appointed Him," should have here the words added "Apostle and High Priest." Christ was faithful in this appointment, and in every capacity!

The word "faithful" is meant to speak to the Christian Jews who were on the very edge of apostasy. The idea is, that in the midst of all of their temptations and trials to which they were exposed, they were to consider Christ. What could be a more powerful argument than to direct their attention to the unwavering constancy and fidelity of the Lord Jesus? The importance of such a virtue in the Saviour is manifest. His faithfulness is seen everywhere; and all the great interests of the world depend on it. In effect, the welfare of the entirety of the world and for all time, depended on the faithfulness of the Lord Jesus. Had He failed in that, all would have been lost.

His fidelity was worthy of the more attentive consideration, from the numerous temptations which beset His path, and the attempts which were made to turn Him aside from His devotedness to God. Amidst all the temptations of the adversary, and all the trials through which He passed, He never for a moment swerved from fidelity to the great trust which had been committed to His hands. What better example, to preserve these Christian Jews, and for that matter us as well, from the temptations to apostasy, could the Apostle propose to the Christians whom he addressed? What, in these temptations and trials, could be more appropriate than for them to "consider" the example of the great Apostle and High Priest of their and our profession, i.e., *"confession"*?

MOSES

The phrase, *"As also Moses was faithful in all his house,"* presents the Holy Spirit through Paul handling Moses delicately; however, there are vast differences in the two, which a careful survey of this Passage will reveal.

Moses, Aaron, and Joshua were the three great Princes of the Hebrew nation. Joshua is hinted at (Heb. 2:10), Aaron is also intimated (Heb. 2:17), but Moses is named (Heb. 3:2), for he was the greatest of all the Hebrews, and he is named in order to show his inferiority to the Messiah Who is both the Apostle and High Priest, not only to the Jews, but to the Gentiles as well.

As Apostle He reveals God to mankind, and as High Priest He presents us to God.

The argument here is: that Moses was only a servant in God's house, i.e., *"regarding the nation of Israel,"* but that Christ is a Son over the house; and it is His Own house — Whose house are we.

Jesus being God built all things; therefore, He built the house of Israel, which of course, makes Him greater than the house, and greater than Moses, as should be obvious!

APOSTLE AND HIGH PRIEST

As an Apostle, Christ was faithful in all that was committed to Him. He made the Perfect Sacrifice, and in effect, was the Perfect Sacrifice to blot out man's sin. He was faithful in his appointment to go to the Cross; He was trustworthy. Even with the opportunity of coming down from the Cross, He was faithful in His appointment, in that He did not do that, but chose rather to pay the supreme price.

Jesus' Mission to the Earth was one of reconciliation, for in Him God was *"... reconciling the world unto Himself ..."* (II Cor. 5:19). In this reconciliation, the Lord Jesus fulfilled His purpose in coming: that we *"... might have life, and that they* (we) *might have it more abundantly"* (Jn. 10:10). As a ransom, He laid down His Life, as He was commanded to do by His Father Who had sent Him as Redeemer. In fact He said this concerning His Life:

"No man taketh it from Me, but I lay it down of Myself. I have power to lay it down, and I have power to take it again. This Commandment have I received of My Father" (Jn. 10:18).

At the Cross Christ finished the work His Father had sent Him to do, and He glorified His Father in it. But there still remained the High Priestly Ministry that must be fulfilled on behalf of the Children of God.

As High Priest He continues in that position, even unto this hour, to minister on behalf of man's needs. His Mission of purging our sins, of making Reconciliation and Atonement for man is finished; the Sacrifice of Calvary need never be repeated. However, the implication is, that His High Priestly work will never end. He is at this moment, at the Right Hand of the Father making intercession for the Children of God. Consequently, He is both Merciful and Faithful, exactly as Paul said in Hebrews 2:17.

The subject of Christ's Priesthood will be dealt with in great detail in another of the Chapters to come. It will suffice now to make the following comments:

1. The Priest is the go-between for God and man.

2. The Priest must be able to speak to God for man and to speak to men for God.

3. Jesus is the Perfect High Priest, because He is perfectly man and perfectly God.

4. As man, He was perfected for this Ministry by experiencing all that is common to man.

5. Christ can fully represent man to God and God to man. Through this Jesus, the High Priest, man has access to God, and only through Him.

THE COMPARISON

Paul, in comparing Christ Jesus with Moses the Lawgiver, is contrasting two men who held singular positions in the economy of God. As man, Jesus rose above Moses and, in every respect, became worthy of more honor. Moses only prefigured the Anointed of God Who was to come, Christ Jesus, the Apostle and High Priest.

Both Jesus and Moses occupied Apostolic and Priestly positions before God. That Moses was Divinely sent by God has been shown, and that he was an effective intercessor and mediator also may be seen in Scripture. Though Aaron was the chosen High Priest, it was Moses who was Israel's true advocate with God. Moses was both spokesman and mediator:

"The Lord our God made a Covenant with us in Horeb . . . I stood between the Lord and you at that time, to show you the Word of the Lord" (Deut. 5:2, 5).

Paul very carefully makes a comparison: both the Messiah and Moses were faithful. The similarity of the comparison, however, ends with this:

After Jesus had completed His Redemptive Work; after He, by Himself, had purged man's sins; after He had made reconciliation for man, He ascended to His Father and *". . . sat down on the Right Hand of the Majesty on High"* (Heb. 1:3). But Moses was unable to even enter the Tabernacle because of the Glory of God that rested upon it.

Jesus has been highly exalted by God Himself and made to have the preeminence in all things. He has entered the presence of God on our behalf, which Moses could not do.

THE HUMANITY OF CHRIST

Some may wonder at Paul comparing Moses with Christ, knowing that Christ is Very God as well as Very Man, where Moses was only a man at best. In other words, he was not even a perfect man, as no man has ever been, other than Christ.

Paul is making this comparison because he is referring to Christ as it regards His humanity. In effect he is saying, if we set aside the fact that Jesus is God, which He certainly is, still even as a Man, there is no comparison with Christ. He was the Perfect Man, the One Paul referred to as the *"Second Man,"* meaning that He was what God intended for man to be (I Cor. 15:47).

As a Man, Christ faced every temptation hurled at Him by Satan, met all the opposition and accusations of the religious leadership of Israel, and even as it regards His personal passions, never failed even one time in any capacity. Moses could never say that, as could, or can, no other man.

Adding to that the fact that He was also *"Very God,"* and we find that the idea of any comparison, even with one as great as Moses,

can only be labeled as ridiculous. It is for certain also, that Moses would have said the same identical thing. As a man Jesus Christ was Perfect, and as God He received worship, even as He should have done so! Moses was none of this, and in fact, could not be any of this, as should be overly obvious!

But the Holy Spirit would handle Moses very delicately, in order to show the Jews how foolish they were in attempting to make this comparison, with some of them, even claiming that Moses was greater. And please remember, we are speaking here of Christian Jews!

(3) "FOR THIS MAN WAS COUNTED WORTHY OF MORE GLORY THAN MOSES, INASMUCH AS HE WHO HATH BUILDED THE HOUSE HATH MORE HONOUR THAN THE HOUSE."

The exegesis is:

1. By every measurement that could be counted, Christ was worthy of more glory than Moses.

2. The Builder of the House, can be none other that Deity, because the building of such a House is beyond the capacity of mere humans.

3. As should be obvious, the Builder of the House, Who is Christ, is greater, and has more honor than the House which He has built.

GLORY

The phrase, *"For this man was counted worthy of more glory than Moses,"* finds Paul proclaiming the humanity of Christ, by which measurement he compares Moses. But this does not at all alter his conviction that Christ is also more than man. He is the Founder of the Church, and the Church was continuous with the Old Testament people of God. Paul will come back to this thought in Verse 6.

Moses was the Apostle of the separated people who were partakers of an earthly calling, and Aaron was their High Priest. But Jesus is both the Apostle and High Priest of the Holy Brethren, holy as we have already seen, because set apart to God in Him, and thus partakers of the Heavenly Calling.

He is infinitely superior to Moses because Moses, though faithful in his day, was simply a servant in the House of God, but Christ

Jesus is Builder of the House and is *"Son over His Own House, Whose house are we, if we hold fast the confidence and the rejoicing of the hope firm unto the end."*

The *"glory"* mentioned here, regards respect, honor, acclaim, prestige, power, riches, Grace, magnificence, spectacular, greatness, splendor, etc.

In back of everything on Earth, and we speak of the system of this world, is the thought of *"glory!"* Hollywood creates its spectacular; the rich seek to build and garnish that which they have built, making it glorious, at least in the eyes of men. Who has the most! Who is the biggest! Who is the greatest! All corresponds with glory, at least as man thinks of such.

When Christ came to this world, He was accompanied by glory, and I speak of the Angelic Host, *"praising God, and saying, Glory to God in the highest, and on earth, peace, goodwill toward men"* (Lk. 2:13-14).

Nevermind that Jesus as a baby was born in a cattle stall, because there was no room for Him in the inn; the Angels knew Who He was, even though the religious leadership of Israel didn't!

There was as well, amazing glory that accompanied His Life and Ministry, glory to such an extent, that defies all description; however, it was the Glory of God represented in the healing of the sick, the cleansing of lepers, etc., which was not the type of glory expected by Israel. They were looking for a dazzling display, an amazing spectacular, a glorified stunt, and to be sure, Satan tempted Him in this, and I speak of the pinnacle of the Temple episode (Mat. 4:5-7).

Of the Glory which God bestowed upon His Only Son, Israel wasn't interested. But to be sure, the magnificence of glory which accompanies Him now, is beyond all description, in which will be beheld on a coming glad day. John the Beloved gives us an idea in his account of that glory given in Revelation, Chapters 4 and 5.

THE BUILDER OF THE HOUSE

The phrase, *"Inasmuch as He Who hath builded the house hath more honor than the house,"* proclaims the fact that the Lord built the house of Israel. Moses is a member of

that house. Since the One Who built the house, has more honor than the house, as would be obvious, it follows that He is worthy of more honor than Moses, for Moses is but a member of the house of Israel. Since the Messiah is better than Moses, which again should be obvious, the Testament which He inaugurated must be better than the one Moses was instrumental in bringing in, and for the reason that a superior workman turns out a superior product (Wuest).

Moses is given credit here, because the work was entrusted to him, which among other things was the great Law of God, even though it was only meant to be a stopgap measure until the coming of the New Covenant, which is in Christ, and in effect, is Christ.

In this, Christ is portrayed as the Creator, which He definitely is. But Moses was only a part of that which Christ had made. The Creator of the house stands above the house.

(4) "FOR EVERY HOUSE IS BUILDED BY SOME MAN; BUT HE THAT BUILT ALL THINGS IS GOD."

1. Every house must have a builder.

2. Creation demands that there be a Creator.

3. In the final analysis, God is the builder of all things.

THE BUILDING

The phrase, *"For every house is builded by some man,"* presents the fact, that even though men are the instruments used by God, they are in fact only instruments. In other words, man cannot build what God doesn't want him to build, and can build only what God wants him to build. Man may think he is the architect or the designer of whatever it is that is being built, but let it be surely known that whatever he does, the hand of God in one way or the other is involved.

This doesn't mean at all that God is the designer of evil, etc. But God does allow evil dictators, such as an Adolph Hitler to function for a time, in order to carry out particular purposes. This means that God uses everything, including the Devil. But it definitely doesn't mean that He is a part of the evil committed in any way or capacity, for He definitely isn't!

The world is full of men and women thinking they are doing or building certain things. And they feel very superior in their positions, but it's only because they do not know or recognize the fact that God will always have the final say.

An excellent illustration is found in the actions of Nebuchadnezzar, king of Babylon, then the greatest empire on the face of the Earth. He said:

"Is not this great Babylon, that I have built for the house of the kingdom by the might of my power, and for the honor of my majesty?

"While the word was in the king's mouth, there fell a voice from Heaven, saying, O king Nebuchadnezzar, to thee it is spoken; the kingdom is departed from thee" (Dan. 4:30-31).

It should be obvious here as to whose power is manifested!

GOD, THE CREATOR

The phrase, *"But He that built all things is God,"* verifies the statements we have just made.

In Verse 3, Messiah is seen as the Builder of the house of Israel. In this Verse, Paul guards that fact against any possible misunderstanding on the part of his Readers. Messiah is the Builder of the house of Israel, but not by any independent will or agency of His Own. He as the Son built the house, but it was as one with God Who builds all things, that He built the house of Israel (Wuest).

If this Fourth Verse was heeded by men, the world would be a different place; however, most everything that is done is done without the thought of God. In other words, He is denied existence altogether, or else ignored! And the Truth is, no man, irrespective as to whom he might be, does anything, but that God draws the boundaries.

The idea is, that we seek the face of the Lord and get His Will as it regards all things. But irrespective of that, no man functions and no man works, outside the boundaries drawn by God. Were that not the case, man would have destroyed this world a long time ago!

(5) "AND MOSES VERILY WAS FAITHFUL IN ALL HIS HOUSE, AS A SERVANT, FOR A TESTIMONY OF THOSE THINGS WHICH WERE TO BE SPOKEN AFTER;"

The construction of this Verse is:

1. The Holy Spirit says here that Moses was faithful, and no higher accolade could be given.

2. However, Moses was but a servant, although the highest type of servant.

3. Everything that God gave to Moses as it regards the Law, in one way or the other, pointed to Christ Who was to come.

THE FAITHFULNESS OF MOSES

The phrase, *"And Moses verily was faithful in all his house,"* presents the greatest accolade that could be given to any man, and especially by God. In fact, God has not really called us to be successful, but He has called us to be faithful. That is what the Holy Spirit observes, and that's what we should always remember.

For instance, the Old Testament often uses the word *"faithful"* or *"faithfulness,"* as an attribute of God, to express the total dependability of His Character or Promises. Its first use in describing the Lord is found in Deuteronomy 32:4:

"He is the Rock, His Works are perfect, and all His Ways are just. A faithful God Who does no wrong. Upright and just is He." In fact, many other Passages apply this great Old Testament term to God or to His Words and Works (I Sam. 26:23; Ps. 33:4; 36:5; 40:10; 88:11; 89:1-2, 5, 8, 24, 33, 49; 92:2; 98:3; 100:5; 110:75, 86, 90, 138; 143:1; Isa. 11:5; 25:1; Lam. 3:23; Hos. 2:20).

The Greek word *"pistos"* is translated *"faithful."*

It has both an active and a passive use. In its active sense it means *"trusting, believing."* More often, though, it is passive, meaning *"trustworthy, reliable, faithful."* *"Pistos"* portrays an unshakable loyalty, which is displayed in a number of ways.

We see *"Pistos* (faithful)*"* in the faithful servants of Matthew 24:45 and 25:21-23, who proved trustworthy in carrying out their assignments. Most often, however, the New Testament calls our attention to God and describes Him as faithful. Because God is faithful, He can be trusted completely to carry out His commitments to us in Christ (I Cor. 1:9; 10:13; II Cor. 1:18; I Thess. 5:24; II Thess. 3:3; II Tim. 2:13; Heb. 2:17; 10:23; 11:11; I Pet. 4:19; I Jn. 1:9; Rev. 1:5; 3:14; 19:11).

"Faithful" is also a word used to commend Believers for their quality of steadfast endurance (I Cor. 4:17; Eph. 6:21; Col. 1:7; 4:7).

Paul is particularly aware that God has committed to him, as to every Believer, the responsibility of using his gifts to serve others. *"It is required that those who have been given a trust must prove faithful,"* he writes (I Cor. 4:2).

We know that we can trust God to remain faithful to His commitments. It is wonderful that God entrusts so much to us. Let us use our opportunities to show our loyalty and faithfulness to Him (Richards).

SERVANT

The phrase, *"As a servant,"* proclaims the position of the great Lawgiver as it relates to God.

The Greek word for *"servant"* used here is *"therapon."* There is an ethical character attached to the word. It speaks of service of an affectionate nature, and of a hearty character, performed with care and fidelity. It speaks of service that is of a nobler and a freer character than that of *"doulos* (bond slave)."

The use of the word in our present Passage is indicative of the close relationship which existed between Jehovah and Moses, and of the fact that his services were of an exceptionally high and important character, and valued by Him (Wuest).

In the manner in which the Holy Spirit chose the Greek word *"therapon"* as it related to Moses, portrays to us the fact of the highest accolade that could be given; however, even though at least one of the greatest servants of all, still, he was only a servant, even as all any man could ever be. Paul is aiming toward a particular point, which the next Verse will reveal.

A TESTIMONY

The phrase, *"For a testimony of those things which were to be spoken after,"* pertained to Moses, and the entirety of the Law, with all its ceremonies, rituals, and Sacrifices, pointing to that which was to come, and more particularly, Who was to come, the Lord Jesus Christ. In fact, the entirety of the Old Testament points to Him, and above all that which He would do to redeem humanity, which

speaks of the Cross. That is the *"testimony"* of the Old Testament (Gen. 3:15; 12:3; 22:14; 49:10; Ex. 12:1-13; Lev., Chpts. 1-5; Isa. 7:14; Chpt. 53, etc.).

(6) "BUT CHRIST AS A SON OVER HIS OWN HOUSE; WHOSE HOUSE ARE WE, IF WE HOLD FAST THE CONFIDENCE AND THE REJOICING OF THE HOPE FIRM UNTO THE END."

The exegesis is:

1. Moses was but a servant in the house, while Christ is the Son over His Own house, which means that He built the house, and, thereby, owns the house.

2. The words *"His Own House,"* refer to the fact that God never intended for the house of Israel to be the final product, but had something far larger in mind. That house was earthly, while this house as built by Christ is Heavenly, and includes *"whosoever will,"* i.e., *"both Jews and Gentiles."*

3. God intended for the Jews to come into this greater house, but regrettably, most wouldn't come!

4. The last phrase of this Verse shoots down completely, the unscriptural doctrine of unconditional eternal security. It is staying the course unto the end that guarantees Salvation.

CHRIST THE SON

The phrase, *"But Christ as a Son over His Own House,"* presents a clear distinction that is made between the Old Testament House of God and the New Testament House. The former, as stated, was of this Earth, and composed of Israelites after the flesh. This latter house is composed of *"Holy Brethren"* born of the Spirit. Jesus referred to this House, when He said:

"Upon this Rock I will build My Church; and the gates of Hell shall not prevail against it" (Mat. 16:18).

The title *"Christ"* is used here by Paul, to signify the humanity of our Lord, as well as *"Messiah,"* hence, *"the Anointed"*; however, Paul then uses the title *"Son"* to verify His Deity.

BELIEVERS

The phrase, *"Whose House are we,"* refers to the Church.

God's House, God's Temple, is a dwelling place for God. As He dwelt among Israel of old, so He dwells in the Church. This indwelling by the Spirit sets the Church apart from the world; the Church is a holy body, and those who are a part of it are holy. Paul also said:

"Ye are God's husbandry, ye are God's building . . . Know ye not that ye are the temple of God, and that the Spirit of God dwelleth in you? If any man defile the temple of God, him shall God destroy; for the temple of God is holy, which temple ye are" (I Cor. 3:9, 16-17).

Observe that the term "house" is used here in three senses:

1. The house in which Moses was faithful was the Tabernacle, which symbolized Israel.

2. The Tabernacle was the pattern of things in the Heavens, so the house that God built is the entirety of everything, i.e., "the universe."

3. The house over which Christ is set and to which we belong is that building composed of living stones in which every Believer has a place.

ETERNAL SECURITY?

The phrase, "If we hold fast the confidence and the rejoicing of the hope firm unto the end," proclaims the conditions for Salvation.

The Believer must "hold fast" this grasp of Eternal Life, which can only be done by Faith (Rom. 5:1).

It is Faith that gets us in; it is Faith that keeps us in; however, if Faith is lost, then the person is no longer in (Heb. 6:4-6; 10:26-29).

As well, this must be done to the end (Heb. 6:11).

We as Believers are His House! But to remain in the household of Christ is conditional. The condition is here clearly stated: ". . . If we hold fast the confidence and the rejoicing of the hope firm unto the end."

In this statement, it is obvious that Paul assures the Reader of his position: the Reader has been justified by Faith, is born of the Spirit, and has been placed in the Body of Christ. However, certain conditions must be fulfilled and certain requirements

must be met in order to continue in this unique relationship with God through Christ. The responsibility rests with the Believer, and not with the Lord. We must not forget that the warning here "if we hold fast," is a Divine warning, and must not be taken lightly!

Paul is fearful lest the Readers throw away the precious Gift of Salvation. They had been guilty of heedlessness, neglect, and carelessness, all because of a vacillation regarding Who and What Christ actually is, which Paul addresses in this Epistle.

Two things obviously stand out in this Verse:

1. Being a part of God's household is conditional.

2. The warning implies an actual danger of apostasy from God on the part of the Hebrew Christians, and any Christians for that matter, who forsake the Lord and what He did at the Cross.

The assurance of being in the House of Christ, along with the warning, comes to us today. We are His house "if . . ." (Fjordbak).

THE ONLY ASSURANCE AGAINST APOSTASY IS FAITH IN CHRIST AND HIS FINISHED WORK

First of all, I'm certainly *not* saying that every Christian who doesn't understand the Cross as he or she should, is going to lose their way. But I am saying, that many in this capacity will go into apostasy and be lost, with that number probably being far higher than we realize.

The only Way of Salvation is Faith in Christ and what He did at the Cross on our behalf. The only way of victory is by the same method. It doesn't change at all!

If any other way is enjoined, self-righteousness is the result, which always leads to terrible spiritual declension. In fact, there are untold millions of people who claim Christianity, but who aren't saved, and for this very reason. Either they never were saved to begin with, only becoming religious, or else they lost their way after coming to Christ, which means their Faith is anchored in something other than the Cross. Now that's very important, so let's look at it again.

Without the Christian properly understanding the Cross as he or she should, that Christian of necessity, will have Faith in *"works."* That direction, and a direction sadly and regrettably where most of the Church is traveling, spirals downward spiritually speaking, and fast. There is no Righteousness in that direction, because there is no Righteousness in the Law, at least that can be obtained by Christians (Gal. 3:21). As well, there is no victory over sin in that capacity, because the direction of works which excludes Faith, nullifies the Grace of God (Gal. 2:21), and because such direction stifles the Holy Spirit (Rom. 8:2).

The Believer must understand that everything hinges on the Cross. In other words, Righteousness comes exclusively through what Christ did at the Cross and our Faith in that Finished Work. As well, all that the Holy Spirit does is done totally and completely within the parameters of the Finished Work of Christ. I've said it many times; the Holy Spirit doesn't demand much of us, but He does demand that we exhibit Faith in the Cross, understanding that it is from this Source from which all blessings and help flow. Minus that Faith, there is no Holy Spirit, which means there is no victory!

DECEPTION

Regrettably, when the Cross is mentioned, most Christians dismiss it with a wave of the hand, saying, *"Oh, I know all about that!"* When in reality, they really know next to nothing about that. The knowledge of most Christians as it regards the Cross, is limited to their initial Salvation experience. They know that Jesus died for them, and that He died on the Cross, and that's about the extent of all they know. They know almost nothing about what Romans Chapter 6 teaches, or the Seventh and Eighth Chapters of that Epistle, for that matter. Consequently, they have no knowledge whatsoever as to how to walk in victory.

Let the Reader understand, that his Faith must be built on the following principles:

1. Everything comes through the Cross of Christ Rom. 6:3-14).

2. Understanding that, our Faith must be anchored in the Cross of Christ, with us not allowing it to be moved (Gal. 3:23).

3. With our Faith anchored properly in the Cross, the Holy Spirit will then work mightily upon our behalf, which is the secret of our living victoriously (Rom. 8:1-2, 11, 13).

CAN A BELIEVER LOSE HIS SALVATION?

As long as a person continues to trust Christ, that person cannot lose their Salvation. But if they cease trusting Christ, and begin to trust other things, and for whatever reason, most definitely that person can lose their Salvation.

We have now come to a very serious portion of the Letter to the Hebrews. Paul gives strong admonitions against the sin of apostasy. It is in this Passage of Scripture that we begin to deal with the subjects of the perseverance of the Saints, the security of the Believer, and also the question of the security of the backslider, if one would use that term. It is not really the security of the Believer that actually is in question; it is the security of the person who is in a negative or backslidden state, in other words, on the verge of committing apostasy.

We need not doubt the ability of God to preserve the Believer. God in Christ Jesus has done all that is necessary to bring the Believer to Glory. But it is man who must surrender to God's forgiveness; it is man who must heed the Heavenly Call, and it is man who must *"... deny himself, and take up his Cross daily, and follow ..."* (Lk. 9:23). There is no question as to the Power of God to preserve and keep; rather, the issue is man's faithfulness and perseverance, or the lack of such.

"And the very God of Peace sanctify you wholly; and I pray God your whole spirit and soul and body be preserved blameless unto the Coming of our Lord Jesus Christ" (I Thess. 5:23).

If it wasn't possible to not be preserved blameless, then Paul's statement here makes no sense.

"Jude, the servant of Jesus Christ, and brother of James, to them who are sanctified by God the Father, and preserved in Jesus Christ, and called: Mercy (be) unto you ... (He) is able to keep you from falling, and to present you faultless before the presence of His glory with exceeding joy" (Jude vss. 1-2, 24).

If it wasn't possible for a Believer to fall, which means to quit trusting Christ, then the words that Jude here gives us as well, makes no sense.

"But he that shall endure unto the end, the same shall be saved" (Mat. 24:13).

Jesus said these words, and if one does not endure to the end, which means to hold faithful unto the end, will that person then be saved? No they won't! The Scripture is very clear here about such a situation.

CONDITIONS

There are many references in both the Old and New Testaments that point out the conditional aspects of God's Covenants with man. From the beginning God has not been *". . . willing that any should perish, but that all should come to repentance"* (II Pet. 3:9). But regrettably, most have perished!

God ever deals with man, calling him by the Holy Spirit, and drawing him with love and Grace. God awaits man's response to the Gospel that is preached; what God does for man is conditional upon man's response to God. By way of example, we cite several references from both the Old and New Testaments. Note the conditions:

"And the Lord said unto Cain, why art thou wroth? And why is thy countenance fallen? If thou doest well, shalt thou not be accepted? And if thou doest not well, sin (a Sin-Offering) *lieth at the door* (a lamb is at the door, so go and offer it up, a Sacrifice which God will accept)*"* (Gen. 4:6-7).

"Now therefore, if you will obey My voice indeed, and keep My Covenant, then ye shall be a peculiar treasure unto Me above all people: for all the earth is Mine" (Ex. 19:5).

The conditions to this Covenant should here be obvious!

"Behold, I set before you this day a Blessing and a curse; a Blessing, if you obey the Commandments of the Lord your God, which I command you this day: And a curse, if you will not obey the Commandments of the Lord your God, but turn aside out of the way which I command you this day, to go after other gods, which ye have not known" (Deut. 11:26-28).

"Then said Jesus to those Jews which believed on Him, if ye continue in My Word,

then are ye My Disciples indeed . . . verily, verily, I say unto you, if a man keep My saying, he shall never see death" (Jn. 8:31, 51).

"Behold therefore the goodness and severity of God: on them which fell, severity; but toward thee, goodness, if thou continue in His goodness: otherwise thou also shall be cut off" (Rom. 11:22).

"Moreover, Brethren, I declare unto you the Gospel which we preached unto you, which also ye have received, and wherein ye stand; by which also ye are saved, if ye keep in memory what I preached unto you, unless ye have believed in vain" (I Cor. 15:1-2).

"Wherefore the rather, Brethren, give diligence to make your calling and election sure: for if you do these things, you shall never fall" (II Pet. 1:10).

The Scriptures are very clear about who is not part of the household of God and who will not inherit the Kingdom God has prepared. God is holy and just; His conditions also are holy and just.

Paul said, *"Now the works of the flesh are manifest, which are these; Adultery, fornication, uncleanness, lasciviousness, idolatry, witchcraft, hatred, variance, emulations, wrath, strife, seditions, heresies, envyings, murders, drunkenness, revellings, and such like: of the which I tell you before, as I have also told you in time past, that they which do such things shall not inherit the Kingdom of God"* (Gal. 5:19-21).

All of this means that if a man claims to be of the household of God, and yet practices these acts which Paul has mentioned, then he is a *"servant of sin,"* and has no part in the body of Christ, irrespective that he once was saved. In fact, millions have truly come to Christ, and then have drifted over into these things of which we say, with no intention of getting victory. To be sure, such people have lost their way.

It is certainly true, that untold millions who claim Salvation have really never been saved. In other words, their Faith and trust is in a Church, or their religious acts, and they have never truly been Born-Again. There are far more of this stripe than one realizes.

But yet, there are millions as well, who have truly been saved, but for whatever reason, have turned their backs on Christ, even as these Christian Jews during Paul's day were on the edge of doing. To be sure, if such is done, one loses one's Salvation. Let the following be understood:

A CRISIS OF FAITH

It must be understood that in the writing of Hebrews, Paul is not writing to men and women who are contemplating Christianity, or to those who are mere professors; he is writing to *"Holy Brethren, partakers of the Heavenly Calling"* (Heb. 3:1). That he is not referring to a class of sinners, or as stated, mere professors, but Brethren, indicates a crisis in their Faith. Pressures of life had arisen, with the steadfastness of their Faith being threatened.

An obligation of faithfulness to Christ assumes an understanding of the Blessings promised. The honor of being a part of the House of God and the promised inheritance that awaited them was worthy of their strict attention and absolute faithfulness. They were to *"hold fast."* To hold fast signifies *"resolution and determination."*

With such a strong warning coming from the Holy Spirit, it would be harmful and possibly damnable not to give serious consideration to the matter. There is a distinct possibility in all of this of going back into complete and hopeless apostasy. Paul will say the following in Chapter 6 of Hebrews:

"For it is impossible for those who were once enlightened, and have tasted of the heavenly Gift, and were made partakers of the Holy Spirit, and have tasted the good Word of God, and the powers of the world to come, if they shall fall away, to renew them again unto repentance; seeing they crucify to themselves the Son of God afresh, and put Him to an open shame" (Heb. 6:4-6).

This Passage which we will study in greater detail upon arriving at that particular Chapter, does not mean that one cannot come back to Christ, if they will renew their Faith. It does mean, that if they turn their backs on Christ, which means to repudiate Him and what he did at the Cross, in effect denying His Finished Work, and if they remain in that state of unbelief, there is no way to be saved.

The Jewish Christians of the First Century had given up their Temple, sacrifices,

and Priesthood; they had identified themselves with Christ and had made a profession and confession of Jesus as the Messiah, the Apostle, and High Priest. They had accepted what He had done for them at the Cross, understanding that He paid the price for their sins.

As a result, they had suffered great persecution from the Jewish community and from their former friends and even relatives, as these had endeavored to force them to renounce Jesus Christ and return to the Old Covenant. Under the pressure of persecution, they were admonished to hold fast their boldness and the rejoicing of their hope to the very end. They must not lose their position in Christ and in His house, so to speak!

The warning given them was not to create uncertainty, but to call them out of presumptuous carelessness. The admonitions given were to turn their minds away from the taunts of their relatives and former friends, and as well, from the temptations of the world, and to fix their minds on Christ Jesus Alone. If they heeded, they would be steadfast in holding their confidence and rejoicing to their completion.

AT WHAT POINT DOES CHRIST REJECT THE BELIEVER?

Christ will never reject any Believer, and irrespective of the circumstances. It's not a matter of Christ rejecting anyone, but rather of the individual rejecting Christ. In fact, there's no such thing as a Believer *"falling"* who continues to trust Christ. There is definitely a matter of Christians *"failing,"* but that is a far cry from *"falling."*

A Christian who falls, is one who quits trusting Christ, exactly as Paul mentions in Hebrews 6:4-6.

But what about a Christian, some may ask, who is bound with some type of sin, and cannot quit?

Unfortunately, there are millions of Christians in that very condition! They are bound in some way by the powers of darkness, and despite all of their efforts to do otherwise, they have not been able to break the bondage of this iniquity, whatever it might be. This is because of not having a proper understanding of the Cross, as we've already mentioned.

That person is not lost, for the simple reason that they are continuing to trust Christ. They don't want the particular bondage that binds them. In fact, they are trying to yield their bodily members to Righteousness, but simply have been unable to do so, because they do not understand the Way of the Cross.

That is a far cry, from a person who wants to hold on to particular sins, and at the same time be saved. Now that's at least one of the major problems in the modern Church. Many want Salvation and sin at the same time. Such is not to be, as ought to be obvious!

While there are many Christians who are mired in sin and failure, it's not because they desire to be that way. In fact, and as stated, they have struggled and are struggling with all their might and strength, to have victory. Their problem is, they don't know how to have victory, and what they're doing is not working, which manifests itself in their continued failure. The answer to these Believers is the Cross of Christ, and in fact, it is the only answer.

This means, until these Believers begin to understand the Word of the Cross (I Cor. 1:18), they're not going to have victory. They are saved, and because they are trusting Christ; however, their trust in Christ while proper as it regards Salvation, is improper as it regards their continued walk and victory. In other words, they are frustrating the Grace of God (Gal. 2:20-21). Until they learn the victory of the Cross, they will continue in this failing condition, with the situation even getting worse as time goes on. Their answer is the Cross, which means they must understand that as they received Salvation by simply trusting in what Christ did at the Cross, likewise, they are to walk in victory by the same method — continued Faith in the Finished Work of Christ (Rom. 6:6, 11, 14).

(7) "WHEREFORE AS THE HOLY SPIRIT SAITH, TODAY IF YOU WILL HEAR HIS VOICE,"

The construction of the Verse is:

1. Warning is given here by the Holy Spirit, and should be taken very seriously.

2. The Holy Spirit is warning Christians here and not sinners. That must be clearly

understood. As well, He is warning today, and today it must be heeded.

3. His voice is the Word of God.

THE HOLY SPIRIT SAITH

The phrase, *"Wherefore as the Holy Spirit saith,"* presents the fact, that since Christ has claims on us far greater than those which Moses had, let us hearken to His voice, and dread His displeasure.

Hebrews 1:2 says that God *"in these last days* (has) *spoken unto us by His Son."* Paul is speaking here of the Holy Spirit saying certain things, which is taken from Psalms 95:7-11. This means that when Christ speaks, it is the same as the Holy Spirit speaking and vice versa.

And yet, by Paul using the Name of the Holy Spirit in this instance, proves the most serious of circumstances.

It is the Holy Spirit Who conveys the words of the Father, and the meaning of the great Finished Work of Christ. In other words, it is the Holy Spirit with Whom all of humanity deals one might say. That's the reason that Jesus said, *"And whosoever speaketh a word against the Son of Man, it shall be forgiven him: but whosoever speaketh against the Holy Spirit, it shall not be forgiven him, neither in this world, neither in the world to come"* (Mat. 12:32).

Thankfully, most people do not voice any objection directly against the Holy Spirit; however, to reject anything pertaining to God, is in a sense rejecting the Holy Spirit, simply because everything that God does on this Earth, other than what Jesus did in His Incarnation and at the Cross, is done totally and completely by the Holy Spirit. Even with Christ in His earthly Ministry, the Holy Spirit was attendant upon Him regarding everything.

In the balance of this Chapter, the Holy Spirit is solemnly warning us, that as Believers, we must not take our Salvation for granted, thereby going into unbelief. Such is extremely dangerous, and can conclude in the loss of the soul, irrespective as to what the individual once had in Christ. In fact, how anyone can read Chapters 3 and 4 of this Epistle, and not get this Message, is simply because they don't want to see that which is obvious.

TODAY

The phrase, *"Today if you will hear His Voice,"* takes the Reader of the Book of Hebrews back to Israel in the wilderness. They lost their way because of unbelief. The Holy Spirit through Paul is saying, in essence, that if Believers, whether Jew or Gentile, cease to believe, then they will lose their way, just as Israel of old.

As an aside, we know that the writer of this Psalm was inspired. The Holy Spirit speaks through the Word which He has revealed. The idea is, that this *"Word"* is just as important under the Christian Dispensation as it was under the Jewish. What applies to one, applies to the other! The danger of hardening the heart by neglecting to hear His Voice is as great, and the consequences as fearful and alarming — we should regard the solemn warnings in the Old Testament against sin, and against the danger of apostasy, as addressed by the Holy Spirit to *"us."* In fact, they are as applicable to us as they were to those to whom they were at first addressed; and we need all the influence of such appeals, to keep us from apostasy, as much as they did.

A MOMENT OF OPPORTUNITY

In Hebrews, Chapters 3 and 4, the word *"today"* is used some five times. Each time, it speaks of a moment of opportunity, marked by hearing God's voice speak a word of guidance and direction. And to be sure, the Holy Spirit uses the word *"today"* for a particular reason.

The idea is, this is so important that it must not be put off until tomorrow. All God's Commands relate to the present — to this day — to the passing moment. He gives us no Commands about the future. He does not tell us to repent and turn to Him tomorrow, or ten years hence. The reasons are obvious.

It is our duty to turn from sin, and love Him now. We know not that we shall live to another day. A command, therefore, could not extend to that time, unless it were accompanied with a Revelation that we should live until then — and such a Revelation God does not choose to give. Everyone, therefore,

should feel that whatever Commands God addresses to him are addressed to him now. Whatever guilt is incurred by neglecting those Commands is incurred now.

For the present neglect and disobedience each one is to answer — and each one must give account to God for what he does today.

WILLINGNESS

The Scripture says, *"Whosoever will"* (Rev. 22:17).

Man is a free moral agent, created that way by God. This means that God will not override a person's *"will."* He will deal with the person, speak to the person, even as here, even use pressure as it regards the person, but He will not force the issue, even though He definitely has the power to do so. He always respects the will of the individual.

This means if the person *"wills"* to serve God, to hear the Voice of the Lord, even as spoken here, that all the demons and devils of darkness, cannot stop that person from having what God has promised.

Conversely, if the individual does not will to hear the Words of the Lord, but rather something else, God will allow that person to go in the other direction, even though it will mean total and complete destruction. As well, this completely debunks the unscriptural doctrine of unconditional eternal security. It is the *"will"* of the individual that makes it possible for the Holy Spirit to bring that person to Salvation. And if the person *"wills"* to stop believing, God will honor that, with the individual not being forced to live for God. It is always *"whosoever will . . ."* (Rev. 22:17; Jn. 3:16).

Actually, even as we've already stated in other commentary, the will of an individual is always protected by God, as it regards the acceptance of Christ and His Finished Work. In other words, show me the worst alcoholic in the world who in no way has the willpower to quit drinking, but if that person will yield to Christ, God protects the will in that capacity. In other words, the worst drunk on the face of the Earth, can accept Christ, and there's nothing that Satan can do to stop it. He can force that person's will as it regards the drinking of alcohol or whatever; however, he is not allowed to touch the will of the individual, as it regards the acceptance of Christ. If the individual wants to or *"wills,"* he can accept Christ as his Saviour, and then the Lord can deliver him from this bondage.

When it comes to Christians, it is the same! God protects the *"will"* of the Believer as it regards trusting Christ, and that refers to what Christ did at the Cross. However, the Christian must not think that just because he is a Christian, he now has the power to say *"yes"* or *"no"* to whatever he desires. It doesn't work that way.

If he tries those tactics, he will quickly find Satan overriding his will and causing him tremendous problems. That may come as a shock to many Christians; however, Romans 7:18 completely bears this out.

The will of the Christian is protected by God against Satan, as it refers to the Believer using his *"will"* to trust Christ, as it regards the Cross. But that is the only area of protection guaranteed to the Child of God. The reasons should be obvious:

Trusting in Christ and what He has done for us at the Cross speaks for itself. Trusting in other things, in other words our own strength to be able to choose whatever we so desire, is trust in ourselves, which the Holy Spirit can never honor. Therefore, despite all of our bluster in this capacity, we are left on our own, which guarantees failure. The reason being that the Holy Spirit will not help us in such efforts, and to be sure, His help is totally indispensable in all things. He helps us only as we place our Faith in the Finished Work of Christ, knowing and understanding that this is the Source of all life, all blessings, and all prosperity (Rom. 8:1-2).

HIS VOICE

Does the Reader realize the tremendous significance of *"hearing His Voice"*?

This tells us that not only did Jesus die on the Cross in order to redeem us, but that the Holy Spirit is likewise constantly proclaiming the veracity of this great Finished Work to us, and in essence, the entirety of the world.

Whatever conveys to us the Truth of God, or is adapted to impress that on us, may be regarded as *"His Voice"* speaking to us. He thus speaks to us everyday in some way,

whether by His Written Word, by the preached Gospel, in our own consciences, or even in the events of daily happenings. The greatest thing a Believer can ever do, is to learn to hear that Voice, and to follow the leading of that Voice. This is the key to all life, all victory, all power, all strength, in fact everything that is worth anything.

To think that He stands ready to do this, and in fact is doing it constantly, presents a wonder of wonders. For us not to take full advantage of such is a crime of unprecedented proportions. And to make it worse yet, it's a crime against ourselves.

The Believer must live close enough to the Lord, that these great spiritual things can be heard and understood. Unfortunately, too many Believers are so carnally minded, meaning that their thoughts and ideas are constantly on the things of this world instead of God, that they really cannot hear what the Spirit is saying. That's the tragedy of all tragedies. He lives in our heart; He speaks to us; but yet the noise of unimportant things drowns out His Voice. What a travesty!

To hear His Voice guarantees blessings abundant; to ignore His Voice, which is the warning given here, spells disaster!

(8) "HARDEN NOT YOUR HEARTS, AS IN THE PROVOCATION, IN THE DAY OF TEMPTATION IN THE WILDERNESS:"

The exposition is:

1. This warning is to Christians.

2. Consequently, it is possible for a Christian to become hardened and lose their way.

3. As Israel provoked God in the wilderness, Christians can likewise provoke God by unbelief.

4. *"Temptation"* as it is used here means that Israel put God to the test in the wilderness.

THE HARDENED HEART

The phrase, *"Harden not your hearts,"* proclaims the fact that as Israel hardened their hearts against God in the wilderness, it is likewise possible for modern Christians to do the same. In fact, Paul was warning the Jews who had in fact accepted Christ.

What causes the hardened heart?

Rebellion against God and His Ways is the root cause of the hardened heart. It is one of the most serious concepts associated with sin.

It portrays God as ultimate Sovereign, Who stooped to establish a well-defined relationship with mere human beings.

Israel as an example enjoyed many benefits through her unique Covenant relationship with God. Yet, though God as the superior in the relationship had been absolutely faithful to His Covenant obligations, Israel again and again proved unfaithful. She worshiped other gods, violated the Laws and Statutes that the Lord established, and stubbornly refused to acknowledge any fault.

How does God react to such rebellion?

He offers His people two alternatives, whether Israel of old, or Christians at present — turn to Him for forgiveness and Salvation, or persist in rebellion and be eternally lost.

What protects the Believer presently from rebellious attitudes and actions? According to this Book of Hebrews which we are presently studying, we are to *"fix our eyes on Jesus"* (Heb. 12:2), which means to keep our Faith in the Cross, keep our hearts open to God, and do our very best to obey His Will as revealed in Scripture, which we can only do by the power and help of the Holy Spirit.

Once again, notice how this quotation from the Psalm is introduced, *"As the Holy Spirit saith."* This means that it is not merely the word of David or some other unknown author, but it is the word of the Holy Spirit Himself warning those who profess the Name of the Lord against hardening their hearts and walking in disobedience.

THE PROVOCATION

The phrase, *"As in the provocation,"* refers to what Israel did to embitter the Mind of God against them. It was a course of conduct which was adopted to provoke God to wrath. This is a very serious statement as quoted here by Paul, and should cause the Believer to think twice, because it is to Believers that this warning is given.

Israel provoked God by not believing His Word, thereby trusting in other things. The irony is, while in the wilderness there wasn't much else in which they could trust; therefore, they murmured and complained

constantly, which caused many of their plagues and judgments.

Can modern Christians provoke the Lord?

Most definitely! Even though much could be said on the subject, I think the following will pinpoint the situation.

Even though there are many ways for a Believer to provoke the Lord to anger, all provocation, and without exception, has its roots in the Believer ignoring God's Way, which is the Finished Work of Christ, and instead substituting his own way. It is perfectly understandable as to how God is provoked by the unredeemed who attempt to save themselves by their own machinations, thereby ignoring the Cross; however, He is no less perturbed, and possibly even more so, by Christians who attempt to find victory in ways other than simple Faith in what Christ did at the Cross. In fact, this is the worst rebellion against God, and because among other reasons, it is an insult to Christ Who has paid such a terrible price. And to be sure, the price that was paid was carried out, simply because man in the first place, could not do what was needed. While it's bad enough for the unredeemed to reject the only answer Who is Jesus Christ, it is worse yet for Believers, who ought to know better, to reject the Cross, which is the height of rebellion. Surely one could see how this would provoke the Lord!

In essence, this was Israel's source of rebellion as well! Their deliverance from Egypt had come about by the shed blood of the slain lamb, which was a type of the coming Christ. To be sure, the Law was given some 50 days after deliverance from Egypt, which contained the great Sacrificial system. This was the source of their strength, their leading, their power, and in fact everything they received from the Lord. So in effect, they were rejecting the Cross as well, even though they then did not have light on the subject, as modern Christians.

God has one Way, and that is the Cross! The unredeemed can accept that Way and be saved; the Redeemed can accept that Way and walk in victory; there is no other way. And for man to reject that way, and especially Christians, presents an insult of the highest order. Surely one can see that!

In fact, when one fully sees the Cross as one ought to see the Cross, then all of this becomes crystal clear. The Lord has only one Way, and that is *"Jesus Christ and Him Crucified"* (I Cor. 2:2). Hence Paul said, *"We preach Christ Crucified"* (I Cor. 1:23).

THE DAY OF TEMPTATION

The phrase, *"In the day of temptation in the wilderness,"* points to a particular temptation. The Greek word means in its primary usage, *"to put to the test."* Israel put God to the test by asking, *"Is the Lord among us, or not?"* Instead of trusting God in the midst of adverse circumstances, they demanded that He show His hand in order to demonstrate to them that He was in their midst to help them.

This was very similar to Israel demanding a sign from Christ to prove that He was the Messiah, when in fact, there were signs of every description all around them. Likewise, there were abundant signs regarding Israel in the wilderness.

For instance, the Manna fell every single day, except the Sabbath. This was at least one miracle a day. As well, God over and over again, provided them with water, and even other types of food, in essence, *"setting a table in the wilderness"*; however, unbelief simply cannot see what God is doing, irrespective as to the abundance of evidence.

The sad fact is, the modern Church is very much in the same mode of unbelief. It does not at all see what God is doing, but rather claims things to be of Him, which obviously aren't, and denies that which is actually of Him, claiming the opposite. The Church is in terrible condition, when it doesn't know what is of God and what isn't, and regrettably, this is where the modern Church finds itself. Of course, there are exceptions to this statement, but not many!

The idea is, Israel tempted God in the wilderness, and did so sorely! The Bible says they temped and tried God ten times (Num. 14:22). They did not hearken to His Voice; therefore, instead of entering the Promised Land at once and taking possession of it, they remained in the wilderness for 38 more years, until all that generation of unbelievers had died, and all that generation of the men of war was consumed.

Of those who were already full-grown when they came out of Egypt, only Caleb and Joshua survived to enter Canaan, the place which God had prepared for them.

Their tempting Him was a constant insult flung in His face, and we might quickly add, the face of the all-loving and all-powerful God. They refused to trust His goodness: they despised His goodness. Their hearts were evil and full of unbelief, and they fell away from the Grace of God. They sought to test God in order to approve Him. The Truth is, God did not need proving: it was they who needed the approval of God.

(9) "WHEN YOUR FATHERS TEMPTED ME, PROVED ME, AND SAW MY WORKS FORTY YEARS."

The exegesis is:

1. The tempting of God.

2. The crass unbelief shown in the putting of God to the test.

3. They were basically unchanged even after 40 years of miracles, which means that the generation which went into the Promised Land, was really no better than the ones who had perished in the wilderness.

TEMPTING GOD

The phrase, *"When your fathers tempted Me,"* presents a serious matter indeed!

The idea is, that through unbelief and rebellion, these people were sorely provoking God. The idea continues in the vein that if God had been less than He actually is, in other words human in any capacity, He would have destroyed them totally and completely.

To be sure, God registers passions such as anger, or one might even say a time when His patience runs out. That doesn't mean that He is impatient, for He isn't. To be sure, He is longsuffering; however, men can do so bad in the face of God, that He will take steps to remedy the situation, and that by judgment. It doesn't at all mean that He loses control of His passions, for He definitely doesn't. Consequently, when He does take steps of judgment, it is never in the fashion of the acts carried out by men. Men lose their temper and grow angry, thereby doing terrible things. God never does that, with everything He does always controlled.

This means that whatever He does in the realm of judgment, is done in a measured way, and for an intended result. It is never in the form of the things done by men.

HOW MANY CHRISTIANS ARE PRESENTLY TEMPTING GOD?

Of course only the Lord knows the answer to that question; however, considering the condition of the modern Church, and especially the erroneous direction of many Preachers, and in fact, entire religious Denominations, I would say the situation is grave indeed!

Let not the Believer think that just because this is the Day of Grace, that all judgment has been suspended. In fact, it is the very opposite.

In reality, there is more judgment being poured out upon the world today, than even in Old Testament times. The Holy Spirit through Paul plainly said, *"And the times of this ignorance* (Old Testament Times) *God winked at* (and because they had precious little light)*; but now* (this Day of Grace) *commandeth all men everywhere to repent"* (Acts 17:30).

It is my belief that at the present time, untold numbers of Preachers are staring judgment in the face, even though they little think so. They have desecrated His Word; they have repudiated the Cross of Christ, which Faith in that Finished Work is the only means of Salvation. They have desecrated the Name of the Lord, by claiming things to be of the Spirit, which in reality are of the flesh, and even of demon spirits.

WHAT DOES TEMPT GOD?

Unbelief and rebellion tempt God more than anything else. But let's be a little more specific.

It basically speaks of unbelief in what Jesus did at the Cross, as it regards the answer to man's dilemma, thereby, rebelling against God's Way (Jn. 16:7-11). In fact, the highest form of rebellion, is rebellion against the Cross of Christ, God's supreme answer in the form of the giving of His Son for the sins of man. This works in two ways:

It speaks of the Cross and the Holy Spirit.

About half of the Church world, has attempted to preach the Cross, at least somewhat,

without the Holy Spirit. In other words, they have rejected the Baptism with the Holy Spirit, which is always accompanied by the speaking with other tongues (Acts 2:4). Being impossible to preach the Cross without the Holy Spirit, they are left with nothing, which characterizes that part of the Church world.

Regarding the part of Christendom which claims to believe in the Baptism with the Holy Spirit as accompanied by the speaking with other tongues, which makes up as well about half of Christendom, for the most part (thankfully, with some exceptions), it is attempting to preach the Holy Spirit without the Cross. The results are fanaticism, and attributing to the Divine Spirit that which is actually of the flesh, and to be frank, even of demon spirits. In other words, the Holy Spirit cannot be Scripturally preached and proclaimed, without the foundation of the Cross of Christ.

But dismiss the majority of the Church world which has rejected the Baptism with the Holy Spirit. I do not think I'm too strong in that remark, because almost nothing is being done for God in those circles despite all the religious machinery. Let us address the so-called Spirit-filled variety of the Church.

Having rejected the Baptism with the Holy Spirit, Satan little opposes the non-Pentecostal sector of the Church, simply because they are not going to cause him much trouble anyway. He turns his full brunt of attack toward those who are Spirit-filled. That attack has taken many directions; however, its greatest direction has been the forsaking of the Cross of Christ.

The leadership of every major Pentecostal Denomination in the United States and Canada, at least of which I am aware, has opted totally and completely for humanistic psychology as the answer to man's dilemma. In doing so, they have completely repudiated the Cross, which alone holds that answer. Of course, they would deny that they have repudiated the Cross, but it's impossible, and I mean literally impossible, to accept both ways, especially considering that these two ways are diametrically opposed to each other.

One stems from the wicked hearts of men, which constitutes wisdom which is *"earthly, sensual and Devilish"* (James 3:15), while the other comes directly from God.

It is an abomination when the editors of the Pentecostal Evangel, the weekly voice of the Assemblies of God, the largest Pentecostal Denomination in the world, recommend in that Magazine, 12-step programs as the answer for mankind. It is an abomination in the eyes of God, when the Leadership of the Church of God (Cleveland, Tenn.), the second largest Pentecostal Denomination in the world, is headed up by a practicing Psychologist (at this time, 2000). I'll say it again:

It is impossible to promote both systems, the Cross and psychology, at the same time. One cannot serve God and mammon.

The Holy Spirit through Paul addressed this subject by saying, *"And what agreement hath the temple of God with idols? For ye are the temple of the Living God; as God hath said, I will dwell in them, and walk in them; and I will be their God, and they shall be My people* (and to be sure, humanistic psychology is an idol)."

"Wherefore come out from among them, and be ye separate, saith the Lord, and touch not the unclean thing; and I will receive you" (II Cor. 6:16-17).

To be associated with that which espouses gross error, even though one may not agree with that direction, makes one a part of the sin being committed. In other words, it's not possible for one to absolve oneself of culpability and responsibility, if one is associated in any manner with such erroneous direction.

In the Charismatic world, the situation if possible, is even worse. Not only do they espouse, at least for the most part, the world of humanistic psychology, but many of them openly repudiate the Cross, actually referring to it as *"past miseries."* Or they say that the Cross was the greatest defeat known in human history.

Such terminology shows a gross ignorance of the Word of God, which would be laughable were it not for the fact, that hundreds of thousands, if not millions of so-called Christians, are following these pied pipers, and I might quickly add, following them to spiritual oblivion.

In these circles, we have displays of all types of manifestations, purporting to be of

NOTES

the Spirit, when in reality, it is of the flesh, or even of demon spirits. That means that a great segment of the Church is following demon spirits, thinking it's the Holy Spirit. What a travesty! What a horror!

Now you know why Jimmy Swaggart is not too very much liked or appreciated in the Church world.

WHAT DID JESUS SAY?

Before I address myself to that question, let's see what the modern Church is saying:

It is claiming that these are the greatest days ever known by the Church. It is bigger than ever and richer than ever. More people are attending Churches today than ever before, with more money coming into the till than ever before.

However, the Truth is, a 500 pound man might be big, but he's definitely not healthy. In fact, he is sick, and so sick, that he could die at any moment.

The Truth is, despite the influx of human bodies and money, and to be sure, money is the driving force of this religious engine, there are fewer people being saved today than in the last several hundreds of years. There are almost no Believers being Baptized with the Holy Spirit anywhere. Donnie is probably seeing more people filled with the Holy Spirit presently, than anyone on Earth, simply because almost no emphasis is placed on this all-important subject at this time. Despite all the hype, almost no one is being truly healed. As well, victorious living in Christian lives is almost a thing of the past. In other words, most of professing Christendom is walking in spiritual failure and defeat.

I realize those are not words that people enjoy reading; however, they are the Truth, whether we like them or not.

The problem is, the modern Church anymore, little knows what is of God and what isn't of God. It worships idols thinking it's worshiping the Lord. It accepts manifestations which obviously are of the Devil, thinking they are of the Holy Spirit. God help us!

Jesus said, *"The Kingdom of Heaven is like unto leaven, which a woman took, and hid in three measures of meal, till the whole was leavened"* (Mat. 13:33).

Jesus is speaking of the Church in the last days.

"Leaven" is figurative of sin (I Cor. 5:6-8; Gal. 5:9); false doctrines (Mat. 16:6-12; Mk. 8:15-21); and hypocrisy (Lk. 12:1).

The woman as used here is figurative of wickedness, fallacy, uncleanness, and unfaithfulness (Lam. 1:17); harlotry (Ezek. 16:15, 22, 26, 28-59; 23:1-49; 36:17; Hos. 1:2; 2:2-17; 3:1; Rev., Chpt. 17); wickedness (Zech. 5:5-11; Rev. 17:5); and false religion (Rev., Chpt. 17).

When used in a good sense women represent Israel (Gen. 37:9-10 with Rev. Chpt. 12; Ezek. Chpt. 16); the two Covenants (Gal. 4:21-31); and Righteousness and Purity (II Cor. 11:2; Rev. 19:7-8).

The *"meal"* symbolizes the Word of God (Mat. 4:4; Jn. 6:47-63).

This short parable as given by Christ, illustrates how the Kingdom of Heaven, representing the Church in this age, would become corrupted by false doctrines and unscriptural programs, until the whole is corrupted, which is presently well on its way (Lk. 18:8; I Tim. 4:1-8; II Tim. 3:5; 4:3-4; II Pet. 3:3-4).

All false teachings, religious programs, and professed Christian lives, seek to hide behind the Word of God. In other words, the *"Word"* is freely used in all of this error, but to be sure, it is a corrupted word, which means the Word of God is pulled out of context, and to make it simpler to understand, it is the Word which is not based upon the Cross of Christ. If one doesn't properly understand the Cross of Christ, then one doesn't properly understand the Word. John said as much in the First Chapter of his Gospel (Jn. 1:1, 14, 29).

So, if a repudiation of the Cross is the greatest tempting of God, and it definitely is, then where does that leave the modern Church?

THE GREATEST JUDGMENT OF ALL!

In fact, the greatest judgment of all is about to come upon the modern Church.

In a very short period of time, the Rapture is about to take place (I Thess. 4:13-18). With the True Church taken away, the horror of the Great Tribulation is going to burst upon the apostate Church. To be sure,

NOTES

at first it will seem as if it is the greatest moment in history.

All the voices that cried out against the apostasy of this age will now be gone. The Antichrist will be acclaimed by Israel, at least at the beginning, as their Messiah. The false Church will fall in line, proclaiming the same identical thing; however, after a short period of time, the Antichrist will show his true colors, actually turning on Israel, which will be in the midst of the Great Tribulation Period. Then the Judgment of God is going to be poured out upon this world as never before, which is characterized in Revelation, Chapters 6 through 19.

In fact, and as previously stated, the Church has already entered into the last great apostasy. The Revelation of the Cross, which the Lord has given unto me, is I believe, a presentation of the dividing line between the True Church and the apostate Church. It is the Message of the Cross.

To be sure, that has always been the dividing line; however, I believe it is going to be more pronounced now than ever. If the Message of the Cross is rejected, that individual doing the rejecting will go into apostasy. There is no other way. If it is accepted, it will mean life, as it always has meant life.

However, it's not going to be quite as cut-and-dried as I have just stated. To accept this Message of the Cross, one is going to have to go against most of institutionalized religion, as well as about every other brand. There's not going to be any such thing as *"closet Christians,"* in other words, those who secretly believe in the Cross. The Believer is going to have to come out and boldly take his or her stand.

To take such a stand, is going to mean the loss of friends, even of family, and in reality, of most all things; however, to do so, will gain Christ, which is everything. But due to the fact of having to take such a stand, many will fall by the wayside.

Please read these words very carefully, for that which you are reading, is far more than instruction, but actually a prophetic Word from the Lord.

There will be no doubt as to the Message of the Cross, and there will be no doubt as to its adherents.

PROVED ME

The short phrase, *"Proved Me,"* refers to the fact, that instead of trusting God in the midst of adverse circumstances, Israel demanded that God show His hand and demonstrate to them that He was in their midst. Actually, they insulted Him over and over, especially considering, and as stated, that He was performing miracles for them even on a daily basis. Again, I wish to emphasize the fact, that unbelief cannot see God, irrespective as to what He is doing. And what do we mean by unbelief?

The Greek words translated *"tempted"* and *"proved,"* are *"peirazomai"* and *"dokimazo"* respectively. They are an interesting contrast. *"Peirazomai"* means *"to put to the test to see what good or evil may be in a person."* *"Dokimazo"* means *"to put to the test for the purpose of approving the person if he meets the test."*

The Greek here is *"put Me to the test to see what evil or good there is in Me when they put Me to the test for the purpose of approving Me should I meet the test."* What crass unbelief is shown in such a procedure. What an insult it flings into the face of an all-loving, all-powerful God.

Those to whom Paul was writing, in this instance, Christian Jews, are warned not to take that attitude toward God, and the same warning goes to us presently.

While it is true that they were being bitterly persecuted because of their professed Faith in the Lord Jesus Christ, the idea is, they should trust God in the midst of it all and not harden their hearts against Him (Wuest).

MODERN TEACHING

The so-called modern Faith Ministry has probably done more presently to hurt the Work of God, than anything else. For one thing, it repudiates the Cross, or else greatly reduces its emphasis. Also, it claims that if one has enough Faith, that one can forego all difficulties, problems, hindrances, etc. Consequently, one's consecration, or faith level, is judged by the model of car they drive, the price of their clothing, and lack of problems. I would hope that one could see that such direction has absolutely no similarity

to the Biblical account of the Child of God as given in the Word of God.

However, hundreds of thousands, if not millions of people follow this perfidious teaching, simply because they think it's an easy way to *"get rich,"* etc. Irrespective of these claims, and all the attempts to confess away all problems, adverse circumstances always come sooner or later to the Child of God. In fact, the Lord orchestrates all such things, in order to prove and to test our Faith.

To be sure, the Lord knows all things. He knows the past, the present, and the future, which means that He already knows how we will act; however, these *"tests of Faith"* are given and allowed, for our own benefit. How can we learn to trust God, if there are never any problems to overcome?

But when these problems come, as they always do, the followers of this perfidious teaching, having been told that such will not come if they have the proper confession, etc., many times, get discouraged and simply quit. They are called *"Faith drop-outs."*

No! They are not drop-outs, they are casualties of teaching that is awfully wrong!

In effect, the modern Faith teaching is very similar to what Israel did in the wilderness, as it regards *"proving God."* To be certain, they were not proving Him in a positive way, but rather in a negative way. They were like petulant children who were stamping their feet, demanding that God do certain things, etc. As stated, they were not at all unlike the modern variety.

THE WORKS OF GOD

The phrase, *"And saw My works forty years,"* refers to the fact that Israel didn't believe God, and we're speaking of the wilderness experience, even though God was doing great and mighty things for them, on a constant basis. This means, that for 40 years they tempted God, proved Him, and provoked Him. Forty years was a long period of time to walk with the Lord, and to see God's miraculous hand upon them; yet they remained unchanged.

It is all of an 11-day journey from Horeb by way of Mount Seir to Kadesh-barnea. Yet we read that 40 years later on the first day of the month, Moses spoke God's commands to the Children of Israel. This means, that it took them 40 years to make an 11-day journey! Why?

Because of their presumptuous wickedness. They had tried the Lord, proved Him, but had forgotten His goodness and His great power. In other words, they constantly looked at the circumstances instead of looking at God.

All of this was an insult flung in the face of the all-loving and all-powerful God to tempt and to prove Him. The words they used, as stated, denote a putting to the test in order to see if the God Who brought them out of bondage had evil or good intentions for them. This means that they refused to trust His goodness, over and over again, reading evil into that which He did.

They despised His goodness. Their hearts were evil and full of unbelief, and they fell away from the Grace of God. They sought to test God in order to approve Him. God did not need proving: it was they who needed the approval of God.

The short phrase, *"And saw My works,"* proclaims the fact, that there was no excuse for their behavior. They had seen the wonders at the Red Sea, the descent on Mount Sinai, the supply of Manna, etc.; and yet, even while seeing those works, they rebelled.

And let us remember, Paul is not addressing this to unbelievers, but rather those who pretend to follow Christ, i.e., *"Christians."* As well, please understand, that we must allow these admonitions to be warnings to us. If Israel could lose her way, even as the entirety of a generation did in the wilderness, despite the fact that God was performing for them the mightiest miracles the world has ever known, where does that leave us presently?

Millions of Christians at this very moment, and I think I exaggerate not, are saying in their hearts, that if they could see God do the great things now that He did in those days, they would certainly believe Him. In other words, whether realized or not, they are finding fault with God presently.

GOD, AND HIS DEALINGS WITH HIS CHILDREN

First of all, God *is* doing great and mighty things presently, even greater now than He did then. Unbelief sees what it wants to

see, and Faith sees what it wants to see. As Believers, we must ever remember the following:

Our relationship with the Lord must never be based on Him giving us an abundance of material things, or withholding those things. Neither must it be based upon physical situations. In other words, whether we are physically sick, or physically well.

While all of these things are very important, and while God definitely does supply all of our needs according to His riches in Glory, and while He is definitely the Healer, those things must never be the main emphasis.

The main emphasis must always be the heart being right with God. If I'm in the center of God's Will, it doesn't really matter what else happens. Look at this situation:

Paul and Silas were definitely in the direct center of God's Will, when they went to Philippi to establish a Church. For their trouble, thank you, they were rewarded with a beating that almost killed them, being thrown into prison, with their hands and feet made fast in the stocks, and with the pain being excruciating to say the least! (Acts, Chpt. 16).

I am persuaded that if most Christians presently were put to such a test, that many, if not most, would find themselves cursing God. As stated, much of this spirit can be laid at the feet of the modern Faith Ministry, which in reality is no Faith at all!

So, at this stage, we must ask the Reader, *"What do you see?"* Do you see circumstances, difficulties, problems, hindrances, etc.? Or do you ignore these things, and instead, see the Lord in His great power to save, and to keep in the midst of adverse temptations, with Him doing great and mighty things? Faith must always be tested, and great Faith must be tested greatly. Once again, it is not that He might know, for He already knows, but that we might know. And to be sure, we will find that our Faith is never quite as strong as we think it is, hence the necessity of it being tested.

(10) "WHEREFORE I WAS GRIEVED WITH THAT GENERATION, AND SAID, THEY DO ALWAY ERR IN THEIR HEART; AND THEY HAVE NOT KNOWN MY WAYS."

The construction of this Scripture is:

1. God was offended at the actions of Israel.

2. Israel was led astray with respect to the heart, the seat of one's personal character and of one's moral and Spiritual Life.

3. They knew God's acts, but not His ways, therefore, registered unbelief, despite the acts.

4. This shows us that the *"acts of God,"* regarding miracles, etc., are not nearly as important as the *"Ways of God."*

GRIEVED

The phrase, *"Wherefore I was grieved with that generation,"* refers to God being offended with that particular generation in the wilderness, which because of their unbelief, died in the wilderness.

"Grieved" in the Greek is *"parosochthizo,"* and means, *"to be angry or displeased with."* It also means, *"to loathe, be disgusted, to spew out, to exclude, reject, abhor, repudiate."* Consequently one can see how strong this thing actually was. God, as stated, was offended at the actions of Israel.

For 40 years, God patiently pleaded with Israel, and with miracles, signs, and wonders. He again, and also with miracles, pleaded for a like period from the beginning of the Ministry of Christ, which was in about A.D. 30 until the time of the Judgment in A.D. 70, when their nation was destroyed. During both periods the nation hardened its heart, and the rejecters all perished.

THIS GENERATION

This quotation as given by Paul, is derived from Psalms 97:10. The Hebrew actually says *"this generation."*

Jesus used the same wording concerning the rejection of His Ministry, by saying, *"This generation shall not pass, till all these things be fulfilled"* (Mat. 24:34). As stated, both generations, the generation that came out of Egypt, and the generation during the time of Christ, perished. As well, the generation of the End-times, of which Jesus spoke, will likewise perish.

We must not miss the reference here to the anger of God. The Bible is clear that God is not impassive or indifferent in the face of human sin. He is a *"consuming fire,"* because His Holiness demands such (Heb. 12:29),

and His inevitable reaction to sin is wrath (Rom. 1:18).

Bringing the Reader up to the present time, God looks down from Heaven today and is constantly grieved by the sins of this world, and often grieved by the failure of the Church to obey His Word and the Great Commission.

"Grieved" also signifies *"to be burdened or heavy laden with."* That generation in the wilderness had become a burden to God. Consequently, the Old Testament tells us that God excluded them from the inheritance, even though He endured them for forty years, until their children were old enough to enter the Promised Land.

WALKING BY SIGHT AND NOT BY FAITH

How often, like Israel, because of circumstances, we murmur and complain. We walk by sight and not by Faith, and it manifests within us an evil heart of unbelief.

Had Israel trusted in God and turned to Him, spreading their need before Him, He would have supplied it abundantly. Difficulties, trials, and tests come upon all of us and they reveal the state of our hearts, and they are meant to do just that.

When everything is smooth sailing, it is easy to praise the Lord. But what really proves our metal so to speak, is our reaction during times of difficulties. What do we then do? How do we react?

As someone has well said, it's not so much our actions that show what we are, but rather our *"reactions,"* which speak of our response to adverse circumstances.

Do we get angry and blame God? Or others? The following should always be noted:

1. God is in control of all things. This means, that every single thing that comes our way, has been allowed by God, Who is monitoring the situation very closely. In other words, there are no accidents with God.

2. Whatever adversity the Lord allows, He means it for our good, and never for our harm. We must understand that, thereby, never blaming God.

3. We should allow the test to bring us closer to God, leaning on Him ever more, learning to trust Him, which is the reason for the test.

As well, we must understand that disobedience causes God to allow many more adverse circumstances to come upon us; nevertheless, irrespective as to how difficult those circumstances might be, still, it is all for our good, and we must ever understand it in that capacity. And yet at the same time, perfect obedience will not forestall all difficulties. Even as we've already stated, Paul and Silas certainly were perfectly obedient, but yet, adverse circumstances, and tremendously adverse at that, were allowed to come upon them.

Irrespective, the Lord always has in mind, our betterment, and is ever working toward that goal. We must understand that, thereby never blaming Him, but always knowing that everything will ultimately work out to our good, providing we love the Lord, and are the called according to His purpose (Rom. 8:28).

When the storm breaks, as sooner or later it will, it is not so much that we fail under it, as it is that our habitual lack of leaning upon God, and daily depending upon Him, are made evident. Circumstances do not change us: they expose us.

ERRING IN THE HEART

The phrase, *They do always err in their heart,* proclaims the seat of obedience or disobedience — in this case, disobedience.

The *"heart"* does not refer here to the physical organ, but rather the seat of one's personal character and moral life. The heart of man is his very person: his spiritual core. The conscious awareness each of us has that makes us persons and the spiritual dimension of responsiveness or unresponsiveness to God are both expressed by the word *"heart."* This term occurs in 158 New Testament Passages.

"Heart" denotes the *"inner man,"* the essence of personality; being the seat and center of all life. The spiritual term of nearest equivalence to the old English word *"heart,"* possibly is that of *"ego,"* which represents the *"I, self, person."* It is that term which is formalized, as a logical necessity, to denote that *"center"* to which all of a person's spiritual activities and characteristics refer.

The *"heart of man"* represents, then, that innermost center which is of ultimate importance; that which is basic, central, substantive, and of profound essence.

There is a consistency of treatment with all Biblical uses of *"heart."* The term invariably refers to that which is central. Even when the word is used as a figure of speech, expressive of things and situations apart from mankind, it denotes central location, center, or being in the midst. *"Your borders are in the heart of the seas"* (Ezek. 27:4); *"in the heart of the sea"* (Ps. 46:2); *"in the heart of the earth"* (Mat. 12:40).

The word is employed to express certain important dimensions of man and God's concern and dealings with man. It is used, then, to denote:

1. The *"inner man,"* the *"hidden person of the heart"* (I Pet. 3:4), the central essence of man, with which God is primarily concerned. It is that portion or essence of man on which God the Lord looks, searches, and tries (I Sam. 16:7; Prov. 10:8; Jer. 11:20; 17:10; 20:12). It is the center and source of belief and Faith (Lk. 24:25; Rom. 10:10).

2. That central agency and facility within man whereby he imagines, intends, purposes, thinks, and understands (Ezek. 13:2). In fact, the *"heart"* is where the will is exercised (Eph. 6:6). It is there where ponderings are made (Lk. 2:19), and purposes are formed (Prov. 20:5; Acts 11:23).

Imaginations originate there, along with intents and purposes (Prov. 6:18; Eccl. 10:2; Heb. 4:12).

3. Particular qualities of a man's character originate there. As such a man may be seen to be or possess a *"heart"* that is:

A. Double (I Chron. 12:33).

B. Honest and good (Lk. 8:15).

C. Largeness of heart (I Ki. 4:29).

D. Perfect (mature) (I Ki. 8:61; 11:4; II Chron. 16:9; 25:2; Ps. 101:2).

E. Pure, pureness (Ps. 24:4; Prov. 22:11; Mat. 5:8; I Tim. 1:5; II Tim. 2:22; I Pet. 2:22).

F. True (Heb. 10:22).

G. Understanding (Job 28:36).

H. Wise (Job 9:4).

4. That which is descriptive of a man's attitude as depicted in his actions and behavior:

A. Despiteful, despising (II Sam. 6:16; Ezek. 25:15).

B. Dull (Acts 28:27).

C. False (Hos. 10:2).

D. Gross (Ps. 119:70).

E. Hard (Mk. 3:5; 16:14; Rom. 2:5).

F. Meek and lowly (Jesus, as self-described, Mat. 11:29-30).

G. Searching (Judg. 5:15-16).

H. Stony (Ezek. 11:19; 36:26).

I. Subtle (Prov. 7:10).

J. Whorish (Ezek. 6:9).

K. Willing (Ex. 35:5).

L. Wise (Prov. 10:8; 11:29).

5. That center, essence, and inner substance of man which needs to be reconciled to God, redeemed: being righted with God means that it now may be reconciled to others. As such, the *"heart"* is described as being:

A. Deceitful and desperately wicked (Prov. 12:20; Isa. 44:20; Jer. 17:9).

B. Froward and proud (Ps. 101:4-5).

C. In need of a new creation and cleansing by God (Ps. 51:10).

D. In need of a new heart so as to know the Lord (Jer. 24:7).

E. Set to do evil (Eccl. 8:11; 9:3).

F. Stony, needing removal and a new heart given in its stead (Ezek. 11:19; 18:31; 36:26).

G. Stubborn and rebellious (Jer. 5:23).

H. Turned by the Lord to others, otherwise to be smitten with a curse (Mal. 4:6).

I. Wicked (Ps. 58:2).

6. The core and seat of emotions; the center of emotional reaction, feeling, and sensitivity. As such, the *"heart"* may experience or know what it is to be:

A. Astonished (Deut. 28:28).

B. Broken (Ps. 34:18; 69:20; 147:3; Isa. 61:1).

C. Bitter (Ezek. 27:31).

D. Discouraged (Num. 32:7-9).

E. Failing (I Sam. 17:32).

F. Fearful (Isa. 21:4; 35:4).

G. Glad (Deut. 28:47; Ps. 104:15; Prov. 24:17; 27:11).

H. Greedy (I Sam. 25:31; Ps. 73:21).

I. Heavy (Prov. 12:25; 25:20; 31:6; Mat. 26:37).

J. Joyful (Job 29:13; Eccl. 2:10).

K. Merry (I Sam. 25:36; I Ki. 21:7; Prov. 15:13, 15; 17:22).

THE WAYS OF GOD

The phrase, *"And they have not known My Ways,"* pertains to the fact that there had

NOTES

been a neglect of Jehovah on their part. The knowledge they lacked was experiential knowledge which could only be acquired through experience with the Ways and Character of God, which pertained to relationship with Him. In other words, relationship is never automatic, but comes about as one works at the situation.

In other words, it is impossible for a husband and wife to have a proper relationship, unless they work at it. It is the same with Believers as it regards the Lord.

Regarding these Israelites, they showed constancy of error, *"always going astray."* Their inner state was not right with God. They did not know the Ways of God, therefore, they could not walk in them.

However, it must be fully understood that their ignorance was culpable, not innocent. They were not blamed simply for not knowing, but for not knowing things they ought to have known and acted on. They did not take the trouble to learn. This means, that to neglect opportunity is a serious thing.

Even though the Lord dealt with them constantly, showing them what He wanted and didn't want, still, the warnings and discipline were fruitless. They gained no knowledge of His Ways, because they had no interest in His Ways.

It is a serious mistake to think that God will go on offering His Grace despite all our rejections. We are mistaken if we believe that we can yield to God just when we please. There can come a day when it will be too late.

To err in the heart is to err in the mind, the will, and the real personality of the person. In all, they did not know, learn, or experience the Ways of God in such a way as to change them inwardly.

THE CROSS OF CHRIST

Even though the Israelites in the wilderness would have had no knowledge of the Cross, at least as we understand such, still, they knew that their deliverance from Egypt was by the principle of the slain lamb (Ex., Chpt. 12). As well, some 50 days after their leaving Egypt, they were given the Law on Mount Sinai. The very principle of the Law consisted of the Sacrificial system, which was its very core. So, according to that, they should have known that their deliverance had been by virtue of the slain lamb, and would continue to be by virtue of the slain lamb. So in essence, they knew and understood the Cross, at least as far as it was possible then for it to be understood.

Consequently, the entire principle of their obedience or disobedience, rested upon their knowledge of the Sacrifices, and acting upon that principle by Faith. However, they didn't understand this principle, simply because they had no interest in understanding it. Therefore, they went to their doom!

It is the same presently. The modern Christian has little relationship with Christ, simply because he little understands the meaning of the Cross. Furthermore, in most cases it is not ignorance because of lack of knowledge, but rather, lack of concern. In other words, the Message of the Cross, which is the very core of Christianity, holds no interest for most Christians; therefore, most Christians have little relationship with the Lord! To turn it around to a positive approach the following must be noted:

First of all, the Believer must understand his place and position in Christ, which can only be understood and acted upon, by a proper understanding of the Cross. If that understanding is properly obtained, then everything else can be built upon that proper foundation. Otherwise, no proper results can be brought about.

The *"Ways of the Lord,"* are constituted in His Word. His Word is constituted in the Cross, for that's the story of the Word. So, to understand God's Ways, one must understand the Cross.

As well, when the Cross is properly understood, one will find the entirety of the Bible becoming easier to understand, and because everything is built on that structure (Jn. 1:1, 14, 29).

(11) "SO I SWARE IN MY WRATH, THEY SHALL NOT ENTER INTO MY REST."

The exegesis is:

1. God threatens with an oath.

2. He ultimately grew angry at their rebellion. Let the Reader understand, that under Grace, His wrath is even more pronounced.

NOTES

3. The word *"rest"* here refers to Canaan, but in totality, it refers to Salvation.

THE OATH

The phrase, *"So I swear in My wrath,"* is figurative, and denotes a strong affirmation, or a settled and determined purpose. An oath with us implies the strongest affirmation, or the expression of the most settled and determined purpose of mind.

The meaning here is, that so perverse and obstinate had Israel become, that God solemnly resolved that they should never enter into the land of Canaan. And so they didn't!

Let not the Reader think, that such situations happened only in Old Testament Times, and have no bearing on the present. To be sure, the Holy Spirit through Paul is bringing it over into New Testament Times, which includes the present, and because this is a principle which is apropos for all time. Believers can make God angry, by denying His Ways, which is the Cross of Christ, and then incur His wrath. I realize, that such action is denied behind most modern pulpits; however, that in no way negates the actual facts of what is presently taking place.

The Reader must understand, that sin must incur the Wrath of God. There is no alternative, considering the destructive power of this monster. And if the Reader doesn't understand the significance of what has just been said, then the Reader needs to change Churches. Sin is so awful in fact, that even though God could speak worlds, and in fact, the entirety of creation into existence, He for all His power, could not speak Redemption into existence. So, the Wrath of God must always be aroused by sin, and poured out upon sin. In fact, the Scripture plainly says:

"For the Wrath of God is revealed from Heaven against all ungodliness and unrighteousness of men, who hold the Truth in unrighteousness" (Rom. 1:18).

The only thing that assuages that Wrath, is the Sacrifice of Christ, which is the only solution for sin. And when we say that the Sacrifice of Christ is the only solution for sin, we mean that it is the only solution. So, if men reject that Solution, which incidentally has been brought about at such great price, and a price which God Himself paid, then it should be understandable as to why such wrath is aroused.

Everything boils down to sin which is rebellion against God, and the Solution which is the Sacrifice of Christ. For those who accept the Sacrifice of Christ, God's anger is appeased; otherwise, it is not appeased at all, but rather grows more intense!

REST

The phrase, *"They shall not enter into My rest,"* refers here to a particular *"rest,"* which pertained to the land of Canaan, but which was undoubtedly regarded as emblematic of the *"rest"* which is afforded by Salvation. Into that rest God solemnly said they should never enter. All the means of reclaiming them had failed. God had warned and entreated them; He had caused His Mercies to pass before them, and had even visited them with judgments, all in vain; and He now declares, that because of all their rebellion, they should be excluded from the Promised Land.

In reading all of this, we are to understand it in a manner consistent with the Character of God, and we are not to suppose that He is affected with the same emotions which agitate the bosoms of men. As previously stated, the anger of God is not like the anger of men. In fact, even though the same words may be used, nothing about God is like men.

Everything He does is noble, righteous, holy, and true. Nothing about man is noble, holy, righteous, and true! Most every emotion we have as human beings has been perverted by the Fall, which means that nothing quite works right.

THE MEANING OF *"REST"* AS A WORD

Many different Hebrew words express various aspects of what the Old Testament suggests by *"rest."* Three different terms are commonly translated *"rest"* and express most of these meanings. They are *"sabat," "nuah,"* and *"saqat."*

The word *"sabat"* implies ceasing or coming to an end of activity. Thus, Moses records that God rested when His work of creation was completed (Gen. 2:2-3). The impression of peaceful repose is present only in the 13 instances where this verb is used in a Sabbath context.

"Nuah" suggests being settled down, an absence of movement. It implies security and a sense of inner ease. In the Old Testament, *"nuah"* speaks of a spiritual release from pressures and tensions (as in Isa. 28:12). It is closely associated with the victorious conclusion of conflicts (Josh. 21:44; II Chron. 15:15). The victors enjoy peace as the external threat is removed.

It is very clear from the Old Testament uses of this word that God Alone is able to provide such rest (Ex. 33:14; Deut. 12:10; Josh. 22:4).

TRANQUILITY

The Hebrew word *"saqat"* has the idea of one finding tranquility. It signifies the absence of external pressures and inner anxiety. This kind of rest comes only through a relationship with the Lord. As Isaiah says, *"The wicked are like the tossing sea, which cannot rest . . . thus, there is no peace . . . for the wicked"* (Isa. 57:20-21).

This Hebrew word too is used of the aftermath of victory and of periods of time in which God's people were faithful to Him (Judg. 3:11; 5:31; 8:28). The Prophets look forward to a promised time of rest, when God would deliver His people from bondage. Despite the agony of preceding judgments, God declared, *"I will surely save you out of a distant place, your descendants from the land of their exile. Jacob will again have peace* (saqat) *and security, and no one will make him afraid"* (Jer. 30:10).

In the Old Testament, then, the words that communicate the idea of *"rest"* imply a wide range of benefits. There is security, an absence of danger and anxiety. There is an ease and confidence that has both an outer and inner basis, each of which can be traced directly to one's relationship with the Lord. Only through a relationship with the Lord can we experience the Blessing of the rest that God has for those who trust Him.

THE SABBATH

The seventh day of the week, which divided the Hebrew month into four equal parts, was called the Sabbath. However, it is the spiritual significance of the Sabbath that is primarily important in the Old Testament:

1. The Sabbath was a testimony to God the Creator, Who rested after His six days of shaping our universe (Gen. 2:2-3), which in a sense, foreshadowed the coming spiritual rest, found only in Christ.

The statement about the Sabbath in the Ten Commandments goes like this: *"Remember the Sabbath day by keeping it holy. Six days you shall labor and do all your work, but the seventh day is a Sabbath to the Lord your God. On it you shall not do any work, neither you, nor your son or daughter, nor your manservant or maidservant, nor your animals, nor the alien within your gates. For in six days the Lord made the Heavens and the Earth, the sea, and all that is in them, but He rested on the seventh day. Therefore the Lord blessed the Sabbath day and made it holy"* (Ex. 20:8-11).

2. The Sabbath became a symbol of Israel's Covenant relationship with the Lord. Exodus 31:12-17 identifies it as a lasting sign, celebrating the mutual commitment expressed in the Mosaic Covenant.

Israel's observance of the Sabbath as a day of rest was a clear indication of her spiritual condition, for it showed obedience to the Divine Law (Neh. 13:15-22; Jer. 17:19-27).

This relationship of the Old Testament Sabbath to the Mosaic Law is important, for when Jesus instituted the New Covenant through His Death at Calvary, Sabbath observance, like many other aspects of the Old Covenant, was done away with.

3. The Sabbath is also intimately linked with deliverance from Egypt. God, in repeating the Ten Commandments, says this about the Sabbath:

"Remember that you were slaves in Egypt and that the Lord your God brought you out of there with a mighty hand and an outstretched arm. Therefore the Lord your God has commanded you to observe the Sabbath day" (Deut. 5:15).

A REMINDER OF THE SOURCE

The intimate association of the Sabbath with Creation, Redemption, and Law gives us insight into how the day was to be used.

Each seventh day provided a full-orbed reminder of Who God was to His people. He was the Source of their life. He was the

Provider of their freedom. He was the One Who ordered their lives and gave them meaning. The Sabbath day provided a rest from the normal activities of life in the world and an opportunity for each believing Israelite to contemplate his roots and his identity.

In addition to these theological aspects of the Sabbath, there was an intensely practical aspect as well. The Sabbath was provided for the benefit of all who lived in the sphere of Divine influence. Family members and servants, and even the animals of the land, were to have a time for relaxation and restoration of strength. Even the land was to be given its Sabbath, which came about every seventh year, lest its nutrients be used up. In its rest, the land was to bless the poor and the animals (Ex. 23:10-11).

As Verse 12 goes on to say, *"Six days do your work, but on the seventh day do not work, so that your ox and your donkey may rest and the slave born in your household, and the alien as well, may be refreshed."*

THE SABBATH BY THE TIME OF CHRIST

The humanitarian aspect of Sabbath law was ignored in Jesus' day and gave rise to many of Jesus' conflicts with the Pharisees. These men focused on do's and don'ts that had grown up around and over the basic Biblical principles. Again and again they challenged Jesus' right to heal on the Sabbath (Lk. 6:1-11; 13:10-17; 14:1-6; Jn. 5:9-18; 7:22-23; 9:14-16). In most of these instances, Jesus, Who claimed Lordship over the Sabbath (LK. 6:5), pointed out that it had always been right to do good on the Sabbath. Clearly God's humanitarian concern, expressed in Exodus 23:12 and other Passages, demonstrates that it is not the legalities but the benefits to humankind that the Lord values in this Old Testament holy day.

Theological and humanitarian explanations for the institution of the Sabbath underline a vital Truth found often in Scripture. God's demands communicate His concern for the whole person. Both the spiritual and the physical needs of human beings were intended to be met by the Sabbath day of rest.

After the Resurrection, the Early Church began to meet on the Lord's Day, the first rather than the seventh day becoming the day of worship. What the Believers gathered weekly to remember was the Resurrection.

The Lord's Day replaced the Sabbath, but the meaning of the Sabbath as a time for spiritual and physical refreshment remains significant for us today.

THE GREEK WORDS

The Greek words for *"rest"* are used to translate as many as 16 different Hebrew words. As they are used in the New Testament, they often reflect the Old Testament perspective.

"Anapauo" (used 12 times in the New Testament) means, *"to rest"* in a physical sense; and, as a verb, it also means, *"to calm,"* *"to comfort,"* or *"to refresh."* Significantly, it is this rest that Jesus promised those who are willing to take His yoke (Mat. 11:28-30).

The image is of one person in harness with another, the two tied in tandem as two draft animals were tied, in order that they might work together. In the context of Scripture, human beings always find themselves yoked. Most commonly the yoke involves slavery. In Matthew Chapter 11, as well as Acts Chapter 15 and Galatians 5:1, the yoke is the Law of Moses, which humanity experiences as an unbearable burden. Jesus' invitation was for people to commit themselves to Him. Consequently, when we are bound to Jesus, we can experience rest from this yoke.

"Anesis" another Greek word, indicates a rest that comes from freedom or from the relaxation of a burden. It is found only five times in the New Testament (Acts 24:23; II Cor. 2:13; 7:5; 8:13; II Thess. 1:7).

"Katapausis" another Greek word (nine times in the New Testament) is the rest of repose and is found only in Acts 7:49 and Hebrews. As used in Hebrews, Chapters 3 and 4, it has special theological significance.

Just as the Old Testament shared the conviction that human beings can find rest only through a living relationship with the Lord, so the New Testament expresses the conviction that we can find our rest only in Jesus.

THE USE OF *"REST"* IN HEBREWS

The Third and Fourth Chapters of Hebrews explore the significance of God's Voice

NOTES

in the Believer's experience. Paul argues that only by hearing and responding to the Lord as He speaks to us in our *"today"* can we find rest. Such rest is not cessation of activity but repose in activity.

God's Sabbath rest is defined: God has ceased creating (Heb. 4:9-11). But the God of the Old Testament is certainly active, as should be obvious! How then is He at rest?

He is at rest from bringing into existence and organizing the basic plan and contents of the universe. He knows the end from the beginning, and His purpose will stand (Isa. 46:8-10). Thus, His voice is able to guide us into the paths He intends for us.

The struggle Christians are engaged in is not that of finding their way through life but of entering into His rest, which is the Scripture of our study. That is, we are to be responsive to the Lord and let His Word and Spirit guide us to the solutions He has already provided for our problems.

In knowing God and responding to Him we find true repose.

The real *"rest"* promised by God, and symbolized by the Sabbath, is found only in Christ. And more particularly, this *"rest"* is provided to us by what Jesus did at the Cross on our behalf.

God's recreation aspect of the Earth, found in Genesis, Chapters 1 and 2, and symbolized by Him resting on the Seventh Day, all foreshadow the recreation of humanity, in the Born-Again experience, which then provides a spiritual rest for the Child of God.

The Jewish Sabbath as portrayed in the Law of Moses, was, as stated, but a symbol of that which would be brought about in Christ. It was no more than that, and no less than that. In fact, the entirety of the Old Testament pointed to Christ, and more particularly, what He would do at the Cross. So, the foolishness of some claiming that we are to presently keep the old Jewish seventh day, shows a complete lack of knowledge as it regards the Word of God. We are not to keep the Jewish Sabbath anymore than we are to continue offering up animal sacrifices, etc. All were fulfilled in Christ, and by Christ. That to which all of these laws and symbols pointed, are found totally in Christ, and Christ Alone! Consequently, to go back and attempt to pick these things up, and make them appropriate for the present time, is an insult of the highest proportions to the Person of Christ. As someone has well said, this *"rest"* is found not in a day, but in a Person, and more particularly, the Person of Christ, and more particular still, what Christ did for the whole of humanity on the Cross.

So I think it would be safe to say presently, that if the Cross is ignored, that which God said of Israel so long ago, He is saying the same presently. *"So I swear in My wrath, they shall not enter into My rest."*

(12) "TAKE HEED, BRETHREN, LEST THERE BE IN ANY OF YOU AN EVIL HEART OF UNBELIEF, IN DEPARTING FROM THE LIVING GOD."

The construction of this Scripture is:

1. The Holy Spirit gives a warning through Paul to all Believers. Notice, He uses the word *"Brethren,"* proving that He is speaking to Christians.

2. Unbelief is the cause, and to be more particular, it is unbelief in the Finished Work of Christ which causes the problem.

3. All and without exception come to Christ because they *"will"* to do so, and if they *"will"* to do so, they can depart the same way (Rev. 22:17).

TAKE HEED

The phrase, *"Take heed, Brethren,"* proclaims Paul once again warning the Hebrew Christians, as well as all Believers, that if they follow the example of Israel's unbelief while in the wilderness, they will meet with the same destructive end.

In fact, the warning could not be more clear. The entirety of the Book of Hebrews deals with this very subject.

Many Jewish Christians were growing discouraged, (or for whatever reason,) and were going back into Judaism, which, in essence, meant that they had to denounce Christ.

For them to do this, which is the reason for the writing of the Book of Hebrews, meant the loss of their souls. It is the same presently for Christians who forsake Faith in Christ and the Cross, thereby being diverted to something else.

In fact, this is what the entirety of the Book of Hebrews is all about, and especially

these Third and Fourth Chapters.

The warning was given to the Jewish Christians of Paul's day, which was brought over from the warning given concerning Israel of old, and it is intended for us presently as well!

Many in the Church are very bad about segmenting the Word of God into particular time frames, claiming that such does not apply to us now. While of course, that is true about things which happened in certain dispensations; however, even the warnings given in those particular dispensations, even as proven by Paul's statements, are always applicable to all. In other words, the God Who said *"Thou shalt not steal,"* 3,600 years ago, is still saying, *"Thou shalt not steal!"* In fact, the overall Plan of God doesn't change, even as it cannot change.

Unfortunately, there are untold millions of people who call themselves *"Christians,"* who are not living for God, and in fact, are making no pretense at living for God, with their lives being a constant practice of sin, who have been told the lie of unconditional eternal security, and because of believing that lie, will be eternally lost.

Worse yet, are those who are truly saved, and truly living for God, but yet believe this lie, pumping it out, which is also causing untold numbers to be lost!

UNBELIEF

The phrase, *"Lest there be in any of you an evil heart of unbelief,"* speaks not of a passive or latent state, but an active, pernicious condition.

The Greek order of words is *"a heart evil with reference to unbelief."*

The particular word for *"evil"* here is not *"kakos,"* which is normally used, but rather *"poneros,"* which refers to evil in active opposition to the good. This word is much stronger than *"kakos,"* which means *"evil in the abstract."* It means that the *"kakos man"* may be content to perish in his own corruption, but the *"poneros man"* is not content unless he is corrupting others as well, and dragging them down into the same destruction with himself (Wuest).

The situation had come to the place with some of these so-called Christian Jews, that they were actually taking an active opposition against Christ, which attitude Paul was afraid would result in a deliberate and final rejection of the entirety of the New Covenant, i.e. *"the New Testament."*

We must be careful to discriminate here between a heart in which unbelief is present, and an unbelieving heart. The first may be true of a Christian, but if that Christian actually comes to the place of the second (the unbelieving heart), then the Christian has completely lost his way and is no longer saved. In other words, he is no longer a Believer, but rather an unbeliever.

This refers to a heart solely and entirely controlled by unbelief, in which there is no Faith whatsoever. However, that must be defined:

To be sure everyone has Faith, even the unbeliever. They just don't have Faith in the right object. The individual who comes to the place described here by Paul, is the Christian who no longer believes in the Cross of Christ as the answer to the sin of man, but has diverted his Faith elsewhere. In other words, he is trusting in something else to save his soul, which is the same sin committed by Cain, and untold billions of others since.

When Paul said, *"Examine yourselves, whether ye be in the Faith; prove your own selves. Know ye not your own selves, how that Jesus Christ is in you, except ye be reprobates?"* (II Cor. 13:5), this is what the Apostle was speaking about!

This brings us down to a personal introspection, which it is intended to do. We must look at our own hearts, our own wills; we must see if our hearts are evil. The *"unbelief"* spoken of here, is the type that will damn one's soul.

Therefore, please understand, that we are not speaking here of unbelief as it comes to healing, the Lord answering prayer, etc.; we are speaking of the type of unbelief that registers itself in a vote of no confidence regarding the Cross of Christ. And once again I want to emphasize the following fact:

One cannot trust the Cross, and other things at the same time. This means that the modern Church cannot place its Faith and confidence in humanistic psychology, and at the same time claim to be trusting the Cross. One or the other must go, as one or the other will go! The Israelites were damned in unbelief by resisting the voice of

the Holy Spirit, which is always the case with a denial or rejection of the Cross. The Reader needs to grasp the weight of this of which we here speak.

THE SACRIFICE OF CHRIST

For a Christian to not properly understand the Cross of Christ, is the most serious ignorance which one could ever begin to entertain. Anything about the Word of God is of extreme importance; however, the Cross of Christ is the very heart of Redemption.

In comparing it with the physical body, it is the same as the physical heart. While one may have problems with his foot or hand, etc., which of course will be detrimental; however, if one has problems with his heart, it can kill him, as should be obvious. It is the same with the Gospel!

To be mixed up in one's thinking as it regards the Atonement, to not properly understand the Sacrifice of Christ, is a most serious matter. And please, even at the risk of being overly repetitious, please allow me to state the following, which will give a bare bones description of what the Cross actually means:

1. Every single thing that the Believer receives from the Lord, and without exception, comes through the Sacrifice of Christ. So, this means that the Believer should look exclusively to this which Christ has done, understanding that the Cross is the key to all things (Gal. 6:14).

2. Understanding that, the Believer must anchor his Faith in the Cross, the idea being, that the Cross should ever be the object of one's Faith. Everything that we receive from the Lord is by Faith, but it is by Faith in what Christ did at the Cross. Everyone in the world has Faith of some kind, but it's only Faith which is registered in the Cross of Christ, which will be honored by God. As well, whenever Paul mentions *"Faith"* in his writings, he is, and without exception, referring to Faith in the Finished Work of Christ. The Believer must understand that (Jn. 3:16).

3. With the Believer's Faith properly placed, the Holy Spirit Who always works exclusively within the parameters of the Finished Work of Christ, will then be able to perform His Office work within the heart and

life of the Believer. The Holy Spirit abides in every Believer; however, for Him to do the things which only He can do, our Faith must be in the Cross (Rom. 8:1-2, 11, 13).

To be sure, nothing will be done in the heart and life of the Believer, without the Holy Spirit carrying out this work. In other words, we cannot do these things ourselves, the Holy Spirit Alone being able to do so. But His Work is never automatic. He wants us to understand our inadequacy, thereby leaning on what Christ did at the Cross, trusting in that exclusively, and then He will work.

Unfortunately, millions of Christians, although Spirit-filled, get very little help from the Holy Spirit, at least to the degree that they could receive, and it's because their Faith is in something else other than the Cross.

AN EVERLASTING COVENANT

As stated, this which I've just given you is a bare bones description of what we're speaking about as it concerns the Cross, our Faith, and the Holy Spirit. The Truth is, this subject is so vast, so broad, so wide, so deep, that it will never be exhausted. And the facts are, the more that one learns about this great subject, the more wonderful this Christian life becomes, and for the simple reason, that all Blessings are wrapped up in what Christ did at the Cross on our behalf.

Actually, it's not really possible for the Believer to properly understand the Word of God as he should, unless he properly understands the Cross. So, understanding that, surely we can see how serious it is, when we lose our Faith in the great Sacrifice of Christ, or allow our Faith to be diverted to other things.

If every Believer would avail himself of every opportunity of learning more and more about the Cross of Christ, asking the Lord to teach him these things, the *"more abundant life"* spoken of by Christ, would become a greater reality in one's life, with the *"in Christ"* experience, becoming what it was all the time meant to be (Jn. 10:10).

Living for Jesus is the greatest life there is. In fact, it's the only real life there is; however, it is impossible for one to know this *"Life,"* to understand this *"Life,"* and in effect, to properly have this *"Life,"* unless one properly understands the Cross, which is the

NOTES

Source of all Life, i.e., *"and we speak of Christ and what He did at the Cross."*

DEPARTING FROM GOD

The phrase, *"In departing from the Living God,"* presents the following facts:

As the Jews of old were in the wilderness, we presently are in the wilderness of this world. This same principle is shown under all dispensations, and in all circumstances; and there is no less danger of it under the Gospel, than there was when the Fathers were conducted to the Promised Land.

We too, are exposed to trials and temptations. We meet with many a deadly and mighty foe. We have hearts prone to apostasy and sin. And yet, we are seeking a land of promise — a land of rest.

But at the same time, we are surrounded by the wonders of Almighty Power, and by the proofs of infinite benefits given to us by God. So, the same decision that the Israelites of old had to make, we have to make presently.

It all comes down to *"belief"* or *"unbelief!"* Or as one might say, *"Faith"* or a *"lack of Faith!"*

And I have learned from bitter experience, which is the greatest learning operation of all, although quite expensive, that if our Faith is not in the Cross, we will have for ourselves serious circumstances. In fact, Faith cannot grow unless it is in the Cross, and when it is in the Cross as it ought to be, then Faith begins to grow exceedingly so, and because the Cross is the true object of Faith, in essence, Faith in the Word (Jn. 1:1, 14, 29).

Unbelief causes a person to depart from the Living God. Such begins in the heart, and it's always centered up someway in a rejection of the Cross. It means that the heart of unbelief will manifest its evil in apostasy.

The only way one can have *"an evil heart of unbelief,"* is that this person has once believed, and now is turning away from God. And let the following be understood:

A CLEAR AND PRESENT DANGER

For Christians to repudiate their Apostle and High Priest, Christ Jesus, is an even more dangerous and deliberate revolt against the Living God than that of the Children of Israel against Moses, etc. This means that the apostasy of the Hebrew Christians would be against God's Son, their only hope. It would be a complete abandonment of Faith in God and the Lord Jesus Christ, a relapse from Christianity into Judaism, a turning of their backs on Christ, and a going back into their spiritual Egypt.

It would not merely be a return to a position previously occupied, but a gesture of outright apostasy, a complete break with God. Judaism did provide some vague access to God, as perverted as it had become, but one turning their back upon Christ, would mean turning back from an irretrievable position, that is if they remained in that state. It would be the sin against Light, which is the greatest sin of all!

This danger arises from an evil heart, at least this is its point of beginning. How? Why?

As someone has well said, *"We do what we do, because we believe what we believe!"* And what does that mean?

Whatever a person believes, that's what the person will do. As stated, all of this begins with doubts about the Cross. There have been untold numbers of Christians who have quit living for God, simply because they didn't know the Way of the Cross; therefore, they were unable to live the Christian life. They grew discouraged, and simply quit. That number is legend.

We're not speaking, however, of this group. We are speaking of those who have deliberately opted for something else other than the Cross. Even though I'm being repetitious, the foray of the Church into humanistic psychology is an example.

For years I could not understand as to how men and women who claimed to know the Bible, could opt for this false science, which in reality is no science at all! However, once the Lord began to reveal to me the Word of the Cross, helping me to understand what the Cross actually means, and especially for the Child of God, then I began to see that this defection to humanistic psychology is more than it seems to be on the surface. It is actually a repudiation of the Cross, which is in effect a vote of *"no confidence!"* As I've said repeatedly, there is no other conclusion which can be drawn.

For men who claim to be Spirit-filled, and who claim to be Preachers of the Gospel, to

opt for this humanistic way, means at the same time, that they have abandoned the Cross.

Of course, they would strongly, even vehemently, deny such a position. But considering that the two, the Cross and humanistic psychology are totally opposed to each other, no other conclusion can be drawn. To accept that world, one has to reject the world of Redemption, which is the Cross.

The Message of the Cross is about to be heralded all over the world, and in a way that it's never been heralded before. In other words, no one is going to have any excuse for not knowing. So, the fall-out from that will be, that the Cross will be and in fact is, the dividing line between the True Church and the apostate Church. In fact, it's always been that way, but it's going to be more pronounced now than ever.

God's purpose is for Believers to enter His Rest, yet it is God's power alone that enables us to do such. And as well, that power, which comes exclusively from the Holy Spirit, is able to function only as we have proper Faith in the Cross of Christ (Rom. 8:1-2).

God has placed responsibility upon men to believe. The condition to entering His rest is to believe in Him, and more particularly, what He did at the Cross on our behalf. This means, that this work is of God and not of ourselves, but at the same time, we must appropriate it, and we must do so by Faith, and it must be Faith that's placed in the Cross.

A FURTHER WARNING

To say that the persons to whom Paul is writing apparently had stopped short of embracing the true Christian Faith, but was only contemplating such, is to reject the tenor of the entirety of this Epistle, and especially the two Chapters, 3 and 4.

As well, Verse 1 of this Chapter, is addressed to *"Holy Brethren, partakers of the Heavenly Calling."* The expression *"Brethren"* in Scripture refers to those who are in Christ Jesus. Such terminology is never used of the unredeemed. We are brothers because we have been made one through the Cross.

So, get it out of your mind, as many teach, that the Apostle is here speaking to those who had only considered Christ, and had really not accepted Him. The evidence is so loaded in the other direction, that it's really *"no contest."* Such interpretation is reading into this which isn't there, and at the same time, plainly ignoring what is actually there.

The upshot is, it is quite possible for a Believer to quit believing, thereby departing from the Living God. And if such is done, and that person remains in that condition of unbelief, the only conclusion that one can draw is that the person is eternally lost.

(13) "BUT EXHORT ONE ANOTHER DAILY, WHILE IT IS CALLED TO DAY; LEST ANY OF YOU BE HARDENED THROUGH THE DECEITFULNESS OF SIN."

The exegesis is:

1. Christians are to exhort each other daily, which means to warn each other about the possibility of the deceitfulness of sin.

2. We are to take all of this to heart today, even as the Holy Spirit demands. This refers to the fact, that what we have *"today"* is what we have. We cannot necessarily live on something that we had yesterday, or hopefully will have tomorrow. It is one's Faith *"today"* that is counted!

3. Sin is deceitful, and it hardens one, and we're speaking here of the sin of unbelief, and it is unbelief in Christ, and what He did at the Cross on our behalf.

EXHORTATION

The phrase, *"But exhort one another daily,"* proclaims a constant frequency, and for a particular reason.

"Exhort" in the Greek is *"parakaleo,"* and means *"to call aloud, to utter in a loud voice."* The idea is, that there be no doubt as to what is being said.

This means that the Preacher should preach the Cross, and do so constantly. It means that Believers who aren't Preachers, should as well, *"exhort one another daily,"* as it refers to this all-important principle.

We must consider, that we're speaking here of the issues of life and death, of which there are nothing more important!

To be sure, the Holy Spirit gives us these things for a reason. Beginning sometime in 1998, and because of being instructed by the Holy Spirit, we began to teach exclusively on the Cross, regarding our 90 minute, daily Radio Program, *"A Study In The Word,"*

which goes out all over the United States, and even all over the world via the Internet. Since we have begun to do this, I have noticed Believers who tune in to the Program discussing this all-important subject among themselves, which is the greatest thing a Believer can do.

When Believers discuss the Cross, they are discussing that which is the single most important part of the Gospel. If they understand that, every other Doctrine will fall into place as well, or at least become much easier to understand.

When we begin to take the Word of God at face value, which means to believe exactly what it says, and as well, to try to carry out what it says, then we will begin to notice a positive change within our lives. There is nothing more important than the Word of God; consequently, we must take it to heart, asking the Lord to help us understand exactly what is being said, and then trusting totally in Him to help us carry it out. That is the path of true victory!

TODAY

The phrase, *"While it is called today,"* refers to several things:

1. It is what we have today that counts, and not yesterday, or tomorrow.

2. All of this of which the Holy Spirit speaks, is so important that it must be done today, and not put off until tomorrow.

3. There is still time regarding today, but there may be no time after today.

4. God is ready today to do great and mighty things for any and every Believer, who will truly trust Him. He is a *"today"* God!

5. God is speaking today, so we must answer today!

HARDNESS

The phrase, *"Lest any of you be hardened,"* proves that it's possible for a Christian to come to this state.

It is unbelief that hardens the heart, and more particularly, unbelief as it regards the Cross. To turn it around, the Cross of Christ was the greatest example of humility the world has ever known. When one properly understands the Cross, thereby placing his Faith in the Cross, such a position automatically guarantees a deepening of humility. The very nature of the Cross demands that, which is carried along by our Faith as the Cross is made its object.

When the Cross is replaced with something else, the humility automatically goes, and pride begins to take its terrible effect, which is the result of self-will.

The point I'm making is, if the Cross of Christ is not understood, or if we forsake the Cross substituting something else, hardness toward God is the inevitable result, and for all the obvious reasons. God's great plan of Redemption for sinners, and victory for the Saints, is the Cross. To reject that plan in any fashion, is to reject all that God is, which makes it impossible for the Believer to escape a hardness of heart.

THE DECEITFULNESS OF SIN

The phrase, *"Through the deceitfulness of sin,"* actually says *"the deceitfulness of the sin,"* which refers to a rejection of the Sacrifice of Christ. It is the sin of unbelief, i.e., *"the sin of apostasy."*

The word *"deceitfulness"* is the translation of the Greek *"apate"* which refers to a trick, stratagem, or deceit rather than to the quality of deceitfulness. The idea is, that Believers must be warned against being hardened by a trick which their sin may play upon them. In other words, whatever it is the person is thinking as the Cross of Christ is abandoned, will not materialize. Satan is playing a trick upon the individual, in effect, lying to them!

It is ironic, the word *"today"* as used here by the Holy Spirit through Paul, was very near its close, at least as it regarded the nation of Israel. In fact, this was God's last prophetic message to His ancient people. Hebrews was written just before the Apostle's violent death, and just as the Romans as God's instruments of judgment were being prepared to march against Jerusalem.

That day of God's patience then closed for Israel as a nation; but Grace reigned embracing both Jews and Gentiles, gathering out of them a people to the Messiah's Name; and this action still continues.

Please understand, that when Paul speaks here of the *"deceitfulness of sin,"* he is speaking of a particular sin, and it is the sin of

forsaking Christ as it regards His Cross. The Reader must understand, that it is not possible to know Christ, at least the Christ of Glory, unless one knows Him in the realm of His great Sacrifice. It must always be *"Jesus Christ and Him Crucified"* (I Cor. 2:2). If we think of Jesus in any other manner, we are pure and simple, thinking of *"another Jesus"* (II Cor. 11:4). This is *"the sin"* of which Paul is speaking here!

This means, and beyond the shadow of a doubt, that the Cross of Christ is the dividing line. And that presents itself as a fearful prospect, especially considering that the modern Church, knows almost nothing about the Cross, and that goes for Spirit-filled people as well!

(14) "FOR WE ARE MADE PARTAKERS OF CHRIST, IF WE HOLD THE BEGINNING OF OUR CONFIDENCE STEDFAST UNTO THE END;"

The Scripture structure is as follows:

1. We are made partakers of Christ, as we understand that we *"were baptized into His Death"* (Rom. 6:3). This speaks of us having Faith in what Christ did at the Cross, with the benefits of the Crucifixion awarded to Believers.

2. The condition of Salvation is to hold the original confidence steadfast unto the end.

3. This is a warning to Christians that they can fall into sin and apostasy and be cut off from God by sin, even as Israel was.

PARTAKERS OF CHRIST

The phrase, *"For we are made partakers of Christ,"* actually refers to Romans, Chapter 6, which gives us the manner in which this is done. It is the union of the branch to the Vine, where the branch is supported and nourished by the Vine (Jn. 15:1-5). Of this union, Jesus said, *"At that day* (after the Cross, when the Holy Spirit could come in to abide) *ye shall know that I am in My Father, and ye in Me, and I in you"* (Jn. 14:20).

But of course, the great question is, how is all of this brought about? We find the answer to that in Romans, Chapter 6.

ROMANS, CHAPTER 6

When Jesus died on the Cross, it was all done for you and me. As well, His Death was a Sacrifice, and not an execution. In other words, He did not merely run afoul of Roman law. In Truth, due to the fact that He was born without original sin, and never sinned, death had no claim on Him. Consequently, He could not have died, unless He purposely laid down His life, which He did (Jn. 10:18).

In His life, He perfectly kept the Law of Moses, i.e., *"the Law of God."* Thereby, on our behalf, He gained the Righteousness of the Law, which demanded perfect obedience, and which perfect obedience He presented. But still, there was the matter of the terrible penalty of sin to be dealt with.

As the *"Last Adam"* (I Cor. 15:45-50), He kept the Law perfectly, and as the *"last Adam"* He also paid the penalty for our sin — a penalty which we rightly owed, but could in no wise pay.

He offered up Himself as a Perfect Sacrifice on the Cross, which God accepted as payment for all sin (Jn. 1:29).

Inasmuch as His Death atoned for all sin, Satan lost his legal hold upon man, because sin gave him that legal right; however, with all sin atoned, which it was by the Death of Christ, Satan then lost his legal hold, at least for those who will believe (Jn. 3:16).

Jesus was buried, and then rose from the dead on the third day, as the *"Second Man"* (I Cor. 15:47). The first man, Adam, totally failed, while the *"Second Man,"* the Lord Jesus Christ, totally succeeded and in every manner.

Incidentally, the Holy Spirit used the words *"Last Adam"* as He referred to Christ, simply because there will never be the need for another.

As stated, the Lord did all of this for us. So all we have to do as Believers is to register Faith in this which Christ did. When we do this, in the Mind of God, we were and are, literally baptized into the Death of Christ, which Paul brought out in Romans 6:3. In other words, God looks at us as if we did this thing ourselves, even though of course, it was not done by us, and in fact couldn't be done by us. That's why we refer to Christ as our Substitute or Representative Man. He did for us what we could not do for ourselves.

Romans 6:4 says that we were also *"buried with Him by Baptism into Death."* And

please understand, when Paul uses the word here *"Baptism,"* he is not speaking of Water Baptism, but rather the Crucifixion of Christ, and our being literally, at least in the Mind of God, being baptized into His Death.

The word *"Baptism"* or *"baptized"* are the two strongest words that could be used, which typifies that one is in something, and that certain something is in one. A perfect illustration is a ship which has been sunk in the ocean. The water is in the ship, and the ship is in the water, which aptly describes *"Baptism."*

That's the reason that Jesus said, and as we quoted, *"At that day ye shall know that I am in My Father, and ye in Me, and I in you"* (Jn. 14:20).

Then Paul said that our *"old man,"* which refers to our life before conversion, was literally buried with Christ (Rom. 6:4-6), which means we died to all sin, and in every form. Once again this takes place in the Mind of God, as we evidence Faith in the great Sacrifice of Christ.

We were then raised with Him in *"newness of life"* (Rom. 6:4).

THE EFFECT OF THE CROSS ON OUR DAILY LIVING

Knowing all of this, we then as Believers are to *"reckon ourselves to be dead indeed unto sin, but alive unto God through Jesus Christ our Lord"* (Rom. 6:11).

While the word *"reckon"* means to compute or to account, it also has its roots in the Greek word *"logos,"* which actually means *"word."*

So, the Holy Spirit through Paul is saying here that God's Word tells us that these things are true, and we should believe them.

Continuing to exhibit Faith in the Cross, which we must do all of our days, we are to ever understand that our victory rests completely in what Christ did at the Cross. Consequently, and as stated, our Faith must rest totally in that.

As we continue to exhibit Faith in the Cross of Christ, we will then have the power to yield the members of our physical body as instruments of Righteousness. However, if we shift our Faith from the Cross to something else, we will quickly find that Satan will then be able to override our wills (Rom. 7:18).

In fact, that's where most Christians are presently. They are trying with all their strength not to fail the Lord, but find that their strength is not enough. They are confused and don't know what to do, when in reality, their problem is that they have shifted their Faith from the Cross to something else.

Many Christians have the mistaken idea that since they are now saved, they have the power to say *"yes"* or *"no"* to whatever they desire. No you don't!

You only have the willpower and the strength to say *"yes"* to Christ, and you must never forget that. This means to say *"yes"* to what He did at the Cross on your behalf, which guarantees you total and complete victory, and we might quickly add, perpetual victory. For the Scripture then plainly says, *"For sin* (or the sin, which refers to the sin nature) *shall not have dominion over you: for ye are not under the Law, but under Grace"* (Rom. 6:14).

WHAT DOES PAUL MEAN BY THE STATEMENT, *"FOR YE ARE NOT UNDER THE LAW, BUT UNDER GRACE"*?

If a Christian attempts to function in any other manner other than by the Grace of God, which means he's functioning in law whether he understands it or not, sin will definitely have dominion over him. Anything that's not strictly by the Grace of God, is law, whether it was the Law of Moses which some of the Early Church Gentiles were attempting to keep, or whether it's laws of our own making at present.

What is the Grace of God? And how do we function in the Grace of God?

The Grace of God is simply the instrument whereby the Goodness of God is extended to undeserving individuals. And of course, all are undeserving, irrespective as to whom they might be. The Cross of Christ is the means by which this is done.

The manner and way in which we function in the Grace of God, is to place our Faith strictly in the Cross of Christ, understanding that it is the Cross which makes the Grace of God possible. That's all the Believer is required to do.

Understanding that we could have nothing or receive nothing from God, except by and through the Cross of Christ, with us

placing our Faith exclusively in that Finished Work, makes it possible for the Grace of God to be extended to us. In fact, God cannot extend His Goodness to us by any other means. The Cross made it all possible. And to be sure, it is the Holy Spirit Who superintends all of these things, and He demands that our Faith be in the Cross at all times (Rom. 8:1-2).

So, that's all the Believer has to do, is to understand that everything flows from, by, of, and through the Cross of Christ, which demands that our Faith be in that great Sacrifice, which then makes possible the Work of the Holy Spirit in guaranteeing to us the benefits of the Cross.

What we've just said is not something complicated, difficult, or hard to understand. In fact, it's very simple. But yet, Satan will fight the Cross, and your understanding of the benefits of the Cross, as he fights nothing else. Tragically, he has been very successful in the last several decades in getting the Church to ignore the Cross, or misunderstand the Cross, or outright deny the Cross.

This is the only manner in which the Child of God can walk in perpetual victory. If he attempts to live this life in any other manner than by Faith in the Cross, which enables the Holy Spirit to do His Office work within in our hearts and lives, he frustrates the Grace of God, which means that he is going to live a life of spiritual failure (Gal. 2:20-21).

WHAT IS THE LAW?

If one is to notice, Paul mentions the Law over and over again, and especially in the Epistle to the Galatians. Why did he do this, considering that Jesus fulfilled all the Law, and it is actually no more applicable to Believers?

He did it in this manner, simply because the Holy Spirit desired that it be done, and for great and excellent reasons. In fact, *"the Law"* is the greatest problem for the Child of God, i.e., *"the Church."* And the sadness is, most Christians are neck-deep in law, and have no idea that such is their position. Let us say it again:

If the Believer doesn't properly understand the Cross, which means he takes full advantage of its many benefits, for which Jesus paid such a price, he is going to automatically function in law. Now let's explain that.

Law is any rule that we make up, any particular regimen which we follow, and irrespective as to what it is, that is other than simple Faith in the Cross of Christ. And that means anything!

In fact, there are many things which definitely aren't law within themselves, but which Believers turn into law, by the manner in which it is used. For instance, the laying on of hands is definitely Scriptural, and has nothing to do with law; however, if we think that we can obtain victory over sin by having Preachers or anyone for that matter, lay hands on us, then we've turned it into a law which God can never honor, at least in the respect of the needs we presently have. Please understand that what we're discussing here is victory over sin.

Now when we say that, many Christians, especially those in the Pentecostal and Charismatic camps, automatically turn off, thinking that doesn't apply to them, because they no longer sin. The Truth is, almost all of these people are functioning in spiritual failure, in other words they are sinning in some way, which means the sin nature has dominion over them, which they refuse to admit. If one doesn't understand the Cross, it cannot be otherwise! Somehow we have made ourselves believe, that if no one else knows about our problem, then it's not so bad. But please understand, God knows about the problem, and so do you, whatever it might be!

So what we presently have, and because of the modern Church little knowing or understanding anything about the Cross, is a Church full of hypocrites so to speak. In Truth, most of these people are not hypocrites, because they don't want to be the way they are, and are not purposely living that way, but they simply don't know how to walk in victory. So in a sense, there definitely is hypocrisy, but not so much in the manner in which we normally think of that word.

Sin comes in many shapes and forms, and this monster is of such power, that the only thing that could handle it was the Cross of Christ.

THE CROSS OF CHRIST
WAS A LEGAL WORK

I've made the statement many times, that God could speak worlds into existence, but

He couldn't speak Redemption into existence. To bring about this tremendous work, God would have to become man, live this life perfectly as a man, and then die on the Cross to pay the terrible sin debt, which man owed to God, but could not pay. However, that needs explanation.

As far as raw power is concerned, God could definitely have redeemed mankind with just the word of his mouth, exactly as He called worlds into existence. He has the power to do that. But the Reader must understand, that God functions entirely within the boundaries of Laws, incidentally, Laws which He has made. Which means that in a sense, everything with God is a legal work. And what do we mean by the word *"legal"*?

Law is a binding custom or practice, which refers to a rule of conduct or action prescribed or formerly recognized as binding or enforced by a controlling authority. It is a rule of order, and in this case, devised solely by God.

The word *"legal"* or *"lawful,"* means to be in harmony with established law.

God has created all things by a system of laws. We read in our science books, where Newton discovered the *"law of gravity,"* etc. However, that law, and untold numbers of others, has always been present, because it was devised by God.

When Adam sinned in the Garden of Eden, he broke the law. The penalty for breaking that law was spiritual death, which meant separation from God (Gen. 2:16-17). Satan now enters the picture:

Because man has broken the law, a law incidentally made by God, Satan now has a legal right to place man in captivity, which he did.

God being perfectly righteous, perfectly just, and perfectly holy, means that He cannot ignore the laws which He has made. The penalty of this sin debt is going to have to be paid, that is if man is to be redeemed. In fact, it could be paid in one of two ways:

God could simply allow all of mankind to be eternally lost, thereby being locked up in an eternal hell, which would have satisfied the law. Or else, He could redeem man by paying the debt Himself, which He did, and which could only be done by offering up Himself as a Sacrifice on the Cross. The debt was a legal debt, and the payment would have to be a legal payment. In other words, God could not just simply decree this thing to be done, but would actually have to pay the debt.

So, the work of the Cross was actually a legal work, which satisfied a legal debt, which made it possible for man to be legally justified. In fact, all that man has to do to obtain this legal justification, which means that he is declared perfectly right in the eyes of God, is for him to exhibit Faith in what Christ did on our behalf at the Cross (I Cor. 6:11).

So, when Jesus died on the Cross, He satisfied the righteous demands, i.e., *"the legal demands,"* of a thrice holy God. That's the reason that the Cross was necessary.

WHY A CROSS?

In fact, the Cross is another law made by God.

In Old Testament Law, He had said, *"If a man has committed a sin worthy of death, he is to be put to death, and then hanged on a tree.*

"His body shall not remain all night upon the tree, but thou shalt in any wise bury him that day; for he that is hanged is accursed of God (which means that he has committed a crime so horrible, that this penalty is attached)*"* (Deut. 21:22-23).

So this means that Jesus would have to die upon a Cross, for in the Mind of God, this was the most ignominious death of all.

It must be remembered, that Jesus had to atone for every sin, and in fact every type of sin, even the most vile. So the Cross was demanded, as would be obvious!

When Jesus died, He could not die as the result of being stoned to death, or thrust through with a spear, etc. He had to be placed on a Cross, that is if the vilest sins were to be atoned. Therefore, when the religious leaders of Israel screamed at Pilate, that Jesus must be crucified, they were actually fulfilling prophecy, even though they did not realize such (Jn. 19:15). However, from the prophecies, they should have known (Deut. 21:22-23; Isa. 52:14; Chpt. 53). Actually, the Lord had shown Abraham that Redemption could only be brought about by the death of the Redeemer (Gen. 22:1-14). He had shown Moses exactly as to how this death would be

carried out. It would be on a Cross (Num. 21:6-9). In fact, Jesus told Nicodemus the type of death He should die, by quoting this experience of the children of Israel so long before. He said, *"And as Moses lifted up the serpent in the wilderness, even so must the Son of Man be lifted up* (lifted up on a Cross).*"*

He then said, *"Whosoever believeth in Him should not perish, but have Eternal Life"* (Jn. 3:14-15).

The Cross was an absolute necessity, in fact, an absolute, legal necessity.

WHY WAS THE FORFEITURE OF A LIFE DEMANDED?

In other words, why couldn't the sin debt which man owed to God, not be paid with silver and gold?

The Holy Spirit through Peter, pointedly stated, that *"we were not redeemed* (in fact could not be redeemed) *with corruptible things, as silver and gold . . . but with the precious Blood of Christ, as of a lamb without blemish and without spot"* (I Pet. 1:18-19).

That's not difficult to understand, seeing that human law, which is based on the Law of God, or should be, demands that for certain crimes, silver and gold will not suffice. In other words, if cold-blooded murder is committed, human law oftentimes, demands that the life of the murderer be forfeited. At the very dawn of time, God said, *"Whoso sheddeth man's blood* (to murder the individual in cold blood), *by man shall his blood be shed: for in the Image of God made He man"* (Gen. 9:6). Incidentally, this is another Law devised by God, and because of the sanctity of life.

As well, it must be understood, that every Law made by God, is perfect, right, just, and is meant for the benefit of all creation.

God had told Adam and Eve, that if they partook of a certain tree in the Garden, the tree of the knowledge of good and evil, that *"in the day that thou eatest thereof thou shalt surely die"* (Gen. 2:17).

The *"death"* of which He spoke, was spiritual death, which meant separation from God, which means that man lost his life source at the Fall. Cut off from his life source, he ultimately died physically as well, and in every other way. Actually, because of the Fall, everything is dying, which tells us how bad the sin of Adam actually was. In effect, Adam changed Lords, in that God had been his Lord, but now Satan is his lord, in which position Adam was placed because of default. With God no longer as man's life source, he can be easily taken captive by Satan, which he was, and has been ever since.

The idea is, the crime was so bad, that the only thing that could pay this terrible debt, was a human life offered up in Sacrifice; however, such was impossible for man to do, because due to the Fall, all are born in original sin, therefore, disqualified; consequently, God would have to become man, in order to pay this price on the Cross, because God as God cannot die.

Therefore, one can say that the reason death was demanded, is because the crime of man was a capital crime, in other words, so bad, that nothing else would suffice. As the life of the flesh is in the blood, blood would have to be shed in order for this debt to be paid, which was carried out at the Cross, and in graphic detail. God had said:

"For the life of the flesh is in the blood: and I have given it to you upon the Altar to make an atonement for your souls: for it is the blood that maketh an atonement for the soul" (Lev. 17:11).

That's why Peter said that we were purchased by *"the Precious Blood of Christ"* (I Pet. 1:19).

As well, it had to be a perfect Sacrifice, hence Christ was Perfect, having never sinned, which meant that His Spirit, Soul, and Body, were absolutely Perfect before God, thereby, perfectly sufficient for a Perfect Sacrifice. Again, Peter said of this, *"As of a lamb without blemish and without spot"* (I Pet. 1:19).

CONFIDENCE STEADFAST UNTO THE END

The phrase, *"If we hold the beginning of our confidence steadfast unto the end,"* pertains to the fact that in order to be saved, the sinner had to place his Faith and trust totally in Christ, and to stay saved, the Believer has to continue to do the same. In fact, this is what the entirety of this Epistle is all about.

At least some, if not many Christian Jews, were seriously contemplating forsaking Christ and going back to Temple worship.

In fact, there is no doubt that some had actually done so! So, the Holy Spirit through Paul is plainly telling them, that if they do such a thing and remain in that vein of unbelief, even though previously saved, they will now be eternally lost.

It is absolutely all-important, that the Believer hold firmly to what God has given him. *"The Confidence we had at first"* is that experienced when the believing sinner first came to Christ. They had no doubts then, nor should they have any now. *"Till the end"* points to the end of the Believer's life.

The little word *"if"* here pertains to the perseverance of the Saints. In this expression is the condition of final Salvation. Unbelief caused some of the Christian Jews to turn back, and the penalty for their unbelief was death, which means separation from God, which is all it can mean. Such is the tragedy and the hopelessness of those who turn away from the Lord Jesus Christ today. They are excluded from the *"rest"* which is found only in Christ Jesus.

The Hebrew Christians had made an initial start at following Jesus. They were born of the Spirit, and were members of the Body of Christ: *"partakers of Christ,"* Paul says! However, the following must be noted:

The *"commencement"* of the Christian Life, although totally necessary as would be obvious, within itself is not sufficient; there must be a *"continuation"* and *"completion,"* which refers to a day-by-day, moment-by-moment walk with the Lord. To be sure, His faithfulness is not in question, for the Lord has promised to go all the way with us; it is our faithfulness that is critical.

In other words, the Lord will not forsake us, if we won't forsake Him.

In no way does this mean that the Gospel is of works, but it definitely does mean that human responsibility is involved. The partaker, or sharer, of Christ is to take a firm stand, not forsaking or apostatizing. To begin is good, but within itself, is not enough. Only those who finish the race have any hope of gaining the prize.

CONFIDENCE

The Hebrew Believers had truly begun in the reality of Who Christ is. They began in

Godly confidence. In fact, *"the beginning of our confidence"* is found to be the basis of our confidence in the Person of the Lord Jesus Christ. This confidence, which in reality is Faith, is manifested by perseverance. In other words, we must persevere, which means to hold firm to the end.

The word *"confidence"* is also translated *"title deed."* The word was used in secular manuscripts or documents, denoting ownership of a person's property. Similarly, the Faith of these Jewish hearts needed to be kept in the Lord. They further needed to persist in that Faith to the end of their lives, despite the persecutions they were enduring. The ultimate goal was theirs only if they held it true to the end.

What was the beginning of their confidence?

Without doubt their first Faith in Christ was accompanied by an assurance that Jesus Christ had been their Lord and Saviour. These Hebrew Believers could not have had such a Revelation of Jesus Christ, or entered into this relationship, without Christ first revealing Himself to them. Their Faith in Him would be the evidence of the hope they had in Him. They must hold that unto the end, as we must hold that unto the end.

(15) "WHILE IT IS SAID, TO DAY IF YE WILL HEAR HIS VOICE, HARDEN NOT YOUR HEARTS, AS IN THE PROVOCATION."

The breakdown of this Verse is:

1. This is the third time the Holy Spirit uses the word *"today,"* and does so to emphasize the fact that it is the present when God's Voice is heard. This shows us how serious the matter is. We must hear the Voice, obey the Voice, and do so promptly.

2. To fail to heed the Voice of God is done so because of unbelief, which hardens the heart.

3. Israel in the wilderness was an example, and we should heed that example by all means!

TODAY, HEAR HIS VOICE

The phrase, *"While it is said, today if you will hear His Voice,"* presents the Holy Spirit through Paul, coming to us the third time with this warning. Any time the Lord says something once, it is of extreme significance. If He says it twice, it is serious indeed! But when He says it three times, as here, its significance is beyond comprehension.

The idea is, the Holy Spirit is telling Christians, that unless they heed the Voice of the Lord, they could lose their souls. As we've said repeatedly, this completely shoots down the ungodly, wicked doctrine of unconditional, eternal security, in other words, the idea that after one is saved, one cannot lose their soul irrespective as to what happens or what they might do. In other words, even if they go back into the deepest sin, completely rejecting Christ, they are still secure in Christ, etc. Nothing could be further from the Truth.

The moment a person ceases to trust Christ for Salvation, at that moment that person is lost. And as well, it is not possible for one to live in sin, with no effort made to get out of sin, actually enjoying such a lifestyle, and at the same time claim to trust Christ. The two positions are totally antagonistic to each other. The Holy Spirit through John plainly said, *"If we say that we have fellowship with Him, and walk in darkness, we lie, and do not the Truth"* (I Jn. 1:6).

He then said, *"He that saith, I know Him, and keepeth not His Commandments, is a liar, and the Truth is not in him"* (I Jn. 2:4).

John also said, *"And all liars, shall have their part in the lake which burneth with fire and brimstone: which is the second death"* (Rev. 21:8).

While there are millions of Christians who are struggling with some sin within their lives, and because they do not know God's prescribed order of victory, which is the Cross, still, it's not something they want or desire. That is a far cry, however, from those who desire to live in sin, and in fact, do live in sin. Struggling Christians, and I speak of struggling in the realm of which we have spoken, are definitely saved, although living far beneath their spiritual privileges in Christ. These don't want the problem, and are trying to overcome it, but trying in the wrong way.

THE HARDENED HEART

The phrase, *"Harden not your hearts, as in the provocation,"* presents the third time also, that the Holy Spirit refers to the possibility of the heart being hardened. As well, He continues to use Israel of old as an example.

Paul, under the guidance of the Holy Spirit, isolates the wilderness experience in Israel's history, in which the people heard God's Voice directing them to enter and possess the Promised Land. Israel refused to enter, and because of unbelief.

If the Holy Spirit warns us three times in this one Chapter about the danger of hardening our hearts, then we certainly should understand the distinct possibility of such. Considering what is at stake, and I speak of the loss of our souls, we should read these words with fear, even fear and trembling. In fact, there is no way that I can overemphasize the seriousness of this which is being addressed!

The Holy Spirit uses the unbelieving generation in the wilderness as an example, which at the borders of Canaan refused to follow Caleb and Joshua into the Promised Land, but chose to take the advice of those who did not believe. In the final analysis it was lack of Faith in God and His power to give them victory over the giants, and all other particular situations of that nature. This is the provocation spoken of.

Not only did this unbelieving generation lose its way, but their actions delayed the Plan of God for nearly 40 years. Think of that, all of Heaven was ready for Israel to enter the Promised Land, but the people of God wouldn't do so!

If it happened then, and it most definitely did, then it is most definitely certain that it can happen now, and in a sense, in the same manner. What we as Believers do, affects not only ourselves, but the entirety of the Work of God also. While the actions of some definitely affect the Work of God more than others, still, all actions by Believers, whether good or bad, affect the Work in some way.

(16) "FOR SOME, WHEN THEY HAD HEARD, DID PROVOKE: HOWBEIT NOT ALL THAT CAME OUT OF EGYPT BY MOSES."

The exegesis of this Scripture is:

1. The adult generation that came out of Egypt provoked God. They would not believe, despite all the great miracles they had seen.

2. The provoking included the entirety of the adult generation, with the exception of Joshua and Caleb.

3. Considering they came out under Moses, the idea is they came out right, i.e., *"started right, but didn't continue right."*

PROVOKE

The phrase, *"For some, when they had heard, did provoke,"* should have been translated, *"For who when they had heard did provoke."*

They *"heard,"* which means they heard the Voice of God, but they refused to listen.

And how did they hear the Voice of God at that time?

They heard the Voice of God through Caleb and Joshua. The Scripture says, *"And Caleb stilled the people before Moses, and said, let us go up at once, and possess it; for we are well able to overcome it"* (Num. 13:30).

Ten of the spies, however, said, *"We be not able,"* and it was those whom the people believed.

The far greater majority of the time, God speaks through His servants; and to be sure, whatever He says, will always coincide perfectly with Scripture. If some Preacher says something that's not Scriptural, and to be factual, that which is unscriptural is mostly what is proclaimed behind most pulpits, it is not to be heeded in any fashion. However, if it is Scriptural, that means it's the Voice of God, and must be heeded.

OUT OF EGYPT

The phrase, *"Howbeit not all that came out of Egypt by Moses,"* should have been translated, *"Was it not all that came out of Egypt through Moses?"* which refers to that generation which provoked God.

As we have stated, these people began right, but they did not conclude right, and because they did not continue right. Paul is reminding his Readers that it was the entire generation that committed the sin of apostasy, which is a departure from Truth.

Let me emphasize again, that this present generation, and I speak of the year 2000, has in effect departed from the Cross. While of course there definitely are exceptions, and far more than Joshua and Caleb during the time of Israel's apostasy; however, I think it can be said without any fear of plausible contradiction, that the greater body of the Church has abandoned the Cross. To abandon the

Cross, is to ultimately abandon Christ. So that's the condition of the modern Church!

Regrettably, even those who have not abandoned Christ, as it regards that group, most have little understanding of the Cross as it involves their daily Christian experience; therefore, they walk in defeat! It should be obvious, that the situation is grave indeed!

Thank the Lord, the Holy Spirit is definitely dealing with some about this foundation Message, so I would ask you the Reader to pray, that God would help us to proclaim this all-important Word far and wide. In fact, into this critical situation, I believe the Holy Spirit is going to thrust the Cross as never before; consequently, even as previously stated, it will be the dividing line between the True Church and the apostate Church. But yet, it has always been that way, but will now be more pronounced, I think, than ever.

(17) "BUT WITH WHOM WAS HE GRIEVED FORTY YEARS? WAS IT NOT WITH THEM THAT HAD SINNED, WHOSE CARCASES FELL IN THE WILDERNESS?"

The Scriptural breakdown is as follows:

1. God was grieved with that generation for some 40 years, which spoke of it taking that long for all of them to ultimately die.

2. Their problem was sin, the sin of unbelief!

3. These people died physically in the wilderness, but they had long since died spiritually.

GRIEVED

The question, *"But with whom was He grieved forty years?"*, refers to God's wrath continuing, simply because their unbelief continued. God is always angry at unbelief, which proclaims a lack of Faith in His Word. Considering that He is God, and that as God He cannot lie, and considering that He was constantly proving His Word to them, one can understand His anger.

The question may well be asked, *"Did any of these people repent before they died?"*

Possibly so! However, the indication seems to be, that few, if any, did. Unbelief of this nature is an awful thing. Once people start out on this particular road, they seldom turn around. I'm not saying that none

do, but I am saying that most don't. Experience proves that!

It is one thing not to know something; however, it is something else again, for a Truth to be patiently explained, even with signs following, and then for that Truth to be rejected. To be frank, that's where much of the Church is presently.

The non-Pentecostal segment of the Church has been given the Truth about the Holy Spirit, but to no avail on their part. In other words, even though many did accept, the far greater part rejected the Holy Spirit. Consequently, they have set out on a road of unbelief, which in effect, is completely destroying these old line Denominations, at least as far as true spiritual influence is concerned.

As it regards the Pentecostal and the Charismatic varieties, they for the most part, are abandoning the Holy Spirit also. For both groups, it is somewhat being done in the following manner:

The non-Pentecostal groups have tried to preach the Cross, without the Holy Spirit. As a result, they no longer preach much of anything except a social Gospel, which for all practical purposes is worthless.

Regarding the Pentecostal and Charismatic varieties, they have attempted to preach the Holy Spirit without the Cross. The result is fanaticism, with things claimed to be of *"the Spirit,"* when in fact they are of *"a spirit."*

In both cases, the non-Pentecostal and Pentecostal worlds, if all the layers be pulled aside, it is unbelief in the Cross that has caused the problem.

SIN

The question, *"Was it not with them that had sinned . . . ?"*, refers to the sin of unbelief! The Reader should understand the following:

Even though the Blood of Jesus cleanses from all sin, at least when the Believer asks forgiveness (I Jn. 1:9), which means that it as well, handles the effects; still, even considering that, which is a blessing beyond compare, no one gets by with sin. There is always a residue of some nature that lingers, which causes the Believer problems of some sort. So don't think that the fact of sin can be easily dismissed with a wave of the hand. Unfortunately, due to this being the day of

Grace, many Believers have an erroneous conception of sin, thinking that God doesn't call it to account.

The Truth is, God calls sin to account in this day of Grace, even more than He did under the Law. God winked at ignorance then, *"but now commandeth all men everywhere to repent"* (Acts 17:30).

In fact, in this day of Grace, one can lay at the feet of sin, the cause of much of the inclement weather around the world, plus what is referred to as *"natural disasters,"* etc. Some may claim that these things are the work of Satan and not God; however, it must be understood, that God doesn't answer to Satan, but Satan to God (Job, Chpts. 1-2). Satan cannot do anything unless he has permission from God to do so, and even then, it is the Lord Who draws the boundaries, and not the Evil One.

Sin at all times must be judged! Considering that almost all of humanity has spurned the Grace of God, which means they've not taken advantage of God's solution for sin, Who is Jesus Christ, which means that judgment is the only alternative.

With God's people, sin is even more strictly called to account. We as Believers ought to know better, which refers to God's solution which is the Cross. Unfortunately, most Christians have little understanding of the Cross, which guarantees the eruption of the sin nature, which of course spells failure in one way or the other.

While the Cross is the solution for both the unsaved and the saved, God doesn't expect much from the unsaved in their initial coming to Christ. In fact, the only knowledge they have of the Cross is what is given to them by the Holy Spirit, which is basically limited to the fact that Jesus died for mankind and rose again, and that Faith in Him will guarantee Salvation (Jn. 3:16).

However, when it comes to Believers, the Lord as stated, expects much more. We are to know what the Cross actually means, which information is given to us in Romans Chapter 6. We should as well know and understand what Romans Chapter 8 tells us, as it concerns the Holy Spirit, and how He functions entirely within the parameters of the Finished Work of Christ. In other words, we

greatly tie the hands of the Holy Spirit, so to speak, if we do not understand the Cross, thereby placing our Faith in the great Sacrifice of Christ. While it's impossible for we Believers within ourselves, to overcome much of anything, all things and everything are possible with the Holy Spirit (Acts 1:8).

The Holy Spirit can overcome any demon spirit, and do so easily, plus give strength, power, aid, and help, and as much as is needed to any Believer. All of this is at our disposal, providing we place our Faith in the Cross of Christ. That's all that He calls for and demands (Rom. 8:1-2, 11, 13). But unfortunately, most Christians do not know that; consequently, they keep trying to function through and by laws which they have made up themselves, or else someone else has made up, which the Holy Spirit will never honor. Therefore, that Christian walks in defeat!

SAVED FROM SIN

It must be understood, that the Lord does not save us in sin, but rather *"from sin"* (Gal. 1:4). The moment the believing sinner comes to Christ, the Holy Spirit comes into the heart and life of that particular new Believer (I Cor. 3:16).

The Believer should then proceed to ask the Lord to baptize him in the Holy Spirit, which will always be accompanied by the speaking with other tongues (Acts 2:4). It must be remembered, that there is a great deal of difference in being *"born of the Spirit,"* which happens to every new convert, than being *"Baptized with the Spirit,"* which comes only if one asks the Lord for such (Lk. 11:13).

Even though the Holy Spirit definitely comes in at conversion, with this Baptism, which always follows conversion, the Holy Spirit is then given far greater latitude in one's life. That's why Jesus *"commanded them that they should not depart from Jerusalem, but wait for the Promise of the Father"* (Acts 1:4).

Concerning the Baptism with the Holy Spirit, we should understand that this given by Christ in Acts 1:4, is not a suggestion, but rather a Commandment! That's how important that the Baptism with the Holy Spirit actually is.

However, even though the Believer experiences the Baptism with the Holy Spirit,

His work is not automatic. He must have cooperation from us, and above all, we must anchor our Faith totally and completely in the Cross of Christ. He demands that! (Rom. 8:2, 11).

Immediately upon proper Faith being evidenced in the Cross, He sets about to rid us of any sin, thereby making us more and more Christlike. Even though He will attempt to do that even if our Faith is elsewhere than the Cross, His success will be very limited! The Cross must ever be in view, and with the Cross ever in view, which means that our Faith is properly placed, the Holy Spirit will then bring about the Sanctification process within our hearts and lives, which He Alone can do!

CARCASES

The conclusion of the question, *"Whose carcases fell in the wilderness?"*, refers to the deaths of approximately two million people. It was everyone about 20 years old up, who had been delivered from Egypt.

The word *"carcases"* is the translation of a Greek word which in its singular number means *"a limb."* The idea of dismemberment underlies its use. Paul is referring to Numbers 14:29. This means that the entirety of their travels saw the area littered with the graves of those who could have been in the Promised Land, but rather continued in unbelief. Truly, the way of the transgressor is hard! Their bleached bones were a mute testimony to the stupidity of their action.

(18) "AND TO WHOM SWARE HE THAT THEY SHOULD NOT ENTER INTO HIS REST, BUT TO THEM THAT BELIEVED NOT?"

The structure of this Scripture is:

1. God takes an oath concerning certain things, and to be sure, whatever He says will be carried out.

2. For those who continued in unbelief, they would not enter into His rest, i.e., *"be saved."*

3. Their sin was unbelief, which spoke of a lack of Faith in the Word of God.

TO WHOM DID HE DIRECT THIS OATH?

The beginning of the question, *"And to whom swear He,"* proclaims the fact of the

immutability of the Word of God. In other words, whatever God says is going to happen, will happen!

The Lord directed this oath toward those who claimed to be Believers, but, in essence, *"believed not."*

Now, what do the words, *"believed not,"* actually mean.

This wasn't being directed toward those that we would classify as rank unbelievers, in other words, those who didn't believe in God, etc. This was directed at those who claimed to be saved, using today's vernacular. But the truth is, at heart, they were judged by God as being unbelievers. So, the question must be asked:

How many who presently claim to be Believers are looked at, in actuality, by God as *"unbelievers"*? Of course, only the Lord knows the answer to that. But the truth is:

Most of the people in modern Churches simply aren't saved. They are religious, but unsaved!

THE CROSS

Faith, as judged by God, must be registered in Christ and what Christ has done at the Cross (Jn. 3:16; Rom. 5:1; 6:3-14; I Cor. 1:17-18, 21, 23; 2:2).

If the Cross of Christ is denied, or even ignored, as it is in most circles, such constitutes *"unbelief."*

This being the case, such a person is in serious jeopardy.

Let no person think that God doesn't mean what He says, and that He says what He means. The problem presently with the world, and the Church also, is that it doesn't take seriously the Word of God. In fact, that has always been the problem. We must remember what Jesus said:

"For verily I say unto you, till Heaven and Earth pass, one jot or one tittle shall in no wise pass from the Law, till all be fulfilled" (Mat. 5:18).

The Lord saved me when I was eight years of age and baptized me with the Holy Spirit a few weeks later. At the time of this writing (June, 2000), I am 65 years old. I've learned many things about the Word of God, but one thing I've learned, is that *"Man shall not live by bread alone, but by every Word that proceedeth out of the Mouth of God"* (Mat. 4:4). This means that there is not one single thing in the Word of God, no matter how obscure it might seem to be, but that it is extremely important, in fact, so important that it is beyond our comprehension. And yet, far too often, we treat the Word with disdain, ignoring its precepts; however, we must always remember, that every single thing from Genesis 1:1 through Revelation 22:21, will come to pass in totality, and will also prove to be true in totality. I've learned this one thing, that every single problem I've had in life, I have always and without exception, found that the cause has been a lack of understanding of the Word in some way or manner. If something isn't working right, it's because we don't rightly understand the Word. Consequently, every Believer should constantly pray, *"O Lord . . . teach me Thy Judgments"* (Ps. 119:108).

The Holy Spirit through Paul is here saying in this Eighteenth Verse, that even though Israel was His chosen people, because of their unbelief, He did not allow them to enter into His rest. And to be sure and certain, He is saying the same identical thing to us presently.

TO SWEAR

Swearing and oath taking are found in two contexts in the Bible. On the one hand, the Bible, particularly in Matthew 5:34-37 and James 5:12, warns against swearing *"at all."* This appears puzzling at first, both because the Old Testament recognizes the validity of oath taking and because God Himself adds His oath to confirm His Promises.

Let's see what the Bible actually says about this very important item.

Most of us make a distinction between casual words that express an intention and the more formal expressions of a commitment. When the Bible uses terms like *"oath"* and *"swear,"* it refers to solemn commitment.

THE HEBREW WORDS

Two Hebrew terms are translated *"oath"* and *"swear"* in English versions of the Bible. They are *"alah"* and *"saba."*

Of the two, *"alah"* is used less often. As a verb, it means, *"to make a solemn oath"* and is found in six Passages (Judg. 17:2; I Sam. 14:24; I Ki. 8:31; II Chron. 6:22; Hos. 4:2; 10:4). The Hebrew noun of this word indicates a solemn promise, or sworn testimony given in court. It is often used to indicate the certainty of disaster should God's people not keep their Covenant obligations. In this context, *"alah"* is often translated *"cursed,"* and is found quite often in the Old Testament.

The Hebrew *"saba"* is found 184 times in the Old Testament, and it means, *"to swear,"* and is usually used in a reflexive stem with the meaning *"to bind oneself with an oath."* This strong word means to give one's sacred, unbreakable promise as testimony that one will faithfully keep one's word to do or not do a certain thing.

The oath may be sworn to another person (Gen. 21:22-34), or it may be sworn to God (Ps. 119:106) or *"by the Lord"* (I Ki. 1:17). The Old Testament recognizes the pattern of making a binding oath using God's Name (Deut. 6:13; Isa. 19:18) and shows how compelling this form of commitment was supposed to be to God's people (Josh. 9:19).

TO MAKE THE CERTAINTY OF GOD'S PROMISES EVEN CLEARER

The most striking use of the verb, and the most common, is in relating God's sworn commitment to mankind. Many times God's Covenant commitments to Abraham and his descendants are spoken of as God's Sacred Word, sworn to His people. To make the certainty of God's Promises even clearer, God has at times sworn by Himself or His attributes (Gen. 22:16; Ps. 89:35; Isa. 45:23; 62:8; Jer. 22:5; 44:26; 49:13; Amos 4:2; 6:8; 8:7).

Such an addition to the bare promise was unnecessary; God would surely keep His Word. But God graciously added these strengthening phrases to encourage those who, despite the Promise, might hesitate to trust.

The close link between *"Covenant"* and *"Oath"* is significant. The Covenant is the substance of God's stated intention — the constant reminder that God swore (bound Himself by an oath) in making the Covenant Promise and so underlines His firm commitment to do all that the Covenant defines.

NOTES

THE GREEK WORDS IN THE NEW TESTAMENT

The verb *"to swear"* in the Greek is *"omnyo."* It means to bind oneself by an oath and is used mainly in two types of contexts. In one context there are warnings against swearing any oaths. In the other there are references to the oaths that God has sworn historically.

As we have stated, *"swearing"* and *"oath"* taking are found in two contexts in the New Testament. On the one hand, the Bible, particularly in Matthew 5:34-37 and James 5:12, warns against swearing *"at all."* This appears puzzling at first, both because the Old Testament recognizes the validity of oath taking and because God Himself adds His oath to confirm His Promises.

The best explanation of Passages such as these is found in Matthew 23:16, which reports a series of Rabbinical interpretations designed to distinguish between valid (binding) oaths and invalid (nonbinding) oaths.

For instance, a person might promise and bind himself *"by Jerusalem."* But the Rabbis held that unless that person was actually facing Jerusalem when making the oath, it had no force. In essence, the way oaths were misused in Jesus' day made them a cloak for lies; they had lost that most solemn commitment found in the Old Testament oaths. So Jesus said in concluding His teaching, *"Simply let your 'yes' be 'yes,' and your 'no,' 'no'; anything beyond this comes from the Evil One"* (Mat. 5:37). In other words, stop lying. Be the kind of person whose expression of a commitment is so trustworthy that no one will ask for a binding oath.

GOD USES AN OATH TO UNDERLINE HIS INTENTIONS

On the other hand, a number of New Testament Passages remind us that God swore with an oath (Lk. 1:73; Acts 2:30; Heb. 3:11; 4:3; 6:17; 7:20-22, 28) in Old Testament times. But this we must remember:

God did not use an oath to cloak His real intentions. Rather, He used an oath to underline His intentions and to give us a basis for confidence that everything He has promised will come true. God's bare Word is enough for us. But, in His Grace, *"to make*

NOTES

the unchanging nature of His Promise very clear to the heirs of what was promised, He confirmed it with an oath" (Heb. 6:17). Now we who believe can be *"greatly encouraged,"* for in God's Word of commitment we have hope as an anchor for our souls.

(I am indebted to the scholarship of Lawrence O. Richards, for the material concerning Biblical oaths, etc.)

SHOULD NOT ENTER

The phrase, *"That they should not enter into His rest,"* proclaims an extremely solemn statement, as should be overly obvious. And so it was! As stated, the whole of the Sinai was littered with the bleached bones of those who didn't take God's Word seriously. They had been delivered from Egyptian bondage, and greatly so by the Power of God; however, because of unbelief they did not continue on, and, therefore, died lost.

The word *"rest"* as used here, and as we've already explained, definitely refers to the Promised Land, but it does not merely refer to that geographical location. To cut through all the clutter, it refers to Salvation.

While there certainly may have been some Israelites who repented of their unbelief, and even though they were not allowed to enter the promised Land, they were saved, because of a renewal of Faith in God and His Word; however, such evidence is very sketchy to say the least, with the preponderance of evidence being that most, if not all, died eternally lost. In fact, the entirety of the Book of Hebrews is a warning against Christians losing their Faith in Christ, and more particularly what He did at the Cross, thereby becoming unbelievers, and dying eternally lost. Consequently, let us once again give a note of warning.

THE TWO-EDGED SWORD

The Word of God pierces to the joints that connect the natural and the supernatural. It does not ignore the former. On the contrary, it addresses itself to man's reason and conscience, in order to erect the supernatural upon nature. Where reason stops short, the Word of God appeals to the supernatural faculty of Faith; and when conscience grows blunt, the Word makes conscience, like itself, sharper than any two-edged sword.

Once more, the Word of God pierces to the marrow. It reveals to man the innermost meaning of his own nature and of the supernatural planted within him. The truest morality and the highest spirituality are both a direct product of God's Revelation.

But all this is true in its practical application to every man individually. The power of the Word of God to create distinct dispensations and yet maintain their fundamental unity, to distinguish between masses of men and yet cause all the separate threads of human history to converge and at last meet, is the same power which judges the inmost thoughts and inmost purposes of the heart. These it surveys with critical judgment.

If its eye is keen, its range of vision is also wide. No created thing but is seen and manifest. The surface is bared, and the depth within is opened up before it. As the upturned neck of the Sacrificial beast lay bare to the eye of God, so are we exposed to the eye of Him to Whom we have to give our account (Edwards).

Consequently, we should take very seriously the words given by the Holy Spirit *"they should not enter."* We should also remember that this was spoken of those who had been God's chosen people. Understanding that, now please allow me to jump down to the First Verse of Chapter 4:

"Let us therefore fear, lest, a Promise being left us of entering into His rest, any of you should seem to come short of it."

THEY BELIEVED NOT

The phrase, *"But to them that believed not,"* which is actually the conclusion of the question concerning those who would not enter into His rest, gives us here the reason. As plainly stated, it is because of *"unbelief."*

What was it that they didn't believe?

They didn't believe the Word of God concerning the Promised Land, and their ability to occupy that land by His power.

We must always understand, that when unbelief is registered, it is always and without exception, in the face of the mighty moving and power of God. In other words, there is never a cause for unbelief.

Whenever God requires Faith, He always does so on the foundation not only of His

Word plainly given, but as well an abundance of evidence of His Word having brought forth great and mighty results.

For instance, the children of Israel had the evidence of God laying Egypt waste immediately behind them, and as well performing the greatest miracle the world had ever known by opening the Red Sea. Also, He had healed the bitter waters of Marah, thereby quenching the thirst of millions of people plus all the livestock. He had sent Manna, plus many other wonderful things. In other words, miracles were in abundant supply, and it was in the face of these miracles, that the Children of Israel registered unbelief. It is the same presently!

LET'S LOOK AT THE CROSS

Even though the Children of Israel at that particular time would not have understood the word *"Cross,"* still, that's to what this entire plan was leading. From the loins of Abraham and the womb of Sarah, the Lord was to bring a nation of people into this world, for the sole purpose of giving them the Word of God, and to bring in the Messiah, i.e., *"the Redeemer."* Of course, that Redeemer was and is the Lord Jesus Christ. The way and manner in which man would be redeemed, was by the means of the Cross. In other words, this was the Plan of God even from before the beginning of the world (I Pet. 1:18-20). So in reality, the story of the entirety of the Bible is the story of the Cross. This means that the Children of Israel, even though they would not have understood such at that time, nevertheless, were actually rebelling against the Cross of Christ, inasmuch as this was the ultimate Plan of God.

I think if one looks at the entire scenario of rebellion against God, and from whatever source, and by whatever means, one will find that ultimately the individual or individuals are rebelling against the Cross of Christ. Man doesn't want to go God's way, which is the Cross, but would rather devise his own.

One of my associates at the Ministry was speaking with a Pastor from another State. He was relating to him the Message of the Cross. The Brother agreed with him up to a point, but then ultimately began to claim the necessity of adding things to the Cross.

In other words, he really didn't believe in the Cross, despite his claims to do so. In fact, the modern Church knows next to nothing about the Cross of Christ. There has been so little teaching and preaching on the Cross in the last 50 or more years, that the Church is presently, basically ignorant on this all-important subject — actually the Foundation of the Church. And to the degree that one is wrong respecting their understanding of the Cross, to that degree they will be wrong about their understanding regarding everything else as it pertains to the Word of God. I'm trying to say the following:

If one doesn't properly understand the Cross, one doesn't properly understand the Word. It's just that simple!

Martin Luther the great Reformer said, and rightly so, that as one viewed the Cross, so they viewed the Reformation. In other words, if they were opposed to the Cross, they were opposed to the Reformation.

If the modern Church understands anything at all about the Cross, it is basically limited to the initial Salvation process, and to be frank, even that is falling by the wayside. In fact, the Bible is little preached anymore, and by that I mean, the very Bible Plan for Salvation and all that it means to be a Child of God. While the Bible is used every Sunday Morning, it is basically used in the attempt to buttress particular pet doctrines, etc. In other words, Scriptures are twisted out of context with an effort to make them fit some particular belief system, etc.

The only way that the Word of God can be properly understood and properly explained, is to let the Bible form our doctrines, instead of trying to force the Bible into our Doctrines. And if the Bible is properly understood, it will always be understood in the context of the Cross. It is the story of the Cross, which is the story of Redemption.

REBELLION AGAINST THE CROSS

Since the Lord gave me this Revelation on the Cross, which began in 1997, and actually continues unto this hour, and I trust will ever continue, and for the grand reason that it's impossible to exhaust the meaning of the great Sacrifice of Christ, I have been elated at the testimonies we are receiving

regarding the victory that's being brought about in hearts and lives. Actually, numerically that number is increasing almost daily, and spiritually the results can be concluded as little less than miraculous, for which we give the Lord all the praise and the glory. I'm believing that the increase is going to continue until it's an avalanche all over the world. In fact, the *"preaching of the Cross"* is the Message of this Ministry.

But yet, at the same time I am appalled at the lack of interest evidenced by most Preachers. But yet I think I understand why.

Most of the modern Church has opted for humanistic psychology as the cure-all for the ills of man. And yet, the Bible proclaims the Cross of Christ as the cure and the only cure (Rom. 6:3-6, 11, 14; 8:1-2, 11, 13; I Cor. 1:18, 23; 2:2; Gal. 1:4; 6:14). As a result, it's impossible to herald both. I'll be straightforward! I can't see the leadership of the modern Pentecostal Denominations abandoning the psychological way, especially considering that they have loudly trumpeted this particular direction. In fact, it would take a miracle of God for the situation to change. The two systems, that of the Lord and that of the world, are so diametrically opposed to each other, that it's impossible to claim one without strongly opposing the other. It simply cannot be otherwise. What I'm saying is this:

If one is going to opt for humanistic psychology, or any other way other than the Cross, at the same time that individual, or Church, or Denomination, is going to strongly oppose the Cross. They will do so even though in their heart, they know the Cross is right!

RELIGIOUS LEADERSHIP

One of my associates gave me an interesting quote from A. C. Dixon, who served as Pastor of Moody Memorial Church and the Metropolitan Tabernacle of London (1854-1925). He said:

"Every Preacher ought to be primarily a Prophet of God who preaches as God bids him, without regard to results. When he becomes conscious of the fact that he is a leader in his own Church or Denomination, he has reached a crisis in his Ministry. He must now choose one of two courses, that of Prophet of God or a leader of men.

"If he seeks to be a Prophet and a leader, he is apt to make a failure of both. If he decides to be a Prophet only insofar as he can do so without losing his leadership, he becomes a diplomat and ceases to be a Prophet at all. If he decides to maintain leadership at all costs, he may easily fall to the level of Politician who pulls the wires in order to gain or hold a position."

I might quickly add, that when the Preacher attempts to protect his reputation, and I speak of being well-liked by all, he generally compromises the Message. In fact, if that's the stand he takes, it actually is no stand at all, at least for God! Then he's placed in the position of opposing that which is of God, which always comes about sooner or later. If we seek to please men, we cannot please God! If we seek to please God, we cannot please men!

The upshot is, while many will hear the Message of the Cross, accept it, and be gloriously set free, the greater majority will not. Jesus said so! (Mat. 13:33).

It all comes down to Faith. In what and in whom does one believe?

And if we say that we believe in Christ, what do we mean by that statement? We must be careful to understand, that the Holy Spirit through Paul bluntly proclaimed the fact that there is such a thing as *"another Jesus, another gospel and another spirit"* (II Cor. 11:4).

To fully believe in Christ, at least the manner in which the Bible proclaims Christ, one must believe in the Christ of the Cross, and that the Cross answers all the questions of man. Otherwise, and no matter how loud such a Christ is trumpeted, it is not the Christ of the Bible being proclaimed, but another Christ entirely!

God did swear that those who believed not, and we might quickly add, believed not in Jesus Christ and Him Crucified, *"should not enter into His rest."*

(19) "SO WE SEE THAT THEY COULD NOT ENTER IN BECAUSE OF UNBELIEF."

The division of this short Verse is:

1. The Holy Spirit is emphatic in His statement through Paul respecting the results of unbelief.

2. The pronoun *"they"* refers to those considered to be in the Covenant, or at least they had been in the Covenant.

NOTES

3. Unbelief was the major problem then, and unbelief is the major problem now!

DO YOU SEE?

The phrase, *"So we see,"* proclaims the fact that there is no reason for one not to see.

See what?

1. These people, the Children of Israel, delivered from Egyptian bondage, had formerly been Believers.

2. They now registered unbelief in the Word of God, concerning possession of the Promised Land. They said they couldn't accomplish the task, while God said they could! Because of unbelief they wouldn't go forward, and perished in the wilderness.

3. As should be obvious, the entirety of the Book of Hebrews completely refutes the unscriptural doctrine of unconditional eternal security. The Holy Spirit has made this subject so plain, so clear, so absolutely understandable, that there is no excuse for one not to see what is here being said.

BECAUSE OF UNBELIEF

The phrase, *"That they could not enter in because of unbelief,"* proclaims the seventh time in this one Chapter of Hebrews alone, this statement is made in one way or the other (vss. 6, 8, 11-12, 14, 18-19). For the Holy Spirit to say something one time signifies tremendous importance. For Him to say it seven times, and in one Chapter at that, proclaims an amazing emphasis of gigantic proportions. On top of that, He has said, *"So I sware in My wrath, they shall not enter into My rest"* (vs. 11).

The following is a Message preached by Reverend H. W. Cragg at one of the great Keswick conventions conducted in England at about the mid Twentieth Century.

It will not be italicized, but will conclude this particular Chapter.

THE FINISHED WORK OF CHRIST

I would like to say something this afternoon in relation to the particular purpose of our gathering together, about the Finished Work of Christ. Quite obviously we shall only be able to touch upon that great subject in relation to our own need just now, and not in relation to the vastness of that theme, as seen in Holy Scripture.

I have a text for you, then, from John 19, these great central words of our Faith, in Verse 30: *"Jesus therefore received the vinegar and said, 'it is finished.' And He bowed His head, and gave up the ghost."*

It is finished; or as you know very well, it is in the Greek New Testament just one great triumphant word, *"Finished!"* Or as the New English Bible translates it, *"It is accomplished."* It is finished.

THE SIXTH WORD

You will, of course, know that this is the sixth of the seven words from the Cross. Only one more task awaited Jesus Christ, that of handing back His Spirit to God Who gave it. Everything that He had come to do was done. And so this word *"Finished"* tells us that Jesus had reached the end of the journey.

Look again at the way in which the Apostle Paul writes about that journey in Philippians 2:5, *"Let this mind be in you which was also in Christ Jesus, Who . . ."* and this is that journey *". . . being in the form of God, thought it not robbery to be equal with God, but made Himself of no reputation, and took upon Him the form of a servant, and was made in the likeness of men. And being found in fashion as a man, He humbled Himself, and became obedient unto death, even the death of the Cross."*

The great down-stooping of the Lord of Glory was from Heaven's home to Earth's gloom; and then down to the bitter shame, and death, and sorrow of the Cross. And when He got there He said, *"It is Finished."* I am well aware of what may now be springing to your minds, that there was, of course, a second half to the journey, and we speak of His Resurrection: but I am now concerned with that great stooping of our blessed Lord to the Cross, to bear our sins in His Own Body on the Tree; and when He died He cried, *"It is Finished"*; He had reached the end of the journey.

I HAVE FINISHED THE WORK
THOU GAVEST ME TO DO

What a great deal had been crowded into those 33 short years. Jesus had taken human nature upon Himself, and lived here as a man in the flesh; and while so doing He

had lived as the very Son of God, revealing the Father to men, so that if any generation wants to know what God is like, we may look to Jesus Christ with the record of His earthly life given to us in the four Gospels.

But not only had He entered our life, and revealed the Father, but in so doing He had fulfilled all the Old Testament pictures and promises and prophecies of Himself. He could claim, as He prayed to His Father not long before His Passion, *"I have finished the work Thou gavest Me to do."*

I pause here, for we must contemplate this great Truth before we seek to apply it in any measure to ourselves. How delightfully tidy the end was when it came. For our blessed Lord there were no ragged ends, no tasks undone, no purposes frustrated, such as all of us seem to leave behind when we go. Everything was done that He came to do.

FORGIVENESS

A glance at the first three of these seven words from the Cross shows, just as illustration, how beautifully all was left. You remember there was a relationship of Jesus Christ with those Roman soldiers who nailed Him to the Cross, and in the first of these seven words He prayed, *"Father, forgive them, for they know not what they do."* Everything was right between Jesus and the soldiers when He died. It was finished.

SALVATION

Then the second word from the Cross concerned the thief: and you remember the reply He gave to the prayer of the thief, *"Lord, remember me"* — *"Today thou shalt be with Me in paradise."*

He had answered the prayer of the thief, satisfied the longing of his heart, indicated by a distinct promise that his sin was put away. There were no ragged ends when Jesus died. It was all finished.

CARE AND LOVE

And what is to me the most delightful of all: the third and fourth of these words from the Cross — the care that Jesus had for His Mother, and for John.

You remember that there stood at the foot of the Cross that Disciple whom Jesus loved, and as if Jesus could hardly bare to die without seeing that everything was right and ready for Mary His Mother, He turned to John, and He said, *"Behold thy Mother!"* And turning to His Mother, *"Woman, behold thy son."*

And from that hour that Disciple took her into his own home. It was as if Jesus would not die until all was prepared and ready for Mary, His Mother. How beautifully, it all seems now, as we contemplate it from a distance.

"It is finished," He cried! It was the end of a journey. Everything He came to do had been completely finished.

> *"No work is left undone*
> *"Of all the Father wills:*
> *"His toils, His sorrows, one by one*
> *"The Scriptures are fulfilled."*

Finished!

THE RINGING CRY OF VICTORY

But if these great words mark the end of the journey, I should like to suggest to you, in the second place, that they announce *"the ringing cry of victory,"* the shout of victory.

We only read this word *"Finished"* in John's Gospel. It does not occur in the first three Gospels. Instead, Matthew tells us in 27:50 and Luke tells us in 23:46, that Jesus cried with a loud voice, and after that yielded up His spirit. So both Matthew and Luke tell us that there was a loud cry. John tells us what was in that cry.

So we put the three records together, and we note with great clarity and with unmistakable certainty that when Jesus announced the completion of the task, He cried with a loud voice, *"It is Finished!"*

The whole strength of His Being was behind that cry. It was not whispered in weakness but rather strength; it was announced to the world with a ringing note of victory — Finished! Perfected! Completed! Accomplished! All done!

THE CONFLICT

For a moment we pause on the thought of the *"conflict."* We see it foretold in Genesis 3, where God, speaking to Satan through the serpent, says in Verse 15, *"I will put enmity between thee and the woman, between thy seed and her Seed; it shall bruise thy head, and thou shalt bruise His heel."* So

the conflict was foretold by the Father, way back in the beginning of time.

Then we see that conflict entered upon in terms of Matthew 12:28-29, *"If I cast out Devils by the Spirit of God, then the Kingdom of God is come upon you, or else how can one enter a strong man's house and spoil his goods, except he first bind the strong man, then he will spoil his house."* This is the conflict, foretold of God in Genesis, and now entered upon by Jesus as He enters into the strong man's house to despoil his goods, having first bound the strong man.

We see the conflict working up to its culmination in John 12:31, *"Now is the judgment of this world. Now shall the prince of this world be cast out."*

The struggle foretold; the struggle engaged in; the struggle brought to culmination. *"Now is the prince of this world cast out."*

And we see the conflict also recalled in Hebrews 2:14, *"That through death He might destroy him that had the power of death, that is the Devil, and deliver them who through fear of death were all their lifetime subject to bondage."*

SATAN'S GOODS WERE SPOILED

Foretold of the Father, entered by the Son, brought to culmination at the Cross, and recalled in Apostolic Church Life; and all down the years to pick up the strain of this triumphal cry, that what Jesus did when He came was to enter the strong man's house and spoil his goods, having first bound the strong man.

He who died for sin dealt with Satan; and the last word but one from the Cross was this victory word, *"Finished!"* And ever since that moment the Spirit of God has taken up that Truth in convicting the world of judgment: *"The prince of this world is judged."*

THE CROSS OF CHRIST

Why do I approach my application of the theme in this way? Simply because, dear friends, all you and I can do is enter into the experience of that which Christ accomplished for us; and that in entering into the experience of it, it is good for us to tread the steps by which it was achieved.

We can do no better than come again to the Cross of Christ. As we face the problems, and the sins, and the failures, and the break-downs in our own lives, hear Him say with that great triumphal cry once more: *"When I died, I did it for you. I accomplished victory. I accomplished your deliverance. I purchased your pardon. Take from My hands now what I purchased with My precious Blood then."*

THE OFFER OF REMEDY

It was the end of the journey, and it was the shout of victory. And because it was the end of the journey, and because it was the shout of victory, this great triumphal word is to me and to you today *"the offer of remedy."* How? Why?

I think it is true to say that all men are agreed — that is, all Christian men are agreed — that the Cross of Christ must touch down into our lives at some point. It is not a fact of history only. It is certainly not an ornament or a monument. It is certainly not a great achievement wrought out by God for mankind in general.

The Cross of Christ is something which must touch down somehow, somewhere, into my life. And I believe, dear Brethren, that the shout of victory at the point of contact, there was a battle concluded there that it might be concluded here. He triumphed there, in order that He might triumph here.

It was finished then, that it might be finished now, here. And God begins His work, and God accomplishes His work in the soul, when the victory word of Jesus Christ becomes the victory experience of the human heart: and no man has dealings with God except it be upon the basis of the work that He carried to completion at the Cross.

So there is the offer of remedy today, based upon the announcement of victory. Is this what you see? This is what God offers. This is why Jesus died. This is why we are met: that we might enter into the remedy for sin which Jesus Christ completely accomplished at His Cross, and announced in His gracious Word. The offer of remedy!

THE GUILT OF PAST SIN IS FINISHED

And I want to suggest before we conclude, that there is remedy for two serious matters in your life and in mine. When Jesus Christ

NOTES

cried *"Finished!"* there was wrapped up in that great triumphal cry this glorious Truth, that *"the guilt of past sin can be finished,"* in you, and in me. The guilt of past sin finished. Gone. Gone forever, never to be heard or seen or known again. Is that what you see?

It may well be that some of us have come here burdened with a sense of guilt. You would love to be rid of it. In fact, you are here in order that you may be rid of it; for although you only hope to be rid of it, God plans that you shall be. And God plans that you shall be, not because this is Keswick, and not because this is a sermon or a message being delivered on this theme, but because it was purchased for you, and secured for you, before Keswick was known, or the theme opened up at all.

God has provided in the Finished Work of Christ that your sin may be finished; and the record of it put away forever. *"If we confess our sins, He is faithful and just to forgive us our sins, and to cleanse us from all unrighteousness"* (I Jn. 1:9).

GONE

Come back with me, will you, to Leviticus 16 for a minute, in thought.

Here we come to the Day of Atonement in Old Testament economy. On that great Day of Atonement there were two rams brought, one for the Lord, and the other for the scape-goat; and a Priest laid his hands on the head of the goat that was to be led away, after the other goat had been sacrificed, and there confessing the sins of his own life, and the sins of the people, upon the head of the scape-goat, he ordered that it should be led away to a place not inhabited, from which it could never return, but perished with its load in the wilderness, never to be seen or heard of again.

John the Baptist takes up that graphic picture when introducing his two Disciples to Jesus Christ, in John 1:29. He said:

"Behold the Lamb of God, that beareth away the sin of the world!"

Isaiah has brought the same Truth to the surface in his great Chapter 53, where he tells us:

"The Lord hath laid on Him the iniquity of us all." And if God laid my sins on Jesus, then they are gone.

"Since my discharge Thou hast secured,
"And freely in my room endured
"The whole of wrath divine
"Payment God will not twice demand,
"First at my bleeding Surety's hand,
"And then again at mine."
It is finished!
"Oh, sinner, believe it;
"Oh, sinner, receive it!
"Tis for thee."

THE GRIP OF PRESENT SIN IS FINISHED

And just as if I were preaching to a company of unconverted people, who had never known or heard this Truth before, it is exactly the same for God's people in every way. There is no way to be rid of the guilt of sin that is past, except it be through the Precious Blood of Christ; and if I come through the Precious Blood of Christ, there is no way to hold on to it. It is gone. Is this what you need? Is this the Truth for which God brought you here today, with your burdened conscience and your sorry past? The guilt of past sin is finished.

But that is not all. This offer of remedy in the Finished Work of Christ upon the Cross tells me not only that the guilt of past sins is finished, but *"the grip of present sin can be finished as well."* This brings us to that specific thing for which, in the good purpose and providence of God, this Convention movement has been raised up: that not only do sinners need to know that the guilt of past sin is gone, in the blood of Christ, but Christian people need to know that the grip of present sin, habit, impurity, lack of love, can as well be gone. Do you long to be free? Take your longing to the Cross, beloved.

Do you long to conquer? Take your longing to the Cross. For He Who died to put away my sin, rose again, and is my living Lord and Saviour; and by His Holy Spirit, He comes to indwell those He has first redeemed. And He is able to break the power of sin in your life today.

I must pursue this for a moment or two, for it is important that in making a statement of this kind we should say something to open up its theme and its Truth.

By what principle is the grip of present sin finished, when I come to the Cross?

I think there may be two answers that we should consider at this stage.

UNITED WITH CHRIST BY FAITH

Being united with Christ by Faith, is the great Truth of Romans 6, that central Chapter of the Christian experience which makes it perfectly plain that Christ died once for all:
"Knowing that Christ being raised from the dead dieth no more; death hath no more dominion over Him."

And I am united with the Christ over Whom death and sin no longer have dominion; and because I am united with Christ, then I am brought into a position by Grace through Faith, in which death and sin no longer have dominion over me.

This is the great Truth of this Chapter, and this is the great purpose of God for you and for me: that, because I belong to Christ, I am united with the One over Whom death and sin have no dominion. He died to sin, once. And I have been united with that Lord Jesus Christ, united in His death, united in His burial, united in His Resurrection, united in His Ascension; and according to Colossians 3, to be united with Him in His coming again.

For Faith has linked me on with Jesus Christ, and in a way which God has revealed in Scripture, I know that, at every stage of His Redemption work, I share in that great stage, step by step.

Death, burial, Resurrection, Ascension, and ultimate manifestation; and because of that union with Jesus Christ, the Truth of Romans 6:14 is ours today: *"Sin shall not have dominion over you."*

SHARING IN THE VICTORY OF THE CROSS

Let us be clear about this. It does not mean that sin is no longer a possibility. It does not mean that within me, which responds to the allurements and the temptations of sin, is in some strange way cast out.

What it does mean is that sin shall no longer triumph, and hold me in its grip; that my union with Christ is the secret of sharing in the victory of the Cross and, therefore, the remedy purchased for me in that Cross. The guilt of past sin finished, and the grip of present sin finished. Do you know that?

If my memory serves me rightly, it was the year 1928 when I first came to Keswick. I cycled here 90 miles with three friends. We had a great time at our first Keswick, as most young people do; and we learned lessons we had hardly begun to learn before.

In those days there was a Saturday morning meeting, and we had to push away home on Saturday morning. I remember so well, having pushed our bicycles up the hill that leads out of Keswick on the Ambleside Road, pausing at the top of the hill; in the tent here in the valley there was a song of praise rising, and these were the words — *"Sin shall not have dominion over you."* That is the Truth for which we are met. That is the experience to which we are called. That is the Grace that flows from the Finished Work of Christ: not only forgiveness for the past, but victory in the present, with the grip of sin finished.

THE INDWELLING SPIRIT

By what principle is the grip of sin finished? By my union with my blessed Lord; and second, *"because of His indwelling by the Spirit."*

For He Who died to put away my sin, lives within to put away my sinning. The indwelling Spirit of God applies the triumphal victory of that ringing cry, to the day-by-day needs of my unworthy life, to break the power of sin, to release me from its bondage and its grip, and to bring me the remedy He died to purchase.

If you would like to open up this further at your leisure, I would bid you link together two Verses of John's first Epistle — I John 3:9 and 5:18, and notice this glorious Truth of the Scriptures for every man and woman seeking deliverance from the grip of sin.

John writes here under the inspiration of the Holy Spirit: *"Whosoever is begotten of God doth not continue in a course of sin, for His seed remaineth in him, and he cannot sin, because he is born of God."* Set that with I John 5:18:

"We know that whosoever is begotten of God sinneth not, for He that was begotten of God keepeth him, and that wicked one toucheth him not."

Are you begotten of God? Have you been Born-Again? Then He Who away back in history was begotten, keepeth you. *"He that is born of God does not continue in a course of sin."* The grip, the bondage, broken; while the guilt is also cleansed.

"It is Finished!"

Is it finished?

IT IS FINISHED!

I return to one of my favorite quotations drawn from *"Pilgrim's Progress"*:

"And I saw in my dream that just as Christian came up with the Cross, the burden loosed from off his shoulders, and it fell from off his back, and began to tumble; and so continued until it came to the mouth of the sepulcher, where it fell in, and I saw it no more.

"Then was Christian glad and lightsome of heart, and said with a merry heart, He hath given me rest by His sorrow, and life by His death. Then Christian gave three leaps for joy, and went on singing —

> *"Thus far did I come laden with my sin,*
> *"Nor could aught ease the grief that I was in*
> *"Till I came hither. What a place is this!*
> *"Must here be the beginning of my bliss?*
> *"Must here the burden fall from off my back?*
> *"Must here the strings that bound it to me crack?*
> *"Blest Cross, blest sepulcher, blest rather be*
> *"The Man that here was put to shame for me."*

It is finished! There is nothing more to do, save to enter in by Faith into all that Jesus did, once for all, when He died upon the Cross.

The end of a journey. All done. The shout of victory, and the offer of remedy. This is sin finished, done, complete.

It is finished!

— ◼ —

CHAPTER 4

(1) "LET US THEREFORE FEAR, LEST, A PROMISE BEING LEFT US OF ENTERING INTO HIS REST, ANY OF YOU SHOULD SEEM TO COME SHORT OF IT."

The exegesis is:

1. We must not take our Salvation for granted, knowing that it is possible for one to lose one's way, that is if one doesn't stay close to God.

2. The Promise of finishing this course is given to us, that is providing we keep our Faith; however, the Promise can be forfeited through and by unbelief.

3. It is quite possible for any Believer to come short of this Promise, which means that God has no favorites. All must come His way, which is the way of Faith, and more particularly, Faith in Christ and what He did at the Cross on our behalf.

FEAR

The phrase, *"Let us therefore fear,"* presents that which leads to caution and care. This type of *"fear"* doesn't speak of men cringing before a demanding God. It simply refers to the fact that Salvation can be lost, that is if a person is lax in their consecration to the Lord.

This in no way means that one can earn one's way or place, or that works carry any part of the effort. It means simply as stated, that we must exercise caution and care.

In fact, Hebrews is a Book of Doctrines, Warnings, and exhortations. In it the Person of Christ Jesus is set forth as He really is — preeminent in all things. Jesus Christ is God's fullest and most complete Revelation of Himself to man.

On the basis of the finality of this Revelation, Paul gives many strong admonitions accompanied by persuasive exhortations to remain faithful. The Readers are exhorted *"to give the more earnest heed,"* to *"hold fast the confidence and the rejoicing of the hope firm unto the end,"* to beware of *"an evil heart of unbelief"* and *"the deceitfulness of sin"* that hardens the heart, and to *"hold the beginning of our confidence steadfast to the end"* (Heb. 2:1; 3:6, 12-14).

The use of the word *"fear"* was not meant to bring condemnation or despair. Paul is speaking of a Godly, reverential fear that recognizes the awesomeness of God. In fact, there must be a balance in the Believer's life between Faith and fear; we walk by Faith, but we also walk in the fear of God.

NOTES

IN CHRIST

The Godly fear that the Believer should have is not a fear of God's power or a fear of His judgments, for the Believer is in Christ and as such is not the object of God's wrath but of His Grace; it is not a fear that shrinks back in terror from God, for now through Christ Jesus the Believer has access to God.

It is a fear that influences the actions, thoughts, disposition, and attitude of the Believer; it is a fear that causes the Believer to take into account God's standard of Holiness and Righteousness in each action or decision. There is need for a healthy fear of displeasing God. This fear will move the Believer to Godly obedience, as Noah who acted on Faith and through fear.

Fear is an honest response to the warnings of God. The word translated *"fear"* originally denoted *"flight,"* but later came to signify that which causes flight. It is a word that speaks of motivation.

The Believer must not rest on past confessions, but he must continue in Faith consistent to the end. Our initial confession of Faith, and by that, we speak of Faith in the Cross of Christ, is successful only if we continue in it.

As Westcott has said in his Commentary, *"The Epistle to the Hebrews,"* *"To be in Christ is a beginning and not an end. In such a case 'fear' is a motive for strenuous exertion"* (Fjordbak).

THE PROMISE

The phrase, *"A Promise being left us of entering into His rest,"* pertains to two particulars. They are as follows:

1. It is obvious that God's Promises mean much to Paul. Actually the Greek word *"epangelia"* (*"promise"*) occurs more often in Hebrews that in any other New Testament Book (14 times; next in Galatians with 10).

The Promise in question *"still stands."* That is to say, though it has not been fulfilled, it has not been revoked. In one sense, of course, there was a fulfillment, for the generation after the men who died in the wilderness entered Canaan. But throughout this section it is basic to the argument that physical entry into Canaan did not constitute the fulfillment of the Promise. God had promised *"rest,"* which actually referred to Christ, and that meant more than living in Canaan (Mat. 11:28-30).

2. It seems that these persecuted Jews had expected in Christ, to find freedom from all stress and strain such as they were experiencing in the persecutions (Heb. 10:32-34). The Old Testament Jews were taught to believe that tribulation was a mark of God's displeasure with Israel. They did not understand that which was a mark of God's displeasure with His Own in Old Testament times, was instead a mark of His Blessing and a means of purging and refining the lives of Saints in New Testament times. Consequently, their professed Faith was being sorely tried by the adverse circumstances in which they now found themselves. The idea is this:

They were evidently being taught by Jews who were nonbelievers in Christ that things were better under the Law, and that Christ was an imposter anyway!

Unfortunately, such teaching has made headway in modern Christendom. The so-called modern Faith Ministry taught for years, that if one had proper Faith, which incidentally could be received by proper confession, one could forgo all physical, spiritual, and financial problems. The physical has been pretty well dropped from this teaching, and simply because it doesn't work, with the emphasis now being that of money.

At any rate, this teaching has done its terrible damage in the Church, because the so-called Faith exhibited, is Faith in self, etc., which means that it's not Faith in the Finished Work of Christ. Consequently, it's not Faith that God will honor.

Of course, the Preachers who espouse this false doctrine would never agree to what we've just said, and for all the obvious reasons; however, the only ones who are going to get rich in this spectacle are the Preachers.

LIVING FOR CHRIST

Living for Jesus is not an event free life, neither is such promised in the Word of God. As stated, the *"rest"* which is promised by the Lord (Mat. 11:28-30), is the rest one obtains by being properly in Christ. In no way, however, does this promise a lack of situations, disturbances, and problems. At times

those things come, however, we are taught in the Word of God that we can find and have repose in Christ, in the very midst of adverse circumstances. To be frank, the experiences of Paul are a great example. With backs cut to ribbons, and thrown into the stocks in the inner prison, despite the pain and suffering, Paul and Silas could still *"pray and sing praises unto God"* (Acts 16:22-25).

FAITH BRINGS THE REST

The *"rest"* addressed here represents an experience of the inner Christian life, an offer to come up out of the wilderness into the rest of God. While this word can have several meanings, its basic intent is to point toward Salvation by Faith instead of Salvation by works. It is specifically called *"His rest"*; it is of and from God Alone, and it is eternal.

This rest is a possession that we can lay hold of in this present life, and it is offered to those already converted. Though Israel, because of unbelief, failed to enter the rest, the Promise is still available to the people of God.

There is obviously the underlying assumption that when God gives a Promise, He is bound by an oath to fulfill this Promise, even if it does not occur in our lifetime or even the lifetime of the next generation. Wherever God finds hearts full of Faith and that do appropriate His Word, He will fulfill the Promise.

With the strongest words of admonition thus far, Paul says, and to which we have already addressed, *"Let us therefore fear, lest. . . ."* If the Believer were absolutely assured of preservation by God, irrespective of their attitude, faithlessness, or conduct, these words would be out of place. Keep in mind that God's ability to keep us is never the issue; the real issue is the faithfulness or perseverance of the Believer.

Since this responsibility rests upon the Christian, and since it is possible to fall short of that which God has promised, even to miss Him altogether, then this exhortation is necessary.

DEPARTING FROM THE FAITH

The anxiety that Paul feels in giving this exhortation is expressed in the word *"lest."* The word signifies *"lest ever, lest perhaps, lest at any time."*

Paul knew that the possibility of departing from the Faith was an immediate threat, and that the reality of the heart becoming hardened, of being deceived by sin and unbelief, is an ever-present danger with all Believers.

It is important to remember to whom this warning is written. It is not written to sinners or to those whose position in Christ is doubtful, but to *"Holy Brethren, partakers of the Heavenly Calling . . ."* (Heb. 3:1).

In the previous Chapter in Verse 14, the Readers are shown to be *"partakers of Christ,"* or, literally, they *"have become partakers."*

The Apostle is addressing true Believers who already had acquired the privileges and blessings of Faith in Christ Jesus; through these experiences they had come to know Jesus as Lord and Messiah. In fact, their present position was not in question; however, the security of their future position was definitely at stake. They must continue to *"hold . . . steadfast unto the end,"* if they intended to remain in the promised rest of God. To be sure, Paul includes himself in the exhortation, *"Let us therefore fear. . . ."*

COMING SHORT

The phrase, *"Any of you should seem to come short of it,"* proves that it is possible for such to be done.

The example of the failure of the Israelites under faithful Moses was one that spoke strongly to the Hebrew Christians. In their consideration of Christ Jesus the Son, and the Lawgiver Moses, the servant, they had realized the superiority of Jesus over Moses. Now they were being provoked to consider themselves by comparing their position with that of the generation which had left Egypt with Moses. If that generation perished in the wilderness and did not enter Canaan, what ground did the First Century Believers have for thinking they would remain in God's rest if they persisted in unbelief? It is clear that disobedience on the Believer's part would have the same result as it did in the lives of the Israelites. God has not changed in that He always demands Faith from them who follow Him; unbelief consistently results in the judgment of Almighty God.

God's promised *"rest"* still remains open and available to the Believer. The Christian

may enter into the rest which God provided many centuries ago. Israel's unbelief and failure did not nullify God's Promise; God's faithfulness is not limited by the shortcomings of men. There is still an entrance Promise, but with the Promise comes the exhortation that the Believer must continue to guard himself against the same peril that befell Israel — hardness of heart and unbelief.

To even *"seem to come short"* was a thing to be dreaded; consequently, every Believer must be as consistent with his Christian experience, actually his relationship with Christ, as the athlete is when training for an important event. Paul said as much (I Cor. 9:24-25).

HOW ONE OBTAINS THIS "REST"

Of course, the *"Rest"* of which Paul speaks here, ultimately pertains to Heaven; however, at the same time it pertains to the *"rest"* found in Christ Jesus, which speaks of this present life.

What was Jesus speaking about when He said, *"Come unto Me, all ye that labor and are heavy laden, and I will give you rest.*

"Take My yoke upon you, and learn of Me; for I am meek and lowly in heart: and ye shall find rest unto your souls.

"For My yoke is easy, and my burden is light" (Mat. 11:28-30)?

The *"Rest"* of which Jesus spoke, did not apply directly to Heaven, but rather one's victorious daily walk, which can only be found in Christ.

There are millions of Christians who truly love the Lord, and in fact who are consecrated to Him, but are not living victorious lives. They are trying to live the life they know they ought to live, but despite all their efforts they're not being successful. In fact, their problem, whatever it might be, and despite their efforts, is not getting better but rather worse. Many of these Christians, if not all, are extremely confused, and simply because many of these people, as stated, are trying very hard, but yet with no victorious results.

What is wrong?

The *"rest"* of which Jesus spoke, was rest from self-effort, one's own labors, one's own efforts, etc., and we speak of the attempt to try to live a proper, Christian life. That seems somewhat strange, doesn't it?

The idea would seem to be that we try to live this victorious life, and try to do so by making every effort we know how to make.

That answer is correct, and at the same time, incorrect!

There is only one way that any Believer can have the *"rest"* of which Jesus spoke, and which refers to living a victorious, overcoming, Christian life. One must place one's Faith totally and completely in the Finished Work of Christ, which refers to what Jesus did at the Cross and in His Resurrection. The Believer must understand, that the victory and power which he seeks, cannot be brought about by self-effort of any nature. It cannot be earned, purchased, merited, or obtained by any means of such like effort. It is always a free gift (Rom. 6:23).

To obtain this free gift, which refers to total and complete victory in every capacity, as stated, all one has to do is exhibit Faith in the Cross, and continue to do that, even on a daily basis (Lk. 9:23-24; Rom. 6:3-6, 11, 14; 8:1-2, 13).

One might quickly ask, how such Faith can bring about such miraculous results?

ENTER THE HOLY SPIRIT

To be sure, every Believer has the Holy Spirit; however, most Believers do not obtain near the help from the Spirit which He desires to give, simply because our Faith is misplaced. The secret to a victorious, overcoming, Christian life, and such on a perpetual basis, is found exclusively in the following:

1. Everything we need comes through the Cross of Christ.

2. We must exhibit Faith in the Cross at all times.

3. Once we do this, the Holy Spirit will then work mightily upon our behalf, simply because He works totally and completely within the parameters of the Finished Work of Christ. Consequently, He demands our Faith in that great Sacrifice.

With this done, and we speak of Faith in the proper object, which is always the Cross of Christ, the Holy Spirit will then do His great Office work within our hearts and lives, guaranteeing us the victory for which Jesus paid such a price. In fact, the problem with almost all Christians is misplaced Faith. In other words, they have Faith in this, Faith in

that, and Faith in the other, but not Faith in the Cross; consequently, such type Faith, God will never honor, because it is outside the parameters of the Sacrifice of Christ, which goes right back to Genesis, Chapter 4.

The Scripture plainly says, *"By Faith Abel offered unto God a more excellent sacrifice than Cain* (which Sacrifice of Abel was symbolic of Christ), *by which he obtained witness that he was righteous* (God imputed to him Righteousness, because his trust was in Christ), *God testifying of his gifts* (which means that God accepted his Sacrifices)*: and by it he being dead yet speaketh* (meaning that our Faith must be in the same category, that of the Sacrifice of Christ)*"* (Heb. 11:4).

As everyone understands, Cain offered a sacrifice of his own making, instead of the slain lamb which symbolized Christ, and which sacrifice God could not accept. So, the Christian can either put his Faith and trust in what Christ did at the Cross, or something else. The *"something else"* will always have the same results which accrued to Cain — rejection by God.

Unfortunately, Cain grew incensed at his brother because Abel's sacrifice was accepted, and his rejected; consequently, he killed his brother. That spirit has permeated all who reject the Sacrifice of Christ. They grow incensed at those who evidence Faith in Christ and what He did at the Cross on our behalf, placing total confidence in that Finished Work. So, proper Faith will always be opposed by those who trust in other things. In fact, this is the great battleground of Christianity. We either trust Christ and what He did at the Cross on our behalf, or we trust a salvation of our own making.

If we trust Christ and what He did at the Cross, the *"rest"* of which Jesus spoke, will definitely be granted unto us. Otherwise, it is not possible.

So, the millions of Christians who are struggling to live a holy life, and are failing, is because they do not understand God's prescribed order of victory, which is the Cross of Christ.

ETERNAL LIFE

The phrase, *"Any of you should seem to come short of it,"* refers to the fact of coming short of Eternal Life.

Again and again the Readers are reminded of the danger of unbelief and the possibility of coming short of God's Promise. The purpose of the Apostle is to keep the Readers from being disloyal to Christ, to encourage them to persevere to the end, and to prevent the Hebrew Christians from even appearing to be missing what God desires for them, which certainly applies to all others as well.

They must enter the unique experience of God's rest in complete surrender of will, life, and plans to the Lord Jesus Christ, with constant dependence upon God for the ability to fulfill that which God has called them to perform.

It is clearly pointed out that the promised rest missed by the ancient people of God is still available to the Church today. The *"rest"* is open to those who will believe; it is offered only to those whose Faith is solely in Jesus the Messiah. If the Believer will continue in Faith, and that is the key, he will surely enter that blessedness that God has promised in His Kingdom.

THE HOLY SPIRIT IS EMPHATIC

Notice that the Spirit said through Paul, that even *"to seem to come short of it"* was a thing to be dreaded.

This statement points to the statement made by Christ to the Laodicean Church. Jesus said:

"I know thy works, that thou art neither cold nor hot: I would thou wert cold or hot.

"So then because thou art lukewarm, and neither cold nor hot, I will spew thee out of My mouth.

"Because thou sayest, I am rich, and increased with goods, and have need of nothing; and knowest not that thou art wretched, and miserable, and poor, and blind, and naked" (Rev. 3:15-17).

What a terrible indictment! And yet, I'm afraid that this which Paul has said, and this which Christ has said, applies too readily to the modern Church. One can come short of the Lord in many and varied ways.

For me to list all of these ways would take up too much time and space. Suffice to say, that if one will do the following, one definitely will not come short of this great *"rest"* which the Lord has promised.

NOTES

If any Believer will look exclusively to the Cross of Christ, i.e., *"the Finished Work of Christ,"* totally and completely for all sustenance, understanding that it is the Cross that has made all blessings possible, the Believer will be well on his way to victory and in every capacity.

As well, one should ask the Lord to reveal the meaning of the great Sacrifice of Christ to him, which the Lord most definitely will do respecting every sincere, honest heart.

The Believer will there find everything for which the heart craves. He will find that this is the means by which God brings all things to needy hearts and lives. In fact, there is no other way. It is only by the Cross that God can reveal Himself to His people.

Moses probably wrote Psalm 91. And if he did, he wrote the first of the 150 which were compiled. He said:

"He that dwelleth in the secret place of the Most High shall abide under the shadow of the Almighty.

"I will say of the Lord, He is my refuge and my fortress: my God; in Him will I trust.

"Surely He shall deliver thee from the snare of the fowler, and from the noisome pestilence.

"He shall cover thee with His feathers, and under His wings shalt thou trust: His Truth shall be thy shield and buckler" (Ps. 91:1-4).

"The secret place of the Most High" is the Cross of Christ. That is the shelter which is the *"shadow of the Almighty."* To be sure, I know, for I personally know what it is to not abide under that shadow, and because of trusting in self. To be sure, much of my negative efforts were because of ignorance of the Cross; nevertheless, the results were extremely negative.

And then after seeking the face of the Lord ardently and sincerely for over five years, that He would show me the way to victory, the Lord did exactly that, giving me the Revelation of the Cross which has totally and completely changed and revolutionized my Christian experience.

I now know what it is to *"dwell in the secret place of the Most High."* I now know what it is to *"abide under the shadow of the Almighty."* And to be sure, the safety and protection there afforded, and where alone it is afforded, provides such security and well-being, that it defies all description.

The Reader must understand, that what is impossible with man is not only possible with God, but in fact very easy. By this term I'm speaking of the attacks of Satan. The Evil One is a formidable foe. And to be sure, no Believer within himself is a match for the wiles and stratagems of Satan.

But the Truth is, we aren't expected to be. We are to understand that our safety and protection is in the Cross (Gal. 6:14). And when our Faith is there placed, the Holy Spirit, Who is God, will then do great and mighty things for us. Satan has no problem with us, but he wants no part of the Holy Spirit whatsoever!

So, if the Reader will stay anchored in the Cross of Christ, seeking to learn more and more about this great Sacrifice, he need never worry about *"coming short of the rest promised by the Lord."*

(2) "FOR UNTO US WAS THE GOSPEL PREACHED, AS WELL AS UNTO THEM: BUT THE WORD PREACHED DID NOT PROFIT THEM, NOT BEING MIXED WITH FAITH IN THEM THAT HEARD IT."

The breakdown of this Scripture is as follows:

1. The Good News is preached unto us, which is presently based on better Promises, and because of what Christ did at the Cross on our behalf. The question is, what are we doing with this *"Good News"*?

2. The Good News preached to Israel in the wilderness, was ultimately the same as that preached to us, but temporarily less. The Good News which was announced to the First Century Readers of this Epistle, and to us presently as well, was and is that of a spiritual rest in Christ. The Good News given to the generation which came out of Egypt was that of a temporal, physical rest in a land flowing with milk and honey, offered to a people who have been reduced to abject slavery for 400 years, with all its attendant difficulties. Due to Christ not having yet gone to the Cross, this then was the limit of the Promise of God, at least in the temporal capacity. Of course, upon continued Faith, the Israelites of old, would ultimately make Heaven their eternal home, but which awaited the Cross.

3. For the Word of God to be effective in one's heart and life, it must be received by Faith. Otherwise, there is no profit.

4. To merely hear the Word is not enough. The Word must be believed. We are seeing here the core reason for failure and for defeat as it refers to any individual, that is, concerning spiritual things.

THE GOSPEL

The phrase, *"For unto us was the Gospel preached, as well as unto them,"* presents the Holy Spirit making the Gospel *"one Gospel."* That means it's not five, four, or two Gospels, but only one.

There has ever been one Message, whether to Israel of old, or the First Century Church, or to the modern Church. This must be clearly understood!

What is that Message?, i.e., *"the Gospel?"*

One can sum up the entirety of the Gospel Message, by the word given to Abraham and his response. The Scripture says:

"Abraham believed God, and it was accounted to him for Righteousness" (Gen. 15:6; Gal. 3:6).

What is it that Abraham believed?

He believed many things, but primarily, he believed God as it regarded the Promise of the Lord to send a Redeemer into this world, in order that man might be saved. Abraham simply believed that, and his Faith secured for him the perfect, pure, Righteousness of Christ (Gal. 3:16).

It plainly says, *"And the Scripture, foreseeing that God would justify the heathen through Faith, preached before the Gospel unto Abraham, saying, in thee shall all nations be blessed"* (Gal. 3:8; Gen. 12:3).

To sum it up, the *"Gospel"* is *"Jesus Christ and Him Crucified"* (I Cor. 2:2).

Concerning the Gospel, Paul also said, *"One Lord, one Faith, one Baptism"* (Eph. 4:5).

The *"one Lord"* here mentioned, is the Lord Jesus Christ. It means that He Alone through the Cross affords Salvation, hence, Peter saying, *"Neither is there Salvation in any other: for there is none other Name under Heaven given among men, whereby we must be saved"* (Acts 4:12).

The *"one Faith"* spoken of here refers to what Christ did at the Cross and in His

Resurrection, and Faith in that Finished Work. Any other type of Faith can never be recognized by God. The object of Faith must always be the Sacrifice of Christ. If we attempt to believe in Jesus apart from the Cross, or to espouse Him in any way other than *"Jesus Christ and Him Crucified,"* pure and simple, we are believing, preaching, and teaching *"another Jesus"* (II Cor. 11:4). The *"Faith"* of which Paul speaks here, concerns totally and completely, Faith in the Finished Work of Christ, hence it being spoken of as *"one Faith."*

"One Baptism," refers to the Believer being baptized into Christ as it regards the Crucifixion of the Saviour (Rom. 6:3-5). Paul is not speaking here of Water Baptism as many think. He is speaking of the Baptism into Christ, which is brought about by the believing sinner expressing Faith in what Christ did at the Cross on his behalf (Rom. 6:3). This is the *"Baptism"* that saves, and the only Baptism which saves. Hence it is called *"one Baptism."*

So, if the Preacher is not preaching *"Jesus Christ and Him Crucified,"* he is not preaching the Gospel; hence, if any Believer is not placing their Faith exclusively in the crucified Son of God, then what they have is *"another gospel"* (II Cor. 11:4).

As we have ever stated, the Message has ever been one. At the very outset, even in the Garden of Eden, immediately after the Fall, God told Satan through the serpent, *"I will put enmity* (hatred) *between thee* (Satan) *and the woman* (Satan hates all women, simply because it is through woman that the Redeemer came into the world), *and between thy seed* (humanity) *and her Seed* (the Lord Jesus Christ. There is a built-in animosity in the hearts of all unredeemed against Jesus Christ in some manner)*; it* (He, meaning Christ) *shall bruise thy head* (the Cross), *and thou shalt bruise His heel* (the terrible horror of the Crucifixion)*"* (Gen. 3:15). So we see, that the Cross has been the Message from day one!

NO PROFIT

The phrase, *"But the word preached did not profit them,"* speaks of the Children of Israel in the wilderness who refused to

believe God concerning going into the Promised Land, and, therefore, perished in the wilderness.

Why did the Gospel, which definitely was given to them, not serve as profit to them? Well of course, the answer is in the next phrase, as it regards them having no Faith. But let's look at it in another way:

What is the greatest hindrance to Faith?

Without a doubt, the greatest hindrance to Faith is dead works. And what do we mean by that?

Continuing to use ancient Israel as an example, the Lord gave the Law to these people, which they solemnly promised to keep. Of course, that within itself was a great mistake, and for the simple reason that despite all their boasts, it was impossible for them to keep the Law (Ex. 19:8).

They should have said, *"Lord, we are a weak and needy people, and cannot by any means do this which we need to do; consequently, You must help us!"* But instead, they said the opposite.

As a result, in what few efforts they did make to keep the Law, they came to trust in the ceremony and the ritual only, and not at all in what these things represented, which were the coming Christ. Consequently, they were functioning in the realm of dead works, and not at all in Faith. It is the same with the modern Church.

WORKS, THE GREATEST HINDRANCE TO FAITH

The Reader should study that heading carefully, *"Works, the greatest hindrance to Faith!"*

First of all, let's define works.

Works consists of anything in which we place our Faith and confidence, other than the Finished Work of Christ. Putting confidence in these things, whatever they might be, means that we're trusting in that and not solely in Christ. Consequently, this is the greatest hindrance to Faith.

These things fool us, because many times the *"works"* are good things within themselves. For instance, the Sacrifices of old were certainly good, and in fact had been given by God as a means by which Israel could commune with Him, and be forgiven of sin.

So, the Sacrifices within themselves, plus all the other parts of the Law, were not at all bad or evil. In fact they were good! It was Israel's erroneous attitude toward these things, which turned them into mere rituals and ceremonies, which brought about great hurt. It is the same with the modern Church.

Water Baptism, the Lord's Supper, in fact, the Church itself, are all things within themselves which are holy; however, millions of Christians turn them into *"works"* thinking that by merely engaging in them in some way, Salvation will be afforded. In other words, they're looking to these things instead of Christ. If one is trusting in works, one is not trusting in Christ.

Consequently, it's not even ignorance of the Word which is the greatest hindrance to Faith, or even many other things of which we could name, but rather *"dead works."* In fact, this is the greatest problem with the Child of God. Satan ever seeks to divert our Faith to the wrong object, i.e., *"works."* If he can do this, he will destroy our Faith quicker than anything else in which we might engage.

BUT WHAT ABOUT THESE FIRST CENTURY JEWS WHO HAD ACCEPTED CHRIST?

We know from Paul's terminology, that these individuals were losing Faith. But the question is, was it because of works?

It definitely was!

In fact, the entire argument was over Faith and works. They were thinking of abandoning Faith in Christ, and going back to the dead works of the Temple. This was the entire crux of the matter. They were seriously considering going back to the Sacrifices, the Feast Days, and all the ritual and ceremony of the ancient Mosaic Law.

In its day, it had been right; however, Jesus had now fulfilled all its precepts, and to Whom the Law had ever pointed. Therefore, it was extremely noxious to God, for this Temple worship to continue, seeing that Jesus had already fulfilled all of its symbolism; consequently, He completely destroyed the Temple in A.D. 70, by using the Roman General, Titus, as His instrument. So, the problem definitely was *"works"* as it regards

the First Century Jewish Believers, just as it was Israel of old, and just as it is presently.

FAITH

The phrase, *"Not being mixed with Faith in them that heard it,"* presents the one ingredient that is required in totality, that is if men are to receive anything from God. God demands Faith, and what do we mean by that?

The answer to this question is all-important! If we miss it here, we miss it everywhere.

What does it mean to have Faith in God?

Most would answer that it refers to having Faith in His Word, in other words, believing what He has said. While that certainly is true, the problem is, most Believers don't know what He has said.

In fact, what has God said in His Word?

The answer to that is the answer to this question.

God has said in His Word that man is lost, cannot save himself, and that He (God) has provided a redeemer, Who is the Lord Jesus Christ. In order to bring about this Redemption, Christ died on the Cross, thereby paying the penalty for lost mankind, which was death, thereby satisfying the curse of the broken Law, and affording Salvation to all who would simply place their Faith and trust in what He did at the Cross on their behalf (Jn. 3:16; Rom. 10:9-10, 13; Eph. 2:8-9; Rev. 22:17).

Once again, it is *"Jesus Christ and Him Crucified"* (I Cor. 2:2).

That is the Word of the Lord, and that is the foundation of our Faith, actually that in which we are to believe (Jn. 3:16).

The central core of the Word of God, or as one might say, the centrality of the Gospel, is the Cross of Christ (I Cor. 1:18, 23). So, when we speak of Faith, we must always understand, that it is Faith in Christ, and what He did at the Cross on our behalf. If we attempt to separate Christ from the Cross, or the Cross from Christ, we blaspheme!

Many years ago, I heard the great Pentecostal Preacher, A. N. Trotter say, *"If we go beyond the Cross, we backslide, thereby losing our way."* I will confess, that at that particular time, I knew what he said was right, but I really didn't understand it. What did he mean, *"going beyond the Cross"*?

After many years of living for the Lord, and especially since the Lord has given me the Revelation of the Cross, I now know that he was speaking of Believers trusting in Christ and what He did at the Cross as it regards Salvation, but then removing their Faith to something else after they are saved. In fact, this is where most Christians are presently.

Their Faith isn't in the Cross, but rather other things. They're looking to Preachers, false Faith, themselves, their good works, with the list being almost endless, with very few looking toward the Cross.

In fact, it is impossible to go beyond the Cross, despite all the millions who have tried and are trying. In fact, the Cross of Christ is so absolutely inexhaustible, so great and wondrous in its depth, height, length, and breadth, that Paul refers to it as *"The Everlasting Covenant"* (Heb. 13:20).

When the Holy Spirit closed out the New Testament Canon of Scripture in Revelation 22:21, by saying *"Amen"* as His last word, He in effect was saying, *"There will not be another Testament, for this Testament or Covenant afforded by Christ is perfect."*

As we stated at the beginning of explanation regarding this Second Verse, it is not enough to merely hear the Gospel, we must believe it as well. This means that the implication is clear:

It is not the hearing of the Gospel by itself that brings final Salvation, but rather, it is the appropriation of it by Faith. Genuine Faith must be consistent and persistent. The Word once mixed (*"blended, tempered"*) together with Faith becomes effective and profitable to those who receive it. To neglect this Message is to finally reject it; to believe is to act upon it.

But again we emphasize, that when we speak of *"having Faith"* or *"believing,"* we're speaking of our attitude, mind-set, passion, and confidence, being directed totally to the great Sacrifice of Christ. To believe otherwise, is not to believe at all! Jesus must always be the Jesus of the Cross. The Promises of God must always be understood in relationship to the Cross. In other words, every single thing we receive from God, and irrespective as to what it might be, comes exclusively to us according to what Jesus did

NOTES

at the Cross on our behalf. Grace flows through this medium, as well as Peace, in fact, everything!

REPETITION!

I realize the Reader may grow weary at my constant proclamation of the Cross from every angle in which I know how to approach this vast subject. However, I must remind the Reader, that the great problem of the Church today, is a misunderstanding of the Cross, or else complete unbelief as it regards the Cross. Either way, tragedy is the result!

Considering that this is the single most important subject of the Word of God, actually the very Foundation on which all Doctrine is built, I think it would be very difficult to overstate the case.

Knowing how important this is, and being compelled by the Holy Spirit to address this subject in every way possible, I can do no less.

Last week at about this time (as I dictate these notes on June 9, 2000), along with Frances, Donnie, Debbie and others, we were at the ruins of Corinth in Greece, where Paul built that great Church in the First Century. The great Apostle came to this city, sent by the Lord, fresh from a short stay in Athens. There is some small evidence that Paul was not pleased with the Message he preached on Mars' Hill in that city (Acts 17:22-31). To be sure, it was a great Message containing great Truths, and the Lord definitely helped him in its presentation.

But when he wrote his first Epistle to the Corinthians, he said, *"For I determined not to know anything among you, save Jesus Christ and Him Crucified"* (I Cor. 2:2).

I personally believe that he made this particular statement, and others similar, because the Holy Spirit had told him that this was the Message that must be preached.

It did little good, and it does little good, to attempt to deal with men on a philosophical level, or in fact, any level, other than their condition and its remedy, which is *"Jesus Christ and Him Crucified."* I think that Paul might have said in his heart, *"I made that mistake once, but I won't make it again."* I think from the time of his short stay in Athens, that his Message totally and completely, was the Message of the Cross. To be sure, he had no doubt ministered accordingly from the very beginning; however, as his Ministry progressed, I believe that more and more he saw, even as the Holy Spirit revealed it unto him, the absolute necessity of the Cross of Christ being the centrality of the Gospel. Hence, he would proclaim this Message, and this Message only, even to the end of his days and Ministry. In fact, in his last Epistle which he wrote to Timothy, he said, *"It is a faithful saying: for if we be dead with Him, we shall also live with Him"* (II Tim. 2:11).

By him using the term *"it is a faithful saying,"* refers to the fact that he had preached the Message of the Cross to such an extent, that it had become known as his Message.

When he spoke of being *"dead with Him, and living with Him,"* he was speaking totally and completely of the Crucifixion and the Resurrection of Christ, which was all carried out on our behalf, and which by Faith we literally enter into this great accomplished Work (Rom. 6:3-5).

What an awful thing, that the Gospel was given to ancient Israel in the wilderness, but it served no purpose. They held the pearl of great price in their hands, which meant they were the most privileged people on the face of the Earth, but they simply did not know what was in their midst. They treated it lightly and with disdain!

WHAT IS YOUR TREATMENT PRESENTLY OF THE GOSPEL?

How important is the Gospel to you? Is it something on which your thoughts are directed one hour on Sunday morning, with your mind and attention taken up with other things the rest of the time? How prominently does it figure into your lifestyle?

Of course, the answer to these questions is the single most important answer that one could ever give. When we speak of the Gospel we're speaking of something that is of such worth, such value, that there is no way that one could properly describe its significance.

That's what Jesus was speaking about when He said:

"Again, the Kingdom of Heaven is like unto treasure hid in a field; the which when a man hath found, he hideth, and for joy

thereof goeth and selleth all that he hath, and buyeth that field."*

He then said:

"Again, the Kingdom of Heaven is like unto a merchant man, seeking goodly pearls:

"Who, when he had found one pearl of great price, went and sold all that he had, and bought it" (Mat. 13:44-46).

Do you consider your Salvation as a *"pearl of great price"*? How important is all of this to you? Is God in all of your thoughts? Are you so *"in Christ"* that your every need is supplied by Him?

It is sad, but so many Christians spend so much of their time on the temporal to the neglect of the eternal. As someone has rightly said:

"One life will soon be past,
"Only what's done for Christ will last."

(3) "FOR WE WHICH HAVE BELIEVED DO ENTER INTO REST, AS HE SAID, AS I HAVE SWORN IN MY WRATH, IF THEY SHALL ENTER INTO MY REST: ALTHOUGH THE WORKS WERE FINISHED FROM THE FOUNDATION OF THE WORLD."

The exegesis is:

1. Faith is the key to all the things of God, and more particularly, Faith in what Christ did at the Cross.

2. If Faith is not in evidence, there is no Salvation.

3. As the Lord did swear in His wrath that unbelievers would not enter into His rest, the same oath holds true in reverse. In other words, He swears that those who exhibit Faith will enter in.

4. The whole thing has been planned out from the foundation of the world, which means that we face no problem for which God does not already have the solution.

FAITH BRINGS REST

The phrase, *"For we which have believed do enter into rest,"* proclaims unequivocally, that Faith is the key.

The word *"rest"* emphatically declares that they who enter into Christ, Who is the True Sabbath, enter into God's true rest.

In essence, the Bible presents three *"rests."* They are:

1. His creation rest as evidenced in Verse 4.

2. His Canaan rest which is evidenced in Verse 6.

3. His Redemption rest which is evidenced in Verse 1.

The first two are fore-pictures of the third. It must be understood that it is emphatically *"His Rest."* Into this rest — His Own Rest — God invites sinners to enter. Unbelief shuts it out while belief admits to it. Consequently, the Apostle beseeches the Jewish Christians to be on their guard lest through unbelief they should come short of entering it, just as, through unbelief, their forefathers came short of the promised Canaan rest. They went a certain distance and then perished. They did not continue to the end.

GOD DID SWEAR IN HIS WRATH

The phrase, *"As I have sworn in My wrath, if they shall enter into My rest,"* is derived from Psalms 95:11. As we have stated, the statement although translated correctly, does not convey its full meaning on the surface. The idea is, that God has sworn in His wrath, a wrath incidentally caused by the unbelief of Israel. No matter that they were His chosen people, and that He had delivered them with a high and mighty hand out of Egyptian bondage, failing Faith they would not enter into the Promised Land; however, carried in the Text is also the idea, that God has sworn that Faith in Him will guarantee one entering into His Rest.

It's very difficult to properly say it in English, but the essence is that His wrath, incidentally brought on by unbelief, while shutting the door, at the same time opens the door. To attempt to explain it more clearly, that is if it's possible to do so, it is somewhat as if God said in His anger, that He will protect Faith at any cost!

THE FINISHED WORK

The phrase, *"Although the works were finished from the foundation of the world,"* refers to this great Plan of Salvation having been finished even before the world was created.

It actually speaks of Christ and the Cross, with Peter saying, *"Forasmuch as ye know that ye were not redeemed with corruptible things, as silver and gold, from your vain conversation received by tradition from your fathers;*

NOTES

"But with the Precious Blood of Christ, as of a Lamb without blemish and without spot:

"Who verily was foreordained before the foundation of the world, but was manifest in these last times for you" (I Pet. 1:18-20).

The Greek word for *"finish"* is *"ginomai,"* and means *"to come into being, or happen,"* and at times meaning *"to accomplish, or carry out."*

The way the word *"finish"* is used in this Third Verse, records God's promise of rest to those who listen to His Voice and obey it, for His works have been *"finished since the creation of the world."* The thought is that the whole of history is implicit in God's original creative act: the end exists in the beginning, one might say.

For us this means that we face no problem for which God does not already have the solution; consequently, we need not struggle against circumstances, but within our situation we can rest. We can rely upon Jesus to guide us to the solution God has provided from the very creation of the world.

THE MAGNITUDE OF GOD

Does the Reader actually realize what he or she is actually reading here? This one phrase as given by Paul in the latter portion of this Third Verse proclaims the fact that whatever circumstances might arise, the Lord has already addressed the situation, and that no circumstance can arise, but that it has already been addressed. In other words, Satan cannot spring anything on you, that would be foreign to the Lord, or a surprise to Him. And even above that, the solution of victory is already a foregone conclusion, that is if you will believe God. Our trouble is this:

We forfeit the victory that's already won, already accomplished, already brought about, already a sealed fact in the mind of God, simply because we refuse, or at least, fail to believe God in some way. These Chapters are literally riddled with the proclamation that God demands Faith of His people.

WHAT IS FAITH?

All of us are well acquainted with the Hebrews Passage, *"Now Faith is the substance of things hoped for, the evidence of things not seen"* (Heb. 11:1).

However, this Passage moreso than anything else, describes the presence of Faith, rather than the definition.

Perhaps the word *"believe,"* or *"believing"* as used over and over again in these passages, define Faith as nothing else. The Holy Spirit didn't use these words carelessly. He used them for a reason.

To believe, is to simply have a firm conviction as to the reality of that in which one believes. Consequently, we are now talking about the *"object of Faith."* Almost without exception, the object of Faith in the New Testament is Jesus. Only 12 Verses have God as the object of Faith.

Why? The reason is clearly expressed by Jesus Himself: *"I am the Way and the Truth and the Life. No one comes to the Father except through Me"* (Jn. 14:6).

God the Father has revealed Himself in the Son. The Father has set Jesus before us as One to Whom we must entrust ourselves for Salvation. It is Jesus Who is the focus of Christian Faith.

Consequently, in the context of our Faith and in our relationship with Jesus, *"believing"* has come to mean the following:

1. The happy trust that a person places in the Person of Jesus Christ.

2. The allegiance to Him that grows out of that very personal commitment.

WHAT DOES BELIEVING IN JESUS ACTUALLY MEAN?

Of course, anything that Jesus is, that we must believe. And this refers to what the Bible says about Him; however, the main core of our believing must focus on the following:

We must always and without fail make Jesus and the Cross the object of our Faith. To merely believe in Jesus is not really enough. We must believe in the Sacrifice which He actually was.

The very purpose of Christ, His mission, His work, His very appearing, were all for the purpose of going to the Cross, and there to pay the price for dying humanity, thereby redeeming us from the powers of darkness. Paul plainly said:

"Who gave Himself for our sins, that He might deliver us from this present evil world, according to the Will of God and our Father" (Gal. 1:4).

In fact, the entirety of the New Covenant can be explained in the meaning of the Cross, which Paul gave to us in the entirety of his 14 Epistles, but more specifically in Romans, Chapter 6.

As it regards symbolism, the Holy Spirit gave the meaning of the New Covenant to Paul as it refers to that which we call *"The Lord's Supper."* Jesus said:

"Take, eat: this is My body, which is broken for you: this do in remembrance of Me.

"After the same manner also He took the cup, when He had supped, saying, 'This cup is the New Testament (New Covenant) *in My Blood: this do ye, as oft as ye drink it, in remembrance of Me'"* (I Cor. 11:24-25).

So, that which God demands of all Believers, is that your Faith be centered up in the phrase as given by Paul, *"Jesus Christ and Him Crucified"* (I Cor. 2:2). This must ever be the object of our Faith.

(4) "FOR HE SPAKE IN A CERTAIN PLACE OF THE SEVENTH DAY ON THIS WISE, AND GOD DID REST THE SEVENTH DAY FROM ALL HIS WORKS."

The structure is:

1. The seventh day is important only because God had finished His works.

2. Rest implies a completion. One may rest only when work is completed.

3. This which God did on the Seventh day as it regards Rest from all His works, is a perfect portrayal of Redemption.

Because of a sinful disruption, the world was in chaos. God brought it back to a habitable state, and now rests from that effort.

Likewise, man was ruined because of sin. Through what Christ did at the Cross, man was redeemed; consequently, it is a *"Finished Work,"* hence the Lord is *"sat down on the Right Hand of the Majesty on high"* (Heb. 1:3).

THE SEVENTH DAY

The phrase, *"For He spake in a certain place of the Seventh day on this wise,"* is taken from Genesis 2:3.

The entirety of the manner in which the Holy Spirit uses the phrase *"Seventh day,"* as it is linked with *"Rest,"* proclaims the simple meaning of the *"Rest"* which one finds in Redemption in coming to Christ. To attempt to make that particular day which is Saturday, into more than God here intends, is to corrupt the text. The Holy Siprit is not extolling a day, but rather a *"work,"* and the work in which He extols, is that of Redemption. If we attempt to make other out of these statements, we do violence to the Word of God, thereby reading into the Text that which actually isn't there.

GOD DID REST

The phrase, *"And God did rest the seventh day from all His works,"* does not imply being wearied with His toil, but merely that He ceased from the work of creation, simply because the creation was finished. The idea is this:

The notion of *"Rest"* of some kind runs through all dispensations. It was seen in the finishing of the work of creation; seen in the appointment of the Sabbath; seen in the offer of the Promised Land, and is seen now in the promise of Heaven. All dispensations contemplate *"Rest,"* and there must be such a prospect before men now.

Rest in the Old Testament was moreso in the sphere of promise than actual possession; however, in the New Testament there is fulfillment.

Christians, by Faith in Christ, have entered into Rest (Heb. 12:22-24). He is our peace. To all who come to Him He gives Rest, and to be sure, Rest that is relief, release, and satisfaction to the soul (Mat. 11:28-30).

But *"Rest"* in Scripture has also an eschatological content. *"There remains a Sabbath Rest"* for the Christian as for Israel (Heb. 4:9). The Celestial City and the Heavenly Country (Heb. 11:10, 16) are still in the future. Today there is the task (I Cor. 3:9), the good fight of Faith (Eph. 6:10-20), the pilgrimage (Heb. 11:13-16). And even the Rest to which death is the prelude (Rev. 14:13) is not fullness of Rest (Rev. 6:9-11).

But those who have entered into the Rest provided by Faith, and Faith in Christ, and more particularly, Faith in the great Sacrifice of Christ, by casting anchor so to speak, within the veil where Christ has gone, know

that the final state of Rest which is yet to come, is secure.

(5) "AND IN THIS PLACE AGAIN, IF THEY SHALL ENTER INTO MY REST."

The exegesis is:

1. The word *"if"* proclaims the fact that some will and some won't!

2. If one enters into this *"Rest,"* there are conditions to be met.

3. If those conditions are met, which are all centered up in Faith, and which anyone can comply if they so desire, and because the Scripture plainly says, *"whosoever will,"* that person will definitely enter into this glorious *"Rest"* provided by God through His Son, the Lord Jesus Christ.

THE WORD OF GOD

The phrase, *"And in this place again,"* refers to Psalms 95:7-11.

If one studies Paul very closely, one finds that the Apostle always anchored that which he taught squarely in Old Testament Scripture. As someone has well said, *"The Old Testament is the New Testament concealed, while the New Testament is the Old Testament revealed."* The idea is, that one cannot really understand the New Testament, unless one understands the Old Testament. The Old is the foundation of the New.

Not having a proper understanding of the Old Testament is at least one of the reasons for much false doctrine. In fact, that's why many Charismatics go off on tangents. Most have little knowledge of the Old Testament; consequently, they have little foundation. As a result, many foolish concepts are brought forth which in fact, have no Scriptural validity.

If one searches, one will find the entirety of the New Testament mirrored somewhere in the Old. And because of the great significance of what is being addressed here, allow me please to say it another way:

If what we derive from the New is not mirrored in the Old, pure and simple, we are espousing false doctrine. As stated, again and again, Paul anchored everything he taught squarely in the Word of the Old Testament, and because that is the Word of God. While many things in the Old Testament have been fulfilled, and are not meant to be repeated, still, the symbolism these Passages portray, help explain the reality presented in the New Testament.

IF

The phrase, *"If they shall enter into My Rest,"* proclaims by the word *"if,"* as stated, that conditions are to be met before one can enter into this *"Rest"* provided by God. Notice, that God refers to this as *"My Rest."*

Salvation, and in its entirety, is all of God, and none of man. Now please read those words very carefully, because they are very important. Actually, this is where the battleground commences. Man has ever attempted to insert his own way, his own means, in other words, his own salvation. Man being sinful, depraved, and, therefore, corrupted, it is obvious that he can provide no Salvation. In other words, not only can he not save others, he cannot even save himself.

These personal efforts of Salvation fall into many ways and means. In fact, the Church is the greatest means of all as it refers to man. Why not? Satan does his finest work inside the Church.

The Church is of God; however, man has ever attempted to make it more than it actually is.

A short time ago, Frances and myself, along with others, were in Rome, Italy. While there we visited the Vatican. This is the center of Catholicism. A 108 acre enclave, comprising a nation so to speak, all its own. Again, why not? Its goals are earthly instead of Heavenly.

The Catholic Church constitutes the Church as the means of Salvation. Consequently, this Church says that the Bible is what they say it is. In other words, they can change its meaning as they so desire, which obviously means that the Bible is subservient to the Church, i.e., *"actually to man."* The Bible not being the rule of principle as it regards the Catholic Church, means that this Church is totally of man, therefore, and to be blunt, a work of the Devil.

However, many Protestant Churches fall into the same category. Many teach and actually believe, that association with their particular Church affords Salvation, or else some type of spirituality in some way. This means that if one doesn't belong to that particular Church, then one is not a Christian or else is

less than one ought to be. I would trust that one could see the fallacy of such thinking.

Once again we come back to the emphatic, even dogmatic statement of God, *"My Rest!"* This means that Salvation is not of man, has never been of man, will never be of man, and in fact, man has nothing to do with its precepts and principles. Salvation is all of God, and is meant for man to receive and never to originate. It is not of man but rather for man, and if man gets the two confused, he can lose his soul.

ENTER

Having settled the fact that this great Redemption is all of God, now we come to the great Truth as to how it is to be received by man. In other words, how does one *"enter into God's rest"*?

Again, this is where Satan attempts to cloud the issue. Jesus told us how: He said, *"I am the Way, the Truth, and the Life: no man cometh unto the Father, but by Me"* (Jn. 14:6). Now exactly what does He mean by this statement?

1. *"I am the Way"*: Now the great question is, exactly how is He the Way? Is He the Way simply because He is God? Is He the Way because He is the Healer? The Miracle Worker? In a word, no!

The word *"Way"* implies direction. Jesus is the *"Way"* not because He is God manifest in the flesh, or that He is the Healer or Miracle Worker, or anything else of that nature. He is the Way, because of what he did at the Cross and in His Resurrection, all on our behalf. This is why we keep saying that when one speaks of Christ, and more particularly Faith in Christ, it must always be understood that one is speaking of what Jesus did at the Cross on our behalf. That's what He means by *"the Way."*

2. *"The Truth"*: As *"Way"* is a direction, *"Truth"* is a possession. Jesus doesn't merely have Truth, He is Truth, which puts things in an entirely different perspective. This means that Truth is not a philosophy, but rather a Person.

But to be more specific, He is Truth in regards to what He has done, and we refer again to the Cross. This in no way is meant to imply that He needed something added to

Him such as the Cross, in order that He might be Truth, for Truth as it refers to Christ cannot be improved upon. He is Perfect, and, therefore, His Truth is Perfect.

The idea is, no person can even begin to comprehend this Truth, Who Christ really is, and what Christ really is, unless one first understands the principle of all Truth, at least as it is given here, which refers to the Cross. We can only know God through Christ, and we can only know Christ through the Cross. The Cross is the only means by which God can commune with man, and the Cross is the only means by which man can commune with God. This which Jesus did, and we refer to His great Sacrifice, is the *"Truth"* mentioned here.

3. *"The Life"*: Christ is not merely the Giver of Life, although He definitely is that, but moreso, He is the Source of all Life. However, once again we come back to the Cross!

The Life which comes from Him to believing sinners, thereby transforming us from darkness to light, is brought about and made possible entirely by what Jesus did at the Cross, and our Faith in that. We can only *"enter"* into this Life, i.e., *"this Rest,"* by placing our Faith and trust exclusively in Christ, and more particularly, His great Sacrifice, all on our behalf.

Christ has always been the Source of Life. In fact, He is the only Source; however, that mere fact changed man not at all. Before this life could be imparted to men who were *"dead in trespasses and sins,"* certain things had to be done.

The terrible sin question had to be addressed, in other words, its penalty had to be paid. Life could not be imparted to a receptacle of death, for that's what man was. There had to be a way by which man could be changed, and how could that be done?

THE WAY AND THE MEANS

God showed Abraham the way, which was by death, and more particularly, the death of the Son of God. It is all characterized in Genesis Chapter 22, concerning the proposed offering up of Isaac, with God then telling the Patriarch that *"He would provide."* The Scripture says:

"And Abraham called the name of that place Jehovah-Jireh: as it is said to this day,

in the mount of the Lord it shall be seen" (Gen. 22:14).

"Jehovah-Jireh" means *"God will provide,"* and it speaks of providing a Redeemer, Who was and is, the Lord Jesus Christ.

However, even though God showed Abraham the way by which it would be done — by death — He did not show him the means. That was shown to Moses.

The Scripture relates how that Israel sinned bitterly against God. As a consequence, *"the Lord sent fiery serpents among the people, and they bit the people; and much people of Israel died"* (Num. 21:6).

So here we have the problem of humanity. Man sins against God, with Satan then having a legal right to *"bite man,"* in other words, to place him in Satanic captivity.

The answer to this terrible dilemma, as God told Moses, was the serpent on the pole.

"And the Lord said unto Moses, make thee a fiery serpent, and set it upon a pole: and it shall come to pass, that everyone that is bitten, when he looketh upon it, shall live" (Num. 21:8).

As God had shown the way of Salvation to Abraham, now he shows the means of that Salvation to Moses, which portrays the manner in which Christ would die. It would be on a *"pole,"* i.e., *"tree."*

Jesus referred to this when He told Nicodemus, *"And as Moses lifted up the serpent in the wilderness, even so must the Son of Man be lifted up"* (Jn. 3:14). This referred to Jesus being lifted up on a Cross.

The Master then said, *"that whosoever believeth in Him should not perish, but have Eternal Life"* (Jn. 3:15).

"Believing in Him," even as we've already stated, refers to believing in what He did on the Cross on our behalf. The most oft quoted Scripture in the world says, *"For God so loved the world, that He gave His only Begotten Son, that whosoever believeth in Him should not perish, but have Everlasting Life"* (Jn. 3:16).

Every time in the Word of God, it speaks of the *"Gift of God"* or that *"God gave,"* it is referring to the Sacrifice of His Son, all as a Gift to man, and that which He showed both Abraham and Moses. That's at least one of the reasons we keep saying, that when we proclaim our Faith in Christ, it must always be with the thought in mind of the Cross. If we attempt to separate Jesus from the Cross, or the Cross from Jesus, we do great violence to the Word of God.

So, one can enter into God's rest, only by believing in Christ, and what He did at the Cross on our behalf. And I might quickly add the following:

As one *"enters"* in by Faith, one *"stays"* in by Faith. This means that we must never take our eye off the Crucified Christ. As Faith in that Finished Work got us in, Faith in that Finished Work keeps us in.

The Believer is to ever look to the Cross, hence all the days of his life, hence Jesus commanding us to always *"deny ourselves,"* which means to deny our own efforts and abilities regarding this Christian life, and instead, to *"take up the Cross daily and follow Him"* (Lk. 9:23). This is the only means by which one can live a victorious, overcoming, Christian life. It is by Faith in the Cross, and I must quickly add, continued Faith in the Cross, which then gives the Holy Spirit latitude to work within our hearts and lives (Rom. 8:1-2, 11, 13).

So, we enter in by means of the Cross, and we stay in by means of the Cross (Rom. 6:3-5).

EXACTLY HOW DOES THE CROSS EFFECT A CHANGE IN MAN?

There was no way that man could be rehabilitated. Due to the Fall, he was totally corrupted, totally polluted, totally depraved. He was *"dead in trespasses and sins,"* meaning, that there was no Spiritual Life in him whatsoever.

So, all that he was and had been, had to pass out of existence, and how could this be done?

It is all done in Christ, and all done by Faith. This is the way it works:

Paul said, *"Know ye not, that so many of us as were baptized into Jesus Christ were baptized into His death?"* (Rom. 6:3).

This is not speaking of Water Baptism as many teach, but rather the death of Christ on the Cross. The Holy Spirit here used the word *"baptized,"* because that is the strongest word that could be used. The very meaning

of the word implies that one is in that into which one is baptized, and that into which one is baptized, is into the one being baptized. Perhaps a sunken ship would illustrate it better:

When a ship is sunk beneath the waves, the ship is in the water and the water is in the ship. That's an apt description of *"Baptism."*

Upon the believing sinner exhibiting Faith in Christ, and what Christ did for him at the Cross, in the mind of God, the believing sinner is literally baptized into Jesus' death. This is what we mean by Jesus being our Substitute, or Representative Man, or as Paul referred to Him, *"the Last Adam"* (I Cor. 15:45). In other words, He took our place, actually acting in our stead, with God granting us all that he did on our behalf, which we receive by simply exhibiting Faith in Him (Eph. 2:8-9). But it doesn't stop there:

Paul then said, *"Therefore we are buried with Him by baptism into death"* (Rom. 6:4). Not only did we die with Christ, but that which died was so awful, so terrible, so wretched, so sinful, so wicked, so beyond salvage so to speak, and of course, we speak of ourselves and not Christ, that it had to be buried. This means that the old man referred to in the Sixth Verse, with all of its passions, pride, sin, and wickedness, was buried, never to be exhumed again, at least in that state.

All our sins are gone! All the past life is gone! All the old me and the old you are gone! And one might say, thank God, gone forever! But it doesn't stop there.

Paul then said, *"That like as Christ was raised up from the dead by the Glory of the Father, even so we also should walk in newness of life.*

"For if we have been planted together in the likeness of His death, we shall be also in the likeness of His Resurrection" (Rom. 6:4-5).

This means that we are raised in *"newness of life,"* actually a *"new man."* This is the reason that Jesus is referred to by Paul as *"The Last Adam"* Who paid the price for our iniquity, and also as *"The Second Man,"* which refers to His Resurrection Life. As well, we are in effect a *"second man,"* i.e., *"new man,"* all in Christ Jesus (Eph. 4:24).

DEAD TO SIN

When Christ died, in the mind of God we died, that is if we exhibit Faith in what Christ did. When that happened, we were set free from the old man, i.e., *"from sin."* Satan had a legal claim on the *"old man,"* but he has no claim at all on this *"new man,"* who is in Christ Jesus. And now Paul plainly says:

"Now if we be dead with Christ (meaning that by Faith we died with Him in His Crucifixion, which was actually all for us to begin with), *we believe that we shall also live with Him* (meaning that we now have a new life, all in Christ Jesus)*"* (Rom. 6:8).

In view of the fact that all of this has taken place, we are to also *"reckon ourselves to be dead indeed unto sin, but alive unto God through Jesus Christ our Lord"* (Rom. 6:11).

The word *"reckon"* means to *"compute, to conclude, to consider, to read the bottom line."*

All of this has come about because of what Jesus did for us on the Cross and in His Resurrection, and our Faith in that. That's the reason I keep telling you, that our Faith must ever be in the Cross. The Cross was the only means by which man could be free, and it is the only means by which man can stay free. So the idea, that we park the Cross after conversion is foolish indeed! Actually, that is the understatement of eternity.

To forsake the Cross after conversion, even as most of the modern Church has presently done, guarantees a life of defeat, of failure, of sinning and repenting, sinning and repenting, etc. We are to ever understand, that we can function *"in the likeness of His Resurrection,"* only if we fully understand and continue to understand, that *"we have been planted together in the likeness of His Death"* (Rom. 6:5).

The secret of all Salvation is found in the Cross of Christ, as the secret of all victorious, overcoming, Christian living, is found in the Cross of Christ. And as well, when we speak of the Cross, we are at the same time presupposing the Resurrection, even the Exaltation of Christ (Eph. 2:6), and even the Second Coming, when we will as well come

NOTES

with Him (Rev. Chpt. 19), as well as Reigning with Him (II Tim. 2:12).

So we have *"dying with Him"* (Rom. 6:3), *"buried with Him"* (Rom. 6:4), *"resurrected with Him"* (Rom. 6:4), *"exalted with Him"* (Eph. 2:6), *"coming with Him"* (Rev. Chpt. 19), and *"Reigning with Him"* (II Tim. 2:12).

THE HOLY SPIRIT

Regarding the Child of God, three things enter into all of this, in fact, the three single most important things in one's life. They are:

1. The Cross.
2. Our Faith.
3. The Holy Spirit.

After we are brought to Christ, actually becoming a new creation (II Cor. 5:17), let us not think that Satan will suddenly vanish into the mist, never to trouble us again. In fact, the Evil One is going to do everything he can to hinder as long as we live. Peter addressed this by saying:

"Beloved, think it not strange concerning the fiery trial which is to try you, as though some strange thing happened unto you" (I Pet. 4:12).

Of course, we might ask the question, why does the Lord allow this, especially considering, that Satan cannot do these things without permission from the Lord? Peter answered that as well:

"That the trial of your Faith, being much more precious than of gold that perisheth, though it be tried with fire, might be found unto praise and honor and glory at the appearing of Jesus Christ" (I Pet. 1:7).

This in effect tells us several things:

1. Our Faith will be tried. As someone has said, Faith is always tested, and great Faith is tested greatly. Faith being the vehicle by which all good things from God are obtained, and by that we mean Faith in Christ and what He did at the Cross, Faith is where we are attacked by Satan. It really doesn't matter if the attack is spiritual, physical, domestical, or material, it is all for the purpose of destroying our Faith, or at least seriously weakening it. And God, as stated, allows the Evil One to do these things, but only within the parameters drawn off by the Lord (Job, Chpts. 1-2). Of course, Satan means it for our harm, while God means it for our good.

This tells us that the only way that Faith can be strengthened, is for it to be tried.

2. Our Faith is much more precious than gold that perishes, for true Faith will never perish, though it be tried with fire. The actual meaning is, that the fire of tribulation and testing will not destroy our Faith, but will rather strengthen our Faith.

3. All of this is to bring praise, honor, and glory to God, in essence stating that what Jesus did at the Cross on our behalf was not a failure, but rather the most crowning victory of all, which it definitely was!

4. This *"trial of our Faith,"* will continue until *"the appearing of Jesus Christ,"* which means all of our lives.

However, in the midst of all of this is the Holy Spirit. He is present to lead us, guide us, help us, empower us, anoint us, strengthen us, and to do whatever is necessary, in order that we might have total and complete victory. However, the means by which He does all of this, is once again, the great Work which Christ carried out on the Cross. In other words, He will not work outside of those boundaries. Whatever Jesus did at the Cross, whatever victory He there won, whatever price He there paid, the Holy Spirit works within those confines, meaning that it is absolutely necessary for us to have Faith in that Finished Work, and to continue to have Faith, even on a daily basis, in that Finished Work.

THE WAY OF THE HOLY SPIRIT

First of all, there is no way that the Believer, even though a new creation in Christ Jesus, can hope to have what he ought to have from Christ, and be what he ought to be in Christ, without the aid, help, and power of the Holy Spirit. In fact, the indwelling presence of the Spirit is such a part of this great process, and such an absolute necessity, that it is all linked together in the great Justification process.

Paul said:

"Christ hath redeemed us from the curse of the Law (which was death), *being made a curse for us* (meaning that He died for us)*: for it is written, cursed is everyone that hangeth on a tree* (Christ took the penalty that we should have taken).*"*

Paul then said, *"That* (meaning that Jesus taking the curse on our behalf was absolutely

necessary) *the Blessing of Abraham* (Justification by Faith) *might come on the Gentiles through Jesus Christ* (what Jesus Christ did)*; that we might receive the Promise of the Spirit through Faith* (in other words, as we are justified by Faith, which means to believe in what Jesus did for us at the Cross as stated here, that same Faith also gives us the Spirit, Who was Promised by God through the Prophet Joel [Joel 2:28-29])*"* (Gal. 3:13-14).

In explaining how the Holy Spirit works within our lives, Paul said, *"For the Law of the Spirit* (this is a Law of God, which means that it will not be broken) *of life* (meaning the only manner and way in which life can be imparted) *in Christ Jesus* (this is very important, telling us that this *'Law of the Spirit of Life'* is all predicated on what Christ did at the Cross and the Resurrection on our behalf) *hath made me free from the law of sin and death* (meaning that *'the law of the Spirit of Life in Christ Jesus'* alone, is powerful enough to make us free from this law of sin and death)*"* (Rom. 8:2).

The Holy Spirit emphasizes through Paul, that this is a *"Law,"* meaning that it is ironclad, ironbound, and as stated, from which it will not be deviated.

This further means that if the Believer doesn't function according to the Holy Spirit, which refers to having Faith in the Cross of Christ, that the Holy Spirit although abiding within us, simply will not work on our behalf. He absolutely refuses to help us function in the capacity of self-will or self-dependence, and for all the reasons which should be obvious. Jesus paid a terrible price for our Redemption, which includes a victorious, overcoming, Christian life, and the Holy Spirit will not tolerate for one moment, us deviating from this great Plan of God. This is the only way we *"enter"* into this Rest, and the only way we *"stay"* in this Rest.

WALKING AFTER THE SPIRIT

Paul said, *"There is therefore now no condemnation to them which are in Christ Jesus, who walk not after the flesh, but after the Spirit"* (Rom. 8:1).

All of this great thing told us in Romans 8:2, can only be brought about if we *"walk after the Spirit."* But of course, the great question is, how do we do that?

The Truth is, most Christians, sadly and regrettably, are *"walking after the flesh,"* even though they probably think they are *"walking after the Spirit."*

To cut through all the fluff, if one is truly *"walking after the Spirit,"* one will not have to ask if he or she actually is! When one is truly *"walking after the Spirit"* the evidence is so obvious as it regards a victorious life, so obvious as it regards joy unspeakable and full of glory, that there is no shadow of doubt as it regards this tremendous *"walk!"*

Now the way and manner that we walk after the Spirit, is to simply exhibit Faith *"in Christ Jesus,"* i.e., *"to trust completely in what Christ did for us."* The *"Spirit"* Who is God, always and without exception, leads one to the Cross of Christ. As stated, He works exclusively within the boundaries and the parameters of the Finished Work of Christ. This gives Him the legal right to help you, work for you, fight for you, etc. To say it a little better:

At Salvation, the Holy Spirit fights for us, while in Sanctification, the Holy Spirit fights in us.

If our Faith is properly placed, which means to be placed in Christ and what He did at the Cross, Paul then said, *"But if the Spirit of Him* (of God, meaning that the Spirit proceeds from both the Father and the Son) *that raised up Jesus from the dead dwell in you* (which He definitely does if we are saved), *He* (God) *that raised up Christ from the dead shall also quicken your mortal bodies* (this present life) *by His Spirit that dwelleth in you"* (Rom. 8:11).

This great Eleventh Verse as given by the Holy Spirit through Paul, gives us the greatest Promise that one could ever begin to imagine. We are here told, that the same power that raised Jesus from the dead, will at the same time give us power over Satan and all the powers of darkness. What a Promise! What a victory!

With that type of power there is no way that we can lose. All it requires is our Faith in the Cross.

THE STATE OF MOST CHRISTIANS PRESENTLY

As I dictate these notes, even at this very moment (June 13, 2000), millions of Christians are struggling and fighting, trying to overcome some particular sin within their lives. Let's not beat around the bush! Let's not be dishonest!

The great problem in the hearts and lives of Christians is sin. We might try to claim it's lack of Faith, or a bad confession, or some such like thing, but the fact is, the problem is sin. Satan wants to drag us down with sin, and he uses every method and tactic at his disposal in order to bring this about.

Our problem is, being ignorant of the Cross, we attempt to oppose him by our own abilities and means, and as religious as those abilities and means might be, we always fail, as fail we must. In fact, we not only fail, but the harder we try in that capacity, the worse the failure gets. And what do we mean by all this?

We mean that whatever means and ways that a Believer is attempting to use to bring about victory in his life, other than Faith in the Cross of Christ, is going to bring about failure, and I don't care what means he uses.

The Church is casting about presently in every direction, trying to find an answer to this dilemma. Most of it has succumbed to humanistic psychology, which is worse than no help at all. Other Christians by the thousands are running all over the world, looking for some Preacher to lay hands on them, in order to rid them of their problem, whatever that problem might be.

While the laying on of hands is definitely of God, and while many manifestations which accompany such are of God, still, that is not the answer to man's dilemma.

Man has one answer to his dilemma, and one only, and that is the Cross of Christ. Why can't we see that! Why can't we understand that!

The answer is not in some great Church, or some great Preacher, or in other religious things we can think of, but only in the Cross. That is God's answer to a hurting world, to mankind in every capacity, and to you as a Christian. The answer is the Cross, and the only answer is the Cross.

The other day in Rome while at the Vatican, I observed hundreds of people crawling up a long series of steps, crawling on their hands and knees, I suppose thinking they were atoning for sin, or bringing about some spiritual work within their lives. As I stood there grieved at their action, I had to admit within my heart, that many things which I had done in the past, were actually no different in the eyes of God. And at the same time, I must admit that most of the things presently done by most Christians in this respect, are just as fruitless as those dear people crawling up those steps in Rome.

In fact, there is absolutely nothing that man can do to bring about anything from God, except simply believe in what Jesus has already done at the Cross. When you do that, the Holy Spirit will then mightily help you. That's what Jesus meant when He said, *"You shall know the Truth, and the Truth shall make you free"* (Jn. 8:32).

That *"Truth"* is what He did at the Cross on our behalf, and our Faith in that.

(6) "SEEING THEREFORE IT REMAINETH THAT SOME MUST ENTER THEREIN, AND THEY TO WHOM IT WAS FIRST PREACHED ENTERED NOT IN BECAUSE OF UNBELIEF:"

The structure is:

1. The phrase, *"Seeing therefore it remains that some must enter therein,"* should have been translated, *"It remains for some to enter therein."* In fact, the Scholars say there is no word in the Greek, at least not as used here, for *"must."*

2. The words *"it remaineth,"* means that the door is open to all who will believe. This completely debunks the erroneous manner in which predestination is taught in many cases. God has not predestined some to go to Heaven and some to go to Hell, with them having no choice in the matter. It is left up to *"whosoever will"* (Rev. 22:17).

3. When we boil it down to the bottom line, the reason that people do not enter in, and by that we speak of Salvation, is because of *"unbelief."* And by the word *"unbelief"* we are speaking of a lack of Faith in Christ and what He did at the Cross on our behalf. In other words, men do not believe that the Cross of the remedy, but rather opt for something else instead!

THE DOOR IS STILL OPEN

The phrase, *"Seeing therefore it remaineth that some must enter therein,"* means that God is still holding the door open wide,

that *"whosoever will may come."* In fact, John wrote:

"And the Spirit and the Bride say, Come. And let him that heareth say, Come. And let him that is athirst come. And whosoever will, let him take the water of life freely" (Rev. 22:17).

As it regards coming into this great *"Rest"* provided by God, the Holy Spirit is constantly saying to all, *"Come!"* Every Believer in the form of the *"Bride"* is also saying, *"Come!"* And then the one who hears this great Word, is to also say to himself, *"Come,"* meaning, *"I can come, if I only will!"* This includes everyone, and excludes no one.

And then the Scripture says that all who are thirsty (spiritually thirsty) may come. This includes every human being on the face of the Earth, because there is a thirst, i.e., *"spiritual thirst,"* in the heart of every person. Unfortunately, they try to slake that thirst at the brackish waters of this world, but find no satisfaction. Hence Jesus saying:

"If any man thirst, let him come unto Me and drink, and he that believeth on Me, as the Scripture has said, out of his innermost being shall flow rivers of Living Water" (Jn. 7:37).

And then, in case that anyone might feel excluded, the Holy Spirit cries, *"Whosoever will,"* which broadens it so much, that no one could misunderstand the invitation, and then says, *"let him take the water of life freely."*

As priceless as it is, as wonderful as it is, as glorious as it is, still, it is all *"free!"* Hence the Prophet would say:

"Ho, everyone that thirsteth, come ye to the waters, and he that hath no money; come ye, buy, and eat; yea, come, buy wine and milk without money and without price" (Isa. 55:1).

There seems to be a contradiction in the statement as given by Isaiah, with him saying *"buy,"* and then *"without money and without price."* What is he actually saying?

The idea is, that which is given to us freely, of which we do not have to purchase, and in fact it is so precious, that man has nothing with which he could purchase such a commodity so to speak. But yet, it has been purchased, and by the precious Blood of the Lord

Jesus Christ, hence Isaiah using the word *"buy"* (I Pet. 1:18-20).

UNBELIEF

The phrase, *"And they to whom it was first preached entered not in because of unbelief,"* proclaims from Verse 2, that the Israelites of old had the same Gospel preached unto them as we do, but to no avail. Unbelief caused them to not enter into the *"Rest"* spoken of in Verse 5.

Some three times in this Fourth Chapter, Paul refers to preaching. In fact, in one way or the other, the entirety of the Chapter speaks of the proclamation of the Word of God by the means of preaching. This is God's method of spreading His Word. When preaching in a Church or Denomination becomes weak, such signals the death knell. Skits, plays, dramas, singspirations, discussion groups, etc., or any other such like effort can never take the place of the preaching of the Gospel. Preaching is God's way.

However, having said that, what Message must the Preacher preach and proclaim?

Of course, the stock answer is, *"The Word of God."* And naturally, that is certainly correct. But please allow me to venture the following:

THE PREACHING OF THE CROSS

While every subject of the Word of God must be proclaimed, and constantly, the foundation of all preaching, in other words the foundation on which every Message is based, must be the Cross of Christ. In other words, we must preach the Cross.

Paul said, *"For the preaching of the Cross is to them that perish foolishness; but unto us which are saved it is the Power of God"* (I Cor. 1:18).

And then he said, and we must remember he is speaking by the inspiration of the Holy Spirit, *"For after that in the wisdom of God the world by wisdom knew not God, it pleased God by the foolishness of preaching* (preaching the Cross) *to save them that believe"* (I Cor. 1:21).

And then, *"But we preach Christ crucified"* (I Cor. 1:23).

And then finally, *"For I determined not to know anything among you, save Jesus Christ, and Him Crucified"* (I Cor. 2:2).

If we understand Paul at all, we understand that his Message was the Cross of Christ. That's what he preached, and that's what he preached continually. Of course, and as stated, he broached every subject in the Word of God, but all were built on the foundation of the Cross of Christ. In fact, the Word of God cannot be properly understood without one first having a proper understanding of the Cross. This is absolutely imperative!

Whenever the Cross of Christ is preached, the Holy Spirit brings men to a decision. They either have to accept it and be saved or reject it and be lost.

This pertains not only to unbelievers, but it pertains to the Church as well. The Cross must be preached to the Church, i.e., *"Believers,"* that is if they are going to walk in victory. But here's where the problem comes in.

THE CHRISTIAN AND THE CROSS

Thus far in this Volume, we have attempted in every way possible to proclaim the absolute necessity of a proper understanding of the Cross as it regards the Christian experience. In other words, if the Believer doesn't properly understand the Cross, and how it affects his everyday living, it is absolutely impossible for him to walk in victory.

As I've already said several times, in 1997 the Lord in answer to soul-searching prayer, began to open up to me the great Word of the Cross. In fact, to make it very brief, He revealed to my heart that the answer which I sought, which was the way that the Christian could walk victorious over the world, the flesh, and the Devil, was found in the Cross, and was found only in the Cross. It was the most revolutionary, the most gripping, the most glorious moment of my life, other than the day I was saved and baptized with the Holy Spirit. He did this through the great and glorious Sixth Chapter of Romans.

This which He did for me, I immediately began to preach to our people at Family Worship Center, as well as over the two Radio Stations owned by the Ministry.

Now to be sure, I had always preached the Cross and strongly so, as it regarded the Salvation of the lost; however, I did not know or understand the part the Cross plays in our everyday living. And shamefully, I did not know any other Preacher who knew this great Truth as well. Satan has been so successful at steering the Church away from the Cross, that anymore its great Truth is hardly known.

The sadness is, this is not a new Message. It is actually the story of the Bible. It is the foundation of all that we are in Christ Jesus. That's the reason that Paul said, *"But God forbid that I should glory, save in the Cross of our Lord Jesus Christ, by Whom the world is crucified unto me, and I unto the world"* (Gal. 6:14).

In this one Scripture, the Holy Spirit through Paul, tells us that the only way we can overcome the world, is by appropriating that which Jesus did for us at the Cross, and continually having Faith in that Finished Work.

To make the story brief, this Message revolutionized our Church. And then the Lord informed me that I was to greatly enlarge our Radio Ministry, which we immediately set out to do by acquiring translator Stations all over the nation. In fact, we will possibly install as many as 2,000 of these Stations.

As well, the Lord instructed me to once again put our daily Telecast, *"A Study In The Word"*, back on the air, which we also immediately did. Even though as I dictate these notes (June, 2000), the daily Telecast has only been airing about three months, the results have been and are absolutely fantastic. The Lord instructed me to teach on the Cross, which we have done and will continue to do, until He says otherwise.

People are calling and saying, *"This Message witnesses with my spirit."* Others are saying, *"For the first time in my life, I now have hope,"* etc.

The Church is presently entering into the last great apostasy, actually that which was foretold by the Apostle Paul, and which will lead up to the Rapture of the Church, the rise of the Antichrist, and the great Tribulation period (II Thess. 2:3; I Tim. 4:1; Rev. 3:13-20). At this time, the Cross, I believe the Lord has revealed to me, is going to be the dividing line between the True Church and the Apostate Church. In fact, it has always been that way, but is going to now be more pronounced than ever.

The only way for the Christian to walk in victory, and that speaks of victory as we've

already stated, over the world, the flesh, and the Devil, is that the Christian properly understand the part the Cross plays in his everyday experience. As we've stated many times, the Christian without fail, must place his Faith squarely in the Cross of Christ, not allowing it to be moved from this all-important work, which will then guarantee the help of the Holy Spirit on his behalf. God has provided no other source or means of victory, because no other source or means are necessary.

Little knowing this great Truth, the Church has cast about in all directions, jumping from one fad to the other, attempting to find victory. When Frances and I first began in Evangelistic Work back in the mid 1950's, we soon found that Preachers were advocating the idea that all problems were caused by demon spirits, and that the Christian must have these spirits cast out of him, etc. Consequently, there were long lines of people at some Churches, trying to get some Preacher to cast the demon of lust, avarice, gossip, or whatever out of them.

In those days, I didn't know the correct answer, but I knew that wasn't Biblical. While demon spirits definitely do get involved in all failure, the answer to the problem is not in that direction. What did Jesus say?

"You shall know the Truth, and the Truth shall make you free" (Jn. 8:32). As one of my associates said, *"The Church needs the Truth a whole lot more than it needs a touch."* And how correct that is!

Hundreds of thousands of Christians are running all over the world, even presently doing so, trying to get a touch, when they really need the Truth — the Truth of the Cross.

Don't misunderstand, I definitely believe the Bible teaches the laying on of hands and manifestations which will follow. But as valuable as those things are, and as helpful as they are, they cannot take the place of Truth; however, coupled with Truth, the laying on of hands, etc., become very valuable assets for the Child of God.

In the 1970's the Church began to go pell-mell into humanistic psychology; consequently, some of the leading Preachers began to advocate the method which I refer to as the *"buddy system."* In other words, each Christian is to have a friend with whom they can reveal their problems and difficulties, and supposedly, both of these people together can bring about a solution. Once again, there's absolutely no Scriptural foundation for such foolishness.

And then in the 1970's and the 1980's, the Faith Message began to take hold, which seemed like music to the ears of the Church; however, as well, it was and is unscriptural. The reason is simple: the Faith which is advocated, is not Faith in the Cross of Christ, but something else altogether; consequently, this Message has degenerated basically into what I refer to as the *"greed gospel,"* i.e., *"money."*

In the early 1990's, the *"laughter"* phenomenon swept the world. If everyone could be touched by the Holy Spirit it was alleged, thereby going into convulsions of laughter, which would last for great periods of time, this would be the answer to all problems. It wasn't and it isn't!

Of course in all of this, and I speak of the Pentecostal and Charismatic camps, *"being slain in the Spirit"* has been held up as the great manifestation. If this could happen, then once again, the problem is solved.

To be sure, the Lord definitely does move upon people at times, with them being *"slain in the Spirit,"* as to how it is commonly referred; however, if this happens, and the person still doesn't know the Truth, unfortunately he or she is going to get off the floor exactly as they went down — defeated. Once again we go back to what Jesus said about *"knowing the Truth"* (Jn. 8:32).

There is only one way and means of victory for the Child of God, and that is the victory provided by Christ by the work which He carried out at the Cross and in His Resurrection.

SELF-HELP OR CROSS-HELP?

The great battlefield for the Christian is whether he attempts to find victory by his own machinations, or trust completely in what Christ did at the Cross? In fact, this is the same battlefield for the unredeemed. Do they trust in their own efforts to save themselves, or do they trust in what Jesus did at the Cross? The Cross ever stands at the intersection of life, and for all people, and for all situations.

NOTES

Of course we know and understand that the unredeemed cannot be saved, unless they trust in what Christ has done at the Cross on their behalf (Jn. 3:16). Admittedly, they don't have to understand much about it, but they must evidence Faith, at least in some degree. Of course, the Holy Spirit supplies them the Faith as they hear the Word of God. But when it comes to the Christian, the following can happen, to which Paul addressed the entirety of the Epistle to the Galatians. Theologians refer to this problem as *"Galatianism."*

It simply means that people come to Christ by trusting in what He did at the Cross, but after being saved, then transfer their Faith from the Cross to something else entirely. Even though they of course remain a Child of God, simply because they continue to trust Christ as it regards their initial Salvation, by no means, however, can they walk victorious. So we have *"Salvation by Faith,"* and *"Sanctification by works,"* which as stated, is the greatest problem for the Child of God.

In fact, the Galatians had been brought to Christ through the Ministry of Paul. Of course, they were taught correctly as would be obvious. But then, false teachers came into these respective Churches, telling the people, that they must add Law to their experience. In other words, now that they had accepted Christ, they must also engage in circumcision (for the boys and the men), and Sabbath keeping, etc. This was the way to deeper life, etc., they claimed!

If it is to be noticed, Paul's Letter to the Galatians drips with scorn, and in fact, is His most strident Epistle. In fact, the Apostle is downright angry, and rightly so!

He knew that if the Galatians followed that error, they were going to lose their victory, and possibly even their souls. So, the Holy Spirit had him to write the Epistle to the Galatians to address this terrible error.

Unfortunately, the problem didn't die with the Galatians. It remains with us today, and in fact, it is the greatest problem faced by the Child of God.

After coming to Christ, which means that we now have a new nature within us, which of course is provided by the Holy Spirit by and according to what Jesus did for us at the Cross (Jn. 7:37-39), we instinctively know that we must live right, and in fact, we want to live right. But the great question is, how is this done?

If we don't know the Message of the Cross, which is God's prescribed order of victory, and I might quickly add, His only prescribed order of victory, then we will cast about attempting to find a method of victory on our own. That's what I meant by Salvation by Faith, and Sanctification by works.

And let it please be understood, that if we do not know the Truth of the Cross, this Truth is just not going to simply fall on us. The Word of God concerning this great foundational Truth in some manner, in some way, must be ministered to us. This is the only way we can come by Truth. As stated, it cannot be given by laying on of hands or any other manner, except the preaching and teaching of the Gospel. So what do we presently have?

Due to the fact that almost none of the modern Church knows or understands the great Message of the Cross, the far greater majority of the Church walks in defeat.

But there's another problem attached to all of this:

SELF-RIGHTEOUSNESS

"Works" always produce self-righteousness. In fact, that's why the Religious Leaders of Israel crucified Christ. The whole Jewish system by the time of Christ had degenerated into *"works"*; consequently, self-righteousness was paramount at that time, and self-righteousness always must kill the Righteousness of the Lord. In fact, we have a perfect example of this in Genesis Chapter 4 with Cain killing Abel.

The Cross produces humility, even as the Cross alone can produce humility, while works always produce self-righteousness.

However, *"works"* are very subtle. Most of the time they are cloaked with all manner of religiosity, which makes us think that what we're doing is of the Lord. In fact, the greatest weapon that Satan uses is to actually take that which is of God, such as prayer, fasting, or manifestations of the Spirit, even as we've already addressed, and make us think that the doing or the engaging in these things will bring about the victory which we must have.

While to be sure, these things we've mentioned, plus many we haven't mentioned, are very necessary in the life of the Child of God; still, if we try to use them in the realm of the source of victory, we will find that we have turned them into works, which God can never bless or recognize.

I am victorious totally and completely, not because of the things I do, but totally and completely because of what Christ has done at the Cross. That and that alone, which demands my Faith, brings victory to the Child of God, and in every capacity I might quickly add. Proper Faith in the Cross, which guarantees the help of the Holy Spirit, is the only manner, the only means, the only way, that the Child of God can walk in victory. And to be certain, there is no power of darkness that wasn't defeated at the Cross of Christ.

THE VICTORY OF THE CROSS

Paul in his Epistle to the Colossians spelled it out as to exactly what Jesus did for us at the Cross. He said:

"Blotting out the handwriting of ordinances that was against us (the Law), *which was contrary to us, and took it out of the way, nailing it to His Cross;*

"And having spoiled principalities and powers, He made a show of them openly, triumphing over them in it" (Col. 2:14-15).

Two things were here done:

1. The demands of a thrice Holy God were satisfied.

2. Satan was completely defeated.

Now let's see how all of this was done.

The Law of God as given to Moses, sometimes referred to as *"the Law of Moses,"* proclaimed the Standard of Righteousness which God demanded of all men. Unfortunately, man in his depraved, fallen condition, could not live up to this Law, and no matter how hard he tried. In fact, in the entirety of these some 1,600 years of the Law, not one person succeeded in satisfying its demands, except Christ.

In fact, as it regards the moral Law (the Ten Commandments), it is still incumbent upon humanity, at least all who do not know the Lord. As stated, this is God's Standard of Righteousness.

Unable to keep the Law, it condemned us, even as all Law must. In other words, it declared us guilty, and demanded the penalty, which was death (Rom. 6:23).

However, Jesus came as the *"Last Adam,"* referred to by Paul in that manner, because He would do what the first Adam did not do, and would as well do it so perfectly, that another would never be needed, hence Him being referred to as the *"Last."*

He kept the Law perfectly in every respect, doing it all on our behalf, even as our Substitute. One might say that he did all of this as the *"Representative Man"* (I Cor. 15:45-50).

He not only kept the Law, and as stated, did so perfectly, but as well, He suffered its terrible penalty of death — all on our behalf.

When He did this, the price was paid, with the record that was against all of us, being completely and totally *"blotted out."* The Scripture plainly says that He *"nailed it to His Cross."*

Now we are seeing why the Cross is so very, very important.

This which He did satisfied the demands of a thrice Holy God. The Reader must understand, that the Cross was not carried out in order to satisfy the Devil, etc., but rather to satisfy the demands of God. It was either us die, which meant that we would never be raised from the dead, and because we were an imperfect sacrifice, or for God to become man, which He did, thereby taking our place.

However, having done this, what Jesus did at the Cross, also spelled defeat for Satan and all his henchmen.

Satan has a legal right to place man into captivity because of sin. But with all sin atoned, even as Jesus did at the Cross, Satan lost that right, at least as it regards those who will believe (Jn. 3:16).

In other words, Satan has no more legal right over me and because I am now *"in Christ,"* which means I have trusted Christ and what He did at the Cross on my behalf, which cleanses me from all sin. Sin being the means by which Satan holds men in captivity, with sin being gone and washed away, and by the precious Blood of Jesus, as stated, Satan has no more right.

As a result, this spoiled all principalities and powers, which refers to all demon spirits and fallen angels, which includes Satan as their federal head, with the Scripture

plainly saying that Jesus *"triumphed over them in it,"* meaning, that what He did at the Cross totally defeated them.

So this means, that every single demon spirit is defeated, every fallen angel is defeated, even the mightiest of them and in totality are defeated, and above all, Satan as their federal head is defeated.

As we've said previously, the work which Jesus did at the Cross by the giving of Himself in Sacrifice, was actually a legal work. It satisfied the legal demands of a thrice Holy God. Man had committed a terrible crime, and that crime had to be addressed, with its penalty satisfied. It was satisfied in Christ.

All these things we've just said, are the reason that the Cross is the Source of all Victory, and of course, we are speaking of what Jesus there did. That's the reason our Faith must ever be in the Cross. And this I might quickly ask:

Many Preachers claim that we must go beyond the Cross, especially many of those of the Charismatic variety. What do they mean by going beyond the Cross? Actually, where is one to go?

The Work of Christ at the Cross, is called a *"Finished Work,"* which is portrayed by Paul in Hebrews 1:3, by Jesus being *"sat down on the right hand of the Majesty on high."* As well, Paul referred to this great work as *"the Everlasting Covenant"* (Heb. 13:20).

Some may claim that we leave the Cross after conversion, thereby going on to the Holy Spirit. However, when we understand, that the Holy Spirit will not work within our hearts and lives, at least to the full degree which He can, without our Faith being properly placed in the Cross, then we realize that it's impossible to separate the Holy Spirit from the Cross. That's what we explained in Romans 8:2. Everything the Holy Spirit does, He does within the framework and the parameters of what Jesus did at the Cross. In fact, before the Cross, He could not even come into the hearts and lives of Believers to abide. This could only be done after the Cross, which satisfied the sin debt (Jn. 14:16-17).

The great Ministry of the Holy Spirit is to *"glorify Christ"* (Jn. 16:14). And how does He glorify Christ?

He does so, by constantly pointing to the Cross (I Cor. 2:2).

Actually, in the last two Chapters of Revelation, which speak of the perfect age to come, when Satan is locked away in the Lake of Fire, along with all his demon spirits and fallen angels, and in fact, there is no more sin, we find the Holy Spirit referring to Christ some seven times as *"the Lamb"* (Rev. 21:9, 14, 22-23, 27; 22:1, 3).

Seven of course speaks of God's perfection, and *"Lamb"* refers to the Crucified Christ (Jn. 1:29).

The Holy Spirit does this, so that we will never forget, that it was the price paid by Christ on the Cross, which has afforded, and does afford all of these great and glorious things. In fact, the entirety of the story of the Bible is the story of man's Redemption, which in effect, is the story of the Cross.

(7) "AGAIN, HE LIMITETH A CERTAIN DAY, SAYING IN DAVID, TODAY, AFTER SO LONG A TIME; AS IT IS SAID, TODAY IF YE WILL HEAR HIS VOICE, HARDEN NOT YOUR HEARTS."

The structure is:

1. The Call of God to dying humanity, although remaining open in general, and even expanded, is not open to each individual forever. There is a limited time which men have in order to accept, with death ultimately closing the door.

2. In David's day, some 500 years after the experience of the Children of Israel in the wilderness, the Holy Spirit is still using the word *"today."* It refers to the fact, that today is the time to accept the Lord, because there might not be a tomorrow for some, and in fact, will not be a tomorrow for some!

3. The Holy Spirit is here emphatic, that we must hear His voice *"today."* Once again, this places limitations on the Call, not due to the fact that the Call is limited, but that man has a limited time in which to accept.

4. Hardened hearts brought about through unbelief, keep people from hearing that voice, and from accepting, and more than all, from accepting *"today."*

A LIMITED TIME

The phrase, *"Again, He limiteth a certain day,"* proclaims in no uncertain terms that

even though the Call of God is unlimited, the opportunity to accept that Call is definitely limited.

Man is cut off by death, or by other situations, even while alive.

God stands ready to save at any and all times; however, there are definitely times, in which the Holy Spirit is moving greatly, while at other times, He might not be doing so.

If men do not accept the Gospel when it is first heard, hence the Holy Spirit constantly using the word *"today,"* it becomes increasingly harder for them to accept thereafter. This in no way means, that if one is not saved the first time they hear, that they will not be saved. It just means that the door of opportunity becomes more and more narrow.

The word *"limiteth"* doesn't refer to God, but to man. God is not limited, and His Call is not limited, and in fact will never be limited. It is still, *"whosoever will"* (Rev. 22:17). But the facts are, that man is definitely limited.

In effect, the Holy Spirit is here giving an Altar Call. It could not be more plain, or more clear as to what He is doing. And in fact, as we shall see in the next phrase, He has been giving that Altar Call from the very beginning.

TODAY

The phrase, *"Saying in David, today, after so long a time,"* once again proclaims Paul alluding to Psalm 95.

Here, and sharply, the Holy Spirit characterizes the word *"today."* He could not be more specific, more clear, and even more dogmatic. He told Israel in the wilderness, *"today,"* and by David's time, some 500 years later, He is still saying *"today,"* and according to the structure of this Passage, He is continuing to say *"today"* unto this very hour.

That's the reason I grieve, when I see so much that passes for Christian Television, wasted on frivolity and nonessentials. People are dying without God, dropping into an eternal Hell, where they will never have another opportunity to be saved, with the Holy Spirit crying *"today,"* and then we waste the opportunity given us to proclaim this glad Message. God help us!

To be sure, every single Preacher of the Gospel is going to give account to God for all the opportunities he or she has had to proclaim this glad Message. What are we doing with the opportunity God has given us? Are we taking full advantage of the opportunities?

We have seen untold thousands brought to a saving knowledge of Jesus Christ through our Telecast. Untold testimonies have come to our office, telling of how they staggered home at one or two o'clock in the morning, drunk, or high on drugs. They would turn on the Television set, and our program would be on. Many found Christ at this time, and continue to do so unto this hour. Now this question must be asked:

What if they had turned on our Telecast, and I had been using this time to promote foolishness? Or better yet, what if what I had been doing was not foolishness, but something important, but not yet the Gospel? Worse still, what if the Gospel we had been preaching had not actually been the Gospel, but something else entirely?

Of course, the answer to all of these questions is, that these people would not have been saved. Now we can take the attitude that God would have brought them in somehow, but that is totally wrong.

If in fact, that erroneous belief was correct, then all the Children of Israel in the wilderness would have been saved. But the Scripture emphatically tells us here that they were not saved. Most of them died lost!

That's the reason that over our Telecast, or our Radio Stations, we do everything within our power, to make certain that what time we have, is dedicated totally and completely to the presentation of the Gospel, and by that I mean, the Gospel that saves, which means that it's presented by the power of the Holy Spirit.

On our Radio Stations, which operate 24 hours a day, we have no advertisements, no foolishness, no entertainment, with the entirety of the Programming being in the form of worship, teaching and/or preaching. Altar Calls are given constantly, with the Spirit of God moving constantly, which holds the door open for dying humanity.

One day I will stand before God. At that time, I will have to answer for this Call of God upon my heart and life. I will have to answer

NOTES

for every Message preached, and every opportunity given. I want to be able to stand before Him, and to say that I did my very best to hold that door open, and to say exactly as the Holy Spirit has said and continues to say unto this hour, *"today, if you will hear His Voice."*

TODAY — HEAR HIS VOICE

The phrase, *"As it is said, today if you will hear His voice,"* proclaims as stated, an Altar Call of unprecedented proportions. In fact, the Holy Spirit is the only One Who can really give what we refer to as the great invitation. And to say it even in a greater way, He has been giving this invitation from the very beginning. That invitation is, *"Today!" "Today!" "Today!" "If you will hear His Voice."*

As we have stated, even though the Call of God is unending, which means it's just as pronounced at one time as it is the other, that is not at all true as it regards individuals. That's the reason that the sinner must accept Christ *"Today!"* That's the reason the Christian must make things right with God *"Today!"* While the Call of God may be here tomorrow, you as an individual may not. In fact, even as I've already stated, there will be no tomorrow for several millions of people who are alive today. Death will claim them, which means their opportunity has ended.

So, the Gospel and its reception, is never yesterday or tomorrow, but always *"today."*

As it refers to hearing the Gospel, Jesus repeatedly said, *"He that hath ears to hear, let him hear"* (Mat. 11:15).

What did He mean by that statement?

First of all, He wasn't speaking of their physical ears. He was speaking of them hearing with their spirit, with their heart, and thereby accepting and receiving.

The word *"hear"* has the connotation of the ability to receive. Some hear what is being said, and some don't! Some heard Christ, but some didn't!

Oh yes, they heard the words, but they really didn't hear with their spirits. This is because of a lack of Faith.

If people refuse to believe, then they simply cannot *"hear."* As stated, while they hear the words, they really do not believe what they hear. Hence the Holy Spirit saying, *"if you will hear His Voice."*

As Paul said in Verse 2, if the Word preached and heard is not mixed with Faith, it will profit nothing. That's the key, *"Faith!"*

HEARING AND THE CROSS

Once again, allow us to take this opportunity to proclaim the Message that must be preached and thereby heard. Too often, people hear that which is wrong and sadly, believe it! Faith in the wrong thing, however, does not turn out to positive results, but rather the very opposite.

If the Preacher is not preaching the Cross, then the person hearing the Message is not hearing the right Message, thereby, even if he receives it, such a Message will be to his detriment. The Preacher must preach the Cross of Christ. This is the only avenue of Salvation for mankind; therefore, it must ever be the preaching of the Cross!

A short time ago I was listening to a Preacher over Television. He concluded his Message by telling the people that they must be baptized in water in order to be saved. That's not the Gospel, and those who are deceived thereby are not wise!

I heard another one say that the Blessing of Abraham was not at all Justification by Faith, but rather money. Now think of that! That's the first time in my life I found myself standing on the floor screaming at the Television set. What a perversion of the Word of God. The sadness is, this man pastors a Church running several thousands of people, which means they are not hearing the Gospel.

This thing is twofold: It's what we preach, and what they hear! If we don't preach that which is right, which is the Cross, they cannot hear that which is right, and cannot be saved. It's hard enough, even though we preach what is right. If not, it becomes impossible! We must preach the Cross.

A FAMINE OF THE WORD OF GOD

During the days of the Prophet Amos, the Holy Spirit through him said, *"Behold, the days come, saith the Lord God, that I will send a famine in the land, not a famine of bread, nor a thirst for water, but of hearing the Words of the Lord:*

"And they shall wander from sea to sea, and from the north even to the east, they shall

run to and fro to seek the Word of the Lord, and shall not find it" (Amos 8:11-12).

That happened to Israel of old, and it is happening today as well. There is a famine of the Word of the Lord in the land, with people running all over the world trying to find that Word, but instead getting something else.

Without going into detail, in 1988, the Church Leaders of the world, with some few exceptions, in essence said that they didn't want the Word of God. They wanted humanistic psychology! They wanted so-called contemporary Christian music. They wanted fads and fancies, and that's exactly what they have received.

Presently, there are thousands upon thousands of people attending meetings, where no one gets saved, no one is Baptized with the Holy Spirit, no one is healed, and no one is delivered; and yet, they call all of this a great Move of God!

People crowing like roosters and barking like dogs, all of this going on in meetings, and claimed to be movings and operations of the Holy Spirit, characterize exactly what I say. Others are claiming that their teeth are being filled with gold, or that gold dust is appearing in their hair and on their clothes, etc. I think it should be obvious as to the utter stupidity of such claims. But what makes it so bad, it's all claimed to be of the Spirit.

To be sure, it is *"a spirit,"* but it's not *"the Spirit!"* As stated, there is a famine of the Word of the Lord in the land!

Paul emphasized the words *"His Voice,"* proclaiming that this is the only Voice that is legitimate. This actually speaks of the Holy Spirit.

His Voice must speak through the Preacher, must teach through the Teacher, must sing through the singer, must witness through the witness, must pray through the prayer, must minister through the Minister. If not, there is nothing!

If it's not *"His Voice,"* then it's the voice of man, which in a sense means that it's the voice of Satan. It is only the call and the cry of the Holy Spirit, which will bring men to Christ. This is done through the preaching of the Word, and I might quickly add, a Word that is uncompromised. If the Anointing of the Holy Spirit isn't upon the person, and especially the Preacher, nothing is going to be done for God. No souls will be saved! No lives will be changed! No bondages will be broken! The Scripture plainly says through the Prophet Zechariah, *"Not by might* (human might), *nor by power* (human power), *but by My Spirit, saith the Lord of Hosts"* (Zech. 4:6).

That's at least one of the reasons we have two Prayer Meetings a day at Family Worship Center. Among all the other needs, I cry to the Lord constantly, that we might be a fit temple through which the Holy Spirit might work and function. I realize that I cannot make this temple what it ought to be by my own efforts and abilities. In other words, I can will to be consecrated, but I cannot bring about the actual work, that being a Work of the Spirit, as I place my Faith in the Cross of Christ. But my constant prayer is, that He will make me what I ought to be, and thereby use me, to reach hurting hearts and lives.

I know, that every soul that's been saved, every life that's been changed under this Ministry, has been brought about by the Work, Moving, Operation, Anointing, and Person of the Holy Spirit working in, by, and through this Evangelist.

Consequently, there must be nothing in my heart and life that's displeasing to the Lord, for God cannot bless sin, cannot anoint sin, and cannot work where sin is present. Sin must be washed by the Blood and forsaken, which is the Work of the Holy Spirit, as He brings to measure the great benefits of the Cross within our hearts and lives.

If people hear my voice they've heard nothing; however, if they can hear *"His Voice,"* then they've heard the Voice of God, and can be saved, healed, or delivered! And remember, His Voice is constantly crying, *"Today!"*

THE HARDENED HEART

The phrase, *"Harden not your hearts,"* refers to the result of unbelief.

That's the reason that we have said, that if a person doesn't hear the Voice of God today, that it becomes increasingly harder as time goes on. The reason is not with God, but with the human heart. If we do not accept, that means we reject, for God is never placed in a neutral position.

This means that in some mysterious way, with each rejection, which means a refusal to accept today, the door closes just a little more. The Lord is still calling as loudly as ever, but His Voice is now not so easily heard. To be sure, this applies to Christians just as well as to unbelievers.

As the Holy Spirit constantly deals with the unsaved, He constantly deals with Believers also. In fact, this of which Paul speaks here, refers to Believers. And the implication of failure to properly hear is awful indeed!

The Holy Spirit is constantly drawing Christians closer to Christ, or rather is attempting to do so. If they do not hear His Voice, they never remain in a static position. In other words, their situation is left somewhat weaker than before they heard.

Unfortunately, many Christians seek out a Church where His Voice is not heard. By that manner, they appease their conscience, but they also cut off the Word of God to themselves. While it is true that they are no longer made to feel uncomfortable, it is also true, that they are on a slide downward, which will ultimately result in spiritual oblivion. For the only thing worse than a lack of Faith in hearing the Gospel, is refusing to hear it at all. And that's where most of the Church is presently. They don't want to hear the Gospel, so they seek out Churches which appeal to their wrong direction. Let me say it again:

It is a terrible thing not to exercise Faith when the Gospel is heard, which means to not believe it. But there is one thing worse than that, and that is refusing to hear the Gospel at all!

Either way, such a road leads to spiritual disaster!

(8) "FOR IF JESUS (JOSHUA) HAD GIVEN THEM REST, THEN WOULD HE NOT AFTERWARD HAVE SPOKEN OF ANOTHER DAY."

The exegesis is:

1. Jesus is the Greek derivative for Joshua. And it should have been translated Joshua, for he is the one here addressed. This Greek word refers to the Lord Jesus in the New Testament except in two places where the context clearly indicates that it speaks of Joshua, Acts 7:45 and in this Passage.

2. The argument is, that if Joshua had given Israel a complete and final Rest in Canaan, then God would not, some 500 years afterward, have spoken of a Rest for Israel, as He did in Psalm 95.

3. Joshua couldn't give Israel Rest, so he spoke of another day, which actually refers to the coming Christ. The Rest into which Joshua led Israel was a temporal, physical, and material Rest, whereas Jesus leads into an eternal and spiritual Rest. Since Jesus is better than Joshua, the New Testament is superior to and takes the place of the First Testament.

JOSHUA

The phrase, *"For if Joshua had given them Rest,"* refers to the fact that even though he was able, by the power of the Holy Spirit, to lead Israel into the land of Canaan, that was only a symbol of the true Rest which was to come, namely the Lord Jesus Christ.

We need only to read the sad account in the Book of Judges of the events after Joshua's death to see the unrest of God's people.

Now the First Century Hebrew Christians were in danger of missing the mark and falling short of the Rest offered through Christ. The example of Israel under Moses and Joshua served as a strong example exhorting them to believe and to obey.

As stated, Jesus is better than Moses; He is better than Joshua. As the Messiah, the Son of God, the Perfect Sacrifice, He offers a perfect Rest to God's people.

ANOTHER DAY

The phrase, *"Then would He not afterward have spoken of another day,"* speaks of God pointing to a coming day, of which Canaan was merely a symbol. Actually, the pronoun *"He"* refers to God and not Joshua.

The Holy Spirit through Paul is carefully delineating the Revelation of God all through the centuries, leading up to Christ. Jesus is the fulfillment of all the prophecies, all the predictions, and all that went before Him. He is the One to Whom the Old Testament constantly points. So, for these Hebrew Christians to leave Christ, and go back to Temple worship, was a sin of extraordinary magnitude, as should be obvious. That's like

trading electricity for coal oil lamps. It's like trading an automobile for a donkey.

The idea here is that if everything was given in the Law at the time of Moses, then why was the Lord during the time of David, some 500 years after Moses, continuing to point to One Who was to come? During the time of David, the Lord spoke of *"another day."* Let the Reader understand, that this day has arrived.

So, as the Christian Jews of Paul's day had no excuse, neither do we! The superiority of Christ is so obvious and so evident, that it is hands down, no contest. He can provide what the Law never could provide, or anything else for that matter.

WHY WON'T EVERYONE ACCEPT?

That's a good question, but the answer is fairly obvious.

The unsaved are spiritually dead, which means they have no conception of God whatsoever. They don't know what He's like, or Who He is.

And as well, God cannot be understood scientifically, intellectually, or any other way conceived by man. God must reveal Himself to individuals, which He does through His Word, and more particularly through Jesus and what He did at the Cross for us.

So, the unredeemed, having absolutely no conception of God whatsoever, as well have no conception as to what it means to live for God. To the unsaved, going to Church all the time, is about the most boring thing they can think of. The same could be said for reading the Bible, or anything of this nature.

About the only thing the unsaved thinks about as it regards coming to Christ, is that if they do so, their life will be over. In other words, they think they'll never have any more fun, they'll never have another good time, that while they might live right in living for Christ, it will be such an awful existence, that they don't think they could stand it. If they think of this at all, these are primarily the thoughts which enter their minds.

Of course, they think these things erroneously, and because they are deceived. They don't know what living for the Lord actually is, and in fact cannot know, until they accept Christ. That's the reason the Psalmist said:

"O taste and see that the Lord is good: blessed is the man that trusteth in Him" (Ps. 34:8).

But it remains for the unsaved to *"taste"* which refers to accepting Christ.

And then of course when one comes to Christ, a whole new world opens up. As the Holy Spirit through Paul plainly said, *"Therefore if any man be in Christ, he is a new creature: old things are passed away; behold, all things are become new"* (II Cor. 5:17).

To be frank, living for the Lord is the greatest life in the world. There's absolutely nothing that can compare with what Jesus can be to an individual. And the beautiful thing about this is, that a person can draw as close to God as they desire, with everything becoming more and more wonderful the closer one gets.

Man is not only a physical being, he is also a spiritual being. However, at the Fall, man was cut off from God, which means that his life source was cut off. Satan has tried to fill that void with *"things,"* but of course, such an effort is impossible.

That's the reason as one man said, *"Before I was saved, I would go to every bar, until they were all closed, and then continue to seek one that was still open."* The reason this is done is because nothing of this world can satisfy the craving of the human heart.

Man being created by God, means that he cannot function as he should without God. Whether he realizes it or not, his heart is constantly crying out for God. He tries to fill that void with baubles, trinkets, gadgets, etc., but all to no avail. The Master said it perfectly:

"Whosoever drinketh of this water (the things of this world) *shall thirst again* (meaning that one's thirst is never slaked by this method)*:*

"But whosoever drinketh of the water that I shall give him shall never thirst; but the water that I shall give him shall be in him a well of water springing up into Everlasting Life" (Jn. 4:13-14).

But men do not accept, at least easily, because they are deceived. That's the reason that many have to come to the end of their way, the end of their efforts, the end of their abilities, with their backs proverbially speaking to the wall, before they will finally say *"yes"* to Christ. But yet in the midst of it all,

NOTES

the Holy Spirit is still calling out *"today, if you will hear His Voice!"*

(9) "THERE REMAINETH THEREFORE A REST TO THE PEOPLE OF GOD."

The breakdown of this short Passage is:

1. The word *"remaineth"* refers to the fact that all which went before Christ was not that *"Rest,"* but only pointed to that *"Rest"* which was to come, which was and is the Lord Jesus Christ.

2. Paul uses here a different Greek word for *"Rest."* In his previous references to the idea of Rest, he used the Greek *"katapausis,"* which means *"a cessation from activity."* Now, he uses *"sabbatismos,"* the word used of the Sabbath Rest. The word points back to God's original Rest, and speaks of the ideal Rest.

It is a Sabbath Rest because the Believer reaches a definite stage of attainment and has satisfactorily accomplished a purpose, as God did when He finished the work of creation.

3. This is not the Believer's Rest into which he enters and in which he participates, but in God's unique, personal Rest in which the Believer shares, all in Christ Jesus.

REMAINETH

The phrase, *"There remaineth,"* pertains as stated, to the fact that all which went before Christ, were merely symbols pointing to Him. No man could provide this Rest, not even Abraham, Moses, or David, or any other person for that matter. As well, neither could the great acts which God performed during all of those times provide that for which the soul longingly sought.

God's miracles before Christ were absolutely necessary, but they within themselves could not bring about that which would satisfy the longing and the craving of the human soul. That remained for Christ to accomplish, which He did at the Cross. But thank God we can now say the following:

Christ has now come, which is the greatest thing that ever happened to the human race, and ever will happen to the human race.

A REST

The phrase, *"Therefore a Rest,"* refers as stated to this completed Rest. And yet, even though we do have a completed Rest, which refers to a completed Salvation, still, we do not yet have all the benefits of this *"Rest."* That remaineth until the coming Resurrection of Life, when we will then be glorified, even as we are now Sanctified and Justified.

We have died with Christ, been buried with Christ, been resurrected with Christ, and in fact have been exalted with Christ (Eph. 2:6). But we have not yet ruled and reigned with Christ, which will take place in the coming Kingdom Age (Rev., Chpts. 19-20). As someone has well said, *"We have been saved, we are saved, and we are being saved."*

As well, *"Rest"* does not mean that there will be no temptations or trials, or that infirmities will no longer come. In fact, we are in a warfare; there will be conflict with Satan day-by-day.

Israel's Rest which was a type of our Rest, was not a cessation of activity but one of conquest and victory. They needed only to believe and obey; God promised to drive the enemy out before them.

Israel failed to take the land through unbelief, compromise, neglect, rebellion, idolatry, and sin. This tells us, there remains yet much Rest-land to be possessed by the Child of God.

The Rest promised involves ceasing from our own labors, even as the next Verse proclaims.

THE PEOPLE OF GOD

The phrase, *"To the people of God,"* proclaims to us, that it is only the people of God which will have, and which do have this *"Rest!"*

The world tries to find this Rest with all its various ways and means, but never succeeds, because such is impossible. It is only for the people of God, and that refers to those who have accepted Christ.

Consequently, Paul is telling the Hebrew Christians, that if they turn their backs on Christ, they will as well, forfeit this *"Rest,"* which means, that the enmity which had formerly been between God and themselves, will be revived, which is an unthinkable thing. In other words, there will cease to be any Peace with God, and because they are no longer trusting in Christ, Who Alone God honors.

(10) "FOR HE THAT IS ENTERED INTO HIS REST, HE ALSO HATH CEASED

FROM HIS OWN WORKS, AS GOD DID FROM HIS."

The structure is:

1. The person who has entered into God's Rest can only come by Faith in Christ and what He did at the Cross on our behalf.

2. Salvation is by Faith, which refers to Faith exclusively in Christ and His Cross, and not at all by works.

3. As the Believer came in by Faith, he remains in by Faith as well. This means that he ceases trusting whatsoever in any and all works, which we will deal with more directly in further commentary.

3. God ceasing from His Works refers back to the third Verse. All the great Plan of Redemption was settled totally and completely even before the foundation of the world, which refers to Christ and what He would do on the Cross, and it has not been changed, and it will not be changed. Now we should understand the seriousness of attempting to enter in some other way than by the Cross. No wonder Jesus referred to such as a *"thief and robber"* (Jn. 10:1).

ENTERING GOD'S REST

The phrase, *"For he* (the individual) *that is entered into His* (God's) *Rest,"* speaks of course of the Salvation process.

The only way that any individual, even from the very beginning, has ever entered into God's Rest is by placing Faith and trust in the Lord Jesus Christ, and more particularly, what Christ did at the Cross. As we've said repeatedly, when one thinks of Christ, one must ever think of the Cross at the same time, because it was through the Cross that every blessing and all Grace have come. All of this is very crucial and very important.

In fact, Satan will do everything within his power to move one's Faith from Christ and the Cross, or as Paul said it, *"Jesus Christ and Him Crucified,"* to something else entirely. To be sure, Satan doesn't really care as to what the object of one's Faith is, providing it's not in the Cross. He is perfectly content for you to be very religious in all of your efforts, just as long as you do not understand the Cross of Christ, thereby placing your Faith totally and completely in that Finished Work. Sadly, he has been very successful in this effort. In fact, I personally think that this constitutes 90 percent of all his efforts, and I speak of his attempts to move one away from the Cross to something else entirely.

I read once where a Preacher stated that God had one Plan of Salvation for the Jews and another for the Gentiles. How absurd! There has never been but one way of Salvation, and that has been by Jesus Christ and Him Crucified. And it's always been by Faith in that great Sacrifice.

Before the Cross, people were saved by looking forward to that coming work, in other words, a prophetic Jesus. Now people are saved by looking back to that Finished Work, thereby an historical Jesus. But everything centers up in the Cross, it being the centrality of the Gospel.

CEASING FROM WORKS

The phrase, *"He also hath ceased from his own works,"* refers to the fact that the believing sinner must not trust works at all as it regards coming to Christ, but must come exclusively by Faith, and as well, must be sanctified in the same manner. This one Passage, if understood correctly, can save untold sorrow and heartache. Please believe me I know exactly that of which I speak, for I have personally walked this road, in fact, as has every single other Believer.

To which we've mentioned in previous commentary, millions of Christians come in by Faith, which is the only way they can come in, but then they attempt to sanctify themselves by works. In other words, it's Salvation by Faith, and Sanctification by works. Now let's look at this more fully, because this is very, very important.

GETTING CLOSER TO GOD

Looking at the heading, *"getting closer to God"* very carefully, the question must be asked, exactly how can this be done?

Even though I have addressed this in previous commentary, it so very, very important, that I must without fail do everything within my power, to get you the Reader to understand this of which we speak.

The problem with us is we have to unlearn so much, so much error I might quickly add, before we can actually learn the Truth.

NOTES

We are products, and in most cases, victims of what we've heard behind the pulpit all of our Christian lives. Some of it has been very good, but some of it has been deadly, and to be sure, we suffer the effects of the error we believe. As someone has said, *"We do what we do, because we believe what we believe!"*

If one were to ask most Christians as to exactly how they could get closer to the Lord, I suppose the first response would be from most, that they should be more faithful to Church, give more money to the Work of the Lord, pray more, witness to lost souls more, etc.

While all of these things are very, very good, and to be sure, that which good Christians will always do, none of that mentioned will draw anyone closer to the Lord. In fact, it is impossible for any Christian to sanctify themselves, or to get closer to the Lord, by any works of any nature, irrespective as to what those works might be. Now please don't misunderstand what I'm saying:

These things mentioned are very definitely very important, and will definitely bless one greatly upon being engaged, etc., but they won't draw one closer to God.

Taking prayer for instance, we have two Prayer Meetings a day here at the Ministry, and have conducted these Prayer Meetings ever since the Fall of 1991. I have attended every single one of them, with the exception of the times I've been out of town, or something has come up. So by that, you might know how we value prayer. In fact, the Lord told me to institute these Prayer Meetings, which we immediately did in obedience. As stated, this was in the Fall of 1991.

Now while the Lord will definitely reveal to the person in prayer as to how all of these things can be done, the mere act of prayer itself, will not draw one closer to the Lord, as valuable as it is in other ways.

No, this is not a mere play on words, and if you the Reader think it is, then I'm stating the case poorly. The Truth is as follows:

FAITH IN WHAT JESUS DID AT THE CROSS

The only means by which one can receive anything from God, and I mean anything, is by simply placing one's Faith and trust in Christ and what He did at the Cross.

That's it! It's at the same time, the simplest thing on the face of the earth, and the most complicated.

It's simple, because it means exactly what it says (I Cor. 1:18, 23; 2:2; Gal. 6:14). It's complicated, because Satan fights this in every way possible, using every tactic at his disposal.

If the Believer will cease from all his works, exactly as Paul says here, and place his Faith and Trust entirely in the Finished Work of Christ, he will find himself getting closer and closer to the Lord.

WHAT DOES IT MEAN FOR ONE TO CEASE FROM ALL HIS WORKS?

Does it mean quit going to Church? Quit giving any of our financial resources to the Work of the Lord? Quit praying? Quit witnessing?

Of course not!

However, it definitely does mean, and in capital letters, that even though these things mentioned, plus many we haven't mentioned, are indeed very important, the idea is, that we are not to depend on them whatsoever as earning us any merit with God. We do these things because we are close to the Lord, and not in order to get close to the Lord. We do these things not to get victory over the world, the flesh, and the Devil, but because Christ has already given us victory over the world, the flesh, and the Devil.

One of the reasons this is so complicated, is because most Christians love their *"works!"* They relish in these works! They are the labor of their hands, and very precious in their sight, exactly as Ishmael was precious in the sight of Abraham, and because that boy was the product of Abraham's ingenuity. But that means, if something is the product of our efforts, then it's not the product of God's efforts.

I have found in preaching the Cross, that many Christians grow angry at these statements. Why would they do that? Really, the answer is very simple.

They get angry, because as stated, they love their works. They like to feel that doing these things, and, yes, trusting in these things, earns them something with God. But even beyond that, it makes them feel superior. In

other words, I do this or that, while others don't, so I'm superior to them.

TRUSTING IN ONE'S WORKS CAN ONLY BREED SELF-RIGHTEOUSNESS

This is one of the reasons that most of the Church is so mean that we can put the unsaved world to shame in this respect. Who do you think it was who crucified Christ?

It wasn't the drunks, or the harlots, or the thieves, etc. It was the religious leadership of Israel who crucified Christ. They did so in their smug self-righteousness, in their air of superiority, in their holier than thou demeanor. And this should show you exactly how deadly, how damnable this thing actually is.

I can understand people getting angry with me, but I cannot understand anyone getting angry with Christ. The only perfect man who ever lived, they put on a Cross. The only One Who evidenced nothing but love, they put on a Cross. And again I emphasize, it was the *"Church"* of that day that did this, and not those on whom the Church looked down on.

If you as a Believer want anything from the Lord, and as previously stated, I mean anything, you are going to have to place your trust totally and completely in what Christ did at the Cross, and not at all in you, or your doings, or all your religiosity! Dependence on works must cease totally and completely. Your Faith and Trust is to be totally and completely in what Christ did at the Cross.

That's the reason that these Commentaries are so very, very important. In fact, the teaching on the Cross that I'm giving you here is without a doubt the most important feature of these Commentaries. This means, that you should learn everything you can about the Finished Work of Christ. Considering, that the Cross is the Source of all your Blessings, the Source of all your fellowship with the Lord, the Source of all the benefits which God has for you, you should want to know every single thing you can know about this all-important Sacrifice.

And please understand, when we speak of the Cross, we are actually speaking of its benefits. We're not speaking of putting Jesus back on a Cross, or you climbing up on some Cross so to speak. We are speaking of the benefits of what Jesus did there for you, thereby paying such a price. And considering that the Cross was an accomplished fact in the Mind of God, even from before the foundation of the world (I Pet. 1:18-20), and that the Cross was ever the destination of this great Plan, and that the very reason for the Incarnation was the Cross, and that Jesus came for this very purpose, i.e., *"to die on the Cross,"* then we should try to learn everything we can learn about this all-important Finished Work. In fact, this must be the center of our understanding of the Bible. It must stand as the foundation of all the great Plan of God. This means that every single Doctrine must spring from the Cross, and if it doesn't, then in some way, it's unscriptural.

WHERE ARE MOST CHRISTIANS PRESENTLY AS IT REGARDS THE CROSS?

The sad Truth is, most Christians have not at all ceased from their works, which means they are not trusting in Christ, but rather something else altogether. This is so, simply because there has been so little teaching and preaching on the Cross in the last several decades, that the modern Church has little knowledge whatsoever as it regards the Cross of Christ. In fact, what little knowledge they have is only in the capacity of sentimentality. In other words, they know that Jesus died for them, that is if they believe the Bible at all, but that's about as far as it goes.

There's not one Christian out of thousand, and I think I exaggerate not, who understands the Cross as it refers to their Sanctification process. In other words, what it takes to have victory over the world, the flesh, and the Devil, the modern Christian has no idea whatsoever. That's the reason for Christians running all over the world trying to get Preachers to lay hands on them, thereby performing some magic work, in order that they may have the victory for which they seek.

In a few of the recent happenings which the Church has labeled as great moves of God, many people were heard to say, *"If I don't get something here, I don't know what I'm going to do,"* or words to that effect!

In fact, one of my associates was in one of these Meetings. They asked him to help catch

the people who were being *"slain in the Spirit,"* which he did. He mentioned to me, that quite a number of them, whispered in his ear just before prayer was offered for them, that they needed help desperately. Many times it would be in the realm of pornography or immorality of some sort, or alcohol, or whatever. Now we may blanch somewhat at Christians being afflicted with these gross sins of which I have just mentioned. However, consider the following:

It doesn't matter who the Believer is, if that Believer doesn't understand the Cross, he has pretty much made himself a target for Satan. In fact, many times, and again I do not think I exaggerate, the Preachers praying for the people, are not walking in victory themselves. In other words, many of them are attempting to deliver people when they desperately need deliverance themselves.

Now by saying that, I'm not trying to fault the Preachers. Most of these individuals I would surely think, are very sincere, which means they love the Lord. I am not impugning their consecration, their dedication, their motivation, or their love for God. In fact, I've been there, so I know what I'm talking about!

But the Truth is, if that Preacher doesn't understand the Cross, and I don't care how big the crowds are attending his meetings, or how much he is heralded all over the world as *"God's man of Faith and power,"* in some way he is walking in spiritual failure. It is impossible for it to be otherwise!

God has only one way of victory, and that is through what Jesus did at the Cross. And if the Believer, be he Preacher or otherwise, doesn't know that, it is impossible for that individual to live the life he ought to live, no matter how hard he or she may try.

SIN

When we speak of sin, the minds of Christians automatically go to the vices. And to be sure, those things definitely are sin. But here's what the Believer needs to understand:

In reality, the vices, or even sins of pride, etc., are actually the result of the greatest sin of all, and that is rebellion against God in the realm of what He has done on our behalf, and I speak of the Cross. Let's say that again:

The real sin is in trying to bring about what we need in ways other than the Way furnished by Christ at the Cross. It is the sin of rebellion, and it is the greatest sin of all, opening the door for all things. Listen to what Paul said:

"Whatsoever is not of Faith is sin" (Rom. 14:23).

Exactly what did the Apostle mean by that statement?

Paul is not speaking here of Faith as we think of such, but rather *"the Faith."* To cut through all the fluff, it refers to what Jesus did at the Cross on our behalf.

In reference to this, Paul also said, *"But before Faith came, we were kept under the Law,"* (Gal. 3:23).

Once again, he's referring to *"the Faith,"* which refers to Christ, and more specifically, what He did at the Cross.

So, when Paul says, *"Whatsoever is not of Faith is sin,"* he is speaking of *"the Faith,"* or more particularly, the great Sacrifice of Christ. He is saying that if we do not place our Faith and trust totally and completely in the great Finished Work of Christ, we sin. In fact, such an attitude is the highest act of rebellion against God. And tragically, that's where most Christians presently are! Admittedly, for most it is because of Scriptural ignorance; nevertheless, the end result of hurt and harm is the same as if it was rank unbelief.

So, you as a Christian are making a mistake, if you zero in on the sin the person has committed. The great question is, why did they commit the sin? And of course I'm speaking of Christians.

The stock answer for all of this is, *"They wanted to do that!"* Now the Truth is, some few possibly did want to *"do that,"* but not many. Most Christians are failing, because they do not know God's prescribed order of victory, and not knowing that prescribed order which is the Cross of Christ, they're going to trust in their own works, which is guaranteed of defeat.

That's why Paul also said, *"Brethren, if any man be overtaken in a fault, ye which are spiritual, Restore such an one in the spirit of meekness; considering thyself, lest thou also be tempted"* (Gal. 6:1).

We must remember, that Paul wrote the Epistle to the Galatians because of the very thing which we are here discussing. The Galatians had been set upon by false teachers, claiming they needed to add the Law to Grace, which of course would bring nothing but spiritual defeat. In other words, the Galatians had actually come to Christ under the Ministry of Paul, and had definitely come in strictly by Faith. But now they were trying to live a victorious life, by the method these false teachers had proposed, and we speak of *"works."* Again, they had been saved by Faith, but now they were trying to sanctify themselves by works.

So Paul is telling them, if someone has failed the Lord, they should be told how they failed and why they failed, which means they were trusting in works and not in the Cross of Christ.

There's no point in taking this person and punishing him or her. That's not going to do any good. In fact, it's an insult to Christ. Jesus took all of our punishment at the Cross, and for us to levy more punishment on others, shows that we have no understanding whatsoever of the great Plan of God for victory.

No, we are to show the individual that they have failed the Lord simply because they have trusted in their own efforts and not in what Jesus did at the Cross; consequently, such direction as repeatedly stated, is guaranteed of failure!

And if we meet with some Christians, who do not want to hear what we're saying, and in fact, do not want to repent of their false direction, and it becomes obvious that they are rebelling against this of which Christ has done on their behalf, then there's nothing left but to disfellowship that person, exactly as Paul mentioned in the Fifth Chapter of I Corinthians. But, if the Truth of the Cross is patiently explained to them, and they accept it, which will quickly become obvious as it regards their sincerity, they are to be instantly Restored. This is God's way.

Everyone must understand, that every single Believer who has ever lived, has had to learn this of which we speak. In fact, the great Paul had to learn it exactly as we do, as is outlined in Romans Chapter 7. He came to the end of his own efforts, by saying, *"O wretched man that I am, who shall deliver me from the body of this death?"* (Rom. 7:24).

To be sure, the Lord did deliver him, and in fact, gave him the meaning of the New Covenant, which is the meaning of the Cross, which the Apostle gave us in Romans, Chapter 6. Let me say it again:

Every Believer has had to learn this great Truth which we are here teaching, that is those who actually do know this Truth, and they must always remember, that before this light of the Cross came their way, that they too walked in failure.

You as a Believer, must cease from trusting in your own works, thinking that such efforts will bring you closeness with God, or victory in some manner or way. The Apostle is emphatic, even dogmatic, in this statement, and it must be heeded. Now let's look at the clincher:

GOD HAS CEASED FROM WORKS

The phrase, *"As God did from His,"* refers to the fact that God has totally and completely, formulated and finished this great Plan of Redemption, which in His Mind, was done from before the foundation of the world (Heb. 4:3; I Pet. 1:18-20). The idea is, that there is not going to be another Covenant, hence Paul using the term, *"The Everlasting Covenant"* (Heb. 13:20).

This also means, that He is not going to allow any other way to be set forward. In fact, when individuals attempt to do so, through ignorance or otherwise, it angers God greatly, as should be obvious. That's why He said, *"So I sware in My wrath, they shall not enter into My Rest"* (Heb. 3:11).

The failure of Christians as it regards sin, is not nearly as noxious to God, as it is the rebellion against His Plan of Redemption, which has brought about that failure. That's what angers God! And to be sure, it should be understandable, considering the great price that He paid in order to give us this glorious and wonderful Redemption.

But the problem is, many Christians don't want to cease from their works. Hence we hear the terms, *"easy grace,"* or *"greasy grace,"* which are little short of blasphemy!

People use such terms, because they are totally ignorant of the Word of God, or else

they are in a state of rebellion against the great Plan of God. Either way, the results are going to be catastrophic!

LET'S LOOK AT WORKS AS IT REGARDS DELIVERANCE

Most of the Church world at present needs deliverance in one manner or the other, and I think I exaggerate not! And please understand, bondage as tendered by Satan, comes in many shapes, forms, and sizes.

When most Christians think of bondage, they think of alcohol, immorality, drugs, nicotine, gambling, etc. To be sure, those things definitely are bondage, and cause individuals untold degrees of difficulties and problems, even destroying them. In fact, untold millions are destroyed by these vices; however, there are bondages of other nature as well.

In fact, religion is the greatest bondage of all. And that's exactly what we are here addressing. People are in bondage to their own works, to their own false ideas, to their own machinations.

Someone has said that the doing of religion is the worse narcotic there is, and in fact, that is the Truth. What do we mean by that?

As drugs make one feel that things are fine and right, when they are nothing of the sort, likewise, the doing of religion, makes people think everything is fine, when it's the very opposite. To be frank, an individual has to be delivered from the bondage of religion just the same as a person has to be delivered from nicotine or alcohol, etc.

But the great question is, *"How are they to be delivered?"*

When it comes to *"deliverance,"* most Christians think of hands being laid on such a person, by a great man or woman of Faith, and then the work being accomplished. In other words, some magical thing happens, and that person is no longer bound by that particular problem, whatever it might be.

That's basically our idea of deliverance! Most non-Pentecostals not believing in the laying on of hands, recommend humanistic psychology. In fact, most of the Pentecostal and Charismatic worlds fall into the same category at present.

Why?

Of course, *"why"* is a big word; however, the method used by we Pentecostals and Charismatics regarding the *"laying on of hands"* as it concerns deliverance, simply doesn't work, and because it's unscriptural. And of course, the world of psychology holds no answers whatsoever.

Now, while the laying on of hands is definitely Scriptural in its own right, and I speak of blessing for individuals and healing, it must be limited to that (Gen. 48:14; Num. 8:10; 27:23; Deut. 34:9; Mat. 19:15; Mk. 5:23; 6:2, 5; Lk. 4:40; 13:13; Acts 5:12; 13:3; 14:3; 19:11; 28:8; I Tim. 4:14; II Tim. 1:6; Heb. 6:2).

WHAT DID JESUS SAY ABOUT DELIVERANCE?

He said, *"The Spirit of the Lord is upon Me, because He hath anointed Me to preach the Gospel to the poor; He hath sent Me to heal the brokenhearted, and to preach deliverance to the captives"* (Lk. 4:18).

Please notice, that He said *"preach deliverance to the captives."* He never said anything about us *"delivering the captives."*

In fact, for years I read this statement, and thought in my mind that it should have been translated, *"He hath sent me to heal the broken hearted, and to deliver the captives."* But that's not what He said!

So, why did He say, *"preach deliverance"*?

He used the phrase in this manner, simply because deliverance has already been effected and in totality, and for every person. It was done at the Cross. There Jesus *"spoiled principalities and powers, making a shew of them openly, triumphing over them in it"* (Col. 2:15). What I'm trying to say is this:

At the Cross, Jesus Christ by His Death and Resurrection, set every single captive free. That means that in the mind of God, every single alcoholic is free; every single drug addict is free; every single individual hooked on nicotine is free; every person under the bondage of religion is free; and of course, it also speaks of any other problem of which one might think.

So, how does the person obtain the benefits of this deliverance which has already been afforded?

Everything is obtained in the same identical way as it regards the Lord. The person

is to believe in what Christ has done at the Cross on his behalf, understanding that it was all there accomplished, and that the only thing that God requires of us, is to have Faith in that Finished Work. The Believer must understand this, believe this, act upon this, center his Faith on this, and he will find victory unparalleled. Any other way will lead to hurt and harm, and possibly disaster!

God has Rested from the formulation and the carrying out of this great Work, and no other work will be allowed or even entertained, as should be obvious. In the first place, what can man do anyway? The answer is obvious to that as well, nothing!

Salvation is all of God and God is all of Salvation, which means that man has no part in it whatsoever, with the exception of receiving its benefits. We must cease from all our works, which means Faith and trust in those works. At the same time, there must be good works which follow the Child of God constantly, but as stated, always in the capacity of being a *"result"* of what we are in Christ, instead of being a *"cause."*

(11) "LET US LABOUR THEREFORE TO ENTER INTO THAT REST, LEST ANY MAN FALL AFTER THE SAME EXAMPLE OF UNBELIEF."

The exposition is:

1. The word *"labour"* as used here, means, *"to give all diligence."*

2. If we do not enter into that *"Rest"* after the manner of Faith, and stay in that *"Rest"* in the same way, we will fall, i.e., *"lose our souls."*

3. The culprit for not going God's Way is *"unbelief."*

LABOUR

The phrase, *"Let us labour therefore to enter into that Rest,"* does not mean that it can be earned by works. Not at all! The words *"let us labour"* are the translation of the Greek *"spoudazo,"* which means *"to hasten, make haste, to exert one's self, endeavor, give diligence."* It is used in the sense of *"do your best, take care, hurry on the doing of something."* It speaks of intensity of purpose followed by intensity of effort toward the realization of that purpose (Wuest). So exactly, what does this mean that the Believer should do?

First of all, the Believer must settle it in his mind once and for all, that every single thing from the Lord comes to him totally and completely through the Cross of Christ, i.e., *"the Finished Work of Christ."* Understanding that and believing that, he must earnestly seek the Lord that the Holy Spirit would open up to him the meaning of the Cross, giving him continued light on the subject. In fact, this must be a continued prayer, and for the simple reason, that the Holy Spirit desires that we totally depend on Him for all things. As well, it is literally impossible for one to exhaust the meaning of the Cross, meaning that whatever light we have, there is always more light to be gained.

Having done that, and continuing to do that, the Believer must avail himself of every opportunity at his disposal, such as these Commentaries, or Teaching Series that we might have on the subject, or anyone else for that matter. Once the Believer makes the Cross the object of his Faith, he will find the entirety of the Word of God becoming more and more clear, and more and more easy to understand. In fact, he will find that the entirety of his relationship with Christ will take on a brand-new perspective.

As well, he will also find that a proper understanding of the Cross will at the same time make erroneous teaching much more obvious. In fact, if one has a proper understanding of the Cross, one is not going to fall for error. Actually, that is the only safety and protection that one actually has — a proper understanding of the Cross, which is really a proper understanding of the Word of God, for the latter is actually the story of Redemption which should be obvious.

The trouble with too many Christians is, they are just plain lazy. That's the reason the *"laying on of hands"* is so popular. People want some Preacher to instantly solve all their problems for them, with what I refer to as a *"quick victory."* Such is not to be! However, this I can promise:

When one embarks upon what I refer to as the *"Cross-life,"* one has just embarked upon the greatest life there is. It is the most rewarding, the most fulfilling, and it will quickly become obvious as to the validity of what I'm saying (Lk. 9:23-24).

WHAT JESUS SAID

The Master said: *"The thief cometh not, but for to steal, and to kill, and to destroy: I am come that they might have life, and that they might have it more abundantly"* (Jn. 10:10).

In 1956 (if I remember the year correctly), the Lord made this Passage very, very real to me. In fact, so real that I can remember the moving of the Holy Spirit upon my heart at the very time it happened, *"I am come that they might have life, and that they might have it more abundantly."* Unfortunately, it took me 40 years to know exactly what our Lord was saying.

Walking in failure and defeat, which is the lot of every Christian life, if one doesn't understand the benefits of the Cross, is not exactly *"more abundant life."* What I'm saying is this:

One can definitely be saved, and still live in defeat. It's not a very pleasant prospect, but that's exactly what's going to happen, and what in fact is happening in every heart and life that doesn't understand the great Sacrifice of Christ.

In 1996, with the greater thrust coming in 1997, the Lord began to open up to me the Revelation of the Cross, which to say the least, was an answer to prayer. In fact, that Revelation has continued unto this hour, meaning that He is continuing to shed more and more light on this subject of all subjects, which has totally and completely revolutionized my life. As well, the Lord has instructed me to proclaim this Word in every manner possible, which we are doing readily with both Radio and Television, as well as the printed page, etc.

I now know what *"more abundant life"* actually is, and it's the most rewarding, the most fulfilling, the most glorious, the most wonderful life that one could ever know, have, or experience. And in fact, this is the only manner, and I speak of the Way of the Cross, in which it can be experienced. God has provided no other, because no other is needed.

When Jesus said, *"Come unto Me, all ye that labour and are heavy laden, and I will give you Rest,"* He meant exactly what He said (Mat. 11:28).

Now when He said *"Rest,"* He wasn't speaking of the opposition that Satan brings against us as it regards our Work for God, which will definitely continue, but rather the Rest and repose that we have in Christ as it regards our living for God. There is a vast difference in our *"living"* for God, and our *"work"* for God. The Reader must understand that.

If we use Paul as an example, which in fact is an excellent example, we will see that Satan opposed him in every capacity that one could think; however, that pertained to his work, and not his personal victory in the Lord. Even in the midst of a prison, with their backs cut to pieces by a Roman whip, he and Silas could pray and sing praises to God (Acts 16:23-25).

You as a Believer can walk with Christ and in Christ so to speak, having total and complete victory within your heart and life, over the world, the flesh, and the Devil. In other words, exactly as Paul said, *"Sin will not have dominion over you"* (Rom. 6:14).

UNBELIEF

The phrase, *"Lest any man fall after the same example of unbelief,"* proclaims in no uncertain terms, the cause of failure.

In the first place, it's impossible for one to fall from something, which they've never had. So this means that Paul is speaking to Believers, and telling them, that if they do not register continued Faith in Christ and what He did at the Cross, which means they are placing their Faith in something else, that ultimately they are going to fall. The only way one can walk in victory is by Faith in the Finished Work of Christ. God has provided no other method, because no other method is needed. Jesus paid it all, and that means that every single thing we need, and in every capacity, is found in the Cross of Christ.

ENTER THE HOLY SPIRIT

I have dealt with this subject over and over again, but knowing how difficult it is for some people to grasp and understand something other than what they have been taught all their life, is not always easy.

The Holy Spirit is the One Who makes possible to our benefit, all that Jesus paid for at the Cross (Rom. 8:1-2). And to be sure, He will work mightily on our behalf, which He in fact, has been sent to do, if only we will exhibit Faith in the Cross of Christ.

Please understand, that the Holy Spirit couldn't even come into the hearts and lives of Believers to abide, until the advent of the Cross. That's why Jesus said to His Disciples concerning the Holy Spirit, *"For He* (the Spirit) *dwelleth with you* (before the Cross), *and shall be in you* (after the Cross)" (Jn. 14:17).

The reason the Holy Spirit could not come in to abide permanently was because the sin debt had not yet been lifted. The reason was simple, the blood of bulls and goats could not take away sin (Heb. 10:4).

When Jesus went to the Cross, sin was definitely taken away and in totality (Jn. 1:29). Consequently, the Spirit can now abide permanently within the hearts and lives of all Believers.

It is the Spirit Who makes possible all things provided by Christ regarding His great and glorious Sacrifice. So, this Christian walk, to use an oversimplification, can be summed up in three words:

A. The Cross.

B. Our Faith in the Cross.

C. The Holy Spirit Who works with us and for us, as it regards the Cross, and our Faith in that great Sacrifice.

So it comes down to the simple question, do you believe that which we have said?

And to be more particular, do you believe that everything we receive from the Lord comes through the Cross?

Do you believe that the Cross must be the object of your Faith, and the sole object of your Faith?

Do you believe that the Cross of Christ, i.e., *"the Sacrifice of Christ,"* is in effect, the ground upon which the Holy Spirit works, which means that He requires Faith on our part in that great Sacrifice?

The Truth is, you either believe it or you don't! If you don't believe that which we've said, and which we believe the Bible totally and completely teaches, then what do you believe?

(12) "FOR THE WORD OF GOD IS QUICK, AND POWERFUL, AND SHARPER THAN ANY TWOEDGED SWORD, PIERCING EVEN TO THE DIVIDING ASUNDER

OF SOUL AND SPIRIT, AND OF THE JOINTS AND MARROW, AND IS A DISCERNER OF THE THOUGHTS AND INTENTS OF THE HEART."

The exegesis is:

1. The Word of God is alive, which means it's different than any literature or writing anywhere else in the world. Actually it is actively alive, constantly alive.

2. In its life it has power, because it is the Word of God, and because it is backed up and empowered by the Holy Spirit.

3. The Word of God has an incisive and penetrating quality, hence being *"sharper."* It lays bare the self-delusions of man.

4. It will bless those who follow the Lord, and at the same time, it will curse and condemn those who don't. Consequently, as stated, it is *"two-edged."*

5. *"Piercing,"* coupled with the phrase *"the dividing asunder of soul and spirit,"* do not mean, *"the dividing asunder of soul from spirit."* Nor is it *"the dividing asunder of joints from marrow."* It refers to *"going through the soul, and going through the spirit."* In fact, joints and marrow are not in contact with one another, and cannot, therefore, be said to be divided asunder.

The idea is, that the Word of God pierces every part of man's soul, spirit, and being, laying bare every facet of the individual.

6. The word *"discerner"* further emphasizes this which we have just said. This means that the Word of God alone can properly divide or separate, thus *"to judge."* It sifts out and analyzes evidence. The ideas of discrimination and judgment are blended. Thus, the Word of God is able to penetrate into the furthermost recesses of a person's spiritual being, sifting out and analyzing the thoughts and intents of the heart (Wuest).

THE WORD OF GOD

The phrase, *"For the Word of God,"* must be understood in the context of the Holy Bible. This means that there is no Word of God other than that. This also means, that the Book of Mormon is not the Word of God, or the Koran, or any other pretender.

Also, we need to remember that God's Word is ever the standard of judgment, and not our knowledge of it. Therefore, the

importance of becoming thoroughly conversant with the Truth as revealed in the Holy Scriptures, is altogether imperative.

As we here have the *"Written Word,"* it will be followed by the *"Living Word,"* both being identical, i.e., *"the Word and Christ"* (Jn. 1:1).

Linking Paul's statement here of the *"Word of God,"* with the word *"unbelief"* in the previous Verse, we learn where the unbelief is centered. Pure and simple, the Apostle is speaking here of unbelief in the Word. However, in almost all cases of error, most would claim they do not register unbelief in the Word, in fact claiming they are right, about whatever it is that's under discussion.

During Paul's day, the Christian Jews, at least those who were contemplating going back into Temple worship, would have argued with him, claiming that they were fully abiding by the Word of God in doing this. They would have been speaking about the Old Testament, and in effect, denying the Epistles he had written as being the Word of God.

Quite possibly they would have even been very sincere in what they believed; however, sincerity alone has nothing to do with what is right or wrong.

There was overwhelming evidence in Christ, His Life, Work, and Ministry, which gave total credence to that which Paul taught, to substantiate what was being said. In other words, there was no excuse for their *"unbelief."*

Presently, there are untold millions who claim Christ, and claim to believe the Bible in totality, but do not believe in the Baptism with the Holy Spirit, with the evidence of speaking with other Tongues (Acts 2:4). As well, there are many who believe in the unscriptural doctrine of unconditional eternal security, despite the Word of God being emphatic otherwise. And to pursue the subject, there will be many who will read these words we have written concerning the Cross of Christ, or hear them preached, and still will not believe.

WHY DO SOME CHRISTIANS BELIEVE ERROR INSTEAD OF TRUTH?

Possibly the Lord Alone knows the answer to that, and quite possibly, the answers are as varied as the number of individuals involved.

However, I think there are definitely some telltale signs. They are:

1. If one doesn't understand the Cross of Christ, then one cannot understand the Word of God, at least as one should. While of course, it can be understood up to a point, the full picture is brought together only when one understands the Finished Work. I personally think this is the biggest problem in the Church, and the reason for so much error.

Once the Cross becomes understandable, which means the entirety of the Plan of God for the human race, then everything else starts to fit together as well. As one dear lady said, one may think that something is definitely of a particular color, until it's placed beside that which is the real color. Then the phony is shown up for what it is. That's the way it is with the Cross.

When one begins to understand the Cross, then everything else must match up to the Cross, and if it doesn't, then it quickly becomes obvious as to what it actually is. That's the reason that Paul plainly and clearly said, *"I determined to know nothing among you save Christ and Him Crucified"* (I Cor. 2:2).

That's the reason he also said, *"For the preaching of the Cross is to them that perish foolishness, but to we who are saved it is the Power of God"* (I Cor. 1:18).

That's the reason that John recorded Jesus as saying, *"For God so loved the world, that He gave His only Begotten Son, that whosoever believeth in Him should not perish, but have Everlasting Life"* (Jn. 3:16).

In this one Verse, plus many others which could be accordingly quoted, we find the entirety of the Plan of God, which is actually the Word of God.

So if one's interpretation of the Word doesn't match up to what the Word says about the Cross, then the interpretation is wrong.

2. Self-will is that which subverts God's Will. If one truly wants the Will of God, and truly asks the Lord to lead them accordingly, the Holy Spirit will definitely lead them into all Truth (Jn. 16:13).

3. Pride is a militating factor in all error. There are untold numbers who know they are wrong concerning what they believe

about the Bible, but they have too much pride to admit it. They think they will look bad in front of their friends, or possibly they've said so much in the other direction, they think they'll look like a fool now that they are backing down.

To have and to hold the True Word of God is the single most important thing in the world. In fact, this is so important that there is no way that mere humans could properly comprehend its vast significance. So, the idea is, irrespective of how much we have to swallow our pride, irrespective of our self-will, we must ardently seek that which the Lord wants and desires, and nothing else. If we will honestly do that, the Holy Spirit has promised, as stated, to lead us into all Truth.

ALIVE

The word *"quick,"* in the Greek is *"zon,"* which is a present participle of the verb *"zao"* which means, *"to live, be alive."* That means, as stated, that it is constantly active. And what do we mean by that?

It means first of all, that it's absolutely impossible to exhaust the potential of the Word. In some mysterious way, the Word of God is the written form of the Living Christ. As such, it is energized at all times by the Holy Spirit, which means in some mysterious way, that the Holy Spirit literally inhabits the Word.

Because of this, the Bible cannot be understood, at least as far as its spiritual content and intent are concerned, by the unredeemed. This means that it is not carnally discerned, hence the Scripture saying, *"But the natural man receiveth not the things of the Spirit of God: for they are foolishness unto Him: neither can he know them, because they are spiritually discerned"* (I Cor. 2:14).

The idea is, that it is the Holy Spirit Alone Who abides within us, Who helps us understand the Word of God.

In living for God these many years, and in studying the Word all of these years, and especially since writing these Commentaries, more and more, I have come to understand how alive, how absolutely important is each single word of the Bible. In fact, the Scripture plainly tells us that God *"hast magnified Thy Word above all Thy Name"* (Ps. 138:2).

God's Word is what He is, while His Name is what He does. One can only do what one is, which means what one is of course, is greater than what one does.

POWERFUL

The word *"powerful"* in the Greek is *"energes,"* from which we get our word *"energy,"* and which means *"active, energizing."*

This speaks of power in the spirit world, and goes in both directions. By that I mean the following:

God always honors His Word, and Satan always respects God's Word. In fact, that's the reason that Christians attempting to live a victorious life outside of Faith in the Cross, meet with failure. Satan does not respect our efforts as it regards our own *"works."* He only respects the Word of God, which in effect proclaims the Sacrifice of Christ. Consequently, whenever we abide by the Word, which means we put our Faith and Trust in the Cross, to be sure Satan respects that, simply because the Holy Spirit is backing it up in its entirety.

Only the Lord knows in years past, the times I would use the Word, or the Name of Jesus, with no results, and I knew in my heart there would be no results. But I didn't know why!

In those days, I didn't understand the Word in relationship to the Cross, neither the Name of Jesus in that respect; consequently, what I was doing was not based on the proper foundation and, therefore, could not garner the help of the Holy Spirit.

Now, my use of the Word and the Name, are based strictly on the Sacrifice of Christ, and carries a new meaning altogether, and above that, it carries *"power."* The reason is obvious: the Holy Spirit guarantees it.

SHARPER

The phrase, *"And sharper than any twoedged sword,"* refers to the ability of the Word of God to *"cut."* In reference to this, the Scripture says concerning Christ:

"And He had at His right hand seven stars: and out of His mouth went a sharp twoedged sword" (Rev. 1:16).

And then the Lord said of Himself, *"These things saith He which hath the sharp sword with two edges"* (Rev. 2:12).

NOTES

The Roman sword was commonly made in the manner of two edges. The fact that it had two edges made it easier to penetrate, as well as to cut in every way. No doubt, the Holy Spirit had Paul to use this word *"two-edged"* in this respect. Nothing can stop its penetration, and only unbelief can stop its effectiveness.

The expression *"two-edged"* which literally says *"two-mouthed,"* as stated, emphasizes the twofold affect of the Word of God. To the one who believes, every Blessing awaits him; to that person, their life becomes active in producing righteous behavior. To him who refuses it, the Word is consuming with judgment. In fact, our response to the Word of God determines our eternal destiny.

There can be no indifference to the Word; by its very nature, the Word demands a choice on our part. Our choice to obey and to trust may mean that the sharp sword of the Word may sever the dearest of ties. This means that the Word with its sharpness must cut and separate.

It is designed to cut away that which is unholy, and to separate us from all that is unscriptural.

PIERCING AND DIVIDING

The phrase, *"Piercing even to the dividing asunder of soul and spirit, and of the joints and marrow,"* proclaims the extent to which this two-edged sword can cut. As we have stated, *"the dividing asunder of soul and spirit,"* doesn't mean, *"the dividing asunder of soul from spirit."* Nor is it *"the dividing asunder of joints from marrow."*

"Piercing" is the translation of the Greek *"diikneomai,"* and means, *"to go through."* The Word pierces the soul and the spirit, adequately proclaiming what man ought to be, and can be only in Christ.

As well, the phrase, *"the joints and marrow,"* is not meant merely as symbolism to give weight, but actually refers to the physical. By that we mean this:

Paul said, *"But if the Spirit of Him* (God) *that raised up Jesus from the dead dwell in you, He that raised up Christ from the dead shall also quicken your mortal bodies by His Spirit that dwelleth in you"* (Rom. 8:11).

Of course, the Spirit does all that He does do, strictly according to and by the Word of

God. He will not stray from those parameters, which once again goes back to the Cross, i.e., *"the Finished Work of Christ."*

"Mortal bodies" has to do with our physical bodies, and speaks of help, even great help.

The idea with the word *"quicken"* is that the Word of God acted upon by the Holy Spirit makes alive our physical bodies, respecting victory over sin, and even Divine Healing.

However, all of this is done, providing we do not *"live after the flesh,"* but rather *"through the Spirit"* (Rom. 8:12-13).

HEALING

The word *"dividing"* as Paul uses it here, is not that of dividing one thing from another, but of one thing in itself by the action of something separating its constituent elements from one another by piercing it. In other words, the Word of God lays bare all the recesses of the *"soul and spirit,"* and as well *"of the joints and marrow."*

So, when it comes to Divine Healing, which I definitely believe this statement includes, especially as it mentions *"the joints and marrow,"* we once again go back to the Cross.

To help define this, one might say that the great Sacrifice of Christ is the Word of God being portrayed in action, as it refers to Redemption. As well, in some way, every particle of the Word, every nuance of the Word, in some way, points to this Finished Work. I really cannot see how anyone can interpret the Bible otherwise, especially if he reads it in the light of the Cross.

As an example, Israel was raised up from the loins of Abraham and the womb of Sarah, in order to give the world the Word of God, which is the story of man's Redemption, and to bring the Messiah into the world, Who would bring about this Redemption by His Sacrificial death on the Cross. This means that the entirety of the story of Israel, with all its twists and turns, ultimately arrive at the Cross.

Concerning Healing and the Cross, the Scripture plainly tells us, *"Who His Own Self bear our sins in His Own Body on the Tree, that we, being dead to sins, should live unto Righteousness: by Whose stripes ye were healed"* (I Pet. 2:24).

NOTES

How much clearer can it be! Physical healing is part of the Redemptive Work of Christ (Isa. 53:5; Mat. 8:17).

Jesus suffered a physical beating, which in the mind of God paid for the healing of our physical bodies.

This doesn't mean, as should be obvious, that each and every Christian is guaranteed total freedom from any and all sickness. The Bible doesn't proclaim that. Christians continue to get old, and ultimately die. As well, there are times when sickness comes. But in the midst of it all, Jesus Christ is the Healer, and actually paid for this work by what He did at the Cross.

This means, that even though we do live in a physical body, with all of its attendant problems and difficulties, which will continue unto the coming Resurrection; still, we should feel free to ask the Lord for healing when it is needed, and should expect healing. As stated, a price was paid for this, and considering that, we should experience healing to a far greater degree than most of us do. Once again, it goes back to unbelief!

THE WORD OF GOD AS A DISCERNER

The phrase, *"And is a discerner of the thoughts and intents of the heart,"* refers to that which is outstandingly unique in the annals of literature or writings of any kind. Of course, it being the Word of God, is what makes this uniqueness.

"Discerner" in the Greek is *"kritikos,"* and means *"to divide or separate,"* thus *"to judge."* It carries the idea of *"sifting out and analyzing evidence."*

The manner in which this is done is by the Power of the Holy Spirit, which means that the Spirit of God is never absent from His Word.

So piercing is the Word of God that it separates and shows up the true nature that is inherent in man's earthly body, in his life, and in the condition of his spirit. Our soul life, our thoughts, and emotions, as well as the inner substance of them are penetrated, laid bare, and exposed by the Word. The Word of God is the only power that can penetrate so deeply and expose so completely the inward nature of man. The Word recognizes and exposes the vanity and sinfulness of our earthly thoughts, strivings, and achievements. All that opposes the Spirit is seen by the Word, and all that opposes the Word, is condemned by the Spirit.

THE WORD AND THE SINNER

Time and time again, the sinner has said, *"The Preacher was preaching right at me!"*

No, he really wasn't. It was the Word of God which he was preaching, which did exactly as Paul said here it would do. It was literally discerning the thoughts and intents of the heart, which made it seem like the Preacher knew the individual, and was telling his heart and life.

I've had countless people to mention such to me, and one comes to mind presently. He is a dear friend, and is now a Preacher of the Gospel, a man who loves God, incidentally, with all his heart.

When the Lord saved him, he was an alcoholic.

He related to me how that he would listen to the Telecast, and that I would describe him so intently, along with the terrible bondage of alcohol, that he would sit amazed, wondering who had told me all about him. Well of course, at that time I didn't even know the man, but to be sure, the Holy Spirit did.

What was happening was exactly what Paul has outlined here. The Spirit of God so to speak, was reading his mail.

That's at least one of the reasons that the Apostle said to Timothy, and all other Preachers for that matter:

"I charge thee therefore before God, and the Lord Jesus Christ, Who shall judge the quick and the dead at His appearing and His Kingdom;

"Preach the word . . ." (II Tim. 4:1-2).

Preaching philosophy, or the latest book report, or any other such foolishness, will have little effect on anyone. Preaching the Word will save the souls of men.

When the Word is preached under the Anointing of the Holy Spirit the sinner sees himself as lost, ruined, and Hell-bound; he recognizes his need of a Saviour. God's Word exposes his thoughts and brings the sinner to the foot of the Cross, for that's what the Word is designed to do!

As well, the Word serves as a mirror for the Child of God, showing him what he is,

and what he ought to be, and what he can be in Christ. That's the reason that habitual Bible reading and study must be a part of our everyday living and life. It is a shame when many Christians, if not most, have not even read the Bible through once. Every single Book in the Word of God was designed by the Holy Spirit. In other words, not to know and understand the Message of each and every Book and Epistle, is to miss out on at least a part of what the Holy Spirit has for us. Nothing could be more hurtful for the Christian.

The Word of God passes judgment on men's feelings and on their thoughts. Nothing evades the scope of this Word. What man holds as most secret he finds subject to its scrutiny and judgment. And because it is the Word of God, it never makes a mistake. In other words, it judges correctly.

(13) "NEITHER IS THERE ANY CREATURE THAT IS NOT MANIFEST IN HIS SIGHT: BUT ALL THINGS ARE NAKED AND OPENED UNTO THE EYES OF HIM WITH WHOM WE HAVE TO DO."

The exposition is:

1. God is the Creator of all; therefore, He knows and understands all creatures, as would be obvious.

2. Due to God being the Creator, He knows every nuance of all creatures, even to the extent of laying bare, to uncover, to expose.

The word *"opened"* carries the idea of *"seizing and twisting the neck or throat."* It means, *"to bend back the neck of the victim to be slain, to lay bare or expose by bending back."* It carries the idea of drawing back and exposing the neck of the sacrificial victim of the Altar. Consequently, the metaphor of the victim's throat bared to the sacrificial knife is a vivid illustration of the total exposure of the human heart to the eye of God Whose inspired Word is as keen as a two-edged sword (Wuest).

3. The words *"with Whom we have to do,"* means that ultimately, every single human being will give account.

MANIFEST IN HIS SIGHT

The phrase, *"Neither is there any creature that is not manifest in His sight,"* refers to God as the Creator of all things, whether animate (relating to human and animal life as opposed to plant life) or inanimate (plant life, lacking consciousness or power of motion). Of course, the Lord is the Creator of all material substance, and of every nature, as well. As stated, He Alone is the Creator of all things.

Consequently, and as would be obvious, He knows all things about all things which He has created. Therefore, it is impossible to hide anything from God and in any capacity. Nothing in all creation remains invisible to God. Consequently it was foolish for Adam and Eve to attempt to hide themselves from the Presence of the Lord, and of course, we're speaking of their actions after the Fall (Gen. 3:8).

When the Lord called to Adam, saying, *"Where art thou?"* it was not meaning that He didn't know where Adam was, but the question was rather posed to the fallen man, that he might take serious stock of his situation. To be sure, God is still saying the same to all of mankind, *"Where art thou?"* To be sure, He knows, but the problem is, we do not all the time know!

"His sight" covers the whole of creation, and in every capacity, referring to the Truth of the old song, *"There's an all-seeing eye watching you!"*

NAKED AND OPENED

The phrase, *"But all things are naked and opened unto the eyes of Him,"* refers to a degree of exposure which we as human beings, cannot even begin to comprehend. No thought of unbelief or disobedience escapes His eye: the first beginnings of apostasy are manifest before Him.

The Holy Spirit through Paul used Psalm 95 to illustrate that which He desired to say. Consequently, the Christian Jews of Paul's time, were warned that this Psalm is the Word of God — a death-dealing sword from whose double edge nothing escapes. And what is true of Psalm 95 is true of the entirety of the Bible. It is living and effective. It is living, for it is the Word of the Living God; and effective, for when He said, *"they shall not enter,"* exactly what He said came to pass. Their carcasses fell in the wilderness.

Consequently, that Word is a perfect instrument for exposing and judging the most secret emotions of the heart and nature.

To the Believer this is exceedingly precious for he rejoices in that which infallibly exposes and judges the deepest emotions of his being.

And we might quickly add, this two-edged and piercing sword of the Word of God, is held by the hand that was pierced at Calvary.

The Catholic Church says that the Word of God is what the Church says it is, making themselves superior to the Word. However, I remind all and sundry, that the Word of God is what Christ says it is, for He is the Living Word (Jn. 1:1).

THE WHOLE OF CREATION WILL ANSWER TO GOD

The phrase, *"With Whom we have to do,"* in the Greek Text, carries the idea of *"with Whom is our reckoning,"* or *"to Whom we must give account."* The idea is that of reckoning. This means that there is a day of reckoning coming, when all will stand before God to give account (Wuest).

Regarding this coming time, the Holy Spirit uses the two words *"naked"* and *"opened."*

"Naked" refers to being fully exposed, and can refer to judgment.

The idea is, all who ignore the Word of God and its binding precepts, are naked to the Judgment of God, which judgment will one day be brought to bear.

When the Scripture says of Adam and Eve after the Fall, *"And they knew that they were naked,"* it refers to far more than a lack of covering regarding clothing. It actually meant that they were naked or exposed to the Judgment of God (Gen. 3:7).

It's a fearful thing to realize that almost all the world, and for all time, lays naked and exposed to Judgment! The only way this *"nakedness"* can be covered is by the Precious Blood of Christ. This means that God has poured out His Judgment upon Christ in our stead, which means He took the blow that we should have taken. Isaiah said:

"Surely He hath borne our griefs, and carried our sorrows: yet we did esteem Him stricken, smitten of God, and afflicted" (Isa. 53:4).

The idea is this: We can either accept the Sacrifice of Christ, which means that He took the judgment on our behalf, or else we will take the judgment ourselves. And to be sure, as the former was not a pretty picture, neither will be the latter. Once again, we come back to the Cross.

This means that the entirety of mankind and for all time, will either face Jesus as the Saviour or the Judge. There is no alternative! That's why the Cross is the centrality of the Gospel, and why it stands at the very center of human history.

In fact, it is stated that Jerusalem is at the exact center of the earth. If in fact that is correct, this means that the Cross stood as well, at the exact center of this earth, because Jesus was crucified in Jerusalem. This means, that there is equal access to all!

The word *"opened"* is from the Greek word *"trachelizo,"* and actually means *"neck or throat."* The verb means, *"to seize and twist the neck or throat,"* bending it back, therefore, exposing the face to the spectators. As well, it exposed the victim's throat to the sacrificial knife, and carries the idea not only of exposure but also of judgment.

Once again we go back to Christ. Either we will accept the bloodletting of the Son of God, which was shed on our behalf, or we will be opened up in judgment by the knife of God's Word.

To be frank, the manner in which the Holy Spirit expresses the Word of God through Paul, provides a tremendous Blessing for those who accept Christ, but at the same time, a fearful prospect for those who reject Christ.

When the Holy Spirit used the words *"naked"* and *"opened,"* it carries the meaning of far more than mere exposure. The two words go all the way to Christ and the Cross. To accept Him, is to accept life. To reject Him, is to make oneself *"naked"* and thereby *"opened"* to the Judgment of God.

(14) "SEEING THEN THAT WE HAVE A GREAT HIGH PRIEST, THAT IS PASSED INTO THE HEAVENS, JESUS THE SON OF GOD, LET US HOLD FAST OUR PROFESSION."

The structure is:

1. Having shown that Jesus is superior to the Prophets, the Angels, Moses, and Joshua, Paul now proceeds to prove on the basis of Old Testament Scripture, that He is better than Aaron (Wuest).

2. All other High Priests in the Jewish economy were mere humans, as are obvious, therefore, flawed! This High Priest, the Lord Jesus Christ, being both God and man, is unflawed, therefore, *"great."*

3. The phrase, *"That* (Who) *is passed into the Heavens,"* refers to the fact that His earthly mission was finished and completed, in that He atoned for all sin at the Cross. As well, His expiatory and vicarious work was accepted by God in the Heavens, which means it is irrefutable. Him being in the Heavens, means that He has opened the door to Heaven, by what He accomplished as our Great High Priest. As the Jewish High Priests offered up the blood of a slain animal on the Mercy Seat on the Great Day of Atonement, likewise, Jesus as our Great High Priest offered up Blood on the Mercy Seat of Heaven, but the difference being, this was His Blood, which was sufficient to atone for all sin, whereas the blood of bulls and goats could never do that.

4. Jesus as the Son of God is vastly superior to all earthly Priests, who in effect, were mere symbols of Him. By Paul using the Name *"Jesus,"* which actually means Saviour, refers to the fact, that what Jesus did effects Salvation for all who will believe. Inasmuch as He was and is the Son of God, this means that His work was perfect, whereas the work of all other High Priests was of necessity, flawed.

5. We must hold fast our *"profession"* or *"confession"* of Christ as the One to Whom all the Prophets pointed. As well, every iota of the Tabernacle and the Temple, with all its sacred furniture, as well as the Priests and Sacrifices, all and without exception, pointed to Him. As such, we must without fail, confess Him, and not be misled into confessing other things, which merely pointed to Him.

Likewise, we must be careful presently, that we understand that Jesus is all in all, meaning that our Salvation totally and completely comes by and through Him and what He did at the Cross on our behalf, meaning, that we must not confess other things such as the Church, the Ordinances, etc.

THE GREAT HIGH PRIEST

The phrase, *"Seeing then that we have a Great High Priest,"* speaks of a present tense.

All the other High Priests of Jewish history are dead and gone, but Christ lives, and will ever live. In fact, they were but symbols pointing to Him Who was ultimately to come, and thank God, did come!

The Incarnation, the temptation, the death, and the High Priestly Ministry of Jesus have always stood out as seriously unique.

Why was the Incarnation necessary? Why was it necessary that Jesus be tempted? Why must He now stand as an Advocate or Intercessor in behalf of the Child of God? Is it right for the innocent to suffer for the guilty? Is suffering inconsistent with the merciful nature of God?

Paul does not attempt to prove the humanity of Christ; he accepts it as a fact, as it was! As well, there is no attempt made to justify the suffering of Christ by philosophical argument. Rather, Paul sets out to demonstrate Christ's identification with man, for if Jesus were to serve as a Substitute for all of mankind, He must not only come in the flesh, but He also must suffer and be tempted as man. By this suffering, Christ Jesus would fully take our place, thereby, becoming the Perfect Mediator and High Priest.

Before the destruction of Jerusalem in A.D. 70, the Ministry of the Priests who officiated in the Temple was fundamental and basic to Judaism. Each evening and morning, Sacrifices were made on the Temple Altar, while prayers were made to God on behalf of the sins of the people.

The concept of the necessity of such a Priestly Ministry for the people had existed in Israel from earliest times. The Old Testament recorded the Sacrifices made by Abel, Noah, and the Patriarchs, Abraham, Isaac, and Jacob, who often built Altars to God. It was God Who gave directions from the beginning of the way to approach Him; it was God Who gave instruction for the building of the Tabernacle and later the Temple.

The Priesthood, Sacrifices, and Altars had been a part of Israel's heritage.

Because Israel understood the necessity of proper representation of man before God, and that is the key, surely, these Hebrew Christians would understand the high and holy position given to Jesus as the *"Great High Priest."* Consequently, Paul boldly proclaims

Jesus to be the High Priest, and not only that, *"The Great High Priest."*

This Priest is no ordinary man, but is Jesus the Son of God.

If the Son were to properly represent man before God, then it was necessary that Christ be man. Here Paul touches on the need of the Incarnation and the Virgin Birth. This One Who stands between God and man is Himself both human and Divine, conceived of the Holy Spirit, yet is the seed of a woman.

By woman, Satan plunged the human race into spiritual oblivion, and by woman, God will elevate the human race back to what He originally intended. Oh, how I can sense the presence of God even as I dictate these notes.

What love, that God would become man, would step down from His royal throne of creation, walk down the starry steps from Heaven, and be born of woman in a stable, and be raised in the home of a carpenter, actually functioning Himself as a carpenter. There was no pretense here, no façade, no show, but rather the very epitome of humility. The Son of God, the Crowned Prince of Glory, the Creator of the ages, reduced to a creature! It is beyond our comprehension, but that's what happened, and that's why we have so great a Salvation.

THE ROLE OF THE HIGH PRIEST

A Priest is appointed to act on behalf of men in relation to God. At least that was the Old Testament role, and was in fact, the only time that the role of the Priest was legitimate, all of that having been fulfilled now by Christ.

Under that old economy, the purpose of the Priest was to bring men to God and thereby bring them to perfection or completion, which Paul amply brings out in this Epistle to the Hebrews (2:10; 9:9; 10:1, 14; 11:40; 12:23).

The Priest does not take this prerogative upon himself; he must have Divine appointment (Heb. 5:4). The way he brings men to God is by offering Sacrifices for sins (Heb. 5:1; 8:3; 9:7, 13). The Priest, too, is a man and, therefore, a sinner; consequently, he must offer up Sacrifices for himself as well (Heb. 5:2-3; 7:27; 9:7). This turns out to be the basic limitation of the Old Testament system.

An imperfect Priest can only offer imperfect Sacrifices (Heb. 9:11-14; 10:1-4). Therefore, both the Covenant on which his Priesthood is based (Heb. 8:6) and the Holy Place in which it is performed (Heb. 9:11) are imperfect. Finally, the net result is imperfect as would be obvious. Consequently, the old system *"can never . . . make perfect those who draw near"* (Heb. 10:1).

Thus Priests, because of their sinfulness, are subject to death; they come and go (Heb. 7:23). Their Sacrifices are repeated daily and annually; but man is not perfected by these Sacrifices, because as stated, they are imperfect. In other words, all of the Old Testament system was an imperfect system, in which it only could be (Heb. 9:9-10). Therefore, the old is only a type (a shadow) of the real Who was to come (Heb. 9:23-24; 10:1).

In this frame of reference Paul views the genuine, but sinless, humanity of Christ in light of His Exaltation, and in an argument at once deeply perceptive and richly varied sees Him as both the ultimate Priest and the end of the Priestly system.

THE ULTIMATE PRIEST

Christ is the ultimate Priest because by His death He ratified a new Covenant (Heb. 9:15-22), toward which the Old Testament itself had looked (Heb. 8:8-13).

Moreover, God had promised that the Messianic King would also be *"a Priest forever, after the order of Melchizedek"* (Ps. 110:4). Such a promise indicates the imperfection of the old Aaronic order (Heb. 7:11-14). It is Jesus Who perfectly *"fulfills"* this Promise.

Melchizedek appeared and disappeared in the Old Testament without *"beginning of days nor end of life,"* simply meaning that it wasn't recorded, thus prefiguring the eternal Son of God (Heb. 7:3). Melchizedek's *"order"* is also superior to Aaron's because according to the Jewish theory of ancestry, Levi was in Abraham's loins when Abraham paid tithes to Melchizedek — and the lesser always pays tithes to the greater (Heb. 7:4-10).

Furthermore, Jesus is a Priest *"forever"* in contrast to the Aaronic Priests, who *"were prevented by death from continuing in office"* (Heb. 7:23). This is Paul's main interest

in Jesus' humanity. Other Priests could not continue because of sin; but Jesus, though *"made like His Brethren in every respect"* (Heb. 2:17), was sinless; therefore, He is a Perfect and eternal High Priest (Heb. 4:15; 5:7-10; 7:23-28; 9:14). This genuine humanity also makes Him a Perfect Priest in that He can fully *"sympathize with our weaknesses"* (Heb. 2:14-18; 4:15).

Jesus is the ultimate Priest also because He offers the Perfect Sacrifice — Himself. The clearest evidence that the blood of goats and calves was inadequate was that such offerings were continually repeated (Heb. 10:1-4). By offering Himself, Jesus offered a Perfect Sacrifice *"once for all,"* one that need not be repeated (Heb. 9:23-28). Furthermore, He offered it in the eternal Holy Place, having entered *"into Heaven itself, now to appear in the Presence of God on our behalf"* (Heb. 9:24).

The end result, therefore, of Jesus' Priestly Ministry is death to the old system, because He now indeed *"brings men to God."* Not only are sins done away, but an *"eternal Redemption"* is also secured whereby one has continual and confident access to God (Heb. 4:16; 6:19-20; 7:25; 10:19-22).

PASSED INTO THE HEAVENS

The phrase, *"That is passed into the Heavens,"* has to do with a legal process.

In Israel, the Atonement for sin was not complete at the Brazen Altar, and of course, we're speaking of the offering up of the Sacrifice. Not until the High Priest had carried the atoning blood into the Holy of Holies, and had sprinkled it on the Mercy Seat, was the Atonement complete.

Likewise, our Lord's Atonement was not complete at the Cross. Not until He had entered Heaven as the High Priest, and actually applied His Blood onto the Mercy Seat of Heaven was the Atonement complete.

Paul said, *"Neither by the blood of goats and calves, but by His Own Blood He entered in once into the Holy Place, having obtained eternal Redemption for us"* (Heb. 9:12).

The Apostle then said, *"For Christ is not entered into the holy places made with hands (the Holy of Holies in the Tabernacle or Temple on Earth), which are the figures* (types) *of the true* (the true Mercy Seat in Heaven)*; but into Heaven itself* (where He applied His Own Blood to the Mercy Seat), *now to appear in the Presence of God for us"* (Heb. 9:24).

Concerning this, Paul continued to write and say, *"Nor yet that He should offer Himself often, as the High Priest entereth into the Holy Place every year* (the Great Day of Atonement) *with blood of others* (bulls and goats)*;*

"For then must He often have suffered since the foundation of the world (meaning that He did not have to offer up His Blood many times)*: but now once* (after the Crucifixion) *in the end of the world* (the end of the old Law) *hath He appeared to put away sin by the Sacrifice of Himself"* (Heb. 9:25-26).

Christ, as the Glorified High Priest, presented Himself at the Mercy Seat in Glory. There is some discussion as to whether He actually presented His Blood on the Mercy Seat, or rather presented Himself. We do know that His Glorified Body contained no blood, but flesh and bones only. It could be that His presenting Himself in His bloodless body, which blood had been shed at Calvary, the evidence that sin had been paid for, is the meaning of His appearance there.

JESUS THE SON OF GOD

The phrase, *"Jesus the Son of God,"* presents in the manner the Name is used, that not only is the Saviour the High Priest, but He is as well the Son of God, or as one might say, *"God the Son, Jesus of Nazareth, the One Who was rejected and crucified by the nation of Israel, its Messiah."*

Paul here brings to bear upon the heart and conscience of his Jewish Readers, the acid test of their Faith.

When the phraseology *"the Son of God"* is used, the question arises as to how that could be, except there be more than one Person in the Godhead; and that Person become incarnate in human flesh as Jesus of Nazareth, Deity and humanity united in one Person, the Jewish Messiah. The Jewish mind had to come to terms with this, which in fact, was ever before the nation of Israel during the three and a half years of Jesus' public Ministry.

It is the same thing with which our Lord confronted the Pharisees when they asserted

that the Messiah would be the Son of David. He asked, *"How then doth David in spirit call Him Lord?"* (Mat. 22:43). That which was involved in our Lord's question was the Incarnation of the Jewish Jehovah in the Person of the Messiah. This would mean that Jesus was and is the God of the Old Testament; consequently, Jesus took them much further than they had originally believed. The Messiah they thought, would be a very charismatic man, but they never reckoned Him as God; however, their erroneous thinking was of their own making, because the Scriptures were abundantly clear that in fact, He would be God (Gen. 3:15; 17:6-8; 22:13-18; 49:10; Deut. 18:15-19; II Sam. Chpt. 7; Isa. 7:14; Chpt. 53).

Whatever it is we think of the Gospel as Christians, that which we think of Christ is, as should be obvious, of utmost importance. Jesus Christ is God! As God He became man, in order to redeem man, which He would do, by going to the Cross. In fact, He will wear the physical body of humanity forever and forever, which within itself, will ever be the greatest reminder of the price that He paid for our Redemption, especially considering the wounds which will also remain in His glorified, physical body. In other words, His Very Person, will forever and forever speak of the price of our Redemption, which was the Cross.

HIGH PRIESTLY WORK

Paul is just now beginning to enlarge upon the position of Christ as High Priest; in the next few Chapters he will have much to say concerning this Ministry. In fact, to enter in upon this Ministry — the Ministry of the High Priest — was the purpose of Christ's Ascension. He now sits at the right hand of God; from that high and holy position He invites us to Rest with Him.

Actually, in order for man to be saved, Jesus not only had to die and rise again, but He also had to ascend to the very Presence of God, where His Personal Presence, as stated, guaranteed the applied blood to the Mercy Seat.

In the light of His position, how could Jewish Believers take offense at the suffering of the Son of God? How could they forsake the

Son as High Priest Who had offered Himself as a meritorious Sacrifice for sins? How could they find it possible to return to Judaism with its animal sacrifices?

The Son, as High Priest, not only offered Himself for our sins, but He in His High Priestly role, now sits at the right hand of God, making intercession on our behalf (Heb. 7:25).

This means that our High Priest has ascended into the Heavens, into the actual Holy of Holies, the very Presence of God Himself. Consequently, and as should be overly obvious, He is vastly superior to the Prophets, to Angels, to Moses and Joshua, and as well, the Old Testament Priests.

There is a rising scale of importance in this Message. The Prophets gave Israel the Word, but here was the Logos, the Word, before them — in other words, the Living Word!

It is true that when the Lord Jesus Christ arose from the dead and ascended into the Presence of God, He took the Old Testament Saints with Him, out of Paradise to Heaven with Him. In fact, they are there now in this place of Rest, awaiting the Rapture of the Church, i.e., *"the Resurrection."*

No Priest who had ever lived had been able to lead the people into the actual Presence of God. Only Jesus the Son of God could provide the deliverance for the Old Testament Saints that years of sacrificing had foreshadowed, and only He could pass through the Heavens into the very Presence of God, and thereby, make intercession on behalf of the Saints still alive on Earth. Truly, He is the Great High Priest, and in fact, as no mere mortal has ever been!

THE ATONEMENT

The Atonement of the Old Covenant was not complete until the Priest had presented the Blood in the Holy of Holies and sprinkled it on the Mercy Seat. Likewise, our Lord's Atonement was not complete by the Cross alone; it was completed when He entered Heaven and sat down in the Presence of God as man's High Priest, even as Paul began this Epistle by relating (Heb. 1:3).

He, as the Glorified High Priest in His body of flesh and bones, presented Himself at the Mercy Seat. In fact, as stated, it was a

bloodless body, for He had spilled His Blood on the Cross for mankind.

Jesus could do all of this, simply because He atoned for all sin, past, present, and future. In fact, had there been one single sin left unatoned, due to the fact that the wages of sin is death, He could not have risen from the dead. But the very fact of Him rising from the dead states that all sin was atoned, and in every capacity; consequently, He could now present Himself in the Presence of the Father, with His very presence serving as the applied blood, and in a manner in which the animal sacrifices could never accomplish. For our Redemption to be complete, He must stand before Almighty God at the Heavenly Mercy Seat, which He did.

A TRIUMPHANT PROCESSION

In fact, it was a triumphant procession that entered into the Presence of God at Christ's Ascension. We visualize in our hearts all Heaven arising, all the Angels standing in silence, as Jesus Christ, God's Son, again enters Heaven, walks to His Father, and presents Himself in a body as the eternal Sacrifice for man's sin. It is there that God accepted the work of Calvary, and our Salvation became full and complete.

Like a conquering general's marching and leading of a procession of victory, so our Lord triumphed over the enemies of Righteousness and entered the Presence of God on our behalf.

In fact, Psalm 24 written by David, expresses this great moment. The sweet singer of Israel said:

"Lift up your heads, O ye gates; and be ye lift up, ye everlasting doors; and the King of Glory shall come in.

"Who is this King of Glory? The Lord strong and mighty, the Lord mighty in battle.

"Lift up your heads, O ye gates; even lift them up, ye everlasting doors; and the King of Glory shall come in.

"Who is this King of Glory? The Lord of Hosts, He is the King of Glory" (Ps. 24:7-10).

A FINISHED WORK

That Jesus has passed through the Heavens means that all earthly Priesthood, ceremony, and Temple are now abandoned by

God during this dispensation. In fact, all of that was merely a shadow in any case, all pointing to Him. Now that He has come, these sacrifices and rituals of the Old Testament need not be repeated, for Christ's one death was sufficient.

Actually, each time we partake of the Lord's Supper we speak of His death and bear witness of the hope we have in Him.

Because of Christ's Ascension, the worshiper is brought nigh to God. The Believer is now privileged to come before a High Priest Who understands and sympathizes. The Believer has the same rights and privileges that belong to the Son; we are heirs and joint-heirs with Him. We may enter His Presence at any time, and to be sure, the Holy Spirit guarantees access, that is if we come by virtue of Who He is (our Saviour), and what He has done on our behalf (paid the price at the Cross). And to be sure, Christ's Priestly Ministry gives us that access, for the role of Priest is on behalf of the Believer. Christ Jesus does not pray for sinners; He prays for the Believer.

MEDIATOR, ADVOCATE, AND PRIEST

It becomes important to understand this Ministry and what it means. It is important to distinguish between Mediator, Advocate, and Priest.

A Mediator reconciles God to man and man to God, which was the role of Christ in His Incarnation. In other words, God would have to become man, in order to properly serve as a Mediator.

An Advocate is something like a Lawyer. Christ serves in this position, according to what He did at the Cross on our behalf. *"Advocate"* is a legal term, and as well, the Cross was a legal work. Consequently, as our Advocate, He claims and demands the merits of His Finished Work, all on our behalf, at least for those who will believe.

As High Priest, He intercedes for us, and does so constantly, and in fact will continue to do so, until we stand in His Presence.

In fact, His intercession on our behalf has to do with sin. He actually prays for us, and to be sure, His prayers are always answered.

A beautiful description of His High Priestly work which is exampled even before the Cross concerns Simon Peter.

NOTES

"And the Lord said, Simon, Simon, behold, Satan hath desired to have you, that he may sift you as wheat:

"But I have prayed for thee, that thy Faith fail not: and when thou art converted (see your wrong direction), *strengthen thy Brethren"* (Lk. 22:31-32).

The Jewish High Priest went into the Holy of Holies before God and went in alone, only once a year, on the Great Day of Atonement. When He had completed his Priestly duties and the Atonement was accomplished, the Priest came out to bless the people.

Christ bids us come with Him even into the Holy of Holies, and in fact, to do so boldly, which Verse 16 of this Chapter will proclaim.

As well, the expression, *"Jesus, the Son of God,"* is an explanation denoting the power, glory, and dignity of our Great High Priest. He is not of the house of Aaron; He is the Son of God; as Great High Priest, He is able to do more than any earthly Priest; He is able to bring His followers into immediate fellowship with God, for Christ is seated by the very Throne of God, and there He occupies a place of supreme power and greatness.

"Jesus" is His human name, indicating His full identity with man. *"Son of God"* indicates the Divine and points out His qualifications to be the Mediator between God and man. His human nature gives the assurance of sympathy; His Divine Nature gives the confidence of strength. His Divine Nature did not disqualify Him from sharing in our needs and becoming sympathetic with our weaknesses. As a man, He endured great trials and overcame them. He remained steadfast to the end and has become an example worthy of our consideration, that we might remain true to His Word.

PRIESTHOOD

There were those of the Jewish community of Paul's day, who claimed that Christianity had no Priesthood. Well actually it does, but not in the manner of old.

Paul not only claims that such a High Priest exists, but that He also exerts His great power and authority on behalf of God's people.

In Judaism the office of the High Priest was the highest religious office. Paul seeks to show that Christianity, too, has a High

Priest, but a Priest Who is superior in every way to the Priests of Judaism. It is made clear that the High Priest of Judaism was a type of the Great High Priest, Jesus Christ (Fjordbak).

HOLD FAST OUR PROFESSION

The phrase, *"Let us hold fast our profession,"* refers to the fact, which is actually the very tenor of this Epistle, that the opposite can be the case, that is if we take the things of God lightly.

In Hebrews 3:6, Paul basically said the same thing with the words, *"But Christ as a Son over His Own house; Whose house are we, if we hold fast the confidence and the rejoicing of the hope firm unto the end."*

The idea is, the Holy Spirit was not only warning the Jewish Christians of old, but is warning us as well, to take heed that we not fail God as many in Israel did and were cut off. The very words *"hold fast"* imply the fact that Satan will do everything within his power, to loosen our grip, so to speak. This is in fact, as stated, the drift and scope of the entirety of this Epistle — to show Christians that they should hold fast their profession, and not apostatize. Considering that we have a Great High Priest Who is interceding on our behalf, there is no excuse for us to fail, must less to fall.

HOW DO WE HOLD FAST?

We could say many things in respect to that, but to be brief, and to go to the very heart of the matter, if the Believer will continue to look to the Cross, continue to depend on what the Cross provides, continue to place his Faith in that Finished Work, Satan will not be able to move you. That's why Paul said:

"But God forbid that I should glory, save in the Cross of our Lord Jesus Christ, by Whom the world is crucified unto me, and I unto the world" (Gal. 6:14).

That's the reason he also said:

"For the preaching of the Cross is to them that perish foolishness; but unto us which are saved it is the Power of God" (I Cor. 1:18).

The Cross tells us that man could not accomplish Redemption by his own efforts, in fact, not in any capacity. It also tells us just how bad man's situation actually was. The

NOTES

Believer constantly looking to the Cross, portrays the fact that He knows and recognizes these things which we have just said. In other words, he must look exclusively to Christ and what Christ did for us on the Cross in order to be saved, and in order to walk victoriously. Any other direction, breeds pride, self-will, and self-righteousness, in fact, the very thing that promotes sin and failure.

The Christian makes a lethal mistake, if he thinks that he can carry out anything spiritual within his life, by his own efforts, Faith, or abilities. The Reader must understand, that there is absolutely nothing we can do within our hearts and lives as it pertains to God, by our own machinations. No matter how religious our efforts might be, no matter how spiritual we may think they are, we must ever understand, that every single thing which we have from God, comes to us totally and completely through the great Sacrifice of Christ, and by that way alone. If we fail to understand this, then we fail to understand Christianity.

In fact, this is the great problem of man. He thinks he doesn't need the Sacrifice of Christ, hence the attitude and actions of Cain of old (Gen. Chpt. 4). And then if he finally recognizes his need for the Sacrifice of Christ as a sinner, then too often, after getting saved, he launches out on a self-willed program of self-sanctification, which never brings about Sanctification, but only self-righteousness.

It is the Sacrifice of Christ which affords all, and that we must never forget. Understanding that, our Faith must always Rest in that Finished Work. The Cross as our object of Faith, and as our constant object of Faith, and in fact, as our never-ending object of Faith, must ever be the realization of our Christian experience. Only then can we *"hold fast our profession."* In fact, in this manner, the Holy Spirit does all of this for us, which He in fact, Alone can do (Rom. 8:1-2, 11).

THE DUAL NATURE — THE FLESH AND THE SPIRIT

Every Believer has a dual nature, which Paul constantly refers to as the flesh and the spirit. To deny that, is to deny the obvious! In fact, the greater bulk of Paul's teaching is in this capacity. The Holy Spirit through him, constantly tells us how to walk in victory, overcoming the flesh, which means that the Divine Nature within us, be prominent at all times.

Many Bible Teachers deny the fact of the dual nature, or that the Believer continues to have a sin nature, even after conversion. But the Scriptures and the facts proclaim the opposite.

Whenever the believing sinner comes to Christ, he is crucified with Christ, buried with Christ, and in fact, resurrected with Christ (Rom. 6:3-5).

The Scripture plainly tells us that *"our old man* (sinful nature) *is crucified with Him, that the body of sin might be destroyed, that henceforth we should not serve sin"* (Rom. 6:6).

This actually speaks of the domination of the sin nature, which of course characterizes all who are unsaved, as would be obvious.

However, we must understand what Paul is actually saying in Romans 6:6. When he says, *"our old man is crucified with Him,"* he is speaking of domination of us by the sin nature. This means that it no longer holds supremacy within our hearts and lives.

What we must understand is, that this Verse doesn't say that the sin nature is destroyed or that it is dead. In fact it says otherwise. What it does say is this:

"Likewise reckon ye also yourselves to be dead indeed unto sin," or as the Greek says, *"unto the sin,"* or *"the sin nature."* Notice, the sin nature is not dead, but we are to be dead to it (Rom. 6:11).

Some Teachers attempt to make the sin nature dead, which puts us into the Resurrection with Glorified Bodies, which is obvious that we have not yet obtained. No, the sin nature is not dead; it still resides in us, but we are to be dead to it.

Claiming that the sin nature is dead and gone as it regards the Believer, is to ignore the obvious teaching of the Word of God. Let me give another example:

Paul said, *"Let not sin* (the Greek says, the sin, or the sin nature) *therefore reign in your mortal body, that ye should obey it in the lusts thereof"* (Rom. 6:12).

If there was no such thing as a sin nature present, why is the Holy Spirit through the Apostle telling us that we are not to allow it

to rule and reign in our lives, and that we must not obey it?

No, the sin nature is definitely present within us, but it is not to rule and reign in our mortal bodies, and we are not to obey it.

Again I emphasize, if such does not exist, then what Paul says make absolutely no sense.

Yes, every Believer has a dual nature within him. He has a sin nature, which in fact is to be dormant, and will be dormant, if He continues to look to the Cross, while at the same time, He has the Divine Nature, which is provided by the Holy Spirit.

LOOKING TO THE CROSS

As we stated, Paul referred to this as the warfare between the flesh and the spirit (Rom. Chpt. 8).

When the Apostle speaks of the *"flesh,"* he's not speaking of the meat on our arms or legs, etc., but rather our self-effort, self-ability, etc. He is speaking of trying to live for God, or to be holy or righteous, or to be what God wants us to be, by our own efforts outside of the help of the Holy Spirit. When we function in this capacity, which refers to *"walking after the flesh,"* (Rom. 8:1), spiritual failure is the inevitable result. When this happens, the sin nature springs to life, and we will find ourselves with the sin nature ruling and reigning, despite all of our efforts otherwise.

That's the reason that many Christians are greatly confused, considering they are trying so hard not to fail, but failing just the same. What they don't understand is, they are attempting to overcome after the *"flesh,"* i.e., *"self-efforts,"* which is impossible to do, with failure being the obvious result, and in fact, the situation getting worse and worse. As stated, in this state, the sin nature begins to rule and reign, with the Christian then being placed in bondage to some vice, or sin of pride, etc. The sin nature, which many Preachers claim doesn't exist, is now ruling and reigning, and in fact, due to most Christians not understanding the victory of the Cross, this is where most of the modern Church actually is.

Most Christians function in this manner, simply because they don't know, as stated, the Truth of the Cross, and not knowing, they resort to the only thing they do know, which is to try to bring about victory by their own religious efforts, etc. Such a direction is impossible!

The Believer in order to have perpetual victory within his heart and life, must *"walk after the Spirit"* (Rom. 8:1). But how to do that? many might ask.

The Spirit of God always functions within the capacity of the Finished Work of Christ. In other words, His license to do what He does, so to speak, is the Sacrifice of Christ. Consequently, if the Believer desires to walk after the Spirit, then the Spirit will always lead the Believer to the Cross (Rom. 8:2). This means that the Believer, should look to the Cross for everything he receives, understanding that all victory was won there. When Faith is placed in the Cross, and is left in the Cross, that is *"walking after the Spirit,"* and then the Holy Spirit will do great and mighty things within the Believer's life. This is the manner in which the sin nature is dominated and remains dominated, which means that the Divine Nature functions properly, with us growing in Grace and the knowledge of the Lord, even on a daily basis.

In fact, this is why Jesus said that we must *"deny ourselves, and take up the Cross daily in our following Him"* (Lk. 9:23).

ERRONEOUS DOCTRINES

Many of those who claim there is no such thing as a sin nature in the hearts and lives of Believers, which actually refers to a tendency to do wrong, claim that problems come about in the lives of Christians, simply because of wrong thinking, or a bad confession, as some put it.

First of all, if this problem of sin was only a small difficulty, which could be handled with correct thinking or a correct confession, well then it means, that sin is not so very bad, and Jesus needlessly died on the Cross.

Others claim that once they are Born-Again, that their spirit is perfect, which actually claims *"sinless perfection,"* and if there is a problem, it's only their physical body responding wrong, because their soul has not quite yet been brought into line. In other words, their spirit is perfect, and their soul is being made perfect, they claim! Therefore, sin is no problem to them. Actually, they

NOTES

claim that sin should not be mentioned, and most definitely should not be mentioned behind the pulpit or preached against, etc. They claim that to do such, only creates a *"sin consciousness,"* which causes people to sin.

Those who claim that sin is a problem only because of wrong thinking, whether they realize it or not, are merely functioning in the realm of humanistic psychology, which in effect denies the fact of sin.

Those who attempt to deny sin, claiming that it should not be mentioned, and if that course is followed there will be no problem, have succumbed to the mind science religions of the East.

If all of that is true, then the Holy Spirit spent an awful lot of time explaining the situation, telling us how to overcome sin, etc.

No, sin is a deadly monster, which could only be conquered by Christ and the Cross; consequently, it can only continue to be conquered by the Believer, by continued Faith in the Cross of Christ (Rom. 8:1-2, 11).

Of course, those who teach these false doctrines, pretty well deny the Cross of Christ altogether, or else they claim a need for the Cross as it regards the initial Salvation experience, but then abandon it for other things. Either way, as should be obvious, is the road to disaster.

The Believer must look to the Cross at all times, which is the way and manner of the Holy Spirit. And by looking to the Cross, of course I'm not speaking of some wooden beam. And neither am I speaking of putting Jesus back on the Cross. Such thinking is ridiculous!

I'm speaking of what the Cross affords, in other words, what the great Sacrifice of Christ purchased for you and me. It is the benefits of the Cross on which we rely, and must rely constantly. To fail to do this, is to deny man's need for a Sacrifice.

THE STRUGGLE BETWEEN THE FLESH AND THE SPIRIT

There are some of these false Teachers who perpetuate these doctrines, who claim they have no problem or trouble whatsoever with the world, the flesh, or the Devil.

In fact, they aren't lying, they're telling the Truth!

They don't belong to Christ; consequently, there is no struggle. To be sure, if the Holy Spirit (not another spirit — II Cor. 11:4), abides within their hearts and lives, there is definitely going to be a struggle between the flesh and the spirit, even as Paul strongly brings out in Romans, Chapter 8 and elsewhere. So, if the struggle is not there, and a constant struggle one might add, then that means the Holy Spirit isn't present.

There are quite a number of examples of this in the Old Testament, given to us in symbolic form.

When Moses smote the rock, with the account given to us in Exodus Chapter 17, and the water poured out, this foretold the Living Water, the Holy Spirit to be sent forth by the smitten Saviour. The Holy Spirit was shed forth as the fruit of Christ's Sacrifice (I Cor. 10:4; Gal. 3:13-14).

The reception of the Holy Spirit immediately causes war. The Scripture says, *"Then came Amalek and fought with Israel"* (Ex. 17:8). Up to this point God had fought for Israel. They were to stand still and see His Salvation; but the command now is to go out and fight with Amalek (Ex. 17:9).

There is an immense difference between Justification and Sanctification. The one is Christ fighting for us; the other, the Holy Spirit fighting in us. The entrance of the new nature is the beginning of warfare with the old.

Amalek pictures the old carnal nature. He was the grandson of Esau, who before and after birth tried to murder Jacob, and who preferred the pottage to the Birthright. This carnal nature wars against the Spirit, *"It is not subject to the Law of God neither indeed can be"*; and God has declared war against it forever, which war we are fighting at present regarding the struggle between the flesh and the spirit (Ex. 17:16).

God did not destroy Amalek, in other words put him out of existence, but determined to have war with him from generation to generation. He was to dwell in the land, but not to reign in it. Romans, Chapter 6 says, and as we have quoted, *"Let not sin therefore reign in your mortal bodies."* This command would be meaningless if the sin nature did not exist in the Christian. The

NOTES

sin nature dwells in a Believer, but is not to rule and reign in the Believer. In fact, it dwells and reigns in the unbeliever, as should be obvious.

In fact, it is remarkable that the first mention of the Bible should be in connection with the hostility of the natural man (Amalek) to the spiritual man (Israel) (Ex. 17:14-16).

Again I state, if the Holy Spirit truly resides within the heart and life of any Believer, there is going to be war between the flesh and the spirit. If there is no war, there is no Holy Spirit, which means there is no Salvation, despite the claims.

There will be war between the flesh and the spirit as it regards the Child of God, and the answer concerning victory, is Faith in the Cross of Christ, and not at all in ourselves.

(15) "FOR WE HAVE NOT AN HIGH PRIEST WHICH CANNOT BE TOUCHED WITH THE FEELING OF OUR INFIRMITIES; BUT WAS IN ALL POINTS TEMPTED LIKE AS WE ARE, YET WITHOUT SIN."

The structure is:

1. Even though Jesus is the Son of God, He is also human, and as such, can empathize totally with us.

2. He can empathize with us, because He has suffered our infirmities.

3. He has suffered every temptation we have experienced, but without sin; consequently, He knows what it is to be tempted.

THE FEELING OF OUR INFIRMITIES

The phrase, *"For we have not an High Priest which cannot be touched with the feeling of our infirmities,"* refers to the kind of High Priest He is.

Paul, having spoken of the exalted and victorious High Priest, and of the fact that He is Very God of Very God, now hastens to assure his Readers that, whatever they, because of these facts, have thought to the contrary, this High Priest, despite the fact of being Very God of Very God, is quite approachable and of a sympathetic nature (Wuest).

The *"feeling of our infirmities"* means "to suffer with" another person, thus to sympathize with him to the extent of entering into his experience and feeling his heartache yourself. The use of the word here means more than a knowledge of human infirmity. It points to a knowledge that has in it a feeling for the other person by reason of a common experience with that person.

The *"infirmities"* mentioned here, are not sufferings but rather weaknesses, both moral and physical, that predispose one to sin, the weaknesses which undermine our resistance to temptation and make it difficult for us to keep from sinning (Wuest).

It is difficult for us to comprehend the degree of this of which we speak as it concerns Christ. We like to think of Christ as being above the fray; however, that is not correct. He was a man, and as a man, He suffered all the temptations which are common to man. He suffered every attack by Satan which Hell could devise, and for all the obvious reasons. He has *"touched"* our infirmities, and has been *"touched"* by our infirmities. The last phrase tells us how.

TEMPTED LIKE AS WE ARE

The phrase, *"Tempted like as we are, yet without sin,"* has reference to two things:

1. The Holy Spirit through Paul made this statement in this manner, to preclude the common fancy that there was some peculiarity in Jesus which made His temptation wholly different from ours. In other words, that He was exposed only to minor temptations, so to speak.

2. He was the *"Last Adam"* and, therefore, had to suffer every single temptation Satan could throw His way, and to a far greater degree than we have ever suffered. Some claim that inasmuch as He was also God, that He could not have sinned. That is basely incorrect.

While He definitely was God, and never ceased to be God, still, in His Incarnation, He laid aside the expression of His Deity. For instance, He grew tired and He grew hungry, and God cannot do either.

The Reader must understand, that while Jesus definitely was Very God, He was also Very Man. And during His Incarnation, which lasted for about 33 and one half years, He functioned 100 percent as man, and not at all as God, even though He never ceased to be God. In other words, He definitely could have sinned!

The one difference between our temptations and those of Christ is that His were

without sin.

The words *"without sin"* mean that in our Lord's case, temptation never resulted in sin. They could mean also that temptation never sprang in our Lord's case, from any sinful desire on His part. As well, He had no sinful nature as we do (Wuest).

Some have pointed out, and I think rightly so, that the Sinless One knows the force of temptation in a way that we who sin do not. At times, we give in before the temptation has fully spent itself; only he who does not yield knows its full force. He Alone knew its full force at all times, and because He never yielded.

As well, Jesus did not face temptation only once, but every day of His life, until the moment that He died upon the Cross. He was assailed, tested, and tempted.

THE GOOD SHEPHERD

Jesus said in the Gospel of John, *"When He putteth forth His Own sheep, He goeth before them"* (Jn. 10:4).

This means that Jesus has walked the sheep's path, and they follow Him. Everything that a Christian will go through, each temptation, Christ faced to perfection.

The very body, mind, and spirit of Jesus were so pure and holy that whenever Satan or temptation assailed Christ, it found no place of sin in Him. Because of His Holiness, His temptations were far more bitter and severe than ours would ever be.

Even though every single pressure and temptation was brought to Him by the Evil One, yet there was not the slightest yielding in Jesus. In fact, and as stated, the extent and degree of His temptation were far beyond anything that man could ever encounter.

All of this means that the temptation was very real. It included every temptation of joy and sorrow, hope and fear, health and sickness, a tax on the mind, the body, and the spirit. Although no inclination to evil ever defiled His pure spirit, the lust of the flesh, the lust of the eyes, and the pride of life came to try Him, but found no place in His affections. Tempted by the Devil through all avenues and desires of the human heart and will, He was still without sin.

At times we are tempted, and at times we yield. Christ, knowing this, has become our interceding Priest. It is because we know our High Priest to be sympathetic and victorious that we can draw near to Him in confidence and assurance. His throne is the seat of Divine and omnipotent power, and yet the source of boundless Grace. He is truly the Good Shepherd!

WE HAVE A GREAT HIGH PRIEST

It was almost impossible for the Jewish mind to accept the fact of Jesus' High Priesthood. They had all their lives come to God through the advocacy of a Priest. A Jewish man would provide his own sacrifice, but he would not make his own sacrifice; the Priest did this for him.

What kind of person could this One be as to fulfill completely all the Divine requirements of a Holy God? Did this One meet all the requirements of the eternal Priesthood, that He might walk with us boldly to the Throne of Grace? Yes, He did!

The message is clear: Because the High Priest is all that has been indicated, we are to make use of Him for our individual needs daily. There should be within our hearts, the consciousness of spiritual possession; we have a Great High Priest! (Fjordbak).

(16) "LET US THEREFORE COME BOLDLY UNTO THE THRONE OF GRACE, THAT WE MAY OBTAIN MERCY, AND FIND GRACE TO HELP IN TIME OF NEED."

The exposition is:

1. Because of what Jesus did on the Cross on our behalf, the Holy of Holies is now open for all to come. This means we can come into the very Presence of God, and because of our Mediator, and Great High Priest, the Lord Jesus Christ.

2. Thank God that this Throne is referred to as *"The Throne of Grace,"* and not *"The Throne of Judgment."* Were that the case, every human being in the world would be in serious trouble.

All of this means that God strongly desires to show Mercy and Grace to all who come to Him. In fact, it is the Cross which makes Grace possible, and the Cross alone.

Due to the Cross, this means that all Believers can come to the Throne of Grace any time they so desire, and as many times as they so desire. If one comes in Faith, one will never be denied. The Cross of Christ demands

NOTES

this, and demands it eternally (Heb. 13:20).

3. We may be assured of always finding Mercy at this Throne of Grace.

4. The *"need"* expressed here, covers everything from forgiveness to strength, to comfort, to anything else of which we might think.

Beyond the shadow of a doubt, we will receive help.

THE THRONE OF GRACE

The phrase, *"Let us therefore come boldly unto the Throne of Grace,"* presents the Seat of Divine and omnipotent power, and yet the source of boundless Grace. Several things are said here:

1. This is a Throne of Grace and not Judgment. In fact, there is no Judgment for the Child of God, that having been handled at the Cross. To say it in a clearer sense, Jesus took the Judgment we should have taken, and Faith in Him, stops all Judgment. There may be chastisement, but never Judgment.

2. It is a Throne of Grace, meaning that Grace is the means by which the Goodness of God is dispensed to undeserving individuals.

3. As a Throne of Grace, and of course we're speaking of the Grace of God, it proclaims the very highest tribunal.

4. Even though it is the very highest, it is open to all, with the pronoun *"us"* including every single Believer.

5. The word *"come"* presents a beckoning hand. In other words, not only is this Throne of Grace open to all Believers, but there is actually a desire for all Believers to come, and to come as much as desired.

6. As well, we should not come timidly, but rather *"boldly,"* meaning, that we have the right of access.

7. All of this is made possible by and through the Atoning Blood of Christ Jesus (Heb. 10:19-20). This means that we come not depending at all upon our own merits, but because a sufficient Sacrifice has been offered for human guilt, and where we are assured that God is merciful.

The Great High Priest of the Christian calling, having shed His Own Blood to make expiation, is represented as approaching God, and by His very Presence, thereby making it possible for all to enter. For God not to show mercy, would mean that the Sacrifice is not accepted. Considering that the invitation is extended to all, tells us that the Sacrifice which Christ offered of Himself on the Cross, has been accepted totally and completely by all of Heaven. The debt has been paid; therefore, the door has been thrown open, for all to come.

MERCY

The phrase, *"That we may obtain Mercy,"* presents that which we want first. All of us need Mercy, even though none of us deserve Mercy.

This means that all the past has been forgiven and washed clean. It means that God as stated, has accepted the Sacrifice of Christ; therefore, on the merit of the Sacrifice accepted, God can show Mercy, which He desires to do, but can only do on the merits of Christ.

This tells us, that despite the fact that we can enter *"boldly,"* we are to never enter the Presence of God with arrogance. We deserve nothing good, and we must always understand that.

When we speak of entering the Presence of God with arrogance, such needs to be understood as it regards what is being said. The arrogance mentioned does not speak of demeanor, but rather attitude.

We must know and understand, that all access to God, has not come about because of our great Faith, or our great consecration, or our great doctrines, etc. We have access to the Throne of Grace, solely and totally because of what Jesus did at the Cross on our behalf, and for no other reason. But for Christ, God wouldn't even look at us, and in fact, couldn't even look at us. It is because of what Jesus did at the Cross, that makes all of this possible, in fact, makes everything possible.

So, when the Holy Spirit had Paul to place *"Mercy"* first, He did so for purpose and reason. A man who comes to God, not feeling his need of Mercy, must fail of obtaining the Divine favor; and he will be best prepared to obtain that favor who has the deepest sense of his need of forgiveness. Jesus said as much:

He told the illustration of the two men who went to the Temple to pray, a Pharisee and a Publican. In the eyes of Israel, a Publican was about the same as one today being a member of the Mafia.

The Lord went on to tell how the Pharisee

in his prayer, praised himself, etc. He then said this of the Publican:

"And the Publican, standing afar off, would not lift up so much as his eyes unto Heaven, but smote upon his breast, saying, God be merciful to me a sinner."

Jesus then said, *"I tell you, this man went down to his house justified rather than the other: for everyone that exalteth himself shall be abased; and he that humbleth himself shall be exalted"* (Lk. 18:9-14).

GRACE

The phrase, *"And find Grace to help in time of need,"* refers to the goodness of God extended to all who come. The invitation is extended during any *"time of need."* How wonderful! How glorious!

PRAYER

This one Passage of Scripture should make us very desirous of taking everything to the Lord in prayer. We should understand, that when we go to prayer, and do so with total dependence on the Lord, that we are in fact, entering into the Throne of Grace. There we are promised help in time of need for any and every problem.

To be sure, God doesn't limit this Throne of Grace. In other words, we can ask Him for anything from forgiveness for sin, to financial help, to physical healing, to comfort, strength, leading, guidance, in fact, anything that is needed.

The only thing required of us, is that we understand that we deserve nothing, and that we are actually asking for Mercy, of which is guaranteed to be granted, that is if we come with humility.

To be frank, many times when I enter the Throne of Grace, which I do every time I go to prayer, I spend most of the time, just thanking the Lord for what He has done. He has been so good to us, so generous, so kind, that we could thank Him forever, and never actually thank Him enough.

As stated, *"Grace"* is the goodness of God extended to undeserving souls. So, one might say that the Throne of Grace is in fact, a *"Throne of Goodness."* So we should as well, feel free to ask the Lord for whatever it is that we need. Actually, we are invited to do so.

AN EMPTY THRONE OF GRACE?

First of all, let my quickly say that the Throne of Grace is never empty. But at the same time, only a few Christians take advantage of this invitation of all invitations. Most only take a few things to the Lord, and that only in times of crisis, much less taking everything to Him!

Why?

The only answer I can give is, that most simply do not believe that God answers prayer. Others I fear, harbor sin within their lives, and sin I might quickly add which they do not want to give up, which means that they don't want to pray. As should be obvious, the moment a person begins to pray, the Holy Spirit is going to start reminding us of wrong directions, etc.

But whatever the case, what a shame! I watch the Lord perform miracle after miracle, even on a daily basis, but most Christians do not seem to have much desire to take advantage of the greatest opportunity and privilege that one could ever know.

Great is the Lord, and greatly to be praised!

"Awake, my soul, in joyful lays,
"And sing thy great Redeemer's praise;
"He justly claims a song from me,
"His loving kindness is so free."

"He saw me ruined in the Fall,
"Yet loved me notwithstanding all,
"And saved me from my lost estate,
"His loving kindness is so great."

"Through mighty hosts of cruel foes,
"Where Earth and Hell my way oppose,
"He safely leads my soul along,
"His loving kindness is so strong."

"Often I feel my sinful heart,
"Prone from my Jesus to depart;
"And though I oft have Him forgot,
"His loving kindness changes not."

—◼—

CHAPTER 5

(1) "FOR EVERY HIGH PRIEST TAKEN FROM AMONG MEN IS ORDAINED FOR MEN IN THINGS PERTAINING TO GOD,

NOTES

THAT HE MAY OFFER BOTH GIFTS AND SACRIFICES FOR SINS:"

The exegesis is:

1. The Jews had not been familiar with the idea of the Messiah being High Priest. He had not come from the family of Aaron. He was a Priesthood of another order, that of Melchisedec. In fact, the Messiah while on Earth did not have access to the Jerusalem Temple so far as officiating as a Priest was concerned. So Paul will explain somewhat further about this new Priest to Whom they were to go for Salvation (Wuest).

2. For a Priest to officiate on behalf of men, he must be taken from among men. A Priest must partake of the nature of the person for whom he officiates. His work is to minister to men in things that involve man's relation to God.

Jesus fit this description in every capacity. In fact, that was at least one reason for the Incarnation, i.e., *"God becoming man."*

3. He offers *"gifts"* and *"sacrifices for sins."* *"Gifts"* can refer to any type of gifts, while *"Sacrifices"* refer to blood Sacrifices, offered up to atone for sin. If the Priest is to do this efficiently, he must have a genuine compassion for the sinful.

HIGH PRIEST

The phrase, *"For every High Priest,"* pertains of course, to the Jewish economy. The remarks, as are obvious, relate to the Jewish system. The Jews had one High Priest regarded as the successor of Aaron (Ex. 29:9).

However, it should be quickly added, that by the time of the Romans, the Mosaic regulations had been disregarded, with individuals holding the office who had no relationship to the lineage of Aaron. In other words, the office by this time was bought and sold. In fact, at this particular time, there were several persons at one time to whom was given the title of High Priest.

According to the Mosaic regulations, the High Priest was the head of all spiritual affairs, at least as it regarded Temple worship. He was the ordinary judge of all that pertained to religion, and even of the general justice of the Hebrew commonwealth (Deut. 17:8-12; 19:17; 21:5; 23:9-10). He had the privilege of entering the Most Holy Place in the Temple (the Holy of Holies) once a year, on the Great Day of Atonement, where he was to make expiation for the sins of the people (Lev. Chpt. 16).

He was to be the son of one who had married a virgin, and was to be free from any physical defects (Lev. 21:13). As well, the dress of the High Priest was much more costly and magnificent than that of the inferior order of Priests (Ex. 39:1-9).

PERTAINING TO GOD

The phrase, *"Taken from among men is ordained for men in things pertaining to God,"* pertains to several things:

1. The High Priests who served in Israel were men, as would be obvious, with the implication leaning toward their frailty.

2. There is an allusion here to the fact that the great High Priest of the present time, Who is Christ, has a higher origin, than that of being mere human. While He was and is definitely human, He was selected from a rank far above men.

3. To be *"ordained for men"* is to be set apart or consecrated for the welfare of men. The Jewish High Priest was set apart to his office with great solemnity (Ex. Chpt. 29).

4. He was to be dedicated totally to God and the things of God. This meant that he was not to be a Civil Ruler, a teacher of science, or a military leader, but his business was to superintend the affairs of the Word of God.

5. The High Priest of Israel served as a Mediator between God and Israel. In other words, he was a type of Christ. The idea was, that the weight of significance rested in his office more so than in his person. Being a mere man, he fell woefully short as a Mediator; however, he would serve as a type until Christ came.

GIFTS AND SACRIFICES FOR SINS

The phrase, *"That he may offer both gifts and sacrifices for sins,"* refers regarding the former to Thank-Offerings, or oblations, which would be expressions of gratitude, with the latter referring to bloody offerings, i.e., *"offerings consisting of the sacrifice of animals."* It was for sin, with the Blood sprinkled by him on the Mercy Seat. As stated, this was done once a year, as he went into the

Holy of Holies, carried out on the Great Day of Atonement.

PREACHERS AND PRIESTS

It is improper since the Cross, to give the name *"Priest"* to a Minister of the Gospel. The reason is, that he offers no sacrifice; he sprinkles no blood. The Minister is appointed to *"preach the Word,"* but never to offer sacrifice, that having already been done by Christ.

Accordingly, the New Testament preserves entire consistency on this point, for the name *"Priest"* is never once given to the Apostles, or to any other Minister of the Gospel.

However, among the Catholics there is a gross and dangerous error in their use of the word *"Priest."* They believe that these *"Priests"* offer up *"the real body and blood of our Lord,"* referring to the Mass, which means that the bread and wine are changed by the words of consecration into the *"body and blood, the soul and divinity, of the Lord Jesus."* They teach that this is really offered by him (the Priest) as a sacrifice.

Accordingly, they *"elevate the host"*; that is, lift up, or offer the sacrifice, and require all to bow before it and worship; and with this view they are consistent in retaining the word *"Priest."* Now please let me say it again:

This which is done by Catholic Priests can be construed as nothing other than blasphemy. As Ministers of the Gospel, we have no sacrifice to offer before God, simply because, the great Sacrifice — the one sufficient Atonement — has already been offered; and true Ministers of the Gospel are appointed by the Holy Spirit to proclaim this Truth to men, not to offer sacrifices for sin.

That's the reason that I state unequivocally, that when Catholics truly come to Christ, as some few of them actually do, without fail, they must leave this erroneous doctrine, for how can one continue to blaspheme, which the engagement of the Mass actually is, and still be a Christian? To be sure, the Holy Spirit and without fail, will always guide one to all Truth (Jn. 16:13).

THE WORD OF THE LORD UNTO ME

In 1982, the Lord spoke to my heart, telling me that I must deliver a Message to the Catholic Church, as well as to the Protestant

Church. At that time, we had the largest Television audience in the world, at least as it regards Gospel, airing our Program in some 35 or 40 countries of the world.

When the Lord began to speak this to my heart, and especially about Catholicism, I was somewhat taken aback. Actually, at that time, I knew next to nothing about Catholic doctrine, and beside that, Catholic Charismatics were contributing millions of dollars each year to our Ministry, which we desperately needed. But the Holy Spirit was adamant, even as the Holy Spirit can be adamant!

To be sure, I sought the Lord earnestly for several months, determining in my spirit that I had the Mind of the Lord, and that what I was being given was not from an erroneous source, etc. It was from the Lord, and if I was to obey the Lord, then I must do what He was telling me to do.

The Message I was to deliver over our vast network of Programs was actually, relatively simple. I was to tell the Catholic people, and to do so with kindness, that their Justification was and is by Faith, and not at all by the Church. I was also to tell them, that if they truly came to Christ, they were going to have to leave the Catholic Church. To be sure, this last word was that which drew fire.

Oddly enough, most of the criticism, and it was like an avalanche, came from Protestant circles, and mostly from Pentecostals and Charismatics. By and large, their message was that the Catholics who had truly come to Christ, could stay in that Church, etc.

One Pentecostal Leader wrote me, saying, *"With one Message, you have destroyed all that I have taken many years to build."*

Because this man was older than me, I wrote him back a very kind and gracious letter; however, the thought did cross my mind, that if one Message destroyed all that he had taken years to build, then that must have been one more powerful Message, or else he had not built very much. He was telling the Catholics to stay in the Catholic Church! I considered that to be blasphemy, and still do, even more so today than ever.

Yes, the opposition was fierce, and as I have stated, mostly from Protestant circles, but the Truth is, we saw many Catholics brought to a saving knowledge of Jesus Christ.

THE CROSS OF CHRIST

What we're speaking of here, and I refer to the Catholic Church, is the great Sacrifice of Christ. If we confuse that issue, which Catholics do, and regrettably, many Protestants do as well, then we have confused the greatest issue of all. If we misunderstand what Christ did on the Cross, the upshot can be, that we can lose our souls. Whatever our ideas as it concerns other nuances of doctrine, that which we believe about the Cross, must be totally Biblical, and because this is the very heart of the Gospel.

As I have previously stated, if one injures their finger or hand, while it certainly might bring pain and difficulty, it shouldn't be life-threatening. However, if one has a problem with one's heart, such a problem can kill the individual. Such is the Cross!

You and I may argue over whether speaking with other Tongues is the initial physical evidence that one has been Baptized with the Holy Spirit. And to be sure, whoever is wrong on the issue will suffer loss. But if we misunderstand what Jesus did at the Cross, and what the Cross actually means, one can lose their soul. The following constitutes where the Church is presently:

1. Many in the modern Church place no confidence at all in what Jesus did at the Cross, which means, that they believe a modernist gospel, which in fact, is no gospel at all (Gal. 1:6-7).

2. Those who understand the necessity of Faith in the Cross as it regards the initial Salvation experience, but have no knowledge of the part the Cross plays in our everyday living before God. In fact, this makes up a large percentage of the modern Church.

3. There are few who understand the part the Cross plays not only in their initial Salvation experience, but as well, in their everyday living before God. As stated, this number is very small, which means that the majority of the modern Church is walking in spiritual failure, and because of *"walking after the flesh"* (Rom. 8:1). If a Believer doesn't understand the part the Cross plays in our everyday living, and by that I speak of our victory, our overcoming strength, and on a perpetual basis, then of necessity, that

individual is walking after the flesh and not after the Spirit. Consequently, it is impossible but that in some way, he is lacking in victorious, Christian living.

Christ is our great High Priest, simply because He offered up Himself in Sacrifice, shedding His Life's Blood in order to pay the terrible sin debt. This means that He not only officiated as the High Priest, but He also was the Sacrifice. That's why Paul said the following:

"Who gave Himself for our sins, that He might deliver us from this present evil world, according to the Will of God and our Father" (Gal. 1:4).

Where the High Priests of old could only offer *"gifts and sacrifices"* which were at best a stopgap measure, Jesus Christ, our Great High Priest, in the offering up of Himself, brought about the total cleansing of all sin, which the blood of bulls and goats could never do. And as well, and even as we will study in coming Passages in this great Epistle to the Hebrews, this One Sacrifice was enough, and in fact, will be enough forever, hence Paul referring to it as *"The Everlasting Covenant"* (Heb. 13:20). Consequently, isn't it understandable how that the Catholic System is blasphemy? As well, isn't it understandable, that much of the action of the Protestant world falls into the same category, considering the attempt to place before God our *"dead works,"* in place of His Glorious Sacrifice! No wonder the Apostle said, *"For he that is entered into His Rest, he also hath ceased from his own works"* (Heb. 4:10).

(2) "WHO CAN HAVE COMPASSION ON THE IGNORANT, AND ON THEM THAT ARE OUT OF THE WAY; FOR THAT HE HIMSELF ALSO IS COMPASSED WITH INFIRMITY."

The structure is:

1. The High Priest should have compassion on others, simply because he is a man, and has endured and does endure, the faults and frailties of life and living. Jesus as a Man underwent the same thing and can, therefore, empathize accordingly.

2. The word *"compassion"* also speaks of a state of feeling toward the ignorant and the erring which is neither too severe nor too tolerant. The High Priest must be careful

NOTES

lest he become irritated at sin and ignorance. He must also take care that he does not become weakly indulgent.

3. The word *"ignorant"* has to do with sins of ignorance. In other words, the individual didn't know that what they were doing was wrong. It shows that sin and defilement might exist unsuspected, that God saw evil where men did not, and that His test of purity was stricter than theirs. The idea is, even though it was a sin committed in ignorance, it was still a sin, and still had to be atoned for.

4. *"Out of the way"* speaks of those who have truly sinned, and know they have sinned. In other words, they have missed God's Way. They need Atonement!

5. The High Priest is able to be moderate and tender in his judgment toward others' sins, because he himself is compassed with infirmities. Although Christ was not compassed with infirmity, which speaks of moral weaknesses, He definitely was tempted in those respects; therefore, He knows the situation, actually as no other knows the situation.

COMPASSION

The phrase, *"Who can have compassion on the ignorant,"* refers to having a fellow feeling for those on whose behalf he officiates. Sensible of his own ignorance, he is able to sympathize with those who are ignorant; and compassed about with infirmity, he is able to succor those who have like infirmities.

"Compassion" in the Greek as used here, is *"metriopathein,"* and means, *"to deal gently with."* It refers to taking the middle course between apathy and anger. A true High Priest is not indifferent to moral lapses; neither is he harsh. He *"is able"* to take this position only because he himself shares in the same *"weakness"* as the sinners on whom he has compassion.

No part of the Mosaic economy was more beautifully portrayed to the minds, the imaginations, and the affections of the Jews than that of the Priesthood of Aaron. The system of ritual worship over which the High Priest resided must have been a very beautiful scene — the gorgeous apparel, apparel incidentally which had been originally designed by the

Holy Spirit, the solemn vestures, the mysterious sacredness of the High Priest, the splendor of the religious rites which he performed, the beauty and grandeur of the Temple — all of these things created a powerful and exciting image in the mind of these Jewish believers.

They longed for much of the beauty and the rituals of the days that had gone by when they worshiped in the Temple. There was much in the form and ceremony to be admired; why not; it had been originally designed by God. In fact there was much that laid hold to the emotions of men as they considered the Temples and its Altars, the Holy Place, and the Holy of Holies.

They recalled the rich and inspiring reading of the Law and the Prophets, they remembered the teaching of the Scribes and the traditions of the Elders, but the dignity of the Priesthood was uppermost in their minds.

However, I might quickly add, that the Hebrew Christians had a mistaken loyalty to Judaism that was leading them farther from the simplicity of Christ, and which could easily conclude with them in apostasy.

THE SUPERIORITY OF CHRIST

Because of the honor that had been placed upon the High Priest both by God and by man, the comparison of Jesus with the Old Testament Priests would be particularly meaningful to the Readers. The contrast between the imperfections of the Levitical High Priest and the perfections of the New Covenant High Priest would point out the superiority of the Priesthood of Christ and its worthiness of the devotion and faithfulness of the Hebrews.

The human nature of Jesus was superior to that of the High priests of Judaism because the Lord Jesus was sinless. The aim of Paul was to encourage the Jewish Believers to draw near at all times to the Throne of Grace in the Name of Jesus, the Great High Priest through Whom we have access to God Himself.

Paul, understanding the high honor that rested upon the High Priest in the Old Testament, now identifies Jesus as the High Priest of the New Covenant. The Priesthood of the Lord Jesus Christ and the Priesthood of Aaron

are compared, so that the Reader may better comprehend the high and holy position given to Jesus by His Heavenly Father.

THE MESSIAH

The Jews had not been familiar with the idea of the Messiah being a High Priest; their ideas and traditions concerning the Messiah had been limited; consequently, the High Priesthood of Jesus Christ would also seem strange to Jewish Christians.

For instance, there was no record of Jesus having ever once officiated in the Temple; never did He assume any Priestly functions while on the Earth. In fact, Jesus was not even born of the Priestly Tribe of Levi. He was of the Tribe of Judah, the Kingly Tribe. How could He lay claim to the Priesthood?

As Paul describes Jesus as High Priest, it all seemed in direct contradiction to the Jewish concept of the meaning of the Priesthood. It was necessary, therefore, to set forth the qualifications for the Priesthood and to explain the Ministry of the Priests.

THE QUALIFICATIONS OF CHRIST

Under the Law, it was required that the High Priest, as stated, be of the Tribe of Levi and, therefore, a descendent of Aaron. It was necessary that the Priest be taken from among men; he must himself be a man, a partaker of human nature. This means that no Angel could be qualified for the Priestly office. The Priest must be ordained or appointed to officiate on behalf of man. He must mediate for man, for the work of the Priest was vicarious (substitutionary); meaning it was done for the benefit of another.

The humanity of Jesus, His Incarnation, and His Virgin Birth, were basic and essential if He were to be the High Priest. Christ identified Himself with man, totally involving Himself with man and with man's needs.

The suffering that Jesus endured enabled Him to "... *be touched with the feeling of our infirmities ...*" and the temptation that He faced made Him "... *able to help them who are tempted*" (Heb. 4:15; 2:18).

All that man meets in life and death has been met and conquered by the Captain of our Salvation, Christ Jesus, *"the Apostle and High Priest of our profession"* (Heb. 3:1). He is qualified more than any other to be the True High Priest of God for man. In fact, the first prerequisite of the Priesthood is found in Christ: He is the Perfect Man, He is God *"manifest in the flesh"* (I Tim. 3:16).

Though stress is placed upon the manhood of Christ, the High Priesthood of Christ also emphasized His Deity. Earthly Priests were chosen from among men, but the One Who is our High Priest, Who was as well chosen from among men, also came from the Godhead. He was fully God and fully Man. More than any man, Jesus was better equipped to minister in the things which pertained to God and to man. He is the *". . . merciful and faithful High Priest in things pertaining to God, to make reconciliation for the sins of the people"* (Heb. 2:17). As God, He was chosen to represent God to man, even as Man, He was chosen to represent man to God!

Man brought sin into the world; therefore, it was necessary that deliverance should come by man. Jesus, the Son of Man, fully paid man's sinful debt on the Cross.

(I am indebted to Reverend Everitt M. Fjordbak for the material above on the Priesthood of Christ.)

THE COMMITTING OF SIN

The phrase, *"And on them that are out of the way,"* refers to those who have sinned, and who know they have sinned. In other words, they have missed God's Way and succumbed to their own way.

The High Priest was to have compassion on these sinners, because in fact, he was a sinner himself. Knowing and understanding this, he could have *"compassion"* on such an individual.

The two statements *"ignorant"* and *"them that are out of the way,"* go hand in hand. While sins of ignorance were committed under the Old Covenant, we may erroneously think that such cannot be done under the New Covenant, especially considering that we now have the Holy Spirit within us, *"Who guides us into all Truth"* (Jn. 16:13).

However, despite that, which of course is a wonderful help, even beyond comprehension; still, sins of ignorance continue to be committed even unto this hour. In fact, I

am persuaded that this is the greatest cause of sin presently among Christians.

MODERN SINS OF IGNORANCE

First of all, please allow me to say that sin, even though committed in ignorance, is still sin, which means that the person is still guilty, still responsible. In fact, even under the Old Economy, when the sins of ignorance were brought to light, the guilty one had to offer up Sacrifices (Lev. 4:2; Num. 15:22-29). All sin is sin in the eyes of God, irrespective as to who commits it, or how it is committed.

However, as it regards the individual who is sinning in ignorance, which we will momentarily address, God definitely looks at the heart differently than He does those who willfully sin. While they are still culpable, the individual doesn't want to do what is being done, and to be sure, the Holy Spirit will bring such a person to a place of victory.

At this present time, the vast majority of the modern Church, and I speak of those who truly love the Lord, is by and large, ignorant of God's prescribed order of victory as given in His Word, which is the Cross of Christ. As a result of not knowing the great benefits of the Cross the Christian will resort to Law, whether he understands such or not; consequently, despite all his efforts otherwise, despite trying so hard not to fail, he is doomed to failure, with in fact, the situation becoming worse, even as he tried harder to do otherwise. In fact, millions of Christians are in that very shape presently, and simply because they do not know the Truth of the Cross.

First of all let me state, that God has only one avenue of victory, and that is the Cross of Christ. As we've said repeatedly, this is the way the Holy Spirit works within our hearts and lives, and I speak of Him working according to the great Sacrifice of Christ, and within those parameters. As we have repeatedly stated, there are three principles as it regards victorious, Christian living. They are:

1. The Cross (Rom. 6:3-5).

2. Our Faith in the Cross (Rom. 6:11, 14).

3. Faith in the Cross guarantees the help of the Holy Spirit (Rom. 8:1-2, 11).

Now if the Christian doesn't know and understand these things which we've just said, it is impossible for that Christian to live a victorious, overcoming life. It simply cannot be done. No matter how hard one might try, no matter how much effort one may put forth, no matter how consecrated one might be, without understanding that everything we receive from God comes totally and completely through the Cross of Christ, and we speak of its continued benefits, and that we must have a constant Faith in that, we cannot have the help of the Holy Spirit, which means we are doomed to failure. So what am I saying?

I'm saying, that due to ignorance of the Cross, ignorance as to what it all means, ignorance as it regards God's prescribed order of victory, the Christian will fail. That doesn't mean he'll lose his soul, but it does mean that life will be far less than what the Lord intends for it to be, and which it can be in Christ.

WHY DOES THIS IGNORANCE PREVAIL?

The Scripture plainly says, *"So then Faith cometh by hearing, and hearing by the Word of God"* (Rom. 10:17).

This simply means, that if the Cross isn't preached, the people will be ignorant of this great foundational Truth. And the Truth is, the Cross has been so little taught and preached in the last several decades, that most Christians have only a sentimental knowledge of the Cross. Jesus died on a Cross for them, and that's about all they know. Most have absolutely no idea of the part that the Cross of Christ plays in their daily living.

Possibly one of, if not the greatest hindrance to this great foundational Truth, is the modern Faith Message. On the surface this Message seems to be right; however, once it is understood that the Faith being projected, even though it is claimed to be Faith in the Word, is more so Faith in self, with the Word being perverted. Whatever, it's not Faith in the Cross of Christ, which is the only Faith that God will honor.

Merely having Faith is not enough. We must understand that it is the object of Faith that is so very important. And the object of Faith must always be the Cross of Christ. To give Chapter and Verse for that, one need only to just open the Bible at random. In fact, the entirety of the Word of God from Genesis through the Book of Revelation is the story

NOTES

of man's Redemption, which of course, was carried out at the Cross. Actually, the meaning of the New Covenant, which the Lord gave to Paul, is in reality, the meaning of the Cross.

The original Apostles did not at the beginning preach the Cross of Christ, but rather Jesus and His mighty Name. In fact, the greater thrust of their Message was that *"He is risen!"* (Acts 3:12-16).

God honored what they preached, even though they were not actually preaching the Cross, and because the light on that great Work had not yet been given; however, when it was given to Paul, the Cross became the Message, with the original Twelve then taking up that Message (I Pet. 1:18-20).

And then again, getting back to our original subject, most of the institutionalized Church has opted totally and completely, for humanistic psychology. In other words, they have registered and are registering a vote of *"no confidence"* in the Cross of Christ. Let it ever be understood, that one cannot have both humanistic psychology and the Cross at the same time. One or the other must go! Psychology constitutes leaven, and to be sure, this leaven will ultimately take over the whole, which in fact, it has already done. I speak of all the major Denominations. In fact, I'm not aware of any Denomination, at least in the United States and Canada, that hasn't opted completely for this human wisdom, that is *"earthly, sensual and devilish"* (James 3:15).

As a result of this debacle, and a debacle it is, the modern Church has little or no understanding of the Cross of Christ and is consequently, doomed to spiritual failure of some nature. Ignorance of this foundational Truth puts them in a very vulnerable position.

HOW DOES ONE EXHIBIT
FAITH IN THE CROSS?

Faith is what it's all about! First I'll state what must be done:

1. We must understand that every single, solitary thing that comes to us from God, and I mean everything, and for all time, comes exclusively, totally, and completely through the Cross of Christ and by no other means. We must understand and believe that (Rom. 6:3-5, 11, 14).

2. We must understand that the Holy Spirit works entirely from the premise of the Finished Work of Christ. In other words, we cannot really do anything as Christians without the Holy Spirit. And when we learn that He functions entirely according to the great Sacrifice of Christ, then we've learned a great Truth (Rom. 8:1-2).

3. He demands that we have Faith exclusively in the Cross, which in a sense, gives Him permission to work for us, so to speak! To be sure, we must have Faith in Him as well; however, the primary ground for all Faith, must rest in the Word of God, which in effect is the story of the Cross, which in essence means that we have Faith in the Cross (Gal. 6:14).

Now let me ask a few questions:

Do you as a Believer really understand and believe that everything comes through the Cross, or that other things must be added to the Cross? Are you wavering in that respect? If so, you're really not going to receive anything from the Lord. James referred to such as *"wavering Faith."* He then said, *"Let not that man think that he shall receive anything of the Lord."*

He then added, *"A double-minded man is unstable in all his ways"* (James 1:6-8).

If you claim to believe in the Cross, and at the same time are placing your Faith in Water Baptism, or the Lord's Supper, or in the Church, or whatever for that matter, you will find that even though these things are very Scriptural in their own right, when we place our Faith in them in the capacity mentioned, we in effect turn them into works, which God cannot honor.

As a Believer, you are what you are in Christ, totally and completely because of what Jesus did for you at the Cross. This means that your Church, or any of the sacred ordinances for that matter, have absolutely nothing to do with what you receive from God.

Again I emphasize, these things mentioned are definitely important in their own way, but only in their own way. For instance, Water Baptism is a perfect symbol of the Cross of Christ and His Resurrection. Of course, the Lord's Supper falls into the same category, respecting the Crucifixion. These are symbols, to ever remind us of the great significance of the Cross, and that we should

look to it exclusively. But when we change our Faith from the reality to the symbol, we're doing the same thing that Israel of old did — changing our Faith from Christ to the rudiments of the Law, which could not save. What and Who the Law represented, namely Jesus Christ, definitely could save, but not the Law within itself.

THE OPPOSITION OF SATAN

The Evil One will fight the Cross as he fights nothing else. He will oppose your understanding of the Cross as he opposes nothing else. In fact, Satan doesn't really care too very much about what you believe, just as long as it's not in the great Sacrifice of Christ. He knows if you put your Faith in other things, you're not going to receive anything from the Lord. He knows you have cut yourself off for all practical purposes, from the Holy Spirit. So, in effect, he promotes many false doctrines, and in fact, all false doctrines.

So, once you embark upon this *"walk after the Spirit"* you will find Preachers opposing you, relatives opposing you, friends opposing you, and maybe even your Church turning against you. Don't be alarmed, that's nothing new.

In fact, the entirety of this situation began, at least as it is drawn out, with the situation regarding Cain and Abel recorded in Genesis, Chapter 4. Cain killed Abel, because God accepted his Sacrifice, which of course was a type of Christ, and rejected Cain's. So he killed his brother, and war has been declared on the Cross from that day until now, and for all the obvious reasons.

One will find that the *"enemies of the Cross of Christ,"* are abundant. They were very evident in Paul's day, and they are evident now (Phil. 3:18-19). So, don't think the opposition as being strange; however, if you will stick to your guns, so to speak, keep your Faith anchored in the Cross, knowing and understanding that it is from this Source that all Blessings flow, you will find exactly what Jesus promised:

"I am come that they might have Life, and that they might have it more abundantly" (Jn. 10:10). You will as well find the following:

"Come unto Me all ye that labor and are heavy laden, and I will give you Rest" (Mat. 11:28).

In fact, the Way of the Cross is the only Way to the Blessings of God. But that way is not without opposition, as we have stated!

INFIRMITY

The phrase, *"For that he himself also is compassed with infirmity,"* refers to the condition of all men, even the High Priest in the old Judiastic economy.

The Greek word translated *"is compassed"* presents a graphic picture here. The word is *"perikeimai,"* which means literally *"to be lying around."* The idea is, the High Priest has infirmity, which refers here to sinful tendencies lying around him. That is, he is completely encircled by sin, since he has a sinful nature which if unrepressed, will control his entire being, and of which he is well aware.

This is denied in the case of Jesus, which in fact makes Him better than Aaron.

"Infirmities" in the Greek is *"astheneia,"* and means *"moral weakness which makes men capable of sinning,"* in other words, the totally depraved nature (Wuest).

Despite being denied by some Preachers, Christians also have a *"sin nature."* This refers, as stated, to the capability of one sinning. As long as we totally lean on Christ, trusting in what He did at the Cross on our behalf, and not at all in ourselves, which gives the Holy Spirit latitude to work, we need not fear the sin nature whatsoever. But if we drift outside of Faith in the Cross of Christ, thereby trusting in ourselves, which in fact is so easy to do, we will find ourselves failing the Lord, which then causes the sin nature to spring into life, which then can cause us real problems to say the least! To deny this is to deny the very Word of God.

In fact, and to which we have already alluded, when Paul mentioned *"sin"* so many times in Romans, Chapter 6, he is actually saying in the original text *"the sin."* This does not refer to acts of sin, but rather to the fact of sin, or the principle of sin. It means, that this danger is always there as it regards the Child of God. If the Believer constantly looks to the Cross, there will be no danger; but if the Believer starts to look elsewhere,

then he's going to have a problem with the sin nature, whether he believes that it exists or not!

(3) "AND BY REASON HEREOF HE OUGHT, AS FOR THE PEOPLE, SO ALSO FOR HIMSELF, TO OFFER FOR SINS."

The exposition is:

1. The very purpose of the High Priest of old, was to administer the affairs of the Priests under him, as well as his duty regarding the Great Day of Atonement, when he personally went into the Holy of Holies to offer up Blood on the Mercy Seat.

2. Not only did he offer sacrifices for the people, but being sinful himself, he also had to offer sacrifices for himself as well.

3. His primary function was sacrifice for sins. In this, he was a type of Christ, Who would later come, offering up Himself on the Cross, which would do away with the need for the Priesthood.

HIS TASK

The phrase, *"And by reason hereof he ought,"* refers to the very purpose of his being, which is to offer sacrifice for sins.

A High Priest could not make a fitting Atonement for sins if he were filled with feelings of indignation, exasperation, and judgment against those who were guilty; neither can we help those in need, unless we seek to understand and bear with them. Jesus as High Priest in no way condemns those who follow Him; instead, He makes intercession for us and our weaknesses.

As Moses went into the Presence of God to make intercession and secure pardon for the people and Aaron when they had broken God's Law with the golden calf, so our High Priest stands before God interceding and praying for us. How assuring to know that Jesus, being holy, guileless, and undefiled, need never offer a preliminary sacrifice for Himself, but that He can immediately enter into God's Presence on our behalf. Though He bore the sins of many, He Himself did not sin; He is the Perfect High Priest in that He is not *"compassed with infirmity."*

FOR THE PEOPLE

The phrase, *"As for the people,"* proclaims the High Priest serving as a Mediator.

We have already noted Aaron's sin in the making of the golden calf; and yet, Aaron was called of God to fulfill the office of High Priest. Perhaps the incident had served as a lesson to him of God's compassion and Mercy so that as High Priest he might be merciful.

One of the qualifications of the High Priest was that he must be able to sympathize and to understand those whom he represented, but another qualification was that the High Priest be personally called of God to service. Aaron was called by God from among men and appointed of God for men.

Aaron officiated as High Priest not because he was a worthy man, but because he was chosen by God and called. Then this office went to his descendants as heirs and successors.

FOR HIMSELF

The phrase, *"So also for himself,"* refers to the fact that he was a sinful man as well, despite the fact that he was the High Priest, in effect, the highest spiritual office in the land.

There are some who presently tend to forget this fact. Consequently, they seem to feel they have the right to judge and always, to judge harshly, very harshly! They seem to forget that they have had to ask the Lord innumerable times to forgive them of sin. Actually, the problem presently is self-righteousness!

Knowing human nature, I'm certain that some of the High Priests suffered from this malady of self-righteousness. That being the case, as I'm sure it was at times, those who had the misfortune of living in Israel at that time, were not blessed to say the least, especially by such a High Priest.

It is worse yet, when modern preachers occupy a man-devised office, which means they were elected by popular ballot, and then they become afflicted with a double problem:

First of all, many of them treat this man-devised office as a spiritual office, which it isn't! And then when you add self-righteousness to that, you have a double-barreled problem. And regrettably, that characterizes so much of modern Christendom, and I speak of that which refers to itself as leadership. What I've said definitely doesn't

characterize all, but I'm afraid it does characterize most!

FOR SINS

The phrase, *"To offer for sins,"* refers to offering a sacrifice, which would make Atonement that would provide reconciliation with God.

As sin was the problem with Israel, requiring sacrifices, sin is the problem of the Church presently, which means that the Sacrifice of Christ is always an immediate necessity. Unfortunately, many modern Christians think of the Cross as something in the past, and the past only! However, the true meaning of the Cross is that which happened in the historic past, but definitely has continued benefits, and incidentally, benefits which will never be discontinued. I am dependent on those benefits every day of my life, and so is every other Christian. This is what makes the Cross of Christ so very, very important! We are to constantly rely on what Christ did at the Cross, understanding that it is through the Cross only that God can deal with humanity.

Thank the Lord that we as Christians do not now have to take a sacrifice, and I speak of a little animal, to a designated place, and then have it offered up. All of this was done away with by the One Sacrifice of Christ. His was sufficient for all, for all time, and for all sin. Now, all we have to do is to exhibit constant Faith in that One Sacrifice, and its benefits will ever accrue to us.

(4) "AND NO MAN TAKETH THIS HONOUR UNTO HIMSELF, BUT HE THAT IS CALLED OF GOD, AS WAS AARON."

The structure is:

1. The High Priest must be Divinely called to his office.

2. One who is compassed with infirmity would hesitate to offer sacrifice for sin unless called by God to do so, as would be obvious.

3. Aaron, Moses' Brother, was the first High Priest in Israel. The lineage was to remain in his family until the Messiah would come. Unfortunately, the High Priesthood ultimately became so corrupted, that by the time of Christ, the office was bought and sold like merchandise.

MAN COULD NOT CALL HIMSELF TO THIS OFFICE

The phrase, *"And no man taketh this honor unto himself,"* means that it was all ordered by God, and not at all by man. In fact, this manner of government continues even in the New Testament. The Scripture plainly says, *"And He* (Christ) *gave some, Apostles; and some, Prophets; and some, Evangelists; and some, Pastors and Teachers"* (Eph. 4:11).

If it is to be noticed, the pronoun *"He"* refers to Christ, and means that these are all Callings which come from the Lord, and never from man. Woe is the congregation presided over by a man who is not called of God.

The modern manner of most Church Government, which model is taken from the world and not at all from the Bible, serves as the greatest destroyer of the Work of God. While there is certainly nothing wrong with forming Denominations or belonging to Denominations, these ideally serving as a tool, as there is nothing wrong with various different Church offices of administrative capacity. In fact, most of the present Church Government would not be wrong were it handled Biblically. But that too often is not the case.

The wrong comes in, whenever men attempt to make these man-devised offices, incidentally with the occupant elected by popular ballot, into a spiritual office, and then demanding spiritual obedience. That is the corruption of modern Church Government.

In the New Testament Economy, God has set the *"Apostle"* in the Office of spiritual leadership. And the occupants of this office are not elected by popular ballot, but rather Called of God.

And yet, the words *"spiritual leadership"* should be handled very loosely, and for the simple reason, that Christ is the Head of the Church and not man. As well, He does all His work through the Person of the Holy Spirit, Who uses Apostles and others. Of course we're speaking here of Spiritual Leadership; however, everything the Lord does in the Church is done in this fashion. He works through the fivefold Calling, but as well, He functions and flows through the entirety of the Body of Christ. In other words, all are used by God, or at least the Lord desires to use all, if they will only consecrate themselves.

When men *"take this honor unto themselves,"* which means they attempt to function in the realm of Spiritual Leadership by the ballot box, they are sinning, and as stated, this has been, and is the greatest hurt to the Work of God. Any time we leave the Scriptures, thereby making policy on our own, it always and without fail, ultimately tends toward wreckage.

CALLED OF GOD

The phrase, *"But he that is Called of God,"* refers here to the high and holy Calling of the Jewish High Priesthood.

Paul probably emphasized this fact simply because, the office of the High Priest at that time in Israel, as previously stated, was now bought and sold like so much merchandise. It was no longer of the Aaronic lineage, as previously ordained by God.

So, he was telling the Hebrew Christians who were contemplating going back into Temple worship, that not only had Christ fulfilled all of this, meaning that it is no more applicable, but as well, it had become so corrupt, and so far removed from the way God originally designed the thing, that to go back into that presented itself as a travesty of common sense.

The Way of God is never an event-free way. To be sure, it is fraught with situations, problems, and difficulties. One can guarantee that Satan will see to that; however, with all the attendant difficulties, it is still so far ahead of anything else, that it beggars description.

When I speak of the *"Way of God,"* I'm speaking of all the many streams that flow out within the Church. Only one stream is the *"Way of God,"* with all the others being counterfeits and imitations, all ultimately fostered and nurtured by Satan.

HOW DOES ONE KNOW THE WAY OF GOD?

That's not easy, simply because Satan has many counterfeits, and all of them made to look exactly like the real thing. Paul referred to them as *"angels of light"* (II Cor. 11:13-15).

If one properly knows the Word of God, and is striving to follow the Lord as closely as possible, to be sure, the Holy Spirit will definitely *"guide into all Truth"* (Jn. 16:13). But the tragedy is, most Christians have only an elementary knowledge of the Word of God, and are not striving to closely follow the Lord. So they are easy targets for the subtly of Satan.

For instance, at this present time (June, 2000), many Christians who label themselves as Spirit-filled are running all over the world attending particular meetings, where certain things are happening, which are purported to be of the Spirit. To be sure, many times *"a spirit"* is definitely involved, but it's not *"the Spirit!"*

For the most part, the Preachers involved, would have to be labeled as *"false apostles, deceitful workers, transforming themselves into the apostles of Christ"* (II Cor. 11:13).

Much of this flows out of a large Television Network which goes under the guise of *"Christian,"* but in reality, is doing the Work of God greater harm, than anything else in the world at this particular time. It is Satan's masterstroke. Untold millions of dollars pour into this *"angel of light,"* with people thinking they are giving to the Work of God, when they are actually supporting the work of Satan. And the tragedy of it is, it's not even a very good *"angel of light!"*

Paul in writing to the Corinthians, and about this very subject, and I continue to speak of false apostles, said to the Church in that great city, *"Ye suffer fools gladly!"* (II Cor. 11:19). Some of the things the modern Church is supporting, is in fact so obviously wrong, that the only conclusion one can draw is that the Church is in terrible condition. In fact, it presently boasts the very opposite.

The modern Church claims to be bigger than ever and richer than ever. For all practical purposes, that is true; however, a 500 pound man may be big, but he's definitely not healthy.

No! The modern Church mirrors perfectly the Laodicean Church of old. Of this Church, Jesus said:

"I know your works, that you are neither cold nor hot: I would that you were cold or hot.

"So then because you are lukewarm, and neither cold not hot, I will spew you out of My mouth.

"Because you say, I am rich, and increased with goods, and have need of nothing; and you know not that you are wretched, and miserable, and poor, and blind, and naked" (Rev. 3:15-17).

What an indictment!

All of the modern spectacle is because of the Church following that which is not of God, which means it's not been called of God. Let me ask this question:

Do you the Reader, think that the Judaizers, or as Paul labeled them *"false apostles,"* were called of God? Of course they weren't! However, many of the people in the respective Churches built by Paul, thought they were.

WHAT DOES IT MEAN TO BE CALLED OF GOD?

It means that God has designated a person to fill a certain role, whether *"Apostle, Prophet, Evangelist, Pastor or Teacher"* (Eph. 4:11). He then gives them the Holy Spirit to fill that role, or I should say, He makes the Holy Spirit available. That's the reason it is said, *"And, being assembled together with them, commanded them that they should not depart from Jerusalem, but wait for the Promise of the Father, which, saith He, ye have heard of Me.*

"For John truly baptized with water; but ye shall be baptized with the Holy Spirit not many days hence" (Acts 1:4-5).

First of all, there must be a distinct Call from God, and to be sure, the individual will definitely know if God has called him or her. If they have to ask, they aren't called!

If perchance, the individual has not yet been baptized with the Holy Spirit, which we teach is always accompanied by the speaking with other Tongues, as I have just quoted, that person is commanded to be filled with the Spirit. To be sure, this is not optional, and for the following reasons:

First of all, it is impossible to get anything done for God, without the Holy Spirit working through us. In fact, He has to do everything as far as leading, guidance, direction, and empowerment are concerned.

As well, when the Call comes to an individual, the Scripture plainly says, *"the gifts and calling of God are without repentance"* (Rom. 11:29). In other words, that Call is never rescinded. The individual may fail God, may not follow the Lord as he or she should, but the Call remains.

As it regards those who are truly Called of God, the Scripture plainly says, *"Touch not My anointed, and do My Prophets no harm"* (Ps. 105:15).

Can one who is truly Called of God go wrong?

Of course they can! However, if they are truly wrong, and it is obvious that this is so from the Scriptures, then they should not be followed; nevertheless, that should be the limit of your activity. You must not lift a hand against that individual or try to hurt them in any manner. If they need chastisement, God will perform the act, and not you. In fact, God has not given any Christian the liberty to chastise another Christian. That prerogative lies within the domain of God altogether, and never of man (Rom. 12:18-21). While God may use the unsaved at times to carry out such a task, they will always do so unwittingly. But let it ever be understood, that God never uses Christians to punish other Christians.

AN UNSCRIPTURAL IDEA

The modern Church has the idea, that men elected by popular ballot to Church offices which are administrative only, and definitely not spiritual, which means they as well have no spiritual authority, that these men have the right to punish other Preachers, etc. There's nothing in the Word of God that even remotely sanctions such a thing. In fact, it totally militates against such action.

If sin is involved, the Scriptures are very clear on the subject:

If an individual will not repent, and it's not difficult at all to detect true repentance, then the individual is to be excommunicated from the Church (I Cor. Chpt. 5). However, even then, no further steps are to be taken, with prayer continued to be offered for the Brother or Sister, that they hopefully will repent and come back to God.

If the individual shows a spirit of repentance, that person is to be shown why they went wrong, which refers to a departure from the Cross, and which means a dependence on self (Gal. 6:1), and immediately restored

in the Church (II Cor. Chpt. 2). That is the Biblical way!

No punishment is allowed, simply because Jesus took our punishment at the Cross. If we try to add more punishment, we are in effect saying that Jesus didn't suffer enough, and we have to add more suffering to that which He has already endured. I am certain that one can see the utter fallacy of such action.

As well, there's no such thing as probation in the Bible. Isn't it tragic!

If Simon Peter had lived presently, considering his denial of Christ, he would have been put on probation for at least two years, which means that he would not have preached the inaugural Message on the Day of Pentecost, or much of anything else for that matter. But did the Lord do that to him?

Of course, we all know the answer to that question. He was restored immediately, even as he should have been. The point I'm attempting to make in all of this is:

The Call of God on an individual's life, and that Call incidentally will be obvious, is a very high and holy thing. As stated, irrespective of what happens, that Call is never rescinded by the Lord. And woe be unto the individuals who lay their hands negatively on such a person. To be sure, concerning His Prophets, and those whom He has called, God said exactly what He meant, and meant exactly what He said. Don't do them any harm! Anyone who does such a thing, and that goes for entire Denominations, will find themselves on the angry side of God, incidentally, a side on which no one wants to be. And to be sure, anyone who helps the individual who is truly Called of God will obviously be blessed by the Lord.

A BIBLICAL EXAMPLE

As all know, David miserably failed the Lord as it regards Bathsheba and her husband, Uriah.

At an opportune time, sensing that David was very weakened, his own son, Absalom, rose up against him, drawing away much of Israel, and even many of David's close advisors.

But the Scripture carefully delineates those who helped David, among them, one by the name of Barzillai.

The Scripture says that when David was fleeing Jerusalem, and it was not known whether he would survive or not, that *"Barzillai"* plus others, *"brought beds, and basins, and earthen vessels, and wheat, and barley, and flour, and parched corn, and beans, and lentils, and parched pulse,*

"And honey, and butter, and sheep, and cheese of kine, for David, and for the people that were with him, to eat: for they said, 'The people are hungry, and weary, and thirsty, in the wilderness'" (II Sam. 17:27-29).

The Holy Spirit was very careful to name the individuals, and even that which they gave to David, which to be sure, was precious in the sight of God.

As well, when David had put down the uprising, Barzillai is mentioned again (II Sam. 19:31-36).

It should be well understood, that God in no way condoned David's great sin, and as well, he paid dearly! But the chastisement would come from the Lord, and not from man. Those who lifted hands against him did not fare very well, even as they never do, while those who blessed and helped David, even at this crucial time, were greatly honored by the Lord.

I AM CALLED OF GOD

I realize that my heading is a bold statement; however, it is the Truth, and I would be wrong not to state the fact. My Calling, even as Paul, is *"not of men, neither by man, but by Jesus Christ, and God the Father, Who raised Him from the dead"* (Gal. 1:1).

Paul said this, and said it strongly, because some in the Early Church were denying his Call. As well, many have denied my Call; nevertheless, that in no way alters the fact of what God has called me to do. And I also say with Paul:

"For I am the least of the Apostles, that am not meet to be called an Apostle, because I persecuted (failed) *the Church of God.*

"But by the Grace of God I am what I am: and His Grace which was bestowed upon me was not in vain; but I labored more abundantly than they all: yet not I, but the Grace of God which was with me" (I Cor. 15:9-10).

In 1982 (if I remember the year correctly), the Lord spoke to my heart and told me, *"Your own will turn against you."* Little did I then realize the far reaching effects of that

NOTES

statement. And to be sure, I'm glad that I then did not know.

At that time, we had the largest Christian Television audience in the world, by far. The Lord was helping us to see hundreds of thousands brought to a saving knowledge of Jesus Christ, and I exaggerate not! Nevertheless, that which the Lord said would happen, happened exactly as He said. I realize that the Church world thinks that it was because of the very untoward things which happened; however, that was not the case at all:

It was what I preached, and as well, the Anointing of the Holy Spirit on what I preached, which caused the animosity.

But in the early Spring of 1992, the Lord also spoke to my heart, saying, *"Behold, all they that were incensed against thee shall be ashamed and confounded"* (Isa. 41:11).

As the first came to pass, I believe this will come to pass as well!

Beginning in 1996, with the greater thrust coming in 1997, and continuing unto this hour, the Lord in answer to soul-searching prayer, incidentally, the seeking of His face which lasted for over five years, began to give me a Revelation of the Cross. To be sure, the Cross is not new, actually being the very Foundation of the Church; however, the Church has drifted so far away from the Cross in the last several decades, that anymore it hardly knows its past, its present, or its future. This *"Word"* has been so revolutionary, that it has dramatically and gloriously changed my life. That for which I had so long sought the Master, He gloriously and wondrously gave, and in such an abundant way that it defies all description.

He took me straight to the Word of God, first of all to the great Sixth Chapter of Romans, and then to the Seventh and Eighth Chapters. Romans Chapter 6, which incidentally I had read any number of times previously, I learned, is the great Emancipation Proclamation of the Child of God.

To be brief, the Lord showed me that every answer that I sought, every question that I asked, every solution for which I reached, all and without exception, are found in the Cross. As the Cross is the answer for the unsaved, it is the answer as well for the Christian.

All along, I had known that the Cross and the Cross alone was the answer for the unsaved. I preached it strongly, believing it with all of my heart, which saw one of the greatest harvest of souls, possibly in the history of Evangelism. However, I didn't understand the Cross as it pertains to the Christian experience. I didn't know that the Cross plays just as much a part in our everyday walk before God, as it did in our initial Salvation experience.

I learned that my Faith was to rest in the Cross at all times, in other words, that the Cross must ever be the object of my Faith.

And then the Lord taught me the manner in which the Holy Spirit works. He showed me that He works exclusively within the parameters of the Finished Work of Christ. In other words, what Jesus did at the Cross, is of such significance, that the Holy Spirit demands that we have Faith in that great Sacrifice, or else He will not function on our behalf, at least to the degree which He can. That being the case, the Christian is going to live a life of spiritual failure. But with His power, the Christian can have total and complete victory, over the world, the flesh, and the Devil. But the Christian must realize, that all of this comes through what Jesus did at the Cross and in His Resurrection.

WHAT I BELIEVE THE LORD IS ABOUT TO DO

In fact, I believe that He has already begun the great work of which I am about to mention.

This great Revelation which has been given unto me, was definitely for me, but not only for me. It is meant to be given to the entirety of the Church, which we immediately have set out to do.

That's at least one of the reasons I plead with you the Reader, to give these Commentaries to Preachers of your acquaintance. The tragedy is, most Preachers don't know the great victory of the Cross, any more than those who sit under them. In fact, the reason that the Laity doesn't understand the Cross is because the Preachers don't understand the Cross. If they can see this in the Scriptures, then they can greatly influence others, as would be obvious.

We are now beginning to receive letters from Preachers, for which we are so thankful,

NOTES

telling us how that the Lord has opened their eyes as it regards the Message of the Cross. Churches are experiencing revival because of this Message, which in fact, is the only way that true Revival can actually come.

Revival actually means, that the Church is brought back to the foot of the Cross. Concerning the Reformation, Martin Luther said, *"According to one's view of the Cross, according to that view will they judge the Reformation,"* or words to that effect!

As well, the Lord has opened to us once again the privilege of airing our Program, *"A Study In The Word,"* on a daily basis over nationwide Television. He has instructed me to teach exclusively on the Cross, even as we preach about the Cross on our weekly, Evangelistic Telecast.

Also, the Lord has instructed me to apply for F.M. Radio frequencies from the F.C.C. in Washington, respecting translator stations, which we have already begun to do. Actually, even as I dictate these notes (June, 2000), we have over 250 before the F.C.C., with nearly 100 already granted, and with some 17 already constructed. Actually by the end of 2000, we should have well over 100 on the air. It is possible that we'll erect as many as 2,000 of these Stations.

The Gospel is aired 24 hours a day on these Stations, all coming from Family Worship Center, in Baton Rouge, Louisiana. Along with the music and the worship, and of course, the Preaching of the Gospel, some six hours a day, seven days a week, are dedicated to *"preaching the Cross"* (I Cor. 1:18, 21, 23).

The results have been, and are, absolutely astounding, for which we give the Lord all the praise and all the glory. I believe that He's going to help us, to take this Message of the Cross to the entirety of the Church world, where it is so desperately needed. For a long time, I literally grieved, thinking *"Lord, they won't accept it from me"*; however, I didn't choose this Calling, but the Lord chose me. And as well, the Church doesn't have a choice as it regards the Messenger. They have to accept the one sent by the Lord!

AARON

The phrase, *"As was Aaron,"* refers as stated, to the very first High Priest, which means, that as far as this office was concerned he was the first Mediator between God and men, which means that he was a type of Christ. Aaron was from the Tribe of Levi, from which all Priests would come. However, these Priests and especially the High priests, all and without exception, would point to the Great High Priest Who was to come, namely the Lord Jesus Christ, which Paul is describing here. When Jesus came, the entirety of the Mosaic system came to an end, and for all the obvious reasons. Why is the symbolism needed, when the reality is present?

Under the old Mosaic system, which was merely a guardian unto the time of Christ (Gal. 3:24), access to God was very limited. Only the High Priest could go into the Holy of Holies, and then only once a year, at which time he must take blood to offer upon the Mercy Seat. None of the other Priests could come into this Most Holy Place. They could come no further than the Veil.

The rank and file of Israel, and we speak now of men only, could only come to the *"Court of Israel,"* which was the closest to the Brazen Altar, where the Sacrifices were offered.

The women did not even have access to that, but were rather commanded to remain in the *"Court of Women,"* which was behind the Court of Israel at the Temple enclosure.

Back further than all, was the *"Court of Gentiles,"* which was as close as Gentiles could come, even as the name implies. God dwelt in the Holy of Holies, between the Mercy Seat and the Cherubim, which was on top of the Ark of the Covenant.

However, when Jesus came, offering up Himself on the Cross as a Perfect Sacrifice, in order to atone for the sins of all humanity, this opened the door for all to come. Paul plainly said:

"For ye are all (both Jews and Gentiles) *the Children of God by Faith in Christ Jesus.*

"For as many of you as have been baptized into Christ (into His death by Faith — Rom. 6:3) *have put on Christ.*

"There is neither Jew nor Greek, there is neither bond nor free, there is neither male nor female: for ye are all one in Christ Jesus" (Gal. 3:26-28).

With Christ having opened up the way, Paul also says, *"Let us therefore come boldly unto*

the Throne of Grace (the Holy of Holies in Heaven), *that we may obtain Mercy, and find Grace to help in time of need"* (Heb. 4:16).

ACCESS IS ONLY BY THE CRUCIFIED CHRIST

There is one requirement to this unlimited access. We not only must believe in Jesus, accepting Him as our Lord and Saviour, but as well, we must understand that all of this was made possible by what Jesus did at the Cross. That's at least one of the reasons that Paul also said, *"But God forbid that I should glory, save in the Cross of our Lord Jesus Christ"* (Gal. 6:14).

As it regards this access, the Holy Spirit through the Apostle said, *"But now in Christ Jesus ye who sometimes were far off* (that speaks of Gentiles) *are made nigh by the Blood of Christ* (by what Christ did at the Cross on our behalf)" (Eph. 2:13).

He then said, *"And that He might reconcile both unto God in one body by the Cross, having slain the enmity thereby* (meaning that the sin debt was removed, at least for all who would believe)" (Eph. 2:16).

And then last of all, he said, *"For through Him* (Christ and what He did at the Cross) *we both* (Jews and Gentiles) *have access by one Spirit unto the Father"* (Eph. 2:18).

The idea is, that if the Believer doesn't come to the Father, at all times understanding that such access is made possible by what Jesus did at the Cross, the Holy Spirit will bar the way, so to speak.

Oh dear Reader, can you not sense the Presence of God even as we make these statements! Isn't it all so clear as to what the Cross has done! That's the reason that the Cross is the centrality of the Gospel. It is the intersection for all things, the foundation for all Faith, the repository of all Doctrine. Whatever is not built on this foundation, which is the Rock, Who is Christ Jesus, of necessity must be building on the sand, which ultimately will be swept away (Mat. 7:24-27).

The tragedy is, much of the modern Church world is trying to obtain access by means other than the Cross. Such cannot be done! This means that all in the so-called Faith camp, who denigrate the Cross, as many of them do, can have no access to God, despite their claims. This means that the Modernists who place no value on the Sacrifice of Christ, have no access to God. This means that those who advocate humanistic psychology have no access to God. In fact, anyone who places Faith in anything, irrespective as to what it might be, or how good it may seem to be on the surface, other than *"Jesus Christ and Him Crucified"* has no access to God. All access is strictly limited, to those who place their full trust and confidence in Christ, and what He did at the Cross, on our behalf.

If we do not understand Christianity in that fashion, then we do not understand Christianity! If we do not understand the Bible in that fashion, then we do not understand the Bible! God has access to us only through the Cross of Christ, and to be sure, we have access to God only through the Cross of Christ.

(5) "SO ALSO CHRIST GLORIFIED NOT HIMSELF TO BE MADE AN HIGH PRIEST; BUT HE THAT SAID UNTO HIM, THOU ART MY SON, TO DAY HAVE I BEGOTTEN THEE."

The exegesis is:

1. In keeping with the demeanor of Christ as a human being, as well as God, and giving Himself over completely to the Will of the Father, Christ didn't take this honor of High Priest of His Own volition, but was appointed such by the Father.

2. The Call to Priesthood was based upon the fact that the Messiah was God's Son.

3. He was begotten by God for this very purpose, which was one of the reasons for the Incarnation.

THE FATHER GLORIFIED CHRIST

The phrase, *"So also Christ glorifying not Himself to be made an High Priest,"* proclaims the fact that this was no personal ambition on the Messiah's part that resulted in His becoming a High Priest, but rather the fact that God called Him to that position (Wuest).

Again, at least one of the reasons that Paul may have made this statement in this fashion is because of the degeneration of this Office in Israel's history. As stated, it was now bought and sold like merchandise; consequently, the Apostle is saying to the Christian

NOTES

Jews, *"Do you want to turn your back on the Great High Priest, the Lord Jesus Christ, in favor of these scoundrels who have purchased this Office, by bowing to Rome?"* It is the same presently:

Why would the modern Church forsake Christ, to Whom we can go at anytime, and Whoever lives to make intercession for us, in favor of humanistic psychology? There is no help other than Christ! In fact, there are only two reasons that one would do such a thing:

1. Ignorance of the Word: If the Christian doesn't understand the great part that the Cross plays in our everyday living, that Christian is going to live a life of spiritual failure. No matter how hard he tries otherwise, the end result will be the same, a lack of overcoming power.

2. Unbelief: I am persuaded that millions presently, and I speak of the Church, simply do not believe that what Jesus did at the Cross is the answer to hurting humanity. Not believing that, they resort to humanistic structures, which includes the psychological way.

A few days ago, someone sent me a clipping from one major newspaper. The writer had written about particular Churches, who were advocating some particular type circles, which were about 50 feet in diameter, with particular lines drawn in these circles. People were being urged to come and walk the different patterns of these circles, doing so slowly, even stopping at particular designated places to mediate, which was supposed to bring them peace and serenity.

Actually, this stupidity comes from ancient, cultic mysticism, which means that it was originated by demon spirits. Incidentally, whether the practitioners know it or not, this foolishness comes under the heading of parapsychology.

All of this would be bad enough, but to consider the fact that Churches are promoting this stupidity, tells us how far removed such Churches are from Christ.

MY SON

The phrase, *"But He that said unto Him, Thou art My Son, today have I begotten Thee,"* refers to two things:

1. The Priesthood of Christ was planned by God from the very beginning.

2. The phrase, *"Today have I begotten Thee,"* refers to the Incarnation, i.e., *"when Jesus was conceived in the womb of Mary by the Holy Spirit"* (Mat. 1:18), but was instituted in the Mind of God from before the foundation of the world (I Pet. 1:18-20). Among all the things that Christ would do, the High Priestly Ministry was one of them, meaning it was in the very Plan of God from the beginning.

There are those today who deny utterly Christ's Priestly service on behalf of the Church. They say (to use the exact language of one of the Teachers of this school), *"Christ is not my High Priest; He is a High Priest for Israel only, not for the Church which is His Body."*

They then say, *"All Believers now are part of the High Priest and it will be our place to intercede for Israel by and by."*

What an absurd idea!

Christ, the Head of the Body, the Church, is one aspect in which our Blessed Lord is presented in the Word, but Christ as the High Priest is another aspect altogether. The two differences are according to the following:

1. As members of the Body, which refers to His Body crucified on the Tree, we are seen in a peculiar relationship to Him, and because we are literally baptized into His death (Rom. 6:3), which does not involve the thought of failure or infirmity. In other words, we are perfect in Him, at least in the Mind of God.

2. But as a pilgrim passing through a sinful world, we know that our actual condition is far removed from our actual position; however, we have a Great High Priest ever representing us before God in Heaven and ministering to our needs as they arise from moment to moment. To rob the Christian of this blessed Truth is to leave him poor indeed.

Who is the Christian who thinks he doesn't need the High priestly Work of our Lord? Who does he think he is? as James uses the term (James 4:12).

THE PRIESTHOOD OF THE HEAVENLY SANCTUARY

In Hebrews, Verse 14 of Chapter 4, which subject extends to Verse 39 of Chapter 10, which of course, is the largest part of the Epistle, we have opened up to us a vast system

NOTES

of precious Truth, namely, the Priesthood of the Heavenly Sanctuary, a Priesthood, incidentally, far superior to the Aaronic system, not only because of the more excellent character of the Priest Himself, but because of the infinitely better Sacrifice upon which it rests, which is the offering of the Body of Jesus Christ once for all upon the Cross for our sins.

Properly speaking, Priesthood has to do with the Heavens. Our Blessed Lord was anointed to fulfill three Offices — those of Prophet, Priest, and King. While to a certain extent these Offices overlap, yet generally speaking we may say that He was Prophet on Earth, He is Priest in Heaven, and He will reign as King when He returns in glory.

This, however, is not to deny that He was just as truly the King when He presented Himself to Israel in the days of His flesh. In fact, He was rejected in that special character when they exclaimed, *"We have no king but Caesar,"* thus fulfilling the expression in the parable, *"We will not have this man to reign over us"* (Lk. 19:14).

And so too it was as High Priest that He lifted up His eyes unto Heaven and offered that wonderful intercessory prayer recorded in John Chapter 17. And as High Priest, fulfilling the type of the Great Day of Atonement, He offered Himself to God as a Sacrifice on our behalf.

Then, too, we see Him in the role of Prophet when, on the Isle of Patmos, He appeared to the beloved Apostle and gave him a marvelous Revelation concerning things which must shortly come to pass.

The High Priest of the Old Testament must of necessity be a man, one who could enter into the trials of his Brethren, and so our Lord Jesus has already been demonstrated to be True Man as well as Very God, that He might thus enter practically into all the sorrows and difficulties of His people.

His title *"Son"* speaks of His relationship both with God and man; He is Son of Man and Son of God. The comprehensive dignity of this Sonship is expressed in His atoning death, His Resurrection, and His Ascension; it is verified in His Ordination and appointment by God to the Office of Eternal High Priest.

This means that His Sonship and His Priesthood are interconnected. As the Son of God, in time, He was so saluted at His In-carnation (Ps. 2), and at His Ascension He was saluted as a Priest forever (Ps. 110:4).

(6) "AS HE SAITH ALSO IN ANOTHER PLACE, THOU ART A PRIEST FOR EVER AFTER THE ORDER OF MELCHISEDEC."

The structure is:

1. Paul, as is his custom, continues to use the Old Testament as the ground on which he bases his Doctrine.

2. The Priesthood of Christ is forever.

3. The Priesthood of Christ falls into the line of the Priesthood of Melchisedec, who was king of Jerusalem during the time of Abraham. Abraham paid tithes to this man, meaning that he was greater than Abraham, and because he was a type of Christ. Being a Canaanite which he was, and which he was a type of Christ, made the Priesthood of Christ applicable to both Gentiles and Jews. Jesus was a Jew, so He satisfied that requirement, and with Melchisedec as a Gentile, that re-quirement was satisfied also, making Jesus as High Priest, accessible to all!

A PRIEST FOREVER

The phrase, *"As He saith also in another place, Thou art a Priest forever,"* is taken from Psalms 110:4, and speaks of Christ. The Fourth Verse of this particular Psalm, is the kernel of the Psalm, and supplies the theme for a large portion of this Epistle, especially Chapter 7. As the Promise of II Samuel, Chapter 7 was the prelude to the Revelation of the Second Psalm, the Divine declaration recorded in Exodus 19:6 may have prepared the way for the Promise of Psalms 110:4. David to whom the Promise was given by the Lord, as promised in II Samuel, Chapter 7, was a type as should be obvious, of the Son of David; which Israel, had she been faith-ful, would have remained the representa-tives of all nations before God, as they will yet do in the coming Kingdom Age, headed up by Christ, Who will not only be Prophet and King, but will also continue to be the High Priest.

Two conditions are first laid down regard-ing a Priest:

1. He must be a man, even as we've al-ready stated.

2. He must be appointed by God.

The argument of this section shows that Christ satisfied these two conditions. As man, Christ did not appoint Himself High Priest. His Sonship and His Priesthood as stated, are interconnected. As the Son of God, in time, He was so saluted at His Incarnation (Ps. 2), and at His Ascension He was saluted as a Priest forever (Ps. 110); for He could not be a Priest on Earth, at least He will not be, until the coming Kingdom Age.

CHRIST THE PRIEST

When Paul used the term *"Thou art a Priest forever,"* this was a powerful way of bringing out certain aspects of Christ's sav-ing work for men. All that a Priest does in offering sacrifice for men Christ has done and does. But whereas they did such only sym-bolically, He really effected Atonement.

"Forever" is another contrast, as it regards Christ. Other Priests had their day and have passed away. Not Christ! His Priesthood abides, and will do so forever. He has no suc-cessor, a fact which will be brought out later.

The First Chapter of this Epistle proclaims the Lord's appointment of Christ to His Kingly Office as *"Son"*; now Paul shows that this Kingly Office carries with it, also by Di-vine appointment, an eternal Priesthood.

Christ's entry into this Kingly Priesthood is best conceived as inaugurated by His Resur-rection, after accomplishment of human obe-dience, whereby He fitted Himself for Priest-hood. Before this He was the destined High Priest, but not yet the *"perfect"* High Priest, *"ever living to make intercession for us."*

It is not during His life on Earth, but after His Exaltation, that He is spoken of as the High Priest of mankind. In His sufferings and death He was consecrated to His eternal Office. This appears from Verses 9 and 10, and also from Psalm 110, quoted in this Verse, where the Priesthood after the order of Melchizedek and the Exaltation to the right hand of God are regarded together. In fact, the application of Christ to the text, *"This day have I begotten Thee,"* points to this.

THE COMBINING OF THE KINGLY AND PRIESTLY OFFICES

When the Holy Spirit had David to pen Psalm 110 it was much more than a typical prophecy. The Holy Spirit through David had a distinct view of One far greater than David, actually of the Son to come, Whom he calls his *"Lord."*

Even though David organized and controlled the Priesthood and the services of the Sanctuary, though both he and Solomon took a prominent part in solemn acts of worship, yet neither they nor any other king assumed the Priestly office, which, in its essential functions, was scrupulously confined to the sons of Aaron. In fact, the Judgment on Uzziah (II Chron. 26:16-22) is a notable evidence of the importance attached to this principle. Yet this Sixth Verse of this Fifth Chapter of Hebrews, assigns a true Priesthood to the future King. For Melchizedek, as he appears in Genesis, is evidently a true Priest, though prior to the Aaronic Priesthood, uniting in himself, according to the system of the Patriarchal age, the royalty and the Priesthood of his race: as a true Priest, he blessed Abraham, and received tithes from him.

But of him, historically and symbolically, we will take up more fully in Chapter 7.

Enough here to observe that in Psalm 110 a true and everlasting Priesthood is assigned to the Son in union with His exalted royalty at the Lord's right hand, and this by Divine appointment, and even confirmed by the Lord's oath as given in Verse 4 of this Fifth Chapter of Hebrews.

THE ORDER OF MELCHISEDEC

The phrase, *"After the order of Melchisedec,"* continues from Psalm 110, and is the distinguishing characteristic of this order of Priesthood, and proclaims it as an eternal one.

The Hebrew Christians would still be curious about the Priesthood of Christ. Indeed, Jesus met the qualifications for the High Priesthood; He met them perfectly. His qualifications were superior in every way to that of any Priest who had ever come before. But one barrier remained:

The fact was that Jesus came from the wrong Tribe; He came from the Tribe of Judah and the Priest had to be from the Tribe of Levi, and in fact, the High Priest must be descended from Aaron. Paul now addresses this.

The Priesthood of Jesus was a Priesthood *"after the order of Melchisedec,"* not after the

order of Aaron. Messianic prophecy, even as Psalm 110 proclaims, had pointed to the Priesthood of the Messiah, but it had declared explicitly that the Messiah's Priesthood would be similar to that of Melchisedec and not that of Aaron.

There are some who claim that the word *"order"* should have been translated, *"after the same kind,"* as it regards Melchizedek. They say there was no succession of Priests from Melchizedek and thus no *"order."* Jesus, therefore, was Priest of this kind, not like Aaron and his successors.

That definitely is correct; however, if the word *"order"* is used in the sense of *"kind"* in which it actually is used here, then the translation is correct.

(7) "WHO IN THE DAYS OF HIS FLESH, WHEN HE HAD OFFERED UP PRAYERS AND SUPPLICATIONS WITH STRONG CRYING AND TEARS UNTO HIM THAT WAS ABLE TO SAVE HIM FROM DEATH, AND WAS HEARD IN THAT HE FEARED;"

The exegesis is:

1. *"The days of His flesh,"* refers to His Incarnation, actually the approximate 33 and one half years of His earthly life, and more particularly, the last three and a half years, which constituted His public Ministry.

2. The prayer life of Christ, in which He submitted everything to the Father, seeking only the Father's Will, presents itself as an example to us. What about our prayer life?

3. He knew He would die on the Cross, for that was the very reason He came, and His prayer was for Resurrection. We must understand, that even though Christ was Very God, He was also Very Man, of which the latter constituted totally His earthly walk. In other words, even though never ceasing to be God, He did nothing as God, but all things strictly as man, but man filled with the Holy Spirit.

4. He was heard by His Heavenly Father, and in fact, was always heard by His Heavenly Father.

5. The *"fear"* mentioned here is not at all connected with His Deity as should be obvious, but altogether to His manhood. As stated, He was total man, and as such, experienced fear, at times even as we do, which meant that He took those particular things

causing fear, always to the Father. Again, this should be a graphic example for us.

THE DAYS OF HIS FLESH

The phrase, *"Who in the days of His flesh,"* proclaims the Incarnation, God becoming man, *"the Man Christ Jesus"* (I Tim. 2:5), which was necessary, in order that man might be redeemed. Jesus must come as the *"Last Adam"* (I Cor. 15:45), to undo what the first Adam had done. As a Man, Christ Jesus must keep the Law of Moses perfectly, and as well must offer up Himself as a perfect Sacrifice on the Cross, thereby taking the curse of the broken Law upon Himself, which we rightly deserved, which Sacrifice God would accept, and which Sacrifice alone God would accept!

In all of this, Christ is regarded, not as executing His Priestly Office, but as being prepared and consecrated for it. His Eternal Priesthood, as stated, is conceived as entered on after the human experience which is the subject of these Verses.

In all of this, Paul points out Jesus' oneness with mankind. In realistic language he brings out the genuineness of His humanity.

By the use of the word *"flesh,"* he speaks here of man's ability, man's strength, etc., which in fact, are extremely small, at least as it compares with God, and is given here in this fashion to draw attention to the weakness that characterizes human life.

In fact, Paul uses the word *"flesh"* constantly in his writings, to denote man's helplessness as it regards the spirit world. This means, that if man, even redeemed man, attempts to overcome the world, the flesh, and the Devil, by his own means alone, which means without the Holy Spirit, and which constitutes *"the flesh,"* he will surely fail. It must ever be understood, that if Jesus had to have the Holy Spirit to live the life He must live, where does that leave us? The Truth is, as Believers, we must rely totally and completely upon the Holy Spirit in order for the things of God to be carried out within our hearts and lives. He does this, and will only do this, predicated on our Faith in the Cross, which made possible the Spirit's work within our lives (Rom. 8:1-2).

In fact, in Verses 7 through 10, the Spirit emphasizes the reality of His Manhood and

His participation in all the sinless experiences of His people. *"In the days of His flesh,"* when He was here on Earth in human condition, He trod the path of Faith and took the place of dependence on the Father, *"offering up prayers and supplications,"* accompanied by *"strong crying and tears, unto Him Who was able to save Him out of death"* (Ironside).

THE MAN

Jesus Christ was a Man among men, and it was because He was a Man that He could fully and perfectly understand the needs of men; He was *"in all things . . . made like unto His Brethren"* (Heb. 2:17).

"The days of His flesh" does not mean or imply that His Manhood was terminated with His Exaltation to the right hand of God. The expression serves to emphasize that this was a period of humiliation and complete identification with man during which time He was exposed to all the experiences that man must endure. He is still and will ever be the God-Man; He is our Representative in the Godhead. At this moment, our Lord Jesus Christ is functioning as High Priest in all our temptations, heartaches, sorrows, and failures.

In fact, the experiences of Jesus of Nazareth are recorded in the four Gospels. He was not, by some strange set of circumstances, being also Son of God, above or exempt from the trials that befall mankind. The Priest must be one with men; if Christ were to be the Perfect High Priest, which He definitely was, then He had to pass through man's experiences in order to be sympathetic.

The superiority of His qualifications for the Priesthood is seen in this; He is better qualified for the Priesthood in that He is Man and God, and because He endured the experiences of men to the fullest — even tasting death for every man. Jesus was One with man as Priest and Sacrifice. Consequently, He has the ability to bear with people without being irritated or annoyed, for He is merciful and faithful. His attitude, in fact, toward men, is one of love, compassion, and understanding (Fjordbak).

THE PRAYER LIFE OF CHRIST

The phrase, *"When He had offered up prayers and supplications with strong crying and tears unto Him,"* presents the prayer life of the Master.

It was customary for Jesus to spend long hours in prayer, often spending an entire night in prayer. His prayer life, in fact, was so impressive, that His Disciples desired that He should teach them how to pray.

Actually, the extent of His humiliation is seen in the strength of His prayers. His praying expresses human need and human distress. While He tabernacled among us upon Earth, in the *"days of His flesh,"* His physical body was subject to those things to which all men's bodies are subject — hunger, thirst, weariness, pain, and death.

The *"fears"* speak of the attacks upon His mind, exactly as Satan does with all Believers presently.

However, even though this Passage refers to His prayer life in general, it more specifically refers to Gethsemane and the Cross.

To explain the horrors of Gethsemane and the Cross would do no justice to the matter, considering that Christ entered into a position of suffering, of which we cannot comprehend. I think it would be wiser, if we dwelt on His prayer life, as it concerned not only Gethsemane and the Cross, but rather the entirety of His earthly sojourn (Mat. 5:44; 6:7-9; 9:38; 14:23; 17:21; 19:13; 21:13, 22; 26:36-41, 53; Mk. 1:35; 6:46; 9:29; 11:17, 24; 13:33; 14:32, 38; Lk. 5:16; 6:12, 28; 9:28-29; 10:2; 11:1-2; 18:1, 10; 19:46; 21:36; 22:32, 40-41, 44-46; Jn. 14:16; 16:26; 17:9, 15, 20).

If the Reader would take the time to read all of these Passages just quoted concerning the prayer life of Christ, I think it would be obvious as to the extent of His supplications before the Lord. We must understand, that Christ was the True Man, and as such, portrayed the manner in which man must walk, that is, if he is to have the approval of God.

The greatest hindrance to man is his personal will. That will must be swallowed up in the sweet Will of God. In order to do that, the Face of the Heavenly Father must be sought constantly, in order that His Will may be ascertained in all things. Anything that we do on our own, which means without the leading and guidance of the Holy Spirit, will always bring hurt. Everything that is done by the Holy Spirit within us, portrays the Will

of the Father, and as such, proclaims the *"more abundant life"* (Jn. 10:10).

Jesus epitomized all of this perfectly, in His lifestyle, His character, His way of doing things, His manner and demeanor, etc. Consequently, in that which we commonly refer to as the Lord's Prayer, He epitomized this, by telling us to pray, *"Our Father which art in Heaven, hallowed be Thy Name. Thy Kingdom come. Thy Will be done, on Earth, as it is in Heaven"* (Lk. 11:2).

It is impossible for the Believer to know the Will of God, without having a strong prayer life, and at the same time, thoroughly knowing and understanding the Word of God.

As well, I personally believe, that our constant Faith in the Cross is also demanded. I don't really think that one can really ascertain or know the Will of God without such Faith being expressed. In other words, the Cross must ever be the object of one's Faith, and not other things, irrespective as to how good those other things might be.

The sadness is, most Christians don't pray at all, much less have a qualified prayer life. Again I emphasize, if Jesus had to have a constant prayer life, and He definitely did, then where does that leave us?

DEATH

The phrase, *"That was able to save Him from death,"* presents the prayer for Resurrection.

There are two words in Greek which mean *"from."* The first one *"apo"* means *"from the edge of."* The second one *"ek"* means *"out from within."* This is the one that is used here. The Messiah prayed to be saved out from within death, in other words, to be resurrected. Had Paul used the word *"apo,"* he would have reported our Lord as praying to be saved from dying a physical death, which He did not do. In fact, at no time in His life did He pray that type of prayer. His very purpose for the Incarnation was to die on the Cross in order to redeem humanity.

Furthermore, if He prayed for escape from physical death, His prayer was not answered. Paul says that this prayer spoken of in Hebrews 5:7 was definitely answered, which shows that escape from physical death was not in this wording.

The prayer here was a petition to be saved out from under death. It was a prayer for Resurrection, quite possibly uttered on the Cross. It is believed, and with good reason, that our Lord uttered the entirety of Psalm 22 while hanging on the Cross. In Psalm 22, is His Own description of what took place there.

Verses 1-13 speak of His heart suffering; that due to God turning away His face from Him, outlined in Verses 1-6, and that mankind spurned Him recorded in Verses 7-13. His physical sufferings are described in Verses 14-18. His prayer for Resurrection is recorded in Verses 19-21, and His thanksgiving for answered prayer in Verses 22-31.

Actually, while the four Gospels portray His actions, the Psalms portray His heart. In fact, all of the Psalms, and not only those claimed to be Messianic, portray Christ. So if one desires to investigate the prayer life of Christ, the Psalms perfectly portray that action.

FEAR

The phrase, *"And was heard in that He feared,"* tells us two things:

1. The word *"heard"* proclaims the fact that God heard and answered His prayer.

2. The word for *"fear"* in the Greek text used here is not *"phobos,"* the ordinary word for fear, but *"eulabeia."* The verb of the same root means *"to act cautiously, to beware, to fear."* The picture in the word is that of a cautious taking hold of and a careful and respectful handling. Hence, it speaks of a pious, devout, and circumspect character, Who in prayer, takes into account all things, not only His Own desire, but the Will of the Father (Wuest).

It was not the act of being fearful as we think of such, but in a careful, cautious attitude toward the Will of the Father, in other words, fearing that He would not properly uphold that Will in all things. What a lesson for us!

To be fully equipped as a Priest, it was necessary that He should, during His lifetime on Earth, feel to the utmost possible degree as man the fear and horror of death. It was impossible that He could be exempted from a consciousness of any form or degree of the suffering afflicting men.

Yet He never sinned while feeling the anguish, the terror, the pain, and the horror of death, as well as temptation. He prayed to be saved *"out of death"* and was heard because of His perfect submission to the suffering of that supreme horror. It was answered, as stated, in Resurrection.

One might say that the word *"fear"* describes the attitude of Jesus, as it refers to the Will of God. As a servant He submitted Himself to the Will of His Father in every respect so that all Scripture pertaining to Him might be fulfilled.

He was cautious and circumspect in all that pertained to God's Will; He wanted everything to be done as God had declared. The eternal destiny of man was at stake, and He must not veer from His course in any detail.

TEARS

In this Seventh Verse, we are told as to the manner in which Christ prayed. It was with *"strong crying and tears!"* What a testimony those tears were to the reality of His Manhood! Three times we read of His weeping.

He wept at the grave of Lazarus as He contemplated the awful ravages that death had made, tears of loving sympathy.

He wept as He looked upon Jerusalem and His prophetic soul saw the tribulations through which the devoted city must pass.

And He wept in Gethsemane's garden as His holy soul shrank from drinking the cup of Divine indignation against sin, when He should hang upon the Cross.

(8) "THOUGH HE WERE A SON, YET LEARNED HE OBEDIENCE BY THE THINGS WHICH HE SUFFERED;"

The exposition is:

1. Jesus Christ was and is the Son of God.

2. He did *not* learn to be obedient, for that would have meant that He had been disobedient, which He never was. He rather learned *"obedience,"* which refers to obeying everything the Father desired.

3. He learned this obedience through His sufferings.

THE SON OF GOD

The phrase, *"Though He were a Son,"* stresses Deity, but at the same time, it stresses Christ in the role of *"Son of Man."* This refs to His submission to the Will and Discipline of God which is now unfolded. Such submission does not mean that there was ever at any one time any idea or thought of not submitting. The entire emphasis is in the other direction.

The idea was, that Christ as the Omniscient God knew what obedience was, but He never experienced it until He became incarnate in human flesh. Before His Incarnation, He owed obedience to no one. There was no greater than He to Whom He could have rendered obedience. But now in Incarnation, God the Son became obedient to God the Father. He learned experientially what obedience was.

As a Son it was necessary that as a Priest He should, through suffering, learn obedience — not, as stated, learn to be obedient, for that would prove Him to be a sinner — but being sinless He learned obedience in order to have compassion on the ignorant and to sympathize with the feeble. Thus, being perfected or fully equipped as a Priest, He, because of His eternal Priesthood, endows with eternal Salvation all who believe upon Him.

THE LEARNING OF OBEDIENCE

The phrase, *"Yet learned He obedience,"* doesn't mean that He had to learn to obey. In fact, He said, *"I do always those things that please Him"* (Jn. 8:29).

Vincent says *"He required the special discipline of a severe human experience as a training for His Office as a High Priest Who could be touched with the feeling of human infirmities."* He did not need to be disciplined out of any inclination toward disobedience; but as Alford puts it, *"The special course of submission by which He became perfected as our High Priest was gone through in time, and was a matter of acquirement and practice."* In fact, this is no more strange than His growth in wisdom (Lk. 2:52). Actually, growth in experience was an essential part of His humanity (Wuest).

In the life of Jesus, obedience was an outflow of His love for His Father. It was an expression of His willingness and determination to please God in all things. Likewise, true obedience on our part is an outflow of love to God.

NOTES

Obedience brings submission, patience, and trust. In fact, this great Salvation is given only to *"all them that obey Him"* (Heb. 5:9). It is not as if our obedience and submission are meritorious in any way on our behalf, but rather that our submission and obedience are representative of our Faith in and yieldedness to the Divine Purpose, Plan, and Will of God. Obedience is subjection to the will, authority, and pleasure of another, meaning the Lord.

BEFORE HIS INCARNATION

Before the Saviour became man, He had, Himself, occupied the place of authority — supreme authority. As stated, His seat had been the throne of the universe. It was He Who had issued the commands of creation. All of the Angelic hosts had obeyed Him.

Now He has taken the place of a servant; He has assumed the place of the creature. He became a Man. In this role He must submit further to the Divine Will of God.

He had come to work out a perfect Righteousness for man. He must become the perfect representative of man before God; therefore, He, too, must obey God's Laws, which He did do in every respect. He must magnify and honor the Word of God, and He must voluntarily comply to all that God had said.

If the animals prescribed for Sacrifice were to be without spot and blemish, so must also this One be without spot or blemish.

In fact, when the Incarnate Son of God entered into the experience of obedience, He denied Himself, renounced His Own will, and *"pleased not Himself"* (Rom. 15:3).

He lived the life of discipline. He learned what Divine Righteousness required of Him. He learned the extent of that obedience which God's Holiness demanded.

THE SUFFERING OF CHRIST

The phrase, *"By the things which he suffered,"* refers to the entire course of His earthly sufferings from the day of His birth to the day of death. He passed through each test and trial by means of obedience. In His obedience He demonstrated meekness, lowliness, self-denial, patience, and Faith. As His sufferings increased, so His obedience grew in extent and intensity.

The pressures brought upon Him by the enemy and allowed by God only increased His fervent determination to accomplish the Will of God. The greater the conflict, the higher His submission to Almighty God (Fjordbak).

His suffering doesn't mean that His will had to be subdued, but that from the moment when He assumed humanity, He entered into new experiences, and He Who had always commanded learned from a practical sense what obedience meant.

How carefully the Holy Spirit guards against the least suggestion of defilement in His nature while insisting upon the reality of His humanity. Great indeed is the mystery of Godliness, for He, the Holy One, has been manifested in flesh. And now as the exalted Priest, He enters into all the sorrows of His people; and because He has entered into all these sorrows, He sympathizes with us in all of our infirmities, simply because He has experienced these infirmities as well!

He does not sympathize with our sins, and indeed, we would not wish Him to do so, but He does feel for us in all our weakness and is waiting to supply needed strength for every trial (Ironside).

The sufferings God allows to come into our lives have a purpose, because God controls all things, and we should learn from them. We must remember that God loves us and that we are His Children, but this relationship does not exempt us from suffering, even as it did not exempt Him from suffering.

Though Jesus was truly God's Son in the infinite expression of God's love to the world, God did not spare Him. God allowed His only Begotten Son to be tempted and to suffer. In fact, discipline is the mark of sonship.

The Deity of Jesus might seem to have exempted Him from the necessity of obedience and suffering, but such was not the case. He suffered that He might be the perfect High Priest, interceding for mankind.

EXACTLY WHAT DID CHRIST SUFFER?

First of all, He suffered temptation and onslaught from Satan as no human being has ever suffered. As well, every evidence is, that this continued for the entirety of His life, and especially during the times of His Ministry, letting up only for short periods of time (Lk. 4:13).

Going back to Hebrews 4:15, and the phrase *"yet without sin,"* this has been frequently taken to mean, *"yet without sinning,"* as though it simply implied that He did not fail when exposed to temptation; however, the exact rendering in the Greek is *"sin apart."* That is, His temptations were entirely from without. He was never tempted by inbred sin as we are. He could say, *"The prince of this world cometh and hath nothing in Me."* When we as Believers are tempted from without, we have a traitor within called the sin nature, which ever seeks to open the door of the citadel to the enemy. But it was otherwise with Him.

If we ask, how then could His temptations be as real as ours? Let us remember that when temptation was first presented to Adam and Eve, they were sinless beings, but being merely human, they yielded and plunged the race into ruin and disaster.

"Tempted in all points," means of course that appeals were made to Him by Satan from the three standpoints whereby alone any of us can be tempted:

1. The lust of the flesh:
2. The lust of the eyes:
3. The pride of life:

Tempted on these three points, Eve capitulated completely. *"She saw that the fruit of the tree was good for food"* — the appeal to the lust of the flesh; *"it was pleasant to the eye"* — the appeal to the lust of the eyes; *"and a tree to be desired to make one wise"* — the appeal to the pride of life (Gen. 3:6). She failed on every point.

To our Lord in the wilderness the same appeals were made. *"Make these stones bread"* — an appeal to *"fleshly desire"*; *"he showed Him all the kingdoms of Earth in a moment of time"* — the *"lust of the eyes"*; then in the suggestion that our Lord should cast Himself down from the pinnacle of the Temple to be borne up by Angels before the wondering eyes of the populace, we have the appeal to the *"pride of life."*

However, to Christ it meant much more than that, not stopping there. All of these temptations were efforts as well, to divert Him from the Cross.

His Mission was to come to Earth and die on the Cross, which was the Will of God. To turn the stones to bread, would have been entirely upon His will, and not the Will of God, which would have diverted the purpose altogether.

The kingdoms of the Earth, and the falling down and worshipping Satan, with such kingdoms given to Him, was aimed at diverting Him from securing these kingdoms by the means of the Cross.

To gain acceptance by the religious crowd, by using His power to thrust Himself from the Temple, etc., was as well, a direction other than the Cross.

The Incarnation was Satan's greatest opportunity against Christ, and to be sure, he made the most of that effort. As Deity he had no chance whatsoever against Christ, but as Man, the door was wide open, so to speak!

We could speak of the manner in which His own family turned against Him. We could talk about the religious hierarchy of Israel hating Him with a passion. We could talk about His Own Disciples, little understanding Him. We could speak of Him being made the butt of every cruel joke; the end result of all unbelief; the hatred expressed against His Person. He was truly *"a man of sorrows, acquainted with grief, and we hid as it were our faces from Him"* (Isa. 53:3).

Yes He suffered, and in every way possible, so whatever it is that we might have to suffer, we can be certain that He has faced this thing before us.

(9) "AND BEING MADE PERFECT, HE BECAME THE AUTHOR OF ETERNAL SALVATION UNTO ALL THEM THAT OBEY HIM;"

The structure is:

1. *"Being made perfect,"* refers to being brought to the goal fixed by God. As God He was already Perfect; as Man, He to be sure was Perfect in character and integrity, but in order to be fitted for the Priesthood, He had to learn obedience. As stated, this was done by the things which he suffered.

2. Being made Perfect, He was now ready for the Cross.

3. The death of Christ on the Cross is the cause of our Salvation. It is that from which our Salvation proceeds.

4. The words *"that obey Him"* are descriptive of those who are saved. They do not

present the grounds of our Salvation, but has reference to the fact, that if we truly have made Him the Lord of our lives, we will definitely obey Him.

MADE PERFECT

The phrase, *"And being made perfect,"* refers to all that He did, in order to be a fit Sacrifice which was necessary in order for man to be redeemed.

It included Him becoming man, i.e., *"the Incarnation."* It included Him keeping the Law of Moses perfectly, not failing even one time, or in any one point. It included Him suffering every temptation that Satan could throw His way, and doing so without failure of any nature.

At the end of all this, He was declared Perfect by the Holy Spirit, meaning that He was now ready for Sacrifice, which meant that as a High Priest, He would offer up Himself.

The statement about Jesus being *"made perfect,"* does not mean that He was imperfect and that out of His imperfection He became perfect. There is a perfection that results from having actually suffered; it is different from the perfection that is ready to suffer. *"He became,"* indicates a change of relationship that follows the perfecting.

To use a piece of equipment as an example, the manufacturer might declare it to be *"perfect"*; however, until it is perfectly tested, it has not been proven.

To be sure, God had absolutely no doubt about the outcome of this which Christ endured. He knows the beginning from the end and the end from the beginning. But still, for Him to be perfectly fitted for His role as the High Priest of all mankind, at least those who will believe Him, the suffering was an absolute necessity. Remember, all of this had to be done as a man, which means that everything is thought out differently, looked at differently, and done differently, than Deity, as should be obvious!

THE AUTHOR OF ETERNAL SALVATION

The phrase, *"He became the Author of Eternal Salvation,"* proclaims a perfect Salvation, because He was and is the Perfect Redeemer. Because His Priesthood ever endures, the Salvation He obtains for those who obey Him ever endures. All of this which he did, His sufferings as it regards His life and living, the overcoming of all temptations, everything and all things were but for one purpose, and that was to make Him a fit Sacrifice, that which God could accept. In other words, the Cross was ever before Him. Even though all that He did was totally necessary; still, it was the Cross which was ever intended to be the crowning result. That's where man was cleansed, was delivered, was set free, was given Eternal Salvation. The Cross is where all sin was atoned by His death, which destroyed the legal right of Satan to hold men in captivity, at least those who will believe. To not understand this, is to not understand the Word of God.

"Author" in the Greek is *"aitios,"* and means, *"that in which the cause of anything resides."* Jesus in His Death on the Cross is the cause of our Salvation. And that means in totality and in every way!

When the word *"Salvation"* is used, as far as Redemption is concerned, it refers not only to the initial Salvation experience of being *"born again,"* but as well, it speaks of a life of victory, ultimate Resurrection, and then to come back with Him to rule and reign in what we refer to as the Second Coming (Rev. Chpt. 19). We must not *"minimize"* our Salvation by limiting it to the Born-Again experience, as wonderful as that is. And as well, we must not *"trivialize"* our Salvation, by limiting it to baubles, trinkets, and gadgets. Jesus died for much more than for us to trade our Neon for a Cadillac!

OBEDIENCE

The phrase, *"Unto all them that obey Him,"* does not make obedience the ground of Salvation, as it seems here on the surface, that being Faith (Eph. 2:8-9). The idea is, and as stated, that those who truly know Him as Lord, will certainly desire to obey Him in every respect.

As well it should be said, He is not the Author of Eternal Life to them who obeyed Him once but have since lapsed into disobedience and apostasy; it is to them who are presently obeying Him that He is the Author of Eternal Salvation. Our walk must be continual, a present tense walk of obedient Faith.

Just as the obedience of Christ was required by Almighty God, so the obedience of man is also required by Almighty God; hence, all the conditions of Salvation are to be obeyed in the Name of Jesus Christ, the Lord. To obey fully is to acknowledge and confess that Jesus is Christ and Lord, the Author of Eternal Salvation, and that no one else fits that bill, as no one else can fit that bill.

(10) "CALLED OF GOD AN HIGH PRIEST AFTER THE ORDER OF MELCHISEDEC."

The exegesis is:

1. *"Called"* here, means that He was now saluted by God, as having passed through and completed His earthly discipline.

2. He was saluted as the eternal High Priest.

3. Being after the order of Melchisedec, this means that His Calling, is an eternal Calling, i.e., *"an Eternal Priesthood."*

CALLED OF GOD

The phrase, *"Called of God,"* in this instance, carries a somewhat different meaning than the phrase *"Called of God"* in Verse 4. Verse 4 refers to a work which is beginning, while Verse 10, refers to a work that is completed.

"Called" is the translation of the Greek *"prosagoreuo,"* which means, *"to address or accost by some name, to publicly give a name, to salute, to style."* He was addressed and saluted by God as having finished the course, one might say!

HIGH PRIEST

The phrase, *"An High Priest,"* presents the word *"Priest"* as used in Verse 6, now extended to *"High Priest."* The purport remains the same; or, rather, it is by this change of word that the meaning of Psalms 110:4 is fully expressed.

What is to become His characteristic designation throughout this Epistle is a title not given by men, nor assumed by Himself, but conferred on Him by God the Father. Consequently, this Calling is the highest that any Calling could ever be.

MELCHISEDEC

The phrase, *"After the order of Melchisedec,"* is repeated here from Verse 6 for a purpose.

Any time the Spirit says something, it is by its nature of extreme importance; however, whenever He repeats something, which is always done for emphasis, it is meant without fail to be understood with all solemnity.

In this case, the Holy Spirit through the Apostle is drawing attention to this fact, in order that the Hebrew Christians would understand the Priesthood of Christ. While it was true that He was not of the Tribe of Levi, from which the Jewish Priesthood came; this was done for purpose and reason.

Christ was not to be a Great High Priest merely for the Jews, which would have insinuated such, had He been of the Tribe of Levi, but rather High Priest for all men, both Jew and Gentile. Being after the order of Melchisedec satisfied both demands, simply because Melchisedec preceded Israel as a people, and because the Holy Spirit showed Abraham the meaning of this, hence him paying tithe to Melchisedec (Gen. 14:18-20). As well, the Holy Spirit, as stated, also proclaimed all of this through David, about a thousand years before Christ (Ps. 110:4). So, Paul's contention was based on solid Scriptural Truth!

(11) "OF WHOM WE HAVE MANY THINGS TO SAY, AND HARD TO BE UTTERED, SEEING YE ARE DULL OF HEARING."

The exposition is:

1. The pronoun *"Whom"* does not refer here to Melchisedec, but rather to Christ. The idea is, that there is much yet to be expressed about Christ, which these Hebrew Christians evidently did not know.

2. The Apostle fears that it's going to be hard for many of these individuals to understand what he is saying about Christ.

3. The reason for it being hard for them to understand is because of unbelief, i.e., *"they were dull of hearing."*

MUCH ABOUT CHRIST

The phrase, *"Of Whom we have many things to say,"* refers as stated, not to Melchisedec, even though he will say more about him in Chapter 7, but rather about Christ.

Here we have before us the Apostle Paul, who knew more than anyone in the world about the New Covenant, which was actually

the meaning of the Cross of Christ, and it seems that many of these Hebrew Christians had little interest in what he was saying. The reason as we will momentarily study, was unbelief.

Let it be ever understood, that if one is confused as it regards the great Sacrifice of Christ, then one is going to be confused, basically, about everything else concerning Christ, which includes the Word of God. The Cross, and a failure to properly understand this Finished Work, is the cause of all error, all false doctrine, etc.

And the tragedy is the modern Church, at least as a whole, knows little more about the Cross, than these Hebrew Christians of old. Consequently, it's very easy for Satan to substitute *"another Jesus and another gospel, all promoted by another spirit"* (II Cor. 11:4).

HARD TO BE SAID

The phrase, *"And hard to be uttered,"* was not brought about because the subject was itself inexplicable, or that Paul was incompetent to explain this; his difficulty was in adapting the interpretation to the capacity of his Readers. From this, it is obvious that the Hebrew Christians had regressed in spiritual perception. In fact, this is very easily conceivable.

As through the teaching of Paul, the tie between Christianity and Judaism became more and more broken, there was likely to be a certain reaction among the Jewish Christians, who were very reluctant to go all the way with Christ. They were left, consequently, straddling both sides of the theological fence, with one foot on the foundation of Christ and the other on the foundation of Law, so to speak. Thus inclined, they are more liable to cling the more fondly to their old associations from the fear of losing them altogether, than going all out for Christ.

Jesus had plainly addressed this when He spoke of *"putting a piece of new cloth onto an old garment,"* or *"putting new wine into old bottles"* (Mat. 9:16-17). Both present an unworkable situation.

The old pulls away from the new, thereby renting the garment, and the new wine put in old bottles of skin causes the skin to inflate, and thereby burst. He said that the *"new wine must be put into new bottles, and then both, the wine and the bottles, are preserved."*

There was no reason for the position that many Jewish Christians were taking, considering that the Old Testament was replete with the idea, that the Law of Moses was merely transitorial, always pointing to One Who was to come, namely Christ. Nevertheless, they were having great difficulties accepting Christ totally: Messiah? Yes! but merely One to make the Law stronger, and never to replace the Law. They wanted to hold onto the symbol while they had the reality, with such a stance being spiritually and Scripturally impossible!

When Paul used the words *"hard to be uttered,"* he in effect was addressing all of his Epistles. While it shouldn't have been hard as it regarded the Gentiles, it was hard for some, simply because the minds of some Gentile Christians, had been somewhat subverted by this very Law/Grace issue. As fast as Paul could preach Grace and Faith, false apostles were busily sowing seed of proposed Law-keeping. In other words, they were trying to foster the Law of Moses off on the Gentiles. Had they been successful, it would have completely destroyed the great Message of Grace, thereby destroying the effectiveness of this great Salvation, purchased at such great price by the death of Christ on the Cross. As we should understand, every single error, in some way, always goes back to an attack upon the Cross.

DULL OF HEARING

The phrase, *"Seeing ye are dull of hearing,"* refers to that which is *"slow and sluggish."* It is used of the numbed limbs of a sick lion, and the stupid hopes of the wolf that heard the nurse that threatened to throw the child to the wolves.

These Jewish Christians were slow, sluggish, stupid, and numbed in their apprehension of the teaching of New Testament Truth. This made it difficult to teach them. The difficulty lay not with Paul, but in them.

They had not always been in this condition, as is shown by the word translated *"are."* It means, *"to become."*

These Jewish Christians had at one time a spiritual apprehension of New Testament Truth sufficiently clear that they saw that the

NOTES

New Testament Sacrifice displaced the First Testament Offerings. Paul tells us that also in the words, *"who were once enlightened"* (Heb. 6:4). Consequently, the inability to apprehend and understand was not a natural, inherent, and pardonable weakness, but a culpable incapacity which was the result of past neglect of and a gradual working away from New Testament Truth (Heb. 2:1-3). It was the hardening of the heart against the ministrations of the Holy Spirit (Heb. 3:7-8).

HOW HAD THEY COME TO THIS PLACE?

The first problem began with them lending a listening ear to unsaved Jews, who were ridiculing Christ, etc. Instead of refusing to hear such lies, they not only listened, but continued to listen.

It's impossible for any Christian to entertain such fabricating work of Satan, without being evilly influenced. If the ear is leant to such false doctrine, to be sure, the heart will follow.

The idea of all of this as tendered by Satan is to generate unbelief. If the first leaven of unbelief can be planted, of necessity, leaven will then do its work, and ultimately engulf the whole.

Once a Believer knows the way, and he knows the way simply because it is obvious as to its Scripturality, and it is obvious as to its results, he should then refuse to listen to anything else which contradicts the Word of God. It makes no mind that it may be cleverly presented, as most false doctrine always is. If it's not strictly according to the Word of God, it must not be entertained.

When it is entertained, the spiritual hearing becomes *"dull,"* meaning, that the person no longer hears correctly. Millions have been lost in this manner, and to be sure, the greatest attack, in fact reserved for the end time, has actually already begun (I Tim. 4:1).

(12) "FOR WHEN FOR THE TIME YE OUGHT TO BE TEACHERS, YE HAVE NEED THAT ONE TEACH YOU AGAIN WHICH BE THE FIRST PRINCIPLES OF THE ORACLES OF GOD; AND ARE BECOME SUCH AS HAVE NEED OF MILK, AND NOT OF STRONG MEAT."

The exegesis is:

1. These Jewish Christians had been living for the Lord long enough, that they should by now be teachers of the Word, when in fact they are only students, and not very good students at that!

2. They needed to learn again the *"first principles of the Oracles of God,"* which pertain to the old Law, which refer to what it actually meant. And if they understood the true meaning, they would know that in its entirety it pointed to Christ Who was to come, and in fact, had now come.

3. They were babies in the Word; however, they were not true babies but rather those which were deformed. The terminology used here refers to a child who is 11 or 12 years old, or even older, but has not developed mentally to that age, but rather remains in that sense as a two year old.

SCRIPTURAL IMMATURITY

The phrase, *"For when for the time ye ought to be teachers,"* refers to the fact that they had been saved long enough that they should by now be mature in the Word. Incidentally, this phrase completely shoots down the erroneous claims by some, that these Jews had not really accepted Christ, but were only thinking of doing so. Paul would never refer to unsaved people as lacking in spiritual and scriptural maturity. Such thinking is silly! As is glaringly obvious, these Jews had definitely accepted Christ, had in fact, been living for Him for some time, and according to the words of the Apostle, should now be equipped to teach others, but instead, needed teaching themselves.

Regrettably, the far greater majority of the modern Church falls into the same category. Oh to be sure, it has had much teaching, but most of it has been wrong, leaving Christians presently in possibly the saddest shape that the Church has experienced in several centuries.

In the last several decades, actually going back to the middle of the Twentieth Century, the Church has been taught almost nothing about the Cross of Christ. In fact, these last several decades have majored in *"Faith,"* but due to the fact that it's not been Faith in the Cross of Christ, but something else entirely, it has left the Church in far worse shape than if it had no teaching at all.

Whenever a teaching is unscriptural, it quickly becomes obvious by the fruit that it produces (Mat. 7:15-21).

From this teaching no souls have been saved, no Believers have been Baptized with the Holy Spirit, no people have been truly healed, and no one has been delivered. Now please understand what I have said.

Yes, in the Churches which espouse this doctrine, and they number in the tens of thousands, there have definitely been a few people here and there who have come to Christ, and a few who have been baptized with the Holy Spirit, etc. However, and to be sure, they were not saved or filled with the Spirit, or in fact received anything from the Lord as a result of this teaching, but rather because of hungry hearts. Error cannot produce Truth, and the modern Faith teaching is error pure and simple!

Any teaching which does not anchor itself in the Cross of Christ, which in effect is the culmination of the true Word of God, is error. In fact, the Cross is not really a Doctrine, but rather the foundation of all Doctrine. Christ and what He did on the Cross, is the story of the entirety of the Bible. So for something to be Biblical, it must anchor itself in the Cross of Christ. In fact, the very interpretation or meaning of the New Covenant, which the Holy Spirit gave to us through Paul, is actually the meaning and understanding of the Cross. Please allow me to repeat myself again:

About half the Church world has attempted to preach the Cross without the Holy Spirit, which is impossible, and which has left that segment of Christianity as preaching neither the Cross nor the Spirit. The other half has tried to preach the Holy Spirit without the Cross, and once again, the results are the same, neither the Cross nor the Holy Spirit is being preached. Consequently, the Church has never been in worse condition, at least in the last century.

A MODERN SPECTACLE

Just last night (June 19, 2000), for a few minutes I turned on a so-called Christian Television Network. What I saw could be described as none other than an abomination.

It is bad enough for the non-Pentecostal Church world to ignore the Spirit, and in some cases deny the Spirit, but worse yet, to operate totally in the flesh, and in many cases, by the power of demon spirits, and then call it the Holy Spirit. What I saw was so obviously unscriptural, so obviously wrong, so obviously awful, which incidentally, is typical of that particular Network, that it would be impossible for me to properly describe the situation. But to add insult to injury, the building was packed with people who call themselves Christians, screaming and yelling, offering praise to demon spirits, which they thought was the Lord. They were so spiritually dull, so spiritually inept, so Scripturally illiterate, that sadly, they didn't even know the difference!

Don't misunderstand, Satan can come as an *"angel of light,"* which so closely resembles the Lord, that immature Believers can be fooled (II Cor. 11:13-15). However, what I saw, was not an angel of light, but rather that which was so obviously wrong, that anyone, the saved and the unsaved, would know that it's not right. And yet, and as stated, the place was packed to capacity, cheering on this travesty!

Regrettably, the situation is not going to get better but rather worse. The Church has entered into the last great apostasy, and the departure from the Cross of Christ is the glaring sign that this is already happening. But at the same time, the Lord is going to see to it that the Message of the Cross is proclaimed to such an extent at this time, heralded far and wide, and with such power, that for those who truly love the Lord, they will know, see, and hear, thereby knowing the right way. In other words, the Cross is going to be the dividing line between the True Church and the apostate Church. In fact, it has always been the dividing line, but now it is going to be more pronounced than ever.

THE FIRST PRINCIPLES

The phrase, *"Ye have need that one teach you again which be the first principles of the Oracles of God,"* actually pertains to the Old Testament, and what it really means, instead of the way it was being erroneously taken by these Christian Jews. Some claim that Paul is here speaking of the elementary doctrines of Christ regarding the Salvation experience,

NOTES

etc.; however, we know from the first two Verses of the following Chapter, that Paul is speaking of the Old Testament. In other words, if these Christian Jews had been interpreting the Old Testament correctly, they would have known that it pointed exclusively to Christ, and that in fact, Christ fulfilled all of the precepts of the Old Law, etc.

However, inasmuch as we have mentioned the Old Testament, please allow us to state, that it's absolutely imperative for every Believer to understand the Old Testament, that is if they are to understand the New. In fact, I don't think it's possible for one to understand the New, unless they do understand the Old, which is the foundation of the New. In fact, every single thing that's in the New Covenant, is found somewhere in the Old Testament, which as stated, provides a foundation.

As an example, the Cross of Christ is so obviously proclaimed in the Old Testament, and I speak of the Sacrifices and in effect, the Sacrificial System, which were actually the very heart of God's moving and operation in Old Testament Times. If one properly understands that, one will properly understand the Cross. In fact, every single thing about the old Law, and we speak of the Feast Days, the Sabbath, Circumcision, and the manner of worship, all and without exception, point directly to Christ and what He did at the Cross. The problem was, as it regards Paul's Letter to the Hebrews, these Christian Jews didn't have a proper understanding of the Old Testament.

As well, even as we have already stated at the beginning of commentary on this Epistle, the decision made by James as it regards the Gentiles not being bound by the Law, which was right, should have included the Jews as well (Acts 15:19-20). To teach that the Christian Jews should continue in the Law, which seems to be what James did, had its ultimate result in this problem addressed by Paul, Christian Jews contemplating, with some probably actually having done so, going back into Temple worship and thereby, forsaking Christ. The idea of the Epistle to the Hebrews is, that one, whether Jew or Gentile, couldn't have both the Law and Christ at the same time. One or the other must go!

MILK AND MEAT

The phrase, *"And are become such as have need of milk, and not of strong meat,"* refers to their lack of immaturity. The immaturity had resulted from unbelief in Christ.

In effect, what Paul is saying here is that these Christian Jews were torn between *"works and Faith."* There is no greater hindrance in the pathway of righteous living than attachment to a traditional religion consisting in ordinances. It sets up a barrier between the soul and God. The heart — easily deceived — rests in these religious ceremonies; and the spiritual intelligence is so impaired as to be unable to discern between good Doctrine and evil doctrine. In fact, works of any nature have that tendency.

This is even more deadly when the forms and symbols are of Divine Ordination. In other words, I speak of things which are truly of God, such as Water Baptism, the Lord's Supper, or even prayer for that matter, being turned into works, which so easily can be done. With these Christian Jews of old, it was Temple worship, which had originally been given by God, was of God, etc. But as stated, all of these things had been fulfilled by Christ and were now no more necessary. Actually, they would be extremely detrimental to one, if engaged, and for the simple reason, that it's impossible for one to place Faith in other things, as right as they may have been, or even as right as they presently are, and Christ at the same time. While the present ordinances of which we speak, such as Water Baptism, etc., are definitely of the Lord, and definitely should be engaged; still, there is no Salvation in those things, Salvation being totally in the Finished Work of Christ.

Now the Work of Christ is a Finished Work, or else it isn't. But of course, we know that it is a Finished Work, and that means that nothing must be done that would unfavorably address itself to that Finished Work. Faith must exclusively be in the Sacrifice of Christ as it regards all things pertaining to God, and nothing else!

WHAT DOES PAUL MEAN BY THE WORD *"MILK"*?

When a person first comes to Christ, it is obvious that they know nothing about the

Lord or His Word. Consequently, a teaching and training process must begin. During this time, the Lord most assuredly has patience with us, and for all the obvious reasons.

It's like a newborn baby which has come into the world, with its stomach being unable to take solid food. It has to begin its nourishment with milk, before it graduates to more solid food.

The tragedy is, as Paul uses this metaphor of *"milk,"* is that these Christians were remaining in the babyhood stage. They had definitely been saved, but they had not progressed at all in the deep things of the Cross, rather staying too close to where they got in.

WHAT DID PAUL MEAN BY *"STRONG MEAT"*?

Regrettably, most of the modern Church is still in the *"milk stage,"* and how do I know that?

The *"strong meat"* of which Paul spoke here consists of the Believer learning and thereby understanding all that Christ did for us at the Cross and in His Resurrection. I say *"all,"* when in actuality, it is impossible for one to exhaust the benefits of the Finished Work of Christ. But in learning this, one is on the right road, and will go from Faith to Faith.

I made mention just this morning over our daily Radio Program, that I had learned more about the Holy Spirit, since the Lord began to give me the Revelation on the Cross, than I had known in the balance of my Christian experience put together. In other words, the learning and understanding of the Cross, as the Holy Spirit began to teach this to me through the Word, has taken me to spiritual heights and spiritual depths, such as I have not known previously. As well, and as stated, there is no limit to this, the Cross of Christ actually being inexhaustible (Heb. 13:20). This is what Paul meant by *"strong meat!"*

At this stage, the Reader may desire to ask the following question:

Am I saying that one cannot really know the *"strong meat"* of the Gospel, unless one knows and understands the Cross?

That's exactly what I'm saying! That's the reason I'm also saying that most of the modern Church is still in the *"milk"* stage, simply because I know that most of the modern Church doesn't know very much about the Cross of Christ. The extent of most knowledge as it regards the Finished Work of Christ, is the trust in Christ and the Cross relative to the initial Salvation experience. That's about as far as it goes with most Christians. Anything else that they know and understand about the Cross is mostly in the realm of sentimentality. In other words, the Cross was a terrible thing, and Jesus suffered there greatly, etc.

While all of that is true, most know almost nothing about the benefits of what He did. He died for us, not only to give us Salvation, but as well, that we may walk in victory regarding our Sanctification, and do so constantly. In fact, the only way that the Christian can have victory over sin, in other words, victory over the world, the flesh, and the Devil, is through Faith in the Cross of Christ, which demands an understanding of this great Sacrifice. As I've said over and over again, that's at least one of the reasons, these Commentaries are so very, very important. This great Revelation which the Lord has given me concerning the Cross, which incidentally is not something new, but actually the foundation of the Church, also provides the foundation for all the teaching in these Commentaries.

(13) "FOR EVERY ONE THAT USETH MILK IS UNSKILFUL IN THE WORD OF RIGHTEOUSNESS: FOR HE IS A BABE."

The structure is:

1. These Jewish Christians despite having been saved for quite some time were still on a diet of elementary doctrine. The idea is that they had not learned much at all.

2. They were unskilled in the Word of Righteousness, which refers to the Cross of Christ, even though they were in fact, claiming great skillfulness of the Word. Regrettably, this is usually the case with such people.

3. They were still functioning as a baby Christian, even though they had been saved for quite some time. In other words, their situation was grossly abnormal.

USING MILK

The phrase, *"For everyone that useth milk,"* does not, as stated, in this case, refer

to people who have just been saved, but rather those who have been saved for quite some time, and should have advanced in the Word of the Lord.

The idea here is, that something had come in to hinder, which was the cause of the situation. That which had come in was false doctrine, obviously being propagated by non-Christian Jews, who were moment by moment, denigrating Christ. And again, even that which we have just mentioned, the practice of these Christian Jews in continuing to try to keep the Law, as well as a faithfulness to Temple worship, exacerbated their situation drastically. In fact, they had never given up Temple worship. So, when we speak of going back into Temple worship, we are actually speaking of the fact that these individuals were seriously considering the repudiation of Christ altogether. This is borne out in Chapters 6 and 10, which we will comment on more directly upon arrival at those Passages.

A lack of Spiritual Growth is always caused by something. If things go right, every single Christian will grow in the Lord. So, it's sin, self-will, apathy, or false doctrine, which hinders Spiritual Growth. In the case of the Christian Jews, it was self-will and false doctrine.

UNSKILLFUL IN THE WORD OF RIGHTEOUSNESS

The phrase, *"Is unskillful in the Word of Righteousness,"* refers to the benefits of the Cross, from which Righteousness is derived.

The idea is, these Christian Jews had discounted the Cross of Christ as being of no consequence. In other words, they placed no Faith in that great, Finished Work. While some possibly may have continued to believe in Christ as the Messiah, the greater emphasis of unbelief lay in the fact of the Cross and what it represented. Once again, this is borne out in Chapters 6 and 10.

Righteousness comes by individuals placing their Faith and Trust in Christ, which refers to what He did at the Cross on our behalf. In other words, upon Faith, God awards the believing sinner, a spotless, pure Righteousness, actually, the Righteousness of Christ, all made possible by the Cross.

Jesus kept the Law perfectly, and thereby gained its Righteousness. However, there remained the curse of the broken Law to be addressed, which He did by and through the Sacrifice of Himself (Gal. 1:4).

So, the *"Word of Righteousness"* pertains to that which Jesus did at the Cross on our behalf, and our Faith in that. It is impossible to divorce Righteousness from the Cross, or the Cross from Righteousness.

Man was and is woefully unrighteous, at least within himself. As well, there is no way within himself, that he can change this situation. As such, God cannot accept man and for all the obvious reasons. So, a way had to be brought about, in which a spotless Righteousness could be given to man, and a way in which man could obtain this Righteousness.

Man ever seeks to bring about his own Righteousness by his own good works, etc. Of course, this is Righteousness which God can never accept. And this is the major contention in the great Gospel of Christ.

God contends, even as we've already addressed, that man has no Righteousness, and cannot come by any Righteousness by his own machinations. To alleviate this situation, in effect to redeem mankind, God became man, in effect, becoming the *"Last Adam"* (I Cor. 15:45), to do for us what the first Adam could not do. Incidentally, He is referred to as the *"Last Adam,"* simply because what He did in His Life, Ministry, and Sacrifice, will never need to be repeated, hence Him being the *"Last!"*

THE MINISTRY OF CHRIST AS OUR HIGH PRIEST

As we've said repeatedly, the Ministry of the Priest was to offer up sacrifice for sins. This was his chief purpose and role regarding his office. The High Priest officiated over all the other Priests, demanding that their work of Atonement be carried out to perfection. As well, he was the sole one who could go into the Holy of Holies once a year on the Great Day of Atonement, to offer up Sacrifice for himself and for the entirety of the nation.

So, while the entirety of all that Jesus did was of supreme importance as should be obvious, and played its part in this great process, it must be understood, that His Virgin Birth, His Life, His Ministry and Miracles, in

fact, everything He did, all led up to the grand finale, which was the Cross. This is where the price was paid, the curse of the broken Law satisfied, and where Satan and all his cohorts were totally and completely defeated. Paul plainly said:

"Blotting out the handwriting of ordinances that was against us, which was contrary to us, and took it out of the way, nailing it to His Cross;

"And having spoiled principalities and powers, He made a show of them openly, triumphing over them in it" (Col. 2:14-15).

Satan's legal hold upon humanity is sin. This means that he has a legal right to place man in captivity because of sin; however, when Jesus satisfied the demands of the broken law, which had condemned man, which should be obvious, simply because man could not keep its precepts, Satan's legal hold was broken. The Law of Moses, which in effect was the Righteousness of God, condemned all of mankind, simply because they could not keep its precepts. Law being law, not only portrayed these statutes and precepts, but as well, demanded that they be kept, with a severe penalty attached if they were not kept, which of course, applies to all law.

Man woefully failed to keep the Law, simply because he was incapable of doing so, as a result of the Fall. So the penalty was demanded!

Jesus came, perfectly kept the Law in every respect, doing so on our behalf, thereby gaining its Righteousness, again on our behalf, meaning that Faith in Him, grants us the privilege of Law-keeper instead of Law-breaker, which we actually were. He then went to the Cross to satisfy its penalty, which was death. But being a Perfect Sacrifice, and having atoned for all sin, which He did by His death, death could not hold Him. The wages of sin is death, but if there is no sin, there is no death; consequently, death has lost its power; consequently, Jesus rose from the dead, once again, all for us.

Simple Faith in Him, and what He did, which speaks of the Cross, grants to us a spotless, pure, perfect Righteousness, i.e., *"the Righteousness of Christ,"* and in brief, that is the *"Word of Righteousness."*

Trust in Christ and what He did at the Cross is the only way in which men can become righteous. It is the only way and manner of Salvation. There is no other! And that is what Satan has ever contended.

He tries to insert other ways and means, which of course are false, and he does his greatest damage from inside the Church. He is subtle, slick, cunning, and will propose that which looks to be right, but which isn't. He will seek to add something to Faith. In other words, to get someone to trust in something else other than the Finished Work of Christ. For instance, the Church of Christ people claim that an individual must be baptized in water in order to be saved. Pure and simple, their Faith and Trust are in that ordinance, and not at all in Christ. And to be sure, anyone who places his or her Faith accordingly, is not saved. That goes for trust in anything else as well.

For instance, the Catholic Christ teaches that the Church saves, or in other words, faithfulness to the Church will bring about Salvation, which of course, is a Salvation by works, which God cannot accept. This means that Catholics who trust explicitly in the Catholic system, simply aren't saved. It also means, that if a Catholic truly comes to Christ, which some definitely do, they must then leave out of this erroneous Doctrine.

As well, many of you may weary of me constantly mentioning psychology, but only because you do not know the dangers involved. Psychology claims to hold the answers for the ills and aberrations of mankind, while the Bible makes the same claims. The former is totally from the ingenuity of man, with the latter originating totally with God. The two cannot be mixed.

When the attempt is made to mix the two, even as the modern Church as a whole is doing, the Way of Christ is totally abrogated, irrespective of claims otherwise. Again, the two cannot mix.

This means that the foray of the Church into humanistic psychology, presents itself as a vote of no confidence in the Cross of Christ. Either Jesus paid it all at the Cross, or else, He didn't, and what He did needs to be replaced with something else, or at least what He did needs help. Of course, all of this is utter blasphemy.

The only way that man can be free from sin and all of its results is by Faith and Trust

in Christ and what he did at the Cross on our behalf. There is no help in psychology, or any other of the ways of man. There is help and hope only in the Finished Work of Christ.

WHAT IS RIGHTEOUSNESS?

Righteousness is simply that which is right. But the definition of *"right"* is that which God says it is, and not what man says it is. As stated, man keeps trying to develop his own Righteousness, which God can never accept.

That which is *"right"* pertains to that in which there is absolutely no sin, and we speak of moral perfection in every capacity. This can only be found in Christ, and He can only give it to man, as man exhibits Faith in Christ and what He did at the Cross. Always remember, Christ must never be separated from the Cross, as the Cross must never be separated from Christ. What we mean by that is this:

The Cross is an historical fact pertaining to that which took place in history, and will never need to be repeated; however, what was done there, has continued results, and in fact, results which will never be discontinued. So when we speak of the Cross, we have to understand it in that fashion.

We're not speaking of worshiping some wooden gibbet, or even an historical event. We're speaking of what Christ did there, which makes possible all that we now have in the Lord. It is something like the Emancipation Proclamation instituted by Congress under the administration of Abraham Lincoln. This is something that happened in the past, but it has continued results, guaranteeing the freedom of all people in this country, etc. Likewise with the Cross of Christ!

A BABY

The phrase, *"For he is a babe,"* refers to the individual who does not understand or thereby know all the benefits of what Jesus did at the Cross. Failure to understand the Cross of Christ leaves the Believer in an immature state. In fact, I personally believe that it's impossible for a Christian to grow in the Lord, at least as they should grow in the Lord, without a knowledge of the Cross of Christ. And this is the problem with the modern Church. It knows so little about the Cross, and the irony is, it thinks it knows everything about the Cross.

Knowledge of the Finished Work of Christ is the foundation of every Doctrine in the Bible. In fact, it is the story of the Bible, of God's dealings with man. The Bible points exclusively to the Cross of Christ, making that event the cause and the reason for all of God's dealings with mankind, and mankind's dealings with God.

If the Cross is not understood, the same problem will present itself, as it did with the Christian Jews of Paul's day. Then, the visible Temple was that to which they were turning, while presently, it is humanistic psychology, or the *"money gospel,"* or something else, etc. All of this is the result of improper knowledge of the Cross, or else of unbelief.

From the manner in which Paul addresses this subject, at least as it regards here the Christian Jews of his day, it was both a matter of lack of knowledge and unbelief; however, the lack of knowledge was not because the knowledge was not available, but simply because through neglect they had failed to bring this understanding to themselves, which resulted in unbelief, even as it always does. But let the following be understood:

An improper understanding of the Cross of Christ always and without fail, leads to dire, spiritual circumstances. Think of the following:

Before the Holy Spirit could come in a new Dispensation, which He did on the Day of Pentecost, the Cross of Christ had to first be a fact. Likewise, before the great latter rain outpouring of the Spirit, as prophesied by Joel (Joel 2:23), and which began at approximately the turn of the Twentieth Century, the Cross had to be strongly preached, which it was for some 200 years in the great Holiness movements. And one of the reasons, that we're seeing very little outpouring of the Holy Spirit presently (June, 2000), is because the Cross is not being preached. In fact, for the last decade, the Church has wandered somewhat like a drunken man not knowing where it's been or where it's going. It has lost its moorings, and I speak of the foundation of the Cross of Christ. But thank the Lord, the Cross is once again beginning to be preached, which signifies that a great outpouring of the

NOTES

Holy Spirit is coming, which I believe is much closer than we realize, and for reasons which I will not now take the time to enumerate.

(14) "BUT STRONG MEAT BELONGETH TO THEM THAT ARE OF FULL AGE, EVEN THOSE WHO BY REASON OF USE HAVE THEIR SENSES EXERCISED TO DISCERN BOTH GOOD AND EVIL."

The exegesis is:

1. The *"strong meat"* is the *"Word of Righteousness,"* which is the meaning of the Cross of Christ.

2. Those who are of *"full age"* speak of those who have a proper understanding of the Word of God, which always has as its foundation the Cross of Christ.

3. Only those who properly understand the Finished Work of Christ, have proper discernment, as it regards *"good and evil."* This is the basic reason that the modern Church hardly knows the difference between that which is of the Spirit and that which is not of the Spirit. They have little discernment, because they have little knowledge.

STRONG MEAT

The phrase, *"But strong meat belongeth to them that are of full age,"* refers as is obvious, to those who are mature in the Lord. And as we have repeatedly stated, maturity comes about, as it can only come about, according to one's understanding and knowledge of the Cross of Christ. The Finished Work of Christ must be the foundation on which all understanding of the Word of God is based. Otherwise, the understanding will be skewed in some manner.

Since the Lord began to give me the Revelation of the Cross, I sensed at the beginning that this was larger, much larger, than what immediately appeared on the surface. How right I was!

I remember in those days, the early part of 1997, I think it was, seeking the Lord, asking Him to enlarge this Revelation, and in fact, that it ever be enlarged. The Lord beautifully and wondrously answered that prayer, with the Revelation continuing unto this hour. By that I mean that the Scriptures just keep opening up as it regards the Cross of Christ, with the entirety of the Word of God being affected. Actually, I have come to believe, that it's impossible for a person to properly understand the Word, that is if they do not properly understand the Cross. In fact, the story of the Bible, which is the Redemption of man, is in effect, the story of the Cross.

THE FULL SCOPE

I've had many to hear the Message of the Cross, and then come to the conclusion that they believe it, or else they say, *"I'll try it,"* etc.

In the first place, when Faith is first evidenced in the Cross, which in reality, is the only Faith that God will recognize, the individual must understand, that this is only the beginning. Such an individual will find that everything, and of course we're speaking of the Word of God, is going to have to be rethought. Actually, this will automatically take care of itself, as the Spirit of God begins to bring everything in line with the great Sacrifice of Christ. As Faith is properly anchored, it is more so the individual just watching all of this take place, as the Holy Spirit begins to work, rather than having to set out on some particular course of action. In fact, the course of action has already been set out with one's proper Faith in the Cross. In other words, it is the object of one's Faith that's really important, and the Cross is that object, which gives the Holy Spirit latitude.

PROPER DISCERNMENT

The phrase, *"Even those who by reason of use have their senses exercised to discern both good and evil,"* proclaims the results of proper maturity, which comes about with one's proper Faith in the Cross of Christ.

This statement as given by the Holy Spirit through Paul, plainly tells us that if one does not properly understand the Word, then one cannot have a proper discernment as it regards what is right and what is wrong. Consequently, this is the reason that the modern Church, and we speak of the segment that claims to be Spirit-filled, seems to be chasing after every fad of which one could think. Not having a proper understanding of the Cross of Christ, which means they do not have a proper understanding of the Word of God, there is little or no discernment whatsoever as it regards *"good"* and *"evil,"* in other words, that which is right or that which is wrong!

"Discern" in the Greek is *"diakrisis,"* and means *"to discriminate, to properly distinguish, or to properly pass judgment."*

WHY IS THE CROSS THE STRONG MEAT OF WHICH PAUL HERE SPEAKS?

When one begins to understand the Cross, the answer to this question becomes overly obvious. The reason that the Cross is the fountainhead, or the foundation of all that the Bible teaches, is because it is God's Plan of Redemption, carried out through His Son, the Lord Jesus Christ. If one properly understands the Cross, one will at the same time properly understand the Lord, and one will properly understand himself. As it regards one's self, the idea is, we must understand, that every answer which we seek, and every solution we seek, are found totally and completely in the Cross of Christ, and are found *only* in the Cross of Christ. We soon learn that there is nothing we can do within ourselves that will bring about that which we must have from the Lord. In fact, we quickly learn, that if we attempt to advance something in this capacity, that God will not accept our efforts. Everything is in Christ and in totality. That means that whatever we receive from the Lord, and in whatever capacity, must be received by and through Christ, and that means what He did at the Cross. Any other manner, way, or direction that we might take, constitutes a work of the flesh, which God can never recognize.

So, a proper understanding of the Cross, teaches one a proper dependence on Christ, and that Christ Alone is the Source. That's the reason that Paul used the short phrase *"in Christ,"* or one of its derivatives such as, *"in Him,"* etc., some 170 times in his 14 Epistles.

The whole thing boils down to the fact of us believing that Christ did it all at the Cross, or else we can bring about some of these things by our own efforts and abilities. Of course, the latter is impossible, but mankind, even Christian man, keeps trying.

To close this Chapter, please allow me to say it again:

The Christian Jews of Paul's day, were in serious, spiritual difficulty, simply because they had lost Faith in the Cross of Christ.

This problem regrettably, is still with us presently, perhaps even worse than ever. While this of which we speak affected greatly the Christian Jews of Paul's day, presently, it also affects much of the modern Church. Much of the so-called Faith community, which in reality is no Faith at all, at least that which God will recognize, openly repudiates the Cross. The Leadership of the major Pentecostal Denominations in the United States and Canada, at least at the time of this writing, have long since openly embraced humanistic psychology, which is at the same time, a repudiation of the Cross. Due to a paucity of teaching on this all-important subject, actually the very foundation of the Church, the modern Church has little knowledge of the Cross; therefore, it is an open target for the most absurd doctrines and practices, simply because it has little or no discernment.

But in the midst of it all, there is a glimmer of hope. The Message of the Cross is once again being preached, and I speak of our own particular Ministry. Even with the open door of the Media as it regards Television and Radio which God has given us, it is still, however, only mercy drops around us falling; nevertheless, I'm believing that this is going to quickly broaden into a downpour all over the world. I believe the Lord has spoken to me, that the Cross of Christ is going to be the dividing line in these last days, between the True Church and the apostate Church. As I've already said several times, this in fact, has always been the case, but I believe that presently, it is going to be more pronounced than ever.

If in fact what I've just said is true, and I definitely believe that it is, then the Holy Spirit will have to place special emphasis on this of which we speak. I believe He will do that, and in fact, has already begun to do that.

"O my soul, bless thou Jehovah,
"God of Love and Grace art Thou:
"Thou Alone art wise and holy;
"At Thy feet I humbly bow."

"Thou Thy Son hast freely given,
"All our sins to bear away;
"On the Cross He made Atonement,
"Then to Glory led the way."

"He for us received the Spirit,
"Precious gift of love Divine;
"Shed Him forth upon Thy children;
"Now forever He is mine."

"Jesus soon again returneth,
"Evermore with Him I'll be,
"Like Him thro' the endless ages,
"Saved for all eternity."

CHAPTER 6

(1) "THEREFORE LEAVING THE PRINCIPLES OF THE DOCTRINE OF CHRIST, LET US GO ON UNTO PERFECTION; NOT LAYING AGAIN THE FOUNDATION OF REPENTANCE FROM DEAD WORKS, AND OF FAITH TOWARD GOD,"

The structure is:

1. The *"Doctrine of Christ"* covers the entirety of the Bible, both Old and New Testaments. The story of the Bible is the story of Christ, and what He did to redeem humanity, as it refers to the Cross.

2. The principles which we are to leave, speaks of the *"first principles"* of Verse 12 of the previous Chapter, and refers to the Old Testament.

3. The *"perfection"* addressed here, speaks of that which comes about totally and completely through the Cross of Christ and our Faith in that Finished Work, which places the Believer in Christ.

4. The *"dead works"* mentioned here, refers to the old Sacrificial system, which had been replaced by the Cross of Christ.

5. Before Christ came, *"Faith toward God"* was the only Faith then possible. It refers more so to what God would do as it regards the sending of His only Son to redeem mankind. Now that the *"Son"* has come, our Faith is to ever have as its object, Christ and His Cross (Acts 20:21).

THE DOCTRINE OF CHRIST

The phrase, *"Therefore leaving the principles of the Doctrine of Christ,"* actually reaches back to Verse 12 of the previous Chapter, and speaks of the *"first principles,"* which speaks of the Old Testament.

The words, *"The principles of the Doctrine of Christ,"* are literally in the Greek, *"the word of the beginning of the Christ."* The phrase, *"Of the beginning,"* does not limit *"Christ"* for He had no beginning. It, therefore, modifies or limits *"word."*

The phrase, *"The beginning word of the Christ,"* to say it in a clearer way, therefore, refers to the teaching concerning Him which is first presented in the Bible. And what is that but the Truth concerning His Person and Work found in the symbolism of the Levitical Sacrifices. In fact, the Tabernacle, Priesthood, and Offerings all speak of Him in His Person and Work. And this interpretation is in exact accord with the argument of the Book of Leviticus. All dependence upon the Levitical Sacrifices is to be set aside in order that the Christian Jews can go on to *"perfection,"* as we have it here, all in Christ.

Actually, the first mention of Christ, but in a yielded way, came about immediately after the Fall, when the Lord told Satan through the serpent, that the *"Seed of the woman,"* Who, incidentally, is Christ, would bruise the *"head of the serpent"* (Gen. 3:15).

To properly understand the Bible, one must first of all understand that the Old Testament is the story of the Promise of Christ and what He would do to redeem humanity, all captured in the Law of Moses, with its Sacrifices, etc. If we think of the Old Testament in any other capacity, we misunderstand the intention of the Holy Spirit.

PERFECTION

The phrase, *"Let us go on unto perfection,"* speaks of the New Testament Sacrifice, the Lord Jesus, and the Testament He inaugurated by His Work on the Cross.

"Perfection" in the Greek is *"teleios,"* and refers to that which is *"complete."* In fact, Paul uses the same Greek word in Hebrews 7:11, where he argues that if perfection were under the Levitical Priesthood, then there would be no further need of another Priesthood. But since God has brought in a Priestly line after the order of Melchizedek, which of course is in Christ, it logically follows that completeness is obtained only in Christ and what He did at the Cross. In fact, he states in Hebrews 7:19 that the Law of Moses, namely

the Sacrificial Law, made nothing perfect. That is, the Levitical Offerings were not complete in that the blood of bulls and goats could not pay for sin. Neither was there completeness in what they could do for the offerer.

But *"this Priest* (the Lord Jesus), *after He had offered One Sacrifice for sins, sat down in perpetuity on the Right Hand of God"* (Heb. 10:12). His Sacrifice was complete.

Thus, Paul exhorts these Hebrews to abandon that which was incomplete for that which is complete, the type for the reality (Wuest).

PERFECTION IN CHRIST OR MAN?

"Perfection" as it is used here, pertains only to Christ. Everything He did was perfect. So when we read the phrase, *"Let us* (all Believers) *go on unto perfection,"* it is not meaning that we as Believers can go on unto perfection, but that we place our Faith and confidence in that which is perfect, namely Christ, and His Finished Work. Let no man think that he is perfect, at least in the manner in which this is spoken, for no man is. Only Christ is Perfect, and the *"perfection"* here addressed, pertains only to Him, and more particularly, what He did at the Cross on our behalf. It is actually speaking of His Finished Work, which refers to what He did at the Cross and in His Resurrection. It is a perfect work, which means that it will never have to be done again. We are to place our Faith in that, in fact, ever making that, and I speak of the great Sacrifice of Christ, the object of our Faith. This is what Paul is saying.

DEAD WORKS

The phrase, *"Not laying again the foundation of repentance from dead works,"* refers to these Jewish Christians going back to the old Sacrificial System, etc. If they would go back to the First Testament Sacrifices, they would be laying again the foundation of the First Testament, and building upon it again. In fact, that was the problem of these Jewish Christians, and the very reason this Epistle to the Hebrews was written.

Some of them had either already gone back into Temple worship and as well had abandoned Christ, or at least, were seriously contemplating doing so. The Apostle is saying, that any activity of this sort, even as he will boldly proclaim in this Sixth Chapter, will cause these people to lose their souls.

ANOTHER JESUS

Since Christ has now come, as would be obvious, fulfilling all of the *"first principles of the Oracles of God,"* any attempt to go back to these things, can be constituted only in the category of *"dead works."* Naturally, God could not under any circumstance, accept these *"dead works."*

Even before Christ came, if the Jews did not properly understand the Law of Moses, which of course included all the Sacrificial System, meaning that they placed Faith in these particular ceremonies and rituals, instead of the One to Whom they pointed, they were then turned into *"dead works"* as well. In fact, this was Israel's major problem of old, not properly evaluating the Law of Moses, understanding that all of this pointed toward Christ, Who must ever be the object of their Faith. It is the same thing presently. Christ and what He did at the Cross, all on our behalf, must ever be the object of our Faith.

In fact, the far greater majority of modern Christendom conducts itself in basically the same manner as Israel of old. Instead of Christ and His Cross being the object of Faith, the Church becomes the object of Faith, or Water Baptism, or the Lord's Supper, and believe it or not, in many circles, Faith is the object of Faith.

Actually, this is Satan's greatest effort and where he spends the greater part of his energy, in attempting to divert our Faith from Christ to something else. To be sure, in all of these things which men erroneously do, the Name of Christ is used, and claimed; however, in these capacities, it is not really the Christ of the Bible Who is being worshipped, but rather *"another Jesus"* (II Cor. 11:4). Regrettably, the problem didn't die with Israel of old, or the Jewish Christians of Paul's day. It continues with us unto the present, and in fact has always been the greatest problem, and I speak of the problem of *"dead works."*

FAITH TOWARD GOD

The phrase, *"And of Faith toward God,"* refers to Faith toward God in an improper manner. Paul is not denigrating Faith toward

God, but rather in attempting to evidence Faith toward Him in an improper way.

There was no way that Faith could properly be evidenced in God, by these Jewish Christians going back to the Old Testament Sacrifices. God would not honor such Faith, especially considering, that such an act is an insult of all insults toward His Son, Who gave His Life on the Cross, in order that men might be saved.

The Old Law only served as a guardian until Christ came (Gal. 3:24). It was never meant to save men, and in fact could not save men. All of it pointed totally and completely to Christ. And the idea of going back to that, especially considering what Christ had done on the Cross for all of mankind, which fulfilled all of the Law of Moses, would be as stated, the insult of all insults. This is not Faith that God would recognize, thereby making it impossible to have proper Faith in God from that source. It is the same presently:

Millions claim to believe God, or to trust in God, as it regards their Salvation, when their Faith is really not in God, but in *"dead works,"* of some nature. While that certainly might be Faith, it definitely is not Faith that God will recognize.

As I've stated many times, every human being in the world has Faith. In fact, the Scientists who boast that they do not function on the basis of Faith, but rather fact, whether they realize it or not, are operating on Faith constantly. They have Faith in their experiments; Faith in their calculations; Faith in themselves; Faith in their efforts, etc. So, everyone has Faith, even the Atheist who boasts of his lack of Faith. In fact, his Faith is in the fact that he has no Faith. So, to say that one has Faith doesn't exactly mean a lot.

THE OBJECT OF OUR FAITH

Now this is the key point, *"the object of our Faith."* Our Faith must ever have as its object, *"Jesus Christ and Him Crucified"* (I Cor. 2:2).

Having the Cross as the object of our Faith, and ever the object of our Faith, means that we understand that every single thing we receive from God, comes exclusively from, by, of, and through the Sacrifice of Christ. It is impossible for man to receive anything from God in any other manner. The Believer must understand that, must believe that, must act upon that.

When we say that we have Faith in Christ, we must understand what we're saying. If it's not Faith in Christ, meaning what He did at the Cross on our behalf, then in fact, it is Faith in *"another Christ"* (II Cor. 11:4). In the mind of the Believer, Christ must always and without exception, be linked to the Cross, and the Cross without exception, linked to Christ.

Now when we say that, we are not speaking of Christ still being on a Cross, as He is portrayed by the Catholics. We are speaking of what He accomplished at the Cross, the benefits of the Cross, that which the Cross made possible. Christ is not still on a Cross; in fact, He is seated presently at the Right Hand of the Father, making intercession for the Saints, and in fact we are seated with Him in these Heavenly Places (Eph. 2:6; Heb. 1:3; 7:25).

The great problem of mankind has always been, and still is, attempting to have Faith toward God by doing things which God can never honor.

GOD IS PLEASED ONLY WITH CHRIST

When Jesus was baptized in the River Jordan, God said of Him, *"This is My beloved Son, in Whom I am well pleased"* (Mat. 3:17).

This means that He is not pleased with anyone else, and irrespective as to what they might do, unless their Faith is anchored solely and completely in Christ and what Christ has done at the Cross. That being the case, that individual is *"in Christ,"* and as such, God is pleased with the person, but only because he is properly aligned with Christ.

For instance, if Mother Teresa was trying to please God by her good works, instead of pleasing Him, such action rather greatly displeased Him, and for the simple reason, that it was bypassing the Finished Work of Christ. Such actions, with which the world is filled, in effect says, *"I don't need Christ and what He did at the Cross. My works are sufficient within themselves."* It is the same problem which existed at the very beginning between Cain and Abel. Abel followed the instructions of the Lord, and offered up a Sacrifice of a clean animal, which included the shedding of

NOTES

its blood, which was all a symbol or a type of the Lord Jesus Christ, which God could accept, i.e., *"which pleased Him."* Cain did the very opposite:

He offered up the labor of his hands, spurning that which God had demanded, which God could not accept. Regrettably, man has been on this erroneous road ever since.

He thinks that his good works, his religious activity, his Church attendance, or a hundred and one other things we might name, please God. They don't! While they may be good in their own right, they are not the coin which spends in God's economy.

The only coin which spends in His realm is Faith in Jesus Christ, and what He did at the Cross. That is it, pure and simple!

LEAVING THE CROSS?

It is Hebrews 6:1 which many use, claiming that we should leave the Cross, going on to greater things, because the Cross is elementary, etc.

As I would trust by now is overly obvious, such thinking shows a complete misunderstanding of what this Passage says, and if such misunderstanding continues to be followed, will lead to spiritual disaster.

As we've already explained, the phrase *"leaving the principles of the Doctrine of Christ,"* has absolutely nothing to do with leaving the Cross, as claimed by some. It is speaking of the Old Testament, which all of this is actually all about.

If in fact, we believe that this First Verse is teaching us to leave the Cross, then at the same time, we must also leave the *"Doctrine of Baptisms,"* and of *"laying on of hands,"* and as well the *"Resurrection of the dead,"* etc. I would hope we could see how foolish this would be. So let's ask it in another way:

Do these people who teach that Hebrews 6:1 means that we should leave the Cross, at the same time, teach that Water Baptism or the Baptism with the Holy Spirit is no longer for us, or that *"laying on of hands"* is unscriptural, or that we should not any longer believe in a Resurrection? Of course not! However, we must understand, that we cannot have it both ways.

No, Hebrews 6:1 is not telling us to leave the Cross, and neither is Hebrews 6:2 telling us to lay aside Water Baptism, or the *"laying on of hands,"* etc. So what is Verse 2 actually saying?

(2) "OF THE DOCTRINE OF BAPTISMS, AND OF LAYING ON OF HANDS, AND OF RESURRECTION OF THE DEAD, AND OF ETERNAL JUDGMENT."

The structure is:

1. The *"Doctrine of Baptisms"* as given here by Paul, refers to the Old Testament doctrine of the ceremonial washings of Judaism. In fact, the Apostle uses the same Greek word translated *"washings"* in Hebrews 9:10.

2. The *"laying on of hands"* once again refers to the Old Testament practice, of the one offering up sacrifice, laying his hands on the head of the animal, confessing all his sins, just before the animal was killed.

3. The *"resurrection of the dead"* as taught in the Old Testament was very limited. For instance, it wasn't then understood that there would be two Resurrections, which are taught under the New Covenant.

4. *"Eternal judgment"* should have been translated *"eternal condemnation."* Condemnation, at least to a certain extent, characterized even Believers in Old Testament Times. The reason being, the blood of bulls and goats could not take away sins (Heb. 10:4). But now in Christ, there is no more condemnation (Rom. 8:1).

THE DOCTRINE OF BAPTISMS

The phrase, *"Of the Doctrine of Baptisms,"* would have been better translated, *"the Doctrine of Washings,"* for this is what the Greek word used here more pointedly means.

The *"washings"* as instituted in the Law of Moses, were quite prominent. For instance, in the Law of the Red Heifer, water was used extensively. It was called *"the water of separation"* (Num. 19:9).

In the dedication of the Levites to the service of the Lord, they were sprinkled with water, and it was called *"the water of purification"* (Num. 8:7). There were many such like uses.

We could go into long descriptions, but suffice to say, Paul was bringing out the fact, that all of that was made unnecessary, by what Christ did at the Cross. He bluntly and plainly says to the Christian Jews, we must leave this

NOTES

"Doctrine of Baptisms," or *"washings,"* because they have all been fulfilled in Christ.

LAYING ON OF HANDS

The phrase, *"And of laying on of hands,"* as well, goes back to the Levitical Offerings of the Old Testament.

The Law plainly said, *"Speak unto the Children of Israel, and say unto them, if any man of you bring an Offering* (Sacrifice) *unto the Lord, ye shall bring your Sacrifice of the . . . flock."*

It must be *"a male without blemish: he shall offer it of his own voluntary will at the door of the Tabernacle . . . And he shall put his hand upon the head of the Burnt Offering"* (Lev. 1:1-4; 3:2, 8, 13; 4:4, 24, 29, 33). At that time, he was to also confess his sins, in effect, transferring them to the innocent animal which would be slain (Lev. 16:21).

When we as Christians think of *"laying on of hands,"* we're thinking of doing such in the Name of Jesus, etc. (Mk. 16:18). But we must remember, that Paul was speaking to Jews, and while they understood perfectly well the New Testament Doctrine of laying on of hands, they were also very familiar with the Old Testament Doctrine, which was completely different than the New. In fact, to go back to that, was in essence saying that what Christ did at the Cross carried no meaning and, therefore, brought about no forgiveness of sin.

We are to leave this Old Testament way, which in fact, was one of the *"first principles of the Doctrine of Christ,"* in that all of these Old Testament things pointed to Christ. As the animal took the sins in Old Testament times, Christ has now taken our sins, of which the animal sacrifice was but a type.

RESURRECTION OF THE DEAD

The phrase, *"And of resurrection of the dead,"* refers to Resurrection as taught in the Old Testament. The doctrine there was very incomplete, even as all doctrine in the Old Testament was incomplete. In fact, until Jesus came, it could be no other way.

In Old Testament Times, the doctrine of Resurrection was shadowy at best. While the Jews definitely believed in a coming Resurrection, at least some of them, they had very little idea as to how all of this was to be done.

For instance, they knew nothing of a Rapture, which is the same as a Resurrection (I Thess. 4:13-18). They knew nothing of how the human body would be changed and glorified, even as Paul explained in I Corinthians, Chapter 15.

There was no point in the Holy Spirit explaining this during those times, due to the fact that Jesus had not yet come, Who would make it all possible. As stated, they knew a Resurrection was coming, but how, when, and what it all exactly meant, they were not sure. Job said, *"If a man die, shall he live again? All the days of my appointed time will I wait, till my change come"* (Job 14:14). He plainly speaks here of a coming Resurrection, but of its particulars, he had no knowledge.

Jesus Christ is actually the *"Firstfruits"* of the Resurrection, being the first One resurrected to Eternal Life. His Resurrection guarantees the Resurrection of all Saints, including those who lived in Old Testament times. Before Jesus came, Who incidentally is the Resurrection, there wasn't much point in the Holy Spirit explaining this very complicated Doctrine. In Christ it's very easy to understand. Before Christ, it would have been very difficult, if not impossible.

In fact, and as we've stated, the entirety of the Old Testament was but a shadow of that which was to come. It all awaited Christ! If it is to be noticed, He is all of these things. He is cleansing from sin, therefore, all the washings of the past are no longer needed. He has taken our sin away, therefore, the animal sacrifices are no longer needed. He is our Resurrection, which now makes it easy to understand. As well, He took our judgment, so there will be no Judgment for the Believer in Christ.

ETERNAL JUDGMENT

The phrase, *"And of eternal judgment,"* presently presents itself as more fully understood, than it was in Old Testament Times. In those times, God was looked at much more as a Judge than anything else. Presently, and because of what Christ has done at the Cross, God, that is if rightly understood, is looked at as a Saviour.

While God definitely must judge all sin, He has already done so in Christ, which

refers to Christ offering up Himself on the Cross. In other words, He took the Judgment of God, which I should have taken. He died in my stead!

Actually, in Old Testament Times, when a Saint died, they didn't go to Heaven, but rather were taken captive by Satan into the heart of the Earth, into the place referred to by Christ as *"Abraham's Bosom"* (Lk. 16:22). While it was a place of peace, with Satan not being able to put them into the place of fire, because of their Faith in Christ, due to the fact that Jesus had not yet come, they were held captives by Satan. The reason for all of this was, that the sin debt was still hanging over the heads of all Believers in Old Testament Times, simply because the blood of bulls and goats could never take away sins (Heb. 10:4).

The moment that Jesus died on the Cross, thereby taking all sin away (Jn. 1:29), He at that time went down into this place, and liberated all the Old Testament Saints, taking them to Heaven (Eph. 4:8-10). Now when Saints die, they instantly go to Heaven, to be with Christ (Phil. 1:23).

In a sense, the Old Testament Saints were still under condemnation, or one might say, under judgment. To be sure, they were definitely saved, and saved in the same manner as we are presently, which is by Faith; however, inasmuch as Christ had not yet come, they could not at all have the benefits which we presently have since Christ has come. In fact, that's what the Book of Hebrews is all about, to show the superiority of Christ over all of that which preceded Him.

Due to the fact that the blood of bulls and goats could not take away sins, there was a certain condemnation which plagued the Old Testament Saints. Since Christ, which speaks of Faith in His Name, which refers to what He did at the Cross on our behalf, *"there is therefore now no condemnation to them which are in Christ Jesus, who walk not after the flesh, but after the Spirit"* (Rom. 8:1). Consequently, who would want to go back to that time of *"judgment"* and *"condemnation"*?

(3) "AND THIS WILL WE DO, IF GOD PERMIT."

The exposition is:

1. This which Paul said we will do, pertains to leaving the first principles of the

Doctrine of Christ, which refers to Old Testament ways.

2. We will go on to perfection, which refers to the Perfect Way of Christ.

3. We will do this *"if God permits,"* meaning that we can do nothing without His help.

WHAT WILL YOU DO?

The phrase, *"And this will we do,"* proclaims that which is said in the manner of complete necessity. In other words, if we don't do this, and it refers to the going on to the perfection of Christ, the results will be disastrous, i.e., *"the loss of one's soul."*

The question must be asked of the Reader, *"Is this what you are doing?"*

Are you going on into the perfection of Christ, which refers to what He did at the Cross for you, or are you trusting in *"dead works"*?

THE HELP OF GOD

The phrase, *"If God permit,"* refers to the fact that all dependence must be in Christ and totally in Christ. God will not honor any other type of Faith. In fact, everything we have from God is given to us as a gift. As well, it all comes through the Sacrifice of Christ on the Cross. This means we must look to the Lord, depend on the Lord, trust the Lord, and do so for all things.

God resists the high and haughty spirit, but gives Grace to the humble, which one must have, if one is to succeed.

So, even though Christ has done all of this for us, still, I must have the help of God in securing these great and wonderful things, which help is supplied by the Holy Spirit.

Even though Jesus has paid all the price on the Cross, which makes possible all the benefits for which He died, still, it is the Holy Spirit Alone Who can make all these things possible in our hearts and lives. And He does so, according to our Faith in the Cross of Christ (Rom. 6:3-5, 14; 8:2).

(4) "FOR IT IS IMPOSSIBLE FOR THOSE WHO WERE ONCE ENLIGHTENED, AND HAVE TASTED OF THE HEAVENLY GIFT, AND WERE MADE PARTAKERS OF THE HOLY SPIRIT,"

The exegesis is:

1. It is impossible for a Christian, and of course we speak of one who has truly been

saved, to quit believing in Christ and what He did at the Cross, and remain saved.

2. To be enlightened speaks of one who has accepted the Light of the Gospel, thereby having been saved.

3. The Heavenly Gift is the Lord Jesus Christ.

4. For one to be a partaker of the Holy Spirit, one must be Born-Again.

5. Verses 4 through 6 prove the fallacy of the ungodly, unscriptural doctrine of *"unconditional eternal security."* While the Bible definitely teaches eternal security, it definitely doesn't teach unconditional eternal security.

ENLIGHTENMENT

The phrase, *"For it is impossible for those who were once enlightened,"* refers to those who have accepted the Light of the Gospel, which means accepting Christ and His great Sacrifice. Jesus Christ is the Light of the world. Consequently, Paul is here speaking of true Christians. He is speaking of individuals who have accepted Christ as their own personal Saviour. In fact, the entirety of the Book of Hebrews is directed toward Christian Jews, meaning they had truly and factually accepted Christ as their Saviour, but were now seriously considering abandoning Christ, and going back into Old Testament, Temple worship. In fact, it is impossible not to see that, as one reads this Epistle. And if one doesn't see that, one is purposely blinding oneself, to what is plainly said here.

I say these things because of those who contend that these Jews had not really accepted Christ, but were rather only contemplating doing such. Of course, these are the promoters of the unscriptural doctrine of unconditional eternal security.

For one to twist these Scriptures in such a fashion, portrays a blindness to the obvious and a deafness to the Truth. In other words, it is impossible to sensibly claim that these individuals were only merely contemplating Christ, and had not actually ever accepted Him as Saviour. Such thinking is silly!

"Enlightened" in the Greek is *"photizo,"* and means *"to shine, to brighten, to illuminate, to give light, to make to see."*

All unsaved people being spiritually dead, i.e., *"totally depraved,"* means that they have no enlightenment whatsoever as it refers to the Lord; consequently, the word *"enlightenment"* as it is used here, would never be used of the unsaved.

As well, it doesn't mean that the light was shone to them and they rejected it. One cannot be enlightened by merely being shown the light. One has to accept what the light produces, which in this case, is the Gospel of Christ, and only then, can one be said to be *"enlightened."*

The Apostle is addressing Christians here, and endeavoring to keep them from apostasy. The kind of exhortation appropriate to those who were not saved, would be to come to Christ; not to warn them of the danger of falling away. A person cannot fall away from something they've never previously had.

"Impossible" in the Greek is *"adunatos,"* and means *"unable, could not do, not possible."* The idea is, even as Paul addresses the issue here, and strongly so, that if a Christian turns his back upon Christ, thereby no longer believing in Christ and His great Sacrifice, that person is then considered to have fallen away from Faith, and if remaining in that condition, is no longer a Christian, and is thereby eternally lost. There is no other way these Scriptures can be properly interpreted.

UNCONDITIONAL ETERNAL SECURITY?

In an attempt to buttress the unscriptural doctrine of unconditional eternal security, some have asked the following questions:

Can a saved man ever be lost?

Can a Believer ever be lost?

The answer to both questions is a resounding *"no!"*

However, a saved man can turn his back on Christ, even as these Passages in Hebrews prove, and if he stays in that condition, he is no longer saved, and will definitely be lost.

As well, a Believer can quit believing, even as Paul is addressing here, and if remaining in a state of unbelief, will be eternally lost.

We do not question the position or the security of the Believer. Those who are in Christ are secure under the Blood Covering, but there are conditions God has clearly set down that must be met to obtain and retain Eternal Life:

"... if we hold fast the confidence and the rejoicing of the hope firm unto the end ... if we hold the beginning of our confidence steadfast unto the end" (Heb. 3:6, 14).

THE RESPONSIBILITY OF MAN

We repeat, we have no doubt as to the ability of God to preserve and keep the Believer. The real issue here is with the responsibility that rests upon man, as Paul is addressing here in his Epistle to the Hebrews.

God has done all that is possible for Him to do in the Salvation of man. God has given His Son and provided us with cleansing and forgiveness; now God awaits our response.

Considering all of this, we must ask ourselves some serious questions:

On whom, then, does the responsibility for security rest?

Under what conditions, if any, may this security be obtained or lost?

May a person choose to depart from this position as freely as he chose to enter?

The Scriptures definitely teach that it is possible for one to depart from the Faith and to become devoid of Faith. It is possible for one to deny his Lord and to apostatize, even as Paul is addressing here.

In fact, this setting of Scripture (Heb. 6:4-6) brings us face-to-face with the doctrine of apostasy, i.e., *"the falling away from Truth."*

To falsely teach the Word of God presents a frightful prospect. Such never leaves people unaffected.

To teach that once one is in Grace, it's impossible to fall from Grace, is not what the Bible teaches (Gal. 5:4). The Bible doesn't teach such Grace, and it doesn't teach such Faith, and it doesn't teach such security. As we've already stated, it, however, definitely does teach conditional security.

CONDITIONAL SECURITY

Conditional security does not take away peace of heart, mind, or of spirit. On the other hand, it causes a deepening of our love and respect for the Holiness and Righteousness of a just God. The Word of God teaches that man is an absolutely free moral agent; he serves the Devil or God as he freely chooses.

If a man wants to turn from Satan to God, he is always free to do so (Jn. 3:16). And if man chooses to turn from God to Satan, this same freedom of choice is also granted to him.

Man is not forced to live a holy life. He is free to dedicate or consecrate to that end, or he can live a life of self-gratification.

A saved man has the same power of choice that he had before Salvation. His desires are definitely changed at Salvation, but he can permit his former desires to take hold of him again, should he so choose. The flesh can gain ascendancy over him, and he can choose once more to live in the old paths of sin, even as Paul graphically brings out in Romans, Chapters 6, 7, and 8.

If he chooses to forsake Christ, which means to choose to forsake dependence on Christ and what He did at the Cross, and to go into sin again, he thus incurs the same death penalty and wrath of God as though he had never been saved. Again, that's exactly what Paul is addressing here.

Whether these Christian Jews went back into Temple worship, depending solely on that for Salvation, or whether a Christian presently and with purpose goes into sin, actually speaks of the results of something else far worse.

Even though Paul mentions the going back to the old way, even as we have just mentioned the going back into sin, the real problem is forsaking Christ, which means that one no longer trusts Him and what He did at the Cross on their behalf. That is the real sin! And that is what will cause a person to be eternally lost, even though they may have once known the Lord. In fact, this is the entirety of the warp and woof of this Epistle to the Hebrews.

BUT WHAT ABOUT A CHRISTIAN WHO IS IN BONDAGE TO SIN BECAUSE HE DOESN'T UNDERSTAND THE CROSS?

As long as a person is trusting Christ, regardless of the problems, that person is saved. However, it must be fully understood, that we're speaking of Christians who, although in bondage to sin of some sort, in fact hate that sin, and are attempting to get victory. Romans, Chapter 7 describes this person perfectly.

This is the individual who does not know the victory of the Cross, and who is struggling to live a righteous and holy life by his

own efforts, but rather obtaining the opposite results.

That person is saved, but definitely will suffer very negative results, as a result of sin. Sin always takes a deadly toll. This type of person is living a life of sinning and repenting, sinning and repenting, which is miserable to say the least! Sadly and regrettably, because of not knowing the great Message of the Cross, this is probably the state of the far greater majority of modern Christians.

FREE MORAL AGENCY

The doctrine of free moral agency, constitutes the freedom of the individual to make a choice, whether right or wrong. In other words, God will not coerce or force a person's will. The Doctrine of Scripture always is, *"whosoever will"* (Jn. 3:16; Rev. 22:17).

However, most Christians still do not understand this doctrine, with most thinking that it means that a person can choose whatever he or she likes, etc. Such a statement as given here, and mostly thought, is blatantly wrong.

Man is a free moral agent, but only in the sense of being free to accept God and His Way, or to reject God and His Way. If he accepts God and His Way, all is well. If he rejects God and His Way, then he soon finds, that his will is overpowered by Satan, irrespective as to whether he is a Christian or not.

Preachers talk about Christians *"choosing to sin."* That is really an incorrect statement.

Christians actually choose to accept God's Way of the Cross, or not to accept that Way. If they don't accept the Way of the Cross, which refers to the great Sacrifice of Christ, which alone gives one power to overcome sin, then the Believer is left to his own strength and willpower, which are always woefully inadequate and insufficient. In other words, in that state, even though he chooses not to sin, Satan can force his will, making him do things he does not desire, even as Paul outlines in Romans 7:18. That may come as a shock to most Christians, but it is true.

In fact, at this very moment, there are millions of Christians who are fighting with all their strength not to do something that's wrong, but failing. They are left confused and bewildered, simply because they don't understand. They don't want to do this thing they are doing. In fact, they hate it, again even as Paul said (Rom. 7:15).

Actually Paul said in this very Scripture, *"For that which I do I allow not."* The word *"allow"* in the Greek actually means, *"understand."* Consequently, it should have been translated, *"For that which I do I understand not."*

This means that he was trying with all of his strength not to fail, whatever it was of that of which he was speaking, but despite all of his efforts, was failing just the same. As stated, that's the condition of most modern Christians.

Romans, Chapter 7 describes the personal experience of Paul immediately after he was saved, baptized with the Holy Spirit, and even called to be an Apostle. At that time, he did not know the victory of the Cross, consequently, trying to live a holy life by his own efforts and machinations, which most Christians do presently.

As someone has well said, desperation precedes Revelation. It did with Paul, and it has with untold others as well.

The Apostle greatly sought the Lord about this matter, with God giving him the secret of the victorious, overcoming, Christian life, which the Apostle gave to us in Romans, Chapter 6. In fact, the meaning of the New Covenant is actually the meaning of the Cross. It refers to what the Cross did, or better said, what Jesus did for us on the Cross, which of course, includes His Resurrection.

Most Christians understand the Cross as it refers to their initial Salvation experience, but have absolutely no understanding whatsoever as it refers to their everyday living. In fact, the Cross plays just as great a part in our daily living before God, and I speak of our overcoming victory, as it does in our initial Salvation experience. Regrettably, as stated, most Christians don't know that.

When it comes to Christians, and we speak of those who are not mere professors, but those who truly know the Lord, they, and without question, hate sin (Rom. 7:15). In other words, even though they may be sinning, they do not choose to sin. Their choice is taken from them, by them not trusting in Christ. In other words, whether they realize

NOTES

it or not, whether it's done through ignorance or not, they have made a choice to accept their own way, rather than God's Way, which is the great Sacrifice of Christ. That's where the choice lies, and that's only where the choice lies.

UNBELIEF AS IT REFERS TO THE CROSS

Please allow me to repeat the fact that every Christian is responsible for sin, even though it may be committed because of ignorance of the Word of God as it refers to the Cross. Sin is sin, however committed, and the person committing the sin is responsible. For things to be made right such a person has to seek forgiveness from the Lord, as proclaimed in I John 1:9.

Nevertheless, there is a vast difference in the person who hates acts of sin, and is thereby trying to conquer it, although in the wrong way, than the Christian who registers unbelief in his or her heart, and I speak of unbelief in the Cross, even as the Christian Jews of Paul's day were doing. These Christian Jews had once registered Faith and confidence in the Finished Work of Christ, or else they could not have been saved to begin with; however, because of whatever reason, they had now come to the place, at least those who did, that they no longer registered Faith in the Cross of Christ, and were thereby seriously contemplating going back into Temple worship. Let it be understood, that if a Christian abandons Christ, and by that I speak of abandoning God's solution for the world which is the Cross, that Christian, whomever he or she might be, will at the same time opt for a solution devised by man. In fact, that is the state of the far greater majority of the modern Church presently.

The embrace by the Church of humanistic psychology, is at the same time a forsaking of the Cross. One cannot have it both ways. The Lord either addressed every single problem that man has at the Cross, or else He didn't, and we must turn to other sources.

Of course, the history of the Cross proclaims the fact that God definitely did address man's problem at the Cross, and in totality, as proven by the hundreds of millions down through the centuries, who have had their lives gloriously and marvelously changed by the Power of God, as is registered in the Cross of Christ (I Cor. 1:18). So, why does the modern Church seek to forsake the Cross?

The problem is unbelief. In other words, despite what they say, their actions prove that they no longer believe as they once did. When they originally came to Christ, and I continue to speak of those in the modern Church, they came by accepting Christ and what He did at the Cross on their behalf, for that's the only way in which one can be saved. But somewhere on the path, even as the Christian Jews of Paul's day, they lost their Faith in the Finished Work of Christ. Of course, they would deny that; however, again, I maintain that it's impossible to embrace the Cross and at the same time embrace that which is humanistic.

It is the same as with Ahaz of old, king of Judah. He saw an Altar in Damascus, an Altar incidentally designed for the worship of Baal, and was so enamored with its design, that he gave instructions for one to be built according to its pattern, and for it to replace the Brazen Altar designed by the Lord, which sat in front of the Temple.

He moved the Altar of the Lord to the side, replacing it with the heathen altar, which means that he now had two altars sitting side by side. That is the condition of the modern Church.

The modern Church hasn't totally abandoned the *"Altar,"* i.e., *"the Cross of Christ,"* meaning it's still there; however, it is no longer in use. Sacrifices and burnt offerings were all offered by Ahaz on the heathen altar, which of course, God could never accept.

The modern Church pays lip service to the Cross, but lip service only. It places its trust and confidence in a heathen way, i.e., *"that devised by man"* (II Ki. 16:10-15).

HOW DOES A CHRISTIAN COME TO UNBELIEF?

That's a good question! Why did the Christian Jews come to unbelief? Why have millions down through the many centuries come to unbelief? Why does much of the modern Church register unbelief?

The unbelief of which we speak, always, and without exception, centers up in the great Sacrifice of Christ. Does that Sacrifice suffice, or do we need to look for something else?

Concerning this, Jesus said that the Holy Spirit *"will reprove* (convict) *the world of sin."* He then said, of what type of sin it was of which He spoke, *"because they believe not on Me"* (Jn. 16:8-9).

This doesn't mean that necessarily the person of Christ would be denied, but that His Sacrificial, Atoning Work would be denied. In fact, many if not most, in the Faith movement presently deny the Cross. They don't deny its existence, or that it truly happened, but rather its veracity. In other words, they claim that it carries no meaning, which of course, is a blatant denial.

They claim that the Cross was just an incident in the Life and Ministry of Christ, which of course denies the Blood Atonement, claiming that man is saved by trusting in what Christ did in Hell, of all places.

They claim that Jesus took upon Himself the nature of Satan while on the Cross, and because of that, upon His death, went to Hell, and again, we speak of the burning side of the Pit. They claim that demon spirits celebrated in hellish glee, claiming that they had defeated Christ, and that Satan would now take the Throne of God. But after a period of time in this condition, God said, *"It's enough,"* with Jesus then throwing off the shackles, and was *"born again,"* and of all places, in Hell.

He then came out of the Pit, they claim, resurrected from the dead, with Salvation brought on by Faith in that particular process.

They seem to not understand, that there is not a shred of what they teach found in the Bible. In other words, it's made up out of whole cloth. However, that doesn't seem to deter them, as they continue to preach their fallacious doctrine, with hundreds of thousands, if not millions, believing what they say.

Why would people believe that, especially considering that it's not found in the Bible?

To be frank, that's not the central thrust of their message. They only bring that up occasionally. The central thrust of their message is *"money!"* In other words, they teach that money is the answer to all things, and if a person is to truly glorify God, they must be rich, etc. And of course, a major thrust of their message is, that money is to be given to them, which will ensure riches, etc. The only ones getting rich, however, are the Preachers.

There is no Saving Grace in that process, and because there cannot be any Saving Grace in that process. The only way that a person can be saved is by trusting in what Christ did at the Cross, and if that is ignored or denied, Salvation and even the opportunity for Salvation, are forfeited (Jn. 3:16).

The reason that hundreds of thousands, if not millions, follow this doctrine just mentioned, is because of *"greed."* Never mind that they will lose their souls if they continue on that particular road!

And then we have many others in the modern Church plunging into humanistic psychology, thereby forsaking God's Way which is *"Jesus Christ and Him Crucified."* However, this one thing is certain:

Unbelief blinds and ultimately blinds completely. That's the reason that very few ever pull back. It's like a downward path with the downward degree ever increasing. In fact, and as stated, this is the very reason this major Epistle to the Hebrews was written. Hopefully, it would pull some back from the precipice!

THE HEAVENLY GIFT

The phrase, *"And have tasted of the Heavenly Gift,"* pertains to Christ and what He did at the Cross. When the Scriptures, at least in this context, speak of a *"Gift,"* it is always and without exception, speaking of the Sacrifice of Christ. For instance, Paul wrote:

"For the wages of sin is death; but the Gift of God is Eternal Life through Jesus Christ our Lord" (Rom. 6:23).

Although God gives all type of gifts to humanity, the teaching of the New Testament makes it clear that the ultimate Gift of God is Jesus Himself. Of course, and without fail, that speaks of what Jesus did for humanity, concerning His Vicarious Offering of Himself in Sacrifice, that we might be saved.

As a result of that, all other gifts which we receive from the Lord, come to us exclusively through the Son, and more particularly, what the Son did on the Cross, and more particular still, our Faith in that which He did.

Accepting Christ, we step into the relationship with God that Paul describes in

NOTES

Romans 8:32: *"He Who did not spare His Own Son, but gave Him up for us all — how will He not also, along with Him, graciously give us all things?"*

"Tasted" in the Greek is *"geuomai,"* and means *"to experience, to eat."* It does *not* mean, as some teach, who incidentally are espousing unconditional eternal security, that these Jews only tasted with their tongue, and really did not experience or eat that which was offered. The Greek text is emphatic as to what was done. Figuratively speaking, they ate of this Heavenly Gift, they experienced this Heavenly Gift, which means they experienced Christ, which means they were saved.

David wrote: *"O taste and see that the Lord is good: blessed is the man that trusteth in Him"* (Ps. 34:8).

The implication here is, that one who does *"taste"* is at the same time, one who *"trusts."*

PARTAKERS OF THE HOLY SPIRIT

The phrase, *"And were made partakers of the Holy Spirit,"* refers to every individual who is saved, i.e., *"comes to Christ."*

The Holy Spirit is the One Who gives the Word to the Preacher or whomever, to deliver, anoints what is delivered, convicts the sinner of their sin upon hearing that Word, and then gives Faith to the sinner in order that he or she might believe. He will not force the issue, but He definitely makes it possible. It is then up to the sinner as to whether they will accept or not. Regrettably, many, if not most, do not receive, but some definitely do (Rom. 10:13-17).

If the person heeds the Call of the Spirit, and accepts Christ as their Saviour, they then are *"made partakers of the Holy Spirit,"* i.e., *"born of the Spirit"* (Jn. 3:5).

It is impossible for the unsaved to be *"partakers of the Holy Spirit."* Anyone who knows anything about the Word of God knows that. Of this, Jesus plainly said, *"Even the Spirit of Truth; Whom the world cannot receive, because it seeth Him not, neither knoweth Him"* (Jn. 14:17).

I think it is clear, that the Word of God proclaims the fact that great responsibility rests upon the Believer, following his conversion to Christ. The Scriptures teach that the Christian is *"kept by the Power of God,"* but the responsibility of Faith rests upon the Christian. Peter said, "(We) *are kept by the Power of God through Faith unto Salvation ready to be revealed in the last time*" (I Pet. 1:5). To continue in Faith, which refers to Faith in Christ and what He did at the Cross, is to continue in God's blessings. To cease to walk this walk of Faith is to come under the Judgment of God. Jude said:

"*I will therefore put you in remembrance, though ye once knew this, how that the Lord, having saved the people out of the land of Egypt, afterward destroyed them that believed not*" (Jude vs. 5).

We believe and teach that Salvation is by Grace and Grace alone, that man can do nothing to merit Salvation. We believe that, while Grace is offered, however, man must, by his own volition, accept this Grace by Faith; thus, believing is a conditional factor. Man has the capacity to believe or not to believe.

We also believe that, because of God's predetermined counsel and foreknowledge, having ordained that man be a free moral agent with freedom to accept or resist the Spirit, man's destiny is dependent upon his answer to this question:

"*. . . What shall I do then with Jesus which is called Christ?*" (Mat. 27:22) (Fjordbak).

THE SECURITY OF THE BELIEVER

While we examine the doctrine of the Believer's security in the light of the Scriptures, pointing out the possibility of faithlessness on the part of the Christian, and if continued, the loss of the soul, we need to be careful that we do not go to another extreme.

Great responsibility rests upon us to be honest with the Word of God. There is great danger here. It is never enough just to denounce emphatically a doctrine believed to be false. After reproof and correction, instruction must come. The Believer must be led into Righteousness by the teaching of the Truth.

With the excision of error must come the careful uncovering of the counterbalancing Truth. Let us never forget that to substitute the opposite extreme of insecurity in Christ is no less heretical than the *"once saved, always saved"* extreme. Between these two extremes are the green pastures and still

waters of the Believer's security in Christ. The Scripture teaches this to be the normal walk and life of the Christian.

We must preach the entirety of the Word of God, which refers to all of its Doctrines, including the Doctrine of Christ-centered security. We must not default on preaching any Passage because it may be habitually abused or misused in other theologies. We must live by every Word that God has given. In fact, the Word of God is our only guide to Righteousness.

One of the tragedies of our times is the alarming number of people in the Church who never become rooted in Biblical Truths, and are, therefore, not stabilized in Christ.

As we have taught over and over, they have accurate knowledge of the forgiveness of sins through the provisions made in the Atonement, but they still try to manage their day-by-day living for God, in the security of their own strength. Like those who labor to keep the Law, and in fact, they are in a sense attempting to keep a law, albeit one devised of themselves or others, thereby, becoming weary and heavily burdened.

They live under a cloud of trying to offer to God their own righteousness, but as soon as one sets about to establish his own righteousness as a basis for God's approval, he sets for himself an impossible task. Its end can only be frustration and consequently, insecurity.

THE SECURITY OF THE BELIEVER IS CHRIST AND HIS CROSS

What Jesus did at the Cross not only made it possible for the sinner to be saved, but for the Believer as well, to live a righteous, holy life, even on a daily basis. Most Christians, regrettably, do not understand that. They limit the Cross to the initial Salvation experience, not understanding that its benefits extend as well to our daily living. And, any Christian who doesn't understand this, and regrettably, this makes up the far greater majority of Christendom, despite all of their efforts otherwise, will live in some measure, a defeated life. Victory is found only in the Cross, which demands our Faith to be in this Finished Work, and only then, will the Holy Spirit work on our behalf.

Even though much of the Church would deny such, the biggest problem with the Christian is sin. Satan is ever seeking to drag the Christian into failure in one way or the other. While it might be the sins of vice (of the flesh) with some, it's sins of pride with others, but nevertheless it is sin.

As well, the Believer must understand, that acts of sin are actually the result of the initial sin, and what is that initial sin?

The initial sin that the Believer commits, which brings on acts of sin, is the sin of trusting self instead of the Cross. Admittedly, most do this, simply because they have no understanding of the victory of the Cross; consequently, they resort to other methods, simply because they don't know any better; nevertheless, and even as we have already explained, Scriptural ignorance does not forego responsibility.

With the Believer trusting self, or whatever method other than the Cross, such a Believer is doomed to commit acts of sin in some fashion. There is no victory in that direction. But again I state, the initial sin, is the sin of not trusting in the Finished Work of Christ, which in a sense, whether committed ignorantly or not, is the highest form of rebellion.

The Lord has but one way, or one manner of victory for the Saint, and that is the Cross of Christ. There is no other! (Rom. 6:3-5, 11, 14).

HOW IS THE CROSS THE MANNER OF VICTORY?

As we have stated, sin is the problem of mankind, and the problem of the Christian as well. When Jesus died on the Cross, He died as the *"Last Adam,"* which means that there will never have to be another (I Cor. 15:45).

After living a Perfect Life, thereby gaining the Righteousness of the Law, this all being done totally and completely on our behalf, in other words, as our Representative Man, He now had to address the terrible sin debt, which refers to the debt owed by man to God. Man had broken God's Law, and the wages and penalty of that crime was and is death (Rom. 6:23).

The Righteousness of God demanded that this debt be paid, and due to the fact that man could not pay the debt, that is if he was to survive, then God would have to pay it

Himself, even at a frightful price. That price was the death of the Last Adam on the Cross, the Lord Jesus Christ. Because He was Perfect in every way, and we mean Perfect in every way, He could offer up Himself in Sacrifice to God, shedding His Life's Blood as an Atonement for all sin, a Sacrifice, incidentally, which God would and did accept. In fact, He accepted it as payment for all sin, past, present, and future, that is, for those who have placed their Faith and Trust in Christ and what He did at the Cross (Jn. 3:16).

Satan's legal hold upon mankind is sin. Because of sin, he has a legal right to place man into captivity, which he has done on a worldwide basis. With Jesus atoning for all sin, and with Faith evidenced by sinners in this Atonement, Satan loses his legal hold upon all who express such Faith (Rom. 10:9-10, 13; Eph. 2:8-9).

Because all sin was addressed and atoned for, Satan could not hold Christ in the death world, and He thereby, was raised from the dead. And I might quickly add, He was raised from the dead as the *"Second Man"* (I Cor. 15:47).

THE SECOND MAN

What did Paul mean by the term, *"Second Man,"* as it refers to Christ?

Adam was the *"first man"* (I Cor. 15:47), and his Fall brought about the Fall of all who followed him, simply because in essence, every human being was in the loins of the first Adam.

As all of humanity was in the first Adam, all who express Faith in Christ are likewise, in the *"Second Adam,"* hence Paul using the term some 170 times in his 14 Epistles, *"in Christ Jesus,"* or *"in Him,"* etc. This is our place of power and victory, but we must understand what being *"in Him"* actually means.

We were placed in Him at conversion, and of course, we remain in Him. And that means all He is, and all He did for us, are now ours. There's only one thing that we must do, in order to have all of these tremendous Blessings, which He has purchased for us:

FAITH

We are to have Faith in the Cross, which refers to what He did, and do so constantly.

That's why Jesus plainly stated, *"If any man will come after Me, let him deny himself, and take up his Cross daily, and follow Me"* (Lk. 9:23).

What Jesus said here, is the key to all blessings, all power, all overcoming strength, and all victorious living. Let's see exactly what He said:

When He said, *"deny himself (yourself),"* He was not speaking of asceticism as some think. This word refers to a denial of all things which are pleasurable, etc. That's not what Christ was talking about.

He was meaning that you as a Believer are to deny yourself as it refers to all your personal efforts to live a victorious life, etc. You are instead, to place total Faith in what Christ did at the Cross on your behalf, not trusting in yourself at all.

When He spoke of taking up the Cross, if it is to be noticed, He said that it must be done *"daily."*

In a sense, this means that we are to look to the Cross, i.e., *"the Finished Work of Christ,"* every single day of our lives. It is somewhat like renewing our Faith each and every day, but more particularly, renewing our Faith in the Cross each and everyday, understanding, that it's what Christ did there, which gives me the strength and the power this very day, to live the life I ought to live.

This means that you as a Believer are to exhibit Faith in the Cross of Christ each and everyday of your life, understanding that it was by the great Sacrifice of Christ, that everything from the Lord was and is made possible. You must know that and understand that. Knowing and understanding that, your Faith will be anchored in the Cross, in other words, the Cross will be the object of your Faith on a constant basis.

Satan will do everything within his power to shift your Faith to other places. In fact, he really doesn't care too much where you put your Faith, or how religious it might seem to be, just as long as it's not in the Cross of Christ. He doesn't mind you putting your Faith in your Church, in a Preacher, in yourself, or your Denomination, etc. He knows that you're not going to get any help there. He just doesn't want you to understand these things we are telling you, and thereby placing your

NOTES

Faith in that which will bring you guaranteed results — the Cross of Christ.

Please understand, that there is really nothing magic about your Faith being in the Cross. The idea is, that you understand that you cannot do these things yourself, but in fact, it was all done for you at the Cross. That's what it means to be *"in Christ."*

However, it is the Holy Spirit Who makes all of this possible.

THE HOLY SPIRIT

The moment you were Born-Again, the Holy Spirit came into your life. As well, you were then commanded by the Lord to be Baptized with the Holy Spirit, which is always done after Salvation, and is always accompanied by speaking with other Tongues as the Spirit of God gives the utterance (Acts 2:4).

Due to the amount of Light given on this subject since the turn of the Twentieth Century, the Command of Christ in this respect must not be ignored (Acts 1:4). Without this Baptism, the Spirit is greatly hindered regarding His work within your heart and life. This means that every Believer desperately needs the Baptism with the Holy Spirit.

Even then, and I speak of being Baptized with the Spirit, these things of which we are about to speak, aren't automatic. In other words, just because a person is Baptized with the Holy Spirit and speaks with other Tongues, does not guarantee victorious living. Even having Gifts of the Spirit, and the Lord working through you, doesn't guarantee any victorious living. In fact, there are millions of Christians right now, who are definitely Spirit-filled, but aren't living victorious as they ought to be. It is very confusing to them as to why this is happening, but to be sure, it is happening in most Spirit-filled lives, simply because they don't know the way of the Cross. Let me say it another way, so we'll be sure to understand.

The Believer can speak in Tongues every day of his life, sense the Power of God greatly as the Spirit works within him, and as stated, even be used of God, and still not live victoriously. In fact, the two aren't actually connected. And this is what confuses many Spirit-filled Christians. They know that the Lord is working within them, and with some,

He is working mightily. But yet, they are failing in some respect, and despite all of their efforts to do and be otherwise.

As we mentioned some pages back, that's what Paul was talking about when he said, *"For that which I do I allow not: for what I would, that do I not; but what I hate, that do I"* (Rom. 7:15).

Remember that we told you, that the word translated *"allow"* should have been translated *"understand,"* because that's exactly what the Greek word used means. In essence, Paul said:

"For that which I do I understand not."

It must be remembered that at this particular time, which was not long after his conversion, he was Spirit-filled, even called to be an Apostle, but still, despite these things, was definitely not living a victorious life. He was trying with all of his strength, but failing still! Consequently, he didn't understand what was happening in his life, and why he was failing, considering that he was trying so hard not to fail. As stated, that's the very condition that most Christians are in presently.

Paul was in this state, because at that time, he did not know or understand the victory of the Cross. In other words, that great Truth had not yet been revealed unto him. But out of this desperation, a desperation that cried, *"O wretched man that I am! Who shall deliver me from the body of this death?"*, the Lord gave him the answer to this dilemma (Rom. 7:24).

The answer is the Sixth Chapter of Romans which gives us, as one person has said, the mechanics of the Holy Spirit. In other words, the Holy Spirit showed Paul the meaning of the Cross and what the Finished Work of Christ actually does for the Believer.

He then showed Paul in the Eighth Chapter of Romans, just how the Holy Spirit works, with that Chapter being called *"the dynamics of the Holy Spirit."* The point is this:

All of these things of which we speak, have to be done by the Holy Spirit, and I speak of victorious living, power for a consecrated life, and Blessings of every stripe and condition.

The Believer doesn't have to be a theologian in understanding all of this. To be sure, the more you can learn about it the better off you are, and a thousand times over. In fact, it's impossible to exhaust the potential of what Christ did for us at the Cross. So, you ought to learn all you can; however, the only real requirement that the Holy Spirit makes of me and you is, that we evidence Faith at all times in the Cross of Christ (Rom. 8:1-2, 11). But the following will happen, once you begin to evidence Faith in the Cross:

TELL ME MORE ABOUT THE CROSS!

Once you as a Believer begin to evidence Faith in the Cross, and do so on a daily basis, actually taking up your Cross daily, which refers to trusting in its benefits, you will want to learn more and more about the great Finished Work of Christ.

Going back to the statement made by Christ, when He said that we must take up our Cross daily, most people take this all wrong. They think that He's speaking of suffering; consequently, even though they know that Christ said these words, they sort of close their minds to what is said because no one wants to suffer. And most Christians have it in their minds, that taking up the Cross means going through some horrible, terrible ordeal.

No! That's not what the Lord is speaking about at all. When He told us to take up the Cross daily, He wasn't meaning that we have to suffer daily. Actually, He was speaking of the very opposite.

He was talking about experiencing the benefits of what He had done for us, even on a daily basis. Yes, there was suffering involved, most definitely! But it was the suffering that Christ experienced on the Cross, that we might enjoy this more abundant life (Jn. 10:10). Unfortunately, Satan has made Believers think that taking up the Cross daily, is some horrible experience, that consequently, nobody wants to go through. Listen to what Jesus said:

"The thief cometh not, but for to steal, and to kill, and to destroy: I am come that they might have life, and that they might have it more abundantly" (Jn. 10:10).

Do you think that horrible suffering everyday, can be constituted as *"more abundant life"*? Of course not!

Taking up the Cross daily is experiencing the great benefits of what Christ did for us, which is *"more abundant life."*

Jesus also said: *"For whosoever shall save his life shall lose it: but whosoever will lose his life for My sake, the same shall save it"* (Lk. 9:24).

What does He mean by this?

He means that if you try to handle your life on your own terms, by your own efforts, by your own abilities, you're going to lose it — even if you're a Christian. He's not actually speaking here of the soul, but rather our lives. In other words, if we try to live this life outside of the Cross, it's going to be miserable to say the least!

But if we lose our lives, and I speak of doing away with our own efforts and abilities at trying to be what we ought to be by our own machinations, but rather place our Faith and trust in Christ, in effect, actually placing our lives in Him, which is intended, we will then save our lives.

To help us properly understand the situation, it simply means that Christ now becomes our all in all. We are in Him, which means that our lives are totally and completely in Him, with Him providing all things for us, which He did by His Sacrifice at the Cross.

In doing this, we are ceasing to have Faith in ourselves, and other things, but rather exhibiting Faith in Him totally and completely, which refers to what He did for us at the Cross, which speaks of taking up the Cross, and doing so daily.

Living for Jesus is the greatest, most wonderful life there is. In fact, there is no life outside of Christ; however, all of this of which we speak, the greatness, the glory, the grandeur, the power, the strength, the Blessing, and actually everything, are all found, and in totality, in what Christ did at the Cross, all on our behalf, which demands that our Faith be ever placed in His great Sacrifice. When this is done, the Holy Spirit will work mightily on our behalf, guaranteeing us all of these benefits for which Jesus paid such a price.

Our victory and security are totally and completely in the Sacrifice of Christ.

(5) "AND HAVE TASTED THE GOOD WORD OF GOD, AND THE POWERS OF THE WORLD TO COME,"

The exposition is:

1. They had originally believed the Word. This means they had experienced the Word.

2. The *"powers"* mentioned here, speaks of the Holy Spirit.

3. By accepting Christ, they had been made ready for the world to come, speaking of Heaven, and above all, ruling and reigning with Christ forever.

THE GOOD WORD OF GOD

The phrase, *"And have tasted the good Word of God,"* is not language that is applied to an impenitent sinner, as some claim. The unsaved have no relish for the Truth of God; see no beauty in it; derive no comfort from it. It is only the true Christian who has pleasure in its contemplation, and who can be said to *"taste"* and enjoy it.

This language describes a state of mind of which every sincere Christian is conscious. It is that of pleasure in the Word of God. The Believer loves the Bible; he loves the Truth of God that is preached and proclaimed. He sees an exquisite beauty in that Truth. It is not merely in its poetry; in its sublimity; in its arguments; but he has now a taste or relish for the Truth itself, which he had not before his conversion. His love is now for the Truth, which of course, is the Word of God.

The word *"tasted"* as used here has a little bend in the Greek, which suggests that it means, *"tasted that God's Word is good."* These Jewish Christians had heard and received this Word, and had proved for themselves its excellence. An unsaved person cannot do that, as should be overly obvious.

I say these things, because the proponents of unconditional eternal security claim that these Jews to whom Paul speaks, had never really been saved. They claim that *"tasting"* means they didn't really eat it or experience it. But the Greek, as we've already proven, shows the exact opposite.

THE PURPOSE OF THE HOLY SPIRIT

It is agreed upon, that this Epistle was written for the Jews. I do not see how anyone could deny that.

However, it makes no sense whatsoever that the Holy Spirit would write this Epistle in this manner, to individuals who had never accepted Christ. In other words, they had never been saved. Such a person would have no understanding whatsoever as to what Paul was saying. Not being capable of understanding such terminology, it would have been wasted on them, again, as should be overly obvious.

No! Paul wrote this Epistle to Jews who had truly been saved, which means they had truly accepted Christ as their Lord and Saviour, and were living for Him. Paul would not tell unsaved people, *"For when for the time ye ought to be teachers, ye have need that one teach you again . . . and are become such as have need of milk, and not of strong meat"* (Heb. 5:12).

That's not terminology that one would use for unsaved people. The unsaved are never referred to as *"teachers,"* and neither are the terms *"milk"* or *"strong meat"* used of the unsaved. These terms without exception, are used of Believers.

Unsaved people have to first give their hearts to God, before these terms would apply to them. No, Paul is speaking here, as stated, to Jews who had accepted Christ, but now were seriously contemplating turning their backs on Christ, actually denying what He had done for them at the Cross, and going back into Temple worship, etc. If they do this thing, and remain in that state, as Paul will plainly say in coming Verses, they will lose their souls. Of course, this completely refutes the unscriptural doctrine of unconditional eternal security.

THE WORLD TO COME

The phrase, *"And the powers of the world to come,"* refers to the Work of the Holy Spirit within their hearts and lives, which as well opened up to them, as it does all Believers, the *"world to come,"* i.e., *"that which God has prepared for them who love Him"* (I Cor. 2:9-10).

The Scripture plainly says, *"But the natural man receiveth not the things of the Spirit of God: for they are foolishness unto him: neither can he know them, because they are spiritually discerned"* (I Cor. 2:14).

This plainly tells us that no unsaved person can *"taste the good Word of God, and the powers of the world to come."* As the Scripture plainly says, *"They are foolishness unto him."*

All of this given by Paul plainly describes a person who has come to Christ. They first of all are:

1. Enlightened.
2. They then partake of the Gift of Heaven.
3. They are made a partaker of the influences of the Holy Spirit.
4. They then experience the excellence and loveliness of the Word of God.
5. There is a participation in the powers of the new dispensation, of that which is to come.

(6) "IF THEY SHALL FALL AWAY, TO RENEW THEM AGAIN UNTO REPENTANCE; SEEING THEY CRUCIFY TO THEMSELVES THE SON OF GOD AFRESH, AND PUT HIM TO AN OPEN SHAME."

The exegesis is:

1. This refers to Believers who have quit believing in Christ. They have fallen away from Faith, and it's impossible to fall away from something that one has never had.
2. If they stay in that state of unbelief, it's impossible for them to be saved. Repentance before God is accepted only, if one has Faith in Christ (Acts 20:21).
3. To crucify the Son of God afresh, is to express hatred toward Him, exactly as did the Jews who crucified Him.
4. To *"put Him to an open shame"* is to deny Him, which means, to deny that He was and is the Son of God, and is in fact, a deceiver.

FALL AWAY

The phrase, *"If they shall fall away,"* should have been translated, *"and having fallen away."* There is no *"if"* in the Greek.

This is not an affirmation that any had actually fallen away, or that, in fact, they would do so; but the statement is, on the supposition that they would fall away, it would be impossible to renew them again to repentance, that is, if they remain in that state.

"Fall away" in the Greek is *"parapipto,"* and means, *"to apostatize,"* which means, *"to fall away from Truth."* Again I emphasize, that it's impossible for one to fall away from something which they never had. In fact, it's impossible for an unsaved individual to apostatize. Apostasy means, *"a falling away from Truth."* It's impossible for one to fall away from Truth which they have never possessed to begin with.

No! As is overly obvious, Paul is speaking here to Jews, and anyone for that matter, who had once known the Lord or else, knew Him presently in the realm of Salvation.

We must remember that no man has the power to remove any Believer from the hand of God. As well, there are no circumstances or powers of Hell that can move us. However, we can remove ourselves, if we are so inclined to do so. The responsibility to maintain our relationship with God through Christ rests not upon Christ, inasmuch as He has already done His part, and in fact, continues to do His part, and will ever do His part, but rather rests upon us (Jn. 10:28; Rom. 8:35-39).

The security of the Believer rests in his continued relationship to Christ by Faith, exactly as it did with these Christian Jews of Paul's day. Consequently, such a position which we presently have regarding our standing before God is secure as long as we persevere in Faith and obedience, for the Scriptures declare *"the just shall live by Faith"* (Rom. 1:17).

These Christian Jews were losing Faith in Christ, which is the one thing that can jeopardize and even destroy one's position in Christ.

All of this means, that our participation in His life, which is the life we presently have, which is Eternal Life, is dependent upon our abiding and remaining in Christ.

Eternal Life is in Christ; to know Him is to have Eternal Life. This means that we must continually abide in Him in order to have Life. If we choose to turn from Him, and if we cease to abide in Him, we forfeit Eternal Life (Jn. 5:24; I Jn. 5:11-13).

REPENTANCE

The phrase, *"To renew them again unto repentance,"* centers up on the two words *"renew"* and *"again."* The word *"renew"* plain and simple means that the individual had once before repented. This is proven as well by the word *"again."* People cannot renew something that they have not previously had, and as well, the word *"again"* would not be used if there had not been a previous experience.

Concerning *"repentance"* the Scripture plainly says, *"Testifying both to the Jews, and also to the Greeks, repentance toward God, and Faith toward our Lord Jesus Christ"* (Acts 20:21).

One's repentance unto God is accepted solely on the basis of one's Faith toward and in the Lord Jesus Christ, and more particularly, what Christ did at the Cross on our behalf, for that's what it means. The idea is, these Jews were claiming that they would continue to serve God, but Paul is telling them, that it's impossible to get right with God or to serve God, except one goes through the Lord Jesus Christ. In fact, Jesus plainly said, concerning this very thing, *"I (Jesus) am the Way, the Truth, and the Life: no man cometh unto the Father, but by Me"* (Jn. 14:6).

So, our Catholic friends or our Mormon friends, who pay lip service to Christ, but rather try to go to God through the Church, aren't saved. It's just that simple. I don't mean to be blunt, but I don't know of any other way it can be said. In fact, it goes for anyone else, and anywhere else. If the sinner doesn't place his Faith exclusively in Christ and what Christ did at the Cross on his behalf, he cannot be saved. And as well, if the Christian places his Faith in Christ and the Cross respecting his Salvation, but in something else concerning his Sanctification, while he is saved, he definitely will not walk in victory. *"Jesus Christ and Him Crucified,"* is the answer for all men, for all time, and for all things.

WHAT DOES THE WORD *"IMPOSSIBLE"* MEAN, AS USED IN THE FOURTH VERSE?

Does it mean that these individuals who would do such a thing, and we refer to denying Christ, have blasphemed the Holy Spirit, and can, therefore, never come back to God?

With some, *"yes!"*, and with others *"no!"* Let us explain:

Concerning blaspheming the Holy Spirit, Jesus said, *"And whosoever speaketh a word against the Son of Man, it shall be forgiven him: but whosoever speaketh against the Holy Spirit, it shall not be forgiven him, neither in this world, neither in the world to come"* (Mat. 12:31-32).

First of all, it's not possible for an individual who has never known Christ to blaspheme the Holy Spirit. It is possible only for those who have once known the Lord, or else have made a great profession of knowing Him as the Pharisees and Sadducees of old, but actually didn't.

There's never been an individual in history, who wanted to come to the Lord, or back to the Lord, but that the door was always open. Jesus plainly said, *"Him that cometh to Me I will in no wise cast out"* (Jn. 6:37).

If a person has actually blasphemed the Holy Spirit, that person will not try to come to the Lord, and in fact, will have no desire to come to the Lord. The very fact of a desire in one's heart to come to God proves the drawing power of the Holy Spirit. To be frank, a person cannot even really desire to come to the Lord, unless the Holy Spirit instigates such a desire. And to be sure, He would not do such, were it not possible for that person to be saved. The Godhead doesn't work against itself, as should be obvious. So, the idea *"I want to, but I can't,"* doesn't hold water!

So what does the word *"impossible"* as used in the Fourth Verse actually mean?

It means that if a person refuses to believe that Christ is the Saviour, and in fact, the only Saviour, and that such Salvation is provided by His Sacrifice of Himself on the Cross, that it's impossible for that person to be saved, or to come back to God, etc. It doesn't mean that they cannot come back, but that if they remain in that state, it's impossible for them to do so.

Paul is not speaking here of a particular act, as much as he is a state of being. These Christian Jews were at the point of losing Faith in Christ. And of course if they did that, thereby going back to Judaism, or whatever, they would lose their Salvation, which could not be renewed if they remained in that state. In fact, the next two phrases of this Verse tell us how this is brought about.

CRUCIFY THE SON OF GOD AFRESH

The phrase, *"Seeing they crucify to themselves the Son of God afresh,"* refers to their action of denying Him, and thus agreeing with His murderers. It speaks of those who, with a distinct conviction of the Divine mission of Jesus, have deliberately joined His foes, uniting in denouncing Him as a *"deceiver"* (Mat. 27:63), and rejoicing in His shame, and thus *"for themselves, at least in spirit, crucifying a second time the Son of*

God." With some, in the doing of this, should such a horrible thing be done, they would also speak against the Holy Spirit, which would then seal their doom. In other words, they no longer can be saved, and in fact, will have no desire to be saved, that is by Christ. Of course, at the same time, just as with the Pharisees and Sadducees of old, they will no doubt continue to claim Salvation, etc. But whatever type of Salvation they claim, which of course is bogus, it will be without Christ, which of course, makes Salvation impossible.

At the same time, there quite possibly would be some who would do such a horrible thing as turning their backs on Christ, but at the same time, would not speak against the Holy Spirit, and at some later time would desire to come back to Christ. No doubt that happened! And if so, they would be accepted.

The impossibility always rests in the action of an individual attempting to be saved in another way other than Christ.

To which we have already alluded, these Christian Jews who were contemplating such a thing, and we speak of forsaking Christ and going back into Judaism, in no way considered themselves to be forsaking God; irrespective, whatever it was they considered, that's exactly what they were doing.

THE TRUE WAY OF THE LORD

Let us not think that this which Paul addressed so long ago has no present meaning. In fact, it is heavy with meaning pertaining to the present time.

There aren't many good Churches which totally and completely preach and proclaim the Gospel of Christ, in other words, *"Jesus Christ and Him Crucified."* Such a Church would be led by the Spirit, empowered by the Spirit, and would experience a move of the Spirit on a constant basis.

As stated, not many of these type Churches exist, and anyone who has the privilege of being associated with such a Church is privileged indeed!

To leave such a Church, and to do so in the wrong spirit, thereby attending another Church that does not enjoy the Spirit of God, presents itself as a serious matter indeed! While such a person would not be openly repudiating Christ, their actions in fact are doing just that! Consequently, their Spiritual Growth has just stopped, and the end result could be the loss of their souls, even as it has with many. To do such a thing, as stated, is serious indeed!

It's bad enough to have the availability of such a Church, and not associate one's self with such a Church. But to be a part of such a Church, and then leave for malicious reasons, presents itself as a very serious thing.

While this of which we speak is not as serious as this of which Paul speaks, it definitely is a step in that direction.

The question should be asked, *"Why do we attend a particular Church?"* Is it because that's the Denomination with which we've always been associated? Is it because we enjoy the social activities? Is it because all our friends attend there? Is it because we like the sports program of the Church?

These things we've named, and many we haven't named, should have no bearing whatsoever on why a person attends a particular Church. There must be two reasons and two reasons alone:

1. Is the Word of God truly preached in your particular Church?

2. Does the Spirit of God move in that Church, resulting in souls being saved, Believers being Baptized with the Holy Spirit, the sick truly being healed, and lives truly being changed?

The sadness is, due to the fact that most Churches do not enjoy this of which we have just said, most Christians have no idea whatsoever as to what the Word of God actually is, or what the moving of the Spirit actually is. Some few know; most don't!

Such a climate makes Satan's work very easy, and we speak of the ease of deception. Considering that we're speaking here of the issues of life and death, we should do exactly as Paul said, *"Examine yourselves, whether ye be in the Faith; prove your own selves. Know ye not your own selves, how that Jesus Christ is in you, except ye be reprobates?"* (II Cor. 13:5).

OPEN SHAME

The phrase, *"And put Him to an open shame,"* means to hold Christ up to public ridicule. In fact, this is what the nation of

Israel was doing concerning Christ, and has continued to do so to this moment.

They claim that His birth was the result of Mary being associated with a drunken, Roman soldier. Consequently, they refer to Him as *"the Bastard!"*

Considering that He was crucified, they also refer to Him as *"the hung!"*

Paul is telling these Christian Jews, that their apostasy and rejection of the Saviour would be like holding Him up publicly as deserving the infamy and ignominy of the Cross. In fact, a great part of the crime attending the Crucifixion of the Lord Jesus, consisted in exhibiting Him to the passing multitude as deserving the death of a malefactor. To reject Him, at least in such a circumstance, is to hold Him up to contempt.

Some would claim that it's not possible for a Believer to do such a thing. That is infallibly correct; however, it is certainly possible for a Believer to cease believing, in effect to lose his Faith in Christ, as many have done, and then anything is possible.

Jesus addressed this when He said, *"When the unclean spirit is gone out of a man, he* (the unclean spirit) *walketh through dry places, seeking rest, and findeth none.*

"Then he saith, I will return into my house from whence I came out; and when he (the evil spirit) *is come, he findeth it empty, swept, and garnished.*

"Then goeth he, and taketh with himself seven other spirits more wicked than himself, and they enter in and dwell there: and the last state of that man is worse than the first" (Mat. 12:43-45).

This is what happened to the nation of Israel after the Ministry of Christ. In rejecting Him, they became seven times worse, figuratively speaking, and were destroyed. It is the same with the person who has known Christ, and then turned his back upon Him. Their state is even now worse, far worse, than before they knew Him.

(7) "FOR THE EARTH WHICH DRINKETH IN THE RAIN THAT COMETH OFT UPON IT, AND BRINGETH FORTH HERBS MEET FOR THEM BY WHOM IT IS DRESSED, RECEIVETH BLESSING FROM GOD:"

The exposition is:

1. The Earth receives rain, which Paul uses as an analogy of a Believer receiving the Word of God.

2. Due to the rain, the Earth brings forth herbs, and as the Earth does this, the Believer is expected to bring forth fruit as a result of the imparted Word.

3. *"By whom it is dressed,"* refers to the ones cultivating the Earth and expecting a harvest due to the rain. Likewise, God expects a harvest of Spiritual Growth as a result of Him giving the Word.

4. As the rain upon the Earth is a blessing from God, likewise the Word being given to Believers is a Blessing from God, in which and from which He expects results.

THE RAIN

The phrase, *"For the Earth which drinketh in the rain that cometh oft upon it,"* presents Paul using natural things to represent spiritual realities which is common throughout Scripture. Vines, vineyards, and the planting of seeds are illustrations frequently used to describe the individual's relationship with God.

The rain here as used by the Apostle, represents spiritual enlightenment and renewal; the rain *"cometh oft,"* and as the ground *"drinketh in the rain"* it produces fruit to the satisfaction of those who have planted and cultivated.

The lesson is clearly seen. The Gospel had come to the Jewish community; many had believed and accepted it. Enlightenment had come to them as the Word was preached and confirmed. Now some were in danger of bearing no fruit; as a result of this, there was a possibility of their becoming unacceptable. Many of them were responding, as did their forefathers, who did not, and in fact, could not enter into God's rest because of their unbelief.

Let it be understood, even as we've already stated, that these Jews being written to by Paul had been born of the Spirit. If in fact that had not been the case, why would the Jewish community as a whole have rejected them and persecuted them if there had not been a conversion from Judaism to Christianity? Furthermore, the construction of the Greek Text demands that we understand

NOTES

these descriptions as facts, in other words, that these Jews were in fact Believers in Christ, and not merely just someone who had heard the Gospel, but had rejected it.

One has to seriously distort these Passages to conclude that these described never had known the Holy Spirit in a personal dynamic way. The Holy Spirit's work in illuminating them to the things of Christ, and their response in tasting, actually eating and experiencing the Gospel, had brought them into a new communion with God the Holy Spirit; they were now participants and sharers of the Holy Spirit.

The problem here, as is overly obvious, is to voluntarily profess Christ and to accept Him in Faith, and then to voluntarily abandon and reject Him, is apostasy. It is a total desertion of the principles of Faith. Paul plainly said, on which we have already commented:

"Take heed, Brethren, lest there be in any of you an evil heart of unbelief, in departing from the Living God" (Heb. 3:12).

In all of this, the Apostle, by the inspiration of the Holy Spirit, clearly shows the real danger of apostasy, and also sets forth the terrifying consequences.

We must also keep in mind that all of these Passages are not referring merely to shortcomings, faults, or failures of the Believer; neither does it refer to sins we may commit. It is speaking of a desertion of the Faith, which means that one turns their back upon Christ and what He did at the Cross on their behalf, by which alone an individual can be saved.

The moment an individual comes to Christ, at that moment the Holy Spirit proceeds to give them an understanding of the Word of God, which is designed for a particular result, actually that stated in the next phrase.

SPIRITUAL GROWTH

The phrase, *"And bringeth forth herbs,"* presents that which is the natural result of ground which is properly cultivated and receives proper rain. There will be a harvest.

Paul compares Believers who persevere in Faith to fertile land which produces rich, abundant fruit. Faithful Believers bring forth fruit and herbs, continuing to use the analogy in a spiritual sense. Their lives are filled with the fruit of Righteousness. In fact, Jesus dealt with this very extensively in Saint John, Chapter 15. He said:

"I Am the True Vine, and My Father is the Husbandman.

"Every branch in Me that beareth not fruit He taketh away: and every branch that beareth fruit, He purgeth it, that it may bring forth more fruit."

He then said, *"Abide in Me, and I in you. As the branch cannot bear fruit of itself, except it abide in the vine; no more can ye, except ye abide in Me.*

"I am the Vine, ye are the branches: he that abideth in Me, and I in him, the same bringeth forth much fruit: for without Me ye can do nothing."

He then said, which coincides exactly with what the Holy Spirit through Paul is teaching, *"If a man abide not in Me, he is cast forth as a branch, and is withered; and men gather them, and cast them into the fire, and they are burned"* (Jn. 15:1-6).

BRINGING FORTH FRUIT

The idea is, we as Believers bring forth fruit according to the Word of God, which is brought about by our abiding totally and completely in Christ, which refers to totally and completely trusting in what He did at the Cross on our behalf and not at all in ourselves, or else we wither and die, which refers to ultimately going into apostasy.

When we get to the bottom line of all of this, it refers to Faith being transferred from the Cross, the great Sacrifice of Christ, or as we might say, *"the Finished Work of Christ,"* and rather placing it in something else. Whatever the results, and whatever the difficulties, and however it might appear to be on the surface, when Christians lose their way with God, it is always and without exception, because their Faith is transferred from the Cross to other things. In fact, the surface may appear to be something else, but if one goes to the root of the problem, one will always find this of which we speak.

The entirety of the matter speaks of our Faith. When one loses Faith, it is a loss of Faith in the great Sacrifice of Christ. In some way, the individual no longer believes that all he is in the Lord has come through the great Offering of Christ of Himself, and one's

NOTES

Faith in that, which in essence means that he has cast a vote of no confidence in the Cross of Christ.

When Jesus speaks of abiding in Him, He is saying the same thing that Paul was saying in his use of the term *"in Christ,"* which he used about 170 times in one manner or the other, in his 14 Epistles.

To be *"in Christ,"* and to stay *"in Christ,"* refers to what Christ did at the Cross on our behalf, and our Faith in that, which is done on a continuing, even everyday basis (Lk. 9:23).

These individuals who think they outgrow the Cross, and have, therefore, gone beyond the Cross, have done two things, whether they realize it or not:

1. First of all, they are denying what Paul has said, about the great Cross of Christ being absolutely inexhaustible. He referred to the great Sacrifice of Christ as *"the Everlasting Covenant"* (Heb. 13:20). This means it will never be replaced, and that its potential can never be exhausted. These poor individuals are claiming that they have in fact, exhausted its potential!

2. Going beyond the Cross is in effect, doing the same thing that Cain did, which refers to one making his own sacrifice. I would hope that one could see the fallacy and absolute destructive power of such a course.

First of all, for any Believer to come to the place, that he thinks he no longer needs the efficacy of the Cross, in other words what it provides, is in fact, apostasy, which is a departure from Truth.

What these Christian Jews actually thought of Christ is anyone's guess. More than likely in their hearts, they did not consider themselves as abandoning Christ. They may have been continuing to claim Him as a Messiah of sorts, or whatever, even though had they gone back into Judaism; however, they would have ultimately been forced to repudiate Him totally. The first step downward doesn't seem to be so serious, but it must always be remembered, that a downward trend cannot stop at a certain place, but must always go to the bitter end, which is total destruction.

However, irrespective as to what they thought of Christ, or in what type of posture they were attempting to place Him, the Truth was, they definitely were rejecting what Christ did at the Cross as the answer to man's dilemma, be he Jew or Gentile. There was no getting around that!

Understanding that, we must also come to the conclusion, that to divorce Christ from the Cross, or the Cross from Christ, is blasphemy. In other words, when one thinks of Jesus, one at the same time should think of His great Sacrifice. And when one thinks of the great Sacrifice, one must at the same time think of Jesus. The two are synonymous! That's why the Holy Spirit through Paul, used the term *"Jesus Christ and Him Crucified"* (I Cor. 2:2).

To the Reader who doesn't quite know what I'm talking about, it may seem as though I am belaboring the point; however, once the seriousness of this matter begins to sink in, and one comes to the place that one properly understands the Cross of Christ, then it becomes abundantly clear, that it's not possible to belabor this point. The Sacrifice of Christ is what the Bible is all about, and that is because the Cross stands at the very center of history. Everything that man receives from God, and in any capacity, comes exclusively through the great Sacrifice of Christ. And the simple manner, in which all of this is carried out, is Faith in that Finished Work. That's the reason that Satan fights the Cross to the extent that he does. If he can turn the Believer's Faith to something else, even as he was doing with these Christian Jews, he can drive the person to total apostasy, and thereby, the loss of their eternal soul. That's the reason that all of this is so very, very serious!

THE HOLY SPIRIT WHO CULTIVATES

The phrase, *"Meet for them by Whom it is dressed,"* refers to individuals who do the cultivating of land, planting the seed, etc. Pulling it over to the spiritual sense, it refers to the work carried out by the Holy Spirit within our hearts, Who expects a harvest. Why not!

The land has been properly cultivated and God has sent rain. So there is no reason for a lack of harvest. Jesus dealt with this concerning Israel. He said:

"A certain man had a fig tree planted in his vineyard; and he came and sought fruit thereon, and found none.

"Then said he unto the dresser of his vineyard, behold, these three years I come seeking fruit on this fig tree and found none: cut it down; why cumbereth it the ground?" (Lk. 13:6-7).

The Ministry of Christ to Israel was about three years. Spiritually speaking, He cultivated the ground and watered it, all to no avail. It brought forth no fruit! Consequently, it was cut down, because it was only cluttering the ground.

All of this is exactly what is being said by the Spirit through Paul in his Letter to the Hebrews.

To fail to bring forth fruit brings about that which the Apostle gives us in the next Verse.

BLESSING FROM GOD

The phrase, *"Receiveth Blessing from God,"* presents the inevitable result, of proper Faith.

The term *"blessing from God"* is given in this fashion, in order that the Believer might know and understand, that everything we receive from the Lord, is totally and completely of the Lord, and not at all of us. This means, that it is impossible for a Believer to draw closer to the Lord, or to bring about a work of the Lord within his heart, by his own efforts, abilities, religiosity, or machinations. All and without exception, is a Work of the Spirit, which is brought about within our hearts and lives, by our constant dependence on Christ, and more particularly, what Christ did for us at the Cross.

DEPENDENCE ON CHRIST

The phrase, *"dependence on Christ"* which makes up our heading, is used constantly by most all Christians. The Truth is, however, most don't actually know what it means.

Most think rightly that He is the Lord of Glory, which He definitely is, but that the mere fact of Him being that, guarantees them some type of spiritual success. It doesn't!

Christ has always been God; however, man was not redeemed on this fact alone. God had to become man, and die on a Cross, in order for all of this to be brought about.

So, when we speak of *"depending on Christ,"* or *"trusting in Christ,"* we must understand what that exactly means. It means that we place our total and complete trust in what He did on our behalf by giving Himself as an Offering before God on the Cross.

We do not have all of these *"Blessings from God,"* simply because Jesus is God, or He was Virgin born, or that He was a great Healer, or Miracle Worker, or anything else of that nature which we might think. Even though these things were absolutely necessary, and play a very important part in all that Christ did, still, we were not redeemed until Christ went to the Cross. Everything He was and did, pointed to His great Sacrifice. Everything was pushing toward that one goal.

On the Mount of Transfiguration, the Scripture plainly tells us, that when Moses and Elijah appeared there with Christ, in full view incidentally of Peter, James, and John, that they (Christ, Moses, and Elijah) *"spake of His decease which He should accomplish at Jerusalem"* (Lk. 9:28-31).

The death of Christ on the Cross, in order to redeem lost humanity, was the topic of conversation between Christ and these two Old Testament Faith worthies, simply because, this was the core of the very mission of Christ on Earth.

Following the great confession made by Simon Peter concerning the identity of Christ, *"the Son of the Living God,"* Jesus told how that *"He must go unto Jerusalem, and suffer many things of the Elders and Chief Priests and Scribes, and be killed, and be raised again the third day."*

The Scripture then says, *"Peter took Him, and began to rebuke Him, saying, Be it far from Thee, Lord: this shall not be unto Thee.*

"But Jesus turned, and said unto Peter, 'Get thee behind Me, Satan: thou art an offense unto Me: for thou savourest not the things that be of God, but those that be of men'" (Mat. 16:14-16, 21-23).

That's when Jesus also said, *"If any man will come after Me, let him deny himself, and take up his Cross, and follow Me"* (Mat. 16:24).

Christ was showing His Disciples, and all others for that matter, that it was and is the Cross, which would and did make all of this

possible, and we speak of Eternal Life, and victorious, overcoming living.

In other words, every single *"Blessing"* from God in its entirety, comes exclusively by and through the Cross of Christ. The Christian must understand that and must ever act upon that. This must ever be the object of one's Faith — the great Sacrifice of Christ.

(8) "BUT THAT WHICH BEARETH THORNS AND BRIERS IS REJECTED, AND IS NIGH UNTO CURSING; WHOSE END IS TO BE BURNED."

The exegesis is:

1. If no fruit is forthcoming, but rather thorns and briars, that person is then rejected.

2. The curse of the broken Law then comes upon them. The curse was taken by Christ (Gal. 3:13-14). However, it is taken and removed from us, only because of what Christ did at the Cross, and our Faith in that. If Faith is lost, the curse once again, descends.

3. The burning here reflects judgment and, therefore, destruction. Let it ever be understood, while God definitely chastises all His children, He never sends judgment upon them, that being already taken by Christ at the Cross; however, if a Believer ceases to believe, which many have done, thereby depreciating the great Sacrifice of Christ, that person ceases to be a Child of God, and is, therefore, a subject of Judgment. To say the least, it's not a pleasant prospect! The end result is eternal Hell.

REJECTED!

The phrase, *"But that which beareth thorns and briers is rejected,"* presents Paul continuing to use the analogy of the Earth producing or not producing. If it brings forth no fruit, but rather *"thorns and briers,"* such are rejected, as would be obvious. It is the same in the spiritual sense!

As land that produces nothing but thorns and briers, and despite the work lavished on it, is rejected, and as would be obvious, likewise, the Christian falls into the same category. One can't have it both ways.

If we try to claim these people had never been saved, even as some do, then our conclusion makes no sense. The *only* thing that the unsaved bring forth is *"thorns"* and *"briers."* They are incapable of bring forth any fruit for the Lord, as should be overly obvious.

No! Paul is speaking to Christian Jews, individuals who had accepted Christ, having made Him their Lord and Saviour, and were now seriously contemplating turning their backs on Him, thereby repudiating the Cross, and going back into Law-keeping as their means of Salvation, which for certain would bring destruction.

One writer said that it is impossible for a Christian to apostatize, but if they did, this is what would happen. How nonsensical can we be!

Why would the Holy Spirit through Paul desire to have an entire Epistle written, concerning something that was impossible? And what difference does it make concerning what would happen, if it's impossible for such to happen!

"Rejected" in the Greek is *"adokimos,"* and means *"unapproved, rejected, worthless, castaway, reprobate."* Again I emphasize, all unbelievers are in this state. So it is pointless to bring out all of this teaching, if these Jews to whom Paul is addressing this Epistle are unsaved. The Truth is, these Jews had definitely been saved, with many of them still in that state. The Lord had dealt with them graciously, but unbelief was beginning to pull them in the wrong direction, with its spiral concluding by them being totally and completely rejected, that is, if they continued on this path. The entirety of this Epistle is written, in order to make them see what is happening, and hopefully, to turn them around. As well, the Reader should understand, that this graphic teaching applies to all others and for all time.

God must reject all who refuse to accept Christ as their eternal Saviour, which refers to all unsaved, that is if they remain in that state, and as well, He must reject all efforts by Christians which take them away from the Cross. Continuing to speak to Christians, this means, that all good works are rejected, at least as a means of bringing one closer to God, or attempting to bring about Holiness and Righteousness in one's life.

When the Believer attempts to effect his walk with God, by self-effort, which means

that his Faith is no longer in the Cross of Christ, God must reject that effort. He cannot do otherwise! In fact, the entire Epistle to the Galatians was written in respect to this one thing. The Galatians had been saved by *"Faith,"* and we speak of Faith in Christ and what He did at the Cross, but were now attempting to bring about Sanctification through *"self."* Such a road could not help but lead to disaster, and because God must reject such efforts (Gal. 3:2-3).

God will even reject a person's prayer life, at least if it is an attempt to make one holy and pure by this method. While a proper prayer life is definitely demanded of all Christians, it must always be used in the right manner, and never as a means to attain a spiritual place and position with God. All such things are found only in Christ, and are given to us due to what He did for us at the Cross. It only requires Faith on our part in Him and in what He did, for these results to be brought about. Then and only then will the Holy Spirit work on our behalf.

But when we attempt to use even good things such as prayer, or fasting, etc., as a means to bring these things about, of necessity, God must reject our efforts, which means to say the least, that we will have no satisfactory result.

MODERN CHRISTIANS

If the Believer doesn't know and understand the great veracity of the Cross of Christ, in other words, what the Sacrifice of Christ actually means, of necessity, he will resort to other things, attempting to bring about desired results in his life. In fact, that's where most of modern Christendom is presently. Knowing almost nothing about the Cross, at least beyond sentimentality, which includes the Preachers as well, they must resort to other means. But the sad fact is, there are no other means, because God rejects all efforts otherwise.

He rejected the offering of Cain, and for all the obvious reasons. It is ironic, that Christians read this account in Chapter 4 of Genesis, and never once think that they possibly might be doing the same thing.

The Truth is, if we're not depending totally and completely on Christ and what He did at the Cross, we are of necessity, offering up efforts of our own making, which constitutes the same thing as done by Cain. It is only the Sacrifice of Christ which God will honor. And to interject irony again, most Christians think they know all about the Cross, actually dismissing it as elementary. The Truth is, they know almost nothing about the Cross!

As a result, almost all of the modern Church is rejected by God. This doesn't mean that these people are necessarily lost. However, it definitely does mean, that such a direction, which as stated is rejected by God, will bring forth very negative results. And the simple fact is, that many of these people will conclude by being eternally lost.

A wrong direction cannot be corrected, unless the person truly repents. And let's look at that a moment.

REPENTANCE

Some years ago, one British Preacher made the statement, that Christians need to repent not only of evil things which they do, but as well, of the good.

When I read those words, I knew instantly that he was right, but at that particular time, I didn't know why he was right. What did he mean by repenting of that which is good?

He was speaking of Christians depending on their good works, their efforts, their faithfulness to the Church, or a hundred and one other things we might name, instead of depending exclusively upon Christ and what He did for us at the Cross. The man was saying, that we need to repent of our dependence upon these things. That's what he was talking about!

More than likely, most Christians would nod their heads in agreement with this which I've just said, but at the same time, most would continue right on depending on their good works.

All of this happens, simply because Believers do not understand the Cross, even though they fully believe they do understand the Cross.

Most Christians will read Romans 8:1 which says, *"There is therefore now no condemnation to them which are in Christ Jesus, who walk not after the flesh, but after the*

Spirit," and then ask the question, *"How does one walk after the Spirit?"*

If one has to ask, then one is not walking after the Spirit. It is that simple! It is somewhat like asking if one knows that a 2,000 pound elephant is in his house.

When one truly begins to walk after the Spirit, the results will quickly become obvious. The Spirit will always lead the Believer to the Cross. He does so because this is the manner in which He works. Everything the Spirit of God does within our hearts and lives, is predicated totally and completely on what Christ did at the Cross. In other words, the Finished Work of Christ is the parameters.

Understanding this, the Holy Spirit demands of us, that we exhibit simple Faith in what Christ did there, and do so on a constant basis. With this done, and continuing to be done, the Holy Spirit then works mightily upon our behalf, giving us the victory which He Alone can give. Everything else is rejected, as everything else must be rejected, and irrespective as to what it might be.

THE CURSE

The phrase, *"And is nigh unto cursing,"* refers to judgment.

When Jesus died on the Cross, He redeemed us from the curse of the Law, being made a curse for us (Gal. 3:13).

The curse of the broken Law was and is death (Rom. 6:23). Consequently, considering that all had broken the Law of God, the sentence had already been pronounced on all. But Christ took this curse upon Himself, which means that He died for us, which means that He took our place. Not having any curse upon Himself, simply because He had never sinned, He had to be *"made a curse for us."*

He was made a curse by being crucified, with the Scripture saying, *"Cursed is everyone that hangeth on a tree"* (Gal. 3:13).

All of this, as striking as it was and is, simply means, that our Faith in what Christ did there, removes the curse totally and completely from us. However, if we remove our Faith from the Finished Work of Christ, thereby placing it in something else, even as these Christian Jews were contemplating doing, and if we remain in that state, we have forfeited the Grace of God, because the Grace of God can only function through the Cross, and our Faith in that (Gal. 2:20-21).

If we remain, as stated, in that state, which means that our Faith has been pulled away from Christ and His Finished Work, the end result can only be that the curse of God descends back upon us once again. To deny that, is to deny the obvious.

The only thing that stops the curse is our Faith in the Finished Work of Christ. So if such Faith is absent, the removed curse is allowed to come back. This means that instead of Jesus having died for our sins, we will die for our own sins, which of course, avails us nothing! In other words, our physical death cannot atone for our sins, because we are an imperfect sacrifice. The only Atonement is the Cross of Christ.

DESTRUCTION

The phrase, *"Whose end is to be burned,"* refers to the simple fact, that if a person who was once a Believer remains in that state, he will lose his soul.

"Burned" in the Greek is *"kausis,"* and means exactly what it says, *"to be burned, to be consumed."*

The Lord has but one Sacrifice. If that Sacrifice is rejected, there remains no other manner or way of Salvation. Consequently, the end result has to be Hell fire, which means the eternal loss of one's soul, and despite the fact that the person has once known Christ. Again we state, this is the entirety of the reason for this Epistle to the Hebrews.

All of these warnings aren't given merely to individuals who had been under conviction by the Holy Spirit and had never accepted the Lord. It is obvious as to their state and their conclusion, that is if they remain in that state.

No, all of these warnings, admonitions, teaching, and instruction, are given to individuals who had indeed, accepted Christ as their own personal Saviour. But for whatever reason, they had not grown in Grace. In fact, Paul plainly told them that by now they should be Teachers, but instead, they were in need of teaching themselves, even elementary teaching (Heb. 5:12). In fact, the next Verse continues to prove that Paul is speaking to Believers.

(9) "BUT, BELOVED, WE ARE PERSUADED BETTER THINGS OF YOU, AND THINGS THAT ACCOMPANY SALVATION, THOUGH WE THUS SPEAK."

The exposition is:

1. By using the word *"beloved,"* we are again given proof upon proof, that Paul is speaking to Believers. In fact, Paul uses the word *"Brethren"* several times regarding these Christian Jews, which he certainly would not have done had they been unsaved, as many claim (Heb. 3:1, 12; 10:19; 13:22).

2. The phrase, *"We are persuaded better things of you,"* refers to Believers. The Apostle would have expected nothing from the unsaved!

3. The earmarks of Spiritual Growth were absent in these people.

4. This is the reason that Paul is writing as he does.

BELOVED

The phrase, *"But, Beloved,"* presents the fact that these Christian Jews were the object not only of God's love, but also of Paul's care and concern. The warning he has written has been for their good. He is bound to them by the ties of Christian love.

If there was anyone in the world who knew their plight as Jews, and of course, Jews who had accepted Christ, Paul was well acquainted with the entirety of this situation. Of all people, he knew the animosity that the nation of Israel had against Christ. In fact, they had leveled much of their animosity against him, actually trying to kill him.

As well, he knew the Mosaic Law as no other human being on the face of the Earth. In fact, he was probably the most learned scholar in that capacity of anyone else in the world. So, if anyone had weight in this respect, Paul did! Consequently, if they wouldn't listen to the Apostle, they wouldn't listen to anyone!

Therefore, when he uses the word *"beloved"* of these Hebrews, such terminology comes from his heart. It is not an act of flattery.

YOU

The phrase, *"We are persuaded better things of you,"* makes the pronoun emphatic.

In other words, he is speaking specifically to those who were seriously contemplating turning their backs on Christ. He has gone into great detail, explaining to them the supremacy of Christ. And of course, the Holy Spirit was inspiring Paul in all that he said, which means that this Epistle is the Word of God.

As is obvious, the Apostle has also said some very strong things to these particular Jews. He has had no choice but to do so. They must be made aware of what is going to happen if they continue on the course of apostasy.

Incidentally, he uses the word *"better"* here, which is one of the staple words in the entirety of this Epistle. He spoke here of *"better things,"* as he spoke of a *"better hope,"* a *"better Testament,"* a *"better Covenant,"* *"better Promises,"* a *"better country,"* and a *"better Resurrection,"* etc. In fact, everything of Christ is *"better!"*

SALVATION

The phrase, *"And things that accompany Salvation,"* proclaims that which is *"better,"* that is, if the individual grows in the Lord.

"Salvation" is a word that encompasses far more than the initial Born-Again experience, as wonderful as that is! While it definitely includes that, it also includes much more.

Salvation pertains to that which Jesus did at the Cross on our behalf, in other words, all of its benefits.

It speaks of the sinner being Washed, Sanctified, and Justified, all done at the initial conversion experience (Rom. 6:3-5; I Cor. 6:11). It then speaks of victorious, Christian living on an everyday basis. This is portrayed, by Believers actually being seated with Christ, spiritually speaking, in Heavenly Places (Eph. 2:6).

As well, what Christ did at the Cross as it regards Salvation, includes the coming Resurrection, when then, every Saint will be glorified (I Cor. 15:51-54; I Thess. 4:13-18).

The Salvation process, also includes every Saint of God coming back to this Earth with the Lord, which of course will take place *after* the Rapture, and is referred to as the Second Coming, when all Saints will rule and reign with Christ forever (Rev. Chpt. 19).

As is obvious, we do not yet have all that Salvation affords; but just as surely as we have

NOTES

been Sanctified and Justified, we shall be Glorified. The Resurrection of Christ guarantees that. Christ is the *"Firstfruits!"*

THAT WHICH WE SPEAK

The phrase, *"Though we thus speak,"* refers to him saying this which he knows. In other words, he is not speaking from guesswork, but from many years of experience. As stated, due to Paul's wide ranging experience, if these Jews wouldn't listen to him, they wouldn't listen to anyone.

(10) "FOR GOD IS NOT UNRIGHTEOUS TO FORGET YOUR WORK AND LABOUR OF LOVE, WHICH YE HAVE SHEWED TOWARD HIS NAME, IN THAT YE HAVE MINISTERED TO THE SAINTS, AND DO MINISTER."

The exposition is:

1. God does not deal unfairly, ever!

2. It is the Character of God, the perfectly just Judge of all, that gives rise to confidence.

3. God will not forget anyone's work and labor of love.

4. The Name of the Lord sums up all of that which He is.

5. To prove that these people had been truly saved, their love reached out to other Saints, which will always be the hallmark of true Christians. Unsaved people don't do these type of things.

GOD IS NOT UNRIGHTEOUS

The phrase, *"For God is not unrighteous,"* although brief, proclaims itself as one of the grandest statements ever made. God will always be kind, merciful, compassionate, loving, and just in His dealings with man. God truly is *"good!"* In fact, His goodness, and we speak of goodness extended even to sinful man, is of such magnitude, that it is beyond the comprehension of mere mortals.

God will always do right by a person. That's at least one of the reasons, that it is so wrong, for so-called Christian Psychologists to tell people to forgive God. Compounding their problems, to be sure, doesn't help!

The Lord has never done anything untoward, unjust, or unfair to anyone. While man has done much evil, which God has time and again forgiven, God has never done anything that's wrong, that would require man to forgive Him. Such thinking borders on the edge of blasphemy!

Satan has been very successful at painting God as a villain; however, the villain is Satan himself.

If one wants to know what God is like, one only has to look at Jesus Christ, Who in effect is God, and is a perfect replica as well, of the Father. In fact, this was one of the Ministries of Christ, to show Israel and the world, exactly Who God was and is, and exactly what God was and is. To be sure, the picture He presented is beautiful indeed!

As I dictate these words on June 28, 2000, I am 65 years old, and have served the Lord, since the age of eight. There have been countless times that I have wronged Him, and have had to plead His Mercy and Grace, which without question and without fail He has always extended. In conjunction with that, I can truly say, that He has been so much better to me than I could ever begin to deserve. In fact, I deserve nothing good, but because of His Love, Mercy, and Grace, He has given me everything. He has been and truly is, a Friend that sticketh closer than a brother.

If I remember correctly, it was Polycarp who made the following statement, while being burned at the stake. Again, if I remember correctly, he was nearing 100 years of age. He said:

"For 86 years I have served Him, and He's never done me any wrong. I only regret that I don't have another life to offer Him in His Service."

PAUL

A few weeks ago, as I dictate these notes, Frances and I, along with Donnie, Debbie, Gabriel, Matthew, and others, were in the city of Rome, Italy. (Jennifer couldn't go, she was finishing up College.)

While there, we had the occasion to visit the Mammertine Prison, where Paul spent his last months on Earth.

This was a prison cell, that is of one could call it that, carved out of solid rock, and was actually underground. Even though steps have been made into this small cell presently, when Paul was incarcerated there, it had no windows and no doors. There was a hole in the floor above, where they let down his food

during the day, and actually let him down with a rope, when he was first placed in this cell. It was there that he wrote II Timothy, his last Epistle. It is believed that it was in late A.D. 67 or early 68, that he was hoisted out of this dank cell, and executed. Tradition says that he was martyred on the Ostian Way leaving out of Rome. He suffered death by decapitation.

Some may argue that the Lord didn't treat Paul who wrote this Epistle very well, considering that this man was one of the greatest men of God who has ever lived; a man incidentally, who labored tirelessly for the Lord, who was actually the Masterbuilder of the Church.

No! The Lord treated Paul in a most excellent fashion, as the great Apostle himself testified over and over again. We must never forget, that the Lord's Ways aren't our ways. He has a purpose and a plan for everything He does, and to be sure, that which incorporates His Children, is always good.

Among other things, and as it concerns Paul, and all other Believers as well, the Lord wanted the world to know, that living for God was and is the greatest life that one could ever have, and by far, so great and grand in fact, that it was and is worth dying for.

As a number of us that day in Rome gathered in this small cell carved out of rock, I could almost see the great Apostle hunched over a small table, with the flickering light of a candle providing slight illumination, as he penned II Timothy. Or possibly, the Roman authorities allowed Luke to serve as his Scribe (II Tim. 4:11).

As I looked around that small cell that day, I knew and know that the world has little idea as to the contribution made to all freedom everywhere, by the one known as *"Saul of Tarsus!"* Maybe one could say without fear of contradiction, that no man lifted up Christ as Paul! No man served his Master better! Consequently, when he came to the end, he could say:

"For I am now ready to be offered, and the time of my departure is at hand.

"I have fought the good fight, I have finished my course, I have kept the Faith:

"Henceforth there is laid up for me a Crown of Righteousness, which the Lord, the

Righteous Judge, shall give me at that day: and not to me only, but unto all them also who love His appearing" (II Tim. 4:6-8).

As all of us stood there that day in that prison cell, I really cannot tell you exactly how I felt. As I attempted to relate a few things about Paul to the small group, I reached a place to where I could no longer continue. The Presence of God filled my heart, and filled that room. The tears came, which at times express one's feelings even better than words.

"Saul (Paul) *of Tarsus!"*

GOD DOES NOT FORGET

The phrase, *"To forget your work and labor of love,"* presents a glorious and wonderful promise.

To be sure, man's work cannot in itself merit reward from God but the Righteous God cannot neglect His Own Promise and Law that such works shall receive reward. Of that we can be certain! Everything we do for Him, every dollar given toward His Work, every sacrifice made, every labor extended, to be certain and to be sure, will without fail, receive its reward. Jesus said so:

"For whosoever shall give you a cup of water to drink in My Name, because you belong to Christ, verily I say unto you, he shall not lose his reward" (Mk. 9:41).

Let's look at the word *"forget"* as it is used in the Bible.

FORGET

The Hebrew verb *"sakah"* for *"forget"* is used 102 times in the Old Testament. At times a literal lapse of memory is intended, as in the story of the released butler who forgot his former fellow prisoner Joseph (Gen. 40:23).

At times God is the subject of this verb. It may seem at times to Believers, that God has forgotten, and they may express their apparent abandonment in cries to Him (Ps. 10:11; 42:9). But God never neglects or ignores His Own.

What is more likely is that human beings forget the Lord. Thus, the Hebrew word *"sakah"* is often used in warnings. God's people must not forget the Lord or His Covenant. They must not forget His Laws and Statutes. Nor may they forget the helpless.

These illustrations help us realize that the Old Testament idea of forgetting indicates not a mere mental state, but rather, a moral one. The focus is on a person's choices, not memories.

To forget God's Laws and Statutes, which man is so prone to do, is to choose to ignore them; it is to act without considering God's revealed will.

In this context, *"forget,"* indicates a complacent neglect of the Lord, perhaps linked with a material prosperity that dulls awareness of our need of His constant Blessings (Deut. 8:11-19).

In the New Testament, the words translated *"forget"* are *"epilanthanomai,"* and used in this sense in the following Verses: (Mat. 16:5; Mk. 8:14; Lk. 12:6; Phil. 3:13; Heb. 6:10; 13:2, 16; James 1:24), and *"eklanthanomai,"* with this word used in Hebrews 12:5. These may indicate a literal forgetting, but often they suggest neglect or overlooking.

We may neglect or overlook important issues. But God is incapable of overlooking even the death of a small sparrow (Lk. 12:6). How good to know that we, who are so precious to the Lord, can never be forgotten by Him, although he definitely does *"forget"* our sins, and for that, we will be eternally grateful.

MOTIVES

First of all, we must ever remember, that what we do for God is to be strictly out of love for Him, and not for the purpose of reward, although reward is promised and faithfully given. In fact, I personally believe that this is one of the great hallmarks of true Christianity, and as well, a constant test as provided by the Holy Spirit.

Why do we do for the Lord, what we do? What is our purpose? What is our motive? Concerning the giving of money, the Holy Spirit through Paul said that we should give *"to prove the sincerity of our love"* (II Cor. 8:8).

Even though we certainly have the right to expect God to bless our efforts, especially considering that His Promises are abundant in this capacity; however, if we give for that purpose alone, we are exhibiting greed, which shows that our motives are altogether wrong.

As I have said, this is a constant test provided by the Holy Spirit, Who knows our hearts. We can claim loudly whatever it is that we desire, but God knows the motive of our hearts, as He Alone knows these motives.

So, the point in all of this is, that every effort expended for Christ, everything done for Him, must be done from the position of our love for Him. While we can never repay Him, and in fact, we must not even try, simply because God has nothing for sale; still, understanding that He has done so much for us, we should desire to do all we can for Him, simply because, as stated, we love Him.

TOWARD HIS NAME

The phrase, *"Which ye have showed toward His Name,"* reflects that everything must be done in His Name, signifying many things.

First of all, due to the fact that Christ has saved us, and did so at great price, we in effect belong to Him. Paul was fond of using the term *"bond slave"* as it referred to our position in Christ. (The Greek word for bond slave was often translated *"servant."*)

Christ owns us, and what a privilege it is to be owned by Him, and considering that, everything we do must be done in His Name.

As well, His Name signifies Who He is and What He does! Once again, we go back to what Jesus said about giving the cup of water in His Name (Mk. 9:41).

As well, doing all that we do in His Name, signifies, that He has made it possible for us to do these good things, whatever they might be, and that without Him it could not be done. In fact, without Him, our condition would be dire indeed!

Also, we must not forget, that doing things in His Name, in a sense, says that He is doing them, and not actually us. He gets the Glory, as He Alone is worthy of the Glory; consequently, always being cognizant of this fact, keeps down pride in our hearts, and exalts Him, Who Alone should be exalted.

Do not misunderstand, God is not on an ego trip! Is a human being on an ego trip, when he accepts the affection of a little dog that licks his hand in gratitude? Of course not!

Pride is man's problem, and the doing of all things in the Name of the Lord, as stated, helps assuage this problem.

NOTES

MINISTERING TO THE SAINTS

The phrase, *"In that ye have ministered to the Saints, and do minister,"* refers to the fact that they had been doing this, and were continuing to do so. While we as Believers are to be gracious and kind to all men, we should especially make evident acts of kindness toward fellow Believers. We are all members of the Family of God. It is sad indeed, when the Church neglects this true sign of the Love of God being evident in one's heart and life. John plainly said, *"We know that we have passed from death unto life, because we love the Brethren"* (I Jn. 3:14).

We might also hurriedly say, that love has no conditions attached. While a Christian might get on the wrong track, and might even lose his way with God, even as Paul is addressing these Christian Jews, with some possibly refusing to repent. If this happens, as it does in many cases, while love cannot then be shown as one would desire, still, we can pray for the individual. Wrong direction by a Child of God, stops the *flow* of God's Love as it regards Blessings, but not the *fact* of His Love.

THE CROSS OF CHRIST

When the Church, and as well, individual Christians, cease to make the Cross the center of their Christianity, but rather turn to other things, the first thing that happens is self-righteousness. To be sure, this is the greatest hindrance to love that there could ever be. A self-righteous person has no love for the Brethren or anyone for that matter.

Such is made abundantly evident in the actions of the Elder Brother, toward the Prodigal Brother who had come home (Lk. 15:11-32). Concerning the return of the Prodigal, and the understandable joy made evident by the Father, the Scripture says of the Elder Brother, *"He was angry."*

I personally believe, that it is impossible for any Christian to avoid self-righteousness, if that Christian doesn't understand the principle of the Cross. The Cross speaks volumes as it concerns God's Love for us, and our obvious helplessness at being what we ought to be in Christ. In other words, a proper interpretation of the Cross automatically humbles one. It speaks of the fact that the individual knows and understands, that were it not for what Jesus did for him at the Cross, he could never have been saved. He also knows and understands, that even though he is saved, he cannot live a life of victory, in other words, to walk as he should before the Lord, without the benefits of what Christ did for him at the Cross. He knows that Faith in that, is what gives him the strength to be what he ought to be, which gives the Holy Spirit latitude to work, and keeps the flow of Grace coming (Gal. 2:20-21).

That of which we speak, is not one of the side issues of Christianity, but rather the Foundation of all that we are in Christ, and all that Christ is to us.

As I've already said several times in this Volume, if the Believer doesn't properly understand the Cross of Christ, at the same time he cannot properly understand the Word of God. This means that in some way, his thinking is skewed as it concerns proper interpretation. A proper understanding of the Cross, pulls the entirety of the Word of God into focus and thereby, into place. In fact, I don't think it would be improper to say, that the Word and the Cross are synonymous.

In the Gospel according to John, we are told in the very First Verse, that Jesus is the Word. And then in John 1:14, we are told that the Word became flesh and dwelt among us.

And then in John 1:29, we're told that this Word which was made flesh, went to the Cross and there atoned for all sin. So, when we say *"Word"* or *"Jesus"* or *"Cross,"* we are in a sense, speaking of one thing. If we divide them in any way, we do violence to the Word of God.

After seeking the Face of the Lord for some five years, doing so day and night, and with tears, asking Him to show me the manner of victory for the Child of God, in other words, how one could be victorious all the time, over the world, the flesh, and the Devil, He spoke to my heart and said, *"The answer is in the Cross!"* And then He said, *"Everything you seek is found in the Cross!"*

Just days before, He had taken me to Romans, Chapter 6, which began this journey of victory, in a manner that I had never previously known. And the beautiful and

NOTES

wonderful thing about all this is, that this door just keeps opening wider and wider. In other words, I have found that all that Christ did at the Cross is absolutely inexhaustible as far as its benefits are concerned, or even our understanding is concerned. It's like a flower, with the petals which just keep blooming and multiplying. Consequently, I believe the Lord will allow me to say the following:

THESE COMMENTARIES

If a Believer will obtain these Commentaries on the Epistles of Paul, study them carefully, asking the Lord to reveal these things to his heart and to his spirit, the teaching contained therein as it regards the Cross, will lead the Believer I believe, to such spiritual heights and depths, as never previously known.

I believe the Lord has given us a depth of knowledge as it regards the Cross, which includes the working of the Holy Spirit, that is not commonly found. In fact, I have never seen the extent of this Truth, which the Lord has given to us, in any other Book or Commentary, or heard it preached anywhere. But yet, when you begin to study these things according to the Word of God, I think they will become very clear to you, as the Holy Spirit quickens these Truths to your heart and life. As stated, and to be sure, if every Believer would do this, and I mean study these Truths diligently as it regards the great Sacrifice of Christ, I personally believe that your life will be so changed as to be indescribable.

If you believe that Jesus did it all at the Cross, then you should desire to know exactly what it is that He did. And as well, you must know how to obtain these benefits, which in fact, the Holy Spirit strongly desires that we have. Of course He does, especially considering the great price paid by Christ!

(11) "AND WE DESIRE THAT EVERY ONE OF YOU DO SHEW THE SAME DILIGENCE TO THE FULL ASSURANCE OF HOPE UNTO THE END:"

The exegesis is:

1. All Christians are to function in the Love of God, thereby showing that Love to others.

2. We must be diligent, always working toward this end, understanding that we ever represent Christ.

3. We must not let down in these endeavors, but continue to do so until death, or the Lord comes.

ALL CHRISTIANS

The phrase, *"And we desire that every one of you,"* proclaims the fact, that true Salvation in true hearts, will bring forth true results as it regards all true Christians.

While I do not want to belabor the point, I must emphasize the fact, that all of this is possible, only as the Believer understands his rightful position in Christ. And one can understand that only as he understands the great Sacrifice of Christ.

Unfortunately, many Christians tend to believe that this great Sacrifice, i.e., *"the Cross,"* is merely, the door, with other things coming to the fore after one enters the door. That is totally wrong!

While the Cross of Christ is definitely the door to Salvation, it is also the door to every single good thing that God has for His people. In fact, Jesus said this of Himself:

"Verily, verily, I say unto you, I am the door of the sheep . . . by Me if any man enter in, he shall be saved, and shall go in and out, and find pasture" (Jn. 10:7-9).

How is Jesus the Door?

Always and in every capacity, when Jesus speaks of Himself in this manner, He is referring to the Cross. It is there that He will make all things possible. So, this means, that this Door which one enters, is Christ, and more particularly, what Christ has done on the Cross for the entirety of the world. Therefore, whatever we receive after we enter the Door, is always and without exception, made possible by what Jesus did at the Cross. That's the reason that our Faith must ever be anchored in this great, Finished Work.

Please allow me to go back to the first three Verses of this Sixth Chapter. It is these Passages, as stated, which are used by the detractors of the Cross, claiming that we should leave the Cross, after we are saved, and go on to other things. The question should quickly be asked, *"To what other things are you going?"*

They would probably answer that they are going on to the things of the Holy Spirit; however, everything the Holy Spirit does within our hearts and lives, is done strictly within

the parameters of the Finished Work of Christ, which in fact, has made His Work possible. He says this plainly in Romans 8:2. He is the *"Spirit of Life,"* but all of this great Life which He gives unto us, is made possible in totality, by what Christ did at the Cross, hence Him using the words *"in Christ"* — *"The Law of the Spirit of Life in Christ Jesus"* (Rom. 8:2).

Understanding this, if we attempt to come by any Work of the Spirit, without going through the Cross of Christ, we will not only not come by His Work, but will at the same time, attract unto ourselves evil spirits. And to be frank, that's the major problem of the Pentecostal and Charismatic worlds presently. They're chasing after that which they think is the Holy Spirit, when in reality, much of the time, it is *"spirits!"*

No, and again I emphasize, Paul is not telling us in Hebrews 6:1-2, that we are to leave the Cross of Christ, but rather *"the first principles of the Doctrine of Christ,"* which has to do with the Old Testament, and proven by His statements in the latter portion of Verse 1 and in Verse 2. In fact, the entirety of the Epistle to the Hebrews was written to Christian Jews, who were seriously contemplating going back to the Old Testament Covenant, with the Apostle telling them that if they do this, they will lose their souls. And let me follow up by saying this:

For any Believer who thinks he can leave the Cross, let him understand, that he is actually leaving his Salvation if he does such a thing. While modern Believers aren't going back to the Old Testament Covenant, still, the greater danger is not so much the false doctrine embraced, or the wrong direction taken, but rather the leaving of the Cross of Christ, which is *"the secret place of the Most High,"* and the *"Shadow of the Almighty"* (Ps. 91:1).

These Christian Jews who were contemplating such a thing, in no way thought they were forsaking God or denying God by their actions, but this is exactly what they were doing. When we deny Christ, and more particularly, deny the veracity of His Finished Work, by going to other things, we at the same time, forsake God and all that Salvation actually is. Everything is through Jesus Christ, and more particularly, what He did at the Cross on our behalf.

One can only have *"the full assurance of hope unto the end,"* if one fully and completely places that hope in the great Sacrifice of Christ. That is the foundation of all Faith, the centrality of the Gospel, the Door to all things of God.

WHY DO WE SEE THE CROSS IN EVERYTHING PERTAINING TO GOD?

We see the Cross in everything, because the Cross is in everything. And until you see the Cross in everything, you're not properly interpreting this great Offering of Christ.

While it is true that Paul did not mention the Cross in every single thing he said, and for all the obvious reasons. Had he done so, even as I am here attempting to do, the Bible would have been several times thicker than it actually is.

However, the Holy Spirit through him did give these great Truths in such unmistakable fashion, that there is no excuse and reason for us not to know.

In Romans, Chapter 6, Paul plainly tells us what happens to us at conversion, and thereafter. He explains in detail, how all of this is made possible by the Cross of Christ.

In Romans, Chapter 8, he proclaims to us the manner and way in which the Holy Spirit works in our hearts and lives, all made possible by what Christ did at the Cross. To help us understand it a little better, consider the following:

When Paul wrote these Letters, he did not write them in Chapters and Verses as we now see. They were Letters, exactly as we have said, and written exactly as we write letters.

When he began a thought as the Holy Spirit inspired him, he didn't necessarily stop that thought at the end of the particular Chapter as it's sectioned off in our modern Bibles. Sometimes a Chapter will end a thought, but many times it doesn't.

In Romans, Chapter 1, Paul proclaims the destitute state of the Gentile world. In Chapters 2 and 3, he places the Jews in the same category, which incidentally, they didn't at all appreciate!

In Chapters 4 and 5, he explains Justification by Faith. And then in Romans, Chapter 6, he brings out as to how this process was done, by explaining to us the Crucifixion of Christ, and our part in His death.

In Romans, Chapter 7, he explains his own personal experience immediately after being saved and Baptized with the Holy Spirit, when he tried to live a Godly life and couldn't. At that time, he didn't know the great victory of the Cross. But in desperation, the Lord gave him the solution to his problems, which he gave to us in Romans, Chapters 6 and 8. In the Eighth Chapter, as stated, he tells us how the Holy Spirit works, which is all predicated on our Faith in the Cross of Christ.

In Chapters 9 through 11, he reverts back to the Jews, and because they have rejected Christ, and Justification by Faith, thinking that the mere fact of them being Jews guaranteed them some type of Salvation. In these three Chapters, he plainly says to the Jews that if they are to be saved, they must accept Christ and what He did at the Cross; however, even though his Message in these three Chapters is primarily to the Jews, it also speaks loudly to the Gentile world, that if Israel cannot be saved by her *"works,"* how do we Gentiles think that we can be saved by our works, which in fact, are nonexistent as they compare to those of Israel?

In Chapters 12 through 16, he picks up again with the Gentiles, and to be more exact, the Church, giving instructions as to how we should live, considering that we have come to Christ. In other words, we have a responsibility before God and before the entirety of the world, to be Christlike, which in fact, we can only do, by properly understanding the Cross, and reaping its benefits (Lk. 9:23-24).

(12) "THAT YE BE NOT SLOTHFUL, BUT FOLLOWERS OF THEM WHO THROUGH FAITH AND PATIENCE INHERIT THE PROMISES."

The structure is:

1. As Christians, we must be diligent and not slothful, implying that the Holy Spirit cannot help lazy Christians.

2. We are to look at those who have gone before us, and did so in victory, using them as examples.

3. Through Faith and patience they inherited the Promises, and if we exhibit Faith and patience, we will do the same. In other words, the Holy Spirit set the pattern through them.

SLOTHFUL

The phrase, *"That ye be not slothful,"* presents a command!

"Slothful" in the Greek is *"nothros,"* and means *"sluggish, lazy, dull, stupid."* It's bad enough to be lazy, but the Holy Spirit is telling us here, that for a Christian to be slothful, means he is also spiritually stupid.

We are presently living in an age, when Christians want Preachers to lay their hands on them, and solve all their problems. Sorry, but it doesn't work that way!

You as a Believer are expected of the Lord, to learn the Word of God yourself. You can only do that by taking the time to study its contents, which most Christians don't do. That's slothful! Such a position will fall out as stated, to spiritual stupidity as well!

If the Reader will allow me to mention these Commentaries once again, most Christians don't bother to obtain them, simply because they are too lazy to study their contents. Now think about that for a moment!

We're speaking here of the issues of life and death. We're speaking of eternal consequences, which outweigh anything the world has to offer, and a thousand times over. In fact, a person's soul is more important and worth more than the entirety of the world.

But when it comes to spiritual things, we too often let them slide. We spend all of our time and attention mostly on things, which have no significance whatsoever, all to the detriment of our spirituality.

Why?

Lazy!

I get amazed at Christians going from one disaster to the other, but yet will not take the time to learn that which could stop all of these disasters, and change their lives gloriously and wondrously. They're just too lazy to take the time to do so, which falls out to Scriptural and thereby, spiritual stupidity, which falls out to the disasters we have mentioned.

JESUS TOLD US TO KEEP KNOCKING

In the Spring of 1992, if I correctly remember the season, the Lord gave me from His Word, a Promise inculcated in that which I refer to as *"the Parable of the three loaves"* (Lk. 11:5-13).

It concerned an individual who went to a friend at midnight, asking to borrow three loaves of bread. An unexpected guest had shown up, needed sustenance, and the man had nothing to give him.

Because of the lateness of the hour, the friend answered that he could not arise, in other words, come back tomorrow.

But Jesus told of the individual who was desperate, and kept knocking on the door, until his friend arose, and gave him as much as he needed. The Master then gave us the great Truth of persevering prayer. In other words, keep knocking until the answer comes.

He then proclaimed the fact, that the Holy Spirit would guarantee the answer, if we would only persevere (Lk. 11:13).

During the next five years, the Lord over and over again, would bring this Promise back to me. In fact, I stood on that particular Word for all of that time, believing exactly what the Lord had said, and by that, I mean that He would answer my petition.

To be sure, at times I grew very discouraged. Five years is a long time. During that time, the Devil would say over and over again, and using any number of fabricated reasons, that the Lord was not going to answer. But I kept *"asking,"* kept *"seeking,"* and kept *"knocking!"*

And then in 1996, the answer began to come, with the greatest thrust being given in 1997. However, if slothfulness had been a problem during all of this time, I never would have received an answer from the Lord. I had to keep praying, keep believing, and keep standing on His Promises.

Why did it take so long?

I cannot answer that question. However, irrespective of the time factors, the answer did come, and in fact, continues to come, and other than my Salvation and the day I was Baptized with the Holy Spirit, is the greatest thing that's ever happened to me. Of course, I'm speaking of the Revelation of the Cross.

FAITH, PATIENCE, AND THE PROMISES

The phrase, *"But followers of them who through Faith and Patience inherit the Promises,"* refers to the Faith worthies of the Old Testament, with a long list given in Chapter 11, and with Paul referring now to Abraham. We learn several things from this statement:

1. We are to allow these people to serve as our examples. They faced the same problems that we face, but persevered just the same, and because they didn't quit. God cannot help a quitter!

In fact, He's not nearly as troubled by failure as He is by quitting, as should be obvious.

While the Lord can get a person up who has failed, there's not anything He can do with an individual who has quit. The latter refers to the loss of Faith, hence they discontinue the journey. In fact, there has never been a Christian who hasn't failed in one way or the other. Unfortunately, it seems to go with the territory. The great problem, as stated, is just simply giving up and quitting, which many have done.

For instance, Peter failed, but he didn't quit. Judas failed and quit!

The Lord doesn't promise an event-free life, but He does promise that He'll see you through, if you won't quit.

2. God has given every Believer Promises. In fact, the Holy Spirit through Peter referred to them as *"exceeding great and precious Promises: that by these ye might be partakers of the Divine Nature, having escaped the corruption that is in the world through lust"* (II Pet. 1:4).

In other words, God has promised that He'll see us through; however, at the same time, He has given us individual Promises, exactly as I have mentioned concerning my own personal experience. I think this is true with every Child of God.

As well, and without exception, all of His Promises come to us through His Word. Now let's see how these Promises are brought to reality within our hearts and lives.

3. Faith is the ingredient through which God works. It is the simple act of believing something, and in this case, believing what God has said about Himself, and what He would do for mankind, and more particularly, what He would do for us personally.

However, it must ever be understood, that the only Faith that God will recognize, and to boil it down to the bottom line, is Faith in the Cross of Christ, i.e., *"the great Sacrifice of Christ."* If one investigates these Old Testament worthies, one will find, that the object of their Faith, was in some way, the Cross

of Christ. Of course, when I say *"Cross of Christ,"* they would have had no knowledge of the word *"Cross."* They would not have known what such a word meant, or the part it would play in all of this of which we speak. But they did know, that all the Promises which God made to them, the great Revelation which He gave them, and in whatever manner, were all centered up in some way, in the Sacrifices. They also knew that the Sacrifices pointed to One Who was ultimately to come, who would redeem humanity, with Abraham being an excellent example, which Paul addresses in the next Verse.

Therefore, for Faith to be the Faith which God will recognize, and which gets an answer, the Cross of Christ must ever be its object.

4. The Holy Spirit now directs us to *"patience."* Even if our Faith is as it ought to be, the Promises do not develop immediately, even as I mentioned concerning my own experience, and I think which will bear out as well, with the Faith Worthies listed in Chapter 11.

Patience speaks of delay, and why the delay?

I'm sure that God has many reasons, and to be sure, the reasons are always His.

First of all, the very character of Faith is patience. Faith demands that we hold on, whenever we cannot see the answer. It takes patience to do that, hence the Holy Spirit promptly displaying this attribute.

Second, the delay tries our Faith, and all Faith must be tried in some way. As someone has well said, *"Faith must be tested, and great Faith must be tested greatly."*

Delays as it regards Faith, are never wasted. The Holy Spirit uses this time to work out things in our lives, which makes us ready to receive the Promise. While it doesn't take the Lord any time at all to do these things, it takes us a lot of time to get prepared.

PERSONAL

I remember a very foolish act of my own carried out many years ago. It was only a simple statement that I made, but I blush every time I think about it.

If I remember correctly, it was in about 1970. The Lord was preparing me for Radio, for the Crusades, and for Television. It was a time of great soul searching, of great intercession and prayer. I've always had a strong prayer life, but this particular time was exceptional. The Spirit of God moved mightily during those days.

At a given point in time, and concerning a particular thing which I will leave nameless, but as it regarded Ministry, in prayer one morning, I informed the Lord, *"I am now ready."*

The Truth was, I was about as unready as one could ever be.

Concerning what the Lord is now doing, someone asked me the other day that very question, *"Are you ready?"*

My answer was very quick, *"No, I'm not ready, and I don't think any person could ever be ready."*

The Truth is, whatever the Lord wants us to do, He has to provide everything that is to be done. While we can consecrate ourselves, there is still so much yet to be done in our lives, which only He can do, that no human being can even think of himself in the realm of being ready. Whatever is done with us, about all we can do is provide a *"willing mind and obedient heart,"* with the Holy Spirit then having to do everything else.

WHAT MIGHT THE CHRISTIAN JEWS HAVE BEEN THINKING?

The manner in which Paul makes these statements, lets us know that these Christian Jews had some erroneous thoughts in their minds. Being Jews, and knowing that the Prophets had predicted that the Messiah would rule over the entirety of the world, quite possibly, and due to unscriptural information being fed to them somehow, they evidently had come to the place that they did not believe that Christ fulfilled this role. In other words, the Cross didn't fit into all of this. And then Paul had informed them, as well as the entirety of the Church of that day, that quite a number of things had to happen before the Second Coming of Christ, even as he related it all in the two Epistles to the Thessalonians. Having discounted the Cross, which means they had no Faith in what the Cross would produce, their imagined scenario, at least in their minds, would fit better in Judaism. Little did they know or

NOTES

realize, that in a matter of months, Jerusalem would be completely destroyed, with nothing left of the Temple, with even its foundation destroyed.

It is easily observed from this, what God thought of Temple worship continuing. Christ had come and fulfilled all the demands of the Law, as well, He fulfilled all the symbolism and types; consequently, to continue with this, was an insult to Christ of the highest order, especially considering the great price that was paid at the Cross for man's Redemption. In fact, Israel's continued Temple worship as a nation, not to speak of these backsliding Christian Jews, was that which God could no longer tolerate. So He took it out, and took it out in a way, that it could not be reestablished.

He will allow Israel one more stab under the Antichrist, but that will be short-lived, which in fact, is not long coming in the future.

The Apostle is telling these Christian Jews, that if they will exhibit Faith and Patience, that all the Promises will be inherited, which means, that Christ will ultimately rule and reign over this Earth, with Israel completely restored, but of course, it will be God's way, and not the way of recalcitrant Israel.

(13) "FOR WHEN GOD MADE PROMISE TO ABRAHAM, BECAUSE HE COULD SWEAR BY NO GREATER, HE SWARE BY HIMSELF,"

The exegesis is:

1. God kept every Promise He made to Abraham, as He has kept every Promise made to anyone.

2. God's Promises are more than the Promises of man. In fact, they are ironclad.

3. These Promises are ironclad, because God has sworn by and of Himself, that they will be carried out, which in effect, places all the resources of Heaven behind each and every Promise.

THE EXAMPLE OF ABRAHAM

The phrase, *"For when God made Promise to Abraham,"* presents the Patriarch as chosen for special mention as the most illustrious example of those who *"inherit the Promises"* (Jn. 8:58).

Why Abraham?

It was to Abraham that God explained the method of Salvation by Faith, and to be more particular, that man would be justified only by Faith, and never by works. He even told Abraham, by one of the most poignant object lessons ever shown to any man, that this would be brought about by the death of His (God's) Son. All of this took place in the Lord telling Abraham to offer up Isaac, which was of course, stopped at the last minute.

However, in all of this, even though Abraham knew that Redemption would come by death, and the death of the Son of God, he did not know exactly how this death would be brought about. It was to Moses that it was revealed that such a death would be on a Cross, as symbolized by the serpent on the pole (Gen. Chpt. 22; Num. Chpt. 21; Jn. 3:14-16).

For all of this to be brought about, and we speak of God becoming man, a lineage would have to be provided which would in effect begin with Abraham, even though it actually began with Adam. In other words, for this lineage to begin, Abraham and Sarah would have to have a son, and through this lineage many times removed, ultimately would be born the Son of God. So, to carry this out, God promised Abraham a son. This was a problem, at least as far as Abraham and Sarah were concerned, simply because Sarah was barren, meaning that she could not have children. But God has made a Promise to Abraham. . . .

THE OATH

The phrase, *"Because He could swear by no greater,"* refers to the solemnity and power of this Promise; actually, it is so powerful, that it is in the form of an oath, meaning that all the resources of Heaven, and more important still, the very Character of God backs up this Promise.

As we said in previous Commentary, there is a close link between Covenant and Oath. The Covenant is the substance of God's stated intention — the constant reminder that God swore (bound Himself by an oath) in making the Covenant Promise and so underlines His firm commitment to do all that the Covenant defines. In other words, to use some street language, whatever God says, you can take it to the bank. In fact, the entirety of

the Word of God falls into this category. It is *"immutable,"* which means, it is not capable of change. As well it is *"imperishable,"* which means that it is not subject to decay and will endure permanently. Also, it is *"indestructible,"* which means it cannot be torn down. It is *"indecomposable,"* which means it is not capable of being broken up into component parts. It forms a whole. It is *"indefeasible,"* meaning that it's not capable of being annulled or voided or undone. It is *"indefectible,"* meaning that it is flawless.

AN OATH BASED UPON HIS CHARACTER

The phrase, *"He sware by Himself,"* refers as stated, to all the resources of Heaven, which of course is the creation of God, but more particularly, it refers to the Character and nature of God, which refers to Who He is.

Jehovah is God and there is nothing greater. Regarding that, He had to appeal to Himself.

Fjordbak said, *"One of the hardest things to do after God has given a Promise is to sit down, be patience, and wait for the fulfillment. It is hard not to keep reminding the Lord, 'Lord, I thought You were going to do this for me!' The answer comes back from God, 'Be patient; have Faith.'"*

Abraham learned to walk with God and to trust God to fulfill the Promises He had made. God is sovereign. The Promises God made to Abraham will be completely fulfilled, even if He takes centuries to do so. It must come to pass, because God has spoken it, and there is almighty power behind and in the Word of God. In fact, Abraham's faithfulness and patience are an example for us to follow.

HOW CAN A PROMISE HELP SOMEONE COMING TO PASS HUNDREDS OF YEARS LATER?

First of all, even though this Promise was to Abraham personally, it actually involved the entire Plan of God for the entirety of the human race, as it regards Redemption. So, it could not come to pass during Abraham's lifetime, and actually wasn't even meant to do so; however, God definitely did give to Abraham and Sarah, the part of the promise which pertained to them, and which figured so prominently in the great Plan of God, which refers to the Incarnation of Christ, by giving them Isaac, who was the Son of Promise. Always remember the following:

Even though God makes staggering Promises, in other words, Promises which are so large, so great, so wonderful, that they actually defy description; still, let the Reader understand, that the actual possession of the Promise, is always much greater than the Promise itself. The idea is, no one ever need fear that what God promises, is going to be less than stated. It is always more, much more, far more, than He has promised. In fact, that is His characteristic! If you the Reader, actually feel that God has truly promised you something, and many of you would definitely fall into that category, you can be sure, that though He tarry long, the Promise will be fulfilled and in great magnitude.

In this earthly sojourn, I've learned a few things. I've learned that the waiting is part of the process. And I've also learned that it is never wasted time. While the Lord is bringing about events, He at the same time, is drawing us nearer to Him, and thereby reshaping our very natures and lives.

(14) "SAYING, SURELY BLESSING I WILL BLESS THEE, AND MULTIPLYING I WILL MULTIPLY THEE."

The exegesis is:

1. The word *"saying"* proclaims the Word of God, i.e., *"the Promise."*

2. He promised a Blessing, which in this instance referred to the birth of Isaac, who in a sense, would begin the lineage of Christ.

3. He promised to make of Abraham and Sarah a great nation, a nation incidentally, which would be used to give the world the Word of God and to serve as the womb of the Messiah.

BLESSING

The phrase, *"Saying, surely blessing I will bless thee,"* is taken from Genesis 22:17. And what a Blessing this was!

Abraham, the ancestor of the Hebrews, the first personal recipient of the Promises, the Father of the faithful, is now used by the Holy Spirit as an example.

This Blessing consisted of God giving Abraham the meaning and manner of Salvation, which was and is *"Justification by Faith,"*

NOTES

called *"the Blessing of Abraham"* (Gal. 3:14). This great *"Blessing of Abraham"* made possible the advent of the Holy Spirit in an entirely different dimension, actually abiding in the hearts and lives of Believers, which was all made possible by what Jesus did at the Cross.

As well, the Lord revealed to Abraham as to exactly how all of this would come to pass, which would actually mean, God becoming man, i.e., *"the Incarnation."*

There couldn't be any Blessing any greater than this! For God to give all of this to this man, in effect, and as stated, to make him the Father of the faithful, presents itself as a Blessing of unprecedented proportions.

A GREAT NATION

The phrase, *"And multiplying I will multiply thee,"* refers to his seed becoming a nation. Actually, in the original Text it says, *"and in multiplying, I will multiply thy seed"* (Gen. 22:17).

The slight change from *"thy seed"* to *"thee,"* is done by the Holy Spirit, no doubt, to fix the thought on the Blessing promised to Abraham personally. He would be the Father of many nations, but more particularly, he would be the Father of Israel, hence the Holy Spirit saying, *"in Isaac shall thy seed be called"* (Gen. 21:12). This was meant to specify that the lineage would be in Isaac, the fulfillment of the Promise, and not Ishmael, the son of the Egyptian servant girl, the latter being a work of the flesh.

Truly enough, God gave Abraham and Sarah exactly what He had promised.

He told them that they (their seed) would inherit the land of Canaan, *"for an everlasting possession"* (Gen. 17:8). But He also told them that it would be some 400 years before it would actually become their possession (Gen. 15:13).

These 400 years are to be reckoned from the confirmation of Isaac as the seed when Ishmael was cast out (Gen. 21:12; Gal. 4:30). This was five years after the birth of Isaac.

The actual time from the departure of Abraham from Haran at the age of 75, some 25 years before Isaac was born or 30 years before Isaac was confirmed and Ishmael cast out, was 430 years. They spent about 215 years of that time in Canaan as pilgrims and strangers, which means they did not then possess it. They then spent about 215 years in Egypt, before being led out by Moses.

At that time, they were about three to four million strong, which was the approximate number as well which entered the Promised Land. Truly, God had gloriously and wondrously multiplied them, exactly as He said He would — all from Abraham and Sarah.

(15) "AND SO, AFTER HE HAD PATIENTLY ENDURED, HE OBTAINED THE PROMISE."

The structure is:

1. Faith requires patience.

2. In time, the Promise will come.

3. The Holy Spirit used Abraham as an example of patient Faith, from which we are meant to learn.

PATIENTLY ENDURED

The phrase, *"And so, after he had patiently endured,"* proclaims much more here than meets the eye. There is always a distance between the Promise and the Possession, and that distance is never uneventful.

The record of Abraham's patient enduring is recorded in the Book of Genesis. The Truth is, which as well should be a great lesson to us, patient enduring is never easy. For all of these things, these Blessings, to be brought about, a son had to be born to Abraham and Sarah. Through him the Messiah would ultimately come, the Redeemer of the World. As stated, this was quite a Promise and quite a Blessing!

But Sarah was barren (Gen. 11:30). So, how could all of this be brought to pass?

With every Promise of God, it seems as if the Lord allows Satan a certain amount of latitude to hinder that Promise. Of course, Satan desires that we give up altogether, while God allows the activity of the Evil One for an entirely different purpose. As we've said many times, Faith must ever be tested, and great Faith must be tested greatly. Will we continue to believe God, despite circumstances? despite problems? despite difficulties? Or when facing these things, will we fold under the pressure and quit? As stated, getting from the Promise to the Possession is never uneventful!

NOTES

In this test of Faith, Abraham and Sarah took matters into their own hands, and a son, Ishmael, was born, a son incidentally, who was rejected by God. God had given a Promise of an heir — God would bring it to pass. The fulfillment of God's Promises must ever be of God and not at all of man. The moment we attempt to bring these things about by works of the flesh, we always produce an Ishmael as Abraham, which always causes problems. The idea is:

The God Who gave the Promise is able to bring the Promise to pass, irrespective of whatever type of difficulties and circumstances may come our way. We are to trust God! To believe God! To stand upon His Promises! As stated, whatever hindrances there are, the Lord is actually the One Who allowed them. Let me say it a little more clearly:

It was the Lord Who allowed Satan to make Sarah barren. Never think for a moment that Satan can do anything to one of God's Children without having total permission from the Lord, and as well, with all parameters drawn by the Lord. The Lord is in charge of the situation from beginning to end. That's not the question! In fact, the question always is, how will we react to problems and difficulties?

GOD WON'T GIVE UP ON YOU, IF YOU WON'T GIVE UP ON HIM

When Abraham and Sarah sinned by attempting to help God out, the Lord didn't wash His hands of them, but kept dealing with them, and even encouraging them. The Truth is, God will never give up on a person, if that person won't quit.

God cannot help quitters, but He can do mighty and glorious things with those who refuse to quit, despite the fact that they may fail at times along the way.

I'm afraid in today's spiritual climate, that the modern Church would have washed Abraham out long before the finish line. In fact, he would have never gotten past Hagar. But the tragedy is, those who do such things, are in far worse condition spiritually, than the ones they are washing out. As someone has well said, *"It's not over till it's over!"* And the Truth is, it's not over till God says it's over. And again I emphasize, that God will never say it's over, as long as that person is evidencing Faith.

If we stumble and fail, the Lord will pick us up, dust us off, and start us back on our way, if we'll only allow Him to do so. Consider this:

GOD HAS NEVER FAILED!

The heading, *"God has never failed,"* means that if a person will keep believing, victory will come. While man fails and fails repeatedly, God has never failed. So if you the Believer will keep believing, despite the circumstances, despite the problems, and yes, despite the failures, God will see you through. God has never dishonored Faith. To be sure, He will close the door on doubt and unbelief, but He will never shut the door on Faith. And guess what?

If every person in the world gives up on you, and God doesn't, guess who's going to win out! I'll say it again:

God has never lost a battle, and if you the Believer will stick it out, will keep believing, will hold to His hand, He's going to see you through, and no matter what it takes to do so.

Please understand, the words that I am dictating are not mere hype. I've been there! I know what it is to have the whole world against you, and even the entirety of the Church. But I also know what it is to hear Him say to me the following: *"Fear thou not; for I am with thee: be not dismayed; for I am thy God: I will strengthen thee; yea, I will help thee; yea, I will uphold thee with the right hand of My Righteousness."*

And then He said, *"Behold, all they that were incensed against thee shall be ashamed and confounded: they shall be as nothing; and they that strive with thee shall perish"* (Isa. 41:10-11).

No, it's not easy, and the Lord never said it would be easy; however, whatever it is that we have to endure for the Promise to ultimately materialize into the possession, is worth every effort a thousand times over.

THE PROMISE

The phrase, *"He obtained the Promise,"* proclaims itself as much larger than it seems on the surface.

In fact, the Promise was so grand, so glorious, so far reaching, that he could receive only a small portion in his lifetime, which he did with the birth of Isaac. The ultimate fulfillment of the Promise was the coming of the Promise, the Lord Jesus Christ, which took place about 2,000 years after Abraham. As well, he became the Father of many nations, according to that which was spoken.

In fact, the Lord had promised him, *"In thee shall all families of the Earth be blessed"* (Gen. 12:3). What a Promise!

This came about, as stated, with the birth of Christ. And when I read that word concerning *"all the families of the Earth,"* of course, I think of my own family. Thank God, this glorious Promise given to Abraham some 4,000 years ago, has reached even unto me and my family, even as it has reached to you and your family. As stated, what a Promise! But more particularly, what a mighty God we serve.

(16) "FOR MEN VERILY SWEAR BY THE GREATER: AND AN OATH FOR CONFIRMATION IS TO THEM AN END OF ALL STRIFE."

The structure is:

1. Men swear an oath by something greater than themselves, in order to bind the promise.

2. When this is done, there is no more argument concerning the contract.

3. To bring this up to today's terminology, this of which Paul says, is the same thing now as a contract with the law of the land binding such contract, which of course is greater than the principles entering the contract, which thereby confirms it.

THE GREATER

The phrase, *"For men verily swear by the greater,"* could pertain to many things. As stated, in modern vernacular, it would refer to a contract which is backed up by law. But it can also mean an appeal to God. Men never swear by one who is inferior to themselves. And to be sure, God is the highest authority to which one could appeal.

The object of the Apostle in this declaration is to show that, as far as it is possible for him to proclaim such a thing, he is stressing the immutability of the Word of God. God could not indeed swear by one greater than Himself, but He could make His Promise as certain as an oath taken by men was when they solemnly appeal to Him. He could appeal to His Own existence and veracity, which were at any time the most solemn form of an oath, and thus put the mind to rest in regard to the hope of Heaven. This is the argument that Paul is using as it regards these wavering, Christian Jews.

CONFIRMATION

The phrase, *"And an oath for confirmation is to them an end of all strife,"* means in our modern terminology, that a contract has been agreed upon, and has been signed by all parties, which ends all strife. All parties rest satisfied with such a contract, and they feel assured that the agreement will be complied with.

The idea of all this is, God's Word can be relied upon. And if these Christian Jews would just simply believe what God had promised Abraham, which in fact, and Who in fact, was the Lord Jesus Christ, they could then rest easy in Christ, and put away their ideas of going back into Judaism.

They no doubt were claiming that they must abide by the Old Testament, so Paul confronts them with the Old Testament, in effect, telling them that Jesus Christ is the fulfillment of the Promises made to Abraham, in effect, fulfilling all the Old Testament.

The thing is, if an earthly contract made by men can put away strife, it would certainly seem that the great Promises of God would do the same. Or is it true, that men believe the Promises of God a lot less than they do the promises of other men? I'm afraid the answer is in the affirmative for many!

(17) "WHEREIN GOD, WILLING MORE ABUNDANTLY TO SHEW UNTO THE HEIRS OF PROMISE THE IMMUTABILITY OF HIS COUNSEL, CONFIRMED IT BY AN OATH:"

The exegesis is:

1. Since the oath has this convincing power among men, God disregards the insult implied in man's doubting His Word, and condescends to human infirmity, confirming His Word by an oath.

2. The word *"willing"* as it concerns God, means that faced with human infirmities, He was minded to do thus and so.

3. The word *"immutability"* guarantees that God will not change His position as to His Promise. Having made the Promise, He will stand by it.

GOD IS WILLING

The phrase, *"Wherein God, willing more abundantly to show unto the heirs of Promise,"* refers to the Lord working in accordance with this universal custom. Since the oath has this convincing power among men, God lowers Himself, one might say, down to the level of men, at least in this sense.

Why was God abundantly willing to function in this fashion, and we speak of Him swearing that He will keep His Word? God had no need to swear an oath. Nevertheless, He did it to make absolutely clear to His servant that His Promise would be fulfilled.

Knowing that our ability as creatures to properly comprehend all that God intends, and as well, His reasoning for doing things, are in fact very limited; still, perhaps the following will be of some help:

The oath that God took upon Himself as it regards the Promise made to Abraham (Gen. 22:16-18), concerned the entirety of the Plan of Salvation for the human race. Of course, nothing could be greater or larger than this. It was not that God needed to make the oath, but that Abraham needed to hear the oath. What the Lord was promising was so staggering, so all-encompassing, so grand and glorious, that actually, it defied all description. Could it be?, was no doubt the great question of Abraham.

To calm the fears of the great Patriarch, God took an oath, based upon Himself, because there was nothing greater!

The Promise that God made to the Patriarch, required him to look far beyond his own world, and that's not easy for a man to do. But he did do it. Jesus said of him in speaking to the Jews, *"Your father Abraham rejoiced to see My day: and he saw it, and was glad"* (Jn. 8:56).

HEIRS OF PROMISE

These words *"heirs of Promise,"* refer to the children of Faith, which Paul described in Romans, Chapter 4. He there also used Abraham as an example. The idea is, we get the Promise, which refers to Justification by Faith and thereby, the infilling of the Holy Spirit, totally and completely by and through the principle of Faith; however, we must understand as to what type of Faith the Holy Spirit is speaking.

First of all, Paul said *"Therefore it is of Faith, that it might be by Grace; to the end the Promise might be sure to all the seed; not to that only which is of the Law* (the Jews), *but to that also* (the Gentiles) *which is of the Faith of Abraham; who is the father of us all"* (Rom. 4:16).

When Paul used the term *"the Faith,"* he was speaking of a particular type of Faith. It was exclusively Faith in what Christ would do at the Cross on behalf of lost humanity. In fact, the entirety of the story of Abraham, is that he believed that God would send a Redeemer into the world to save lost humanity, and would do so by that Redeemer dying, which God graphically portrayed to him, by the proposed offering up of Isaac (Gen. Chpt. 22).

And then Paul, sealing this doctrine, and saying of Jesus, *"Who was delivered for our offenses* (the Cross), *and was raised again* (the Resurrection) *for our Justification"* (Rom. 4:25).

One must not read Romans 4:25 wrong. The emphasis is always on Christ being delivered up, i.e., *"the Cross,"* which purchased our Justification. While the Resurrection, as would be obvious, was an absolute necessity, it was not the Resurrection which settled the sin debt, but actually Christ dying on the Cross.

WHAT ROMANS, CHAPTER 6 ACTUALLY MEANS

Romans, Chapter 6 portrays both the Death and the Resurrection of Christ, but more particularly, gives us the meaning of this great Finished Work. And if the Believer doesn't understand Romans, Chapter 6, then the Believer cannot really understand God's prescribed order of victory for the Saint.

Romans, Chapter 6 and Romans, Chapter 8 as well, are a direct result of the agony of Romans, Chapter 7. Immediately after Paul came to Christ, and was Baptized with the Holy Spirit some three days later, as recorded in Acts, Chapter 9, he sets out to live the

Godly life he wants to live and because he is now a new creation in Christ Jesus; however, he finds out to his dismay, as he tries to keep the Law that he keeps failing, and despite the fact that he is saved and Spirit-filled.

The reason for this was that he did not know or understand the meaning of the Cross, and in fact, neither did anyone else at that particular time. As a result, he tried to live the life he knew he must live, and in fact wanted to live, by the means of his own efforts and machinations. To be sure, these efforts were noble and true, but due to the sin nature still residing even in the hearts and lives of Believers, Paul found to his dismay, that he couldn't do the things which he desired to do, i.e., *"be righteous"* (Rom. 7:15, 18). In other words, he was trying to live this life by the strength of his willpower, which in fact most Christians continue to try to do presently, but which always brings failure.

The idea is, he didn't know the manner and the way in which the Holy Spirit worked, even though he was definitely filled with the Spirit. And once again, that's also the plight of most modern Christians. While millions are Spirit-filled, the mere fact of that great experience doesn't guarantee victory at all. We must know how the Spirit works, which refers to Him working totally and completely within the framework of the parameters of the Finished Work of Christ. All He asks of us is that we have Faith in that great Work, but it's difficult for most Christians to do this, when they have very little knowledge of the Finished Work of Christ; therefore, most Christians forfeit the help of the Holy Spirit, which leaves the Believer in a perilous condition indeed!

WHAT THE BELIEVER MUST KNOW

Some 13 times in Romans, Chapters 6, 7, and 8, Paul mentions things that the Believer should know. In other words, he uses the words *"know"* or *"knowing"* or *"known,"* some 13 times. The sadness is, most Christians don't know!

Know what?

The knowledge of which he speaks, and which we must know, and which is the single most important thing in the world, is what He did for us at the Cross and in His Resurrection.

First of all, he tells us that Jesus came to this world and died on a Cross as our Substitute. What we couldn't do for ourselves, He did for us.

He uses the term, *"Know ye not, that so many of us as were baptized into Jesus Christ were baptized into His Death?"* (Rom. 6:3).

He is not speaking here of Water Baptism as many think, but rather the Death of Christ on the Cross. The idea is, that our Faith in this which Jesus did, places us, at least in the Mind of God, in the very death of Christ. It is as if we died, hence the Holy Spirit through Paul using the term, *"baptized into His Death."*

When He died on the Cross, which in fact He came to this world to do, which means that the Crucifixion was not an incident or an accident, but rather a Sacrifice, He satisfied the terrible sin debt which man owed to God. A debt, incidentally, which man could not pay. The wages of sin is death (Rom. 6:23), and those wages or penalty, had to be satisfied. Only death could satisfy the demand, and, therefore, Jesus had to die.

SATAN?

Please know and understand, that Jesus didn't go to the Cross to satisfy Satan. In fact, Satan had absolutely nothing to do with the Cross. Jesus went there to satisfy the demands of a thrice Holy God. In other words, the Holiness and Righteousness of God demanded that sin be addressed. That means that it was a debt which could not be written off. It must be paid! As stated, it was a debt owed to God.

When Jesus died on the Cross being actually made a Sin-Offering, this satisfied the demands of God, and of course, it was all done on behalf of sinful man. If one wants to know how absolutely horrible sin actually is, one only has to look at the Cross. He can look there at the Judgment of God expended upon the suffering Son of God, all incidentally on our behalf, and say *"sin did this!"*

The Holy Spirit through Paul used the word *"baptized"* in describing this action, because that's the strongest word that could be used. The word *"Baptism"* actually means, *"to dip under."* In its total analysis, it is the same as a sunken ship in the sea. The ship is in the sea and the sea is in the ship. That's what *"Baptism"* actually means.

The idea is, being baptized into Christ at His Death, means that we were in Christ when He died, at least in the Mind of God, and as a result of our Faith in that Finished Work, Christ is in us. That's the reason that Jesus said, *"At that day* (after the Cross and the advent of the Holy Spirit) *ye shall know that I am in My Father, and ye in Me, and I in you"* (Jn. 14:20).

But notice, we were *"baptized into His Death,"* and not into His Life. In fact, life would come out of this death, and a new life at that, but the death was demanded first. That's the reason we should never in any shape, form, or fashion, minimize the Cross. We were saved by His Death and not by His Life (Jn. 3:16).

When Christians boast of being Resurrection people, that is in fact correct; however, if they are saying and believing such a thing by minimizing the Cross, they are totally wrong. Salvation was effected at the Cross. While the Resurrection, as would be obvious, was an absolute necessity, it was not what redeemed humanity. Redemption came through Jesus Christ shedding His Life's Blood on the Cross (Rom. 3:25; 5:9; I Cor. 11:25, 27; Eph. 1:7; 2:13; Col. 1:14, 20).

As we've said previously, the Death of Christ was not an incident or an accident, but rather a planned Sacrifice, actually planned from before the foundation of the world (I Pet. 1:18-20). Understanding all of this, we must anchor and center our Faith in the Cross of Christ. This is where the work was done, which guaranteed not only our Salvation, but also, our victorious walk in Christ on a daily basis. In fact, ever single thing we receive from the Lord, be it Salvation, the Baptism with the Holy Spirit, Sanctification, Grace, Power, Divine Healing, financial prosperity, everything, and without exception, comes through what Christ did at the Cross. If we don't understand that, then we don't understand the Gospel. Therefore, understanding that, we must at the same time, as stated, center our Faith in that great Sacrifice of Christ, and not allow it to be moved from this great, Finished Work.

On this basis, and I speak of the Sacrifice of Christ, the Holy Spirit works. As stated, He only demands that we exercise Faith in the Cross, understanding, that the Cross made and makes everything possible (Rom. 6:3-5, 11, 14).

BURIED WITH HIM

We were not only *"baptized into His Death,"* but we were also *"buried with Him by baptism into death"* (Rom. 6:4). Once again, this is not speaking of Water Baptism, but rather what Jesus did for us on the Cross.

This speaks of the *"old man"* being crucified with Him, which refers to what we once were, and then being buried with Him. This means that all the old life, the old way, the old sinful way, the old ungodly way, all and without exception, died with Him, and more particularly, died in Him, and as well, was *"buried with Him."* This also means that we are totally and completely dead to all the old way, the old life, and to sin in general (Rom. 6:7).

DEAD TO SIN

It is very important that we understand this. It doesn't say that sin was dead, and in fact it's not dead, but very much alive, and by that we refer to the *"sin nature,"* because that's actually what it means. When Paul said, *"For he that is dead* (crucified with Christ) *is freed from sin"* (Rom. 6:7), he actually said in the original Greek Text, *"the sin,"* which refers to the *"sinful nature."* While the *"sin nature"* continues to be present in the life of the Believer, it is for all practical purposes disarmed. In other words, it should not cause us any problem whatsoever, and because we are dead to its impulses; however, the moment we attempt to live this life by our own efforts, instead of having Faith in the Cross, which denies the help of the Holy Spirit, the sin nature will come to life quickly, with the Believer finding himself in serious trouble, which regrettably is the lot of most modern Christians, and because they do not understand these things we are teaching here. (The sin nature, which is a result of the Fall, is simply the bent or ease of sinful direction.)

Let me emphasize again, that the Bible nowhere teaches that sin is dead in the life of the Christian, but rather that we are dead to sin. This was all done by what Jesus did at the Cross, and our Faith in that. However, the moment our Faith shifts to something

else, that's the moment the sin nature revives, and we are in trouble. As long as we continue to have Faith in the Cross of Christ, and this means on a daily basis (Lk. 9:23), we will remain dead to sin, and the Holy Spirit will guarantee such; however, the moment our Faith wanders to something else, that's the moment we are in trouble.

RAISED IN NEWNESS OF LIFE

We not only were baptized into His Death, and we were buried with Him, we were also raised with Him *"in newness of life,"* which refers to His Resurrection, which in a sense refers to our Resurrection, at least this new life, which completes the process. Let me emphasize again, that Christ did all of this strictly and totally for us, and not at all for Himself. Consequently, every single thing He did at the Cross and in His Resurrection is of vital significance. Of course, anything and everything that Christ did in totality throughout His Life is vastly important; however, we must understand, that everything He did in His Life, led up to, and without exception, that which He would do at the Cross.

To *"walk in newness of life,"* which refers to our living this life on a daily basis, is the grandest, most glorious life there could ever be. This is the *"more abundant life,"* of which Jesus spoke (Jn. 10:10). It is also the *"rest,"* of which He spoke (Mat. 11:28-30). However, to maintain this *"newness of life,"* i.e., *"Resurrection Life,"* we must always understand and abide by the following:

Paul plainly said, *"For if we have been planted together in the likeness of His Death, we shall be also in the likeness of His Resurrection"* (Rom. 6:5).

The idea is, that we cannot have Resurrection Life, unless we properly understand *"His Death,"* and what it all meant, which we have been attempting to explain here. Unfortunately, many Christians zero in on the Resurrection Life, without properly knowing and understanding the Cross, which means, despite what they say, they really do not have Resurrection Life. All Resurrection Life is based 100 percent on the Cross of Christ, which refers to what He did there. In fact, the Cross always has the preeminence. That's why Paul also said:

"But God forbid that I should glory, save in the Cross of our Lord Jesus Christ, by Whom the world is crucified unto me, and I unto the world" (Gal. 6:14).

RECKON OURSELVES

Concerning all this, the Apostle then said, *"Likewise reckon ye also yourselves to be dead indeed unto sin, but alive unto God through Jesus Christ our Lord"* (Rom. 6:11).

This means that you as a Believer are not to look at yourself, but rather to Christ. You are to understand that the Death of Christ on the Cross, and His Resurrection, and our Faith in that, handled the sin question. Consequently, we are not going to be victorious, we are in fact, already victorious, and because of what Christ has already done. We are not to think of ourselves as going to be an overcomer, but rather that we are already an overcomer. Likewise, we shouldn't think of ourselves as going to be delivered, but rather that we have already been delivered. In other words, all of this is a past tense action, which took place at the Cross of Christ. Our Faith in that, guarantees this of which we speak.

Any Christian who is *"trying to be victorious,"* or *"trying to be an overcomer,"* is never going to make the grade. Such a life, even though it sounds right on the surface, will always lead to total failure. The reason is because of the following:

In trying to do these things, in other words, always putting them into the future, we are in essence saying, that what Christ did is not enough, and we must add something to His great Work. Such thinking is totally wrong, and thinking incidentally, which the Holy Spirit cannot bless, and as well, is an insult to Christ. In fact, such thinking shows that we do not understand the Cross.

Every single thing that we need for our life and living was handled at the Cross of Christ. Our Faith in that is all that God demands, which guarantees the help of the Holy Spirit (Rom. 8:1-2, 11).

BUT WHAT IF I'M NOT ACTUALLY VICTORIOUS?

The Truth is, no Christian is victorious in a practical sense, immediately after being saved, even as Romans, Chapter 7 proclaims.

NOTES

And the trouble is, most Christians are still not victorious, even after living for Christ for many, many years, and because they do not understand God's prescribed order of victory. But what you are to do is this:

Quit thinking of yourself as being defeated, and do exactly what the Scripture says as it regards the Cross of Christ, which means to *"reckon ye also yourselves to be dead indeed unto sin, but alive unto God through Jesus Christ our Lord."* Start out on this basis, because that is the actual Truth. Remember, Jesus said:

"You shall know the Truth, and the Truth shall make you free" (Jn. 8:32).

Begin counting yourself, or reckoning yourself, as being exactly this which the Word says you are, which means to be dead indeed unto sin, but alive unto God. Now that your Faith is rightly placed, the Holy Spirit can help you. However, you must understand, that it is absolutely necessary that you begin on this basis. This is so important, that I must be allowed to say it again:

Do not look at yourself and your failures. Do not look at your own shortcomings and weaknesses. But look totally to the Cross of Christ, understanding that He addressed every single problem that you might have in His Death, Burial, and Resurrection, which also includes His Exaltation at the Right Hand of the Father (Eph. 2:6). I can sense the Presence of the Lord even as I dictate these notes.

Too many Christians look at themselves instead of the Cross. And to be sure, when you look at yourself, at least in the manner you are presently, you're not going to see very much. Don't look at yourself, but rather look at the Cross of Christ, understanding that every problem was handled there.

DID CHRIST ACTUALLY ADDRESS EVERYTHING AT THE CROSS?

I don't care who you are, or what your problem might be. Jesus unequivocally, totally, and completely addressed every single problem at the Cross. In other words, everything that man lost in the Fall, and I mean everything, was addressed at the Cross of Christ. Listen to what Paul said:

"Blotting out the handwriting of ordinances that was against us (this is the Law

of Moses), *which was contrary to us, and took it out of the way, nailing it to His Cross."* This means that Jesus satisfied the Law in every respect, which refers to Him keeping it perfectly, and as well suffering its consequences and penalty, all on our behalf.

And then the Apostle said, *"And having spoiled principalities and powers, He made a show of them openly, triumphing over them in it"* (Col. 2:14-15).

This means that Jesus satisfied the demands of a thrice Holy God by His Death on the Cross, and by doing that, He also at the same time defeated Satan in every capacity, which is proclaimed in Verse 15.

Satan's legal hold upon humanity is sin. With all sin removed, as Jesus did at the Cross (Jn. 1:29), Satan also lost his legal hold. In other words, if he holds any person in bondage presently, it's because they have not taken advantage of what Christ did at the Cross. That refers to all of humanity who aren't saved, and it also refers to Christians who do not know and understand God's prescribed order of victory, which we are teaching.

A homosexual wrote me just the other day, asking if this great Price paid by Christ at the Cross included him. Most definitely it does! It doesn't matter what the sin is, what the bondage is, or what demon power we might be addressing. Christ addressed it all at the Cross, meaning that all can go free. Everyone is included in this victory, which means that none are excluded. The only thing that excludes anyone is unbelief, which Paul addressed powerfully in Hebrews, Chapter 4.

THE DOMINION OF SIN IS BROKEN

Paul now says, *"For sin shall not have dominion over you: for ye are not under the Law, but under Grace"* (Rom. 6:14).

He actually said in the original Greek, *"For the sin shall not have dominion over you,"* speaking of the sin nature. The Bible doesn't teach sinless perfection, but it does teach that sin will not have dominion over us, meaning that we are free from its power. While the sin nature still remains in the Believer, it is never to *"reign in our mortal body, that we should obey it in the lusts thereof"* (Rom. 6:12).

In the unsaved, the sin nature *"dwells"* and *"reigns."* In the Believer, while it might dwell in us, it definitely is not to reign in us, even as Paul here reiterates. And how do we keep it from reigning in us?

We do so, by understanding this Sixth Chapter of Romans, which explains to us the meaning of the Cross of Christ, and that we should ever have our Faith in this which Christ has done on our behalf.

Most of the modern Church knows little about the Cross. They know that Jesus died there, but that's all they know. In fact, if they know anything else, it's mostly in the realm of sentimentality. Consequently, it's hard to have Faith in something, of which you know almost nothing, and tragically, the modern Church knows almost nothing in this respect.

Understanding these things which we have taught you, you can now properly place your Faith in the Finished Work of Christ, which will guarantee the help of the Holy Spirit, which will then guarantee victory on a daily basis. In fact, this is what Jesus was speaking of, when He talked about denying ourselves and taking up the Cross daily, to follow Him (Lk. 9:23).

The sad Truth is, most Christians are being dominated by the sin nature in some way. It may be in the form of one of the vices, which are sins of the flesh, or it may be in the form of sins of pride, which are apathy, unforgiveness, greed, etc. But the fact is, if the Believer doesn't understand the Cross of Christ, the sin nature is going to dominate that Believer in some way. It is impossible for it to be otherwise. And understanding, that most of the modern Church little knows or understands the Cross of Christ, this means that most of the modern Church is presently being dominated by the sin nature. That is tragic but true!

This is proven by what the Church is presently doing. Let's look at that for a moment.

DELIVERANCE

Paul said, *"Who gave Himself for our sins, that He might deliver us from this present evil world, according to the Will of God and our Father"* (Gal. 1:4).

Deliverance is what Christ effected for us at the Cross, which means that we were delivered from the powers of darkness, and brought unto and into Christ. But most Christians misunderstand *"deliverance."*

Preachers are running all over the world attempting to deliver people, with thousands of others laying hands on people, attempting to do the same thing. Now don't misunderstand. The *"laying on of hands"* is definitely Scriptural; however, it must be understood and used in the right context.

The Truth is, and addressing ourselves now to Christians, every single Believer in the world has been delivered totally and completely, and yet at the same time, most Christians need deliverance. No! That's not a contradiction. In fact, in a sense it is a contradiction, but not in the way we have made the statement. Let's look at the latter first.

It is a fact that millions of Christians need deliverance, and it is a travesty that this fact exists. Actually, Christians by the tens of thousands are running all over the world trying to find a Preacher who they think God is using, as stated, who can lay hands on them, and deliver them from their problem, whatever it might be. They're not going to find any help in that manner.

While it may be true that the Preacher in question is definitely of God and definitely being used of God, and it also may be true that the person may be greatly and wonderfully blessed whenever hands are laid on them in this fashion; however, they will find when it's all over, despite the Preacher being used of God, and the Blessing, that their problem is still with them.

Seeking deliverance in this fashion is not Scriptural, and if it's not Scriptural, there will be no positive results.

In fact, the whole atmosphere of Christianity has become so warped by much of the Faith teaching of the last several decades, that the Church hardly knows where it is anymore. It really doesn't know what it believes, why it believes what it believes, or what it's supposed to believe. It goes from one fad to the other, with each effort becoming more and more ridiculous. When we deviate from the Word of God, *"ridiculous"* is usually the result. And that's what the Church has done in these last several decades. It has drifted from its foundation, which is the Cross of Christ.

NOTES

Many Pentecostal and Charismatic Preachers believe and teach that if a Christian has a problem, it is caused by a demon spirit, and the Christian should have this spirit rebuked, etc. To be sure, demon spirits definitely do get involved in every type of spiritual failure; however, this of which these Preachers teach is not Scriptural. Christians fail not because demon spirits overcome them, even though they may definitely be involved, they fail because the Christian has shifted his Faith from the Cross of Christ to something else. To be sure, and as stated, Satan definitely takes advantage of all of this, but the cause is not in that capacity, but rather in the incorrect object of one's Faith.

Back in the 1970's, this teaching was very big, consequently with Christians lining up at various Churches all across the nation, in order to have the demon of lust, or of greed, or of temper, etc., cast out of them, etc. One book took the Christian world by storm, entitled *"Pigs In The Parlor,"* referring to Christians being controlled by demon spirits, etc.

As stated, demon spirits always get involved in all types of sin and failure, etc. That's a given! However, laying hands on Christians with problems, and rebuking these type of things, is not going to do the Christian any good. It is an unscriptural manner and will not work. In fact, even though many Preachers claim to still believe this, the long lines of Christians being prayed for in this respect, have long since ceased. The reason is, it simply doesn't work!

MANIFESTATIONS

There's a new twist to the situation now, and it refers to manifestations. While the Lord definitely does give manifestations of the Spirit, and while they are definitely a great blessing to people, manifestations aren't the answer either.

I am speaking primarily of Christians once again, getting Preachers to lay hands on them, with the idea being, that if they can be *"slain in the Spirit,"* or have some such type manifestation, that their problem will be solved. While the manifestation might be real and, therefore, a great blessing, still, it will not solve the problems of which we speak. In other words, after the manifestation, and after the blessing, when the person gets home, they're going to find that their problem is still with them. In fact, this latter effort has been going on now for several years, but is presently dying down, and because, as well, it doesn't work.

I don't want the Reader to misunderstand. I believe in manifestations, that is if they are truly from the Lord, and I definitely believe in the laying on of hands. Both of these things are Scriptural; however, these things and others we have not mentioned, can be used in the wrong way, and in fact are being used in the wrong way by many Preachers and the Laity as well.

Your victory as a Child of God doesn't come from any of these things, as Scriptural as they might be in their own right. Your victory totally and completely, comes because of what Christ did at the Cross on your behalf. That's what I mean by the fact that every Christian has been delivered totally and completely. It was all done at the Cross of Christ, and is a *"Finished Work"* (Heb. 1:3).

Christians trying to get delivered when in fact they have already been delivered, shows that their understanding of the Scriptures is wrong. The Truth is, such Believers, and they number almost the entirety of the Church, don't know their place and standing in Christ, which is a place and standing given to us by what Christ did at the Cross. Consequently, if we do not walk in the victory provided there, it's because our Faith is not properly placed in the Cross, but is rather in something else, which is in fact, the situation regarding the far greater majority of the modern Church.

WHAT DID JESUS TEACH ABOUT DELIVERANCE?

Let's look carefully at what He said:

"The Spirit of the Lord is upon Me, because He hath anointed Me . . . to preach deliverance to the captives" (Lk. 4:18).

If one is to notice, which we've already explained elsewhere in this Volume, Jesus didn't say that the Lord had anointed Him to deliver people, but rather to *"preach deliverance to the captives."*

Of course when He made this statement, He had not yet gone to the Cross; but still,

He made this statement in the past tense simply because His coming Work at the Cross would soon be accomplished.

Again I emphasize that He didn't tell us to go around delivering people, but rather to *"preach deliverance."* And what did He mean by that?

For us to try to deliver people, as many Preachers attempt to do, in effect says that Christ didn't finish the work, and we have to do something ourselves. It should be obvious that such efforts and thinking are an insult to Christ. But yet, most preachers do this, simply because they don't know any better. They are trying to help, and many times what they do does actually help some, but it really does not bring about the victory for which the individual seeks, and because it cannot bring about such victory.

When Jesus used the phrase *"preach deliverance to the captives,"* He was actually referring to what I'm doing right here, and what any Preacher does, or anyone for that matter, when they proclaim what Jesus did at the Cross. Telling what He did at the Cross on our behalf, is in effect, *"preaching and teaching deliverance."* It's telling people how that deliverance is already come, and how it is already theirs, that is, if they will have Faith in what Christ did at the Cross on their behalf.

Deliverance is found totally in the Cross, and deliverance is found only in the Cross. So it's not some particular act or manifestation that is needed in order for Believers to enjoy this victory, but merely that they know and understand the Truth. Again I emphasize, this is why Jesus said, *"Ye shall know the Truth, and the Truth shall make you free"* (Jn. 8:32).

When the Believer begins to properly place his Faith in the Cross of Christ, which is where all Faith properly belongs, he will then find the Holy Spirit beginning to help him, and that is the key.

THE HOLY SPIRIT

When Paul said, *"For the preaching of the Cross is to them that perish foolishness; but unto us which are saved it is the Power of God,"* we should find out exactly where this power is (I Cor. 1:18).

In fact, there was no power inherent in the wooden Cross, on which Jesus died, or even in the Death of Christ on that Cross. Where the *"Power"* comes in, is by the Holy Spirit.

The Holy Spirit Who abides in the heart and life of every Believer, has all power, and because He is God. In fact, His abiding within us is the greatest thing that can ever happen to a Christian (Jn. 14:16). In fact, His abiding in us, which means that He will be there forever, is all because of what Christ did at the Cross. That's what Paul was speaking about when he said, *"Christ hath redeemed us from the curse of the Law, being made a curse for us . . . that we might receive the Promise of the Spirit through Faith"* (Gal. 3:13-14). So, the Power is registered in the Spirit (Acts 1:8).

The idea is, the Holy Spirit works exclusively within us according to the parameters of the Finished Work of Christ. Paul again said:

"For the Law (it's a Law which cannot be broken) *of the Spirit* (Holy Spirit) *of life* (all life comes from the Spirit through the Son) *in Christ Jesus* (which refers to what Christ did at the Cross) *hath made me free from the law of sin and death"* (Rom. 8:2).

As stated, the Power is in the Spirit, and the way and manner this power becomes available to us, is by our Faith in the Cross of Christ.

Paul also said, *"But if the Spirit* (Holy Spirit) *of Him* (God the Father) *Who raised up Jesus from the dead dwell in you, He Who raised up Christ from the dead shall also quicken your mortal bodies by His Spirit Who dwelleth in you"* (Rom. 8:11).

When Paul speaks of our *"mortal bodies,"* he's not speaking of the coming Resurrection, but rather our everyday life and living. Also, the word *"quicken"* means to *"make alive."* It is by the Power of the Holy Spirit Who dwells in us, that we have victory over the world, the flesh, and the Devil. However, and as repeatedly stated, this comes about, and without exception, through our Faith in the Cross of Christ.

To say it another way, the Holy Spirit will not *"quicken your mortal bodies,"* as it regards you having a Preacher lay hands on you and your trusting in that or accompanying manifestations, etc. While the Spirit might help and bless you in other ways in

this respect, He will not give you victory over sin in this respect. And to be sure, it is sin which we are talking about, because sin is the problem.

SIN

Most Christians have the idea that if they are not vexed by one of the *"vices,"* that everything is all right with them. (By the vices I speak of alcohol, gambling, drugs, immorality, nicotine, etc.) However, sin comes in many and varied colors, shapes, forms, and fashions.

In fact, the committing of sin, whether it's in the capacity of which we have just mentioned, or the capacity of self-righteousness, etc., is really a symptom of the real problem. Unfortunately, most of the Church not knowing what the real problem actually is, has a tendency to try to address the problem by addressing the symptom. It cannot be done in that way. In fact, that's doing the same thing that the world of psychology does, which doesn't know the cause of sin or the cure.

The real sin, which brings on all of these other things that we have mentioned, is a departure from Faith exclusively in the Cross of Christ. The Believer's safety and protection always is in the Cross. Even though the Cross was an act performed in the distant past, it has continuing results, and in fact, results which will never be discontinued. That's why Paul referred to it as *"The Everlasting Covenant"* (Heb. 13:20).

Because it's so important, please allow me to say it again:

The real sin, which always leads to failure in other ways, is rebelling against God's prescribed order of victory, which is the Cross of Christ (Rom. 6:3-5, 11, 14; 8:1-2, 11; I Cor. 1:18, 21; 2:2; Gal. 6:14).

While it is true that most Christians do this through ignorance, in other words they simply don't know the veracity of the Cross, still, the results are the same — failure. And as repeatedly stated, that's where most Believers are presently.

Having little or no understanding of the Cross of Christ, they try to obtain victory in many and varied ways other than God's Way, which always brings defeat. To be frank, this makes the Christian life far less than it ought to be. Not living up to what Christ did for us at the Cross, for which He paid such a price, is a travesty. But that's exactly what is happening. The people perish for lack of knowledge.

When one properly understands the Cross, one will properly understand sin. We will know that this problem is so acute, so bad, so awful in fact, that God would have to address it by becoming man, and giving Himself as a Sacrifice on the Cross. When we understand it in that light, then we see how bad sin is, and that it is impossible for it to be handled any other way. Let the Reader understand perfectly and well, that sin was handled at the Cross, and because it could only be handled at the Cross. That means, we cannot handle it any other way, and in fact, must not try to handle it in any other way. To do so spells disaster! And yet at this very moment, millions of Christians are attempting of overcome sin in ways other than Faith in the Cross. No matter how hard they try, they will not succeed in this endeavor. In fact, the problem, whatever that problem might be, will only get worse and worse!

SELF-RIGHTEOUSNESS

There is another side issue to the wrong object of Faith, that causes so many problems in the Church. It is the problem of self-righteousness.

Any time that any Believer attempts to live this life other than by constant Faith in the Cross, the only thing that will be developed in that person's life is acute self-righteousness. In fact, that's what happened to Israel. In attempting to find Salvation by the Law, they just kept adding more and more law, which did nothing but bring about self-righteousness.

In that terrible spirit and attitude, they crucified the Lord of Glory. Actually, that's what self-righteousness always does. It is never content with going its own way; it feels that it must also stamp out the true Way of Christ. That is ironical, when Christ is claimed by all parties concerned; however, it must always be understood, that any Christ claimed other than the Christ of the Cross, is pure and simple *"another Jesus"* (II Cor. 11:4).

It's the same problem with Cain and Abel all over again. Cain, lifted up in his own self-righteousness, grew angry with God and Abel because Abel's sacrifice was accepted and not his. Consequently, not able to do anything to God, he instead killed his brother Abel. That spirit has functioned in that same capacity from then until now! Ishmael tried to kill Isaac, even as Saul tried to kill David. Joseph's brothers tried to kill him, even as the Jews killed Christ. This spirit is no less prevalent today, and is brought about solely through a departure from the Cross of Christ to other things.

Therefore, when we talk about sin, we must also understand that we're speaking not only of the *"vices,"* which are the sins of the flesh, but as well we're speaking of sins of pride, which always evidence themselves in self-righteousness. To be frank, the problem of the *"vices,"* as sordid as they might be, can be handled rather easily. The problem of self-righteousness is not handled so easily at all. This is what Jesus was speaking about when He said to the religious leaders of Israel:

"Verily I say unto you, that the Publicans and the harlots go into the Kingdom of God before you.

"For John came unto you in the Way of Righteousness, and ye believed him not: but the Publicans and the harlots believed him: and ye, when ye had seen it, repented not afterward, that ye might believe him" (Mat. 21:31-32).

Again allow us to emphasize the point, that all of this, whether the sins of the publicans and harlots or the sins of the religious leaders of Israel, came about and come about, because of a departure from Faith in the Cross of Christ.

CARNALITY

If we were to ask most Christians to define carnality, I think that most would define it as *"watching too much television,"* or *"not reading the Bible enough,"* etc.

No! That's not carnality, and neither does it have anything to do with carnality.

"Carnality" is trust in the flesh, instead of the Finished Work of Christ. In other words, it is the Christian attempting to bring

about Righteousness and Holiness, in fact, Christlikeness, by his own religious efforts, etc.

"Spirituality" is the Believer trusting exclusively in what Christ has done for him at the Cross, in order to bring about these desired things. This is *"spiritual"* simply because our Faith in the Cross gives leeway and latitude to the Holy Spirit to bring about the desired work. The Believer should understand, that no matter that he is saved and Baptized with the Holy Spirit; still, there's nothing that he can do within himself, that will draw him closer to God. In fact, if he tries to do anything other than having simple Faith in the Finished Work of Christ, that is carnality, and Paul plainly said, *"So then they that are in the* flesh (attempt to do things by their own strength and efforts) *cannot please God"* (Rom. 8:8).

But many Christians would protest, claiming, *"I'm not trying to be holy in the flesh, but by Faith in God."* But the Truth is, if the Believer doesn't know and understand the Truth of the Cross, which we've been teaching for the last few pages, in fact more or less throughout the entirety of this Volume, he can do nothing but function in the flesh, no matter how hard he tries to do otherwise.

What deceives most Christians is, the things they are doing to attempt to bring about victory, are good things. And because they are good things, such as more Bible reading, more prayer, more faithful Church attendance, giving more money to the Work of the Lord, etc., we think surely, this will perform the task.

While these things are good, and in fact that which all Christians should do, and will bring about blessing, the doing of such in this fashion, which means to have dependence on these things, will not bring about the victory for which we seek. That can only come about by one's Faith in the Cross of Christ and in nothing else. Anything that's done outside of Faith in the Cross is constituted by God as carnality, which means that we are attempting to do something by our own efforts, etc.

FAITH

God demands one thing and one thing only of Believers, and that is Faith. However, when

Paul speaks of Faith, he is in effect speaking of *"the Faith,"* which refers to what Jesus did at the Cross on our behalf, in other words, the great Sacrifice of Christ. We are to always understand Faith in that capacity.

In fact, and as we've already stated several times in this Volume, everybody in the world has Faith. The problem is, they have it in the wrong thing. For it to be Faith which God will recognize, it must always be Faith in the great Sacrifice of our Lord. This is the only Faith which God will recognize, and which obtains for us the Victory.

When the Scripture says that *"Abraham believed God, and it was counted unto him for Righteousness"* (Gen. 15:6), the word *"believed"* refers to the fact that Abraham had Faith in God. However, it must be understood, that the Faith which is addressed here, is not the mere fact that Abraham believed there was a God, but rather, that he believed that God was going to send a Redeemer into this world, to lift man out of his dilemma. In other words, he believed a certain way and in a certain thing, that way being the Way of the Lord, and that certain thing being the Sacrifice of Christ.

Since about the midpoint of the Twentieth Century, the Church has had more teaching on Faith than perhaps all the balance of the centuries put together since the Day of Pentecost; however, for the most part, and in fact, almost altogether, it's been Faith in the wrong thing. It's been Faith in self, Faith in Preachers, or Faith in Faith, but it's not been true Faith in God.

While these Teachers claim that it's Faith in the Word, it is in fact, the Word which has been perverted, in other words, being pulled out of context.

The idea was, that individuals could find a Scripture which seemed to go along with their need, and then their constant repetition of the quotation of this Scripture, along with their claiming to have Faith in this, would guarantee them some type of success. As stated, that is a perversion of the Word. That's taking the Bible completely out of context, making Faith the principle force instead of the One in Whom we are supposed to be evidencing Faith, namely Christ. Let it ever be understood, that God will never allow His

Word to be used against Himself. And that's exactly what has happened:

This particular teaching has degenerated to the place, that its present thrust is about money altogether. I call it the *"money gospel."*

As stated, if it's not Faith in the Finished Work of Christ, then it's not Faith which God will recognize. In fact, the entirety of the Bible is the story of Christ and Him Crucified. If one reads the Bible correctly, this becomes quickly obvious. The centerpiece of the whole of the Mosaic system was the Sacrifices. The Sacrificial System in all of its complex ceremonies and dealings pointed exclusively to the coming Christ, and what He would do on the Cross for sinning and dying humanity. In fact, the whole of the Old Testament pointed to Christ, and without fail, it pointed to what He would do as it regards His Finished Work (Isa. Chpt. 53).

The New Testament, which is the New Covenant, which is in fact the meaning of the Cross, explains to us what Christ did for us, and how it affects our hearts and lives for time and eternity. The Cross of Christ is the centrality of the Gospel. To not understand that, is to not understand the Gospel!

IMMUTABILITY

The phrase, *"The immutability of His counsel,"* refers to the fact that God will not change His position as to His Promise. Having made the Promise, He will stand by it. He is not a turncoat. He will not change His position as to His Promise, because that Promise rests upon His Counsel, and that is immutable, i.e., *"unchangeable."*

"Counsel" in the Greek is *"boule,"* which means *"to desire, and more particularly, a desire which comes from one's reason."* The idea is, the Triune God in counsel convened brought forth this principle to the effect that the soul might find a sure refuge in the Lord Jesus. This counsel is immutable (Wuest).

The idea is, it is impossible for God to break Faith. By His providential care, He is able to bring to pass all those things He has promised. Those who are heirs may rest assured that God will make them sure. God is abundantly willing, the Promises unchangeable, and it is confirmed with an oath by God Almighty Himself (Fjordbak).

Andrew Murray says:

"God points to Himself, His Divine Being, His glory, His power, and pledges Himself, gives Himself as security, as hostage, if you will, that, as sure as He lives, He will fulfill His Promise.

"And now let us pause and realize what all this argument about the blessing and the oath of God means. In the Christian life there is lack of steadfastness, of diligence, of perseverance. Of all the cause, the greatest is simply, lack of Faith. And of this again the cause is, the lack of the knowledge of what God wills and that it is of His purpose and power to bless most wonderfully, and of His faithfulness to carry out His purpose."

In other words, Believers do not have Faith, because they do not properly understand the Word, and more particular still, they do not understand the Cross of Christ. To properly understand the Cross, means to properly understand the Word, which means to properly understand the Will of God, which means to properly understand the Promise and how it is effected.

God's Will does not change and because it doesn't need to change. He has His purpose and He works it out, that is if we believe it.

WILL GOD WORK IT OUT IF WE DO NOT BELIEVE?

While He might work it out with someone else, if we lack Faith, which means we quit believing, He definitely will not work out the Promise with us, whatever the Promise might be. Actually, that's what Paul was dealing with these Jews about.

If they lost Faith in that What Christ had done on their behalf, and Who Christ actually was, then the great Salvation promised them, plus all the other benefits that go along with Salvation, would be forfeited. That's the gist of the entirety of this Book of Hebrews.

However, even though they might forfeit the great Promise of God, even as many have, the Promise still held true for all who believed.

While the Work of God may definitely be hindered and even delayed because of unbelief, as it no doubt has many times, ultimately and eventually, God will get somebody to believe Him, with the Work then progressing forward as it should. It's all hinged on Faith.

God doesn't require much of us, actually only one thing, and that is Faith. He does demand that, which again, is what this Epistle to the Hebrews is all about. As long as the Believer keeps believing God, the Promise will ultimately be realized. It's when the Believer quits believing, that the problem occurs, which is what Paul is addressing.

This shoots full of holes the idea that it is impossible for a Believer to quit believing. In fact, that is the problem with everything as it pertains to God and His Word. If we believe, we can enter in. If not, we cannot enter in, which is what the Scripture plainly tells us (Heb. 4:1-11). It is always the Faith of the individual that is in question.

CAN A CHRISTIAN CONTINUE IN SIN AND STILL CLAIM TO HAVE FAITH?

No!

While the Bible does not teach sinless perfection, it definitely does teach that the Christian is to have victory over sin, or to say it another way, *"sin shall not have dominion over you"* (Rom. 6:14).

It is definitely true that there are millions of Christians who are struggling with sin of some nature, simply because they do not understand the Cross of Christ. They don't want the sin in their lives, and they are doing all they know to do to get it out of their lives, even though what they are doing is wrong. These people are saved, and in fact, might even be close to God, and if the latter is the case, the Lord will ultimately show them the right way, which is the Cross. But for an individual to think that they can claim to trust Christ, and at the same time purposely and willingly continue right on in a sinful lifestyle, claiming to have both Faith and sin at the same time, that person is fooling themselves.

The Holy Spirit through Paul plainly said, *"Know ye not that the unrighteous shall not inherit the Kingdom of God? Be not deceived: neither fornicators, nor idolaters, nor adulterers, nor effeminate, nor abusers of themselves with mankind, nor thieves, nor covetous, nor drunkards, nor revilers, nor extortioners, shall inherit the Kingdom of God"* (I Cor. 6:9-10).

Again I emphasize, this is not referring to Christians who are having a struggle with sin,

and because they do not understand the Cross. These people hate sin, and as stated, are trying to do all within their power to rid themselves of this monster. The problem is, they don't know God's prescribed order of victory. In fact, almost all of the modern Church falls into this category. And that also refers to Preachers, even those who are being used of God. If they don't know the victory of the Cross, it is impossible for them to walk in victory. They may walk in victory some of the time, or part of the time, but they definitely cannot walk in victory all of the time. As I've said many times, if we're fighting and winning, after awhile we will fight and lose.

But these people, at least those in the category of which we speak, are definitely saved, they love God, and are trying to walk true before the Lord. They're just trying in the wrong way.

But again to emphasize, I'm speaking of the millions who call themselves Christians, because they claim to trust Christ, when at the same time they are purposely living a sinful lifestyle, and are making no efforts to change. In fact, they attempt to twist the Word of God to make allowance for their sin, by claiming unconditional eternal security, or some other type of foolishness! While God Alone knows the hearts of individuals, it becomes obvious and very quickly, as to the sincerity of an individual regarding what they actually believe. Because of the seriousness of the matter, allow us to say it again:

No! If one truly has Faith in the Lord Jesus Christ, one will at the same time truly attempt to walk holy before the Lord.

CONFIRMATION

The phrase, *"Confirmed it by an oath,"* refers to the guarantee of the Pledge or Promise.

"Confirmed" in the Greek is *"mesiteuo,"* which means *"to act as Mediator between litigating or covenanting parties, to accomplish something by interposing between two parties."* One might say, *"God placed Himself between Himself and the inheritors of the Promise, in effect, guaranteeing by Himself and of Himself, what He has promised."* Such a statement may seem somewhat confusing, but there's really no other way to explain it.

Delitzsch says: *"God descended, as it were, from His Own absolute Exaltation, in order, so to speak, to look up to Himself after the manner of men, and take Himself to witness; and so by a gracious condescension, confirmed the Promise for the sake of the inheritors."*

Davidson said: *"He mediated or came in-between men and Himself, through the oath by Himself."*

Incidentally, the word *"promise"* is preceded by the definite article in the Greek Text, meaning that it originally said *"the Promise,"* pointing to a definite, particular promise defined in the context. It actually is the Promise to Abraham and his posterity found in Verse 14, which in effect, had its fulfillment in Christ.

We cannot doubt, as we read this whole Passage, that there is a special reason for the emphasis thus laid on God's oath to Abraham. Paul dwells on this confirmation of the Divine Word of Promise, not merely because it is the first recorded in sacred history, but because he has in thought the declaration of Psalms 110:4.

To this as yet he makes no reference; though he has quoted from the Verse repeatedly, it has been without mention of the Divine Oath: but throughout the section before us he is preparing the way for his alter argument in Hebrews 7:21 (Ellicott).

(18) "THAT BY TWO IMMUTABLE THINGS, IN WHICH IT WAS IMPOSSIBLE FOR GOD TO LIE, WE MIGHT HAVE A STRONG CONSOLATION, WHO HAVE FLED FOR REFUGE TO LAY HOLD UPON THE HOPE SET BEFORE US:"

The exegesis is:

1. The two immutable things are the Promise to Abraham (Heb. 6:13-14), and making Christ a High Priest forever after the order of Melchizedek (Heb. 7:21).

2. God cannot lie, so what He has promised will be done.

3. We can be consoled in the fact that God can back up anything that He has promised.

4. When a person flees to Christ, he can be guaranteed of the hope which he has.

TWO IMMUTABLE THINGS

The phrase, *"That by two immutable things,"* actually pertains to the entirety of

the Plan of God as it regards the Redemption of mankind. They are:

1. God promised Abraham that He would bless him, and multiply his seed. This was not merely a personal Promise, although it definitely was that, but had a far larger intent. It spoke of a great people who would come from the loins of Abraham and the womb of Sarah, who would ultimately bring forth the Christ, Who would redeem mankind by His Death on the Cross.

2. The One Who was to come, and in fact did come, would not only redeem humanity from sin, but as well, would serve as a High Priest for all who were redeemed, forever and forever (Heb. 7:21). So, these *"two immutable things,"* which means they cannot be changed, contain the entirety of the Promise of God as it regards the Salvation of mankind. What a Promise!

Some say that these *"two immutable things,"* are the *"Promise"* and the *"Oath."* While that definitely is true, it becomes easier for us to understand, if we know what the Promise and the Oath actually are. They are the Promise to Abraham of the coming Redeemer, and the Oath given as it regards Christ being a Priest forever after the order of Melchizedek.

GOD CANNOT LIE

The phrase, *"In which it was impossible for God to lie,"* refers to the moral impossibility of such. The meaning here is, that such was and is the love of God for Truth, such as His Holiness of Character, that He could not and cannot speak falsely. So we actually have two confirmations as well concerning the immutability of the Promises of God:

1. God has Himself pledged that the Promise will be kept. This is almighty power.

2. It is impossible for God not to do what He has said that He will do.

Concerning this, it would seem to me, that the Apostle has nailed down the guarantee of the Word of God. Men lie, but God cannot lie.

A PROMISE MADE TO ME PERSONALLY

In the Fall of 1991, with the Ministry in crisis, and not knowing if I could continue on, I earnestly sought the Lord about the matter. In fact, a goodly number of us were earnestly seeking the Lord. What were we to do?

To be sure, I will never forget that night. There must have been about eight or ten of us gathered in our home. We had gone to prayer to seek the Lord about this very thing. As stated, the situation was grave indeed!

During the time of prayer, the Spirit of God fell mightily in the room, and the Lord spoke through me a word of prophecy. It was very simple and to the point. He said:

"I'm not a man, that I should lie; neither the son of man, that I should repent . . . what I have blessed, nothing can curse" (Num. 23:19-20).

The Lord was simply saying, *"Men may lie, but I don't lie. I called you for this Ministry, and I didn't lie about the Call. As well, men may change their minds, but I don't change My Mind. The Call that I gave you is still valid. And in fact, that which I have promised I will do, and Satan cannot stop it."*

As I dictate these words on July 6, 2000, it is a verifiable fact, that this which I have spoken was definitely given to me by the Lord, and to be sure, the Lord has done and is doing, exactly what He has promised. It doesn't matter what men may say, it's what God says that counts! In fact, much of the Church world (apostate Church) has attempted to prove God wrong. But that is impossible to do, because God cannot lie.

A STRONG CONSOLATION

The phrase, *"We might have a strong consolation,"* refers to assurance.

"Consolation" in the Greek is *"parakaleo,"* and means *"to call earnestly, thus to exhort, to encourage."*

"Strong" in the Greek is *"ischuros"* and refers to *"indwelling strength embodied or put forth either aggressively or as an obstacle to resistance, as an army or a fortress."* Thus, the encouragement which God's Promise and God's Oath afford is a strong army or a fortress against doubt and discouragement.

This *"consolation"* concerns itself with the Word of God, but as that Word has played itself out in the hearts and lives of untold millions before us. Of course, the greatest

example to which we can refer constantly, concerns the Bible Characters who, before us, exhibited the same Faith, in the same God, relying upon the same Word, which never failed them. That's at least one of the reasons we should study the Bible constantly. It affords encouragement and strength through the experiences of those who have preceded us. It shows how the Word of God worked within their lives, and here Paul by the inspiration of the Holy Spirit, tells us that God guarantees the same results in our lives as well. What more could we ask for!

REFUGE

The phrase, *"Who have fled for refuge to lay hold upon the hope set before us,"* carries the idea of the Old Testament principle of the sinner fleeing to one of the Cities of Refuge in Israel afforded for this very purpose, from the penalty of sin. In effect, he was fleeing to the High Priest who has offered Atonement for him and his sin (Deut. 4:42). Using that as a type, we are to flee as well to our High Priest, the Lord Jesus Christ, of which the High Priests of old were a type.

Abraham had to rest on Promises which he did not possess. Likewise, Jesus promises Eternal Salvation to all who trust Him. He, as such, Personally guarantees the fulfillment of the Promises to all guilty and broken of heart who seek refuge in Him, and lay hold upon Him as a Hope and Anchor which neither breaks nor drags, and which is cast within the Veil. This Anchor which we will study in the next Verse, unites Earth to Heaven.

However, having said that, it is incumbent upon us to say as well, that the oath of God's wrath (Heb. 3:11) is as eternal as the oath of God's Grace. A Gospel which excludes either of these oaths is a false gospel.

Through this Passage, Paul is telling the Christian Jews that they have sinned as it regards their lack of Faith in the Atoning Work of Christ, and that they must flee to Him as a refuge, of which they were well acquainted with that word, knowing and understanding the Old Testament example. As the cities of refuge in Old Testament times were open to all Jews who had committed certain types of crimes, and who were afraid for their lives, cities of refuge incidentally where they could find safety and protection, likewise, they must now run to Christ, Who is the perfect fulfillment of those ancient types. He will forgive; He will cleanse; He will pardon!

CITIES OF REFUGE

In Old Testament Times, the cities of refuge as ordered by the Lord, were six in number. Three were westward of Jordan, and three eastward.

These cities were designated as places of refuge (Num. 35:9-34; Josh. 20:1-9), for those who had accidentally killed someone; however, this did not include the murderer.

In the City of Refuge the manslayer found safety, at least as long as he remained in its confines. He was to stay there until the death of the High Priest.

The Avenger of Blood (the one seeking revenge) symbolized the Law. It demanded the death of the manslayer. The death of the High Priest satisfied this claim and liberated the manslayer, which was a type of the Death of Christ which liberated the sinner from his chains. The idea is, Christ's death, not His life, rent the Veil, and frees the sinner from the curse of the broken Law.

The manslayer was then at liberty to return to his home and possessions.

In a coming glad day, when Israel shall look upon Him Whom they have pierced, it will be then revealed to them that His death restores them to the land and family of God.

Thus, a City of Refuge stood almost at every man's door; but to enjoy its safety the manslayer had to flee thither. Had such a man said, *"If I am to be saved I shall be saved,"* etc., and not fled to the nearest City of Refuge, he would have perished.

In all of this as we have stated, the murderer by intention could find no refuge. Sinners who flee to Jesus, by doing so prove that they are not willingly guilty of His Blood; and they, therefore, find in Him both safety and liberty. But sinners who refuse thus to seek Mercy in Him, demonstrate by their refusal that they are verily guilty of His Death, in other words, that they place no stock in His atoning Sacrifice of Himself; and for these there is no protector or Salvation.

Regarding sinners and Christ, the idea is not the sin, but the refusal to come. All who come will find safety and refuge (Rev. 22:17).

THE CROSS OF CHRIST

The refuge for sinners has always been, and is, the Sacrificial, Atoning Work of Christ on the Cross. As we have just stated, as the death of the High Priest in Old Testament Times, signal freedom restored to the manslayer, likewise, it is the Death of Christ and not His Life, as wonderful as that Life was, which gives freedom to all who believe (Jn. 3:16).

The modern Church has a tendency to forget this. The Church far too much majors in the Life, Ministry, and Miracles of Christ, to the exclusion of His Atoning Work on the Cross. This is not in the least meant to minimize anything that Christ did, holding all things in great regard, but it must ever be remembered, that it was, and is, His Death on the Cross, and that alone, which provided and provides Salvation for all who come. This is stressed far too little and the result is, a Church which presently little knows and understands the veracity of the Cross of Christ, which is the very foundation of Christianity.

The Cross is our *"refuge,"* and the Cross is as well, our *"Hope."* It is *"set before us"* in unmistakable clarity, that none will misunderstand; however, due to the fact that Satan fights the Cross more so than anything else, many are led away from its safety to other things, with the other things incidentally, whatever they might be, and however good they might be in their own right, providing no safety at all! It is only the Cross of Christ which is our *"Refuge"* and our *"Hope."* All else is sinking sand.

(19) "WHICH HOPE WE HAVE AS AN ANCHOR OF THE SOUL, BOTH SURE AND STEDFAST, AND WHICH ENTERETH INTO THAT WITHIN THE VEIL;"

The structure is:

1. The hope of the Cross is the anchor of the soul.

2. It is sure and steadfast, meaning that it will never lose its power.

3. Only by the shed Blood of the Lamb, can we enter into the Holy of Holies, which is that within the Veil.

THE ANCHOR OF THE SOUL

The phrase, *"Which hope we have as an anchor of the soul,"* presents the Apostle changing the allusion from safety in the Cities of Refuge to a ship reaching harbor after a tempestuous voyage, knowing that her anchor is sure and steadfast. So it is with the Believer who has the hope of Eternal Life anchored safe in Heaven. Once again, as the Cities of Refuge were types of the Cross, likewise, the *"Anchor"* is presented as well.

While the metaphor of the anchor is widely used in antiquity, it occurs only here in the New Testament. The ship firmly anchored is safe from idle drifting. Its position and safety are sure.

Paul is not saying simply that *"hope"* secures the spiritual aspect of man, he is also affirming that hope forms an anchor for the whole of life. The person with a living hope has a steadying anchor in all he does. It is undisturbed by outward influences and is *"secure"* in its inherent character.

No matter how stormy the sea of life may become, we are anchored, who are *"in Christ."* Never once has this Anchor given way. Never once has that chain broken. We are anchored to Him.

Paul is telling these Christian Jews that their only hope is Christ, and more particular, what Christ did at the Cross on their behalf. If they go back into Judaism, thereby forsaking Christ, they have destroyed their Anchor. To be sure, nothing can destroy that Anchor, if the person remains firm regarding Faith in Christ; however, as is here very obvious, the Believer can quit believing, which means to cease placing Faith and confidence in the Finished Work of Christ, thereby going to other things which destroys the hope, and the anchor. We go back once again to the Cities of Refuge.

As these Cities of Refuge were not for the willful murderer, likewise, for the sinner who refuses to believe Christ, or the Christian who loses Faith in Christ, for those there is no safety or protection. Faith in Christ is the one requirement, and as we've already stated, it is not possible for one to have proper Faith in Christ, and at the same time, continue to live a life of willful sin. Proper Faith in Christ

brings victory to the soul, safety, and shelter from the storm.

All of this portrays to us the fact that Jesus is not only High Priest, but also Captain, of the redeemed host, leading us on and opening the way for us to enter after Him into the Sanctuary of the Promised Land.

Thus, as we shall see in the next phrase and in the next Verse, with the help of metaphor heaped upon metaphor in the fearless graduation of conscious strength and gladness, the Apostle has at last come to a great conception of Christ in the Sanctuary of Heaven. He has hesitated long to plunge into the wave it seems; and even now he will not at once lift the veil from the argument. The allegory of Melchizedek must prepare us for it.

SURE AND STEADFAST

The phrase, *"Both sure and steadfast,"* presents the use of two adjectives to describe this Anchor.

"Sure" in the Greek is *"asphale,"* and means *"not to make totter, not to baffle or foil."* It speaks, therefore, of something that cannot be made to totter when put to the test.

"Steadfast" in the Greek is *"bebaian,"* and means, *"sustaining one's steps in going."* Thus, it speaks of something which does not break down under the weight of something that steps on it. This hope which the believing soul has in the Lord Jesus is an anchor of the soul which cannot be made to totter nor break down when put under stress and strain (Wuest).

WITHIN THE VEIL

The phrase, *"And which entereth into that within the Veil,"* refers to the Holy of Holies. Even though Paul is referring to the Old Testament type, as it refers to explanation, he is actually speaking of the reality of the Holy of Holies in Heaven itself. The Anchor of the Believer is, therefore, fastened within the Veil of the Holy of Holies of Heaven.

We have some rich figures here. This present life is the sea; the soul, a ship. The soul is seen as storm-tossed on the troubled sea of life. The soul of the Believer, as a tempest-tossed ship, is held by the anchor within the Veil, fastened by Faith to the blessed reality within the Veil. There our Anchor is, and our faithful High Priest stands in our behalf.

> "Upon life's boundless ocean where
>   mighty billows roll,
> "I've fixed my hope in Jesus, blest
>   Anchor of my soul;
> "When trials fierce assail me as storms
>   are gathering o'er,
> "I rest upon His Mercy and trust Him
>   more."
>
> "I've anchored in Jesus, the storms of
>   life I'll brave,
> "I've anchored in Jesus, I fear no wind
>   or wave,
> "I've anchored in Jesus for He hath
>   power to save,
> "I've anchored to the Rock of Ages."

We have this hope, this Anchor, because of the unchangeable Promises of God. God the Father, God the Son, and God the Holy Spirit in eternity past took an oath. The oath is this:

If Jesus Christ would come to Earth in the form of a man, in the flesh, and die, giving His Life upon the Cross, God would honor that Sacrifice. Jesus came on that oath, knowing full well God would keep His Word. When Jesus died, He could confidently say, *"It is finished."* Mankind has, therefore, been given hope. The gates of Hell cannot shatter nor break this Divine Oath.

WHAT THE OATH AND THE HOPE MEANS

When we accepted Jesus Christ as Lord and Saviour, God confirmed it to us by His oath. God said, *"If you will believe, and if you will confess that Jesus Christ is Lord, believing in your heart that God raised Him from the dead, I give you My oath, you will be saved"* (Rom. 10:9-10). The very moment that we said, *"Lord, forgive me, I'm a sinner,"* God fulfilled His oath. God cannot lie. God keeps His Word.

When we allow Jesus to enter our hearts and lives, we were anchored securely to Him. We may hold on and endure to the very end, for we are anchored to Him Who is within the Veil. We hold on to this end of this Anchor in Faith, for there is a Divine Hand holding to the other end. That is our assurance.

We need not go through life with worry or fear that our Lord will leave us behind when He comes, or at death. Our souls are secure, anchored in Him. When we die in the Lord, He simply pulls the ship of life into the harbor. We go home to be with Jesus.

What this old, troubled world needs today is this Anchor, for the world is rocking in every direction. It needs the Divine Anchor of the Lord Jesus Christ. If this world would turn to Jesus and would anchor itself and its Faith in the Lord, God would steady it. It is when we try to steer our own ship, run our own lives, that we get into trouble.

The Anchor is steadfast. It is sure. It cannot give way, neither will it break down under any weight or strain. The word, therefore, speaks of the place within the Veil. The wording used here reminded the Readers of the Old Testament.

They thought of the Veil that separated the Holy Place from the Most Holy Place in the Temple. However, Paul, as stated, is actually speaking of the Heavenly Holy of Holies where Jesus stands as our hope and security. He is our assurance.

To those outside Christ we say there is refuge in Christ. We may come to Him. He will not reject us nor cast us out. In Him we will find rest for our souls. Trials may come, tests may come, but remember, *"our light affliction, which is but for a moment, worketh for us a far more exceeding and eternal weight of glory"* (II Cor. 4:17).

An anchor as is obvious, is used for securing a ship, particularly in a time of storm, to prevent it from sinking or drifting. The anchor is invisible; it sinks down beneath the water, firmly gripping the ground below.

As well, the winds of life may roar against us, the waves may beat against our ship, but if our anchor is in Christ Himself, He will sustain us, hold us. Just as He sustains all creation and upholds it, so He sustains and upholds us in every trial.

God is not looking for great ability, but for patience and Faith. In return, God gives hope and assurance. Let us surrender to His Will and to His Plan. His Plan is the Cross, and His Will is that we trust in that which has been provided by Christ through His sacrificial, atoning Work on the Cross. To be sure, our response to that is all-important. To respond in Faith is to be anchored securely to Him Who is working in our lives by His Spirit. It can be done no other way! (Fjordbak).

(20) "WHITHER THE FORERUNNER IS FOR US ENTERED, EVEN JESUS, MADE AN HIGH PRIEST FOR EVER AFTER THE ORDER OF MELCHISEDEC."

The exegesis is:

1. Our forerunner is Jesus.

2. He has gone before us and done everything that needs to be done; consequently, our Faith in Him gives us all that He has Personally accomplished.

3. He is our High Priest forever, meaning that these Promises will always stand.

THE FORERUNNER

The phrase, "Whither the forerunner," speaks of Jesus.

Here an entirely new idea is introduced, foreign to the ideas of the Levitical economy. The Aaronic High Priest did not enter into the Holy of Holies as a forerunner, but only as the people's representative. He entered a place where the one on whose behalf he ministered, could not follow him. He entered the Holy of Holies in the stead of the Believer, not as one cutting a pioneer path for him.

Paul in Verses 19 and 20, proclaims the privilege we have of entering the Holy of Holies personally, which we do by Faith, and which Christ has paved the way for us (Heb. 4:16). Because Jesus has entered the true Sanctuary (Heb. 9:24), at the same time, He may give His people entrance there (Jn. 14:2-3; Heb. 10:19).

FOR US ENTERED

The phrase, "Is for us entered," presents once again the imagery of the Great Day of Atonement, when the High Priest entered the Most Holy Place on behalf of the people. Our forerunner, Jesus, has entered the Holiest for us. As stated, this is something more than the Levitical High Priest could do though he entered the Most Holy Place and made Atonement on behalf of the people, at the end he and they were still outside. But to call Jesus our "forerunner" implies that we will follow in due course.

NOTES

"For us" or "on our behalf" indicates that Jesus did something for us. He not only showed the way but also atoned for us. So we come to the thought that He has become "a High Priest forever, in the order of Melchizedek." The thought had been introduced in Hebrews 5:6, but Paul had gone on to other things. Now he comes back to that thought and proceeds to develop it.

It must be understood, as I'm certain it is, that all of this was and is made possible by what Jesus did at the Cross. There He atoned for all sin, making it possible for the sinner to be saved, and the Believer to walk in victory. The sin debt being removed, also allowed the Holy Spirit to come in and abide within the hearts and lives of all who have trusted Christ as their Saviour, which actually means that trust has been placed in what He did at the Cross.

AN HIGH PRIEST FOREVER

The phrase, "Even Jesus, made an High Priest forever after the order of Melchisedec," presents Christ as not in the line of Aaron, but another order altogether. In fact, the line of Aaron as instituted by the Lord originally, had a beginning as well as an ending. To the contrary, Christ is an Eternal High Priest. His Priesthood had no beginning nor will it have an ending. This High Priest is the Rock of Salvation into which the Anchor of the Believer's soul is fastened, which Anchor is his Faith in the Atonement his High Priest has offered.

The High Priest in Israel of old, arrayed in his gorgeous robes, would enter the Sanctuary, wearing on his shoulders 12 onyx stones upon which were inscribed the names of the 12 Tribes of Israel, and upon his Breastplate, 12 precious stones with the names of the Tribes of Israel upon them. Thus, he would carry upon the shoulders of his strength and upon the heart of his love, the saved of Israel into the Presence of God.

Just so, this Heavenly High Priest, the Lord Jesus Christ, after the order of Melchizedek, carries upon the shoulders of His Omnipotence, and upon the heart of His infinite love, those who place their Faith in Him, into the very Presence of God. Thus, does Paul encourage these Christian Jews, not to abandon their Faith in the New Testament Sacrifice. To go back to the First Testament Sacrifices which were set aside by God at the Cross, and for all the obvious reasons, is a sin, even a crime of the highest proportions.

THE HUMAN WILL

Instructive in this Chapter is the view presented of Divine purpose in relation to human will. The Divine purpose may have been evinced by supplies of Grace so abundant as to remove all doubt of the possibility of success; yet through the human will there may be failure: the very Divine Oath may have ensured fulfillment of the Promise; yet, as to Abraham, so to individual Christians, Faith and patience are the conditions of fulfillment.

It is evident that the Divine purpose and the Divine promise are all along referred to, not to dishearten any for fear that they may not be included in them, nor to encourage remissness in any on the ground of certainty of attainment, and as well, not to suggest any idea of arbitrary selection irrespective of the attitude of the supposed Believer, but simply to incite to perseverance on the ground of assurance of success, if the human conditions are fulfilled. Those conditions are Faith in the Finished Work of Christ, and one might say, continued Faith in that Finished Work.

The idea is, God has done His part by supplying His Son; Christ has done His part by going to the Cross; the Holy Spirit has done and is doing His part, by convicting of sin, of Righteousness, and of judgment, so it is now up to the individual to do his part by simply believing in this which has been done. God does not save anyone against their will, nor does He keep anyone against their will. It is still, *"whosoever will"* (Rev. 22:17).

"Wondrous it seemeth to me, Jesus so
    gracious should be,
"Mercy revealing, comforting, healing,
    blessing a sinner like me."

"Heart of mine never could know, Jesus
    such peace could bestow,
"Till the dear Saviour showed me His
    favor, cleansed my heart whiter than
    snow."

NOTES

"Once I was full of all sin, now thro'
    the Blood I am clean;
"Willing to save me, pardon He gave
    me, and I am happy within."

"He doth my new heart control,
    cleansing and keeping me whole,
"Banishing sadness, with joy and
    gladness, filling and thrilling my
    soul."

CHAPTER 7

(1) "FOR THIS MELCHISEDEC, KING OF SALEM, PRIEST OF THE MOST HIGH GOD, WHO MET ABRAHAM RETURNING FROM THE SLAUGHTER OF THE KINGS, AND BLESSED HIM;"

The composite is:

1. Melchizedek was a type of Christ in His Eternal Priesthood.

2. A brief history of Melchizedek is given in Genesis, Chapter 14.

3. When Abraham came to Salem (Jerusalem), he found a Gentile Priest of God, ministering to Believers in that city.

MELCHIZEDEK

The phrase, *"For this Melchisedec,"* is the one referred to in Genesis 14:18-20.

Melchizedek was a Type of Christ in many respects:

Even though Melchizedek certainly had parents, the Scripture doesn't give his genealogy, and for a pointed reason (Mic. 5:2; Heb. 7:3, 6). His Priesthood had nothing to do with his parents or forefathers, as did the Aaronic Priesthood. So, in essence, he could serve as a Type of endless Priesthood which would characterize Christ (Ps. 110; Heb. 5:10; 6:20; 7:3, 17, 21, 23-28).

As well, the man functioned not only as a Priest, but also as a King, so, in effect, as Christ, he was a King-Priest (Zech. 6:12-13; Heb. 7:1).

In fact, there was a great contrast between the Priesthood of Melchizedek and that of Aaron. The latter was intended only for a period of time, in fact, only until Christ would come. The former was an Eternal Priesthood, hence only one man, Melchizedek, who was closer to a perfect Type of Christ, at least as it regards the Eternal Priesthood. Therefore, in His High Priestly work which is eternal, Christ followed the Melchizedek order, and for reasons which we have already addressed, and will continue to address.

JERUSALEM

The phrase, *"King of Salem,"* presents another name for Jerusalem (Ps. 76:2; 122:3).

Jerusalem is one of the oldest cities in the world. It is believed to have been founded in approximately the year 4200 B.C. It has been called, as stated, by the name, *"Salem,"* and, after that, *"Jebus."* The latter name came into being through the Jebusites conquering Salem, thereby changing the name.

David made Jerusalem his capital (II Sam., Chpt. 5).

It served in the capacity of the capital of Israel or Judah until it was destroyed by the Romans in A.D. 70.

The name, *"Jerusalem,"* actually means *"habitation of peace."*

Most of the world presently don't look at Jerusalem as the capital of modern Israel, claiming that part of it belongs to the Arabs, etc. In fact, that argument will not be settled until the Second Coming of the Lord Jesus Christ. Some three and a half years before the Second Coming, Jerusalem will be occupied by the Antichrist.

After about three and one half years of his treaty that he will sign with Israel, he will turn on the ancient people, defeating them in war for the first time since their becoming a nation again in 1948, and make Jerusalem his capital for at least part of the last three and one half years of the Great Tribulation (Rev. 11:1-2).

As well, Jerusalem is God's chosen place for the Capital of His eternal Earthly Kingdom under the Messiah, which will take place at the Second Coming (II Chron. 6:6; 33:4; Isa. 2:1-4; 9:6-7; 44:26; 62:7; Jer. 17:25; 43:7; 48:35; Joel 3:20; Zech. 14:1-21).

PRIEST

The phrase, *"Priest of the Most High God,"* tells us what he was, but gives us almost no information other than that. Incidentally, this account of Melchizedek in Genesis 14:18, is the first mention of the word *"Priest"*

NOTES

found in the Bible.

Some have ventured that Melchizedek may have actually been Shem, Noah's son, who in fact, was contemporary with Abraham for about 75 or 80 years (Gen. 11:10-32). In other words, Shem was alive the first 75 or 80 years of Abraham's life, which meant that he died at about the time, or a few years after, that God spoke to Abraham (Gen. 12:4). Some have even ventured that Shem is the one who witnessed to Abraham. In fact, Abraham was definitely in the lineage of Shem, but whether God actually used this man to speak to the Patriarch, we aren't told. And as well, that Shem was actually Melchizedek is speculation at best.

While *"Melchisedec"* is a Canaanite name, and as well, the man could probably be concluded as a Canaanite, this in no way means that he was a devotee to Canaanite gods. In fact, he wasn't.

We do know that Melchizedek worshiped God, the Creator of all things, while the Canaanites worshiped things created by God. In other words, Melchizedek regarded God (El Elyon) as the Creator of matter, the cosmos (Gen. 14:19), a concept foreign to the polytheistic religions (worship of many gods) of the ancient Near East, which did not distinguish spirit from matter and, therefore, worshiped the elements of the cosmos.

Moreover, it is clear that Abraham regarded Melchizedek as worshiping the same God as he. By unhesitatingly giving Melchizedek a tithe of everything, Abraham not only showed his support of this Priest-King and his Sanctuary but also publicly demonstrated that he recognized him as a person of higher spiritual rank than he, a Patriarchal Priest.

By contrast Abraham declines a gift from the king of Sodom to indicate publicly that he has no theological or spiritual affiliation with him. In fact, Abraham emphasized to the king of Sodom that his God (Abraham's) and Melchizedek's are one and the same.

The idea is that God revealed to Abraham just who Melchizedek actually was. How this man knew of God, or that God revealed Himself to him, we are not told. As well, it is evident at least at that time, if Melchizedek was a Priest, which the Scripture plainly says that he was, there were others also who were following the Lord. A Priest serves as a mediator; consequently, there would, of necessity, have to have been others following the Lord in Salem (Jerusalem).

DAVID

In Psalms 110:4, David proclaimed the coming Messiah as being *"a Priest forever after the order Melchizedek."*

F. F. Bruce claims that the background for this acclamation is provided by David's conquest of Jerusalem in about 1000 B.C., which was also about 1,000 years after Abraham, in that David and his house became heirs to Melchizedek's dynasty of Priest-Kings. We do know from II Samuel, Chapter 7, that David was chosen by the Lord as the one through whom the Redeemer would come.

So again, as the Lord revealed to Abraham the spiritual position of Melchizedek, He also revealed the same to David.

BLESSING

The phrase, *"Who met Abraham returning from the slaughter of the kings, and blessed him,"* presents Melchizedek in a superior, spiritual position.

It is difficult for us to grasp the fact that this man was greater than Abraham, even as Paul reiterates in Verse 4. But the reason is this:

Anyone connected with Christ in any manner automatically places that person in a unique position. And of course, there are different associations regarding Christ.

For instance, one could conclude, I think, that David is placed in a higher posture and position even than Abraham. While the lineage of the Incarnation definitely came from Abraham, it more specifically came through David, with Christ even being called *"the Son of David."* Hence, the New Testament opening with the words, *"The Book of the Generation of Jesus Christ, the Son of David, the son of Abraham"* (Mat. 1:1). As is obvious here, David's name is mentioned first. Actually, as the name of David is the first human name mentioned in the New Testament, it is also the last (Rev. 22:16).

Regarding relationship with Christ, at least according to that of which we speak, David would be at the top spot, with Melchizedek second, and Abraham third. Melchizedek would be greater than Abraham,

simply because he was a type of Christ as High Priest. That position regarding Christ would take second place only to Christ as *"King of kings and Lord of lords,"* of which David was a type (Rev. 19:16).

A BLESSING BESTOWED

Paul will plainly say in Verse 7 that *"the less is blessed of the better."* We should learn something here of this.

While it's quite proper for any all Believers to lay hands on others regarding prayer for the sick (Mk. 16:17-18), as it regards the bestowal of blessings, the better are not blessed by the less, as ought to be obvious. What do I mean by that statement?

The Lord has set in the Church, *"Apostles, Prophets, Evangelists, Pastors, and Teachers"* (Eph. 4:11). Those who stand in these Callings and Offices, which incidentally are of God, can properly bless others by the laying on of hands, etc. Consequently, it is not exactly proper for the Laity under normal circumstances to lay hands on those of these Callings, with the idea in mind of blessing them, unless asked to do so. While it's definitely proper regarding prayer for the sick, it, I think, should not go beyond that. To do so, ignores God's order. It would fall out to the same I think, as it regards one who stands in the Office of the Teacher, presuming to lay hands on the one who stands in the Office of the Apostle, in order to bless that person. Again we state, the better are not blessed by the less.

Now when the Holy Spirit used the words *"better"* and *"less,"* He wasn't referring to character, etc., but only the Office. The Office must be recognized in a sense, as superior to the one holding the Office, simply because it is God Who has designated the Office.

Oftentimes, I have witnessed junior Preachers presuming upon themselves to lay hands on one of higher Office, claiming to bless them, when in reality they are making mockery of the Calling of God. Only presumptuous pride, ignorance, or a failure to recognize a proper Office, would dare do such a thing.

Many years ago (as I dictate these notes in July, 2000), I happened to be in the presence of a particular Minister of the Gospel, whose name would be recognized by all. Whenever our meeting concluded, he politely asked me if I would lay hands on him and pray for him. I declined to do so. At that particular time, I did not know the Scriptural reason as to why I shouldn't do so, but in my spirit I knew it wasn't right. I politely asked him instead, to lay hands on me and pray for me, which he did. In my spirit I knew that was right, and it was!

While everyone and anyone has the right to pray for everyone and anyone, the laying on of hands in order to bless is something else altogether. The Lord seldom, if ever, uses the less to bless the better (Heb. 7:7).

Let the Reader understand the following: It is not the person so much being honored, nearly as much as the Office that person occupies, and because such Office was instituted by the Lord as well as the Call to that Office. To fail to recognize God's Call upon someone, or His designated Office respecting that person, whomever the individual might be, is a serious offense indeed. As stated, it's not so much an offense against the person as it is against God. But let the Reader also understand, that this applies only to the God-designated Offices of *"Apostles, Prophets, Evangelists, Pastors, and Teachers,"* and not at all to man-devised offices. For instance, I will respect a man who is a Catholic Priest, but I will not respect his office, because I know the office is man-devised, which means that it is not devised by God, and, therefore, not recognizable by God. Therefore, what God doesn't recognize, neither do I.

Regarding man-devised offices in Protestant Denominations, I will definitely respect the individual who holds these offices, who most of the time is a Minister of the Gospel, which means that he falls under one of the fivefold Callings. However, I will recognize in a spiritual sense only his Calling as a Minister of the Gospel, and not the man-devised office he holds in the Denomination. Those particular types of offices are administrative only, and carry no spiritual connotation whatsoever. Unfortunately, men have attempted to force the issue, claiming that such offices are spiritual, but there's nothing in the Word of God which substantiates such thinking.

WHAT ABRAHAM LEARNED FROM MELCHIZEDEK

Melchizedek shared something with

Abraham about God which Abraham had not previously known. The Patriarch had known God as *"Almighty God,"* also known as *"The El Shaddai, the One Who overshadows, or the Breasted One Who nourishes."* To some degree as well, he knew God as *"Jehovah, the Covenant-Keeping God."* However, the Name *"Jehovah"* was not fully understood by any of the Patriarchs until the Revelation of God to Moses (Ex. 6:2-3).

Through Melchizedek Abraham was to learn that God was also *"El Elyon,"* which means *"The Most High God, Possessor of Heaven and Earth"* (Gen. 14:19).

In effect, Melchizedek by using this title of God before Abraham was saying, *"Abraham, you don't need the riches of the king of Sodom. El Elyon is Possessor of all. He is Most High. God is Sovereign and has authority over all Heaven and Earth"* (Fjordbak).

THE SLAUGHTER OF THE KINGS

The account of Abraham as a warrior is found in Genesis, Chapter 14.

Both Melchizedek and Abraham along with Lot, Abraham's nephew, lived in the land of the Canaanites. The religions of Canaan were idolatrous and immoral. There the cities of Sodom and Gomorrah were located. In fact, the Sodomites were the most wicked and ungodly people of that day. But, in the midst of depraved wickedness, God had men who lived for Him! He had Abraham, father of the faithful; and Melchizedek, king of Peace and Righteousness. He had Lot as well, but who was not the example he should have been, which precipitated the action of Abraham as warrior. As stated, it is recorded in Genesis, Chapter 14.

The Text tells us that Amraphel king of Shinar, along with other kings, made war with some of the Canaanite kings (Gen. 14:1-2). This was a protracted situation which lasted for a number of years, but which in the final analysis, saw the Canaanite kings defeated, and Lot, Abraham's nephew, taken captive. Lot was residing in Sodom, where he should not have been (Gen. 14:12).

"And when Abraham heard that his Brother (nephew) *was taken captive, he armed his trained servants, born in his own house, three hundred and eighteen, and pursued*

them unto Dan" (Gen. 14:14).

This tells us how great and powerful that Abraham actually was. Beside that, the Lord, of course, helped him greatly.

The Scripture says that he rescued Lot along with all his goods and the people that had been taken captive with Lot (Gen. 14:16).

In this instance, Abraham is a type of Christ Who rescues His children taken captive by Satan.

(2) "TO WHOM ALSO ABRAHAM GAVE A TENTH PART OF ALL; FIRST BEING BY INTERPRETATION KING OF RIGHTEOUS-NESS, AND AFTER THAT ALSO KING OF SALEM, WHICH IS, KING OF PEACE;"

The exegesis is:

1. By Abraham paying Tithe to Melchizedek, he was acknowledging him as a Priest of God, and also as superior.

2. Melchizedek was the King of Righteousness, which means he was a type of Christ.

3. He was also the King of Peace, as well a type of Christ. The Righteousness of Christ brings Peace.

TITHE

The phrase, *"To whom also Abraham gave a tenth part of all,"* refers to the tenth part of the spoils of battle. By doing this, Abraham acknowledged Melchizedek as a Priest of the Most High God. Incidentally, this is the first example of paying Tithe given in the Word of God. It was practiced 430 years before the Law.

This means that if Abraham paid Tithes to Melchizedek, his natural and spiritual seed, which of course includes every Believer, we should continue to pay Tithes to this Priesthood since it has now replaced the Aaronic Priesthood.

Should God require tithing under this Priesthood at the first and then discontinue it when Christ became a Priest after this order? Does Grace lessen the obligation of man or increase it? Has this Priesthood come to a self-supporting place, where it needs nothing from those under its benefits?

Was it right that Abraham pay Tithes to this Priesthood and for Melchizedek to receive them for his support? It was right! And if it was right then, could it be wrong now to continue this same program? The question is:

Should a mere typical Priesthood be supported, which was that of Melchizedek, and not the Eternal Priesthood itself?

The answer to all of that is obvious. No Scripture even mentions a substitute program for tithing in the New Testament. As the stage for Faith was set by Abraham, the stage for Tithing was set for Abraham as well. If Faith continues, and it definitely does, then Tithing continues also.

When we Tithe we are saying, *"God, I acknowledge that You are the 'El Elyon,' the Most High God, the Possessor of Heaven and Earth. You are God. You are my Saviour. It is through You that I have my health and strength. It is through You that I am furnished employment or the means to make a living. It is You Who has given me the mentality to perform my task in this life."*

THE TEST

When the king of Sodom heard of the marvelous victory of Abraham over the enemy kings, he went out to meet him. Abraham at this time was placed in great danger, but yet a different type of danger.

The king of Sodom would tempt Abraham by trying to get him to take the goods which had been taken in battle, and which evidently had previously belonged at least in part, to the king of Sodom. But God sent Melchizedek at the right moment, to the right place, to keep Abraham from committing sin and falling prey to the snare of temptation that lay before him.

Abraham was to learn from this man that he didn't need the riches of the Sodomite king, but that the God Whom he served, was Possessor of all things. Abraham needed no one else; God would be all-sufficient.

As stated, Abraham would here learn a new Name of God *"El Elyon,"* which means *"The Most High God, Possessor of Heaven and Earth."*

Again we emphasize that when a Christian pays Tithe, he is saying to all concerned, *"I serve 'El Elyon,' The Most High God, Possessor of Heaven and Earth' and He will meet my every need."*

After his meeting with Melchizedek, Abraham's answer to the king of Sodom was a simple matter. If Abraham was to be known as one blessed of God, then he must not let others make him rich. They must not be able to say, *"I helped make Abraham rich."* All glory must go to God.

Consequently, Abraham refused the offer of the King of Sodom; therefore, he returned all goods and people (Gen. 14:21-24).

KING OF RIGHTEOUSNESS

The phrase, *"First being by interpretation King of Righteousness,"* places emphasis on the word *"first."* The word *"first"* refers to the first designation with reference to this mysterious individual. The name *"Melchizedek"* which is the first designation which Paul uses, means *"King of Righteousness."* This is in keeping with Melchizedek as a type of Christ, for Christ is the true *"King of Righteousness."*

Concerning Christ, it is said, *"Thy Righteousness is like the great mountains"* (Ps. 36:6).

David also said in his great prayer of repentance, *"Deliver me from bloodguiltiness, O God, Thou God of my Salvation: and my tongue shall sing aloud of Thy Righteousness"* (Ps. 51:14). In fact, the Psalms which actually portray the heart of Christ, abounds in proclamations of His Righteousness (Ps. 5:8; 7:8, 17; 22:31; 23:3; 31:1; 33:5; 35:24, 28; 36:6, 10; 37:6; 45:7; 48:10; 50:6; 51:14; 69:27; 71:2, 15-16, 19, 24; 72:1-2; 85:10-11, 13; 89:16; 96:13; 97:2, 6; 98:2, 9, etc.).

KING OF PEACE

The phrase, *"And after that also King of Salem, which is, King of Peace,"* refers to the product of Righteousness.

While Melchizedek was High Priest in Jerusalem, it was named *"Salem,"* which actually means *"Peace."* So, *"King of Salem,"* would mean *"King of Peace."* One day Jesus will rule from this very city, actually ruling the entirety of the world, and will rule in Righteousness, with the world for the first time in its history, experiencing total and complete peace. Of this time, the Scripture says:

"And Righteousness shall be the girdle of His loins. Of the increase of His Government and Peace there shall be no end" (Isa. 11:5; 9:7).

Back in Verse 1 where it says of Melchizedek

"who met Abraham returning from the slaughter of the kings, and blessed him," the statement has a greater spiritual significance than meets the eye. Whatever thoughts that Melchizedek had are one thing; however, such portrays the coming day when Jesus Christ, King of Righteousness and Peace, will meet the children of Abraham, i.e., *"the Jews,"* and will welcome them. This will take place at the Second Coming. The Prophet Zechariah describes this in Chapters 12 through 14 of his Book.

(3) "WITHOUT FATHER, WITHOUT MOTHER, WITHOUT DESCENT, HAVING NEITHER BEGINNING OF DAYS, NOR END OF LIFE; BUT MADE LIKE UNTO THE SON OF GOD; ABIDETH A PRIEST CONTINUALLY."

The composite is:

1. Melchizedek was without recorded lineage, in that he could be a type of Christ.

2. Melchizedek was purposely intended by God to be a type of Christ.

3. He was a type of Christ as High Priest.

WITHOUT FATHER OR MOTHER

The phrase, *"Without Father, without Mother,"* doesn't mean that the man didn't have a Father or Mother, but rather that there was no record made of his parents.

This is significant, for it indicates a different type of Priesthood from the Levitical, in which a person's genealogy was of first importance. In Israel, no man was allowed to exercise Priestly functions unless he belonged to the family of Aaron, which meant he was of the Tribe of Levi.

From these words, some have ascribed to Melchizedek a mysterious and superhuman existence and character. It has been maintained that he was actually the Son of God Himself, or the Holy Spirit, or an Angel, etc. None of this is correct!

He was a man just like any other man, which the Bible declares. He is described in such a manner in order to portray that which God intended — a symbol of the High Priesthood of Christ, which David also proclaimed in Psalms 110:4. While we certainly must not make less of this description, at the same time, we must not make more.

In describing this man in this manner, the Holy Spirit through Paul proceeds to show that the order of his Priesthood is better than the Levitical Priesthood. Therefore, the Messiah's Priesthood, being on the order of the Priesthood of Melchizedek, must be superior to that of the Levitical system and of Aaron. Since the Messiah's Priesthood is superior to that of Aaron, the Covenant Jesus instituted through and by His Death on the Cross, is better than the Old Covenant under which Aaron served.

The idea is, the New Covenant in Jesus' Blood is superior to and takes the place of the Old Covenant made in the blood of animal sacrifices.

All of this is designed to show the recalcitrant Jews that they were not at all bettering themselves by going back to Judaism, but rather the very opposite. Hence, and as we have previously stated, Paul will constantly use the word *"better"* as it describes Christ and His Finished Work.

OUR PRESENT POSITION IN CHRIST

Lest we look at these Jews of Paul's day with a jaundiced eye, I'm not so sure our situation presently is any better, if as good. Most modern Christians having little or no knowledge of the Cross at all, are doomed to live so far beneath their spiritual privileges in Christ.

The tragedy is, most every Christian thinks they know all about the Cross; however, the Truth is, most such knowledge is superficial at best. The following must be noted:

It is impossible for any Believer to live victorious without having a proper understanding of the benefits of the Cross. Having a proper understanding, one will place his total Faith and Trust in the great Sacrifice of Christ, which is what the Holy Spirit intends all along.

Man's problem has always been himself. As someone has well said, *"We have met the enemy and he is us."*

Unfortunately, this problem of *"self"* is not only pertinent to the unsaved, but it continues to be the problem with Believers. When unbelievers are brought to a state of helplessness by the Holy Spirit, they can then accept Christ as their Saviour, which many do. Unfortunately, most do not understand that they must remain this way in order to continue receiving from Christ. That's why

Paul said, *"For when I am weak, then am I strong"* (II Cor. 12:10).

This was in reply to the answer given to him by Christ concerning the removal of the thorn, *"My Grace is sufficient for thee: for My strength is made perfect in weakness"* (II Cor. 12:9). The idea is, as pride is the problem with unbelievers, unfortunately, it continues to be the problem with Believers.

Totally and completely, we must look to Christ for everything, and more particular still, we must look to what Christ did at the Cross on our behalf. Our Faith must constantly rest in that great Sacrifice, that great Finished Work. When this is done on a constant basis, ever making the Cross the object of our Faith, the Holy Spirit can then work mightily on our behalf (Rom. 8:1-2, 11). He doesn't require much of us, but He does require that — Faith to be in the Cross of Christ exclusively.

This is why Satan fights the Cross so hard. In fact, at this present time, many in the Charismatic community, and especially those of the so-called *"Word Churches"*, openly repudiate the Cross. Songs about the Cross, the Blood, and the great Sacrifice of Christ, etc., are banned from their Churches. Actually, they refer to the Crucifixion as the greatest defeat in human history.

This portrays a total misunderstanding of the Cross, which portrays a total misunderstanding of the Word of God, and nothing could be more serious!

As we've said over and over again in this Volume, the Cross of Christ is the centrality of the Gospel. To fail to know this, and to understand this, is to fail!

GENEALOGY

The phrase, *"Without descent, having neither beginning of days, nor end of life,"* simply means that the Holy Spirit intended for Melchizedek to be without genealogy. The idea is that the historical record would be silent regarding his birth and death.

In the records of Israel, it is noted that the birth and death of famous individuals are always mentioned. Under the Mosaic dispensation everything respecting the duration of the Priestly Office was determined accurately by the Law. Under the Law, Levites were required to serve from the age of 30 to 50, with the former being lowered to the age of 20 by the time of David (I Chron. 23:24, 27).

THE SON OF GOD

The phrase, *"But made like unto the Son of God,"* actually means *"to be likened to the Son of God,"* in the sense that his history was so written up that he appeared to have no father and mother, and no end of days.

Westcott says, *"The resemblance lies in the Biblical representation, and not primarily in Melchizedek himself."*

One could not have a type that was in itself eternal, for then one would have the reality, not the type. Thus, an accommodative type, so to speak, must be used.

It is important to note that the likeness of Melchizedek is not to Messiah as Son of Man but to Him as Son of God. As Son of Man Jesus was born and died. As Son of God, neither could be said of Him (Wuest).

As well it should be said, it is the Son of God Who is the Standard, not this ancient Priest-King. Paul says that Melchizedek is *"made like"* the Son of God, not that the Son of God is like Melchizedek. Thus, it is not that Melchizedek sets the pattern and Jesus follows it. Rather, the record about Melchizedek is so arranged that it brings out certain Truths that apply far more fully to Jesus than they do to Melchizedek.

With the latter, these Truths are simply a matter of record; but with Jesus they are not only historically true, they also have significant spiritual dimensions.

As well, Paul is speaking of the Son's eternal nature, not of His appearance in the Incarnation.

A PRIEST CONTINUALLY

The phrase, *"Abideth a Priest continually,"* refers to Christ of Whom Melchizedek was a type.

Of course, we know that Melchizedek was born like any other human being, and that he died as well; however, there not being any record of such, his type was eternal, but actually carried on in Christ. Melchizedek is in Heaven today, and the One of Whom he was a type, is now seated by the Right Hand of the Father, constantly making intercession

for the Saints in His High Priestly Office, which He will carry forth forever (Heb. 7:25).

(4) "NOW CONSIDER HOW GREAT THIS MAN WAS, UNTO WHOM EVEN THE PATRIARCH ABRAHAM GAVE THE TENTH OF THE SPOILS."

The exposition is:

1. Paul now proceeds to show that Melchizedek carried a higher office than Abraham, in order that he might show that he also carried a higher office than Levi, and thus better than Aaron.

2. The word *"consider"* speaks of a critical, discriminating inspection, which means that because Melchizedek was a type of Christ, and especially in a High Priestly role, this alone gave him his position.

3. Understanding that it was Abraham the Patriarch who paid Tithes to Melchizedek, lets us know, at least in the Eyes of God, how great this man really was.

CONSIDER

The phrase, *"Now consider how great this man was,"* tells us several things:

1. The Text plainly tells us here that Melchizedek was a man. This means that he was not an Angel, or a preincarnation appearance of Christ, as some have contended.

2. This man was greater than Abraham, which the Text plainly says here, and considering who Abraham was, that is quite a statement.

3. His greatness was not so much in who he was, but the Office and Role which the Lord had granted to him, as it regarded him being a type of Christ. Anything connected with Christ in any way, is of utmost significance, as should be obvious. However, the manner in which he was a type, which pertains to the High Priestly Office of Christ, places him, as previously stated, in a greater position than any other man in the Old Testament, other than David.

THE PATRIARCH ABRAHAM

The phrase, *"Unto whom even the Patriarch Abraham gave the tenth of the spoils,"* tells us as well:

1. By the Holy Spirit using the word *"Patriarch"* as it regards Abraham, we know that He is speaking of Abraham's position as

"father of the faithful." In fact, Paul also reiterated in Romans, Chapter 4, how God gave to the Patriarch the entirety of the Plan of Salvation, as it refers to "Justification by Faith." And as well, considering that every single Believer who has ever lived, at least since the days of Abraham, has come to Christ through the means and method of Faith which God portrayed to Abraham, which means in a sense that we are all children of Abraham, lets us know how great that Abraham actually was. But yet, Paul says that the rank accorded Melchizedek was even greater (Gal. 3:7).

2. To prove all of this, the Scripture plainly says that "Abraham gave the tenth of the spoils," which pertain to a Tithe. This not only portrayed the greatness of Melchizedek, but as well, set the standard as to how the Work of God would be financed from then until the present, and even forever. In view of the fact that the Office of High Priest as it regards Christ is eternal, means that this method of financing will be eternal as well.

Also, the Lord has chosen this method in order that He might bless us. In fact, as it regards our giving to God, this is the only principle of which God allows us to prove His Word. He said through the Prophet Malachi:

"Bring ye all the Tithes into the storehouse, that there may be meat in Mine house, and prove Me now herewith, saith the Lord of Hosts, if I will not open you the windows of Heaven, and pour you out a blessing, that there shall not be room enough to receive it."

He then said, "And I will rebuke the devourer for your sakes, and he shall not destroy the fruits of your ground; neither shall your vine cast her fruit before their time in the field, saith the Lord of Hosts" (Mal. 3:10-11).

In the New Testament, Jesus said, "Give, and it shall be given unto you; good measure, pressed down, and shaken together, and running over, shall men give unto your bosom. For with the same measure that ye mete withal it shall be measured to you again" (Lk. 6:38).

THE ARGUMENT OF THE BOOK OF HEBREWS

It is plain in all these things said by Paul that the Priesthood of Melchizedek is superior

NOTES

to the Priesthood of Aaron. Since that is the case, the Priesthood of Christ, being in the order of the Priesthood of Melchizedek, must be better. That of course, makes Christ better than Aaron and, therefore, the New Testament He instituted, better than the Old Testament, which Aaron was instrumental in bringing in. And that is the argument of the Book of Hebrews, namely, that the New Testament in Jesus' Blood is superior to and takes the place of the First Testament, which only had animal blood.

Now some may wonder why the Lord of Glory, the Creator of all things, would have to have a poor, frail human being, to serve as a type, even as He did with Melchizedek.

The problem goes back to the first Adam. Total and complete dominion was given to him by God immediately after his creation (Gen. 1:28; Ps. 8:3-9). Tragically, Adam forfeited that dominion to Satan.

Consequently, to remain in the boundaries of the Laws that He had Himself formulated, in order to take this dominion back, God would have to become man, in effect, "The Last Adam" (I Cor. 15:45). As a man, "The Man, Christ Jesus," He would have to undo what the first man did and do what the first man failed to do. That is the reason these human types in the Old Testament are brought into play.

As Melchizedek was a type of Christ as High Priest, David was a type of Christ as King. There were other human beings who served as types also.

Abraham was a type of Christ as it regards the Salvation Plan of Justification by Faith. Joseph was a type of Christ as it regards Israel. All the sons of Jacob were, in fact, types of Christ, as it regards what Christ did for all of humanity respecting His Life, Living, Death, and Resurrection. Also, Boaz was a type of Christ as our Kinsman Redeemer. Jonah was also a type of Christ as it regards His Death and Resurrection. In fact, the list is long, even incorporating inanimate objects as types, such as the Tabernacle and Temple, with all of their furnishing, etc.

However, the types were found only in the Old Testament. With the Advent of Christ, types were no longer needed; consequently, such are not found in the New Testament, and for all the obvious reasons.

(5) "AND VERILY THEY THAT ARE OF THE SONS OF LEVI, WHO RECEIVE THE OFFICE OF THE PRIESTHOOD, HAVE A COMMANDMENT TO TAKE TITHES OF THE PEOPLE ACCORDING TO THE LAW, THAT IS, OF THEIR BRETHREN, THOUGH THEY COME OUT OF THE LOINS OF ABRAHAM:"

The composition is:

1. Tithing as it was instituted under the Law was different than this mentioned here regarding Abraham and Melchizedek.

2. Abraham voluntarily paid Tithe, while those under the Law had no choice but to obey, for that is the principle of Law.

3. When we pay Tithe presently, we do not do so under the auspices of Law, but rather Grace. In other words, Christians pay Tithe, solely on the basis or principle from which Abraham paid Tithe to Melchizedek.

SONS OF LEVI

The phrase, *"And verily they that are of the sons of Levi,"* proclaims the Apostle now showing the difference between Law and Grace. The former is vastly inferior to the latter.

Paul speaks of *"the descendants of Levi who became Priests"* as *"collecting a tenth from the people."* In the Law it was provided that the people were to pay Tithe to the Levites (Num. 18:21, 24). The Levites were responsible for the upkeep of the Temple, etc. But the Levites as well, were to pay Tithes to the Priests (Num. 18:26).

THE PRIESTHOOD

The phrase, *"Who received the Office of the Priesthood,"* specify those of the Tribe of Levi who were Priests; all were not! He is saying it this way for a reason, showing these Christian Jews, that the Priesthood after the lineage of Aaron, in which they put great stock, was inferior to the order of Melchizedek. Now what would have been their objections to that?

They would have argued, as some no doubt did, that to compare the lone figure of Melchizedek to the glorious Priesthood of Israel, was facetious indeed! However, if they did that, they were then faced with Psalms 110:4, where the Holy Spirit through David had addressed this by saying, *"The Lord hath sworn, and will not repent, Thou* (the

Messiah) *art a Priest forever after the order of Melchizedek."*

This is proved to be a Prophecy pointing to the Messiah because the very next Verse says, *"The Lord at Thy right hand shall strike through kings in the day of His wrath"* (Ps. 110:5).

This spoke of the coming day when Jesus would sit at the Lord's right hand, even as Paul outlined in Hebrews 1:3, where Jesus would *"uphold all things by the Word of His Power,"* which He is even now doing.

Consequently, their argument would fall to the ground, simply because no son of Aaron has ever sat by the Right Hand of the Father, and none ever would, even Moses!

ACCORDING TO THE LAW

The phrase, *"Have a Commandment to take Tithes of the people according to the Law, that is, of their Brethren,"* refers to the fact that the people were forced to pay Tithes to the Priesthood, under the old Mosaic economy, that is if they were to obey God. But as we shall see in the next Verse, the Tithe which Abraham gave to Melchizedek was on an entirely different basis.

ABRAHAM

The phrase, *"Though they come out of the loins of Abraham,"* is meant by Paul to show these Christian Jews the inferiority of the Mosaic Priesthood. As descendants of Abraham they were required by Law to pay Tithe to the Aaronic Priesthood. And considering that Abraham, whom they revered highly, and in fact should have done so, paid Tithe to Melchizedek, this showed that the Priesthood of the Melchizedek Order was much higher than that of the Aaronic order, which proved the superiority of Christ over the Aaronic system.

The Jews were fond of boasting that they had Abraham as to their father, meaning they were his descendants. So, using him as an example, Paul proves that the Aaronic system was much inferior to the order of Melchizedek, or else Abraham would not have paid Tithes to this man.

A VERY SENSITIVE SUBJECT

That which I will presently address, would not be of that much interest to the Laity. It involves Church Government, of which the Laity are little involved, pertaining mostly to Preachers. But yet, anything that pertains to the Work of God should be known and understood by all. In fact, one of the great sins of the Church has been the division between the laity and the Ministry. Even though there definitely is a difference, the true model must always be the account given in the Book of Acts and the Epistles. We find in those accounts that the Laity were aware of all things, even as they should have been. So should it be presently.

I teach that the Local Church is the highest spiritual authority in the ecclesiastical order. This simply means that no outside religious influence should seek to usurp authority over the Local Church. While outside so-called authority may recommend, that is as far as it should go. Once again, this seems to be the pattern laid down in the Book of Acts and the Epistles.

The Local Church should be free to make its own decisions by the guidance of the Holy Spirit and under the leading of the Head of the Church, the Lord Jesus Christ.

Regrettably, modern, religious Denominations seek to usurp the authority of the Local Church, or else they deny that authority altogether. This is grossly unscriptural. Again I state, while Denominational Headquarters should be free to advise and counsel, that's as far as it should go.

THE USURPATION OF AUTHORITY

When the leadership of Church Denominations take authority over Local Churches, as most do, many of these Denominations then demand that the Local Churches pay tithes to this political order.

I use the term *"political order,"* because it's not a spiritual order, simply because it's not sanctioned by the Word of God. Many of these Denominational Leaders have the idea that if their particular type Government is sanctioned by popular ballot, that makes it Scriptural. It doesn't! It makes it Scriptural no more than the Supreme Court of the United States legalizing abortion, makes that Scriptural. The Word of God is never given over to the whims and the capriciousness of man. When the Holy Spirit laid down

NOTES

the form and type of Government in the Book of Acts and the Epistles which He intended it to be, He in no way meant for it to be changed. The idea that we're living in different times, which calls for different measures, is an old, old trick, nurtured and fostered by Satan. Such attitude in effect says that the Holy Spirit didn't know what He was doing, and we are thereby free to change what Almighty God has designed. This is the height of Scriptural and Spiritual rebellion!

For a Church Denomination to demand Tithe of the Local Churches which happen to be in that particular Denomination, is in effect saying that spiritual authority does not rest in the Local Church, but rather in Denominational Headquarters. As stated, this is a violation of the Word of God.

We have an organization called *"World Evangelism Fellowship."* There are quite a number of Churches associated with this fellowship. These Churches are not Scripturally obligated to pay Tithe to World Evangelism Fellowship, nor do we have the Scriptural right to demand that they do so. To do so, as stated, is to abrogate the spiritual authority and autonomy of the Local Church, which is never Scriptural. Even Paul didn't do such a thing, even though he personally planted most of the Churches to which he wrote. He could suggest; he could plead; he could even threaten the Judgment of God if they did not do certain things, but he could not force them to do anything. Once again, that was left up to the Local Church. Thankfully, most of the Churches, if not all, acquiesced to his instruction, as they certainly should have done. But the point is, they were not forced to do so.

IS IT RIGHT FOR CHURCH DENOMINATIONS TO BE SUPPORTED?

First of all, there's nothing Scripturally wrong with forming a religious Denomination or belonging to one. In the truest sense of the word, there were no such things as religious Denominations in the Early Church; however, if they are used in administrative capacity, which means they are a tool, there's nothing Scripturally wrong with such, or the offices contained therein. However, it must always be understood, that all offices in religious Denominations are administrative only, and do not carry over into any type of spiritual office. In fact, there are only five spiritual offices, one might say, in the Work of God. Those five are *"Apostles, Prophets, Evangelists, Pastors, and Teachers"* (Eph. 4:11). And to be sure, men are not elected to these Offices by popular ballot, but by the Call of God. And them being elected by popular ballot to some religious administrative office, in no way enhances the Call of God upon their hearts and lives.

While I definitely do respect men who are elected by popular ballot to these administrative offices, I do so only because of the Call of God upon their lives, and not at all because of that particular office, which carries no spiritual connotation whatsoever. But regrettably, many who hold these administrative offices elected by popular ballot, conclude them to be some type of spiritual offices, and demand total obedience, which is as blatantly unscriptural as anything could ever be.

If a Denomination functions as a tool, in other words, making every effort to proclaim the Gospel of Christ, and to carry forth the Work of God, they definitely should be supported, both prayerfully and financially; however, this must always be on a voluntary basis and never enacted by force. As we've already stated, the moment that Churches are forced to do such, the spiritual authority of that Local Church has just been abrogated, which is a serious offense in the Eyes of God. What am I saying?

I am saying, even as Hebrews 7:7 proclaims, that the less must never usurp authority over the better. In other words, the Headquarters of Religious Denominations must always function in the capacity of a *"servant,"* exactly as demanded by Christ, which means that they are less than the Local Church (Mk. 10:40-45).

(6) "BUT HE WHOSE DESCENT IS NOT COUNTED FROM THEM RECEIVED TITHES OF ABRAHAM, AND BLESSED HIM THAT HAD THE PROMISES."

TITHES FROM ABRAHAM

The phrase, *"But he whose descent is not counted from them received Tithes of*

Abraham," refers as is obvious to Abraham paying Tithes to Melchizedek, which is as well, the foundation of the Doctrine of Tithing as it regards Christianity.

To which we've already briefly addressed, many argue that Tithing is not in the New Covenant, that being a part of the Old Law. While it definitely was a part of the Old Law, even as Paul has just spoken, he also clearly brings it out that Tithing began before the Law, actually with Abraham. The idea is this:

1. All Believers are Children of Abraham. The Scripture plainly says, *"Know ye therefore that they which are of Faith, the same are the children of Abraham"* (Gal. 3:7). The Holy Spirit through Abraham set the standard. The Patriarch paid Tithes, and his children are to do the same.

2. Abraham, a type of all the children of Faith, paid Tithes to Melchizedek, who was a type of Christ. Consequently, when we as Believers pay Tithes, as we certainly should, we are actually paying Tithes to Christ, Who is the Head of the Church. As a result, we must make very certain, that where we give our money is actually of Christ, because if not, God doesn't honor the giving, as should be obvious.

Many Christians erroneously think that their obligation to God in this respect begins and ends with the fact of their giving. It doesn't!

The Truth is, the giving of most Christians doesn't go to the Work of God, but to something else entirely. Having had much experience in this of which I speak, I dare say that barely one percent, if that, actually goes to the true Work of God.

GIVING AND THE WORK OF GOD

It should obviously be understood, that all giving to that which constitutes unscriptural doctrine is not going to further the Work of God, but actually something else entirely. God cannot bless error, and neither can He bless sin. All false doctrine in one way or the other is instituted by demon spirits. So we certainly shouldn't think that the Lord could bless such.

I'm not meaning by this statement that every single Preacher must have total light on all Biblical subjects. In fact, there is no human being in the world who has all the light on any Biblical subject. All of us are in a state of learning and growing in Grace according to the knowledge of the Lord. However, that is far different than the espousal of that which is obviously unscriptural and thereby false.

For instance, Churches which deny the vicarious, atoning Work of Christ on the Cross, as the only means of Salvation, must not be supported, that is if a person wants to obey God. Any money given to such, is not only money wasted, but is money going to further the work of Satan. And the Reader must understand, that Satan does his greatest work from inside the Church.

Churches which deny the Baptism with the Holy Spirit, with the evidence of speaking with other Tongues, should not be supported. Without the Holy Spirit we can do nothing. And to deny the Holy Spirit, which such Churches do, is to deny the Power of God. Regarding this, Paul said, *"Having a form of Godliness, but denying the power thereof: from such turn away"* (II Tim. 3:5).

Also, those who fall for the bait of various scams, even though such Preachers do claim to be Spirit-filled, such giving can never be honored by the Lord. I speak of the present *"money gospel!"* To be sure, this covers a wide brush, and speaks of anything which seeks to separate a person's money from himself, by the use of wild, unscriptural gimmicks.

For instance, one Preacher says that if you will give a certain amount of money, all of your bills will be paid by a certain time. He says this, claiming that God has told him such.

Another one says that if you will give $1,000, you will have your house paid for at the end of the year.

Another says that the Glory of God is Christians becoming rich. And then on top of that false doctrine, they claim that the people must give the money to them (this particular Preacher).

All of this, and one hundred and one other scams I haven't mentioned, fall under the heading of gross dishonesty. In fact, such gimmicks are far worse than someone taking a .38 caliber revolver and holding up a store. At least the latter doesn't bring God into his perfidious act.

NOTES

It's bad enough to lie, but the sin is compounded when these charlatans claim that God has told them this.

It should be overly obvious, that giving to such chicanery, such obvious dishonesty, such ill-motivation, can never be blessed by God. As well, the money is not only thrown away, it actually goes to further the cause of Satan. To be sure, God, despite the claims made, could never be a party to such!

The Lord definitely does bless and bless abundantly; however, the motivation must be right, or else God cannot bless the effort, no matter how much religious phraseology is heaped upon the appeal.

The criteria must always be, *"What is this money going to do for God?"*

Is it merely going to make the Preacher rich? Is it going to further some work that will really enhance the Work of God very little, if any at all? Is it going to win souls?

Every person who gives to the Work of God, and every Believer certainly should, is responsible not only for his giving, but as well, for knowing exactly how his money is used for that which proposes to be the Work of God.

It should be obvious that every Preacher claims all sorts of things. So that within itself doesn't say much; however, it doesn't take much investigation for a person to know, and to know exactly, what his money is doing. Is the Gospel being preached, truly Scriptural? Is the evidence of that Scripturality, souls being saved, Believers being Baptized with the Holy Spirit, the sick being healed, and lives being truly changed?

Once again, all Preachers claim this evidence, but a little checking will prove if the claim is true or not!

Millions of Christians give untold millions of dollars to Denominations, thinking that their money is going to further the Work of God. Sometimes it does; most often it doesn't! If that particular Denomination has lost its way, as most have, then it's impossible for them to further the Work of God, which means that every dollar given to that Denomination is totally and completely wasted. I don't want to leave the impression that every Denomination has gone astray, for all haven't. Around the world, there is one here and there which is trying to do the Work of God, but those are few and far between.

Giving to God is a very serious business, and should be handled accordingly. It must be done with the right motivation, and it must be done with the right investigation.

THE BLESSING

The phrase, *"And blessed him that had the Promises,"* proclaims the fact, that Melchizedek blessed Abraham, despite the fact, that it was Abraham who had been given all the great Promises by God. And of course, we speak of the Promises of Salvation.

The only way that one could be greater than Abraham, is that he would be a type of Christ, which Melchizedek actually was. The idea is this:

Abraham paid Tithe to Melchizedek, because it was the Will of God, and because this man was a type of Christ, which was meant to portray far more than meets the eye. What happened there that day was meant to set the stage for the Work of God throughout the ages, which it has!

If you as a Believer want the *"Blessing,"* exactly as is stated here, you must make certain that you honor Christ as He should be honored. Abraham honored Melchizedek by giving to him a Tithe. However, this giving was not a mere exchange of money or valuables. It was a recognition of the One Whom Melchizedek represented, i.e., *"Christ."* We cannot expect the Blessings, if we fail to properly honor Christ. And to be sure, we dishonor Him greatly, if we do that which is displeasing in His sight, i.e., *"support that which is false doctrine."*

What would have happened, if Abraham had refused to pay Tithes to Melchizedek, in fact, demanding that Melchizedek pay him Tithes? I think the answer to that would be obvious! We would have never heard of Abraham! And to be sure, much of that which is presently supported which claims to be the Work of God, will not even be heard of 100 years from now, or less time!

(7) "AND WITHOUT ALL CONTRADICTION THE LESS IS BLESSED OF THE BETTER."

The exegesis is:

1. That which the Holy Spirit is saying through Paul cannot be contradicted, in that

the better blessing the less is practiced by all of mankind.

2. The less being blessed by the better as given here by Paul, pertains to the spiritual; however, the principle is held to in every walk of life.

3. We learn from these statements what actually constitutes the *"better."*

CANNOT BE CONTRADICTED

The phrase, *"And without all contradiction,"* means that what he is saying cannot be contradicted in the natural sense of the word, much less in the spiritual.

"Contradiction" in the Greek is: *"antilogia,"* which means literally, *"a word spoken against,"* and thus it comes to mean *"a dispute."* Paul is saying that such a universally held Truth that the inferior is blessed by the superior, leaves no room for dispute about the matter (Wuest).

This being the case, the Christian Jews had no argument. The Priesthood of Christ was far superior to the Aaronic Priesthood, which now in the Mind of God the latter had actually passed away.

While in fact, the Jewish system was still being continued at this particular time, in A.D. 70, the Lord would use as His instrument the Roman General Titus, to completely destroy Jerusalem, and to actually raze the Temple to the ground, not even leaving the foundation. Consequently, the Jews from then until now, have not been able to continue the means of Judaism.

When Jesus died on the Cross, thereby fulfilling all of the Types of the Old Testament, thereby putting an end to that system, a system incidentally which had lasted for about 1,600 years, there was no more place for its practice. Paul would be executed about two years before the destruction of this system; nevertheless, he knew that in the Mind of God, the system had come to its end with the death of Christ on the Cross and in His Resurrection, all coupled with His Exaltation, which made it possible for Him to send back the Holy Spirit, which He did!

In Paul's day, he was about the only one of any note, who was crying out against this system, and because he saw the inherent dangers. He knew that Law could not be mixed with Grace, even as many were attempting to do at this particular time, for if such was attempted, as with all false doctrine, ultimately the only thing which would be left would be Law. In fact, he likened this type of false doctrine, or any false doctrine for that matter, as *"leaven,"* which ultimately corrupts the whole (I Cor. 5:6-8).

THE BETTER

The phrase, *"The less is blessed of the better,"* in this instance refers to Abraham being blessed by Melchizedek. However, the greater thrust pertains to Christ. Melchizedek was a type of Christ; therefore, Paul is saying that Christ is the better of all systems, and is the only One Who can properly bless. Anything else contains no blessing.

The words *"less"* and *"better"* in the Greek Text, express in their widest form that the Blessing carries with it not only the verbal expression of goodwill, but also goodwill achieving actual results. The idea is:

One can only have proper results in Christ. And to be more particular, one can only have proper results as one understands the great Finished Work of Christ, thereby exhibiting Faith in His great Sacrifice of Himself. That and that alone guarantees result for the seeking soul, which is actually the thrust of Paul's Message.

As the Holy Spirit lays out the principle through Paul, it is not so much the idea that *"my system is better than your system,"* but that no favorable results can be expected or received, in any other system except that of *"Jesus Christ and Him Crucified."* That means, that every religion in the world promises only false hopes and delivers the same. It even means that all Christianity which has turned away from the Cross to other things, can expect no favorable results whatsoever, but in fact, only negative results.

When this is followed through to its conclusion, which actually means, that the only way that *"Blessing"* can be received by anyone, is by their Faith in the Cross of Christ, and then realizing that most of the modern Church has little understanding of the Cross, we are quick to see the reason for the present condition of the modern Church. In fact, it perfectly fits the description as given by Christ when He said:

"So then because thou art lukewarm, and neither cold nor hot, I will spew thee out of My mouth.

"Because thou sayest, I am rich, and increased with goods, and have need of nothing; and knowest not that thou art wretched, and miserable, and poor, and blind, and naked" (Rev. 3:16-17).

The *"Better"* is Christ, and He Alone, can bless the *"less,"* which constitutes we poor mortals.

THE GREATNESS OF MELCHIZEDEK AS A TYPE OF CHRIST

Paul points out the greatness of Melchizedek in this short Verse. That one who blesses is considered the greater (or, the better) seems self-evident. Yet Abraham's position was also one of high honor. He was more eminent than any of his descendants, even Aaron. Yet he himself was indebted to the high and holy king of Jerusalem and Priest of the Most High God, and because he (Melchizedek) was meant to be by God, a type of Christ. The idea is, if Abraham's position was one of such prominence, yet he received blessings of another, how great must this Melchizedek be?

Those of the Tribe of Levi, as Paul explains it to these Christian Jews, who, as descendants of Aaron, were Priests, died, and passed from the scene. They were succeeded by others in the Office of High Priest. However, there is no record of a successor to Melchizedek. He was *"made like unto the Son of God,"* so as to be a perfect type of Christ's eternal Priesthood.

This man appears on the scene with no record of his beginning or end; he appears to remain *"a Priest continually."* The Tithes of Israel were paid to dying men and their successors, but Abraham paid Tithes to one who had no successor.

ANOTHER WORD ABOUT TITHES

Going back to what Paul said in Verse 6, we learn from this that the Melchizedek Priesthood received Tithes of Abraham. As well, the Levites later received Tithes of all Israel.

Abraham paying Tithes to Melchizedek set the example for the principle of Tithing to continue. Paul said, *"Know ye therefore that they which are of faith, the same are the Children of Abraham"* (Gal. 3:7). This means that if Abraham paid Tithes, we also, even in this Dispensation of Grace, are to pay Tithes.

Inasmuch as Melchizedek was a Type of Christ, this means that Believers are to continue to pay Tithes to support the Eternal Priesthood of Christ. We do this by contributing to the Work of God.

Of course, the answer to that is obvious. Abraham set the stage, and that stage was meant to be continued, which is God's way.

(8) "AND HERE MEN THAT DIE RECEIVE TITHES; BUT THERE HE RECEIVETH THEM, OF WHOM IT IS WITNESSED THAT HE LIVETH."

The structure is:

1. If temporary Priests received Tithes, as they did under the Mosaic Covenant, should not Christ receive Tithes, Who lives forever?

2. Melchizedek received Tithes of Abraham, setting the pattern for the superiority of Christ, and as well, as a side issue, the financing of the Work of God.

3. Inasmuch as Melchizedek was a type of Christ, and that Christ lives eternally, this program hasn't changed, and in fact, will not change.

THE INFERIORITY OF THE LEVITICAL PRIESTHOOD

The phrase, *"And here men that die receive Tithes,"* refers to the Levitical Priesthood, which in fact, was still being carried on at the time Paul wrote these words; however, it continuing to the time of Paul had no bearing on anything. Paul is merely using this as an example, which in fact, was carried on for nearly 1,600 years. So, if God ordained that Tithes be paid under the old Mosaic economy, which He did, and which was vastly inferior to that which Christ would do, the argument is, that most certainly such practice would be continued under the new system which is perfect, with all perfection of course, being in Christ. Once again, we go back to the *"less being*

blessed by the Better," Who is Christ. And once again we state the fact, that even though the paying of Tithes is not the main thrust of these Passages, that being the superiority of Christ; still, the Truth of continued Tithes paying regarding the eternal Priesthood of Christ, is definitely brought out, and must not be overlooked.

The whole idea is, that if men paid Tithes to a very inferior system, and which they were obligated by God to do so and for all the obvious reasons, how much more should we give of our resources to that which is eternal, i.e., *"Christ!"*

THERE

The phrase, *"But there he receiveth them,"* refers back to the Passage in Genesis, where Melchizedek is recorded to have been receiving Tithes. The words *"here"* and *"there"* as used by Paul, do not refer to any specific places, but rather the occasion.

HE LIVETH

The phrase, *"Of whom it is witnessed that he liveth,"* refers to the eternal Priesthood of Christ.

Inasmuch as the death of Melchizedek is not recorded, nor the end of his Priesthood, we have in him an illustration of a Type of Christ (Isa. 9:6; Mic. 5:2; Heb. 1:8; Rev. 1:8-11).

The expression, *"Of whom it is witnessed that he liveth,"* has caused some to say that Melchizedek is still alive. They have used this as a basis for verifying the teaching that Melchizedek was really Christ in the Old Testament.

In the making of this statement, and as was given by the Holy Spirit, Paul did not mean that Melchizedek absolutely or personally still lived, but that he lives typically, as a representative of Christ. Thus, the record testifies in that way to the fact that in Christ he is still alive, and that the office of Melchizedek did not pass on to another after him (Fjordbak).

(9) "AND AS I MAY SO SAY, LEVI ALSO, WHO RECEIVETH TITHES, PAYED TITHES IN ABRAHAM."

The structure is:

1. *"Levi"* represents and is the Levitical

Tribe which furnished the Priestly Order of Israel.

2. Levi was in the loins of Abraham in that he was descended from him; consequently, when Abraham paid Tithes to Melchizedek, Levi paid him Tithes as well!

3. Once again, in using this analogy, Paul proves that Melchizedek was superior to Levi. It follows that since Melchizedek is better than Aaron, the Messiah is better than Aaron also, for He belongs to a superior order of Priesthood.

TO SPEAK A WORD

The phrase, *"And as I may so say,"* presents a statement, although understandable by us, would have been a very telling statement as far as the Jews were concerned.

The tendency in Jewish theology was to view heredity in this realistic manner. So, when Paul speaks of Levi paying Tithes to Melchizedek, and doing so through Abraham, and because Levi at that time was in the loins of Abraham, the Jews would have understood perfectly that of which he spoke.

LEVI

The phrase, *"Levi also, who receiveth Tithes,"* is not intended to prove him superior in the minds of Jews. In other words, just because Tithes were paid to Levi, i.e., *"the Priestly Order,"* in no way means that this was the superior order. In fact, the entire Levitical system was only meant by God to serve as a stopgap measure, and to do so until Christ came, Who would be the fulfillment of all these things.

ABRAHAM

The phrase, *"Paid Tithes in Abraham,"* would have struck a telling blow in his argument regarding the superiority of the Priestly order of Melchizedek.

The idea is, if Abraham paid Tithes to Melchizedek, which he did, and which he was instructed by the Lord to do so, considering that Abraham is the father of the Jewish people, which means that Levi was in his loins, this means that Levi also paid Tithes to Melchizedek. Abraham performing this task, and as stated doing so upon instructions from the Holy Spirit, placed the whole

of the Jewish system as second to that of Christ, which should be obvious.

Paul wants his Readers to be in no doubt as to the superiority of Christ to any other Priests and sees the mysterious figure of Melchizedek as powerfully illustrating this superiority.

(10) "FOR HE WAS YET IN THE LOINS OF HIS FATHER, WHEN MELCHISEDEC MET HIM."

The composition is:

1. Abraham is looked at here as the father of Israel, and as well, of all Born-Again Believers, which of course includes Gentiles.

2. Levi being in the loins of Abraham, which he was, said certain things, which we will address momentarily.

3. When Abraham met Melchizedek, this was about 150 years before Levi would be born; nevertheless, Abraham paying Tithes to Melchizedek was in a sense, the same as Levi paying Tithes to him.

THE LOINS OF HIS FATHER

The phrase, *"For he was yet in the loins of his father,"* speaks as is obvious, of ancestry.

Roots and lineage are extremely important to Bible history. Their importance is illustrated in the many genealogies found in the Old Testament and in constant references to the forefathers. Their importance is particularly found in the distinctive Covenant relationship that God established between Himself and the descendants of Abraham.

THE HEBREW WORDS

The Old Testament tells the story of God's dealings with one family called out of all humankind to be the avenue through whom God would redeem humanity. God established a special relationship with this family and formalized the relationship in great Old Testament Covenants. Membership in the Covenant community, therefore, was a matter of physical descent from the family founders — Abraham, Isaac, and Jacob. The identity of the individual, and his claim to special relationship with God, rested on ancestry.

The word most commonly translated *"ancestor"* or *"forefather"* in the Hebrew is *"ab."*

This word occurs over 1,200 times in the Hebrew Old Testament and means *"father."*

Usually used of one's parent or more remote ancestor, the term is also applied out of respect to someone in authority. It may be used of a founder, such as of a guild of musicians, or metal workers (Gen. 4:21).

The phrases *"tribes of their fathers"* and *"inheritance of the fathers"* are thus appropriately rendered *"ancestral tribes"* in Numbers and *"ancestral inheritance"* or *"ancestral property"* elsewhere.

A few times the Hebrew word *"yalad,"* which means, *"to bear, beget,"* is used of ancestry. The idea is that by giving birth to a child, one becomes the ancestor of all who descend from the child (Num. 1:18).

A final word, translated *"ancestry"* in Ezekiel 16:3, is a noun from the Hebrew *"yalad."* It can be understood as *"relatives,"* or sometimes as *"birthplace."*

Each of these terms fits solidly within the pattern of Hebrew thought about the vital importance of one's ancestry.

THE SIGNIFICANCE OF ANCESTRY

God made a promise that illustrates the importance of ancestry to the Hebrew people. In Leviticus, Chapter 26, Moses reviews God's promise of reward for obedience to the Mosaic Law and God's warnings about punishment for disobedience. After describing the troubles sin would bring, God said that if the Israelites would confess their sins, this is what He would do:

"I will remember My Covenant with Jacob and My Covenant with Isaac and My Covenant with Abraham, and I will remember the land. I will remember the Covenant with their ancestors whom I brought out of Egypt in the sight of the nations to be their God" (Lev. 26:42, 45).

The basic promise was given to the ancestors. Each generation might appeal to God, but it must be on the basis of the ancient promises. Ancestry became the foundation on which the community and the individual might have confidence that God would hear their confession and appeal.

THE FAMILY OF ABRAHAM

Membership in the family of Abraham did

not guarantee an individual a personal relationship with God. That was won by Faith and was demonstrated in obedience to the Mosaic code. But those outside the Jewish family had no claim on God and no basis for guaranteed access to Him.

Paul describes their situation as *"excluded from citizenship in Israel and foreigners to the Covenants of the Promise, without hope and without God in the world"* (Eph. 2:12).

It is clear, then, that ancestry is a basic and absolutely essential aspect of Old Testament Faith and life. God is the *"God of Abraham, of Isaac, and of Jacob."* Relationship of the Old Testament Believer to God was mediated by physical descent from these ancestors, but was not the bottom line so to speak, that being Faith.

BIBLICAL GENEALOGIES

Since physical lineage is so important in the Old Testament, it is not surprising to find a number of genealogies recorded in Scripture. These provided evidence that an individual or group had the right to membership in the community of Israel, a right that could be established only by proof of descent from the Patriarchal ancestors.

The compelling urgency of racial purity is illustrated in a report recorded by Ezra. There some who claimed to be of Priestly descent *"searched for their family records, but they could not find them and so were excluded from the Priesthood as unclean"* (Ezra 2:62).

This demand for racial purity explains why those returning from captivity rejected the offer of the people who were then settled in Palestine to help in building a Temple to the Lord. The settlers argued that they should help, because they said, *"like you, we seek your God and have been sacrificing to Him since the time of Esarhaddon king of Assyria, who brought us here"* (Ezra 4:2).

But these were a mongrel people who followed the common custom of paying tribute to whatever gods were associated with the land in which they lived. Their ancestry did not go back to Abraham, Isaac, and Jacob. Thus, they had to be excluded; and the animosity caused by this exclusion is reflected in the hostility that still existed in Jesus' day between the Jews and the Samaritans (descendants of these resettled peoples).

Genealogies, therefore, were essential. They alone could guarantee the right of Jewish individuals and families to membership in the community and in relationship with God.

THE SIGNIFICANCE OF GENEALOGIES

Key Old Testament genealogies are found in Genesis (Chpts. 5, 11). They trace history from Adam to Noah and from Noah to Abraham. Also, the first ten Chapters in I Chronicles provide a detailed ancestry list, with genealogies collected from various records.

There are two genealogies of Jesus in the New Testament (Mat. Chpt. 1; Lk. Chpt. 3). Matthew records Jesus' lineage from Abraham through David and his descendants, while Luke goes back to Adam to demonstrate Jesus' full humanity. It is generally accepted that the Matthew genealogy is of the line of Joseph and the Luke genealogy of the line of Mary.

Biblical genealogies are frequently schematic and, therefore, incomplete. Often only chief persons, not every individual in a line, are recorded in Biblical records. Generally these names have been arranged in easily memorized groups of 10 or 14. The fact that genealogies are incomplete is illustrated by comparing Exodus 6:16-20, which reports only four links between Levi and Moses, with Numbers 3:39, which states that some 22,000 male descendants of Levi were living in Moses' day, which hardly could have happened with only four links.

NEW TESTAMENT REFERENCES TO ANCESTRY

Four Passages in the Epistles speak of ancestry. In two the Greek word is *"pater,"* usually rendered *"father."* Romans 9:5 and Hebrews 7:16 use *"ancestry"* to express the meaning of the phrase *"fleshly descent."*

Hebrews 7:10 portrays Levi as *"still in the body of his ancestor"* (Abraham) at the time of Melchizedek, the Scripture of our study. This reflects the Jewish concept noted above:

In giving birth to a child, one becomes the ancestor of all who descend from him. Levi was the child of Abraham's grandson Jacob. In fact, Paul's argument from this

fact is fascinating. The theme of Hebrews is that Jesus is superior in every way to the old Mosaic system. It follows that His must also be a superior Priesthood.

To prove this, Paul relates an incident reported in Genesis, Chapter 14. Abraham met and paid Tithes to a person named Melchizedek, who then blessed Abraham. Paul argues that from Genesis, Chapter 14 and Psalms 110:4 (which speaks of a Melchizedekian Priesthood) that the Bible shows Jesus' Priesthood to be superior to the Levitical Priesthood of the Old Testament. Abraham, whose descendant Levi received Tithes from Israel, paid Tithes to Melchizedek.

Levi, *"in"* the loins of his ancestor, participated in paying Tithes and receiving the blessing given his ancestor. If the one who is paid Tithes under the Mosaic system himself paid Tithes to another, it follows that the other Priesthood is superior. As the Priesthood of Melchizedek was a universal Priesthood, so Christ's Priesthood, following the interlude of the limited Priesthood of Aaron, is also universal — that is, it includes the Gentiles in full participation of the Covenant, and as well, it is everlasting.

This reasoning may not be so clear for us presently to understand. But in the context of the way God's Old Testament people thought of ancestry, it is a valid and compelling argument.

PRESENT APPLICATION

In our day, relationship with God is viewed, and rightly so, as an individual issue. What our parents did or did not believe does not change the fact that each of us must make a personal Faith-commitment to Jesus and what He did at the Cross on our behalf, thereby establishing our own personal relationship with Him. However, we must also understand that Faith was the basis for a personal relationship with God in Old Testament times as well!

But due to the fact that Jesus had not yet come, Faith existed then more so in the context of Covenant than anything else. In other words, God had made a Covenant with Abraham, in that a Redeemer was to come, and Faith in that Covenant granted

Salvation to the Believer.

On down through the centuries, the individual knew that God had made Promises to the ancestors, and it was because the individual was a member of the Covenant family that he or she had the right to call God his or her own.

The great historic promises of God were made to Abraham, to Isaac, and to Jacob. It was the individual's descent from these Patriarchs that made it possible to share in the Blessings God committed Himself to make available to the chosen people.

This means that Salvation has always been by Promise, which is had by Faith (Gal. 3:6-7).

MELCHIZEDEK

The phrase, *"When Melchisedec met him,"* refers to Abraham. Considering all this, it makes the New Testament better than the Old Testament, which is the argument of the Book. This kind of reasoning would appeal to Jewish Readers, for they emphasized strongly the solidarity of the Jewish race. The whole Jewish Law, its Ordinances and Priesthood, is regarded as potentially in Abraham. Consequently, the argument as brought forth by Paul, and inspired by the Holy Spirit, is telling indeed! In other words, if his Jewish Readers could not see the logic of all this, it is only because they did not desire to see.

(11) "IF THEREFORE PERFECTION WERE BY THE LEVITICAL PRIESTHOOD (FOR UNDER IT THE PEOPLE RECEIVED THE LAW,) WHAT FURTHER NEED WAS THERE THAT ANOTHER PRIEST SHOULD RISE AFTER THE ORDER OF MELCHISEDEC, AND NOT BE CALLED AFTER THE ORDER OF AARON?"

The exegesis is:

1. There was no perfection in the Levitical Priesthood, it always pointing to that which was to come, namely Christ.

2. Under the Levitical Priesthood the people received the Law, but they did not receive Grace, that coming by Jesus Christ.

3. We know from the Word of God that the Eternal Priesthood of Christ was typified by Melchizedek. It existed some 400 years before the Levitical Priesthood. Moreover, some 600 years after the Levitical

NOTES

Priesthood, David mentioned the fact, and did so by the Holy Spirit, that a perfect Priest would arise after the order of Melchizedek.

4. So, to look for the original Priesthood, we cannot look to the Law. We must look back to Melchizedek (Gen. 14:17-20).

COMPLETION

The beginning of the question, *"If therefore perfection were by the Levitical Priesthood . . . ?",* in effect says this was not the case.

The word *"perfection"* in the Greek is *"teleiosis,"* which signifies the act or process of consummating. It speaks of completeness.

The purpose of the Priesthood was to remove the obstacle, sin, which kept man from God, and make a way of access for man to God. The Levitical Priesthood could do that in a typical but not in an actual way. The Priesthood and the Sacrifices were an index finger pointing to the Messiah and His Substitutionary Death on the Cross. Because the Levitical Sacrifices and Priesthood could not actually provide a Salvation for sinful man, it follows that a new Priesthood must be instituted that would. And because a Salvation needed to be provided, a new Priesthood was brought in, and a new Priest, the Messiah, the Lord Jesus Christ, a Priest forever after the order of Melchiz-edek (Wuest).

INFERIOR

If the Levitical system was inferior, and it definitely was, then a change would be necessary. If a better Covenant was to be established, and if Christ Himself was to be the High Priest of that Covenant, a change, as would be obvious, was required.

It is somewhat easy to see why Paul delayed the discussion of the order of Melchizedek until after the exhortation in Chapter 6. The things he was saying concerning Melchizedek were indeed difficult for the Hebrew Christians, who had become *"dull"* in their hearing, therefore, not capable of understanding as they should.

The Truth is, there is no reason why they should not have understood all of this perfectly. In fact, none of this explanation would have been necessary had these Jewish Christians viewed Christ and His Finished Work in the right manner.

These Jewish Christians knew that God had placed great honor on the Priestly and Sacrificial systems given by Moses. Had not they come directly from God Himself? How could they be changed? There were many hard questions, especially considering their present thought concerning Christ.

In fact, the Lord had made no reference to His Priestly Ministry during His days upon Earth. During the time of His Ministry and Teaching, there is no record that He ever spoke of it to the Apostles.

However, He did not speak at all of the meaning of the Cross either, although he did speak of it as a fact.

Jesus said to Nicodemus, *"If I have told you earthy things, and ye believed not, how shall you believe, if I tell you of heavenly things?"* (Jn. 3:12).

He said to His Disciples, *"I have yet many things to say unto you, but ye cannot bear them now.*

"Howbeit when He, the Spirit of Truth, is come, He will guide you into all Truth: for He shall not speak of Himself; but whatsoever He shall hear, that shall He speak: and He will show you things to come" (Jn. 16:12-13).

In fact, as is obvious here, it would have done no good for Jesus to have told them all of these things, seeing that they could not then have understood them, that awaited the coming of the Holy Spirit.

While the Holy Spirit didn't speak all of these great Truths to all who lived at that particular time, He did give the meaning of the New Covenant to Paul, and as well, He gave the knowledge to all other Believers to know and recognize the Truth which the Apostle was giving even as here. If they didn't understand, it was only because they didn't desire to understand.

Paul himself knew that the Priestly Position of Christ would have to be validated on the basis of the Revelation given in the Old Testament, or Christ's claims would be impossible to confirm. Hence, he demonstrates both the High Priesthood of Christ and the change of the Priesthood by the use of Old Testament Scriptures, which should have been incontrovertible, and especially to

NOTES

Jewish Christians.

AN IMPROPER UNDERSTANDING

The problem with Israel, even as it is the problem with the modern Church, is that they didn't view the Law as it should have been viewed. Faith was ever the principle of Salvation, even as this Truth was given to Abraham (Gen. 15:6). But when the Law of Moses was given, the people attempted to make Salvation out of the Law, or rather out of its ceremonies and rituals, just as many in the modern Church attempt to make Salvation out of its ordinances.

The great Covenant of Faith was the first Covenant given, at least in this capacity. When the Law was given, Israel should have placed the Law alongside Faith, ever understanding that their Salvation rested in Faith, of which the Law was a description. In other words, the Sacrificial System gave them a more appropriate picture of that, or more particular, of Whom the Sacrifices represented. The Law should have made it easier for them to have Faith, it being an ever present object lesson; however, they transferred their Faith from the One to Whom the Sacrifices pointed, to the Sacrifices and rituals themselves. Actually, they inverted the whole process.

Instead of continuing with Faith as the foundation, they made the Law the foundation, and ignored Faith. Had Faith continued to be the foundation, they would have seen the Law of Moses for what it actually represented. All of it constituted symbols, which means it was all temporary, until the One would come, to Whom it had always pointed.

THE PROBLEM HAS ALWAYS BEEN FAITH

God has always worked on one principle, and that's been the principle of Faith. In fact, if man was to be saved, that's the only way it could be done, at least as far as we know. We are given this example in the experiences of the first family, even as recorded in Genesis, Chapter 4.

The Lord had told the first family as to how they could have communion with Him, and it would be by blood sacrifices. He even specified the type of animal that was to be used, which would typify the One Whom He would ultimately send, the Lord Jesus Christ.

While the offering up of the animal contained no Salvation, Faith in What and more particularly, Who it represented, definitely could and did afford Salvation. However, it must be understood that the emphasis is not on the Faith, but in the One to Whom the Faith pointed, and in a more defined way, what He would do in order to redeem man. In fact, the Holy Spirit through Peter said that due to the Omniscience of the Lord, all of this was *"foreordained before the foundation of the world, but was manifest in these last times for you"* (I Pet. 1:18-20).

Faith puts everyone and everything on the same level. In other words, if God had placed it on the level of riches, that would have left out most of the world. If it had been on the level of education, or social status, the results would have been the same.

Faith places everyone on the same level, incidentally which many do not like, and it as well, involves the same procedure for all, whether great of small, etc.

Once again we emphasize, that when we use the term *"Faith,"* we're not meaning that Faith itself is to be the object. The object is to always be, *"Jesus Christ and Him Crucified"* (I Cor. 2:2). It is the object of Faith that is ever held in view as it regards the Word of God (Gen. 15:6).

The Holy Spirit throughout the Word of God has a way, of capsuling the entire program of God, oftentimes in one Verse. Romans 8:2 is one of those Verses. The Holy Spirit through Paul said:

"For the Law of the Spirit of Life in Christ Jesus hath made me free from the law of sin and death."

In this one Passage, the Holy Spirit tells us exactly how He works. The life is found in Him, and comes through Him. In fact, all of this that He says is actually a Law, meaning that He will not deviate from its precepts.

And yet, He is quick to say, that all of this which He can do and in fact, does, are made possible totally and completely by what Jesus Christ did at the Cross. He used the term *"in Christ Jesus,"* which always refers to the Finished Work of Christ.

IN CHRIST

Actually, Paul uses the term *"in Christ,"*

NOTES

or one of its derivatives such as *"in Him,"* or *"in Whom,"* some 170 times in his 14 Epistles. In fact, he uses this short phrase some 14 times in the First Chapter of Ephesians alone. Actually, several more times in that one Chapter he infers the same, even though he does use other phraseology.

What does it mean to be in Christ?

The full explanation is found in Romans, Chapter 6. Even as we've already explained, all of it is done by Faith, and in a more defined way, Faith in what Christ did at the Cross on our behalf. Our Faith in His Finished Work, which Paul amply describes in this Sixth Chapter of Romans, literally places us in Christ.

The idea is, man's plight was and is so terrible, with there being no way to extricate himself, that whatever was to be done, God would have to do it on man's behalf, which He did! God would literally become man, and do for man what man had not been able to do, and in fact, was not able to do. That's the reason that Paul refers to Christ as the *"Last Adam"* (I Cor. 15:45).

We in the Church look at the world, and boldly proclaim the fact that they cannot earn their Salvation, but must depend exclusively upon Christ, etc. But yet far too often, we as Christians turn right around, and attempt to do the very same thing we tell the world they cannot do — earn Holiness! Let it be clearly said, as the world cannot earn Salvation, likewise, the Believer cannot earn Holiness. Oh, but how we love to try!

We try to earn forgiveness! We try to earn Mercy! We try to earn Grace! We try to earn power! We try to earn favor!

I said to our Prayer Meeting group just this morning (July 10, 2000) that oftentimes we lose our patience. When the Lord doesn't move quite as quickly as we think He ought to, we then try to bring about by the flesh that which He can only bring about by the Spirit.

I made mention to our group, *"At times whenever it seems like things are not moving quite as fast as I would like, the flesh in me wants to relate to the Lord, as to how we've been having two Prayer Meetings a day for over eight years, and surely that has merited us something!"*

To be sure, I don't do that, but the flesh in me, which speaks of self-will, is sorely tempted at times.

However, inasmuch as God has nothing for sale, that type of action or even that type of thinking provides no positive results. If it's of Faith, and it is, then it cannot be by works.

POSSIBLY LESS FAITH TODAY THAN EVER BEFORE

That is ironical, considering that there has been more teaching on Faith since the middle of the Twentieth Century, than ever before. So, if in fact the Church presently has less Faith than ever, what's wrong?

The problem is, the Faith which has been taught for the most part is actually not Bible Faith, but Faith in something else altogether. To be sure, the Bible has been used, but only used! What was presented was *"another Jesus, another gospel, and another spirit"* (II Cor. 11:4).

In all of this teaching, the object of Faith was always something else other than the Cross. It was Faith in Faith, Faith in oneself, and the greatest claim of all *"Faith in the Word"*; however, that which they spoke of was actually a perverted word. It was the Scriptures pulled out of context, in effect, trying to force the issue. The Will of God was little entertained in all of this, with the idea being, that if one can muster up so much Faith, one can then bring to pass almost anything. As should be obvious, this is merely an effort to use the Word of God against God. By that I mean, if we disregard the Will of God, attempting to take particular Scriptures and make them fit our particular circumstances, this means that in effect, we are using God's Word against Himself, which of course, God will never allow. So, the Faith which has been taught the Church, has in effect, almost destroyed the Church. It has pulled the Church away from the Cross, and has done so very effectively.

The proof of this is twofold:

1. The Faith Message, which never really saw anyone saved and precious few Baptized with the Holy Spirit, with precious few healed, and despite the wild claims, in fact saw no lives changed, except for the worse, has now deteriorated to what I refer to as the

"money gospel." Actually, it has degenerated to such total error, that even some of its leading principals are disavowing that to which it has deteriorated, and I speak of *"the greed gospel."* Jesus said we would know a tree by the fruit that tree bears (Mat. 7:15-21).

2. The Cross of Christ is to ever be the object of our Faith, even as the Scriptural context begins in Genesis, Chapter 4. In fact, that is the thrust of the entirety of the Bible. The Patriarchs were Altar builders. As well, the Mosaic Law was centered up in its Sacrificial System, which was a most glaring type and symbol of the Cross of Christ. The four Gospels proclaim the Life, Death, and Resurrection of Christ, while the Epistles proclaim the reason for all of this, which is in effect, the reason for the Cross, which is the meaning of the New Covenant.

So, the modern Faith Message is totally wrong, because it has as its object something else altogether, other than the Cross of Christ. As a result, the modern Church is almost totally bereft of true Faith, consequently, little knowing where it's been, where it is, or where it's going. To be sure, this *"leaven"* of the so-called Faith Message, has influenced the entirety of the Church to a great degree, whether Pentecostal or otherwise.

THE LAW

The phrase, *"For under it the people received the Law,"* proclaims the fact, that if one was changed (the Priesthood), of necessity, the other (the Law) must be changed as well.

For the Jew there was an air of finality about the Law; it was God's definitive Word to men. Also, there was for the Jew the presumption that the Aaronic Priesthood was superior to that of Melchizedek, for the Law came later than Melchizedek and could be thought to be God's way of replacing all previous Priesthoods.

But Paul points out that the Priesthood of Melchizedek was spoken on in Psalms 110, well after the giving of the Law. That God spoke through David about the Melchizedekian Priesthood, while the Aaronic Priesthood was a going concern, shows that the Priests of the line of Aaron could not accomplish what a Priesthood actually aimed at. And because the Priesthood and the Law went together, that meant a change in the Law as well.

Paul sees it as significant, which of course it was, that Jesus did not come from the Priestly Tribe of Levi but from the royal Tribe of Judah. This fits in with the fact that Jesus' Priesthood is of the order of Melchizedek in that he (Melchizedek) was king as well as Priest.

In viewing all of this, we must not think of the Law and the Priesthood of the old Mosaic economy as two quite separate things that happened to be operative at the same time among the same people. In fact, the Priesthood is the very basis of the Law. Without the Priesthood it would be impossible for the Law to operate in its fullness. Thus, the declaration by David which Paul recorded in Verse 17, that there would be another Priest, was within itself, a startling announcement. The Aaronic Priesthood was not succeeding, and in fact, was never meant to succeed, and thus had to be replaced by a more effective Priesthood, which it was in Christ.

ANOTHER PRIEST

The continuing of the question, *"What further need was there that another Priest should rise after the order of Melchisedec . . . ?"*, is centered up in the words *"another Priest."* The word *"another"* in the Greek is *"heteros,"* and means *"of another kind."*

Since the Levitical Priesthood brought nothing to completion, not merely another Priest was needed, but another Priest of a different kind altogether. It could not be another Priest in the line of Aaron, but one of a different order of Priesthood. This is the argument of Paul. Since there was a need for a Priesthood of a different order than Aaron, it follows that a new order of Priesthood has arisen, that of Melchizedek, which had been foretold in Psalms 110:4. Consequently, Paul proves his proposition again, namely, that the New Testament is superior to and takes the place of the First Testament. There was a need for a different Testament since the first one could not offer a Sacrifice that paid for sin (Wuest).

The purpose of the Old Testament Priesthood was to remove the obstacle of sin, which kept man from God, and to make a way of access for man to God. The Levitical

Priesthood, as stated, could do this in a typical, but not in an actual way. The yearly sacrifices on the Great Day of Atonement, merely set aside the sins of the people until the perfect Sacrifice could be offered. In fact, the Priesthood and Sacrifices were constantly pointing to the Substitutionary Death of Christ upon the Cross.

Because the Levitical Sacrifices and Priesthood could not actually provide Salvation for man, it followed that a new Priesthood must be instituted that would. Since the Levitical Priesthood brought nothing to fulfillment or completion, it was not merely another Priest who was needed, but a completely different kind of Priest and Priesthood.

Due to the Aaronic Priesthood constantly having to continue to offer up Sacrifices, this within itself proved that the line of Aaron was insufficient. There had to be one of a different order altogether, one who could forever wipe out the terrible sin debt owed by man to God, and do so with one Sacrifice.

THE NEW COVENANT

Paul's argument may be summarized as this: There was a need for a New Covenant, since the Old Covenant would not offer a sacrifice for sins sufficient to bring man to perfection, and in fact, could not do so. Consequently, such a Covenant would necessitate a change in the Priesthood. There was no other way that it could be done. The old must give way to the new which God had brought to pass in and through His Son Jesus Christ.

Only by means of the New Covenant and the Priesthood of Christ could man be brought into the completeness that God had planned for him. The Levitical Priesthood had served only to point out man's need of Salvation, but it could not effect man's Redemption by its animal offerings of blood sacrifice; man, therefore, remained alienated from God. But the perfect and eternal Sacrifice of Jesus is able to produce a satisfactory and complete relationship between God and man.

A Priesthood that could bring about this perfection would be superior in every respect. The Priest was a Mediator who drew near to God on behalf of others; his work was to present to God a Sacrifice that would satisfy

Divine Justice. The Sacrifice was offered that man might stand with a clean and pure conscience before a thrice holy God and be at peace with Him. Had the Levitical Priesthood been able to obtain these things? Had Aaron and his successors obtained God's remission from the consequences of sin? Had they brought a complete and lasting Redemption?

The answer is, a resounding no!

The whole Message of the Book of Hebrews is to prove the superiority of Jesus Christ over any and everything in the Old Testament, and to show that the New Testament was the fulfilling of God's Promises made in the Old. The New had brought what the Old could only promise and typify; Christ, as High Priest, had provided a reconciliation that no Priest of Aaron's line could ever achieve. The Priesthood of Christ was, consequently, worthy of far more honor than that of the Levites, as should be obvious!

THE PRECIOUS BLOOD OF CHRIST

What was that perfection which the Lord Jesus Christ brought to us?

Perfection came to man because Christ was able, through His Precious Blood, to remove sin, to take it away (Jn. 1:29). Neither the priesthood of Melchizedek nor that of Aaron would perfectly atone for sin. We will learn in Chapter 10 that it was not possible that the blood of bulls and goats should take away sin, but the Blood of the Messiah could and did!

Thus, the New Testament was substituted for the First Testament. Jesus' Blood took the place of the Blood of animals, therefore, the Law governing the Priesthood as found in the Mosaic economy must give way to another order of Priesthood. The Aaronic Priesthood had served its purpose and was superceded by that of Christ, of which the order of Melchizedek was an example.

THE ORDER OF AARON

The conclusion of the question, *"And not be called after the order of Aaron?"*, presents the fact, that the order of Aaron must give way to the order of Melchizedek, which it was always meant to do.

Paul is laboriously explaining the fact, that this is not something new. It had been proclaimed in the Old Testament, not only

NOTES

by the plain statement given by David in Psalms 110:4, but as well, in the endless Sacrifices of the Levitical System, which within themselves, were a glaring example, that the task was not being completed.

However, man loves ritual and ceremony, and especially religious man. So, as the Jews were loathe to give up that with which they were comfortable and accustomed, likewise, the modern Church follows in the same footsteps, preferring to hold onto rituals and ceremonies, and laws of its own making, which have nothing to do with Faith. Let us not think that the problem which Paul is addressing here ended with these Christian Jews. To be sure, it most definitely continues on unto this present hour. It is the age-old battle and conflict of Salvation totally by Faith, and to be more particular still, Faith in what Christ did at the Cross, or in a Salvation of one's own making.

It seems so easy, to just simply have Faith in the great Finished Work of Christ; however, Satan is very subtle at clouding the issue of the Cross. He does so basically in two ways:

1. He stops the Truth of the Cross from being taught to the people, leaving the Church ignorant of the Finished Work of Christ, and what it all means. In fact, that has been his method for the last nearly half century or more. He has succeeded very, very well!

2. Barring that, we attempt to disguise law under the umbrella of *"good things,"* making us think that the doing of these things, constitute Godliness. He doesn't really too much care what we do, if we simply do not have Faith in the great Sacrifice of Christ. He's perfectly willing for you the Believer, to depend on the Church, to depend on Sacraments and Ordinances, or whatever, and because all of these things are very good, we are deceived into thinking this is the path to victory, when it's the very opposite.

So in Truth, Faith is a very simple process, and intended by God to be so; however, due to Satan's subtlety, the true vision of the Cross is often obscured.

PROPER UNDERSTANDING OF THE CROSS

Millions of Christians look at the Cross as an elementary process regarding Salvation. In other words, they give the Cross its place as it regards the initial Salvation experience, but only that place. It is then left for them to go on to other things. But of course, the question must be asked, to what other things are they going?

In fact, there is absolutely nothing that one can go to outside of the Finished Work of Christ, and why would one desire to do so anyway?

Every single thing that man lost at the Fall, Jesus addressed at the Cross. In fact, the great Sacrifice of Christ covers every single thing that men might need. It has Salvation for the sinner, and Victory for the Saint. It is of such consequence, that Paul referred to it as *"The Everlasting Covenant"* (Heb. 13:20).

No! The Truth is, the modern Church despite its thinking otherwise, knows almost nothing about the Cross of Christ. And being ignorant of the very foundation of all that we are in Christ, provides an open target for the powers of darkness. Man's only recourse is the Cross of Christ! I speak of the sinner being saved, or the Believer living in victory. God has provided no other means, no other way, and because no other means or way are needed.

(12) "FOR THE PRIESTHOOD BEING CHANGED, THERE IS MADE OF NECESSITY A CHANGE ALSO OF THE LAW."

The structure is:

1. The Priesthood was changed from the order of Aaron to the order of Melchizedek.

2. The Law governing the Priesthood as found in the Mosaic economy must be abrogated in favor of another which would provide for an order of Priesthood that would function successfully in the very thing in which the Aaronic Priesthood had failed (Wuest).

3. The change was, that Christ became this Priesthood. In fact, Christ is everything!

THE PRIESTHOOD WAS CHANGED

The phrase, *"For the Priesthood being changed,"* refers to the Priestly order of Aaron now being abrogated, to make way for the original Priesthood that preceded it, which in effect had predicted this very thing.

"Being changed" in the Greek is *"metatithemi,"* which means *"to transpose, to put one thing in the place of another."* Thus,

NOTES

the Priesthood after the order of Melchizedek was put in the place of the Priesthood after the order of Aaron.

As we've already stated, there was a reason for all of this. The blood of animals could not pay for sin, but the Blood of the Messiah could. Thus, the New Testament was substituted for the First Testament, Jesus' Blood, the reality, for animal blood, the type.

But that could only be done by changing the Law governing the Priesthood. Thus, if a transfer to a new and different order of Priesthood was to be effected, it must be by reason of a transfer to a new basis. In fact, everything had to be changed.

A CHANGE OF THE LAW

The phrase, *"There is made of necessity a change also of the Law,"* refers to the fact that the connection between the Priesthood and the Law means that a change in one involves a change in the other. Paul is speaking here of more than a transference of the office of Priest from one person to another. He is speaking of a change from one kind of Priesthood to another. Priesthood like that of Melchizedek differs fundamentally from that after the order of Aaron. Christ is not another Aaron; He replaces Aaron with a Priesthood that is both different and better. And with the Aaronic Priesthood went the Law that had been erected with that Priesthood as its basis. Lacking that Priesthood, that Law had to give way. It had lost its basis, its actual reason for being. So, Paul proclaims the fact, that there must be a change of Law, which there was.

The idea is, the Law of Moses which had regulated the old Aaronic Priesthood, had to be replaced, and, therefore, ceased to be binding.

This is a very important point in the introduction of Christianity, and hence it is that it is so often insisted on in the writings of Paul. And we speak of the Law of Moses being fulfilled totally in Christ.

As we've already stated, it was very obvious during the 1,600-odd years of the Law, that this was only, one might say, a temporary measure. It was not meant to be eternal. In fact, every single thing about the Law of Moses pointed to something better that was coming. So, there was no excuse for the Jews not to know this and understand this. The Prophets predicted that something better was coming, and more particularly, Someone, that being the Messiah, Who would fulfill all the symbols of the Law (Ezek. 11:19; 36:26-27).

A PROGRESSIVE REVELATION

Everything that God does is progressive. Even the New Covenant, while never being replaced, still, continues to lead Believers to ever higher spiritual heights and ever greater spiritual depths. What Jesus did at the Cross addresses itself to every single problem that man brought upon himself as a result of the Fall; however, even though all Believers presently have the application of the New Covenant, we do not even remotely have all that the New Covenant affords, that awaiting the coming Resurrection (Rom. 8:18-25).

As one studies the Bible, it quickly becomes obvious as to the progress of Revelation. At the very outset, and I speak of the Fall in the Garden of Eden, the Lord promised a coming Redeemer (Gen. 3:15). In fact, from Genesis, Chapter 4, we know that the instructions given by the Lord to the first family were elaborate, telling them that through Blood sacrifice, the sacrifice of a clean animal incidentally, which would be a type of the coming Redeemer, they could have Communion with God — but only through Blood Sacrifice. In fact, the pattern of the Cross was established from the very dawn of time. This was portrayed by the Patriarchs through the Altars which they built, on which these Blood Sacrifices were offered.

And then God took humanity a step closer, by giving the great Revelation of Justification by Faith to the Patriarch Abraham. This was about 2,000 years after creation. About 400 years after this great Covenant was established, the Lord then gave the Law, which we refer to as *"the Law of Moses."* This was to serve many purposes, and was intended to last until the coming of the Redeemer, which it did. But regrettably, Israel had great difficulty in giving up the Law in favor of Grace. In fact, the nation of Israel as a whole rejected Christ hands down, crucifying Him, judging Him to be an imposter. This act destroyed their nation and in fact, themselves

NOTES

as a people. Even the Christian Jews, who had personally accepted Christ, still had difficulty in laying aside the Law, that in part, being the reason for Paul writing his Epistle to the Hebrews.

Even on a personal basis, and above all on a personal basis, the Holy Spirit works tirelessly to bring the Believer ever closer to the Lord. The Spirit is constantly revealing more and more of Christ to the individual, at least if He receives cooperation, which is not too abundant in many cases.

There is definitely a hunger and a thirst for more and more of God in the hearts and lives of all Believers, placed there by the Holy Spirit at conversion. So every Believer starts out on the same basis. Do you remember when you first gave your heart to Christ?

Regarding most of you, and perhaps all of you, you couldn't get enough of reading the Bible, of attending Church, of talking about the Lord, and because that hunger and thirst were ever present. In fact, such are supposed to remain with you all the days of your life, with Christ Himself exclaiming, *"Blessed are they which do hunger and thirst after Righteousness: for they shall be filled"* (Mat. 5:6).

Regrettably, such hunger and thirst have been pushed aside by the things of the world in the hearts and lives of many Believers; consequently, all Spiritual Growth stops in such cases. However, the very fact that you are studying this Commentary tells me that there is definitely such hunger and thirst in your heart and life. And remember this:

It is absolutely impossible for one to exhaust the potential of the Grace of God, which has been furnished by the great Sacrifice of Christ at the Cross. As someone has said, the Book of Ecclesiastes proclaims the thirst of the soul endeavoring to be filled by the things of the world, which is a fruitless task. To the contrary, the Song of Solomon is the very opposite. In both Books, Christ and the world are contrasted. In the first Book the heart is too large for the portion; in the other, the portion is too large for the heart.

You as a Believer can remain stale and stagnant, if you happen to be that way, or you can progress in the Lord, and such progression is always *"joy unspeakable and full of glory."* It's up to you! The Holy Spirit is ever seeking to change us, and of course, the change He is bringing about is the Image of Christ within us. At least that's what He seeks to do!

(13) "FOR HE OF WHOM THESE THINGS ARE SPOKEN PERTAINETH TO ANOTHER TRIBE, OF WHICH NO MAN GAVE ATTENDANCE AT THE ALTAR."

The structure is:

1. The One of Whom all of this is spoken, is Jesus.

2. He was not from the Tribe of Levi, which produced all the Priests of Israel, but rather from the Tribe of Judah, the kingly Tribe.

3. The Tribe of Judah had absolutely nothing to do with the Altar or the Sacrifices laid thereon.

JESUS

The phrase, *"For He of Whom these things are spoken,"* pertains of course to Christ. They pertain to His Office as Priest, and to be more particular, as *"High Priest,"* and to be more particular still, as *"High Priest forever!"*

Paul assumes it as a point concerning which there could be no dispute, that these things refer to the Lord Jesus, which seems to be overly obvious.

ANOTHER TRIBE

The phrase, *"Pertaineth to another Tribe,"* speaks of the Tribe of Judah, which in effect, was the kingly Tribe. In fact, Jacob's dying blessings on his sons referring to the particular Tribes brings this out. He said:

"The Sceptre (the scepter or rule of Government) *shall not depart from Judah, nor a Lawgiver* (Commander in Chief, referring to being responsible for the Law in all aspects of Israel) *from between His feet* (for one to straddle something, in ancient folklore, referred to them being in charge), *until Shiloh come* (an epithet of the Messiah)*: and unto Him* (the Messiah) *shall the gathering of the people be"* (Gen. 49:10).

Paul now comes to the crucial objection of the Jews concerning the Priesthood of Christ. Jesus, as was obvious, was not born of the Priestly Tribe of Levi or of the house of Aaron. Jesus came from the Tribe of Judah, a Tribe of which Moses said nothing concerning the Priesthood. In fact, Jesus not one time had ever taken part in any Temple ceremonies of

the Priesthood, nor in fact should He have done so.

To what, then, did Paul point out as validation of Jesus' right to the High Priestly position? First, the Priesthood of Christ was not based upon the *"carnal Commandment."* The Law had interested itself only with the Priesthood of Aaron and his descendants, and for all the obvious reasons.

Christ was not associated with that in the least, nor should He have been so. He was made a Priest based upon *"the power of an endless life."* Second, God Himself testified to the right of Christ to be the High Priest, as was given in Psalms 110:4. In fact, the Scripture is emphatic:

*"The Lord hath sworn, and will not re*pent (meaning that He will not change His mind), *Thou art a Priest forever after the order of Melchizedek."*

God had decreed this, so it was irrefutable!

THE SPIRITUAL STATE OF THE NATION OF ISRAEL

The Jewish community which had rejected Christ, and which included almost all of Israel, was greatly opposed to anything pertaining to Christ. They sought every opportunity to question His Person and the validity of His Teachings. And now with Paul proclaiming Christ as our *"Great High Priest,"* to this they took great exception. Naturally, the Priesthood of Christ would have been an object of their hostility. Teaching that the Mosaic system with its laws, rituals, Priesthood, and sacrifices must be set aside was strenuously opposed by the Jews.

They had stoned Stephen to death because he had preached Christ; they accused him of blaspheming Moses, God, the Temple, and the Law.

As well, many Jews who had in fact accepted Christ as Lord and Saviour, were also very slow to accept the fact that a change had been made concerning the Law. Actually, most of them taught that to be saved one must not only accept Christ, but also practice the Law. In fact, these Judaizers harassed the Gentile converts, insisting upon circumcision and subjection to the ceremonial rituals of the Law, which caused Paul and the Early Church endless problems. They seemed to ignore the Scriptures which portrayed the coming of the Messiah and the radical changes that would come as a result of His Ministry and Work, in fact, that He fulfilled all the Law, thereby making it unnecessary.

Going back to Psalms 110:4, where David said by the inspiration of the Holy Spirit, *"Thou art a Priest forever after the order of Melchizedek,"* we learn from this, that if the Levitical Priesthood had been able to bring the people to perfection, such a Prophecy would never have been given. The same God Who said, *". . . Thou art My Son; this day have I begotten Thee"* (Ps. 2:7), and Who also said, *". . . Sit Thou at My right hand, until I make Thine enemies Thy footstool"* (Ps. 110:1), also said, *". . . Thou art a Priest . . ."* (Ps. 110:4).

In other words, the Scripture was emphatic upon the point, but despite that fact, many Jews, even Christian Jews, were very slow to accept this great Truth, which in effect, actually meant a denial of Christ. Consequently, we're talking about a very serious thing!

THE ALTAR

The phrase, *"Of which no man gave attendance at the Altar,"* carries the obvious meaning that none of the Tribe of Judah officiated at the Altar, that being the domain of the Levites exclusively.

While David and Solomon, who were of the Tribe of Judah, are said to have offered Sacrifices (II Sam. 6:12-13, 17-18; 24:25; I Ki. 3:4; 8:62), there is no record, however, that these two kings actually functioned in the hands-on offering of Sacrifices, that being performed by Priests, but rather served in the place and position of seeing that these things were carried out. In other words, they functioned exactly as Jacob prophesied in Genesis 49:10, *"The Sceptre shall not depart from Judah, nor a Lawgiver from between his feet."*

(14) "FOR IT IS EVIDENT THAT OUR LORD SPRANG OUT OF JUDA; OF WHICH TRIBE MOSES SPAKE NOTHING CONCERNING PRIESTHOOD."

The exegesis is:

1. Jesus was of the Tribe of Judah, the Kingly Tribe.

2. The Law of Moses did not portray the

Tribe of Judah as having anything to do with the Priesthood, that being exclusively the domain of the Tribe of Levi.

3. Instead of this being a negative, it was actually a positive. The law of Moses could not speak to that which would follow, but only that which was included in its domain.

JUDAH

The phrase, *"For it is evident that our Lord sprang out of Juda,"* presents a fact that was not questioned, even by the most ardent of the enemies of our Lord. The genealogies of both Matthew and Luke establish this fact. However, these genealogies were also recorded, no doubt, in the Temple for all to see. This much is certain:

During the time of Christ, no one ever questioned His tribal ancestry, or the fact that His ancestry went back to David through both Joseph and Mary. Through Joseph, His foster father, the lineage went back through Solomon, and through Mary it went back through another son of David, Nathan. So, as should be obvious, the ancestry as it regards our Lord and His lineage to David, which were absolutely required for the Messiah, were all above question.

"Evident" in the Greek is *"prodelos,"* and means *"openly evident, known to all."*

"Sprang" in the Greek is *"anatello,"* and means *"the rising of a heavenly body or star."*

Christ came from the Tribe of Judah, as predicted by Jacob (Gen. 49:8-12).

"Lord" is the translation of the Greek *"Kurios,"* which is the translation of the august title of God, Jehovah. In the Jewish setting in which it is found, the use of this name is significant. Paul predicates Deity to Jesus of Nazareth. He calls Him our (the Jewish) Jehovah, the One to Whom the Jews laid claim as their God (Wuest).

PRIESTHOOD

The phrase, *"Of which Tribe Moses spake nothing concerning Priesthood,"* presents itself as plainly obvious in the Old Testament, and in the Law of Moses. The Tribe of Judah had nothing to do with the Priesthood, and the Priesthood had nothing to do with the Tribe of Judah.

However, even though nothing was mentioned in Old Testament Law about the Priesthood of Christ, at least not in particular, still, the very fact that there was an order of Priests, and above that, a High Priest, who served as Mediators between God and men, that within itself, was a glaring statement that such were needed. As well, the fact that the duties of the Priests were never ended, but required constant repetition, was also a statement that what was being done was not sufficient. In other words, all of this pointed to the One Who was to come, and the leaders of Israel should have known that. When one considers that David, some 600 years after the Levitical Law had been established, prophesied that One was coming Who would be a Priest forever, but not after the order of Aaron, but rather after the order of Melchizedek, what more proof was needed? (Ps. 110:4).

The problem then was the same as the problem now. Men want to be religious, but they don't want to accept God's Way, rather establishing a way of their own. We enjoy adopting from the Word of the Lord that which is convenient and quietly discarding that which is inconvenient, rather replacing it with our own gloss. Man being incurably religious delights in all of these things. But to go God's Way, entirely and completely, daily seeking His Face, that we might know His Way, and that He might help us to walk therein, for we surely cannot do it of ourselves, of that, there are few takers.

AN INSTANT FIX?

Since the Lord began to give me the Revelation of the Cross, and which I immediately began to preach and teach, even as we are attempting to do so in these Commentaries, and knowing it is the only answer, not only for fallen humanity, but for Believers as well, it has been most interesting to watch the reaction of many Christians.

Little by little, many in the modern Church have been led to believe in the *"quick fix!"* To be sure, when the Lord saves us, it is immediate, but all the rudiments of Salvation, and I refer to all the benefits of Salvation, do not come to us quickly or easily. Naturally, the Evil One hinders every step of

NOTES

the way, seeking to push us off the track, or to get us to quit completely.

But due to the Faith teaching of the past several decades, which I believe has been the chief cause, many Christians have been led to believe that if they have the proper Faith, they will have instant gratification or whatever it is for which they seek. Nothing could be further from the Truth.

I watch Christians exclaim as it regards the Cross, *"I've tried it, and it doesn't work!"* or words to that effect. That's like someone entering a class in school on Geology, a class incidentally which will last for nine months, attending only one day, and then summarily announcing, *"I've tried it, and it doesn't work!"* As ludicrous as that is, as ludicrous it is for those who exclaim the same as it regards the Cross.

Actually, at least as far as most of the Pentecostal and Charismatic worlds are concerned, they want the Preacher to lay hands on them and instantly solve all their problems. While the *"laying on of hands"* is definitely Scriptural, and will definitely help, it was never meant by God to serve as a magic talisman, in other words, to make up for our own lack of Faith, or else, our misplaced Faith, etc. So, the Truth is, most efforts in that category, and because of misplaced Faith, simply don't work. Again, there is no such thing as a *"quick fix!"*

The Way of the Lord, as the Bible makes abundantly evident, is the Way of the Cross. Jesus settled every account at the Cross, and addressed there every single problem that man has. We must know that and understand that and believe that. As well, such understanding and believing are not just for the initial Salvation experience, but must remain all the days of our lives, or until the Lord comes. Every answer and every solution are found in the Cross. Every need is met at the Cross.

However, once the Believer knows and understands this, the lesson is just beginning. Only then can the Holy Spirit truly go to work within our lives, and for the simple reason that He works exclusively within the parameters of the Cross, i.e., *"the Finished Work of Christ."* Knowing that (Rom. 8:2), He demands that we have Faith exclusively in the Cross of Christ, which refers to the fact that

Jesus did it all for us, and simply because we couldn't do it for ourselves, and our Faith is ever to be in that. In fact, He demands that!

But once He begins work, it is just that, *"the beginning!"*

We may erroneously think that He doesn't have much to do within our lives, but to be sure, there is much to be taken care of, and things incidentally, which only He can do. It's a tragedy, but most Christians who have been Spirit-filled for years, have made little progress in the Lord, if any, which means they have experienced no growth, simply because their Faith has been in something else other than the Cross, which has closed the door to the Holy Spirit. Once again I go back to the statement of Paul:

"For when for the time ye ought to be Teachers, you have need that one teach you again which be the first principles of the oracles of God; and are become such as have need of milk, and not of strong meat.

"For everyone that useth milk is unskillful in the Word of Righteousness: for he is a babe" (Heb. 5:12-13).

So the idea that you place your Faith in the Cross, and then a few days down the road your foot stumbles, and you then exclaim that you've tried it, and it just doesn't work, is ludicrous indeed!

One doesn't try the Cross. That's not Faith, but rather fiction! In other words, such action and attitude are little more than a joke.

A BEGINNING

Until the Believer gets his Faith properly in the Cross, he hasn't even really begun to experience any growth in the Lord. In other words, he's been in spiritual limbo, which regrettably and sadly, characterizes the far greater majority of the modern Church. So, the growth begins only when one's Faith is properly placed in the Cross, for that gives, as stated, the Holy Spirit latitude then to work.

Once the process begins, and it most definitely is a process, the time will definitely come, and with some sooner than others, but it will come, that sin will not have dominion over you, and you will walk in total and complete victory (Rom. 6:14). No! The Bible doesn't teach sinless perfection, but it

NOTES

definitely does teach victory over all types of sin. And I might quickly add, not victory part of the time, or some of the time, but victory all of the time!

There is no such thing as a quick fix, but there is such a thing as total and complete victory. As stated, it doesn't come quickly or easily, but if your Faith is properly placed in the Cross, giving the Holy Spirit latitude to work within your heart and life, to be sure it will come. And there is one more thing:

The Way of the Cross is the only way. It's not one of several ways. It's the only way that God has perfected for our Salvation and for our life and victory. So, if you think you're going to something else, there's nothing else to which one may go. It is only *"Jesus Christ and Him Crucified"* (I Cor. 2:2).

THE FINISHED WORK OF CHRIST

The Levitical Priesthood and economy were now a thing of the past as far as God's recognition of them was concerned. The Finished Work of Christ in Redemption and His preeminent position were far superior to anything done under the Law.

The *"Altar"* at which this High Priest attended, where the perfect Sacrifice was made, which will never have to be offered again, was the Cross on Mount Calvary. This was the only such Sacrifice ever offered. It was the giving of the Life of the Lord Jesus Himself in the shedding of His Blood for a complete Atonement. God excluded the house of Aaron from sharing in this Holy Office, and for many and varied reasons.

As we've already stated, the facts concerning the Life and Teachings of Jesus of Nazareth were well-known from the records of the Gospels. Also, it was clear to all that Jesus came from the Tribe of Judah. However, this well-known fact caused the Christian Jews to be antagonistic against Christ assuming the Office of High Priest. Yet, if it was true that Jesus came from Judah, as the Prophets had said He would (Gen. 49:10; II Sam. Chpt. 7; Mic. 5:2), for the Messiah must be of David's lineage of the Tribe of Judah, then the prophecies referring to the Messiah's Priesthood were equally true. Scriptures had foretold His Priesthood, not a Priesthood after the order of Aaron, but after the order of Melchizedek.

Jesus was the only Person to offer Himself as a Sacrifice, at least in all the offerings which pertained to Israel. Since He had no sin, He did not need to make sacrifices in His Own behalf, but, as the sinless Saviour, He could give Himself as a spotless Lamb for the sins of the world (Jn. 1:29).

However, His Death was not the end of His Ministry, for He arose to newness of life; He lives forever as our interceding High Priest. The High Priest after the order of Aaron served as long as he lived; his office was ended in death, and another descendant of Aaron succeeded him. One by one they died and were buried, their names recorded in the annals of Israel's history; however, the Priesthood of Jesus knows no successor.

THE OLD TESTAMENT HIGH PRIESTS

The Levitical Priests received their right to the Priesthood from the family or Tribe into which they were born. Also there were certain physical and mental qualifications which must be met. First of all, they must be without bodily blemish and must be ceremonially pure. However, a Priest would often be spiritually unfit for the office, yet the Law made him Priest because of his pedigree. He served his official duties, regardless of his spiritual laxity, as the Law commanded.

The Old Testament High Priest was made Priest by reason of the Commandment, but Jesus was made High Priest because He died and rose to eternal life. He has a Priesthood, consequently, that death cannot touch; He is the Possessor of an endless life. Our High Priest, the Lord Jesus, performs His Priestly functions, not because of duty, necessity, or command, but because of love, compassion, and concern for mankind.

Christ's Priesthood, due to its perfection, has set aside the old Priesthood. His Covenant has superceded the Mosaic Covenant by fulfilling it. The work of Redemption accomplished in Jesus Christ has cancelled the old Commandment that was feeble, inefficient, and unprofitable in that it could make nothing perfect.

(15) "AND IT IS YET FAR MORE EVIDENT: FOR THAT AFTER THE SIMILITUDE OF MELCHISEDEC THERE ARISETH ANOTHER PRIEST,"

NOTES

The structure is:

1. It is evident that God designed the Levitical Priesthood to be changed.

2. It was to be changed to another order entirely, the order of Melchizedek.

3. Melchizedek was not only a Priest but also a Prophet and a King; consequently, he was a perfect type of Christ, Who as well, would be a Priest, a Prophet, and a King. None of the Levitical Priests exercised a double or a triple office, as manifest in Jesus Christ.

EVIDENT

The phrase, *"And it is yet far more evident,"* refers to something being plainly obvious, and speaks here of the Priesthood of Christ.

The words *"far more evident"* in the Greek are *"katadelion,"* and means *"thoroughly evident."* The idea is, the Levitical Priesthood did not measure up to the purpose for which a Priesthood is instituted, namely, to offer a Sacrifice that would pay for sin and make a way for sinful man to be saved (Wuest).

Paul says that this is *"far more evident,"* but does not exactly say what the evidence is. He undoubtedly is speaking of the entirety of the Mosaic institution, of which its every function spoke loudly of the fact that it was temporary. As stated, it would have been obvious to all, had they interpreted all of this correctly; however, Israel twisted the Law to their own choosing. By the time of Christ, the Holy Spirit referred for instance, to the great Feast Days originally given by God, as now merely *"a feast of the Jews"* (Jn. 5:1). In other words, they had so perverted its true meaning, that the Holy Spirit no longer claimed this particular feast as being of the Lord. Unfortunately, the modern Church falls greatly into the same category. What men refer to as *"Church,"* God seldom does!

Is it possible that now, at least as far as the Lord is concerned, that with much of present day efforts, it's only *"a meeting of the Baptists,"* or *"a meeting of the Pentecostals,"* or *"a meeting of the Charismatics"*?

Let's put it this way: It was evident and obvious to all who knew their Bibles, that the old Aaronic Priesthood was going to be replaced, and be replaced by that of Christ, but it was not evident at all to those who did not rightly interpret the Scriptures, which accounted for most!

ANOTHER PRIEST

The phrase, *"For that after the similitude of Melchisedec there ariseth another Priest,"* refers to the necessity of such, and that God had chosen Melchizedek to be the type, who would bless Abraham. Such a type is fitting!

Christ Who was a fulfillment of the type, blesses all who come under the Abrahamic Covenant, which every Born-Again soul does.

Paul has stated this several times, referring to Psalms 110:4. He does so because it is a telling argument, in fact, overly conclusive!

These are things that these Christian Jews should have known; however, depreciating Christ in their minds and spirits, they could in no way see all that He was. It is likewise presently:

Millions, who call themselves Christians, see Christ only in a very limited way. And I'm not sure that if we do not see Christ as He really is, Saviour, Baptizer with the Holy Spirit, Healer, Miracle Worker, and the changer of men's lives, which He has brought about through His sacrificial, atoning death at the Cross, that we actually cannot see Him at all! Millions attempt to accept Christ as Saviour, while denying Him as Baptizer with the Holy Spirit, or Healer, etc.

Paul would ask the question, *"Is Christ divided?"* (I Cor. 1:13).

It is obvious that He isn't; consequently, while God Alone is the Judge of men's hearts, I greatly suspect that many so-called Christians are worshiping *"another Jesus,"* instead of the true Saviour of men (II Cor. 11:4).

If Jesus died on a Cross that, among other things, we might be Baptized with the Holy Spirit, and we reject this Baptism, of which to be sure He is the Chief Principal (Mat. 3:11), I do not see how we can then accept Christ as the Saviour! If He is Saviour, He is as well, all of these other things. To reject one, I'm afraid, is to reject all.

Again I emphasize, that many of these Christian Jews to whom Paul was writing, had done this very thing. They had demeaned Christ, denying many of His attributes of Ministry. The end result of that was obvious for all to see.

(16) "WHO IS MADE, NOT AFTER THE LAW OF A CARNAL COMMANDMENT, BUT AFTER THE POWER OF AN END-LESS LIFE."

The exegesis is:

1. Christ was *"made"* a High Priest through His sacrificial, atoning Sacrifice of Himself.

2. *"Carnal commandment"* speaks of weak, frail flesh, which characterized the Levitical order. Christ was not after that order.

3. He was rather made a High Priest after the power of Resurrection, and thereby, of an endless life.

MADE

The phrase, *"Who is made,"* refers to something that Christ had not been, but would now become, and in fact, had become. All of this has to do with the Cross. As a High Priest, He offered up Himself in Sacrifice to God, the very purpose for which He came, and as well, a Sacrifice which was of such magnitude, that it would never have to be repeated. Furthermore, He now sits in the very Presence of God, actually at His Right Hand, and will do so forever, His very Presence guaranteeing the veracity of His Sacrifice on our behalf, hence being able to make intercession for all who come to Him (Heb. 1:3; 7:24-25). So, it is the Cross which effected all of this!

A CARNAL COMMANDMENT

The phrase, *"Not after the law of a carnal commandment,"* does not in this case by the use of the word *"Carnal"* refer to something that is evil. It rather refers to something that is feeble, frail, or more particular, that which is human. The idea is, the Levitical Priesthood was made after the law of a carnal commandment, hence it being weak, frail, and thereby in need of replacement.

ENDLESS LIFE

The phrase, *"But after the power of an endless life,"* refers to the power that raised Him from the dead, which gives Him a completely different foundation. As stated, He was not made a High Priest after the weak, Aaronic order, but rather after the power of immortality or endless life.

The words *"carnal commandment"* and *"endless life"* stand in contrast. The First

Covenant was a Commandment addressed to carnal man; the Second Covenant, a life in man both powerful and endless.

The argument of the Apostle as the Holy Spirit anointed him to write is absolutely irrefutable. There is no doubt that these words pulled back some of the Christian Jews from the brink, but more than likely not all! The human heart once deceived, is very difficult to change. It cannot see the obvious, simply because it refuses to see the obvious. Pride is a factor, along with many other things. In fact, there are millions of Christians in this very state presently. They have been deceived, and even though the Holy Spirit will strongly pull at them, the Truth is, only a few will favorably respond.

(17) "FOR HE TESTIFIETH, THOU ART A PRIEST FOR EVER AFTER THE ORDER OF MELCHISEDEC."

The composition is:

1. David testified through prophecy of the High Priesthood of Christ (Ps. 110:4).

2. The order of Priesthood would be changed from Aaron to Melchizedek.

3. This is the Word of God, so it is irrefutable.

THE TESTIMONY

The phrase, *"For he testifieth,"* pertains to the Word of God (Ps. 110:4), which means that it is above all things, to be heeded. The testimony of the Word of God, as stated, is irrefutable, and is the final authority on all things. This means that the first thing anyone must ask and about anything is, *"Is it Scriptural?"*

I have had the Lord speak to me many, many times, and every single time, it has been directly through His Word, or else something that definitely pertained to His Word. For instance, I've had the Lord to speak to me through the words of songs, but the phrases He would use, would always be totally and completely Scriptural in every respect. In other words, even though not a direct quotation, it was definitely the spirit of the Word. Let me give an example:

ASSURANCE

About two weeks ago as I dictate these notes (July, 2000), we experienced a difficulty

regarding the SonLife Radio Network, which had the potential of causing great problems. I do my best to make it a habit to take everything to the Lord in prayer, and of course, this was no exception.

That particular night as we gathered together for the evening prayer meeting, I began to implore the Lord for leading, guidance, and direction. I laid out the problem before Him, reminding Him of His Promises. Of course, He doesn't have to be reminded, but it does us good to recall these Promises.

To be frank, I should not have needed any assurance. But just the same, I remember very distinctly asking the Lord that if it would be pleasing to Him, would He let me know in some manner that the problem would be solved without any difficulty.

I went on praying about other things. But in about 15 minutes or less, I sensed the Spirit of God beginning to move upon me. And then all of a sudden, the Lord brought to my mind the words of a little Chorus which we sing constantly at Family Worship Center. The words are as follows:

"We are able to go up and take the country,
"And possess the land from Jordan unto the sea.
"Though the giants may be there our way to hinder,
"Our God has given us the victory."

To be sure, that little Chorus was a Rhema Word to me from the Lord, and more specifically the last line, *"Our God has given us the victory."*

Over and over again, the Spirit of God made that real to me, letting me know that the problem was solved. As a result, a deep peace filled my heart about the matter, and all concern left.

Incidentally, it's a situation which could well take several years to come to a favorable conclusion, but I have no doubt that it will. The Lord has already spoken to my heart.

Actually, the line *"our God has given us the victory,"* was taken from the words of Caleb when he said, concerning the taking of the Promised Land, *"Let us go up at once, and possess it; for we are well able to overcome it"* (Num. 13:30).

A PRIEST FOREVER

The phrase, *"Thou art a Priest forever after the Order of Melchisedec,"* presents the fifth time that Paul has made this statement (Heb. 5:6, 10; 6:20; 7:11, 17). He will say it again in Verse 21.

When the Holy Spirit repeats something this many times, He does so for purpose. While we must not ignore anything that God says, considering that something is said a number of times, we should understand the significance of it, realizing that the Holy Spirit doesn't want it to be lost in our thinking. Such is this statement concerning Christ being a *"Priest forever after the Order of Melchisedec."*

(18) "FOR THERE IS VERILY A DISANNULLING OF THE COMMANDMENT GOING BEFORE FOR THE WEAKNESS AND UNPROFITABLENESS THEREOF."

The exposition is:

1. The Law was completely disannulled, or one might better say abolished, by the coming of Christ, Who met all its demands.

2. The Law was weak in that it depended only on the flesh, with no outside power forthcoming.

3. Regarding all of its demands, it was unprofitable, in that the demands couldn't be kept, and which it was as well unable to perfect a holy life.

THE ABOLISHING OF THE LAW

The phrase, *"For there is verily a disannulling of the Commandment,"* presents the end of the Law, which was all done by Christ, and which was intended all the time.

"Disannulling" in the Greek is *"athetesis,"* and means, *"the doing away of something established."*

This goes back to Verse 16, where it speaks that Jesus was not made a Priest according to the law of a carnal commandment, which involved the annulling of that Commandment. For a fact, the Law was always meant to be annulled, which was very obvious in all its doings; however, the Jews seldom looked at it in that manner, too often attempting to make Salvation out of its precepts and statutes, which they couldn't keep anyway.

The Law was actually made up in three parts, the Civil, the Ceremonial, and the Moral. One might say it was made into two parts, if we look at one part of it being the Moral (the Ten Commandments), and the balance of the Law falling into the category of that which is nonmoral, which included both the Civil and the Ceremonial.

At any rate, the question must be asked, if the disannulling of the Commandment included the Ten Commandments, which was and is the Moral Law?

The answer is somewhat incongruous. In other words, *"yes"* and *"no!"*

THE MORAL LAW

When Jesus died on the Cross, He disannulled the entirety of the Law, which includes the Moral Law as well, and we speak of the Ten Commandments. By disannulling all of this, we refer to the fact that He kept it perfectly in every respect, and satisfied its just demands. In other words, He was the fulfillment of all the Feast Days, the Sabbath, etc., which includes all of its ceremonies and rituals. As well, and without fail, He kept the Ten Commandments perfectly, which of course, is the Moral Law. And then by His voluntary death as a Sacrifice on the Cross of Calvary, He also satisfied its just demands by paying its penalty. In other words, the Law demanded death as a penalty, and Jesus, therefore, died.

So, when Paul said, *"Blotting out the handwriting of ordinances that was against us, which was contrary to us, and took it out of the way, nailing it to His Cross,"* he meant exactly what he said. Or I should say, the Holy Spirit meant exactly that! (Col. 2:14).

And yet all of us know, that the criteria for Christianity, and by that I refer to the standard by which we must abide, is a standard of Holiness and Righteousness, which in effect, is the highest moral standard that man has ever known. In fact, only in Christ was the Law perfectly kept. This means that it was not kept by one single individual in all of the some 1,600 years since it was given to Moses on Mount Sinai, until Christ.

So what does that mean for the Christian?

THE BELIEVER AND THE LAW

The Scripture plainly tells us as Believers, that we are *"dead to the Law"* (Rom.

6:14; 7:4). Now if one is to notice, the Scripture doesn't say that the Law is dead, but only that the Believer is dead to the Law. The idea is this:

The Moral Law is still very much alive and demanded of all humanity. In fact, moral law cannot change, as should be obvious. When God some 3,000 years ago, said it was wrong to steal, He, to be sure, is still saying the same thing today, etc.

So what does that mean, that we are *"dead to the Law,"* but the *"Law is not dead"*? How does that affect the Child of God? The idea is this:

If one is dead to something, one does not think about that particular thing. In other words, the Law doesn't exist as far as the Believer is concerned. The reason is this:

Jesus has fully kept the Law in every respect, and as well, satisfied its just demands by dying on the Cross. Also, this which He did was not an incident or accident, but rather a planned program, actually planned from before the foundation of the world (I Pet. 1:18-20), and planned in its entirety for you and me. In other words, everything that Jesus did, was done totally and completely for humanity, and not at all for Himself. If man was to be saved, these were things that man had to do, but of course what man couldn't do. So, Jesus did for us, what we couldn't do for ourselves. As stated repeatedly, this was the greatest act of love the world has ever known.

This is the reason that Paul referred to Christ as the *"Last Adam"* (I Cor. 15:45). The idea is, that He had to do what the first Adam didn't do (render a perfect obedience), and as well, undo what the first Adam did do (to pay the penalty for the first Adam's disobedience).

Whenever the believing sinner evidences Faith in Christ, which refers to the initial Salvation experience, at that moment he is actually placed *"in Christ"* (Rom. 6:3-5; 8:1). As a result, he now becomes a recipient of all that Christ has done. To say it in another way, Faith in Christ and what He did at the Cross on our behalf, grants to the individual all that Christ did, which is the intention of God. Simple Faith in Christ puts us in Christ, and thereby, a recipient of all that He has done, and all that He is. That's the reason

that Paul used the phrase *"in Christ"* or one of its derivatives such as *"in Whom,"* some 170 times in his 14 Epistles. No two words express the Salvation experience, and the experience of victory, more than these.

THE CROSS, OUR FAITH, AND THE HOLY SPIRIT

The moment the sinner comes to Christ, at that moment he is placed *"in Christ,"* and he is to remain there all the days of his life, and actually, forever. It is all done by the person evidencing Faith in Christ and His sacrificial work at the Cross (Rom. 6:3-5).

Now that the Believer is in Christ, he must continue to exhibit Faith in what Christ did at the Cross, which will guarantee the help of the Holy Spirit, which will then guarantee total and complete victory, which refers to one keeping the Moral Law in every respect. To say it another way, our business is not to keep the Ten Commandments, simply because Christ has already done that, and in effect, did it all on our behalf. Our business is to continue to trust Christ and His Cross, and then the Moral Law is guaranteed to be kept. Simple Faith and Trust in Christ and what He did at the Cross on our behalf, guarantees all of this, because those are the parameters in which the Holy Spirit works.

THE CHRISTIAN'S GREATEST DANGER

Once the believing sinner comes to Christ, the Divine Nature becomes a part of the Child of God. This is what Paul was talking about when he said, *"Therefore if any man be in Christ* (notice the "in Christ"), *he is a new creature: old things are passed away; behold, all things are become new"* (II Cor. 5:17).

However, while we definitely should make everything of this Passage which Paul has said, at the same time, we must not make more of it than has been said. What do I mean by that?

Even though the Believer is definitely a new creation in Christ, the Sin Nature still remains in the Child of God. And what is the Sin Nature?

The *"Sin Nature"* or *"Evil Nature,"* as it may be also called, is simply the propensity to go in the wrong direction. Before the Fall, man went totally and completely toward God.

After the Fall, he went totally and completely in the opposite direction, i.e., *"toward evil and Satan."*

Now when we say that the Sin Nature still remains in the Believer, we are referring to it in a dormant state. In other words, it should not cause any problem for the Child of God whatsoever. But the fact remains, it can definitely cause a problem for the Believer, hence Paul over and over again referring to this very thing.

For instance, he said, *"What shall we say then? Shall we continue in sin, that Grace may abound?"* (Rom. 6:1). In the Greek Text, it actually says, *"Shall we continue in 'the sin'?"* He says the same thing in the following Verses (Rom. 6:2, 6-7, 10-14, 16-18, 20, etc.).

This is referred to in the Greek Text as *"the definite article."* It actually means in this case *"the fact of sin,"* or *"the principle of sin."* In other words, it's not speaking of particular acts of sin. Actually, acts of sin are the result of the principle of sin.

Now once again notice what Paul said:

"Likewise reckon ye also yourselves to be dead indeed unto sin, but alive unto God through Jesus Christ our Lord" (Rom. 6:11).

The Holy Spirit through the Apostle didn't say that *"the sin (Sin Nature)"* was dead, but that we were dead to the sin. Once again, it's the same thing He said about the Law.

Now, if the Believer doesn't have a Sin Nature, as many Preachers claim, what is Paul talking about here?

The Truth is, all Believers do have a Sin Nature, which means it's definitely possible for the Believer to sin, and in fact, to be ruled by sin, providing they do not know and understand the victory of the Cross. In the unredeemed, the Sin Nature dwells and rules. In the Redeemed, it dwells, but it is not to rule (Rom. 6:12).

In fact, John said, *"If we say that we have no sin (no Sin Nature), we deceive ourselves, and the Truth is not in us"* (I Jn. 1:8).

While it is true that the definite article in the Greek is not in front of the word *"sin"* as used here by John, irrespective, this is what John is speaking about.

When the Believer comes to Christ, the power of the Sin Nature is broken within his

NOTES

life; consequently, he now has the wherewithal to obey the exhortation of Paul, *"Let not sin (the Sin Nature) therefore reign (rule) in your mortal body"* (Rom. 6:12). *"Reign"* in the Greek is *"basileuo,"* and means, *"to exercise kingly power."* This means that the sinful nature is a dethroned monarch. The Believer has the responsibility of keeping it from mounting into the throne of his heart, the place where the Lord Jesus Alone should occupy. And as well, the Believer is able to do this, simply because Christ has broken the power, as stated, of the Sin Nature. But yet it is done only in one way:

FAITH IN THE CROSS

The Holy Spirit is the One Who guarantees the victory within our hearts and lives. In other words, even though we are saved and new creations in Christ Jesus, it is still the Holy Spirit Alone Who can make us Christlike, in other words, perfect Righteousness and Holiness in our hearts and lives, which He immediately sets out to do upon our conversion (Rom. 8:1-2, 11).

However, He definitely does require one thing of us, and that is that we evidence Faith totally and completely in the Cross of Christ, understanding that it is there where all Spiritual Life and all victory were purchased. This means that the Cross of Christ must ever be the object of one's Faith. We must not allow our Faith to be moved to our Church, our Denomination, a Preacher, our own good works, our own efforts, etc. Our Faith must ever remain in the Cross.

If in fact our Faith veers from the Cross, and irrespective as to where else it goes, or how religious or spiritual the other efforts might be, the Holy Spirit will simply stop His work on our behalf, which means we are then doomed to failure. And that's the problem in the modern Christian.

The modern Saint, knowing little or nothing about the Finished Work of Christ, above the fact that Jesus died for us, as a result, places his or her Faith elsewhere, which denies the help of the Spirit. Such a direction is catastrophic, but that's where most of the Church presently is. There has been so little teaching and preaching on the Cross of Christ in the last several decades, that the modern

Christian has almost no knowledge of these Truths of which we speak. But yet, most automatically think they do, and because the term *"the Cross,"* is such a familiar term.

And to be sure, if the Believer shifts his Faith to other things, and as stated, irrespective as to what those other things might be, he has just denied himself the help of the Holy Spirit, which guarantees that in some way he's going to sin. When he does this, it is the same thing as throwing fuel on the fire. The Sin Nature then springs to life, and the Believer can find himself being ruled by the Sin Nature, exactly as he was before conversion. And again, that's exactly where many, if not most, Christians presently are.

THE PROBLEM IS SIN

Unfortunately, the modern Church hides its head in the sand, and thinks by doing so it can avoid the problem. And what problem is it of which I speak?

I'm speaking of the problem of sin. The modern Church faces this monster in one of two ways:

1. Not knowing the victory of the Cross, Believers cannot live a victorious life. So they give up to sin, in other words, they claim that one has to *"sin a little bit everyday,"* and they somehow try to live with this monster. This is a sure road to disaster.

2. The other half of the Church, as well not knowing the victory of the Cross, tries to deny that the problem is sin. They claim that the problem is a lack of money, which is the message of the prosperity doctrine, etc. Others claim it's a lack of proper, psychological counseling. In most of this second group, they lie about the situation, claiming victory, when in fact there is no victory. These are the super Christians, who mostly fall into the ranks of the Pentecostals and Charismatics. Claiming a superior position, sin surely cannot be a problem with these, especially considering that they are Baptized with the Holy Spirit and speak with other Tongues, etc. But the Truth is the opposite:

Actually, I'm not certain if there's that much difference in these two groups as far as sin is concerned. They're both failing, no matter what they say, and because it's impossible not to fail, if one doesn't know and

NOTES

understand the victory of the Cross, which is God's prescribed order of victory.

This is at least one of the reasons that hundreds of thousands of Christians are running all over the world, trying to find a Preacher whom they think God is using, who will lay hands on them and solve all their problems. Consequently, they jump from one fad to the other.

In the 1970's, they were told that the cause of their problem was demon spirits. So, Christians by the thousands lined up in particular Churches, to have a demon of fear, lust, greed, temper, etc., cast out of them. That soon fell by the wayside, simply because it's unscriptural.

In the 1980's, psychology began to rear its head as the answer to these problems, with most Pentecostal and Charismatic Denominations and Fellowships, succumbing to this foolishness, and foolishness it is!

In the early part of the 1990's, the *"laughing fad"* swept the nation, and other parts of the world. The idea was, laughing uncontrollably for an hour or two, was the answer to these problems, which according to the promoters, was a work of the Holy Spirit. In the last half of the 1990's, being *"slain in the Spirit,"* was the great thruway to victory. And oh yes, rebuking the *"family curse"* was another fad that became quite popular.

The idea of this latter was and is, that Christians are having problems because their great, great Grandfather did something terrible, with a curse of demon spirits coming down upon them through the third and fourth generations, etc. After one comes to Christ, they then must have this family curse rebuked, they are told, which will then set them free.

This is totally unscriptural. And in fact, even though some of the things mentioned above definitely do carry some Scriptural validity, as they were being used, and are still being used in some circles, they are unscriptural.

All of these things are being done, simply because the Preachers do not know and understand the victory of the Cross; consequently, they jump to other methods and fads, which seem to be right, but actually produce no positive results.

Victory over every power of darkness is found only in the Cross of Christ. This is what Paul was talking about when he said:

"Nailing it to His Cross; and having spoiled principalities and powers, He made a show of them openly, triumphing over them in it" (Col. 2:14-15).

This means that every single demon spirit, every fallen angel, and Satan himself, were totally and completely defeated at the Cross of Christ. When Jesus paid the sin debt by and through His Death, this destroyed Satan's legal claim upon humanity, at least for those who will believe (Jn. 3:16). The idea is:

MANIFESTATIONS?

Every single Believer who understands his place and position in Christ, and that it was all done through the Cross, which demands our Faith, which guarantees the help of the Holy Spirit, has victory totally and completely, which is the only way that victory can be had (Rom. 6:14).

I don't want the Reader to think that we are demeaning manifestations, or anything that the Lord does. We aren't! We are drawing attention to the fact of these things being used in the wrong manner and the wrong way. If done in this fashion, such efforts deny the Finished Work of Christ, which of course, the Holy Spirit cannot tolerate.

For instance, while we definitely believe in Christians being *"slain in the Spirit,"* in other words, that the Spirit of God at times, definitely does knock a person off their feet, plus do many other things as well; however, as wonderful as that is, and as much as it will bless us, it will not give us victory over sin. Nor will any other manifestations, as Scriptural as they might be in their own right. It is only what Christ did at the Cross which guarantees our victory, and our Faith in that (Rom. 6:3-5, 11, 14; 8:1-2, 11; I Cor. 1:18, 21; 2:2; Gal. 6:14).

When the Believer places his Faith in the Cross of Christ, and keeps his Faith in the Cross of Christ, which guarantees the help of the Holy Spirit, to be sure, every single Commandment will be kept, and simply because they have already been kept. The Believer will walk in Righteousness and Holiness, i.e., *"Christlikeness!"*

So, when we said the answer to the keeping of the Commandments is *"yes"* and *"no,"* quite possibly, the statement now becomes a little clearer.

To be sure they are to be kept by the Believer, but the Truth is, they have already been kept in Christ, and our Faith in Christ and what He did at the Cross, automatically makes us Law-keepers, instead of Lawbreakers. It is all in Christ. And our constant Faith in His Finished Work will make us what we ought to be (Jn. 8:32).

BACK TO THE SIN NATURE

Many Preachers use Paul's words in II Corinthians as their basis for claiming that the Believer has no Sin Nature. Let's quote it again:

"Therefore if any man be in Christ, he is a new creature: old things are passed away; behold, all things are become new" (II Cor. 5:17).

They claim from this, that there is no Sin Nature in the Believer.

So what does Paul mean by this statement? When he said, *"old things are passed away,"* is he meaning that we will never again have any problem with sin? When he said, *"all things are become new,"* is he meaning that it will be nothing but perfect bliss from here on out?

Everything Paul said, of course, is exactly as he said; however, we must not get the cart before the horse.

The Believer is now *"washed, sanctified, and justified"* (I Cor. 6:11); however, the Believer is not yet *"glorified."* And due to the fact that the Believer is not yet glorified, which incidentally will not come until the Resurrection, the Believer still has a sin nature. When the time comes that the Trump sounds, and *"we are changed,"* we will no longer have a sin nature. Paul then said:

"We shall be changed. For this corruptible (the Sin Nature) *must put on incorruption* (no more Sin Nature), *and this mortal* (death) *must put on immortality* (no more death)*"* (I Cor. 15:52-53).

The problem with we Christians is, that we either make less of what the Lord has done, or we get ahead of ourselves, trying to make more than what is intended at the moment.

The Truth is, *"I have been saved, I am saved, and I am being saved."* We too much either deny what the Lord has done for us, or we try to claim for the present, that which is coming in the next dispensation.

When Jesus died on the Cross, He addressed every single thing that man lost at the Fall; however, even though we presently have some of the benefits of what He there did, we don't have all of these benefits as of yet, and in fact, will not have them all until the coming Resurrection, which should be overly obvious.

And then again, as we refer to the Sin Nature, or whatever name that one might want to put upon *"the sin,"* Paul clearly and plainly tells us, that this potential and problem still exists, even in the hearts and lives of the greatest of Christians. However, so as that statement should not be taken wrong, please allow me to repeat the following:

The moment the believing sinner comes to Christ, he definitely becomes a new creation, which means that the power of the sin nature is broken. In its place, the Divine Nature comes in, giving the Believer a totally new direction. But yet, the sin nature is still present, although dormant, hence all the teaching by Paul. It need never cause the Believer any problem, and in fact, will not cause a problem, if we continue to trust in what Christ did at the Cross.

WHY WAS THE SIN NATURE ALLOWED TO REMAIN?

In the first place, the sin nature, as we've already stated, should not be any problem at all for the Child of God. Its power is broken, and it is actually dormant. But again, let us reiterate:

The sin nature is not something that's physical nor is it an object of some nature. It is simply the propensity or inclination to sin. As long as the Believer keeps his Faith in the Cross, there is no problem whatsoever with the sin nature. So why did the Lord allow this propensity or inclination to remain?

The sin nature was allowed to remain, in order that the Believer may ever understand that its constant danger and potential are present, and, therefore, will constantly lean on the Lord, ever looking to Him.

NOTES

One of the great effects of the Fall is pride. It is pride in self or self-will. That's the reason that most of the world and for all time, has died without God and gone to Hell.

In speaking to a very wealthy business man the other day, I asked him about the condition of his soul.

His answer was so typical of the world. He stated, *"I believe that I'm right with God!"* His reasoning was, *"I supply employment for a great number of people, and this is a good thing."*

Unfortunately, this same problem creeps over into the thinking and believing of the Christian. It doesn't take very much for us as Believers, to begin to look to ourselves and not to Christ. Consequently, we have to have something that forces us to continually look to the Saviour. The sin nature is one of those things.

After a little while, the Believer definitely sees the danger of the sin nature, and how that he can easily fall therein, thereby causing himself untold problems. The idea is, that seeing and knowing this, he totally and completely looks to Christ, and more particularly, what Christ did at the Cross on his behalf, knowing and understanding, that this is the only means and way that victory can be obtained and maintained.

There is no Believer who has ever lived, that hasn't had trouble with the sin nature, whether he understood it or not. The idea was and is, that he ever realize the danger which lurks there, and thereby, ever depend upon Christ. This is the reason that Jesus said the following:

TAKING UP THE CROSS DAILY

"If any man will come after Me, let him deny himself, and take up his Cross daily, and follow Me" (Lk. 9:23).

Most Christians have a totally erroneous view of this Passage. Considering that it is Jesus Who said this, they certainly don't deny what is said, but they somewhat skirt the issue.

In other words, they think that He's talking about suffering greatly in some way. Consequently, they will see some Christian who has had a very difficult time in some manner, and they will think, *"That's his*

Cross!" And then they will retort by saying, *"I pray that the Lord never asks me to have to do that,"* whatever *"that"* might be!

As well, they think the words *"deny himself,"* refer to denying oneself all pleasure, or anything that is good or enjoyable. As stated, they know that Jesus said these Words, but most just get around them by simply ignoring them.

None of that which we've stated is what Jesus meant. The following is what He actually said:

First of all, He said *"if any man will come after Me,"* which means, that every single Believer in the world, that is if they follow Christ, is going to have to *"deny himself, and take up his Cross daily."* There are no exceptions; consequently, ignoring the issue doesn't make it go away.

The Truth is, what Jesus said here about denying ourselves, and taking up the Cross daily, is the single most glorious and wonderful thing that could ever happen to a person. Let me explain:

"Denying ourselves" has nothing to do with denying all good things, that is, one making oneself suffer, etc. In fact, all of that is foolishness!

By *"denying himself* (denying ourselves)*,"* Jesus was simply meaning that we are to deny ourselves respecting our own strength and ability as it regards living this Christian life. The idea is, that we cannot do it of ourselves, but must depend totally and completely upon Christ. That's all that He means here.

He is speaking of self-will, which is the greatest problem for the Child of God. Self must be so hidden in Christ, that we actually become a part of Christ, as He becomes a part of us. That's what He meant by the words, *"For whosoever will save his life* (try to do it himself) *shall lose it: but whosoever will lose his life for My sake* (lose self in Christ) *the same shall save it"* (Lk. 9:24).

If we as Believers attempt to order our lives by our own efforts and machinations, instead of trusting in what Christ did at the Cross, we will lose our lives, i.e., *"the more abundant life promised by Christ."* But if we lose our lives in Christ, which means that we look to Him totally and completely, we will then save our lives. This is what He

meant by *"taking up the Cross daily."* Let's look at that:

The phrase, *"Taking up the Cross daily,"* doesn't refer to suffering for Christ. It refers to looking to the Cross on a daily basis, which means to trust totally and completely in what Jesus did there on our behalf. As well, this is not a one-time thing done at conversion, or even at some other spectacular point in one's life, but rather on a daily basis. Once again we go back to the problem of *"pride."*

THE CROSS AND HUMILITY

Have you noticed that in the Bible, there is no place where it tells us how to be humble? The Truth is, man within himself cannot be humble, and that even includes Christians. Actually, a fake man-devised humility which characterizes some Christians, is about the worst situation which one would ever have to confront. That type of Christian, while appearing so humble on the surface, if crossed, will show you their other side, which is not pleasant to say the least. All of this is a contrived humility, which means that it's not of the Spirit, but rather of the flesh.

Taking up the Cross daily, which means to look to the Cross on a daily basis for all that we need, meaning that Jesus there brought about by His Sacrificial Death everything for our needs and requirements, within itself, perfects humility in the Saint. In fact, it can be brought about in no other way. It is only by constantly looking to the Cross, understanding its meaning, and taking its benefits unto ourselves, and doing so on a *"daily"* basis, can we know what humility actually is. As stated, the Cross of Christ is the greatest act of humility the world has ever known and in fact, ever will know (Gal. 6:14).

Whenever the Believer constantly looks to Christ and His Cross, even on a daily basis, he is in effect, placing all self in Christ, which guarantees the Righteousness of Christ. Otherwise, the Believer takes upon himself self-righteousness, which is the bane of far too many Believers.

I think by now, the Believer should understand, that every single thing we need, and in every capacity, comes by and through what Jesus did at the Cross. The actual Truth is, God could not even look at the human race were it not for the Cross, and as well, man would have no access to God, were it not for the Cross, and of course, we speak of what Jesus did there.

WEAKNESS AND UNPROFITABLENESS

The phrase, *"Going before for the weakness and unprofitableness thereof,"* refers to the problems with the old Law. As stated, the word *"Commandment"* used in the first phrase of Verse 18, and which has to do with the *"weakness"* and *"unprofitableness,"* could have better been phrased *"a foregoing Commandment."* The word *"foregoing"* does not emphasize mere precedence in time, but rather the preliminary character of the Commandment as destined to be done away by a later ordinance. It was to be set aside because of its *"weakness and unprofitableness."*

The Levitical economy under Moses was perfect for the purpose for which it was instituted, that of being an index finger pointing to the Coming, Great, High Priest, the Lord Jesus Christ. But when it came to the place that a Sacrifice would be demanded of it that would pay for sin, and do so totally, to where no other Sacrifice would ever be needed, it was found, as would be obvious, to be *"weak and unprofitable"* (Wuest).

This doesn't mean that the Commandment or Law of Moses was weak or unprofitable within itself, but because of that on which it had to act. Actually, a powerful engine in a weak ship is useless because the ship breaks up under its vibrations.

The Law within itself was not weak and unprofitable, but due to the fact that it had no power incorporated within its commands to enable the Believer to keep its precepts, a favorable result could not be accomplished.

THE MODERN CHRISTIAN AND LAW

By the use of the word *"Law"* in the heading, I'm not referring to the Law of Moses; however, I am definitely referring to law. The idea is this:

If the Believer is not functioning in Faith, he is functioning in Law, whether he understands it or not. Of course, it's not the Law of Moses, but rather a Law of his own making or devising, or that made up by other men, etc. What do we mean by that?

NOTES

First of all let's look at Faith. When we speak of Faith, we are speaking totally and completely of Faith in Christ and what He did at the Cross. This must be defined, because most Christians don't actually even know what Faith really is.

Let the Believer understand, that when Paul uses the word *"Faith,"* and without fail, he is always using it in the context of Faith in the Cross of Christ, i.e., *"the Finished Work of Christ."* All Believers claim to have Faith, and in fact all Believers do have Faith. The Truth is, every person in the world, whether redeemed or unredeemed, has Faith; however, it's not Faith in the great Sacrifice of Christ, but something else altogether. The problem is and, in fact, always has been, the correct object of Faith. That object must always be the Cross of Christ.

Now having said that, if the Faith mentioned is not Faith in the Cross of Christ, it is in fact in law, whether the Believer knows or realizes that or not. As stated, it's not the Law of Moses of which we speak, but it is definitely law. And the results of that will always be *"weakness and unprofitableness."*

Such a direction is *"weak,"* because it doesn't have the help of the Holy Spirit, and because it cannot have the help of the Holy Spirit. The Spirit of God will function and operate only within the parameters of the great Sacrifice of Christ. This means that the Believer, as we have repeatedly stated, must ever have his Faith in the Cross (Rom. 8:2).

If the Believer moves his Faith outside of the Cross in any fashion, and no matter how spiritual the other objects might be, the Holy Spirit won't help, and the result will be *"weakness."* Without the power of the Spirit, we cannot have what we ought to have, or be what we ought to be in Christ.

Without the Spirit, we are left only to our own strength and ability, and to be sure, that is woefully insufficient.

The results of all of this will be *"unprofitableness,"* which means exactly what it says.

In fact, millions of Christians, even the far greater majority, are in the position of *"weakness and unprofitableness,"* simply because they don't know God's prescribed order of victory, which is the Cross. And please understand the following:

If the Children of Israel couldn't keep the Law of God, how in the world do you think you can keep some laws that you have made up, or those made up by another human being? Whenever we do this, whether we realize it or not, we are actually saying that what Christ did at the Cross was not sufficient, in other words, that He did not finish the task, and we must add to whatever it is that He has done. I'm sure with a little forethought, that we can see the absolute insult of such thinking. But yet, all of us have fallen into this trap at one time or the other.

There is no *"weakness or unprofitableness"* in Christ. But there is nothing but *"weakness and unprofitableness"* in us, at least when we function without Christ. And to be sure, when we place our Faith in something else other than the Cross of Christ, we are then operating only within our own power and ingenuity, which are woefully insufficient for the task. We can only live this life through and in Christ which is done by exhibiting Faith in His great Finished Work, which then gives the Holy Spirit the latitude to do in our lives what He Alone can do (Rom. 8:1-2, 11).

CONTINUED OPPOSITION BY SATAN

Let not the Believer think that even though he knows and understands God's prescribed order of victory, which is Faith in the Cross, that Satan is going to cease all operations. To be sure, he will continue to probe, to push, to try to find an opening where he can cause us problems. However, please understand that the Cross which of course, is the Finished Work of Christ, culminating in His Exaltation (Eph. 2:6), is our protection. In fact, it is our only protection. The Christian can bluster and blow and spout all type of religious phraseology, but if he's doing so outside of the Cross, the bluster and blow are empty, and Satan, to be sure, knows that it's empty.

So, let not the Christian think that if he knows and understands the Cross, that Satan will cease all activity. Such is not the case at all. The Evil One will oppose the Child of God in every way possible, all the days of the life of the Believer.

The attacks by Satan without exception will all be headed up against our Faith. He seeks

NOTES

to prove the weakness of our Faith, simply because he knows that our victory is in our Faith, i.e., *"our Faith in the Cross."*

I remember many years ago hearing the great Preacher, A. N. Trotter say, that every attack by Satan tendered against us whether it be physical, material, domestical, or spiritual, is for but one purpose, and that is to destroy our Faith in God, or at least, to seriously weaken it.

When I heard him say that, I knew it was right, but at that time, I didn't fully understand exactly what was being said. But through the years, and by bitter experience, to be most sure, I have learned. Satan wants to discourage you, to influence you in some way, that you may lose your Faith in the Finished Work of Christ. And let the Reader understand the following:

If you fail in any way, it is always as the result of a weakness in your Faith. The idea is, our Faith is never as strong as we think it is. The Evil One understanding that, keeps probing and pushing, trying to find the opening for which he seeks. But remember this:

Even though Believers may at times fail, the Cross never fails! We make a great mistake when we fail to properly understand this.

If there is failure, and in any capacity, the Believer should immediately begin to check his Faith, asking the Lord to show him the reason for the failure. To be sure, the Lord will do exactly that. Of this the Believer can be sure: Any and every failure in the life of a Christian is always and without exception a failure of Faith in some way — a failure of Faith in the Cross.

As I have previously said, this Christian experience, at least as it regards Sanctification, is a process. It doesn't come easily or quickly, but of this one thing we can be certain:

If we keep believing, keep pressing on toward the knowledge of the great Sacrifice of Christ, the Holy Spirit will guarantee total and complete victory. What I'm saying is this:

Whatever it is that's troubling you, that's causing you problems, that's weakening your Christian experience, no matter the difficulties you've had with this thing in the past, whatever it might be, you will get total and complete victory if you keep believing in what

Christ has already done for you and what you already are in Christ.

THE VICTORIOUS OVERCOMER

The Holy Spirit is ever striving to push you closer and closer to Christ. That is His goal and ultimate destination for your heart and life. If He is given the opportunity, He will not fail in this which He has set out to do. The first step that you as a Believer must engage upon is the correct steps of Faith, and what do we mean by that?

First of all, quit trying to be an overcomer; in Christ, you are already an overcomer. Quit trying to be victorious; in Christ, you are already victorious. I've already made the following statement in this Volume, but because of its extreme significance, please allow me to repeat it again:

You must *"reckon yourself to be dead indeed unto sin, but alive unto God through Jesus Christ our Lord"* (Rom. 6:11).

The word *"reckon"* means, *"come to the proper conclusion, to confess, to read the bottom line."* Whatever you feel like, whatever your actions might actually be, the Scripture says that if you are in Christ, and if you are saved, you definitely are in Christ, you are then *"dead unto sin."* As we've already explained, sin is not dead, but you are definitely dead unto sin. So, start believing that; start confessing that; start acting like what you actually are!

Christians who are *"trying to be victorious,"* or *"trying to be overcomers,"* will be trying until the day they die. This means, they will never succeed. And the reason they will never succeed, at least in that fashion, is because they are in effect, whether they realize it or not, denying what Christ has already done for them.

We don't get to be victorious, or get to be an overcomer, due to our own efforts, ability, or machinations. Please understand the following:

There is absolutely nothing you can do as a Christian within your own strength and ability, that will help you achieve the goal of which we have just mentioned. It lies beyond your ability and strength. In fact, there's never been a single human being in history who has ever reached that attainment on his own

strength. It can only be done one way, and that is in Christ.

The moment you evidence Faith in Christ as a Believer, you are instantly victorious and instantly an overcomer. That is your position in Christ, for God cannot accept anything less. In other words, He can only accept perfection, and perfection is found only in Christ, and when you exhibit Faith in Christ, which means to exhibit Faith in what He did for you at the Cross and in His Resurrection, God immediately awards you the perfection of Christ (Rom. 6:3-5).

However, we all know and realize, that even though this is our *"position,"* that it's not exactly our *"condition."* Consequently, it's the business of the Holy Spirit to then bring our *"condition"* up to our *"position."* And that's where the struggle comes in.

This can be accomplished only by our continued Faith in the Cross, knowing it was there that Jesus paid all the price, and consequently, won all the victory. I have already quoted to you Colossians 2:14-15, where Jesus nailed everything to His Cross. So, your Faith in that, and your Faith in that alone, will guarantee you all of these things which you must have and must be in Christ.

As Christians, it is so easy for us to look at ourselves, which means to look at our failure, our mistakes, our wrong direction, etc., and if we dwell on that, we will take our eyes off Christ, which guarantees continued defeat. Quit looking at yourself, and start looking at Christ and His Finished Work, knowing and understanding, that it was all done on your behalf. Now let's say that again:

IT WAS ALL DONE ON YOUR BEHALF

This means that every single thing that Jesus did, He did totally and completely for us, and not at all for Himself. As well, He came to this Earth, taking upon Himself the frailty of man, but for one purpose, and that is to do for us what we could not do for ourselves. So, considering that He paid such a price in order that this be done, doesn't it make sense that He would want us to have the benefits of all of this which He has done? Of course it does!

As well, the Holy Spirit stands ready to do all that needs to be done, and to be sure, He will get this work done within our hearts and lives, which means to guarantee our victory in every capacity, if we will only do the one thing which He demands, and that is to constantly exhibit Faith in the great Sacrifice of Christ (I Cor. 1:18, 21; 2:2; Gal. 6:14). The key is in three things:

1. The Cross: Every single thing streams from the Cross.

2. Our Faith: We must ever exhibit Faith in this great, Finished Work of Christ, from Whom and Which all Blessings flow.

3. Continuing to exhibit Faith in the Finished Work of Christ, the Holy Spirit, who always works within the parameters of that Finished Work, will then work mightily upon our behalf (Rom. Chpt. 8).

THE DOMINION OF SIN IS BROKEN

Paul then said, *"For sin shall not have dominion over you: for you are not under the Law, but under Grace"* (Rom. 6:14).

This Passage is not teaching sinless perfection, but it is definitely teaching the fact that the dominion of sin is broken. This means that the sin nature will no longer rule within your heart and life. However, we must understand the following:

This *"dominion of sin"* was totally and completely broken the moment you came to Christ (Rom. 6:3-5).

Naturally, Satan will do everything within his power to reestablish that dominion, which regrettably and sadly, he succeeds in doing in the lives of many, if not most, Christians, and for the simple reason, that he is successful in getting them to transfer the object of their Faith to something else, other than the Cross. The object of Faith must always be the Cross of Christ, and without exception. But if the Evil One can get you to transfer your Faith to other things, no matter how good those other things might be, you have just embarked upon a sure road of spiritual failure. In other words, you will not grow in Grace and the Knowledge of the Lord, with sin in some way dominating you, and in fact, getting worse with passing time. On that particular road, it doesn't really matter how hard you struggle, how hard you fight, how much you oppose that which is seeking to drag you down, you will not succeed in

winning this victory, at least not in this manner. In fact, the situation will not only not get better, but will actually get worse, and despite all of your efforts otherwise.

This is very confusing to many Christians, especially considering that they are struggling with all of their strength to live right, to do right, and to be right. However, please understand and read these following words very carefully:

There is no way that you as a Believer can be right, can do right, can act right, and we speak of being what you ought to be in Christ, unless you know and understand that all of your victory is in what Christ did at the Cross, and your Faith in that.

Even as I dictate these words, I know within my heart, that there are millions of Christians at this very moment, who are struggling with sin within their lives. They're fighting it with all of their strength, but despite that fact, they are losing. They are not hypocrites, in fact, some of them are very dedicated to the Lord. That may come as shock to some Christians, to understand that some are very dedicated and at the same time failing. But let the Reader understand, that this is not an isolated thing, in fact, it characterizes most dedicated Christians, simply because, most, at least at this particular time, do not know and understand the great victory of the Cross. Not knowing this, and despite their consecration and dedication, in some way, that Christian is doomed to failure, which refers to sin having dominion over him or her in some manner.

While the *"sin"* of which we speak, may not be one of the vices, it definitely will be a lack of development of the Fruit of the Spirit in one's life. The Holy Spirit simply cannot function in the doing of His Office work on our behalf, if our Faith is placed in something else other than the Cross. And regrettably, that *"somewhere else"* is where the Faith of most Christians is presently placed.

Perhaps the Reader may think that I press the point too strongly. Perhaps the Reader thinks that I'm too repetitive; however, once we consider that we're dealing here with the issues of life and death, then perhaps you can understand the reason for my dealing with this all-important issue in every manner and way possible. But let me say one more thing:

If perhaps you think that I am being overly repetitive, then this is a sure sign that you really haven't caught the vision of the Cross yourself. If you do properly understand the Cross and all that it means, you will not only *not* think that I'm being too repetitive, but you will long for the moment when I address this issue again and again.

Paul said that you must *"obey from the heart that form of doctrine which was delivered you"* (Rom. 6:17). Mere lip service will not suffice; there must be a heart understanding of these things of which we say, which the Holy Spirit will definitely give, that is if the Believer will humble himself before the Lord.

Please allow us to say it again:

If one seeks to find fulfillment in Christ through efforts other than Faith in the Cross of Christ, one will only find *"weakness and unprofitableness."* Conversely, if one trusts completely in what Christ has done in His great Sacrifice, one will find total and complete victory.

(19) "FOR THE LAW MADE NOTHING PERFECT, BUT THE BRINGING IN OF A BETTER HOPE DID; BY THE WHICH WE DRAW NIGH UNTO GOD."

The exegesis is:

1. The Law made nothing perfect, because it could not provide a Sacrifice which would pay for sin.

2. The bringing in of a better hope, Who and What is Jesus Christ, Who was able to offer a better Sacrifice, definitely did bring everything to perfection.

3. The Work of Christ, being a perfect Work, makes it possible for the Believer to draw nigh unto God, and let us quickly say, by that way alone.

NO PERFECTION IN THE LAW

The phrase, *"For the Law made nothing perfect,"* would have drawn the line with these Christian Jews. The statement in no way presents itself as offensive to us, because we know and understand the total Truth of what Paul is saying; however, this very thing, the Law of Moses, was the point of contention with the Jews. By forsaking Christ, that is if they would do so, thereby going back to the Law as a means of Salvation, would doom them, for there could be no other conclusion.

NOTES

Even though the Law of Moses was righteous, holy, Divine, and true, still, there was no way that anyone could keep the Law, because it offered no power within its precepts; consequently, due to man's fallen condition, it was impossible for him to perform as the Law demanded. So, man was helpless to obey its demands.

Of course, this was not something of which God was not aware. He knew that man could not obey the precepts of the Law, even though it was demanded that he do so, even with the threat of an awful penalty. The recourse of the Jews, as it regards this perplexing problem, was the Sacrifices. They were to offer up Sacrifices to the Lord, which were types of Christ, which in effect stated that even though they could not abide by the precepts of the Law, and no matter how hard they tried, they could have forgiveness and communion with the Lord, through the Sacrifices, which as stated, were types of the coming Redeemer. In other words, their Hope and Salvation were never in the Law, but always in the One which the Sacrifices represented, the Lord Jesus Christ. So, these Christian Jews during Paul's time, threatening to go back into the Law and thereby denying Christ, which it seems that some of them had already done, presented itself as a sin of unimagined proportions. In fact, if they did this thing, which means to deny Christ and His Work, and they remained in that state, they would lose their Salvation, with no way to be saved. The Way of the Cross being the only means of Salvation, with that denied and repudiated, there remains no other way.

THE LESSON FOR US TODAY

Let not the Reader glance at the phrase, *"For the Law made nothing perfect,"* and then automatically place the statement in the realm of having no meaning for us presently. In fact, it has great meaning for us presently.

The Truth is, not knowing the victory of the Cross, virtually all of the Church struggles in the realm of *"law,"* trying to bring themselves to perfection, i.e., *"maturity,"* by this means, which is a hopeless task. The sadness is, most Christians, although wallowing neck-deep in law, do not actually realize this is what is happening to them. And when we say *"law,"* we're not speaking of the Law of Moses as Paul was, but rather law of our own making.

Christians all over the world, are attempting to walk close to the Lord, or obtain more of the Lord, or obtain victory over sin within their lives, by means and methods devised by themselves, or Preachers, or their Church, or Denomination, etc. While some of these devised things may be good, they will not bring victory. The idea is this:

If the Believer is not functioning totally and completely within the parameters of the Finished Work of Christ, then the only other recourse is law. He may not understand such, and may actually think he's doing exactly what he ought to do, but the Truth is, he is engaging in law. Let me say it again:

If one is not placing his hopes and aspirations totally and completely in what Christ did at the Cross on his behalf, then he is engaging in law. There is no third course. It's either Grace, which comes exclusively by what Jesus did at the Cross, or else it is law. And if it is law, whether the Law of Moses, or a law of our own devising, failure is a guaranteed result.

A PERSONAL EXPERIENCE

This of which I say, I have lived. In other words, at frightful price, I have purchased this knowledge by experience. In fact, I empathize 100 percent with Paul as it regards the Seventh Chapter of Romans. I have been there.

I have always had an excellent prayer life, without which, I don't think I would have survived. But yet, I turned prayer into works, not deliberately, but nevertheless that was the end result, and because of not knowing or understanding God's prescribed order of victory.

Regarding attacks by the powers of darkness, and at the same time winning hundreds of thousands of souls to the Lord Jesus Christ, not understanding the Cross as it refers to our Sanctification, all I knew to do was pray.

To be sure, I understood the Cross perfectly as it regards the Salvation of the sinner. I preached it strongly! In fact, I preached it about as strong as it was possible for one to preach such a subject. There was and is

NOTES

no other way of Salvation except by the sinner trusting in Christ and what He did at the Cross on their behalf. The Lord rewarded my efforts, with the Salvation, as stated, of hundreds of thousands of souls, and I exaggerate not, along with thousands Baptized in the Holy Spirit.

But as it regards Sanctification for the Believer, I had no knowledge of this process and work, which is God's prescribed order of victory. Oh to be sure, I had read Romans, Chapter 6, at least 50 times. Actually, I've read the entirety of the Bible completely through, approximately 50 times.

I look back at those times, and I wonder as to why I did not then see this great Truth of the Cross as it regards the Sanctification of the Saint. I have no answer, except to know that it was my fault and mine alone.

But yet, I did not at that time know of a single Preacher who in fact did know this great Truth. I'm sure that some few did, but I also know that most didn't, and in fact, even in a present sense, most don't. That's the reason for Christians running all over the world, trying to find some Preacher to lay hands on them, which will solve their problem. This is the reason for so much failure. And to be sure, for every one Christian, Preacher, or otherwise, of whom we know who fails, there are scores living in failure of whom we do not know anything about. But God knows all about it, to be sure! That's at least one of the reasons for the foray of the Church into psychological counseling. Not knowing the victory of the Cross, the seeking soul reaches out to whatever straw that can be found; however, please understand, that none of these other ways and means, will bring about victory in one's life, that alone being the Cross.

Not knowing God's prescribed order of victory, as stated, the only thing I knew to do was pray. To be sure, the Lord blessed me and helped me greatly as it regards my consecrated prayer life. But the Truth is, confidence in this provided no barrier to the attacks by Satan.

Thirty minutes of prayer each day, and continued faithfully, not being enough, at least providing no victory, I increased it to an hour a day. I finally increased it to approximately two hours a day, an hour during the day and an hour during the night.

Countless times, I would get up at 1:00 or 2:00 in the morning, stagger out of bed, to try to spend at least an hour with the Lord in prayer. I was desperate! In effect, I was fighting for my life.

This didn't go on merely for a matter of days, but rather for a protracted period of time. As stated, these are the issues of life and death, with everything being at stake, and regrettably, it seems that we do not come to the Truth very easily. And that's a fact that should be thought about very carefully.

In such a situation, trying to do all within one's power to live right, walk right, and to be what God wants one to be, and as stated, having the Lord to use me in seeing hundreds of thousands brought to a saving knowledge of Christ, and then at the same time to fail, and to have almost all the Church pointing fingers of accusation, actually making fun, is not a very pleasant prospect. In fact, had I not known the Lord as strongly as I did, and been as consecrated as I was, it would not have been possible to have stood such an onslaught. It's bad enough to have the world laugh at you, but to have almost all the Church do the same, is about as bad as anything could be. Let me say it another way:

When one is down, which means that he cannot defend himself, and anyone can do any negative thing to him they so desire, knowing and understanding also that they will not be reprimanded, but rather applauded, one then finds out just how many true Christians there actually are. Regrettably, that number is small.

THE WAYS OF THE LORD OR THE WAYS OF THE WORLD

During this time, the only thing proposed to me by the Church, was the ways of the world. Now that may seem somewhat confusing to the Reader, so let me explain.

Almost all of the Church world, and I speak of the Church in general, either not knowing the Way of the Cross, or having deliberately rejected the Way of the Cross, has adopted the ways of the world. Despite what they say, and I speak of most of its Leaders, there is little Faith or confidence in the Word

NOTES

of God. In fact, in so many words, they said to me at that time, that if I trusted in the Bible, they would blackball me from all their Churches, etc. They meant exactly what they said, and did everything within their power to carry out that threat.

So, at a very crisis time in my life and Ministry, I had to make a decision. I knew the answer of victorious living was in the Word of God, even though I didn't know exactly what that answer was. At the same time, I knew that the world held no answers.

The Reader must understand, that most of the Church has opted for psychological counseling, as the answer to the ills of mankind. I maintain and I know beyond the shadow of a doubt, there is no answer from that source. In fact, that is the wisdom of the world, which the Holy Spirit says is *"earthly, sensual, Devilish"* (James 3:15).

Paul plainly said in I Corinthians that *"the world by wisdom knew not God."* In other words, man's wisdom cannot find God, does not know God, and can have no part in God. Everything from God to mankind is always and without exception, by Revelation. This means that the Holy Spirit reveals the Word of God to seeking souls (I Cor. 1:21).

Paul then said, *"For the preaching of the Cross is to them that perish foolishness; but unto us which are saved it is the Power of God"* (I Cor. 1:18).

We are here plainly told, that the answer to the ills of man is the Cross of Christ. We are also told that the wisdom of the world holds no answers, which includes modernistic psychology.

In fact, I had preached that strongly up to the time in question, which had garnered strongly against me the animosity of the institutionalized Church. But yet that needs some explanation.

As stated, I preached the Cross strongly as it regards the Salvation of sinners, and that psychology held no answer; however, at that particular time, I did not properly understand what Paul was talking about as it regards the answer being in the Cross for the Sanctification of Saints. To be sure I believed it, but I didn't understand it. And not understanding it, caused me problems of unprecedented proportions.

I BEGAN TO SEEK THE LORD

On that critical day in October of 1991, I laid my Bible on the table in front of me. There were several people in the room. I made the statement that I did not know the answer as to how the Christian could walk in perpetual victory before the Lord, but I did know that the answer was found somewhere in the Word of God. Whatever it costs, whatever it took, I stated at that particular time, that I would find that answer.

As I've mentioned prayer, quite strongly, beautifully, and wondrously enough, the Lord at that time, instructed me to begin two prayer meetings a day. However, these prayer meetings were not to be conducted in order to earn something from the Lord, but rather to have communion with Him, and that alone. In fact, the Lord pointedly told me, *"Do not seek Me nearly as much for what I can do, but rather for Who I am."* And that I set out to do.

At that time, and I speak of the late Fall of 1991, I really did not know what the Lord wanted me to do. Should the Ministry continue? Should we remain on Television? Should I continue to try to Pastor the Church?

I placed all of these things before the Lord, seeking His guidance and leading totally and completely. To be sure, almost the entirety of the Church world was telling me that I must quit preaching. So, I could listen to that voice, or listen to the voice of the Word of God.

The Lord plainly and pointedly told me, that the Ministry was to continue, and I was to stay on Television, and to continue to Pastor the Church. To be sure, it was not easy, and that is a gross understatement. The vituperation and the scorn of the Church world were scathing to say the least! Their position was:

"You have refused to obey us, so that makes you fair game for anything we desire to do."

DIRECTION

As stated, in such a situation, one quickly finds out just how many true Christians there actually are.

Even though the Lord had instructed me as to what to do, financially speaking, I did

not know how in the world it could be accomplished. A media Ministry, which God had definitely called me to do, and through which we had seen hundreds of thousands brought to Christ, requires large sums of money. Tremendous numbers of people are reached, and even though the cost per person is actually very small, still, in the aggregate, the sum is large. I didn't know how in the world we could function financially.

Importuning the Lord about this matter in prayer, He directed me to Matthew, Chapter 17.

This incident concerns taxes which some of the Religious Leaders of Israel claimed that Jesus owed. Peter was approached about this matter, with him taking it to the Lord.

Jesus in effect, told him that no taxes were owed, but concluded by saying, *"Notwithstanding, lest we should offend them, go thou to the sea, and cast an hook, and take up the fish that first cometh up; and when thou hast opened his mouth, thou shalt find a piece of money: that take, and give unto them for Me and thee"* (Mat. 17:27).

The Lord spoke to my heart that morning hour in October of 1991, saying, *"As I provided on that occasion, I will provide for the Ministry as well."*

The Presence of the Lord was on me greatly at that time, and I knew beyond the shadow of a doubt, that I had definitely heard from the Lord; however, the manner in which the Lord said that He would provide, was somewhat frightening. In fact, it is about the most unorthodox way to raise funds that there could ever be.

My avenue of support in fact, was cut off, at least to continue the Ministry as the Lord had told me to do. So, the Lord would have to work a miracle each and every day for us to survive. And that's exactly what He has done.

Over and over again, we have come to the brink, not knowing how we could pay our bills, in effect, not knowing how we could continue, when the Lord at the last minute would perform a miracle. And as the Lord always does, He used this as a teaching ground for me personally and for this Ministry.

When the Children of Israel were miraculously led out of Egypt, they were then led purposely into the wilderness. This was done deliberately by the Lord, in order that they may learn total and complete trust in the Lord. In this wilderness, there was no means of sustenance whatsoever, which meant that God would have to provide totally and completely, which He did! And to be sure, in the wilderness where we had been placed, there was no means of survival as well! But God would show me, even on a day-to-day basis, that He was not subject at all to circumstances, and that He could set a table in this wilderness, which as stated, He abundantly and gloriously has done.

At the same time, I must also state, that my family stood by me in every way that one could conceive. In fact, it would not be possible for me to ask for greater love and help than that provided by those who were mine.

Also, even though many people left Family Worship Center, at the same time, many stayed. This Church which of course speaks of its people, has provided a comfort and a strength that would be difficult to describe. Their love and their help have been absolutely beyond compare.

And then again, I must speak of the Believers scattered all over the world, although few in number, who saw this thing as it actually was, and not as it appeared to be on the surface. They stood with us, and they stand with us, and to be sure, I personally believe that their reward will be great in Heaven. As Barzillai stood with David at a most crucial time, they have stood with me (II Sam. 17:27-29).

THE CROSS

After some five years of seeking the Face of the Lord, in desperation I might quickly add, the Lord began to answer my prayer. He began to reveal to me the victory of the Cross, in effect, telling me, that every answer which I sought, every solution which I sought, every need which I had, all and without exception, were found in the Cross of Christ. If the Reader is to notice, I said that the Lord began to give me this Revelation. This was in 1996, and it continues to enlarge even unto this hour, and I personally believe will continue to enlarge forever. The reason being, that the great Finished Work of Christ, is absolutely inexhaustible, hence Paul referring to it as *"The Everlasting Covenant"* (Heb. 13:20).

This Revelation began one morning, actually as I was writing the Commentary on Romans. When I came to the Sixth Chapter, the Spirit of the Lord began to open up that Chapter as I had never known it before, even though through the years, I had read it, I suppose 50 times or more. A few days later in one of our morning prayer meetings, the Holy Spirit further opened it up by telling me pointedly and specifically, that every answer for which I had sought, comes through the Cross of Christ, and in fact, comes exclusively through the Cross of Christ. I will never forget that moment as well.

I can still see myself sitting on the floor seeking the Lord, with tears rolling down my face, as the Presence of God rested upon me so heavily, knowing that this for which I had so long sought, was now beginning to open up.

At about this time, I knew in my spirit that something wonderful and beautiful was happening. Of that there was no doubt. I sensed a victory in my life that I had never known before. And let me explain that.

VICTORY

Sometime ago, someone asked me the question, *"What is victory?"*

That's a good question!

For the Child of God, victory is *"walking after the Spirit"* (Rom. 8:1-2). Now let's see what it isn't.

Victory is not merely *not* doing something that's wrong. Now please read that line very carefully, because it's very, very important. It is so important in fact, that I must say it again:

Victory is not merely not doing something that's wrong, but rather, not even having any desire to do that which is wrong. There is a vast difference between the two.

Millions of Christians at this very moment are struggling with something in their lives. I speak of sin in some form or fashion. They are trying not to do the thing, whatever it is. Their struggle is intense, and to these people, not knowing the victory of the Cross, victory is going for a period of time without yielding to the impulses of the flesh. But if one is to notice, after awhile, there will be failure of some sort. Let me put it in this way:

If you are fighting and winning, after awhile you will fight and lose!

The reason that all of this takes place is because of the Passage of our study, *"For the law made nothing perfect."*

I realize that the Reader would say, *"I'm not trying to keep the Law of Moses,"* etc. While that is certainly true, however, most Christians definitely are trying to keep a law of some nature, whether of their devising, or the devising of someone else. If it's not Faith in the Cross, then it's a law of some type, there being no other alternative. And in that mode, it's impossible for the Believer to walk in victory. It simply cannot be done. And please let me state that again:

It doesn't matter how consecrated that the Believer is, how dedicated, even how much that person loves God, even how much that person is struggling and trying, the end result without Faith in the Cross of Christ, is going to be failure. In other words, that Believer will *"walk after the flesh,"* and as a result, and despite all of his efforts to do otherwise, will reap the bitter results (Rom. 8:8).

Whenever the Child of God begins to believe and understand this of which I am teaching, and I speak of the great victory of the Cross, how that every single answer is found in the Cross, then the Holy Spirit will begin to work in that Believer's heart and life, bringing forth a work that heretofore was impossible. To be sure, the Holy Spirit is present in the hearts and lives of all Believers; however, He is unable to do very much in those hearts and lives, simply because the Believer is frustrating the Grace of God by his efforts which are carried out outside of the Cross of Christ (Gal. 2:20-21).

"Walking after the Spirit" is placing one's Faith totally and completely in the Cross of Christ, believing that what Jesus did there meets every need and answers every question, as it regards the individual heart and life (Rom. 8:1-2, 11). That is victory, and it's a victory that is of God, and not at all of man.

When this takes place, the only struggle and fight that is left, is the *"good fight of Faith"* (I Tim. 6:12).

THE GOOD FIGHT OF FAITH

The only fight in which the Christian is supposed to engage, is the *"good fight of Faith."* And what does that mean?

It speaks of our Faith which must be exclusively in the Cross of Christ and in nothing else. In other words, and as we have repeatedly stated, the object of our Faith must always be the Cross. In fact, every human being in the world, even all unbelievers, has Faith. In fact, the entirety of the world, whether it understands it or not, operates on the principle of Faith.

To be sure, for the world which knows not God, the Faith they have is not Faith in the Lord, but nevertheless, it is Faith. In fact, that's what makes the free enterprise system the envy of the world, and why the economies of the world which do not operate on this principle, just about starve their people to death.

The free enterprise system operates on Faith, which is the manner in which God intended for all things to operate and function. The word *"Faith"* simply means that we place our trust in something, whatever it might be. As stated, the Faith the world has, is not Faith in God, even though it, in fact, is Faith.

Now the Faith of which the Bible speaks, as it regards the Child of God, is to always and without exception, be Faith in the great Sacrifice of Christ. The entirety of the Word of God bends toward this tremendous Truth. This is why the Cross of Christ is not a mere Doctrine, but actually the foundation on which all Doctrine is built. In other words, the Cross of Christ is the foundation of Faith (Heb. Chpt. 11).

Every Christian has Faith (Rom. 12:3). And yet, the Church has been taught in the last few decades, that they must increase their Faith, and if they can succeed in doing so, they can bring all type of things to pass.

That particular teaching is wrong. Let's look at what Jesus said:

Operating on the basis of increased Faith, *"the Apostles said unto the Lord, 'increase our Faith.'"* And this is the answer that the Lord gave to them:

"If ye have Faith as a grain of mustard seed, ye might say unto this sycamine tree, be thou plucked up by the root, and be thou planted in the sea; and it shall obey you" (Lk. 17:5-6).

If it is to be noticed, Jesus answered their question by using as a symbol *"a grain*

NOTES

of mustard seed," which is at least one of the smallest of seeds. What was He saying to them?

He was in effect telling them, that it was not increased Faith which they needed, but rather the proper object of Faith. And that's where the Church is presently.

The Church is trying to increase its Faith, when that's not the answer to the problem at all. Faith is so strong and powerful, that it doesn't take much to get great things done. So the object is not more Faith, but rather Faith properly placed.

By the phrase *"Faith properly placed,"* we are speaking of Faith in the proper object, which must be the great Sacrifice of Christ, i.e., *"the Finished Work."* This means that you must understand the following:

Almost all the teaching on Faith in the last several decades has centered up on self instead of Christ. While Christ and the Word of God were used, it was by and large used only to bolster self. Consequently, the emphasis was not at all on Christ or His Word, but rather on our own personal ability and strength. Hence, the effort to increase our Faith. God can never honor that. He honors Christ and Christ alone (Mat. 3:17).

When one places their Faith totally and completely in the Cross of Christ, then the emphasis is on Christ where it belongs, and it is Faith which God will always recognize.

Satan knowing and understanding this will do everything within his evil power to switch your Faith to other things, hence, it being called *"the good fight of Faith."* However, if you keep your Faith anchored in the Cross of Christ, you are guaranteed of victory, hence Paul referring to this fight as something that is *"good."* In other words, the end result will always be victory on your part, which of course, is *"good!"*

THE STRUGGLE AGAINST SIN

There is no place in the Word of God that you as a Believer are told to fight or struggle against sin. And yet, this is where almost all of the modern Church actually is. Now that may sound strange to the Reader, because the first thought that comes to our mind is that we are to fight against sin in every fashion.

Of course, we are to oppose sin in totality; however, we must understand some basic Truths first:

First of all, whenever you as a Believer attempt to fight against sin, you are in effect, whether you understand it or not, saying that Jesus didn't finish the work at Calvary, and He needs your two cents worth added. No!

Jesus conquered sin totally and completely at the Cross. He smashed the fact of sin, destroyed its power, and thereby, took away its effect. The Scripture plainly says:

"He that committeth sin is of the Devil (is doing what the Devil wants)*; for the Devil sinneth from the beginning* (is the originator of sin)*. For this purpose the Son of God was manifested, that He might destroy the works of the Devil"* (I Jn. 3:8).

Now this plainly tells us that Jesus destroyed the power and effects of sin, i.e., *"the works of the Devil,"* which He did at the Cross (Col. 2:14-15). So, if Jesus has already done this thing, and to be sure, He definitely has, then for us to try to do it all over again, which we cannot accomplish anyway, is an insult to the great Sacrifice of Christ.

No! There is no place in the Bible that we are told to fight sin. We are to rather fight the good fight of Faith, which speaks of what Christ did at the Cross, all on our behalf. He has totally and completely conquered sin, and we enter into His victory, when we understand what the Cross is all about, even as explained in Romans, Chapter 6, and we reap its benefits, which refers to all of its great victory, by having Faith in this which Christ has done (Rom. 6:3-5).

Therefore, if you as a Believer are struggling against sin in any fashion, you are fighting a battle that has really already been fought and won, which was done by Christ at the Cross, and at any rate, it's a battle that you cannot win. So why not do as the song says, *"Give up and let Jesus take over."*

GOD'S PRESCRIBED ORDER OF VICTORY

If the Cross is God's prescribed order of victory, then due to the fact that precious few in the modern Church have any understanding of the Cross, this means that most of the Church is presently walking in defeat, i.e., *"walking after the flesh"* (Rom. 8:1). To be sure, that statement, as blunt as it might be, and as shocking as it might be, is the Truth.

Let the Reader understand, that God doesn't have four ways of victory, or even two. He has only one way of victory, and that is the great Sacrifice of Christ, i.e., *"the Finished Work of Christ."* To give Chapter and Verse, just begin at Genesis 1:1 and go through Revelation 22:21. The entirety of the Word of God has as its central focus, the Cross of Christ. If one properly reads the Bible, that's what one will read and see.

And yet, most of the Church thinks it knows and understands everything about the Cross. In fact, it looks at this all-important subject as being very elementary. The Truth is, about all the Church knows about the Cross is *"Jesus died for me."* While that is certainly true, we need to know exactly why He died, and what He accomplished by and through His death, and how it refers to us. We also need to understand that His Death on the Cross is actually the centrality of the Gospel.

Whenever Believers ignore the Cross, shouting loudly that they are Resurrection people, they are getting the cart before the horse, a position incidentally, which God will not recognize.

While we definitely are Resurrection people, we are that pure and simple, because of what Jesus did at the Cross. It was at the Cross where the price was paid by the great Sacrifice being offered, which made all of Redemption possible. Please understand the following:

Paul didn't say, *"But God forbid that I should glory, save in the Resurrection of our Lord Jesus Christ,"* but rather, *"God forbid that I should glory, save in the Cross of our Lord Jesus Christ"* (Gal. 6:14).

To be frank, after what Jesus did at the Cross, the Resurrection was a given.

When Jesus died on the Cross, He atoned for all sin, past, present, and future, at least for those who will believe (Jn. 3:16). Sin is the legal hold that Satan has on the human race. Please notice that I said *"legal hold."* In other words, the Scripture says that the *"wages of sin is death"* (Rom. 3:23). This means that sin on man's part, gives Satan the legal right to place man in captivity, thereby bringing about his spiritual death, which refers to eternal separation from God.

However, when Jesus died on the Cross, offering up Himself as a spotless Sacrifice, the terrible sin debt was then paid. Let the Reader understand, that what Jesus did at the Cross was not in any way to appease Satan. In fact, Satan had absolutely nothing to do with the Cross, referring to what Jesus did there. As well, Jesus didn't go to the Cross to fight with the Devil. The Lord would not lower Himself to engage in such a task. He is the Creator of all things, and Satan is a mere creature. So such a fight would be no contest, as should be obvious.

Jesus did in fact, destroy all the works of the Devil, but He did so not by entering into any type of combat with Satan, but rather by satisfying the Righteousness of a thrice holy God. The Cross was necessary to satisfy the Holiness and Divine Nature of God. God cannot overlook sin, cannot condone sin, cannot abide sin in any form or fashion. Due to the fact of the Fall, man was and is a sinner. In fact, he is literally born in sin, which means he is polluted even at his conception. This is due to the fact that Adam was the original fountainhead of humanity. Consequently, when Adam fell, the entirety of the human race, which in essence was in his loins, fell as well!

God could satisfy man's obligation to Him, by condemning man to Hell forever and forever, or He could redeem man, which would be at a frightful price. In fact, the price would be so great, that there is no way that man could or can properly comprehend this which the Lord did on our behalf. God would literally have to become man, which He did, hence Paul referring to Christ as the *"Last Adam"* (I Cor. 15:45), keep the Law perfectly on our behalf, which is what the Righteousness of God demanded, and then go to the Cross, offering up Himself in Sacrifice, which would then pay the terrible sin debt (Gal. 1:4).

With all of the sin debt legally paid, and that means every single sin, past, present, and future, Satan then lost his legal hold upon man. That's how Jesus defeated the Devil. One might say, that the defeat of Satan was a by-product of what Jesus actually went to the Cross to do, which was to satisfy the Righteousness of God.

As we've said over and over again, this great thing that Christ did at the Cross, paid man's terrible debt, thereby destroying the legal hold that Satan had on humanity, which guarantees Redemption for all who will believe.

If the wages of sin is death, and they definitely are, and if in fact, Jesus has paid those wages, then death had no claim on the Son of God. In other words, Jesus had the legal right to come from the dead. If there had been one single sin left unatoned, He would not have had that legal right. But due to the fact that no sin remained, Jesus was resurrected from the dead, actually serving as the *"Firstfruits"* of all who will follow thereafter.

The Cross is God's prescribed order of victory, which should be obvious!

A MESSAGE WHICH MUST BE PROCLAIMED

If what I'm saying about the Cross is correct, and I speak of it being God's only prescribed order of victory, and to be sure it definitely is, then I think one can readily see the absolute necessity of all Believers knowing and understanding this great Truth. In other words, the Lord didn't give this Revelation to me for me only. While it definitely was for me, it is meant for the entirety of the Church. Therefore, I feel that I have a mandate from the Lord to proclaim this Word to the entirety of the Church world, which we are attempting to do posthaste and with all diligence. And yet it is not easy, and because of the problem of deception.

Spiritual deception is like a drug. It takes the Power of God to break through this shell, this downward spiral, in order to bring a person to their spiritual senses. This can only be done by the Word of Truth being proclaimed with great force, power, and conviction, which speaks of the Anointing of the Holy Spirit. Even then, it's almost like a hammer, that has to keep beating upon a shell before it will finally crack.

Even though Christians are going in a wrong direction, or at least most of them, and because of wrong believing, still, they do not turn around easily. This religious drug, this intoxicant of false doctrine which leads to false direction, is empowered by Satan. So, to get that individual to turn around, that person has to be awakened out of the

NOTES

spiritual stupor in which they are presently capsuled. That's the reason that Paul said:

"Knowing the time, that now it is high time to awake out of sleep: for now is our Salvation nearer than when we believed" (Rom. 13:11).

That's the reason I plead for people to get these Commentaries, and then to read and study them after they are obtained. I grieve when I see Christians who have access to the Truth, and because of neglect or apathy, they simply won't take the time to avail themselves of the very thing that can make the difference between life and death. Yes, it is that critical!

It's impossible for any Christian to walk in victory, unless they understand the Victory of the Cross. While it certainly is possible for some Christians to not be placed in bondage to the vices, it is not possible for a Christian to know and enjoy *"more abundant life,"* or the *"rest"* promised by Christ, unless they avail themselves of the tremendous benefits of the Finished Work of Christ. This means that every single Christian in the world who doesn't know the Victory of the Cross, which includes almost all, is suffering one or both of the following maladies:

1. Millions of Christians are bound by sin in some way, and we speak of the vices. They are living in bondage.

2. Even if the Christian is not afflicted with this of which we have just spoken, it is impossible to enjoy and have the *"more abundant life"* promised by Christ without a proper understanding of God's prescribed order of victory (Mat. 11:28-30; Jn. 10:10).

Most Christians have no way to compare this of which I speak, simply because they've never known what true victory actually is. Yes, they are saved! Yes, they know the Lord! But unless one knows and understands the Cross, one cannot know and understand all that Jesus has done for us, and at such great price. And to be sure, and as I've stated over and over again, considering the price that He paid, it stands to reason, that He wants us to have all that He has done for us. That should be obvious!

A BETTER HOPE

The phrase, *"But the bringing in of a better hope did,"* refers to Christ, and more specifically, what He did at the Cross on our behalf.

Once again, please allow me to reiterate, that this which Paul says in this particular Verse, should not be construed as something that pertained only to the Jewish Christians of old, with no bearing on our present-day situation. In fact, it is just as apropos presently, as it was then.

The far greater majority of the modern Church, even as we've already stated, is struggling with Law, whether they understand such or not, and are, therefore, suffering defeat. This is tragic, when the *"better hope"* is available to us. What needs to be done, and in fact, what must be done in our hearts and lives, cannot be done in any fashion by law. It can only be done by Grace, and please understand the following:

The Grace of God, which is actually the Goodness of God extended to undeserving people, comes totally and completely by the means of the Cross. This simply means, that if the Believer places his or her Faith in the Cross of Christ, that such will guarantee an uninterrupted flow of Grace, which as stated, all of us must have, and even on a continuing basis. In fact, this is not difficult to understand.

It simply means, that all that we need and which Christ can afford is in no way deserved by us. Actually, there's nothing we can do to deserve this *"better hope."* And when we place our Faith totally and completely in the Cross, we are admitting that we do not deserve this which is so freely given, which in fact, God demands. That's why Paul said the following:

"Now to him that worketh (tries to earn his Salvation) *is the reward not reckoned of Grace, but of debt."* This means that when a Believer attempts to try to receive from the Lord by the means of law, he is in effect saying that God owes him something, which of course, is ludicrous!

And then Paul said, *"But to him that worketh not* (does not try to earn it by keeping laws), *but believeth on Him that justifieth the ungodly* (does so by one's Faith in the Cross), *his Faith is counted for Righteousness"* (Rom. 4:4-5).

Any Believer can have this *"better hope"* Who and What is Christ, if the Believer will only place his Faith unreservedly in the Great Sacrifice of Christ.

NOTES

THE POSITION OF MOST CHRISTIANS

With most everything I've said, most Christians would agree wholeheartedly. And it's because they think that all of this is automatic after they come to Christ. It isn't!

As stated over and over again, God does not require much of us, in fact only one thing. That one thing is that we evidence Faith in the Cross of Christ. At the same time, most would claim that they do this; however, the evidence of their lives and living is that they aren't doing this. They aren't doing what is demanded of them, simply because there has been so little teaching and preaching on the Cross of Christ in the last several decades, that the modern Church, despite their claims, is basically Cross illiterate.

I sometimes think this problem is as bad, or even worse in Spirit-filled Believers than anyone else. Most Spirit-filled Christians have it in their minds that due to the fact that they are Spirit-filled, that the work of the Spirit is automatic within their lives. It isn't! If it was, there would be no failure among Spirit-filled Christians, and as well, all Spirit-filled Christians would be instantly mature.

However, we all know that none of this is correct. In fact, many Spirit-filled Christians are in just as much trouble as their nonspirit-filled counterparts. And I'll have more to say about that in a moment.

The fact is, the Holy Spirit will always do anything and everything that He can do; however, what He can do is predicated to a great extent on our cooperation with Him. As stated over and over again, He doesn't require much of us, but He does require one thing, and He is adamant about that.

He requires that we place our Faith at all times in the Cross of Christ, which means that the Cross is to ever be the object of our Faith, and without Fail. Whenever this is done, the Holy Spirit can then work within our lives, and do so in an amazing way.

The Holy Spirit is God; consequently, there is nothing He cannot do. But He will never do anything in our lives by force. In other words, He will not force the issue. Even though He is symbolized in many ways, such as by fire, wind, water, etc., the greatest manner in which He functions within our hearts and lives is symbolized by the *"Dove,"* which of course, denotes extreme gentleness, etc. (Mat. 3:16). If we try to function in the realm of law, even though we might not even understand that's what we are doing, He, although continuing to abide, will not force the issue. In other words, He will allow us to continue on that path, even though He tries constantly to get us into the right direction.

That's not as easy as some folk may think. Of course, the Holy Spirit could force the issue in a moment, but as stated, He will never do that. He deals with us, talks to us, witnesses to us, but most of us are not easy to turn around. Whether we admit it or not, we are prideful, stubborn, opinionated, and self-righteous. I realize that's not a very pretty picture, but it just happens to be the Truth! But if the Believer is sincere, and truly seeks the Face of the Lord asking for direction, to be sure, the Holy Spirit will get that Believer to the right place.

In fact, these very Commentaries are means by which the Holy Spirit is attempting to bring Believers to God's prescribed order of victory. They aren't the only means, but they are definitely a means.

THE BAPTISM WITH THE HOLY SPIRIT

Considering all the light that has been given on the subject of the Baptism with the Holy Spirit, especially in the last 100 or so years, there is no excuse for any Believer not knowing and understanding what the Bible teaches about this all-important subject.

The Bible teaches that immediately after the believing sinner comes to Christ, that the new convert should ask the Lord for the Baptism with the Holy Spirit. This is an experience which is always received after conversion, and which is always accompanied by the speaking with other Tongues, with no exceptions (Acts 2:4; 10:46; 19:1-7).

Due to this Light amply given, even abundantly so, I personally feel that it is virtually impossible for any Believer to fully appropriate the benefits of the Cross without this experience. To be sure, millions of Spirit-filled Christians do not, as stated, come even close to that of which they can be in Christ, but that's not the fault of the Spirit, but rather theirs. The potential is there, if they will only

"walk after the Spirit," which is the Way of the Cross (Rom. 8:1-2).

In fact, that's been the major problem of the non-Pentecostal world — they have attempted to have the benefits of the Cross, at least the few who have, without the power of the Holy Spirit, which is impossible. Regrettably, many in the Pentecostal and Charismatic realms, have attempted to function according to the Holy Spirit without the Cross. Neither way will come out to victory. The non-Pentecostal world cannot have the benefits of the Cross, I think, without the moving, leading, guidance, and power of the Holy Spirit, which demands that the Believer be baptized with the Spirit (Acts 1:4). As well, Pentecostals and Charismatics cannot have the work of the Spirit within their hearts and lives, although truly Baptized with the Holy Spirit, unless they place their Faith properly in the Cross of Christ, which regrettably, most don't do. I'm not meaning by this that the Holy Spirit will not work at all, but that the life of victory cannot be had, without proper Faith in the Cross, which provides the latitude for the Holy Spirit to work.

Every single thing done in the heart and life of the Believer, is done solely by and through the Person and Power of the Holy Spirit. This must ever be understood. Whatever we receive from the Lord, it will come by the way of the Spirit (Jn. 16:7-15). But the key to all of these things is the Cross, and our Faith in that great Sacrifice.

I realize that our non-Pentecostal friends teach that one receives the Holy Spirit at conversion, and there is, therefore, no further experience to be received. While it is certainly true that all Believers definitely do receive the Holy Spirit at conversion, without which it is impossible for anyone to be saved; still, that is far different than being Baptized with the Spirit. In other words, being born of the Spirit is one thing, while being Baptized with the Spirit is something else altogether.

There is no way that one can read the Book of Acts, and come away with any other conclusion than the fact that the Baptism with the Holy Spirit is an experience subsequent to Salvation, and as well, and as stated, which is always accompanied by the speaking with other Tongues (Acts 2:4).

The Baptism with the Holy Spirit opens up the Believer to the Spirit, which cannot be had any other way. To be sure, this has nothing to do with one's Salvation, that coming by initial Faith in Christ. As well, the Baptism with the Holy Spirit is also received by Faith, understanding that it is all made possible by what Jesus did at the Cross. Being born of the Spirit is for the unsaved, while being Baptized with the Spirit is for the redeemed. In fact, the Baptism with the Spirit is something that the world cannot receive, which means that a Believer is the only one who can in fact, receive such an experience (Jn. 14:16-17). And if it's automatically received at conversion, as some claim, why were Peter and John sent to Samaria to pray for those people to receive the Spirit, who had already been saved under the preaching of Philip? (Acts 8:5-17), or why was Ananias sent to pray for Paul in order that he might receive the Spirit, incidentally some three days after he was saved on the road to Damascus? (Acts 9:17), or why did Paul ask the Ephesian Believers, *"Have ye received the Holy Spirit since ye believed?"*, if in fact, they were Baptized with the Holy Spirit at conversion as many teach? (Acts 19:1-7).

The Truth is, while all Believers are definitely born of the Spirit at conversion, no Believers are Baptized with the Spirit at the moment of Salvation. To be sure, some may be Baptized seconds after they are saved, but not at the same moment. The Believer has to first be justified, which means to be perfectly cleansed by the Blood of the Lamb, and his Faith in that Finished Work, before he is a fit subject for the Holy Spirit. In fact, this is the very reason that Believers were not Baptized with the Spirit before the Cross, at least as they are presently. There was no way that the blood of bulls and goats could take away sin, that awaiting the Sacrifice of Christ.

There is an abundance of Scriptural evidence, that the Baptism with the Spirit is a work separate and apart from Salvation, which follows Salvation, and which is commanded of all Believers (Acts 1:4). As well, the same proof is abundant that speaking with other Tongues is the initial physical evidence that one has been truly Baptized with the Spirit. To deny these two factors, even as much as

NOTES

the modern Church does, is to deny the Spirit, which leaves the Believer without any ways and means of Spiritual Growth. And as well, I might quickly add, even as I've already stated, that even if the Believer is Spirit-filled, they must understand the means and the ways of the workings of the Spirit, which is by and through the Finished Work of Christ, requiring Faith in that great Sacrifice on the part of the Believer. Only then, can the Spirit work in the heart and life of the Believer as He so desires.

TO DRAW NEAR UNTO GOD

The phrase, *"By the which we draw nigh unto God,"* verifies what I've just said.

By the Atonement and the New Covenant we have personal approach to God which no man had by the Law, and which no man can have by Law. The idea is, that it's impossible for a person to get close to God, unless they properly understand what the *"better hope"* actually is.

Due to the sin debt not being paid, and because as stated, the blood of bulls and goats could not take away sin, those under the old economy of God were very limited in their access or nearness to God. In other words, they could only get so close, which by today's standards, were not very close at all.

Due to these barriers being removed, which Jesus did at the Cross, a person can have as close a relationship with God as he so desires, and that refers to any and all Believers, irrespective as to whom they might be.

Under the Old Covenant, no Levitical Priest could bring any person closer to God, though the Priest stood before God on behalf of man. Now our Great High Priest, due to what He did at the Cross, which opened up the way to Heaven's Gate, invites us to come into God's Presence, for we now have access through Him. He has put away our sins and brought us near to God. In fact, this is the glorious Truth of the Gospel! But always remember, all of this was done totally and completely by the means of the Cross.

GOD IS NOT AS CONCERNED WITH OUR BACKGROUND AS HE IS WITH OUR PRESENT POSITION

God is able to raise up men and women from the most humble circumstances and make them mighty for Himself. He will never allow our backgrounds to keep us from being all that He intends for us to be, for in Christ we are new creations; the old is gone and the new has come.

The standards the world has for greatness are these: position, honor, fame, power, wealth, etc. But true greatness does not consist of these, for when death comes, God levels all men. There are no Presidents in eternity, there are no kings, there are no millionaires; all are on the same level. The pauper and the rich stand side by side in the presence of death. The only riches that we will have on the other side will be what we have given to God.

Whatever greatness we may possess in eternity lies not so much in what we have or what we have done, but in the Grace and the Wisdom of God, Who by His kindness and Mercy, has made us kings and priests unto Himself.

Putting things down on a more mundane level, but yet that which is extremely holy before the Lord, let us consider that Abraham counted it a very precious honor and privilege to give to Melchizedek, God's servant. We as well, should count it a great honor and privilege to bring the Tithes of our income to God. Our voices should declare, *"Lord, thank You for the honor of giving to You. Thank You that I have the strength, the health, and the means to give something to You."*

Remember, God owns everything. He really does not need what we possess; yet, when we give, He graciously reaches down, thanking us and blessing us. This means that we are to never give out of sentiment or impulsively, but rather cheerfully and freely. Tithing becomes a plan and a principle by which to give, and in reality, our giving should exceed Tithes.

A PLACE OF RECONCILIATION

Since *"the Law of Moses made nothing perfect,"* a change had to come. God desired to bring man into a place of Reconciliation; this was impossible under the Law. To be sure, God honored the Law and the Priesthood, He actually being the originator of both. Consequently, for those who would rebel against the Law or dishonor the Priesthood, there was sure judgment. God was

sensitive about the Law as should be obvious, for it was holy; yet, under it men fell short of God's purpose for them, which in fact, was all they could do. Consequently, the Law was to be only temporary; it acted as a guardian to bring Israel to Christ.

Jesus was the only One ever to fulfill the Law and, by so doing, give man hope and access to God. He lives the life that the Law demanded, and became the needed Sacrifice to redeem mankind. With His Own Blood He made a New Covenant with man and, by virtue of His Sacrifice, Resurrection, and Eternal Life, He became the High Priest Who was far superior to either Melchizedek or Aaron. Jesus Christ Alone provides Eternal Life to all who believe in Him (Jn. 3:16). As well, all of these men we have mentioned, Melchizedek, Levi, Aaron, and all the other Priests, plus all others for that matter, had to come to this Great High Priest in order to have Eternal Life, for He Alone is the only One Who could provide such.

The human Priests referred to by Paul possessed many sins and failures. Consequently, and as would be obvious, they were subject to death. Death made all Priests equal; it brought their ministries to an end. These Priests were powerless to bring men near to God, and they were unable to sympathize fully with the needs of men. But Jesus, *"the High Priest of our profession,"* was without sin and failure. He officiated in sacrificing Himself and in dying, freely giving His Own Life. But He returned from death as Victor, because all sin had been atoned. Consequently, as stated, with all of sins wages paid, which is death, Christ was guaranteed of Resurrection.

As a result, only He could say that all power and authority belonged to Him, for He was and is more than Priest; He is King, Lord, Saviour, and Christ (Fjordbak).

(20) "AND INASMUCH AS NOT WITHOUT AN OATH HE WAS MADE PRIEST:"

The exegesis is:

1. Earthly Priests were not sworn in by an oath, simply because they were temporary.

2. When Jesus was made a High Priest, God took an oath guaranteeing the unending character of His Priesthood.

3. This shows the inferiority of the Aaronic Priesthood to that of Melchizedek.

BY AN OATH

The phrase, *"And inasmuch as not without an oath,"* refers back to Verse 17. There were reasons for this oath, and some of them are as follows:

1. In the Mind of God, Jesus had already paid the price for man's Redemption, even before it had happened, in fact, even before the foundation of the world (I Pet. 1:18-20).

2. The High Priesthood of Christ was predicated on His great Sacrifice, which only He could accomplish.

3. God swore an oath, because the price was paid.

4. The oath sworn by God as well, pertained to the fact that the Priesthood of Christ was and is eternal.

PRIEST

The phrase, *"He was made Priest,"* was added by the translators, not being in the original Text. However, it fits the statement.

He was made a Priest due to the fact of what He did, in the offering up of Himself as Sacrifice. This means that He was not always a Priest, but became such, because of His atoning Work at the Cross.

A Priest, in the truest sense of the word, is a Mediator between God and men; however, he is a Mediator only by the virtue of blood sacrifice. Jesus by the offering up of Himself in Sacrifice, which means that it was willingly and freely done, and done on behalf of mankind, which in fact no other Priest could do, placed Him in a position unequaled in the annals of human history. In fact, one could possibly say without fear of contradiction, that such was unique even in the annals of the history of God, that is, if one would be allowed to use such terminology. While God definitely has a history, the difference in His history and the history of mankind, is that His history had no beginning.

(21) "FOR THOSE PRIESTS WERE MADE WITHOUT AN OATH; BUT THIS WITH AN OATH BY HIM THAT SAID UNTO HIM, THE LORD SWARE AND WILL NOT REPENT, THOU ART A PRIEST FOR EVER AFTER THE ORDER OF MELCHISEDEC:"

The structure is:

1. God swore no oath regarding these human Priests, simply because their office was temporary.

2. The Levitical Priesthood and the Law of Moses were not established by the Lord with an oath. As a result, as should be obvious, He could change or abolish them at His pleasure.

3. The Priesthood of Christ was sworn to by an oath, and for the reason, which we have already stated, that Christ fit the order demanded by God, and thereby, His Priesthood would now be eternal.

4. In His oath, it is given in such a way, that it cannot be rescinded.

5. The oath declares that Jesus will be a Priest forever.

6. It will be after the order of Melchizedek, which was designed as a type in order to portray the coming Priesthood of Christ, and the fact that it is eternal.

WITHOUT AN OATH

The phrase, *"For those Priests were made without an oath,"* refers to the fact, even as Paul brings it out, that such was done simply because God never intended that the Levitical order be eternal. The entirety of the Levitical process was by its very design, temporal. However, as is here very obvious, the Jews were in no mood whatsoever to lay aside the old Levitical order, with even the Christian Jews falling into this category.

THE OATH

The phrase, *"But this with an oath by Him that said unto Him,"* declares the purpose of God in an absolute fashion. It allows of no qualification on account of human weakness or sinfulness or anything else. So Paul contrasts the Priesthood that has the security of the Divine oath to that which lacked it. Christ is contrasted with the Levitical Priests, and the importance of the oath is thereby stressed.

It was not simply that an oath was sworn at the same time He was made Priest, but that the oath was the very essence of what was done. This is the point of the argument.

THE LORD WILL NOT CHANGE HIS MIND

The phrase, *"The Lord sware and will not repent,"* means that the Lord will not change His mind. In fact, men being very fickle change their minds constantly, but when God gives His Word, it will not change.

In fact, this is the third oath of the Epistle:

1. The Oath of Imprecation (Heb. 3:11).
2. The Oath of Consolation (Heb. 6:18).
3. The Oath of Consecration (Heb. 7:20).

These oaths establish immutability.

THE ORDER OF MELCHIZEDEK

The phrase, *"Thou art a Priest forever after the order of Melchisedec,"* is derived as previously stated from Psalms 110:4. As is Paul's custom, he bases the entirety of his teachings on Old Testament Scripture.

Of course, the Old Testament is the Word of God the same as the New. But by Paul basing all doctrine on the foundation of the Old Covenant, lets us know just how immutable was that great Word. Consequently, his argument cannot be refuted, at least as it regards those who desire to be honest with the Word.

(22) "BY SO MUCH WAS JESUS MADE A SURETY OF A BETTER TESTAMENT."

The composition is:

1. The argument here is that Jesus is the surety of a Better Covenant because God took an oath that His Priesthood would be an everlasting one.

2. In this Verse, Paul states the proposition which he proves, namely, that the New Testament in Jesus' Blood is better than and takes the place of the First Testament in animal blood.

3. Jesus is the guarantor or pledge of a Better Covenant or Testament.

JESUS

The phrase, *"By so much was Jesus,"* proclaims the fact, that all of Redemption is bound up totally and completely in Christ. That's the reason that Biblical Christianity is not a religion.

Actually, a religion is a system devised by man in order to reach God, or to better himself in some way.

Biblical Christianity has no part of man in its composition. It is entirely of Heaven, and more specifically, it is entirely of a Person, the Son of God.

This means that no Church or man can add anything to one's Salvation, or take from one's Salvation, such being totally and completely in Christ; however, man loves to claim that he can do such, and unfortunately, some

NOTES

poor people seem to believe such fabrications. What man cannot give, man cannot take away.

The entirety of Salvation, and in every capacity, is wrapped up totally and completely in *"Jesus,"* and more particularly, what He did at the Cross on our behalf.

MADE

"Made" in the Greek is *"ginomai,"* and means, *"to cause to be, to generate, to become, to come into being."* This plainly tells us that Jesus, although always God, had not previously been a High Priest. In the realm of Deity and the order of Heaven, such are not needed. A High Priest being the offerer of a Sacrifice and in reality, a blood sacrifice, and as well a Mediator between God and men, solely as Deity this couldn't be done. Consequently, God in effect, would have to become the God-man, which refers to the Incarnation, for such a thing to be carried out. The idea is, an Angel could not serve as a Mediator, simply because they are of another creation. As well, God strictly as God, could not function as a High Priest, because of the Laws that He had Himself formulated.

At the original creation of man, God placed all of His creation into man's hands, because of the magnitude of man (Gen. 1:28; Ps. 8). Satan by subterfuge, actually because of default on the part of Adam, gained this dominion. Just how far Satan's dominion functions we aren't told; however, we do know that it incorporates the entirety of this Earth (II Cor. 4:4). Even though all of this was done by Satan through subterfuge, trickery, and chicanery, still, God recognized the legal claim of Satan. This means that the Evil One now held God's choicest creation in captivity (Eph. 4:8-10). Therefore, to keep within the legal bounds of the Laws which God Himself had formulated, He would have to redeem man by becoming man, which He did.

The idea is, inasmuch as God had placed so much authority into the hands of the original Adam, He in effect, would have to come to the Earth as man, i.e., *"the Last Adam,"* in order to redeem man (I Cor. 15:45). So, as the Last Adam He did this thing, and by that we refer to the fact that He kept the Law of God perfectly, all on our behalf, and then went to the Cross to satisfy the penalty of the broken Law, again on our behalf, which He did by offering up Himself as a Sacrifice (Gal. 1:4).

To portray how this would be brought about, He instituted the Levitical Priesthood, which would show by example the manner in which this great work would be carried out. Therefore, when He died on the Cross, and was raised from the dead, and ascended back to the Father with His mission total and complete, there was no more need for the Levitical order, because He in effect, had been *"made"* a High Priest, which role He will fill forever.

SURETY

"Surety" in the Greek is *"engyos,"* and means, *"guarantee."* In fact, this is the only time this word is found in the New Testament, and it brings before us an unusual idea.

The Old Covenant was established with a Mediator, actually the High Priest of that order (Gal. 3:19), but with no one to guarantee that the people would fulfill their undertaking. But Jesus stands as a continuing Guarantor and that in two directions. He fulfills both roles of God and man, for He is both. Consequently, this is the reason that the New Covenant cannot fail.

In fact, the Old Covenant was doomed to failure to begin with, because it demanded a proper performance from the people which, in fact, they could not render. But yet, God being God could demand no less. His Divine Nature demands perfection. Such perfection to be sure, can only be found in Christ. And the following is the way the New Covenant works:

Christ guarantees to men that God will fulfill His Covenant of forgiveness, cleansing, and Redemption, and He guarantees to the Father that those who are in Him are acceptable; however, we are acceptable only on the basis of the perfection of Christ and more particularly, His Finished Work. That's actually the reason that Paul uses the term *"in Christ"* or one of its derivatives, about 170 times in his 14 Epistles.

There is no way that anyone can approach God, can have anything from God, or can know anything of God, except by being *"in*

Christ." That is brought about by the *"born again"* experience (Jn. 3:3).

This (the Born-Again experience) refers to the fact that Jesus died on the Cross on our behalf, and we were literally baptized into His death (Rom. 6:3). Of course, it is obvious that we were not there; however, our Faith in what He did at the Cross, in the mind of God, Whose Mind Alone actually matters, actually places us there. We were baptized into His death, buried with Him, and raised with Him in newness of life (Rom. 6:3-5). As stated, Faith in Christ, and what He did at the Cross on our behalf, awards us all that Christ did. It literally places us *"in Christ."* The word *"surety"* is the guarantee of God that this is done!

In fact, all of this which we have just said is actually a *"Law"*; however, let not the Reader confuse this *"Law"* with the Law of Moses. This of which we speak is the *"Law (a Law made by God) of the Spirit* (the Holy Spirit Who guarantees this Law) *of life* (the only manner in which life can be derived) *in Christ Jesus* (meaning that all of this has come about through what Jesus did at the Cross and in His Resurrection) (which) *hath made me free from the law of sin and death"* (Rom. 8:2).

The idea of all of this is, Christ became the guarantor that the benefits of the New Covenant (which is actually the meaning of the Cross) would be given to all men who meet the terms. In this sense He is the Mediator.

A BETTER COVENANT

The phrase, *"Of a better Testament,"* actually should have been translated, *"a better Covenant."*

This is Paul's first use of the term *"Covenant,"* a word incidentally, which importance for him may be gauged from the fact that he uses it in this Epistle some 17 times, whereas in no other New Testament Book is it found more than three times.

In non-Biblical Greek it denotes a last will and testament, but it is normally rendered in the Hebrew as *"Covenant."*

However, we do agree that Paul used the word *"diatheke"* which is not normally used for Covenant, but rather the Greek *"syntheke."* Possibly he used the former word, because the latter might suggest an agreement made on more or less equal terms. While a Covenant does carry that connotation, a *"will"* or *"testament"* by contrast, proclaims something that is absolute. One cannot dicker with the testator. And in like manner, man cannot bargain with God. God lays down the terms, and we must go God's way, which spells out the word *"Testament"* much more than it actually does *"Covenant."*

So, quite possibly, the Holy Spirit wanted Paul to use the Greek word *"syntheke,"* to express this very point. While what Jesus did is definitely a Covenant, it is at the same time much more. What He brought about at the Cross and in His Resurrection, is an immutable contract, meaning it cannot be broken. This is so because as stated, Jesus is both God and man.

BETTER

Even as we've already stated, Paul uses the word *"better"* again and again in this Letter to the Hebrews. He does so because the New Covenant is a better one as compared with the Old Covenant or the Law of Moses.

The former Covenant was that which God made with His people under the Mosaic dispensation: the New Covenant is that made by the means of Christ. This is better, because:

1. The terms are simpler and easier.

2. The observances and rites are much less onerous and hard.

3. It relates to all men, not being confined to the Jewish people.

4. It is now sure. The former was administered through the instrumentality of the Levitical Priesthood. The New Covenant is administered by the Son of God. The former was transitory and changing, the latter is permanent and eternal.

(23) "AND THEY TRULY WERE MANY PRIESTS, BECAUSE THEY WERE NOT SUFFERED TO CONTINUE BY REASON OF DEATH:"

The structure is:

1. There had to be many Priests under the Old Covenant, because the Priests being merely human, died.

2. The fact of them dying showed, as should have been obvious, an incomplete program.

3. The very fact of *"death,"* made the Levitical Priesthood vastly inferior.

MANY PRIESTS

The phrase, *"And they truly were many Priests,"* does not testify of better, but rather of less. Many Priests under the Mosaic economy were needed, because the sacrifices were vastly inferior. There had to be different types of sacrifices for different types of sins, and as well, the sacrifices had to be repeated for each and every sin. Only on the Great Day of Atonement could one sacrifice suffice for the entirety of the nation, but even then, it was only symbolic. The blood of bulls and goats, which Paul will outwardly say in the Tenth Chapter, could not take away sins.

During the time of Christ, Jericho had become known as the *"City of Priests."* It is believed that as many as 20,000 resided there. Of course, these were Priests who functioned in the Temple services in Jerusalem. As well, there were many other Priests who lived in Jerusalem proper, plus others who lived in other towns in Israel. So, when Paul wrote, *"they truly were many Priests,"* that was no overstatement.

THE MORTALITY OF THE PRIESTS

The phrase, *"Because they were not suffered to continue by reason of death,"* automatically portrayed the inferiority of this system.

Wuest says, *"Another proof of the superiority of the New Testament over the First Testament is found in the continued life of its High Priest, the Lord Jesus Christ. Due to this fact, He was and is able to make intercession for the Believer forever, and thus able to save us completely, whereas the Aaronic Priests were compelled by death to transfer their ministry to the next Priest in succession."*

Due to the fact of death, these Priests could not continue as would be obvious.

The many sacrifices continuing to be offered, the great number of Priests required, and the mortality of these Priests, proclaims in glaring, obvious detail, the inferiority of this order.

Even as it regards the High Priests, they of course were as well, mortal. Josephus says that there were 83 High Priests from Aaron to the destruction of the Temple in A.D. 70. The Talmud says there were 18 during the first Temple and more than 65 during the second.

(24) "BUT THIS MAN, BECAUSE HE CONTINUETH EVER, HATH AN UN-CHANGEABLE PRIESTHOOD."

The exegesis is:

1. *"This Man"* is the Lord Jesus Christ.

2. His Priesthood is eternal.

3. It is an unchangeable Priesthood, meaning that it will not change to another system, as the Levitical Priesthood did, and because this system is perfect, and because it is totally in Christ.

THIS MAN

The phrase, *"But this Man,"* refers to the Lord Jesus Christ, but in a more particular way, it refers to what He did at the Cross on behalf of lost humanity.

When one begins to properly understand the Cross, i.e., *"the Finished Work of Christ,"* the entirety of the Word of God takes on a brand-new perspective. In other words, the Cross becomes the centrality of the Gospel, and because the Cross is the centrality of the Gospel.

When the writer speaks of Faith, it is instantly understood, that he is speaking of Faith in the great Sacrifice of Christ. The same is with hope, or Grace, etc. When Jesus is addressed, it is always with the thought in mind, of His great Sacrifice. To think of Him in any other manner, is to do violence to His Life, Work, and Ministry, which actually proclaims *"another Jesus"* (II Cor. 11:4).

The Disciples were guilty of portraying Christ in a role other than that which was intended, consequently, objecting when He mentioned being killed in Jerusalem, and being raised again the third day.

Upon this announcement, Peter actually *"began to rebuke Him, saying, be it far from Thee, Lord: this shall not be unto Thee.*

"But He turned, and said unto Peter, 'Get thee behind Me, Satan: thou art an offence unto Me: for thou savourest not the things that be of God, but those that be of men'" (Mat. 16:21-23).

That which is of men, presents a portrayal of Christ in a way other than that intended, which was the Cross. That which was of God,

beyond the shadow of a doubt, was the Cross, which was the destination of the Saviour. So again I emphasize, that when we think of Jesus, we must think of Him in relationship to His great Sacrifice.

EXACTLY WHAT DO WE MEAN BY THAT?

We are not speaking of putting Jesus back on the Cross. Nor are we presenting any power being attached to the wooden beam on which He was crucified. As well, we're certainly not speaking of the idea that Christians are to suffer, and the more they suffer, then the more they are bearing the Cross, etc. None of that is Scripturally correct.

When we speak of the Cross, we are speaking of the benefits which were brought about by what Jesus did at the Cross.

For instance, when we speak of the equality of all people in this country, we're speaking of a bloody Civil War which was fought in order to bring this about, and as well, the legal document of the Emancipation Proclamation. In other words, the freedom of all minorities in this nation, reside in that legal document mentioned, plus the war which was fought to guarantee its benefits, which were also passed by Congress.

However, when we speak of the freedom enjoyed by all as it regards this legal work which was brought about in the Nineteenth Century, we're not meaning that we should go back and fight this war all over again, or draw up another document. We are merely speaking of the benefits which all of this has brought to this nation. And so it is with the Cross.

The Cross is an accomplished fact which took place in the distant past, and will never have to be repeated again. It has continued results, and in fact, results which will never be discontinued.

After plainly rebuking His Disciples, Jesus then said unto them, *"If any man will come after me, let him deny himself, and take up his Cross, and follow Me"* (Mat. 16:24).

The idea is, all of these things which we want from God, can only be obtained by and through what Jesus did at the Cross. If your Pastor isn't preaching that, then he's not preaching the Gospel.

AN EVERLASTING PRIESTHOOD

The phrase, *"Because He continueth ever,"* proclaims the Priesthood of Christ as eternal, while death was inevitable as it regarded the Aaronic Priests.

Why is this so important?

Of course, the reasons are almost innumerable.

First of all, all the Priests in the Levitical order were merely human, whereas Christ is not only human, but as well is God. That one statement alone, changes the complexion to such an extent, that it makes the difference absolutely indescribable. Men being mortal, have their severe limitations, while Christ has no limitations. As well, many of these men, even though Priests, and even though a High Priest, were sinful and wicked; of course, with Christ that was not only *not* the case, it was and is impossible for such to be. He is, as Paul will say in Hebrews 7:26, *"Holy, harmless, undefiled, separate from sinners, and made higher than the Heavens."* So, there is no contest as it regards the difference in the old order and the New.

AN UNCHANGEABLE PRIESTHOOD

The phrase, *"Hath an unchangeable Priesthood,"* refers to not only that which is eternal, but as well, that which will not change as far as its principle is concerned. What He is now, He will be tomorrow, and forever!

Death was inevitable for the Aaronic Priests and it meant the cessation of their exercise of the High Priesthood. But with Christ it is different. He remains forever and thus His Priesthood never has to be continued by another.

The word rendered *"unchangeable"* or *"permanent"* is found nowhere else in the New Testament. It is often understood to mean *"without a successor,"* but this meaning as given here does not seem to be demonstrated.

It actually means, *"that which cannot be transgressed,"* that which is *"inviolable,"* and so unchangeable.

The idea is, the quality of His Life means a quality of Priesthood that cannot be matched by the Levitical Priests, or anyone or anything else for that matter.

(25) "WHEREFORE HE IS ABLE ALSO TO SAVE THEM TO THE UTTERMOST

THAT COME UNTO GOD BY HIM, SEEING HE EVER LIVETH TO MAKE INTERCESSION FOR THEM."

The composition is:

1. Christ is able to save the worst sinner from the worst sins, because He has atoned for all sin.

2. Anyone who comes to God must come by and through the Lord Jesus Christ.

3. This High Priest ever lives, meaning that His Priesthood is eternal, meaning that it will never change.

4. The very presence of Christ guarantees intercession for all Saints as it regards sin.

HE IS ABLE

The phrase, *"Wherefore He is able also to save them to the uttermost,"* proclaims the fact, that Christ Alone has made the only true Atonement for sin. He did this at the Cross. In this Atonement, He addressed all sin, past, present, and future, meaning that there was not one single sin left unatoned; however, to take advantage of this which Christ has so graciously done, one must exercise Faith in His Finished Work. This means, that this Atonement is not automatic for the entirety of mankind. While in fact it is done, its benefits can only accrue to those who exercise Faith in Him (Jn. 3:16).

ATONEMENT

Actually, the word *"Atonement"* is used only one time in the New Testament (Rom. 5:11), and in actuality, it should there have been translated *"Reconciliation."* It is used a little over 75 times in the Old Testament. Nevertheless, Atonement is what Jesus effected at the Cross.

I personally believe that the reason Atonement was used so readily in the Old Testament is because it pointed to that which was to come. In the New Testament, the word would have been inappropriate, because, even though what Jesus did at the Cross definitely was the Atonement, it also included so very much more! At the Cross, He not only effected Atonement, but as well, forgiveness, cleansing, Justification, Sanctification, Reconciliation, Grace, Hope, plus making it possible for the advent of the Holy Spirit in a completely new dimension. In other words, the Cross was and is the means by which man receives from God, anything and everything which he receives.

To be sure, the Sacrifices of old, while speaking to Atonement, spoke to little else, and in fact, effected Atonement only in a partial way.

The word means *"a making it one,"* and points to a process of bringing those who are estranged into a unity, which the Sacrifices of old, could only do in a limited way.

Atonement signifies a harmonious relationship or that which brings about such a relationship, i.e., *"a Reconciliation."* It is principally used of the Reconciliation between God and man effected by the work of Christ. The necessity for such Reconciliation is the breech in the relationship between the Creator and the creature occasioned by man's sinful rebellion.

It is important to note with respect to the Sacrifices of the Old Testament that they bear witness to the rupture of fellowship between God and man the sinner, that they acknowledge the Righteousness of the Divine judgment upon man as a sinner, and, finally, that they constitute a provision for man's forgiveness and Reconciliation to God which has been Divinely appointed.

In fact, all of these ideas are basic to the thinking of the writers of the New Testament. Of course, in the New Testament the thought is added that the sacrifice of bulls and goats could never fully cleanse the conscience from the defilement of sin and as well, appease an offended Deity. Therefore, the Old Testament Sacrifices have their fulfillment in the Death of Christ, Who is the True Lamb of God (Jn. 1:36) Whom God has set forth to be a propitiation through Faith in His Blood (Rom. 3:23-26). It is He Who has obtained eternal Redemption for mankind by His Own Blood, having entered once for all into the Holy Place not made with hands (Heb. 9:11).

One may then say that Sacrifice, and more particular, Blood Sacrifice at that, is the basic New Testament category used to describe the Death of Christ. Because this is true, Atonement — which the Old Testament Sacrifices wrought in a ceremonial way — is the term commonly employed by theologians to describe the Work of Christ.

By the same token, because the meaning of Christ's death is central in the New Testament, a much wider range of Biblical teaching than that bearing on Sacrifice has been included in the meaning of Atonement, to which we have already alluded.

What the Scriptures have to say about the Nature of God, the significance of the Law, the character of sin, the power of demonic forces, the meaning of Salvation, and the coming Resurrection of the Redeemed — all these are Scriptural themes which have been more or less central in the various meanings of the word *"Atonement."*

THE OLD TESTAMENT GREAT DAY OF ATONEMENT

Before elaborating this larger array of ideas involved in interpreting the meaning of the Death of Christ as an Atonement, one must deal, at least in a cursory way, with the meaning of Atonement in the Old Testament, which is foundational to the New Testament Doctrine of Christ's atoning work. The crucial material in this regard concerns the *"Day of Atonement,"* or as it is sometimes referred to *"the Great Day of Atonement."* Of the Several Passages alluding to this day (Lev. 23:26-32; Num. Chpt. 18; 29:7-11), Leviticus, Chapter 16 is of capital importance.

This Chapter gives us a detailed set of instructions, given by the Lord to Moses, concerning the preparations and ceremonies then enacted. It is eminently clear that on this day there was the highest exercise of the High Priest's Mediatorial office.

THE MANNER OF THE HIGH PRIEST

Being a sinner himself and representing a sinful people, he discarded his gorgeous High Priestly garments and, having bathed himself, he assumed an attire which was destitute of all ornament as fitting one who was suing for forgiveness.

On this particular day, which came about once a year, his attire was white, symbolizing the purity required of those who would enter into the Presence of the Holy One of Israel. Being thus prepared and properly dressed, at least in this humble manner, he performed the Sacrifices which climaxed the whole system of purification in Leviticus. By these

Sacrifices, which involved the confession of sin (the High Priest laid his hands on the head of the scapegoat, confessing Israel's transgression, so putting them upon the head of the goat, Lev. 16:21), and the sprinkling of the shed blood seven times toward the Mercy Seat where the Presence of the Lord dwelt, the Priest made Atonement for the sins of the people.

In fact, he went into the Holy of Holies twice on this one day, once for himself, because he was a sinful man, and once for Israel. He offered up blood both times on the Mercy Seat. In fact, the Holy of Holies which was situated immediately behind the Holy Place, separated by a Veil, could be entered only once a year, and it was on this particular Day of Atonement. As well, it could only be entered by the High Priest.

Thus, by a ceremonial act at the central Sanctuary, peace and fellowship with the God of the Covenant were restored. The entire removal of the cause of God's alienation was symbolically set forth, both by the giving of the life of one animal and the sending of another into the wilderness.

ATONEMENT IN THE NEW TESTAMENT

It is the ceremonial of the Great Day of Atonement which constitutes the principal Doctrine as Paul outlines it in Hebrews, regarding his interpretation of the Death of Christ. In his use of the Levitical example to illumine the meaning of Christ's death, one has a striking example of redemptive history. What Christ did is analogous to what the High Priest did in the Old Testament.

As an aside, Paul knew nothing of the approach favored by some, which contrasts the supposed Old Testament view of God, as an angry Deity appeased only by the shedding of Blood. Paul never even alludes to such a thing.

He rather portrayed God as a loving Father Who dispenses the favor of forgiveness freely to all His erring children, at least to those who come to Him through the atoning Work of Christ. Paul plainly says, *"Without the shedding of blood there can be no remission of sins"* (Heb. 9:22).

TYPES

All the symbols and ceremonies in the Old Testament teaching regarding the Atonement

find their true meaning and fulfillment in the New Covenant in Christ's Blood, which Paul constantly proclaims (Mat. 26:28; Heb. 12:24). Christ is the suffering servant of the Lord Who brings Redemption to all mankind.

Along with this fundamental continuity of Redemptive Revelation, there is also a discontinuity, which speaks of some things dropping off.

The Covenant in Christ's Blood is a New Covenant; in fact, Paul in the Book of Hebrews sharply contrasts the work of the High Priest in the Old Testament with that of Christ in the New Testament, particularly in terms of its effectiveness. Whereas every year the ritual of the Day of Atonement was reenacted as the Priest entered the Holy of Holies with the blood of the appointed victim, Christ has entered once and for all into the True Sanctuary, not made with hands, into the Presence of God, to make intercession for us with His Own Blood. He has secured a lasting deliverance for mankind. Access to God is no longer granted to the High Priest alone, who himself was limited to restrictions of time, place, and circumstance. Rather Christ, the Great High Priest, has opened a new and living way to God, a way by which all whose hearts are purged from the guilt of sin may at all times have free access to the Father. Having made Atonement for sin, He has reconciled man to God (Heb., Chpts. 7-10).

Actually, the same basic interpretation of Christ's Death prevails throughout the New Testament. According to Paul, one is justified by the Blood of Christ (Rom. 5:9), for God has set forth Christ to be a propitiation through Faith in His Blood (Rom. 3:25).

As well, both Jews and Gentiles have been reconciled to God by the Cross (Eph. 2:16). Christ has made peace by the Blood of His Cross, reconciling man to God in the body of His flesh through death (Col. 1:20-22).

Christ suffered for all, bearing our sins in His Own body on the Tree, healing us by His stripes (Isa. Chpt. 53; I Pet. 2:24).

Therefore, one can understand the saying of the Lord that the Son of Man came to give His Life a ransom for many (Mat. 20:28), and join with the redeemed in the Book of Revelation in ascribing praise to Him *"Who loves us and has freed us from our sins by His Blood"* (Rev. 1:5-6).

THE DOCTRINE OF THE ATONEMENT

The first point to be made is that the Atonement originated with God; it was He Who provided it. One may trace the development of blood sacrifice, because it was blood sacrifice which was demanded, among the Hebrews, and one will find in both the Priestly and Prophetic writings of the Old Testament it is God Who appointed the various Rites, giving to Moses and those who followed him, instructions concerning the manner in which they were to be rendered which they secured to the worshiper. So it is in the New Testament as well.

The Atonement for sin provided by the Death of Christ had its source in God. It is He Who *"was in Christ reconciling the world to Himself"* (II Cor. 5:19).

LOVE

The ultimate reason for this initiative is not to be found in any necessity laid upon God, but in His free and sovereign will. *"For God so loved the world that He gave His only Begotten Son, that whosoever believes in Him should not perish but have Eternal Life"* (Jn. 3:16). In fact, this is the ultimate of Revelation; i.e., the Atonement finds its ultimate explanation in an unfathomable urge in God toward His sinful and alienated creatures. He has been pleased, for reasons known only to Himself, to set His Love upon those who are unworthy. The Lord has loved men with an everlasting love (Jer. 31:3), and in due time commended that love to us in that while we were yet sinners Christ died for us (Rom. 5:8). This, then, is the final reason for the Atonement.

When Scripture says that God is love (I Jn. 4:7-8), it teaches that love is no incidental aspect of God's Being, something which He may choose to be or not to be at His pleasure. Rather, it is the very essence of His Being.

Though people, at least if they properly evaluate themselves, can discover no reason in themselves, no value or worth which would evoke such love, yet He loves us because He is God Who is love.

The Lord says that He set His love upon His people, not because they were greater in number than any other — for they were the fewest — but because He loved them (Deut. 7:6-8). That is, He loved them (and us) because He loved them; the reason for His love is hidden in Himself Whose Name is, *"I Am Who I Am"* (Ex. 3:14).

AGAPE LOVE

The principle word which the New Testament uses for the Divine Love is *"agape."* Significantly, *"eros,"* the most oft used word for love in Greek philosophy, does not even occur one time in the Bible.

The most plausible explanation is that erotic love, whether it describes the relation of the sexes, or, as in Plato, the aspiration of the soul for ideas, it is the love of the worthy, a love based on value.

By contrast, God's Covenant Love for His people (agape), which moved Him to provide an Atonement for sin, is a love for the unworthy. Even when His people, like an unfaithful wife, went whoring after other gods, the Lord loved them still (Hos. 11:8-9).

"In this is love," wrote John, *"not that we loved God but that He loved us and sent His Son to be the expiation for our sins"* (I Jn. 4:10). This *"Love Divine, all loves excelling"* cannot be frustrated; it is a love, says Paul, from which nothing can separate us (Rom. 8:38-39). The reason for this is that this love is not dependent upon anything in man; it is a love which is sovereign and free.

And yet, even though nothing can separate one from the Love of God, these Passages in Romans, Chapter 8, say nothing about an individual purposely separating himself from God, which one can do, if one is so inclined. In fact, that's what the entirety of the Book of Hebrews is all about.

THE NATURE OF ATONEMENT

How one interprets the Atonement is of great significance, even as should be obvious. To misinterpret the Atonement, i.e., *"the Finished Work of Christ,"* is to misunderstand the entirety of the Plan of God for the human race.

In Mark 10:45 and Matthew 20:28, Jesus said concerning Himself, *"For the Son of Man also came not to be served but to serve, and to give His Life as a ransom for many."*

To ransom someone means to redeem him by purchasing his release through the payment of a price.

From these Passages, some have claimed, and we refer to the Jesus died spiritually doctrine, that Christ gave His soul, in lieu of man's, to the Devil which paid the ransom price of the delivery from his powers. The theory is that since the first parents had sold their souls to the Devil, he had a legal claim over men, which God, in justice, must satisfy. Hence, Jesus gave His soul as the ransom price for man's release and *"descended into Hell,"* and by that statement, they are claiming that He went to the burning side of the Pit. There it is claimed by these Teachers, that Jesus was Born-Again, with it then becoming impossible for Satan to hold Him in Hell. The third day He rose in triumph, taking with Him all whom He had redeemed.

WHAT DID JESUS SAY?

Such teaching is a serious misunderstanding of the Atonement, and any misunderstanding of the Atonement is serious indeed! In fact, there's nothing in the Bible about this which we have just portrayed.

First of all, Jesus did not say that He came to give His Life a ransom to the Devil, and nowhere does the New Testament, in elaborating the Plan of Redemption, make such an affirmation.

It is true that the concept of ransom presupposes bondage, the need of release, and the payment of a price to obtain this release. But the primary emphasis of Scripture is upon what man was and is redeemed from, rather than to whom the ransom is paid. In fact, the overall implication of Scripture is that Christ's atoning work finds its ultimate objective in God; in other words, it is God Who is reconciled; it is His righteous demands which are satisfied, and not the Devil's. To be frank, even though Calvary affected the Devil in a powerful, negative way, the Atonement was not carried out because of Satan, but rather because of God. Man owed a terrible debt to God, not Satan, and it was only by Blood Sacrifice, actually the shedding of the Blood of the Son of God, that this debt could be paid.

NOTES

The entirety of Scripture plainly proclaims that the death of Christ as ransom, was done in order to render payment to God and because men owed Him an uncompromised obedience, which none had rendered. Consequently, this was a debt that man could not pay, but one which was paid by Christ, and paid to God on man's behalf, through His Own obedience unto death, *"even death on a Cross"* (Phil. 2:8).

WHAT THE ATONEMENT BROUGHT ABOUT

Though Scripture in no way proclaims the *"ransom-paid-to-the-Devil"* theory, it definitely does teach that the redeemed are safe from the power of the Devil, which was effected at the Cross. By Jesus atoning for all sin, Satan lost his legal hold upon man, for sin provided that legal hold.

The Devil has sinners under his power; as a cruel taskmaster he drives them to sin. But Christ by His Death redeemed man from this terrible thralldom.

Paul said in Hebrews 2:14 that Christ partook of mankind's flesh and blood, that through death He might destroy him who has the power of death, that is, the Devil. The Holy Spirit through Paul refers to this triumph over principalities and powers, which Christ obtained at the Cross, actually making an open display of them (Col. 2:15).

WHY WAS THE ATONEMENT NECESSARY?

It is a Scriptural and historical fact, that God expressed His love by way of Atonement. In other words, the Cross of Christ was the greatest act of love that mankind has ever known. However, even though prompted by His love to redeem us, God must do so in a manner consistent with His justice. The necessity of the Atonement, then, is an inference to the Character of God.

Sin is a revolt against God, and He must inevitably react against it with wrath. Sin creates an awful liability and the inexorable demands of the Divine Justice must be met.

However, we must understand, that the love which God is, does not stand alone in the Bible. The God of the Bible also exhibits wrath toward His enemies (Nah. 1:2); the Heavenly Father which Jesus portrayed, is as well, to be feared as One *"Who can destroy both soul and body in Hell"* (Mat. 10:28). *"The wrath of God,"* wrote Paul *"is revealed from Heaven against all ungodliness and wickedness of men"* (Rom. 1:18).

In fact, for love to be love, it must be counterbalanced over against hate. If one truly loves, one will also truly hate that which can destroy love.

Therefore, the Death of Christ is the way in which God shows that He is righteous in forgiving sins and justifying him who has Faith in Jesus (Rom. 3:24-26). God justly demands satisfaction for one's sins, and since by Christ's Death satisfaction is given, the sinner is forgiven and the punishment remitted, at least for those who will believe.

What we've just said regarding the Atonement, is actually the Doctrine of substitutionary satisfaction. In other words, God's Righteousness and Holiness had to be satisfied in that sin had to be punished, and it was satisfied by Christ offering Himself as a Substitute in place of mankind.

As well, regarding the type of Atonement which God demanded, and which man could never pay, it was only the God-man, the Lord Jesus Christ, Who could render such Atonement.

CHRIST OUR SUBSTITUTE

According to Isaiah, Chapter 53, which is a beautiful portrayal of the Atonement, the Suffering Servant was wounded for *"our"* transgressions, *"He"* was bruised for *"our"* iniquities, the chastisement of *"our"* peace was upon *"Him,"* and with *"His"* stripes *"we"* are healed.

In the same vein is Paul's affirmation that He *"Who knew no sin was made sin for us, that we might be made the Righteousness of God in Him"* (II Cor. 5:21).

Christ was *not* made a sinner in the sense of being inwardly polluted, for that cannot happen, unless one personally sins, which Christ did not do. Rather He was reckoned a sinner, which means that He would suffer the penalty for sin, even though He had never sinned; consequently, man's sin and its penalty were imputed to Him, even as His Righteousness was imputed to men. In Himself He bore the condemnation of sin so that to

those who are in Christ Jesus there is now no condemnation (Rom. 8:1).

He was *"made a curse for us,"* which means that He was due no curse, and, therefore, had to make such. In other words, He took the curse of the broken Law upon Himself in our stead, which means He died for us. He did this, in order to make man the Righteousness of God in Him (Gal. 3:13).

Christ rendered a vicarious (substitutionary) satisfaction for sin. It was not by substituting something in the place of the penalty, but rather by a vicarious enduring of the penalty which was death.

CALVARY

Calvary was the one great super act of history which relieved God of any necessity to punish the sinner. However, even though the emphasis in Scripture is on the Death of Christ, it should not be overlooked that His Death, according to Scripture, is the climax of His life of perfect obedience. *"He . . . became obedient unto death, even death on a Cross"* (Phil. 2:8).

"Although He was a Son, He learned obedience through what He suffered" (Heb. 5:8).

In Romans 5:12-19, there is an express reference to Christ's one act of *"obedience,"* in contrast to the disobedience of the first Adam, an act of obedience by which the many are made righteous. And so Christ becomes the Perfect High Priest, having not only removed the sanction of the broken Law by being made a curse, but also having fulfilled the requirements of the Law by His sinless life, thus achieving a perfect Righteousness.

THE RESULT OF THE ATONEMENT

The Christian response to the Death of Christ is to *"rejoice in God through our Lord Jesus Christ, through Whom we have now received our Reconciliation"* (Rom. 5:8-11). Hence Paul can describe the Work of Christ on the Cross, in the beautiful figure of a Ministry of Reconciliation. As an Ambassador of Christ who had been entrusted with the Message of Reconciliation, he and all Believers for that matter, should beseech all men, on behalf of Christ, to be reconciled to God (II Cor. 5:18-21). The Atonement and the Atonement alone, made Reconciliation possible!

While Atonement makes possible the Love of God shed abroad in the hearts and lives of all Believers, delivering to us the Grace of God with all of its hope and power, still, the greatest accomplishment of the Atonement, is the privilege of the sinner once again being reconciled to God.

At the Fall man was separated from God, and because of sin, i.e., *"disobedience."* In fact, sin is a direct affront to our Maker. It is in effect saying that we know more about life and all things for that matter, than the Creator. Once we see it in that light, we see how foolish it is for the creature to think that he can know more than the Creator.

In all of this, it must be remembered that it is God Who has been offended. It is God Who has been slighted, i.e., *"insulted."* Consequently, God feels this insult while man feels it not at all.

In fact, man being spiritually dead as a result of the Fall, has no feelings whatsoever toward God. He doesn't know God, doesn't understand God, and because, as stated, he is spiritually dead.

Because of love, as we have stated, God set about to redeem man, because in fact, love must redeem man. And it must do so, irrespective of the price that must be paid. In fact, the price was so high, that man could not hope to pay such a debt, which remained for God to carry out the payment. That payment was the Cross.

SIN DID THIS

Look upon the horrible scene of Calvary. A scene so horrible that it's impossible for man to even begin to contemplate the darkness of that moment when Christ took upon Himself the penalty for lost mankind. He paid a debt He did not owe, a debt in fact, we could not pay.

And when you look at the suffering of this agony, the horror of what Jesus had to do in order to pay this debt, knowing that His physical suffering was only a minor part of all that He endured, we can only say *"sin did this!"* In fact, *"my sin did this."*

Calvary is the only thing that stood and stands between mankind and eternal Hell. If we don't understand that, then we don't understand the Plan of God.

NOTES

That's the reason that if we misinterpret the Cross, we have misinterpreted what all of this is all about. To misunderstand anything in the Bible is serious, but to misunderstand the Atonement, is to misunderstand the very heart of the matter.

If the Atonement is to become a personal reality in the individual life, there must be this radical, inward change, the response of love to love on the part of the sinner, which can only be brought about by and through the *"born again"* experience (Jn. 3:3). And that can be brought about only by one evidencing Faith in Christ and what He did at the Cross, i.e., *"the Atonement."*

THE PERFECTION OF THE ATONEMENT

Many have argued the question as to whether this or that is in the Atonement, etc. The Truth is, everything that man lost in the Fall, and we mean everything, was included in the Atonement. In other words, it was a perfect Atonement which excluded nothing, and included all things which pertains to life and living, which pertains to God and man.

However, even though that is true, and I speak of a perfect Atonement, we have not yet realized all the benefits of the Atonement, and in fact, will not realize all the benefits until the coming Resurrection.

While Jesus definitely atoned for all sin, the Truth is, Believers, even the Godliest, at times sin. But that in no way negates the fact, that Jesus atoned for all sin.

As well, Jesus paid the price for our total and complete health, in other words, Divine Health. And yet, Christians, even the Godliest, still get sick and ultimately die. In fact, Paul plainly tells us that the body is not redeemed (Rom. 8:23). This refers to the fact that the full benefits of what Jesus accomplished at the Atonement, will be carried out only in the coming Resurrection. That's why Christ is referred to as the *"Firstfruits."* From His Resurrection and His being glorified, we have a general idea as to what the coming Resurrection will be.

The foolishness over arguing whether this or that is in the Atonement, is foolishness indeed! As stated, everything that man lost in the Fall is in the Atonement. And to be sure, the Atonement of Christ was not a limited Atonement as some teach. It was full and complete, total and absolute, and in every respect.

At times, certain individuals attempt to bring all the benefits of the Atonement which can only be had in the coming Resurrection, over into the present. But misinterpretation should not be misunderstood as weakness of the Atonement, but only the brashness of particular individuals who should know better.

To limit what Christ did at the Cross is a sin. Pure and simple it is a sin, and can be defined in no other way. It just remains for us to understand when all things will be fulfilled, even as Paul explains in Romans, Chapter 8. He said:

"For I reckon that the sufferings of this present time are not worthy to be compared with the glory which shall be revealed in us" (Rom. 8:18).

Even though all the glory of which the Apostle speaks has not yet been revealed, to be sure, the Atonement made it possible for that Glory to be revealed, which it definitely shall be at that coming day.

And one more thought:

The Atonement is also universal; that refers to men from every nation, tribe, people, and tongue, to which the door has been opened, who take advantage of the great invitation. And to be sure, many will. They (we) shall one day stand before the Lamb clothed in white with palms of victory in our hands (Rev. 7:9).

If it is to be noticed, John used the appellative *"Lamb,"* when describing this great scene in Heaven.

It is because all of this great and glorious Salvation has been made possible by what Jesus did at the Cross. We must never, never forget that!

COME TO GOD BY HIM

The phrase, *"That come unto God by Him,"* proclaims the only manner in which men can come to God, which is through and by the Lord Jesus Christ. And to be more particular, it is by and through what He did at the Cross on our behalf, and our Faith in that.

Once again, we go back to the great Truth, that when Paul mentions Christ, and in any capacity, it is always in connection with the Cross. If we as well, do not think of Christ in that manner, then we are not properly interpreting Christ. The Scripture is abundantly clear upon this principle.

Man is not able to come to God through Jesus Christ simply because Christ is God. That's the horrendous mistake that the Catholics make in regard to their worship of Mary, thinking that she is access to Christ or the Father, etc. If man could not come to God through Jesus Christ simply because He was and is the Son of God, and understanding the magnitude of that, how in the world does he think he can come to God through a mere human being such as Mary or any other mortal?

No! We do not have access to God through Christ because He is the Son of God, or because He was and is the greatest Healer, or the greatest miracle worker, or that He is Perfect, etc., but rather because of the great Sacrifice of Himself. That and that alone gives us access to the Father.

Paul also said, *"But now in Christ Jesus ye who sometimes were far off are made nigh by the Blood of Christ"* (Eph. 2:13). This plainly tells us, that it was and is the great Sacrifice of Christ which made it possible for us to come to God.

The Apostle then said, *"For through Him we both* (Jews and Gentiles) *have access by one Spirit unto the Father"* (Eph. 2:18).

The idea presented here is access to the Father is allowed by the Spirit only on one basis, and that is through our Faith in the Shed Blood of Christ. If we try to come any other way, the Holy Spirit bars the entrance.

The short phrase *"one Spirit,"* is somewhat strange. It means, that it is the Spirit Alone Who grants entrance. He does so strictly on the basis of the great Sacrifice of Christ, and our Faith in that. In other words, if we try to come to God through any other method, or by any other way, other than Faith in the Finished Work of Christ, the Holy Spirit will bar the entrance.

Jesus Himself addressed this when He said, *"Verily, verily, I say unto you, he that entereth not by the door into the sheepfold, but climbeth up some other way, the same is a thief and a robber"* (Jn. 10:1).

As well, the Believer must understand, that the *"door"* mentioned here, is a *"bloody door."*

The Master no doubt, was going back to the deliverance of the Children of Israel from Egypt, when they were told to kill a lamb, and then *"take of the blood, and strike it on the two side posts and on the upper door-post of the houses"* (Ex. 12:7). He then said:

"And the blood shall be to you for a token upon the houses where ye are: and when I see the blood, I will pass over you, and the plague shall not be upon you to destroy you" (Ex. 12:13).

The blood had to be applied to the doorposts, and then the individuals must go in the house and remain there. The blood which represented the Crucifixion and Death of the coming Redeemer was their safety and protection. It has not changed from then until now, and in fact, never will change.

Again I go back to what Paul said: *"But now in Christ Jesus you . . . are made nigh by the Blood of Christ"* (Eph. 2:13).

INTERCESSION

The phrase, *"Seeing He ever liveth to make intercession for them,"* actually refers to *"intervention."* It includes every form of Christ identifying Himself with humanity, and includes the idea of intercession, but is far more.

We must be careful not to infer from this Verse, or from the last phrase of Hebrews 9:24, that Paul thought of our Lord as having to maintain a kind of continuous liturgical action in Heaven for our benefit, in other words, constantly having to ask the Father to forgive us on His behalf (the behalf of Christ). Nothing like that takes place.

The meaning is that our Lord's very Presence in Heaven, seated at God's right hand, and awaiting the full manifestation of His already achieved victory, itself constitutes His effective intercession for us. In other words, His very person in the Presence of the Father says that He has already finished the work, and guarantees what is needed by any and all Saints. Christ does not have to do anything more.

If we maintain, that He has to engage in some type of action, or even conversation with the Father, in order to gain something for us, the very fact of such thinking says that He has not yet finished the task. And we know, that such thinking is wrong.

It must be stressed that there is no thought of Christ in this statement as given by Paul as conducting Himself as some type of humble supplicant on our behalf. Rather, He is supreme and His very Presence in Heaven in His Character as the One Who died for mankind and rose again is itself as intercession. Again, His very Presence before the Throne of God, which proclaims a work completed, is within itself all that is needed.

As well, the Intercession Ministry of Jesus is not now, nor will it ever be, on behalf of the unredeemed. This intercession is for Saints, and pertains to sin or failure on the part of the Saint. But there is a condition:

We must come to Him, repent of sin, confess Jesus Christ as Lord, and believe in our hearts that He will cleanse and forgive (I Jn. 1:9).

The idea is, no matter what has happened, no matter how vile it has been, no matter what sins have been committed, or how wicked our actions have been, for all sin is wicked with no exceptions, the Truth is, *"if we confess our sins, He will be faithful and just to forgive us our sins, and to cleanse us from all unrighteousness."* We need never fear that this will not be done.

However, no Believer must ever get the idea, due to the fact that forgiveness is available, that sin is not all that serious. Even though forgiveness is definitely always available, to be sure, sin is very serious. No person leaves unscathed and unmarked, even though Christ does forgive.

INTERCESSION BY THE HOLY SPIRIT AND INTERCESSION BY CHRIST

The intercession provided by the Holy Spirit and the intercession provided by Christ are two different things.

Concerning the Holy Spirit Paul said, *"Likewise the Spirit also helpeth our infirmities: for we know not what we should pray for as we ought: but the Spirit itself* (Himself) *maketh intercession for us with groanings which cannot be uttered"* (Rom. 8:26).

The type of intercession that the Holy Spirit does for us as stated here, has to do with prayer. He guides us in praying, telling us how to pray, and for what to pray. And there are even times that we cannot put what we need into words, and He in fact doesn't give us anything to say, except an intense, longing desire, described as *"groanings"* which are interpreted by the Lord, and which meets the need.

"Infirmities" as used in this Verse are *"asthenia,"* and means *"want of strength, weakness."* The weakness spoken of here is defined by the context which speaks of prayer, one of the things in the spiritual realm in which our weakness needs His power. The infirmities here, therefore, are not physical, but spiritual. As stated, they have to do with prayer.

This is the reason that a proper prayer life as it regards each individual Believer is very important. And the tragedy is, many, if not most, Christians have little prayer life, if any, which negates this all-important help which the Holy Spirit gives.

Countless times, as I go to prayer, the Spirit of God will literally take over, and help me to pray about certain things which I could not do without His leading and guidance.

Just last night in our evening prayer meeting, which we conduct every night with the exception of Service nights, the Holy Spirit brought something to my mind concerning what the Lord had done in my life and in this Ministry in the last few years. I speak of the Revelation of the Cross. He then told me that if this was brought to pass, and I continue to speak of this Revelation, then the other things, for which I have so long sought, would also come to pass. Concerning this, there was a deep peace that filled my heart, along with an assurance. In fact, this happens constantly, but never often enough.

Whereas the Intercession provided by the Holy Spirit is more in the realm of help, the Intercession provided by Christ is, as previously stated, totally different.

The intercession provided by Christ, pertains solely to His Finished Work on the Cross and in His Resurrection, and has to do with sin. While the Spirit is definitely involved in this, as He is involved in everything, it is Christ, and actually His very presence which guarantees such intercession on behalf of the Saints, and because He is the One Who paid the price at Calvary's Cross.

So we have two members of the Godhead interceding for us, the Holy Spirit as it regards prayer, and Christ as it regards sin.

(26) "FOR SUCH AN HIGH PRIEST BECAME US, WHO IS HOLY, HARMLESS, UNDEFILED, SEPARATE FROM SINNERS, AND MADE HIGHER THAN THE HEAVENS;"

The exegesis is:

1. Jesus Christ is the type of High Priest that we need, meaning that God literally became man in order to meet our needs.

2. The Character of this High Priest is perfect, whereas those under the Levitical order were anything but perfect.

3. Even though He took the penalty for sin, He has never sinned, which completely destroys the *"Jesus died spiritually doctrine."* While Jesus definitely died physically, He did not die spiritually. He was separate from sinners when He came to this world, lived separate from sinners in His earthly life, but yet suffered the penalty of the sinner on the Cross, which was death. In fact, He could not have suffered such a penalty, which would have been accepted by God, had He not been *"separate from sinners."* The Sacrifice had to be perfect.

4. He is *"higher than the heavens"* simply because He is the Saviour; *"Wherefore God also hath highly exalted Him, and given Him a Name which is above every Name"* (Phil. 2:9).

SUCH AN HIGH PRIEST

The phrase, *"For such an High Priest became us,"* presents the fact that no one less exalted could have met the necessities of the human race. The idea is, there was and is an essential fitness in the provision God made in Christ as High Priest of the Believer. That essential fitness consists of the qualities mentioned in Verses 26-28. That is, we sinners, being sinful and dependent upon the mediation of a Priest, needed a sinless one.

As would be obvious, this was a great contrast to the Aaronic Priests who were themselves sinners and who needed in the last analysis a High Priest to mediate Salvation for them. This One, the Lord of Glory, needs no Mediator, and because He is *"holy, harmless, undefiled, separate from sinners."*

The idea in all of this is not that He should be of a rank superior to that of the Jewish Priesthood, although He certainly is that, but that there was a special propriety that He should surpass all others in *"moral"* purity. Other Priests were mere mortal men, and it was necessary that their office should pass to other hands: as well, and as stated, they were sinful men also, and it was necessary that sacrifices should be made for themselves as well as others. However, humanity as a whole needs something totally different.

We need not only one who ever lives, but one who is perfectly holy, and who has no need to bring an offering for himself, and all the merit of whose sacrifice, therefore, may be ours, and because the need is ours. Such a High Priest we have in the Person of the Lord Jesus; and there is no Truth more interesting, and no proposition more susceptible of proof, than that *"He is exactly fitted to man."*

In His moral Character, which is perfect incidentally, and in the great work which He has accomplished, He is just such a Saviour as is adapted to the wants of ignorant, fallen, wretched, sinful man.

He is kind, gracious, benevolent, and pities our woes; wise, and is able to enlighten our ignorance; compassionate, and ready to forgive our faults. But above all, He has made such a Sacrifice as was necessary to put away our guilt, and offer such intercession as we need to have offered for us in order that we may be preserved from falling (Barnes).

PERFECT

The phrase, *"Who is holy, harmless, undefiled, separate from sinners,"* describes the spotless, pure, perfect character of the Son of God, our Great High Priest. This statement by Paul is given in order to demonstrate the difference between Christ and the Jewish Priests, who were not at all of this caliber, who in fact, couldn't be of this caliber, with some of them being downright evil. The idea is this:

The Holy Spirit through the Apostle describing Christ in this fashion, which actually includes the entirety of the Book, leaves the Reader with one choice. He either believes that Jesus Christ is the Son of God, therefore, in a league and class by Himself, at least as it refers to human beings, which in that case settles the question, or else he believes that Christ is an imposter and blasphemer,

which would mean that He, character wise, would be much less than the Jewish Priests. There is no middle ground! This means that the Holy Spirit is pulling these Christian Jews to a decision. If they desert Christ, they cannot do so claiming that He is a good man, etc., but that they merely prefer the old order; instead, if they take that leap into the dark, and a leap into the dark it will be, they have to completely renounce Christ, and do so in every capacity, which is actually what Paul said in Chapter 6.

As well, let us understand, that this great decision which had to be made, was not incumbent only upon those Christian Jews of Paul's day, but the same question must be answered by all even at the present time.

Who is Jesus Christ?

The Word of God, and the testimonies of untold millions, graphically proclaim exactly Who and What He is. He is the Son of the Living God, the Saviour of mankind, and in fact, the only Saviour. So, there is no excuse whatsoever for anyone in the world, not knowing Who and What Jesus actually is.

This means that to reject Him is to do so in full face of an abundance of light, meaning there is no excuse!

HIGHER THAN THE HEAVENS

The phrase, *"And made higher than the Heavens,"* refers to the fact that He is seated at the Right Hand of the Father, which is the most exalted position in Heaven or Earth.

QUALIFICATIONS

In Verses 23-28, the contrast is between the dying Priests of the old order and the ever living High Priest at God's Right Hand. There was a constant succession of Priests in olden days, for death was continually taking its toll of them. But our Lord's Priesthood is unchangeable because He continues *"unto the ages,"* the strongest expression in the Greek language for eternity.

Thus, as the ever-living One, He is able to deliver completely those who draw near to God by Him, seeing He ever liveth to make intercession for them.

And thus our souls are stirred to worship and thanksgiving as we realize how suited our Great High Priest is to the need of those who were once unholy, harmful, and defiled, sinful and degraded; for He gives us a perfect representation before the Throne of God. He is everything that we were not and should have been. He is holy, harmless, undefiled, and separate from sinners and higher than the Heavens, and He is all this for us.

What could the Spirit of God Himself say to make clearer the superiority of the Priesthood of the new dispensation over that of the old?

(27) "WHO NEEDETH NOT DAILY, AS THOSE HIGH PRIESTS, TO OFFER UP SACRIFICE, FIRST FOR HIS OWN SINS, AND THEN FOR THE PEOPLE'S: FOR THIS HE DID ONCE, WHEN HE OFFERED UP HIMSELF."

The composite is:

1. Daily sacrifices under the old economy were demanded, and because those sacrifices were imperfect.

2. The High Priest even when going into the Holy of Holies, had to offer up two sacrifices, the first for himself, because he as well was a sinful man, and the second for the people.

3. Christ offered up only one Sacrifice, the Sacrifice of Himself, which need never be repeated, and as well, demanded the cessation of all other sacrifices.

DAILY SACRIFICES

The phrase, *"Who needeth not daily,"* refers to the daily sacrifices offered by the Priests. The morning sacrifice was at 9:00 a.m., with the evening sacrifice at 3:00 p.m. In fact, Jesus was put on the Cross at 9:00 a.m., and died at 3:00 p.m., therefore, satisfying both sacrifices. (The sacrifices were doubled on the Sabbath, offering up two animals instead of one each time.)

Some have attempted to attach the High Priest to the entirety of this Verse; however, I feel that Paul while addressing the High Priest, is as well, addressing the entire Priesthood, and their functions. The High Priests did not offer up daily sacrifices, that being the domain of the regular Priests.

Jesus did not have to offer up a sacrifice daily, or any other time for that matter, at least as it referred to personal sin. While He did *"keep the Feasts,"* that was as far as He

went regarding sacrifices. As well, those sacrifices offered up on the Feast Days, such as the Passover, etc., were actually symbolic of the coming Messiah. These Sacrifices more so specified the Ministry and Work of the coming Redeemer, than they did personal sin.

NO SACRIFICE REQUIRED FOR CHRIST

The phrase, *"As those High Priests, to offer up sacrifice, first for his own sins, and then for the people's,"* refers to the work of the High Priest on the Great Day of Atonement, which specified their unworthiness. Christ did not have to function accordingly.

When the High Priest went into the Holy of Holies on this specific day, which He did once a year, he had to go in twice with the blood of two sacrifices, the first time for himself, and the second time for the people of Israel.

This portrayed in glaring detail, that even though he was the High Priest, which in effect was the highest spiritual office in Israel, the fact was, he was also a sinful man requiring sacrifice.

Every Jew knew this; so why would they desire such a frail, flawed, mortal, in place of Christ?

Why do men and women presently seek to find the Peace of God in a human institution such as the Church, while having no relationship with Christ, especially considering that He is available to all?

ONE SACRIFICE

The phrase, *"For this He did once, when He offered up Himself,"* refers to His Death on the Cross, which atoned for all sin and for all time, past, present, and future, making no further sacrifices necessary.

The High Priests of old, had to offer up sacrifices for themselves, for they were themselves unclean, and then they offered on behalf of the people. But these sacrifices never settled the sin question.

He, by His one offering up of Himself upon the Cross, has completed the work that saves, and settled the sin question for all eternity.

The Law constituted men High Priests who were themselves infirm and unreliable, but the Divine Oath has proclaimed Jesus to be a Priest forever, He Who is as to the mystery of His Person, the Son of the Eternal Father.

With the Priesthood, of course, is linked the entire sacrificial system. No Jew ever found settled peace or a purged conscience through recourse to the Altar and the Priest of the Tabernacle or the Temple. Undoubtedly wherever there was real Faith, God met His people in Grace and by the Spirit, gave them an inward sense of acceptance and joy in Himself, but this was not based upon the Levitical system.

All of this was in view of the eventual coming into the world of the Seed of the woman, Who was to bruise the serpent's head and to be Himself wounded for His people's transgressions and bruised for their iniquities.

The pious Israelite obeyed the Commandment of the Law and acted in accordance with the Mosaic ritual because God had so ordained for the time then present. Faith would lead them to do exactly as the Lord had said, as it regarded the Levitical system, but the ground of peace rested not on the typical system but on that which it illustrated, the Finished Work of Christ. In other words, the sacrifices of old never saved anyone. But Jews who evidenced Faith in the One to Whom the Sacrifices pointed, did find Salvation, which God had all along intended.

It was hard even for Christian Jews to fully realize this, hence the care with which the Holy Spirit through the Apostle takes up each detail in His effort to deliver them from Judaism and bring them out into the full light of the Glory of Christ.

THE SIN-OFFERING

Paul used the phrase *"He offered up Himself,"* in this Verse, and then in Hebrews 9:14, He also said, *"Christ Who through the Eternal Spirit offered Himself without spot to God."* Both phrases speak of the Cross. There He voluntarily became the great Sin-Offering.

It is important to remember that the Death of Christ was not merely man's answer to the Grace of God as seen in Christ. None could have put Him to death had He not of His Own volition yielded up His life. He Himself declared, *"No man taketh My life from Me, but I lay it down of Myself. I have power to lay it down, and I have power to take it again.*

This Commandment have I received of My Father" (Jn. 10:18).

In the fullest possible sense He laid down that life voluntarily when He allowed wicked men to nail Him to that Cross. There He took the sinner's place and bore the sinner's judgment. We speak of this as the Finished Work of Christ.

But when we think of His High Priesthood we are on other ground altogether.

This is His unfinished work, the work that will never be completed as long as any of His Redeemed are in the place of testing and in need of help (Ironside).

(28) "FOR THE LAW MAKETH MEN HIGH PRIESTS WHICH HAVE INFIRMITY; BUT THE WORD OF THE OATH, WHICH WAS SINCE THE LAW, MAKETH THE SON, WHO IS CONSECRATED FOR EVERMORE."

The structure is:

1. The Levitical order was grossly inferior, because it could rise no higher than the performance of man, which was and is inadequate.

2. The *"Word of the Oath"* is the Word of God as it pertains to the Promise of a coming Redeemer, Who would as well be the Great High Priest.

3. The promise was given that all of this would replace the Law, with the Oath actually being given some 500 years after the Law was given.

4. This High Priest is the Son of God, thereby greatly superior.

5. He is consecrated to this task of Redemption and all that it pertains.

6. His Priesthood is eternal, so man doesn't have to worry about there being a change. This New Covenant is an *"Everlasting Covenant"* (Heb. 13:20).

THE INFERIORITY OF MEN

The phrase, *"For the Law maketh men High Priests which have infirmity,"* refers to the fact that it was an imperfect system, and it was obvious that it was imperfect, which demanded that it only be temporary.

The word *"infirmity"* as it is here used in the Greek is *"astheneian,"* and means infirmity as a general characteristic. In other words, due to the Fall, the weakness was such, that there was no way the Levitical Order could adequately suffice. While it may serve as a stopgap measure, it was at best only that.

So Paul is saying to these Christian Jews, *"Do you want to go back to that? Do you not see the inadequacy of that system? Do you not realize that by the obviousness of this inadequacy that God only meant for it to be temporary?"*

It is very difficult for men to trade what they can see for that which they cannot see. And what do we mean by that?

The Levitical System was obvious with all its rituals and ceremonies, which have a tendency to impress the beholder; however, the Priesthood of Christ is invisible, but yet the following must be noted:

The Levitical Priesthood being only a symbol, actually addressed the true spiritual need of the supplicant very little. Rituals and ceremonies simply can have no effect on man's spiritual needs. As well, the blood of bulls and goats could not take away sin. Proper Faith in what all of this represented, no doubt was a blessing to the Israelites who eagerly sought to follow the Lord, but that was as far as the system could go.

This is not to be misunderstood, in that true Believers under the old economy definitely were saved; however, it should be overly obvious that they didn't have the benefits that we presently have under Christ.

Even though the Priesthood of Christ is presently invisible, still, the results of that Priesthood are obvious to all. It keeps the way open between the Believer and God, always providing instant access. As well, it guarantees the effectiveness of the Shed Blood which was carried out at the Cross, and our Faith in that.

Again I emphasize, that even though this Priesthood cannot be seen, its effects can definitely be felt and seen and constantly.

THE OATH

The phrase, *"But the Word of the Oath,"* pertains to Psalms 110:4. It was the Promise of God that He was going to institute a Priesthood that would be far superior to the old, Levitical Order.

Even though it was definitely a Promise, it was in effect, far more than that. It was a guarantee if you will, that this thing would

NOTES

be done. And so it was, because God always keeps His Word.

This means that the Oath has the last word, not the Law.

SINCE THE LAW

The phrase, *"Which was since the Law,"* refers to the fact that the Oath was given some 500 years after the Law was given to Moses.

The Law served its purpose, but it was not sufficient for the final transaction.

For instance, on the Great Day of Atonement, the High Priest under the old Law, washed his hands and feet; he put off his precious and colorful robe, and clothed himself in spotless linen. There was brought to him a bullock which he had purchased with his own money.

He laid his hands upon the bullock's head to transfer his sin to the bullock, and thus he made confession. The High Priest prayed the prayer of transgression and forgiveness; he confessed his sins.

The greatest of all the Levitical Sacrifices began with the Sacrifice for the sins of the High Priest himself. This is an offering our Lord never needed to offer.

Consequently, Paul reminds the Readers that the Law had made weak, ineffective men to be Priests, which is all it could do, but the Priesthood of Christ was and is vastly superior.

Christ is not infirm or weak. He is able to save to the uttermost, for He lives eternally, making intercession for the Saints. His was the only Priesthood of such perfection that God confirmed it with an oath.

This means that our High Priest is able to save the Believer: body, soul, and spirit. He is able to do all that is necessary to bring us to Eternal Salvation. He has identified Himself with man completely so as to be the Perfect High Priest. His once-for-all Sacrifice of Himself has given Him a basis upon which to intercede on our behalf and to intervene in our needs (Fjordbak).

So, the Law, unable to bring men to perfection, must give way to the One Who can, the Lord Jesus Christ.

THE SON

The phrase, *"Maketh the Son,"* refers of course to the Saviour.

The idea is, the Oath appointed the Son. Actually, Psalms 110:4 which speaks of the Oath, does not mention the Son, Who is referred to in Psalm 2. But Paul sees both Psalms as referring to Jesus; so he has no difficulty in applying terminology taken from the one to a situation relating to the other.

CONSECRATED

The phrase, *"Who is consecrated,"* means that He and He Alone, can function in this capacity. He has been consecrated by God to serve as our High Priest; He has done so, and He is doing so, and He ever shall do so!

FOREVER

The short phrase, *"For evermore,"* means that this Covenant is perfect, and because the Son is Perfect, and because what He did is perfect.

Three essentials belong to Priesthood:
1. Appointment.
2. Sanctification.
3. Consecration.

These appear in type in the Book of Leviticus. In the Messiah, Sonship and Priesthood are united. God's original purpose proclaimed Priesthood in the firstborn. This gave way to the Levitical Priesthood which was, as stated, also a temporary institution.

On Aaron's appointment as High Priest he was first baptized and then anointed (Lev. Chpt. 8). His sons were not anointed until after a Sin-Offering had been made for them. So Christ was baptized and then anointed (Mat. 3:16-17). He needed no Sin-Offering.

Consecration is the completion of Sanctification. He sanctified Himself (Jn. 17:17) — *"I sanctify Myself in order that they may be truly sanctified."*

This was the final act in His consecration as High Priest of His people. Hence He is not ashamed to call them Brethren (Heb. 2:11) for they and He are one, just as Aaron and his sons were one. His Priestly garments which the Spirit put upon Him are described in Luke 4:18. They were the Holy garments, so to speak.

PRIESTLY WORDS

"Sanctify" and *"consecrate"* are Priestly words (Ex. Chpt. 28; Lev. Chpt. 8). The one is the completion of the other (Heb. 7:9, 28; 10:14).

Sanctification means separation wholly to God — consecration means *"a filled hand"*; and when the hand is full it needs no more. Hence the word *"perfection"* in respect of Christ's Priesthood in this Epistle.

Having accomplished the one great satisfying obligation for sin, Christ passed through the Heavens and entered upon His Ministry there as a perfected High Priest; and there He remains.

Aaron entered the Most Holy Place, but only once a year and then withdrew immediately. Christ entered the Heavenly Sanctuary and sat down, there to remain forever. There was no seat for Aaron in the earthly Tabernacle, for his ministry could never settle the question of sin and its judgment.

MELCHIZEDEK

Abraham was the greatest of the Patriarchs due to the Call of God on his life, but Melchizedek was greater than he, due to the fact that his Call was even higher. In blessing Abraham he brought forth bread and wine. These signified the fullness of creation blessing in Heaven and Earth.

Corn springs from the Earth; the grape hangs down from above. Melchizedek represented the Most High God, Possessor of Heaven and Earth. At the Last Supper the true Melchizedek brought forth bread and wine and spake of the Kingdom of Millennial Blessing which they signify (Mat. 26:29; Mk. Chpt. 14; Lk. 22:15; Rom. 8:21).

THE SACRIFICE

Two great statements now appear — the nature of the Sacrifice and where it entered.

No such sacrifice as this, was ever seen in the universe before, nor could be seen. It was the offering for sin of Him Who was both God and Man in One Person. This Sacrifice did not, like the Aaronic, enter into an earthly sanctuary, but into Heaven itself. This great Sacrifice resulting in the blessing and restoration of the fallen creation was purposed by God from before the foundation of the world, as appears from Job, Chapter 28 and many other Scriptures (I Pet. 1:18-20).

At the last Passover Christ as Melchizedek signified, in the first cup, the deliverance of creation; and as the Passover Lamb He signified in the last cup, the deliverance of His people. Both these deliverances are secured by His offering up Himself.

Melchizedek suddenly appears after the slaughter of the kings. Up till then he was hidden. The true Melchizedek is now hidden but will appear in blessing after the destruction of the kings of Revelation, Chapter 19. As King of Righteousness He will judge the wicked, and as King of Peace He will bless the Earth.

Peace does not displace Righteousness but is based upon it. These are all Millennial Glories reserved for Israel and the redeemed nations; but the Church being one with Him will share all His glories whether heavenly or earthly (Williams).

*"Ask ye what great thing I know, that
delights and stirs me so?
"What the high reward I win? Whose
Name I glory in?
"Jesus Christ, the Crucified."*

*"What is Faith's foundation strong?
What awakes my lips to song?
"He Who bore my sinful load,
purchased for me peace with God,
"Jesus Christ, the Crucified."*

*"Who is life, in life to me? Who the
death of death will be?
"Who will place me on His right with
the countless hosts of light?
"Jesus Christ, the Crucified."*

*"This is that great thing I know; this
delights and stirs me so;
"Faith in Him Who died to save, Him
Who triumphed o'er the grave,
"Jesus Christ, the Crucified."*

CHAPTER 8

(1) "NOW OF THE THINGS WHICH WE HAVE SPOKEN THIS IS THE SUM: WE HAVE SUCH AN HIGH PRIEST, WHO IS SET ON THE RIGHT HAND OF THE THRONE OF THE MAJESTY IN THE HEAVENS;"

The composition is:

1. The first phrase should have been translated, *"Now of the things which we have spoken, the following is the sum."*

NOTES

2. We have a High Priest Who has met every requirement and supplied every need of the human race.

3. The very fact that He has sat down at the Right Hand of the Throne of God, proclaims the fact, that His Work is a Finished Work.

THE SUM

The phrase, *"Now of the things which we have spoken this is the sum,"* refers to what Paul will now give as it regards the meaning of all this.

The two Priests having been contrasted in the prior Chapter, the two Covenants, the two Sanctuaries, the two Mediators, the two Ministers, and the Better Promises and their foundation are now set out, and the superiority of those founded upon the Messiah as High Priest declared (Williams).

In this Chapter Paul uses several very important expressions to establish the excellence of Christ's Ministry over that of the Earthly priesthood of Israel. He says:

1. Christ as High Priest *"is set on the Right Hand of the Throne of the Majesty in the Heavens."*

2. Our High Priest is *"a Minister of the Sanctuary, and of the True Tabernacle."*

3. Our High Priest *"is the Mediator of a Better Covenant."*

4. The Covenant that He mediates is based on *"Better Promises."*

In contrast, Paul points out that the earthly Priesthood of the Aaronic order, with its sacrifices and holy places is only *"the example and shadow of heavenly things."* Christ's Ministry as Priest is more excellent because He fulfilled all the types in Himself (Fjordbak).

SUCH AN HIGH PRIEST

The phrase, *"We have such an High Priest, Who is set on the Right Hand of the Throne of the Majesty in the Heavens,"* is said in this manner, not merely to prove His present place and position, but rather what it all means. The points below will explain at least some of what it means:

1. The very fact that Christ is now seated in the Heavens at the Right Hand of God, proves that His Work is a Finished Work, which means that nothing will ever have to

be added. This means that we are to look totally and completely to Him and more specifically, what He has done, for all that we need. This is so very, very important.

This means the sinner cannot save Himself, but he can be saved by looking to Christ and what Christ did at the Cross on his behalf. That is exactly what the Lord was talking about, when He told Moses to make a replica of a serpent out of copper, and to put it on a pole. He then said, that this pole was to be lifted up high for all to see. And all who had been bitten by serpents, if they would only look, they would live (Num. 21:9). Jesus in addressing the Born-Again experience, told Nicodemus the same thing, *"And as Moses lifted up the serpent in the wilderness, even so must the Son of Man be lifted up:*

"That whosoever believeth in Him should not perish, but have Eternal Life" (Jn. 3:14-15). It is the same for Christians:

The Believer cannot be victorious, cannot be holy, cannot be righteous, cannot be Christlike, or in fact, receive anything from the Lord, except in one way, and that is by trusting in what Jesus did at the Cross on his behalf. The Christian can no more make himself holy, than the sinner can save himself. When we look exclusively to the Sacrifice of Christ, the Holy Spirit, Who works exclusively within the parameters of this great Sacrifice, can then work mightily on our behalf (Rom. 8:1-2, 11).

2. Christ is the High Priest, not by virtue of appointment or by succession as was the Aaronic Priesthood, but rather because of what He did on the Cross as it regards the Redemption of mankind. He has purchased the right to be High Priest of all humanity, due to the price He paid, which was His Shed Blood, which was shed incidentally on behalf of fallen humanity. This atoned for all sin, past, present, and future, which broke the back of Satan, and which satisfied the Righteousness of a thrice Holy God.

3. The very words *"sat down"* involve a contrast to the continued and ever incomplete services of the Priests of old, who *"stood before God"* continually, in His earthly Sanctuary, because their work was never complete. The Work of Christ is total and complete, hence Him having *"sat down."*

NOTES

4. Christ, *"Who is set on the Right Hand of the Throne of the Majesty in the Heavens,"* proclaims the fact of the most elevated position in Heaven. Again, He earned this, which means, it was not given to Him, simply because He was and is the Son of God. This is the place and position of the highest honor in all the universe.

In fact, this is the very reason that we as Believers can approach the very Throne of God, and even do so *"boldly,"* that we may *"obtain Mercy, and find Grace to help in time of need"* (Heb. 4:16).

5. Our Faith in Christ, and what He did at the Cross, places us literally *"in Christ,"* which also means that He *"hath raised us up together, and made us sit together in Heavenly Places in Christ Jesus"* (Eph. 2:6). But we must never forget, that as He occupies this position totally and completely because of what He did at the Cross, and we're speaking of the Redemption of humanity, we as well occupy this position of victory and blessing, totally and completely because of our Faith in what He did at the Cross on our behalf. This exalted position is not attained at all by any type of works on our part. In fact, if we attempt to present such to God, it will be instantly rejected. Paul plainly said, *"So then they that are in the flesh* (trying to earn their way by the self-will of works) *cannot please God"* (Rom. 8:8).

6. As well, Christ occupies this position not only because of what He has done, but as well to perform a service for all Saints, which is to continually make intercession for us (Heb. 7:25).

7. His position is an eternal position, which further testifies to the completeness of His Work as it regards the Redemption of the human race, at least those who will believe (Jn. 3:16).

8. Jesus Christ is portrayed here in both a Priestly and Kingly manner. He is specifically called *"an High Priest,"* but He is seated *"on the Right Hand of the Throne of the Majesty in the Heavens,"* which also gives Him a Kingly position. Because of His Victory on the Cross, He is Lord of all things. He is Sovereign, with all power and authority given to Him, which speaks of a King (Mat. 28:18). As Paul said, *"We have such an High Priest."*

9. The Jewish High Priest each year on the Great Day of Atonement, passed through the Veil, and that with a sacrifice of blood, then presented it before God. He stood before the Mercy Seat with holy awe and, upon offering the blood, he immediately withdrew from God's Presence.

But Christ, after He had offered His Sacrifice to God, a Sacrifice incidentally of Himself, He entered into the Heavenly Sanctuary itself, not to stand before the Throne, but to sit at God's Right Hand, which speaks greatly so of the superiority of His Sacrifice in relationship to the animal sacrifices.

10. He sits at the Right Hand of the Father, because He has been invited to sit there, and because God has accepted His Perfect, spotless, pure, Righteousness, which He effected by His spotless, pure Life and the keeping of all the Law. As well, in His Perfection, He atoned for all sin by dying on the Cross, which paid the penalty of sin, a penalty incidentally, demanded by God.

Incidentally, how can anyone claim that the penalty is too high, considering that God paid it Himself?

11. The fact that this Throne is *"in the Heavens,"* means this is where the authority resides. At the same time, it means that it does not reside in earthly, Religious Denominations, or particular Churches, or Preachers of any nature, or any human being for that matter. So that means that the Pope is dead wrong in claiming such authority, which goes the same for any and all human beings.

THE CROSS

The point I have already attempted to make innumerable times in this Volume, and in fact will continue to do so, is that Christ occupies this exalted position, not because of Who He is, nearly as much as because of What He has done, and we speak of the Cross. This must ever be paramount in the heart and life of the Believer. This must be the thinking of our minds, our spirits, and in fact, all that we are. It is impossible for one to make too much of the Cross. Actually, the Cross is the very centrality of the Gospel.

As it regards the statement we've just made, this means that the Cross of Christ is not merely a Doctrine, but in reality is the very Foundation of the Church, which means, that all Doctrine flows from this Foundation. Consequently, if one misunderstands the Cross, or interprets it wrongly, or registers unbelief in any capacity as it regards the great Sacrifice of Christ, every single thing that he or she believes in some way, will be skewed. In fact, that's the very reason that the modern Church is in the mess that it's in presently, if you will pardon the crudeness of my expression.

The modern Church has attempted to shift the center of gravity as it regards the great Plan of God to other things. Some have tried to make the Holy Spirit the center of gravity, which means that He will have nothing to do with such an effort, which leaves the individuals functioning not according to His leading and power, but rather according to the leading and power of *"spirits."* And that's exactly what is happening presently.

Others have attempted to shift the center of gravity to the Church, and I speak of Religious Denominations, etc. Others have tried to shift it to Ordinances of the Church, such as *"the Lord's Supper,"* or *"Water Baptism,"* etc. Others have tried to shift the center of gravity to works of all nature, etc.

In fact, if the center of Scriptural gravity is placed anywhere other than the Cross of Christ, irrespective of wherever else it might be, it is going to bring ruin and disaster. Everything we have is in the great Sacrifice of Christ. If we forget that for one moment, we not only deceive ourselves, but we also start down a road of spiritual destruction. It cannot be any other way!

UNBELIEF

In 1996 when the Lord began to give me this Revelation of the Cross, with the greater thrust given in 1997, and which I might quickly add was given after some five years of intercessory prayer, to be frank, my whole world changed. I now had the answer for which I had so long sought. I now knew what Paul was saying when he gave the following great Truth:

"The Law (the Sacrifice of Christ was actually a legal work) *of the Spirit* (Holy Spirit) *of Life* (while all life flows from Christ, and because of what He did at the Cross, it is the

Holy Spirit Who makes all of this real to us) *in Christ Jesus* (refers to the Holy Spirit giving the glory to the Son of God for the great Work carried out at the Cross which makes everything possible) *hath made me free from the law of sin and death*" (Rom. 8:2).

Now I know what it means to *"walk after the Spirit,"* and as well, by the Grace of God, I now know how to *"walk after the Spirit"* (Rom. 8:1).

My reason for not knowing before was Scriptural ignorance. In other words, even though I knew very well the part the Cross played as it regarded our initial Salvation experience, I had no knowledge whatsoever of the part that it plays in our Sanctification. And furthermore, I didn't know anyone who did know. As I've said over and over again, there has been so little teaching on the Cross of Christ in the last several decades, that the modern Church is almost Cross illiterate. It's bad enough to have a lack of understanding regarding anything in the Bible, but if we have a misunderstanding concerning the Cross, we are in effect, committing spiritual suicide.

At the outset, and I speak of the time the Lord began to give me this Revelation back in 1996, I believed that the reason for all of these problems in the Church was basically due to just simply not knowing, as it had been with me. However, I have changed my thought somewhat since that particular time. I personally believe there is far more unbelief involved than anything else.

HOW COULD ANYONE WHO CLAIMS TO BE A CHRISTIAN REGISTER UNBELIEF IN THE CROSS?

While it is definitely true that the far greater majority of the modern Church little knows or understands the veracity of the Cross, still, most of the reason for this Scriptural ignorance, I have now come to believe, is because of unbelief. Listen to what the Prophet Hosea said:

"My people are destroyed for lack of knowledge." Now read carefully what He said next:

"Because thou hast rejected knowledge, I will also reject thee" (Hos. 4:6).

The idea is, Israel not only did not have the knowledge of God, which means they did not know the things they should have known,

all of this was because they did not want or desire the Knowledge of God. To be ignorant is one thing; however, to be ignorant because that's the way one wants to be, is something else altogether. And that's the state of the far greater majority of the modern Church. It is not only true that they have no knowledge of the Cross, the added Truth is, most don't want the knowledge. This means they are ignorant of this knowledge, simply because they want to be ignorant of this knowledge.

I realize this is a very serious indictment, but sadly I believe it to be true.

THE WAYS OF THE WORLD AND THE WAYS OF GOD

Due to the Fall, man has no good in him. This means he is totally depraved, which refers to being spiritually dead. Consequently, he cannot produce any type of Righteousness in any form. If man is to have Righteousness, it remains for God to supply that Righteousness, which He has done through Christ Jesus, and what Christ did at the Cross. But this is where the great problem resides.

The world claims it can save itself by its own machinations, and regrettably, the Church does pretty much the same. And what do we mean by that?

When it comes to the world and their claims, that's fairly understandable by all Believers; however, when it comes to the Church, it gets to be a little more difficult to understand.

To sum it up, the Believer, no matter that he is Spirit-filled and possibly even has Gifts of the Spirit, still, there's absolutely nothing he can do himself, which means by his own strength and ability, etc., that will draw him closer to God, or will effect anything with God whatsoever. He can only receive from God, and that goes for anything, by exhibiting simple Faith in the great Sacrifice of Christ, which then gives the Holy Spirit the latitude to do all of these great and wonderful things, which Jesus paid for at the Cross. But regrettably, most in the modern Church don't want to go that way.

THE EFFORTS OF THE FLESH

Paul used the word *"flesh,"* over and over again. He was referring to the very best that man can do by his own strength, ability, and efforts, which means he doesn't have the help of the Holy Spirit.

I think I can say without any fear of exaggeration, that every single Christian who has ever lived, has tried in one way or the other, to effect spirituality by efforts of the flesh, or as Paul put it, *"walking after the flesh"* (Rom. 8:1). The sadness is, all the time this is being done, and I speak of walking after the flesh, most all Believers think they are *"walking after the Spirit."* Let me give you an example:

Were I to ask most Christians as to how they know they are right with God, and to give details, most would answer, I think, according to the following:

They would refer to their faithfulness to Church, their giving of money to the Work of the Lord, their prayer life, their witnessing to souls, or their involvement in the Church in whatever type of activities it might provide. In other words, their thinking would go to works or personal efforts.

While these things mentioned might very well be very good in their place, the Truth is, they do not earn us anything with God whatsoever. If we think we are right with God, or whatever terminology we would like to use, as it regards all of these things, then we are totally misunderstanding the great Plan of God for the human race. But that's where the greater majority of the modern Church finds itself. That's sad, but true!

Every Believer is what he is in Christ, is close to God, and receives things from the Lord, solely and completely on the basis of the great Sacrifice of Christ, and his Faith in that. That and that alone provides access to God, things from God, and our way with God!

The Truth is, we as Believers, rather enjoy depending on these things I've mentioned, and many I haven't mentioned, simply because it gives us a feeling of superiority. It's something we've done, and we love our fair works of the flesh. As Abraham loved Ishmael, we love our works of religion in the same capacity. And as Abraham was loathe to send Ishmael and his Mother away, we are loathe to part with our own efforts of the flesh also.

Ishmael was a result of the ingenuity, planning, and efforts of both Abraham and Sarah. To say that this was all to no avail, and worse

yet, that it was actually very detrimental and harmful, is very difficult for even Abraham to grasp. But the fact remains, and as stated, that *"they who are in the flesh cannot please God"* (Rom. 8:8).

Please notice, that it didn't say *"cannot please the Lord some of the time,"* but just flat out *"cannot please the Lord."* There's only one thing that pleases God:

Faith totally and completely placed in Christ and what He did at the Cross on our behalf pleases God, and that alone.

Paul said, *"By Faith Enoch was translated that he should not see death; and was not found, because God had translated him: for before his translation he had this testimony, that he pleased God."*

The Apostle then told us what it was that pleased God. He said, *"But without Faith it is impossible to please Him"* (Heb. 11:5-6).

And remember, when we speak of *"Faith,"* always and without exception, we are speaking of Faith in the great Sacrifice of Christ.

FAITH?

The terrible Truth is, most of the Leadership of the modern Church, and I think I exaggerate not by the use of the word *"most,"* simply do not believe that the Cross is the answer to all the sinful aberrations of man. They just simply do not believe this to be the case. And that's why I said that I've come to the conclusion, that the problem is unbelief more than anything else.

Having been in the Ministry now not too much short of one half century, and having seen literally hundreds of thousands brought to a saving knowledge of Jesus Christ under this Ministry, and tens of thousands Baptized with the Holy Spirit, I think I have at least some knowledge of this of which I speak.

From experience, and from what I now know about the Cross, I know that most Preachers are not truly preaching victory to their congregations, simply because they don't know God's prescribed order of victory. They propose many and varied things, many which may be good in their own right, but none which will bring victory in the daily walk to the Child of God. And what do we mean by victory?

We're actually speaking of *"walking after the Spirit"* (Rom. 8:1). Every Believer in the world is either *"walking after the Spirit,"* or *"walking after the flesh."* And if the Believer doesn't understand the Cross as it refers to our Sanctification experience, then of necessity, the only place else to be is *"after the flesh."*

Whenever Believers have problems of some nature, and I speak of failure of some sort, most pastors don't have the foggiest idea as to what to tell these people. Deep down in their hearts, they know that what they are telling them, whatever that might be, doesn't work. I realize that's a flat out statement, but I know it to be true. Anything other than the Cross simply doesn't work!

And yet, the far, far greater majority of Preachers, even knowing that what they're doing is not working, will not bother to read these Truths laid out in these Commentaries, even though it would be given to them. Some few will, most won't!

Why?

The reasons are many and varied. With many, it must come from their particular Denomination or circle, or they simply won't accept it, no matter how true it is. With others, if they don't like the messenger, they reject the message. With others it's self-will and pride. Many preachers are loathe to admit that they are teaching something wrong, and that somebody else might have more light than they do on the subject.

But then with most, I am led to believe that it is sheer unbelief. They just simply do not believe that what Jesus did at the Cross avails for the needs of humanity. But in respect to this, we must remember the following:

The Holy Spirit through Paul strongly says, *"Take heed, brethren, lest there be in any of you an evil heart of unbelief, in departing from the Living God"* (Heb. 3:12).

And remember, when the word *"unbelief"* is used, it is pointedly speaking of unbelief in the Sacrifice of Christ. In other words, they began to doubt the veracity of the Cross. When Paul mentions *"Faith,"* without exception, he's always speaking of Faith in the Cross of Christ. When he mentions *"unbelief,"* he is doing the same thing.

The facts are, if Preachers believe in the Cross, they are going to want to learn everything they can about the Cross, and they are going to preach the Cross to their people. It

is pure and simple! If they don't believe it, they have little regard for learning anything about it, and they won't preach it to their people; consequently, the door remains shut as it regards anything of the Lord.

That's primarily the reason that we cannot have true Revival, until we have a Reformation. The thinking of people must be reformed, and I speak of being reformed as it regards the Finished Work of Christ.

(2) "A MINISTER OF THE SANCTUARY, AND OF THE TRUE TABERNACLE, WHICH THE LORD PITCHED, AND NOT MAN."

The exegesis is:

1. Christ, being the Mediator between God and men, represents believing man to God.

2. The Tabernacle and Temple on Earth were temporary, while the True Tabernacle in Heaven is eternal.

3. This building is of the Lord and not man, which refers to the great Plan of God for the human race.

CHRIST, THE PERFECT MINISTER

The phrase, *"A Minister of the Sanctuary,"* tells us what Christ is now doing.

"Minister" in the Greek is *"leitourgos,"* and means *"belonging to the people."* It was used of a person in the service of the State who held public office. Here as Paul uses the word, it speaks both of Priestly service to God, and of service to man (Wuest).

"Sanctuary" in the Greek is *"ton hagion,"* and means *"holy places, the Heavenly Sanctuary."*

This phrase is strange but yet beautiful. It speaks of Christ in His capacity as a Servant, which is striking, as it immediately follows the reference to His High Place in Heaven.

As a Servant, what does He do?

He is there to serve all Believers, and does so by making intercession for us, and does so constantly (Heb. 7:25).

This gives us an exceedingly blessed Truth: The Lord Jesus Christ is not only glorified, exalted, and dignified as our High Priest, He is also our Minister in the Sanctuary. Under the Old Covenant everything centered around the High Priest's Ministry in the Tabernacle. When the Priest failed, the people had no other approach to God.

Everything centers around our High Priest under the New Covenant also, but our High Priest can never fail His people. He has *"a more excellent Ministry"* in the True Tabernacle the Lord has prepared, instead of the one prepared by Moses.

RELATIONSHIP

The problem of establishing a dwelling place with man is of supreme importance to God. The communion of God and man was broken by the terrible tragedy of the Fall that took place in the Garden of Eden. The relationship and fellowship between God and man were interrupted. There came a day when sin intervened, disrupting that peaceful and sweet fellowship Adam had known with God. Since that time God has sought to reestablish a relationship with man and reconcile man to Himself.

Sin will always have the effect of separating man from God. Sin in fact, would have separated man from God eternally unless a remedy could be found to avert its effect and penalty. Man chose to disobey God, and it was necessary for man to suffer the disastrous results of his disobedience. But thanks be unto the Lord, God has provided a perfect remedy for sin by the Perfect Sacrifice of Jesus Christ.

From the time of the Fall in Genesis to the New Jerusalem scene in the Book of Revelation we find the God of all patience solving the problem of making a new dwelling place with man. It was not and is not an easy task, for, unless God brought man up to His Holiness and Righteousness, how could a Holy God dwell with sinners?

God's answer to the whole question may be expressed in these words: *"... The Blood of Jesus Christ His Son cleanseth us from all sin"* (I Jn. 1:7). The answer is found in the Cross of Christ, and the answer is found alone in the Cross of Christ. The Cross is the answer of the infinite wisdom of God on behalf of man. It is God's answer to sin, and God's response to man's lost estate.

However, the Cross does more than save the sinner. It gives him peace and hope (Col. 1:19-20).

The Cross was God's Way of removing the barrier that stood between man and God. By the Cross men are brought back into

fellowship with God. And let it be understood, that Faith in Christ and what He did at the Cross is the only way that men can be brought back into fellowship. There is no other way (II Cor. 5:18-19, 21).

RESTORED FELLOWSHIP WITH GOD

The Cross of Christ gives meaning to God's universe and to His dealings with man. The Cross furnishes a basis of restored fellowship with God on a higher and permanent basis.

Through the Cross and the Blood of Jesus, God has satisfied every demand of His Holiness. The Preaching of the Cross and the Crucified Saviour are the wisdom and power of God (I Cor. 1:18, 23-25).

The centrality of the Cross was vital to both the Old and New Testaments. It was vital because the Cross became a basis for God's dealing with men who lived in Old Testament times before the Sacrifice of Calvary. They were saved then by looking forward to that coming time when Jesus would die on the Cross, which was typified by every single Sacrifice offered. God established Blood Sacrifices and ceremonies as types of the work that would be fulfilled in Christ. In fact, Christ and His Cross are in type the Old Testament Tabernacle with its ceremonies and Sacrifices. Actually, even before Christ came He was the Lamb slain from the foundation of the world, for He is the eternal Sacrifice for sin. He is the only Sacrifice that brings the sinner into fellowship with God (I Pet. 1:18-20).

The death of Jesus was more than just an event that took place 2,000 years ago; it was the purpose of God from eternity. Jesus' death shows God's infinite wisdom and love in bringing men back into relationship, fellowship, and reconciliation with Himself.

Before Golgotha, the Cross was in the mind of God, which means that the death of Jesus was in the purpose of God. The Tabernacle of old, speaks of Him in its every shade of color, the minutest thread, the smallest tent stake, in every ceremony, ritual, or vessel.

As stated, all men were saved before the Cross by looking forward to that event, of which all of these things were types and symbols, and especially the Sacrifices. Men are saved presently, by simply looking back to what Jesus did and exhibiting Faith in that Finished Work (Eph. 2:8-9). But it must always be remembered:

The Cross is the centrality of the Gospel, the centrality of all that God is doing and has done for man, the centrality of the great Plan of God. If we misunderstand that, then we misunderstand the Gospel, which will bring upon ourselves great difficulties and problems.

WHY IS INTERCESSION BY CHRIST NOW NECESSARY ON BEHALF OF THE SAINTS?

It is necessary simply because Christians unfortunately, still sin. We don't have to sin, we shouldn't sin, and in fact, the Word of God emphatically tells us not to sin (I Jn. 2:1), but then it says, *"And if any man sin, we have an Advocate with the Father, Jesus Christ the Righteous:*

"And He is the Propitiation for our sins: and not for ours only, but also for the sins of the whole world" (I Jn. 2:1-2).

The moment a Believer sins, he is instructed to immediately *"confess his sins to the Lord, knowing that He is faithful and just to forgive us our sins, and to cleanse us from all unrighteousness"* (I Jn. 1:9).

The Presence of Christ at the Right Hand of the Father, automatically guarantees that such will be carried out, for the very Presence of Christ is our intercession. As previously stated in other commentary, Christ does not have to do something at this time. It has already been done. His very Presence guarantees all that we need, and provides all intercession. In fact, if He had to do anything else, that would mean that His Work was unfinished, which of course is erroneous. The great Work of Christ at the Cross is a *"Finished Work,"* hence, Him being *"sat down on the Right Hand of the Majesty on high"* (Heb. 1:3).

WHAT IS THE MOST OFT COMMITTED SIN AMONG CHRISTIANS?

The answer will come as a surprise to most. First of all, it's not particular acts of sin as we would think, that being more than anything else, a result of *"the sin."*

The most oft committed sin among Christians is the sin of placing our Faith and confidence in something else other than the Cross. In fact, that is the sin that opens the door to all type of acts of sin. The only way

NOTES

the Christian can be safe, and remain safe, which means to have perpetual and constant victory, is for the Christian to keep his Faith in the Cross of Christ, understanding that it was there that all victory was won, which then gives the Holy Spirit the latitude to work within our hearts and lives, bringing about the Christlikeness which is His purpose (Rom. 8:1-2, 11).

If I remember correctly, I have already stated the following in this Commentary; however, due to its great significance, and to stir your pure minds, please allow me to deal with it again.

Years ago in reading behind a particular English Preacher, incidentally, long since with the Lord, he said something which startled me. I knew he was right, because the Spirit bore witness with my spirit; however, I actually didn't understand what he said, even though I knew it was right and as well, extremely important.

He said, *"Christians need to repent of their good just as much as they need to repent of their bad!"*

Now all of us can well understand the necessity of repentance as it regards acts which we know are sinful and wicked; however, repenting of our good as well, is not so easily understood. What did he mean?

Since the Lord has opened up to me the meaning of the Cross, it becomes very obvious as to what he was saying.

When he spoke of repenting of the *"good,"* he was meaning repenting of these good things which we do, and our dependence on them, whatever they might be, to make us holy and righteous before God. In other words, if we are depending on anything, no matter how good it may seem to us, other than the Cross of Christ, we are committing sin, and a grievous sin at that. Let me emphasize again, the things which we are doing, may be very, very good in their own right, and I speak of things such as faithful Church attendance, the giving of money to the Work of the Lord, prayer, fasting, witnessing to souls, etc.; however, those things should be a result of our walk with God, and never as a cause of our walk with God. God will not honor Faith placed in these things, but only Faith placed in the Cross of Christ.

As I said some pages back, were you to ask most Believers as to what constituted their close walk with God, most would immediately begin to enumerate things I've just mentioned. But the Truth is, none of that draws us closer to God, such being accomplished only by our Faith in the Finished Work of Christ.

Does the Reader understand what I'm saying?

Let me show you how this erroneous way is engrained in our hearts and lives.

A PERSONAL EXPERIENCE

One of my close associates the other day was telling how that his six-year-old son responded to the following question:

"Joseph, what do you think it means to be 'in Christ'?" Now please remember, this little fellow is only six years old.

He immediately began to enumerate the good things he was doing, and the bad things he wasn't doing. Unfortunately, that was not only the response of this child, but is the response of most of Christendom as well!

Again I state, the most oft repeated sin in Christendom is the sin of placing our Faith in the wrong object.

WHAT HAPPENS WHEN BELIEVERS PLACE THEIR FAITH IN THINGS OTHER THAN THE CROSS?

The Believer has then placed himself in serious jeopardy. Let the following be understood:

Every single thing that we receive from God is done by and through the Purpose, Office, Ministry, and Person of the Holy Spirit. In other words, it doesn't really matter that you are saved, thereby a new creation in Christ Jesus, Baptized with the Holy Spirit, with some of you even having Gifts of the Spirit operative within your lives, which means you are being used of God; still, if your Faith is not in the Cross of Christ, irrespective of the things mentioned, you will still walk in spiritual failure. And it doesn't really matter who you are, whether the Pastor of the largest Church in the world, or someone who just got saved yesterday. Faith in the Cross of Christ is the only means of victory in the heart and life of the Believer (Rom. 8:1-2, 11).

Unfortunately, many Spirit-filled Believers,

and I speak of those who believe in the Baptism with the Holy Spirit, with the evidence of speaking with other Tongues, believe that victory is automatic within their lives. Nothing could be further from the Truth. In fact, there are millions of Christians who are truly Spirit-filled, but are not walking in victory at all.

What is wrong?

The mere fact of the Baptism with the Holy Spirit, although extremely important, does not really guarantee a victorious walk before God. To be sure, the potential is there, and greatly so, but the work of the Spirit is never automatic.

Were it automatic, no Spirit-filled Believer would ever fail, and all would be instantly mature; however, we know that none of that is correct, so what is the problem?

ALL THE WORK OF THE SPIRIT IS PREDICATED ON THE CROSS

Even though the Holy Spirit did great and mighty things in Old Testament Times, His perpetual abiding in the hearts and lives of Believers awaited the Cross (Jn. 14:17).

Due to the fact that the blood of bulls and goats couldn't take away sin, the sin debt still attached itself to all of humanity in Old Testament Times, even the great champions of Faith. As well, due to this, when the Saints of Old Testament Times died, they did not go to Heaven, but rather were taken captive by Satan down into Paradise (Lk. Chpt. 16). To be sure, Satan couldn't get them over into the burning side of the Pit, that place being separated from Paradise by a great gulf; still, the Evil One no doubt, hoped to ultimately do exactly that.

When Jesus died on the Cross, thereby satisfying the terrible sin debt owed by man to God, He then went down into Paradise and rescued these captives, for that's exactly what they were (Eph. 4:8-10), and then took them with Him to Heaven. Now when Saints die (since the Cross), they instantly go to be with Christ (Phil. 1:23).

This means that every single thing that the Holy Spirit does within the heart and life of the Believer, is predicated on what Christ did at the Cross. In response to the Words of Christ, *"If any man thirst, let him come unto Me and drink,"* John said, *"But this spake He of the Spirit, which they that believe on Him should receive: for the Holy Spirit was not yet given; because that Jesus was not yet glorified"* (Jn. 7:37-39).

Of course we now know that the Holy Spirit has been given, and because Jesus has been glorified. But let the Reader understand, that Jesus being glorified, was all as a result of the Cross and His Resurrection. It refers to the fact that God accepted the Sacrifice, which was actually the Shed Blood of Christ.

When the believing sinner exhibits Faith in Christ and what He did at the Cross, the Holy Spirit can then perfect the work of Regeneration within his heart, and actually come in to abide forever. It is called the *"born again"* experience (Jn. 3:3).

To which we've already addressed ourselves, the Believer should then ask the Lord to baptize him with the Holy Spirit, which the Lord has promised that He will do (Lk. 11:13).

The Baptism with the Holy Spirit signifies a surrender of the Believer to God as it regards the Will of God. As we've also stated, the Baptism with the Holy Spirit is always accompanied by the speaking with other Tongues as the Spirit of God gives the utterance (Acts 2:4).

After this experience, which is always subsequent to Salvation, the Believer is to ever understand, that he must continue his Faith in the Cross of Christ, which is always demanded by the Holy Spirit (Rom. 8:2). If the Believer does this, and continues to do this, which then gives latitude to the Spirit to work, to be sure, He will do great and mighty things within the heart and life of the Believer. He doesn't demand much of us, but He definitely does demand that we understand that everything we have from the Lord always and without exception, comes through the great Sacrifice of Christ. He will function on that basis and that basis alone! Thereby, when Christians move their Faith from the Cross of Christ to something else the Holy Spirit simply will not work, because to do so would literally be breaking the Law of God, which He will never do (Rom. 8:2). And again to be sure, when we place our Faith in anything other than the Cross, we definitely break the Law of God as well, which

means that God is very displeased with us (Rom. 8:8).

THE TRUE TABERNACLE

The phrase, *"And of the True Tabernacle,"* actually refers to the true dwelling place of God.

Paul uses the term *"True Tabernacle,"* because the Christian Jews would have known exactly that of which he spoke. Their minds would have gone to the Tabernacle constructed by Moses in the wilderness, where God dwelt between the Mercy Seat and the Cherubim. That of necessity, was a temporary dwelling place for God among men, which should have been obvious, awaiting the time when Jesus would go to the Cross, thereby making it possible for God to literally dwell in the hearts and lives of all Believers, which He now does.

Let not the Reader think that by Paul using the term *"True Tabernacle"* that he is actually speaking of some type of building. While there no doubt are many buildings in Heaven, this is not what Paul means here. In fact, the word *"true"* in this case, does not mean that which is false or counterfeit, but rather refers in contrast to that which is a mere copy or representation of the heavenly, which in fact was the Tabernacle of Moses. The genuine is in Heaven, hence Paul using the word *"true."*

Actually, John in his vision of the New Jerusalem said, *"And I saw no Temple therein: for the Lord God Almighty and the Lamb are the Temple of it"* (Rev. 21:22).

As well, after all vestige of sin has been removed from the universe, and Satan and all his cohorts have been locked away in the Lake of Fire, where they will remain forever and forever, and there is no more disobedience to God, John tells us that the New Jerusalem is going to come down from God out of Heaven, and dwell with men. He said:

"Behold, the Tabernacle of God is with men, and He will dwell with them, and they shall be His people, and God Himself shall be with them, and be their God" (Rev. 21:3). The idea is this:

Before the Cross, God was with men; since the Cross, God is in men; in that coming glad day, He will be both with men and in men.

THE PLAN OF GOD

The phrase, *"Which the Lord pitched, and not man,"* refers to the fact that Moses pitched the earthly Tabernacle, but God formed the True Tabernacle.

And yet, even the one pitched by Moses, was done so under the strict guidelines of the Lord, actually with every single feature about the Tabernacle designed totally and completely by the Lord, and not by Moses, or any other man. But yet, it was imperfect and, therefore, temporary.

WHY WAS THE TABERNACLE OF OLD IMPERFECT?

It was very obvious as to its imperfection, by the very fact that the Priests who officiated within its confines, never were able to finish their work. Due to the fact that the blood of bulls and goats could not take away sins, they had to keep offering more and more sacrifices. This within itself, plus all the other accoutrements of the Tabernacle and the Temple as well, which would come about 500 years after the Tabernacle, were all temporary. In fact, and even as we've already stated, every single thing about the Tabernacle and Temple portrayed Christ in some way, signifying that He Alone could truly cleanse from all sin (Jn. 1:29).

These very words, *"Which the Lord pitched, and not man,"* presents a glaring reminder, that man is unable, even believing man, to effect anything within his heart and life that pertains to God. Everything that man receives from God is of God totally and completely, which means it's not of man at all, which means that it can only be received by Faith.

The moment we attempt to earn something from God, or to secure such by merit, we forfeit the Grace of God, which leaves us in a serious predicament as should be obvious. Everything and without fail that God gives to man as it regards Salvation, or anything else, is all of God in totality, and not at all of man (Gal. 2:21).

And the manner and the way that God gives all these things to men is through the Cross of Christ, i.e., *"the great Sacrifice of Christ."* God cannot look at man in any way except through the Shed Blood of Christ, and man cannot approach God in any manner except through the Shed Blood of Christ.

So, if anyone holds anything up other than the Cross, as a way of Salvation, or a way of Victory, or a way of acceptance with God, such a way is obviously false. And it's a way as well, which the Judgment of God must ultimately fall upon.

That's why the present position of the modern Church is so precarious. The Church probably knows and understands less about the Cross presently than it ever has in its history, or at least since the Reformation. That's quite a statement, but I believe it to be true.

Satan has been very successful in the last few decades, at shifting the object of Faith from the Cross to other things. In fact, I personally believe that the so-called modern Faith message has been the greatest vehicle at moving Faith from the Cross, although it has not been the only means. Modernistic psychology has cut a wide swath as well!

However, the undergirding factor in all of this is unbelief — and I speak of unbelief as it regards the Cross. The Church has departed from the Cross, primarily because of unbelief. It simply doesn't believe that what Jesus did there, is the answer to the ills of the world. While it may pay lip service to the great Sacrifice of Christ, its direction proves that its Faith is placed in other things.

For the Church to have the moving and operation of the Holy Spirit once again, it must and without fail, come back to the Cross of Christ. There is no other way! (Phil. 3:18-19).

(3) "FOR EVERY HIGH PRIEST IS ORDAINED TO OFFER GIFTS AND SACRIFICES: WHEREFORE IT IS OF NECESSITY THAT THIS MAN HAVE SOMEWHAT ALSO TO OFFER."

The exegesis is:

1. The purpose of the High Priest is to offer Gifts and Sacrifices.

2. Christ offered Himself, which was the one Perfect Sacrifice, which constituted all Gifts, which met all the needs of man.

3. His One Gift is far superior to the many gifts and sacrifices of the Priests of old. The very fact of their plurality states that they were insufficient. The very fact of the One Sacrifice of Christ, states that it was and is all-sufficient.

PRIESTS OF OLD

The phrase, *"For every High Priest is ordained to offer gifts and sacrifices,"* portrayed these men as the mediators between God and men. As stated, the very fact that they had to continue to offer sacrifices, states the ineffectiveness of the old system. Due to the fact that the blood of bulls and goats could never take away sins, but actually only serve as a stopgap measure, it was obvious that something else was required.

As is blatantly and overly obvious in this Epistle to the Hebrews, Paul keeps placing the Priesthood of Christ over against the old Levitical order. He does, so that the Christian Jews, and all others for that matter, might see the overwhelming supremacy of Christ. In fact, the Priesthood of Christ was so overwhelming, which the Holy Spirit helped Paul to adequately portray, that it was and is impossible for anyone, at least if they will be honest, not to see the vast difference. And yet I'm afraid, the problem continues!

While the modern Church is not trying to go back to the Levitical system, as some of the Christian Jews of old, and for the simple reason that it no longer exists; still, the defection is just as serious. As Satan ever sought to diminish Christ in the eyes of those to whom Paul addressed, he still seeks to do the same presently. As a result, millions put the Church in the place of Christ. Or a Denomination! Or their own good works! In fact, in the latter half of the Twentieth Century, millions placed Faith itself on a pedestal. Some may wonder as to how such could be done?

If it's not Faith in the Cross, which keeps Christ supreme, and the Faith of which I speak definitely wasn't in the Cross, then it becomes sin. Anything that puts Christ in an inferior position, even as the Catholics do the Church and Mary, it becomes a gross sin.

Satan doesn't care how much we worship, or how religious we might be, if Christ is not properly addressed. In fact, he will help us to be very religious and to worship accordingly, providing it's in the wrong direction. And to sum it up, we must note the following:

If the Christ we serve is not the Crucified One, with all emphasis placed upon His great Sacrifice, understanding that all Salvation and all Blessings, come from His great Finished Work, then the Christ we are serving is labeled by Paul as *"another Jesus"* (II Cor. 11:4). The Truth is, and as stated, millions serve their Church, attempting to equate the Church and Christ as one and the same. They aren't!

TO PROVE THE POINT

I personally believe that the Revelation which the Lord began to give me in 1996 was meant to be far more than for me alone. I believe, and firmly so, that He intends for this Message to be heralded to the entirety of the Church, and I speak of the Church worldwide. To be sure, the Message which we proclaim is not by any means new; actually, it is the very foundation of the Faith, but a foundation, from which the modern Church has sorely drifted.

The Lord is giving us the means to propagate this Message on a nationwide, and even a worldwide basis. It should be clearly understood, that He has done this, and is doing this, for purpose. He means for the Church to come back to the Cross.

But the Church has a problem in all of this. If the Message doesn't come from its own source, i.e., *"its Denomination or circle of fellowship,"* will it accept the Message?

The Truth is, most won't; however, the searching heart, of which there definitely are some, will hear, believe, and receive.

Where does that leave the others?

When light is rejected, light is then withdrawn, which means that the apostasy deepens. Jesus addressed this by saying:

"When the unclean spirit is gone out of a man, he walketh through dry places, seeking rest, and findeth none.

"Then he saith, I will return into my house from whence I came out; and when he is come, he findeth it empty, swept, and garnished.

"Then goeth he, and taketh with himself seven other spirits more wicked than himself, and they enter in and dwell there: and the last state of that man is worse than the first" (Mat. 12:43-45).

THE SACRIFICE OF CHRIST

The phrase, *"Wherefore it is of necessity that this man have somewhat also to offer,"* speaks of the offering of Himself.

We now see in Christ a High Priest Who through His Own inherent right has taken a place which no Levitical Priest could ever take. Instead of merely being permitted to enter once a year into the Holy of Holies, and that only for a few moments, not daring to sit down in the Presence of God, our Lord Jesus Christ, as the ascended Man, has entered into the Heavenly Sanctuary and is seated there on the Right Hand of the Throne of the Majesty in the Heavens. There He ministers in the Holiest in that glorious Tabernacle of which the earthly tent was but a type.

How important it is for us to realize that we are represented before God by a Man in the glory, for though we no longer know Christ after the flesh, yet He has gone up to Heaven as the Representative Man to appear in the Presence of God on our behalf.

The earthly High Priest of old was appointed to offer both gifts and sacrifices. By gifts we understand to be those offerings which were the expression of the grateful, adoring hearts of the people of Israel. The Sacrifices, on the other hand, had to do directly with making expiation for sin.

Our Lord did the latter when He offered up Himself on the Cross. But now that He is ministering in the Heavenly Sanctuary, it is of course necessary that He have something to offer. He presents before God our prayers and praises. Our heartfelt worship ascends to the Father by Him, and because of what He did at the Cross which makes it possible for us to approach God, which we do, by evidencing Faith in the great Sacrifice of Christ.

PERFECTION

We may often be discouraged as we realize something of the imperfections even of our highest and best efforts to glorify God. Like William Cowper, we may exclaim:

"Sin twines itself about my thoughts,
"And slides into my prayers."

But it is blessed to know that nothing reaches God that is not perfect. Our Great High Priest takes out of our prayers and praises everything that is unholy or of the flesh, everything that is contrary to the nature of the God we adore. Then to what is left, He adds His Own infinite perfections and

thus presents all to the Father on our behalf.

Oh how I sense the Presence of God, even as I dictate these words. How so imperfect we are, but yet, how Perfect He is. And because He is Perfect, He somehow takes our imperfections, and places them in His Perfection, with nothing left that is not perfect.

How so much we must look to Him! How so much we must understand, as the Priests of old, took a Censer into the Holy Place, filled with perfume placed over blazing coals from the Brazen Altar, which was a type of Calvary, filling the air in that place with a beautiful fragrance, all typical of our prayers and praises; likewise, when Christ finishes with our humble efforts, that which remains comes up into the nostrils of God as a sweet and adoring fragrance. The example of the Priests of old tells us that God cannot accept any prayer, petition, or praises, unless it comes by the way of the Cross. In fact, when *"Nadab and Abihu, the sons of Aaron, took either of them his censer, and put fire therein, and put incense thereon, and offered strange fire before the LORD, which He commanded them not, there went out fire from the LORD, and devoured them, and they died before the LORD"* (Lev. 10:1-2).

The fire that these two Priests took and placed in their Censers was not fire from the Brazen Altar, but some other ignition altogether, which God could never accept.

The Brazen Altar stood for the Cross, was symbolic of the Cross. This means that these Priests could not approach Him by any means other than the Cross of Christ, for that's what it all meant. Should that not be a powerful lesson for us presently?

THE CROSS, AND THE HIGH PRIESTLY ROLE OF CHRIST

Christ is High Priest, and will be so forever, because of what He did at the Cross on our behalf. This means that we must come to Him, and do so at all times, with the understanding that such is made possible totally and completely by His great Sacrifice of Himself. Only with that understanding, and our Faith lodged in that Finished Work, can He take our prayers and praises and thereby turn them into a holy fragrance before God the Father. But the sadness is, most Christians little understand this of which we say, thereby approaching God on the basis of things other than the Sacrifice of Christ, which God can never honor.

Let us never forget, that there is only one thing which pleases God, and that is His only Son, and the great Sacrifice He made of Himself on the Cross. That alone pleases Him; that alone satisfies Him; that alone gives Him pleasure! Consequently, when we place our Faith in Christ regarding His Finished Work, always understanding that this is the basis by which we can approach God, and in fact, the only basis by which we can approach God, this and this alone pleases God (Mat. 3:17).

(4) "FOR IF HE WERE ON EARTH, HE SHOULD NOT BE A PRIEST, SEEING THAT THERE ARE PRIESTS THAT OFFER GIFTS ACCORDING TO THE LAW:"

The structure is:

1. Christ could not be a Priest on Earth after the Levitical order, inasmuch as that order was after the Law.

2. The Priesthood of Christ of necessity must transcend the Law, because it must be superior, which the Law could never do.

3. In fact, even though His Priesthood was made possible on Earth by His Sacrifice, its administration is carried forth in Heaven, even before the Throne of God.

CHRIST, NO EARTHLY PRIEST!

The phrase, *"For if He were on Earth, He should not be a Priest,"* refers to the fact that He was not of the Levitical Order, and due to His Sacrifice of Himself, no more earthly Priests are now needed. In fact, the very idea of a Priest presently, is in effect saying that what Christ did on the Cross is not sufficient and needs something added, which is an insult of the worst sort toward God.

If one is to notice, the name *"Priest"* is never once given to Ministers of the Gospel in the New Testament. They are called Ministers, Ambassadors, Pastors, Bishops, Overseers, etc., but never *"Priests."* Nor should they be so called in the Church.

In fact, the name *"Priest"* as applied to Christian Ministers, has been derived from the Catholic Church. They hold that the Priest does offer as a Sacrifice the real Body and Blood of Christ in the Mass, and holding this,

the name *"Priest"* is given to the Minister who does it consistently. It is not indeed right or Scriptural — for the whole doctrine on which it is based is absurd and false — but because of that doctrine they have the order of Priests.

Thank God, due to what Christ did at the Cross, the order or office of *"Priest"* is no longer necessary. In fact, it is not only no longer necessary, it is abominable to hold to such, seeing that Christ Alone is Priest, and because no other is needed.

The only manner in which it could be held that an earthly Priest is necessary, is the idea that the Sacrifice of Christ was insufficient. And in essence, this is exactly what the Catholic Church does. But in a strict sense of the word, when we place anything ahead of Christ, whether intentional or otherwise, in other words, placing Faith in something other than Christ, or equating things with Christ such as the Church, etc., we are in effect doing the same identical thing as the Catholics. The great sin of the Church is *"not holding the Head"* (Col. 2:19).

Christ is the *"Head"* of the Church, and is so by virtue of what He did at the Cross on our behalf. The idea is, if we're not understanding Christ in that capacity, and I speak of *"Jesus Christ and Him Crucified,"* as being the basis and foundation of all Doctrine, then we aren't properly *"holding the Head!"*

THE LAW

The phrase, *"Seeing that there are Priests that offer gifts according to the Law,"* tells us several things:

1. Christ, as stated, was not of the Levitical Order, so could not be a Priest on Earth.

2. The Law was temporary; therefore, it could not furnish a perfect Priesthood.

3. The very fact that it had to offer continued sacrifices, proved its imperfection.

4. The One Sacrifice of Christ, which was the offering of Himself on the Cross, satisfied all the types of the Old Covenant and abolished all its offerings for sin. Consequently, they are no longer needed!

5. If Christ came back to Earth, which He will soon do, He will not again offer a Sacrifice for sin. Even though He will continue to serve as High Priest, and in fact will do so

forever, His High Priesthood is based totally and entirely on His One Sacrifice of Himself on the Cross, which will never again have to be repeated. In fact, animal sacrifices will once again be offered in the coming Kingdom Age; however, they will not be for sin but rather as a memorial of what was typified before the First Coming of Christ. Such sacrifices were never to take away sins and they will never do so in the future; but it is interesting to note that such a program will be carried on in the presence of all coming generations throughout eternity, to demonstrate to all what Christ had to go through in order that man might be saved (Ezek. 43:18-27; 45:13-25; 46:11-15).

(5) "WHO SERVE UNTO THE EXAMPLE AND SHADOW OF HEAVENLY THINGS, AS MOSES WAS ADMONISHED OF GOD WHEN HE WAS ABOUT TO MAKE THE TABERNACLE: FOR, SEE, SAITH HE, THAT THOU MAKE ALL THINGS ACCORDING TO THE PATTERN SHEWED TO THEE IN THE MOUNT."

The composition is:

1. All the Old Testament rituals and ceremonies were but examples and shadows of the reality which can be found only in Christ.

2. All that which God gave to Moses, as grand and glorious as it was, were only replicas of the real, which were in Heaven.

3. Consequently, Moses was dogmatically instructed that he was not to deviate from the pattern given by God.

TYPES AND SHADOWS

The phrase, *"Who serve unto the example and shadow of heavenly things,"* refers to a suggestive replica, which in fact, had no substance within itself. It had no independent existence. These things were merely proof of the fact that there was reality back of it all.

This means that the earthly Priests served in a Sanctuary which they valued highly; however, they were to never forget, that all of this was a mere copy and shadow of what was in Heaven. While the Old Covenant was but a shadow of heavenly things, Christ is the eternal substance!

When we study the Jewish ritual of the Mosaic Law, and read these words as given by Paul as it concerns *"examples"* and *"shadows,"*

we are not to think in our minds that Heaven is a place of sacrifices, with Altars, Tables, and Arks, etc. None of that exists in Heaven. It all has its meaning in Christ! He is the Sacrifice; He is the Brazen Altar; He is the Brazen Laver; He is the Table of Shewbread; He is the Golden Lampstand; He is the Altar of Incense; He is the Ark of the Covenant; He is the Mercy Seat. In fact, He is the Tabernacle, even as He is the Temple. As well, He is every nail, every cord, every peg, the gold, the silver, the precious stones, the Veil, the foundation stones, the walls, the roof, the pillars. He is everything! Actually, it is to Him to Whom the Cherubim point and praise! It is Christ! It is the Lord Christ! It is the Lord Jesus Christ! He is the *"King of kings and Lord of lords!"*

When one day we pass through the portals of that place called *"Glory,"* and we look upon His Face, we will then see the Sacrifice, the Tabernacle, and the Temple! We will see the Intercession, for He is the Intercession. We will see Eternal Life, for He is Eternal Life!

Oh, Saint of God, why would you want to trade Him, the Creator of all the ages, for mere *"examples"* and *"shadows"*?

THE TABERNACLE

The phrase, *"As Moses was admonished of God when he was about to make the Tabernacle,"* proclaims the fact that this was but a poor replica of the reality Who is Christ.

Again we emphasize, that John said as it regards his vision of the New Jerusalem, *"And I saw no Temple therein, for the Lord God Almighty and the Lamb are the Temple of it"* (Rev. 21:22).

THE PATTERN

The phrase, *"For, see, saith He, that thou make all things according to the pattern shewed to thee in the Mount,"* means that this pattern was not to be deviated from in the slightest. It also means, that all of this was all of God and none of man, which refers to the fact, that Salvation is all of God and none of man. This was why God was so particular in regard to all its details.

There was no room for human ingenuity or for Moses' own thoughts. All must be as ordered of God, for He Alone knew the Son and the work He was to accomplish.

The allusion here is to a pattern such as an architect or sculptor uses; a drawing or figure made in wood or clay, after which the work is to be modeled. The idea is, that some such drawing or model was exhibited to Moses by God on Mount Sinai, so that he might have an exact idea of the Tabernacle which was to be made. In fact, a similar drawing or model of the Temple was given to David which he would give to Solomon, who would in fact construct the Temple (I Chron. 28:11-12).

However, we are not to suppose that there was, in the case of the pattern shown to Moses, any miniature model of wood or stone actually created and exhibited; but that the form of the Tabernacle was exhibited to Moses, possibly in a vision, or it was so vividly impressed on his mind that he would have a distinct view of the edifice which was to be constructed.

A TYPE OR SYMBOL

A type in the Old Testament is a person or thing in the Bible which God designed to represent or prefigure some person, thing, or event that would appear in the future. Actually in some way all of these things prefigured Christ.

It is also interesting to note the use of symbols throughout the Bible; for instance, the use of numbers represents certain Truths. The number *"seven"* is used to signify Divine Perfection in contrast to human imperfection, which is represented by *"six."* (Six falls short of seven by one; man has fallen short of God's glory.)

There were seven men in the Bible who lived to be over 900 years of age. We also find seven *"Blessed's"* in the Book of Revelation (Rev. 1:3; 14:13; 19:9; 20:6; 22:7, 14).

The number *"seven"* is used often in the Book of Revelation. It is as if God has placed His signature upon the Book.

There are seven candlesticks (Rev. 1:13-20), seven stars (Rev. 1:16, 20), seven Letters to the Churches in Asia (Rev. Chpts. 2-3), seven spirits (sevenfold Spirit of the Lord) (Rev. 4:5), seven seals (Rev. Chpt. 5), seven Angels appearing before the Throne (Rev. Chpt. 8), seven trumpets (Rev. Chpt. 8), seven thunders (Rev. Chpt. 10), and seven vials of

NOTES

judgment (Rev. Chpt. 15).

An interesting study may be made also of the number *"eight."* This is the number of new beginnings, or of Resurrection. Jesus arose from the dead on the eighth day (the first day of the week). As well, eight persons were saved from the flood in the Ark. Noah was the eighth man after Adam, and as such, was a fitting person for God to use in the new beginning after the waters of the flood subsided.

There are eight cases recorded in the Bible of persons being restored to life (I Ki. 17:17-24; II Ki. 4:8-37; 13:20-21; Mk. Chpt. 5; Lk. 7:11-18; Jn. Chpt. 11; Acts 9:36-43; 20:7-12).

There is an abundance of types and symbols in the Old Testament and even some in the New. However, one of the most precious types of all concerns the High priestly Ministry of the Lord Jesus Christ.

It is easy to see why the Lord cautioned Moses to follow the pattern he had been given. Each detail had to be exact, just as God had given it. There is a practical application of this for every Christian.

We should exercise the utmost care and diligence to ascertain the revealed Mind of God. We should seek that which He requires from us in our worship and service to Him. It was not Moses who drew up the blueprint for the Tabernacle. Moses did not draw plans or submit them to the people for their approval. It was not left to Moses or to Israel to decide; God gave the pattern.

And the pattern to be sure, was given in every detail carefully — the color of the curtains, the type of tent pins to use, the number of boards, the size and shape of the articles of furniture — nothing was left to the imagination of man. This was to be God's dwelling place, it had to please Him and meet all His requirements.

As stated, this shows us that Salvation and Victory are all of God and none of man. Consequently, to have what He has promised and in fact, has given, we must follow His instructions very carefully and never try to insert additions or glosses of our own.

JESUS IS NOW THE PATTERN

Whereas the Tabernacle and Temple in Old Testament Times were then the pattern, Christ is now our Pattern and our Example; we only need to follow in His steps. He is high, He is holy, He is undefiled, and He is unstained.

As Christians we must follow His example very carefully, even as He left for us in His Word. When construction is begun on a building, the builder must be very careful to follow the plans. If he deviates from the blueprints, somewhere later he will find himself in trouble. The plan must be followed if the goal of completion is to be reached.

The Word of God provides the only set of blueprints that will bring us to maturity and perfection. In other words, the pattern is found in the Word of God. This means that the Bible is our Book of instructions. In it we see Jesus, our Pattern. In it the Voice of the Holy Spirit speaks to us and directs our paths. The Spirit becomes our Teacher to show us the Way of Christ.

God has a pattern, a design for our lives. Whenever we veer from this plan, God will discipline us so that we might follow through to completion His Will. To be frank, we do not like the school of discipline; sometimes we even despise it. It seems easier to walk in our own ways, but we soon find out, that the only way in which our lives will fit together perfectly is in God's Perfect Plan.

GRACE AND LAW

The Holy Spirit plainly told us through Paul, *"Ye are not under the Law, but under Grace"* (Rom. 6:14). So what am I saying?

In a sense, the Law was the pattern in Old Testament Times, which was much more involved, much more complicated, and which demanded an exact performance of man, which man in fact, in no way could do. In the New Testament, the pattern is Christ, Who Alone provides Grace. So, how do we follow this pattern according to New Testament guidelines?

As difficult as the pattern of Law was, simple is the pattern of Christ Who gives Grace. That which was extremely complicated, has become extremely simple and easy.

In this Book of Hebrews, Paul is actually speaking of the *"victorious, overcoming, Christian life."* Salvation and the Baptism with the Holy Spirit have already come to these Saints. If they can in fact walk in overcoming victory, the idea of forsaking Christ

NOTES

in favor of Judaism will be totally and completely forgotten. It is the same presently:

If the Believer can understand God's prescribed order of Victory, and follow it minutely, which is actually His Pattern, results will be guaranteed. So what is the Believer to do?

As stated, the Pattern is very simple:

EVERYTHING COMES THROUGH THE CROSS

This is step number one. The Believer, even as we've already stated in past commentary, is to understand that every single thing he needs, the answer to every question, the solution to every problem, are all found, and in totality, in what Christ did at the Cross. The Believer must settle that in his mind that this, the Cross, is the Source of all Blessings (Rom. 6:3-5, 11, 14).

OUR FAITH

The second step is that we place our Faith in the Cross of Christ, and leave our Faith in the Cross of Christ. God's means of dealing with the human race is through the vehicle of Faith; however, it is to always be understood, and without exception, that it is to ever be Faith in the Cross of Christ. It was there that Jesus paid it all, and it is there in which we must place our Faith (Eph. Chpt. 1).

THE HOLY SPIRIT

The third and final step to all of this is, the Work and Ministry of the Holy Spirit. He Alone can guarantee all the benefits of the Cross. And considering, again as we've already stated, that He works exclusively within the parameters of the Finished Work of Christ, it remains only that we exhibit Faith in that Finished Work (Rom. 8:1-2, 11).

The Holy Spirit doesn't demand much of us; however, He does demand this of which I have said (Rom. 8:1-2, 11).

As stated, this pattern of Grace is very, very simple, actually leaving no room for excuse on our part.

So that being the case, why is it so difficult for Believers to follow this pattern?

I suppose it's the same reason that Israel had such a difficult time following the pattern of the Law. Even though that was much more difficult than the pattern of Grace, still, the problem is the same. And what is that problem?

It's the problem of taking God's blueprint which He has laid down, and then changing it to something else which we think we want or desire. While we always do it in a very religious manner, and even load it down with Scriptures, still, the end result is, that we have changed God's pattern, which He can never condone. To be sure, in such a case, we will always reap the bitter fruit of such action. If we go God's Way, we reap very positive results; otherwise, the picture is not pretty!

(6) "BUT NOW HATH HE OBTAINED A MORE EXCELLENT MINISTRY, BY HOW MUCH ALSO HE IS THE MEDIATOR OF A BETTER COVENANT, WHICH WAS ESTABLISHED UPON BETTER PROMISES."

The composition is:

1. This is a pivot Scripture in the Book of Hebrews.

2. The Priesthood of Christ is far superior to the Priesthood of Aaron.

3. The Covenant under Christ is far better than the Aaronic Covenant.

4. The New Covenant is established on better Promises.

A MORE EXCELLENT MINISTRY

The phrase, *"But now hath He obtained a more excellent Ministry,"* closes the first major argument. The Epistle to the Hebrews was written to prove the following proposition:

The New Testament in Jesus' Blood is superior and takes the place of the First Testament in animal blood. Paul has proved this to be true on the basis of pure logic and the Old Testament Scriptures.

Using the logical argument that a superior workman turns out a superior product, he has shown that Messiah, the Founder of the New Testament is better than the founders of the First Testament, who were the Prophets, Angels, Moses, Joshua, and Aaron. Therefore, the Testament He brought in is superior to and takes the place of theirs (Wuest).

The words *"more excellent Ministry"* refer primarily to the more excellent Ministry which Christ has than that of the Aaronic Priests, which he has amply proved.

"Ministry" in the Greek is *"Leitourgia,"*

and means *"service."*

The blood of bulls and goats could never take away sin, but the one Sacrifice of Christ on the Cross, has taken away every sin, past, present, and future, at least for those who will believe (Jn. 3:16). Consequently, the guilt of sin is removed, which it never was under the Old Covenant, and as well, the terrible sin debt has been paid also, which it never was under the Old Covenant. Reconciliation between man and God is now afforded, which it was not under the Old Covenant, which means that Justification by Faith as was promised to Abraham, is now a fact.

And then, the culmination of all this is the new dimension of the Holy Spirit afforded by the Finished Work of Christ, which among other things, guarantees the Baptism with the Spirit, as well as His abiding forever in the hearts and lives of Believers, which could not at all be done under the Old Covenant (Jn. 14:16-17).

The Covenant of old depended upon man's ability to carry out its requirements. God in effect said, *"If you will do thus and so, I will do certain things."* Thus, the promise of blessing rested upon man's ability to claim that Blessing on the ground of his obedience to the Law. The trouble was, no man ever could obtain the Promises on that basis.

And so our Lord Jesus took upon Himself the curse of the broken Law, was made a curse for us, became the great Sin-Offering, and now has become the Mediator of a Better Covenant, in which all the Promises on God's part and man receives every blessing as pure Grace.

A BETTER COVENANT

The phrase, *"By how much also He is the Mediator of a Better Covenant,"* proclaims the fact that Christ officiates between God and man according to the arrangements of the New Covenant.

"Better Covenant" denotes a disposition, arrangement, or ordering of things; and, in the Scriptures, it is employed to describe the arrangement which God has made to secure the maintenance of His worship on Earth, and the Salvation of men.

This is a Better Covenant in many ways, inasmuch as it relates mainly to the heart; to the pardon of sin; to a spiritual, and holy life. The former related more to external rites and observances, and was destined to vanish away.

THE BIBLICAL CONCEPT OF COVENANT

The notion of a Covenant is unfamiliar today. But the concept of Covenant is utterly basic to our understanding of Scripture.

In Old Testament Times this complex concept was the foundation of social order and social relations, and it was particularly the foundation for an understanding of humanity's relationship with God.

THE BIBLICAL CONCEPT

The concept of Covenant is not found exclusively in the Bible. Other cultures in early Biblical times used the Covenant concept as a basis for a wide range of interpersonal and social relationships. Between one nation and another, a Covenant was a treaty (Gen. 14:13; 31:44-55).

Among individuals, a Covenant expressed a pledge of friendship (I Sam. 18:3; 20:8; 23:18) or served as a business contract. When a ruler and his subjects were the parties to a Covenant, such a Covenant served as a national constitution and spelled out the responsibilities of the ruler and the ruled (II Sam. 3:21; 5:3; I Chron. 11:3). It should not be surprising that in a world in which Covenant was such a fundamental idea, God would select the concept of Covenant to clarify the relationship that He sought to establish with His people.

A Biblical Covenant is a clear statement of God's purposes and intentions expressed in terms that bind God by solemn oath to perform what He has promised.

OLD TESTAMENT ROOTS

The nature of the Biblical Covenant as a statement of God's intentions is seen in each of the four major Covenants (Abrahamic, Davidic, Mosaic, New). In each of these Covenants, God states what He will do. In three of the four, the purposes announced will be accomplished at history's end. Consequently, one might say these are eschatological (Endtime Covenants).

In the other Covenant (the Mosaic, or Law

Covenant), God's purpose is essentially conditional. He states the Blessings He will give when the people of Israel obey and the disasters that will come when they disobey.

The nature of the Biblical Covenant as something in which God binds Himself by solemn oath is seen in the rituals followed in making the Covenants. In Old Testament times a Covenant was *"cut,"* perhaps referring to the fact that the most binding Covenants were enacted in a ceremony that involved the offering of a sacrifice. Genesis, Chapter 15 describes how God followed this cultural form, passing between the halves of Sacrificial animals as Abraham lay in a deep sleep. In this way God bound Himself to keep the Promises made to Abraham.

PROMISE

The Mosaic Covenant followed another binding pattern, that of a treaty made between a ruler and his subjects. The written Law served as the Constitution of the nation thus formed.

The use of these culturally binding forms to express relationship into which God entered with human beings provided a foundation for the Believer in that God has made a full commitment to His Word. He bound Himself to Israel by solemn oaths.

The nature of the Biblical Covenant as promised is stressed in the New Testament by the Apostle Paul (Rom. 4:13-17; Gal. 3:15-18). The Promises that God makes are not dependent on human reaction to them: He will do what He has promised.

We see something of this sense of binding commitment in Israel's response to the Gibeonites, who had tricked them into a political Covenant (*"treaty"*). Despite the deceit of the Gibeonites, the Covenant once made was not set aside, and the people of Israel kept their promise to help when the Gibeonites were attacked (Josh. Chpt. 10).

Throughout history, Israel's own repeated sins often brought God's discipline on the nation. But even the sternest warnings were tempered with restatements of the Promises that one day God would act to fulfill the Covenant Promises given to Abraham and the Patriarchs. This pattern in sacred history cannot be explained if the Biblical Covenants are conditioned on human behavior.

As Paul writes in Romans after reviewing Israel's history of unfaithfulness:

"As far as election is concerned, they (Israel) *are loved on account of the Patriarchs, for God's Gifts and His Call are irrevocable"* (Rom. 11:28-29).

Of course, this speaks of the nation as a whole, which will one day be brought back; however, as it regards individuals, not meeting God's conditions, they were eternally lost.

In fact, the condition has always been Faith, whether under Old Testament directives or the New. Admittedly, the results of Faith presently, are far more pronounced, due to the great Work of Christ; nevertheless, God has always demanded Faith, and still demands Faith. The absence of Faith can forfeit the Promises.

THE NEW TESTAMENT COVENANT

The Greek word for *"Covenant"* is *"diatheke."* It is used over 270 times in the Greek translation of the Old Testament called the *"Septuagint."* It is the Greek word for the Hebrew *"brit."*

Although *"diatheke"* occurs only 33 times in the New Testament, many other Passages base arguments on different aspects of the Covenant that God established with Abraham and his descendants (Rom. Chpt. 5; Gal. Chpt. 3). One cluster of New Testament uses of *"diatheke"* is connected with the Lord's Supper. Other uses are found in Paul's Epistles and especially in the Book of Hebrews, which we are now studying.

From early times the Greeks used *"diatheke"* in the sense of a will. In contrast to the Greek word *"syntheke,"* which spelled out terms of a partnership, a *"diatheke"* permitted an individual to dispose of possessions any way that person chose. The decision, once expressed in a will, could not be annulled by another party. But the will became effective only after the person making it died.

Paul, in Hebrews 9:13-20, builds on this aspect of the Old Testament Covenants. He points out that the Old Covenants were confirmed with blood. Jesus' death instituted a New Covenant — a Covenant that serves as Jesus' Own unbreakable will, *"The promised*

eternal inheritance" (Heb. 9:15).

Paul also speaks in Hebrews of the Abrahamic Covenant as an oath. This is understood to be a legally binding guarantee. As Paul said, *"Because God wanted to make the unchanging nature of His purpose very clear to the heirs of what was promised, He confirmed it with an oath"* (Heb. 6:17).

This, combined with Paul's insistence that *"Promise"* sums up the essential aspect of the Abrahamic Covenant, gives us strong evidence that the Bible regards a Covenant as a statement of God's purposes and intentions, expressed in terms that bind God, by solemn oath, to perform what He has promised.

THE ABRAHAMIC COVENANT

Presumably before God revealed Himself to Abraham, he was a pagan, a worshiper of Nanna, the moon-god, in the city of Ur. God told him:

"Leave your country, your people and your father's household, and go to the land I will show you" (Gen. 12:1). God gave Abraham Promises that were later formally confirmed, with Him working in line with the human custom of making a binding Covenant (Gen. 15:1-21). Still later, Abraham was given a sign of that Covenant (Circumcision) and was told that all his male offspring must as well be circumcised (Gen. 17:1-22).

The Call of Abraham is one of Scripture's theological turning points. Prior to that time, God dealt with the human race as a whole. From that point on, God's Plan was carried out through the family of Abraham. Through that family, God gave His Biblical Revelation to humanity, and from that family the Saviour of all has come.

The Covenant Passages in Genesis show a typical interplay between human beings and God as Sovereign Lord. God announces His purposes, which no action of man can thwart. Abraham responds to God's Revelation with Faith and obedience. Thus, Abraham personally experienced the Blessings that God promised.

CIRCUMCISION

The interplay is implicit in Circumcision: *"Any uncircumcised male, who has not been circumcised in the flesh, will be cut off from his people,"* God announces. *"He has broken My Covenant"* (Gen. 17:14).

The failure of an individual to respond with Faith and with obedience to the stipulations in God's Covenant removed that Covenant-breaking individual from an experience of Covenant Blessings. But the failure of an individual or an entire generation of Israelites did nothing to alter God's commitment to do what He had announced. Human disobedience affects human participation in a Covenant but does not release God from His Covenant oath, at least on a general basis, even though that particular individual might drop out.

What are the provisions of that initial, Abrahamic Covenant? These are the Promises given to Abraham, most of which will be fulfilled only at history's end:

"I will make you into a great nation and I will bless you; I will make your name great, and you will be a blessing. I will bless those who bless you, and whoever curses you I will curse; and all peoples on Earth will be blessed through you" (Gen. 12:2-3). When Abraham arrived in Canaan, God reappeared and added one other clause of Promise, *"To your offspring I will give this land"* (Gen. 12:7), later confirmed by a Covenant oath (Gen. 15:7-21).

The conviction that God spoke to the forefather Abraham, and that Israel inherited the Covenant Promises through Isaac and Jacob is basic to the Old Testament account. It was also basic to the sense of special identity that has preserved Israel as a separate and distinct race to this day, awaiting the coming fulfillment of the Covenant, which delay has been caused by Israel; nevertheless, it will ultimately be fulfilled, even though great numbers of generations of Israelites and untold millions of the past and present, will not be a part of the Covenant, and because of unbelief (Heb. 3:11-12).

THE MOSAIC (LAW) COVENANT

Moses led Israel out of Egypt and through the wilderness on their way to the land that God had promised to Abraham so many centuries before. But from the beginning, the Israelites proved almost impossible for Moses to manage (Ex., Chpts. 15-17). It was while

NOTES

they were at Sinai that God, the Divine Ruler, established a Constitution for the nation-to-be.

That Constitution, the Mosaic Law, follows the pattern of the treaties of the ancient Middle East. The features of such documents are:

1. Preamble: Author identified and His titles given (Ex. 20:1).

2. Historical Prologue: The recounting of the deeds of the ruler on behalf of his people (Ex. 19:4-5).

3. Stipulations: Principles that govern relationships between the parties (Ex. 20:2-7; 21:1-23:19).

4. Blessings and cursings: Announcement of results of keeping and of breaking Covenant conditions (Ex. 23:20-33).

5. Oath: Promise given by the people as they accept the Covenant (Ex. 24:1-8).

The Book of Deuteronomy also seems to follow the structure provided by such a treaty.

The Law Covenant is detailed. It regulates the personal, social, and civil life of Israel, and spells out religious obligations.

There are a number of things about the Law Covenant that are important for us to understand:

GOD

Like The other Biblical Covenants, the Mosaic includes an announcement by God of what He intends to do. As such, Law is an unconditional Covenant.

OBEDIENCE

Unlike the other Biblical Covenants, the Mosaic Law had a particular focus. The other Covenants announce what God will do at history's end. This Covenant announces how God will respond during history during each generation of Israelites, his response being based on their obedience to the Law.

What God intends to do is to bless those generations that keep His Covenant and to discipline severely those generations that failed to do so.

PERSONAL

Unlike the other Biblical Covenants, the Mosaic Covenant was to be confirmed (renewed) by the people. And by that we mean the following:

Each generation had to commit itself to live by the Law given on Sinai (Ex. Chpt. 24; Deut. Chpt. 29; Josh. Chpt. 24).

Each new generation had to choose whom it would serve. And even today in the Jewish tradition a twelve-year-old makes his personal choice. When he becomes *"bar mitzvah"* a *"son of the Commandment,"* he accepts responsibility to live in accord with the stipulations laid down in the ancient Mosaic code.

TEMPORAL

Unlike the other Biblical Covenants, that of the Law was never intended to be permanent. Paul argues that Law is not even implied in the Abrahamic Covenant, which is different in nature from the Covenant of Law. It was introduced some 430 years after Abraham's time. It is a performance code and not a gift offered and confirmed by promise. It neither replaces nor modifies the initial Promise (Gal. 3:15-25). And the Old Testament itself contains God's announcement that there was to come a day when a New Covenant would replace the Covenant of the Mosaic Law.

"'The time is coming,' declares the Lord, *'when I will make a New Covenant with the house of Israel and with the house of Judah. It will not be like the Covenant I made with their forefathers when I took them by the hand to lead them out of Egypt'"* (Jer. 31:31-32).

The Mosaic Covenant has been replaced today by the New Covenant and is the only Biblical Covenant that is not currently in force.

THE DAVIDIC COVENANT

David was Israel's model king. Under David the tiny land expanded some ten times and became a powerful state and came to occupy most, but not all, of the land that God had promised to Israel under the Abrahamic Covenant. As II Samuel Chapter 7 reports, the Prophet Nathan came to David with a Promise from the Lord: *"Your house and your kingdom will endure forever before Me; your throne will be established forever"* (II Sam. 7:16). This was a commitment made by Israel's sovereign Lord, Whose words are trustworthy (II Sam. 7:28). David and the Prophets who followed Nathan viewed this

NOTES

Promise as a Covenant. The Psalmist celebrates both Abrahamic and Davidic Covenants: *"He remembers His Covenant forever, the word He commanded, for a thousand generations, the Covenant He made with Abraham, the oath He swore to Isaac. He confirmed it to Jacob as a decree, to Israel as an everlasting Covenant:*

"'To you I will give the land of Canaan as the portion you will inherit'" (Ps. 105:8-11); and *"'I will declare that your love stands firm forever, that you established your faithfulness in Heaven itself.' You said, 'I have made a Covenant with My chosen one, I've sworn to David My servant, I will establish your line forever and make your throne firm through all generations'"* (Ps. 89:2-4).

Because of this Covenant Promise, the Jewish people of Jesus' day believed firmly that the Messiah was to be a Davidic ruler who would establish the long-promised kingdom. In fact, the genealogies of Jesus in Matthew and Luke are important to authenticate not only His claim to be truly human but also His descent from David and thus His right to the Promised Throne of the Eternal Kingdom.

THE NEW COVENANT FORETOLD

The Promise of a New Covenant to replace the Mosaic Covenant was made at a critical point in Israel's history. The Prophet Jeremiah transmitted God's Promise during a time of national disaster.

It was about 1450 B.C. that God's people received the Mosaic Law. But Israel consistently disobeyed and, therefore, experienced the promised disciplines. Finally the Northern Kingdom, Israel, established at the breakup of David and Solomon's unified land around 931 B.C., was defeated by the Assyrians; the people were deported in 722 B.C.

The Southern Kingdom, Judah, survived. But despite sputtering revivals under a few Godly kings, these people too drifted into idolatry, immorality, and injustice. Jeremiah followed up generations of prophetic warning by announcing that the foretold judgment was to fall on his own generation. Jeremiah's words came true. Judah was devastated, the Temple in Jerusalem was destroyed, and a final group of people were carried captive to Babylon (586 B.C.).

For the first time since the conquest of the Promised Land (1400 B.C.), God's people were torn from the land, the place associated with God's Covenant Promises. One question must have dominated the thoughts of the frightened captives: Had Israel's sin at last caused God to withdraw the Promises made to Abraham and David?

THE ANSWERS AS GIVEN BY THE PROPHET JEREMIAH

Jeremiah said:

1. The exile had initiated a *"time of trouble for Jacob."*

2. *"He will be saved out of it"* (Jer. 30:7). However, it should be noted, that this Passage just quoted as well has to do with the coming Great Tribulation when Israel will undergo extreme persecution, actually coming close to total destruction.

But back to the original meaning, the people who had broken God's Covenant would be punished, but afterward they would be restored. This is God's Promise:

"I have loved you with an everlasting love; I have drawn you with lovingkindness. I will build you up again" (Jer. 31:3-4).

Jerusalem would be rebuilt by another generation, and the land would be Israel's as God had promised (Jer. Chpts. 30-33).

"'Only if the heavens above can be measured and the foundations of the earth below be searched out will I reject all the descendants of Israel because of all they have done,' declares the LORD" (Jer. 31:37).

Nestled among these words of comfort is this unique and unexpected announcement: *"The time is coming when I will make a New Covenant with the House of Israel"* (Jer. 31:31). The Law, relying not on promise but on human performance, had been shown to be unable to produce Righteousness. Now God will replace it with a more effective approach. Like the other Promised Covenants, this Covenant states boldly and clearly what God would do:

"I will put My Law in their minds and write it on their hearts. I will be their God, and they will be My people. No longer will a man teach his neighbor, or a man his brother, saying 'Know the LORD,' because they will all know Me, from the least of them

NOTES

to the greatest," declares the LORD. *"For I will forgive their wickedness and I will remember their sins no more"* (Jer. 31:33-34).

THE NEW COVENANT INSTITUTED

The New Covenant, though prophesied by Jeremiah about 600 years before Christ, was not actually made at that time. The Covenant was made, and confirmed, at the Cross.

At the Last Supper, the night before the Crucifixion, Jesus explained the symbolism of the Communion Cup. He said:

"This is the Blood of the (New) *Covenant, which is poured out for many for the forgiveness of sins"* (Mat. 26:28; Mk. 14:24; Lk. 22:20; I Cor. 11:25). Just as the other Covenants were oath-confirmed, so the New Covenant would be made by a Covenant-initiating Sacrifice. But this time the Offerer and the Sacrifice were One, and the Blood that sealed God's commitment was that of His Own Son. The New Covenant has now been made and confirmed. The Promise of forgiveness is assured. Although only at the Resurrection will we realize the full meaning of what Jesus has done, we can today experience the promised forgiveness and transformation made available in the New Covenant.

THE DIFFERENCE

The difference between the Old and New is striking. The Old Covenant knew a Law that was carved in cold stone. The New Covenant takes the Righteousness that was expressed in Law and supernaturally infuses that Righteousness into the very character of the Believer. Thus, Hebrews quotes the Old Testament foreview as something that is now, through Christ, our own:

"I will put My Laws in their hearts and I will write them on their minds . . . their sins and lawless acts I will remember no more" (Heb. 10:16-17).

There is none of the Law's cold *"do this and live"* in the New Covenant. Instead we meet again the great *"I will"* of God, Who promises that He Himself will transform us from within.

Paul carefully explains that all of God's Promises are appropriated by Faith. Today, to us who, like Abraham, are *"fully persuaded that God had* (has) *power to do what He promises"* (Rom. 4:21) comes the promised Salvation, and with it comes forgiveness and inner transformation. Such are the benefits of Covenant relationship with the Lord.

HUMAN RESPONSE TO COVENANT

In Romans, Chapter 4 and Galatians, Chapter 3, Paul argues that the essence of Covenant is Promise. What can we do to respond to the Promise of God?

We can do only one thing. We are to believe the Promise and consider God's Word trustworthy. We are to consider God's Word so trustworthy that we step out to act on what He says.

It was this Faith that saved Abraham, long before either Circumcision or Law were introduced. It is Faith alone — Faith in Jesus, and more particularly, Faith in what Jesus did for us on the Cross, the seal of God's New Covenant — that saves us today, and in fact has been the manner of salvation for all time.

But what is the relationship of Faith to obligations under the Old Covenant, such as Circumcision and Israel's obligation to keep the Mosaic Law? What is the relationship of Faith today in keeping Jesus' Commandments?

Scripture argues that it is the nature of true Faith to express itself in action.

Those Israelites who heard and believed God's Covenant Promises to Abraham obeyed and were circumcised. Those who loved God in the age of Law followed the Law's commands willingly; and when they sinned, they offered the required Sacrifices.

Under the New Covenant, we who trust Jesus also find our Faith expressing itself in similar loving obedience to Christ, through obedience to Scripture and the Spirit.

We are to place our Trust and our Faith totally and completely, in what Jesus did for us at the Cross, which enables the Holy Spirit to properly help us, and because He functions totally and completely within the parameters of the Finished Work of Christ, which will then give us the victory and overcoming life.

Faith enables human beings to appropriate God's Promises and experience their benefits personally; however, we must always understand, that when we use the word *"Faith,"* or possibly I should say, when Paul uses the

NOTES

word *"Faith,"* he is speaking, and without exception, of Faith in the great Sacrifice of Christ, which makes all things possible.

But whether or not we believe in God's Promises, in no way negates the Promises, even though a lack of Faith will definitely negate them on our part; irrespective, the Covenant Promises stand for those who will believe them. God will always accomplish his purposes in history and in all who believe.

God's Way has always been Faith. He has never deviated from that particular manner. But again, when we say *"Faith,"* always and without exception, we're speaking of Faith in the Finished Work of Christ. It has always been this way, even under Law.

The Sacrifices under the Old Testament economy could not really save anything, or atone for sin in any manner, in the sense of removing sin. However, Faith in Who the Sacrifices represented, namely the Lord Jesus Christ, Who was to come at a particular given time, and Who would give His Life as a ransom for many, actually constituted the Salvation process of that time. From the day that man fell in the Garden of Eden, it has always been Faith in Christ, and more particularly the giving of Himself in Sacrifice, which constituted Salvation. Admittedly, the benefits of Salvation under the New Covenant are far more pronounced than under the Old, and because the Cross is now a fact. Before the Cross, men looked forward to a Prophetic Jesus. Now, men look backward to a historical Jesus.

(We are indebted to Lawrence O. Richards for much of the material on Covenants.)

BETTER PROMISES

The phrase, *"Which was established upon Better Promises,"* presents the New Covenant which is explicitly based on the cleansing and forgiveness of all sins, which the Old Covenant could not actually do. The Old Covenant of Law was a Covenant of types and shadows and was abolished when the realities of those shadows appeared:

1. The First Covenant was given by Moses; the Second by Jesus Christ (Mat. 26:28; Jn. 1:17; Gal. 3:19; Heb. 9:15).

2. The first is *"the Law of Moses"*; the other *"the Law of Christ"* (Acts 13:39; Gal. 6:2).

3. The first is *"the law of sin"*; the other is *"the Law of Righteousness"* (Rom. 7:7-25; 8:1-4; 9:31).

4. The first is the *"Law of the flesh"*; the other is *"the Law of the Spirit"* (Rom. 7:5-6; 8:1-4; Gal. 5:16-26).

5. The first is *"not of Faith"*; the other is *"the Law of Faith"* (Rom. 3:27; Gal. 3:12).

6. The Old Covenant brought death, because that's all it could bring, while the New Covenant brings life (Rom. 8:1-4; II Cor. 3:6-18; Gal. 3:21; Heb. 9:15; 10:1-18).

7. The First Covenant demanded Righteousness, which man could not supply; the New Covenant gives Righteousness, actually the Righteousness of Christ to all who will simply believe (Lk. 10:28; Rom. 8:1-4; Gal. 3:1-29; 5:1-26).

8. The First Covenant was powerless to save from sin; the New Covenant saves to the uttermost (Heb. 7:11-28; 8:7-13; 9:9-28; 10:1-18).

9. The First Covenant had continuing Sacrifices; the New Covenant which is based on better Promises, had only one Sacrifice, the Sacrifice of Christ which is eternally sufficient (Rom. 6:6-13; Heb. 9:9-14; 10:14).

10. The First Covenant had a sinful mediator, the High Priest (Gal. 3:19); the New Covenant has a sinless Mediator, the Lord Jesus Christ (I Tim. 2:5; Heb. 7:26; I Pet. 2:22).

11. The First Covenant was ratified by animal blood, which was woefully insufficient (Ex. 29:1-8; Heb. 9:16-22); the New Covenant is ratified by the Blood of Christ, which is totally sufficient (Mat. 26:28).

12. The First Covenant was based on performance, to which no one could subscribe; the New Covenant is based on Grace (Jn. 1:17; Rom. 3:24-31; Gal. 3:10-12; Eph. 2:8-9).

13. The First Covenant could not redeem, while the New Covenant can (Rom. 8:1-4; Gal. 3:10-14; Eph. 1:7; Col. 1:14; Heb. 7:25).

14. The First Covenant was too weak to overcome sin; the New Covenant gives victory over sin (Rom. 6:1-23; 8:1-4; Eph. 2:8-9; I Jn. 5:1-18).

WAS ANYTHING OF THE OLD COVENANT BROUGHT OVER INTO THE NEW?

First of all, Jesus fulfilled all of the Old Covenant in totality, and that speaks of all

NOTES

Ceremonial Laws along with Rituals, which includes the Sacrifices, etc., and as well all the Commandments. The Scripture plainly says, *"Having abolished in His flesh* (the Crucifixion) *the enmity* (the law of bondage and death), *even the law of commandments contained in ordinances. Blotting out* (making void) *the handwriting of ordinances that was against us, which was contrary to us, and took it out of the way, nailing it to His Cross . . . Let no man therefore judge you in meat, or in drink, or in respect of an holyday, or of the new moon, or of the Sabbath days: which are a shadow of things to come; but the body* (or reality of those things were mere shadows) *is of Christ"* (Eph. 2:15; Col. 2:14-17).

So the idea is, every single thing of the Old Law was fulfilled in Christ and done away; however, nine of the ten Commandments were actually reestablished in the New Covenant. Let's see what the Scriptures say: We will place the Old Commandments on the left, which are all found in Exodus Chapter 20, and then immediately following where this is found in the New Testament:

1. Thou shalt have no other gods before Me: (Rom. 5:8; I Cor. Chpt. 13; I Jn. 3:1-4:21).

2. Thou shalt not make unto thee any graven image: (Acts Chpt. 15; Rom. 2:22; I Cor. 5:10; 6:9-11; 8:1-10; 10:7, 19-28; II Cor. 6:16; Eph. 5:5; I Jn. 5:21).

3. Thou shalt not take the Name of the Lord thy God in vain: (Acts 26:11; Rom. 2:24; Col. 3:8; Titus Chpt. 3).

4. Remember the Sabbath day to keep it holy: This is not commanded in the New Covenant, of which we will say more momentarily.

5. Honor thy father and thy mother: (Eph. 6:2-3; Col. 3:20; II Tim. 3:2).

6. Thou shalt not kill: (Rom. 13:9; I Pet. 4:15; I Jn. 3:15).

7. Thou shalt not commit adultery: (Rom. 2:22; 13:9; I Cor. 6:9-11; Gal. 5:19-21; Heb. 13:4; etc.).

8. Thou shalt not steal: (Rom. 2:21; 13:9; Eph. 4:28).

9. Thou shalt not bear false witness: (Rom. 13:9).

10. Thou shalt not covet: (Rom. 13:9; I Cor. 5:10-11; 6:9-11; etc.).

WHY WAS THE FOURTH COMMANDMENT, *"REMEMBER THE SABBATH"* LEFT OUT OF THE NEW COVENANT?

The Old Testament command to *"remember the Sabbath,"* is not found anywhere in the New Covenant. If the Holy Spirit had wanted it to be a part of the New Covenant it was in His power to command that it be so, even as it was in the Old Covenant. But since the Spirit of God, Who gave the Word, did not require the fourth Commandment to be a part of the New Covenant, and since the New Covenant teaches that men are to be persuaded in their own minds as to what day they want to observe, it is folly to practice that which the Lord does not demand.

As well, the old Jewish Sabbath was a particular *"sign"* and *"token"* of the Old Covenant between God and Israel (Ex. 16:23; 20:8; 31:13-18; Deut. 5:2-3; 29:13-15; I Chron. 16:17; II Chron. 5:10; Ezek. 20:12-20).

The Old Covenant was one between God and the nation of Israel and it never was between God and the Gentiles who were not a part of Israel.

HOW DO CHRISTIANS PRESENTLY KEEP THE SABBATH?

Under the Old Covenant, keeping the Sabbath, along with Circumcision, were the standards of obedience to that Covenant. When Christ came, of which both the Sabbath and Circumcision were types, following Him is now the same thing as keeping the Sabbath and engaging in Circumcision.

The *"Sabbath"* represented the *"rest"* which Believers now have in Christ. In fact, the Sabbath was meant to be a day of rest. Sunday now is a day of worship, or at least it is referred to as such. This was not really the case with the Sabbath of old, it being entirely a day of rest. As such, it was meant to symbolize something, and that something was the *"rest"* which all find in Christ, once He is accepted as Saviour and Lord. In fact, there is no *"rest"* outside of Christ.

Circumcision, on the other hand, is a type of the Cross. When the little baby boy was circumcised at eight days old, blood was shed, and separation was effected. This typifies the Blood that was shed by Christ at the Cross,

which separates believing man from his sins, and which alone can separate believing man from his sins.

Inasmuch as Christ has now come, for an individual to attempt to continue to keep the Sabbath, which, incidentally is Saturday, or to circumcise their little baby boys, at least for any reason other than health reasons, is, in effect, a statement saying that Christ did not finish the work, and this symbolism needs to continue. In other words, such would be a gross insult to Christ.

THE CROSS OF CHRIST

Christ is the Source of all things, and the Cross is the means by which all things come to us. The Law was meant to be temporal. It was meant in its every circumstance to point to Christ, and in every capacity. So, when Christ came, He fulfilled the Law in every respect, both in the keeping of its precepts, and doing so perfectly, and also in satisfying its just claims upon man, because all men had broken the Law. On the Cross of Calvary, Jesus, Paul said, *"has redeemed us from the curse of the law, being made a curse for us: for it is written, cursed is every one who hangs on a tree"* (Gal. 3:13).

That means that Christ satisfied the demands of the broken Law, and did so in every respect. It also means that the Sacrificial System is no more; the Levitical Priesthood is no more; all the rituals and ceremonies, which include the Sabbath and Circumcision, are all done away with. They are no more! The Cross answered every single question, met every demand, and satisfied the Righteousness of God in every respect.

In effect, when Christians presently try to keep the old Jewish Sabbath of Saturday, they are denying the Cross, which, in effect, means they are denying Christ. Nothing could be more serious than that! It's certainly not wrong to go to Church on a Saturday, or any other day; however, when that becomes an object of faith, even as it does with many, pure and simple, those engaged in such are committing sin by carrying out these things.

While the world has ever been trying to invent another god, the Church, sadly and regrettably, has ever been trying to invent another sacrifice. Paul also said:

"But this Man, after He had offered one Sacrifice for sins forever, sat down on the right hand of God;

"From henceforth expecting till His enemies be made His footstool.

"For by one Offering He has perfected forever them who are sanctified" (Heb. 10:12-14).

This plainly tells us that the Cross is the basis of our Sanctification, and not the keeping of some ritual, such as the Sabbath, etc.

THE OBJECT OF FAITH

In all of this, it is Satan's desire, in fact, his strong demand, that the Christian switch his Faith from Christ and the Cross to something else. And, to be sure, the Evil One doesn't really too much care what the something else actually is. He doesn't care how religious it is, or anything else, just so the object of faith is something other than the Cross. In fact, probably one could say, without fear of contradiction, that this is the great sin of the Church – the making of something other than the Cross of Christ the object of their faith.

We could go into detail as to why the Early Church didn't keep the old Jewish Sabbath, which they most certainly did not. We could talk about how Sunday replaced Saturday. But the main reason for all of this is that which we have discussed. It is that Jesus satisfied all of that in His Life, living, and, above all, His Sacrificial, Atoning, Mediatorial Death on the Cross of Calvary. As stated, Believers presently keep the Sabbath, which is the only way it can be kept, by placing their Faith exclusively in Christ and what He did at the Cross, all on our behalf, which affords a *"rest for the people of God."* Also, as stated, this is what the old Jewish Sabbath was all about. It was meant to serve as a Type of One Who was to come, and that One was, and is, the Lord Jesus Christ.

One cannot truly find spiritual rest in keeping a particular day. It can only be found in Christ.

So, this is the real reason that the early Christians gathered for worship on the first day of the week (Acts 20:7; I Cor. 11:17; 16:1-2; Heb. 10:25). It was to honor Christ and what He did for us at the Cross.

NOTES

IF NINE OF THE TEN COMMANDMENTS ARE IN THE NEW COVENANT, AND THEY DEFINITELY ARE, DOESN'T THIS PUT CHRISTIANS BACK INTO THE MODE OF LAW-KEEPING?

No! That is if it's addressed correctly. Before we state how this should be addressed, please allow the following comments concerning Law.

In fact, the Christian's greatest problem is law. There are two reasons for that:

1. First of all, there is something in Christians, even in the best of us, whomever that might be, which likes law. I speak of rules and regulations of any kind. Somehow, the attempt to keep these types of things make us feel holy or righteous, etc.

To prove my point, as I've already mentioned in this Volume, if most Christians were to be asked as to what it means to be *"in Christ,"* or to be *"close to God,"* etc., most would think of the things they do, such as faithful Church attendance, etc. That brings us to the next point.

2. The doing of spiritual things makes Christians think that such constitutes *"walking after the Spirit,"* etc. The Truth is, if we do these things, and depend on that to draw us closer to God, we've just entered into Law, whether we realize it or not. And that's the second point; we engage in law, and we don't even really know that it is law. While it's not the Law of Moses, but rather laws we have devised ourselves, or others have devised, it is still law in the eyes of God, which negates the help of the Holy Spirit.

While it is true that nine of the Ten Commandments were brought over into the New Covenant, and while it is also true that such are incumbent upon all Believers, in order to address it correctly, we must understand the following:

Even though we are under the New Covenant which is based on much better promises, still, if we try to keep these Commandments as we would normally think of doing such, we will not succeed. We must understand that these are moral Commandments, and as such, they cannot change. If it was wrong to steal 3,000 years ago, it's wrong to steal presently. So most definitely, these

Commandments, as stated, are incumbent upon all Believers. The following is the way it should be done:

JESUS

1. Jesus has already kept all of these Commandments. He kept them in totality and in perfection. As well, He did it all on our behalf, simply because we could not do it for ourselves.

2. We as Believers are *"in Christ,"* and that means that the position of law-keeping has been awarded us, simply because of what Christ did on our behalf. In other words, God looks at me as a keeper of the law in every respect, and because of what Jesus has done on my behalf, and my Faith in that.

3. As a Believer, I am to understand that all that I have in Christ was made possible by what Jesus did on the Cross.

4. Understanding that, my Faith is to rest exclusively in the Finished Work of Christ.

5. When this is done, the Holy Spirit will then help the Believer be exactly what he should be. As we've said repeatedly, we must have the help of the Holy Spirit. He Alone can bring about in our lives what is needed. As well, He works exclusively within the parameters of the great Sacrifice of Christ, meaning that He demands that we exhibit Faith at all times in the Cross of Christ.

6. As a Believer, I have a position in Christ, awarded to me because of what Christ did at the Cross on my behalf, and my Faith in that Finished Work.

7. Understanding all of this, I do not worry about keeping any type of Law whatsoever. In fact, even though the Law is very much alive, because of my being in Christ, I am *"dead to the Law"* (Rom. 7:4). As a Believer, it has no effect on me, because Christ has already kept it in totality, and as well, has suffered its penalty, all on my behalf. Consequently, my Faith in Christ and what He did for me at the Cross, which gives me the help and power of the Holy Spirit, will cause me to live the life I ought to live with all of the Commandments being kept, plus anything else that's needed. As stated, it's all done by the Spirit (Rom. 8:11).

8. Whenever the Believer starts trying to keep Commandments or to obey rules and regulations of some nature, he at that moment

takes himself out from trust in the Cross, which as well stops the help of the Holy Spirit, which then demands failure. Actually, the entirety of the Seventh Chapter of Romans portrays Paul, although saved and baptized with the Holy Spirit, attempting to live the life he ought to live, but not being able to do so. He was trying to do it without Faith in the Cross, which denied the help of the Holy Spirit, which left him in a perilous situation, even as it does all Believers who follow that course (Rom. Chpt. 7). However, it must be understood, that Paul at that time didn't know and understand God's prescribed order of victory, and neither did anyone else in the world of that day; however, the Holy Spirit explained to the Apostle what the Cross actually means to Believers, which Paul gave us in Romans, Chapters 6 and 8.

9. What do we mean by the *"Law"* not being dead?

As stated, Believers are dead to the Law, but the Law itself is not dead, meaning that it is very active. However, it being active has no effect on me whatsoever, as long as I understand that Christ has already satisfied its demands, and that my being in Him guarantees me all that He is, which refers to total victory. Consequently, the Law has no effect on such a person.

However, if the Believer ever attempts to try to keep law, whether it's a law of his own making, or whatever, he will find out very quickly that the law is very much alive. The first thing that happens is this:

REBELLION

A. The very idea of the Believer switching his Faith from Christ and what Christ did for us at the Cross, to something else, automatically constitutes sin. In fact, the Christian trusting in anything other than the Cross, constitutes the highest form of rebellion. When this happens, the Believer has just put himself under law, simply because there's no other place to go if one moves his Faith to other things. And please understand, Satan is very subtle in all of this. The *"other things"* to where we move our Faith, are generally very spiritual things, which makes us think that everything is as it should be; however, to be sure, if it's Faith in anything other than the Cross, of necessity, and no matter what those things might be, it all must come under the Judgment of God.

B. The greatest struggle for the Believer is to keep his Faith anchored in the Cross of Christ. The temptation is ever strong for it to be moved elsewhere. And to be sure, Satan does his best work inside the Church. This means that fellow Christians will oftentimes attempt to lure you away, but to do so, is rebellion against God, which puts the Believer under Law, and which can only bring spiritual catastrophe. And regrettably, because of not knowing and understanding the great Truth of the Cross, that's where most Believers presently are — under Law! And it should be quickly said, if the Believer doesn't understand the Cross, and almost none do, there there's no place else to go but law.

(7) "FOR IF THAT FIRST COVENANT HAD BEEN FAULTLESS, THEN SHOULD NO PLACE HAVE BEEN SOUGHT FOR THE SECOND."

The exposition is:

1. The First Covenant served its purpose, which was to point to the coming Messiah.

2. It could not properly atone for sin, therefore, it was faulty.

3. Jesus Christ in His Substitutionary Atonement was and is the answer to lost humanity, and in fact, was ever planned by the Godhead to be the answer (I Pet. 1:18-20).

THE FIRST COVENANT

The phrase, *"For if that first Covenant had been faultless,"* proclaims the fact that the First Covenant definitely was not faultless. In fact, it was faulty in every manner of its operation:

1. The Priests were human, therefore, faulty. Christ, while becoming human, was also God and, therefore, Perfect.

2. The sacrifices of animal blood could not take away sin. The Sacrifice of Christ took away all sin.

3. The animal sacrifices had to continue to be offered, whereas the Sacrifice of Christ was only once, and because that was all that was necessary.

4. The High Priests of the old system could only bring people to God dimly. By contrast, Jesus opened up the way in totality for humanity to come into the very Holy of

Holies (Heb. 4:16).

5. The High Priesthood of the old system was ever changing, because of the mortality of the Priests, while Christ ever liveth (Heb. 7:25).

Had that First Covenant been perfect, it would never have been set to one side and a New Covenant brought in. But because of its imperfection on account of the weakness and frailty of the flesh, God had declared long before the Coming of our Lord Jesus Christ into the world that a New Covenant was to be consummated with Israel and Judah.

A FAULTY COVENANT?

Let not the Reader think that Paul is claiming that the First Covenant was faulty as it regarded the design of the Lord. In fact, the Lord has never made anything faulty of imperfect. For what it was designed to do, it was perfect in that respect; however, the idea of this is, that it was not designed to take away sin, or to provide a foundation of Grace on which the believing sinner could stand, and thereby be justified by Faith.

The First Covenant did exactly what the Lord designed it to do, and did so admirably! It was actually only meant to be a preparatory Covenant, and that it was in detail, ever pointing a finger at the Second Covenant which was to come.

THE SECOND COVENANT

The phrase, *"Then should no place have been sought for the Second,"* proclaims the necessity of the New Covenant.

The New Covenant, or as Paul refers to it here as the *"Second,"* was ever in the Mind of God from the very beginning (I Pet. 1:18-20). In essence, the Holy Spirit through the Apostle is saying, that it should be obvious that the First Covenant was inadequate, and in more ways than one. The idea is, how in the world could these Christian Jews, who had in fact, *"tasted of the Heavenly Gift, and were made partakers of the Holy Spirit,"* even remotely consider forsaking the *"Second"* for the *"First"*?

(8) "FOR FINDING FAULT WITH THEM, HE SAITH, BEHOLD, THE DAYS COME, SAITH THE LORD, WHEN I WILL MAKE A NEW COVENANT WITH THE HOUSE OF ISRAEL AND WITH THE HOUSE OF JUDAH:"

The exegesis is:

1. The pronoun *"them"* refers to the fact that God is speaking here of the Israelites, and not the Covenant itself. The true cause of failure lay in the character of the people, not in the Law, which was holy, righteous, and good.

2. Paul quotes from Jeremiah 31:31-34.

3. The New Covenant was with the Houses of both Israel and Judah, and that because of the Promises.

FAULT

The phrase, *"For finding fault with them,"* presents a subtle delicacy of language in the insensible shifting from the Covenant to the people. As we've already stated, the fault wasn't actually in the Covenant per se as we would think of such. It was faulty in the sense that it could not take away sin; however, it was never designed in the first place to take away sin. Actually, it could not function in this capacity, due to the fact that the blood of bulls and goats is woefully insufficient.

Going back to the phrase, *"Finding fault with them,"* the First Covenant was actually designed to glaringly portray the fault of the people. It was somewhat like a poultice which pulls corruption to the surface. The fact of the corruption is not the fault of the poultice. The medicine only drew to the surface what was already there; and so it was with the Law. It drew to the surface what was already in the hearts of people, and we speak of the ugliness of sin.

However, it had no power to cleanse from sin or to destroy the power of sin. So it was faulty in that respect, but not according to the design of God, but only because it was designed in that fashion.

While a pickup truck can definitely haul some things, it definitely cannot haul the giant load that a dump truck can haul. It was not designed to do that; likewise, the Law wasn't designed by God to redeem humanity. But what it was designed to do, it carried out and functioned perfectly.

THE DAY IS COMING

The phrase, *"Behold, the days come, saith the Lord,"* now presents Paul quoting from Jeremiah 31:31-34. It is an astute move. He puts the Jewish recipients of this Letter in the

place where they will have to accept the New Testament and the Testimony of their own Prophet to the effect that God would bring in a New Testament, or, if they reject the New Testament, they will be forced to reject their own Prophet. Thus does Paul build his argument upon the Old Testament Scriptures, even as he was very oft to do — the very Word of God his Readers professed to believe (Wuest).

A NEW COVENANT

The phrase, *"When I will make a New Covenant with the House of Israel and with the House of Judah,"* proclaims the Northern Kingdom which was Israel, and the Southern Kingdom, which was Judah. Israel broke apart and was divided during the reign of Rehoboam, the son of Solomon. The Northern Kingdom consisted of some nine Tribes, and called itself Israel, while the Southern Kingdom consisted of Judah, which was the largest Tribe of all, and Benjamin, as well as Levi. Also, Simeon had its inheritance within the borders of Judah, so would remain with the Southern Kingdom.

This was the beginning of 260 years of division and strife between the two nations of Israel. Wars, bloodshed, and intrigue became the program of a once united and Godly people.

God's plan for a united nation being a blessing to all other nations of the Earth had now come to a definite standstill and both Kingdoms faced ruin and dispersion among the Gentiles, which would ultimately come to pass for both Kingdoms.

ISRAEL, THE CHOSEN CHANNEL

It is important to note that the New Testament is actually not Christianity. This means that the Book of Hebrews is not an argument the purpose of which is to prove that Christianity is superior to Judaism as seen in its Founder, the Lord Jesus Christ.

The First Testament (Old Covenant) was a Covenant made with Israel. The New Testament (New Covenant) is also a Covenant made with Israel. In fact, God made no Covenants with the Gentiles. Israel is the chosen channel through which He brings Salvation to the human race.

The First Testament consisted of a system of Sacrifices, symbolic in their import.

The New Testament is as well, a Sacrifice, the Lord Jesus at the Cross, actual in its character, and efficacious (effective) in its merits.

The First Testament, one might say, began at Genesis 3:21, and ended at the Cross. The New Testament began at the Cross and is an everlasting one (Heb. 13:20).

Christianity refers to the Mystical Body of Christ of which He is the Head. This Body is composed of all who are saved from Pentecost to the Rapture. The New Testament actually made Christianity possible.

The Saints of the Church Age are saved through the Blood of the Sacrifice which was offered under the New Testament. This is the relationship between the New Testament and Christianity (Wuest).

It was intended by God that Israel would be the recipient of the New Covenant and thereby, be a channel through which the entirety of the Gentile world could be saved, at least those who would believe, which would actually be a fulfillment of the Abrahamic Covenant (Gen. 12:1-3).

Sadly and regrettably, Israel rejected the Covenant and thereby destroyed themselves; however, this in no way negated the Covenant. The door remains open to all, both Jews and Gentiles. Due to the fact that most of the Jews have rejected the Covenant, the Church thereby is made up almost altogether of Gentiles.

The idea is, Israel's rejection of the Covenant in no way destroyed the Covenant, even though it did delay the total advent of the Kingdom of Heaven, which Jesus proclaimed in Matthew, Chapter 24. Nevertheless, there will come an hour, when Israel will accept the Covenant in totality, and that hour is not so far off.

Then Israel will no longer be divided, thereby one again, and will serve the purpose for which God originally intended. This will be in the coming Kingdom Age.

NEW

The word *"New,"* as in *"New Covenant,"* establishes the verbal inspiration of the Scriptures, for on that one word occurring once (Jer. 31:31) is based the whole of the argument of this Chapter. God said He would do it some 600 years before Christ, and that's exactly what He did!

NOTES

(9) "NOT ACCORDING TO THE COVENANT THAT I MADE WITH THEIR FATHERS IN THE DAY WHEN I TOOK THEM BY THE HAND TO LEAD THEM OUT OF THE LAND OF EGYPT; BECAUSE THEY CONTINUED NOT IN MY COVENANT, AND I REGARDED THEM NOT, SAITH THE LORD."

The structure is:

1. The New Covenant is far different from the Old Covenant in nature and contents.

2. To *"take them by the hand"* refers to the immaturity of the people.

3. Israel refused to obey the Covenant made by God.

4. Because of disobedience, even willful disobedience, the Lord allowed them to be made captives of heathen nations.

THE NEW COVENANT TOTALLY UNLIKE THE OLD

The phrase, *"Not according to the Covenant that I made with their fathers,"* refers to the Law of Moses, which was given some 50 days after they were delivered from Egypt.

The word *"Covenant"* as used here, means *"to place between two."* Thus, a Covenant is something placed between two, an arrangement between two parties.

Paul uses the same word in Hebrews 9:16-20 where the meaning of the word is that of a testament in the sense of a last will or testament, the legal instrument by which something is bequeathed to someone. Thus, the words *"Covenant"* or *"Testament"* refer in this Epistle to one thing, the Act of God providing for the Salvation of the believing sinner through the Blood Atonement offered on Calvary's Cross by the Lord Jesus.

It is a Covenant in the sense that it is an agreement on God's part that He will give Salvation to the sinner who will receive it by Faith in the High Priest He has appointed. It is a Last Will or Testament in the sense that God bequeaths Salvation to the sinner who will receive it on the terms of the will, Faith in the Blood of Jesus. Christ, the Divine Testator, dies to make the will effective (Wuest).

The First Covenant pointed constantly to the New Covenant, which could bring about this great Salvation, which in fact, it (the First Covenant) could not bring about.

A MINOR

The phrase, *"In the day when I took them by the hand to lead them out of the land of Egypt,"* speaks to the immaturity of Israel; consequently, she was treated as a minor.

Paul addressed this very thing when he said, *"Now I say, that the heir, as long as he is a child, differeth nothing from a servant, though he be lord of all;*

"But is under tutors and governors until the time appointed of the father" (Gal. 4:1-2).

As a result, God put the nation under laws and regulations. If Israel behaved itself, it was rewarded, and if it misbehaved, it was punished. Israel was taught by object lessons as one would teach a child; for instance, the Tabernacle, Priesthood, Offerings, the gorgeous vestments of the High Priest, etc.

Under this Covenant, the Believer and Israel were declared righteous (Gal. 3:6), that is, if they properly exhibited Faith in Whom the Sacrifices represented, namely, the Lord Jesus Christ.

Men have always been saved the same way, and that's by Faith. Long before the Law, God gave to Abraham the Covenant of Faith (Gen. 15:6). This and this alone was the way of Salvation.

However, Israel inverted the process, making Faith subservient to the Law, instead of the Law subservient to Faith. In other words, they tried to make Salvation out of keeping the Law, which they could not do to begin with; nevertheless, there were some in Israel who evidenced Faith in God, just as the Lord had told Abraham that man must do, and were definitely saved. But regrettably, that number was few!

But again we state, under the Old Covenant, even for those who evidenced true Faith, the Believer was treated by the Lord as a child, and for many reasons. The Old Covenant was very limited in what it could do, which especially centered up in the fact, that even though the Holy Spirit could definitely help all Israelites who evidenced Faith, He could not dwell in them, as He would do after the Cross (Jn. 14:17).

The Holy Spirit could not come in to abide forever in Believers before the Cross, because the sin debt had not yet been paid, and was,

therefore, still attached to each individual, and would not be paid until the Cross. The blood of bulls and goats simply could not take away this debt (Heb. 10:4).

Due to that fact, only so much progression could be made, hence the immaturity of Israel under the Old Covenant.

THE DISOBEDIENCE OF ISRAEL

The phrase, *"Because they continued not in My Covenant,"* presents the obvious, Israel abandoning the Ways of the Lord.

When Israel failed to be true to the Covenant, God's solicitude and concern for His chosen people gave place to one of righteous indignation, which attitude culminated with the captivities. How serious was Israel's defection is seen in the words that Delitzsch quotes from Schelling:

"The Law appears to be the mere ideal of a religious constitution, as far as Israel was concerned. The Jews for the most part, conducted themselves as if it never existed. In practice, they were almost throughout polytheists (worshippers of many gods). The substance of their national feeling was formed by heathendom: the accidents only (going to the right way by accident) by Revelation. From the queen of Heaven down to the abominations of the Phoenicians, and even Cybele, the Jews passed through every grade of paganism."

Delitzsch adds, *"In fact, there is no period in the history of Israel before the captivity, in which more or less idolatry was not united with the worship of Jehovah, except the time of David and the first years of Solomon, during which times the influence of Samuel still continued to be felt. And when by the captivity into Babylon, idol-worship was completely eradicated from the people, as far at least as regards that part of Israel which returned, it is well-known that a hypocritical letter-worship (they worshiped the letter of the Law, instead of God Who gave it) got the mastery over them, which was morally very little better."*

CONTINUE

"Continue" in the Greek is *"emmeno,"* and means, *"to persevere, to hold fast, to be true to, abide by."*

Jesus said the very same thing in His day to those Jews who believed on Him:

"If ye continue in My Word, then are ye My Disciples indeed" (Jn. 8:31).

As should be obvious, this one word *"continue"* shoots down the fallacious theory of *"unconditional eternal security."* The idea is, it's not the one who begins the race, but the one who ends the race. While the Lord will never throw anyone over because of failure, they will in effect throw themselves over, if they fail to continue in the Word of God, which in effect, means to keep believing. In fact, the entirety of this Book of Hebrews deals with this very thing.

Paul is writing to Christian Jews, which of course refers to Jews who had accepted Christ as their Lord and their Saviour, but were now very seriously considering abandoning Christ, and going back into ritual worship. The Apostle, on which we have already commented, told them that if they did this thing, continuing to repudiate Christ, it would be impossible to *"renew them again unto repentance; seeing they crucify to themselves the Son of God afresh, and put Him to an open shame"* (Heb. 6:4-6).

Actually, there is no way that one can read the Bible, which includes the history of the Jews, as well as the New Covenant to the Church, and honestly continue to believe in the doctrine of unconditional eternal security. The evidence is so overwhelming otherwise, even as we are studying here, that it is irrefutable. The Reader should always remember the following:

If a Biblical Doctrine is correct, it will always fall out to the betterment of one's character. Otherwise, it will fall out to the detriment of one's character. The doctrine of unconditional eternal security in no way betters the character of any individual, but in fact, does the very opposite. There are untold millions at present, who claim Salvation, whose lives are ungodly, and actually getting more ungodly by each passing day, with these individuals making no effort to have the situation changed, because they believe the lie of *"unconditional eternal security."* As should be obvious, the character of such a person definitely is not improving, with this doctrine at least being partially to blame.

NOTES

Now that doesn't mean that everyone who believes in unconditional eternal security falls into such a category, but it does definitely pertain to most, I think!

REJECTION

The phrase, *"I regarded them not, saith the Lord,"* refers to the fact of Israel rejecting God's Covenant, so God rejected them. God would reject them as His people, and give new laws better adapted to save men. Instead of regarding and treating them as His friends, which He longingly desired to do, because of their rejection of His Covenant, He would have no alternative but to punish them for their offenses, and visit them with calamities.

From this, we also learn that God guides everything as it regards His children. And let not the modern Believer think that just because we're living in the age of Grace, that the principle of obedience and disobedience no longer holds true.

The Truth is, God has always blessed for obedience, and has always rejected Believers in some fashion, because of disobedience. It cannot be otherwise!

And what do we exactly mean by *"blessing"* or *"rejection"*?

Blessing covers every aspect of individual needs, be they physical, material, financial, domestical, but above all spiritual. Rejection means that God withholds these blessings.

However, we must understand, that *"blessing"* does not mean that one is exempt from all difficulties and problems. The Scripture plainly says, *"Many are the afflictions of the righteous: but the LORD delivereth him out of them all"* (Ps. 34:19).

Using Paul as an example, as is known, he suffered severe persecution; however, such definitely was not allowed by God because of failing on Paul's part or disobedience in any manner, but rather for other reasons altogether.

REASONS?

Some Christians have the idea that the Blessings of God refer to a lot of money and no problems. While that certainly may be the case at times, it is not the case most of the time. The greatest blessings of all are Spiritual Blessings, which refers to the Holy Spirit drawing one closer to God. Nothing could be greater than that! But there's something else we need to look at, continuing to use Paul as an example.

As stated, it should be obvious that Paul did not suffer the extreme persecution which he in fact did suffer, because of sin in his life or disobedience of any nature. Knowing that nothing can happen to a Believer but that the Lord causes it or allows it, we know that the Lord allowed the persecution that came Paul's way.

Why?

I think Paul himself answered the question when he said, *"Lest I should be exalted above measure through the abundance of the Revelations, there was given to me a thorn in the flesh, the messenger of Satan to buffet me,"* and then he says again, *"lest I should be exalted above measure"* (II Cor. 12:7).

Pride is a great problem in all of us, even in the great Paul. Perhaps there are other ways of the Lord combating this problem in some of us, but I think that in most of us, it requires this, at least in some measure, which the Lord allowed regarding Paul. Such persecution keeps an individual humble, keeps them praying, and keeps them trusting God.

That being the case, what I'm about to say, although seldom said, yet I believe to be true.

BLESSINGS?

If in fact, nothing can happen to a Believer but that the Lord causes it or allows it, which we know to be true, and if in fact such similar problems come upon us and not because of sin or disobedience, then we must conclude these things as well as *"Blessings."* The idea is, anything that will keep us trusting the Lord, or will draw us closer to God, can only be construed as Blessing. I realize it's difficult for us to think of such as *"Blessings,"* but they definitely are!

Even if we have sinned or disobeyed the Lord, with the problem continuing long enough that it would require chastisement from the Lord, even acute chastisement, that as well, can be construed as none other than Blessing, and of course, I speak of chastisement. No sin or disobedience could ever be looked at as Blessing in any capacity; however, the chastisement from the Lord which brings us back to God, or one might say, back

to the right way, is definitely a Blessing.

Israel's situation was somewhat different. The Lord had chastised them in many and varied ways, all to no avail. So their rejection of His Covenant was not a momentary lapse, but rather a wholesale turnabout. In other words, they in effect told the Lord that they no longer desired Him, that they rather desired to worship idols. That is when God rejected them. It must be understood, that God will not reject any individual until that individual rejects Him. In fact, that's exactly what was happening to some of the Christian Jews of Paul's day. They were on the verge of rejecting Christ, and which some of them had already done so.

(10) "FOR THIS IS THE COVENANT THAT I WILL MAKE WITH THE HOUSE OF ISRAEL AFTER THOSE DAYS, SAITH THE LORD; I WILL PUT MY LAWS INTO THEIR MIND, AND WRITE THEM IN THEIR HEARTS: I WILL BE TO THEM A GOD, AND THEY SHALL BE TO ME A PEOPLE:"

The composition is:

1. The Covenant mentioned here is the *"New Covenant."*

2. *"After those days,"* refers to the time of the Old Covenant.

3. Whereas the Old Covenant dealt with externals, the New Covenant deals with the mind and the heart, which is the only manner in which a person can actually be changed.

4. Only in this fashion can there be a proper relationship.

THE NEW COVENANT

The phrase, *"For this is the Covenant that I will make with the House of Israel,"* refers as stated, to the *"New Covenant,"* under which we presently live, and in fact, which will last forever (Heb. 13:20).

The Lord's Supper which presents the emblems of the New Covenant was definitely made with the House of Israel, because it was to these people that the promises were given. But as stated, the religious leaders of Israel rejected the Covenant and rejected the Giver of the Covenant, actually crucifying Him.

They were so Biblically confused, that they thought by crucifying Him, such would prove to the people of Israel that He was an imposter; however, they only succeeded in ratifying the Covenant, which the Crucifixion was meant to do.

It was predestined that Christ would go to the Cross, that being the way that the Justice of God would be satisfied and man thereby redeemed, with all of this planned from before the foundation of the world (I Pet. 1:18-20); nevertheless, God definitely did not coerce the religious leaders of Israel into doing this terrible thing, that being by their own volition. Of course, God knowing all things, past, present, and future, knew what they would do. But again, I emphasize that even though it definitely was predestined that Christ would go to the Cross, it was not predestined that Israel would be the ones to put Him there. They did that of their own volition.

CHRISTIANS

Every evidence is, that God had always intended for the Gospel to go to the entirety of the world, which of course refers to both Jews and Gentiles. He plainly said this through the Revelation given to Abraham (Gen. 12:1-3). And He intended for Israel to be the leading people in World Evangelism. In Truth, even though the nation of Israel rejected Christ as a whole, it definitely was Jewish Apostles and Preachers who helped found the Church, with Christ at its head. As well, the Lord looks at all Believers now, both Jews and Gentiles, as Spiritual Israel. Paul said:

"For they are not all Israel, which are of Israel:

"Neither, because they are the seed of Abraham, are they all children: but, in Isaac shall thy seed be called."

He then said, *"The children of the Promise are counted for the seed,"* which refers to all Born-Again Believers, Jews or Gentiles, who have accepted the Lord by Faith, exactly as did Abraham (Rom. 9:6-8).

The Apostle then said, *"For he is not a Jew, which is one outwardly; neither is that circumcision, which is outward in the flesh:*

"But he is a Jew, which is one inwardly; and circumcision is that of the heart, in the spirit, not in the letter; whose praise is not of men, but of God" (Rom. 2:28-29).

AFTER THE OLD COVENANT

The phrase, *"After those days, saith the Lord,"* refers to the Old Covenant having run

NOTES

its course, which it did at the time of the Cross, with the New Covenant taking its place.

At the time that Jeremiah uttered these words (Jer. 31:31-34), the Holy Spirit turned the eyes of the Prophet from the present conditions, to the future, but at that time did not locate it with any precision. The repeated *"saith"* or *"declares the Lord,"* keeps before the Reader the Truth that a Divine and not a human act is in mind.

At the time the Prophet uttered these words, Judah was in sad shape indeed! The nation was on the very brink of disaster, but despite that fact, would not heed the words of the Prophet, and if anything, they increased their rebellion against God. The Prophet, knowing what was coming, was destitute of spirit. Where will this leave the Work of God? What about the Promises of the coming Messiah?

In this terrible time, which in fact did end with total destruction of Judah, with the Temple being totally and completely razed to the ground, with most of the people led away into captivity, the Lord would strike a note of prophetic tones in the heart of Jeremiah, proclaiming the coming of a glad day. In other words, He was telling the Prophet, that this which He has planned, and we speak of the coming of the Messiah, would not be hindered by the terrible state of Judah.

THE NEW COVENANT

The phrase, *"I will put My Laws into their mind, and write them in their hearts,"* proclaims in abbreviated detail, the glorious fact of what the New Covenant would do.

Three Blessings are contained in this Better Covenant. They are:

1. Sanctification, which is proclaimed in this Verse: This is done by the Holy Spirit, and can only be done by the Holy Spirit. As a result of the Cross which paid the terrible sin debt, man could now be *"Justified by Faith"* in practice, as he had been previously in theory. Due to this legal work being carried out in the heart and life of all Believers, and because of the great Work of the Cross, the Holy Spirit could now come into the heart and life of the Believer to abide forever, which He couldn't do before the Cross (Jn. 14:17).

2. The Knowledge of God, as proclaimed in Verse 11: Once again, this can only come about

by the Work of the Holy Spirit in one's life.

I think it can be said without fear of contradiction or exaggeration, that the weakest Saint at present, has a greater knowledge of God, even than the Prophets of old as it regards the Old Testament. In fact, I think that Jesus addressed this when He said, *"Verily I say unto you, among them that are born of women there hath not risen a greater than John the Baptist: notwithstanding he that is least in the Kingdom of Heaven is greater than he"* (Mat. 11:11).

What did Jesus mean by the word *"greater"*?

He wasn't meaning greater in the realm of character or even Godliness. He meant greater in the realm of privileges, due to the New Covenant, which John the Baptist or no other Old Testament Saint were privileged to have.

While it is true that the Holy Spirit helped them in those times, and while it's true that God used many of them greatly, even in a far greater way than most New Testament Saints, but as far as their actual knowledge of God was concerned, which demanded relationship, they actually couldn't have such to the degree as New Testament Saints, due to the fact that the Holy Spirit abides within us presently, and does so on a continual basis. That is the basic difference.

3. The removal of the sin debt as mentioned in Verse 12: While sins were definitely forgiven in Old Testament Times, the sin debt which man owed to God was not removed, because the blood of bulls and goats could not take away sins. This within itself carries a wealth of meaning, which we will address more fully in commentary on Hebrews 10:4.

ALL MADE POSSIBLE BY THE CROSS

Everything we have in the New Covenant was made possible by the great Sacrifice of Christ. This means, that the very meaning of the New Covenant is the meaning of the Cross, in other words, what the Cross provided for us. That's the reason we refer to it as the centrality of the Gospel.

The Cross is really not a doctrine. It is rather the foundation on which all Doctrine is built, that is if it's correct Doctrine. Anything that's incorrect or we might say, unscriptural, is that which doesn't have the Cross as its foundation.

Everything that man needed, man within himself was helpless to supply. So if man was to have these things, and we speak of Justification by Faith, and the Baptism with the Holy Spirit, among other things too numerous to mention, God would have to provide it for man, which He did at the Cross. Now what we've said is very important.

Due to the fact that the Cross was in the Mind of God from before the foundation of the world (I Pet. 1:18-20), we know the Cross was the only way this thing could be done, or at least the best way. The Cross tells us how bad the situation with man actually was, and at the same time, how good that God is. Salvation for the sinner comes exclusively through what Christ did at the Cross, and victory for the Saint comes in the same way. Most Christians understand the first part, but they don't understand the latter. As a result, most Christians live in defeat of one kind or the other.

To approach a great subject in a very abbreviated way, the way to perpetual victory in the Lord, is according to the following:

1. The Believer must ever understand that all things in totality come through the Cross of Christ. This is the Source of all blessings, all help, all strength, and all power (I Cor. 1:18, 23; 2:2).

2. Understanding that, the Believer is to constantly exhibit Faith in that Finished Work. This is very, very important. So important that I must say it again:

The Saint of God must ever have the Cross of Christ as the object of his Faith (Gal. 6:14).

3. When this is done, and continues to be done, the Holy Spirit Who resides in the heart and life of the Saint, will then use His mighty power to guarantee for the Saint all the benefits of the Cross (Rom. 8:1-2, 11). The Holy Spirit will not work outside of the parameters of the Finished Work of Christ; consequently, to have His help, which we absolutely must have, He demands that we ever have Faith in the Cross of Christ (Rom. 8:1-2, 11).

RELATIONSHIP

The phrase, *"And I will be to them a God, and they shall be to Me a people,"* refers to relationship under the New Covenant that was not possible under the Old Covenant. As repeatedly stated, all of this was and is made possible by the Cross of Christ, and one's Faith in the Cross.

This last phrase of Verse 10 is very similar to the old way which said, *"I will take you as My Own people, and I will be your God"* (Ex. 6:7). So, what is the Holy Spirit through Paul saying differently here in Verse 10, than He said in Exodus?

The idea pertains to Revelation. *"I will be your God"* acquires fuller meaning with every further Revelation of the Character of God. The Life, Death, Resurrection, Ascension, and Exaltation of Jesus mean that God has acted decisively to save a people. The God Who saves people in Christ is the God of His Redeemed in a new and definitive way. When people have been saved at the awful cost of Calvary, they are the people of God in a way never before known, as should be obvious, and should be understood.

WHAT DO WE MEAN BY *"VICTORY"* AS IT PERTAINS TO THE CHILD OF GOD?

To answer that question, we would have to go back to the phrase, *"I will put My Laws into their mind, and write them in their hearts."*

We know as Believers under the New Covenant, that we are *"dead to the law by the body* (Crucifixion) *of Christ"* (Rom. 7:4). So, what was Paul talking about regarding the *"Law"* in Verse 10, which is actually the moral Law that's found in Exodus Chapter 20?

To cut straight through to the chase, Jesus has already perfectly kept the Law, as well as taking its terrible penalty, all on our behalf, which fulfills Romans 7:4, as it regards us being *"dead to the Law."* It means that it doesn't have a claim on us anymore, because all claims were satisfied in Christ.

However, at the same time, it is in our mind and heart to keep the moral Law, in fact, now more than ever. But it's *how* that we keep it which decides whether we walk in victory or not.

Every single Christian in the world *has* victory, because Christ has victory, and we are in Christ; however, all Christians are not *walking* in victory, even though they do have victory.

That may seem like a play on words, but please believe me it's not! So the great question, if I have victory, why is it that I'm not walking in victory? Again let's cut to the chase:

Even though every single Christian has victory, if their Faith is not anchored squarely in the Cross of Christ, understanding that this is the Source of all blessing and victory, then they cannot walk in victory. It's just that simple!

And when we speak of having Faith in the Cross of Christ, this refers to far more than giving a mere nod toward the Cross.

One must understand that the Cross of Christ is as we have stated, the very centrality of the Gospel. In other words, the Holy Spirit has to reveal the great significance of the Cross to each Believer, which He most definitely will do, if the individual exhibits proper Faith in that direction.

Again we state, while *"walking after the Spirit,"* is the way to victory, one's Faith in the Cross is the victory.

The Believer must never allow himself to be maneuvered by Satan into believing that his victory is in not doing certain wrong things. If that is the case, his Faith will be on himself instead of on Christ, which will only make a bad matter worse. My victory is in the Cross of Christ, irrespective of what else might happen. And to be sure, if my Faith remains in the Cross as it should, the lapses and failures will be less and less, and ultimately, *"sin will not have dominion over me"* (Rom. 6:14).

(11) "AND THEY SHALL NOT TEACH EVERY MAN HIS NEIGHBOUR, AND EVERY MAN HIS BROTHER, SAYING, KNOW THE LORD: FOR ALL SHALL KNOW ME, FROM THE LEAST TO THE GREATEST."

The structure is:

1. Under the New Covenant, the Word of God is far more easily understood.

2. The Passage is not meaning that Teachers are not needed, but rather not needed in the capacity as under the Old Covenant.

3. The Priesthood and the Scribes were the privileged few under the Old Law, with there being no such distinctions under the New Covenant. The Word of God is now open to all.

KNOWLEDGE OF THE WORD

The phrase, *"And they shall not teach every man his neighbor, and every man his brother, saying, know the Lord,"* refers to the constant need of such which prevailed under the Old Covenant. Under the Old Covenant, none but the educated Scribe could understand the details of the Law. The elaborate ritual made it impossible for the private individual to know whether a ram or a pigeon was the appropriate sacrifice for his sin, etc. In fact, a Priest had to be consulted.

Under the New Covenant intermediates are abolished. Due to the advent of the Holy Spirit in the hearts and lives of all Believers under the New Covenant, and especially considering the Baptism with the Holy Spirit, the great Teacher actually abides within the heart and life of every Believer.

As well, considering the present proliferation of the Word of God, which was not at all accessible under the Old Covenant, except to a privileged few, there is no excuse presently for any Believer not knowing and understanding the Word of God. And yet, so few Believers take advantage of this greatest opportunity afforded mankind.

However, let not the Reader think that this Passage means that God-called Teachers aren't necessary. Such would be a contradiction of the Word of God (Eph. 4:11). The idea is, that Teachers are not needed presently near the degree they were needed under the Old Covenant.

THE HOLY SPIRIT MAKES ALL EQUAL

The phrase, *"For all shall know Me, from the least to the greatest,"* presents the fact that the Holy Spirit will teach the Word to any and every convert, just as much as He does one who is an Apostle, etc. That was not so under the Old Covenant!

Once again this does not negate the value of Teachers of the Word, but only infers that the Holy Spirit is available to all Believers. In fact, one of the greatest works of the Holy Spirit is to help Believers, whomever they might be, to understand the Word (Ps. 119:102, 105, 108; I Cor. 2:9-10).

Again, I emphasize the fallacy of every Believer not taking advantage of learning the Word of God, which is the greatest education one could ever have, and as well, the only Lamp and Light in the world today.

COMING KINGDOM AGE

The total and absolute fulfillment of these Passages, at least as it pertains to Israel, will take place only in the coming Millennium.

NOTES

Under the New Testament, Israel in the Millennium, its individual members cleansed in the fountain filled with blood through the sovereign Grace of God, indwelt by the Holy Spirit Who will both sanctify and teach the individual (Zech. 12:10-13:6), will have no need of any intermediate between the individual Believer and God. At that time, and for many and varied reasons, the tremendous restrictions Israel experienced under the Old Covenant, will be no more. Equipped with the great Teacher, the Holy Spirit, all, from the least to the greatest among them, shall have a personal, direct relationship to God.

While there will be Priests offering Sacrifices at that time, yet the people will be on a level with the Priests of Israel so far as their understanding of God and His Word is concerned. This knowledge of God will be without any distinction of age or station in life.

As well, the Reader should understand, that Sacrifices then offered, which they definitely shall be (Ezek., Chpts. 40-47), will be carried out only as a memorial. They will not be meant to take away sin, and in fact, never could take away sin.

(12) "FOR I WILL BE MERCIFUL TO THEIR UNRIGHTEOUSNESS, AND THEIR SINS AND THEIR INIQUITIES WILL I REMEMBER NO MORE."

The exegesis is:

1. Due to the Cross, the Mercy of God is far more available under the New Covenant than it was under the Old.

2. The Cross made it possible for all sin to be taken away, thereby remembered no more.

3. As should be obvious, all of this, plus everything which comes from God, is made possible by the Cross.

MERCY

The phrase, *"For I will be merciful to their unrighteousness,"* proclaims unlimited Mercy, but it's predicated on two things:

1. The Cross made it possible for the Mercy of God to be extended to man in a greater way than ever. In fact, God is no more merciful now than He was under the Old Covenant. The idea is, the Cross made it possible for Mercy to be tendered in unlimited quantities. It is the same with the Grace of God. All are made possible by the Cross.

The Believer must understand this, which is really the bedrock of his Faith. To any degree that this is not understood, and I speak of the Cross being the Source of all things from God, to that degree the Believer will suffer loss.

2. Mercy is extended only to those who exhibit Faith in the Finished Work of Christ. In fact, it cannot be extended to those who continue in rebellion against God, especially those who deny the Finished Work of Christ. God has always required Faith, and there will never be a time that He doesn't require Faith; however, the Faith which He requires, is always and without exception, Faith in the great Sacrifice of Christ, which was carried out at great price, and which makes all things possible.

ALL SINS TAKEN AWAY

The phrase, *"And their sins and their iniquities will I remember no more,"* refers to the fact, that due to the Cross, such no longer exists.

As it refers to the Old Covenant, and due to the fact that the Sacrifice of animals could not actually take away sins (Heb. 10:4), the sin debt still hung over the heads of men. This refers to man's crimes against God.

While unredeemed man doesn't understand that he's constantly sinning against God, i.e., *"committing crimes against God,"* this nevertheless is what is happening. God's Standard of Righteousness was and is the Ten Commandments. Man is constantly breaking those Commandments, which is the cause of all the problems in the world. And whether man realizes it or not, these crimes are directed against God, because it's God's Standard as the Creator which has been broken, and in fact, is constantly being broken. The penalty for that is death (Rom. 6:23). And the type of death of which this speaks is spiritual death, which happened to Adam and Eve upon their failure in the Garden of Eden. Due to the fact that every human being who would ever live, was in effect in Adam's loins, this one act by Adam doomed the human race.

When a baby is born into the world, it is born in original sin, actually made that way by the failure of the first parent. In this fallen, depraved condition, it can do nothing but come short of the Glory of God.

As we've previously stated, unredeemed man might conclude that such a condition is not his fault, that is if he thinks about it at all. If he goes far enough in his thinking, he might also conclude that God is not fair in punishing him for something over which he had no control, that is if he believes there is a God. Whatever the conclusions, unredeemed man being spiritually dead, it is impossible for him to have any correct thoughts about God or what God does, etc.

First of all, God is not unfair in anything He has ever done. In fact, God is love. And by that statement, we mean that He is far more than merely having love, but in fact, is love. Actually, if one wants to know Who God is, and What God is, and How God is, one need only look at Jesus Christ Who was the Perfect replica of the Father. When Philip said to Christ, *"Lord, show us the Father . . . Jesus said unto him, 'Have I been so long with you, and yet hast thou not known Me, Philip? he that hath seen Me hath seen the Father'"* (Jn. 14:8-9).

So, even though Satan has been very successful at painting God as some type of vengeful monster, the Truth is, He is the very opposite. It is Satan who is the monster.

THE CROSS, GOD'S SOLUTION TO MAN'S DILEMMA

While it is true that man would be eternally lost because of his fallen condition, the further Truth is, that God has done something about the situation. In fact, what He has done is of such moment, such power, such magnitude, that it literally defies description. I speak of God becoming man, and then dying on a Cross in order to redeem man, thereby paying a price that is absolutely incomprehensible as it regards the thinking of humanity.

The Scripture tells us, that God's condemnation against man is not about his fallen condition, over which in fact he had no control, but rather because of his rejection of God's solution to the dilemma, *"Christ and Him Crucified"* (I Cor. 2:2).

Jesus said, and speaking of the Holy Spirit, *"And when He is come, He will reprove* (convict) *the world of sin, and of Righteousness, and of judgment."*

He then said, *"Of sin, because they believe not on Me"* (Jn. 16:8-9).

So we know from this, that the accusation against unredeemed man at the Great White Throne Judgment (Rev. 20:11-15) will not so much be the fact that he is a sinner, but that he has rejected God's solution to his problem. In other words, he has rejected Jesus Christ, and more particular, has rejected what Christ did for him in order that he might be saved as it refers to the Cross.

The great price that Jesus paid at the Cross, which was the giving of Himself in the shedding of His Own Life's Blood, completely takes away all *"sins"* and *"iniquities,"* at least for all who will believe (Jn. 3:16).

HOW DID THE DEATH OF CHRIST TAKE IT ALL AWAY?

When Adam and Eve fell in the Garden of Eden, they forfeited the Life of God. Due to their rebellion, which in effect means they threw in their lot with Satan, the archenemy of God, this terrible crime which actually threatened the entire Creation, placed a barrier between God and man. That barrier is sin, which is the cause of all of man's problems. Now, man who is a physical being, an intellectual being, and a spiritual being, is deprived of the most important part of his being, his spiritual side. God had filled that part before the Fall, which constantly infused man with the Life of God, which in effect, was Eternal Life. With the Life of God now gone, man is spiritually dead, which will ultimately bring on death of every nature, including physical death.

Considering the magnitude of this crime, which as stated, threatened the entire Creation of God, and which has filled this world with unimaginable sorrow, death, dying, sickness, and heartache, man was and is helpless within himself to assuage this terrible dilemma in which he now finds himself.

Once again let us emphasize the fact, that if one wants to know how horrible this crime actually was and is, one need only look at all the sorrow and heartache that fills the world today. This which Adam did has killed every single human being who has ever lived, with the exception of Enoch and Elijah, and those who are alive today, but we are dying.

NOTES

Therefore, if the whole thing was to be salvaged, God would have to do it Himself, which means that all Salvation, all Redemption, all and in its entirety, originated with God, and, therefore, comes from God. In other words, man has had absolutely nothing to do with Redemption, as man can have nothing to do with Redemption. So, the moment that man attempts to insert anything into God's Plan, it destroys that which must be exclusively of the Spirit. And that's the great crime of the Church! Far too often, it seeks to add something to the Finished Work of Christ, or take away from that Work, or to ignore it altogether, substituting its own brand, which is always abominable in the eyes of God. Polluted man cannot furnish true righteousness in any case.

When God came to this world, the Cross was His intended destination. The Cross is that which had to be, at least if man was to be redeemed. The most ignominious and horrifying death, which Crucifixion in those days was, was that which God demanded, and because of the magnitude of the crime. However, there was a catch to all of this:

In God becoming man, in which the Holy Spirit through Paul referred to Him as the *"Last Adam"* (I Cor. 15:45), He would have to face all the powers of darkness, not as God, but rather as a man, *"The Man Christ Jesus."*

If He failed even one time, then man would be eternally lost. I realize that many Preachers claim that Christ could not have sinned; however, for Him to be the Last Adam, which He definitely was, and which was demanded, He definitely had to be subject to failure (I Cor. 15:45).

But He didn't fail! Not in anything! Not at any time! Not in any capacity!

He had to go to the Cross as a Perfect Sacrifice, which means there could be no imperfection about Him, and certainly there must be no sin of any nature. Consequently, when He died, actually giving Himself, which means that His Death was a Sacrifice and not at all an execution, etc., it was a Perfect Sacrifice which God could and did accept.

In fact, the pouring out of His Life's Blood was absolutely required, simply because the life of the flesh is in the blood (Lev. 17:11).

That's why Paul said, *"But now in Christ Jesus ye* (Gentiles) *who sometimes were far off are made nigh* (can come to God) *by the Blood of Christ."*

The Apostle then said, *"And that He might reconcile both* (Jews and Gentiles) *unto God in one body by the Cross, having slain the enmity thereby* (tore down the barrier created by sin between God and man)*"* (Eph. 2:13-16).

When we see the Cross, we see the Love of God as nothing else could express that Love. But we also see something else:

We see the horror of man's fallen condition, actually how fallen he really is. Actually, that's one of the reasons why the world rejects the Cross. It as nothing else shows the world for what it actually is.

THE GREAT SIN OF THE CHURCH

This is at least one of the reasons that the foray of the Church into humanistic psychology is a sin and crime against God of unprecedented proportions. This perfidious act says several things:

1. It is a vote of no confidence as it regards the Cross. In other words, the part of the Church which has embraced humanistic psychology, which includes almost all, is in effect saying, that the Cross is not sufficient for the ills, aberrations, perversions, and sins of man; consequently, we must turn, they say, to psychology.

2. To cover their tracks, many claim that psychology is a science exactly as medicine. However, psychology is not a science, and in no stretch of the imagination can be concluded as such. In fact, it is a religion, the religion of humanism. As such, it not only holds no answers for man, but it actually makes a bad matter worse.

3. Anyone who knows anything at all about psychology, and at the same time knows something about the Bible, knows that the two are opposites. Their directions are totally different, with their teachings being totally contradictory. In other words, it is not possible for a Christian to embrace the Bible and psychology at the same time. As stated, how can such be done, if these two directions are opposites?

This is at least one of the reasons that the Leadership of most so-called Pentecostal Denominations hate Jimmy Swaggart. At least two of these Denominations, the two

largest, the Assemblies of God and the Church of God, have totally embraced this humanistic philosophy, which means, that they have forsaken the Cross. Let me emphasize again, the Words of Christ, *"No man can serve two masters: for either he will hate the one, and love the other; or else he will hold to the one, and despise the other. Ye cannot serve God and mammon"* (Mat. 6:24).

This statement as given by our Lord is crystal clear. If one embraces humanistic psychology which opposes everything the Bible teaches, that simply means that he hates the Cross.

The main reason for all of this is the forsaking of the way of the Spirit.

THE WAY OF THE SPIRIT

The Way of the Spirit is the way of the Word of God. As we've already stated, Salvation in its totality is all of God and not at all of man. This means that man's problems, whether the Salvation of the lost, or victory for the Saint, can only come about, by the way of the Spirit. That is the Way of the Cross (Rom. 8:1-2, 11). That alone is the answer for humanity, and to be sure, that alone suffices for the ills of humanity. The Cross is the answer for every unsaved human being in the world. It's the answer for every alcoholic, every drug addict, every gambler, everyone who is in bondage to immorality of any stripe, to the thief, the liar, the cheat, the pervert, etc. Not only is the Cross of Christ the answer, it is the only answer, which means there is no other answer. That is the Way of the Spirit (Rom. Chpt. 8).

So, when Churches attempt to use the music of the world to attract young people, most definitely they will attract young people, but it won't be to God. Please let the Reader take careful note of the following.

THE SPIRIT OF GOD OR THE SPIRIT OF THE WORLD

There is no way that the Church can use the spirit of the world, and thereby attract people to Christ. Such thinking pure and simple is of Satan. But that's exactly what much of the Church is attempting to do.

The sad Truth is, the Church has never been in worse spiritual condition than it is presently, since the time of the Reformation. For the most part, it has left the way of the Spirit, and has embraced the ways of the world.

Most of the modern Church tells the Entertainer that they can keep playing in the night clubs, and still be a Christian. As stated, they attempt to attract the youth with the spirit of the world, and they attempt to solve the problems of man with humanistic psychology. Consequently, the Church in its promotion of psychological twelve-step programs, now has such programs for the alcoholics, gamblers, homosexuals, and perversions of every nature. They are referred to as *"rehabilitation programs,"* when in fact, this word is not even found in the Bible.

DELIVERANCE

The Spirit of God, through what Jesus did at the Cross, doesn't rehabilitate anyone. He delivers them (Gal. 1:4). In fact, the entirety of mankind was delivered some 2,000 years ago through the Price that Jesus paid on the Cross. That's the reason that He said:

"The Spirit of the Lord is upon Me, because He hath anointed Me to . . . preach deliverance to the captives" (Lk. 4:18-19).

That deliverance, and in fact, all true deliverance, comes simply by the individual understanding that Jesus paid it all at the Cross, and our Faith in that Finished Work, gives us the help of the Holy Spirit, which then guarantees the benefits of the Cross, which is freedom from the dominion of all sin (Rom. 6:14). That is the answer for humanity, and the only answer for humanity. That's the reason that Paul said:

"For the preaching of the Cross is to them that perish foolishness; but unto us which are saved it is the Power of God" (I Cor. 1:18).

The Holy Spirit through him then said, *"For after that* (after God made foolish the wisdom of the world by the Cross) *in the wisdom of God the world by wisdom knew not God* (cannot find God in this manner, which shoots down the efforts of most Churches), *it pleased God by the foolishness of preaching* (preaching the Cross) *to save* (deliver) *them that believe"* (I Cor. 1:21).

The Apostle then said, *"We preach Christ Crucified,"* which means, that it's not enough

to merely preach Christ, the Message must be *"Christ Crucified"* (I Cor. 1:23).

Considering all this, the Apostle then said, *"For I determined not to know anything among you, save Jesus Christ, and Him Crucified"* (I Cor. 2:2).

I would ask the Reader, does any of that sound like humanistic psychology? In fact, the Holy Spirit through the Apostle in this First Chapter of I Corinthians, completely denigrates the wisdom of this world, as being incapable of affecting man in a positive sense whatsoever, of which is humanistic psychology (I Cor. 1:19).

As I've already stated several times in this Volume, I believe the Lord has told me that the Cross is the dividing line between the True Church and the apostate Church. Actually, it has always been the dividing line, but is going to be more pronounced now than ever, and made so by the Holy Spirit. The idea is this:

Concerning the Reformation, Martin Luther said, *"As one viewed the Cross, so they viewed the Reformation."* It is the same presently.

As one presently views the Cross, so such a one will come down either on the side of the True Church or the apostate Church.

The crowd will not be large in the True Church, as it has never been large in this capacity. But as Joshua of old, I want to say it loud and clear:

"And if it seem evil unto you to serve the LORD, choose you this day whom ye will serve . . . but as for me and my house we will serve the LORD" (Josh. 24:15).

Paul said:

"For the Law of Spirit of Life in Christ Jesus hath made me free from the law of sin and death" (Rom. 8:2).

This means that the Holy Spirit works exclusively through and by what Jesus did at the Cross, hence the Apostle saying *"in Christ Jesus."*

John 3:16 tells us that the Cross is the only answer for the unredeemed. Paul tells us here that the only answer for the Christian is as well, the Cross!

(13) "IN THAT HE SAITH, A NEW COVENANT, HE HATH MADE THE FIRST OLD. NOW THAT WHICH DECAYETH

AND WAXETH OLD IS READY TO VAN-ISH AWAY."

The structure is:

1. God gave the Word to the Prophet Jeremiah, that a New Covenant was coming.

2. This prediction clearly proclaims the fact that the First Covenant is coming to an end, which it did at the Cross.

3. The Old Covenant would serve its purpose, which it did, and then *"vanish away."*

A NEW COVENANT

The phrase, *"In that he saith, a New Covenant"* is derived from Jeremiah 31:31.

There were two great differences in the first or *"Old"* Covenant and the second or *"New"* Covenant. Those two differences are *"the Cross"* and *"the Holy Spirit."*

The Cross did away with all of the animal sacrifices as well as the Levitical Priesthood, which of course, did away with the Temple and all forms of ceremonial or ritualistic worship. In fact, all of those things were symbols of what Christ would actually do at the Cross.

While the Holy Spirit was definitely present in the Old Covenant, and did work mightily; still, He was limited in what He could actually do, simply because He could not come into the hearts and lives of Believers to abide permanently, due to the fact that the sin debt still hung over the heads of men, even the stalwarts of the Faith. The blood of bulls and goats couldn't take away sin, hence the continuing problem. But once the Cross was a fact, which atoned for all sin, thereby taking it away, the Holy Spirit could now come into the hearts and lives of Believers to abide forever (Jn. 14:16).

Due to the fact that the Holy Spirit could not abide permanently within the hearts and lives of Believers under the Old Covenant, they were unable to properly live up to the conditions which God required. In other words, irrespective of the fact that they greatly loved the Lord, without the help of the Holy Spirit there was no way they could properly function.

But now with the Holy Spirit, and the fact that He resides within our hearts and lives permanently, meaning that we are actually Temples of the Holy Spirit (I Cor. 3:16), there

NOTES

is no excuse for us not properly following the Lord.

THE HOLY SPIRIT OR THE SPIRIT OF THIS WORLD

To briefly address the latter first, we know that the Spirit of this world is fostered by *"the god of this world"* (II Cor. 4:4), who is Satan.

Paul also said, *"Now we have received, not the spirit of the world, but the Spirit which is of God; that we might know the things that are freely given to us of God"* (I Cor. 2:12).

As is plainly said here, the Spirit of God is given unto us, that we might recognize the spirit of the world and not be led thereby. So, we learn from these Passages, that the Saint of God can be led by either the Holy Spirit or the spirit of this world. Of course, if the Saint is led by the spirit of this world, it won't be long until there will be spiritual wreckage. And that's the condition of much of the Church presently. It is being led by the spirit of this world instead of the Holy Spirit.

Much of the Church world doesn't even believe in the Holy Spirit as it refers to the mighty Baptism (Acts 1:4; 2:4). Of consequence, they are led by the spirit of this world, because they cannot be led any other way. So let me make a strong statement here:

If the Preacher or Church doesn't believe in the Baptism with the Holy Spirit, with the evidence of speaking with other Tongues, there is no way they can have the leading of the Spirit. So, all people who attend such Churches are basically serving God in name only. The Truth is, most of those Churches and Denominations have only embraced the philosophy of Christianity. That means it is a Christianity without Christ, and more particularly, the Christ of the Cross, which leaves it as nothing but mere humanism. They are left with a mere ethic, which is actually no more than the ancient Law of Moses, with the ethic possibly stating the right way, but offering no power to do the things required. So what am I saying?

I'm saying that it's impossible to know Christ without the Holy Spirit, and if one is properly led by the Spirit, one will be led not only to Christ, but the *"Crucified Christ"* (I Cor. 1:23).

Second, as it regards the Churches and Denominations which claim to believe in the

Baptism with the Holy Spirit, as we've already stated, most of these Churches whether claiming to be Pentecostal or Charismatic, either ignore the Holy Spirit, or else preach *"another Jesus"* (II Cor. 11:4). In other words, there are precious few of these particular Churches that are truly led by the Spirit. There are a few, but not many!

As well, it is my belief, that if Preachers are going to truly follow the Lord, they're going to have to separate themselves from most religious Denominations, at least those in the United States and Canada. Most of these Denominations are led by the spirit of the world, and not by the Spirit of God. That's a blunt statement, but regrettably and sadly, I know it to be true.

As we've repeatedly stated, there is no way that any Christian can follow humanistic psychology, and at the same time be led by the Holy Spirit. The two directions are diametrically opposed to each other. But the road of humanistic psychology, which is a denial of the Cross, is a road well traveled by most of the modern Denominations.

If any Believer truly desires to be led by the Spirit, which one must be if one is to truly know and follow the Lord, one will find that every single time, the Spirit will lead directly to the Cross of Christ. It is within the parameters of the great Sacrifice of Christ, i.e., *"the Cross,"* in which the Holy Spirit works (Rom. 8:1-2). So I feel like it is proper to say the following:

If one is truly led by the Spirit, one will be led unalterably to the Lord Jesus Christ, and more particularly, to the Christ of the Cross (Jn. 16:7-15).

WORSHIP

The barometer of any Church or any Believer for that matter, is *"worship,"* and more particularly, the manner in which one worships. All worship is not of God.

Untold millions of Catholics as well as millions of Protestants attend Church each and every week, going through rituals and ceremonies which they conclude to be worship, but which isn't.

As well, millions of Pentecostals and Charismatics do the same thing, but in a different way.

Praise is what we do, while worship is what we are. While all praise is worship, all worship isn't praise, at least that is vocal. The latter means that our whole being should be one of worship of God, which incorporates everything we do, everything we think, and everything we are. The whole of the life should be worship. Consequently, anything in our lives that cannot be placed in that category, as should be obvious, is very much wrong.

All praise and worship must be generated from the spirit of the individual, over which the Holy Spirit controls (Jn. 4:23-24).

I personally believe, that it's virtually impossible for the Saint to truly worship the Lord, unless the Saint has been Baptized with the Holy Spirit (Acts 2:4), especially considering all the light that has been given on this subject. In fact, without the Baptism with the Holy Spirit, one is left with little more than form and ceremony, which is no worship at all, at least of God!

As well, one can be Baptized with the Holy Spirit, actually speaking in Tongues very often, and still not be led by the Spirit. In fact, that is the awful condition of most modern Charismatics and Pentecostals. To cut to the chase, they are little led by the Spirit, because they haven't placed their Faith totally and completely in the Cross of Christ, but something else altogether.

MUSIC

One of the greatest barometers of praise and worship is music. If one is to notice, the largest Book in the Bible is the Book of Psalms, which is, as is obvious, a Book of Songs. These were songs given to David and other writers of the Psalms, which are given over to Praise and Worship of the Lord. Considering that this is the largest Book in the Bible, the very fact of such, should say something to us. It tells us two things:

1. The value that God places on praise and worship.

2. How much music and singing constitute the barometer of our spirituality. I realize that is quite a statement, but I know it to be true. If the Spirit of God is allowed to have His way in our music and singing, He will pretty well be able to have His way in everything else also. At least this much will

be true, the people concerned will definitely want and desire the Will of God in all things.

Some Churches have the mistaken idea, that a particular style of music constitutes Spirit-led music and singing, i.e., *"praise and worship."* In other words, if the music is fast, some constitute that as worship, while with others, if it's slow, they constitute such as worship. None of that really has anything to do with anything.

While style definitely does matter, as the Holy Spirit to be sure, has a particular style by which He functions, a mere copying of the style will not guarantee the flow of the Spirit. And to be sure, Churches that adopt Contemporary Christian Music, which by definition refers to similarity with that of the world, most definitely aren't being led by the Spirit. But regrettably, that characterizes most of the Church world, which lets us know where they are spiritually.

Then others attempt to have what they consider to be correct as far as their regular Services are concerned, but promote the music of the world as it regards the young people in their Churches. They claim that this draws the young people. While it certainly might draw young people, it definitely doesn't draw them to the Lord. And if we're not to draw them to the Lord, what is our purpose? As we've already stated, the Spirit of God doesn't use anything that the world has in His Work. To be sure, if anything of this world, and I speak of the spirit of the world, is mixed by man into the Work of the Spirit, the Holy Spirit will have none of that effort.

How foolish and even stupid can we be, thinking we can pull so-called Christian rock groups, who do their very best to ape the rockers of the world, into our Churches, thinking that by using these methods we are *"winning the youth."*

A short time ago I was told of a particular Church in our city of Baton Rouge which claims to be Spirit-filled, but which employs rock groups in its youth services, rock groups incidentally, which perform in night clubs during the week, and occasionally in Churches on the weekends. To say that such is an abomination is an understatement, in fact, a gross understatement! Actually, I don't know

if there's anything in any vocabulary that could properly express the utter, absolute stupidity of such action.

Is such a Church led by the Spirit? I think the answer to that ought to be obvious. Irrespective of their claims, such a Church knows nothing about the Lord, is not preaching Christ, but rather another Christ, fostered by another spirit, which presents another gospel (II Cor. 11:4). But I'm afraid, that this which I've just stated is more so the norm than not. All these Churches are doing is pushing young people a little closer to Hell.

The other day someone sent me a copy of an article that was in a so-called Christian Magazine, promoting a particular Church in California, which had set up a pseudo-night-club for its young people. They *"serve drinks over the bar,"* which although nonalcoholic, were designed to ape the real thing. Oh yes, they also had a dance floor, etc.

As well, this particular Church claims to be Spirit-filled and thereby Spirit-led. To be sure, they are spirit-led, but it's not by the Holy Spirit, but rather by *"spirits."* Once again, this which I've just described is far too often the norm.

The young people who attend such Churches will not be led to the Lord, but rather the very opposite. Virtually all of them will conclude with wasted lives, wrecked and destroyed, simply because the spiritual leadership of such Churches are leading them wrong.

Let the Reader understand, that what we're talking about here, plays out either into lives gloriously blessed by the Lord Jesus Christ, or totally wrecked and destroyed. There is no in-between.

Now again, I think you can see why most of the Churches hate Jimmy Swaggart. I regret that; however, my business is not to please people, but rather to please God. And if I am to please Him, I must tell the Truth!

For this very reason, most of the Preachers in the world have attempted to demonize this Evangelist. Most people think it's because of something that happened many years ago; however, that was only an excuse. While there are certainly exceptions, the majority of the Church world doesn't like what I preach; consequently, they are afraid of any influence I might have, so they do all they can to wreck and destroy that influence.

The Church presently is in the same shape of Israel of old, with the Scripture saying, *"And Jesus, when He came out, saw much people, and was moved with compassion toward them, because they were as sheep not having a Shepherd: and He began to teach them many things"* (Mk. 6:34).

This means that the loss of millions of souls, as it regards the youth in our Churches, as well as the wreckage of their lives, can be laid at the feet of the modern, religious leadership of our time. In other words, the Preachers are to blame!

THE FIRST HAS BEEN MADE OLD

The phrase, *"He hath made the first old,"* means that the Old Covenant was designed by God to have a particular lifespan. That lifespan ended at the Cross, with the New Covenant brought in.

By the very fact, that the Holy Spirit through Jeremiah used the word *"new,"* He has permanently antiquated the First Covenant.

Considering that Jeremiah uttered this Prophecy some 600 years before Christ, gave the people and its religious leaders ample time to properly discern and understand what God was doing. But when the time came that the First Covenant was to be set aside, Israel did not let go easily. Even Christian Jews did not easily let go, which among other things, necessitated the writing of this very Epistle to the Hebrews.

TO VANISH AWAY

The phrase, *"Now that which decayeth and waxeth old is ready to vanish away,"* speaks of the time in which Paul lived. In fact, in the Mind of God, the ancient Law of Moses had already vanished away. Jesus fulfilled all of it with His Coming, His Life, and Ministry, and above all, His Death on the Cross, along with His Resurrection, Ascension, and Exaltation (Rom. 4:24-25; Eph. 2:6). Actually, it started vanishing away long before the Cross, even during the time of Jeremiah.

During his day, the Temple in Jerusalem was totally destroyed by Nebuchadnezzar, with Israel being taken into captivity.

NOTES

They remained some 70 years in Babylonian captivity, with the latter part of that time being under the Medes and the Persians, who had defeated Babylon. During this time, they had no Temple and no Sacrifices.

Upon coming back to Israel at the end of the 70 year dispersion, they eventually rebuilt their Temple; however, there was no Ark of the Covenant placed in the Holy of Holies, that having been lost. So, even though Sacrifices could now be carried out once again, the High Priest could not go into the Holy of Holies once a year, on the Great Day of Atonement, to offer up blood on the Mercy Seat, because such didn't exist. This was the same with Herod's Temple, during the time of Christ. However, by that time, the whole of Judiastic worship, had become so corrupted, that it little resembled anymore the original Law of Moses. As stated, Jesus fulfilled all of the Levitical Law by His Life and Death; consequently, soon after the writing of this Letter to the Hebrews by Paul, the Temple at Jerusalem was totally destroyed by the Roman Tenth Legion under Titus, and with it the Ministry of the Old Covenant perished forever.

THE TWO COVENANTS

These two Covenants, the Old and the New, were made with Israel. A Covenant, as already explained, is a principle of relationship between man on the Earth and God. Such is Israel's glory as an earthly people. The First Covenant was established with them at Sinai; the Second was established with Christ, which they rejected.

So this means, that the Gospel is a Covenant, a Revelation of the Salvation of God. The Church enjoys all the fullness of the New Covenant, and much more. The foundation of her Blessings are based upon the foundation of the New Covenant. As well, all of this will be fulfilled with Israel in the coming Millennium, when she shall then accept Christ as Lord and Saviour.

"Free from the Law! Oh, happy condition!
"Jesus hath bled, and there is remission;
"Cursed by the Law and bruised by the Fall,
"Christ hath redeemed us once for all."

CHAPTER 9

(1) "THEN VERILY THE FIRST COV-
ENANT HAD ALSO ORDINANCES OF DIVINE
SERVICE, AND A WORLDLY SANCTUARY."

The exegesis is:

1. Paul is contrasting the First Covenant
with the Second or New Covenant.

2. The First Covenant had Ordinances of
Divine Service, which means that it was of
God, although meant to be temporary only.

3. The phrase *"worldly sanctuary"* does
not have an evil connotation as used here,
but rather means that it was of the Earth,
while the Sanctuary of the New Covenant is
in Heaven.

THE FIRST COVENANT

The phrase, *"Then verily the First Covenant,"* is meant to describe the Tabernacle
in which the Service of God was celebrated
under the former dispensation, and to show
that it had a reference to what was future, and
was, therefore, only an imperfect representation of the coming reality.

It is important to show this, as the Jews
regarded the Ordinances of the Tabernacle and
of the whole Levitical service as of Divine appointment, and of perpetual obligation. The
object of Paul is to prove that they were to
give place to a more perfect system, and hence
it was necessary to discuss their real nature.

The word *"Covenant"* is not in the original Text, but is rightly placed, because that
is what Paul is actually talking about. It
means, that while the First Covenant was
definitely of God, meaning that it was given
by God, and was to be held as sacred, still, it
was to only have a temporary existence.

The two Covenants having been introduced
and contrasted, the imperfection of the Atonement under the First Covenant is in Hebrews
Chapters 9 and 10 contrasted with the perfection of the Atonement under the Second
Covenant, and the unrelieved conscience of
the worshiper under the one set over against
the perfected conscience of the worshiper
under the other — that is, a conscience perfectly relieved from a sense of guilt in the
Presence of God.

The Scriptures proving these contrasts are
quoted by Paul, and a warning (Heb. 10:26-
31) added as to the judgment certain to fall
upon those Jewish Christians who rejected
this Second Covenant and the Atoning Sacrifice that ratified it.

God is a God of order. This is verified by
the details to which He has gone in man's
Redemption. From the very beginning God
has prescribed ways for man to enter into
His Presence. When man fell in the Garden
of Eden an animal was slain to provide a covering for Adam and Eve as they went from
the Garden into the world. This act illustrated the seriousness of their sin, and
showed that the shedding of innocent blood
in Sacrifice (of clean animals) was the only
means of access into the presence of God.
Without the Blood there will be no remission of sins.

When God instituted the Mosaic economy,
He ordained the order for service and worship. He gave Moses detailed instructions,
carefully outlining the Priestly functions, the
Sacrificial system, and the construction of
the Tabernacle.

GOD'S ORDER

It is interesting to note the time God spent
in giving plans for the building of the Tabernacle and in giving instructions for worship.
He had taken only six days to re-create the
world, but when He began to design His house,
He took 40 days (Ex. 24:18). This comparison tells us that God is concerned deeply
about His house, whether the Tabernacle and
Temple of old, or our present hearts and lives
(I Cor. 3:16).

He is concerned that the service be in order, that the house of the Lord be fitting in
His sight. Consequently, it is perfectly in order to begin a worship service with singing,
hence the Book of Psalms being the largest
Book in the Bible, following that with praying and giving, and concluding with preaching and more praying. God has an order
(Fjordbak).

ORDINANCES

The phrase, *"Had also Ordinances of Divine Service,"* means *"ordinances adapted for
Divine Service."*

The Greek word for *"Ordinances"* means *"laws, precepts, ordinances."* The idea is, that there were laws regulating the worship of God.

Has the Reader noticed the number of times that the Holy Spirit through Paul uses the word *"Law,"* as it refers to the great Plan of God? Please note the following:

In the creation which includes everything from man, to Angels, to the planets, etc., God has done all of this by a system of Laws, Laws incidentally, which He has formulated Himself.

The following are some of these Laws, all of which pertain to the moral and the spiritual. However, the world of science is governed in the same manner, but of that we will not attempt to address ourselves:

1. The Law of Moses: This was the Law which was given to Moses and the Children of Israel on Mount Sinai. Except for the moral part of that Law listed in Exodus Chapter 20, this Law is no more in force, actually meaning by God to have been temporary.

(Nine of the Ten Commandments were brought over into the New Covenant, excluding only the fourth Commandment, *"Remember the Sabbath,"* etc., which we have addressed in previous commentary.)

2. The Law of Faith (Rom. 3:27): The Law of Faith pertains to the Finished Work of Christ, in other words, what Christ did for us on the Cross. Everything that humanity needs to be saved and to live victoriously comes by the means of what Jesus did at the Cross and in His Resurrection on our behalf. Our Faith is supposed to be within those parameters, in other words, believing in what Christ has done for us. This means that all Faith, in one form or the other, is to refer to the Cross. If it's Faith in something else, while it might truly be Faith, it's not Faith that God will recognize.

3. The Law of the Sin Nature (Rom. 7:21): The sin nature is the evil impulse which fills the heart of man as a result of the Fall, and propels man toward that which is wicked and wrong. When the believing sinner comes to Christ, the sin nature although remaining, is throttled so to speak. In other words, it becomes dormant; however, it can spring to life very quick, if the Believer attempts to trust in other than the Cross.

NOTES

4. The Law of God (Rom. 7:22): This is the Divine Nature which comes into the Believer at conversion. It is the opposite, as would be obvious, of the sin nature, and is now to control the Believer, and does so by the Power of the Holy Spirit. This is actually what takes place at Regeneration.

5. The law of self-will (Rom. 7:23).

6. The Law of my mind (Rom. 7:23): This is actually the law of the inward man, which has been renewed by the Power of the Holy Spirit. It is supposed to be very similar to *"the Law of God."*

7. The law of sin (Rom. 7:23): This is the same as *"the law of sin and death"* as given in Romans 8:2. It is the Law which will kick in, and without fail, if the Believer attempts to walk holy and live holy by other than the means of the Cross. In other words, if the Believer places his faith in things other than the Cross, he will sin, which will then kick in the sin nature.

8. The Law of the Spirit of life (Rom. 8:2): This is the Law by which the Holy Spirit functions, which pertains to the Finished Work of Christ. In other words, all that Jesus did on the Cross was done for sinful humanity. Whatever those parameters consist of, in that the Holy Spirit works. This is a Law that He will not break, meaning that He will not work outside of those parameters.

9. The Law of Righteousness (Rom. 9:31). This Law pertains to the moral part of the Law given to Moses, and described in Exodus Chapter 20. It is referred to as the *"Ten Commandments."* The only One Who ever fully kept this Law was Christ; however, all who place their trust in Christ and what He did at the Cross on our behalf, are instantly imputed this Righteousness.

LAW

The Holy Spirit used the word *"Law"* for a reason. Law means *"a statement of an order or relation of phenomena that so far as is known is invariable under the given conditions."* It is *"a rule of construction or procedure."*

As we've already stated, every single law in the universe whether it be scientific or moral, was created by God, and to be sure, will hold true. Science struggles to find these laws and then to understand how they work.

Fortunately, science cannot change these laws, and are thereby forced to abide by the ramification of those which they presently understand.

The Bible contains the moral laws and to be sure, they are just as exact as the laws of true science. Actually, that's what we are studying here — the moral Laws of God.

To explain how they work, the following must be noted and understood:

THE WORKING OF GOD'S MORAL LAWS

Every moral Law made by God is of course, of extreme significance. Because they are Laws made by God, they cannot be bent, broken, or ignored. Whether one believes in them or not, they are very similar to the laws of science, they invariably function. As stated, that's the reason the Holy Spirit referred to them as *"laws."*

The Believer has to contend with the following:

1. The law of the sin nature.
2. The law of self-will.
3. The law of sin and death.

Again we emphasize, these are laws, and they will definitely kick in if the Believer doesn't address them correctly.

First of all, *"the law of the sin nature"* should not cause any Believer a problem, as it has been rendered powerless by the Divine Nature — that is, if we address it correctly. However, if we do not address it correctly, it can cause the Christian untold problems (Rom. 7:18).

The *"law of self-will"* is an ever-present factor in the life of every Believer, and actually our greatest problem. *"Self-will"* refers to the Believer encountering one of two problems, or both. The first problem pertains to attempting to force our will into the mix instead of God's Will. And this speaks of anything as it pertains to life and living. The second factor pertains to the Believer attempting to walk in Righteousness and Holiness by his own self-efforts, instead of God's prescribed order.

The secret of the victorious, overcoming, Christian life, is *"the Law of the Spirit of Life."* This is a greater law than the law of sin and death, or the law of self-will. However, if we as Believers attempt to push forward the law

of self-will, the Holy Spirit Who operates the Law of Life, will simply refuse to function. In other words, if the individual demands to have his or her way, instead of God's Way, the Holy Spirit will allow the Believer to do just that; however, the results, and to be sure, will be bitter!

HOW DOES THE CHRISTIAN GET THE LAW OF THE SPIRIT OF LIFE TO WORK FOR HIM?

This is the secret of all victory in Christ.

If one is to notice, the Holy Spirit through Paul tells us, that this *"Law of the Spirit of Life"* is *"in Christ Jesus."* This refers to what Jesus did at the Cross and in His Resurrection, all on our behalf. In other words, this Law which is the Source of our victory, functions totally and completely within the parameters of the Atonement, i.e., *"the Sacrifice of Christ."* The account of that is found in Romans 6:3-5.

All the Believer has to do, is what we've been saying in this Commentary and in fact in several Commentaries, over and over again; the Believer must exhibit Faith in the great Sacrifice of Christ, and must do so on a continuing basis. That's what the Holy Spirit demands of us (Rom. 8:1-2, 11).

FAITH

It must always be remembered, that God works exclusively with us on the basis of Faith. And that means it is never of works or merit of any nature, but always, and exclusively, on the principle of Faith. In fact, and as we've already stated, it is called *"the Law of Faith"* (Rom. 3:27). This pertains totally and completely to what Jesus did at the Cross in order to redeem humanity, and our Faith in that Finished Work.

When one exhibits Faith in the Sacrifice of Christ, such effort and direction says that the one exhibiting Faith knows and understands, that Jesus did all that we need, and which we could not do for ourselves, at the Cross. At the same time, it also states that the Believer knows and understands that he cannot do any of these things which needs to be done, but they can only be done by Christ, and in fact have already been done by Christ at the Cross. Faith in that Finished

Work proclaims that which God demands on behalf of all who come to Him.

When the Believer does this, and continues to exhibit Faith in the Finished Work of Christ, the Holy Spirit will then work mightily on the Believer's behalf, which is the *"Law of the Spirit of Life which is in Christ Jesus."* This is secret of all victory and all overcoming strength. In fact, it is the only way that the Believer can live the life he ought to live (Rom. 8:1-2, 11).

The biggest problem in the Church presently, and in fact which has always been the biggest problem, is the Christian attempting to be what he ought to be in the Lord by efforts and means of his own ability and machinations outside of the Cross of Christ, which God will never honor. It doesn't matter how spiritual or how religious these efforts might be, the Holy Spirit simply will not honor them, which guarantees defeat on the part of the Believer. Sadly and regrettably, and because of not knowing the Victory of the Cross, i.e., *"the Law of the Spirit of Life in Christ Jesus,"* the majority of Christendom presently, walks in defeat. That's the reason that I've tried in every way that I know how, asking the Lord to help me to explain the victory of the Cross, and even to explain it over and over again, even in different ways, praying that the Reader will grasp the Truth that is given here. In fact, there is no Truth more important than this of which I say. Without the Believer understanding this which has been provided by our Heavenly Father, and at such great price, it is impossible for the Believer to *"walk in victory,"* or to experience the *"more abundant life"* promised by Christ, or to live and experience this *"rest"* also promised by the Saviour (Rom. 8:2; Jn. 10:10; Mat. 11:28-30).

SANCTUARY

The phrase, *"And a worldly Sanctuary,"* is not meant to imply by the word *"worldly"* that something here is amiss. The word *"worldly"* is used as contrasted to the Heavenly world. The Tabernacle as constructed by Moses was on Earth, while the Heavenly Sanctuary, as would be obvious, is in Heaven.

Paul is contrasting here two whole ways of approach to God. He is talking about the

Old Covenant that has been superseded now that Jesus has set up the new one. But the old one, Paul points out, had been set up with a full set of regulations for worship and the like. In other words, the method of worship was not left haphazard, but was Divinely prescribed. This means that the old way must be seen as originating in the Divine initiative, which it most definitely was. Then the new is its fulfillment, not its contradiction.

The old way not only had regulations, but also a Sanctuary described as *"earthly."* The meaning is not that the Sanctuary as described here, is worldly in the bad sense, but simply that it belonged to this world in contrast to the Heavenly Sanctuary where Jesus now Ministers. The First Covenant, then, was established with its due regulations for worship and its holy place of this Earth where worship could be carried on. We will find that Paul will go on to stress the *"earthly"* nature of it all, in contrast to the Heavenly Sanctuary.

(2) "FOR THERE WAS A TABERNACLE MADE; THE FIRST, WHEREIN WAS THE CANDLESTICK, AND THE TABLE, AND THE SHEWBREAD; WHICH IS CALLED THE SANCTUARY."

The composite is:

1. Paul is speaking here of the Tabernacle which design was given to Moses by the Lord.

2. The first part of the Tabernacle was the *"Holy Place,"* which contained the sacred vessels mentioned. Immediately behind the *"Holy Place"* was the *"Holy of Holies"* which contained the Ark of the Covenant.

3. The word *"Sanctuary"* usually refers to the whole edifice; however, if the word is used in its most strict sense, it refers only to this first room.

TABERNACLE

The phrase, *"For there was a Tabernacle made,"* refers to that which Moses had made in the wilderness, which specifications were given to him by God. If we use 18 inches to the cubit, which seems to be the measurement most agreed upon, the entire frame of the Tabernacle was 45 feet long and 15 feet wide. As well, it was 15 feet high.

The first room or the *"Holy Place,"* in which the Priests attended their duties constantly, was 30 feet long. The *"Holy of Holies"* which made up the second room or tent as it was referred to, was 15 feet long. This room contained the Ark of the Covenant, on which there were two Cherubim, one on either end, looking down upon the Mercy Seat. God dwelt between the Mercy Seat and the Cherubim. No one went into this room except the High Priest, and that only once a year on the Great Day of Atonement, when the blood of the Sacrifice was sprinkled on the Mercy Seat. Actually, he went into this room twice, the first time for himself, and because, even though he was the High Priest of Israel and a type of Christ, still, he was a sinful man. He went in the second time for Israel, both times on the same day.

(Actually, the exact size of the two rooms in the Tabernacle is not specified in the Scriptures, but it is commonly supposed that the Tabernacle was divided in the same manner as the Temple was afterwards; that is, two-thirds of the interior constituted the *"Holy Place,"* and one-third the *"Holy of Holies."*)

WHY THE TABERNACLE AND NOT THE TEMPLE?

It will be noted throughout that Paul has the Tabernacle in view rather than the Temple. This is not, as some have supposed, because the construction of the Temple was any less Divinely ordered than that of the Tabernacle. David plainly declared to Solomon, and giving him the plan of the more permanent Sanctuary, *"All this the Lord made me understand in writing by His Hand upon me, even all the works of this pattern"* (I Chron. 28:19).

However, the Temple types evidently prefigure Millennial Glory and Blessing and will be fully entered into and understood in that day of Jehovah's power.

The Tabernacle, on the other hand, which was a temporary dwelling place, picturing truth for a pilgrim people, has its application to the present times when the Holy Spirit, typified by the cloudy pillar of old, is leading the new dispensation company through the wilderness of this world, on to the rest that remains for the people of God (Ironside). So, while the Tabernacle pictures the Church on Earth before the Resurrection, hence the Holy Spirit using this example, the Temple represents the coming Millennial Reign.

TYPES

A study of the Tabernacle and its furnishings would show how Christ is portrayed in this structure with all its rituals, ceremonies, and ordinances. This study is called *"typology."* A study of the types will bring additional light to many Passages of Scripture.

This is very important, because it continually focuses our attention on the Blessed Lord Jesus, His life and work. Over and over in the Types He is lifted high; He is exalted and magnified. By studying these *"types"* we will see the meticulous care with which God planned Redemption and, in so doing, gave to His Son, the Lord Jesus Christ, the pre-eminence throughout all Scripture.

A *"type"* as found in the Bible is a person or thing which God has designed to represent or prefigure some person, thing, or event that would appear in the future. Usually, if not always, the type appears in the Old Testament and the person, thing, or event to which it refers appears in the New Testament. In a way, types were a sort of prophecy, giving an advance view in symbolic picture form, of what was to come.

In fact, *"types"* and *"symbols"* are so closely related, sometimes it is difficult to distinguish between them. In fact, the dictionary uses these two words as synonyms for each other. There is a slight difference, however, though their purpose and intent are much the same.

A *"type"* is a sort of model of the thing to which it refers, containing some of the qualities and characteristics of the real thing.

In comparison, a *"symbol"* is an object that reminds us of something else, not by resembling it exactly but by having certain features or characteristics that remind us of it (Fjordbak).

THE SACRED VESSELS

The phrase, *"The first, wherein was the Candlestick and the Table and Shewbread,"* refers to the Holy Place where these sacred vessels were situated. It was, as stated, the *"First Room."*

Into this area, the Priests went constantly as they attended their duties; but, as stated, it was only the High Priest who could go farther which was past the Veil into the Holy of

Holies, and that only once a year, and not without blood.

THE CANDLESTICK

The *"candlestick"* would have been better translated *"Lampstand."* It was much more than a mere *"Candlestick."*

There was no window in the Tabernacle, for the light of nature cannot reveal spiritual things. It was, therefore, illuminated from this Holy Vessel, which was placed on the south side, or left side, as one walked in.

The *"Lampstand"* is a type of Christ who provides illumination for the world.

Jesus Christ came into a world that was darkened by sin and despair. He came as a Light, so that *"The people which sat in darkness saw great light; and to them which sat in the region and shadow of death light is sprung up"* (Mat. 4:16).

The Gospel was meant to dispel the darkness. Though men may reject the Light and refuse it, they can never extinguish it. The Light still shines today in and through the lives of Believers.

LIGHT

But men loved darkness rather than light. They rejected the Light, and so far as they were concerned, extinguished it. Since Christ was put to death by wicked hands, the world has never again gazed upon the Light. He is now hidden from their eyes. But He Who was slain by the world rose again, and then ascended on high; it is there in the Holy Place in God's Presence, in which that Presence is the Holy Place, that the Light now dwells. And while there — Oh marvelous privilege — the Saints have access to Him.

As a result of Israel's rejection of Christ, black shadows rest upon the world which has cast out the Light of Life: *"The way of the wicked is as darkness"* (Prov. 4:19).

Regarding the Crucifixion, even though Israel was the chief instigator, still, Rome participated in this event, thereby, symbolically speaking, Christ was rejected by the entirety of mankind.

It is now night, for the *"Dayspring from on high"* is absent. The Lampstand tells of the gracious provision which God has made for His Own beloved people during the interval

of darkness, ere the Sun of Righteousness shall rise once more, and usher in for this Earth that morning without clouds.

Its seven branches and lamps constantly fed by oil, represented the fullness of Light that is in Christ Jesus, and which by Him is communicated to His whole Church.

The *"oil,"* representing the Holy Spirit, was poured into its lamps and then shed forth light from them. Such was and is the economical relation of the Spirit unto the Mediator.

First, Christ was *"anointed"* with the Spirit *"above his fellows"* (Ps. 45:7; Jn. 3:34), and then He sent forth the Spirit (Acts 2:33). Objectively, the Spirit conveys light to us through the Word; subjectively, by inward and supernatural illumination (Pink).

LIGHT AND OIL

In studying the candlestick, two symbols are of great interest: Light and Oil. These two symbols are used throughout the Scriptures. As we have seen, Jesus Himself is called *"the Light."* God dwells in light *"which no man can approach unto,"* and God is called the *"Father of lights,"* from Whom is *"every good gift and every perfect gift"* (I Tim. 6:16; James 1:17).

The two figures of light and oil are very beautiful and interesting, even in their natural symbolism. Light was the first restored object of the natural world, and it is its chief glory. It is essential, in a great measure, to the existence of life. It is that which clothes everything with beauty and color. It is that which gives the glory to the rainbow and the ruby. It is that which makes the diamond anything but a little bit of charcoal. It is that which makes the human face so full of loveliness; and it is that which gives us everything that is beautiful in our human relationships, and in all the wonders of the natural world.

Nor have we only the light which comes from without, but the light which comes from within; the sense of sight, the power of wisdom which brings into our consciousness and perception the objects of nature around us.

The Holy Spirit is also the Source of light. And the vision of Revelation closes with the light that is brighter than the sun, and a Rainbow gathering up all of its beautiful effulgence around the Throne forever.

As well, the figure of oil expresses many interesting thoughts. It is the source of artificial light. It contains in itself the elements of life and healing and, in contact with fire, the elements of light. We find it employed for many other purposes than light.

It was used in connection with the consecration of the Priesthood, and in healing, but it was especially set apart for the lighting of God's Sanctuary. And it was specifically prescribed by God Himself, and by the most awful sanctions, guarded from being counterfeited. If anyone should endeavor to imitate or counterfeit it, he was to be cut off from among the people. Its ingredients were compounded together in some mysterious way for its sacred use to light God's Holy Sanctuary (Simpson).

GOLD

The substance of the material for the furniture of the Tabernacle was different in the Holy Place. In the outer court, copper was the prevailing material. Copper had to do with the judgment of sin. In the Holy Place, gold was the material that predominated. This was no accident or chance occurrence.

The gold speaks of the Deity of Christ. It was the only object that set forth in such a visible way its Deity.

Two objects of furniture, the Lampstand and the Mercy Seat, were made entirely of gold. The Lampstand was the perfect symbol of Christ as the Son of God — *"That was the True Light, which lighteth every man that cometh into the world"* (Jn. 1:9). He was a *"Light of the Gentiles"* (Isa. 42:6).

Had He been philanthropic and had He not come out from God, He would have been merely another teacher who *"darkened counsel by words."* He would have only added another ethical system to the already multitudinous and multifarious systems, and He would have been but the harbinger of darkness *"through philosophy and vain deceit."* But as the Son of God, *"He is Light, and in Him is no darkness at all."*

A TYPE OF CHRIST

The Lampstand was handmade, of beaten work, and was highly ornamented. Although gold, this beaten work speaks of His humanity.

There was a central shaft with three branches on the side, making seven branches in all. The central shaft spoke of Christ, with the three branches to the side speaking of the Church. The six branches are short of perfection, made perfect by the central shaft, hence the number *"seven,"* which denotes perfection and completion.

It is said that the Lampstand was one piece of pure gold. In other words, the six branches were not fused to the central shaft, but rather the entirety of the piece was made of one slab of gold, beaten into its design. This signifies, as Jesus said of Himself and the Church, i.e., each individual Believer, *"I am in My Father, and ye in Me, and I in you"* (Jn. 14:20).

Each branch contained three sections, each section being beaten into the shape of an almond blossom, a blossom, and a knop. On top of each shaft was an open almond blossom. This speaks of the Fruit of the Spirit, which should be predominant in the lives of all Believers.

On each of these almond blossoms at the top, were placed the Olive Oil Lamps. Even though the Almond Blossoms looked like wood, they in fact were gold, reminding us of Aaron's rod that budded.

This represents the Incarnate Christ as the Light of the world, and filled with the Spirit without measure.

As well, we must remember even as stated, that the branches represent Believers, but Believers in Christ, which are but reflections of His Light. We have no light within ourselves per se, all Light being of Christ.

HUMANITY AND DEITY

There were no measurements given for the Lampstand of pure gold. That which speaks of His Deity alone cannot be measured, for Deity is beyond the computation of man, neither can a tape be placed along that which speaks of God.

Again, the Priesthood of Christ, which is conditioned on the fact that He became a man, is made to rest on His Deity.

There is not recorded any incident in the Life of Christ in the Gospels which does not instantly record His Deity with every mention of His humanity, yet never confusing or fusing the two. In the shortest verse of the

Bible, *"Jesus wept"* (Jn. 11:35), there is recorded a perfectly human incident in His life. It is a characteristic of humanity to weep; it is perfectly natural. But the tears were not dry upon His cheeks before He commanded, *"Lazarus, come forth."* And Lazarus came forth. That was perfectly Divine — only Deity has the power over death.

THE WORK OF THE SPIRIT

One technical point about the Lampstand is of interest — it was a light-holder. The olive oil lamps were placed upon the Lampstand. The Lampstand supported the flame, but the flame revealed the beauties of the golden Lampstand. The olive oil lamp is a scriptural symbol of the Holy Spirit. The analogy is striking.

Christ sent the Holy Spirit into the world and He supports the Spirit in His work. But the Spirit takes the things of Christ and reveals them unto Believers. As the olive oil lamps were supported by the Lampstand and they in turn revealed its beauty, thus Christ is the foundation and support for the work of the Spirit, but the Spirit in turn reveals the things of Christ (Jn. 16:12-15).

IN SPIRIT AND IN TRUTH

The Lampstand gave light in the Holy Place — it not being possible for natural light to percolate or penetrate there. The Priest inside walked by Divine Light, but he had to go outside for natural light.

True worship today is in spirit and truth; it is where the Spirit takes the things of Christ and reveals Him unto the Believer. Walking by the light of reason, intellect, science, or the Golden Rule may be fine and proper for the natural man, but these never lead the soul into the place of fellowship with God. Natural light is the extent of these, and by virtue of the appeal to the natural man, they are indeed dazzling. The moths are attracted, and the light that draws them is their destruction.

But true worshipers behold only Christ, and this is never discerned by the natural man, but only with the aid of the Holy Spirit. The beauties of Christ are never beheld by the natural man, but are revealed only by the Holy Spirit.

NOTES

Divine light was only found in the Holy Place. Only as worshipers in the present age pass by the Cross and Laver (Word of God) and come to Christ for light are they truly worshiping God. Christ is the Lamp unto our feet and the Holy Spirit is the Light unto our path. Christ said, *"I am the light of the world."* True Believers alone know that to be true.

Going back to the open almond blossom on top of the branch where was placed the olive oil lamps, the following sheds light on that:

Believers today have been sent into the world as lights: *"Ye are the light of the world."* However, and as stated, this means that we are merely reflectors, to reflect His light. Only as we walk in Him can we be lights in the world. A reflector must be where light is in order to reflect it. *"Come ye, and let us walk in the light of the Lord"* (Isa. 2:5) (McGee).

THE ONE PURPOSE OF THE LAMPSTAND

The one purpose of the Lampstand was to shine. To do this there had to be oil in the cups which were part of the Lampstand. One of the Ministries of the Priests was to make sure there was oil in the Lampstand. If the oil became used up, the light would go out. The oil was a type, as stated, of the Holy Spirit.

Without the presence of the Holy Spirit, we cannot shine as lights in the world. We can be thankful for the New Testament arrangement. The oil for the Old Testament Lampstand had to be replenished continually. But in the New Testament era, the Holy Spirit dwells within Believers and is available with His help whenever needed; however, that help is forthcoming only as we maintain our Faith in the Cross of Christ which must never be forgotten (Rom. 8:1-2, 11).

It must not be forgotten, that of all the sacred pieces of furniture and vessels of the Tabernacle, the Brazen Altar was first and foremost, and was a type of the offering up of Christ on the Altar of the Crucifixion. Without that, everything else in the Tabernacle, even the Ark of the Covenant, were moot.

MINISTRY

Each branch of the Lampstand was equal in height to the others. None was considered better than another. There are various ways we can shine for Christ. There are different kinds of ministries, because talents and abilities vary, along with the Call of God. But to God all Ministries are of equal value. As the children's chorus of long ago said:

"Each one should shine,
"You in your small corner,
"And I in mine."

In order for the Lampstand to be effective, it required constant care. The oil had to be replenished. The wicks had to be trimmed. The wicks were the means by which the light was shed, as they were soaked with the oil.

Remember this, our abilities and talents are like the wick of the candlestick. We are not to serve in such a way that people say, *"Oh, what a beautiful wick!"* Rather, they should admire the Lampstand — Christ. The only time the wick calls attention to itself is when it's not burning properly. If people notice us, that means they're not noticing Christ, and it means we are not properly presenting Christ, i.e., *"Not burning properly."*

The tongs and the snuff dishes (Ex. 25:38) were used in caring for the Lampstand. When the Priest checked the Lampstand each morning to see how it was doing, he would also trim the wick if necessary. Sometimes the Lord has to deal with us in similar fashion, so that we can shine for Him more brightly.

Many Christians need trimming so-to-speak, in order that they might burn properly, and not merely cast forth a dirty soot, which a dirty wick does (Harris).

DIVINE

The Light which God gives to us is all Divine, and in no sense human. The oil . . . was made from materials Divinely specified. And so it teaches us that the Light we need does not come from man, not from the reasonings of the wise, not from our own soundest judgment even; but it comes to us from the Holy Spirit, through Jesus Christ and His precious Word. And all the light that God gives a soul in its Heavenly journey must be Divine.

SOLE ILLUMINATION

The Candlestick was the sole illumination of God's Sanctuary. And so it teaches us that

we have no other light but God. When we trust Him, we must wholly trust Him. *"Trust in the Lord with all thine heart, and lean not to thine own understanding."*

Have you this light? Have you taken all of your ideas of things from the Bible and from the Spirit, and from God? Is your Tabernacle partly lighted by the golden lights, and partly by the murky light of the world? I do not wonder that it gets dark sometimes. Let us look and see if we have the Light after the pattern of Christ. A great many Christians go astray here. They are not careful to have all their light from above.

THE SEVENFOLD LIGHT

Again, we learn from the ancient Lampstand that the Light which God gives us is a perfect light. It was a *"sevenfold light,"* and seven . . . stands for completeness. There was not one only, but there were seven, and they afforded all the Light that was required. And so God gives you Light that has no darkness in it. When He leads you . . . it is always in the right path . . . When He teaches, you can lean your whole weight on Him, for He cannot fail. *"God is light, and in Him there is no darkness at all."*

So the Holy Spirit is called *"the seven Spirits before the throne."* Isaiah tells us what that is:

"And the Spirit of the LORD shall rest upon Him, the Spirit of wisdom and understanding, the Spirit of counsel and might, the Spirit of knowledge and of fear of the LORD" (Isa. 11:2).

1. The Spirit of the Lord.
2. The Spirit of Wisdom.
3. The Spirit of understanding.
4. The Spirit of counsel.
5. The Spirit of might.
6. The Spirit of knowledge.
7. The Spirit of fear of the Lord.

These are all different forms of Light, but they are all the same Divine Light.

So God has a great many kinds of Light. He has the light by day, and the light by night. He is the Light that guides, and the Light that glorifies. He is the Light that shines in with awful power upon your sins and makes you weep. And then He is the Light that shines upon His Own sweet face, His Own precious Cross, and Blood, and lifts you out of your sin, and makes your heart happy in His joy. Sometimes the Light shines from His Truth, then sometimes from the Spirit's presence in the inner life. And sometimes we cannot keep it in, but it shines out and sheds its glory on others — the sevenfold Light of God in the heart.

THE BREAD OF LIFE

This Light revealed the other objects in the Tabernacle. It showed the Priests the beautiful and precious things in the Holy Place. It revealed to them the Table, covered with the Bread, and the Frankincense.

The best thing in the Light was that it showed, not the Light, but the Bread. And so when this Light comes, it is not that you have such a light that you gaze until your eyes are dazzled; but the Light comes to show you the Bread of Life, the Lord Jesus Christ, to show how the promises are for you, how you are to understand, how you are to take, how you are to hold fast and be strong.

The main business of the Spirit is to glorify Christ (Jn. 16:14-15). This means that if what is happening in our lives as it regards what we think is the Spirit, which is to make Christ greater and greater, then it's really not the Spirit of God, but another spirit altogether. And furthermore, the Spirit will also portray to the Believer, and in a way that is paramount, not only Christ as the Son of God, but *"Christ crucified"* (I Cor. 1:23).

While He does many glorious things within our lives, even as we've already portrayed, it is the glorification of Christ and more particularly, what Jesus did at the Cross on our behalf, which are always paramount. Again I state the following:

If we are dazzled by displays of sensationalism or emotionalism, which causes us to get our eyes on other things, this is not the Spirit of God, not the True Light, but rather *"an angel of light,"* i.e., *"Satan"* (II Cor. 11:14).

THE WORK OF THE LIGHT

As stated, the Light was portrayed not to dazzle the beholder, but rather to portray the *"Bread,"* i.e., *"Bread of Life."*

So that we will not be bedazzled by other things, how can we as Believers assure

NOTES

ourselves, that the light we have is not darkness? (Mat. 6:23).

If the Believer will understand and follow three particular things, the Light will always shine properly. These things are:

1. Understand that the Cross is the Source of all things from God (Rom. 6:3-5).

2. Understand that your Faith at all times must have the Cross as its object. This must never change! (I Cor. 1:18, 23; 2:2).

3. With Faith properly placed in the Cross, which means that we properly understand that the Cross is the Source of all Blessings and all help, the Holy Spirit will then be able to function properly within our hearts and lives (Rom. 8:1-2, 11).

To be sure, I have already given several times these three simple steps in this Commentary, and have done so with purpose. There is nothing more important for the Christian than that which we've just stated. I want to make certain that you understand exactly what is being said, and if so, I know that your path will be that of victory. Otherwise, it will be anything but victory!

BELIEVERS AND THE LIGHT

The Lampstand did not have inherent light; it was only the bearer of the light; it only held the Light, but the oil gave the light. We must remember, that the branches on either side represent Believers. So this means, that we aren't the light, but only a bearer of the light.

In fact, Jesus Christ and Jesus Alone is our Light, and we simply receive and reflect Him.

While it is true that the oil represents the Holy Spirit, still, the Holy Spirit does all things by and through what Jesus did at the Cross. Hence, Paul saying the following:

"The Law of the Spirit of life in Christ Jesus, has made me free from the law of sin and death" (Rom. 8:2).

If the Believer is to notice, this great and wonderful promise of all Life and Victory is brought about by the Spirit, but all that is done is *"in Christ Jesus,"* which means what He did at the Cross on our behalf.

THE TABLE AND THE SHOWBREAD

As the Priests entered the Holy Place, the Table with its twelve loaves of bread sat on the right or north side of the Sanctuary. The

Table was small, and of course we're speaking of the Tabernacle and not the Temple, measuring some three feet long, 18 inches wide, and 27 inches high. It was made of acacia wood, covered with gold. A golden border surrounded the table with a crown of gold.

Though intimately connected, yet these two objects (the bread and the Temple) may be distinguished in their typical significance. The natural relation of the one to the other helps us to perceive their spiritual meaning: The Bread was placed upon and thus was supported by the Table. The Table speaks of *"communion"* (I Cor. 10:20-21).

The *"Showbread,"* or twelve loaves on the Table, also spoke of Christ. *"My Father giveth you the true bread from Heaven"* (Jn. 6:32).

The word *"Showbread"* in the Hebrew is literally *"bread of faces,"* faces being put by a figure for its *"presence"* — pointing to the Divine Presence in which the Bread stood, *"Showbread before Me always"* (Ex. 25:30) (Pink).

TO PARTAKE OF THE BREAD

The Golden Showbread Table contained an array of twelve loaves of fine flour, sprinkled with sweet-smelling frankincense, and eaten only by the Priests, and were replaced on the seventh day by a fresh supply.

Here again . . . is that mysterious blending of Christ and His people. Christ is the True Bread of Presence. He is the Bread of God.

Jehovah finds in His obedience, life, and death, perfect satisfaction; and we too feed on Him. His flesh is meat indeed. We eat His flesh and live by Him.

The Table was portable, so as to be carried in the journeyings of the people; now we can never thrive without taking Him with us wherever we go. This is the Heavenly Manna, our daily Bread, our Priestly prerequisite.

HOW CAN ONE EAT OF THE FLESH OF CHRIST?

Actually, the Showbread eaten by the Priests was meant to represent Christ and our partaking of Him.

This is what Jesus was talking about when He said, *"Verily, verily, I say unto you, except ye eat the flesh of the Son of Man, and drink His Blood, ye have no life in you.*

NOTES

"Whoso eateth My flesh and drinketh My Blood, hath eternal life; and I will raise him up at the last day.

"For My flesh is meat indeed, and My Blood is drink indeed.

"He that eateth My flesh, and drinketh my Blood, dwelleth in Me and I in him" (Jn. 6:53-56).

What did Jesus mean by this?

First of all, He wasn't speaking of literally eating His flesh and drinking His Blood. He was referring to the Cross, and the Faith that one must have in that Finished Work.

When Jesus died on the Cross, it was His physical body which died, hence the *"flesh!"* As well, He shed His Blood at that time.

When one exhibits Faith in this great Sacrifice of Christ, one is literally partaking of what Jesus did at the Cross on His behalf. In fact, this is what Paul was talking about when He said:

"Know ye not, that so many of us as were baptized into Jesus Christ were baptized into His Death?" (Rom. 6:3).

By the use of the word *"baptize,"* Paul was *not* speaking of Water Baptism, but rather, the Death of Christ on the Cross. When the believing sinner exercises faith in what Jesus did there, in the Mind of God, the sinner is placed in Christ, and more particularly, in His Death. Jesus, serving as our Substitute (Last Adam) and our Representative Man (Second Man) (I Cor. 15:45-47), did for us what we could not do for ourselves. Faith in Him and what He has done, establishes such a union with the Price that He paid, that the Holy Spirit through Paul used the word *"baptize,"* which explains this union more than any other word.

THE CHRISTIAN AND THE CROSS

As we've said over and over again, almost all Christians understand the Cross as it refers to our initial Salvation experience; however, almost none have understanding as it regards the part the Cross plays in our ongoing experience. In fact, the Cross is just as important in our everyday living for God, and will be until the Lord calls us home, as it was in our initial Salvation experience.

Jesus said, *"As the Living Father hath sent Me, and I live by the Father: so he that eateth Me, even he shall live by Me"* (Jn. 6:57).

The words *"even he shall live by Me,"* refer to our everyday lives. As well, the words, even as we've already explained, *"so he that eateth Me,"* refers totally and completely to the Cross, and one's Faith in that Finished Work. So, Jesus is plainly saying here, that our *"living,"* i.e., *"victory and overcoming power,"* will come from what He did at the Cross, and is made available to us by Faith in that great Sacrifice.

When the Believer understands this, and evidences faith in the Finished Work of Christ, knowing that this is the Source of all Blessings and all help, then the Holy Spirit performs mighty things in our hearts and lives (Rom. 8:1-2, 11). In fact, I don't know how much clearer all of this could be.

THE CROSS, A REQUIREMENT

The Table was not merely to be admired for its beauty. The Bread on the Table was not a decoration. Before the Priests could derive nourishment from it, they must actually eat.

This means that it is not enough to admire and appreciate Christ; we must partake of Him and do so in the manner mentioned, which refers to believing in what He did at the Cross on our behalf, and thus make His death and life a part of our lives.

The purpose of the Table was to exhibit the Bread. This is the purpose and ministry of the Church and the Christian; this is what we have been appointed to do.

The Table was not made to show itself, nor have we been made to show ourselves. Our Ministry today is to show forth Christ, and by that, we mean to preach and teach *"Christ Crucified,"* as the answer for dying, hurting humanity (I Cor. 1:23).

If we present Christ in any other way other than *"Jesus Christ and Him Crucified,"* we are, in fact, presenting *"another Jesus"* (I Cor. 2:2; II Cor. 11:4).

CHRIST, THE SOURCE OF ALL LIFE

Jesus said: *"The thief* (the Pharisees and religious leaders of Israel — Satan) *cometh not, but for to steal and to kill and to destroy: I am come that they might have life, and that they might have it more abundantly"* (Jn. 10:10).

He also said: *"Come unto Me, all ye that labour and are heavy laden, and I will give you rest.*

"Take My yoke upon you, and learn of Me; for I am meek and lowly in heart: and ye shall find rest unto your souls.

"For My yoke is easy, and My burden is light" (Mat. 11:28-30).

When Jesus said that He had come that we might have *"life,"* and that He would give us *"rest,"* He was as well, speaking of the means by which this would be brought about, which would be the Cross.

Millions of Christians, although they have this *"Life,"* do not really at all enjoy it, and as well have this *"Rest,"* but do not experience it. Any person who is in Christ, by virtue of being in Christ, has these things of which we speak. But if the Believer doesn't know and understand the veracity of the Cross, the Believer will not enjoy *"Life,"* even though he has it, and neither will he experience *"Rest,"* even though he has that as well. In fact, most Christians presently live in Romans Chapter 7, and if the truth were known, they would have to say with Paul before he learned God's prescribed order of victory, *"O wretched man that I am! who shall deliver me from the body of this death?"* (Rom. 7:24). To be sure, very few will admit to this; nevertheless, that is the actual fact.

What's wrong?

VICTORY AND THE CROSS

What is wrong with modern Christendom, is the same thing that was wrong with Paul in Romans Chapter 7, before he learned the secret of the victorious, Christian experience, which he gave to us in Romans Chapter 6. They are trying to live the Christian life 180 degrees from the manner in which they became Christians.

Every single person who's ever been saved did so by having simple Faith in Christ. In fact, if they attempted to find Salvation in any other manner, they were unsuccessful!

But after coming to Christ, most Christians, simply because few know any better, then try to *"live"* for God, through a regimen of works, in one way or the other. They do so, because they have little or no understanding whatsoever of the victory that's found in the Cross. In fact, victory can only be found in the Cross. Now let us state again the following:

Every single person in this world who truly knows Christ has the victory and is an overcomer. The problem is, they're not walking in victory, and not living as an overcomer, even though they do have these attributes, exactly as they have *"life"* and *"rest."*

Every single thing that Christ did at the Cross, and to be sure, He covered everything that man lost in the Fall, is given automatically to every individual immediately upon their coming to Christ — at least all that we can have this side of the Resurrection.

That means there's really nothing else that Christ can do for us, meaning that He has already done it all.

Despite that fact, millions of Christians are seeking deliverance in one way or the other, when the truth is, their deliverance was effected at the Cross nearly 2,000 years ago. In other words, it's already done, and done in totality!

So, most Christians would then ask, *"If it's already done, why am I having problems?"*

We're having problems simply because we're trying to appropriate these things all in the wrong way. In this mode, in which the vast majority of Christendom finds itself, the Holy Spirit simply will not help. In fact, for Him to do so would actually mean that He would be breaking the Law (Rom. 8:2).

REVIVAL OR REFORMATION?

Many Christians are talking about the need for Revival, when the actual need is Reformation. And what do we mean by that?

First of all, Revival cannot actually come until there is a Reformation.

By Reformation, we're speaking of the fact that Christians need to change the way they believe. This means that the thinking process of the Church must be reformed.

Reformed in what way?

Our Faith must be anchored squarely in the Cross of Christ; however, for that to be successfully done, most Christians are going to have to change their thinking.

We must realize, first of all, that every single Blessing, every single help that we need,

NOTES

comes exclusively from, by, of, and through the Cross of Christ. Jesus said:

"You shall know the Truth, and the Truth will make you free" (Jn. 8:32).

The Believer must understand that the Cross of Christ is the centrality of the Gospel, not your Church, not your works, not anything else, rather the Cross and the Cross alone! That's where Jesus paid it all, which means the price was paid, and which means that He paid for all that we need. In fact, if we attempt to win victory by our works, or anything we might do other than Faith in the Cross, we will find ourselves having the very opposite of victory.

When the Believer understands what we're saying (Rom. Chpt. 6), and begins to act upon that, he will find that the *"more abundant life"* which Jesus spoke about, along with the *"Rest,"* and as well a victory and overcoming power, will begin to be realized within his heart and life, which will then translate into his everyday walk. It may not come instantly, and in fact, seldom does; however, if one is on the right road, and the Cross is the right road, the desired destination will ultimately be reached (Rom. Chpt. 8).

Now the Reader should consider very carefully these things we have said. Considering that we are speaking of the issues of life and death, we should realize the utter significance of what is being taught here.

And please believe me, the moment that one begins to make the Cross of Christ the object of his faith, which then secures the help of the Holy Spirit, one will instantly know that he's on the right road. No one will have to tell him, no one will have to explain it to him, he will know!

Of course, Satan will do everything within his power to discourage any and every Believer who begins this *"good fight of Faith,"* but the Believer is to keep his eyes on the Cross, never deviating from that great Sacrifice. If he does happen to suffer a setback, he is to simply ask the Lord to forgive him (I Jn. 1:9), and as well, ask the Lord to show him the discrepancy in his faith, which the Lord will always do. To be sure, every problem we have is because our Faith is deficient in some way. It's either totally misplaced, as it is with most Christians, or else it's not as strong as we think it is, which is true of most also!

Faith must ever have as its correct object the Cross of Christ. The Believer must ever understand and act upon that.

SANCTUARY

The phrase, *"Which is called the Sanctuary,"* should have been translated, *"which is called the Holy Place."* The name *"Sanctuary"* was commonly given to the whole edifice.

The Tabernacle pictured Israel under the First Covenant, having no assurance as to the forgiveness of sins and no access to God, except on a very limited basis.

Only the Priests had the right of entrance into the *"Holy Place,"* and the High Priest alone once a year for a few moments into the *"Holy of Holies."* Such was the relationship of the nation with God.

They could not draw near to Him, or stand in His Presence. The First Covenant in its highest and nearest access to God placed a Priesthood between God and the people, and the *"Holy of Holies,"* the holiest of all, characterized the inadequacy of that access (Williams).

(3) "AND AFTER THE SECOND VEIL, THE TABERNACLE WHICH IS CALLED THE HOLIEST OF ALL;"

The exposition is:

1. There were two Veils in the Tabernacle. The first separated the Holy Place from the Tabernacle court and prevented the people from looking into the Holy Place (Ex. 26:31-38). The second Veil was placed between the first room, which was the Holy Place, and the second room which contained the Ark of the Covenant, which was the Holy of Holies.

2. The *"Holiest of all,"* was actually the second room, or the *"Holy of Holies,"* as stated, where the Ark of the Covenant was located.

3. Access was extremely limited to this particular room, with only the High Priest allowed in, and that only once a year, and then only for a few moments.

THE SECOND VEIL

The phrase, *"And after the second Veil,"* pertains to that which hid the Holy of Holies from the Holy Place. The Holy of Holies was a small room 15 feet square — a perfect cube. Inside the Holy of Holies was the Ark of the

Covenant, overshadowed by the Cherubim on the Mercy Seat of gold.

Inside the Ark, were the rod of Aaron, a golden pot of Manna, and the Tables of Stone on which were written the Ten Commandments given to Moses.

The Holy of Holies was the Throne Room of God, a place where He manifested His Presence by the Shekinah. From this place the pillar of fire and cloud arose. As such, it was a picture of Heaven.

Comparing Christ with the High Priest who entered into the Holy of Holies just once a year, Paul said:

"For Christ is not entered into the Holy Place made with hands, which are the figures of the true; but into heaven itself, now to appear in the Presence of God for us" (Heb. 9:24). As God, i.e., *"the Holy Spirit"* once dwelt in the Holy of Holies, so now He dwells in another temple, who is in fact, the Believer (I Cor. 3:16).

WHY THE VEIL?

Why was there this barrier?

It shut God in. He is Holy, and because the people were sinful, they could not fellowship with Him. Sin is always a barrier between man and God.

An encouraging feature of this barrier was that it was a curtain and not a wall. This suggested that though God was hiding Himself from man and there was no direct access to Him, a time was coming when the Veil would be eliminated. Also, this barrier was not entirely closed, for once a year, as stated, a representative of the people, the High Priest, could enter with the blood of Sacrifice.

The Veil was made of fine twined linen embroidered like the roof of the Tabernacle with Cherubim in blue, purple, and scarlet colors. Hebrew historians tells us it was about four inches thick and very strong, at least the one which hung in the Temple, and that it would have taken four yoke of oxen to tear it apart. Exactly how thick the one was which hung in the Tabernacle, if not the same, we aren't told.

THE COLORS OF THE VEIL

First of all, we know and understand, that everything in the Tabernacle spoke of Christ, and when we say everything, we mean *"everything!"*

First of all, the Veil was of fine linen. As well, linen is white.

The word *"fine"* speaks of Christ's spotless innocence and faultlessness. Peter says of Him that He *"did no sin, neither was guile found in His mouth"* (I Pet. 2:22).

The linen, as is all linen, unless it's dyed, was white, which speaks of the purity of Christ.

The word *"twined"* as in *"fine twined linen,"* pictures the perfect unity of the human and the Divine in Jesus. He was perfectly human, with feelings and desires like any other man. But He was also perfectly Divine. As one Greek scholar said, *"When God became man, i.e., 'incarnate,' He never lost the possession of His Deity, but did lose the expression of His Deity."*

The white linen was embroidered in blue, which spoke of the Heavenly origin of all Salvation, i.e., *"Christ."*

It also had purple and scarlet colors in it, with the purple speaking of the Kingship of Christ, and the scarlet speaking of His Blood, which would be shed for the sins of man. Both colors, the purple and the scarlet, outlined the figures of Cherubim on the Veil.

JESUS AS THE DOOR

The entirety of the Veil represents the Person of Christ, and as some have said, it represents His Body. To enter the Holy of Holies where God resided between the Mercy Seat and the Cherubim, one would have to pass through the *"Veil."*

Jesus said of Himself, *"No man cometh unto the Father but by Me"* (Jn. 14:6).

As well, He said, *"I am the door of the sheep"* (Jn. 10:7).

It must also be remembered, that the *"door"* is a *"bloody door"* (Ex. 12:3-7), signifying the Crucifixion, the price which Christ would have to pay in order for man to have access to God.

When the Veil in the Temple was torn (Mat. 27:51), at the time that Jesus died on the Cross, it was done supernaturally. It was torn from the top to the bottom: from the top to show that God did it; to the bottom to show how complete a Sacrifice Jesus' death actually was.

The torn Veil represented His torn body, i.e., *"the Crucifixion,"* which opened up the way to God.

As we've stated over and over again, it is impossible for the Believer to fully understand the New Testament unless he understands the Old. In symbolic and picture form, the Old Testament pictures Christ totally and completely, in His atoning work, regarding Who He is, and what He did, i.e., *"the Cross."*

THE HOLY OF HOLIES

The phrase, *"The Tabernacle which is called the Holiest of all,"* is in fact the Holy of Holies, which contained the Ark of the Covenant and the Mercy Seat, overlooked by Cherubim on either end, who looked down upon the Mercy Seat. As we've already stated, no one could enter this room except the High Priest, only once a year, and then only for a few moments. As well, he had to enter with blood from the Sacrifice, which would represent the Blood that would be shed by Christ on the Cross. He actually entered in twice, the first time for himself, because he was a mere human and, therefore, sinful, and the second time on behalf of Israel. He sprinkled the blood on the Mercy Seat, and as well part of the blood was sprinkled on the horns of the Altar of Incense. It was done so seven times on the horns, signifying that the Redemption which would be afforded by the coming Redeemer would be a perfect Redemption (Lev. Chpt. 16).

(4) "WHICH HAD THE GOLDEN CENSER, AND THE ARK OF THE COVENANT OVERLAID ROUND ABOUT WITH GOLD, WHEREIN WAS THE GOLDEN POT THAT HAD MANNA, AND AARON'S ROD THAT BUDDED, AND THE TABLES OF THE COVENANT;"

The composite is:

1. The *"Golden Censer"* was actually the *"Altar of Incense,"* and was looked at as being a part of the *"Holy of Holies,"* even though it actually sat in front of the Veil in the *"Holy Place."*

2. The Ark of the Covenant was in the Holy of Holies proper, and was where God dwelt between the Mercy Seat and the Cherubim.

3. A golden pot of Manna was kept in the Ark and of course was a type of Christ as the Bread from Heaven.

4. *"Aaron's Rod that budded,"* speaks of the Resurrection of Christ.

5. *"The Tables of the Covenant,"* refer to the two stones containing the Ten Commandments, i.e., *"five Commandments each."*

THE ALTAR OF INCENSE

The phrase, *"Which had the Golden Censer,"* should have been translated *"the Golden Incense Altar."* The Greek word here used for *"Censer,"* is *"thumiasterion,"* and is the ordinary word for an *"Incense Altar,"* and should have been translated accordingly. It is not at all the same as the word used in Revelation 8:3, 5 for a censer which is *"libanotos."* Any ordinary reader of English can see how utterly different the two words are. There can be no question then, but that *"Censer"* means the Incense Altar.

But why does Paul plainly connect it with the Holy of Holies, when matter of fact it clearly stood in the Holy Place?

First of all, the Apostle does not say it was in the Holiest, but he does declare it belonged to the Holiest. It belonged to the Holiest because it typified Christ's Person and intercessory work in the Holiest of all.

But during all the Old Testament Dispensation it must stand outside the Veil where it could be approached by the Priests, and yet so near the Veil that the moment this curtain was parted for the High Priest to enter once a year, the fragrant smoke of the Incense entered the Holiest.

However, the High Priest did take a *"Censer"* full of burning coals of fire from off the Altar (Brazen Altar) before the Lord. He then took Incense and put it upon the fire, *"that the cloud of the Incense may cover the Mercy Seat that is upon the Ark"* (Lev. 16:12-13).

But as well, we must note that this was not a Golden Censer, neither was it kept in the Holy of Holies. And as we've already stated, the Greek word which Paul used, actually meant *"Golden Altar,"* and not *"Censer."*

THE LAW

At any rate, the ritual carried out by the High Priest on this Great Day of Atonement,

as it regarded the Mercy Seat, the Censer, and the Golden Altar, presents the acceptability of Christ's Person to God and the efficacy of His intercession. The beautiful type of this entire procession as denoted in Leviticus Chapter 16, presents the satisfaction that Christ made unto God, and completed at the Cross. His mediatory intercession is a sweet savor unto the Father, and effective unto the Salvation of His Church.

The fact that the smoke of this Incense covered the Ark and the Mercy Seat wherein was the Law, and over which the symbol of the Divine Presence abode, denoted that Christ has magnified the Law, met its every requirement, and is the end of the Law for Righteousness unto everyone who believes.

The Ministry of the Altar of Incense and the yearly Ministry before the Mercy Seat were very similar. A Veil stood behind the Altar of Incense and before the Ark so that the interceding Priest was separated from the Presence of God. The High Priest could not make direct intercession, at least as it regarded his own person.

God's Holiness demanded such a barrier because of man's sinfulness, yet there were Divine provisions made for access through the shed Blood of the Sacrifice. At that time, the barrier remained, reminding them that the way into the very Presence of God had not yet been provided. Perfect access would come only through the shedding of the Blood of the Lamb of God, the Lord Jesus Christ Himself. By His Death, He removed all barriers that stood between God and man. The Veil is now rent.

F. B. Meyer says, *". . . The way into the Holiest lies open. It is new and living and blood-marked; we may, therefore, tread it without fear or mistake, and pass in with holy boldness to stand where angels veil their faces with their wings in ceaseless adoration."*

THE MANNER OF THE ALTAR OF INCENSE

Along with the Golden Lampstand and the Table of Showbread in the Holy Place, stood the third article which was the *"Altar of Incense."* It stood at the west end of the Sanctuary before the Veil that separated the Holy Place from the Holy of Holies.

It was made of acacia wood overlaid with gold. It had a golden crown around the top with four horns on the corners. It stood three feet high, 18 inches wide, and 18 inches long. As obvious, it was small.

Incense was to be offered on the Altar to the Lord each morning and each evening. The sweet Incense smoke ascending and filling the Holy Place represented the priestly intercession of Christ on our behalf. His very Person is a sweet fragrance unto the Lord. We must always remember that! For that means, that if we try to come to the Father in any other way except through and by the Name of Jesus, access will not be granted (Jn. 16:23).

As well, Incense was to be burned upon this Altar both morning and evening. The idea is according to the following:

Coals of fire were to be taken from the Brazen Altar, which represented the Crucifixion of Christ on our behalf, where in effect, He took the judgment of God upon Himself which we should have taken, all represented by fire. These coals then laid upon the Altar of Incense, signified that God will accept no worship, no petition, in fact no access whatsoever, unless it comes through Christ and the Cross.

The Incense which burned on the Golden Altar had a special significance. It had certain prescribed ingredients which were to be used only for this purpose. In fact, every item in the Incense spoke of Christ in some manner, whether in His Life or Death. There were four spices. They are as follows:

1. Statce: This was a type of gum that came from a tree that had been cut. It typifies the shedding of the Blood of Christ.

2. Onycha: This comes from a shell found on the shores of the Red Sea and the Indian Ocean, and signifies the Baptism of death that Christ underwent on our behalf.

3. Galbanum: This was the juice or *"bleeding"* of a shrub, which spoke of being crushed, and again, which signified what Christ underwent on the Cross.

4. Pure Frankincense: This seems to be the most important of the aromatic gums and is regarded by itself as a precious perfume. It comes from a tree that grows abundantly in India. The word *"pure"* used here refers to the free-flowing and liberal giving forth

NOTES

of its odors. It speaks of what the death of Christ would produce, which was and is Eternal Life.

Nothing else was offered on this Golden Altar except the Blood of Atonement, which as stated was administered once a year. Blood was placed on the four horns at either end of the Altar, signifying several things:

1. Access into the Presence of God was provided only by what Jesus did at the Cross, and our faith in that Finished Work.

2. All that God does for us as Believers can only come through what Christ did at the Cross.

3. The Blood on the horns of the Golden Altar signifies the absolute necessity of the Believer continuing to have Faith in the Finished Work of Christ, understanding, as necessary as it was to have Faith in the Cross to be saved, as necessary it is to continue to have faith in the Cross in order to walk in victory.

The Reader must understand, that it was God the Holy Spirit Who resided in the Holy of Holies, between the Mercy Seat and the Cherubim. This tells us, along with the Blood being applied to the horns of the Golden Altar, that the Spirit will not work within our lives, unless our Faith remains steadfast in the Cross of Christ (Rom. 8:1-2, 11; I Cor. 3:16).

DISTURBED CHRISTIANS!

The Scriptural Truth we have just given regarding the manner and way in which the Holy Spirit works, is the very reason that many Christians live less than victorious lives, and despite all of their efforts otherwise. Most Christians do not know or realize, the part the Cross plays in their continued living for God. In fact, most Christians only think of the Cross as it relates to their initial Salvation experience. They little know the part that the Finished Work of Christ plays in their ongoing living for God, therefore, placing their faith in other things. As a result of this, the Holy Spirit, Who always demands that we have Faith in the Cross, as typified by the Blood on the horns of the Golden Altar, simply will not work within our lives. And to be sure, without His help, it is literally impossible for the Believer to live as he ought to live, and be what he ought to be in Christ (Jn. 14:16).

THE ALTAR OF GOLD AND SACRIFICE

The Altar of gold was the place where Incense was burned. Sacrifice of any kind was forbidden, only Incense could be offered; however, the Blood which was applied to the four horns once a year definitely was symbolic of Sacrifice, but rather a Sacrifice already offered. Even though this was an Altar, no Sacrifice was to be offered on it, as it generally is on Altars, for the simple reason, that the one Sacrifice of Christ would be forever sufficient; however, the very fact that it was referred to as an Altar, tells us, that our Faith is to ever be in that one completed work. Whereas no more Sacrifice will ever be needed, yet, we are to ever have Faith in that one Sacrifice.

This Altar was made of shittim wood overlaid with gold. This type of wood was indestructible in the sense that it would never rot, nor due to its fragrance, could it be infested with worms, etc. It speaks of the humanity of Christ which was a perfect humanity. The gold of course, speaks of His Deity.

OUR GREAT INTERCESSOR

The Altar of gold is first of all a figure of Christ as our great Intercessor. It was where the Priests ministered both morning and evening, and above all, where the High Priest ministered once a year on the Great Day of Atonement, when the blood was applied. All of this was a figure of Christ, our High Priest in Heaven. *"We have such an High Priest, Who is set on the right hand of the Throne of the Majesty in the heavens"* (Heb. 8:1).

What type of Intercession does Christ make for us, and how is it made?

As it regards Intercession, and irrespective of the type, Christ in effect, does such by His very Presence at the Throne of God. That means that He really doesn't do anything, simply because it has already been done at the Cross and in His Resurrection. The Scripture plainly says, *"For Christ has not entered into the Holy Place made with hands* (the Tabernacle and Temple of old), *which are the figures* (symbols) *of the true; but into heaven itself, now to appear in the Presence of God for us"* (Heb. 9:24).

In other words, His very appearance *"in the Presence of God for us"* guarantees

Intercession of all types. He doesn't really have to say or do anything, His Presence alone, signifies that it has already been done and accepted by God.

THE TWO ALTARS

The Brazen Altar sat outside the Tabernacle, and was actually the first thing seen when approaching the Tabernacle. At this Altar, God deals with the sinner. The Altar of Gold inside the Tabernacle is where God deals with the Saint. The Altar of Brass speaks of Earth while the Altar of Gold speaks of Heaven. The Altar of Brass has to do with sin, while the Altar of Gold has to do with Holiness. The Altar of Brass, is a figure, representing what Christ did for us on Earth in the giving of Himself on the Cross; the Altar of Gold, is a figure, representing what Christ does for us in Heaven; however, what He does for us in Heaven, is made possible by what He did for us on Earth.

THE CROWN

The Golden Altar had a golden crown on its outside edges. It refers to Christ as our High Priest, but yet a crowned Priest. In other words, He is both King and Priest. Consequently, He combined both offices in Israel of King and Priest. In fact, He combined the Offices of King, Priest, and Prophet.

These three offices provided the titular leadership of Israel. The King was the head; the Priest was the Intercessor; the Prophet was the Spiritual Leader. These were all types of Christ, and in fact, Christ was and is all of these offices. This means that He is the True Israel, just exactly as He is the True Church, and as well, the True Man.

THE HORNS

On all four corners of this Altar were four horns. They pointed outward, north, south, east, and west.

This signifies the fact, that this is not a *"Western Gospel,"* or an *"Eastern Gospel,"* but rather, Salvation for the entirety of the world.

As well, it signifies that Christ died for the whole of humanity (Jn. 3:16), and that His sacrificial, atoning work, suffices for all.

Also, these horns signify, and by the blood being applied to them once a year, even as we've already stated, that the way to everything that Christ has done for us, is through the Cross, and our Faith in that great Sacrifice.

I have before me a Commentary written by a famous name in Christendom, who without a doubt was a great man of God; however, the things he said about this Altar and the Intercession of Christ, tells me that he didn't quite understand the mode of Intercession or how it is brought about.

He said, *"He* (Christ) *is pointing this very moment to your need, saying, 'Father, deliver; Father, give the victory'."*

Now most of the Church would applaud that statement, but it is wrong!

In the first place, all deliverance and all victory were purchased totally and completely by Christ at the Cross. It is not a matter of Him or the Father, or even the Holy Spirit having to do anything else in order for anyone to have victory over anything within their hearts and lives.

When Jesus died on the Cross, He died for the entirety of mankind. That means, that every single person can be saved if they will only accept.

At the same time, His Death and Resurrection guaranteed total and complete victory for every single, solitary Believer. In other words, it's already done. As we've already stated in this Volume, this means that every single Christian has victory, even though most Christians are not walking in victory. Every Christian is an overcomer, even though most Christians are not living an overcoming life.

This refers to what Christ did for us at the Cross, and our faith in Him, literally placing us in His life and victory (Rom. 6:3-5, 11, 14). If Christ, or the Father, or the Divine Spirit, have to do anything else in order for us to have anything that we need, this means that the Work of Christ is not actually a Finished Work.

But it definitely is a Finished Work! So, that being the case, why is it that all Believers do not walk in victory, especially considering, that all Believers are *"in Christ,"* which means, that we have everything that Christ did for us at the Cross?

IT IS A MATTER OF FAITH

Christians do not walk in victory and do not live an overcoming life for one reason

NOTES

— their lack of Faith in the Cross of Christ. As we've stated over and over again, most Christians know and understand the part the Cross plays in their initial Salvation experience, but they have little or no knowledge at all, as it regards what the Cross means to their everyday living. Consequently, they place their Faith in other things, which God will never honor.

It is not a question of Christians having Faith, but rather a question of their Faith being misplaced. Now please read the following thought very carefully:

It is only Faith in the Cross of Christ, which refers to His Finished Work, which God will recognize (Gal. 2:20). If it's Faith in anything else, we have actually turned this great commodity into a *"work."* And what did the Holy Spirit say about that?

"And if by grace, then is it no more of works: otherwise grace is no more grace. But if it be of works, then it is no more grace" (Rom. 11:6).

Paul also said, *"For by Grace are ye saved through faith; and that not of yourselves: it is the Gift of God;*

"Not of works, lest any man should boast" (Eph. 2:8-9).

So, while faith continues to be faith irrespective as to what is its object, still God classifies it as *"works"* if it's not Faith in the Finished Work of Christ, which is specified by the word *"Grace."* Grace is simply the goodness of God extended to undeserving man. However, it is the Cross of Christ, and our Faith in that Sacrifice, which makes it possible for God to extend Grace to undeserving souls.

Inasmuch as the four horns on the Golden Altar signify Kingship and, therefore, victory, this means that it is for all; however, it must come by the way of the Cross, signified by the Blood applied to those horns once a year on the Great Day of Atonement, which means that our Faith must ever rest within the Finished Work of Christ. Then, and as stated, the Holy Spirit Who then resided between the Mercy Seat and the Cherubim, will guarantee to us all that Christ carried out on our behalf in His Finished Work. It is the Divine and Eternal Spirit, Who guarantees all that Christ did, and does so on our behalf (Jn. 16:7-15).

THE ARK OF THE COVENANT

The phrase, *"And the Ark of the Covenant overlaid round about with gold,"* presents the most glorious and mysterious Vessel of the Tabernacle. Actually, it was the first thing made (Ex. 25:10-11). In fact, in a sense one might say, the whole Sanctuary was built for no other purpose but that it may house the Ark of the Covenant (Ex. 26:33).

The Ark was the outstanding symbol that God Himself was present among His people and that His Covenant-Blessing was resting upon them. It was the coffer in which the Tables of the Law were preserved. Its preeminence above all the other Vessels was shown in the days of Solomon, for the Ark alone was transferred from the Tabernacle to the Temple. But yet we must not forget that it was the Brazen Altar alone which made access possible to the Ark of the Covenant.

Once again, the Ark was an outstanding figure of the Son of God. It too was made of Shittim wood, overlaid with gold. The wood which was incorruptible was a type of His sinless humanity. Of course, the gold, as stated, was a type of His Deity.

The two materials of which the Ark was made symbolized the *"union"* of the two natures in the God-Man, the Lord Jesus Christ. The Scripture says, *"God was manifest in the flesh"* (I Tim. 3:16).

The Ark formed God's Throne in Israel: *"Thou that dwellest between the Cherubim"* (Ps. 80:1).

Christ is the only One Who perfectly enthroned God, honoring His Government in all things.

A TYPE OF CHRIST

As everything else in the Tabernacle is a type of Christ, the Ark of the Covenant falls into the same category. Some of the ways are as follows:

1. From it God communed with Moses, the leader of His people. Christ is the manner in which we reach the Father. In fact, no man can come to the Father except by and through Christ (Jn. 14:6).

2. It symbolized guidance. *"And they departed from the Mount of the LORD three days' journey: and the Ark of the Covenant of the LORD went before them in the three days' journey to search out a resting place for them"* (Num. 10:33).

3. While it is the Holy Spirit Who leads and guides us presently (Jn. 16:13), He does so strictly and solely through the Finished Work of Christ. The Holy Spirit resides in all Believers, but He is able to do that only because of what Jesus did at the Cross.

4. As the Ark of the Covenant symbolized guidance, it also represented Divine Leadership, which refers to Christ as the *"Head"* of the Church (Eph. 1:22).

When Israel was about to pass over Jordan into Canaan, the Priests carrying the Ark went first. And it was when their feet touched the water that Jordan was rolled back and the people of Israel could march over on dry ground (Josh. 3:14-17).

To say this in New Testament terminology, *"When He putteth forth His Own sheep, He goeth before them"* (Jn. 10:4). As we've already stated, He not only brings victory, He is our Victory.

GOD'S PORTRAIT OF CHRIST

As we come in closer to the dwelling place of God, the emphasis is removed from the *"Work of Christ,"* as represented all the other Sacred Vessels, to the *"Person of Christ,"* represented by the Ark. There were actually two articles of furniture in the Holy of Holies, the Ark and the Mercy Seat; however, they were so joined as to be one. We will direct our attention first to the Ark.

Israel was a theocracy, meaning that Jehovah Alone was their king. At least this held true until they demanded a king, with the first one being Saul, who was not the choice of God but rather the people. David was God's choice, and was meant to be the first king of Israel; however, Satan used the people of Israel to attempt to thwart the Plan of God, which he so often does. Let me say it a little clearer:

God has a Plan for His Church, and more particularly, He has a plan for every individual member of His Church. Unfortunately, unspiritual men too often usurp authority over the Headship of Christ, and insert their own plans instead, which always brings great hindrance to the Work of God.

Even when David became king of Israel, and even with the members of his family who followed him, this more than anything else was to represent the Kingship of Christ. Jehovah was still King or at least was meant to be!

In this they were unlike the nations around them. The Ark was God's Throne; however, in no way do we mean to insinuate that there was some type of physical presence in the Holy of Holies, for there wasn't. But yet, He dwelt, as far as His presence was concerned, between the Cherubim (Ps. 99:1). Actually, and as we've already stated, as far as the Godhead was concerned, it was the Holy Spirit Who actually resided in the Holy of Holies (I Cor. 3:16).

Of all the articles of furniture that made up the Tabernacle, the Ark of the Covenant was the most important. The instructions for it were the first given of any part of the Tabernacle. The fact that it was God's Throne lent importance to it. And yet, no Israelite ever saw it, so sacred was it. Only the High Priests were permitted to behold it.

On the wilderness march it was carefully wrapped, first in the Veil and then with badger's skins . . . it was thus a True Symbol of the Lord Jesus Christ setting forth both His Deity, represented by the gold, and His humanity, represented by the wood; for the Ark was made of wood (incorruptible wood) and overlaid with gold. In this it spoke of Him as *"Very God of Very God and Very Man of Very Man."*

The Ark could not be spoken of as merely a wooden box, for it contained gold; and it could not be called a golden chest, for it contained wood. It required both to maintain the symbolism pointing to Christ as the God-Man. As we've stated over and over again, every single thing in the Tabernacle and the Temple as well pointed to Christ and symbolized Him in some way.

To overlook this duality is to entertain a monstrous notion of His Person. There is no doctrine of Scripture so filled with infinite mystery, so far removed from the pattern of man's thinking, so foreign to the realm of explanation, than this union of God and Man in Christ. Yet, there is no symbol so simple as the Ark — merely a box made of wood and gold — yet it speaks of things unfathomable.

Truly, God chooses the simple things to confound the wise. That simple box tells the

whole story, so far as man can take it in, of the unsearchable mysteries of the Blessed Person of the Lord Jesus Christ.

GOLD AND WOOD

The gold was both inside and out. *"For in Him dwelleth all the fullness of the Godhead Bodily"* (Col. 2:9). This means that He was not merely an emanation of God, *"He was God."* He spoke as God. He put Himself on the same plane with God: *"Ye believe in God, believe also in Me."* And again, *"He that hath seen Me hath seen the Father."*

Likewise, He was Perfect Man. He grew tired and sat down at a well in Samaria. He slept, He ate, He drank, and He laughed and wept. And beyond all that, He suffered. All these are human characteristics.

The gold and the wood in the Ark were both required; yet neither was mingled with the other, nor was the identity of one lost in the other. Christ was both God and man, but these two natures never were fused or merged, one might say! In other words, He never functioned at the same time as both God and man. Actually, I think one could say without fear of contradiction, that He never functioned as God in His earthly Life and Ministry, although He never ceased to be God. As one Scholar said, *"As the God-Man Jesus Christ, He never lost His possession of Deity, but in fact He did lay aside freely His expression of Deity."*

Some confuse His performing of miracles with Deity; however, He did all of this as a Man filled with the Spirit, in fact as no other man had ever been filled, thereby performing miracles by the Spirit (Lk. 4:18-19).

ISRAEL AND THE ARK

Containing the Law, and being the place where the Symbol of the Divine Presence was manifested, the Ark was regarded as peculiarly holy; and in the various wars and revolutions in the Hebrew commonwealth, it was guarded with peculiar care.

After the passage over the Jordan it remained for some time at Gilgal (Josh. 4:19), with it then being removed to Shiloh (I Sam. 1:3). From hence the Israelites took it to their war camp, apparently to animate them in battle, but it was taken by the Philistines (I Sam. Chpt. 4).

The Philistines, however, oppressed by the hand of God because of their taking the Ark, resolved to return it, and sent it to Kirjath-jearim (I Sam. 7:1).

In the reign of Saul, it was at Nob. David, attempting to bring it to Jerusalem, but doing so incorrectly, brought death to at least one member of the entourage, and instead conveyed it to the house of Obed-edom, and ultimately to his palace on Mount Zion (II Sam. Chpt. 6).

At the dedication of the Temple it was placed in the Holy of Holies by Solomon, where it remained for many years. Subsequently, it is said, the wicked kings of Judah, abandoning themselves to idolatry, established idols in the Most Holy Place itself; and the Priests removed the Ark, and bore it from place to place to secure it from profanation.

When Josiah ascended the Throne he commanded the Priests to restore the Ark to its place in the Sanctuary, and forbade them to carry it about from one place to another as they had done before (II Chron. 35:3).

It is supposed that the Ark remained in the Temple of Solomon until immediately before its (the Temple's) destruction. There is no record that it was taken by Nebuchadnezzar to Babylon, along with some of the other vessels (II Chron. 36:18-19).

Some think that Nebuchadnezzar may have destroyed it upon his invasion and destruction of Jerusalem and the Temple; however, that is unlikely! The Babylonians were prone to take the *"gods"* of vanquished nations to Babylon, where they were put on display in the temple of the god Bel. In effect, this stated, at least in their minds, that Bel was stronger than the other gods of other nations. Of course, the Ark was not an idol, but Nebuchadnezzar no doubt would have taken it as symbolic of the God of Israel, had it been present in the Holy of Holies when his soldiers overran that sacred place.

Legend says that Jeremiah hid the Ark, with its hiding place remaining a secret. This much is certain, there is no evidence that it was ever placed in the second Temple built by Zerubbabel, after the return of the Jews from Babylonian captivity. As well, when the soldiers of Titus broke into the Holy of Holies in the destruction of the third Temple

NOTES

built by Herod in A.D. 70, Jewish history tells us that the room was empty. In other words, there was no Ark there.

Some claim that it is in a subterranean room under the Temple Mount, with some claiming it is presently in Ethiopia. I think one can say with certitude, that these claims are false!

MANNA

The phrase, *"Wherein was the Golden Pot that had manna,"* presents that which was a type of Christ as the Bread of Life (Jn. 6:32-33, 35).

This tells us that a small quantity of Manna was preserved as a perpetual remembrance of the food which they had eaten in their long journey in the wilderness, and of the Goodness of God in miraculously supplying their wants. As the Manna, also, would not of itself keep (Ex. 16:20), the fact that this was to be laid up to be preserved from age to age was a perpetual miracle and proof of the presence and faithfulness of God. Again we state, the Manna was a type of Christ as the Bread of Life.

At some point in time, this item seems to have been removed from the Ark (I Ki. 8:9); however, I think the evidence is clear, that it definitely was kept in the Ark during the wilderness journeyings, and possibly even some time after they came into the Promised Land. It was of this time, of which Paul speaks. It is for sure, that at some particular time, the *"Golden Pot"* as well as *"Aaron's rod that budded,"* were lost.

AARON'S ROD

The phrase, *"And Aaron's Rod that budded,"* represents Christ Alone as Savior, and to prove that, God raised Him from the dead.

Aaron's rod budded as a proof that God had chosen him to minister as High Priest. The princes of some of the Tribes of Israel while in the wilderness, were disposed to rebel, and to call into question the authority of Aaron. To settle the matter, each one was required to take a rod or staff of office, and to bring it to Moses with the name of the Tribe to which it appertained written on it. These were laid up by Moses in the Tabernacle; and it was found, on the next day, that the rod marked with the name of Levi had budded and blossomed, and produced almonds, all done overnight. In perpetual remembrance of this miracle, the rod was preserved in the Ark (Num. Chpt. 17).

In effect, these rebels in Israel were denying Christ. Aaron being a type of Christ, they were in effect saying, that they could come before God without a mediator, claiming they were worthy. Their judgment was severe (Num. Chpt. 16).

Let it be understood presently, that any and all who attempt to place anything ahead of Christ, be it Church, Denominations, Ordinances, so-called Sacraments, Mary, the Mother of our Lord, good works, etc., will be judged accordingly.

CHRIST AS PRIEST

Aaron's Rod in the Ark in the strict sense of the word, speaks of the Work of Christ as Priest. The Prophet spoke for God before man; the Priest spoke for man before God. As a Priest, Christ offered Himself. As a Priest, He passed into Heaven and even now sits on God's right hand.

We have spoken previously of the Work of Christ as Priest. Suffice to say here that there is a Man in Glory at this very moment for us, i.e., *"representing us."* As Aaron's Rod which budded (the authority of His Priesthood) was in the Holy of Holies, thus today there is in Heaven at God's right hand the Man Christ Jesus, Who was raised from the dead. He is the unique example of Resurrection up to the present hour. He is there for us.

Going back to the Golden Pot of Manna, this as stated represents Christ as the Bread from Heaven. This means that He was the consummate Prophet. Christ not only spoke for God, He was also God's Message to man. He was the Logos, the Word of God, the very Alphabet of God, and the Alpha and Omega.

Christ was God's final Message to man . . . God has no addendum to place after Christ. There can be no postscript to the letter where Christ is the embodiment of that letter. God has told His heart in Christ.

THE TEN COMMANDMENTS

The phrase, *"And the Tables of the Covenant,"* proclaims two Tables, with each Table

NOTES

containing five of the Ten Commandments. It is said that the first five pertain to man's obligations toward God, with the second five pertaining to his obligations toward his fellowman.

As the Golden Pot of Manna spoke of Christ as Prophet, and the Rod that budded spoke of Him as Priest, the Tables of the Covenant speak of the Kingship of Christ. This Earth needs a ruler; a man needs a king; and someday He is coming as *"King of kings and Lord of lords."*

The phrase, *"And the Tables of the Covenant,"* is drawn from Deuteronomy 10:1-5. The preservation of the two Tables of stone (on which were inscribed the Ten Commandments) in the Ark, foreshadowed Christ magnifying the Law and making it honorable (Isa. 42:21). The fulfillment of this type is stated in Psalms 40:7-8 where we hear the Mediator saying, *"Lo, I come: in the volume of the Book it is written of Me; I delight to do Thy Will O My God; yea, Thy Law is within My heart."*

The Representative of God's people was *"made under the Law"* (Gal. 4:4), and perfectly did He *"fulfill it"* (Mat. 5:17).

Therefore, it is written, *"By the obedience of one shall many be made righteous"* (Rom. 5:19). Thus may each Believer exclaim, *"In the Lord have I Righteousness and strength"* (Isa. 45:24).

We learn as stated, that while the Golden Pot of Manna and Aaron's Rod that budded, were ultimately lost from the Ark, meaning that Christ had totally fulfilled these types, the two Tables remained. In fact, the Law, and we speak of the Moral Law of God, can never be done away with. It is holy, just, and good. Not one jot or tittle can pass away from it. It is at the heart of all things.

Beneath all surfaces, below all the coverlets, deeper than the foam, tumult, and revolution of the world, rests the righteous, inexorable Law. We must all yield to its imperial sway. Even the atheist must build his walls according to the dictates of this plumb line, or they will inevitably crumble to ruin, as history has proven over and over again.

While Christ definitely fulfilled all the Law, meaning that He kept it perfectly, and even satisfied its just demands by His righteous death on the Cross, still, the world in general continues to be answerable to the Law, whether they realize it or not! In other words, one day when all the unredeemed stand at the Great White Throne Judgment (Rev. 20:11-15), it will be according to that Law that they will answer. Regrettably, they will all be found wanting.

The only way that one can escape the *"found wanting,"* is to place one's faith and trust totally and completely in Jesus Christ and what He did at the Cross on our behalf. As stated, He satisfied the Law regarding all of its demands, and the only way that the Law can have no claim on anyone, is for that person to express Faith in Christ and nothing or no one but Christ. That being the case, all the ordinances that were against us, are blotted out. In fact, Jesus *"nailed all of these to His Cross"* (Col. 2:14-15).

As well, the Law is kept in Christ, and our being In Christ, makes us *"Law-keepers,"* instead of *"Lawbreakers."* But the Reader must remember, that all of this is predicated on our Faith in Christ, and more particularly, what Christ did at the Cross for us, in other words, on our behalf (Jn. 3:16).

Every single person in the world will answer to the Law of God, whether in Christ, or whether on their own, in which the latter no one wants to do, at least if they are in their right mind.

(5) "AND OVER IT THE CHERUBIMS OF GLORY SHADOWING THE MERCYSEAT; OF WHICH WE CANNOT NOW SPEAK PARTICULARLY."

The exegesis is:

1. There were two Cherubims attached to the Ark of the Covenant, one at either end facing each other, and looking down upon the Mercyseat.

2. The Mercyseat was the lid of the box called *"the Ark of the Covenant."*

3. All of this typifies the Throne of God, of which Paul now says that he will not take the time to go into detail.

CHERUBIMS

The phrase, *"And over it the Cherubims of Glory,"* presents these strange beings. *"Cherubims"* is a transliteration of the Hebrew word meaning *"Living Creatures."*

NOTES

The Cherubims, as stated, were two in number, made of gold, actually of one piece with the Mercy Seat, the golden cover of the Ark. They are described as the Cherubims of Glory because they are closely attached to and attended upon, the place of the manifestation of the Divine Glory representing the Throne of God.

These Cherubims had outstretched wings, meeting in the center, thus overshadowing and, as it were, proclaiming the Holiness of the thrice holy God.

There is profound significance connected with their figures, which is made clear from the prominent place which they occupy in connection with the description of the Mercy Seat given in Exodus 25:17-22. Mention is there made of the Cherubim, in either the singular or plural number, no less than seven times. As well, the mention of them in Genesis 3:24 suggests that they are associated with the administration of God's Judicial authority. In Revelation 4:6-8 and Ezekiel 1:5-10, they are related to God's Throne.

Notice that the Cherubim look down upon the Mercy Seat of the Ark which it covered. They symbolize, it seems, the Righteousness and Justice of God. A broken Law demanded judgment, but God made a provision.

Once a year the Mercy Seat was sprinkled with Blood. This meant that God, represented by the Cherubim, saw not the broken Law but the Blood of Atonement. His grace covers all our sin (Harris).

When the Temple was built, the Cherubim placed in the Holy of Holies at that time, were of huge size. They were made of olive wood, and were 15 feet high. They were overlaid with gold, with each having two sets of wings. One set touched the wall on one side of the Holy of Holies, with the other Cherubim touching the other wall. The other set of wings met together over the Ark (I Ki. 6:23-28).

It is almost certain, that their design in the Tabernacle was somewhat different, with their second set of wings folded down by their sides, that is if such wings were shown.

Also, there is evidence that the smaller Cherubim attached to the Ark of the Covenant remained in their position as it regards the Temple, but with the giant Cherubim towering above them, actually filling up the entirety of the room. Incidentally, the Holy of Holies in the Temple was 30 feet square and 30 feet high. The two giant Cherubim were 15 feet high, with all four sets of wings spanning the entirety of the length of the room. As stated, one set touched the walls behind, with the second set of wings of each Cherubim stretching out in front, meeting in the middle over the Ark.

Whereas the Cherubim attached to the Mercy Seat, and made of the same mass of gold, looked downward upon the sprinkled blood, the Cherubim made of olive wood looked outward. God's perfect judgments will, in the Millennium, which these Cherubim in the Temple represent, be enabled to look out from Calvary upon a Kingdom wherein shall dwell Righteousness. This is not now possible, for Righteousness retreated to Heaven when Christ went to the Father (Jn. 16:10); however, in the coming Millennium, Christ will Personally reign from Jerusalem, hence Righteousness then filling the Earth (I Ki. Chpt. 6).

We find the Cherubim connected with Eden at the beginning (Gen. 3:24), and we see them again at the Throne of the Lamb at the close of Bible History (Rev. 4:6-9).

STRANGE BEINGS

In Ezekiel Chapter 10 we find the chariot-throne of God being borne up by Cherubim, and actually going from place to place. Representations of these winged creatures were also embroidered on the Curtains and the Veil of the Tabernacle, and even on the walls of the Temple (Ex. 26:31; II Chron. 3:7).

These Beings were also carved in the form of a frieze around the wall of Solomon's Temple, and they appeared together with animal representations on decorative panels forming part of the base of the huge brass basin (Molten Sea or the Brazen Laver) which contained water for ritual ablutions.

The Old Testament does not describe the appearance and general nature of these Cherubim clearly. They were generally represented as winged creatures having feet and hands. In Ezekiel's vision of the restored Jerusalem, the carved likenesses of Cherubim had two faces, one of a man and the other of a young

lion (Ezek. 41:18-19), whereas in those seen in his vision of the Divine Glory, each of the Cherubim had four faces and four wings, each with the face of a man and the face of a lion on the right side, and the face of an ox and of an eagle on the left side (Ezek. 1:6-11).

In Revelation, John described them a little differently. He said they were *"full of eyes before and behind."* As well, each of these Living Creatures had only one face, one with the face of a lion, the other of a calf, the third of a man, and the fourth like an eagle. As well, whereas the ones Ezekiel saw had four wings, those observed by John each had six wings (Rev. 4:6-8).

I think it is obvious from the Scriptures, that there are different types of these creatures. Actually, in Isaiah's vision, he told of seeing creatures which the Holy Spirit told him were *"Seraphims."* These as well had six wings, but like the Cherubim seen by John, only had one face. As well, those seen by Isaiah cry, *"Holy, holy, holy is the LORD of Hosts: the whole earth is full of His Glory"* (Isa. 6:3), while those seen by John also say, *"Holy, holy, holy, LORD God Almighty, which was, and is, and is to come"* (Rev. 4:8). Ezekiel mentioned, it seems, that they said something, but he doesn't say exactly what (Ezek. 1:24-25).

It seems from what little description we are given, that these strange creatures have many duties, and as well, are greatly connected with the Glory and Holiness of God. They as well seem to be attached to the Throne, but beyond that we have little knowledge. To speculate further, would be only speculation, and of little value.

THE MERCY SEAT

The phrase, *"Shadowing the Mercy Seat,"* of which we cannot now speak particularly, refers to the golden lid which covered the Ark, and down upon which the Cherubim gazed.

The words *"Mercy Seat"* are the translation of the Greek *"hilasterion,"* and means *"propitiation"*; however, the manner in which this Greek word is used, does not suggest as it normally does *"something offered to placate or appease anger,"* but rather refers to Atonement or Reconciliation through covering, and in that way getting rid of the sin which stands between God and sinful man. The chief idea in the word is not that which is related to an offended party, but to sin or uncleanness (Wuest).

Vincent says, *"As here used of the Mercy Seat, it is not that of appeasing one who is angry with a personal feeling against an offender, but of altering the character of that which, from without, occasions, a necessary alienation, and interposes an inevitable obstacle of fellowship."* The idea is, that obstacle between God and man, namely sin, was removed by our Lord's atoning death on the Cross. The Sacrificial Blood sprinkled on the cover of the Ark fully satisfies the demands of the broken Law, and comes between the tablets of the Law reposing in the Ark and the High Priest who represents the people and in whom the people stand. Thus, did the Blood of Jesus interpose itself between the Law of God and the guilty sinner.

This is where mercy is offered on the basis of justice satisfied. It is the place where a Holy God will meet sinful man and save him (Wuest).

THE SIGNIFICANCE OF THE MERCY SEAT

There were two articles in the Holy of Holies. The appearance of them seemed as one, but careful examination revealed two, for the Mercy Seat furnished a top for the Ark. They would appear to be the same thing, but they were separate and distinct. However, the instructions for both are given together. The blueprint of the Mercy Seat is contained in Exodus 25:17-22, following the blueprint for the Ark.

The Mercy Seat was the top for the Ark, but it was actually a separate piece of furniture. It was made of pure gold. It was about 3 ¾ feet long, and about 2 ¼ feet wide. As stated, the Cherubims were actually a part of the Mercy Seat, all of it made out of one piece of gold, and was probably the special work of Bezaleel.

Perhaps we could say, that the Mercy Seat was the most important article of furniture, and where all were God-appointed, it was supreme.

In the instructions, God interjects this revealing declaration, *"And there will I meet with thee, and I will commune with thee from above the Mercy Seat."* On the Great Day of Atonement God issued a warning to Aaron not to come within the Veil, except at the appointed time, *"For I will appear in the cloud upon the Mercy Seat."*

On the wilderness march it was from above the Mercy Seat between the Cherubim that God directed Israel.

The fact that the Mercy Seat was gold declares the Deity of Christ again. There is a resurrected Christ upon the Throne of the universe today. The Man in Glory is sitting at the Father's right hand, waiting until the time when His enemies shall be made His footstool and when He will receive the Throne of David, which will take place at the Second Coming (Rev. Chpt. 19).

THE BLOOD

As we approach the teaching of the Mercy Seat in its primary import, it is essential to see what made it a Mercy Seat. In order to ascertain this, a consideration must be made of the Great Day of Atonement, for only on this day did the High Priest approach the Mercy Seat.

Aaron, after casting lots for the scapegoat, which was a type of Christ bearing away the sin of man, offered the other goat on the Burnt Altar. After offering a bullock for himself, an analogy which finds no parallel in Christ, and because there was no sin in Christ, Aaron brought the basin of blood within the Veil and sprinkled it upon the Mercy Seat. In fact, the Blood made it a Mercy Seat. God did not look down upon the merit of Aaron, or upon the goodness of the people, but rather He looked down upon the blood.

This means that the sinning nation was made nigh by the blood. Christ is the Mercy Seat today, *"Whom God hath set forth to be a propitiation through Faith in His Blood, to declare His Righteousness for the remission of sins that are past, through the forbearance of God"* (Rom. 3:25) (McGee).

COVERING

Even though the Greek word used for the Mercy Seat means *"propitiation,"* the Hebrew word actually means *"covering."* They are very close in meaning, but the word *"covering"* probably says it best.

The Mercy Seat covered the Tables of the Law which were in the Ark, and which Commandments had been broken by all people. Consequently, the people needed a covering to shield them from the condemnation for their sins. The Mercy Seat was this covering.

The idea is, that the Blood of Jesus covers all sin, actually cleansing it (I Jn. 1:7, 9; 2:1-2). He brings atonement through His Own Blood, not that of bulls or of goats. Every human being on the face of the Earth has sinned, but when the Blood of Christ is applied, our being in Christ, which we are, means that God sees the Blood of His Son, which He has shed for us, which also means we have no more sin.

A NECESSITY FOR ALL

I get sadly amused at times at the manner in which many Christians speak of sin.

One Brother wrote just the other day, and his letter is indicative of many, mentioning that he had *"had a problem,"* which I suppose he was speaking of a *"moral problem."* Many Christians use these terms as if they only apply to a few. The truth is the following:

While many definitely will not commit certain sins, the Truth is, the entirety of the human race, and without exceptions, *"have a problem,"* and that problem is sin. And to be sure, it is all a *"moral problem"* in one shape, form, fashion, or the other. That's why Jesus had to come down here and die on a Cross. As well, I think it would be proper to say two or three other things:

Also, some Christians are rather fond of referring to certain people as *"fallen,"* when the Truth is, the only Christians who are fallen are those who have discontinued their faith and trust in Christ. No one is fallen because of sin of any nature, and I speak of having dutifully confessed it before the Lord, thereby receiving forgiveness and cleansing (I Jn. 1:9). If in fact, *"sin"* of any nature, other than rebellion against God's Way which is the Cross, constitutes one as *"fallen,"* this would then mean that the entirety of Christendom is fallen. No! The only ones who are judged by God as *"fallen"* are those who no longer trust Christ (Heb. 6:4-6).

As well, any Christian who attempts to hang a sin around the neck of a Christian who has

long since repented of the thing and forsaken such error, is doing a terrible despite to the Spirit of Grace. This is an insult to Christ of the greatest proportions. There is no such thing as a 50 percent justification by faith, or 75 percent justification by faith, or a partial justification by faith in any sense. One is either totally justified by Faith, which is the only thing that can be done, or is not justified at all!

And last of all, there is only one way that sin can be handled, and that is by taking it to the Cross. Whenever men demand that something else be done, such as entering into some type of *"works"* regimen in order to attempt to atone for sin, one has just negated the Grace of God. Unfortunately, many Religious Denominations fall into that category. They are not willing to accept God's provision, but rather manufacture provisions of their own, which change with the political climate. Such efforts and ways are an abomination to God, and as well, do terrible despite to the Spirit of Grace (Heb. 10:29).

And it should be quickly said that any Preacher or person, who subscribes to such a regimen, is cutting off the Grace of God unto themselves. One cannot trust God for Mercy and Grace, and at the same time trust man as it regards a regimen of *"works."* There is one atonement, and that's the Blood of Jesus. Whenever we try to enter something else into the mix, we sin greatly against God. And that goes for the ones demanding such works, and the one agreeing to abide by such works. This is the same thing as a sinner trying to be saved by trusting in Christ and Mary, the Mother of our Lord, at the same time.

Again I emphasize, there is only one answer for sin, one solution for this dread monster, and that is the Cross of Christ, and one's Faith in that Finished Work. To add anything else is abominable before God.

It must always be understood, that there is no such thing as a probationary time with God, no partial forgiveness of sins, no partial justification; there is nothing of that sort in the Word of God. And if such is insinuated or suggested, it is always of man and never of God, and must never be heeded at any cost.

(6) "NOW WHEN THESE THINGS WERE THUS ORDAINED, THE PRIESTS WENT

ALWAYS INTO THE FIRST TABERNACLE, ACCOMPLISHING THE SERVICE OF GOD."

The structure is:

1. The word *"ordained,"* means they were designed by God, and speak of the Tabernacle Service.

2. The *"Priests"* were mediators between God and Israel, and as such, served as types of Christ.

3. The words *"first Tabernacle"* actually mean the first part of the Tabernacle, or that referred to as the *"Holy Place."*

4. What they were instructed to do, was *"the service of God,"* all designed by God that He could commune with His people.

5. It was all temporary, in fact, pointing to something better which was to come.

ORDAIN

The phrase, *"Now when these things were thus ordained,"* refers to the fact that all of this was of God, and that every part and parcel of the Tabernacle in some way pointed to Christ. In fact, Paul plainly intimates that every part of it had a specific significance as typical of the Lord Jesus and His Ministry.

TABERNACLE MINISTRY

The phrase, *"The Priests went always into the First Tabernacle,"* refers as stated, to the first room of the Tabernacle called the *"Holy Place,"* which the Priests went into daily and which, with the exception of the High Priest, they could go no further.

In fact, as long as the old dispensation lasted, the Priests had no access into the Holiest. They went only into the First Tabernacle and accomplished the liturgical service. Once a year the High Priest alone was permitted to enter the Sacred Inner Chamber where the Shekinah hovered over the Mercy Seat. Nor could he approach without atoning blood, which he offered first of all for himself as being but a sinful man, and also for the failures of the people.

The Tabernacle was actually a place of communion, a place of fellowship, a place of worship, and a place for forgiveness of sins. The people could come freely to the gate of the Outer Court; it was always open as an invitation to any who needed to come. They could come into the Outer Court where Sacrifices were made on behalf of their trespasses and sins. However, the people did not enter the Tabernacle itself, but the Priests entered on their behalf.

THE SERVICE OF GOD

The phrase, *"Accomplishing the Service of God,"* refers to what was done there. From the Sanctuary Paul moves to the ritual. He is particularly interested in what was done on the Day of Atonement, and he uses the limitations attached to the High Priest's entry into the Holy of Holies to bring home the inferiority of the whole Levitical system. But he begins with the Ministry of the lower Priests.

When the Tabernacle system was established, the Priests did their work in the first room of the Tabernacle. This included such things as burning incense (Ex. 30:7-8), setting out the holy loaves (Lev. 24:8-9), and trimming the lamps (Ex. 27:20-21; Lev. 24:3-4). There was a sharp distinction between the duties and place of service of the Priests and those of the Levites (Num. 18:1-7).

The Levites, who of course were also of the tribe of Levi, were to be under Aaron and the succeeding High Priests in any service they were allowed by Law to perform in the Tabernacle service. They were limited to certain duties in the Tabernacle Court and around the Brazen Altar, to transporting and erecting the Tabernacle, and to some other services.

They were not to come near the vessels of the Sanctuary and the Golden Altar inside the Tabernacle itself. In fact, breaking the Law on this point carried the death penalty.

The Priests were to have charge of all Sacrifices of the Brazen Altar and all services inside the Holy and Most Holy Places.

(7) "BUT INTO THE SECOND WENT THE HIGH PRIEST ALONE ONCE EVERY YEAR, NOT WITHOUT BLOOD, WHICH HE OFFERED FOR HIMSELF, AND FOR THE ERRORS OF THE PEOPLE:"

The construction is:

1. The word *"second"* refers to the second room in the Tabernacle, which was the *"Holy of Holies."*

2. Only the High Priest was allowed in this particular room.

3. He was allowed to go in only once a year, and that on the Great Day of Atonement.

4. When he went inside this room, he had to take with him the blood of the Sacrifice, *"which he offered for himself, and for the errors of the people."*

THE HOLY OF HOLIES

The phrase, *"But into the second went the High Priest alone,"* refers as stated, to the *"Holy of Holies,"* and has great significance as it regards Christ.

ALONE

As we look at this, and I speak of the Tabernacle Ministry being a type of Christ, let's first of all look at the word *"alone."*

When Jesus came to Earth, He came alone. He walked among men, but He walked alone. He went into the Garden with His three chosen Disciples, but He was really alone. The work He came to accomplish could be done only by Himself alone; the Redemptive Work of Jesus was done alone. *". . . He had by Himself purged our sins . . ."* (Heb. 1:3).

No angel or any man could do what Jesus did. Nor could any assist Him. He alone bore the sin of the whole world; He alone made reconciliation.

Around the Cross was a multitude — but He was alone. That day when He hung on a Cross on Calvary's hill, drops of blood flowed from His wounded hands and feet; His brow and back were bloodstained from thorns and from scourging. He cried out, *"My God, My God, why hast Thou forsaken Me?"* (Mat. 27:46). He felt the separation that sin brings, and He cried out in agony under sin's burden (Mat. 27:50-51).

Alone, Jesus died for the sins of the world. Alone, He carried the sins of men. Alone, He purged, He reconciled. He became the Captain of our Salvation and *"the Author of Eternal Salvation unto all them who obey Him"* (Heb. 5:9).

As we've already stated, the *"Veil"* signified separation, emphasizing the sinfulness of man and the holiness of God; however, when Jesus died on the Cross, that Veil was rent; it was torn apart. This means that the way into the Holiest was made open; access through the Blood of Christ was now provided. No longer did anyone need to stand outside, but whoever would, could enter. The rent Veil is

NOTES

God's way of saying, *"Enter into My Presence; walk with Me into the Holy of Holies."*

HE ALONE IS WORTHY

As He alone paid the great price, this means that He alone is worthy! He alone has been exalted as Lord over all things, and simply because He alone paid the price. This also means, that He alone is the faithful, merciful, sympathetic High Priest.

YEARLY

The phrase, *"Once every year,"* pertaining to the Great Day of Atonement (Lev. 16:14; 23:27), tells us several things. They are as follows:

1. As is obvious, the way was not open for all to enter. Not even the Priests could enter, save only the High Priest.

2. He could only enter on one particular day each year, the Great Day of Atonement.

3. The very fact that he had to keep entering each year, testifies that whatever sacrifices had been previously offered, did not suffice, and because they could not suffice. The blood of bulls and goats could not take away sin.

4. The very fact that this arrangement was made, which as is obvious was imperfect, tells us that it was only temporary.

BLOOD

The phrase, *"Not without blood, which he offered for himself, and for the errors of the people,"* presents him going in twice on this one day.

Some say he actually entered three times on this day, the first time with Incense, then with the Blood of the bullock which atoned for his own sins and those of his house, and finally with the blood of the goat for the sins of the people.

The word *"errors"* is the translation of *"agnoema,"* and means *"a sin committed through ignorance or thoughtlessness."*

Whenever a known sin was committed, each Israelite was to journey to the Tabernacle, or Temple for that matter, and offer up the proper sacrifice, according to the sin committed. Actually, there were five different types of Sacrifices, *"the Whole Burnt-Offering, the Sin-Offering, the Trespass-Offering, the Peace-Offering, and the Thank-Offering."*

Of course, Jesus fulfilled by His one offering of Himself, all five Sacrifices.

However, even for the few who tried to be diligent in their service to the Lord, still there were sins of ignorance or thoughtlessness committed, which required this one great Sacrifice each year.

"For" in the Greek is *"huper,"* and speaks of *"substitution."* It means *"for the sake of, in behalf of."* It speaks of the substitutionary character of the Atonement. Here the blood is offered as a type pointing to the coming Atonement of our Lord.

THE HIGH PRIEST WITHIN THE HOLY OF HOLIES

Having made a brief reference to the structure of the Tabernacle and its two compartments, and the furniture belonging to each of them respectively, the Apostle now turns to consider the uses for which they were designed in the Service of God.

When the things mentioned in Verses 2-5 had been made and duly ordered, they stood not for a magnificent show, but were designed for constant use in the Service of God. Hereby, we are taught that for any service to be acceptable to God, it must be in strict accord with the pattern He has given us in His Word.

Actually, everything was fully prepared for Divine service before that service was performed. So in modern public services and Divine worship, there must be fit persons who, under the Spirit, are to lead it — *"able Ministers of the New Testament"* (II Cor. 3:6); fit arrangements and order (I Cor. 14:40), not mere human tradition (Mat. 15:9); a fit message unto edification (I Cor. 14:26) (Pink).

However, of all the priestly duties carried on by the many Priests in the first room of the Tabernacle, they could not at all enter the Holy of Holies, which was the second room, that being reserved for the High Priest, who alone could enter only on one particular day of the year, the Great Day of Atonement.

PREPARATION

Even though all the Priests of the Mosaic Order were types of Christ, the High Priest held a special position in this regard.

First of all, all High Priests were afforded very special garments. They were called *"holy*

NOTES

garments for glory and for beauty" (Ex. 28:2). These garments were made of gold, blue, purple, scarlet, and fine linen (Ex. 28:5). Actually, they were designed by the Holy Spirit. All of these colors spoke of Christ in a special way: gold for deity, blue for Heaven, purple for royalty, scarlet for His Blood, and fine linen for His Perfect Righteousness.

However, when he went into the Holy of Holies, he was to divest himself of these beautiful garments, leaving only the coat made of fine linen which was worn next to the body. The fine linen as stated, speaks of the Righteousness and spotless purity of Christ. As well, him divesting himself of his *"garments of glory and beauty,"* tells us that He did not purchase our Redemption through His Deity, but rather through His humanity, and that by dying on a Cross.

THE MINISTRY OF THE HIGH PRIEST

On this very special day of the year, the Great Day of Atonement, after the usual morning Sacrifice, the High Priest as stated, removed the beautiful robes he usually wore, and dressed himself in pure white linen garments, the symbol of purity. Here is a picture, also as stated, of Christ laying aside His Divine prerogatives and coming down to Earth that He might work Atonement for us.

First of all, the High Priest offered a bullock for a Sin-Offering for himself and his family. Usually this blood was poured out entirely at the base of the Brazen Altar. But on this occasion it was placed in a basin which he carried into the Holy Place. From the Brazen Altar he took coals and he obtained some Incense which he placed in a Censer. As he pulled aside the Veil that hung between the Holy Place and the Holy of Holies, the smoke from the Incense upon the coals billowed up, hiding the Mercy Seat from view. If he had failed to do this, he would have died (Lev. 16:13).

With his finger, he took of the blood of the bullock and sprinkled it upon the Mercy Seat and in front of it seven times. It was only because he had blood for Atonement to present that he dared to come into the Holy of Holies.

After the High Priest had made Atonement for himself, he returned to the door of the Tabernacle. Here two goats were led before him. They represented two parts of one offering, picturing the means and the results of Atonement. By casting lots, one was chosen to be offered upon the Altar. It was called the Lord's goat. The other one was called the goat of the people.

Taking the Lord's goat, the High Priest killed it and offered it upon the Brazen Altar. Then taking some of its blood, he entered the Holy of Holies and sprinkled the blood of sacrifice there seven times. He also put part of that blood and the blood of the offering he had made for himself upon the Altar of Incense. Then the body of the bullock which had been offered for a Sin-Offering was burned outside the camp.

A BEAUTIFUL PICTURE OF ATONEMENT

On the Cross of Calvary, Jesus became our Sin-Offering. The pouring out of His Blood on the Cross, and then Him presenting Himself before the Father, means that He was accepted there on our behalf.

The Blood on the Altar of Incense, which represents intercession and worship, means that because of Jesus' Death, we have access into the very Presence of God. Fulfilling the type perfectly, Jesus died outside the Holy City, Jerusalem, just as the animal was burned outside the camp.

SCAPEGOAT

The goat for the people was called the scapegoat, and represented Christ taking our sins away.

At the door of the Tabernacle the High Priest laid his hands upon it and confessed the sins of the people over it. Then the scapegoat was sent away into the wilderness never to return.

Jesus not only died for our sins and cleansed us from them; He also sends them away, not to be remembered against us anymore. They have been put away forever. Like the Israelite who watched the scapegoat disappear from view, we can say, *"There go my sins!"*

In the time of all of this, when the High Priest entered into the Holy of Holies, the people knew that if he were to disobey any of the provisions of God about coming into His Presence, he would die. But as they listened,

NOTES

finally they would hear the tinkling of the bells on the skirts of the garments of the High Priest, of which he had once again clothed himself, and by that they knew he was alive. The entire procession had been accepted by God, and that means that Atonement had been made.

After Jesus died on the Cross for our sins, He ascended on high and presented Himself to the Father. He had shed His Own Blood on our behalf. God accepted that, which means that Atonement was now made for all time and for every human being, at least those who would believe (Jn. 3:16).

As the people waiting anxiously outside of the Tabernacle heard the sound of the bells, likewise on the Day of Pentecost, there was heard a sound from Heaven. The coming of the Holy Spirit not only brought Divine power and joy, but also indisputable proof that Jesus was alive, and that His great Sacrifice had been accepted as full Atonement for man's sins (Harris).

(8) "THE HOLY GHOST THIS SIGNIFYING, THAT THE WAY INTO THE HOLIEST OF ALL WAS NOT YET MADE MANIFEST, WHILE AS THE FIRST TABERNACLE WAS YET STANDING:"

The exegesis is:

1. Paul states that the Holy Spirit is both the Divine Author of the Levitical system of worship and its Interpreter.

2. The first Tabernacle or the first room is the *"Holy Place."*

3. As long as that part of the Levitical institution was still in effect, Israel was to understand that the way into the Presence of God had not yet been opened.

4. The division of the Tabernacle into the Holy Place and the Holy of Holies showed the limitations of the Levitical system, and kept the people from coming directly to God.

THE HOLY SPIRIT

The phrase, *"The Holy Spirit this signifying,"* proclaims several things:

1. Every single thing done on this Earth by the Godhead, with the exception of the Birth, Life, Ministry, Death, Burial, Resurrection, and Ascension of the Lord Jesus Christ, was done and is done exclusively by the Holy Spirit.

2. That being the case, the Holy Spirit was both the Divine Author of the Levitical system of worship and its Interpreter.

3. The Holy Spirit is actually the Member of the Godhead Who dwelt between the Mercy Seat and the Cherubim in the Holy of Holies.

4. The very manner in which the Spirit designed the Levitical system portrays the fact that it was only temporary.

5. As long as the Veil stood between the Holy Place and the Holy of Holies, access to God was cut off.

6. Until the Cross, the Holy Spirit could not be approached, as is here painfully obvious, but since the Cross, He now literally abides permanently within the hearts and lives of all Believers (Jn. 14:17).

As John recorded it, Jesus said, *"For He dwelleth with you, and shall be in you."* And that's exactly the way it was!

As we are studying here, He dwelt with Israel, but definitely not in Israel, i.e., *"abiding permanently within their hearts and lives."* The Cross changed all of this, in that Jesus there paid the terrible sin debt, which made it possible for Believers to be justified in fact as well as theory.

7. The Holy Spirit is a Person, actually a Member of the Godhead, and not merely an emanation from God. In other words, the Holy Spirit is God, just as the Father is God and the Son is God (Mat. 28:19).

THE MINISTRY OF THE HOLY SPIRIT

Paul is demonstrating one aspect of the Holy Spirit's Ministry in the Old Testament. It is the Ministry of the Spirit to testify of Christ; the Spirit glorifies Christ. Even in the Old Testament the Spirit used the Mosaic system to point to the Redemptive Work of Christ.

Paul is showing the Reader the privilege that is now his to come boldly into the Presence of God. The Saints of the Old Covenant never knew such a blessed privilege. The Believer may now draw near to God in confidence because of the Atonement made by Christ. We are accepted by the Father on the basis of the Finished Work of Christ.

Now we begin to understand the words of Jesus: *"I am the Way, the Truth, and the Life: no man cometh unto the Father, but by Me"*

(Jn. 14:6). There is no other sacrifice for sin but the sacrifice of Jesus Himself; there is no other name in which we find Salvation. The way into the Most Holy Place is by the Blood of Jesus, God's only begotten Son.

THE CROSS

So, the Holy Spirit ever points to the Cross. He did so in every Sacrifice offered. He did so in all the blood that was spilled from the Sacrifices, with it being poured out at the base of the Brazen Altar. He did so in the doctrine of the Sabbath and the Feast Days. He did so in the Rite of Circumcision. He did so in the very work of all the Priests, and especially the ministry of the High Priest. He did so in all of the apparatus of the Tabernacle, including its furniture and sacred vessels, even down to the tent pegs. Everything and without exception pointed to Christ, but more particularly Who He was, and what He would do in order to redeem mankind, which was to go to the Cross.

That's at least one of the reasons that many Christians come up with all type of false doctrines. They do not know the Old Testament, which in effect, actually lays the foundation of the New Covenant, and in fact is the foundation of the New Covenant. In types and shadows and in symbolism, over and over again, the portrait of Christ is painted in the sense of Paul's statement, *"Jesus Christ and Him crucified"* (I Cor. 2:2).

It is the Cross and the Cross alone, which tore down the Veil that separated man from God. It was the Cross alone, which gave access into the very Holy of Holies. It was the Cross alone, which made it possible for the Holy Spirit to come in and abide permanently within the hearts and lives of all Believers. It was the Cross alone, which made it possible for men and women to life victorious over the world, the flesh, and the Devil. That is God's Way, and His Way alone!

When Jesus said, *"I am the Way, the Truth, and the Life: no man cometh unto the Father, but by Me"* (Jn. 14:6), He was in effect saying, that His Way was the Cross; His Truth is the Cross; the Cross is that which provides the Life. As well, when men come to God, they must come by the way of the Cross. There is no other way.

Millions presently attempt to portray Jesus other than the Cross. In other words, they completely ignore Paul's statement which said, *"We preach Christ crucified"* (I Cor. 1:23), thereby, presenting and preaching *"another Jesus"* (II Cor. 11:4).

Let the Reader understand, if it is not the Jesus of the Cross, it is pure and simple, another Jesus, which is the ruination of the Church.

Every single person in this world who has ever been saved, has been saved by the virtue of Faith expressed in Christ and what He did at the Cross on their behalf. Of course, as a believing sinner, their knowledge of Christ was very scanty. In fact, all unbelievers are spiritually dead, meaning they have no concept of God whatsoever, at least a concept that is Scripturally correct; consequently, the Holy Spirit has to provide Faith to them in order that they may believe, which He readily does upon presentation of the Word. But the Faith He provides is that which anchors in the Cross.

As well, every single victory and blessing had by any Believer after coming to Christ, is altogether obtained by and through what Jesus did at the Cross on our behalf. Faith in the Cross of Christ is the secret of all victory, all overcoming strength, all power, and all blessings. It is the secret of all Spiritual Growth, all growing in grace and the knowledge of the Lord.

DECEPTION

It is August, 2000, as I dictate these notes. And what I'm about to say is not said with any joy, but rather with a broken heart.

Due to the fact that the Church has had so little teaching on the Cross in the last several decades, any more it hardly knows where it's been, where it is, or where it's going. In fact, there are less people being saved at this hour, than at any time since the Reformation. Also, there are less people being Baptized with the Holy Spirit than any time since the outpouring of the Latter Rain at the turn of the 20th Century. In fact, there are fewer people actually being healed, and that despite all the hype otherwise. As well, there is less true victory within hearts and lives than ever before. Why?

It is because of a departure from the Cross, which is the foundation of the Faith (Rom., Chpts. 6, 8; Eph. Chpt. 1).

The Church is presently being scammed by hucksters as never before. Under the guise of *"faith,"* people are being separated from their money, claiming that for every dollar they give, they're going to get many dollars back, etc. It would be ludicrous if it weren't so sad!

Just two nights ago, I watched a scam artist over Television telling the people, God had told him that for every single dollar they give, they would get two back. The place was filled with slack-jawed gullibles waiting to be fleeced. Unfortunately, there seems to be enough greed in all of us to keep these scams going. The tragedy is, great segments of the Church think this blasphemy is actually of the Lord.

Then the other day I saw another Preacher over Television delivering people, and giving them a word of knowledge, while the band behind him played *"rap."* To cut straight through to the chase, the whole scene was one of sorcery, which means that it was actually being promoted by demon spirits. But yet, the auditorium which belonged to a so-called Christian TV Network was filled with people thinking it was all of God. That's the tragedy!

In such a situation, the people definitely do not leave as they came. They leave with Satan having a greater hold on them than ever. One cannot subject oneself to the operation of the spirits of darkness, even though they come under the guise of *"angels of light,"* and not be adversely affected (II Cor. 11:13-15).

On the other side of the spectrum, auditoriums are filling up with multiple thousands of people, who watch the Evangelist as he produces one *"trick"* after the other, with various manifestations, all claiming to be of the Holy Spirit. To be sure, it is a spirit involved, but it's not *"the Spirit."* If it's not Biblical, then it's not right.

The Church is so easily deceived, simply because it has been lured away from its True Foundation, which is the great Sacrifice of Christ. Other things have been substituted, and these other things are destroying untold millions of souls.

The Holy Spirit will never deviate from the Word, and will always anchor everything He does in the Finished Work of Christ (Rom. 8:1-2). But the problem is, the Church, little knowing the true way, falls for any way that's presented, with money being the fuel that drives this whole sordid mess. And a sordid mess it is!

THE WAY INTO THE HOLIEST

The phrase, *"That the way into the holiest of all was not yet made manifest,"* proclaims the fact, and by the Holy Spirit at that, that while the Law was in force, which included the Priesthood, Tabernacle or Temple worship, Feast Days, Sabbaths, Circumcision, etc., access to God was blocked, except in the most limited way.

As we've said repeatedly, the very means by which all of this was carried on, provided a constant, glaring reminder, that all of this was at best, a stopgap measure, meaning that it was temporary. It was merely pointing to the One Who was to come, namely, the Lord Jesus Christ.

Paul sees the Holy Spirit as using the pattern of the Tabernacle to teach important truths. The limited access into the Holy of Holies was meant to bring home the fact that ordinary men had no direct access to the Presence of God. Paul is actually saying that people get direct access to God through the Finished Work of Christ and that alone, and that before such work was accomplished there was no such access.

Actually the words, *"the way into the holiest of all,"* although definitely referring to the Presence of God, in the final analysis, refers to Heaven, where the true Throne of God actually is. To show you how correct this is, before the Cross, when Believers died, they didn't go to Heaven. They were actually taken down into Paradise which was actually very near the burning side of Hell. Jesus said there was a great gulf that separated the two compartments (Lk. 16:26).

The reason that before the Cross Believers could not be taken into Heaven when they died, but rather taken to the heart of the Earth, is because the sin debt still remained. In other words, due to the fact that the blood of bulls and goats could not take away sin,

NOTES

even though they had exhibited Faith in the coming Redeemer, and were, therefore, saved, still, they could not be taken into the Presence of God, until the sin debt was removed.

When Jesus died on the Cross, thereby saying, *"It is finished"* (Jn. 19:30), Matthew recorded *"the Veil of the Temple was rent in twain from the top to the bottom"* (Mat. 27:51). This meant that due to what Christ had done at the Cross, which was to bear the sin penalty of mankind which was death, the sin debt to God was then paid, with God immediately opening up access to Himself by man. As well, Jesus then went down into Hell itself, at least into the Paradise side, and Paul said, *"He led captivity captive"* (Eph. 4:8).

This means that before the Cross all the Saints were actually held captive by Satan in Paradise. To be sure, they were comforted in this state, but nevertheless captives of the Evil One. Jesus upon His Death liberated all of those righteous souls from Paradise, actually making them His captives, taking them to Heaven with Him. This means the sin debt had been paid, with Satan having no more claim. The Cross did it all.

Now when Believers die, all instantly go to be with Christ in Heaven (Phil. 1:23).

So, when Paul spoke of *"the way into the holiest of all not yet being made manifest,"* which spoke of the time before the Cross, it had a far deeper meaning than is at first realized.

The Cross of Christ was a monumental thing. In fact, it addressed every single problem which man had incurred upon himself as a result of the Fall. While it is true, that we do not yet have all the benefits of what Jesus did at the Cross, and will not have until the coming Resurrection, still, what we do have is enough to walk totally and completely in victory with sin not at all having dominion over us (Rom. 6:14).

THE FIRST TABERNACLE

The phrase, *"While as the first Tabernacle was yet standing,"* shows the limitations of the Levitical system.

When God rent the Veil, as stated, this was God's object lesson to the Aaronic Priesthood that its ministry was now over, that the Temple was to be closed, that a new Priest had arisen after the order of Melchisedec. But, Israel in its apostasy, repaired the Veil and kept on offering sacrifices, until God in His wrath, sent Rome to destroy the City of Jerusalem and scatter His chosen people to the ends of the Roman Empire, and ultimately the Earth (Wuest).

The way into the Holiest of all, into Heaven itself and the Presence of God, had been opened at the Cross. As long as the old dispensation lasted, the Priests had no access into the Holiest. They went only into the first Tabernacle (Holy Place) and accomplished the liturgical service.

Once a year the High Priest alone was permitted to enter the Sacred inner chamber where the Shekinah hovered over the Mercy Seat. Nor could he approach without atoning blood, which he offered first of all for himself as being but a sinful man, and also for the failures of the people.

YET STANDING

By this arrangement, the Holy Spirit was declaring the solemn fact that the way into the immediate Presence of God had not yet been made known, nor could be, so long as that first Tabernacle had any standing before Him.

The expression *"was yet standing"* is misleading. It would suggest the way into the Holiest was not made known until the destruction of the Temple in A.D. 70, and thus many have understood it.

But it clearly means that the way into the Holiest was not opened up so long as God recognized the first Tabernacle. The truth is according to the following:

The moment Christ Jesus died upon the Cross, the entire typical system ceased to have any standing before God. It was but a figure for a time then present, and the gifts and sacrifices offered in connection with it were simply picturing the offering up of the Body of our Lord Jesus Christ upon the Cross. In themselves, they were of no real value. They could not settle the sin question and, therefore, could not perfect the consciences of those who brought them, even as we will study in the next Verse.

(9) "WHICH WAS A FIGURE FOR THE TIME THEN PRESENT, IN WHICH WERE OFFERED BOTH GIFTS AND SACRIFICES,

THAT COULD NOT MAKE HIM THAT DID THE SERVICE PERFECT, AS PERTAINING TO THE CONSCIENCE;"

The exegesis is:

1. The word *"which"* refers back to the *"Tabernacle"* of the previous Verse.

2. *"Figure"* refers to a parable or symbol, which refers to the Tabernacle as an object lesson used to explain spiritual truth. As long as it remained an object lesson, thus a recognized institution, it was clear that the actual Tabernacle to which it pointed was not yet in use.

3. The words *"in which"* refer to the prescribed details of the Levitical ritual which included all the Sacrifices, etc.

4. These rituals could not affect the heart of man, as no ritual within itself ever does.

A FIGURE

The phrase, *"Which was a figure for the time then present,"* refers to the Tabernacle being a representation of important realities, and of things which were more fully to be revealed at a future period. All of this should have been extremely obvious; but at the same time, it is admittedly much easier to look at something after the fact, than to do so from a future perspective. However, there was no excuse for Israel not knowing and understanding all of this after Jesus had come and began His Ministry. They didn't accept Him as the Messiah, because they didn't want to accept Him as the Messiah. They were looking for someone to satisfy their own sinful lusts, instead of the One Whom the Bible had predicted. Had they bothered to investigate His Life and Ministry according to the Scriptures, the evidence would have been irrefutable. But like so many, they saw only what they wanted to see and heard only what they wanted to hear.

In fact, by the time of Christ, the religious leadership of Israel had so perverted the Law and even the rudiments of the Temple, that it now held little resemblance to that which was originally given to Moses by God. The religious leadership of the nation now used the great Law to enrich themselves, to put forth their own agenda, in other words, to use it for their purposes. Its true meaning had long since been forgotten.

GIFTS AND SACRIFICES

The phrase, *"In which were offered both Gifts and Sacrifices, that could not make him that did the service perfect, as pertaining to the conscience,"* portrays the weakness of the First Covenant. These Gifts and Sacrifices could not make the worshipper perfect so far as his conscience was concerned. The word *"perfect"* in the Greek is *"teleios"* which does not mean sinless, but rather complete, finished. The word described that which needed nothing to make it what it should be — complete.

The Levitical ritual as such did not touch the conscience. In fact, no ritual in itself ever does. There was nothing in it that should deal with conscience. Only the working of the Holy Spirit through the Word of God and the efficacy of the Blood of the Messiah could do that.

The Holy Spirit did in Old Testament Times deal as He does today with the consciences of men, but the Salvation which He applied under the Levitical system found its source in the New Testament Sacrifice, the Lord Jesus. In other words, there was no salvation in the Sacrifices, as there could be no Salvation in such. Salvation was found in the Believer having Faith in What and Whom the Sacrifices represented, namely the Lord Jesus Christ, and what He would do at the Cross, of which the Sacrifices were typical.

Therefore, while operating under the jurisdiction of the First Testament, God was giving Salvation to the First Testament Believer by virtue of that which would be accomplished through the New Testament. Since the First Testament could not do that which the New Testament did, it was set aside in favor of the New Testament, even as it had to be! And this is actually the argument of the Book of Hebrews (Wuest).

The old system could not bring Israel, or anyone else for that matter, to the Heavenly purpose God had for them.

THE LAW

The Old Covenant — the Tabernacle, the Sacrifices, the Priesthood — was *"imposed upon Israel until the time of Reformation."* The Mosaic order was placed upon them until the New Covenant could be established in

Christ, and until all that which had been symbolized in the Old could be fulfilled in Christ.

Of necessity, the Law was a burden and a weight to them with its many commands, its gifts, sacrifices, meats, drinks, diverse washings, and carnal ordinances. No person was ever justified before God by doing any of the things required by the Law, for the simple reason, that rituals and ceremonies cannot cleanse the heart of the sinner. How wonderful it is presently that we may worship Him, not under the bondage and weight of legalism, but in spirit and in truth.

We need no longer worship in shadows. We no longer serve in examples, but we have moved from the realm of symbols into the reality of the freedom of Christ, the Minister of the Heavenly Sanctuary of which the earthly was only a figure.

A TABERNACLE IN HEAVEN?

We do know there is a literal Temple in Heaven (Rev. 3:12; 7:15; 11:19; 14:15, 17; 15:1-8; 16:1, 17).

John did say regarding his vision on the Isle of Patmos, *"And I saw no temple therein: for the Lord God Almighty and the Lamb are the Temple of it"* (Rev. 21:22).

But what John was actually saying pertained to the fact of going to a temple to worship, as in the earthly Temple at Jerusalem. God and the Lamb, i.e., *"the Lord Jesus Christ,"* will be visibly present among men forever, with worship continuing forever (Rev. 22:3-5).

But yet, according to John's statement, there is a sense in which Christ is all of these things. In other words, He is the Brazen Altar, the Brazen Laver, the Table of Showbread, the Golden Lampstand, the Altar of Incense, the Ark of the Covenant, the Mercy Seat, etc.

We do know that John also saw in his vision regarding Heaven, *"the Ark of His Testament,"* which is in the Temple in Heaven — the Ark incidentally, after which Moses patterned his Ark of the Covenant (Heb. 8:5; 9:23; Rev. 11:19).

As a part of this vision, John also mentioned that he saw Christ standing *"in the midst of the seven candlesticks"* (Rev. 1:12-13). Whether that exactly means that there is a literal Golden Lampstand in Heaven, we aren't exactly told. We do know that John also said that the Golden Candlesticks or Lampstands, represented the seven Churches which Jesus would address; however, that within itself doesn't negate the idea of a literal Lampstand in Heaven. He does give us another clue by saying, *"And out of the Throne proceeded lightnings and thunderings and voices: and there were seven lamps of fire burning before the Throne, which are the seven Spirits of God"* (Rev. 4:5). There is some evidence that this is the same Golden Lampstand of Revelation 1:13.

As well, the *"Golden Vials full of odours, which are the prayers of the Saints,"* in some way resembled the Altar of Incense, which John also saw (Rev. 5:8). This in a sense is seen again in Revelation 8:3, but this time held in the hands of an Angel.

Consequently, I think at least in some crude way, that one could say that the wilderness Tabernacle was a pattern of the one in Heaven. There is a Sanctuary in Heaven that corresponds to the earthly Tabernacle. The earthly Tabernacle furnishes us with some of the geography of Heaven.

The Reader must understand, that sin has not only entered the human family on this Earth, but considering that one-third of the angels fell with Lucifer in his great revolution against God, it extends to the whole creation of God, even to Heaven itself. No, this doesn't mean there is sin in Heaven; but it does mean that Heaven has been greatly affected by that which happened in the dateless past.

It seems from what little at least we can understand, that God evidently abides in a Heavenly Tabernacle in order to protect the creation from His Holiness. If God dealt only in Righteousness and Justice, He would be forced to destroy in judgment His universe and creatures touched by sin. This Heavenly Tabernacle sets forth His Redemption by the Blood of Christ.

Paul said, *"And, having made peace through the Blood of His Cross, by Him to reconcile all things unto Himself, by Him I say, whether they be things in Earth, or things in Heaven"* (Col. 1:20).

If God dealt only in Righteousness, He would destroy in judgment His universe and creatures touched by sin, but the Heavenly Tabernacle makes it possible for God in Righteousness to salvage His creation. In this Tabernacle, Jesus is the Lamb of God slain from the foundation of the world. When He died on the Cross, He ascended by the virtue of His shed Blood into the Heavenly Tabernacle.

THE SACRIFICIAL SYSTEM

The whole system of the Mosaic Covenant was to provide a means by which sinful man might approach a holy God. This was to be done by means of a sacrificial system, through various types of offerings. By this means men learned the proper way to approach God, and they also found Atonement for their sins.

Looking at all of this from a naturalistic viewpoint, the Sacrifices are a glory spectacle; however, a Spirit-guided inspection of these Offerings will unveil some of the great principles of God's dealings with men and will lead us into the Holy of Holies of Scriptural truth.

The principle in back of the offerings is this: man is doomed as a sinner, and yet God has planned to save him. The Law of God is that sin brings death, yet God has provided a way of escape.

There is one life that has not been forfeited, because it belongs to Christ, Who never sinned. Therefore, His life is accepted by God in place of the sinner's life, at least upon Faith evidenced by the sinner in Christ and what He did at the Cross on the sinner's behalf.

THE BLOOD

Moses said, *"For the life of the flesh is in the blood: and I have given it to you upon the Altar to make an Atonement for your souls; for it is the blood that maketh an Atonement for the soul"* (Lev. 17:11).

Paul said, *"And without shedding of blood is no remission,"* (Heb. 9:22).

The Blood, as is obvious, assumes a very important part in all of this. The Hebrew word *"kaphar,"* translated *"Atonement,"* shows its significance. It literally means, *"to cover."* The Blood of Christ acts as a screen which hides sin from God's eyes, so He does not visit judgment on the soul that has been covered by the Blood. Of course, the Blood of Jesus does even more, cleansing the heart from sin. In the Old Testament economy, the Blood only covered, while under the New Testament economy, which is all in Christ, the Blood not only covers but also cleanses, in effect, doing away with the sin as though it never existed.

Though the animal sacrifices of the Old Testament covered sin, they could not take it away. *"For it is not possible that the blood of bulls and of goats should take away sins"* (Heb. 10:4). An animal, incapable of independent thought and moral feeling, was not a perfect sacrifice for man. Furthermore, the work of Atonement in which the animal was involved was not a voluntary and personal act of the animal, which would be obvious.

The value of the animal sacrifices as ordained by God was the fact that they pointed forward to the coming of a Perfect Sacrifice, One foreordained before the foundation of the world. They all foreshadowed the coming of Christ, Who would give Himself for the sins of mankind.

(10) "WHICH STOOD ONLY IN MEATS AND DRINKS, AND DIVERS WASHINGS, AND CARNAL ORDINANCES, IMPOSED ON THEM UNTIL THE TIME OF REFORMATION."

The exposition is:

1. The Old Covenant sacrifices were carnal, temporary, and powerless to cleanse from sin.

2. However, these rites and Ceremonies were commanded by Divine authority, as proper representations of the Gospel system, which would come and rectify all things.

3. *"The time of reformation,"* refers to the New Covenant which was to come, and which did come, and which is Christ.

RITUALS AND CEREMONIES

The phrase, *"Which stood only in meats and drinks, and divers washings, and carnal ordinances,"* refers to the entirety of the Levitical system.

To go into detail as to the meaning of these things would be pointless. Even though they were then necessary to accomplish, the truth was, all of these rituals could not forgive one single sin or save one single soul, and neither were they meant to do so. In themselves, they were of no real value.

They could not settle the sin question and, therefore, could not perfect the consciences of those who brought them. The idea is this:

The many ordinances in connection with meats and drinks and different washings, whether of persons or things, in fact all the fleshly observances which were connected with the First Covenant, were only intended to serve a temporary purpose and to be in force until the time of reformation; that is, until Christ by His Death and Resurrection fulfilled them all and brought in the present new and glorious dispensation of the Grace of God.

The moment Christ died upon the Cross, the entire typical system ceased to have any standing before God. It was but a figure for a time then present, and the gifts and sacrifices offered in connection with it, were simply picturing the offering up of the Body of our Lord Jesus Christ upon the Cross. In other words, all of these things were only meant to portray in symbolic form that which was to come. It was faith in what they represented that caused one to be saved, and not the actual carrying out of the rituals or ceremonies.

Paul uses the phrase, *"carnal ordinances,"* which refers to religious ceremonies that touched man's body, but went no further. They were as powerless as modern *"sacraments."*

MODERN RELIGIOUS RITUALS

Unfortunately, the problem of dependence on rituals and ceremonies did not die with the old Mosaic Law. It is just as prevalent presently as then.

Millions of people have joined Churches, in effect going through a ritual, which within itself is no harm, but dependence on that for Salvation in fact is great harm. And that's the whole idea! It really doesn't matter what it is.

If the Israelites of old placed their faith solely and completely in these *"divers washings"* and *"carnal ordinances,"* the simple fact was, they couldn't be saved. As already stated, it was only by understanding what these things represented, and having proper faith in that symbolism, which was Christ, which afforded Salvation. It is the same presently.

To attempt to enumerate all of the many things in which men presently place their faith would be too cumbersome. Suffice to say, if we place our Faith in anything other than Jesus Christ and what He did for us at

NOTES

the Cross, we will not find that for which we seek. Salvation is only in Christ and His Finished Work. One can say the same for a victorious walk in Christ after Salvation.

The only way that one can walk in victory, meaning that sin will not have dominion over him, is to place his Faith exclusively in the Cross of Christ, understanding it was there that provision was made for all things. When the Believer does this, and in fact, continues to do this even on a daily basis (Lk. 9:23), then the Holy Spirit will mightily help the Believer, Whose help incidentally we must have (Rom. 8:1-2, 11).

Our difficulty is, we think the doing of spiritual things automatically constitutes *"walking after the Spirit"* (Rom. 8:1). It isn't and it doesn't!

Doing spiritual things, as good and noble as that might be, does not constitute Faith in Christ and Him Crucified, which is an absolute requirement if we are to have what we must have from the Lord. But regrettably, that's where most of the modern Church presently finds itself.

Satan doesn't care how many Preachers lay hands on you, or how much you are *"slain in the Spirit,"* etc. He knows if your faith is in those things, that even though those things within themselves are Scriptural and real and will afford Blessings, still, you're not going to find victory over the world, the flesh, and the Devil, by these methods.

The Reader is not to think that we're demeaning manifestations or anything that pertains to the Lord, just as Paul was not demeaning the rituals and ceremonies required in the Law of Moses. In fact, and as stated, all of these things were given by God, even as many modern things are of the Lord; however, the idea is, if Christians place their Faith in these things, which most do, not really understanding that all they receive from the Lord comes by and through what Jesus did at the Cross, then they will not really receive that for which they seek.

To be sure, Satan is very subtle! He doesn't really care how religious you actually are. He doesn't really mind your involvement in all type of religious or even spiritual things, just so long as you do not exhibit proper faith in the Finished Work of Christ. Much of the modern Church, ignorant of God's prescribed order of victory and life, look to other means, which always brings disappointment.

This is one of the reasons that when Christians hear about something which is supposed to be happening in a certain place followed by particular manifestations, thousands flock to the site. While that which is happening may truly be of God, that doesn't mean that victory will be achieved by one involving themselves in what is actually taking place.

If a Christian doesn't understand the Cross and how it involves itself in our daily walk before God (Lk. 9:23), then spiritual problems of one nature or the other will plague that particular Christian. In fact, that is the case with almost all of Christendom presently! Then to find relief in respect to these situations, which pertain to victory in one capacity or the other, they resort to things which, although Scriptural within themselves, do not turn out to be the victory for which they had hoped.

VICTORY

Victory is not something we get by doing, but rather we do by getting. No, that's not a mere play on words.

Victory is ours by getting it from Christ. And we get it simply by exhibiting Faith in His great Sacrifice. It's not earned or merited, it is rather all in Christ.

When convicted by the Spirit, the human heart cries out to God; however, that cry is not satisfied by being religious or doing religion, it is only satisfied in Christ.

I watch Christians stumble from one scenario to the other, and to be sure, it is painful to observe. And I think the reason that it's so painful, is because I've been there. Consequently, I know the frustration which always leads to fear. I know what it is to work and labor, and then to think, maybe if I'll just do more, this will bring that for which I seek.

Many may think that Christians don't follow this path. But the truth is, almost all of Christendom is doing exactly that. We think the more we do, that somehow it earns something with God. We should understand the following:

God has nothing for sale. So that means we cannot earn anything as it regards the Lord, and neither can we merit anything. It doesn't really matter what we do or how hard we work at it, it doesn't buy us anything with God.

God works strictly on the principle of Faith. And by that, we mean Faith placed exclusively in Christ and Him Crucified. If the Believer thinks of Christ in any other manner or way other than what Christ did at the Cross, then the Believer is misunderstanding Christ. While Christ is many things, we must never forget that it was the Cross that set us free.

That's the reason that Jesus is referred to in the Book of Revelation some 28 times as *"the Lamb."* In fact, He is referred to accordingly some seven times in the last two Chapters of Revelation, which speak of the perfect age to come.

Upon the arrival of that time, there will be no more sin, no more Satan, no more failure, and no more disobedience or rebellion toward God. All of those things are now past, with nothing remaining except Righteousness. And yet, Christ is referred to even in this atmosphere some seven times as a *"Lamb."*

Why?

The reasons should be obvious. The Holy Spirit wants us to understand that this great Salvation which every Saint has and will have, and will enjoy forever, and in a glory and splendor which absolutely defies description, was all purchased by such a great price. We must never forget that, and the Holy Spirit refers to Christ as the *"Lamb"* in order that we not forget that.

And if the Holy Spirit wants the entirety of eternity future to understand that all was acquired by what Jesus did at the Cross, doesn't it stand to reason that it is to be the centrality of the Gospel presently? The Message is, *"Jesus Christ and Him Crucified"* (I Cor. 1:23). We must never forget that, understanding that this is the source of all things that comes from God to us.

THE TIME OF REFORMATION

The phrase, *"Imposed on them until the time of Reformation,"* refers to the entirety of the Law being fulfilled by Christ, and thereby set aside, with the New Covenant taking its place, which is perfect in every respect (Heb. 13:20).

NOTES

To be sure, these ordinances were of value in order to introduce the better system; however, they were not adapted to purify the conscience and remove the stains of guilt from the soul, simply because they could not do so. The fact of sin was too terrible and the damage was too great for these things to answer that problem. It took the Blood of Christ to do that!

The idea is, the First Testament never was satisfactory, so far as offering a sacrifice that could pay for sin was concerned. It could not actually in itself save the Believer. It only pointed to the One Who could save, and that was the One to Whom all the Sacrifices and rituals pointed, namely Christ.

The idea is not that these things were bad. In fact, they were all given by God and for specific reasons. They presented a stopgap measure which would suffice until Christ came. Actually, the Law was intended to do many things, but it was never intended to save, but merely point to the One Who could save. When Christ came, the Law had served its purpose, and was now laid aside.

The problem was never with the Law, but rather with Israel who tried to make Salvation out of its rituals and ceremonies. And now during Paul's day, Christian Jews were still trying to hang onto the Law, along with Christ, with some even repudiating Christ altogether and going back totally into Law and ritual worship, which of course, would spell doom to the soul. In fact, this is the reason for the writing of the entirety of the Epistle to the Hebrews.

(11) "BUT CHRIST BEING COME AN HIGH PRIEST OF GOOD THINGS TO COME, BY A GREATER AND MORE PERFECT TABERNACLE, NOT MADE WITH HANDS, THAT IS TO SAY, NOT OF THIS BUILDING;"

The composition is:

1. Christ has now come, to Whom the Law had pointed.

2. He was not a mere human being born in the midst of humanity. He came from outside of humanity and incorporated Himself with humankind through the Virgin Birth. He came from another world. (Wuest)

3. *"Good things to come,"* should have been translated *"of the good things realized."*

4. Christ was the True High Priest, to which the Levitical order had always pointed.

5. The more perfect Tabernacle was His Personal Body; however, it represented the heavenlies, that is, the Throne of God.

6. The Tabernacle of which He speaks is not of this Earth. It is all Heavenly.

CHRIST HAS COME

The phrase, *"But Christ being come,"* speaks of an advent.

The little word *"but"* is the pivot upon which all the argument swings. Paul speaks of Messiah *"being come."* The Greek word is *"paraginomai,"* which means, *"to become alongside,"* thus, *"to arrive upon the scene,"* here the human scene. As stated, it speaks here of an advent.

Christ was not a mere human being born in the midst of humanity. He came from outside of humanity and incorporated Himself with humankind through the Virgin Birth. He came from another world. He in total was the prediction of the Prophets, actually the One promised by God at the very outset of the Fall in the Garden of Eden (Gen. 3:15). Of course, when we speak of Christ coming, we're speaking of the Incarnation, God becoming man.

HIGH PRIEST

The phrase, *"An High Priest,"* is now presented by the Apostle to show how marvelously the One offering of our Lord Jesus Christ transcends all the types and shadows of old. He is both High Priest and Victim.

As High Priest *"of the good things realized,"* Whose Ministry is linked with a greater and more perfect Tabernacle, that is, with the eternal dwelling place of God, He has by the presentation of His Blood (by it being shed at the Cross) entered in once for all into the Holiest on the basis of an accomplished Redemption. His work abides eternally before God.

Because of the infinite value of His precious Blood, He has fully met all the claims of Divine Justice and thus secured eternal Redemption.

THE GOOD THINGS REALIZED

The phrase, *"Of good things to come,"* as stated, should have been translated, *"of the good things realized."*

Even though some of the things that Jesus accomplished by His Death and Resurrection await the coming general Resurrection, still, as it regards the Blessings already attained, these are grand and many. Because of Christ, we now have free approach to God, a better Covenant, personal communion with God, along with the purging of the conscience. Actually, there is no limit to what Christ has done for us at the Cross, and as well, which is realized presently within our hearts and lives.

Above all of this one might say, the advent of the Holy Spirit, Who abides permanently within our hearts and lives, is of such blessing as to defy all description (Jn. 14:16-17).

The multitude of carnal ordinances that had been placed upon Israel were only temporary. All the blessings of the Old Testament rested upon obedience to the Law, yet no one could keep the Law perfectly. All sinned; all came short of the Glory of God.

The Old Covenant was ineffective; it could not produce an inward change that would enable man to obey the commandments set down by God.

The Old Economy produced despair. But Paul showed his readers hope: *"Christ . . . High Priest of good things now realized."* The New Covenant brought new and eternal life, forgiveness of sins, and the indwelling Presence of God. It is a New Covenant in which God places His Laws in men's hearts; He writes them on our hearts and minds.

It was the tragedy of all tragedies, that Israel did not recognize Him when He came. There was no reason for this, considering that the Prophets of old had perfectly proclaimed Who He would be, and how and what He would be. What Israel wanted was not what Israel needed! They wanted money, place, position, and, oh yes, to be the greatest nation in the world once again. A Messiah of that stripe, which the Word of God did not proclaim concerning the First Advent, they would have accepted. In fact, they will accept the Antichrist when he makes his debut, all in the same spirit. It will prove to be the worst mistake they've ever made, other than the Crucifixion of Christ.

Unfortunately, much of the modern Church follows down the same path. It doesn't want Christ Who makes one holy and righteous, but rather a Christ who will give them money.

God help us!

A GREATER TABERNACLE

The phrase, *"By a greater and more perfect tabernacle,"* presents the contrast of Christ with the Tabernacle of old.

As the Apostle has already said, the first Tabernacle could not cleanse from sin and thereby assuage the guilt, but the new Tabernacle could.

The new Tabernacle is Christ, as proven by the statements of Verse 12. While as well it definitely does pertain to the Throne of God; nevertheless, it is Christ Who had made it possible for all Believers to enter that Holy of Holies. To picture only the Throne without Christ does great violence to the entirety of the Finished Work of the Savior. In effect, Christ is all in all, i.e., *"everything."*

NOT OF THIS BUILDING

The phrase, *"Not made with hands, that is to say, not of this building,"* refers to the fact that the great Plan of God is entirely of God and not at all of man.

While man did have a part in the building and erection of the first Tabernacle, man has no part in this one whatsoever. The idea is, by the means of the shedding of His Own Blood (not the blood of animals), has Christ entered the holiest of all, into the Presence of God. This is an emphatic way of saying that He has won for His people an effective Salvation in that it has nothing to do with earthly sacrifices.

HANDS

The problem that the Lord has with all of us is the problem of *"hands!"* What do we mean by that?

We're speaking of man putting his hands into the great Plan of God and thereby changing it, which makes it ineffective. That's the great problem of the Church, as it has always been the great problem of the Church.

Preachers claim that one has to be baptized in water to be saved. They seem not to realize that this negates faith in the Finished Work of Christ. This is man putting

NOTES

his meddlesome hands into the great Work of God.

When this is done, it has the *"trickle down effect,"* on everything that pertains to the Lord. For instance, if there is failure of any kind on the part of a Preacher, most Denominations, if not all, instead of continuing to trust Christ, once again put their *"hands"* into the mix. Almost without exception, a dog and pony show of some nature is prescribed, which must be ridiculous in the eyes of God. Oh yes, I must quickly add that these rules are changed quite often. That demands a question: If in fact such rules are Scriptural to begin with, how can they be changed? The truth is, men love to make rules and force other men to obey them, and religious men love to do so most of all!

PERSONAL HANDS

The biggest problem for the Child of God, at least as it regards walking in victory, is not knowing God's prescribed order of victory, which is Faith in the Cross of Christ, which guarantees the help of the Holy Spirit. Not knowing this, we resort to the efforts of our *"own hands,"* so to speak! As I've already said several times, we do spiritual things, and we think that this is what brings whatever it is that we need.

The Truth is, we turn these things into the efforts and labors of our own hands, which God can never honor. In fact, trying to bring about victory other than by trusting in what Christ has already done on our behalf, is sin! I realize that's a blunt statement, but it is true.

I had a young Preacher say to me some time ago, *"When I have trouble with the world, the flesh, or the Devil, I go on a three-day fast, and that solves my problem."*

While fasting is definitely Scriptural, it is not Scriptural in this fashion. If that's what it took to walk in victory, then Jesus didn't pay it all at the Cross, and there are other things which need to be added.

No! This young man was turning a perfectly Scriptural principle into *"works,"* i.e., *"hands,"* which is always wrong in the sight of God.

Not knowing the victory of the Cross — this is a world that I lived in for years, which brought untold sorrow to this Evangelist.

But Grace upon Grace, the Lord showed me that this great life lived in Christ, is *"not made with hands,"* but is totally and completely of Christ. The day the Holy Spirit revealed this to me, and then as well told me that all victory was in the Cross, was the greatest day of my life other than the day I was saved and the day I was baptized with the Holy Spirit.

Having walked the path made by the hands of men, and having lived in a building made by the hands of men, I want no more of that direction. Therefore, I say with the Psalmist, *"Through Thy precepts I get understanding: therefore I hate every false way"* (Ps. 119:104).

(12) "NEITHER BY THE BLOOD OF GOATS AND CALVES, BUT BY HIS OWN BLOOD HE ENTERED IN ONCE INTO THE HOLY PLACE, HAVING OBTAINED ETERNAL REDEMPTION FOR US."

The exegesis is:

1. The blood of bulls and goats under the First Covenant could never take away sin.

2. By His Own Blood, which was blood of a unique kind, He purchased our Redemption.

3. His One Sacrifice is sufficient for all time.

4. His Sacrifice opened up the way to the Holy of Holies, i.e., *"the Throne of God,"* to which all can come, who will place their faith and trust in Christ and His Cross.

5. This which He did, *"obtained eternal Redemption for us."*

THE BLOOD OF GOATS AND CALVES

The phrase, *"Neither by the blood of goats and calves,"* proclaims by the fact of the continued need of more sacrifices, that such were not effective. It is estimated that approximately one billion sacrifices were offered up during the approximately 1,600 years of the Law. Josephus, the Jewish Historian, says that as many as 250,000 lambs were offered up during the Passover week when Jesus was crucified. As well, that was typical of most Passovers. Also, there was a constant stream of individual sacrifices carried on perpetually.

The Reader, however, is not to think that these particular sacrifices were of no value. While it is true they couldn't take away sins, still, they were symbols of the One Who was to come. Also, they served to atone or cover

NOTES

the sins of men, even though they could not take them away. This fact alone is extremely important; therefore, we must not minimize the blessing of the covering of sin which then existed. This made it possible for God to commune with His people, at least in a limited fashion, and as well was a portend of that which was to come.

THE BLOOD OF CHRIST

The phrase, *"But by His Own Blood,"* presents the price that was paid.

The moment the Blood of Christ was shed upon the Cross, its efficacy was recognized in Heaven, thus answering to the sprinkling of the blood upon the Mercy Seat. But, spiritually speaking, it is not only seen as sprinkled upon the Throne of God, but also upon the Believer, who is thus purged from all uncleanness.

There is a great distinction set forth in these Verses, which is exactly what Paul intends. Not only was the Ministry of the New Covenant carried out in a different Tabernacle, but also the Blood that had been offered was different.

In the case of Aaron's Priests, it was the blood of goats and calves. In the case of Christ, it was His Own Blood. Now the effectiveness of our Lord's Blood rested not in the mere fact that it was human blood, but in that it was the Holy Blood of God's Son. It was Blood that had flowed in the veins of One Who was, as to His humanity, sinless. But He was also Divine; He was God manifested in the flesh; therefore, the Blood of the New Covenant was more efficacious than that of the Old.

This was the only Blood that the High Court of Heaven would accept as valid Atonement or payment for sin one might say. It was the Sacrificial Blood of the Son of God. And by the word *"Sacrificial,"* or *"Sacrifice,"* we are referring to that which was offered freely. In other words, Jesus was not executed and in effect, no one killed Him. He purposely and freely breathed out His Own life in Sacrifice for dying humanity.

THE BLOOD ON THE MERCY SEAT

When we speak of the Blood of Christ being applied to the Mercy Seat of Heaven, we are not to understand that our Lord took His physical Blood into Heaven. That didn't happen! The Precious Blood of Christ was poured out at the Cross and dripped onto the Earth. But because He shed His Blood, He was able to enter into the very Throne Room of Heaven itself, having accomplished Salvation by the giving of Himself. Now He sits at the right hand of the Father. His is the exalted, bloodless, glorified body which is an eternal testimony that all sin, past, present, and future, has been atoned, at least for all who will believe (Jn. 3:16).

Some translations import the idea of Christ as taking His Blood into Heaven itself. They claim this from one translation that says, *"taking not the blood of goats and calves but His Own Blood"*; however, this is quite unwarranted. The Greek does not say this.

The translation is objectionable because it implies that Christ's atoning work was not completed on the Cross, but that He still had to do some atoning act in Heaven like the earthly High Priest who took the blood into the Most Holy Place on the Day of Atonement.

However, the manner in which Paul makes these statements tells us, that what Christ did on the Cross was final. It needed no supplement. Jesus fully, totally, and completely paid the price at the Cross, which means there was nothing else to be done.

In fact, the price was so complete at the Cross, that God immediately ripped the Veil in the Temple from top to bottom, completely opening up the way to the Holy of Holies, which meant the work is now done (Mat. 27:51).

This completely shoots down the fallacious doctrine, claiming that Jesus died spiritually on the Cross, actually taking upon Himself the nature of Satan, and then went to Hell as a sinner. This doctrine also claims that after being in Hell for a period of time, He then threw off the shackles, and was *"born again"* as any sinner is Born-Again, etc. And by having faith in that, people are saved.

That particular doctrine is an abomination. There is not one single shred of Scriptural proof regarding this erroneous subject. Jesus did not pay for your Redemption in Hell. He paid for it at the Cross, and did so by the shedding of His Own Precious Blood.

In fact, the Resurrection of Christ after the Cross was a given. Jesus had atoned for all sin. Inasmuch as the wages of sin is death, and all sin had been atoned, Satan, death, and Hell had no claim whatsoever on Christ. In fact, if there had been one single sin unatoned, Christ could not have risen from the dead. But God raised Him from the dead, because in fact, all sin had been atoned, and had been done so by the Blood of Christ.

THE RESURRECTION

Many Christians are fond of talking about themselves as *"Resurrection people."* In a sense, that is so; however, most of the time when they say this, they are ignoring the Cross, or even demeaning the Cross. I would remind the Reader of the following:

Paul said, *"But God forbid that I should glory* (boast)*, save in the Cross of our Lord Jesus Christ by Whom the world is crucified unto me and I unto the world"* (Gal. 6:14).

I remind the Reader that Paul didn't say, *"But God forbid that I should glory* (boast)*, save in the Resurrection of our Lord Jesus Christ,"* etc. While of course, the Resurrection of Christ was of extreme significance, that goes without saying; however, everything that we have today in the realm of Salvation and Blessings, comes entirely by and through what Jesus did at the Cross, and by no other means.

As well, it must be understood, that when Jesus shed His Life's Blood, it was not for Himself — for He had no sin — but it was for others, in fact the entirety of humanity, who definitely was polluted with sin. But faith in the atoning work of Christ on the Cross, removes the sin and the guilt, and in truth, is the only thing that can remove the sin and the guilt (I Jn. 1:7).

ONCE

The phrase, *"He entered in once into the Holy Place,"* proclaims Christ doing what no other Priest had done. He offered a Sacrifice that was complete; thereby the Heavenly Tabernacle was opened to Him.

Actually, He might have entered Heaven at any moment during His Perfect Life; He could have gone back to His Father, for He was always pleasing to Him. Yet, had He done so, not one single soul would have been redeemed. He had to willingly offer Himself as a Lamb without spot or blemish. Though He was the sinless One, our sins were laid on Him; He was made to be sin for us, which means to take the penalty of sin, which He did. Only after He had accomplished Eternal Redemption did He return to His Father.

When He did return, He went into God's Presence for us with only one claim on our behalf: His shed Blood. His Blood was the witness that, in the Person of our Substitute, Divine wrath and judgment had been endured on our behalf. Now, according to our Faith in His Finished Work, we might come near to God, having been brought nigh by the Blood of Christ. There is now Reconciliation and Peace because of our great High Priest.

The very word, *"once"* states that what He did, will never have to be done again. His One Sacrifice was sufficient for all people, for all time, in essence for all eternity. There can be no repetition, simply because there doesn't need to be a repetition. The work is final; the work is done!

THE HOLY PLACE

Once again we emphasize, that Christ didn't go into Heaven with His Blood in a basin or a container of sorts and apply it to the original Mercy Seat. Actually, the *"Holy Place,"* as Paul here describes it, is the Throne of God.

The idea is, that He entered Heaven after His Resurrection and appeared at the Throne, where He is now seated by the right hand of Majesty (Heb. 1:3). His Blood having been shed for sin is now the ground of His pleading and intercession for the pardon of sin. It is not something that He must continue to do, but the fact of His very appearance there guarantees all that we have said.

While there is an Ark of the Covenant in Heaven (Rev. 11:19), there is nothing in Scripture that says that He literally applied literal Blood to the Mercy Seat. In a sense, He is the Mercy Seat, exactly as He is the Ark. As such, He serves as our Mercy, or the means by which we have mercy extended to us, and as well He is the satisfier of the Law, which pertained to the Ark of the Covenant, i.e., *"the Law."*

ETERNAL REDEMPTION

The phrase, *"Having obtained Eternal Redemption for us,"* proclaims what was accomplished by the giving of Himself on the Cross.

"Redemption" in the Greek is *"lutrosis,"* and is from the Greek *"lutroo,"* which means *"a ransoming, or a ransom price of redemption; an atonement; a release on receipt of a ransom price."*

Let the Reader understand, that the ransom was paid to God and not Satan. It was to God that the terrible sin debt was owed. It was God Whom man had offended. Man owes Satan nothing, and for sure, God owes Satan nothing.

The ransom was a price that man could not pay due to the fact of it being so high; therefore, God paid the ransom Himself, in the giving of His Only Son, Who suffered on the Cross, which thereby paid the price.

As well, the Greek word *"lutroo,"* means that such a price was paid, that no creature in eternity future, be he demon, devil, Angel, or man will ever be able to say that the price was insufficient. The word *"eternal"* guarantees that the price stands good forever. It is eternal in its merit and efficacy.

UNCONDITIONAL ETERNAL SECURITY

Some would attempt to take the word *"eternal"* as it refers to Redemption and force it into a meaning that Paul did not proclaim here.

Redemption, as afforded by Christ, presents a perfect Redemption, and thereby will never need amendment. This means that it will stand forever; however, man's possession of it is eternal only upon continued faith. So, the word *"eternal"* refers to Redemption as here plainly stated, and as well to possession of Redemption.

There are certain conditions one must meet to get this Eternal Redemption, and certain conditions that one must meet in order to keep this Eternal Redemption (Jn. 6:27).

To cut through all the theology, and to go to the very reason for which this Epistle to the Hebrews was written, the key ingredient is Faith. The Lord doesn't overthrow His children because of sin. Calvary addressed that; however, in no way does that mean that sin is to be looked at with impudence. The facts are, no true Christian wants to sin, and in fact, every true Christian hates sin (Rom. 7:15). Any so-called Christian who sins with impunity, and continues to claim Christ, is simply fooling himself. In other words, that person is not saved, despite their claims.

It is true, that there are many Christians who are in fact bound by sin, and because they do not know God's prescribed order of victory, which is the Cross. But still, those people whomever they might be, and to be frank, they number the vast majority of Christendom, hate the sin that dominates them, and actually continue to try to break out of its grip, although attempting to do so in the wrong way. These people are saved, even though not walking in victory, and for the reasons given.

As should be obvious, I'm not speaking of those particular Christians, but rather those who profess Christ, but with whom there's never been a change within their lives. In other words, it's business as usual. These people number into the millions, and as stated, aren't saved, and in fact have never been saved.

As long as a Christian continues to evidence Faith in Christ, that person is saved. But if they lose their Faith in Christ, even as some of these Hebrews were doing, hence the writing of this Epistle, then one can lose their way and lose their soul.

The Lord never throws a person over for any cause or reason, who continues to have Faith in Him. But when an individual ceases to have Faith in Christ and His Finished Work, there is no basis on which God can continue to deal with that person (Heb. 6:4-6).

Some would attempt to claim that no true Christian would do such a thing; however, once again we go to the Book of Hebrews. The entirety of this Epistle was written by Paul addressing this very problem. These particular Jews definitely were Christians. Paul, as previously stated, refers to them as *"Brethren."* In fact, he refers to them as *"Holy Brethren, partakers of the heavenly calling"* (Heb. 3:1).

Knowing that the Holy Spirit is the One Who inspires the Scriptures, we must come to the conclusion, that being the case, that

either the Holy Spirit lied, or else these Jews were in fact *"Holy Brethren,"* which means they had accepted Christ. Of course, we know the latter to be the correct conclusion. These were Christians who were seriously considering, at least some of them, turning their backs on Christ.

In fact, for these Jews to do this, they would actually have to renounce Christ, actually confessing and saying that He was an imposter and, therefore, a blasphemer, and was worthy of Crucifixion. Paul said if they did this thing, and remained in that state, that it would be *"impossible . . . to renew them again unto repentance; seeing they crucified to themselves the Son of God afresh, and put Him to an open shame"* (Heb. 6:4-6).

It's bad enough to believe the unscriptural doctrine of unconditional eternity security, but it's worse yet to believe this particular doctrine, thinking you can live any way you so desire and still make Heaven your home. Such thinking presents a fool's hope. And in fact, there are millions in this very state presently, and part of the blame can be laid to this unscriptural doctrine.

THE ECONOMY OF REDEMPTION

A Bible Scholar once said: *"What is unfolded in Scripture is one great economy of Salvation, an organism of Divine acts and testimonies, which, with the beginning of Genesis with creation, advances progressively to its completion in the Person and Work of Christ, and is to find its close in the new heaven and earth predicted in the Book of Revelation; and it is only in connection with this whole that the details can be properly estimated . . . He who has not learned to understand the Old Testament and its historical connection . . . lacks the key to its meaning."*

Some modern theologians have a tendency to divorce Old Testament teaching and experience from any direct connection with the New Testament. To this school of thought Jehovah of the Old Testament is a dim and distant Figure Who has gone into retirement.

Of course, such thinking is without fact or foundation. Quite to the contrary, the relationship of the New Testament to the Old is of such nature that they both stand or fall together. The New Testament assumes the existence of Old Testament Law and Prophecy as its positive presupposition.

We cannot have the redeeming God of the New Covenant without the Creator and Covenant God preached in the Old; we cannot discount the Redeemer from the Old Testament predictions which He came to fulfill. The genesis of all the ideas of the New Testament relating to Salvation lies in the Old Testament.

A famous divine says, *"There is not a flower of truth blooming in the New Testament whose seed was not sown in the soil of the Old; and there was not a seed of truth planted in the Old Testament which does not come to full fruitage in the New . . . the very breath of the Old Testament is the same breath that prayed, dying, on Calvary."*

THE PLAN OF REDEMPTION

The Scripture teaches us that the Heavenly Council met in an extraordinary session on behalf of man's Redemption long before the catastrophe of the Fall took place. God the Father, with the Son, and the Holy Spirit, constituting the Trinity, had the bridge of Salvation built before man actually came to it (I Pet. 1:18-20).

While the details of the Plan of Redemption were not known from the beginning, there was no uncertainty as to the facts. The Christ promised in Eden, from that moment was the Savior of the world; making it possible that the first woman who yielded to the temptation of disobedience, might through faith in the Promised Redeemer, become a subject of His Redemptive Grace.

A noted Bible Scholar captures the significance of this truth in these words: *"Before the first man sinned, God provided a way by which he (man) might escape the death penalty and be made perfect again. That was through the atoning work of Christ on the Cross, Who in the reckoning of God was slain from the foundation of the world."*

With regard to Christ's eternal relationship to Salvation, another noted Bible Scholar says, *"Before the foundation of the world God had appointed His Son to be the Mediator of the predetermined counsel of Salvation. The Son is the Lamb, without blemish or fault, before known prior to the*

NOTES

foundation of the world being laid" (I Pet. 1:20). This means that Christ is the Mediator of world Redemption, for it was the good pleasure of the whole fullness to dwell in Him and through Him to reconcile all things unto Himself (Eph. 1:4; 3:11; Col. 1:19-20; Heb. 1:2; I Pet. 1:20). From eternity the Son was willing to carry out the work of Redemption. His Death on the Cross was an offering of Himself to God *"through the eternal Spirit"* (Heb. 9:14), that is through His eternal Spirit, through which Christ performed all His other works also, and in which finally He presented Himself to the Father, in obedience unto death, which death, although carried out in time, is nevertheless an act above time.

ONE GOD

The Bible, from Genesis through Revelation, reveals one God, the Creator of the Heavens and the Earth. The God of creation is presented in the New Testament as a God of love and mercy, and it was this God Whom Jesus came to reveal.

The fact that God is holy and eternally the same, makes it impossible for Him to change. His hatred for sin and His love of Holiness have always been the same; with Him *"is no variableness, neither shadow of turning"* (James 1:17). The Psalmist had this in mind when he said: *"Thou art the same, and Thy years shall have no end"* (Ps. 102:27).

Malachi, as a spokesman for the Lord says, *"For I am the LORD, I change not"* (Mal. 3:6). Parallel to this plain teaching of Scripture is the fact that God does not have two redemptive plans — one for the people in the Old Testament and one for those in the New. After Adam and Eve sinned, God made a redemptive provision for them, and this initial provision was made for all people of every age and dispensation (Rom. 4:13; 9:6-8).

THE BLOOD

After their transgression, Adam and Eve suddenly realized that they were sinful and naked, and immediately they made aprons from fig leaves for temporary covering. Shortly thereafter *"the LORD God made coats of skins, and clothed them"* (Gen. 3:21).

A well-known Scholar says, *"By this we are informed, that the price of the covering for man's nakedness and sin, was the life of the animal . . . thus it would appear, that the Lord permitted those who had been victims of the Fall, and upon whom death had been pronounced, as a sign or pledge of their deliverance, to take the first life, and shed the first blood, as a type of Him Who was Himself the seed of the woman; but who should conquer Satan, destroy His power over humanity, deliver from the curse and prepare man for eternal blessedness and a youthful immortality."* What a wonderful Message of Salvation in the early shedding of blood.

CONSCIOUSNESS OF SIN

Fairbairn, in his *Typology of the Scriptures* makes a striking statement at this point: *"It is the fact noticed at the close of God's interview with our first parents after the Fall: 'Unto Adam also and to his wife did the LORD God make coats of skins, and clothed them' (Gen. 3:21).*

"The painful sense of nakedness that oppressed them after their transgression, was the natural offspring of a consciousness of sin — an instinctive fear lest the unveiled body should give indication of the evil thoughts and dispositions which now lodged within. Hence, to get relief to this uneasy feeling, they made coverings for themselves of such things as seemed best adapted to the purpose, out of the vegetable world which had been freely granted for their use. They girded themselves about with fig leaves.

"But they soon found that this covering proved of little avail to hide their shame, where most of all they needed to have it hidden; it left them miserably exposed to the just condemnation of their offended God. If a real and valid covering should be obtained, sufficient to relieve them of all uneasiness, God Himself must provide it."

THE COVERING

And so He actually did. As soon as the promise of mercy had been disclosed to the offenders, and the constitution of mingled goodness and severity brought in, He made coats to clothe them with, and these were coats of skin. But clothing so obtained argued the sacrifice of life in the animal that furnished them; and thus, through the death

of an inferior, yet innocent living creature, was the needed relief brought to their disquieted and fearful bosoms. One might say, that the outward had respect to the inward and spiritual. The covering of their nakedness was a gracious token from the Hand of God, that the sin which had alienated them from Him, and made them conscious of uneasiness, was henceforth to be in His sight as if it were not; so that in covering their flesh, He at the same time covered their conscience — at least as much as it could be done with such a covering.

All of this was done purposely by God to denote the covering of the guilt from the eye of Heaven — an act which God Alone could have done. But He did it, as we have seen, by a medium of death, by a sacrifice of life in those creatures which men were not yet permitted to kill for purposes of food, and in connection with a constitution of Grace which laid open the prospect of recovered life and blessing to the Fallen.

ADAM

It might be possible to say that Adam and Eve at the beginning, appropriated God's redemptive provision for their fallen condition. It is obvious that Adam at the first believed in the original good news of the coming seed of the woman (Gen. 3:15). This is proven by the name *"Eve,"* which means *"Life,"* which he gave to his wife (Gen. 2:23). This was directly after the original promise, and immediately before the expulsion from Paradise. Sunken in death he nevertheless gave his wife so proud a name, and thereby expressed his faith in the conquest of death by life, and from that time the new name of his wife was for man the reminder of the promise of God's Grace.

That Eve also in faith took her stand on the ground of the word of promise as shown by her statement in Genesis 4:1. The redemptive acceptance is most strongly reflected in Abel, whose Righteousness cannot be doubted (Mat. 23:35; Heb. 11:4; I Jn. 3:12). On the other hand, Cain is presented as one who rejected the redemptive plan, and this rejection is evidenced by the fact that he murdered his brother (Gen. 4:5-15). Abel accepted God's redemptive plan by faith; Cain rejected it by doubt. Abel's faith was evidenced by Righteousness; Cain's sinful rebellion is evidenced by his crime. *"By their fruits ye shall know them"* (Mat. 7:20).

However, at a point in time, the evidence is that Adam and Eve had lost faith. When Cain was born, the first lady said, *"I have gotten a man from the LORD"* (Gen. 4:1).

By her using the name *"Lord,"* which means *"Covenant God,"* it shows that she had faith in the Covenant that God would send a Redeemer. Possibly she even thought that this baby would be that Redeemer. Instead, he turned out to be a murderer, which shows that she did not know or realize just how bad sin actually was and the terrible toll it had taken.

When Seth was born, she said, *"For God hath appointed me another seed instead of Abel, whom Cain slew"* (Gen. 4:25).

She now no longer addresses Jehovah as *"Lord,"* signifying faith in the Covenant, but rather as *"God,"* meaning she had lost faith. This we do know, Adam and Eve are not listed in the great roster of Faith outlined in Hebrews Chapter 11. Every evidence is, that they lost their way with God, because of losing Faith.

THE SHEDDING OF BLOOD

Cain must have been in a position to have the same knowledge of sin and mercy, but the offering which he brought was rejected. In what way did the two offerings differ?

One offering, that of Abel, was of such a nature that it required the shedding of blood. The other was bloodless. Evidently the principle of truth suggested in Hebrews 9:22, *"without shedding of blood is no remission,"* was in force even at this early date.

Here it can be seen that the blood sacrifice, typifying the Blood of *"the Lamb slain from the foundation of the world"* (Rev. 13:8) was sufficient ground for the Faith of Abel.

It is quite evident, that we have an intimation, at least in the sacred records, that the sacrifice and its earliest history was instituted by God Himself, either by example or immediate command . . . The shedding of the blood of the sacrifice, and the yielding up of its life, must repeat continuously to stupid, fallen humanity of every generation,

the message of man's guilt, of Divine justice and God's mercy, until the Promise made in Eden should be fulfilled.

The loss of life is the penalty of sin, and its typical vicarious surrender was necessary to remission (Heb. 9:22) . . . the blood of animals was used in all offerings for sin in Old Testament times (Lev. 17:11).

As well, the *"Blood of Jesus,"* the *"Blood of Christ,"* the *"Blood of Jesus Christ,"* or the *"Blood of the Lamb,"* are figurative expressions for His atoning death (I Cor. 10:16; Eph. 2:13; Heb. 9:14; 10:19; I Pet. 1:2, 19; I Jn. 1:7; Rev. 7:14; 12:11).

Scripture tells us that Noah took clean sacrificial animals into the Ark (Gen. 7:2). Evidently for sacrificial purposes, and after the flood *"Noah built Jehovah an Altar and offered Burnt-Offerings"* . . . To Him must the hearts of the pious lift themselves, to Heaven the height must their offerings and prayers ascend, if they are to reach His Throne.

So as to give this *"upward direction"* to the sacrifice, from now on there were erected on Earth high places and Altars from whence they should ascend Heavenwards in the fire. The Presence of God is indeed everywhere and is not restricted by the boundaries of an above or beneath (Ps. 139) . . . the clean animals offered, as well as the sacrifices from the beginning of the world, themselves point to the Sacrifice of Golgotha, the Lamb without blemish and without spot (I Pet. 1:19-20) Who is in truth the foundation of all preservation and Salvation of the world.

It is also evident that this blood symbolism is reflected in the Old Testament rite of Circumcision. This act was a covenant signed between Abraham and Jehovah.

In order that Abraham might become the *"friend of God,"* it was commanded that he should be circumcised as a token of the Covenant between him and God (Gen. 17:10-11). The blood exuding from the operation was a testimony of Faith in God's Blood Atonement.

The use of blood in the Old Testament is everywhere vested with cleansing, expiatory, and reverently symbolic qualities . . . from the Old Testament to the New Testament we see an exaltation of the conception of blood and ceremonies. In Abraham's Covenant, his own blood had to be shed . . . There must always be a shedding of blood. *"Apart from shedding of blood there is no remission"* (Heb. 9:22). The exaltation and dignifying of this idea finds its highest development then in the vicarious shedding of Blood by Christ Himself (I Jn. 1:7).

SACRIFICE

Noah was a faithful follower of Christ (Jehovah), and of him it was said that he *"found grace in the eyes of the Lord."* He was a *"just man and perfect in his generations, and Noah walked with God"* (Gen. 6:8-9).

He was not only righteous in his conduct, but he was pious and had continual communion with God. In his devotion to God, Noah observed carefully the redemptive pattern given by God to the Adamic generation.

Adam Clark says, *"The old world began with sacrifice, so also did the new. The proper mode of worshipping the Divine Being is the invention or institution of God Himself; and Sacrifice, in the act and design, is the essence of Salvation."*

Without Sacrifice, actually offered or implied, there never was, and there never can be any Salvation. Even in the heavens, a Lamb is represented before the Throne of God as newly slain (Rev. 5:6, 12).

The design of Sacrifice is two-faced: the slaying and the burning of the victim first point out that the life of the sinner is forfeited to Divine justice; second, that his soul deserves the fire of perdition.

The Jews have a tradition that the place where Noah built his Altar was the same in which the Altar stood that was built by Adam. It was by the offering of this blood sacrifice that Noah linked his profession of faith with those who preceded him. By this offering he acknowledged himself a sinner and professed faith in the promised Christ (Jehovah) Messiah. To this faith the writer of Hebrews refers (Heb. 11:7).

FAITH

Abraham was a child of faith. At a point in time, Abraham *"believed God, Who spoke to him."* He did not oppose the light of faith which, through God's doing, was born in him as a superior wisdom . . . by this capacity to welcome within him a new life, by this heroic

faith, was he justified . . . Abraham believed; he had faith in Jehovah, and Jehovah reckoned it to him as Justice, i.e., *"Righteousness."* In fact, this is one of the peaks of Scripture. It is higher than Sinai. It joins together the two Testaments.

Already it reflects the light of Christ . . . Abraham, now at peace, lived on in faith.

The most significant event in Abraham's life was the Revelation he received on a starry night when God concluded with the Patriarch the Covenant of Faith (Gen. 15:5, 18). That was the time when Abraham received the Divine declaration of justification, and it is there that in the annals of Salvation the very first plain and express mention is made of the *"justification"* of a sinner (Gen. 15:6; Rom. 4:2-4).

It is evident, however, that all redemptive responses required an act of faith, and it was by faith in God's redemptive provision that people of all ages have been justified.

Let us hurriedly state, that when we speak of Faith, it is plainly obvious, that always and without exception, it is speaking of Faith in Christ and what He would do at the Cross on behalf of lost humanity. Faith in Christ that leaves out the Cross, is no faith at all, at least that which God will recognize; consequently, every Believer must understand this about Christ, and understand this about Faith. Every thought of Faith, every sinew of Faith, every ligament of Faith, all understanding of Faith, must always be concluded, and without exception, in the parameters of the Cross of Christ. To think of Faith other than the Cross, is again as stated, Faith that God will not recognize. To prove the point, please note the following:

When was faith reckoned to Abraham for Righteousness? Was it before or after his circumcision? (Rom. 4:10).

The answer runs: not less than 13 years before he was circumcised. Because the covenant of circumcision was first introduced when Abraham was already 99 years old (Gen. 17:1-14); but the Covenant of Faith and the Justification took place before even the birth of Ishmael, and, therefore, before his 86th year (Gen., Chpt. 16; 17:1).

Consequently, Abraham had been justified already 13 years before he was circumcised, proving that circumcision had absolutely nothing to do with his Justification, and as well, proving that his Justification was based strictly on the Sacrifice of Christ.

It is significant that Paul builds his case for Justification by Faith upon the Old Testament. In Romans, he draws liberally upon the Hebrew Scriptures to prove that Justification is through faith and faith alone, and again, by that, we refer to Faith in the Cross (Rom. 3:21; 4:1).

Paul graphically points out, that Abraham's justification prior to circumcision is prophetically significant in that through it Abraham was to become father of all such as were without circumcision, but through faith alone should become justified. Through this very fact it became evident that circumcision cannot be a condition precedent to, but only a *"seal"* of the Righteousness that Faith has already provided (Rom. 4:11).

THE ABRAHAMIC COVENANT AND THE LAW

One Scholar points out, and rightly so, that to attain the temple of Salvation, the Gentiles must not first pass through the anteroom of the Jews — that is through the Law — but the Jew must first pass through the anteroom of that faith which Abraham already had while being, so to say, a *"heathen."* Thus, it is set forth that Salvation is without human merit and that Redemption is of Grace, a free gift purely to faith, and proof is given that the Gospel of the Church Age was foreshadowed in the Covenant with Abraham, thus the *"New Covenant"* is the continuation and glorious perfection of the Covenant already given to Abraham (Rom. Chpt. 4; Gal. 3:9, 14).

Exactly what Abraham knew about the coming Christ we are not told; however, we do know that death and resurrection were explained to him, and was made even more pertinent by the object lesson of God's demand that Abraham offer Isaac up to Him in sacrifice.

In this, the Patriarch knew that God would redeem humanity by the death of His Son. As well, the Patriarch also knew that the Redeemer would be resurrected.

His faith in God's resurrection power is manifested in his willingness to sacrifice his

NOTES

son Isaac, upon whom so much depended. And this very act he reckoned *"that God was able to raise him up, even from the dead"* (Heb. 11:19).

Special attention should be directed to the words of Abraham to his servants: *". . . I and the lad will . . . worship, and come again to you"* (Gen. 22:5). Thus, Abraham becomes the type of the New Testament Faith in Resurrection.

All of this is proclaimed by Christ when He said of the Patriarch, and speaking to the Jews, *"Your father Abraham rejoiced to see My day: and he saw it, and was glad"* (Jn. 8:56).

Isaac, Jacob, Joseph, and Moses were men of faith (Heb. 11:20). They knew about the Promise and rejoiced *"concerning things to come"* (Heb. 11:20).

THE LEVITICAL SYSTEM

The sacrifice which represented, in the fullest measure, Christ and His work of expiation and Atonement, was the particularly great offering of the Levitical system. Whether from the herd of cattle, the flock of sheep or goats, or the clean fowl, it was one without blemish. This represents Christ, the choice One of Heaven, the unblemished One, Whose whole life was sacrificed, and consumed as it were upon the Altar of Divine justice, on behalf of sinful men.

As previously stated, from the foundation of the world (Rev. 13:8), offering the Sacrifice was a testimony to saving faith in God's Redemptive Promise. Of these men of faith it is said:

"These all died in faith, not having received the Promises, but having seen them afar off, and were persuaded of them, and embraced them, and confessed that they were strangers and pilgrims on the Earth" (Heb. 11:13).

ALWAYS BY FAITH

Faith has always been the basic fundamental in the sinner's Redemption. Only by faith and faith alone can a sinner be reconciled to God. Faith was the key to Salvation for Abel, Abraham, Isaac, and Jacob, as well as for Paul and Silas, and in fact, every person who has ever come to Christ. Paul said:

"Without faith it is impossible to please Him: for he that cometh to God must believe

that He is, and that He is a rewarder of them that diligently seek Him" (Heb. 11:6). However, and as we've already stated, when the Bible mentions faith, and in any capacity, it is always and without exception, speaking of faith expressed in the atoning merits of the Blood of *"the Lamb slain from the foundation of the world"* (Rev. 13:8).

In the last several decades, the Church has been inundated with teaching on Faith. But virtually all of the teaching has been faith in self or faith in faith, or as they like to put it, *"faith in the Word,"* but the latter is a misnomer, because if it's not Faith in the Cross of Christ, in other words, if Faith doesn't have the Cross as its sole object, then it's not Faith that's taught in the Word of God. Faith, as it's been taught since the middle of the 20th Century, has for the most part been Faith in the Word pulled out of context. In other words, instead of allowing the Word which always addresses itself to the Cross, to mold our lives, these teachers attempted to take the Word and make it serve them. Theirs was the sin of the wilderness temptation.

Satan attempted to get Jesus to do the same identical thing. He wanted Him to use His power for His Own benefit, i.e., *"turn the stones to bread"*; however, Jesus would not at all yield to such, placing the emphasis on the Word instead of the bread by saying, *"Man shall not live by bread alone, but by every Word that proceedeth out of the Mouth of God"* (Mat. 4:1-4). This is so important that I want to state it again:

In the last several decades, false teachers have attempted to make the Word produce for them whatever their lustful desires claimed. In other words, to use it for their own gratification, which of course found a ready audience. Unfortunately, there seems to be enough greed in all of us to keep such false doctrine alive.

The Word of God is meant to mold us into the image of Christ, which the Holy Spirit sets out to do. It is never to be used merely as a provider of *"things."* And the only principle which can throttle such unholy desires within our hearts, is to understand that the Word of God is actually the Cross, as the Cross is actually the Word of God. That means that Faith must be anchored at all times in

NOTES

the Cross, which will then bring about the veracity of the Word within our lives. To do otherwise, is to invite sure disaster! Let's say it this way:

If *"Jesus Christ is the same yesterday, and today and forever"* (Heb. 13:8), His relationship to the redemptive program is the same *"yesterday, and today and forever."*

THE HOLY SPIRIT

It must be understood that God the Creator and Jehovah the Savior are eternally the same. The Spirit of God in the Old Testament is the Holy Spirit in the New; He reveals Divine truth in both Testaments.

It must be noted, however, that the coming of the Holy Spirit upon persons in the Old Testament was limited in the manner in which He could work. Due to the fact that the sin debt was not yet paid, and because the blood of bulls and goats could not take away sin, the Holy Spirit could only abide *"with"* individuals instead of His present capacity as being *"in"* Believers (Jn. 14:17).

While it is definitely true that He did come into certain individuals in Old Testament times for short periods of time, He could not there abide permanently, as He does presently.

As it regards the Word of God, Peter definitely attributes the inspiration of the Old Testament to the Holy Spirit when he says: *"For the prophecy came not in old time by the will of man: but holy men of God spake as they were moved by the Holy Spirit"* (II Pet. 1:21).

In fact, it is only through the Divine self-witness of the Spirit that Divine Revelation penetrates the heart and mind of man. The Spirit is represented as proceeding from Christ, but it must be understood, that a person can also lose the Spirit even as Saul did (I Sam. 16:14). The Scripture also says in Isaiah, *"they rebelled, and vexed His Holy Spirit"* (Isa. 63:10).

The point I'm attempting to make in all of this is, the Holy Spirit superintended every single thing that was written in the Old Testament, and as well, superintended every single thing given by God in that period of time. Consequently, when we observe carefully what He did, we see the Cross of Christ as prominent in the entirety of the great Plan of God in olden times. In fact, the Law portrays the Sacrifices as the centerpiece of that great work, which portrayed the Cross as nothing else.

Peter in speaking to the people of Israel about Christ said, *"This is the Stone which was set at nought of you builders, which is become the Head of the corner. Neither is there Salvation in any other: for there is none other name under heaven given among men, whereby we must be saved"* (Acts 4:11-12). Here again is the language of eternity which projected this truth into every age. It is evident that Salvation has never been available through any other name. Only by Faith in God's Christ, and what He did at the Cross on our behalf, can anyone be saved. This means, that every single person who has ever gone to Heaven, or who will go to Heaven, will be there because of exercising saving Faith in Him.

It is clearly revealed that the God of creation is the God of Abraham, Isaac, and Jacob, as well as of Peter, James, and John. God has a standing offer of pardon to all men who turn from their evil ways and do that which is right (Ezek. 33:11-14). The *"Song of Redemption"* is the keynote of all Christian hymns.

As stated, the Holy Spirit superintended all of this in the Old Testament, which provides the foundation for the New, and centers it all up in Christ, and more particularly, in His Cross (Isa. Chpt. 53).

THE NATURE OF THE ATONEMENT

In the Gospels, Christ Himself related His anticipated *"death on the Cross"* to the culminating phase of the Atonement that was provisionally and foundationally made in the death of *"the Lamb slain from the foundation of the world"* (Rev. 13:8). In effect, the death of Christ was as Anselm said, *"a satisfaction paid to God for the sins of mankind."* Luther and other Reformers attested that the suffering of Christ was the Divine punishment for the sins of the world. The death of Christ presents the fact of the Doctrine of the Atonement predicated upon the assumption that man had sinned and that he could regain favor with God only by becoming justified, i.e., *"restored to a condition as though he had never committed sin."*

Justification in turn was possible only by Faith, and we speak of Faith in Christ and His Cross, a concept stated in the Old Testament and reaffirmed in the New (Hab. 2:4; Rom. 1:17; Heb. 10:38; 11:6).

The Old Testament Church had a prophetic look at the Cross, while the New Testament Church has a historical look at the Cross; however, it is the one and same Cross to which God committed His Son *"from the foundation of the world."*

A pledge from God has always been current legal tender in the Kingdom. The Believer could transact Faith upon this provision and gain personal justification.

Sauer says, *"When the Mediator of Salvation is described as Christ-Messiah, that is, Anointed, this means that the highest offices and dignities (Prophet, Priest, and King) of the whole of the Old Covenant are united in His Person, and that in Him all prophecies have reached eternal fulfillment."*

FULFILLED IN CHRIST

David attested the Lordship of the Christ-Messiah when he said: *"Thou hast crowned Him with glory and honor. Thou madest Him to have dominion over the works of Thy hands; Thou hast put all things under His feet"* (Ps. 8:5-6; Heb. 2:6-9).

Here David is addressing God the Father (Elohim) with regard to His Son, the Lord Jesus Christ (Jehovah) and states in the *"eternal tense"* a truth that was acknowledged by Paul in his writing the Epistle to the Hebrews.

As well, the fact of the personal, conscious, real preexistence of Christ is taught plainly in John 8:58; 17:5; Phil. 2:6-8, where voluntary action is ascribed to the Son of God as before the world was. This excludes a merely *"ideal"* preexistence (Mic. 5:2; Jn. 1:14; Heb. 10:5-7).

All of this means, and makes itself very evident, that all the symbols, doctrines, and examples of Atonement in the Old Testament find their counterpart fulfillment and complete explanation in the New Covenant in the Blood of Jesus Christ (Mat. 26:28; Heb. 12:24).

By interpreting the inner spirit of the sacrificial system, by insisting on the unity and holiness of God, by passionate pleas for purity in the people, and especially by teaching the principle of vicarious sufferings for sin, the Prophets laid the foundation in thought-forms and in spiritual atmosphere for such a Doctrine of Atonement as is presented in the life and teachings of Jesus, and especially His death and Resurrection, and as is unfolded in the teaching of His Apostles as well. Jesus Christ came to elucidate, exemplify, and clarify the eternal truth of the Atonement, and in fact Jesus Christ is the Atonement.

CHRISTIANITY

It is an accepted fact that, *"Christianity"* named as such, had its beginning with the Incarnation of Christ, but provisionally and functionally the principle of *"Christianity"* was a reality from the day God gave the redemptive plan. In fact, one might say, that all Believers of the Old Testament were actually *"Christians,"* and they were *"Christians,"* because they exercised saving faith in Christ (Jehovah) the Messiah. They were Christians before they were so called at Antioch (Acts 11:26).

By assuming the name *"Christian"* the Believers in the Early Church did not subscribe to a new faith, they merely accepted a new name. The foundation for Salvation has always been rooted in the Atonement made for man. As Jesus Christ was in the Divine purpose appointed from the foundation of the world to redeem man by His Blood He, therefore, is in a very imminent sense, *"the Lamb slain from the foundation of the world,"* i.e., *"from creation"* (Rev. 13:8).

Every student of the Bible is aware of the fact that of Christ *"all the Prophets witness, that through His Name whosoever believeth in Him shall receive forgiveness of sins"* (Acts 10:43). Christ is the theme of the Old Testament: He said so Himself (Lk. 24:25-27, 46; Jn. 5:39). Jesus Christ is the King of all Scripture, and it is in this light that the testimony of His preceding heralds can be properly understood: it is only from the New Testament that the question of the Atonement so plainly stated in the Old Testament solves itself.

ONE ATONEMENT

Any intelligent interpretation concerning the Atonement must take into consideration the fact that there is only one Atonement — both in the Old and New Testaments, and that the Blood of animals in the Old Testament

was symbolical of that Blood which was shed by the Lamb of God, which was provisionally, and prophetically, appropriated during the Old Testament.

In all Atonement in the Old Testament and the New Testament, the initiative is solely of God Who not only devises and reveals the way of Reconciliation, but by means of Angels, Prophets, Priests, and ultimately His only Begotten Son applies the means of Atonement and persuades men to accept the proffered reconciliation. It follows that Atonement is fundamental in the nature of God in His relations to men, and that Redemption is in the heart of God's dealing in history. In Jesus Alone we *"behold the Lamb of God taking away the sin of the world"* (Jn. 1:29).

DAY OF ATONEMENT

The *"Day of Atonement,"* as such, did not make its appearance until the era of Tabernacle worship, but its functional principle was patent in the worship system current in earlier days. A progressive element of refinement is to be recognized in redemptive history.

Early worship had as its center the Altar without benefit of a particular building or temple, etc. Later came the Tabernacle, which was followed by the Temple. During the exile, the Synagogue came into being, and it is out of the Synagogue, that the Church arises.

All of these places of worship were different in design but were, for purpose and function, the same. In each of these places of worship there is the idea of God meeting man — a place of meeting where sinful man meets the conditions of Salvation, made possible through the Atonement.

Abraham built an Altar, which of course represented Christ and the death He would die on the Cross, thereby appropriating the benefits of the Atonement through Faith which, in effect, made him a Believer in Christ. In fact, the way in which Abraham responded to the Goodness of God makes him a type of the Christian Believer, and one might even turn it around and say that the Christian evidencing Faith in the Redeemer, makes him a type or child of Abraham. Both have come the same way, which is by Faith in Christ — with Abraham it was Faith in the Christ Who was to come, and with Christians it is Faith in Christ Who has come. In fact, it was the Faith of Abraham in the Divine Promise, which in effect, was in the Atonement, which was not supported at all by the evidence of the senses and, therefore, becomes the type of Faith that leads to Justification (Rom. 4:3). It is in this sense that he is the *"Father"* of Christians, as Believers (Rom. 4:11).

For that Promise to Abraham was, after all, a *"preaching beforehand"* of the Christian Gospel, in that it embraced *"all nations"* (Gal. 3:8). By Faith Abraham appropriated personal Salvation, and he is one with all Believers in God's Christ. Even though the formal *"Day of Atonement"* had not been instituted, Abraham was indeed a kind of spiritual child made possible through the Blood Atonement, laid down in principle even in the Adamic generation (Gen. Chpt. 4).

The Atonement is again symbolized in the Passover. It was instituted in Egypt to commemorate the culminating event in the Redemption of the Israelites (Ex. 12:1, 14, 42; 23:15; Deut. 16:1-3). Sprinkling the blood of the Paschal Lamb symbolized Faith in the blood of the *"Lamb of God, which taketh away the sin of the world"* (Jn. 1:29).

Actually, all of this comes down to us in the Christian era in our taking of that referred to as *"the Lord's Supper."* It should be pointed out that the words used in the narratives of the New Testament institution of this Ordinance, are similar to those in connection with the Passover, i.e., *"body," "blood," "covenant," "given," "poured out," "for you," "for many," "unto remission of sins," "memorial"* (Ex. 24:6-8; Lev. 2:2; 4:5-7, 16-34; 17:11-14; 24:7; Num. 10:10; Heb. 9:11-28; 10:4-10, 19-20). In fact, the immediate background of the Lord's Supper is the Passover, which Jesus Himself instituted (Lk. 22:7-18).

THE NATURE OF THE NEW BIRTH

A very important question revolves around the question of personal Salvation in the Old Testament. Professor Oehler states the question thus: *"Are we to say that the just man not only walked in the faith of a future fulfillment of the Promise and a future Redemption, but also rejoiced in the present possession of Salvation and had an assurance that His sins were forgiven?"*

NOTES

From the evidence gathered in the Old Testament comes the conclusion that personal Salvation was definitely enjoyed by people before the Advent of Christ. It is assumed that the Disciples and others were saved men before the Crucifixion.

Both the Old and New Testaments teach by precept and example that all individuals experience Divine Forgiveness who have repented of their sins and turned to God in saving faith, and that these Believers constitute the Old Testament Church (Ezek. 43:27; Acts 10:34-36). David, as an individual, testified to personal forgiveness and Salvation when he said, *"blessed is he whose transgression is forgiven, whose sin is covered"* (Ps. 32:1). It is assumed that this Testimony closely followed his confession and repentance after his sin with Bathsheba. On another occasion the Psalmist said: *"There is forgiveness with Thee"* (Ps. 130:4; II Chron. 7:14; Isa. 55:7; Ezek. 18:21; Acts 2:38). Many other instances are given in the Old Testament of individuals repenting and being restored to God's favor (II Kings 22:19; Job 42:1, 6; Jonah 3:6-9). The sin of Israel is recognized as the sin of the individual, which can be removed only by individual repentance and cleansing. This is best seen from the stirring appeals of the Prophets of the Exile . . . this cannot be understood otherwise than as a turning of the individual to the Lord.

There was no merit in the animal sacrifice brought by the individual worshipper, for *"the blood of bulls and of goats"* cannot take away sins (Heb. 10:4). It was only as the Sacrifice symbolized and testified to faith in the blood of God's redemptive *"Lamb"* that sins were remitted.

In the teachings of our Lord, based upon the Old Testament, the *"new birth"* or regeneration is assumed. The Old Testament teaching is clear at this point and graphically brought to the surface by Christ in His conversation with Nicodemus (Jn. 3:1-21).

Nicodemus *"was a man of the Pharisees . . . a ruler of the Jews"* (Jn. 3:1). As such, he was well versed in the Law. And yet, despite this fact, Nicodemus was apparently ignorant of the Old Testament teachings on *"the new birth."* He is somewhat typical of the church member, although religious, but who hasn't been *"born again."*

Jesus takes this occasion to rebuke Nicodemus for his ignorance. In fact, Jesus chides him with these words: *"Art thou a master of Israel, and knowest not these things?"* (Jn. 3:10).

Here it is seen that Christ is speaking about a Divine necessity existing before the Crucifixion was actually carried out. Nicodemus could not become a member in the *"Kingdom"* until he had experienced Salvation, i.e., the *"new birth."* The Incarnation did not in any way change the conditions by which Believers entered the *"congregation of the Righteous"* (Ps. 1:5; 40:3; 51:7; Ezek. 11:19; 36:26; II Cor. 5:17; Gal. 6:15).

BACK TO FAITH

Throughout centuries God spoke the word *"Faith"* into the history of Salvation — this is the meaning of the Covenant with Abraham. Through 2,000 years it was an education in faith. Throughout centuries God also spoke the word *"repent"* into the history of Salvation — this is the meaning of the Law of Moses. Therefore, throughout approximately 1,500 years, it was an education in repentance. *"Repent and believe the Gospel"* (Mk. 1:15) says Christ and thereby pulls together both repentance and faith in redeeming oneness. This is the New Testament purpose of the Old Testament.

THE NEW BIRTH

The teaching on the *"New Birth"* in the New Testament reiterates a truth that is, was, and always will be, effective to the end of time. It is written in the language of eternity and is not subject to change. It is anchored totally and completely in the great Sacrifice of Christ, which is found in both Testaments (II Tim. 3:16; I Pet. 1:10-11).

Paul distinctly reaffirms the basic Old Testament concept that a new life is in store for those who have been spiritually dead; that at conversion a spiritual resurrection has taken place. This regeneration causes a complete revolution in man. He has thereby passed from under the law of sin and death and has come under *"the Law of the Spirit of Life in Christ Jesus"* (Rom. 8:2). The change is so radical that it is possible now to speak of a *"new creation,"* of a *"new man, that after*

NOTES

God is created in Righteousness and true Holiness" (Eph. 4:24) and of *"the new man, which is renewed in knowledge after the image of Him Who created him"* (Col. 3:10; II Cor. 5:17); and the Image to which the sinner in the New Testament is renewed is the Image of the Old Testament God.

The idea of all of this is, God has only had one way of Salvation, whether in Old Testament times, or New Testament times. That way has been Jesus Christ and Him Crucified. Every Sacrifice pointed to this. In fact, every single Revelation of God given to men has always centered in this foundation Doctrine, the Gospel of Christ, and more particularly, what Christ did for us that we might be saved.

(13) "FOR IF THE BLOOD OF BULLS AND OF GOATS, AND THE ASHES OF AN HEIFER SPRINKLING THE UNCLEAN, SANCTIFIETH TO THE PURIFYING OF THE FLESH:"

The exegesis is:

1. This Verse speaks of ceremonial defilement.

2. Ceremonial defilement was not in itself sin, but a type of sin.

3. The defilement and cleansing as here enjoined were both symbolic.

THE BLOOD OF BULLS AND GOATS

The phrase, *"For if the blood of bulls and of goats,"* presents Paul turning again to the Levitical Sacrifices. In them he finds the power to effect an external purification, a cleansing from ritual defilement. He refers to the blood of *"bulls and goats,"* which means much the same as that of *"goats and calves"* in Verse 12.

What do we mean by ceremonial defilement?

There were many rules and regulations in the Mosaic Law, which if violated defiled the individual, which necessitated them going through a cleansing ritual. There were no moral connotations involved in these rules, except obedience or disobedience to the Word of God. The idea was, that these rules represented something concerning Christ Who was to come.

Even when sin was committed, and especially when sin was committed, the sacrificial process had to be engaged, of which Paul speaks here; however, the ritual of the animal sacrifices as well did not take away sin, because such sacrifices cannot take away sin. But it did serve as a covering for the sin, and Faith in what the Sacrifices represented, and more particularly, Who they represented, did bring forgiveness of sins.

Now that Christ has come, all of these things which pointed to Him, are now of no necessity. The shadow is no longer a necessity once the reality has appeared.

THE LAW OF THE RED HEIFER

The phrase, *"And the ashes of an heifer sprinkling the unclean, sanctifieth to the purifying of the flesh,"* once again refers to ritual defilement, and as well, the method of cleansing. As we've stated, ceremonial defilement was not in itself sin, but a type of sin. In the case of the red heifer, it was only the flesh of the person which was defiled by contact with the dead. It was likewise only the flesh that was cleansed. Thus, defilement and cleansing were both symbolic. But let's look at it more closely:

The *"Law of the red heifer"* may be somewhat strange to modern thinking; however, it was given to Israel by the Holy Spirit for a specific reason.

If a person touched a dead body, he was ceremonially unclean, and could only be purified by applying the *"water of separation"* to his physical body.

The red heifer was killed and its body was burned. Its ashes were to be taken up, placed in a clean place, and then when needed, a certain amount was to be mixed with water, with it then being called the *"water of separation."* This water was to be sprinkled upon him on the third day after touching the dead body and on the seventh day. As well, any place where an individual died, anyone who walked into the room, would also be considered unclean, and would have to be cleansed by the application of the *"water of separation"* (Num. Chpt. 19).

The reason for all of this had to do with death which is brought about by original sin. It was to be an object lesson as to the horror of this awful malady, and we continue to speak of sin, which has gripped the human race, and brought death to everything.

The *"heifer"* symbolized Christ. It was spotless externally and without blemish internally. It was to be a female, and it was to be red. Christ in His humanity was spotless within and without; he was gentle as a woman; he was never in bondage to any sin; the Law had no claim upon Him as a debtor; and He robed Himself with the red Earth of manhood, with *"red"* also symbolizing His Blood.

The heifer was to be led by the High Priest without the camp; and there was she slain. So was Christ led of the Spirit to Calvary, where He offered up Himself.

The body of the heifer was then to be burned, which signified the Judgment of God which came upon Christ, instead of the human race. While the heifer was being burned, cedar wood, hyssop, and scarlet were to be thrown into the fire. The cedar wood represented the Cross of Christ, the hyssop represented His humanity, and scarlet represented His shed Blood.

The blood of the heifer is only once mentioned in the Chapter. So Christ was once offered. As well, it needed not be that a heifer should be killed every time purification was needed, which was constant. Its ashes would suffice.

PURIFICATION

Purification from the defilements unavoidable during pilgrimage was effected by an application of the ashes of the burnt heifer with running, i.e., living water. Christ's death need not be repeated, in order to the forgiveness of the daily sins of the celestial pilgrim. It only needs that the meaning and perfection of His death, typified by the burnt ashes, should be effectively applied to the conscience by the Living Spirit, symbolized by the running water, and the sense of forgiveness and cleansing is enjoyed.

The last twelve Verses of Numbers Chapter 19, reveal the malignity of sin, and its enduring contagion and defilement. Accidentally touching a bone, even though it were a thousand years old, defiled and procured exclusion from the camp. Restoration was only possible after an application of the ashes of the heifer on the third day and on the seventh day.

The three days prior to the first purging fastened on the conscience, the hatefulness of sin to God; the four days prior to the second and final application of the ashes and running water, instructed the conscience as to the perfection of the purge and the wonders of the grace that provided it.

Possibly the third day pointed to the Resurrection of Christ; the seventh day as to the perfection and totality of Redemption afforded by His Death and Resurrection.

"At even" the defiled person was pronounced clean. The preciousness of Christ's Atoning Blood, and its sufficiency to cleanse from all sin, speak with special sweetness to the heart and conscience at evening, when life is closing and the shadows of death are about to fall.

The presence of death in a house defiled everything in the house, except a covered vessel. The Christian pilgrim necessarily comes in contact with *"death"* every day, i.e., with that which defiles, but he escapes defilement if he is a *"covered vessel,"* that is, if he lives under the covering of the Blood and the Holy Spirit.

The warning duplicated in Verses 13 and 20 of the 19th Chapter of Numbers, predicts the doom of those who deny the need of Christ's Atoning Death (Williams).

(14) "HOW MUCH MORE SHALL THE BLOOD OF CHRIST, WHO THROUGH THE ETERNAL SPIRIT OFFERED HIMSELF WITHOUT SPOT TO GOD, PURGE YOUR CONSCIENCE FROM DEAD WORKS TO SERVE THE LIVING GOD?"

This structure is:

1. Paul now makes a comparison between the effectiveness of the blood of animals and that of the Blood of Christ.

2. The former could cleanse from ceremonial defilement, but only the latter could cleanse from actual sin.

3. The *"Blood of Christ"* was perfect, therefore, acceptable to God, as payment for all sin.

4. The application of that of the animal had to be done constantly, with many animals having to die down through the centuries, while the one Sacrifice of Christ sufficed for all time.

5. The ceremonial cleansing gave no power to live right, while the application of the Blood of Christ, and faith in that Finished

Work provides the power to *"serve the Living God."*

THE BLOOD OF CHRIST

The beginning of the question, *"How much more shall the Blood of Christ . . . ?"*, proclaims beyond question, the price paid for man's Redemption, a price so great, that in fact, it beggars description.

The efficacy (effectiveness) of our Lord's Blood rested, not in the fact that it was human blood, but that it was human blood of a unique kind. It flowed in the veins of One Who was as to His humanity, sinless, and as to His Person, Deity. And the combination of these two, sinless humanity, and Deity, made it unique, efficacious. It was the only sacrificial blood that could be sprinkled on the Mercy Seat in the Heavenly Holy of Holies, so to speak, the only Blood which the High Court of Heaven would accept as payment or Atonement for human sin. It was this blood poured out on Calvary's Cross that gave Christ access as High Priest into the Holy of Holies of Heaven.

However, and as we've already stated, we are not to understand that our Lord took His Blood into Heaven, for that didn't happen. That precious Blood was poured out on the Cross, and dripped into the Earth. But it was by virtue of that fact that He entered Heaven, having accomplished Salvation by the Sacrifice of Himself. It was in that bloodless, glorified human body which is an eternal testimony that the debt of sin has been satisfied, that our Blessed Lord entered Heaven.

DEATH

The words *"how much more"* stress the incomparable greatness of Christ and His Work for us. *"The Blood of Christ"* means Christ's Death regarded as a sacrifice for sin. Though some have suggested that we should see in references to *"the Blood"* allusions to life rather than death, this does not seem soundly based. The word *"Blood"* points to death.

In this context *"Blood"* is not death in general but death seen as a sacrifice. Christ offered Himself in Sacrifice to God.

As well, the Sacrifice offered here, which was the spotless, pure, Perfect Blood of the Lord Jesus Christ, which means that He poured out His Life, in order that we might have life, was so effective, so grand, so total, so complete, that it will never have to be done again.

When Paul mentioned the red heifer in the previous Verse, and more specifically *"the ashes of the heifer,"* this cried aloud as did the expiring Savior, *"It is finished!"* For ashes tell of fire burned out never to burn again. It was done!

This is what makes it so bad for religious men to attempt to add something to the Finished Work of Christ, or to take from that Work. Some of the Christian Jews attempted to add to that Finished Work by attempting to add the Law, which Paul adamantly refused to accept. In fact, this problem continues unto this hour, with men attempting to add the Church to that Finished Work or Water Baptism, or good works of any nature, etc.

Others attempt to take from that Finished Work, by claiming that it is so effective, that we need not worry about sin, in other words, claiming that the Cross gives them license to sin. Paul addressed that by saying, *"shall we sin that Grace may abound?"* His answer was to the point:

"God forbid! How shall we, that are dead to sin, live any longer therein?" (Rom. 6:1-2).

THE ETERNAL SPIRIT

The phrase, *"Who through the Eternal Spirit offered Himself without spot to God,"* refers to the Holy Spirit. It speaks of the Ministry of the Holy Spirit at Calvary. Twice in this Chapter Paul has pointed out the Ministry of the Holy Spirit as it relates to the Ministry of Christ.

In Verse 8, the Spirit used the Old Covenant as a means to point to the Redemptive Work of Christ that would make perfect access possible into the Presence of God. Now, in Verse 14, the role that the Holy Spirit played in the offering of Jesus upon the Cross is unfolded. Jesus offered Himself through the Spirit. Consequently, I think one could say without fear of contradiction, that the Holy Spirit Personally had to grant permission before the Son of God could give His Life on the Cross.

The Blood of Jesus was spilled through the Eternal Spirit, in effect with the Spirit superintending every moment of this moment of all moments. God the Father, God the Son, and God the Holy Spirit are one God; They are the Trinity, the Three in One. In the counsels of Heaven it was agreed by Almighty God — Father, Son, and Spirit — that Christ should become the Sacrifice for man's sin. This means that all felt the pain of Calvary; all fully knew and understood the cost of redeeming mankind from sin. So again we will make the statement, *"The Blood of Jesus was spilled through the Eternal Spirit."*

THE MANNER IN WHICH THE HOLY SPIRIT WORKS

As a result of the Sacrifice of Christ, we find the Spirit not speaking of Himself, but pointing to Him Who died on Calvary's Cross. The Spirit is ever glorifying, magnifying, and uplifting the Son of God. It is through the Spirit that we worship the Lord. In fact, the Holy Spirit bears witness with our spirit as we worship Him in truth and in spirit (Jn. 4:24; Rom. 8:16).

Not only are we told here that the Eternal Spirit superintended the great Sacrifice of Christ, but as well, the Scripture also says, *"To wit, that God was in Christ, reconciling the world unto Himself"* (II Cor. 5:19). As well, it was the Father Who gave His Son because of His love for mankind (Jn. 3:16); it was Christ Who offered Himself freely on the Cross; it was through the Spirit that He offered Himself without blemish. Thus, all three Persons of the Trinity were involved in our eternal Redemption.

When Christ came into this world, He came to do the Will of His Father. Christ's Will was subject to the Will of God the Father and to the Will of the Holy Spirit, with there never being a conflicting spirit.

The Holy Spirit rested upon Him in power and anointing to carry out the Will of God. When Christ humbled Himself and took the form of a servant, when He became a man, He was filled, led, and motivated by the Spirit.

Christ was obedient even unto death. He subjected Himself to the Spirit's leading in every detail, even to being driven into the wilderness of temptation by the Spirit. It was the Spirit Who led a willing Messiah to the Cross, that lost mankind might find Redemption (Fjordbak).

THE REVELATION OF THE CROSS

When the Lord began to open up to me the Revelation of the Cross, He showed me as well, the manner and the way in which the Holy Spirit works.

First of all, He portrayed to me the true purpose and mission of Christ to this Earth, which was to die upon the Cross. That was His destination, His Purpose, actually, the very reason for the Incarnation, i.e., *"God becoming man."* While every aspect of Christ's Person, Life, and Ministry was of extreme significance, everything and without exception, pointed directly to the Cross. In other words, the Cross was His eternal destination, with everything pushing toward that. In fact, all of this had been decided by the Godhead before the foundation of the world (I Pet. 1:18-20).

Consequently, He portrayed to me that every thought of Christ must in some way, be in connection with the Cross. To divorce Jesus from the Cross in any manner, is to present *"another Jesus"* which of course, cannot be acceptable to the Divine Spirit (II Cor. 11:4).

All of the prophecies of the past, all the predictions by the Seers of old, portrayed the Redeemer as giving Himself for the sins of man (Isa. Chpt. 53). The whole of the Sacrificial system of the Mosaic Law, ever pointed toward the eternal Sacrifice.

Consequently, the Lord told me that all Salvation has as its Source, the Cross of Christ. As well, from the Cross flows all Blessings, all Healing, all Prosperity, in fact, everything we receive from God. The Cross is the means by which the Grace of God is extended to undeserving man. This means as well, that to divorce Grace from the Cross, is to completely misunderstand Grace (Gal. 2:20-21).

The basis for my understanding of the Cross is Romans, Chapter 6. In fact, that's where this Revelation began. The Lord began to open up to me the meaning of this tremendous Chapter, which explains what the Cross is all about, and how that it pertains to the

believing sinner upon coming to Christ. (Please see our Commentary on Romans.)

FAITH

As the Revelation continued, the Lord took me to the experience of Abraham as it regards Faith (Gen. 15:6; Rom. 4:3; Gal. 3:6).

He showed me that Abraham believed God, but more particularly, he believed what God would do as it regards the Redemption of humanity. God would send a Redeemer into this world, and Abraham was to have Faith in that exclusively. In fact, the Covenant that God made with Abraham is the foundation of the entirety of the Plan of Salvation for the human race.

As a result of this, the Holy Spirit showed me that my Faith must be the same as that of Abraham, meaning that it must be anchored totally and completely in the Cross. The Cross must ever be the object of my Faith, understanding, as stated, that the Cross is the Source or the Means of all Blessings from God.

He also portrayed to me the error of much of the teaching on faith in the last several decades, and the reason for the error!

The faith which has been proclaimed and taught for the last several decades, has not been Faith in the Finished Work of Christ, not at all! It has been faith in other things, with the greatest claim being that it's faith in the Word; however, let it ever be understood, if it's not Faith squarely in the Cross of Christ, then it's actually not faith in the Word, but something else altogether, despite the claims.

It is impossible to divorce the Word from the Cross, or the Cross from the Word. The Scripture plainly portrays Christ as the *"Living Word"* (Jn. 1:1).

It also tells us, *"And the Word was made flesh, and dwelt among us"* (Jn. 1:14).

Now let it ever be understood, that the Word was made flesh for one reason, and that was to go to the Cross. This is proven by the next statement:

John said of Jesus, *"Behold the Lamb of God, which taketh away the sin of the world"* (Jn. 1:29).

The Holy Spirit had John to use the appellative *"Lamb"* for one purpose, and that was to portray the Cross.

So, if we do not think of the Cross as in a sense being the Word, and the Word as in a sense being the Cross, we misunderstand the Word of God altogether. It can all be summed up in Jesus, but it must ever be understood that it is *"Jesus Christ and Him Crucified"* (I Cor. 2:2).

To have Faith properly in the Word, one is at the same time having Faith in the Cross. And one might even say, that to have Faith in the Cross is to have Faith in the Word. As stated, the two cannot be divorced!

When one begins to understand the Cross, and as well, understanding that this is where our Faith is to ever be, the entirety of the Bible takes on a brand-new complexion. One sees the Cross on every page and in every act. The reason is, one now sees the Bible in the light of the Cross. The Word of God is that which tells us what was done, and the Cross is that which was done. In other words, the Word ever points to the Cross, as the Cross ever points to the Word. So, Faith must be understood in that capacity. It must ever be in Christ and what He did at the Cross on our behalf.

THE HOLY SPIRIT

The Lord then showed me that this is the manner in which the Holy Spirit works. In other words, He demands that we exhibit Faith at all times, in the great Finished Work of Christ. He actually doesn't require much of us, but He definitely does require that. In fact, the Word emphatically states this:

Paul said, *"The Law of the Spirit of Life in Christ Jesus, hath made me free from the law of sin and death"* (Rom. 8:2). Now let us briefly analyze that Scripture:

1. The Law: The Word *"Law"* refers to that which is designed by God, which refers to the manner and means by which the Spirit works, and as well, means that He will not deviate from this way. Laws made by God will always function exactly in the manner in which they are designed. They have the power of Deity behind them, and will never be broken by God. While man may break them, God never shall. And to be sure, if man breaks them, which he constantly does, he must suffer the consequences.

2. The Spirit: Of course, this speaks of the Holy Spirit. This refers to the fact that

the Holy Spirit, the Third Person of the Godhead, works exclusively within the boundaries, i.e., *"the parameters,"* of this particular Law, which we will define momentarily.

3. Of Life: This *"Life"* comes through and is superintended by the Holy Spirit. It is actually the Life of God in an uninterrupted flow coming to the Believer. This is what Jesus was speaking about when He said, *"If any man thirsts, let him come unto Me, and drink.*

"He that believeth on Me, as the Scripture hath said, out of his innermost being shall flow rivers of living water."

John then quickly added, *"But this spake He of the Spirit, which they that believe on Him should receive"* (Jn. 7:37-39). This *"Life,"* which Jesus likened to *"Living Water,"* referring to its uninterrupted flow, is what makes this Christian experience different than anything else in the world. This is the *"more abundant Life"* promised by Christ (Jn. 10:10).

4. In Christ Jesus: This means that this *"Law"* is centered up in Christ, and more particularly, what He did at the Cross on our behalf. The idea is, what Jesus did at the Cross makes everything possible that we receive from God. This actually means that the Holy Spirit works entirely within the parameters of the Finished Work of Christ, and that He will not work outside of those parameters. That's why He demands that we exhibit Faith totally and completely in the Cross of Christ. When this is done, He will do great and mighty things for us and with us. But without such Faith being registered at all times, His work will be very limited within our lives, for the simple reason that He will not break the Law.

REASONS FOR FAILURE

I want the Reader to read very carefully these next few paragraphs, because if properly understood, many questions will be answered.

At this very moment, there are good Christians who in their love for the Lord are witnessing daily in their efforts to win souls to Christ, and in fact, are winning souls to Christ. But yet, sin is dominating them in some fashion, and they do not understand how or why, especially considering that they love the Lord as much as they do, and are working tirelessly for Him!

As well, there are untold thousands of Preachers who are truly called of God, and are anointed by the Holy Spirit to preach the Gospel, which sees wonderful things done for the Lord in the realm of people being saved, etc. But yet, sin is dominating these Preachers in some way. In fact, such a scenario is almost endless.

There are untold thousands of Christians who eagerly seek Preachers who are being used of God, that they may lay hands on them, that God may move upon their hearts and lives. In fact, this is done constantly, with at times great manifestations following such as *"healings,"* etc.

But then these people find themselves continuing to fail spiritually, in other words, with sin dominating them, and they are left very confused.

Most of the modern Church not understanding this, is very quick to claim, that is if the problems of these Preachers or people are found out, that they are not of God, etc. What they don't seem to realize is, that if these people are not of God, then they aren't either. Because if the truth is known, sin is dominating these faultfinders just as much as the others, if not more.

So how do we explain Christians truly being used of God, and truly loving God with all their hearts, but at the same time failing in some way, as it regards some particular sin. In fact, these people, and their number is the vast majority of the modern Church, are living a life of sinning and repenting! Sinning and repenting! Sinning and repenting! Etc.

Many of them mistake forgiveness for deliverance, when such is not the case at all.

FORGIVENESS IS NOT DELIVERANCE

While forgiveness is always available to every Child of God, with the Lord putting no limitation on that whatsoever, we are to never mistake forgiveness for deliverance (I Jn. 1:9).

Forgiveness is merely a restoration of fellowship which has been broken because of sin of some nature. And the Lord has always promised to do this if we will always confess our sin to Him. To be sure, He, exactly as He has stated, will always be faithful to forgive and cleanse.

NOTES

Even though this is available to all Believers, and thank God it is; still, *"sinning and repenting"* on a constant basis are not the Will of God, as should be obvious.

While the Bible does not teach sinless perfection, it definitely does teach that *"sin shall not have dominion over us"* (Rom. 6:14). But the truth is, sin is dominating the hearts and lives of most Christians.

THE SIN NATURE

And when we say *"sin,"* we are actually speaking of *"the sin."*

In Romans, Chapter 6, Paul explains all of this. In the original Greek, most of the time before the word *"sin"* it has what is referred to as *"the definite article."* In this case, it is *"the,"* as in *"the sin"* (Rom. 5:20-21; 6:1-2, 6-7, 10-14, 17-18, 20, 22-23, etc).

It's amazing that some Preachers claim that Believers no longer have a sin nature, when it could hardly be clearer and plainer in Scripture! However, the power of the sin nature is totally and completely broken within the heart and life of the Believer. In other words, it should cause no problem whatsoever; however, if the Believer doesn't understand the veracity of the Cross, in other words, what Jesus did there for him, then it is certainly possible for the Christian to once again be controlled by the sin nature, which in fact millions are.

The sin nature dwells and reigns (rules) in all unbelievers. It definitely does dwell in Believers, but it's not supposed to reign (rule).

Paul said, *"Let not the sin therefore reign in your mortal body"* (Rom. 6:12). Again, I want the Reader to understand that he is speaking here of *"the sin."* This means, he's not actually speaking of acts of sin, so much as he is speaking of the nature of sin. And if all of this weren't possible, why would the Apostle say, *"Let not the sin therefore reign . . ."* He said it, because it definitely is possible, and in fact, is happening right now in the majority of Christian's lives.

THE REASON FOR THE
SIN NATURE RULING

A person coming to Christ doesn't mean at all that Satan is not going to bother them again. In fact, every Christian is a target for Satan.

As well, just because God has called Believers for certain particular things, even to Preach the Gospel, with them being used mightily, doesn't mean that Satan will stop his efforts. Peter said:

"Beloved, think it not strange concerning the fiery trial which is to try you, as though some strange thing happened unto you" (I Pet. 4:12).

There is absolutely nothing that a Christian can do that will stop the attacks of Satan, but there is much that the Christian can do which will guarantee Satan's defeat. In other words, you as a Believer do not have to yield to his advances, his temptations, his efforts, or anything that he does. The Scripture also says:

"Greater is He that is in you, than he that is in the world" (I Jn. 4:4).

I DON'T UNDERSTAND!

Millions of Christians at this very moment, and I speak of those who truly love the Lord and are even being used of God, and some of them in a great way, in their hearts are saying, *"I don't understand!"*

They're saying this simply because they cannot seem to find victory in their own personal hearts and lives, which means, as stated, that sin is dominating them in some way. They have fought this thing, whatever it might be, in many and varied ways. They've tried to overcome by praying more, giving more money to the Work of God, getting more involved in the Work of God, fasting, or many other things that one might name. However, their problem is not getting better, but rather worse.

Paul addressed this by saying:

"For that which I do I understand not" (Rom. 7:15).

While the word *"allow"* is used by the King James translators, the actual Greek word which Paul used should have been translated *"understand."*

Romans Chapter 7 proclaims Paul's experience not long after he was saved and baptized with the Holy Spirit. At that time, he didn't understand the Victory of the Cross, so he tried to live for God in the same manner that most Christians try to live for God, which translates into one's own strength and power, etc. In other words, to try to live this life without the help of the Holy Spirit, which is impossible.

Despite all of Paul's efforts to the contrary, he found himself failing, and failing over and over again; hence him saying, *"I don't understand."* And that's the very condition of the majority of Christendom presently.

And once again, please understand, that I'm speaking of good Christians. These are people who love God, and in fact, are being used of God. They are trying so hard, but despite all of their efforts, they continue to fail in some way.

It doesn't really make any difference that no one may know about their problem, God knows about the problem, and so do they. It is in fact, hurting them to no end, as sin always does! And please understand, that it's sin which we are talking about.

THE LAW

The Holy Spirit will definitely help any Believer do anything, providing He's not called upon to break the Law. Now what do we mean by that?

Every one of these Christians of whom I speak are attempting to overcome their problem, whatever it might be, in one of many ways. Millions have gone to their Pastor, confided in him, asking what they should do. Almost invariably, most Pastors, not actually knowing the answer, will tell them one of several things:

"You must get more involved in the Church!" "You must get in the Altars!" "You must increase your Faith!" Or many at this present time, are referring them to a Psychologist. Actually, some large Churches have a Psychologist on their staff, or else there is a *"Christian Psychologist"* with whom they are acquainted, etc.

While the former advice will help a little, the latter will help not at all!

The tragedy is, most Preachers to whom the people go for help, are not walking in victory themselves. And please understand that I do not say that sarcastically or unkindly. It just happens to be the truth!

What is wrong?

THE CROSS

God's way is the Cross, and it is for everyone. That means that the same solution which He has for the Laity, He as well has for

Preachers. There's only one solution! And the Truth is, most Preachers do not have the slightest idea as to the part the Cross plays in our everyday living for God. Most of them know and understand that the Cross is important as it involves our initial Salvation experience, but beyond that they have little or no knowledge.

Every single failure on the part of a Believer, and it doesn't matter who that person is, or what type of failure it is, is brought about because of not understanding the victory found only in the Cross. As I've repeatedly stated, in the last half century, the Church has had almost no teaching on the Cross; consequently, one might say, and with saddened regret, the modern Church is Cross illiterate.

And then there's the other problem of unbelief! Many in the modern Church simply do not believe the Cross holds the answer for the ills of man. They look to other things, mostly humanistic psychology. In fact, I think I can say almost without fear of contradiction, that any Preacher who recommends psychology, has simply lost faith in the Cross of Christ. While there certainly may be some few who have fallen into this trap because of ignorance of the Cross, I feel the vast majority are traveling that road of humanistic religion because of unbelief.

If the Believer will read carefully the previous pages concerning the Cross, and believe what he reads, asking the Lord to properly reveal it to his heart, he will start down a road that will lead to the greatest life and living he's ever known in all of his experience in following Christ. This doesn't mean that Satan will quit; however, it definitely does mean that sin will no longer have dominion over you. It definitely does mean that you now will begin to enjoy this *"more abundant life."*

The Scripture tells us, *"The husbandman that laboureth must be first partaker of the fruits"* (II Tim. 2:6).

That simply means, that I cannot tell you how to have victory in your life, if I haven't first gained victory in my own personal life.

VICTORY

If there is anyone in this world that's a perfect example, this Evangelist is. I know

what it is to be greatly used of God. I know what it is to love the Lord with all of your heart, and at the same time be failing Him, and not really knowing and understanding why, especially considering, that you're trying so hard to do otherwise!

I also know what it is to be laughed at, ridiculed, with your name becoming a joke, and no one there to help. In fact, not only did most not try to help, but they even tried to hurt. So when I bring these things to you, I bring them from experience.

I'm sure the Believer understands, that the Christian doesn't have a choice as to how Satan attacks him. Those things are decided by God (Job, Chpts. 1-2). Satan is allowed a certain amount of latitude, but thank God it is the Lord Who decides the degree of that latitude and not Satan himself.

As a Believer, and again, being mightily used of God to win untold thousands to Christ, I understood the Cross as it regarded our initial experience of Salvation, but I had no knowledge whatsoever as to the part the Cross plays in our everyday living for God. I didn't know that the Cross was our source of victory. And regrettably, I didn't know a single Preacher in those days who did, and don't know many now who do. As I've stated, Satan has been very successful in pushing the Church away from its True Foundation. He's been very subtle in his approach, making us think it was great faith that we needed, when in reality, what we were being taught about faith wasn't even Scriptural. Of course, it should be obvious by now, I speak of the modern faith message.

And let the Reader understand, even as we've been attempting to explain in the last few pages, it really doesn't matter how much you're being used of God, if you don't know God's prescribed order of victory, you will suffer defeat. That means at this very moment, that most Preachers, even those who are pastoring the largest Churches, even those who are truly being used of God, for the most part, are not living victoriously themselves. Again, I state:

If the Believer, Preachers included, does not understand the Cross as it regards what Jesus there did on our behalf, and how it alone is the source of all things we receive from God, and how our Faith in the Cross gives latitude to the Holy Spirit to do His mighty work within our lives, that individual, irrespective as to whom he is, will live a life of spiritual failure. In other words, and as stated, sin will dominate him or her in some way.

And, considering that precious few presently know and understand the *"Word of the Cross,"* this means that the vast majority of the Church is presently living far beneath what Christ has actually afforded for them. And to be sure, living beneath our spiritual privileges in Christ, does not merely fall out to us having to drive a Neon instead of a Cadillac, but it rather falls out to Satan dominating us with sin in some manner.

Regarding my own personal life, living for the Lord is now the most pleasant, the most wonderful, the most glorious life that one could ever lead, live, or have. Now, I personally know what Jesus was talking about when He said, *"I am come that they might have life, and that they might have it more abundantly"* (Jn. 10:10). I now know what He meant when He said, *"Come unto Me, and I will give you rest"* (Mat. 11:28).

Having experienced both sides of this fence so to speak, and knowing the sorrow and heartache that an improper understanding of the Cross can mean in the life of a Christian, and as well, knowing exactly what it means as it regards all that Jesus did there, and our appropriating His great Life and Victory unto us, and doing so by our Faith in His Finished Work, which gives one the constant help of the Holy Spirit, can I be blamed for doing everything within my power to reveal to you what the Lord has revealed to me, and which is so obvious in His Word!

The Scripture plainly says, *"So then faith cometh by hearing, and hearing by the Word of God"* (Rom. 10:17).

The reason that the majority of the Church knows next to nothing about the Cross of Christ, is simply because, as stated, it has been little preached in these last several decades. And if a great truth is not preached, it's impossible for the people to have faith in that of which they do not know.

If this Commentary that you now hold in your hands could be read by the entirety of

the Church all over the world, and if it would be read with Faith, there isn't a single Christian who could not start down a road of total and complete victory. It remains only for them to know and believe.

That's also the reason that I plead with you the Reader, to get as many copies of these Commentaries into the hands of other Believers as possible, and especially Preachers. Please remember this:

The Cross is the answer to the ills of mankind, and in fact, the only answer. That's the reason that Paul said:

"But God forbid that I should glory, save in the Cross of our Lord Jesus Christ, by Whom the world is crucified unto me, and I unto the world" (Gal. 6:14).

DEAD WORKS

The phrase, *"Purge your conscience from dead works to serve the Living God,"* is exactly what I've been trying to say in these last few pages. This fourteenth Verse, as the Holy Spirit gives it through Paul, plainly tells us that it is only the *"Blood of Christ,"* which will *"purge the conscience,"* which refers to taking away the guilt of sin, and then help us to *"serve the Living God."* Clear and plain, this is exactly what I've been telling you in paragraph after paragraph.

Guilt comes about because of sin, of course, which is failure on our part. This puts the individual under condemnation. And regrettably, that's where most Christians presently are, and because they have tried to bring about Salvation and victory through *"dead works."*

Let the Reader understand, that Paul is speaking here to Believers. While this definitely applies to the unsaved, still, he is addressing himself to those who are already saved, but have drifted back into *"dead works,"* which is the problem that presently grips the modern Church.

What are *"dead works"*?

It is anything other than simple Faith in the Cross of Christ, i.e., *"the Blood of Christ."* And when I say *"anything,"* I mean *"anything."*

Do you the Reader understand, that it's possible for the Believer to turn something as holy as prayer into *"dead works"*? or church attendance? or fasting? or the giving of money to the Work of the Lord? or manifestations of the Spirit?

All of these things I've mentioned, plus many we haven't mentioned, are righteous and good within themselves, and will be a tremendous blessing to any Believer, and are things in which all true Christians will definitely engage themselves; however, if we try to use these things to overcome sin, we turn them into *"dead works,"* which God can never recognize.

Now I ask the Reader, please don't misunderstand what I say. I'm not telling the Believer not to pray. If anything, I'm telling you to pray more. But it must be done in the right way.

Satan wants to drag every Believer down. And when I mention dragging the Believer down, I'm speaking of sin. He does everything within his power to get the Believer to fail God in some way. And if he can do that, he will then try to place the Believer in bondage to that thing, with the sin nature once again running riot in the Believer's life. In other words, and as previously stated, the sin nature will not only then dwell within the Believer, which it does in all, but it will also rule and reign in the Believer, which is a tragedy, but which is the case with most modern Believers.

If that is in fact the case, and it is with most, the Christian is then miserable. In fact, it cannot be any other way.

If you are to notice, some particular Preacher or person in whom great confidence is placed will fail the Lord, and many will say, *"I don't understand!"* Or, *"How could they have done that?"* And please remember, for every one whose sin comes to light, there are scores of others in which the sin doesn't come to light.

Or else, Satan may not choose to attack some Believers with one of the vices, but rather with sins such as *"unforgiveness,"* or *"apathy,"* etc. With others it is *"fear"* or *"unbelief,"* etc. Irrespective, that most Christians don't pay much attention to the latter, they are still sins in the Eyes of God, and will cause tremendous trouble and difficulty in the heart and life of the Believer.

The Cross answers to all sin, irrespective as to what it might be, and in fact, is the only answer for sin.

PRIDE AND HUMILITY

The one sin that is the most prevalent of all, is the sin of pride. Of course, this is the opposite of humility. But it is probably the sin that keeps more Believers from trusting in the Cross than anything else.

It's difficult for Preachers to admit that what they're doing is wrong, and I speak of a particular belief system. All Preachers, and I include myself, are like Abraham, who when told by the Lord that he had to give up Ishmael, wasn't so very happy about doing so (Gen. 21:9-12).

Isaac and Ishmael symbolized the new and the old nature in the Believer. Sarah and Hagar typified the two covenants of grace and works, of liberty and bondage (Gal. Chpt. 4).

The birth of the new nature demands the expulsion of the old. It is impossible to improve the old nature. The Divine Way of Holiness is to *"put off the old man"* just as Abraham *"put off"* Ishmael. Man's way of Holiness is to improve the *"old man,"* that is, to improve Ishmael. The effort is both foolish and hopeless.

Of course, the casting out of Ishmael was *"very grievous in Abraham's sight,"* because it is always a struggle to cast out this element of bondage, that is, Salvation and victory by works. For legalism is dear to the heart. Ishmael was the fruit, and to Abraham the fair fruit of his own energy and planning.

But the Epistle to the Galatians states that Hagar, the bondwoman, represents the covenant of the Law, and that her son represents all who are of *"works of Law,"* that is, of all who seek Righteousness on the principle of works of Righteousness.

But the bondwoman cannot bring forth a free man! The Son Alone makes free, and He makes free indeed. Sarah, the freewoman, symbolizes the covenant of grace and liberty.

WORKS OF RIGHTEOUSNESS

Please allow me to say again that which I've just stated:

All who seek Righteousness on the principle of *"works of righteousness,"* will never achieve that for which they seek, but actually the very opposite. While *"works of righteousness"* are very desirable in the hearts and lives of all Believers, those things in no way make us Righteous. Righteousness, i.e., Holiness, i.e., Victory, etc., can only be achieved by simple Faith in what Christ did on the Cross on our behalf. Simple Faith expressed in Him, and more particularly, in what He did for us, will guarantee all that the Saint needs, and more besides. But if we try to attain these things, as stated, by *"works of righteousness,"* we will fail every time.

And in the failing, we will be very confused. In the doing of spiritual things, we automatically think that we are *"walking after the Spirit"* (Rom. 8:1); however, that is not the case at all.

"Walking after the Spirit," as Paul described, is simply ordering our behavior in the manner of the Spirit, which is the manner of the Cross. Then we will walk in perpetual victory, enjoying all that Jesus has purchased for us at great price.

Don't you the Reader understand and know, considering what Jesus did for us, and the tremendous price that He had to pay, that He certainly wants us to have all that He has done for us! Surely, you realize that!

And as well, don't you think it saddens His heart, when we fall so far short of all this He has done for us! To be sure, it's ours, but only by Faith, and only by Faith in what He did on the Tree nearly 2,000 years ago.

No! We're not trying to put Jesus back on a Cross. In fact, at this moment, He is seated by the right Hand of the Father (Heb. 1:3), and in fact, spiritually speaking, we are seated with Him (Eph. 2:6).

Actually, the Cross is something which happened in the distant past, and which will never have to be repeated, and which has benefits that continue unto this hour, and in fact, will never be discontinued. It's those benefits which we are to have, and that of which I speak!

TAKING UP THE CROSS DAILY

Jesus said, *"If any man will come after Me, let him deny himself, and take up his cross daily, and follow Me"* (Lk. 9:23).

Besides all the teaching of Paul, which incidentally the Holy Spirit gave to him, this one Verse quoted by Christ, proclaims the absolute necessity of the Cross as it involves

NOTES

our daily living before the Lord. Unfortunately, most Christians completely misunderstand this Verse. They don't deny it, simply because it is undeniable. Jesus said it, and besides that, it is so clear and plain as to its intent, that it cannot be explained away. But as stated, most completely misunderstand what He has said here.

The understanding of the Cross as it regards the modern Church, is that of suffering. In other words, they are thinking that Jesus is saying here that we must suffer, and do so, I suppose, on a daily basis. Of course, that's not a very inviting prospect!

Whenever some Christian has to go through a terrible problem, other Christians will look at the situation and their response generally is, *"That's the cross they have to bear, and I pray the Lord never asks me to do that!"*; or words to that effect.

While the Cross definitely did speak of suffering on the part of Christ, and suffering of such magnitude that it defies all description; however, where the Cross spoke death to Him, as it was intended to do, it speaks life to us. In fact, taking up the Cross daily is the most glorious, the most wonderful, the most life-giving, the most fulfilling thing that one could ever do. Such is the source of all blessing, all help, all Grace, all Peace, all riches, all things which are good, etc. Christians should be running to take up the Cross, should be endeavoring to find out exactly how it is to be done, should be clamoring to engage themselves in this process, but because of erroneous understanding, Christians want no part of the Cross. But, notice what Jesus said:

DENY OURSELVES

First of all, He tells us that if anyone is to follow Him, and that means *"anyone,"* they have to first of all *"deny themselves."* What does that mean?

Jesus is not speaking of asceticism. As you know, asceticism is the denial of anything that is good, all pleasure, etc. So, the first misunderstanding occurs with the first command of denying oneself.

Jesus is speaking instead of denying ourselves, as it regards denying our own strength and ability, our own power and personal effort, concerning living this Christian life. In other words, He is telling us that it's impossible for us to live as we ought to live, do as we ought to do, and be as we ought to be, within our own strength. We have to have the help of the Holy Spirit. That's what He is saying! And now He will tell us exactly how we can have that help.

"Taking up the Cross," merely refers to taking upon oneself all the benefits of what Jesus did there on our behalf, and understanding that the Cross is the source of all Salvation and Blessing. That's the reason that I said that bearing the Cross is the greatest, most wonderful life that one could ever begin to live. Jesus paid a terrible price in order that we might have all the things which God desires to give us. This means that we can have nothing from God, but that Jesus made it possible through the Cross. Considering the great price that He paid, it stands to reason, as we've already stated some pages back, that He would want us to have these great benefits. And to be sure, we can only have them by understanding what the Cross actually is, and what it actually means to us, even as Paul proclaims in Romans Chapter 6.

Again, we emphasize that the Cross made everything possible, and I speak of all the good things that God has given us through Christ Jesus. That's the reason that Paul keeps saying *"in Christ,"* or *"in Him,"* etc. So, instead of running from the Cross, every Believer ought to run toward the Cross, for it is there that the fountain of all blessings flow.

DAILY

Now notice that He said to us, that the Cross must be taken up *"daily!"* Why did He say that?

Man has such a problem with pride, even the most ardent Believers, that we have to have constant reminders that all the Blessings we possess, are not at all of our own making, but rather come totally and completely from Christ, and more particularly, what He did at the Cross on our behalf. At the slightest pretext, we are prone to look to ourselves, thinking that it's our ability, our talent, our mental gymnastics, or whatever, that have brought upon us these Blessings. Or else we'll begin to think that it's *"our Faith,"* *"our consecration,"* *"our dedication,"* etc.

NOTES

Satan doesn't really too much care as to what we do or think, just so long as we take our eyes off of Jesus Christ and Him Crucified.

So, the Lord desires that we begin each day with the understanding that our Faith must be freshened and renewed for that particular day, which means that we put yesterday in the past, and not concern ourselves about tomorrow. Remember, that He told us to do just that:

"But seek ye first the Kingdom of God, and His Righteousness; and all these things shall be added unto you.

"Take no thought for the morrow: for the morrow shall take thought for the things of itself. Sufficient unto the day is the evil thereof" (Mat. 6:33-34).

It's like the Manna of old. The Israelites were given instructions to gather each day only enough for that particular day, because there would be a fresh supply the next day. This taught them trust and dependence on the Lord.

It is the same identical thing as to what Jesus says here. We are to take up the Cross daily.

In fact, this is where many Christians have problems. Many will come into the knowledge of the Cross, just as I pray that you the Reader are now beginning to do, with great joy filling your heart, and because of this foundational Truth of all truths, and then you'll stub your toe, and wonder what went wrong?

What goes wrong is one of two things, or perhaps both:

1. We do not take the admonition of Christ seriously enough about taking up the Cross daily; consequently, we little by little begin to trust in ourselves, instead of this which Jesus has done for us.

2. All failure in any capacity is in some way a failure of Faith. And, I'm sure that the Reader can see how these two points are tied together as it regards Faith. Taking up the Cross daily refreshes our Faith, and above all, it secures it in the correct object, which is the Cross, and which is the most important part of our Faith.

SAVING OUR LIVES

To help us more fully understand this of which the Master is saying, He further adds:

"For whosoever will save his life shall lose it: but whosoever will lose his life for My sake, the same shall save it" (Lk. 9:24).

In this Passage, Christ is merely saying, that all life is found in Him, and Him Alone, and more particularly, in what He did at the Cross on our behalf.

When He spoke about us saving our life, and thereby losing it, He is merely saying that if we try to find life in any way other than through and by His Cross, that no matter what we find, it will conclude by us losing life.

If instead, we give our life over to Him totally and completely, actually understanding that we were baptized into His Death when He died, were buried with Him, and raised with Him in newness of life (Rom. 6:3-5), we will in turn save our life.

The idea of all of this is, that all life is found exclusively in Christ, and more particularly, what He did at the Cross, all on our behalf. Jesus has always been God, but that fact alone could not save us. It is the Cross which made possible the life of God being manifested in us. This is what Paul was talking about when he said:

"The Law of the Spirit of life in Christ Jesus, hath made me free from the law of sin and death" (Rom. 8:2).

Once again, I emphasize the fact, that Christ is not speaking about suffering as He speaks here of the Cross, except in an indirect way. He is actually saying, that out of His great suffering, we can have life and have it more abundantly (Jn. 10:10).

ACTIVITY OR POSITION?

If one is to notice, all of this which Jesus says is not arrived at by activity on our part, but rather by position. And what do we mean by that?

Every Believer has a *"position"* in Christ. It is a position of relationship, which the Holy Spirit through Paul referred to as *"sons."* Of course, *"sons"* is used for both men and women, as there is no gender in Christ, no male or female, all are one in Him.

We gain this position not at all by activity, and in fact, it cannot be gained by activity, but only by Faith.

Most Believers understand what I've just said, as it regards the initial Salvation experience, knowing they were saved by Faith and

not by works (Eph. 2:8-9). However, when it comes to our daily living, which is what we are here discussing, most Christians resort to activity, thinking the activity will bring about a victorious life. It doesn't! In fact, it has the very opposite effect!

What do I mean by activity?

We attempt to gain Righteousness or victory, whatever term we would like to use, by *"works of Righteousness."* In other words, by doing things for the Lord, we somehow think this will bring us out to a victorious life. It doesn't!

While every Christian as previously stated, should definitely be engaged in *"works of Righteousness,"* we should ever understand, that this should be a result of our experience with Christ, and never a *"cause."* In other words, no Christian can gain victory over the world, the flesh, and the Devil, by engaging in *"works of Righteousness,"* as important as those works may actually be. Our victory is gained totally and completely by simple Faith in Jesus Christ, and what He did for us at the Cross, and exhibiting that Faith even on a daily basis, which we've already discussed. When we do this, and do it in this fashion, the Holy Spirit then helps us, which is the secret of all overcoming strength (Rom. 8:1-2, 11).

Concerning the Holy Spirit, Paul said:

"But if the Spirit (Holy Spirit) *of Him* (God the Father) *that raised up Jesus from the dead dwell in you, He* (God the Father) *that raised up Christ from the dead shall also quicken your mortal bodies* (your present life) *by His Spirit that dwelleth in you"* (Rom. 8:11).

Most Christians read this Verse and think that Paul is speaking here of the coming Resurrection. No, he isn't!

He is speaking of our living and our lives now. He is speaking of us walking in victory before the Lord, being daily overcomers, and telling us that the Spirit will do this thing in us, and do this thing for us, *"quicken your mortal bodies,"* etc.

But the Spirit will not do this if we attempt to bring it about by *"works of Righteousness."* When we attempt to live our lives in this fashion, we have turned these works of Righteousness into efforts of the flesh. And, Paul also said, *"So then they that are in the flesh cannot please God"* (Rom. 8:8).

As Christians, we have the mistaken idea that our doing spiritual things means that it's after the Spirit. It might be; however, if we're doing these things in an attempt to be what we ought to be in Christ, then it ceases to be spiritual, and becomes *"works,"* and which we might quickly add, works in the wrong way, which constitute the flesh, which God can never bless.

We must go back to Romans 8:2, understanding that our victory over the *"law of sin and death,"* is brought about entirely by our Faith in what Jesus did for us at the Cross. Again, I state, it's called, *"The Law of the Spirit of Life in Christ Jesus."*

So, our victory is not found in *"activity,"* but rather in *"position,"* and by that, I mean our position in Christ, which refers to what He did for us at the Cross.

SONS OR SERVANTS?

Paul said, *"And because ye are sons, God hath sent forth the Spirit* (Holy Spirit) *of His Son* (made possible by what Jesus did at the Cross) *into your hearts, crying Abba, Father.*

"Wherefore thou art no more a servant, but a son; and if a son, then an heir of God through Christ" (Gal. 4:6-7).

First of all, we know and understand, that every single Believer in the world, and no matter how weak or strong that Believer might be, is a *"son in Christ."* This is made possible by what Christ did at the Cross and our Faith in Him.

However, the facts are, that even though every single Believer is a *"Son,"* with all of the inherent rights and privileges, still, most Believers are living instead like *"servants."* And as should be readily obvious, there is a vast difference in a *"servant"* and a *"Son."* And for emphasis, please allow me to add this:

We do not get to be a *"Son"* by earning the position, or as we have just discussed, by some sort of activity. We have this *"position"* simply by Faith in what Christ has already done for us. So, why is it, that most Christians are living like servants instead?

If the Believer doesn't know and understand the Cross of Christ, and that the Cross is the Source of all blessings, in other words, that the Cross made everything possible, then of necessity that particular Believer is going

to exist as a *"servant,"* even though he is a *"Son."* And because most of the modern Church has little or no understanding at all about the Cross of Christ, most are living like servants. Consequently, they keep trying to earn their place and position, which is impossible anyway, and beyond that, Christ has already done everything that is needed.

To live as a *"Son,"* which refers to having all the benefits and privileges for which Jesus paid such a price, we don't have to do one single thing except simply trust in what He did at the Cross for us. And as stated, we must do this on a daily basis! Now why is that so hard?

It's hard, even though it doesn't have to be, simply because of unbelief.

For nearly 50 years (or longer), the Church has been taught *"Salvation by faith"* and *"Victory by works."* In fact, that's the reason that Paul wrote his Epistle to the Galatians.

The Galatians had been saved under Paul, which means they had the benefit of the greatest teaching on the face of the Earth of that particular time. But after Paul founded these Churches, and then went on to other fields of labor, false teachers came in from Jerusalem, Christian Jews incidentally, who professed Christ, but as well taught that the Law must be kept, etc. This is what occasioned the Epistle to the Galatians, and one might quickly add, the most strident Epistle written by Paul. In other words, the Apostle was angry when he wrote the Epistle, simply because he knew if the Galatians believed this false doctrine, it would fall out to their ruin.

FALSE DOCTRINE

First of all, how in the world could anyone get people like the Galatians who had been brought in under such sound teaching, to forsake that teaching, and thereby believe error?

All false doctrine is instigated by demon spirits (II Cor. 11:13-15; Rev. 16:13-15). Consequently, this means there is power behind false doctrine. As well, all false doctrine, will always appeal to some base interest within the heart and life of the individual. I speak of self-will, greed, love of position, etc. However, the appeal is made in a spiritual way, which makes it seem right.

Also, as it regards abandoning Faith in the Cross, and instead placing it in other things, there is something in the heart of every single Believer, which likes to *"do religion."* It's an evil thing, but strangely enough, it makes us feel holy.

Consequently, many Preachers will say, *"Oh yes, I believe in the Cross, but I also believe that we have to do. . . ."* What they're actually saying is, that they don't believe in the Cross, but rather in their own *"works,"* whatever those works might be.

For instance, one Preacher speaking a few days ago with one of my associates said, *"Yes, I believe in the Cross, but I also believe that every person has to be accountable."*

He was actually saying that he didn't believe in the Cross, but rather believed in some regimen cooked up by men, in whom the party in question must engage, and if he does such to their satisfaction, whatever it might be, then he is being *"accountable,"* and thereby accepted!

ACCOUNTABILITY

What is accountability?

That's a good question, and would be answered in any number of ways by as many people. In fact, almost all Preachers would claim that accountability is doing what they tell you to do, which is seldom Scriptural, but some regimen, which we've already mentioned, devised by themselves. And as well, the regimen changes with each Preacher, etc. As I've said before, men love to make rules and make other men obey them, and religious men love to make rules most of all.

While such foolishness might be accountability in their eyes, it is definitely not accountability in God's eyes. And whom do we want to please? God or men?

Accountability is being accountable to the Word of God. Let me direct you to David.

The sweet singer of Israel in the one of the last Psalms he wrote, if not the last one, said: *"For I have kept the ways of the LORD, and have not wickedly departed from My God"* (II Sam. 22:22). In fact, this is the 18th Psalm.

In reading a Commentary the other day, the writer commenting on this particular Verse as given by David said, *"How could*

David have said such a thing, considering the great sin he committed with Bathsheba?"

In the first place, David wasn't merely giving us his thoughts in the Psalms, but was rather writing as the Holy Spirit moved upon him to do so. This means that every single thing he said was absolutely right, and in fact, perfect. So, what did he mean?

In the first place, there is no human being who has never sinned. However, it seems that some Christians conduct themselves as if some have sinned and some haven't. No! *"All have sinned and come short of the Glory of God,"* which means, that all are totally dependent upon the Grace of God, that is, if they are to be saved.

David wasn't claiming that he had never sinned or anything of that nature. He was saying, that whatever had happened in his heart and life, with some of the things being very wicked and very negative, he had not failed to take them to the Lord. In other words, he had not wickedly departed from God in seeking solutions elsewhere. He took his terrible failures to the Lord, which is the only place they can be taken. That is accountability!

When you the Believer hear Preachers talking about accountability, you should ask yourself the question as to what type of accountability it is of which they are speaking. Are they speaking about accountability to God, or to rules and regulations made up out of their own minds?

We as Believers must always remember the following:

In all things, we must go God's way. It may cost us something, but any other way will bring death. Dog and pony shows are for carnivals. Christians shouldn't engage in such.

THE COUNTERFEIT CHURCH

"I know the blasphemy of them which say they are Jews, and are not, but are the synagogue of Satan" (Rev. 2:9).

The conflict between the forces of good and evil in the world is evident on every hand. Every means and method are used by Satan, along with his angels and demon spirits, to frustrate and destroy God's redemptive program (Job 1:7; Lk. 4:6; Acts 26:18; II Cor. 4:3-4; Eph. 6:12; II Thess. 2:9).

Satan's most effective efforts have been made through imitation, half-truths, and counterfeits. Satan has counterfeits for all the good things of God. This means that there is in the world today a Counterfeit Church made up of people who are motivated by Satan. Sadly, this makes up the largest of that which we commonly refer to as *"Church."*

Directing the Counterfeit Church are the false prophets and ministers who perpetuate a counterfeit religious program, with its seductively beautiful allurements — its ritualistic appeal — its religion made up of works, without repentance or abandonment of sin, of which Jesus said, *"Many there be which go in thereat"* (Mat. 7:13; II Cor. 11:13-15).

It is a well-know fact that counterfeits and adulterations are difficult at times to detect, and many are deceived thereby. The Counterfeit Church propounds a kind of humanistic, rationalistic salvation, or at times even a Salvation of signs and wonders, which in effect, is a dependence on man himself for the attainment of the good life ... etc. Whatever satisfaction he is to enjoy he must achieve by his ability to control the physical world about him, or through his manipulation of social forces which can thus be made to serve him, or an effort to force God into some so-called mode by a supposed, superior faith, or by claiming God through signs and wonders, etc., all outside of the Cross.

Despite all the claims, despite the great religiosity, despite the claims of faith, the Counterfeit Church is made up of people who serve and worship Satan. They do it very religiously, but we must remember, that Satan is a religious being. So this means, that of all his efforts in the world to steal, kill, and to destroy, his greatest efforts are from inside the Church.

These people use the forms and terminology of the Church, and of course I speak of the True Church, but at the same time they *"deny the power thereof"* (II Tim. 3:5), which means to deny the power of the Cross, or else they claim great power, but once again it's power outside of the Cross.

To be very frank, much, if not most, of the institutionalized Church is controlled by this group.

In fact, we can see these two lines, the True Church and the Counterfeit Church, running

NOTES

through all the Ages. Actually, the two are so closely related, that it takes one thoroughly versed in the Word and led by the Spirit, to tell the difference at times. Jesus spoke of it as *"wheat and tares"* (Mat. 13:30).

CAIN AND ABEL

When Cain and Abel had their conflict, the Church came into full view for the first time. God's Redemptive Plan implored the shedding of animal blood, which was typical of the *"Lamb that was slain from the foundation of the world"* (Rev. 13:8). By offering Blood Sacrifices as God had commanded, early Believers, and we speak of all those from Abel on, at least until Jesus came, testified and gave evidence of their Faith in God's Redemptive provision. They expressed faith in Christ (Jehovah) and were thus saved. Favor with God has always hinged upon the sinner's acceptance of God's Son, the Lord Jesus Christ.

That's what the Text means regarding Jesus' Baptism, when God said of Him, *"Thou art My Beloved Son, in Whom I am well pleased"* (Mk. 1:11).

At the same time, this means that God is not pleased with any man, not one single solitary person, and that goes for all time. All were born in sin, and it is the sin that greatly displeases God. The only way the sin can be handled, is by one accepting Christ, and when this is done, because God is pleased with His Son, He is at the same time pleased with those who accept Him, but only then!

At the same time, that means that God has no satisfaction in our Church, Denominations, good works, or anything of that nature, at least if we are engaging in these things, and in whatever capacity, thinking they are helping us to be drawn closer to God, etc. While these things in their own way are very important, and even very important with God, we as Believers must always keep first things first. It is Jesus Who is everything, and more particularly, what He did at the Cross on our behalf. At the same time, that means that nothing must be added to Him or taken from Him. To say it in a clearer way, it's not Jesus and the Church, or Jesus and Water Baptism, or Jesus and speaking in other tongues, etc. It's Jesus and Jesus

Alone Who provides Salvation, and does so in every capacity.

When the Savior said, *"No man cometh unto the Father, but by Me,"* (Jn. 14:6), He clearly revealed that He had always been the channel through which sinners obtained favor with the Father. Here the language of eternity is clearly revealed.

ABEL AND THE CHURCH

Here Abel represents the Church one might say. He brought an acceptable Blood Sacrifice. Cain represents the Counterfeit Church. *"Cain offered no firstling Sacrifice, but the first thing that came to hand, something or other that he had just found, or had raised such as vegetables, etc."*

Cain offered merely an expression of his dependence and thanksgiving, and this indeed a self-wrought production of his own strength. Thereby he became the prototype of all who dared to approach the Sanctuary of God without the shedding of Blood (Heb. 9:22).

CAIN AND RELIGION

It is evident that Cain was religious — he had a religion of the flesh, a self-willed worship, a self-justified justification by works, and the insubordinate self-redemption which relies on itself and rejects substitution — this idealizing of one's own power, this theology of the first murderer, this *"faith"* of the serpent's seed (James 2:10); but on the other hand, note the *"way of Abel"* — the humble acknowledgement that sin demands death, the reliance of the guilty on the Sacrifice appointed by God Himself, the enduring of persecution for the sake of the eternal goal, the expectation of the triumphs of the Divine Redemption through the woman's seed.

The highest perfecting of *"Abel"* is Christ . . . but the highest development of Cain is Antichrist and in him the self-deification of the curse-laden sinner (I Thess. 2:4).

MEMBERSHIP IN THE BODY OF CHRIST

Membership in the Church, i.e., *"The Body of Christ,"* has always been restricted to those who have appropriated the *"Blood of Christ"* by faith; whereas membership in the *"Synagogue of Satan"* (Rev. 2:9; Ex. 15:6; Isa. 30:1; Acts 13:10; Rom. 1:18; 9:22, etc.); i.e., the

Counterfeit Church, has been reserved for those who reject Christ (Jesus) as Lord and Savior, which means to reject the Cross. Many attempt to accept Christ without the Cross, but such is not to be. Paul referred to such as *"another Jesus, another spirit, another gospel"* (II Cor. 11:4).

Man is automatically a member of the Counterfeit Church who defaults regarding Christ, even as did some of the Christian Jews of Paul's day, necessitating him writing the Epistle to the Hebrews, and of course many others as well down through the ages, and/or rejecting the redemptive provision made by God *"from the foundation of the world"* (Rev. 13:8; Acts 2:23, 25; I Pet. 1:18-20).

THE COUNTERFEIT CHURCH

The Counterfeit Church goes under quite a number of names in the Bible. It is referred to as the *"Synagogue of Satan"* (Rev. 2:9), *"an angel of light"* (II Cor. 11:14-15), *"those who have a form of godliness, but deny the power thereof"* (II Tim. 3:5), *"the fallen from Grace"* (Gal. 5:4), *"those who depart from the Faith"* (I Tim. 4:1), *"the rejecters of sound doctrine"* (II Tim. 4:3), *"the evil congregation"* (Num. 14:27-37), *"the assembly of the wicked"* (Ps. 22:16).

If it is to be noticed, all of these people claim to know God, with many even claiming to follow Jesus, with all claiming to be saved, whatever is the definition they put upon that word.

PARALLEL COURSES

The True Church and the Counterfeit Church have always held parallel courses, and at times the Counterfeit Church is found within the Church, but never of it. Representing these two institutions in history, even up to this present hour, are the witnesses — the true and the false.

For instance, in Jesus' day, the Church was no longer represented by the Temple leaders, the formal administrators of the religious affairs, the Priests, etc., even though they possessed the key to the Temple precincts, despite all of this, they were imposters and counterfeits. They were *of the Synagogue of Satan, which say they are Jews, and are not, but do lie"* (Rev. 3:9). Of course, as is perfectly known, they crucified the Lord of Glory.

It is evident that God has never been dependent upon any visible ecclesiastical organization for preserving the Redemptive Plan. At times down through history, the Church has been temporarily forced underground while the Counterfeit Church took over, but irrespective of that, God has always had His witnesses in every Age and dispensation.

CHARACTER AND REPUTATION

As someone has well said, *"Reputation is what people think you are, while character is what God knows you are."*

If one is to notice, the religious leadership of Jesus' day, had impeccable reputations over Israel, but yet, their characters were evil and wicked, so evil and wicked in fact, that they would crucify their own Messiah, the Lord of Glory. So how is such to be judged? To be frank, untold millions have died without God and gone to Hell, simply because they judged wrongly. In other words, they put their faith in a particular Church, a Preacher, a Denomination, etc. Or most of all, they listened to what so-called religious leaders told them, believed it, and died lost.

Knowing that Satan does his greatest work from inside the Church, and knowing that he is a master at making people believe something which isn't really true, Jesus gave us the example that must be followed as it regards True Apostles and false apostles. Listen to what He said:

"Beware of false Prophets (Apostles), *which come to you in sheep's clothing, but inwardly they are ravening wolves."* In other words, these people look the part and even sound the part, but inwardly they are anything but that which they claim.

The Master then said, *"Ye shall know them by their fruits"* (Mat. 7:15-16).

First of all, let's notice what He didn't say:

He didn't say that we would know because they were elected to some official office in some religious Denomination. He didn't say we would know them because they pastor a big Church, or draw large crowds. He didn't say that we would know them because they are talented or have great ability. He didn't say we would know them because they perform

signs and wonders. But rather, He said we would know them by their *"fruits."*

FRUIT

When Jesus used the word *"fruit,"* He was using it as a metaphor, which refers to an object or happening that explains something else.

In the New Testament, as in the Old, metaphorical uses predominate. This is particularly true in the Gospels, where human actions and words are viewed as fruit growing out of a person's essential being or character.

One example of this is found in the preaching of John the Baptist (summarized in Mat. Chpt. 3 and Lk. Chpt. 3). John called for repentance and insisted that any inner change produce fruit as evidence of its reality.

Matthew Chapter 7 and Luke Chapter 6, even as we are here addressing, report Jesus' explanation to His followers that true character is recognized in a person's acts. *"The good man brings forth things out of the good stored up in his heart, and the evil man brings evil things out of the evil stored up in his heart"* (Lk. 6:45; repeated almost identically in Mat. 12:35). A parallel passage, Mat. 12:33-37, expands on this theme.

It is in the Gospel of John, and the Epistles of Paul that the concept of fruitfulness shifts from that of the product of character to the product of God's work within us.

In John 15:1-16, Jesus takes the image of the vine, with God as Gardener, from Isaiah. We Believers are carefully tended by the Father, pruned, and cared for that we may *"bear much fruit."* Fruitfulness is possible, He said, if we remain in Him and His words remain in us.

The point Jesus makes is that fruitfulness is rooted in our personal relationship with Him, and our personal relationship with Him is maintained by living His words: *"If you obey My commands you will remain in My love"* (Jn. 15:10).

God has chosen us. It is His intention that we be fruitful. It is for this reason that He has given us the most intimate of relationships and Jesus' Own words to guide us, and it is our responsibility to walk in close fellowship with our Lord, which we can only do by expressing constant faith in the Cross of Christ and what Jesus did there, which has a constant bearing upon our everyday living (Rom. 6:3-5; 8:1-2, 11).

The Seventh Chapter of Romans which describes Paul's personal experience after coming to Christ, explains that human actions are energized from one of two sources. We can, on the one hand, be energized by our sinful nature; but when we are, we produce *"fruit for death."* Or we can be energized by the Holy Spirit. When we are controlled by the Spirit, we bear *"fruit to God."*

But we must ever remember, that the Holy Spirit works within our hearts and lives on one premise, and one premise alone! He demands that we exhibit Faith in the Cross of Christ at all times, understanding that all blessings, all good things, all power, strength, grace, glory, and peace, come exclusively from God by this source. When we exhibit faith in this manner, the Holy Spirit then works on our behalf, producing the fruit within our lives which only He can produce (Rom. 8:1-2; Gal. 5:22-23).

In fact, we can only be controlled by the Holy Spirit in this fashion. If we try to get close to God, or maintain our walk with God, through any other manner, and no matter how serious or dedicated we might be, we will fail, simply because the Holy Spirit will not help us in those endeavors. Remember what we said sometime back:

God is pleased only with His Son, the Lord Jesus Christ, and of course what Christ did, which refers to the Cross. If we are in Him, which every Christian is, maintaining our Faith and confidence in His Finished Work, then the Holy Spirit will grandly help us. If we step outside of the Finished Work of Christ, although continuing to be Christians, we will then find ourselves *"walking after the flesh,"* which will bring forth sin and death, because we're depending on ourselves. And because we are in fact depending on ourselves, the Holy Spirit at that stage will not help us. Always remember the following:

Every Christian must understand, that everything comes to Him through the Cross of Christ.

Understanding that, every Christian must maintain his Faith in the great Sacrifice of Christ at all times, never allowing his Faith to be removed to any other object, no matter how good that other object may seem to be.

NOTES

When we do this, and continue to do this, with Faith as our essential ingredient, and the Cross of Christ as its ultimate destination, the Holy Spirit, Whom we must have within our lives in order to live what we ought to live and be what we ought to be, then will work mightily upon our behalf, but if we step outside of these parameters, which is where most of the Church is presently, the Holy Spirit, although remaining, simply will not help, because if He did in such a circumstance, He would be breaking the Law, and that He will not do (Rom. 8:2).

THE FRUIT OF THE SIN NATURE AND THE FRUIT OF THE SPIRIT

Galatians 5:16-26 defines the fruit of sinful human nature and the fruit of the Spirit energized nature. It is striking that the fruit God seeks, as defined here, is exactly the fruit sought in His Old Testament Believers! Bad fruit, the acts of the sinful nature, are *"sexual immorality, impurity and debauchery; idolatry and witchcraft; hatred, discord, jealousy, fits of rage, selfish ambition, dissensions, factions, and envy; drunkenness, orgies, and the like"* (Gal. 5:19-21).

As we've already said, let the Reader understand, that Paul is speaking here of Christians. In other words, if the Christian doesn't follow the Word of God as he ought to as it regards the Cross of Christ, the works of the flesh will begin to manifest themselves in his heart and life, just as they did before he came to Christ. In fact, it cannot be any other way. And due to the fact that this is so very serious, please allow us to state the case again:

The only way that the *"Fruit of the Spirit"* can be born out in the heart and life of the Believer, which is *"love, joy, peace, patience, kindness, goodness, faithfulness, gentleness, and self-control"* (Gal. 5:22-23), is that the Believer understand at all times, that these things come exclusively by the Spirit. In other words, there is no way that you as a human being, and no matter how consecrated to God you might be, can bring about these things within your own heart and life by your own machinations. It simply cannot be done.

And how does the Holy Spirit do these things in our lives?

He only requires one thing of us, and that is that we exhibit Faith in the Cross of Christ at all times. This is explained to us in Romans 6:3-5, where we are informed as to what happened to us when we got saved. We were literally baptized into the death of Christ, referring to His Crucifixion; we were buried with Him, meaning that the whole sordid mess of our past life before Christ was good for nothing, except to be buried, and then we rose with Him in newness of life.

Now this is what happened to us in the Mind of God, when we exhibited Faith in Christ and His Finished Work, when we were initially saved.

We will then continue to live this resurrection life, which is the most glorious life in the world, providing that we continue to understand that *"we have been planted together in the likeness of His death"* (Rom. 6:5). Let's say it again:

We cannot have and walk in *"the likeness of His Resurrection,"* which means to enjoy all the victory that He there purchased for us, unless at all times, we understand and realize, that all of this has come to pass because *"we have been planted together in the likeness of His death."* We are Resurrection people with all its attendant blessings, only if we continue to understand that we are as well *"Crucifixion people."* The Resurrection must never be placed ahead of the Cross, and the Cross must never be forgotten in the least, as we survey the wondrous blessings which He affords us at all times. We must remember, that all of these wonderful things didn't come about because of the Resurrection, but because of the Crucifixion, and our being in that Crucifixion by Faith. That's why Paul strongly said, *"But God forbid that I should glory* (boast) *save in the Cross of our Lord Jesus Christ, by Whom the world is crucified unto me, and I unto the world"* (Gal. 6:14).

Understanding our death, burial, and resurrection in Him, and always in Him, we must at all times *"reckon ourselves to be dead indeed unto sin* (dead unto the sin nature), *but alive unto God through Jesus Christ our Lord"* (Rom. 6:11).

Understanding this, and continuing our Faith in this direction, and I speak of the direction of the Cross, the sin nature will never dominate us any more, and the fruit of the Spirit will always be developed within our hearts and lives.

The fruit of that is, *"sin shall not have dominion over you: for you are not under the law* (the law has no more claim on you), *but under Grace* (due to what Jesus did for you at the Cross, which is the source of all Grace)*"* (Rom. 6:14).

Once our Faith is properly placed in the Cross, and it remains in the Cross, understanding that the Cross is the Source of all blessings, then it is guaranteed that proper fruit will result. Otherwise, it will be *"works of the flesh."*

THE TRUE CHURCH

To shorten these theological statements down to simple terms where we all can understand it, it simply means that the Cross of Christ is the dividing line between the True Church and the Apostate Church, i.e., *"Counterfeit Church."*

In fact, it has always been that way, but is going to be and is more prominent now than ever. As one views the Cross, whether positive or negative, accordingly will one be a part of whichever Church.

THE LAMB OF GOD

When John introduced our Lord as *"The Lamb of God, which taketh away the sin of the world"* (Jn. 1:29), he introduced *"The Lamb"* Who had been *"taking away the sin of the world"* from the beginning of time. In certain historical periods *"the faith which was once delivered unto the Saints"* (Jude vs. 3) has been hard pressed, but God has never been without a witness. At times *"The Faith"* has made tactical retreats and has taken its abode with small groups and sects, but it has always revived and flowered into revival movements in many localities.

In the religious world, the ideal has at times been lost as far as the visible outline was concerned, even as the Church more and more apostatized, but it continued to *"glow"* in the hearts and minds of the common people. So it has been with *"The Faith"* throughout the history of Redemption.

The entire ecclesiastical hierarchy of Pharisee-Sadducee Judaism of our Savior's day stands condemned before God. Professing themselves to be servants of God, they were instead the disciples of death. Instead of accepting Christ (Jehovah), now in the Person of Jesus, they rejected Him — the *"Chief Corner Stone"* (Acts 4:10-12). Instead of being truly in *"the Church,"* which is achieved by making Christ one's Lord and Savior, these counterfeits served the *"Synagogue of Satan"* (Rev. 2:9).

A further inquiry might be made relative to the identity of these apostles of evil. Did Christ call them by name? The Gospels bear witness to the fact that the servants of Satan were none other than the Scribes (Pastors), the Pharisees, the Sadducees, the Chief Priests, the Elders, and the Rulers who were in charge of the religious program of Israel. In other parts of the Scriptures they are referred to as the *"congregation of evildoers"* (Ps. 26:5), *"congregation of hypocrites,"* *"assembly of the wicked"* (Ps. 22:16). Jesus said of them, *"Ye are of your father the Devil"* (Jn. 8:44; Jer. 15:17; Ezek. 2:3; 5:6, etc.).

Their interest in the Work of God was limited to the extent to which they could use it as a cloak behind which to hide their wicked and corrupt activities. Sin, to them, became a lucrative business. The poor were oppressed and driven into slavery; dishonest trading and exacting bribes were the order of the day; public and private virtue were almost unknown; the courts of justice were notorious; immoralities were practiced without shame or compunction. The appetites of the greedy Temple authorities were such that they made the House of God *"a den of thieves"* (Mat. 21:13; Chpt. 23).

This is why Jesus said of Israel, *"But when He saw the multitudes, He was moved with compassion on them, because they fainted, and were scattered abroad, as sheep having no shepherd"* (Mat. 9:36).

Through faith the *"congregation of the Saints"* (Ps. 89:5), i.e., *"The Church,"* stood up under every form of persecution and abuse at the hands of these *"children of the Devil"* (I Jn. 3:10), i.e., the Counterfeit Church. The faithful Believers were subjected to every disgrace and indignity known to man (Heb. 11:37-40). These accusations were further established by the witness of Christ.

CONDEMNATION

In addressing the Scribes and Pharisees in Jerusalem, Jesus calls to mind the fact that Isaiah had pronounced condemnation upon the religious leaders of his day. Our Lord then applies this condemnation to their descendants: *"this people draweth nigh unto Me with their mouth, and honoureth Me with their lips; but their heart is far from Me. But in vain do they worship Me, teaching for doctrines the commandments of men"* (Mat. 15:8-9).

Isaiah referred to this group as an *"abominable branch"* (Isa. 14:19); *"rebellious children"* (Isa. 30:1, 9). Teaching humanistic theories instead of Divine Truth has always been characteristic of the Counterfeit Church.

One need only look at much of the modern Church to perceive the counterpart of that which Isaiah spoke. The modern Church proclaims humanistic psychology as the answer to the ills of man, which is a vote of no confidence as it regards the Cross of Christ. It can be concluded as nothing else other than *"humanistic theories instead of Divine Truth."*

THE SPIRITUALLY BLIND

Jesus advised the people to ignore the Temple authorities because they did not possess spiritual faculties with which to discern spiritual issues, that's why they hated Him so readily.

Jesus said: *"Let them alone: they be blind leaders of the blind. And if the blind lead the blind, both shall fall into the ditch"* (Mat. 15:14).

Certainly no blind man wants another blind man to lead him across the street, or anywhere for that matter, nor does a sinner care to have another sinner lead him into the way of Salvation, which of course is impossible.

And let me quickly say, any Preacher presently, who attempts to lead people to Christ other than by the Way of the Cross, or attempts to lead them into victory after they are saved, other than by the Way of the Cross, is none other than spiritually blind. He cannot lead anyone anywhere, because he doesn't know the way. He doesn't know the way, because he hasn't found the way himself. So how can he lead others?

HYPOCRITES

On another occasion, the Pharisees and Sadducees came to tempt Jesus with their foolish questions, whereupon Jesus called them *"hypocrites"* (Mat. 16:1-3). This is also a fitting appellative for members of the Counterfeit Church presently.

The *"hypocrisy"* of which Jesus mentioned here, was not so much the putting on of one face while being another, even though it did include that, but rather spoke of these so-called religious leaders leading people in a wrong direction. In other words, they claimed to know the Way of God, while all the time pointing in another direction.

How similar that is with the modern Church. In fact, all Churches claim to know the way; however, it should be obvious, that with so many pointing in different directions, that all of these directions cannot be correct. In fact, there is only one right direction, and that is *"Jesus Christ and Him Crucified"* (I Cor. 2:2). That's why Paul said, *"we preach Christ crucified"* (I Cor. 1:23).

That means *"Christ Crucified"* for all people, all situations, and all circumstances. What is your Pastor preaching?

WARNINGS

Jesus warned the people then about the religious leaders: *"Take heed and beware of the leaven of the Pharisees and of the Sadducees"* (Mat. 16:6). By leaven, Christ meant the poisonous humanistic commandments of men as against the Doctrines of God. As leaven has a tendency to permeate the dough, so this poison was in danger of spreading completely among the people.

Any error believed by any Christian, if not ultimately removed, will ultimately take over the whole, until that's all that is left. And that's the shape of most of the modern Church.

Jesus warned the Israelites of his day against listening to these religious leaders, and I am doing the same here.

Why are you associated with your present Church?

If it's for any other reason than the Word being preached without fear or compromise behind the pulpit, accompanied by a moving and operation of the Holy Spirit, then you are attending for all the wrong reasons.

There aren't many good Churches, which means there aren't many Godly Preachers. There are a few, but not many! And where you go to Church is of extreme importance. If you're hearing wrong doctrine, it will ultimately take effect within your heart and life, bringing forth negative results.

The great problem with this is, false doctrine carries with it deception, which carries with it a spirit of darkness, which is somewhat like placing a person in prison, mentally and spiritually. Only the Power of God can get them out of such a situation, hence the reason that many never make it out of that darkness, even as they didn't in Jesus' day.

THE AUTHORITY OF CHRIST

As evidence of corruption and perversion within the ranks of the Priests and Elders of Jesus' day, attention is called to the way in which they challenged the authority of Christ (Mat. 21:23). The fact that they did not recognize the Savior as the Son of God evidences their ignorance of the Father (Jn. 8:19).

At the present time, it's not so much a direct challenging of the authority of Christ, as it is the authority of the Cross as the means by which all things come to us from God. This is the great problem presently!

The modern Church has drifted so far away from the Cross, that it anymore little knows its place and position in Christ. For one can only know that place and position according to the Cross of Christ, and our Faith in that Finished Work (Rom. 6:3-5, 11, 14).

DEMON POWERS

The demon-possessed nature of these leaders in Israel is further evidenced in the effort of the Chief Priests and Pharisees to lay hands on the Savior in order to harm Him.

Let the Reader understand, that all false doctrine is instigated by demon spirits. That's the reason that deception has such a power behind it, even as we've already briefly mentioned.

To whatever degree false doctrine permeates the heart and life of a Believer, to that degree will demon spirits have some control. No, that doesn't mean the Believer is demon-possessed, for a Believer cannot be demon-possessed; however, they can definitely be demon controlled to a certain extent.

All of this comes about in works of the flesh, even as we've already discussed (Gal. 5:19-21).

In facing this problem, and incidentally a problem which definitely exists, and exists abundantly so, many Preachers have advocated that hands be laid on individuals with these particular demons *"cast out"* or *"rebuked,"* etc. As stated, while demon spirits are definitely involved in the hearts and lives of many Believers, the laying on of hands under those circumstances is not the answer.

Even if the spirit is rebuked, due to the fact that the person does not know the Truth, the spirit will be back very shortly with the roller coaster ride spiritually speaking, continuing.

The answer is telling the individual the reason for their problem, which allows evil spirits to operate within their lives, which is faith and dependence in something else other than the Cross of Christ. Whenever the Believer begins to trust and believe in what Jesus did for him at the Cross, continuing to believe that on a daily basis, even which Jesus demanded (Lk. 9:23-24), the Holy Spirit will then begin to work mightily within the Believer's life, and victory will be his. That's what Paul was talking about when he mentioned, *"walking after the Spirit."*

To be sure, if one *"walks after the flesh,"* one is going to suffer the penalty of *"the law of sin and death,"* which always falls out to works of the flesh (Rom. 8:1-2).

SELF-RIGHTEOUSNESS

In order to further evaluate the status of the Temple authorities, the following facts must be considered:

Jesus called the Scribes and Pharisees a stumbling block to the Kingdom of Heaven; they refused to go in, and they prevented others from doing so as well (Mat. 23:13).

The Scribes and Pharisees devoured widows' houses (literally robbed the widow of her home and living) and then hid behind long sanctimonious prayers in public places (Mat. 23:14).

Their modern counterparts do the same identical thing under the guise of *"faith,"* in other words, if you'll give so much money, all of your bills will be paid at the end of six months, or some such foolishness. Others

claim, that *"money"* is that which brings glory to God. There seems to be enough greed in all of us to fall for this bait, and bait it is!

The only ones who get rich in this modern scheme are the Preachers, and their gains are obtained in the most perfidious way possible. In other words, they do the same identical thing as the Pharisees of old, by robbing the poor under the guise of faith.

While God definitely does bless people and bless abundantly, and while all Believers should give generously to Him, and while the poorest should most definitely give as well, for that is the secret of their Blessing, still it must always be done with a right motive. To give only to get, is unscriptural, and will not bring any rewards of any nature, but will only seek to separate the person from their money, and as well push them further away from God, by causing them to place their hopes in money instead of the Lord. Paul said that we must give to *"prove the sincerity of our love"* (II Cor. 8:8).

The Pharisees took great pains to convert the heathen to their way of life and then *"to make him twofold more the child of Hell"* than they already were (Mat. 23:15). And this is exactly what happens to most people who join modern Churches.

The Pharisees were referred to by Christ as fools who pervert God's Word by their false teachings regarding the Temple and the Altar, and many other such things (Mat. 23:16-18).

The Pharisees, intoxicated with their own self-righteousness, boasted: *"If we had been in the days of our fathers, we would not have been partakers with them in the blood of the Prophets"* (Mat. 23:30). But Jesus counters their claim: *"Wherefore ye be witnesses unto yourselves, that ye are the children of them which killed the Prophets"* (Mat. 23:31). By their acts, their deeds, and attitudes, they witnessed to their true nature. Jesus then called them *"serpents and vipers,"* the key symbol of sin, and asked the question that cannot be answered: *"How can ye escape the damnation of Hell?"* (Mat. 23:33).

Jesus next described prophetically the persecution and murder to which they would give themselves in their conflict with God's righteous forces (Mat. 23:34). In fact, the

Master gave the Scribes and Pharisees a preview of their future wickedness: *"Behold, I send unto you Prophets, and wise men, and Scribes: and some of them ye have killed and crucified: and some of them ye shall scourge in your Synagogues, and persecute them from city to city: that upon you may come all the righteous blood shed upon the Earth, from the blood of righteous Abel unto the blood of Zacharias, son of Barachias, whom ye slew between the Temple and the Altar"* (Mat. 23:34-35).

Paul gives a vivid description of the horrible treatment received by the Saints at the hand of the Counterfeit Church apostles: they were stoned, they were sawn asunder, were tempted, were slain with the sword: they wandered about in sheep skins and goat skins; being destitute, afflicted, tormented; (of whom the world was not worthy:) (Acts 4:1-3; 15:18, 21; Heb. 11:37-38).

Finally the Chief Priests, Scribes, and Elders mocked him as He died on the Cross (Mat. 27:42).

In a final consideration of the religious leaders of Israel, it can be pointed out that their rejection of Christ evidenced the fact that they did not know the Father and that the love of God was not in their hearts (Jn. 8:19).

While the leaders made much over their faith in Moses, still our Lord told them that they stood condemned in the presence of Moses (Jn. 5:45-46). If they had been the true spiritual descendants of Moses, they would have accepted Christ as the Messiah. He said to them: *"For had ye believed Moses, ye would have believed Me for he wrote of Me"* (Jn. 5:46).

These Religious Leaders continued to boast that they had *"one Father, even God"* (Jn. 8:41), but the Master said to them: *"If God were your Father, ye would love Me; for I proceeded forth and came from God, neither came I of Myself, but He sent Me. Why do you not understand My speech? Even because you cannot hear My Word"* (Jn. 8:42-43; Mat. 11:27).

MODERN COUNTERPARTS

In a final address, Jesus drove His indictment home. Says He: *"You are of your father the Devil, and the lust of your father you*

NOTES

will do. He was a murderer from the beginning, and abode not in the truth, because there is no truth in him" (Jn. 8:44).

As well, it must be remembered, that these people were very, very religious. They could quote much of the Law by memory. In fact, they were hair splitters on the letter of the Law. Yet they stood slamming Heaven's doors in sinner's faces.

Jesus said, *"Ye shut up the Kingdom of Heaven against men. Woe unto you. . . ."*

While their adornings were likewise attractive as *"shining brightly"* even while their hearts were full of dead men's bones — gossiping, killing with a dagger-tongue dipped in slime of slander, and writing the death warrant. Jesus called it *"hypocrisy and iniquity"* even though practiced by the chief religionist of that day.

This certainly is a very serious indictment of those who were clad in ecclesiastical garb, and it is well to note that Jesus does not once recognize or identify the fleshly descendants of Abraham as the *"Israel of God"* (Rom. 2:28-29; Gal. 6:16).

Their modern counterparts flourish pretty much in the same manner. While most people do not presently know this of which I say, even as the people of Jesus' day did not know or realize how wicked their religious leaders were as well. As stated, the religious leaders of Jesus' day, had impeccable reputations over Israel, but their characters were as evil as evil could be. Please allow me to state this fact again: *"Reputation is what people think you are, while character is what God knows you are."*

The great wickedness of this hour, and I speak of the present day in which we live, is not the dope-dealers and liquor distillers, or even the gambling interests, as wicked and vile as those things might be. The greatest wickedness of all is *"spiritual wickedness in high places"* (Eph. 6:12). I speak of many of the religious leaders of this nation, and around the world, who are leading people astray by their man-devised rules which have no Scriptural foundation. In other words, whichever way it is looked at, and by whatever degree it is judged, the conclusion is an abrogation of the Cross of Christ. And let me hurriedly state the following as well:

The same murderous spirit that was in the Pharisees and Sadducees of old is in their modern counterparts. The only difference is, those of Jesus' day, had more latitude under the Law to do physical harm than at the present. Still, those of the present day, even though not allowed to murder one physically, still do all within their power to steal, kill, and destroy, with gossip, innuendo, slander, anything to destroy the reputation of those whom they do not like.

Even though most of the laity would not be aware of these things, even as they were not aware in the time of Christ, still the fact remains that this situation is grossly prevalent.

These religious leaders, and I speak of the leaders of most modern Denominations, have little regard for souls, little regard for lives being changed, their one interest being place, position, and money. I realize that's strong, but it's not nearly as strong as that which Jesus said, as he referred to these as *"snakes, vipers, hypocrites,"* etc. (Mat. Chpt. 23). Paul referred to them as well as *"dogs"* (Phil. 3:2).

It's also a known fact, if the so-called religious leaders advocate a certain way, most of the people will follow, no matter how wrong it might be. Again, it was the same in Jesus' day. Despite the miracles and healings which He performed, and which make any modern ministry seem to be small by comparison, that particular rule held. And why did it hold?

In Jesus' day, if the people followed Him, they were threatened with excommunication from the Synagogue (Jn. 9:22), which threatened every part of their livelihood. In other words, most put in this position, lost their employment, plus they were evicted from the places where they were living, and forsaken by their family. Their modern counterparts do the same!

If modern Preachers, at least in most Pentecostal Denominations, violate the man-devised rules of the Denomination, they will not only be drummed out of that particular Denomination, but every effort will be made to hinder and hurt the person even though they are no longer associated with that group. The law of the land prevents physical harm, but were that not the case, and to be sure,

many modern religious leaders, would actually murder those with whom they do not agree. Let me take it a step farther:

If the law of the land allowed, and that's what makes the separation of Church and State a God-given blessing, many modern religious leaders, would shut the doors of every single Church in the nation with whom they did not agree, stop every single Preachers from preaching over Television or Radio, or anywhere for that matter, with whom they did not agree or approve. Let me say it again:

The spirit of false doctrine incorporates itself in the spirit of the person, which falls out to the spirit of murder. And let the Reader understand, that the Commandment which says *"Thou shalt not kill,"* carries with it the meaning not only of the taking of one's life, but the destroying of one's reputation by gossip and slander as well! This is always a characteristic of the Counterfeit Church.

TRUE DOCTRINE AND FALSE DOCTRINE

While it's perfectly proper for the Preacher of the Gospel, and even demanded of him, that he point out false doctrine, at the same time, he is not to denigrate the person preaching the false doctrine. Some people confuse the two. They think opposition to false doctrine is opposition to the person. It isn't!

Every true Preacher of the Word is commanded by the Lord to be a *"watchman"* (Isa. 21:11; Ezek. 3:17). This means that false doctrine must be pointed out; however, there must not be any animosity against the one who holds to false doctrine. In fact, every effort must be made to get these individuals, whomever they might be, back to that which is right. And speaking disparagingly of their person will not render too very much help regarding that.

However, as well, if it is to be noticed, those who are engaged in false doctrine, will very seldom attack the Message, but instead, the Messenger. They will do everything they can to denigrate him, his way, his person, and anything about him that they can.

In fact, that's one of the ways a person can tell what is being preached and who is preaching it. If they attack his Message, what they're saying may be right or it may not be right. But if they attack the Messenger, much of the time, if not all of the time, what they're saying is wrong, or else their spirit is wrong.

FALSE RELIGIONS AND THE COUNTERFEIT CHURCH

It is sometimes assumed that heathen religions are false, and because they are false, there is no factual foundation for their existence; however, this interpretation must be viewed with caution.

The Biblical record clearly shows that good and evil, both, are present in the world, and evidenced in every area of life, including religion. In fact, heathen religions are satanic realities, which must not be minimized. Satan's counterfeit religious system includes the use of all non-Biblical religions, which are designed to *"steal, kill, and destroy"* (Jn. 10:10). Actually, no evangelistic program is more pronounced and evident than the one which is and has been promoted by the *"prince of this world"* (Jn. 14:30).

And of course, the most dangerous of all is Satan as *"an angel of light,"* designed to *"deceive the very elect"* (Mat. 24:24; II Cor. 11:13-15). These, as stated, *"preach another Jesus, another spirit, and another gospel"* (II Cor. 11:4).

This is all done through *"principalities, powers, rulers of the darkness of this world, and spiritual wickedness in high places"* (Eph. 6:12).

Satan has control of a mighty region, even after his fall, and this suggests that the Earth and its surrounding atmosphere, was his place of dominion before the Fall. This finds its definite confirmation in the Word of God. Our Lord Himself recognized Satan as the *"prince of the world"* (Jn. 12:31; 14:30; 16:11). Paul terms him the *"prince over the power of the air"* (Eph. 2:2).

When at the time of the temptation Satan offered to the Lord all the kingdoms of the Earth, and said, *"All this power will I give Thee and the glory of them: for that is delivered unto me; and to whomsoever I will I give it"* (Lk. 4:6), the Lord acknowledged this authority. Thus, the Lord did in no way minimize or discount the power of Satan and evil spirits. The governmental position of Satan over his world-region has continued through the ages. John testifies that *"the whole world*

lieth in wickedness" (I Jn. 5:19). And Paul speaks often of the authority of Satan (Acts 26:18; Eph. 2:2; Col. 1:13).

From the time Satan renounced his allegiance to the Most High a mighty breach runs through the cosmos, and an organized, opposing kingdom of evil, i.e., the Counterfeit Church, confronts the universal Kingdom of God (Mat. 12:26). Satan as a ruler has in turn princes and authorities under himself (Dan. 10:13-20; Eph. 6:12), and the opposition between him and the Kingdom of God is henceforth the theme and the essential subject of the universal superhistory outlined in the Holy Scripture.

THE VICTORY IS IN THE CROSS

Christ, instead of denying the existence of evil spirits, recognized them, and by His power overcame them. However, when we mention Him overcoming Satan, his fallen angels, and spirits of darkness, that must be qualified.

Jesus Christ is the Creator of all things; however, even though He did create Lucifer in the beginning, along with all Angels, He definitely did not create them in their fallen condition. They were created beautiful, righteous, holy, and true (Isa. Chpt. 14; Ezek. Chpt. 28).

At some time in eternity past, Lucifer, possibly the most beautiful and powerful of all of God's Angels, led a revolution against God, which drew away one-third of the Angels to his side. We do know that this revolution must have been powerful for that many Angels to defect (Rev. 12:4). As well, we also know that demon spirits were not created by God in this fashion. They became this way at a point in time.

Some Bible Scholars believe that they were a form of creation on this Earth before the Fall, and when Lucifer ruled this Earth under God in Righteousness and Holiness (Isa. 14:12-15). Throwing in their lot with Lucifer, now known as Satan, they became spirits without bodies, actually seeking a body to inhabit, and all of them evil, hence *"evil spirits."*

Satan then dragged man down in the Garden of Eden, no doubt extremely jealous that God had given Adam dominion over the Earth and in fact, it seems all of God's creation, at least that part of the heavens which affected this Earth, and possibly even the entirety of the creation (Ps. 8).

Consequently, the Lord Jesus Christ being the Creator (Jn. 1:1), and Satan plus all of his fallen Angels being but mere creatures, it should be obvious as to Who is the Head over all things. So, when we speak of Jesus overcoming Satan, we are not speaking of supremacy. Christ already has that, and in fact, has always had that and it is a supremacy which will never change.

That of which we speak is the dominion that Satan had over humanity as a result of the Fall. Adam was given this dominion, and then forfeited it to Satan by disobedience to God.

As we've already stated in previous Commentary, God works entirely from the position of Laws — Laws incidentally which He has instituted Himself. Satan as well works within those Laws, and so does all of humanity. Of course, Satan broke those Laws when he led a revolution against God, and will ultimately be condemned to the Lake of Fire forever because of this disobedience. As well, much of humanity has broken the Laws of God, and will have the same end.

DOMINION

So, for the dominion that man forfeited to be regained, God would have to do it lawfully, and even at great price. The price was the Cross.

But let it be understood, that the ransom paid by Christ was not to Satan at all, but altogether to God. Man had sinned against God, had committed a gross crime against God, and it was to God that the debt was owed. That's the debt that Jesus paid, the debt owed by man by pouring out His Own Life's Blood.

When He did this, He atoned for all sin, which means the debt was paid totally and completely. With all sin being atoned, past, present, and future, at least for those who will believe (Jn. 3:16), Satan lost his legal hold upon humanity; in other words, his dominion over man was broken.

The Scripture plainly says regarding man and Satan, respecting what Jesus did, that He *"blotted out the handwriting of ordinances that was against us* (satisfied the demands

of the Law), *which was contrary to us, and took it out of the way, nailing it to His Cross;*

"And having spoiled principalities and powers, He made a show of them openly, triumphing over them in it" (Col. 2:14-15).

This is the manner in which Jesus conquered Satan. By dying on the Cross and paying the debt that man owed to God, Satan was then deprived of his legal right to hold man in captivity. So, this defeated not only Satan, but also every power and principality, all the rulers of the darkness of this world, and all spiritual wickedness in high places. It was all done at the Cross, and in His Resurrection.

ISRAEL

But due to what Israel did in rejecting Christ when He came, the world has been submitted to nearly 2,000 more years of evil and wickedness, which Jesus referred to as *"the times of the Gentiles."* He said:

"And they shall fall by the edge of the sword, and shall be led away captive into all nations (speaking of the Jews, which they were)*: and Jerusalem shall be trodden down of the Gentiles, until the times of the Gentiles be fulfilled"* (Lk. 21:24).

As stated, this time has now lasted for nearly 2,000 years. The Jews while in control of Jerusalem presently, still do not control the Temple Mount. They will get control of that for a short period of time in the coming Great Tribulation, when they will have accepted the Antichrist, thinking that he is the Messiah.

But they will find to their dismay, that they have just made the biggest mistake of their existence, other than when they crucified Christ. They will come very close to being exterminated by this false Messiah, and in fact would be exterminated, were it not for the Second Coming of the Lord (Rev. Chpt. 19), which will then rescue them, and as well totally defeat the Antichrist and his armies.

Then, Israel will accept Christ not only as their Messiah, but also as their Lord and Savior. In fact, the Scripture plainly tells us that they will then know and realize what they did in the past, and how awful and wrong that it actually was. The Scripture says:

"In that day there shall be a great mourning in Jerusalem . . . and the land shall

mourn, every family apart; the family of the house of David apart . . . (and) *all the families that remain"* (Zech. 12:11-14).

At that time they will say, *"What are these wounds in Thine hands? Then He shall answer, Those with which I was wounded in the house of My friends"* (Zech. 13:6).

They will then accept Him Whom they have so long rejected!

COUNTERFEIT AND IMITATION

But until then, the Counterfeit Church is a present reality in the world today. How could Satan better promote his objectives then through a religion, remarkably genuine on the surface, but inwardly false? Even the conception of idols has its basis in the idea of God. With all its disfigurement, the false god is a caricature of the One True God . . . in heathenism truth and untruth, worth and worthlessness, lie, not only beside each other, but at times, in each other.

Viewed as a whole, this is the false way of myriads of men. Through the centuries it has ruled mankind. *"Professing themselves to be wise, they became fools"* (Rom. 1:22).

Counterfeit and imitation have always been the most difficult deception to detect. The Counterfeit Church has many formal representations in the world — all dominated and directed by Satan and his demon spirits. Paul warned the Corinthian Church of *"false apostles, deceitful workers, transforming themselves into the apostles of Christ . . . for Satan himself is transformed into an angel of light. Therefore it is no great thing if his ministers also be transformed as the ministers of righteousness: whose end shall be according to their works"* (II Cor. 11:13-15).

As the Spirit of God is incarnate in Christ, so the spirit of Satan is incarnate in the many Antichrists in the world today (I Jn. 2:18), many of them, who deny the Father and the Son (I Jn. 2:22). John presents these two forces thus: *"Hereby know ye the Spirit of God: every spirit that confesseth that Jesus Christ is come in the flesh is of God: and every spirit that confesseth not that Jesus Christ is come in the flesh is not of God: and this is that spirit of anti christ, whereof ye have heard that it should come; and even now already is it in the world"* (I Jn. 4:2-3).

The final goal of the Church always must be *"Jesus Christ and Him Crucified"*; the end of nominal Christendom, as such, is Antichrist. Contrary to the belief of some, the Bible unmistakably teaches that *"history is not the product of history, that the Kingdom of God does not reach sovereignty through growth and ascent, but only after world-wide collapse and catastrophe."* What am I saying?

I'm saying, that all of this will not conclude by the world being Christianized as some presently teach, but rather, an increasing enmity in the world unto the expulsion of Christianity from civilization, which will take place under the Antichrist. This is the path foretold by Biblical prophecy.

This means that the *"kingdom now"* message being proclaimed by many in the modern Church is grossly unscriptural. The world will not be won to Christ by electing better men and better women to public, political office. The Bible doesn't even remotely teach such a thing.

As well, it is not because the world is not Christian enough that Christ has not yet come, but He has not yet come because the world is not unbelieving enough (I Tim. 4:1-3; II Tim. 3:1-4; 4:3-4; II Pet. 3:3). It is a basic principle of the Divine Government of the world that all things, the good as well as the evil, must reach ripeness (Mat. 13:29-30; Rev. 14:15, 18).

This not at all means that we shouldn't evangelize, but rather the very opposite. The only way that people are going to be saved, with lives being changed, is through World Evangelism; however, this will not stop the progress of evil, but with this progress steadily increasing, even until the rise of the Antichrist. In fact, the Church has already entered the last day apostasy, which will grow increasingly worse.

Actually, the Bible teaches two thrusts in the spirit world, which will take place in the last days. It teaches a great outpouring of the Holy Spirit, which will usher millions into the Kingdom of God (Acts 2:17-21), and as well, it teaches a great *"falling away from truth"* (I Tim. 4:1-2; II Tim. 3:1-7; 4:3-4), both streams running at the same time, but one might say in opposite directions.

The forces of Satan fight persistently against God's redemptive objectives through the Satan-endowed religions and humanistic-rationalistic, Christ-denying systems of the world.

In Satan's religion, the heathen expresses his godliness. In fact, *"religion"* is the sin, namely, the sin against the First Commandment, the replacing of God by the gods; the most powerful expression of the opposition of man against God and contradiction within himself.

Religion is that which is made up by man, and wholly by man, instituted by Satan, as a way to reach God, or be god, or to better oneself in some way. Because it's not of God, it cannot be condoned in any way by God.

And anything that is not *"Jesus Christ and Him Crucified"* is *"religion."*

THE REVELATION OF CHRIST

The whole history of Salvation is self-revelation of Christ, the Creator of the universe and the Redeemer of mankind. Besides Him there is no other, and consequently all other claims to Deity are in the category of Satanic direction.

As the Church is represented by many Denominations, so the Counterfeit Church is represented by many systems, and each system offers some kind of opiate and/or substitute for *"Salvation by Faith."* All of the false systems follow a single design, that of denying Christ as Lord and Savior. They bypass the *"Way of the Cross"* in favor of some humanly conceived substitute.

Satan is very intent upon promoting *"religions,"* and it makes no difference which one it is so long as it does not demand faith in Christ.

The Counterfeit Church is not disturbed as long as Christ is interpreted only as *"a good man," "a great prophet," "a fine teacher," "a miracle worker,"* or *"a god among many."*

Mahatma Gandhi is quoted as saying, *"All religions are equally true and equally false, and every man should remain in the one in which he was born."*

This notwithstanding, there is a movement among the leaders of the non-Christian religions, in the direction of a missionary-evangelistic nature. Satan, disguised in

the agents of these other religions, is making a desperate bid for the souls of men. The *"tempter"* (Mat. 4:3) assumes various roles and titles, but he is substantially the same, irrespective of the name by which he presents himself.

Some well-intentioned people tell us that the various religions of the world are good, provided the adherents are sincere and follow the precepts laid down, but this viewpoint cannot be valid if Jesus Christ, and only He, is the Savior of the world (Acts 4:12; I Cor. 3:11).

Many people have been sincere in thinking they were right, but later found they were wrong. The best example of this is Saul of Tarsus or Paul (Acts Chpt. 9).

"There is a way which seemeth right unto a man, but the end thereof are the ways of death" (Prov. 14:12).

THE MODERN APOSTASY

I personally feel that the greatest thrust of the Evil One is the present effort to destroy the Spirit-filled church. And Satan has gone a long way toward accomplishing this task.

As I dictate these notes in mid-August of 2000, the non-Pentecostal world has for all practical purposes denied the Baptism with the Holy Spirit, which means there is little or nothing going on in these ranks for the Cause of Christ. While there is much religious machinery, which means there is much activity, it is all, at least for all practical purposes, man-devised, and therefore, not Spirit directed. As a result, nothing can be accomplished for Christ.

In the Pentecostal world, the situation is as bad or possibly even worse. Most of the Pentecostal Denominations at the present time, cannot even boast of 50 percent of their people professing the Baptism with the Holy Spirit. Actually, according to my information, less than one-third of the people who consider themselves to be members of Assemblies of God and Church of God Churches, the two largest Pentecostal Denominations in the world, even consider themselves to be Baptized with the Holy Spirit, with the evidence of speaking with other tongues; consequently, in all honesty, these particular Denominations cannot even rightly refer to themselves anymore as *"Pentecostal!"* Regrettably, most of the other Pentecostal Denominations fall into the same category.

It is bad enough to have the light of the Holy Spirit offered and then rejected, but to reject the Light after it has been received is worse still! And that is what most of the Pentecostal Denominations, at the least in the United States and Canada, are doing.

I had the occasion in 1987 (if I remember the year correctly), to preach to the General Council of the Assemblies of God for the country of Mexico.

I preached that night on the subject *"There Is A River,"* actually ministering on the Holy Spirit. The Lord moved mightily that evening. Actually, I didn't even get to finish the Message, with the Spirit of God falling in the place to such an extent, that Preachers by the hundreds started getting out of their seats, running down the aisles, and falling in the Altars, asking the Lord to refill them with the Spirit.

I didn't know that this particular Denomination in Mexico had been on the verge of denouncing the Baptism with the Holy Spirit with the evidence of speaking with other tongues. Actually, a debate had been going on for quite some time regarding this very issue. The Spirit of God brought forth this Message at the right time, and not a minute too early.

I do not know what the situation is in Mexico since then. I do know that what I've heard has not been good, at least as it regards that particular Denomination.

In fact, the two major Denominations of which I have just spoken have opted totally and completely for humanistic psychology; however, there is no way that one can accept psychology and the Gospel at the same time. One or the other must go, considering that they are opposites.

In fact, to opt for psychology, means that one has registered a vote of no confidence as it regards the Cross of Christ. One cannot have it both ways, especially considering that humanistic psychology is the very opposite of the Word of God. Either Jesus addressed every single problem that man has at the Cross, or He didn't, and we need to turn to the likes of Freud, Maslow, Rodgers, etc.

NOTES

However, I happen to know that the Gospel works, and so does any and every right-thinking Believer. There are hundreds of millions down through time who have seen their lives gloriously and wondrously changed by the power of the Cross. Beside that, not one single individual has ever been helped by humanistic psychology, but rather made worse, because it draws them away from the true help they can get only in the Lord.

So I'll say again, you probably now know why Denominational Leaders do not like Jimmy Swaggart too much. But the truth is the truth, and somebody needs to stand up and say it.

On the other side of the coin, and I continue to speak of the Pentecostals and Charismatics (I am Pentecostal), far too often the Ministry is represented on Television by hucksters and flimflam men, who go under the guise of Preachers of the Gospel. They are *"selling"* miracles and promising all type of financial returns for the people's money. In fact, for much of the Charismatic world, the message today is *"money."* And that is an abomination in the Sight of God. As we've already stated, God readily blesses and blesses abundantly; however, He doesn't have anything for sale, and as well, faith is not bargained out on a dollar sign. Jesus didn't die on a Cross for us to trade in our Ford for a Cadillac. He died to set men free from their sin, but that has ceased to be the Message in most Pentecostal and Charismatic Churches.

Don't misunderstand, there are some Pentecostal and Charismatic Preachers who are definitely preaching the Gospel, and who love the Lord with all their hearts. But sad to say, that number is small, and one might say, few and far between, at least as one looks at the whole. And how do I know that?

I do have some experience; and as well, how many Preachers in those particular ranks are rising up and saying the things I've just said? There are a few, but not many!

The great Message of the Cross is, that He, the Sinless One, offered Himself to take the sinner's place, and this is the power of the Eternal Spirit; and through the shedding of His Blood, our consciences are purged from works of death and we are set free to serve the Living God.

The best the Israelites of old had, who were defiled by coming in contact with the dead, was recourse to the *"water of separation."* That was the best that the Law had to offer.

But since Christ, even though we were defiled by the fact that we ourselves in our unsaved state were dead in trespasses and in sins, now, with all the past completely settled, we can go to Christ, and because of what He did for us at the Cross, we can have the past completely washed clean, not merely the external, but the very recesses of the heart, which gives us a freedom to serve the Living God in Faith and in Power which gives a new life which those under the Old Covenant never had.

They were saved one might say, on credit, while we are saved in fact. All because of Jesus!

That and that alone, *"Jesus Christ and Him Crucified,"* is the answer to a hurting, human race. The world today without God, sees only a besotted yesterday, a hurting present, and a darkened tomorrow. Only in Christ can one have the past completely blotted out, and the present made anew, which guarantees tomorrow. Only in Jesus! And through only what He did at the Cross! And only by our Faith in that Finished Work!

(15) "AND FOR THIS CAUSE HE IS THE MEDIATOR OF THE NEW TESTAMENT, THAT BY MEANS OF DEATH, FOR THE REDEMPTION OF THE TRANSGRESSIONS THAT WERE UNDER THE FIRST TESTAMENT, THEY WHICH ARE CALLED MIGHT RECEIVE THE PROMISE OF ETERNAL INHERITANCE."

The structure is:

1. Christ is the Mediator of a Better Covenant.

2. *"Mediator"* is one who intervenes between two, either to make or restore peace and friendship, to form a compact, or to ratify a Covenant.

3. Here Christ acts as a go-between or Mediator between a Holy God and sinful man.

4. By His Death on the Cross, He paid the debt, thereby removing the obstacle which is sin, which had caused an estrangement between man and God.

5. When the sinner accepts the merits of the Sacrifice of Christ, the guilt and penalty of his sin is his no more; the power of sin in his life is broken; he becomes the recipient of the Divine nature, and the estrangement between himself and God, both legal and personal, disappears.

6. Jesus became the Mediator not only in order that He might pay the penalty of sinners who live since the Cross, but also that He might do so for those who lived before the Cross. Sinners who were saved under the First Testament were actually saved, not by it or by any sacrifice offered under its jurisdiction, but through faith in the coming, atoning work of Christ under the New Testament (Wuest).

MEDIATOR

The phrase, *"And for this cause He is the Mediator of the New Testament,"* refers to the reason that Christ died on the Cross. He did so that through His Death, the Eternal Spirit on the basis of a work completed, a debt paid, could purge the conscience of the sinner from dead works, in order that we might serve the Living God.

It is important to be clear that Christ's saving work operates on quite a different level from that of the Levitical Sacrifices. These were but external and material, and neither could cleanse or effect anything within themselves, even as Paul repeatedly emphasizes. They were only meant to symbolize the One Who was coming, Who in fact could cleanse and effect eternal Salvation within the heart and life of the Believer, irrespective as to how defiled the Believer had previously been. Christ was concerned with sins which trouble and defile the consciences of men. So His Sacrifice was directed to the cleansing of the conscience, which takes away the guilt of man, something the sacrifices under the Old Law could never do (Heb. 10:2). This is a work that cleanses *"from acts that lead to death,"* where the Greek is more literally *"from dead works."*

Paul now having introduced the thought of the death of Christ, proceeds to develop it. This death is the means of redeeming people from the plight they found themselves in as the result of their sin. This Death, at least if accepted by the believing sinner, brings the believing sinner an eternal inheritance, which is absolutely incomprehensible as it regards its eternal consequences.

Paul will go on to bring out the necessity for the Death of Christ, just as the death of the testator is required if a will is to come into force.

However, Christ is the only One Who has ever died and left a will, and then come back to life, in order to see that the will be adhered to in totality. He mediated a New Covenant so that we might receive the inheritance.

CHRIST THE ONLY ONE

There was no mere mortal who could stand in-between God and man as a Mediator, simply because all men were sinners and needed mediation themselves. In other words, Mary herself, even though being the Mother of our Lord, needed a Savior just like all others do. She said so herself (Lk. 1:47). So, the idea that Mary is a co-redemptress, as proposed by John Paul II is preposterous indeed! The only way that such a mediatorship could be arrived at was for God to become man, which He did as it regards the Incarnation. Isaiah prophesied this some 800 years before Christ (Isa. 7:14).

And then to do so, Christ even though virgin born, would have to live a life perfect and free from all sin. In other words, He must be, even as Paul said, *"made under the Law,"* which means that He had to abide by the Law in every respect, which no human being had ever done, that is if He was to be our Substitute and Representative Man (Gal. 4:4). This He did, and then died on the Cross as well, in order to take the curse of the broken Law, which penalty was death, the curse incidentally, we should have taken.

As our Substitute, He did for us what we couldn't do for ourselves, and as our Representative Man He gave to us all the victory that He purchased by the shedding of His Own Precious Blood.

Inasmuch as He atoned for all sin, the legal rights of Satan were broken. Consequently, Christ can stand as the Mediator, and a Perfect Mediator at that, between man and God.

NEW TESTAMENT

There has been much controversy as to whether the change from Covenant to Testament, in the sense of a will, is intended in the Verses that follow. But the two are so

intimately connected that there would seem to be no reason for difficulty in understanding the truth presented.

The Old Covenant was God's will for His people prior to the coming of Christ and was sealed by the blood of calves and goats, which Moses sprinkled upon the Book and all the people saying, *"This is the blood of the Testament which God hath enjoined unto you."*

The New Covenant is the will of our blessed Lord, whereby He decrees that all who put their trust in Him should receive part in that eternal inheritance, which He gladly shares with all Believers. By His Death this Testament came into force. Apart from His death, there could be no such blessing for guilty sinners. A Testament is in effect after men are dead. His death on the Cross puts this New Covenant, or Testament, or Will, into operation, and inasmuch as it is a Covenant of pure Grace, all who believe enter into the good of it even before the day when it is to be openly confirmed with Israel and Judah, as we saw in the previous Chapter.

The blood of the Covenant having already been shed, there is nothing to hinder the outflow of blessing. The sprinkling of the blood under the Old Dispensation confirmed that Covenant, and was a warning to the people that death would result for its violation; while at the same time it typified the shedding of the blood of the New Covenant Victim, which we will study in the succeeding Verses (Ironside).

THE REASON FOR THE FAILURE OF THE OLD COVENANT

The Old Covenant was between God and man. Unfortunately, due to man's fallen condition, man has broken every single covenant that he's ever made with God. So, due to man's inability, that Covenant was terribly broken, meaning that every single human being who lived broke the Law of God, and we speak of the Ten Commandments (Ex. Chpt. 20).

However, the New Covenant is altogether different. While it is true, that it is a Covenant made between God and man, exactly as the Old Covenant, still there is a major difference.

To guarantee this New Covenant, God became man in the form of the Lord Jesus Christ. As well, He died on the Cross to seal the

Covenant, and to do so with His Own Blood, and then was resurrected from the dead.

Consequently, His Blood is the seal of the Covenant, meaning that it will be kept forever, and as well, He is both God and man, so the Covenant is dependent totally upon Him and Him Alone. It cannot fail, because He is both God and Man.

As long as the Believer is *"in Christ,"* he is a beneficiary of the Covenant, and it cannot be broken. The only thing that will take him out of the Covenant is a lack of Faith in the Covenant, which is why Paul wrote the Epistle to the Hebrews. And to be sure, it applied not only to the Christian Jews of Paul's day, some of them who were abrogating their place and position in Christ by faithlessness, but as well to all who have lived since then, and even at the present. It is not so much a question of Christ leaving man, but man leaving Christ. The Lord doesn't demand much of us, only Faith, but He does demand that! If the Believer ceases to believe, he is no longer in Christ and, therefore, the Covenant is broken, but not by God, only by unbelieving man (Heb. 6:4-9; 10:26-31).

Man needs a mediator because of the Fall. Man lost his standing before God and has no ground on which to approach God. Jesus now becomes the means of approach; He is the Mediator between God and man. With sin removed, which Christ did at the Cross, man may have perfect communion with God. Man may enjoy the Love of God and be the recipient of God's Grace and forgiveness; he may now walk in the Spirit and know freedom from condemnation (Rom. 8:1).

Paul is showing here the necessity of Christ's death. The Promises of God made to man and the eternal purpose God had for man could not be realized until Jesus died. In this respect, Jesus was a Testator, whose will or testament was of no effect until He died. We are the beneficiaries. We are the recipients of *"the promise of eternal inheritance."*

It is well understood that the New Testament provided benefits to man; the greatest benefit is the disposition of eternal life on the basis of the acceptance of the atoning merits of the Sacrifice of Jesus Christ.

Moses, as stated, sealed the Old Covenant with animal blood. If the New Covenant is

better and more effective, then it must, of necessity, be sealed with something of greater quality. The New Covenant has been sealed by the Blood of Jesus Christ. Jesus instituted the Lord's Supper by saying of the cup, *"This is My Blood of the New Testament, which is shed for many for the remission of sins"* (Mat. 26:28).

Jesus settled the sin problem and did so forever. He made it possible for God legally to remit all that we have ever done, to give us eternal life and to make us new creatures, all in Christ Jesus, and all in what He did at the Cross on our behalf.

DEATH

The phrase, *"That by means of death,"* speaks of the Crucifixion of Christ, and the only means by which man could be saved, for death was the penalty for sin (Mat. 26:28; Rom. 5:6-11; 6:10; 14:9; I Cor. 15:3; II Cor. 5:14-21; Col. 1:14-22; Heb. 2:9-15; I Pet. 2:24).

If it is to be noticed, it didn't say *"by means of Resurrection,"* but *"by means of death."*

In no way do we mean to belittle the Resurrection; however, when Jesus died on the Cross thereby atoning for all sin, the Resurrection was a given. In other words, there was no doubt that Jesus would come from the grave on the third day. If all sin is atoned, and it definitely was atoned at the Cross, past, present, and future, Satan then had no legal right to hold Christ in the death world; consequently, Resurrection was guaranteed.

In fact, it was so very much guaranteed, that God rent the Veil in the Temple immediately upon the Death of Christ, signifying, that the way was now open (Mat. 27:51). Had there been a single doubt that Jesus wouldn't come from the dead, God would have never rent the Veil at that time.

Some may read these words and claim that His Resurrection was inevitable, simply because He is God. While the latter is certainly true, the former is true only as it regards all sin being atoned.

The Reader must understand, that when God became man, He reduced the entire economy of Heaven down, way down, to the far lower spectrum of flesh and blood. *"God is a Spirit"* (Jn. 4:24). But when God became Man, i.e., *"Jesus,"* as it regards the Incarnation, all of Heaven was reduced to that lowest denominator. In other words, if Jesus had failed, Satan would have won, and that means that he would have been the king of all things, including Heaven, even as he aspired to be (Isa. 14:13-14).

And then again, many claim that Christ could not have failed inasmuch as He was God. While it is definitely true that He was God, and never for a moment ceased to be God, still, to be the Last Adam (I Cor. 15:45), which He was, He had to function in the same capacity. In other words, even as it was possible for the original Adam to fail, it was also possible for the Last Adam to fail. If not, He could not have been our Substitute and our Second Man (I Cor. 15:45-50).

But not one time did He fail, in word, thought, or deed. He was Perfect in His Life in every capacity. When He came to the end of His life, He could say without reservation, *"For the prince of the world cometh, and hath nothing in Me"* (Jn. 14:30).

If it wasn't possible for Satan to have some place in Him, Jesus would not have made such a statement.

But considering that His life was perfect, He could then be offered up as a Perfect Sacrifice, which God could perfectly accept, which He did, thereby that life in death atoning for all sin.

THE CROSS

His death was not an execution or an incident.

In other words, He did not run afoul of Roman or Jewish Law, and was thereby executed. That may have been what they thought they were doing, but He gave His life freely, even as a Sacrifice. In fact, His life and His death, both were a Sacrifice.

Not having been born in sin, and not having ever sinned, death had no claim on Him whatsoever. In other words, had He not voluntarily laid down His Life, He would not, and in fact, could not have died. This means that no one could have killed Him, nor would He have grown aged and ultimately died, as do all other human beings. Sin is the ruination of the human race, and the cause of all death. He had no sin!

Concerning His life, He said, *"No man taketh it from Me, but I lay it down of Myself.*

I have power to lay it down, and I have power to take it again. This Commandment have I received of My Father" (Jn. 10:18).

So, He voluntarily laid down His life as a Sacrifice, and above all, a Sacrifice for sin, which atoned for all sin. The Cross was the reason that He came to this world, and the only reason. While everything about Him was of vast significance, and because He was God manifest in the flesh, the Cross must ever be understood as His destination.

While the Healings and Miracles were of vast significance, still, they would not have saved anyone. While His Words were such as no man had ever spoken, still, that alone would not have saved anyone. He had to go to the Cross, and the Cross was the reason He came.

Peter said, *"Forasmuch as ye know that ye were not redeemed with corruptible things, as silver and gold . . . but with the Precious Blood of Christ, as of a lamb without blemish and without spot:*

"Who verily was foreordained before the foundation of the world, but was manifest in these last times for you" (I Pet. 1:18-20).

This plainly tells us, that the Cross was a planned destination by God for Christ, and was planned by the Godhead even before the disruption or overthrow of the pre-Adamite world. Consequently, we should realize and understand the vast significance of this of which we speak.

Neither was the Cross an incident. By that we mean just one of the many incidents in the Life and Ministry of Christ.

Why would we bring out such a point?

We do so simply because many in the Charismatic community, place little or no significance at all in the Cross of Christ, claiming it as just another incident in His Life, Ministry, Death, and Resurrection.

They claim that Jesus took upon Himself the nature of Satan on the Cross, actually becoming a sinner and thereby, dying as a sinner and going to Hell. And when they say *"Hell,"* they are speaking of the burning side of the pit.

They claim that Jesus went to Hell as a lost sinner, and while Satan gloated over Him, after a period of time, He (Jesus) threw off the shackles of death, and was Born-Again — and of all places, Born-Again, they claim, in Hell itself. He was then resurrected, and it's faith in Him as a *"born again man"* which constitutes Salvation.

Nothing could be farther from the Truth! There is nothing in the Bible that even remotely substantiates such a tall tale, and a tall tale it is!

The Bible repeatedly states, that it was His Death, and the shedding of His Precious Blood, which affected Salvation for humanity, and nothing else (Mat. 26:28; Mk. 14:24; 22:20; 6:53-56; Acts 20:28; Rom. 3:25; 5:9; I Cor. 10:16; 11:25, 27; Eph. 1:7; 2:13; Col. 1:14, 20; Heb. 9:12, 14, 22; 10:29; 13:12, 20; I Pet. 1:2, 19; I Jn. 1:7; 5:6, 8; Rev. 1:5; 5:9; 7:14).

It is by the means of His Death, that we have Salvation, and that we walk in victory as well (Rom. 8:1-2). In fact, it is the Cross alone which stands between man and eternal Hell. We must never forget that!

REDEMPTION

The phrase, *"For the Redemption of the transgressions that were under the First Testament,"* proclaims the fact that the Death of Christ pertained just as much for those before the Cross, as those after the Cross. Sinners, who were saved under the Old Covenant, were actually saved, not by it or by any Sacrifice offered under its jurisdiction, but through the atoning work of Christ under the New Testament (Wuest).

This proves as should be obvious, that there has always been only one way of Salvation, and that has been and is and ever shall be, *"Jesus Christ and Him Crucified"* (I Cor. 2:2).

It is because of Christ's Sacrifice having been such as has been described, that He is the Mediator of that new and better Covenant; it qualified Him for being so. A Sacrifice, a Death, was required for giving it validity, and the character of His Sacrifice implies a Better Covenant than the Old, even such a one as Jeremiah foretold.

Further, the purpose of His Death is said to be *"for the Redemption of the transgressions that were under the First Covenant."* For in the passage of Jeremiah the defect of the First Covenant was based on the transgression of its conditions by man, while under the new one, such transgressions were to be no more remembered. But this could

not be without Atonement for them; the whole ceremony of the Law signified this; and also that such Atonement could not be except by Death. The Death of Christ satisfied this requirement; and so the New Covenant could come in.

The idea of this is, the First Covenant had been broken by *"transgressions"*; consequently, unless there be redemption from these — that is, from the bondage of penalty which has resulted from these — there can be no promise and no New Covenant. In respect of this bondage, this penalty, the Death of Christ was a ransom — an offering to God looked at in the light of a payment in the place of debt, service, or penalty due.

When debt and payment are changed into the corresponding ideas of sin and punishment, the *"ransom"* gives place to the Sin-Offering, of which the principle was the acknowledgement of death deserved, and the vicarious suffering of death.

So far our thought has rested on the removal of the results of the past. The Covenant and the Promise relate to the establishment of a better Covenant, i.e., *"a better future."* Death was necessary alike for both. The offering of Christ's life (Mat. 20:28) was a ransom or an offering for sin; it was also a sacrifice inaugurating a New Covenant, which contained the promise of the eternal inheritance.

THE SIN-OFFERING

This is what Paul was talking about when he said, *"For He* (God) *hath made Him* (Christ) *to be sin for us, Who knew no sin; that we might be made the Righteousness of God in Him"* (II Cor. 5:21).

Some have taken the passage, *"For He hath made Him to be sin for us,"* and tried to turn it into something it doesn't mean. In other words, they claim that Jesus literally became a sinner on the Cross, taking upon Himself the nature of Satan, and died lost like any other sinner. He then went to Hell as stated, they claim, and was Born-Again in Hell, etc. However, such a thing is not given in Scripture, simply because it didn't happen.

As stated, when debt and payment are changed into the corresponding ideas of sin and punishment, for sin demands punishment, the word *"ransom"* comes into play, and gives place to the Sin-Offering, which is what Jesus actually became.

To properly understand the term *"For He hath made Him to be sin for us,"* one must correlate that with, *"That we might be made the Righteousness of God in Him."*

You and I within ourselves had no righteousness, and neither has any other human being who has ever lived. We had to be given the righteousness of Christ, which we obtained by Faith in His Finished Work. With that Righteousness comes *"Life"* (Jn. 10:10).

To get this Righteousness, we did not do anything, obtain anything, perfect anything, or commit anything, with the exception of simply having Faith in Christ. So the Righteousness is all of Him and none of us.

Likewise with the sin! Christ did not sin, did not do anything that pertained to sin, did not commit any act that was sin, but in fact received our sin, which effect is death. The fruit of righteousness is life, which we receive freely from Christ, while the wages of sin is death, which Christ received from us. He was made to be a Sin-Offering which He received from us, while we were made to be a Life-Offering, which we received from Him. The life I now have, I have only because He paid my penalty, which is death.

THE OLD COVENANT AND THE NEW COVENANT

Sinners who were under the First Covenant actually were saved by Faith, looking forward to the atoning work of the Messiah upon the Cross. The types of the Old Covenant pointed to this act. All men, Old and New Testament, will meet together at the Cross. Only the Name and the Blood of Christ can cleanse and purify from all sin. This was the purpose of God in the New Covenant.

Justification and Sanctification can never be separated. When God imputes the Righteousness of Christ, He also imparts the principle of His Holiness; both are necessary before we can enter His Presence in Heaven. Because the Blood of Jesus Christ has fully met every righteous claim of a Holy God against His people, this Blood, by its virtue and purifying effects, when applied by the Holy Spirit, has opened the new and living way to God.

The offering of the Old Testament Saints had looked forward to this event. Jesus' death was the fulfillment of all their hopes and expectations. Each time they offered a sacrifice, it was an act of faith. They were acknowledging the coming Messiah by every symbolic act of the Old Covenant. Each year their sins were set aside until Jesus could come and remove them, which He did!

It is easy to see that the Hebrew Christians would have many questions concerning the Old Testament Saints, very probing and provoking questions. Were their fathers, who had died under the old Levitical system, lost? Was the Plan of Redemption as revealed in the Old Testament sufficient to meet the need of that time? Or could it be that the rewards and blessings of the Old Testament were only earthly blessings?

It became necessary for Paul to remove any doubts these Hebrews might have. He affirms that Old Testament Believers, too, were redeemed by the Blood of Jesus. His Blood covered both the old and the new. It made good the old, and made possible the new. To know their fathers and loved ones had Salvation through Christ must have brought great peace to their hearts and minds. Christ also restored the originally intended nature of their fathers which had been lost in the Fall. He restored their sonship and inheritance — their hope!

THE HOLY SPIRIT

It is amazing how the Holy Spirit understands the needs of man. The Holy Spirit inspired Paul to reassure the Readers concerning the efficacy of Christ's Sacrifice for Old Testament Times. The Saints who had lived under the First Testament were also called, that they too might receive the promise of the eternal inheritance.

THE ETERNAL INHERITANCE

The phrase, *"They which are called might receive the promise of eternal inheritance,"* refers to those before the Cross who had died in the faith, who were referred to as *"the called."* These statements proclaim the fact that all the Old Testament Saints were just as saved as those since the Cross. However, there was a difference:

Even though the sins of Old Testament Saints were atoned or covered by means of the animal sacrifices, those sins were not actually taken away. That could not be until Christ came and paid the sin debt, which He did at the Cross. That's why John the Baptist said, *"Behold the Lamb of God, which taketh away the sin of the world"* (Jn. 1:29).

By His Death on the Cross, Jesus Christ, not only covered our sins, but washed them away as if they never existed, which means that in the sight of God, it is as if we had never sinned. It is called *"Justification by Faith."* And it harks back to the Abrahamic Covenant (Gen. Chpt. 15), which portrayed in simple but yet graphic detail, how that an unjust man could be justified, how that a sinful man, could be brought to the place as if he never sinned, how the guilty could be declared *"not guilty!"* As stated, it is all by Faith, but to be more particular, it is always and without exception, Faith in what Christ did at the Cross, which is what Paul is carefully outlining in this great Epistle to the Hebrews.

WHAT IS THE ETERNAL INHERITANCE?

Does the Reader really know and understand the portend of this which he is reading in the Epistle to the Hebrews? Do you actually realize what is being said?

To answer that question, it is actually impossible for any of us to know in the entirety as to what this eternal inheritance proclaims, simply due to the magnitude of that of which we speak. But first of all, allow me to say this:

Whatever this eternal inheritance is, and to what degree or magnitude it might be, it is the Holy Spirit Who gives us all of these things, making real to our hearts and lives, that which Jesus did at the Cross (Gal. 3:14).

Of course, the moment the believing sinner comes to Christ, the Holy Spirit definitely comes within His heart; however, as we've said quite a number of times, there is a vast difference in being *"born of the Spirit"* than being *"Baptized with the Spirit"* (Jn. 3:3-8; Acts 2:4). While Salvation prepares us for Heaven, the Baptism with the Holy Spirit prepares us for a life of service to the Lord Jesus Christ in this present world. And to be frank, without the Spirit Baptism, which is

always accompanied by the speaking with other tongues (Acts 2:4; 10:44-46; 19:1-7), the Believer is going to receive very little from the Lord. He will find that his efforts are almost totally in the flesh and merely according to human ingenuity. For the Spirit of God to truly work within one's heart and life, there must be a Spirit Baptism, which, incidentally, Jesus demanded (Acts 1:4).

I'm not saying that the Holy Spirit doesn't work at all in those who are not Baptized with the Spirit, but I am saying, that His activity is greatly curtailed. Among other things, the Spirit Baptism portrays a surrender on the part of the individual to the Spirit, which then allows the Spirit to function and work as He desires, at least, if we keep our faith anchored in the Cross of Christ (Rom. 8:2).

ETERNAL

As well, whatever this inheritance is, it is *"eternal!"* This means it will never be lost, stolen, dissipated, or taken from us. And the Reader must understand, that the word *"eternal"* means never ending, and, therefore, time without end, which is actually beyond our comprehension.

Let the Reader also understand, that this one word proclaims volumes to us, as it regards God's dealings with His children. Satan will tell you, *"three strikes and you're out,"* or whatever lie he can get you to believe. But the Reader must understand, that God will never throw over one of His children, as long as faith is maintained in the Finished Work of Christ.

It took a long time for Jacob the supplanter, to be changed to Israel the prince of God (Gen. 32:28). It took a long time for Abraham and Sarah to see the fruition of their Faith as it regards the birth of Isaac (Gen. 12:1-3; Chpt. 21). It took a long time for David to ultimately gain the Throne of Israel (II Sam. 5:1-5). It took some time for the original Disciples to come to the place of victory within their lives (Lk. 22:32). It took a long time for the Apostle Paul to come to the knowledge of Faith in the Cross (Rom. 7:24). But through Faith, they all arrived at the place of victory, even though the time was long. As stated, God will not throw you over. The only thing that can stop you is for you to quit. If you don't quit, you can rest assured that the Holy Spirit won't quit. So what am I saying?

I believe the Holy Spirit through these words is telling me to relate to you, how much that God loves you; how much that He has invested in your Salvation; how determined He is to bring you to the place of victory, which He can do, and definitely will do, if you will only heed His clarion call.

To be frank, this very Commentary which you hold in your hands, is a part of your solution and answer. No, I'm not speaking of the book itself, but rather the teaching contained therein. It shows you that God's way of victory, is the way of the Cross, and as such, is God's answer to your prayers and to your petitions regarding many things within your life.

INHERITANCE

Through our acceptance of Christ, we have been made *"heirs of God, joint-heirs with Christ"* (Rom. 8:17). Due to being *"in Christ"* everything which belongs to Him, now belongs to us as well. In fact, there is such a close relationship, that Paul said, *"And hath raised us up together* (Christ and all Believers), *and made us sit together in heavenly places in Christ Jesus* (meaning, that all of this is in Christ and what He did at the Cross on our behalf)*"* (Eph. 2:6).

As our Substitute, Christ took the punishment which we should have taken (Isa. Chpt. 53), and as our Representative Man, He gave us the victory which He purchased at such a price (I Cor. 15:45-50).

This means that whatever Christ is, we are!

THE CROSS

It should be overly obvious throughout this Epistle to the Hebrews, and in fact, in all of Paul's writings, that the Cross is the Source of all these things of which we speak. In other words, the Cross made it possible for God to give believing man all of these great blessings. I speak of Eternal Life, Grace, Peace, Power, Justification, Sanctification, Reconciliation, Gifts of the Spirit, Fruit of the Spirit, leading and guidance, etc., as stated, all brought about through the Person and Office of the Holy Spirit. But it is the Cross that made it possible for God to do all of these things.

NOTES

As we've said over and over again, the Cross of Christ is the centrality of the Gospel. This means that everything in the Word of God strains irrevocably toward the Cross. Every prediction, promise, and prophecy, in some way, are pointing toward the Cross, or else something is promised because of the Cross.

Consequently, every Believer should always look at the Cross as ground zero, so to speak. In fact, if every doctrine which we believe is not anchored fully in the Cross, then something is wrong with that doctrine. If the Cross is minimized in any way in the thinking of any Believer, then the Believer is thinking wrong.

The reason I'm so adamant as it regards these things, is because I know how that Satan fights the Cross. In fact, he's not so very much interested in what you believe, or how you believe it, and no matter how religious or even spiritual it might be, providing it's not Faith in the Cross. He knows that your source of all victory, all power, all prosperity, in fact, everything that comes from the Lord, is all made possible, by what Jesus did at the Cross; therefore, he fights the Cross, opposes the Cross, as he does nothing else.

And to be sure, he does such from inside the Church, instead of outside. In other words, he uses Preachers and so-called religious leaders more so than he does anything else.

With you knowing and understanding what the Cross actually means, and how this great eternal inheritance is ours because of what Jesus did there, then your Faith must be anchored supremely within this Finished Work. Even at the risk of being overly repetitive, the Cross of Christ must ever be the object of your Faith. As we've already stated, this gives the Holy Spirit, Who is indispensable to your spiritual success, latitude to work in your heart and life.

Please allow me to ask this question:

Is the Cross central in the Church presently? I think the answer to that is obvious. No, it isn't! In truth, much of the modern Church anymore little knows what it actually does believe. The reason for the confusion, the reason for being led astray, is because the Cross is not central in the doctrine of the Church.

In most Churches, if the Cross is mentioned at all, it's relegated simply to the initial Salvation experience. Thereafter, it is abandoned as being of little or no consequence. In fact, in many Charismatic circles, the Cross is openly repudiated.

To be frank, it's bad enough for the Cross to be ignored, but when it's openly opposed, this spells catastrophe for those who are unfortunate enough to sit under such erroneous teaching.

The modern Church little knows and understands the part the Cross plays in our ongoing, everyday living before God. And actually, for me to state that the Cross plays an important part is really a misnomer. In fact, the Cross is everything. One can only find Christ through the Cross. One can only be Baptized with the Holy Spirit, according to what Jesus did at the Cross. Paul graphically spells this out in Romans, Chapters 6, 7, and 8. In fact, everything that Paul says is attached to the Cross.

The very meaning of the New Covenant is the Cross of Christ. To turn it around and say it another way, the meaning of the Cross, is the meaning of the New Covenant (I Cor. 11:23-30).

PROMISE

Old Testament Saints only had the Promise of the inheritance, while New Testament Saints have the foundation of the Promise; however, the entirety of the Promise of this inheritance, will not take place until the coming Rapture of the Church, i.e., *"the Resurrection."* Then we will be Glorified, as we are now Sanctified and Justified.

As well, with God, a *"Promise"* is iron clad. In other words, it is inviolable, i.e., *"unbreakable."*

(16) "FOR WHERE A TESTAMENT IS, THERE MUST ALSO OF NECESSITY BE THE DEATH OF THE TESTATOR."

The composite is:

1. Due to what Christ did at the Cross, the word *"Testament"* and *"Covenant"* here mean the same.

2. God has made a Covenant with the human race through His Son, the Lord Jesus Christ, and with the Death of His Son, the word *"Covenant"* is merged into the word *"Testament,"* with all of its inherent meaning.

3. The Death of Christ is the guarantee of this Covenant, i.e., *"Testament."*

A TESTAMENT

The phrase, *"For where a Testament is,"* presents this which Christ has accomplished through His Death.

The Scholars say that Paul's argument is not easy to follow in English, because we have no single word that is the precise equivalent of the Greek *"diatheke,"* which is translated *"Testament."* The Greek word denotes something like an authoritative laying down of what is to be done, and is the normal word for a last will and testament. But it is also suited to Covenants God makes with people. However, as we use the word *"Covenant"* we must understand that this Covenant is not the result of a process of negotiation, which God talks things over with people and they come to a mutually acceptable arrangement. God Alone lays down the terms. The result is a Covenant characterized by the same kind of finality as we see in a Testament. And to which we have already briefly alluded, the Death of Christ merged the Covenant into a Testament, which is basically the same as a *"Will."*

DEATH

The phrase, *"There must also of necessity be the death of the Testator,"* refers, as is obvious, to the death of Christ. His death guaranteed the veracity of the Redemption process. He paid the price that was demanded by God, which was done at the Cross, thereby carried out through His Death. Upon this being done, the Righteousness of God was completely satisfied, making it possible for Christ to be our Substitute, because He was the Perfect Sacrifice. Consequently, our identification with Him guarantees us all that for which He died. For such a Covenant to be valid, the death of the Testator had to take place. And that it did in Christ!

In Verse 15 we have seen the two-fold reference of the Death of Jesus, to the past and to the future. As High Priest He has offered Himself as a Sin-Offering to cleanse the conscience from dead works; the same Offering is also looked on as a ransom redeeming from the penalty of past transgressions, as it regards the Old Testament Saints. And, still by means of His Death, He has, as Mediator, established a New Covenant. We are reminded at once of the words of Jesus Himself, *"This cup is the New Covenant 'in My Blood'"* (I Cor. 11:25). It is this very thought which Paul proceeds to develop: a Covenant cannot be established without death — cannot exist at all. That among Jews, Greeks, and Romans alike, covenants were confirmed by sacrifice we need not pause to prove; of this usage we have the earliest example in Genesis Chapter 15. The material point here is, that a Covenant must be established over sacrifices, and that in such a sacrifice *"the death of Him that made the Covenant"* must in some manner be *"brought in"* or assumed. There remains only the application to the particular Covenant spoken of here. If this be taken as made between God and man, even as stated, the Sacrificial Death of Jesus in man's stead ratified the Covenant forever.

What makes this so peculiar as it regards Christ, He is set forth as High Priest and Sacrifice, so He is both the Author of the Covenant and the Sacrifice which gives it validity.

THE FORCE OF THIS COVENANT

As would be understood, a Covenant has to be between two or more parties. In this case, it is between God and man; however, it is between God and man in a very peculiar sense. Jesus being both God and Man, in other words, *"very God"* and *"very man,"* serves as both.

To put the Covenant into force, which always requires a sacrifice in some manner, He literally became the Sacrifice, dying as Man. However, His Death even though a Sacrifice, was more than a sacrifice. It was as well a payment, which satisfied the terrible sin debt which man owed to God. The shedding of His Life's Blood, also served as a cleansing agent, which cleanses the stains made by the sin committed. So, not only was the sin removed, as well the effects of sin were removed also. Sin had been the legal right by which Satan kept men in bondage, which is now removed, and the cleansing agent brought about by the Blood, serves as the Sanctification of the former sinner, which refers to being *"set apart"* unto God, which makes Justification possible.

The death of the *"Testator,"* in this case

Christ, put the Covenant into motion; however, Christ did something which had not heretofore been done. Due to the fact that He atoned for all sin, which voided death, He was raised from the dead, thereby coming back to guarantee the force of the Covenant. This makes this Covenant or Testament different than any such legal action that has ever been previously performed, and to be sure, it definitely was a legal action.

Due to the fact that the Covenant is all in Christ, it is a Covenant which cannot fail; therefore, the Covenant is inexhaustible, incontestable, inviolable, guaranteed, backed up by the Promise of God, and the act of Sacrifice regarding Christ, and is, therefore, eternal.

(17) "FOR A TESTAMENT IS OF FORCE AFTER MEN ARE DEAD: OTHERWISE IT IS OF NO STRENGTH AT ALL WHILE THE TESTATOR LIVETH."

The argument is:

1. There has to be a death for a will or testament to become operative.

2. While the party is alive, a will or testament carries no power or validity.

3. In the case of God bequeathing Salvation to the lost sinner, the bequest is only operative by reason of the Death of Christ.

THE FORCE OF THE TESTAMENT

The phrase, *"For a Testament is of force after men are dead,"* presents a legal action. This tells us in no uncertain terms, that the Death of Christ on the Cross was a legal matter. Satan held a legal claim upon man because of sin. That legal claim was captivity.

God as well had a legal claim on man because of sin. The sin of man is a crime against God, meaning that God's claim comes first. When Jesus died on the Cross, He died as a Substitute Man, meaning that He was the Substitute for all of humanity, which thereby, paid the debt incurred by sin, which was owed to God. As stated, it was all a legal work. As well, by the debt being paid, Satan also lost His legal hold upon man, at least for those who will believe (Jn. 3:16).

Due to the fact that Jesus died, which is not open to question, the Covenant is in force. That's why we're told at the conclusion of the New Covenant these words:

"And the Spirit and the Bride say, Come.

And let him that heareth say, Come. And let him that is athirst come. And whosoever will, let him take the water of life freely" (Rev. 22:17).

THE DEATH OF THE TESTATOR

The phrase, *"Otherwise it is of no strength at all while the Testator liveth,"* simply means, as in the case of any testament or will, it is not valid until the individual dies to whom the will belongs.

As stated, and as is obvious, Jesus died on the Cross. Whereas the New Covenant was not in force until the Cross, even though it was predicted in the Old Testament, it definitely was put in force after the Death of Christ. The *"strength"* of this New Covenant, is in fact, the Death of Christ, which Paul reiterates over and over in these Passages. That's what makes everything valid!

That's why I keep repeating that the Cross is the centrality of the Gospel. It was not the Resurrection that made valid the Covenant, as important as the Resurrection was, but rather the Death of Christ on the Cross. We must never forget this, which means that we are to never allow the Cross to be anything but paramount in our thinking and our faith.

(18) "WHEREUPON NEITHER THE FIRST TESTAMENT WAS DEDICATED WITHOUT BLOOD."

The exegesis is:

1. Even the Old Covenant, which was temporary, was dedicated with blood, which is required, if it is to be a Covenant.

2. There are many sacrifices, but if it's not a sacrifice with blood, it is that which God cannot accept. The Cross was a sacrifice with Blood.

3. This is the great dividing line in the Church presently, and in fact has been from the very dawn of time, as evidenced in Genesis Chapter 4. What kind of sacrifice will God accept?

THE OLD COVENANT

In Verse 18 we're told several things. They are as follows:

1. The *"First Testament"* or *"Old Covenant,"* was made between God and man.

2. Man could not perform his part; therefore, the Covenant was broken by every single human being who was in its agreement.

3. The First Covenant, due to its insufficiencies, was temporary. To be frank, anything dependent on man is deficient.

4. Even though it was temporary, it was ratified with Blood, even though it was animal blood, which was absolutely necessary, if it was in fact to be a Covenant.

5. The First Covenant was a mirror of the Second or New Covenant, but with all the deficiencies addressed in the New.

(19) "FOR WHEN MOSES HAD SPOKEN EVERY PRECEPT TO ALL THE PEOPLE ACCORDING TO THE LAW, HE TOOK THE BLOOD OF CALVES AND OF GOATS, WITH WATER, AND SCARLET WOOL, AND HYSSOP, AND SPRINKLED BOTH THE BOOK, AND ALL THE PEOPLE,"

The structure is:

1. Moses explained the Covenant to the people.

2. The Covenant was sealed with the blood of calves and of goats.

3. The *"water"* represented the Holy Spirit.

4. The *"scarlet wool"* represented the Shed Blood of Christ.

5. The *"hyssop"* represented the humanity of Christ.

6. For the Covenant to be valid, the blood of calves and goats mixed with the water, was sprinkled upon both the Book, containing the Covenant, and as well, upon the people. This had to be done, for the Covenant to be valid.

MOSES

The phrase, *"For when Moses had spoken every precept to all the people according to the Law,"* presents the Old Covenant, which included the Law and all of its precepts. It was commonly referred to as *"the Law of Moses."*

The Book of which is here spoken, is the Book of Leviticus in our Old Testament. It would have been broken down as follows:

1. Laws concerning sacrifices (Lev. 1:1 — 7:38).

2. The Tabernacle service put into operation (Lev. 8:1 — 10:20).

3. Laws concerning purity and impurity (Lev. 11:1 — 15:33).

4. The Great Day of Atonement (Lev. Chpt. 16).

NOTES

5. Various Laws (Lev. 17:1 — 25:55).

6. Promises and warnings (Lev., Chpt. 26).

7. Valuation and Redemption (Lev., Chpt. 27).

THE BLOOD OF CALVES AND GOATS

The phrase, *"He took the blood of calves and goats,"* proclaims the seal of the Covenant, which was *"shed blood."* Even though the blood of calves and goats could not remove sin, it did serve as a stopgap measure, thereby performing the work of Atonement. However, the Atonement was only in part one might say, in that the sin was covered and not cleansed. Nevertheless, the blood that would be shed here in the inauguration of the Law, presented the binding of its precepts, which had to be, that is if it was to be a Covenant.

This Passage has been one of perplexity regarding Commentators from the fact that Moses, in his account of the transactions connected with the ratification of the Covenant with the people (Ex. Chpt. 24), mentions only a part of the circumstances referred to here. He says nothing of the blood of calves and of goats; nothing of water, and scarlet wool, and hyssop; nothing of sprinkling the book, the Tabernacle, or the vessels of the ministry. The question has been ventured, therefore, as to where Paul obtained the knowledge of these circumstances. Since the account is not contained in the Old Testament, it must have been either by tradition or by direct inspiration.

The latter is hardly probable, since the information here given is hardly of sufficient importance to have required an original revelation.

He may have derived this information from the Jewish Targums, which in effect, were a commentary on the Old Testament. While there were things in the Targums which were incorrect, no doubt, there was much information which was correct. To be sure, the Holy Spirit would have guided the Apostle in his selection of material regarding these statements; therefore, one can be certain that what Paul said here actually happened.

WATER

The short phrase, *"With water,"* was no doubt done for several reasons. How many calves and goats were slaughtered we aren't told;

however, it is very doubtful that the entirety of several millions of people were sprinkled for that was the number of Israel at that time.

More than likely, it only concerned those of the Tribe of Levi, and even then only those who were involved directly in Tabernacle service. Even this would have numbered several hundreds of people, necessitating the mixing of water with the blood.

Second, knowing that everything that pertained to the Tabernacle and the entirety of the Old Covenant for that matter, pointed to Christ, and actually symbolized Him in some way regarding His Person, Life, Ministry, Death, and Resurrection, the water here also carried a much higher spiritual meaning than the mere necessity of mixing it with the blood of the animals in order to be sprinkled.

Water is one of the symbols of the Holy Spirit (Jn. 7:37-39). As well, very soon after Jesus died, His side was pierced with a spear by one of the Roman soldiers, and the Scripture says, *"And forthwith came there out blood and water"* (Jn. 19:34).

The Scripture also says, *"This is He that came by water and blood, even Jesus Christ; not by water only, but by water and blood. And it is the Spirit that beareth witness, because the Spirit is Truth"* (I Jn. 5:6).

The water witnessed to His full and proper humanity (Jn. 19:34), and the blood witnessed to the nature of His atoning Death (Jn. 19:34), and the Spirit witnessed to the Deity of His Person (Mat. 27:54; Lk. 23:42-44).

This refers to the fact that the Believer's sins are, therefore, fully expiated and He enjoys a perfect purification before God. That which was impure no longer exists, for the old man is crucified with and is dead with Christ; that which is raised with Christ in the spiritual sense, as born of God is perfectly pure. Only death could provide this expiation and purification; and the outflow of water and blood from the Redeemer's side demonstrated the actuality of death. So, the *"water"* represented both the Holy Spirit and the Finished Work of Christ.

SCARLET WOOL

The phrase, *"And scarlet wool,"* is symbolic of the blood which thoroughly cleanses. The brilliant whiteness of wool after thorough washing is used to illustrate purity. The Prophet Isaiah said:

"Come now, and let us reason together, saith the LORD: though your sins be as scarlet, they shall be as white as snow; though they be red like crimson, they shall be as wool" (Isa. 1:18).

HYSSOP

The phrase, *"And hyssop,"* presents a bushy plant, which grew between large stones, and has hairy stems and leaves, which would easily soak up water or blood, and could be used to sprinkle.

Concerning the first Passover, directions were given by God to Moses, to take a bunch of hyssop and dip it into the blood of the lamb that was in the basin, in order to be able to apply it to the lintel and the two side posts of the front door of each house in Egypt, at least those lived in by Israelites (Ex. 12:22).

David in Psalms 51:7 said, *"Purge me with hyssop, and I shall be clean."* This was a figure of speech used by David in his intercessory prayer concerning his sin, which obviously referred to the application of the blood of the lamb, for it is only, Scripture says, with the shedding of blood that there can be remission of sin.

So, the type represented here, would be that of the humanity of Christ, which of course, was necessary, in order to serve as a Sacrifice.

THE APPLICATION OF THE BLOOD

The phrase, *"And sprinkled both the Book and all the people"* would pertain as stated, to the Book of Leviticus, and those of the tribe of Levi ordained for Tabernacle Service.

The sprinkling of the blood was the ratification of the Covenant, and symbolized the Blood of Christ which would be shed, and applied by Faith to the hearts and lives of believing sinners.

(The blood mixed with enough water would have made it possible, for the entirety of the approximate three million people to have been sprinkled; however, it is highly unlikely that this was done, inasmuch as water was scarce in the desert as well.)

(20) "SAYING, THIS IS THE BLOOD OF THE TESTAMENT WHICH GOD HATH ENJOINED UNTO YOU."

The structure is:

1. The blood ratified the Old Covenant.

2. God was the One Who drew the design of the Old Covenant as well as the New.

3. Because it was of God, the ritual had to be carried out with exact precision.

4. Not only was the design entirely by God, each part of the design represented the coming Christ, which gives it a significance of vast proportions.

THIS IS THE BLOOD

The phrase, *"Saying, 'This is the Blood of the Testament',"* presents that which made the Old Covenant valid. As we have stated, all of this represents Christ in some way.

When Moses said, *"This is the Blood,"* even though it was only at that time the blood of animals, it represented the Son of God, and made the statement that this is the only way that man can be saved.

The Sacrifice of Christ, which was the offering of Himself by the pouring out of His Blood, and the sacrifices of other things, have always been the dividing line between the True and the false. *"This is the Blood,"* proclaims totally and completely that which it would take in order for man to be redeemed. It would have to be the precious, shed Blood of the Lamb, i.e., *"Christ"* (I Pet. 1:18-20).

Of course, when we speak of *"The Blood,"* we are at the same time speaking of *"The Cross,"* and at the same time speaking of *"The Gospel,"* and at the same time, speaking of *"The Faith."* They basically all mean the same thing! When we preach the Cross, we are preaching the Blood, and when we preach the Blood, we are preaching the Cross! Surely the Reader can see the vast significance in all of this, and how important it is that our Faith be properly placed.

When man fell in the Garden of Eden, life was forfeited, which speaks of Life from God. In other words, the life force that came constantly from God to Adam, and was intended to continue to come to all who would be born thereafter, was suddenly cut off. Due to Adam's Fall, it was cut off not only to the first man, but as well to all who would follow thereafter, because in effect, all were in Adam's loins. So when he sinned, he sinned for all, and, likewise, when Christ purchased back this *"Life"* with His Own Blood, He did so for all — at least for those who will believe (Jn. 3:16; I Cor. 15:45-50).

DESIGNED BY GOD

The phrase continuing, *"Which God hath enjoined unto you,"* presents the fact, that everything in the First Covenant, exactly as in the New Covenant, is all of God, and not at all of man. In fact, if man adds anything or subtracts anything, he has destroyed this which *"God hath enjoined unto you."* This phrase is derived from Exodus 24:8.

Once again, Paul uses the word *"enjoined,"* which means that he did not regard this as strictly of the nature of a Covenant, or compact. While it definitely was a Covenant, it was not strictly of the nature of a Covenant. When a compact or covenant is made between two parties, one does not enjoin or command the other, it is a mutual agreement.

In the transactions between God and man, though called a Covenant or Testament, it is definitely not a transaction between equals, or an agreement in this capacity. It is in fact, a solemn arrangement on the part of God which He proposes to men, and which He enjoins them to embrace; which they are not indeed at liberty to disregard, but which, when embraced, is appropriately ratified by some solemn act on their part, in this case, the shedding of blood.

The Testator of the First Covenant was God, for it was God Who was the Source of Salvation for Believers in Old Testament Times. But God was not yet ready to come in the Person of His Son and die on the Cross for man. Therefore, He provided a substitute that would typically represent Him in death, a death that would make the First Testament effective. This substitute was an animal. The emphasis in these Verses is that everything connected with the Testament bears the mark of blood, therefore, death.

(21) "MOREOVER HE SPRINKLED WITH BLOOD BOTH THE TABERNACLE, AND ALL THE VESSELS OF THE MINISTRY."

The structure is:

1. Moses sprinkled not only the Book and the people, but as well, the Tabernacle and all the Vessels of the Ministry.

2. God told him to do this.

3. This shows us the absolute necessity of the Blood of Christ as it regards Salvation.

THE BLOOD

This particular Verse portrays the fact of the awfulness of sin, in that it has contaminated everything on this Earth. This of course, is not to leave the impression that some particular type of ritual must be engaged now as it regards cleansing, but that which God enjoined (commanded) under the Old Covenant was typical of the severity of the problem.

As well, in sprinkling both the Tabernacle and all the Vessels of the Ministry, we are told that every single thing that pertains to God as it regards our present Salvation has come to us, and in its entirety, by and through the Shed Blood of Jesus Christ. As well, everything we do for Him, once again, typified by the Tabernacle and the Vessels, must also be anchored in the *"Blood of the Lamb."*

All of this is meant to portray theology in the sense of the significance of what is being presented here. The idea is this:

Not only does Salvation come through the Cross, but as well, the Baptism with the Holy Spirit, all Grace, Peace, Divine Healing, financial prosperity, Justification, Sanctification, Reconciliation, etc. This one Verse, plus scores of others which could be added, proclaims the fact that the Cross is the Source of all things, at least all things that are from God.

Once again, the Reader must understand, that every single thing demanded by the Lord in the Old Covenant, pointed to Christ and His sacrificial work. This is the reason that it is very difficult for one to understand the New Testament, if one doesn't understand the Old. In picture form, and symbolic form, the Old Testament portrays the entirety of the Work of Christ, in order that there be no misunderstanding.

This is what made it so awful that the Jews, who were so intimately acquainted with the Old Testament, did not recognize Christ when He came, especially considering, that the entirety of the Old Covenant pointed directly to Him.

(22) "AND ALMOST ALL THINGS ARE BY THE LAW PURGED WITH BLOOD; AND WITHOUT SHEDDING OF BLOOD IS NO REMISSION."

The exegesis is:

1. *"Almost all things"* refers to some things in Tabernacle worship, which were ceremonially purged with water and fire (Num. 31:23). An example is the ashes of the red heifer, to which we have already addressed (Num. 19:2-10).

2. *"Purged with blood"* presents the fact that these things were ceremonially purged, which means, that the blood of calves and goats couldn't take away sin.

3. The shedding of the blood of animals in sacrifice was symbolic of the Blood which would be shed by Christ, and which would cleanse from sin.

ALMOST ALL THINGS

The phrase, *"And almost all things,"* pertains as we have stated, to some things which were cleansed with water.

Concerning some things cleansed only with water, if the Holy Spirit had anything in mind here in the giving of these instructions more than practical application, it would have pertained to the fact that He (the Holy Spirit), cannot properly do His work, in fact, cannot do any work at all, unless the blood has been applied to the principal objects. To say it another way, the Holy Spirit, typified by the water, works exclusively from the premise of the Shed Blood of the Lamb. Therefore, the leaving of some things to be cleansed only by water could have been a portrayal of the work of the Spirit. Due to the vast significance of this, please allow us to make the following statements:

As we've said several times, every single thing done on Earth by and through the Godhead, is done exclusively by and through the Person, Office, Ministry, and Power of the Holy Spirit. However, He works on one premise alone, and that is by and through the great Sacrifice of Christ, which of course portrays the Shed Blood of the Son of God poured out on behalf of lost humanity. This means that the Sacrifice of Christ is the only means by which the sinner can be saved, and the Christian can walk in victory on a daily basis.

In regard to this, I think I can say without any fear of exaggeration, that the Holy Spirit demands that we as Believers exhibit faith

at all times in the Finished Work of Christ, always understanding, that it is from this Source that everything flows from God to humanity (Rom. 8:2).

If in fact this is the case, and it definitely is, then where does that leave the modern Church which knows and understands this little or not at all? For me as a Believer to be what I ought to be in Christ, I have to have the work and operation of the Holy Spirit within my heart and life. That is absolutely imperative! However, just because I am baptized with the Holy Spirit, with the evidence of speaking with other Tongues, by no means guarantees this work. The potential is there, but it definitely isn't automatic, as many Christians seem to believe.

There are millions of Christians speaking in tongues quite often, which is Scriptural and right, but are still living lives of spiritual failure. There are even many Christians with the Gifts of the Spirit working within their lives, and rightly so, which includes Preachers whom God is using, and because they are called of God, and they are allowing the Holy Spirit to flow through them and function according to that call. But irrespective of that, untold numbers of these that we have just mentioned are living lives of spiritual failure. In other words, sin is dominating them in some way, in some fashion!

Now we've already addressed that in previous Commentary, but due to the fact that it is so important, I have felt led to mention it again. The Church doesn't understand this, and thereby casts about trying to find a solution to the problem. And to be frank, the proposed solutions much of the time, is worthy of a Roman Circus.

No! It doesn't matter who the individual might be. Preacher or otherwise, God has only one prescribed order of victory, and that is the victory of the Cross (Rom. 6:3-5, 11, 14; 8:1-2, 11). And if the individual doesn't know that prescribed order, it makes no difference that he might be pastoring the largest Church in the land, or drawing the largest crowds, etc., he is still going to walk in failure.

The reason is, while the Holy Spirit will help the individual regarding certain things, and because it is within the boundaries of the way He works, as it regards our personal lives, if we step outside of the boundaries of the Cross, the Holy Spirit just simply will not help us and that means that we are left on our own. We're then guaranteed to fail, and regrettably, that's the condition of most of the modern Church world.

As I keep saying over and over again, the Holy Spirit works according to *"The Law of the Spirit of Life in Christ Jesus"* (Rom. 8:2). In simple terms, that Law pertains to what Christ did at the Cross on behalf of humanity. In other words, Jesus did certain things for us through His Sacrifice of the Cross, and the Holy Spirit works within the boundaries and the parameters of that which Christ has done. He demands that we do the same thing. And how do we do that?

It is all a matter of Faith, which means that we believe in what Jesus did there, understanding that this is the means by which the Lord works with humanity. Faith anchored in the Finished Work of Christ, and continued in the Finished Work of Christ, will guarantee victory for any Saint, no matter who the person might be, etc. And as stated, this is God's only prescribed order of victory. He has no other, and simply because no other is needed.

PURGED WITH BLOOD

The phrase, *"Are by the Law purged with blood,"* speaks of a ceremonial purging, which is the most that the blood of bulls and goats could do. These particular sacrifices under the Old Covenant, couldn't take away sins (Heb. 10:4).

However, even though the shed blood of the Old Covenant couldn't take away sins, it definitely served as a pattern for the One Who was coming, Who definitely could take away sins, even as Paul mentions in Verse 23.

In looking at all of this, some may inwardly flinch at the rivers of blood which were shed, necessitating the slaughter of untold millions of animals down through the centuries. Every single day, there was a Sacrifice offered at 9 o'clock in the morning and at 3 o'clock in the afternoon. On the Sabbath, two animals were offered at each Sacrifice.

As stated, this was done on a daily basis, actually never ending, and was in addition to the untold numbers of Sacrifices constantly

offered by the people of Israel, who came to the Tabernacle or Temple. In fact, it was a never ending work.

On top of all of that, tremendous numbers of Sacrifices were offered on the Feast Days of the year, with as many as a quarter of a million Sacrifices being offered during Passover week, according to Josephus.

While the carnal mind may wonder at the necessity of all of this, the spiritual mind knows and understands why it was necessary. This tells us, this river of blood, how awful and bad that sin really is, how destructive it is, and at the same time how difficult it is to roll back its terrible effect of stealing, killing, and destroying (Jn. 10:10).

If one wants to know exactly how awful, how horrible, how terrible that sin actually is, one need only look at the Sacrifice of Christ. The agony, the horror, the terrible price He had to pay, gives us the answer to our question. When we look at His Crucifixion, when we think of His Crucifixion, when we contemplate His Crucifixion, realizing the utter, absolute horror of it all, we can only say, *"sin did this!"* And we might quickly add, that this alone is the remedy for sin.

THE SHEDDING OF BLOOD

The phrase, *"And without shedding of blood is no remission,"* proclaims the Apostle as portraying the Old Law as being symbolic of that which Christ would do, in the shedding of His Blood, which in fact, did cleanse from all sin (Jn. 1:29).

To be more specific, Paul shows here that there can be no Redemption but through the Blood of Christ; and to prefigure this, the Law could not grant any remission of sin without the blood of a victim.

More particular here, Paul is talking about the Shed Blood of Christ, which was an absolute necessity, that is if sin was to be remitted, i.e., *"cleansed and taken away."* This means, as is overly obvious, that one cannot be saved unless one trusts in Christ and what He did at the Cross for us. While the believing sinner may not understand much about this, and what little he does know has been imparted to him by the Spirit, still, it requires faith on his part in the Finished Work, in order to be saved (Jn. 3:16).

Satan has been very successful in pushing other things into the mix, attempting to dilute the one way of Salvation, which is the Blood. He is very successful in this, with many Christians and even Preachers doing this, and deceived into thinking otherwise. It is never Christ plus, but always Christ and Him Crucified, as the order of Salvation.

SIN

Sin is the major problem of humanity, even as it is the major problem of the Church. Unfortunately, such a statement is denied by most of the world and most of the Church. The world doesn't recognize sin for what it is, and many in the modern Church refuse to believe that sin is their problem. However, the type of sin of which is actually the problem is very subtle.

It's not so much acts of sin, as it is rebellion against the Finished Work of Christ. In other words, Satan tries to get the Believer to shift his Faith from the Cross to other things. This is the great sin; it is rebellion against God's Way of Salvation and victory, and in fact, God's only way of Salvation and Victory. Of course, Satan knows when this is done, that acts of sin will then begin to appear, with the sin nature ultimately beginning to once again rule in the heart and life of the Believer.

But when we Believers think of sin, almost all the time we think of acts of sin. That's not what Paul is speaking about in his explanation of this in Romans, Chapters 6, 7, and 8. When we get to acts of sin, we have already traveled down this road of defeat quite a ways. And then when we attempt to start opposing the acts of sin, by making up our own rules and regulations, etc., we get very confused because our efforts do not bring forth any proper fruit. The trouble is we are opposing symptoms instead of the real cause.

The real cause is a shifting of our Faith from the Finished Work of Christ, to something else, and it doesn't really matter what else it is.

Millions have their faith in a particular Preacher. Paul addressed this in I Corinthians Chapter 1. Satan doesn't mind this at all, because he knows that faith so placed will never bring about any victory. Millions of other Christians place their faith in a Denomination. Satan is not bothered by that either,

NOTES

knowing that the Christian will find no help there. In fact, this list is very long, and the Evil One is very content for you to believe in these things until the day you die. He knows that you will find no victory there, and as well, that your spiritual situation will continue to deteriorate.

When Jesus came to this world, He came to address sin. That was His purpose for coming. His purpose for coming was not that you may trade your Neon for a Cadillac, or you may get an increase in pay, etc. Such thinking does tremendous violence to the Word of God.

Man's problem is not physical, or else God would have sent a doctor. Man's problem is not economic, or the Lord would have sent an economist. Man's problem is not scientific, or else the Lord would have sent a scientist. Man's problem is sin, so God sent a Savior. All of this is so important that we must be allowed to say it again:

ONE WAY OF SALVATION

It is universally true that sin never has been, never will be forgiven, except in connection with and in virtue of the shedding of blood, the Blood of Christ. It is on this principle that the Plan of Salvation by the Atonement is based, and on this that God in fact bestows pardon on men. There is not the slightest evidence that any man has ever been pardoned except through the Blood shed by Christ for the remission of sins.

In light of this, it remains to be demonstrated that not one single member of the human family has ever had the slightest evidence of pardoned sin, except through the blood of expiation. In the Divine arrangement there is no principle better established than this, that all sin which is forgiven is remitted through the Blood of the Atonement; a principle which has never been departed from hitherto, and which never will be. Consequently, it follows, therefore:

1. No sinner can hope for forgiveness except through the Blood of Christ.

2. That if men are ever saved they must be willing to rely on the merits of that Blood.

3. That all men are on a level in regard to Salvation, since all are to be saved in the same way.

4. There will be one and the same song in Heaven — the song of redeeming love.

(23) "IT WAS THEREFORE NECESSARY THAT THE PATTERNS OF THINGS IN THE HEAVENS SHOULD BE PURIFIED WITH THESE; BUT THE HEAVENLY THINGS THEMSELVES WITH BETTER SACRIFICES THAN THESE."

The composite is:

1. *"The patterns of things in the Heavens"* refers to the real which is in Heaven.

2. The Tabernacle, although designed by God, and of God, needed cleansing from the defilement it incurred by reason of its presence in the midst of a sinful people.

3. This Rite was observed on the Great Day of Atonement (Lev. 16:16).

4. *"These"* referred to animal sacrifices. Thus, the sacrificial blood of animals was used to cleanse the Tabernacle in Israel from the defilement it contracted by reason of its position in the camp of Israel.

5. We learn from this Verse that sin is so widespread, and has had such an effect, that even the Heaven of heavens had to be cleansed, which was done by the Death of Christ.

PURIFICATION

The phrase, *"It was therefore necessary that the patterns of things in the heavens should be purified with these,"* pertains to several things:

1. The Tabernacle and all of its sacred vessels, were a copy of that which was in Heaven.

2. Consequently, every single thing about the Tabernacle and its Vessels, plus the manner that everything was to be used, were all, and without exception, designed by God, with the understanding, that man must not, under any consideration, insert his thoughts or activity into the process.

3. Everything in the Tabernacle and as it pertained to the Sacred Vessels, plus the manner in which all of it was to be used, portrayed Christ in some manner, as it regarded His Life, Ministry, Death, Resurrection, and Exaltation.

4. All of this was a part of the Law of Moses, intended to portray to Israel the fact that Salvation was in the One Whom all of this represented, namely Christ, and not at all in the rituals, ceremonies, or even the Sacrifices themselves.

NOTES

5. Due to the fact, that man had touched these things, even though they were designed and given by God, they all were defiled and, therefore, needed purification, i.e., *"cleansing."*

6. The cleansing process, could only be done in the manner prescribed by the Lord, which was by the blood of a clean animal, an animal incidentally offered in sacrifice, was to represent the Blood of Christ which would ultimately be shed.

7. In reality, the blood of the sacrificed animals did not really cleanse or purify anything, simply because they were insufficient to do so (Heb. 10:4), but the symbolism pointed to One Who ultimately would cleanse from all sin.

A BETTER SACRIFICE

The phrase, *"But the heavenly things themselves with better Sacrifices than these,"* refers to the fact that the Shed Blood of Christ addressed itself, not only to the sins of man, but to the entirety of the revolution of Lucifer, which began long before man was created (Isa. 14; Ezek. Chpt. 28).

Paul alluded to this when he said, *"That in the dispensation of the fullness of times He might gather together in one all things in Christ, both which are in Heaven and which are on Earth; even in Him"* (Eph. 1:10).

This passage as well, tells us that what Christ did on the Cross, addressed itself to Heaven, as well as it did the Earth. In other words, what Jesus did on the Cross, addressed the entirety of this problem of sin and rebellion, as invented, nurtured, and fostered by Satan himself.

The question at once arises as to why Heaven itself needed to be cleansed?

This revolution against God instituted by Lucifer, which drew away a third of the Angels (Rev. 12:4), is of far greater magnitude than meets the eye. We only know and understand, at least somewhat, the part of this revolution that affects man, with only an inkling of that which pertained to Heaven itself. But we do know that a revolution which would draw away a third of the angels, which instituted this war between good and evil, between God and Satan, has to be of immense magnitude. Many Bible Scholars believe that Lucifer actually ruled this Earth before man was ever created, and did so in righteousness, purity, and holiness, subject to God. But at a point in time, lifted up in himself because of his great wisdom and beauty, he led this revolution against God, which extended all the way to Heaven itself, as would be obvious. Some believe, and it possibly is true, that demon spirits, which we know that God didn't create in this fashion, actually were subjects of Lucifer in the pre-Adamite Earth, and who threw in their lot with the Evil One, with the result being that of which we presently know and understand as *"demon spirits."*

When God created Adam and Eve, as well, his helpmate, giving Adam dominion over God's creation (Ps. 8), and more particularly this refurbished Earth, this must have angered Lucifer greatly so. Consequently, he sets out to wreak havoc almost immediately, which resulted in the Fall of Adam and Eve, which as well, corrupted the entirety of the human race which was to come.

Therefore, when God became man, and came to this Earth to die on a Cross, which was His destination, His Death definitely was carried out in order to redeem mankind, but as well, it addressed itself to the entirety of the world of darkness, which included the totality of the revolution of Lucifer against God. So, the Blood of Jesus not only cleansed man from sin, but also cleansed the heavens themselves, even the very Throne of God, which means that His Death and Resurrection, is of such magnitude as to defy all description.

THE WAYS OF GOD

Even though we have already alluded to the following in previous Commentary, due to its complexity, and vast significance, please allow us to state the case of the legalities of God once again.

As a child, I wondered in my mind, as to why God didn't simply kill the Devil or do with him whatever is necessary, in order to stop all of this problem! Perhaps that question might be in your mind as well.

In the first place, spirit beings cannot die, and Satan as well as all Angels are spirit beings. But of course, that begs the issue. God surely could have just simply locked Satan away, as He will ultimately do in the Lake of Fire (Rev. 20:10-15).

There is a reason that God has not yet locked away Satan, etc. God in His creative processes has fashioned all things according to Laws, which He has devised Himself. In other words, the entirety of this universe, and all that is therein, operates totally and completely according to these Laws laid down by God at the outset of creation (Gen. 1:1). The reason for the great problems on Earth at present is because of the fact that man has broken these Laws, which has brought about untold death, suffering, and destruction (Jn. 10:10).

God not only made these Laws, but He as well, abides by these Laws. Consequently, the situation with Satan would have to be resolved in a legal manner, or else God would be no different than Satan himself.

It is somewhat the same as man presently taking the law into his own hands, thereby ignoring civil authority. If this is done, anarchy soon prevails, and the entire fabric of society is destroyed. Even as nations have to abide by laws, which they do more or less, God does the same thing, as should be obvious.

Without going into further detail, God would have to put down this revolution by legal means, and those legal means were and are, God becoming man, in effect, becoming the *"Last Adam,"* Who would purchase back what the original Adam forfeited in the Fall. He did this, by going to the Cross, which satisfied the righteousness of God, and thereby atoned for all sin. This did away with the legal claims of Satan upon man, simply because sin is Satan's legal right to hold man in captivity; however, when Jesus atoned for all sin, Satan has no more legal right. However, there is a problem inherent in all of this.

OBEDIENCE TO GOD

Looking at the situation, and understanding that the world, at least for the most part, is still held captive by Satan, we might ask the question as to whether the Sacrifice of Christ was effective?

Most definitely it was effective, and in such a way as to defy all description; however, for man to accrue to himself the benefits of all that Christ did for us on the Cross, man must believe that Jesus Christ is the answer, and in fact the only answer, and thereby accept

Him as Lord and Savior. In other words, man has to shift his allegiance from Satan to Christ. Satan is the god of this present world, which means that most of humanity serves him (II Cor. 4:4). Until man avails himself of what Christ has done on the Cross, and does so by Faith, which is the only way it can be done (Eph. 2:8-9), he will remain under the domain of Satan. It remains for man to accept Christ to be liberated from the bondages of eternal darkness.

Of course, Satan fights the Cross in every way possible as it regards the world, shrouding man in unbelief and deception, which keeps most of humanity from accepting Christ (Mat. 7:13-14). However, the Church basically has the same problem as the world, and I speak of total and complete trust in the Cross of Christ.

THE CROSS OF CHRIST

As Satan tries to deceive the world, and I speak of the unredeemed, as it regards the Cross of Christ, he by no means stops his efforts of deception as it regards the Church. As he tries to get man to think he can save himself, he tries to get the Christian to think he can sanctify himself. And in one sentence, there is the great problem of mankind, both as it pertains to the unsaved and the saved.

As the sinner can no more save himself by his own efforts, likewise the Christian can no more sanctify himself by his personal efforts. Both present a hopeless task. So how does Satan go about attempting to accomplish this task of getting the Christian into the realm of self-sanctification?

The Evil One first of all attacks the Cross. He does this in many ways, many of these ways are very subtle, and some very blatant.

His first effort is to get the Preacher to direct his attention to things other than the Cross. Of course, Satan doesn't want the Gospel preached in any capacity, but above all, he doesn't want the Cross preached. If he can stop the preaching of the Cross, He can pretty well dissipate everything else, for the simple reason, that the Cross is the foundation of the Gospel, in effect, it is the Gospel (I Cor. 1:18, 23; 2:2). And that's what's happened the last half-century as it regards the Church. There has been so little preaching

and teaching on the Cross of Christ, until the modern Church is for all practical purposes, Cross illiterate, which means at the same time, it is for the most part, blind to the true things of God. And of course when the blind lead the blind, even as the Master said, both fall into the ditch.

So at the present, we have a Church that has set the Cross aside, opting for other things, not the least of them being humanistic psychology. However, in other circles, the Cross is not merely being politely ignored, it is being blatantly attacked. I speak of great parts of the Charismatic Church, especially those, or at least most of those, who go under the heading of *"Word of Faith,"* etc.

Almost on a daily basis, we get e-mail from individuals all over the world, pointing out the errors of the *"Faith Message."* However, every single one of these descriptions I've seen, basically address themselves to symptoms. In other words, they show the wrong way that the Faith Ministry has gone, but they don't show why it has gone in that direction. Consequently, as stated, they are merely addressing themselves to symptoms.

The reason that the faith world, which in reality, is no faith at all, at least that which God will recognize, has gone in these erroneous directions, which has probably caused more damage to the Church than anything else in the last 50 years, is because its teaching is not based on the Cross. It has ignored the Cross, making other things the object of Faith, which God will never recognize, and because it insults the great Sacrifice of Christ. Any doctrine must have as its firm foundation the Cross of Christ. If not, such doctrine will become more and more off base. And that's exactly what the so-called Faith Ministry has done.

While the error should be pointed out, the cause of the error above all should be pointed out. To show the error, and not show the cause or the solution, leaves the soul hanging in spiritual limbo.

Getting back to the original thought, the Believer must place his Faith in the Cross one hundred percent, as it regards anything and everything that comes from God. The Lord does not deal with the human race in any capacity, except through the Cross, and by that we speak of the Shed Blood of Christ. As well, He doesn't deal with the Church except through the same method. It is always the Cross! The Cross! The Cross!

The Holy Spirit lives within our hearts and lives as a Born-Again Believer, strictly because of what Christ did at the Cross on our behalf. There the great sin debt was paid, meaning that all sin was washed and cleansed, making it possible for the Holy Spirit to come in and abide permanently. However, even as we have said it in every way we know how, He, and we speak of the Spirit, will not work within our lives, unless our Faith is anchored totally and completely in the Cross of Christ. And when I say, *"work within our lives,"* I am speaking of Sanctification, i.e., *"the Fruit of the Spirit,"* etc.

There is no victory for the Saint outside of the Cross. There is no consecration, at least true consecration for the Saint, outside of the Cross. There is no Spiritual Growth outside of the Cross. Over and over again, this is what Paul's Epistle to the Hebrews tells us.

DECEPTION

Satan's efforts of deception are just as powerful within the Church as outside of the Church. It's the age-old problem of self-dependency, or the dependence on anything other than the Cross of Christ. One would think that every Christian would know and understand the veracity of the Cross, but due to the fact that it's been so little preached and taught in the last several decades, most Christians have no understanding at all as to the part the Cross plays in their everyday living before God; consequently, most Christians walk in spiritual defeat in one way or the other.

Even though the statement I'm about to make is strong, and to be sure, I pray that I'm wrong, but I fear that I'm right.

The Church is probably in worse spiritual condition presently than it has ever been since the Reformation. It's like a blind giant that doesn't know where it's been, where it is, or where it's going. In other words, it is vastly deceived.

But this deception of which I speak, has a greater power than just merely an erroneous direction. It is deception that goes down into the very recesses of the soul. Let me explain:

Since the Lord began to open up to me the Revelation of the Cross in 1996, and has continued to expand that Revelation from then until now, and I trust will ever continue, I have had occasion to observe many things as it regards people who are living for God.

For instance, I watch Christians who are in deep trouble spiritually, with their lives about to become unraveled, with everything which they love and hold dear about to disintegrate before their eyes, and because of sin, and they still will not avail themselves of the great Victory of the Cross.

One man called one of my associates the other day, a man incidentally who was and is a stranger to us, pouring out his soul to him, asking for help. He was in a *"Word of Faith"* Church, actually one of its Elders, if I remember correctly what I was told.

He blurted out to my associate, *"I'm a homosexual, and no one knows about this but myself, and I'm seriously considering suicide."* He went on to say, *"I've tried everything I know, but nothing helps."* He then told us how that he had begun hearing our daily program, actually aired seven days a week, over SonLife Radio. He said, *"For the first time, I sense that there is something that can help me."*

My associate, as he spoke with him over the phone, pleaded with him to come to Family Worship Center, where he could sit under teaching that would set him free.

The man said, *"I want to do that, but I'm afraid that I can't."* When asked why? His answer was most revealing, and yet indicative of so many:

"My family won't come with me!" he said.

One would think that one in such a situation of such desperation would pay any price to find help. But as stated, deception is a powerful weapon in the hands of Satan.

While we have many in our own Church, Family Worship Center, who have availed themselves of what the Lord has given to us as it regards the Cross, still, there are some in the Church who haven't. Think of that!

There is absolutely nothing in the world more important to the Child of God than knowing God's prescribed order of victory, which is the Cross. To have the opportunity to learn this, to know this, and understanding that it is the Holy Spirit Who is revealing this, and then not take advantage of such an opportunity, is a tragedy of unprecedented proportions. No wonder that Jesus said, *"For the children of this world are in their generation wiser than the Children of Light"* (Lk. 16:8).

If there were several ways of victory and abundant life, that would be different. But there is only one way, and that is the Cross, and if we miss that way, we've missed everything, for there is victory in no other!

THE PEARL OF GREAT PRICE

Jesus addresses this very succinctly when He said *"The Kingdom of Heaven is like unto treasure hid in a field; the which when a man hath found, he hideth, and for joy thereof goeth and selleth all that he hath, and buyeth that field."*

He then said, *"Again, the Kingdom of Heaven is like unto a merchant man seeking goodly pearls:*

"Who, when he hath found one pearl of great price, went and sold all that he had, and bought it" (Mat. 13:44-46).

Is the *"pearl of great price, which is the Cross"* worth having?

In fact, it is of such value, that Jesus told us that everything else must fall by the wayside, with us doing whatever is necessary to obtain this *"treasure,"* i.e., *"this pearl."*

The tragedy is, most Christians don't recognize the *"treasure"* or the *"pearl"* when they see it! And then others do recognize it, but don't want to pay the price demanded in order for such to be obtained.

(24) "FOR CHRIST IS NOT ENTERED INTO THE HOLY PLACES MADE WITH HANDS, WHICH ARE THE FIGURES OF THE TRUE; BUT INTO HEAVEN ITSELF, NOW TO APPEAR IN THE PRESENCE OF GOD FOR US:"

The exegesis is:

1. Christ did not go into the Holy of Holies of the earthly Tabernacle or Temple, which would have been useless anyway. He went into the Heavenly Holy of Holies.

2. That on the Earth, and we continue to speak of the Tabernacle or the Temple, were only figures of the True.

3. It was not earthly Priests to whom He must answer, but to God Himself, which He

did! It is God who had been grossly offended, and not man; consequently, it was His Righteousness which must be satisfied, and which was.

THE HOLY PLACES MADE WITH HANDS

The phrase, *"For Christ is not entered into the holy places made with hands,"* presents the Apostle telling these Christian Jews, of the true worth of the earthly Tabernacle by comparison to that which was Heavenly. In this explanation, Paul as well gives us the function of the earthly Tabernacle, which was meant to serve as a symbol of the *"True."* Inasmuch as the *"True"* has come, why do we now need the symbol?

Verse 24 is an explanation of the statement in the previous Verse to the effect that the Heavenly things had to be purified by blood superior to animal blood, and that the Messiah did not enter the Holy of Holies on Earth as High Priest, for that would have done no good, but the Holy of Holies of Heaven itself. As we have stated, it was God Who had been offended, and it was, therefore, the Righteousness of God which must be satisfied.

Christ did not enter into a Holy Place made with hands, which of course was the Tabernacle, to offer repeated sacrifices, as the Priests had been doing for nearly 1,600 years, but to present Himself in the perfection of His One Great Sacrifice — so sufficing and effectual that it needs no repetition.

The *"better sacrifices"* of Verse 23, represent the One Sacrifice of Christ, which is the greater Sacrifice, and which suffices for all.

The ground has now been laid which enables the Apostle to open up for us the special truth of the New Dispensation, and to show how fully Christ has superceded all the types of old.

We have already been presented the idea by the Apostle that Christ's Ministry was not in a Sanctuary that is *"man-made,"* and here we come back to it. Not in such Sanctuaries, and we continue to speak of that made by man, even though God did design it, can the Atonement be made that really deals with sin.

COPIES

The phrase, *"Which are the figures of the true,"* presents the fact that the earthly holy places and things are mere representations of the true and the Heavenly, which they were intended to be. The earthly antitype points to the Heavenly reality, *"the true one."*

Unfortunately, as the Christian Jews of Paul's day lost sight of the true meaning of the Tabernacle, likewise, many in the modern Church follow down that erroneous path. As Israel attempted to make Salvation out of the Tabernacle, likewise, many modern Christians attempt to make Salvation out of the Church, along with some of its ordinances, such as Water Baptism, the Lord's Supper, etc.

As there was no Salvation in any of the ceremonies and rituals of the Old Testament Tabernacle and Temple, likewise, there is no Salvation in anything which pertains to the Church. Salvation has always only been in Christ, even as it is in Christ presently, and more particularly, in what Christ did for us in the offering of Himself on the Cross.

Cannot the Reader see here, that it is not merely Jesus, but rather what Jesus did for us in His Great Sacrifice. This sets the Cross ever before us, even as it must set the Cross ever before us.

That's the reason I keep saying, that if we think of Jesus apart from the Cross, we are not thinking of Him correctly. If we think of the Gospel apart from the Cross, we are not actually thinking of the Gospel correctly. If we think of victory apart from the Cross, then we are going to be sadly mistaken. It is not only Who He was, but as well, what He did! That is the *"true,"* and everything else is a mere *"figure."* We must not under any consideration, get the *"figure"* mixed up with the *"true."* And that's our problem!

THE APPEARANCE IN THE PRESENCE OF GOD

The phrase, *"But into heaven itself, now to appear in the Presence of God for us,"* presents the purpose and reason for the Cross.

The word *"now"* speaks of Christ's present Ministry in the New Testament dispensation as contrasted with the Old typical economy, and also refers to a continually present manifestation of Himself in the Heavenly Holy of Holies.

The word *"to appear"* deserves careful treatment.

Vincent translates, *"to be manifested."* He says this word *"exhibits the manifestation of Christ as something brought about as the result of a new and better economy, and distinctly contemplated in the institution of that economy. Christ is made openly manifest before the Face of God.*

"The Levitical Priests were compelled to shroud the Ark and the Shekinah with incense-smoke, that he might not look upon God face to face."

In fact, the darkness and clouds of incense in the old Sanctuary were meant as much to veil the unworthiness of the Priest from God as the Glory of God from the Priest. Now Christ appears before God face to face with no intervening cloud. Perfect fellowship is attained by His perfect and stainless offering of Himself. All is now clear between God and man, and because of what Jesus did for us at the Cross.

It is *"for us"* that He enters into this Presence and Fellowship; not that He Alone may enjoy it, but that we may enter into the rest and blessedness that He purchased for us, by the shedding of His Own Precious Blood.

THE THREE APPEARINGS OF CHRIST

In Verses 24-28 of this Ninth Chapter, we have what someone has very aptly designed, *"the three appearings of our Lord Jesus Christ"*: He hath appeared, He doth appear, He shall appear.

The order, however, is somewhat different, for the Holy Spirit dwells first on His present appearing as our Intercessor, as outlined in Verse 24, then turns our minds back to the time when He appeared to settle the sin question, as given in Verse 26, and in Verse 28, carries us forward to the glad hour when He shall appear the second time for our complete and glorious Redemption, which refers to His Second Coming.

To say it another way, Christ appeared to put away sin (vs. 26); He appeared to silence sin (vs. 24); and He will appear without sin (vs. 28).

He saves from the penalty, the power, and the presence of sin. His One Offering of Himself once offered has made an eternal settlement of the question of sin, and abolished it forever.

Because of the fact of sin no Covenant could be made between God and men who ignored sin. Hence both Covenants were based upon Atonement — the one typically (a type), the other actually. But whereas the Blood that ratified the First Covenant was only the blood of calves and of goats, that which ratified the Second and gave to it its validity, was the Precious Blood of Christ. Apart from the death of a sacrificial victim, a Covenant proposing the establishment of relations between God and men has no real value.

THE GLORIOUS THEME

The extent and value of Christ's Atoning Sacrifice of Himself is, therefore, the glorious theme of these Chapters. Three results appear:

1. Access to God.
2. Purification of the conscience.
3. Eternal Redemption.

These provide fellowship with God in a Righteousness in which no flaw can be found, and in a Redemption possessing eternal value. All is eternal because all is Divine.

The worshipper has a perfected conscience. This is much more than an innocent conscience. That is unconsciousness of evil and of God's Holiness. A perfected conscience knows God and dwells in His Presence with joy because of a consciousness of the value of the Precious Blood that cleanses from all sin.

FOR US

As Christ didn't go to the Cross to die for Himself, for He needed no Redemption, likewise, He did not appear in the Presence of God for Himself. He did it totally and completely *"for us."*

This means, that He has already appeared before God for me. And what did He do there?

His very appearance tells us that God had accepted His Sacrifice of Himself; therefore, every individual who places their trust in Christ and what He did at the Cross for us, is granted a perfect, pure, spotless righteousness, i.e., *"the Righteousness of Christ,"* which alone, God can accept. He went to the Cross *"for us,"* was resurrected *"for us"* (Rom. 4:25), and appeared in the Presence of God *"for us."*

Let it be understood, that *"His appearance in the Presence of God for us,"* signified a

NOTES

"Finished Work!" It was all done, meaning that there was nothing remaining. Everything had been accomplished. And again I emphasize, He did it all *"for us,"* which means that He did it for sinners.

Our Salvation is registered in *"Heaven itself."* And if it's not registered in Heaven itself, but rather some particular Church, then you aren't saved! So the question must be asked: *"Is your name written there, or is it merely written here?"*

(25) "NOR YET THAT HE SHOULD OFFER HIMSELF OFTEN, AS THE HIGH PRIEST ENTERETH INTO THE HOLY PLACE EVERY YEAR WITH BLOOD OF OTHERS;"

The structure is:

1. His one Sacrifice was sufficient.
2. The High Priests of old, having to enter year by year into the Holy of Holies, signified that their work was insufficient.
3. It was insufficient, because it was *"with blood of others,"* i.e., *"animal sacrifices."*

HE OFFERED HIMSELF ONCE

The phrase, *"Nor yet that He should offer Himself often,"* refers to the fact that the One Sacrifice of Christ, which was the Offering of Himself on the Cross, was eternally sufficient for the cleansing from all sin, past, present, and future. Even as the Apostle has stated, the Death of Christ on the Cross, sufficed as well, for all those who were under the First Covenant. Inasmuch, as the blood of bulls and goats could not take away sins, and above all couldn't address the fact of sin, it remained that the Sacrifice of Christ would perform this great act, which it did!

The very fact that the High Priests of old, had to go in year by year was within itself a testimony to its ineffectiveness. This Israel should have seen, but regrettably, they became enamored with the Ritual, just like many today are enamored with the Church.

The Cross work of Christ so to speak, can never be repeated, and because no repetition is required, in that it itself was totally sufficient. He settled the sin question perfectly when He took our place in judgment. And in this we have the great distinction between the legal sacrifices and His One Offering of Himself, when He put away sin by His Mighty

Sacrifice. The Offerings of old had to be repeated again and again because they did not possess value sufficient to settle the sin question. But His Precious Blood poured out for our Redemption was of such infinite value that it is sacrilegious even to think of adding to it in any way.

Having officiated at the Altar, which refers to the Cross, which answered the type of the Great Day of Atonement, He has now gone into the Sanctuary in Heaven in the value of His Own Blood, and by and by He will come out to bless His people as did the Priests of old, which we now refer to as the Second Coming, and which is referred to in Verse 28 of this Chapter.

HIS OFFERING

The word *"offer"* does not refer here to Christ offering Himself on the Cross, but rather to His entrance into the Holy of Holies, as well, on our behalf. He offered Himself there in the Presence of God for us, which was a once-for-all offering, which will never again have to be repeated. The point is, being once in the Heavenly Sanctuary, Christ is not compelled to renew again His presentation of Himself there, since, to do so, would state, that the Sacrifice of Himself was insufficient. His was a once-for-all entrance, based upon and given efficacy and merit by virtue of His Precious Blood, as against the annual entrance of the High Priest in Israel who came into the earthly Tabernacle by virtue of the blood of sacrificial animals.

So, what all of this means is that God accepted Him. That's a simple statement, but it carries far greater meaning than mere surface attention.

It was not so much that God accepted the Person of Christ, because that was a foregone conclusion. He had stated and rightly so, *"This is My Beloved Son, in Whom I am well pleased"* (Mat. 3:17).

The offering of Himself this one time, referred to the offering of His completed Work which had taken place at the Cross. Was it sufficient? Considering what that work had to do, would this one Sacrifice of Himself be sufficient?

We can understand the magnitude of the moment, when we understand the horror of

sin, and how it had polluted the very creation of God, and above all, had wrecked God's choice creation, which was and is man. In fact, the task was gargantuan, of such magnitude in fact, that it is impossible for us to fully comprehend and understand all that was done. That's the reason it's impossible to over magnify the Cross and it's efficacious Work. That's also the reason, that the Holy Spirit through John the Beloved, referred to Christ some seven times as the *"Lamb"* in the last two Chapters of the Book of Revelation. In those two Chapters, all is light, with every stain of sin having been purged and cleansed in the entirety of the universe, and for all time. But yet, the Holy Spirit refers to Christ as the *"Lamb,"* that we may know and understand, that all of this was brought about, the cleansing of man and the cleansing of the Heavenly Tabernacle by what Christ did at the Cross.

As well, considering that He referred to Christ as the *"Lamb"* seven times, and understanding that the number seven is God's number of perfection and completion, we realize, that what Jesus did was perfect, hence it is referred to as well by the Holy Spirit, as *"the everlasting Covenant"* (Heb. 13:20; Rev. 21:9, 14, 22-23, 27; 22:1, 3).

THE BLOOD OF OTHERS

The phrase, *"As the High Priest entereth into the Holy Place every year with blood of others,"* refers to the Great Day of Atonement, which took place once a year, every year. The *"blood of others"* refers to the blood of animal sacrifices, which refers to the fact, that it was not the Blood of Christ, therefore, could not really cleanse from sin. This is a great point in which the Work of Christ differs from that of the Jewish High Priest. Christ entered there with His Own Blood. Paul is showing these Christian Jews, the tremendous difference between the old Levitical order and that of Christ, and how superior was that of Christ.

The idea of all of this is, Christ did not enter a man-made Sanctuary . . . nor did He . . . offer Himself again and again. Paul is here concerned in this Verse to repudiate the idea that Christ might have made an offering from time to time in the manner of the High Priests. It was basic to their ministry, as we've already stated, to offer sacrifices repeatedly, just as it was basic to Christ's Ministry that He did not do so.

THE ONE OFFERING

Two things call for comment:

1. The first is the clear implication that only Christ's Offering can put away sin. The sins of those who lived in old times were also dealt with by Christ's One Offering. The reasoning is if that Offering had not been sufficient, Christ would have had to offer Himself *"again and again."* That is to say, no other offering is in view when it is a matter of really putting sin away.

2. The other point is that when the High Priest entered the Most Holy Place, he did so *"with blood that is not his own."* The superiority of Christ's Offering is seen in that He does not press into service some external means, like the blood of some noncooperating, noncomprehending animal. He uses His Own Blood and with it makes the one sufficient Offering (Morris).

(26) "FOR THEN MUST HE OFTEN HAVE SUFFERED SINCE THE FOUNDATION OF THE WORLD: BUT NOW ONCE IN THE END OF THE WORLD HATH HE APPEARED TO PUT AWAY SIN BY THE SACRIFICE OF HIMSELF."

The composite is:

1. If the One Offering of Christ had not been sufficient, He would have been forced to continue to offer Himself for each generation of humanity.

2. He only offered Himself once, so that shows that this Sacrifice was sufficient for all time.

3. This one Offering of Himself, *"put away sin,"* past, present, and future, at least for all who will believe.

THE FOUNDATION OF THE WORLD

The phrase, *"For then must He often have suffered since the foundation of the world,"* presents the fact that He wasn't functioning as did the High Priests of Israel, who yearly had to offer sacrifice.

Expositors say: *"If His Offering of Himself were not independent of time and valid as a single act, if it were valid only for the generation for whom it was immediately made, then in order to benefit men in the*

past, He must have suffered often, indeed in each generation of the past." But of course that didn't happen!

Vincent says: *"For, from the foundation of the world, sin required Atonement by Sacrifice; and, therefore, if Christ had been a victim like others, which must be offered repeatedly, He would have had to suffer repeatedly from the foundation of the world. If His Sacrifice, like the animal atonements, had availed for a time only, He would have been obliged to repeat His Offering whenever that time expired; and, since His Atonement was designed to be universal, it would have been necessary for Him to appear repeatedly upon Earth, and to die repeatedly from the foundation of the world."*

Inasmuch as this never happened, in that He offered Himself only once, this shows that His Sacrifice was sufficient for all time, as stated, past, present, and future, which made it vastly superior to the offering of animal sacrifices by the High Priests of Israel on a yearly basis.

BUT NOW ONCE

The phrase, *"But now once in the end of the world hath He appeared to put away sin by the Sacrifice of Himself,"* presents the One Sacrifice of Christ as sufficient for all time.

The phrase, *"In the end of the world,"* should have been translated *"in the consummation of the ages."* Jesus appeared on Earth to put away sin by the Sacrifice of Himself *"when the former ages had reached their moral consummation under the old Levitical economy."*

Expositors say: *"If there was to be One Sacrifice for all generations, the occurrence of that Sacrifice itself marked the period of the consummation. It closes the periods of symbolism, expectation, and doubt."*

"Appeared" in the Greek is *"phaneroo,"* and means, *"He has been manifested."* The appearance of Christ at the Cross corresponds to the appearance of the High Priest at the Brazen Altar on the Day of Atonement where the animal for sacrifice was slain. This is Christ's first appearance. He puts away sin. His second appearance, recorded in Verse 24, is in the Holy of Holies of Heaven, where He is presently. He took care of sin at the Cross,

and now He appears in the Presence of God for us who are saved, His appearance bringing Believers into the very Presence of God, which could only be done by the Sacrifice of Himself, and our Faith in that great Sacrifice.

THE FINISHED WORK

God allowed the ages to pass, and thus fully demonstrated that man is corrupt in nature and hostile in will. It was true of the world and it was true of Israel!

This demonstration of man's hopeless corruption magnifies, as a black background, the Grace and efficacy of Christ's Sacrifice of Himself. He appeared to load Himself with the fullness of that corruption; to suffer its doom, which He did by becoming a Sin-Offering, thereby removing the corruption; this redeemed the slaves of sin from sin, as this alone could redeem the slaves of sin from sin.

So effectual was His Atonement that He blotted sin out of the heavens and the Earth, making so complete an end of it as to cause as if it never had existed.

THE CATHOLIC MASS

This is at least one of the reasons, that the Catholic Mass is so wrong. It claims that the wine becomes the literal Blood of our Lord, and the Bread His literal Body, therefore, sacrificing Him all over again, and doing so repeatedly. I would hope that the Reader can see how that this is an abomination!

The Scriptural admonition is, *"but now once,"* meaning that this was sufficient for all time, and nothing must ever be done that would cast reflection on this *"once-for-all Offering."* That's the reason, that the single most important thing in the world is how we look at the Atonement of Christ. If we take from it in any way, which refers to looking elsewhere for Salvation and Victory, or we add to it in any manner, which refers to perverting it, then we do great injustice to the Finished Work of Christ.

While it's easily understood as to how one can easily take from the Atonement, what exactly do we mean by perverting the Atonement?

One manner in which the latter is done is by Christians thinking that the Atonement is such that they can sin all they desire with no repercussions. Paul addressed that when

he said, *"shall we sin that Grace may abound?"* His answer was cryptic and to the point, *"God forbid!"* (Rom. 6:1-2).

In the right and correct sense, it's impossible to make more of the Atonement than we should; however, by perverting it, which many have done and continue to do, it is possible to add to the Atonement that which God never intended. As stated, there is nothing more important than how we address the Atonement. In that lies all our Salvation, all our victory, and all that God has given to us. Therefore, nothing could be more important!

That's the reason I shrink back when I hear some of our Charismatic friends belittle and demean the Cross, claiming that it was the greatest moment of weakness and defeat that the world ever knew. While it definitely was weakness, it was a contrived weakness, meaning that Christ would not save Himself, even though He well could have done so and easily. However, the word *"defeat,"* comes close to blasphemy.

To claim that the Cross was a defeat shows a total misunderstanding of the Atonement, which refers to a total misunderstanding of the Word of God in general. Nothing could be more serious! And to be sure, people who attend such type Churches, will not come away unaffected. In fact, many will be seriously weakened in the spiritual sense, if not in fact, losing their souls!

PUT AWAY SIN

At the beginning of the Ministry of Christ, John the Baptist addressed the sin question concerning Christ, by saying of Him, *"Behold the Lamb of God, which taketh away the sin of the world"* (Jn. 1:29).

Please notice, that the forerunner of Christ referred to the Lord as *"the Lamb of God,"* insinuating the manner and the way in which the sin question would be handled. It would have to be by the Cross, which in fact had been predicted from the very beginning (Gen. 3:15).

Why the exact words *"taketh away sin,"* or as Paul used it, *"to put away sin"*?

As we've said quite a number of times already in this Commentary, and which Paul will also address in Hebrews 10:4, the blood of bulls and goats could not take away sin. The best the animal sacrifices could do, which were symbolic of the great Sacrifice to come, was to merely cover sin, meaning that in fact, the sin was still there. And it was only by the Goodness and Grace of God that this was allowed, because the payment which God demanded, and which He would pay Himself, was staggering, even beyond belief. This portrays to us the Love of God, but it also portrays to us exactly how bad, how awful, how terrible the sin problem actually is.

This is the reason that all Faith must be totally and completely in Christ, which translates into what He did for us at the Cross. That's the reason the Cross is the centrality of the Gospel, and in fact, is the Gospel. That's the reason when we say Faith, we always must understand that it is Faith in what Jesus did at the Cross. If we're talking about any other Jesus other than the Christ of the Cross, or any type of Faith that's not anchored squarely in the Cross of Christ, then what we're actually speaking of is *"another Jesus"* and *"another gospel"* (II Cor. 11:4), which avails nothing with God.

God doesn't demand much of the human race; however, in order to be saved, He does demand that the sinner place his trust exclusively in Christ, and more particularly what Christ did for him at the Cross (Jn. 3:16). When it comes to the Believer, He demands that we continue to trust in what Christ has done at the Cross, understanding that everything we receive from God, and ever will receive from God, comes exclusively through what Christ did for us by His great Sacrifice. If the Believer moves his faith to other things, and no matter how good or wonderful the other things might be, the Holy Spirit will cease all operations regarding help, and to be sure, there is no way that any Believer can make it, without the help of the Holy Spirit (Rom., Chpt. 7; 8:1-2, 11). And this is the major sin of the modern Church.

For several decades now, the Church has been taught to put its faith in this and that and the other, with the Cross being ignored. As a consequence, the Church is presently filled with people who aren't saved, and for those who are saved, nevertheless, for the most part, are walking in spiritual defeat. As I would trust that all of Paul's writings proclaim, and especially his Epistle to the Hebrews, there

is no way that the Believer can walk in victory, which refers to victory over the world, the flesh, and the Devil, without understanding these things of which I say. The Cross of Christ is the central focus of all that God has done for the human race. And by that we mean this:

We're not advocating putting Christ back on a Cross, or for you the Believer to strap yourself to some type of Cross. To be frank, that's silly!

The true meaning of all this of which we speak, is that the Cross is a Finished Work, accomplished in the past, but with continued results, and I might quickly add, results which will never be discontinued. To use an earthly analogy, one may explain it in this fashion:

A WORK ACCOMPLISHED IN THE PAST WITH CONTINUED RESULTS

The Constitution of the United States was framed by its designers regarding this country over 200 years ago. In fact, a war was fought with much blood spilled, in order to validate this Constitution. And yet, every single freedom that we Americans presently have, all prosperity, stems back, at least in a legal sense, to the Constitution of the United States. Those are our rights, and that which guarantees all of our freedoms under our form of government. It is the same identical way with the Cross.

The Cross of Christ is the *"New Covenant,"* in other words, that which makes the New Covenant valid. Consequently, every freedom I now own in Christ, all victory, all prosperity, all Spiritual Growth, all the work of the Holy Spirit, in fact everything, comes totally and completely, through the validation of that New Covenant which is the Cross of Christ. That's why Jesus said the following at what we refer to as the *"Last Supper"*:

"Take, eat: this is My Body, which is broken for you: this do in remembrance of Me.

"This cup is the New Testament (New Covenant) *in My Blood: this do ye, as oft as ye drink it, in remembrance of Me"* (I Cor. 11:24-25).

THE LORD'S SUPPER

This is the one ordinance in the Church, which we are commanded to keep on a continuing basis. The Lord didn't tell us how often we should take *"the Supper."* He merely told us, it was to be a continuing process, however often it would be done. But in this we are told several things:

1. We are to ever remember, that He gave His Body in Sacrifice, which was broken for us, and done so on the Cross.

2. He then specified His Shed Blood, symbolized by the *"cup,"* which in effect ratified the Covenant.

3. He told us that this, and we speak of the Cross, *"is the New Testament,"* i.e., *"The New Covenant."* It is ratified, as stated, *"in My Blood."*

4. He used the words as it regarded the continued taking of the Supper, *"as oft as ye drink it,"* with Paul including the same thing as it regards the *"eating of the bread"* (I Cor. 11:25-26). This tells us that this is to be a continued process, and for reason:

5. Or taking of the Lord's Supper, continues to *"show the Lord's Death til He come."* This refers to the fact, that this is to be ever before us, and if we make less of the Lord's Death than we should, we do ourselves great harm, even as the next verses in I Corinthians Chapter 11 proclaim.

As well, we should notice, that He didn't tell us to *"Show the Lord's Resurrection til He come,"* but rather *"the Lord's Death."* While of course, the Resurrection is of supreme significance, as should be overly obvious; however, we are to ever understand, that it was the Cross which paid the price, and not the Resurrection.

6. We're told that we must not *"eat this bread, and drink this cup of the Lord, unworthily."* If we do so, Paul continues, *"we shall be guilty of the Body and Blood of our Lord"* (I Cor. 11:27).

What does that mean?

It means as He stated in I Corinthians 11:29, that we are not *"properly discerning the Lord's Body."*

What did He mean by that?

In fact, what He meant by that is the single most important thing that any Christian could ever know and understand.

The Holy Spirit through Paul is telling us, *"to properly discern the Lord's Body, which means to properly discern His Death on the Cross, we must understand that every single thing we have from God, comes exclusively to us through Christ, and what He did for us on the Cross."*

Whenever we were told to *"examine ourselves,"* as it regards the eating and drinking of the *"bread"* and the *"cup"* (I Cor. 11:28), it is referring to Faith that must be placed exclusively in the Cross of Christ. It is not telling us that there has to be sinless perfection in our lives in order for us to take the Lord's Supper as Believers. He is saying to us, that we must understand that all Mercy, Grace, Forgiveness, Compassion, and cleansing for all sin, come totally and exclusively, through what Jesus did for us at the Cross, and our faith in that. In *"examining ourselves"* we must make doubly certain, that our Faith is properly placed in the Cross. That is properly *"discerning the Lord's Body."*

7. If we do not properly discern the Lord's Body, which simply refers to having Faith in that Finished Work, we literally *"eat and drink damnation to ourselves."* As should be obvious, this is an extremely serious thing.

It simply means, that if we do not properly discern the Cross, for that's what it means, then we've cut off ourselves from God, because it is through the Cross that God gives us all things. Now you can understand why I'm so adamant as it regards continued Faith in the Cross of Christ, and why I constantly warn you not to listen to false teachers who would pull your faith away to other things. To do such, is to literally wreck yourself, of which Paul will here have more to say.

8. Because of not properly discerning the Lord's Body, i.e., not maintaining Faith in the Finished Work of Christ for all things, the Apostle said *"For this cause* (not maintaining faith in the Finished Work) *many* (many Christians) *are weak and sickly among you* (bring upon themselves unnecessary illnesses), *and many sleep* (meaning, that many Christians die prematurely)" (I Cor. 11:30).

I would hope the Reader understands the implications of these things which Paul has just given us:

SICKNESS AND PREMATURE DEATH

The Believer is not to misunderstand this of which the Apostle says, as to think that there are some type of magic qualities in the Lord's Supper, etc. He is merely telling us, although with very serious consequences, that every single thing we receive from God comes exclusively through the Sacrifice of Christ, which demands our Faith in that Finished Work. If our Faith is moved to other things, then we're not properly discerning the Lord's Body, i.e., *"His Death on the Cross."* All healing comes to us by and through the Cross. Isaiah said, *"and with His stripes we are healed"* (Isa. 53:5). Peter said the same thing, but added more information:

"Who His Own Self bear our sins in His Own Body on the tree, that we, being dead to sins, should live unto Righteousness: by Whose stripes ye were healed" (I Pet. 2:24).

The Apostle links here all that Christ suffered, including the *"stripes,"* i.e., *"the beating He experienced,"* as a part of the Cross experience. But what have we heard in the last few years?

Regarding Healing, the Child of God has been told by the faith teachers, that they must increase their faith more and more, continue to confess particular Scriptures in the Word of God as it regards healing, and then they can walk in perfect health, etc. Thankfully, we don't hear much of that anymore, for the simple reason that it doesn't work, because it's not Scriptural. And why isn't it Scriptural?

It's not Scriptural, simply because the faith that was spoken of and most of the teaching that's been given in the past several decades, has not been Faith in the Cross of Christ, but rather other things. And those other things, are as varied as the mind of man can contemplate; however, it doesn't really matter what the *"other things"* are, if it's not the Cross of Christ in which our Faith is anchored, it's not Faith that God will recognize.

And then Paul said, *"And many sleep,"* meaning, that many Christians die prematurely, because of not properly discerning the Lord's Body (I Cor. 11:30).

Notice, that he used the word *"many,"* which in fact, is chilling indeed!

The doctor may call it something else, but the Holy Spirit here through Paul, is telling us, that if we do not properly understand the Cross of Christ, realizing and recognizing the fact, that everything we receive from God

comes exclusively from, through, and by that great Sacrifice, then the truth is, we can die prematurely. That's how serious that this is, and to be more particular, that's how serious the Holy Spirit is about the Cross of Christ.

Considering all of this, do you think that I am being overly repetitive, by addressing the Cross from every angle, and in every way that I know how? Considering how serious that it is, I think not!

When one considers that the modern Church knows almost nothing about the Cross of Christ, which means it's not properly discerning the Lord's Body, which falls out to disastrous consequences, do you now realize how important these Commentaries actually are? Can you now understand why the Lord has instructed me to write them, and to do so, with a heavy emphasis on the Finished Work of Christ!

Considering the fact, that the modern Church is almost Cross illiterate, we must come to the conclusion that this is the reason for most sickness among Christians. As well, at the same time, we must come to the conclusion, that not properly discerning the Lord's Body is the reason that many Christians die prematurely. They don't lose their souls, but their lives are cut short, and simply because they do not avail themselves of all the things of which the Cross guarantees.

Again I emphasize, that we're not speaking of some magic situation here, but rather, that everything we receive from God as Believers, comes exclusively to us through the Cross of Christ, and our Faith in that great Sacrifice. If we don't know that, and thereby place our Faith in other things, the benefits of the Cross cannot then be ours.

It is somewhat like an individual being physically sick, and there being a particular medicine which can bring relief and help, but yet the person will not take the medicine, whether through lack of knowledge, or unbelief, resulting in the individual getting sicker, and possibly even dying. Perhaps that's a crude analogy, but I think it somewhat explains this of which we speak.

THE CORRECT OBJECT OF FAITH

Even the most newly converted Believer, knows and understands at least somewhat, that God deals with the human race on the basis of Faith. Due to the fact that the Believer is now in Christ, there is a Divine nature within us, that helps us to understand this. I speak of this new nature within us made possible by *"Regeneration,"* which of course, is supplied by the Holy Spirit (Jn. 3:3-8).

Faith simply means that we believe something, and in this case, we believe God, and more particularly, what the Lord did for us at the Cross.

Whenever the Lord began to reveal this to me, and I speak of the correct object of Faith, He took me, as I have previously stated, to Romans, Chapter 4.

The Holy Spirit through Paul used Abraham as the great example, and because he was the great example. It was to this Patriarch, that the Lord gave the great Doctrine of *"Justification by Faith."* It is explained in simple terms:

"Abraham believed God, and it was counted unto him for Righteousness" (Rom. 4:3). Paul derived this from Genesis 15:6.

But when it says that, *"Abraham believed God,"* what did it mean by that?

It didn't mean, that Abraham merely believed that there was a God. Millions do that and aren't saved. It rather had reference, to what God would do in order to save humanity. Paul gave us that in the Third Chapter of Galatians.

He again used the same phrase, *"Even as Abraham believed* God (had Faith in God), *and it was accounted to him for Righteousness"* (Gal. 3:6). He then told us what all of this meant:

Abraham believed that God would send a Redeemer into the world, and that Redeemer would be Christ. He said:

"Now to Abraham and his seed were the promises made. He saith not, and to seeds, as of many; but as of one, and to thy Seed, which is Christ" (Gal. 3:16).

In this particular Scripture which is somewhat complicated, the Apostle is merely saying, that there is one Redeemer, one Savior, *"which is Christ."* And then he told us how that Christ would carry forth this great task:

"Christ hath redeemed us from the curse of the Law, being made a curse for us: for it is written, Cursed is everyone that hangeth on a tree" (Gal. 3:13).

We are here told, that Christ would redeem humanity by and through the Cross, i.e., *"on a tree."*

He then said, *"That the Blessing of Abraham* (that which God promised Abraham as it regarded Justification by Faith) *might come on the Gentiles through Jesus Christ* (what Jesus did at the Cross); *that we might receive the Promise of the Spirit through Faith"* (Gal. 3:14).

So, I think it is clearly obvious here, that the object of our Faith must always be the Cross of Christ. And that's how Satan has been so successful in these last few decades:

He has steered the faith of the Church to other things, and as previously stated, he doesn't really care what those other things might be, just so it isn't the Cross.

As a Christian, the most important thing I think that you could ever learn is that the Cross affords you all blessings, and that your Faith must ever be anchored there. Then and only then, will the Holy Spirit work on your behalf, guaranteeing you all that Jesus has done for you (Rom. 8:1-2, 11).

(27) "AND AS IT IS APPOINTED UNTO MEN ONCE TO DIE, BUT AFTER THIS THE JUDGMENT:"

The exegesis is:

1. The idea of this Verse is, that if men do not accept Christ as their Savior, they will face Him as their Judge.

2. Due to the Fall, it is appointed or laid up by Divine Decree: *"Dust thou art, and unto dust thou shalt return"* (Gen. 3:19).

3. As it is appointed that all men must die, with the exception of those who will go in the Rapture, it is also appointed, that all will be judged.

THE APPOINTMENT OF DEATH

The phrase, *"And as it is appointed unto men once to die,"* in effect, gives us the reason for the great Sacrifice of Christ. Due to the Fall, man brought upon himself the sentence of death. He separated himself from God, Who is man's Life Source, and that separation being effected, death was and is inevitable.

In fact, before the Fall, man was destined to live forever, and this speaks of physical life as well as Spiritual Life; however, with Spiritual Life forfeited, physical life was doomed, hence all the sickness, disease, afflictions, inevitably leading to death.

All of this was brought on by sin, hence, necessitating the Remedy offered by Christ, in the giving of Himself in Sacrifice. Sin had doomed man, providing no way of escape, which means that he was to be separated from God forever and forever. The implications are chilling to say the least!

Man's life and works on Earth end with death: what remains is the result of this life and these works, as determined by God's *"judgment."* Man does not return to die a second time. That some few have twice passed through death does not affect the general law. The emphatic word *"once"* and the special design of the Verse are explained by the words that follow in the next Verse, which we will address momentarily.

As well, we should note from this Verse, that death ends probation. After death is the Judgment, not a second chance to live on Earth and be saved, as some teach as it regards the unscriptural idea of reincarnation. As well, praying for the souls of individuals after they have died is a wasted effort. All opportunities of Salvation are on this side of the grave. There remains no more opportunity after death.

First, second, and third opportunities, etc., to accept Christ are all on this side of the grave. In other words, death ends it all as far as the possibility of accepting Christ is concerned, that is if He has not already been accepted. This means there is no such thing as purgatory, as our Catholic friends teach. It simply does not exist.

When the Believer dies, his soul and spirit instantly go to Heaven, there to await the coming Resurrection of the body (II Cor. 5:8; Phil. 1:21-24; Heb. 12:23; Rev. 6:9-11).

When the unredeemed person dies, instantly their soul and spirit go to Hell, where they will remain until the Resurrection of damnation, which will take place a thousand years after the Resurrection of Life (Isa. 14:9; Lk. 16:19-31; Rev. 20:11-15).

THE JUDGMENT

The phrase, *"But after this the Judgment,"* refers to that which is inevitable, even as death is inevitable!

Looking about us, and understanding that all men must die, and because all have died (with the exception of those who will be alive at the time of the Rapture), man should understand, that a judgment is coming as well.

Paul is speaking here of the *"Great White Throne Judgment,"* outlined in Revelation 20:11-15.

This Judgment will include all the wicked from the time of Adam to the end of the Millennium. In fact, this Judgment will take place at the end of the Millennium (Rev. 20:7-15).

The place will be as stated, *"The Great White Throne"* (Ps. 9:7-8). The Throne is literal and the *"white"* indicates absolute Righteousness and Justice of the Judgment (Ps. 45:6-7; 96:10-13; Jn. 7:24; Acts 17:31; II Tim. 4:8).

The Judges will be *"God the Father"* (Rom. 2:12-16; Heb. 12:23-24; 13:4; Rev. 6:10).

It will also be *"God the Son"* (Jn. 5:19-27; Acts 10:42; II Tim. 4:8; Rev. 19:11).

God will judge by Jesus Christ. The Father will decree, the Son will execute (Acts 10:42; 17:31; Rom. 2:16).

This Judgment will not be a spiritual, invisible, endless process, but rather a definite, literal, visible, and personal trial in God's Court similar to a trial on Earth (Ps. 9:8; Mat. 7:2, 21; Acts 17:31; Rom. 2:12-16; Heb. 9:27; Rev. 20:11-15).

At that time, the sea will give up the dead in it. This could only refer to bodies, or at least to the form of such, for souls and spirits of the wicked dead do not remain in the sea, if in fact, that's where the person dies. They go to Hell and await the resurrection of their bodies, where uncounted millions are at present (Isa. 14:9; Lk. 16:19-31).

At the time of the Judgment, Hell will disgorge all of the uncounted millions who are there presently. This is referred to as the *"Resurrection of Damnation"* (Rev. 20:11-15). At that time, the physical bodies, or at least the form thereof, will be reunited with the soul and the spirit of the unsaved. Every last one who appears at this Judgment, and we continue to speak of the *"Great White Throne Judgment"* will be eternally lost, and placed in the Lake of Fire forever and forever (Rev. 20:10-15).

We are not given the length of time in

judging all the wicked, but we do know that the length of the sentence for all will be eternal. In other words, there will be no Purgatory or probation or second chance after death (Isa. 66:22-24; Mat. 5:29-30; 10:28; 13:42-50; 18:9; 23:15, 33; 24:51; 25:41, 46; Mk. 9:42-48; Lk. 12:5; Heb. 6:2; 10:26-31; Rev. 2:11; 14:9-11; 19:20; 20:10-15; 21:8; 22:15.

THE BIBLICAL TEACHING REGARDING JUDGMENT

Man today rejects out of hand the idea that he must one day render account for his life and its decisions. His loss of conviction concerning an afterlife, combined with the erosion of the notion of moral responsibility on the basis of popular belief of psychological and psychoanalytical theories, has contributed to the moral indifference and pragmatism of our times. In other words, the world has been so psychologized, which teaching is the very opposite of the Word of God, that man no longer believes in a coming judgment. This is at least one of the reasons that the foray of the Church into humanistic psychology is so destructive. It is impossible for it to be otherwise. The idea, that the Church can accept the *"good points of psychology"* while rejecting the rest, or else meld psychology with the Bible, could not be more erroneous. In fact, if anyone knows the Word of God at all, one instantly knows that the two teachings and directions are totally opposite, meaning that they cannot be joined. Also, psychology has no *"good points,"* it entirely being from the diseased minds of men, which can produce nothing good.

According to psychological teaching, moral issues, insofar as they matter at all, relate only to the present moment and to the considerations of personal happiness. The thought that they might relate to some Divine Dimension, or that all men must one day be inescapably summoned to accept responsibility for these very moral decisions in the all-seeing Presence of their Creator, is denied by the teaching of psychology.

Unfortunately for modern man it happens to be true, that man will one day answer. Judgment is inevitable and awaits us all.

In face of this modern tendency to dismiss future judgment, there is the greater

NOTES

and more urgent responsibility placed upon the Church to tenaciously maintain the Biblical perspective. And the Biblical perspective tells us, that man's sins will be judged in Jesus Christ, by man accepting Christ and what He did for us at the Cross, or His sins will be judged by Christ at the Great White Throne Judgment, with the inevitable loss of the soul. As stated, man accepts Christ as Savior, or faces Him as Judge — whichever, man will inevitably face Christ!

(28) "SO CHRIST WAS ONCE OFFERED TO BEAR THE SINS OF MANY; AND UNTO THEM THAT LOOK FOR HIM SHALL HE APPEAR THE SECOND TIME WITHOUT SIN UNTO SALVATION."

The structure is:

1. Christ came first to suffer on man's behalf, which He did at the Cross.

2. His suffering on the Cross was done in order to pay the penalty for man's sins.

3. As He came the first time to *"bear the sins of many,"* He will come the second time *"without sin unto Salvation."* This refers to the Second Coming, and to the fact, that the sin question has already been addressed. He will come the second time to rule and reign!

ONE SACRIFICE

The phrase, *"So Christ was once offered,"* refers to His Crucifixion, which refers to the One Sacrifice of Himself, which sufficed for all time.

This argument is rounded off with a reference to the one death men die and the one death Christ died. There is a finality about both but very different consequences. In effect, Jesus died that men might live, which refers to *"Life Eternal,"* but which man must accept before his death. While death is the complete and final end to life on Earth, it is not, as so many in the ancient world thought, the complete and final end. Death is more serious than that because it is followed by judgment, even as we've already stated. Men are accountable, and after death they will render account to God.

This is the very purpose and reason for the Death of Christ. Man could not save himself. There was absolutely nothing he could do that would avoid the horror of eternal separation from God, which means the Lake of Fire forever and forever (Rev. 20:10-15). So, if man was to be saved, God would have to become man, and then pay the price for man's redemption, which was demanded by God.

While it is true that the price was high, so high in fact that man could not hope to pay; still, man has no argument or complaint, considering that God paid the price Himself. To be sure, it was paid in full, with the Apostle using the Greek adverb *"hapax,"* which means *"once-for-all."* This means that what Christ did at the Cross will never have to be repeated, and because it atoned for all sin, past, present, and future (Jn. 1:29; I Jn. 2:2).

So we won't lose sight of what the Holy Spirit is actually saying here through Paul, we must understand, that the Apostle introduces the finality of men dying without God and a coming judgment, as that which is inevitable. However, this terrible *"appointment"* was broken into by Christ, Who *"was once offered to bear the sins of many."* In other words, the only thing that can thwart this terrible appointment that Paul addresses in Verse 27, is the Sacrifice of Christ, and man accepting that which Christ has done on his behalf. That's the reason I constantly say, that the only thing that stands in-between man and eternal Hell, is the Cross of Christ. That's how important all of this is!

As well, it is not only that, but also, the only Source of all Blessings and Victory for the Child of God after the acceptance of Christ. In other words, the Cross of Christ is everything, which I would think would be overly obvious as the Scriptures proclaim.

TO BEAR THE PENALTY OF SIN

The phrase, *"To bear the sins of many,"* presents as is obvious, what Christ did at the Cross. The Cross was God's answer to man's sin, and in fact, is the only answer.

Sin-bearing is a concept found in the New Testament only here and in I Peter 2:24, but it is quite frequent in the Old Testament, where it plainly means, *"bear the penalty of sin."* For example, the Israelites were condemned to wander in the wilderness for 40 years as the penalty for their failure to go up into the land of Canaan: *"For 40 years — one year for each of the 40 days you explored*

the land — you will suffer for your sins" (Num. 14:34; Ezek. 18:20). Isaiah alluded to what Christ would do by saying, *"He will bear their iniquities"* (Isa. 53:11); *"He bore the sin of many"* (Isa. 53:12). So Paul is saying here that Christ took upon Himself the consequences of the sins of many (Mk. 10:45).

The idea is not that He only suffered the penalty for the sins of some in the world and not for others, but that in fact, He did suffer the penalty for the sin of the entirety of mankind and for all time, but that only some will take advantage of this great Sacrifice. Unfortunately, even though all of humanity can be saved, at least those who are alive presently and those who will be born, at least until the coming Judgment, the fact is, that most spurn the Gospel Call (Mat. 7:13-14).

The phrase *"To bear the sins of many,"* does not mean that Christ was a sinner — for that was in no sense true. The phrase here means simply, that Christ endured sufferings in His Own Person which, if they had been inflicted on us, would have been the proper punishment of sin. He Who was innocent interposed, and received on Himself what was descending to meet us, and consented to be treated as He would have deserved if He had been a sinner. Thus, He bore what was due to us; and this in Scripture phrase is what is meant by *"bearing our iniquities."* However, that which He did bear, pertains only to death, and not going into the burning side of Hell, as some teach. The reason is this:

When a sinner dies, he goes to Hell, because he in fact is a sinner. But the truth is, he has been a sinner all along, and refusing to accept Christ, upon physical death, he must be placed in eternal quarantine.

But Christ was not a sinner and, therefore, the punishment that He bore on our behalf, was that of physical death. That paid the price. He did not go to Hell, because He was not a sinner, had never been a sinner, and would never be a sinner; therefore, to put Him in Hell as some teach, would be a breaking of the Law of God. The Law says, *"the soul that sinneth it shall die,"* and this means to be eternally separated from God, unless Christ is accepted. The soul of Christ never sinned; therefore, did not experience spiritual death in any fashion. This is so important, that I wish to emphasize it again:

"The soul that sinneth it shall die" (Ezek. 18:4, 20), but Christ never sinned, so He never experienced spiritual death. He could experience the penalty for man's sin, which was physical death, but He at no time ever experienced spiritual death, which means separation from God.

Some may contend that His cry on the Cross, which was predicted in the Psalms, *"My God, My God, why hast Thou forsaken Me?"* (Ps. 22:1; Mat. 27:46), is an indication that He was separated from God; however, that's not true at all. The following proves my point:

THE EXPERIENCE OF CHRIST ON THE CROSS

1. Jesus being born without original sin, in fact could not have died, without God forsaking Him for a short period of time. This was the only way that He could expire, and in that, He literally breathed out His life.

2. Just before He died, He said to the thief hanging by Him on another cross, and who had accepted Him as Savior, *"Verily I say unto thee, today shalt thou be with Me in Paradise"* (Lk. 23:43). This plainly tells us, that when Jesus died, that He went to *"Paradise,"* instead of the burning side of Hell, as some claim. In fact, all the righteous souls who had passed away before the Cross, due to the fact that the sin debt could not be removed by the blood of bulls and goats, were taken captive by Satan down into Paradise, which in fact, was next door to the burning side of Hell. Due to their faith, they were in comfort, but still were held captive by the Evil One. Jesus rescued them from this place, due to the fact, that He had cleansed them from all sin as a result of His Death on the Cross (Eph. 4:8-9). There is nothing in the Bible that says that Jesus went to the burning side of Hell; but yet, the part called *"Paradise"* was actually referred to as a part of Hell (Lk. 16:19-31).

3. Just before Jesus died, He said, *"It is finished"* (Jn. 19:30).

This referred to the great Sacrifice that brought about Redemption for mankind, being finished. This means there remains nothing else to be done, which completely debunks the theory that Jesus went to Hell as a sinner,

and was actually *"born again"* in Hell, etc. In fact, the Holy Spirit, functioning on the premise of the words *"It is finished,"* ripped apart the *"Veil of the Temple in twain from the top to the bottom,"* signifying that the way was now open, all brought about by the Cross (Mat. 27:51). Actually, the Holy Spirit did this even before the Resurrection of Christ, simply because it was the Cross which atoned for all sin, which guaranteed the Resurrection of Christ. Had there been one sin left unatoned, Christ could not have risen from the dead, because the *"wages of sin is death"* (Rom. 6:23). But due to the fact that all sin was atoned, the Resurrection, as we have previously stated, was a given; therefore, the Holy Spirit could rip the Veil down, signifying that Atonement was complete and finished.

4. The very last words that Jesus said before His Death were, *"Father, into Thy hands I commend My Spirit"* (Lk. 23:46). In fact, the order of events at those closing moments no doubt were:

"It is finished: Father, into Thy hands I commend My Spirit."

If Jesus had been separated from the Father because of sin, He could not have commended His Spirit to the Father upon His Death. One cannot have it both ways. The truth is:

He was forsaken by God only for a few moments of time, in order that He could die. The moment He died, all sin was atoned, and He was instantly reinstated with the Father. Had He been forsaken by the Father any more than a few moments in order that He could die, He could not have stated that His Spirit would immediately go into the Father's hands. To be sure, the spirit of the unsaved at death, definitely does not go into the hands of the Heavenly Father.

THE JESUS DIED SPIRITUALLY DOCTRINE

The Reader may wonder as to why the detail as it regards the manner of Jesus' Death? The reason is because of the erroneous *"Jesus died spiritually doctrine."*

To which we have already alluded, this doctrine which is very prominent presently, claims that the Cross had nothing to do with Redemption, that being accomplished by Christ being Born-Again in Hell. They claim that the Cross was a mere incident, or one of the incidents on the road to the main event. They claim that Jesus died as a sinner, and as a sinner went to Hell, and we speak of the burning side of Hell. They also teach that demons and fallen Angels rejoiced in triumph at this time, claiming that He was defeated.

But after suffering the agonies of the damned for a period of time, God then said *"it's enough,"* with Jesus then throwing off the shackles of sin and death, and being *"born again,"* just like any sinner is Born-Again. He then came out of Hell, they claim, in His Resurrection. They then claim, that people are saved by trusting in what Christ did in Hell by being *"born again."*

Of course, there is not a shred of Scriptural evidence for such foolishness, which is actually a complete denial of the Atonement of Christ.

They use the Scripture, *"For whom He did foreknow, He also did predestinate to be conformed to the image of His Son, that He* (meaning Jesus) *might be the firstborn among many brethren"* (Rom. 8:29).

This is where they get the idea that Jesus was *"born again,"* but with Him bein0g Born-Again in Hell, being strictly of their own imagination.

"Firstborn" in the Greek is *"prototokos,"* and means *"priority to all creation and sovereignty over all creation."*

In the Passage in Romans, it simply means that Christ, due to His Death on the Cross, has made it possible for sinners to be *"born again."* He is the institutor or originator of such! He is shown here, and acknowledged to be, and glorified as, *"The Son of God,"* preeminent among those who are by adoption through Him sons of God.

Any time the word *"firstborn"* is used as it regards Christ, it is always referring to Him being the Creator or Founder of such, whatever it is.

The *"Jesus died spiritually doctrine"* claims that Jesus became a sinner on the Cross, thereby taking upon Himself the nature of Satan, and thereby died and went to Hell, even as any other sinner goes to Hell. This presents a complete misunderstanding of the Atonement, and is a most serious thing. The tragedy is, millions of people, in following these so-called Faith teachers, believe this lie, and a lie it is, which can have a very serious

NOTES

effect on their Salvation. In other words, such direction is a serious lack of the proper discernment of our Lord's Body. The consequences are dire indeed! The whole of Salvation depends totally and completely upon one's viewpoint of the Cross, and as well, the victory of the Child of God after being saved, is also totally dependent on one's viewpoint of the Cross. That's how important all of this actually is.

THE SECOND APPEARANCE OF CHRIST

The phrase, *"And unto them that look for Him shall He appear the second time without sin unto Salvation,"* refers to the Second Coming.

The Rapture is not in view here, neither the Church. This is Jewish, inasmuch as Paul is writing to Christian Jews.

The latter part of Verse 28, refers to the Second Advent of the Messiah to Israel which will begin the Millennium.

THE HIGH PRIEST AND CHRIST

1. The first appearance of the High Priest on the Day of Atonement was at the Brazen Altar where the sacrifice was slain. This corresponds to the first appearance of Christ on Earth to die on the Cross.

2. The second appearance of the High Priest was in the Holy of Holies. This corresponds to the Messiah's present appearance before God in Heaven now, making intercession for the Saints.

3. The third appearance of the High Priest was out the gate of the court surrounding the Tabernacle, to Israel, having in a symbolic way accomplished Salvation. This corresponds to the appearance of Christ on Earth in the Second Advent to Israel, having actually accomplished Redemption. His return will be apart from sin in that He settled the sin question the first time He came. Now He comes with Salvation for the one who puts his Faith in Him (Wuest).

The Second Coming will herald Christ not only as High Priest, but as well, as King, inasmuch as He will then rule and reign over a restored Israel, and thereby the world. Ezekiel portrays how that Israel along with Jerusalem and the Temple will literally be built anew (Ezek., Chpts. 40-48).

"Lamb of God! Our souls adore Thee,
*   while upon Thy face we gaze;*
"There the Father's love and glory
*   shine in all their brightest rays;*
"Thine almighty power and wisdom all
*   creation's works proclaim;*
"Heaven and Earth alike confess Thee
*   as the ever great 'I Am'."*

"Lamb of God! Thy Father's bosom
*   ever was Thy dwelling place;*
"His delight, in Him rejoicing, One with
*   Him in power and grace;*
"Oh, what wondrous love and mercy!
*   Thou didst lay Thy glory by;*
"And for us didst come from Heaven
*   as the Lamb of God to die."*

"Lamb of God! When we behold Thee
*   lowly in the manger laid,*
"Wandering as a homeless stranger in
*   the world Thy hands had made,*
"When we see Thee in the garden in
*   Thine agony and blood*
"At Thy Grace we are confounded,
*   Holy, Spotless Lamb of God!"*

"When we see Thee, as the victim,
*   bound to the accursed Tree,*
"For our guilt and folly stricken, all our
*   judgment borne by Thee,*
"Lord, we own, with hearts adoring,
*   Thy great love, vast, like a flood,*
"Glory, glory everlasting be to Thee,
*   Thou Lamb of God."*

"Lamb of God, Thou soon in glory will
*   to this sad Earth return;*
"All Thy foes shall quake before Thee,
*   all that now despise Thee, mourn;*
"Then Thy Saints all gathered to Thee,
*   with Thee in Thine kingdom reign;*
"Thine the praise and Thine the glory,
*   Lamb of God, for sinners slain!"*

—■—

CHAPTER 10

(1) "FOR THE LAW HAVING A SHADOW OF GOOD THINGS TO COME, AND NOT THE VERY IMAGE OF THE THINGS, CAN NEVER WITH THOSE SACRIFICES WHICH THEY OFFERED YEAR BY YEAR

NOTES

CONTINUALLY MAKE THE COMERS THEREUNTO PERFECT."

The exegesis is:

1. The Law of Moses, as stated here, was only a shadow of the New Covenant which was to come.

2. It was not the very image of the New Covenant, even though all of the ceremonies and rituals pointed to Christ, but not with such clarity that it was fully recognizable by the people.

3. The mere fact that the sacrifices were constantly renewed, portrayed the insufficiency of that Covenant.

THE LAW ONLY A SHADOW

The phrase, *"For the Law having a shadow of good things to come,"* presents Paul engaging in further explanation of the finality of Christ's One Sacrifice and thus of its superiority to the sacrifices of the Law. A *"shadow"* suggests indefiniteness and insubstantiality; a mere indication that a reality exists.

In the first eighteen Verses of this Chapter, the contrast between the sacrifices under the Law and the One Offering of Christ is brought out more clearly than ever. It is important to follow the argument carefully and notice the close reasoning of the Apostle as he contrasts the one with the other. The Levitical economy was but a shadow of the coming good things.

The preceding sections have brought out the efficacy of the Blood of Jesus as a prevailing Sacrifice, and now stress is laid on the once-for-all character of that Sacrifice. First of all, Paul contrasts the substance and the shadow. He sees the ancient system that meant so much to the Jews as no more than an unsubstantial, shadowy affair. The real thing is in Christ. To leave Christ in favor of Judaism would be to forsake the substance for the shadow. The sacrificial system practiced by the Jews could not deal effectually with sin, even as Paul says in Verse 1. Since it was no more than a shadow, that was quite impossible.

"The Law" refers strictly to the Law of Moses, but here it stands for the entirety of the Old Testament, with particular reference to the sacrificial system.

As we will see from the next phrase, the *"shadow"* is merely the preliminary outline that an artist may make before he gets to his colors, and the finished portrait. Paul is saying that the Law is no more than a preliminary sketch. It shows the shape of things to come, but the solid reality is not there. That awaited Christ, and was fulfilled in Christ.

NOT THE VERY IMAGE

The phrase, *"And not the very image of the things,"* presents the fact that the Law was basically only a suggestion, and not really an image. In fact, it was quite impossible for the Law to present a proper image of Who Christ would be, and What Christ would be, even though the mere mechanics of the Law suggested, that something better had to come.

It's very easy for us to look back and draw the *"types"* and *"symbols"* represented in the Law, for the simple reason that we now look at the situation after the fact. But before Christ came, it would not have been so simple.

However, as we have repeatedly stated, the fact that the sacrifices were constantly renewed, showed that the Law possessed no more than a mere shadow of the coming good which was exhibited in those sacrifices. But yet, no repetition of the shadow can amount to the substance.

THE SPIRIT OF ALL THAT WAS DONE AND IS DONE

What the Lord gave to Israel as it regards the Law, with all of its types and symbolisms, was done exactly as the Divine Spirit desired. While the shadow was there, this was all the Lord intended for it to be. So, the blame for Israel not seeing a perfect representation of the coming New Covenant in the Law, is not to be blamed on the Lord Who gave the Law.

The idea is, if the individual contained the right spirit, and we speak of the right spirit toward God, the Holy Spirit would then reveal to him that which was necessary.

People tend to see what they want to see, and hear what they want to hear. In fact, that which we are discussing as it regards the Law of old, applies in the same manner presently to the Cross.

As the majority in Israel could not see Christ in the Law, the majority presently in the Church cannot see Christ in the Cross. A problem of deception which is with humanity, doesn't

NOTES

change. Everything that is necessary is given by God. If there is failure to recognize that which ought to be obvious, then the failure is on our part and not that of the Lord. His Way is Perfect, while ours is anything but perfect.

The Prophets of old constantly predicted One Who was to come, Who would give peace in the hearts of men, which the Law and the Sacrifices could not give; consequently, Israel should have recognized Him when He came, but regrettably, they didn't!

As well, it should be obvious as to what the Cross means as it regards Christianity, but that also seems not to be the case.

As the sacrifices could not bring peace to the conscience of the Believer of old, neither can ways and directions other than the Cross bring peace to modern Believers. That should be the greatest tip off of all. But yet we seem to be making the same mistakes presently as the Jews of old made in their time.

IMPERFECT SACRIFICES

The phrase, *"Can never with those sacrifices which they offered year by year continually make the comers thereunto perfect,"* presents the fact that the very nature of the sacrifices, and their continued necessity, could not accomplish the task desired. So why did Israel place such stock in all of this?

It is understandable as to Israel's pride in the Law before Christ, but not at all afterward. And I speak specifically of the Christian Jews.

One of the problems is that human beings quickly become enamored with the *"doing of religion,"* which is done most perfectly as it relates to rituals and ceremonies. There is something about these things that makes us *"feel religious,"* and thereby, that something has been accomplished, when in fact, nothing has been accomplished.

Rituals and ceremonies cannot cleanse from sin, cannot bring forgiveness, cannot bring cleansing, and cannot bring peace with God. But still, the *"doing of religion"* excites us.

As we study these texts, we must not relegate these great Truths and warnings only to the Jewish Christians of old, but we must see what the Holy Spirit is telling us presently, and to be sure, He is telling us much. We make a grand mistake, if we feel that we presently are not susceptible to the same difficulties as the Christian Jews of Paul's day. In fact, the problem is just as acute now as it was then, even though the shape of things may be a little different.

IT WAS THE CROSS THEN, AND IT IS THE CROSS NOW

As the problem was the Cross then, the problem is the Cross now! It all boils down to the Cross!

Jesus dying on a Cross, and thereby atoning for all the sins of mankind, did not seem nearly as spectacular to those particular Jews as did the rituals and ceremonies of the Mosaic Law. It was a question of *"activity"* vs. *"Faith"* or the *"doing of religion"* vs. *"trusting that which has already been done."*

Considering the teaching given by Paul, I seriously doubt that ignorance of the Word could have been the greatest problem for these Christian Jews. I think the Text brings it out very graphically. The problem was *"unbelief"* (Heb. 3:12-13).

As I mentioned some pages back, when the Lord first began to open up to me the Revelation of the Cross, which was in 1996, my immediate thought was that the greater problem concerning most Christians was ignorance of the Word; however, I have come to believe that this is not exactly the case. Whereas that definitely exists, the greater problem I fear, is the same as the problem in Paul's day, the problem of rank unbelief. The Christian Jews, at least some of them, were fastly coming to the place that they simply did not believe that what Christ did was sufficient. It is the same presently! There is no way the modern Church can delve wholesale into humanistic psychology, without at the same time registering a vote of no confidence as it regards the Cross. And for the most part, that is the position of the modern Church.

MAKE PERFECT

The words *"make perfect"* are the translation of the Greek *"teleioo,"* which means, *"to bring to a state of completeness."* The idea here is that the ceremonial law could not actually save the Believer. Its work was always short of completeness.

When we think of the word *"perfect,"* we must understand that such perfection is found

only in Christ. In fact, our Salvation is a perfect Salvation, simply because it's in Christ. Our Redemption is perfect, even as our peace is perfect. This means that our cleansing from all sin is perfect, for that's all that God can accept.

He cannot accept partial cleansing, which means that there is no such thing as a partial justification. A person is either completely forgiven or all sin, or he's not forgiven at all! And when the Believer turns to Christ, and confesses his sin (I Jn. 1:9), the Lord totally and completely forgives and cleanses from all sin, which He has promised to do. In fact, there is no limitation on the times of forgiveness and cleansing which can be engaged.

Now the *"perfection"* here enjoined, does not refer to sinless perfection regarding the Believer. No Believer is perfect in this regard, but at the same time, our Salvation is perfect.

This is what makes it so wrong for Churches and Denominations to refuse to accept God's Way, rather attempting to substitute other things of themselves. There is only one answer for sin, and that is Christ, and what He did at the Cross. To claim the great Sacrifice of Christ, and then attempt to add something to that Sacrifice, is a sin of gargantuan proportions. In fact, those attempting to add something to the Finished Work of Christ are committing far worse sins, than the poor victim they are claiming to rehabilitate — which word incidentally, is not found in the Bible, and simply because such does not exist in true Scriptural terms.

The Salvation afforded by Christ on the Cross is a perfect Salvation. Nothing dare be removed from that Sacrifice, and nothing dare be added to that Sacrifice.

(2) "FOR THEN WOULD THEY NOT HAVE CEASED TO BE OFFERED? BECAUSE THAT THE WORSHIPPERS ONCE PURGED SHOULD HAVE HAD NO MORE CONSCIENCE OF SINS."

The structure is:

1. The necessity for the continued offering of the sacrifices under the old Law, proved by that very thing, that they were insufficient.

2. Had there been true cleansing, there would have been no more need for further sacrifices. The very fact of continued sacrifices proved that the sins had not been washed clean.

3. Faith in the Cross of Christ, which Paul is here grandly proclaiming, cleanses from all sin, and thereby, the *"conscience of sins."*

CONTINUED SACRIFICES

The question, *"For then would they not have ceased to be offered?",* presents a tremendous Truth which we should study very carefully. In this is the very heart of the Gospel.

It is obvious here that the old Law, even as grand as it was in its day with all its rituals, ceremonies, and sacrifices, still, could not cleanse from sin. The idea is, even though the sins were covered as it regards these sacrifices, at least if faith was properly placed in the One Whom the Sacrifices properly represented, still, the sins were not taken away. There is a great difference in sins being covered than being completely removed, which latter only the Cross could accomplish, and in fact, did!

The Hebrew Christians were having difficulty accepting this. The simple fact of the Cross up beside the beautiful ritual and ceremony of the Temple, seemed to place the Cross in a secondary position. I think we could say that many of the Hebrew Christians to whom this Epistle was addressed were puzzled. If God had rejected the Temple and the Old Testament ordinances and worship, why was the Temple still standing?

The truth is, in a very short time after this Epistle was written, the Temple was indeed destroyed, with of course, the sacrifices ceasing.

Paul gave no attention to the Temple itself, rather speaking in detail concerning the Tabernacle, the Priesthood, and the Sacrifices of the Old Economy, from which had come the Temple. In fact, the Temple and all of its ritual had been rejected by God, no longer possessing an authoritative standing in the minds of the Holy Spirit and, therefore, as well, of Paul. The Temple sacrifices were continuing to this time because the nation of Israel had refused to accept Christ and His Sacrifice as final. In fact, Israel had rejected Jesus as their Messiah.

POLITICAL AND NOT SPIRITUAL

In the Lord's day the attitude of the Jewish rulers concerning the Messiah was political expectation rather than spiritual, and

national rather than universal. They looked for a Messiah Who would overthrow their enemies, restore the nation of Israel, and set up His Kingdom, all within the house and framework of Israel, and that in the land of Palestine.

They failed to realize how necessary was the removal of sin's barrier. The Law had pointed to the Messiah's redemptive work, but, in their national pride, they had missed the valuable lesson of their guardian, the Law. The significance of the Prophecy that indicated a change in the Priesthood and the establishment of a New Covenant was overlooked in their zeal for a national kingdom.

The Tabernacle constructed under Moses, which of course was the foundation of the Law and later the Temple, had been only a figure or a symbol of that which would come in the Messiah. The rituals of purification given under the Law had only succeeded in ceremonial cleansing, but these rituals could not cleanse moral guilt. All of the offerings could not remove spiritual defilement or the guilt and disdain of sin. Only the atoning work of Christ on the Cross, and Faith in that Finished Work, could purge the conscience. The whole economy of Moses pointed to the Perfect Sacrifice of Jesus Christ, but sadly, this Israel could not see!

NO MORE CONSCIENCE OF SINS

The phrase, *"Because that the worshippers once purged should have had no more conscience of sins,"* proclaims what the proper Sacrifice of Christ could do, and in fact, did do, but which the sacrifice of bulls and goats could not do.

The phrase, *"No more conscience of sins,"* should not be misunderstood as *"No more consciousness of sin."*

The subject here is the perfect peace of conscience resulting from the perfection of the Offering presented to God. Because the Offering, being the Body of Christ, was infinite in its atoning efficacy, therefore, the worshipper enjoys a perfected conscience, that is, perfect peace of conscience — the sense of guilt is removed directly the value of the Offering in expiation is known.

As before pointed out, the conscience of the worshipper is a reflection of the value of the Offering. If the Offering is perfect, the conscience is perfected; if the Offering is imperfect, the conscience is imperfect (Williams).

A failure to understand this of which Paul says, is failure of the highest order. Let's look at it more closely.

THE VALUE OF THE OFFERING

All of this boils down to the value of the Offering. We know with certitude, even as Paul says in many and varied ways, that the Offering or the Sacrifices of the animals, although ordained by God, was only intended to be a stopgap measure. All of this was limited in what it could do.

By contrast, the Offering of Christ, which was the Sacrifice of Himself (Gal. 1:4), was and is an Offering of such magnitude as to defy all description. The idea is this:

If the Believer does not place total Faith and confidence in that *"Offering,"* then the Believer is in effect saying that it is worth far less than it actually is, or else it's worth nothing at all. The question is, *"How much value do we place on the Offering of Christ?"*

Do we feel that the Cross is the answer to every question, the solution to every problem, the strength for every weakness, the life for every death, the salvation for every sin, and the health for every sickness? How you as a Believer look at the Cross, is how you value the Cross. This is very, very serious, so we should think about it very carefully.

The venture of the Church into humanistic psychology is a simple statement which proclaims the fact, that they do not place much value on the Offering of Christ. As I've said again and again, one cannot have it both ways. Either that Offering suffices, or else it doesn't!

If we try to add something to the Offering of Christ, we are at the same time saying that the Offering is insufficient, meaning that we do not place much value on its effectiveness. Let me make the statement again which we have just stated:

"The sense of guilt is removed directly the value of the Offering in expiation is known. The conscience of the worshipper is a reflection of the value of the Offering. If the Offering is properly understood and faith there properly placed, the conscience is perfected;

if the Offering is not properly understood, which means that faith is improperly placed, the conscience will be imperfect as well."

For one to receive the proper benefits of the Cross, in other words that for which Jesus died, one must understand its proper value, and at the same time, properly understand its value.

This is the reason that many say, *"I've tried it, and it doesn't work!"*

In the first place, one doesn't *"try the Cross!"* The very idea of such an effort portrays the fact, that not much value is placed on this One Offering of Christ. Consequently, little value placed, little value received!

THE EFFECTIVENESS OF THE ATONEMENT

The whole design of the Epistle to the Hebrews is to set forth the excellency of Jesus Christ and the efficacy (effectiveness) of His Atonement. By many comparisons and contrasts, Paul is able to show the inadequacy of the old system and the effectiveness of the New. He demonstrates how Christ was able to pay fully for the sins of men.

From the very beginning, the Lord had promised a Redeemer who could fully pay for sins, which meant that the blood of sacrificial animals which was used as a stopgap measure, could not actually pay for sins. If they could, then there would have been no need for Christ!

No matter how often they were presented, the sacrifices of the Mosaic economy were never able to bring men into a righteous standing before God: the worshippers always came short of completion. But yet, there is something else we must say about that:

While this was the condition of the Old Testament worshipper as far as the animal sacrifices were concerned, yet actually, the Israelite who would come to the Tabernacle, and present his animal for sacrifice, thereby looking ahead in Faith to the God-appointed Lamb Who would someday bear his sins, to be sure, that Israelite was saved in Jesus' Precious Blood, meaning that he was just as saved as we are presently. It was by Faith then, as it is by Faith now; however, the great problem then as is the great problem now, was the object of one's Faith.

The Blood of Jesus was just as powerful to save and keep saved for time and eternity before the Cross as since the Cross, for we have a God Who takes things that are not in existence, to bring to naught the things which are.

So, Paul is not saying that sins were not forgiven during those times, for in fact they were. What he is saying, however, is very, very important, and applies to us today just as much, as stated, as it did then.

He is saying that the blood of these animal sacrifices could not save from sin, so to continue in this capacity even after Jesus had come, presents itself as a travesty of the highest order.

Paul is not saying that no one was saved before the Cross. That's not his thinking at all. In fact, he said otherwise in the Fifteenth Verse of the previous Chapter. It is the object of faith which the Apostle is actually addressing, and nothing else.

THE OBJECT OF FAITH

If Israelites brought their sacrifices to the Tabernacle or Temple, placing their faith only in that particular ritual, and thereby ignoring what or who the sacrifices actually represented, these individuals were not saved. Their sins were not forgiven, and in fact, their sins were not even covered. This meant that the object of their faith was wrong, which sadly was the case with the far greater majority.

This is the same thing that was happening with the Christian Jews. Where were they going to place their Faith? Were they going to place it in the sacrifices of animals, or were they going to place it in Christ and what He had done at the Cross on their behalf? That and that alone, decided their Salvation.

It is the same presently. In fact, nothing has changed! Are you as a Believer placing your Faith exclusively in the great Sacrifice of Christ, realizing and understanding its great value, even as we've already addressed, or are you placing your faith in the Church, Preachers, Denominations, your confession, manifestations, etc.?

As a Believer in what Christ has done at the Cross, and placing all of my Faith in that, I know that my sins are purged; therefore, I have no more *"conscience of sins."* I know they are gone, washed away, cleansed, taken

away, etc. I know that they will never condemn me again.

But at the same time, I do have a consciousness of sins, meaning that I am conscience of the fact of sin and as well, of the horror of sin. But because of Christ, my conscience is totally clear and clean of all sin, there being no condemnation (Rom. 8:1).

HOW DOES GOD LOOK AT A CLEANSED BELIEVER?

God looks at cleansed Believers, which in fact, includes every single Believer who has ever lived, as perfect in His sight. Whatever sin they had committed, is now gone and washed away, and I speak of us properly confessing our sins to Him (I Jn. 1:9). That individual is not looked at as a second class Christian, or someone on probation, or half a hundred other foolish positions which Satan can think of. The moment any Christian confesses their sin, that sin is instantly washed, cleansed, put away and forgiven. It is remembered against the Believer no more, because in the mind of God, it does not exist, and because it has been purged. It is all done through Faith in Christ, and because of what He did for us at the Cross, in atoning for all sin, past, present, and future.

So, this means that if any Christian looks at any other Christian in a negative way because of some sin committed in the past, which is now washed, cleansed, and forgiven, that particular Christian is living under Law, and actually bringing upon himself a curse. In fact, he is denying the same Grace to the other brother or sister, which he daily needs himself, and in fact, must depend on constantly.

I'm trying to say that every single Christian who has ever lived, has had to go before the Lord many times, asking for forgiveness for some particular type of sin. If we deny that, then we are denying the obvious.

Some might say, in their efforts to justify their accusations, *"But I haven't done that,"* whatever *"that"* might be! Well what does the Bible say?

"If we confess our sins, He is faithful and just to forgive us our sins, and to cleanse us from all unrighteousness" (I Jn. 1:9).

Now the Holy Spirit here through John said *"all unrighteousness."* He either meant *"all unrighteousness,"* or he didn't! I happen to believe that He told the truth, and you had better believe the same.

Let me say it again in a little clearer way:

If you as a Believer place any Christian in a secondary or second class position, because of a sin they committed in the past, which has been duly forgiven and cleansed by the Lord, you are making a mockery of the Grace of God, doing despite to the Spirit of Grace, and limiting the value of the great Sacrifice of Christ, as far as that individual is concerned. The truth is, you have not hurt or limited them at all, but you have definitely hurt yourself.

Jesus plainly said, *"Judge not, that ye be not judged. For with what judgment ye judge, ye shall be judged: and with what measure ye mete, it shall be measured to you again"* (Mat. 7:1-2).

His statement is very clear: when you limit the Grace of God for someone else, as stated, you have in fact, limited it for yourself. Unfortunately, that is the condition in which entire Denominations presently find themselves. It is sad but true!

FORGIVING YOURSELF?

Unfortunately, the term *"forgiving oneself,"* has crept into the vocabulary of Christians, even though it is from the world of psychology. In fact, very much psychological terminology has made its way into the vocabulary of Christians, which portrays in graphic outline the wrong leanings of the modern Church.

There is nothing in the Bible about Christians, or anyone for that matter, forgiving themselves. Such shows a complete misunderstanding of the basis of forgiveness, and above all the One Who can truly forgive, Who of course is Christ. If one is seeking forgiveness from themselves, they are looking in the wrong place, and looking at forgiveness totally and completely in the wrong manner.

If a Christian does wrong, and unfortunately this happens quite often, the Christian is to immediately take his sin to the Lord. The heavy guilt and condemnation are brought on by sin, which can only be assuaged by properly confessing the sin to the Lord (not other people), asking His forgiveness

and cleansing, which He has promptly promised to do (I Jn. 1:9). If that is done, understanding that what Jesus did at the Cross handled all sin, and as well, understanding that *"He ever liveth to make intercession for us"* (Heb. 7:25), the condemnation will then instantly leave, with fellowship instantly restored. As previously stated, the Lord doesn't put anyone on probation; as well, there is no such thing as a partial justification. When the Lord justifies, He always does so totally and completely, and He will always do so the moment the person comes to Him in Faith believing (Jn. 3:16).

So, when Christians speak of someone and say, *"He won't forgive himself,"* or terminology of that nature, they don't really know what they're talking about. Nothing like that exists in real terms as it regards our relationship with Christ.

Understanding the Grace of God, we should never bring up past failures which the Lord has cleansed and forgiven, except possibly in some remote way in order to teach others, etc. Even then, it must be done in a very limited way, and seldom. In Romans Chapter 7, Paul mentioned past failures on his part, but it was used in order to instruct Believers as to how to have Faith in the Cross and not themselves.

Sin is an abominable thing. A Brother mentioned in prayer meeting just this morning, how that in the last few weeks the Holy Spirit has been dealing with him about the terribleness and the awfulness of sin. He mentioned that the Holy Spirit had used our Commentary on Galatians to bring this to his attention, for which we were grateful. This means that we are to never look at sin with impunity! It is awful beyond description.

God forbid that any Christian should fail in any manner; however, we know that the reality is that failures in one way or the other are more prominent than we would like to think. The major problem is, that most Christians do not understand the Cross; consequently, they attempt to live the life they ought to live by the means of the flesh, when they think they're doing it by the Spirit. The results are always failure and often.

However, even then, the Lord will always forgive and cleanse, no matter how many times the infraction; nevertheless, such an existence is not the Will of God, and will definitely cause the Christian great difficulties, even though the Lord will always be quick to forgive.

But if there is failure of any type, it must be handled correctly. We must always make certain that our thinking and our action never belittles the great Sacrifice of Christ in any manner. This, the Sacrifice of Christ and not our sin, is to always be held in view.

(3) "BUT IN THOSE SACRIFICES THERE IS A REMEMBRANCE AGAIN MADE OF SINS EVERY YEAR."

The composition is:

1. The word *"remembrance"* as it regards sacrifices and sins, tells us that the conscience of the worshippers under the old economy was not purged.

2. The yearly repetition of sacrifices, speaking of the Great Day of Atonement, presented itself as a glaring spectacle that the sin debt was still owing.

3. Despite all of the activity and the rituals and ceremonies of the old Law, in fact, because of all the activity, such were a constant reminder that something else had to be done about sin.

SACRIFICES, REMEMBRANCE, AND SINS

In this Verse, several things are said:

1. Sacrifices: the very fact that the word is in the plural, states that they were woefully insufficient. Hence the Holy Spirit through Paul would refer to them as *"those sacrifices."*

2. A remembrance: the idea is, in these constant offering of sacrifices, there was a remembrance of sins. Where the Bible carries the idea of remembrance, action appears to be involved. When people remember sins, they either repent (Deut. 9:7) or else persist in sin (Ezek. 23:19).

When God remembers sin, and we speak of sin unconfessed and unrepented, He usually punishes it (I Ki. 17:18; Rev. 16:19); when He pardons, He can be said not to remember sin (Ps. 25:7). Under the New Covenant, God doesn't punish Believers, that having already been done in Christ, but rather chastises (Heb. 12:5-11).

By Paul using the expression *"remembrance"* he is reminding us that Jesus said,

"Do this in remembrance of Me" (Lk. 22:19), as He established a Covenant in which the central theme is that God says, *"I will remember their sins no more"* (Jer. 31:34).

As we have stated, the Day of Atonement each year reminded people of the fact that something had to be done about sin. But the ceremonies did no more than that, merely serve as a reminder.

3. Sins: exactly what all of this fully meant to the Israel of old, we have no way presently of knowing. We know then that God definitely did forgive sins; however, there is a difference in sins being forgiven, but with the fact of sin remaining, than sins being forgiven and as well taken away. The former cannot bring a relief of the conscience, while the latter definitely does, and can only be done through Christ.

Even though many of the Jews before the Cross believed in Christ and were definitely saved, still, due to the sacrifices of that time being woefully inadequate, the sin debt still remained. Now, due to what Jesus did at the Cross on our behalf, for all who believe in Him and His great Sacrifice, the sin debt is completely erased. This does cleanse the conscience.

4. Yearly: Paul is not here demeaning what was then done. That's not the idea at all! He is merely saying to the Christian Jews who were considering going back into Judaism, which would have meant the forsaking of Christ, for it's impossible for one to have it both ways, that if they did so, ruin would be the result.

If one leaves the Cross, one has left everything. As He will say in Verse 26 of this Chapter, *"there remaineth no more sacrifice for sins."* It's the Cross or nothing!

(4) "FOR IT IS NOT POSSIBLE THAT THE BLOOD OF BULLS AND OF GOATS SHOULD TAKE AWAY SINS."

The exegesis is:

1. It is not possible for one to be washed, cleansed, and forgiven of all sin except through Faith in the Cross of Christ.

2. There is no relation between the physical blood of animals and man's moral offense, which goes for any other atonement which man may try to make, other than the Cross of Christ.

3. The only thing that God will recognize is that sins are *"taken away,"* which was done by what Christ did at the Cross, and our Faith in that Finished Work.

NOT POSSIBLE

The yearly ceremonies were ineffective because *"it is impossible for the blood of bulls and goats to take away sins."* The word *"impossible"* is a strong one. It means there is no way forward through the blood of animals.

As well, the words *"not possible"* apply to all other efforts made by man to address the problem of sin. In fact, the entirety of the world of religion, whether it be Buddhism, Islam, Catholicism, Hinduism, Mormonism, Shintoism, or that part of Christianity which is corrupt, is but an effort to atone for sin in one way or the other, except God's Way, which is the Cross. And make no mistake about it, the problem is sin.

Man may put one label or another label on the problem, may dress it up in all type of garb, but the truth is, the problem is sin. And the Holy Spirit here emphatically states, that it is impossible for a person's sins to be washed away, except by that person having Faith in Christ and what Christ did at the Cross on our behalf. The reason is, none of these things done by man, have any relation with man's moral offense, which in effect, has been against God.

THE BLOOD OF BULLS AND GOATS

The phrase, *"That the blood of bulls and of goats,"* proclaims the validity of the animal sacrifices, and the fact that God gave this plan until Christ would come. So the idea is, if the blood of bulls and goats couldn't take away sins, which was actually a program devised by the Holy Spirit, how in the world do we think that our own efforts in any manner, could affect a release from sins? The word *"blood"* as it is here used, is a tip off. There are all type of sacrifices offered by men, but it is only the shedding of blood which God will recognize, and because the life is in the blood. Life had been forfeited in the Garden of Eden by man's disobedience, and because life had been forfeited, life must be forfeited again in order that the problem be properly addressed. It is somewhat similar

to an individual murdering in cold blood. They forfeit the life of their victim, and the Bible says that if such is done, and we speak of murder in cold blood, then the life of the perpetrator must be forfeited as well (Gen. 9:6; Rom. 13:4).

Considering that God demanded *"life"* which is in the blood, but that even the blood of bulls and goats couldn't take away sins, this tells us two things:

1. The One Sacrifice which would satisfy the Wrath of God, was only that of His Only Son.

2. It tells us how helpless man is to provide a suitable sacrifice. In fact, and as stated, it is impossible!

TO TAKE AWAY SINS

The phrase, *"Should take away sins,"* pertains to that alone which God would accept. Even though the sacrifices of bulls and goats did serve as a covering for sin, that was not sufficient as it regards the Righteousness of God. Sin, and because it is so awful and horrible, must be completely taken away. This means that man's moral offense had to be dealt with. In other words, what man had done, what man was doing, and what man would continue to do, which constitutes crimes against God, and ultimately the destruction of everything, must be addressed.

Sins being completely taken away, refers to the fact that a correct penalty has been suffered, which means that the Righteousness of God has been satisfied.

Due to the fact that God is omnipotent, and omniscient, He could have easily regenerated man without Jesus having to go to the Cross. But this would in no way have addressed sin and its affects. Even though the Mercy of God could forgive man his terrible sin, the Righteousness of God, which is just as important as His Mercy, demands satisfaction. In fact, satisfaction for sin not being demanded by God, would be the same as a nation dispensing with all of its laws, thereby telling its citizens they were free to commit any crime they liked with no fear of penalty. Of course, such a society would completely destroy itself in a very short period of time. Wrongdoing must be addressed and must be paid for, or else everything self-destructs.

So it was more than the question of God being offended, it was what that offense meant. Sin is the ruination of everything that is good. It is the cause of all suffering, sickness, sorrow, heartache, and death. To ignore it, God cannot do! So the full penalty of sin would have to be paid, which would necessitate the giving of a life, but it would have to be a perfect life, which was carried one might say, by a perfect body, controlled by a perfect mind, which alone could provide a perfect Sacrifice. To do this thing, God would Himself have to become man, which He did! It's called the Incarnation (Isa. 7:14).

That's what John the Baptist was talking about when he said as it regards Christ, *"Behold the Lamb of God, which taketh away the sin of the world"* (Jn. 1:29).

The blood of bulls and goats could not take away sins, but Jesus did. In fact, he did more than that. He not only addressed individual *"sins,"* but as well He addressed the *"sin"* problem in totality. He removed its cause, which addresses the Fall, and He removed its curse, which addressed the penalty. The songwriter said:

"Hallelujah what a thought,
"Jesus full Salvation brought,
"Victory, yes victory!
"Let the powers of sin assail,
"Heaven's grace can never fail,
"Victory, yes victory!"

A PROMISSORY NOTE

The application is simple and clear. It was not possible that the blood of bulls and of goats should take away sins; but every time a believing Israelite brought his sacrifice to the Altar, he was, so to speak, giving his note to God. He acknowledged his indebtedness, his sin, and accepted responsibility for the same.

This was all he could do, but the preincarnate Christ endorsed every one of the notes and in the fullness of time came prepared to settle in full for all, which He did!

Today every Believer can look up and exclaim with all confidence, that all his sins in totality, have been *"taken away."* There is nothing greater than that.

(5) "WHEREFORE WHEN HE COMETH INTO THE WORLD, HE SAITH, SACRIFICE AND OFFERING THOU WOULDEST NOT, BUT A BODY HAST THOU PREPARED ME:"

The structure is:

1. Due to the fact that animal sacrifices could not take away sins, Jesus must come into the world, which He did.

2. He did not come into the world to offer sacrifices of that other than Himself.

3. A physical body was prepared for Him, and done so through the Virgin Birth, for the express purpose of being offered in Sacrifice.

THE ENTRANCE OF CHRIST INTO THE WORLD

The phrase, *"Wherefore when He cometh into the world,"* presents Christ coming as the Savior, Who undertakes in Grace to meet every claim that the Throne of God has against penitent sinners.

His coming was that to which the Prophecies had pointed from the very beginning, actually with the first prediction given in the Garden of Eden by God, as He addressed Satan through the serpent (Gen. 3:15). The prediction was then carried out in type, when *"the Lord God made coats of skins, and clothed Adam and Eve"* (Gen. 3:21). To cover their nakedness to the Judgment of God, they had *"sewed fig leaves together, and made themselves aprons,"* which man has continued to attempt to do ever since, in his efforts to provide salvation for himself (Gen. 3:7).

Due to the terrible affects of sin, it took God some 4,000 years to prepare mankind for the Advent of Christ. This may seem to be an inordinate long time; however, it should portray to us just how bad that sin actually is. Considering the time it took, and even then man was barely ready, and the price that was paid to assuage this monster, we should get an idea as to the destructive power of this thing referred to as *"sin."*

NO MORE OFFERINGS OF ANIMAL SACRIFICES

The phrase, *"He saith, Sacrifice and Offering Thou wouldest not,"* refers to the fact, that He would pay for sin, but not with animal sacrifices. Instead, He would Himself in His physical body gotten through the Virgin Birth from Mary, offer Himself as a supreme

Sacrifice, which would suffice once for all, and for eternity.

The words *"He saith,"* proclaim the fact, that Christ is the Prophetic Word of Scripture. Though not directly mentioned here, it is overly obvious that it is Christ Who has been the subject of the whole context. The words beginning with *"Sacrifice,"* are a quotation from Psalm 40:7-9. It is a Psalm of David.

THANKSGIVING FOR DELIVERANCE

The first part of the Psalm is an expression of thanksgiving to God for deliverance from peril. David has learned the true mode of displaying gratitude, not by offerings of slain animals, but by the sacrifice of the will. So far does the latter excel the former, so truly is the sacrifice of the will in accordance with the Will of God, that the value of the legal offerings is in comparison as nothing. And yet, in all of this, there is no real slighting of the sacrificial ritual, but there is a profound appreciation of the superiority of spiritual service to mere ritual observance.

DAVID AS A TYPE OF CHRIST

In this Psalm we read, *"Mine iniquities are more than the hairs of mine head"* (Ps. 40:12). David comes with a new perception of the true Will of God, to offer Him the service in which He takes pleasure. And yet not so — for such service as he can offer is itself defective, his sins surround him yet in their results and penalties. Hence, in his understanding and his offering of himself he is a type, while his sinfulness and weakness render him but an imperfect type, of Him Who was to come.

By contrast, Jesus came to His Father with a perfect offering of will and self which was foreshadowed in the best impulses of the best of men of God, whose inspired utterances the Scriptures record. The words of David, but partially true of himself, are fulfilled in the Son of David.

And yet, in a sense, all of the Psalms portray Christ, whether in His role as Redeemer, or as Intercessor, as portrayed in Hebrews 7:25. In fact, one can only understand the intercessory role of Christ, by understanding the Psalms, and especially such as that of Verse 12. Christ took our sins, made them His Own, pleaded by His very Presence before the Throne

of God, Mercy, and Grace on our behalf, which are guaranteed because of His Sacrificial Offering. He took our sin, i.e., *"sin penalty,"* that we might take His Righteousness.

THE PREPARATION

The phrase, *"But a body hast Thou prepared Me,"* proclaims the fact that deliverance from sin is not obtained by animal sacrifices, but as stated, by fulfilling God's will.

Vincent says, *"The course of thought in the Psalm is as follows: 'Thou, Oh God, desirest not the sacrifice of beasts, but Thou hast prepared My body as a single Sacrifice, and so I come to do Thy Will, as was predicted of Me, by the Sacrifice of Myself.'*

"Christ did not yield to God's Will as authoritative constraint. The constraint lay in His Eternal Spirit. His Sacrifice was no less His Own Will than God's Will." Paul said, *"Who through the Eternal Spirit offered Himself without spot to God"* (Heb. 9:14).

A BODY

The Body that is prepared for Christ pertains to the Incarnation, God becoming man, that in it He may obey God. God is a Spirit and, therefore, cannot die. So in order to go to the Cross, He would have to take upon Himself a physical body, which the Holy Spirit predicted through David approximately 1,000 years before Christ. However, it is the offering of this body as a sacrifice in contrast to the animal sacrifices of the Law, which Paul emphasizes.

While the Passage in Psalms definitely emphasizes the Will of God, even as the Seventh Verse here proclaims, still, the Passage is far from saying that the essence or work of Christ's offering of Himself lies simply in obedience to the Will of God. While that of course is definitely important as would be obvious, still, the entirety of this which Paul says, and which is taken from David's prophecies, argues that the Son's offering of Himself is the true and final offering for sin, because it is the Sacrifice, which according to prophecy, God desired to be made.

All of this, of course, proclaims the fact that Christ existed long before the Incarnation. In fact, as God He has always existed. As God He is unformed, unmade, uncreated, had no beginning, has always been, always is, and always shall be. Consequently, a human body had to be prepared for Him, which itself tells us, that the blood of bulls and goats couldn't take away sin, or else what Christ did would not have been necessary. And considering what He actually did do, which is beyond comprehension, lets us know just how inadequate were the animal sacrifices, etc.

(6) "IN BURNT OFFERINGS AND SACRIFICES FOR SIN THOU HAST HAD NO PLEASURE."

The composite is:

1. Burnt offerings and animal sacrifices for sin were insufficient.

2. God took no pleasure in the sacrifices, due to the fact that they were inefficient, even though they were necessary at the time.

3. It is only in the Sacrifice of Christ that God would take pleasure, inasmuch, as it would be totally sufficient.

SIN

The phrase, *"In Burnt Offerings and Sacrifices for sin,"* proclaims the root of the problem which besets mankind. It is *"sin!"*

Man refuses to recognize sin as his problem. While he admits, at least after a fashion, that there is a problem, he claims that the lack of education is the cause, or wrong political leanings, or a lack of money, etc.

Approximately 100 years ago, education was touted as the throughway to all solutions. Humanistic psychology has now taken its place. It's ironical, under the former, theology was the queen of the Sciences. Theology has now been replaced with psychology. Humanism has become god, as man worships Himself, and psychology has become its religion.

But despite all of man's efforts, he never seems to be even close to any solution. The facts are, every single heart and life in this world which have been changed from darkness to light, which stands as a monument to the fact that a change can be brought about, all and without exception, have been brought about by Faith in Jesus Christ, and what He has done for the human race at the Cross. This means that Islam has never brought about one changed heart, neither Buddhism, or Mormonism, or Catholicism, or Shintoism,

etc. As well, vaunted psychology, cannot boast of one single solitary individual who has experienced a miraculous change in his or her heart, because of its teachings. Not one!

The problem is sin, and the solution is the Savior, and of course, the Savior Alone is the Lord Jesus Christ. And to be sure, His means is the Cross. That's why a body was prepared for Him, in order that He might offer it in Sacrifice.

This tells man that his problem is far more severe than meets the eye. It is so bad in fact, that man has no solution, as man cannot have any solution. Unredeemed man is depraved, and totally depraved at that, which means that everything he touches he destroys, which is the very opposite of bringing about a solution.

PLEASURE

The phrase, *"Thou hast had no pleasure,"* doesn't mean that God took no pleasure at all in the animal Sacrifices, for He was the One Who instituted this particular means. The idea is, as it regards *"sin,"* these sacrifices were not sufficient; therefore, God took no pleasure in them in that capacity.

But when His Own Blessed Son came into the world to fulfill all these types, and to pay in His Own Person the Redemption Price, it is written: *"It pleased the LORD to bruise Him; He hath put Him to grief: when Thou shalt make His soul an Offering for sin, He shall see His Seed, He shall prolong His days, and the pleasure of the LORD shall prosper in His Hand"* (Isa. 53:10).

(7) "THEN SAID I, LO, I COME (IN THE VOLUME OF THE BOOK IT IS WRITTEN OF ME,) TO DO THY WILL, O GOD."

The exegesis is:

1. Throughout the Old Testament are given prophecies and instructions regarding the Divine Will for the Messiah.

2. This tells us that enough information was given that Israel should have known, and above all, these Christian Jews should know.

3. To rebel against Christ, and His Finished Work on the Cross, is to rebel against the plain and simple Word of God.

THE PREDICTION

The phrase, *"Then said I, Lo, I come,"* proclaims the fact, that the theme of the Old

Testament is the Messiah, i.e., *"The Lord Jesus Christ."* In fact, Paul applies the words *"Then said I,"* directly to Christ, showing that he regarded this Passage in Psalms as referring to Him as the Speaker. The Incarnation of the Son of God becomes the heart of the message found in this Tenth Chapter of Hebrews.

This means that a belief in the Virgin Birth becomes necessary if we are to believe Jesus Christ was truly God manifest in the flesh. It is amazing how many in theological circles do not believe it is any longer necessary to believe in the Virgin Birth of Jesus. It is time to let the world know that Jesus was both human and Divine: God was His Father, Mary was His Mother.

The world would like to reject the Virgin Birth and destroy it. The world would like to do away with the supernatural and the miraculous. However, to remove the Virgin Birth from our message would make Jesus merely a man, and an illegitimate son; it would present Mary as an unholy and unchaste vessel. God would be made a liar. In fact, the evidence is so overwhelming in the Word of God, so plain, so clear, so simple, that either Christ is the Divine Son of God, or He is a fake and a fraud and He deserved to die. One must believe what the Bible says, or one must not believe at all!

IN THE VOLUME OF THE BOOK

The phrase, *"In the volume of the book it is written of Me,"* refers to the fact, that the entirety of the Old Testament points to the Lord Jesus Christ. Every Prophecy pointed to Him. The nation of Israel was raised up for the sole purpose of giving to the world the Word of God, which told of the coming Redeemer, and in fact, to be a womb for the Messiah. All of the Tabernacle and Temple, along with all their Sacred Vessels, spoke entirely of Christ, whether of His Perfect Life and Ministry, or the sacrificial offering of Himself on the Cross. Truly, in the *"Volume of the Book it was written of Him."*

Considering all of this, how could the Hebrew Christians consider returning to the system of sacrifices found under the Old Covenant? Did they not realize that the blood shed in those sacrifices could not purge their consciences from sin? There could be no

NOTES

perfect cleansing outside of the Blood shed by Jesus Christ Himself.

How could anyone compare the Blood of Jesus with that of animals? It was obvious that the blood of man would be greater than that of an animal, and the Blood of the God-Man would be infinitely more effective in cleansing from sin. This Jesus had been raised from the dead, glorified, and taken to Heaven; He had entered into the Presence of God by and through His Own Blood, all on our behalf.

Through the offering of the Body of Jesus Christ once for all, shows that it is the Atonement which explains the purpose of the Incarnation. The Incarnation takes place in order that sin might be put away by the Offering of the Body and the Blood of the Savior. This and this alone, the Sacrifice of Christ satisfies the demands of a thrice-Holy God, thereby making it possible for man to be saved. Nothing else will suffice!

THE WILL OF GOD

The phrase, *"To do Thy Will, O God,"* presents that which all of this is all about — to do the Will of God. The entirety of the Old Testament contains written instructions regarding the Divine Will for the Messiah. It was outlined as to Who He would be, How He would be, and What He would be.

All of this tells us of the veracity of the Word of God, which in fact, is the Will of God. If Christ used the Word, which then was the Old Testament, as His foundation for all things, in fact, that which the Holy Spirit used to guide Him, which certainly set the example for us, shouldn't we do the same?

To which we have already alluded, the Holy Spirit in this given by Paul, used the Psalms to portray this beautiful announcement concerning Christ. Let's look at the Psalms a little closer:

THE PSALMS AND THE MESSIAH

On the road to Emmaus, and in the Upper Chamber, the Messiah, the Lord Jesus Christ, spoke to the Disciples of the things in the Psalms concerning Himself (Lk. Chpt. 24).

The Holy Spirit trained the writers of the Psalms; but He was their Author (Acts 1:16; 2:25, 30; Heb. 3:7). Hence, He says that no

Scripture is of human origination (II Pet. 1:20), but that all Scripture is of Divine Inspiration (II Tim. 3:16).

The Book of Psalms is a volume of prophecy; its principal predictions concern the perfections, the sufferings, and the succeeding glories of the Messiah.

God having been dishonored by human unbelief and disobedience, it was necessary that a man should be born who would perfectly love, perfectly trust, and perfectly serve Him; and Who would be the True Adam, Noah, Abraham, Israel, Moses, and David, etc.

God's moral glory demanded that sin should be judged; that sinners should repent, confess, and forsake sin and worship and obey Him; and being God, His nature required perfection in these emotions of the heart and will.

PERFECTION

Such perfection was impossible to fallen man, and it was equally out of his power to provide a sacrifice that would remove his guilt and restore his relationship with God.

The Psalms reveal Christ as satisfying in these relationships all the Divine requirements. He, though Himself sinless, declares Himself in these Psalms in a sense, to be the sinner, and I speak of His intercessory role; and He expresses to God the abhorrence of sin accompanied by the repentance and sorrow which man ought to feel and express but will not and cannot. Similarly, the faith, love, obedience, and worship which man fails to give He perfectly renders.

HIGH PRIEST

Thus, as the High Priest of His people, He, the True Advocate, charges Himself with the guilt of our sins; declares them to be His Own; confesses them, repents of them, declaring at the same time His Own sinlessness; and atones for them. Thus, those Psalms in which the Speaker declares his sinfulness and his sinlessness become quite clear of comprehension when it is recognized Who the Speaker is, and in what role He is occupying at the time — that of Savior or Intercessor.

The Messiah's other Offices and Ministries as Son of God and Son of Man, as King and Priest, as Servant of Jehovah, as Angel of Jehovah, as the Word of God, and as the Burnt

NOTES

Offering, the Meal Offering, the Peace Offering, the Sin Offering, and the Trespass Offering; and as the Resurrection and the Life, are all sung of, together with the sufferings or the glories appropriate to each Office.

The Gospels record the fact that He prayed; the Psalms, one might say, furnish the words of the prayer.

A DIARY

The Psalter is an inexhaustible source of strength, guidance, consolation, and moral teaching to the people of God, and many valuable Commentaries point out these treasures. It may, therefore, in this aspect be justly regarded as a diary kept by the Lord when on Earth in which are recorded His Own experiences and the experiences proper to those in whom He dwells.

Some of these Messianic experiences were entirely personal, others representative, others sympathetic, and others proper to Him as the True Israel.

The interpretation of the Book of Psalms, therefore, belongs to Him as Messiah, to Israel as His people, and to the nations as His possession. Its application is to all who feel their need of a Savior from sin and from its consequences. Actually, the Church, little, if at all, appears in the Book of Psalms.

(The Author owes a debt of gratitude to George Williams, for the above comments on the Psalms.)

THE INTERPRETATION OF THE PSALMS

I have read after many writers who struggled to separate the Psalms, attempting to point out that which pertained to Christ, and that which pertained to David or other personal writers. As such, they would refer to some of the Psalms as Messianic Psalms, meaning that they overwhelmingly spoke of the coming Christ, etc.

However, if we will understand that the entirety of the Psalms speak of Christ and in their totality, everything will become much more clear. In other words, one, I think can say, that all the Psalms, all 150 of them, are Messianic Psalms, because they all portray Christ.

The reason that it's difficult for most Commentators to see this is because they fail to recognize the different roles in which the Holy Spirit places Christ. As previously stated, at times, He is presented as Savior, with the statements then being crystal clear as pertaining to Him. But other statements speak of failure, of sin, of iniquity, of pleas for forgiveness, etc. These as well speak of Christ, but in His intercessory role. In every sense of the word, He became the True Man.

In these cries and pleas, the Reader is not to misunderstand, thinking that Christ Himself has sinned, for that is not the case at all. But the Truth is, and allow me to say it again, He as the High Priest of His people, as the True Advocate, charges Himself with the guilt of our sins; declares them to be His Own; confesses them, repents of them, while at the same time, declaring His Own sinlessness; in other words, He atones for them. Thus, all of this becomes quite clear, when we recognize the role which He is presently occupying.

TO DO THE WILL OF GOD

In connection with Psalms 40:8, which says *"I delight to do Thy Will, O My God,"* He said in John 6:38, *"I came down from Heaven, not to do Mine Own will, but the Will of Him that sent Me."*

When He spoke of the *"Will of God,"* He spoke of all things, but more particularly, He spoke of the Will of God in His coming to make expiation for iniquity; and by His accomplishment of that Will, which He definitely did do, we who believe in Him are now eternally set apart to God on the basis, not of our promises or feelings or our personal righteousness, but of the offering of the Body of Jesus Christ in Sacrifice once for all.

How slowly truths like these seem to seep into our souls and become part of our very beings. But one may safely say there is no lasting peace until this aspect of Christ's work has been laid hold of in faith.

In His doing the Will of God, and doing it perfectly, He had to be perfectly obedient to the Law in every respect. He could not fail in even the slightest part of the Law, even one time. This was totally necessary, if He was to be a proper Atonement for sin. He would have to become *"obedient unto death,"* but it would have to be a death that was the result of a perfect life (Phil. 2:8).

NOTES

So, the greater thrust in all of this is the offering of Himself in Sacrifice, which is everywhere in the Scriptures held out as being the *"Will of God."* There was Salvation in no other way, nor was it possible that the race should be saved unless the Redeemer drank that cup of bitter sorrows (Mat. 26:39).

THE VALIDITY OF THE CROSS

All of this, as surely should be obvious by now, proclaims to us the validity of the Cross of Christ. And by that, I mean that the Cross is the centrality of the Gospel. The Cross as we've already said several times in this Volume, is not really a Doctrine, but is actually the foundation of all Doctrine. Everything from God to man comes totally and exclusively through the Cross of Christ. Everything that the Holy Spirit does in totality is done totally and completely within the parameters of the legal Work of Christ at the Cross. Yes, I said *"legal!"* And what do I mean by that?

Once again we go to Romans 8:2. The Spirit through Paul there said, *"For the Law of the Spirit of Life in Christ Jesus hath made me free from the Law of sin and death."*

Notice that he said it is *"the Law of the Spirit of Life in Christ Jesus."* That makes it something legal.

Man's bondage in the realm of Satan, is a legal bondage. In other words, due to the fact that the wages of sin is death, Satan had a legal right to hold man in captivity because of man's sin. When Jesus died on the Cross, He died in order to pay the just demands of a thrice-Holy God, which was and is a legal work. By His Death He legally satisfied those demands, which at the same time deprived Satan of his legal right to hold man in captivity. Due to the fact that all sin is atoned, Satan actually has no legal right to hold anyone in the bondage of sin. Of course, most of the world is in the bondage of sin simply because they will not trust Christ. And sadly enough, most Christians are dominated by sin in some way, simply because they do not understand the validity of the Cross of Christ, as we are here explaining it.

You as a Believer must first of all put your Faith exclusively in the Cross of Christ, understanding, as we've already stated, that everything that God gives to you comes through the Cross, and your means of reaching God is totally and completely through what Jesus did at the Cross. When you put your faith there, then the Holy Spirit will begin to reveal to you all of the meaning of the Cross, which in effect, is so vast that it literally beggars description (Rom. 6:3-5, 11, 14).

But if your Faith is misplaced, in other words, somewhat in the Cross and somewhat in your confession, or something else, that produces a double-minded spirit, which God cannot honor, and in fact, which is no faith at all (James 1:5-8).

Paul was given the meaning of the New Covenant, which he gave to us in his fourteen Epistles, which is in effect, the meaning of the Cross. Let me say that another way.

What the New Covenant is all about is what Jesus did for us at the Cross. That explains the Covenant; that in fact, is the Covenant.

Now Satan will do everything within his power to steer you as a Believer away from that Covenant, while all the time making you think you're still in the Covenant. The point I'm making is this:

The Believer, even though having been saved as a result of what Jesus did at the Cross, which is the New Covenant, still, is in danger of being pulled away from the Cross after conversion. Satan is very subtle in this. He claims that for one to go on to deeper life, one must leave the Cross, simply because that's elementary, and he must go on to deeper things. But of course, the definition of those deeper things is always different with different Preachers. The truth is, there is nothing deeper than the Cross! The Holy Spirit, even as we've already stated, works exclusively within the legal boundaries of the Cross, in everything that He does with us and for us. So, for one to say that they're going to go deeper than the Spirit is facetious indeed! Once, as a Believer, we understand that everything that the Holy Spirit does is done totally and completely within the parameters of the Cross, then we begin to understand how important all of this really is.

The Reader may grow somewhat weary concerning my constant applications of the Cross; however, understanding that this is the very center of our Faith, and actually the secret of all Blessings from God, I don't see

how it would be possible for me to overstate the case. I know how subtle that Satan is, in attempting to steer us away from that which is Scriptural concerning God's dealings with us. His major effort is to get us away from the Cross of Christ, because he knows that this is God's prescribed order of Salvation and victory, and more particularly, Faith in that Finished Work.

(8) "ABOVE WHEN HE SAID, SACRIFICE AND OFFERING AND BURNT OFFERINGS AND OFFERING FOR SIN THOU WOULDEST NOT, NEITHER HADST PLEASURE THEREIN; WHICH ARE OFFERED BY THE LAW;"

The exegesis is:

1. The first part of this Verse has to do with Verse 5. All of the Sacrifices and Offerings were but a stopgap measure, until Christ would come.

2. The Lord took no pleasure in these things, even though He had instituted them, for the simple reason, that they could not take away sin. They did serve a purpose, but not the ultimate purpose.

3. All of this is under the Law of Moses, which was the Covenant that was absolved by Christ, even as the next Verse proclaims.

THE SACRIFICES OF OLD COULD NOT TAKE AWAY SIN

The phrase, *"Above when He said, Sacrifice and Offering and Burnt Offerings and Offering for sin Thou wouldest not,"* refers to the fact that animal sacrifices could not cleanse from sin. This could only be done by Christ, in the offering of Himself.

To this end, God prepared a body for the Eternal Logos Who came to do the Will of God and die for the sins of the world (Gal. 1:4; I Pet. 2:24).

God ordained the Sacrifices and Offerings of Leviticus as shadows of the great Substance Offering of Calvary. He found no abiding pleasure in the sacrifices under the Law, but He does find an eternal joy in the Body He prepared for His Beloved Son, in which Body Christ was to make the Great Offering purposed by the Will of God before the world began.

It is awe-striking to be permitted in Psalms 40 to hear the Father and the Son in the past eternities planning the Atonement. The sacrifice of dumb and irrational creatures is here contrasted with the intelligent obedience of Christ's Sacrifice of Himself.

By the words *"wouldest not,"* some have thought that the Spirit is here saying that God didn't want sacrifices; however, that's not what is being said.

In effect, He is saying that animal sacrifices, even though necessary, as stated, as a stopgap measure, still could not redeem humanity in that they could not take away sin. It should be understood, to be sure, considering that God would have to pay the price Himself, that if it were possible that animal sacrifices would suffice, the Lord surely would have accepted them. He didn't because they wouldn't!

NO PLEASURE

The phrase, *"Neither hadst pleasure therein,"* concerns the fact of the insufficiency of the animal sacrifices. If it is to be noticed, Paul mentions about all the types of Sacrifices offered, which were actually five in number — Whole Burnt Offerings, Sin Offerings, Peace Offerings, Meal Offerings, and Trespass Offerings. All involve the shedding of blood, with the exception of the *"Meal Offering,"* which was a thanksgiving Offering of sorts, which involved bread, etc. The Peace Offering was generally used in connection with the other Offerings. In other words, when a Whole Burnt Offering or Sin Offering was Sacrificed, it would be followed by a Peace Offering, signifying that God had accepted the Offering, and there was now Peace with God.

UNDER THE LAW

The phrase, *"Which are offered by the Law,"* refers to the fact that all of these Offerings were included in the Mosaic Law. The description of the Sacrifices is offered in the first few chapters of Leviticus.

It should be noted that it took five different types of Sacrifices to portray the One Sacrifice of Christ. To turn it around and say it in another way, the One Sacrifice of Christ of Himself, fulfilled all five of the Levitical Offerings. The following gives a brief description of what these Sacrifices typified.

THE WHOLE BURNT OFFERING

The first Sacrifice offered, at least of which we have a record, was that offered by Abel (Gen. Chpt. 4). He offered a Whole Burnt Offering, the same as Noah, and Abraham. In other words, it was only Whole Burnt Offerings that were sacrificed up until the Law of Moses.

This was the offering of a Lamb in its entirety, with the exception of the skin that was stripped from its body. It symbolized two things:

First of all, it symbolized that man was a sinner, and that he needed a Substitute, and the Lamb pointed toward the One Who was to come.

Second, by the signification of it being a *"Whole Burnt Offering,"* the statement was made, that God was giving His all in reference to the Redemption of mankind, which this Sacrifice represented, and that God expected man in turn, to give God His all!

When the modern Christian feels a need of consecration to God, and he does so through prayer and the seeking of the Face of the Lord, He is in essence, offering up a *"Whole Burnt Offering"* before the Lord. He is saying, *"Lord You have given me Your all, and now I give You my all!"*

THE SIN OFFERING

Until the Law of Moses was given, the entire Atonement process was signified by the Whole Burnt Offering. It was only when sin was defined, which the Law did, that other offerings were required, and which were instituted in the Mosaic Law.

The Sin Offering means exactly what it says, that man has sinned against God, and was to offer up a sacrifice, which could be a Lamb, a goat, or even a Bullock. However, the far greater majority of the time, it was a lamb that was offered.

Most of the time a Peace Offering was offered immediately following the offering of a Whole Burnt Offering, or a Sin Offering, or a Trespass Offering. This signified that God had accepted the sacrifice, and now Peace was restored.

Whenever the modern Christian sins against the Lord, which is something that should never happen, but which regrettably and sadly, does, and they then confess the sin to the Lord, asking His forgiveness and cleansing, they are in essence doing the same thing as the Believing Israelite of old, when he offered a Sin-Offering.

THE TRESPASS OFFERING

This Offering was required, when one Israelite sinned against another Israelite. He had trespassed against his Brother or Sister in the Lord, which at the same time means that he had trespassed against God, therefore, requiring a Sacrifice.

If a modern Christian sins against a fellow Christian, he has to seek forgiveness from that person, as well as the Lord, which is the same as that which the Israelite did of old as it regarded his Trespass Offering.

THE PEACE OFFERING

As we've stated, this Offering was generally offered after one of the other Offerings. It signified that Peace with God had been restored.

It was the only one of the animal sacrifices, of which the Offerer could partake. In other words, when the Lamb was offered, a part would be given to the Priests, and a part could be taken by the Offerer, with him gathering his family and friends about him, having a feast, in effect celebrating relationship with God which had been restored. Of course, the Peace Offering would always follow one of the other Sacrificial Offerings.

This is the same thing with the modern Christian, whenever repentance has been enjoined, and peace with God has been restored.

All of these were blood sacrifices, in effect, which refers to the shedding of blood upon the killing of the animal. It all typified the great, One Sacrifice of Christ, when He would offer Himself on the Cross, which He did, making these things any more unnecessary. Thank God that we presently, do not have to offer up a Sacrifice to God in this respect, knowing that the One Sacrifice of Christ has made all of that unnecessary. Our trust in that One Sacrifice is all that is necessary for the Believer, and in whatever circumstance.

THE MEAL OFFERING

This was the only bloodless Offering of the five sacrifices. It was somewhat a Thanksgiving Offering to the Lord, for all His many

blessings. It as well could be offered in conjunction with the other sacrifices which it oftentimes was.

It is the same presently as Christians offering thanksgiving to the Lord for His Mercy and Grace.

As stated, all of these Sacrifices are outlined with descriptions given, in the first seven Chapters of Leviticus.

(For greater detail concerning the Sacrifices, please see our Commentary on Genesis — Volume 1.)

(9) "THEN SAID HE, LO, I COME TO DO THY WILL, O GOD. HE TAKETH AWAY THE FIRST, THAT HE MAY ESTABLISH THE SECOND."

The structure is:

1. Once again, the Will of God is proclaimed as the total requirement, which in effect is the Sacrifice of Christ.

2. His Sacrifice of Himself on the Cross, took away the First Covenant, simply because it satisfied all its demands.

3. As well, the Sacrifice of Christ on the Cross established the Second Covenant, which in effect, is the Second Covenant.

TO DO THY WILL, O GOD

The phrase, *"Then said He, Lo, I come to do Thy Will, O God,"* proclaims this statement a second time. Whenever the Holy Spirit says something twice, it is of extreme importance.

The doing of the Will of God as it regards Christ, pertains totally and completely to His Sacrifice of Himself on the Cross, proclaiming the fact, that the Cross was the eternal destination. This means that the Cross was not an incident or an accident. It was a planned work, actually planned from before the foundation of the world (I Pet. 1:18-20).

Inasmuch as the Cross was the Plan of God, some may have the tendency then to think that Israel, that being the case, was not culpable.

While the Cross was the Plan of God and in every respect, to be sure, Israel definitely was culpable. God through His omniscience, which means that He knows everything, past, present, and future, knew that man would fall, and that he would be redeemed only by the Sacrifice of His (God's) Only Son. This

Sacrifice would be carried out on a Cross, and for reasons which we will not now get into.

However, even though this was the Plan of God, it definitely was not the Plan of God for Israel to do this terrible thing. They did this of their own volition, strictly out of their wicked hearts. In other words, God did not force the issue in that capacity whatsoever. Consequently, even though the Cross was the Will of God, Israel would still answer to God for her perfidious action, which she definitely did!

Some may ask the question as to how Christ would have been crucified, had Israel in fact accepted Him, thereby not doing this terrible thing?

Knowing the depraved hearts of men, the Crucifixion was a given. Rome would have been next in line had Israel not done this terrible thing. In Truth, all of humanity crucified Christ. It was my sins and your sins, which nailed Him to the Tree.

CHRIST FULFILLED THE FIRST COVENANT

The phrase, *"He taketh away the first,"* refers to the fact that the Sacrifice of Himself, made the First Covenant unnecessary. He fulfilled all the requirements of the Law, both in keeping it perfectly, and then satisfying its penalty on the Cross. The statement, *"He taketh away the first,"* means that the Offerings of the Old Covenant were temporary and ineffective. The idea is, He took away the Sacrifices of slain animals that He may establish the doing of God's Perfect Will. That such sacrifices as were formally offered are no longer according to God's pleasure follows as an inference from this.

The words *"take away"* are very strong in the Greek, pointing to the total abolition of the former way. Therefore, it is an insult to God for anything of the First Covenant to be carried over into the present, as should be overly obvious. In fact, that's what the argument of the entirety of this Epistle to the Hebrews is all about.

THE CROSS ESTABLISHED THE SECOND COVENANT

The phrase, *"That He may establish the Second,"* has to do with the New Covenant.

This tells us that Christ's One Offering is eternal and satisfactory. So the First is taken away in order to the establishment of the Second. Through the One Offering of the Body of Jesus Christ once for all, the worshipper is sanctified forever and perfected forever.

By the taking away of the First Covenant, the Second is *"established,"* *"made firm."* Neither *"the First"* nor *"the Second"* are defined, but clearly the way of the Levitical Sacrifices and the Way of the Sacrifice of Christ are being set over against each other. This means, they are not complementary systems that may exist side by side. The one excludes the other. In other words, no compromise is possible between them. Again, this is the whole argument of Paul's Epistle to the Hebrews.

This phrase, *"That He may establish the Second,"* is the very reason we state that the meaning of the Cross is actually the meaning of the New Covenant. In fact, the words *"New Covenant"* and *"Cross,"* are synonymous. When one says one, in effect, one says the other. The idea is this:

If one doesn't understand the Cross, one doesn't understand the New Covenant. And if one properly understands the New Covenant, one properly understands the Cross.

(10) "BY THE WHICH WILL WE ARE SANCTIFIED THROUGH THE OFFERING OF THE BODY OF JESUS CHRIST ONCE FOR ALL."

The composition is:

1. The word *"will"* refers here to the Will of God which Christ came to do.

2. The Will of God which the First Testament Sacrifices could not accomplish was the Sanctification of men. Sanctification is accomplished only through the Sacrifice of Christ, and Faith in that Finished Work.

3. *"Once for all"* means that the Sacrifice of Christ totally suffices, and there will never be any other need for any other sacrifice.

ONCE AGAIN, THE WILL OF GOD

The phrase, *"By the which will,"* refers to a specific *"will,"* in this case the Sacrifice of Christ, which took away the First Covenant, which means it satisfied its demands, and established the Second or New Covenant.

In order to perform the Will of God perfectly, Jesus must Himself of necessity be God;

for to do all that which such a *"will"* says must be done, demands perfection of knowledge. All God's Will cannot be accomplished twice. Were it possible to do so it would be a proof of the inadequacy of the first effort; and so of both.

In Psalms 40:6, the actual rendering is, *"Mine ears hast Thou opened,"* with Paul translating it *"But a body hast Thou prepared Me"* (Heb. 10:5).

However, the Holy Spirit moved Paul to translate it in this way, meaning that it is totally and completely translated with every accuracy.

Christ was the One and perfectly obedient Servant — only listening to One Voice, and only speaking the words that He was given to speak (Jn. 8:17). He was so to say, simply an ear. This figure of speech vividly pictures Him as the Perfect Servant Whose ear was opened morning by morning (Isa. Chpt. 1).

The bondservant in Exodus Chapter 21 engaged to serve perpetually his master, his wife, and his children; and his pierced ear witnessed to his affection. Psalms 40 and Hebrews 10:5 may, perhaps, point to this, for Christ in love to God, to Israel, and to her children, took the form of a servant and suffered the painful death of the Tree (Williams).

SANCTIFICATION

The phrase, *"We are sanctified,"* proclaims one being set apart unto God, which can only be done, and can only come about, through what Jesus did at the Cross, and our Faith in the Cross. This one Verse of Scripture proclaims in glaring, concise outline, exactly what I have been teaching throughout the entirety of this Volume. Because it's so important, and to hopefully make it even more clear, let me say it again:

Paul is speaking to Believers, and by that of course, we mean those who have already accepted Christ as their Savior; however, after Salvation, the Holy Spirit sets out to sanctify us, which means to root all sin out of our lives, to develop the Fruit of the Spirit in our lives, and to make us Christlike. As well, this pertains to everything else that we receive from the Lord, be it Divine Healing, financial prosperity, and Blessings of every sort. It is taken for granted, that the Believer

here has as well, been baptized with the Holy Spirit, with the evidence of speaking with other tongues (Acts 2:4).

However, many Charismatics and Pentecostals have the mistaken idea, that once one is baptized with the Holy Spirit, then everything is automatic from there on out as it regards the Sanctification process. Not so! While the potential is there as it regards the Holy Spirit, He demands that we at all times, exhibit Faith in the Cross of Christ, understanding that the Crucifixion of Christ, and our being baptized into His Death, is that which makes all of this possible. Now let's see how it is done.

THE SACRIFICE OF CHRIST

The phrase, *"Through the Offering of the Body of Jesus Christ once for all,"* proclaims the means by which the Sanctification process is brought about, and the only means I might quickly add. Now the Christian can believe this which Paul has said in this Tenth Verse and experience all that Christ has done for him as it regards the Sanctification process, or else he can put his faith in something else, and suffer defeat. It's just that simple!

We are here plainly told that *"we are sanctified through the offerings of the Body of Jesus Christ,"* and how much clearer could it be! We must remember that it is the Holy Spirit Who inspired Paul to write these words.

It is unfortunate, that the word *"Sanctification"* in the modern Church is almost never used anymore. It is not because the word is out of date, but because the Church has moved so far away from Sanctification.

Why?

Perhaps there are many reasons, but the major reason is because we have attempted to engage the process in all the wrong ways. Some Denominations have taught *"Sanctification"* as a definite Work of Grace. Others have taught that Sanctification is arrived at by proper confession, or by some type of super faith, etc. None of that works!

In fact, no Christian can be Sanctified except in one way, and that is by exhibiting Faith totally and completely in the Cross of Christ, which then allows the Holy Spirit to perform the task, Who Alone can do this thing at any rate. There is no way that the Believer can sanctify himself. It doesn't really matter what you do, what effort you make, what things in which you engage, the only manner in which the Sanctification process can be enjoined is by the following way, in which I've already outlined quite a number of times in this Volume:

1. We must understand, exactly as Paul here says, that everything comes through the Sacrifice of Christ.

2. You must exhibit faith in this at all times, and for the simple reason, that God works exclusively on the basis of Faith. In other words, and to make it even more clear, the Cross of Christ must ever be the object of your Faith.

3. When this is done, the Holy Spirit will then work mightily on your behalf, bringing about this process, which only He can do (Rom. 8:2, 11).

If I could get the entirety of the Church to see this simple truth, which is so clearly brought out in the Word of God, untold misery and heartache could be avoided. The Reader should understand, that the Holy Spirit will not deviate from the Sacrifice of Christ. It doesn't matter how sincere you might be as a Christian, or how dedicated you are, or even how much God is using you in other ways, if you do not understand God's prescribed order of victory, which is simply and plainly here given, irrespective as to whom you might be, you will live a life of spiritual failure in some way. And to be sure, we're speaking of difficulties and problems which know no bounds. Satan fights the Cross as he fights nothing else, because He knows this great Truth as well. But if he can keep you in the dark regarding this which Jesus has done for us, and cause our attention to be diverted elsewhere, which pertains to his effort to get us to place our faith elsewhere, he will have then won the battle.

WHAT DO YOU KNOW
ABOUT THE CROSS?

Someone sent us an e-mail the other day stating, *"Why are you talking so much about the Cross? I'm a Christian, and all Christians know all about the Cross,"* or words to that effect.

Unfortunately, that is the thinking of most; however, the truth is, most Christians

don't know anything about the Cross. They know that Jesus died for them, but that's about the extent of their knowledge. Most have absolutely no knowledge as to the part the Cross plays in their everyday, ongoing Christian experience. They read Romans Chapter 6, that is if they read it at all, not really understanding what it actually says. As a consequence, they are being dominated by sin in some manner (Rom. 6:14).

What we are addressing here is the single most important thing in the life of the Believer. We're talking about one's spiritual welfare, one's happiness, one's joy in the Lord, actually everything that truly makes Christianity what Christianity ought to be. So, it's not something that one can pick or choose at one's will. You either know and understand this and walk in victory, or else you don't know this, and live in defeat.

And the words *"once for all,"* tell us that this is God's Way, and that it's a Way that will never change.

(11) "AND EVERY PRIEST STANDETH DAILY MINISTERING AND OFFERING OFTENTIMES THE SAME SACRIFICES, WHICH CAN NEVER TAKE AWAY SINS:"

The composite is:

1. This Verse proclaims the fact that the Temple was yet standing in Jerusalem, which means that this Epistle to the Hebrews was written shortly before A.D. 70, the year that Jerusalem and the Temple were destroyed.

2. The standing position of the Priests is set in vivid contrast to the seated posture of the Messiah, as given in Verse 12.

3. This was apostasy on the part of the leaders of Israel. In defiance of the clear Will of God, in that Jesus had already paid the price, they kept on offering sacrifices.

4. They did all of this despite the fact, that their sacrifices had never been able to take away sins, and couldn't do so at present.

THE STANDING PRIESTS

The phrase, *"And every Priest standeth,"* refers not only to those at the present, but goes all the way back to the beginning of the Mosaic Law, a time-period of some 1,600 years. The reason for their standing posture is because their work was never finished. They had to keep offering more and more sacrifices, and because the blood of bulls and goats, even as Paul has said, could not take away sins.

As previously stated, this was God's way for the period of the Law, which was meant to point at all times to Christ Who was to come, but after Christ had come, the continuing of this system was an abomination in the Eyes of God. In fact, it was a slap to the Face of God, which brought total destruction upon Jerusalem and the Temple, which took place in A.D. 70.

THE SAME SACRIFICES

The phrase, *"Daily ministering and offering oftentimes the same Sacrifices,"* referred to a work that was never completed, simply because the Sacrifices themselves, were insufficient to take away sins.

We must remember that Paul is writing this to Christian Jews with some seriously considering abandoning Christ and going back into Judaism. Of course, being Jews they had been born and raised in Judaism, but at a point in time, had accepted Christ as their Savior. When they did this, they experienced a peace within their hearts, that all the Levitical sacrifices could never offer, and for all the obvious reasons; however, many of these Christian Jews continued on in Temple worship, that is if they lived in Jerusalem, and if elsewhere, following the Law as closely as they could. This more than anything else, the serving of two masters, is what had brought them to this place.

To fully serve Christ, one must totally and completely follow Christ. Everything else must be abandoned.

CHARISMATICS

On January 1, 1969, we went on the air with our Radio Program, *"The Campmeeting Hour."* It was a 15-minute daily, Monday through Friday. Despite so many things we lacked, the Lord began to bless, until we were ultimately on some 600 Stations daily.

About a year after the initiation of the program, the Lord began to deal heavily with my heart about teaching on the Baptism with the Holy Spirit, which we did! I suppose I must have taught for a year or so primarily on this one subject.

NOTES

The Lord used the teaching to touch the hearts and lives of untold thousands of people. In fact, I think we probably had the largest audience in the world at that particular time for a daily Radio Program, at least in the field of Gospel.

During the 1970's, tens of thousands of Baptists, Methodists, in fact, all types of Denominational people were baptized with the Holy Spirit, with the evidence of speaking with other tongues. This was the result of a hunger for the Spirit, and one of the reasons, the Lord instructed us to teach on this very important subject.

Of course, we were only a small part of this Move of God which was taking place around the world, but the Lord did use our efforts. The point I make is this:

Many of these people after being baptized with the Holy Spirit, attempted to maintain their ties with the old-line Churches with which they had been so long associated. It is a posture which will not work.

THE WAY OF THE SPIRIT

The Way of the Holy Spirit is a total way. And to be sure, the Spirit-baptized Way carries no similarities to the old-line Denominations. As someone has well said, *"Salvation separates the sinner from the world, while the Baptism with the Holy Spirit separates Christians from dead, cold, formal churches."*

Those who fit this mold were referred to as *"Charismatics."* While the term actually means something else, it actually came to mean, as here used, old-line Church members who had been baptized with the Holy Spirit, and who elected to remain in their old-line Churches.

Failure to go all the way with the Spirit, which means they were trying to hold onto many unscriptural positions, has produced much error in the last several decades. It is the same problem although in a different way, which these Christian Jews faced. They didn't quite go all the way, trying to hold onto Judaism while at the same time following Christ. Their modern counterparts did the same, at least for the most part, attempting to hold onto the old Denominational line, while at the same time attempting to follow the Spirit. In fact, millions do the same thing as it regards the world. They try to hold onto the world while at the same time attempting to follow Christ.

Serving Christ, means cutting loose from everything else, making Christ foremost in one's life. All religion, all error, everything in fact which is not of the Spirit, must be totally and completely abandoned. Christ must be all in all! This, many of the Christian Jews failed to do, and now were being pulled away from Christ altogether.

THE REMOVAL OF SINS

The phrase, *"Which can never take away sins,"* proclaims to us several things:

1. God cannot tolerate sin in any fashion. It must be taken away. In fact, all sin must be completely gotten out of the universe and in totality, which shall happen at the end of the coming Millennium. Concerning that, Paul said, *"Then cometh the end, when He (Jesus) shall have delivered up the Kingdom to God, even the Father; when He (Christ) shall have put down all rule and all authority and power.*

"For He must reign, till He hath put all enemies under His feet.

"The last enemy that shall be destroyed is death."

Then, *"God shall be all in all"* (I Cor. 15:24-26, 28).

2. The animal sacrifices were a stopgap measure at best, employed temporarily until the Messiah would come. They couldn't take away sins.

3. Only the Blood of Jesus, God's Only Son, shed at Calvary's Cross, could affect this work, which it did!

4. This is the reason that the Cross is of such magnitude.

5. When any individual places their complete trust in Christ and what He did at the Cross on their behalf, without fail, they experience the glorious wonder of every sin being washed clean. It's called *"Justification by Faith"* (Rom. 3:24, 28; 5:1).

6. Then the peace of God comes into the heart, which is the most glorious and wonderful experience that one could ever have, and an experience which will last forever, as our trust in Christ continues (Gal. 1:3; 5:22).

(12) "BUT THIS MAN, AFTER HE HAD OFFERED ONE SACRIFICE FOR SINS

FOREVER, SAT DOWN ON THE RIGHT HAND OF GOD;"

The composition is:

1. *"This man,"* referring to the Lord Jesus Christ, according to the Greek Text should have been translated *"This Priest."*

2. His Offering of Himself on the Cross was an act that has never-ending results and that needs no repetition.

3. Christ is sat down at the Right Hand of God, implying that His Work is a Finished Work, and will never need any repetition, or anything added.

THIS PRIEST

The phrase, *"But this man,"* as stated, should have been translated *"this Priest,"* and because it is related to the word *"Priest"* of Verse 11. At any rate, the emphasis is on Christ and Christ Alone!

Let the Reader understand, that all Salvation is in Christ; all Victory is in Christ; all overcoming strength is in Christ; all Blessings are in Christ. In other words, everything that comes from God to undeserving humanity comes exclusively through Jesus Christ, and more particularly, through what He did at the Cross on our behalf, as Paul reiterates in these Passages over and over again.

What I've just said is a very simple statement; however, it is from this simplicity that Satan seeks to deter us. One of his biggest weapons is to get us to look at our own faith. It's *"my faith this!"* and *"my faith that!"* While Faith is definitely the basis on which God works, more particularly, it is the object of Faith that makes the difference. And by the object of Faith, we are speaking of the Cross of Christ.

As we've said repeatedly, even as Paul here outlines graphically, when we think of Christ, it must always be in connection with His great Sacrifice. That and that alone is the secret of all blessings.

ONE SACRIFICE

The phrase, *"After He had offered one sacrifice for sins forever,"* speaks of His purpose, which was the Cross.

Does the Reader notice in all of this, that Paul doesn't really mention the Resurrection of Christ? While of course, the Resurrection is of supreme significance, still, it was not by the Resurrection that Christ affected man's Redemption, but by the Cross. It was His Sacrifice that made Salvation possible, the Baptism with the Holy Spirit possible, ongoing victory possible, in fact everything!

Does the modern Church believe that?

Greek Scholar Kenneth Wuest says, *"His Offering of Himself on the Cross was an act that has never-ending results and that needs no repetition. This is in contrast to the oft-repeated offerings of the Levitical Priests. It is also true that our Lord seated Himself forever at the Right Hand of God. This is in contrast to the perpetual standing posture of the First Testament Priests."*

The key to all of this is that this *"one sacrifice for sins forever,"* has never-ending results.

When anyone denies that all things come through the Cross, they are in essence claiming that God deals with the human race in some other way, other than by the Sacrifice of Christ. Of course, they don't get that from the Bible, because the Word of God which is glaringly obvious, proclaims the Sacrifice of Christ as the great intersection of God and humanity, and that alone! To project something else, even as many are now doing, is to make up out of whole cloth, one's own brand of Salvation or victory. And the fearful thing about this is, that this blasphemy, and blasphemy it is, is not coming from the modernists so much, as it's coming from the so-called *"Word of Faith"* people. And the tragedy of all tragedies is, hundreds of thousands of people who claim to be saved and baptized with the Holy Spirit are believing this lie of all lies.

Let the Reader understand, that we're not speaking here of side issues, but rather the paramount issue of all things, the salvation of the soul, i.e., *"man's standing with God."*

One of their bright lights in describing the Cross refers to it as *"past miseries."* He then recommends that the Cross be forsaken, inasmuch as it was *"the greatest defeat in human history."*

Pure and simple, these people do not believe in the Sacrifice of Christ as the key to all Salvation.

There are tens of thousands of these Churches all over the world. And the tragedy

NOTES

is, most Pentecostals upon hearing this gross error, and gross error it is, even if they don't accept it totally, do not in any way denounce it. In fact, and I don't think I'm exaggerating when I say this, I personally feel that most so-called Pentecostals actually accept this blasphemy.

For the Cross of Christ to be denounced over world wide television, and to be denounced repeatedly, and no one say anything, or else very little, but rather pour millions of dollars into the coffers of these blasphemers, and blasphemers they are, lets us know the sick condition of the modern Church.

If the Cross is ignored, which is the foundation of all Biblical Doctrine, which the modern Church is now doing, then the Church drifts like a ship without a rudder, not knowing where it's been, where it is, or where it's going.

Jesus asked the question, *"When the Son of Man cometh, shall He find faith on the Earth?"* (Lk. 18:8).

He is speaking here of true Faith, which refers to Faith in His great Sacrifice of Himself. In fact, there has been more teaching on faith in the last 50 years than all the balance of Christianity put together; however, it has not been Faith in the Cross, but rather faith in other things, which means it's not of God. One of Satan's greatest ploys is to present a doctrine that is very, very similar to the real thing, so similar in fact, that many cannot tell the difference. The so-called modern faith message fits that description. Because it claims to be faith in the Word of God, it fools most people. The Truth is, it is not Faith in the Word, but rather in a perverted word, which refers to the Scriptures being pulled out of context. Satan tried the same thing with Christ in the wilderness temptation (Mat. 4:1-10). If it's not faith anchored squarely in the Cross of Christ, even as Paul is proclaiming from every angle, in this Epistle to the Hebrews, then it's not really Faith that God will recognize.

A FINISHED WORK

The phrase, *"Sat down on the right hand of God,"* refers to the great contrast between the Priests under the Levitical system who never sat down, and because their work was never completed. Christ sitting down at the *"Right Hand of God,"* refers to the fact, that His Work is a *"Finished Work."* And what does that mean?

It refers to the fact that everything which God demanded of the human race, Jesus met at the Cross. Nothing was left undone. The Cross also addresses every single thing that man lost in the Fall. While it is true that we do not yet have all the benefits of the Cross, some of those benefits awaiting the coming Resurrection, still, everything was there addressed.

It means as well, that no more Sacrifice or any other type of similar work will ever have to be enjoined, the Sacrifice of the Cross being sufficient for time and eternity. In fact, one Greek word *"lutroo"* which describes Redemption, carries the idea that such a price was paid at the Cross, that no creature in eternity future, be it man, demon, or Angel, will ever be able to say that the price was insufficient.

That great Sacrifice being a *"Finished Work"* refers to the fact, that everything from God to man, and in totality, was made possible by what Christ did at Calvary. This is the Source of all things, and of course, I speak of all things which come from God to man. That's the reason our Faith must ever be anchored in the Cross of Christ. The Holy Spirit demands it, that is, if He is to work within our hearts and lives (Rom. 8:1-2, 11).

(13) "FROM HENCEFORTH EXPECTING TILL HIS ENEMIES BE MADE HIS FOOTSTOOL."

The exegesis is:

1. *"From henceforth"* refers to Christ sitting on the Right Hand of God, until all enemies are subdued.

2. That which He did at the Cross, will ultimately dispel every single enemy.

3. *"Enemies"* constitute all Satanic powers, and as well, all men who look to other than the Cross.

FROM HENCEFORTH

The short phrase, *"From henceforth,"* refers to the idea, that this which the Cross will ultimately affect, is a settled conclusion. There is no doubt about the outcome! As stated, it is a Finished Work, which will do exactly what

it says, *"finish the work."* So that the Reader will not misunderstand, please allow me to say it in another way:

The Work of Christ at the Cross is finished; however, all the things this Finished Work is to accomplish, have not yet been done, but most definitely shall!

EXPECTING

"Expecting" in the Greek is *"ekdechomai,"* and means *"to await," "wait for."* The idea is, that which Christ did at the Cross, with its continued results, will ultimately bring all things to a successful conclusion. It is not a case of *"hope so,"* or *"maybe so,"* but rather, that which is certain, but has not yet come to pass.

ENEMIES DEFEATED

The phrase, *"Till His enemies be made His footstool,"* is actually derived from Psalms 110:1. So it was prophesied by David, that what he had prophesied in Psalms 40:6-8, which was the Sacrifice of Christ, would fall out to the total defeat of all enemies. What does he mean by *"enemies"*?

The enemies of the Redeemer are Satan, the wicked of the Earth, and all the evil passions of the heart. The idea is, that all things are yet to be made subject to His Will — either by a cheerful and cordial submission to His authority, or by being crushed beneath His power. The Redeemer, having performed His great work of Redemption by giving Himself as a Sacrifice on the Cross, is represented now as calmly waiting until this glorious triumph is achieved, and this Promise is fulfilled.

By this, we are not to suppose that He is inactive, or that He takes no share in the agency by which this is to be done, but the meaning is, that He looks to the certain fulfillment of the promise.

The word *"footstool,"* has to do with one putting his foot on the neck of his enemy, signifying that the enemy is totally defeated. The same idea is expressed in I Cor. 15:25 by saying that all His enemies shall be put under His feet. To be sure, this is certain of fulfillment.

(14) "FOR BY ONE OFFERING HE HATH PERFECTED FOR EVER THEM THAT ARE SANCTIFIED."

The composite is:

1. The *"One Offering"* is the Sacrifice of Christ on the Cross.

2. The word *"perfected"* means to bring to a state of completion.

3. The Cross makes possible our Sanctification, and one might quickly say, the Cross alone!

ONE OFFERING

The phrase, *"For by One Offering,"* refers to the Sacrifice of Christ, which addressed every single problem that man has, in other words, all that man suffered in the Fall.

Paul possibly uses the word *"one,"* by contrast to the five Levitical Offerings which were required under the old Mosaic Law. In other words, the One Offering of Christ addressed itself to that which took five Offerings under the Levitical system. However, even that description begs the question. The facts are, the five Offerings of the Levitical system could not take away even one sin, whereas the One Offering of Christ atoned for all sin, past, present, and future. The difference is in the worth of the Offerer. As should be obvious, Christ, the Son of God, is of infinite worth, while the animal sacrifices provide no comparison.

As well, the Levitical Sacrifices had to be offered again and again, actually multiple millions down through the centuries, while the One Sacrifice of Christ sufficed for all time.

PERFECTION

The phrase, *"He hath perfected forever,"* means that everything essential to the Salvation of the individual is included in the gift of Salvation, which the sinner receives by Faith in Messiah's Sacrifice.

The idea of this is, whereas the offerings made under the Jewish Law were so defective that there was a necessity for repeating them every day, the Offering made by Christ was and is so perfect that it needs not to be repeated, and as well, that it secures the complete and final Salvation of all those who avail themselves of it.

SANCTIFICATION

The phrase, *"Them that are sanctified,"* once again brings this word into view.

Those whom Christ calls He sanctifies, that is, He sets apart for Himself. This is an operation of God's Will and not of man's. This Sanctification is affected by the one great Offering. Such was its cost. As an example, God took the unclean Hebrews from among the nations and set them apart for Himself. The blood of the Paschal Lamb affected this consecration; consequently, Faith can joyfully exclaim: *"Christ our Passover is sacrificed for us, therefore let us keep the Feast"* (I Cor. 5:7-8).

This Offering of Christ is *"once for all."* It admits of no repetition. The Sanctification it secures is eternal. It consecrates to God forever because of its eternal and unchanging value.

He Who made this Perfect Offering is seated in the Heavens; and He is Himself there the Righteousness of God. There is a Righteousness suited to the Throne of God. It never can vary or fail. In that Righteousness, the worshipper stands.

THE CROSS AND OUR SANCTIFICATION

Does not the Reader here see, which we have already stated, the connection between the Cross and our Sanctification? Actually, it is impossible for the Sanctification process to be carried out in our lives, which refers to our being completely set apart to God, without the Believer understanding that all of this comes through the Cross, and by no other means. This is absolutely essential!

Unfortunately, most of the modern Church has absolutely no idea of the part that the Cross plays in our everyday living for God, our overcoming victory, in other words, our Sanctification.

Before we can be what we ought to be in Christ, we have to understand that there has been a death in our lives. What do we mean by that?

This death occurred when we first accepted Christ. We were baptized into His Death, meaning that His Death literally became our Death, inasmuch, as He died as our Substitute and in fact, as our Representative Man (Rom. 6:3). This is all done by faith on our part.

In other words, whenever we exhibited Faith in Christ and what He did for us at the

Cross, and I am speaking of our initial Salvation experience, at that moment, at least in the Mind of God, we literally died with Christ.

What died, was so worthless, was so valueless, in other words so wicked and polluted, that it was buried with Christ as well (Rom. 6:4).

We were then raised with Christ *"in newness of life"* (Rom. 6:4).

All of this is what Jesus referred to as being *"born again"* (Jn. 3:3). But yet, a tremendous legal work took place with God, upon our Faith being exhibited in Christ when we were saved. Now that we are saved, we are *"a new creature: old things are passed away; behold, all things are become new"* (II Cor. 5:17).

Now redeemed, it is crucial that we understand, that we continue to have Faith in the Cross of Christ, realizing that this not only afforded us Salvation, but as well, it also affords our Sanctification experience, even as Paul says here in Hebrews 10:10, 14. And of course, this is also what Paul is talking about in the entirety of his Epistle to the Galatians.

The idea is, if we cease to look to the Cross, which alone provides us the liberty to live for God as we should, then *"Christ is become of no effect unto you,"* meaning, that all He did at the Cross is wasted, simply because we're trusting something else (Gal. 5:4). In fact, if we look to anything else other than the Cross of Christ, we then *"fall from Grace,"* which presents itself as a catastrophe of unprecedented proportions (Gal. 5:4).

Every Believer has to have the Grace of God in order to live for God. This is not an option, but a *"must."* The way Grace is obtained, is for us to just simply have Faith in the Cross of Christ and maintain our Faith in that Finished Work, for the simple reason, that it is the Cross which makes the Grace of God possible (Eph. 2:13-20). In fact, if we attempt to look to other things than the Cross, we frustrate the Grace of God, which places us in a perilous situation (Gal. 2:20-21). It is somewhat like a diver underwater, who has his air hose cut. As should be obvious, he quickly finds himself in perilous circumstances. And so it is with the Child of God, who no longer has a plentiful supply of the Grace of God coming to him.

All of this is predicated on our Faith in the Cross, thereby, what Christ did for us.

This is the only way the Sanctification process can work, referring to the fact, of making us what we ought to be in Christ.

THE HOLY SPIRIT

The great Sanctification process, and in fact everything we receive from the Lord, is all done by what Christ did at the Cross, but *"through the Spirit"* (Rom. 8:2; Gal. 5:5).

The facts are, even though we are now saved and even Baptized with the Holy Spirit, if in fact that is the case, still, we cannot within our own strength and power, bring about anything in our lives that pertains to God. It is only the Holy Spirit Who Alone can do all of these things which must be done. If we try to do it, it becomes a *"work of the flesh,"* which God can never recognize, and which will always fall out to our ruin and hurt.

Sadly and regrettably, this is where most of the Church operates. It operates in the flesh, which means according to rules and regulations made up by men, which means it's not of the Spirit, which means it's going to fall out to harm to everyone who comes under such teaching. The Church cannot sanctify you and neither can any Preacher. Every Preacher in the world can lay hands on you until there is no more hair on your head, and even though the laying on of hands is Scriptural, such being done in this manner will not bring you what you need. But unfortunately, most Pentecostals and Charismatics think that Preachers can solve their problems by laying hands on them, etc.

Of course, they pick and choose certain Preachers, thinking that God is using *"this particular one,"* and, therefore, I will get what I need. Even though God definitely does use Preachers, still, there will be no victory achieved by this process. Unfortunately, after people come to Christ, too often, the Church points these converts to itself, instead of to the Cross. That is the sure road to spiritual catastrophe.

If the Church is not pointing you to the Cross, then it's pointing you in the wrong direction, and the end results will not be pretty.

The Holy Spirit doesn't function according to the edicts of the Church, or by the commands of Preachers; He functions totally and completely upon the premise of the Finished

Work of Christ, and our Faith in that Finished Work (Rom. 8:2). As I've said repeatedly in this Volume, the Divine Spirit doesn't expect much of us, but He definitely does expect one thing, and in fact, even demands that one thing, and that is that we exhibit Faith in the Cross of Christ at all times. He demands this, because as stated, He works exclusively within the parameters of that Finished Work.

If you follow this which we have stated, and I speak of a constant Faith in the great Sacrifice of Christ, then *"sin shall not have dominion over you: for you are not under the Law, but under Grace"* (Rom. 6:14). In other words, the Grace of God will continue to flow to you like an uninterrupted river. But if you step outside of these boundaries, which sadly and regrettably, most of the modern Church has done, you will find yourself *"under the Law,"* which means that the Grace of God stops, and you are thereby destined for spiritual failure. In fact, Paul said if you do this, you will *"be entangled again with the yoke of bondage"* (Gal. 5:1).

In the One Offering of Christ, not only was our Salvation perfected, but as well, our *"Sanctification."* This must ever be understood. This means, that in the same manner in which we received our Salvation, in that same manner we receive Sanctification.

(15) "WHEREOF THE HOLY SPIRIT ALSO IS A WITNESS TO US: FOR AFTER THAT HE HAD SAID BEFORE,"

The structure is:

1. The Holy Spirit witnesses to all this which is said. This means it's the Word of God, and cannot fail.

2. The Spirit, Paul says, *"testifies."* The choice of word implies that there is excellent testimony behind what he has been saying about Christ.

3. For a fact, the entirety of the Word of God is inspired; however, when emphasis is added, even as it is here, with the Holy Spirit actually testifying of Himself as it regards Christ, we surely should be able to see the great significance of the Cross of Christ.

THE WITNESS OF THE SPIRIT

The phrase, *"Whereof the Holy Spirit also is a witness to us,"* proclaims the very highest emphasis that can be had. The idea is,

the Holy Spirit is inspiring Paul to place His Name in the text (the Name of the Spirit), which cannot help but give added emphasis.

The Spirit is saying, that the one Atonement made by the Redeemer lays the foundation for the eternal perfection of all who are sanctified. The witness of the Holy Spirit here referred to, is that which is furnished in the Scriptures, and not any witness in ourselves.

I will never forget the day that the Holy Spirit led me to the Word as it regarded the manner and the way in which He works. He took me to Romans 8:2. To live the life that one ought to live, the Believer must have power. To be sure, this contest between good and evil, between light and darkness, is not idle games. Satan plays for keeps, and plays unto the death, the death of himself so to speak, or our death. This means that the powers coming against us as Believers are not mere fancies of our imagination, or mere philosophic inventions. The Child of God is facing the demon powers of darkness, which are trying to drag him down in the realm of sin and spiritual failure. Within one's own ability, which Paul constantly likens to the *"flesh,"* there is no way that the Christian can overcome. He must have the Power and the Help of the Holy Spirit.

However, this help, to which we have already addressed, is never automatic. Even as the Text here tells us, while the Spirit of God has been sent into our hearts and lives to perform a task, He will perform this task only on one basis, and that is within the great victory of the Finished Work of Christ. In other words, these are the legal boundaries in which the Spirit works.

For the Spirit to exhibit His great power, He demands of us that we at all times, exhibit Faith in the Sacrifice of Christ. It is Jesus Who has paid the price for our Redemption. It is Jesus Who has satisfied the sin debt by the giving of Himself on the Cross. It is Jesus Who atoned for all sin, thereby making it possible for the Spirit to abide permanently within the hearts and lives of Believers (Jn. 14:16).

Due to this which Christ has done, without which man could not have been saved, and without which the Believer could not walk in victory, the Spirit glorifies Christ. In fact, Jesus said of the Spirit, *"He shall glorify Me* (and because of what Christ did at the Cross)*: for He shall receive of Mine, and shall show it unto you"* (Jn. 16:14). All of this works through Faith in what Christ has done for us at the Cross (Rom. 3:25; 5:1-2; 9:30; 10:6; Gal. 2:16, 20; 3:2, 5, 14, 24; Eph. 2:8-9; Heb. 12:2).

According to one's own strength, and no matter how consecrated the Believer might be, we are no match for the Evil One; however, with the Holy Spirit working mightily within us, which He definitely will do if our Faith is properly placed, anything and everything is easy for Him. The Holy Spirit is God!

AN ETERNAL VICTORY

The phrase, *"For after that He had said before,"* refers to the fact that the Holy Spirit has always witnessed to the veracity of the Finished Work of Christ. Long before the Cross, which we will see in the next Verse, the Spirit proclaimed through Jeremiah what the Sacrifice of Christ would bring about.

This means that the Way of the Cross is not a new way, but actually the only way that's ever been formulated by God, which was actually planned from before the foundation of the world (I Pet. 1:18-20).

(16) "THIS IS THE COVENANT THAT I WILL MAKE WITH THEM AFTER THOSE DAYS, SAITH THE LORD, I WILL PUT MY LAWS INTO THEIR HEARTS, AND IN THEIR MINDS WILL I WRITE THEM;"

The composite is:

1. The Apostle appeals here to a Passage which he had before quoted (Jer. 31:33-34).

2. Paul places the Jewish recipients of this Letter in the position where they will either accept their Prophet and thus the New Testament, or in rejecting the New Testament, they will at the same time, be rejecting their own Prophet.

3. This is a prophecy proclaiming the New Covenant, which Christ would bring about by His Death on the Cross.

4. This New Covenant would function on an entirely different basis than the Old.

THE NEW COVENANT

The phrase, *"This is the Covenant that I will make with them after those days,"*

proclaims its distinctive feature as being the sanctifying work of the Holy Spirit Who would be caused to take up His permanent abode in the Believer under the New Testament dispensation.

Heretofore, He had come upon or in individuals in order to equip them for a certain Ministry, and then would leave them when the time of that Ministry was over. He did not personally indwell them for purposes of Sanctification.

The Old Testament Saint was regenerated, thus becoming a partaker of the Divine Nature, and thus had that impetus to the living of a holy life. However, the New Testament Saint has both the advantages of Regeneration and the personal indwelling and the sanctifying work of the Holy Spirit. Thus, under the First Testament, God wrote His Laws on stone, whereas under the New Testament, He writes them upon the heart (Wuest).

THE MANNER OF THE NEW COVENANT

The phrase, *"Saith the Lord, I will put My Laws into their hearts, and in their minds will I write them,"* proclaims that which was promised to Israel and Judah through the New Covenant, but is now made true of all who turn to Christ. By a New Birth God puts His Laws in our hearts and writes them in our minds, and then declares without any qualification, *"their sins and iniquities will I remember no more."*

The quotation from Jeremiah Chapter 31 is here repeated. It was first cited (Heb. 8:8) to set aside the Old Covenant; here it is used to prove the perfection of the New Covenant.

(17) "AND THEIR SINS AND INIQUITIES WILL I REMEMBER NO MORE."

The structure is:

1. Sins and iniquities are the reason that Jesus came to this world.

2. By and through His Death on the Cross, He took all of those sins and iniquities away, at least from those who will believe (Jn. 3:16).

3. The sinner is then justified, which refers to *"Justification by Faith,"* which means that the sinner exhibited Faith in Christ and what Christ did at the Cross, and was, therefore, justified. Justification means that God looks at such a person as if they

have never sinned, and will remember their sins no more.

SINS AND INIQUITIES

The phrase, *"And their sins and iniquities,"* pertains to that which is man's problem, and, therefore, why Jesus came to this Earth. As well, these two words, *"sins"* and *"iniquities,"* constitute a far greater problem than most will admit. In fact, the world, while agreeing that there is a problem, claims that it's only slight, and can be addressed by certain particular measures such as education, money, etc. Unfortunately, most in the modern Church as well, do not properly understand the horror of sin.

The entirety of the principle of the Gospel is according to the following:

1. Sin is the problem.

2. Jesus Christ is the answer and the only answer.

3. He is the answer only according to what He did at the Cross on behalf of sinners.

While many other things might be preached, that which we have just said must ever be the foundation of our presentation of the Gospel to the world. If we lose sight of this, we have lost sight of what the True Gospel really is.

Actually, the word *"Gospel"* means *"good news."* That good news is *"Jesus Christ and Him Crucified"* (I Cor. 2:2). That and that alone is the solution to dying, hurting humanity.

If Satan can get the Preacher to place the emphasis elsewhere, and he really doesn't too much care where the elsewhere is, he has then completely destroyed the effectiveness of that Preacher. This means that if the Preacher is truly preaching the Gospel, without fail, He must preach the Cross. Paul said, *"For the preaching of the Cross is to them that perish foolishness; but unto us which are saved it is the power of God"* (I Cor. 1:18).

He then said, *"It pleased God by the foolishness of preaching* (the Cross) *to save them that believe."* Consequently, he further said, *"We preach Christ crucified"* (I Cor. 1:21, 23). The tragedy is, the far greater part of the Church ignores the Cross, doesn't preach the Cross, with some of it even repudiating the Cross! Paul plainly says in the Text as he speaks of *"sins and iniquities,"* that Jesus

"offered One Sacrifice for sins" (Heb. 10:12). How much clearer can it be, that the Cross of Christ is the only answer for the sins of man?!

JUSTIFICATION BY FAITH

The phrase, *"Will I remember no more,"* proclaims in a few words, *"Justification by Faith."*

The Work of Christ is the Cross; the witness to all of this is the Holy Spirit (vs. 15). This means that God is the *"Source"* of this great Salvation, Christ the *"means,"* and the Holy Spirit the *"evidence."*

The guilty conscience that seeks peace with God is shut up to this evidence of the Spirit. There is no other witness. The Spirit has recorded His evidence in the Scriptures, and outside of them there is no other testimony for faith to rest upon. So the certainty that God will never remember the sins and iniquities of the Believer in Jesus is founded on the unchanging Will of God, the perfect Work of Christ, and the sure witness of the Holy Spirit.

This is complete justification from all things. No charge can now be brought against the one for whom Christ has settled everything. The very words *"and their sins and their iniquities will I remember no more,"* presents the crowning promise of the New Covenant of which Jesus is the Mediator. When these words were first quoted in 8:12 some important points in the argument were still untouched. Now the firm basis of the Promise has been shown, for the Covenant has been ratified by the Death of Christ, and the blessings He has won for men are eternal. All of this tells us that the sin question is settled. The once for all Offering of the Messiah shows that sin is paid for and put away. There is no greater wonder, no great blessing, no greater news than this, hence the Gospel being referred to as *"good news."*

(18) "NOW WHERE REMISSION OF THESE IS, THERE IS NO MORE OFFERING FOR SIN."

The structure is:

1. Sins being completely taken away, to never be charged against the sinner again, proves the effectiveness of the Cross of Christ.

2. Consequently, there is no need for any more sacrifice.

3. If we attempt to add anything to the Finished Work of Christ, we sin greatly!

REMISSION OF SIN

The phrase, *"Now where remission of these is,"* settles the argument once and for all. The blood of bulls and goats never could remit sins; however, the One Sacrifice of Christ effectively remitted all sins for all people who will believe (Jn. 3:16). This short Verse emphatically conveys the utter finality of Christ's Offering and the sheer impossibility of anything further. Where sins have been effectively dealt with, there can be no further place for an offering for sin, and because there is no need for a further place for an offering for sin. This is what Jesus came to do, and this is what Jesus did, and He did this by the sacrificial Offering of Himself on the Cross, which makes the Cross the centrality of the Gospel.

A FINISHED WORK

The phrase, *"There is no more offering for sin,"* proclaims a statement of obvious magnitude. On this one short phrase stands or falls the Gospel which we preach. What do I mean by that?

This Text plainly tells us that Jesus paid it all. His Work is a Finished Work, meaning that there is nothing else that must be done, and because there is nothing else that needs to be done. As stated, Jesus paid it all!

That being the case, where does that leave Preachers who attempt to add something to the Finished Work of Christ? By that question I mean this:

As it regards sin, much of the Church world little regards the Sacrifice of Christ, but rather portrays their own program, as it regards Justification. For the sinner coming to Christ, he is advised to *"join the Church,"* which in effect, substitutes the Church for the Offering of Christ. Or else they claim that one is saved when he speaks in tongues or is baptized in water, etc. All of this is substituting something else in place of the Sacrifice of Christ, and Faith by the sinner in that Sacrifice.

When it comes to Christians who sin, the Church has by and large as well, substituted their own program in place of the great Work of Christ.

In such cases, and especially as it regards Preachers, they've placed little stock at all in true repentance, but rather add other things. And what are those other things?

To be sure, these *"other things"* change with the wind; however, it really doesn't matter what these *"other things"* actually are, if anything is substituted in the place of the Sacrifice of Christ, and one's Faith in that Finished Work, then the Sacrifice of Christ has been ignored.

Let us emphasize again, there is no sacrifice for sin except the Sacrifice of Christ. To attempt to force individuals to do other things which are claimed to be necessary in order to effect forgiveness and cleansing is blasphemy pure and simple. Not only do those who insist upon such, sin greatly, but as well, any person who yields to such foolishness, forfeits the Grace of God.

Sin is awful! It is horrible! And because it is so awful and horrible, there is only one way it can be handled, and that's by taking it to the Cross (I Jn. 1:9; 2:1-2). Jesus Christ is the only solution, not the Church, or some silly man-devised rules — only Christ and Him Crucified.

(19) "HAVING THEREFORE, BRETHREN, BOLDNESS TO ENTER INTO THE HOLIEST BY THE BLOOD OF JESUS,"

The exegesis is:

1. The word *"Brethren"* signifies privileges in Christ.

2. *"Boldness"* as here given, refers to full access by all Believers to the Lord.

3. All of this has been brought about *"by the Blood of Jesus,"* meaning that it was at the Cross where He opened up the Way.

BRETHREN

The phrase, *"Having therefore, Brethren,"* refers to the Family of God, all made possible by what Jesus did at the Cross. There is no greater privilege than being in this great Family. Paul also said that Jesus is the *"firstborn among many Brethren"* (Rom. 8:29).

The word *"firstborn"* as it is here used, doesn't mean that Jesus was *"born again"* as are all Believers, but rather, that He is the Founder of the Church and, therefore, the *"Head"* of the Family of God. He is the Creator of this Family!

BOLDNESS

The phrase, *"Boldness to enter into the Holiest,"* harks back to the Holy of Holies of the Tabernacle. The High Priest alone could enter this sacred room where dwelt the Presence of God, and then only once a year. The people, nor any of the other Priests, could enter, except only in the High Priest as their representative. The reason for these limitations then, was due to the fact that the sin debt was not paid, which means that sins still clung to Believers, and because the blood of bulls and goats could not take away sins.

The idea is, that before Christ died and entered into Heaven, there was no such access to the Throne of Grace as man needed. Man had no offering which he could bring that would make him acceptable to God. But now the way is open. Access is free for all, and all might come with the utmost freedom, at least if they come by and through the Blood of Jesus (Eph. 2:13-20).

THE BLOOD OF JESUS

The phrase, *"By the Blood of Jesus,"* proclaims to us, and in no uncertain terms, how all of this has been made possible.

Through what Jesus did for us at the Cross, which refers to His poured out Blood, our Faith in that and that alone gives us immediate access to the Throne of God, and that goes for every single Believer.

This is the reason that I constantly proclaim the validity of the Cross. We have access to the Throne of God, not because of our great faith in ourselves, or our good works, or our supposed spirituality, but through one means alone, and that is the Blood of Jesus. In fact, Paul also said, that if we attempt to gain access by any other manner, that the Spirit of God will bar the entrance (Eph. 2:13-18).

This then entitles the *"Brethren"* of Christ, the new priestly house, to enter with boldness as purged worshippers into the Holiest, the immediate Presence of God, and all the infinite value of the Blood of Jesus through that New and Living Way which He Himself opened for us when, by His Death on the Cross, the Veil was rent in twain, and God no longer was hidden, nor man in Christ shut out.

So intimately are the Redeemed and the Redeemer linked together, so truly are the High Priest and priestly house one before God, that we are urged to enter in spirit where He has gone, and to draw near to God with true hearts and the full assurance of that faith that is based upon the knowledge of an accomplished Redemption; our hearts having been sprinkled by the Blood of Christ from an evil conscience, and like the once-defiled Israelite, *"our bodies having been washed with the water of purification."*

It is to be regretted that so few Christians seem to apprehend all this today. It is safe to say that for thousands who have hope in Christ, the Veil might just as well never have been rent. They do not have any conception of liberty for access into the Holiest, but think of themselves as a people on probation still, who, if only faithful to their profession, and faithful to some type of laws made up by themselves or others, will eventually be fitted for admission into the Presence of God.

How much is thus lost through failure to understand the true Christian position.

God sees every Believer in Him, and the feeblest Saint has title to immediate access into the Holiest through the Atoning Blood (Ironside).

Due to what is being said here about approaching God, for that's what the Text proclaims, let's look at the word *"approach."*

APPROACH

The word *"approach"* usually describes a commonplace event. A man looked up and saw camels approaching (Gen. 24:63). Jesus approached a boat pulled up on the shore (Jn. 6:19). But in some specialized uses, this word is anything but commonplace — particularly in what we are taught about approaching God.

THE OLD TESTAMENT

The Old Testament makes it plain that approach to God (seeking intimate contact with Him) is a distinct privilege, a privilege not lightly granted. God called Moses from the burning bush, but when Moses came over to see the phenomenon, God stopped him and said, *"Do not come any closer,"* or *"Do not approach"* (Ex. 3:5). Moses was told instead to remove his shoes, for he stood on holy ground.

When God thundered from Sinai, the people were warned not to approach the mountain in an attempt to see God, lest they be struck down (Ex. 19:16-25). When the Tabernacle was constructed to serve as the place for Israel to corporately worship God, only the Priests were allowed to enter the Tabernacle or serve at its Altar (Num. 18:1-7), and even they had to approach with extreme care and follow exactly the ritual established by God.

Two sons of Aaron who *"offered unauthorized fire before the LORD, contrary to His command,"* were destroyed in flames that *"came out from the Presence of the LORD and consumed them"* (Lev. 10:1-3). Even the High Priest was warned that he must rigorously follow the established pattern when entering the Most Holy Place, and then just once a year, or he too would be struck down by the Lord (Lev. Chpt. 16).

APPROACHING A THRICE-HOLY GOD

All of these experiences and warnings to early Israel were intended to underline the fact that approaching a Holy God is never to be lightly undertaken. Looking back, the New Testament explains that the rigid walls of ritual, like the inner curtain of the Tabernacle and Temple, were erected because the way into the Holiest — into God's very Presence — had not yet been manifested (Heb. 9:8). Human beings could approach the Lord only with fear, bearing offerings that reminded them of their sin and that God was willing to forgive.

It is clear from the Old Testament that the ritual observances were never enough to insure a welcome from God. So the Prophets spoke, condemning an unwelcome generation who drew near to God with words but whose hearts were far from Him (Isa. 29:13; Jer. 12:2). But even with a pure heart, ritual was required.

THE NEW TESTAMENT ON APPROACHING GOD

It is striking to move into the New Testament and read: *"In Him* (Jesus) *and through Faith in Him we may approach God with freedom and confidence"* (Eph. 3:12); *"Let us then approach the Throne of Grace with confidence"* (Heb. 4:16); and *"This is the confidence we have in approaching God: that*

if we ask anything according to His Will, He hears us" (I Jn. 5:14).

The Old Testament's wall of ritual is gone, even as the curtain that separated the Holy Place from the Most Holy Place in the Jerusalem Temple was supernaturally torn from top to bottom when Jesus died (Mat. 27:51).

That tearing signified that, on the basis of Christ's Death, the way of approach to God is open to all. Jesus' Death dealt finally and decisively with the sins that separated us from God. Now, as forgiven and cleansed persons, we can approach God freely and without hesitation.

This freedom that we have in Christ is emphasized in each of the three theologically significant *"approach"* Passages in the New Testament (Eph. Chpt. 3; Heb. Chpt. 4; I Jn. Chpt. 5). In each, our approach to God is described by the Greek word *"parresia."* The word signifies outspokenness or plainness in speech, openness to others, and confidence and boldness when in the presence of those of higher rank.

We now come into the very Presence of God with joyous confidence (Heb. 10:19), sure that Jesus has opened a new and living way for us to draw near to God (Heb. 10:19-22) (Richards).

(20) "BY A NEW AND LIVING WAY, WHICH HE HATH CONSECRATED FOR US, THROUGH THE VEIL, THAT IS TO SAY, HIS FLESH;"

The exegesis is:

1. This is a new way, made so by Christ, which means it must not incorporate any of the old ways of the Law.

2. It is a *"living way,"* made so by Christ, by contrast to the old way which contained no life.

3. Christ consecrated this way, meaning that He made it possible for us to enter.

4. The *"Veil"* is that which hid the Holy of Holies, but which now spiritually speaking, has been taken down.

5. *"His flesh"* signifies His Death on the Cross, which made all of this possible.

A NEW AND LIVING WAY

The phrase, *"By a new and living way,"* presents the New Covenant. The way to God now is both *"new"* and *"living."* It is *"new"* because what Jesus has done has created a completely new situation, *"living"* because that way is indissolubly bound up with the Lord Jesus Himself. Paul does not say, as John does, that Jesus is the way (Jn. 14:6), but this is close to his meaning.

At the same time, this means that this *"new and living way,"* is not the way of the dead animals of the Old Covenant or the lifeless floor over which the Levitical High Priest walked. It is the living Lord Himself.

By the Holy Spirit using the words *"new"* and *"living,"* He is in effect, telling the Jewish Christians, that they certainly don't want to go back to the old way of animal sacrifices. This new way is fresh, inviting, open to all, requiring only Faith, which is the opposite of the old way.

ISRAEL

I think in all of this, the Jews, even the Christian Jews, were somewhat piqued that all of this was passing them by as an indigenous people. Heretofore, they had been the only people on the face of the Earth who had access to God, as limited as it was! But now, Paul is talking about there being no difference between the Jew and the Gentile, and that the old way is out, with a New and Living Way brought in. As stated, this must have somewhat grated on them.

However, this should not have been the case at all, if in fact they did feel that way. If they had looked at the Law properly, they would have known that it was temporary, and that it was meant to be replaced by something better. They had been used mightily by God to institute this. In fact, they were the recipients of all the Promises, and could take great pleasure in the fact that they had held the breech so to speak, until the Redeemer could come. Their legacy was great, even as their history was great, that is if they looked at it properly.

But instead, many of them were jealous of the Gentiles, and put off that they had to be saved in the same manner as these people whom they had formerly referred to as *"dogs."* However, all of this was a matter of their pride, and not at all because God had in fact, mistreated them in some manner. Actually, He had been more gracious to the Jews than anyone on the face of the Earth. While it is quite true that they had great problems; still,

NOTES

it was because of failure on their part, and not at all on God's part.

CONSECRATED

The phrase, *"Which He hath consecrated for us,"* refers to the fact that this way was opened up by Him, and through the shedding of His Blood, and it is set apart for our service. It is a path consecrated by Him for the service and salvation of man; a way of access to the eternal Sanctuary for the believing sinner which has been set apart by the Redeemer for this service alone.

Paul is here making it clear that he does not have reference to the earthly Holy of Holies, as it refers to the Tabernacle. In the first place, it is by means of the Blood of Christ that we are to enter, not by the means of the blood of animals. The old road to the Mercy Seat of the Tabernacle in Israel was a dead road. There was no life there. It was all symbolism, an index finger pointing to the reality with which this First Century Jew was then faced. In the new road was life, all furnished by Christ.

THE VEIL

The phrase, *"Through the Veil,"* contains an allusion as is obvious, to the Veil which separated the Holy of Holies from the Holy Place in the Tabernacle. No one could enter this Sacred Place where dwelt the Presence of God between the Mercy Seat and the Cherubim, except the High Priest, and then he could only enter once a year, which was on the Great Day of Atonement. The idea of this Text is, that Jesus literally did away with that barrier, i.e., *"the Veil."* In other words, it no more remains!

HIS FLESH

The phrase, *"That is to say, His flesh,"* refers to the Cross. His flesh was torn on the Cross that the way to God might be opened, which it was.

When the Messiah died on the Cross, the Veil of the Temple was rent by the unseen hand of God, showing Israel two things:

1. The Messiah had now provided the actual entrance for the believing sinner into the Presence of God.

2. The symbolic sacrifices were to be discontinued, for the Reality to Whom they pointed had come.

3. In all of this, let us understand that an uncrucified Savior is no Savior. Even though all the things that Christ did were of vast significance, as would be obvious; still, it was not until He died on the Cross, that this way was opened. So, if we minimize the Cross in any way, we are striking negatively at the very heart of the Atonement, which is the foundation of all Salvation. The Reader must understand, that every single thing that pertains to Christ, His Virgin Birth, His Life and Ministry, His Healings and Miracles, everything and without exception, pointed to the Cross. It is only the Cross which redeems lost humanity; only the Cross which opened up the way to the very Throne of God; only the Cross which made Salvation possible.

(21) "AND HAVING AN HIGH PRIEST OVER THE HOUSE OF GOD;"

The structure is:

1. Jesus is now our great High Priest.

2. He is an active High Priest functioning now in the Presence of God on our behalf.

3. His High Priesthood covers the entirety of the Church, i.e., *"all born again Believers."*

HIGH PRIEST

The phrase, *"And having an High Priest,"* in the actual Greek says *"a Priest, a great One."* Not only is He now a High Priest, but He is a great One, and His greatness is shown by the fact that He is the Priest over the actual House of God, the One Who by His Death on the Cross saves all those who belong to the House of God in all dispensations.

THE HOUSE OF GOD

The phrase, *"Over the House of God,"* proclaims the Truth, that despite the fact that Jesus is a lowly Servant, and functioned as such in His earthly Ministry, still, He is *"over"* God's household.

Paul does not forget Jesus' high place. He has taken a lowly place, as it refers to His flesh, and has died to make a way to God for men. But this assumption of the role of a servant should not blind us to the fact that Jesus is the *"Head"* of the Church. Once again we have the highest Christology combined with the recognition that Jesus rendered lowly service.

There is a strong reason for believing that the language of one of the prophecies of

Zechariah is here before Paul's mind. In the preceding Verses (12-14), he has used words which united the Priestly and Kingly imagery.

On the head of Joshua, *"the great Priest"* (Zech. 6:11), are placed crowns of silver and gold in token of royal dignity. Then follows the prediction of Him of Whom Joshua was the type. *"He shall build the House of the LORD: and He shall bear the glory, and shall sit and rule upon His Throne; and He shall be a Priest upon His Throne"* (Zech. 6:13).

A TYPE

In the Verse of our study (vs. 21), are combined several of the characteristic thoughts of the Passage in Zechariah — the Great Priest, the Priestly Ruler, the House of God. The last-mentioned words are repeatedly used throughout the Old Testament, both in the Pentateuch and in later Books, for the Tabernacle or Temple of God.

In Hebrews 3:6 (to which there is a manifest allusion) the meaning is enlarged, but only so that under *"the house"* is also compromised the household of God. Here the two thoughts are combined.

Into the House of God we may enter; over it Jesus rules as *"The Great Priest."* The Family of God subject to His rule includes the whole community of *"the people of God"* in Heaven and upon Earth (Ellicott).

(22) "LET US DRAW NEAR WITH A TRUE HEART IN FULL ASSURANCE OF FAITH, HAVING OUR HEARTS SPRINKLED FROM AN EVIL CONSCIENCE, AND OUR BODIES WASHED WITH PURE WATER."

The structure is:

1. It is only the true of heart who can come into the Presence of God.

2. The proper Faith in Christ and what He did at the Cross on our behalf, gives us a *"full assurance."*

3. That which the Jews of old had in type as it regards the *"sprinkling"* and *"washing,"* we now have in reality in Christ.

A TRUE HEART

The phrase, *"Let us draw near with a true heart,"* not only states that such has to be if one is to enter, but as well, tells us that the Cross of Christ separates the true from the false. The idea is, it is impossible to place one's Faith in the great Sacrifice of Christ, and at the same time be hypocritical, double-dealing, or false in any manner. Many other aspects of that which goes under the guise of Christendom can entertain that which is false and often does; however, the Cross separates the false from the true, and does so perfectly.

In the first place, for one to place their faith and trust in the Cross of Christ, at the same time means that they are no longer trusting in themselves or anything else for that matter. Such a position also proclaims the fact that the individual knows and understands that within himself he can do nothing, and that Christ has done it all, and it is only Faith in what Christ has done that will slake the thirst of the human soul.

Also, the very principle of the Cross speaks of humility, which is the very opposite of pride. In fact, the Cross was and is the greatest example of humility than mankind has ever known and ever will know. So, in order to place one's Faith in the Finished Work of Christ, and to do so exclusively, automatically humbles one, which is an absolute necessity as it regards the *"pure heart."*

In all of this, the Reader must understand, that the desire placed in the heart of the seeking soul by the Holy Spirit, does not mean the heart is pure. In fact, it is not only impure but very impure, as is every heart which hasn't been cleansed by the Blood; however, the Blood, and to be sure, will grandly cleanse the heart of all that is displeasing to God.

FULL ASSURANCE

The phrase, *"In full assurance of Faith,"* proclaims the assurance provided by Faith, and better yet, Faith in the Finished Work of Christ.

Christ as our High Priest deals with infirmity; as Advocate He restores communion (I Jn. Chpt. 2). Power and enjoyment rest upon this double ministry. Man condemns the full assurance of Salvation, claiming that such cannot be; however, such an assurance magnifies the offering upon which it is based, and an absence of assurance discredits the perfection of that offering. The *"full assurance of Faith"* stresses that it is only by trust in Christ, Who has performed for us the High Priestly work that gives access to God, that

we can draw near at all. Once again, *"full assurance of Faith,"* means *"unwavering confidence."* It is a fullness of Faith in God which leaves no room for doubt. Christians are permitted to come thus because God has revealed Himself through the Redeemer as in every way deserving our fullest confidence. No one approaches God in an acceptable manner who does not come to Him in this manner.

THE LAW AND FAITH

The only manner in which one can have a full assurance of Faith, is through and by the Cross of Christ. When one places one's Faith totally and completely in the great Sacrifice of Christ, due to the fact that this is the correct object of one's Faith, assurance is thereby guaranteed. As stated, there is no other assurance.

Conversely, when one attempts to come by the means of Law, i.e., *"good works,"* or by the means of anything else other than the Cross, there is no assurance of faith. In fact, Law as the object of one's faith is the cause of so much consternation, worry, anxiety, and fear on the part of the Christian. The reason is simple, these other objects of Faith, really boil down to *"self."* In other words, irrespective as to what we might think, if the Cross is not the object of our faith, then in actuality, it is *"self."*

WHAT DO WE MEAN BY LAW?

To make it very simple and easy to understand, we're referring to anything other than the Cross of Christ. Most Christians have their faith in their Church. Others have their faith in particular Preachers. Others in all of their religious activity; however, it really doesn't matter what it is, if it's not the Cross, then in some way, it is Law. We may not understand it as such, and to be sure, it's not the Law of Moses; nevertheless, it is Law.

And inasmuch as it is Law, whether formulated out of our own minds, or the minds of others, in some way it comes back to self and for this simple reason:

When we place our Faith in other than the Cross, the Holy Spirit will not help us; consequently, we are left with nothing but our own strength and capabilities, which always are woefully inadequate. As stated, that's the reason that we have no assurance of faith.

When one places one's Faith exclusively in the Finished Work of Christ, understanding that it was all done there, the Holy Spirit will then help us, which gives us an assurance that defies all description. And to be certain, this of which we speak is far more important than we think at first glance.

If Christianity doesn't have an assurance of peace with God, of rightness with God, of place and position with God, all perfected by Christ, then it's really not true Christianity. This doesn't mean an absence of problems, but it does mean a peace and serenity in the midst of problems, whatever those problems might be.

A NEW FAITH FOUNDATION

What we're speaking of here is not a side issue, or just another fad. What we're talking about is a total and complete new way of thinking, and actually, a new way of doing. As I've said many times, the Cross of Christ is not a Doctrine. It is actually the foundation of all Doctrine. It is the foundation on which we build everything that we believe about Christ and our relationship with Him. Again, as I've already said, the Cross and the Word of God are synonymous. When one is spoken of, the other is spoken of as well!

This is one of the reasons that many Christians balk at the Message of the Cross. They realize, once they begin to understand some things about the Cross, that they are going to have to completely reshape their theology. The Message of the Cross incorporates every single thing in the Word of God, and as well the entirety of our relationship with the Lord. This is God's Way! In fact, it is His only way!

Unfortunately, most Christians do not give up their Ishmael's easily. As Abraham of old, it's hard to give up that which is our own fair work of the flesh. And regrettably, that's what most of modern Christianity actually is — works of the flesh. The Church has been pulled so far from the Cross, that most Christians are going to completely have to rethink their whole experience, upon being brought to their rightful place in Christ. The Church is so *"works"* oriented, so enmeshed in law.

NOTES

And the sad thing is, most don't even realize this of what I say.

It sounds simple enough, the placing of one's Faith entirely in the Cross of Christ; however, once this begins, one begins to realize quickly, that there is no end to the height or the depth of this great Message of the Cross. In other words, what Jesus there did for us, is of such moment, such magnitude, as to defy all description. What I'm actually saying is, that it's impossible to exhaust the great Finished Work of Christ.

And yet, when one begins to anchor one's faith in this which Christ did nearly 2,000 years ago, and begins to reap the results which continue to come from that Finished Work, one for the first time will begin to understand the glory and the joy of true, Bible Christianity. This is exactly what Jesus meant when He said, *"I am come that they might have life, and that they might have it more abundantly"* (Jn. 10:10). This is the way of victory over all the powers of darkness, and in fact the only way! This is the road to the *"rest"* promised by Christ (Mat. 11:28-30).

Because of its great significance, please allow me to state this Truth again:

The Message of the Cross is a total way of life. It is the true, Christian way. This is the faith which provides the assurance of which Paul here speaks. In fact, it is the only Faith which God will recognize — I speak of Faith in the Cross and in the Cross exclusively!

THE CLEANSING POWER OF THE BLOOD

The phrase, *"Having our hearts sprinkled from an evil conscience, and our bodies washed with pure water,"* portrays Paul using Old Testament types to represent the reality we now have in Christ.

The sons of Aaron were sprinkled with blood and washed with water. These carnal shadows of the First Covenant were figures of the spiritual realities of the Second. The sprinkling and the washing of this Verse must, therefore, be wholly spiritual — the conscience cleansed by a consciousness of the value of the Blood of Christ, and the conduct cleansed by obedience to the Word of Christ applied by the Holy Spirit.

The reference here is to the Laver at the Door of the Tabernacle, in the Wilderness.

In it the Priests were baptized, i.e., washed, for to baptize means to wash, the water being poured upon them. This symbolized the New Birth.

The most effectual way of cleansing from sin is by putting to death. In the New Birth of Regeneration, the Believer in Christ is put to death, so to speak. He is baptized into death with Christ at Calvary and He rises into a new life with Christ in Resurrection (Rom. 6:3-5). This is an effectual break with sin. It is an effective washing — not the application of material water to the outward flesh, which accomplishes nothing, but the effectual action of the Holy Spirit within the soul which accomplishes everything. Let us make one more statement about the Cross:

THE CROSS AND SPIRITUAL CLEANLINESS

For a Believer to trust Christ for Salvation, and then after conversion to drift into *"works,"* which most do, and because that's where most Churches lead them, presents that Believer in a sense as living under the old Mosaic economy. In other words, even though all Christians have place and position in Christ, still, most function as if they are functioning under the old Law of Moses. As all the ritual washings under the old Law could not truly cleanse the heart and life, likewise, modern works fall into the same category. The truth is, if the Believer is not fully trusting in what Christ did at the Cross on His behalf, and doing so exclusively, which means to the exclusion of all else, then in some fashion, that Believer is living under Law, which can provide no true cleansing of the heart.

I would trust that the Reader by now can see how that the *"Cross Life,"* is in fact a total way of life.

It was one thing for the Jews of old not to be able to enjoy what we presently have in Christ, and for the simple reason that it was not then available; however, it is a shame of unprecedented proportions, for Believers presently to have the availability of Christ, but yet to conduct ourselves as if we are living under the ancient Law. What a travesty!

It is only when one exhibits Faith totally and completely in the Cross of Christ, that

one truly and surely knows the joys of sins forgiven, and the total cleansing which the Blood alone can provide. I realize that every Christian would argue that they do have this of which I speak, even though their faith is elsewhere; however, the reason they argue, if in fact they do, is because in reality, most Christians have never known what it's like to fully enjoy Christ, which can only be done by ever having the Cross as the object of our Faith.

(23) "LET US HOLD FAST THE PROFESSION OF OUR FAITH WITHOUT WAVERING; (FOR HE IS FAITHFUL THAT PROMISED;)"

The exegesis is:

1. *"Hold fast"* refers to having a firm hold which masters that which is held.

2. The *"profession of our faith"* refers to faith in the Cross of Christ, and the Cross of Christ exclusively.

3. *"Wavering"* refers to the fact, that we aren't to weaken in our profession of faith as it regards the Cross of Christ.

4. Everything that God has promised, He will perform, providing our faith doesn't waver.

THE PROFESSION OF OUR FAITH

The phrase, *"Let us hold fast the profession of our Faith,"* refers exclusively to the Finished Work of Christ.

For years, the *"Word of Faith"* teaching has used this particular Scripture as it regards their claims. They were and are touting Faith, but it wasn't and isn't Faith in the Cross. Consequently, their teaching is unscriptural!

As should be obvious in these Passages, Paul is speaking of what Jesus has done at the Cross on our behalf. We are to place our Faith in that, *"holding fast"* its great Truth.

The idea of the words *"hold fast"* proclaim the fact that Satan will do everything within his power to dislodge our faith from the Sacrifice of Christ. But the Spirit here through Paul, tells us that we are to hold so firmly to our faith, that we master that which is held, meaning that we perfectly understand what our Faith actually is, and where it is.

"Profession" in the Greek is *"homologia,"* and means, *"to say the same thing."* The idea is, that our Faith is to be so synonymous with

the Cross, that it says the same thing as the Cross, and the Cross says the same thing as our Faith.

What did Christ do at the Cross? He suffered the penalty of the broken Law on my behalf, and as well, atoned for all sin, past, present, and future. This destroyed Satan's legal right to hold humanity in captivity; consequently, I can now live free from sin, simply because of what Christ has done for me. In fact, at conversion, I was baptized into the Death of Christ, buried with Him, and raised with Him in Newness of Life (Rom. 6:3-5). This means that I literally died to sin and the old life, which also means, it no longer has a hold on me. I can now *"reckon myself to be dead indeed unto sin but alive unto God through Jesus Christ my Lord"* (Rom. 6:11).

This is what my *"profession"* says and, therefore, this is my Faith. As a result, *"sin shall not have dominion over me, for I'm not under Law, but under Grace"* (Rom. 6:14).

As a result, I am now functioning in *"The Law of the Spirit of Life in Christ Jesus."* Consequently, I am free from *"The Law of sin and death"* (Rom. 8:2).

WITHOUT WAVERING

The phrase, *"Without wavering,"* refers to the fact that as a Believer, and having my faith anchored firmly in the Finished Work of Christ, under no consideration must I waver toward anything else. Paul is here urging the Christian Jews not to lean back towards the First Testament. Like the generation which left Egypt, who in their hearts were returning to that place of slavery, so these Christian Jews under stress of persecution were leaning back in their hearts to the First Testament. However, the Holy Spirit, even as Paul says in Verse 15, is constantly pushing them toward the Finished Work of Christ, even as He continues at the present in our own hearts and lives.

THE FAITHFULNESS OF GOD

The phrase, *"For He is faithful that promised,"* refers to the fact that everything the New Covenant promises, will be realized in totality. Because He is unwaveringly faithful, therefore, He should be unwaveringly confessed.

All the Promises of God given through the Prophets in the Old Testament, all and without exception, center up in the Cross. It is there that the Promises were realized and fulfilled. Consequently, it stands to reason, that our Faith must be in that great Sacrifice as well! If that's where the Promises are made possible, then that's where our Faith must be located. This must be our confession, and we must not waver in this confession.

(24) "AND LET US CONSIDER ONE ANOTHER TO PROVOKE UNTO LOVE AND TO GOOD WORKS:"

The composite is:

1. If our Faith is properly in the Cross, we will then properly consider one another.

2. The love here mentioned, has as its example the Cross (I Jn. 4:10).

3. Proper Faith in the Cross will always produce good works, but good works will never produce proper Faith in the Cross.

CONSIDERING ONE ANOTHER

The phrase, *"And let us consider one another,"* harks back to the previous Verse. If we see our Brother waving in the faith, and I speak of Faith in the Cross of Christ, we are to give attentive, continuous care to that particular individual. The exhortation is to take careful note of each other's spiritual welfare which also harks back to our *"profession of Faith."* We are to notice each other as it regards this singularly most important aspect of our Christian experience. Whenever faith is starting to slip, it becomes noticeable and obvious. If that happens, the next phrase presents the step we should then take.

LOVE

The phrase, *"To provoke unto love,"* refers to the manner in which we must deal with our Brother. Love as it is here used, is the characteristic New Testament term for a love that is not self-seeking, a love whose paradigm (example) is the Cross. In fact, there can be no real love, and we speak of *"agape love,"* which is the *"God kind of love,"* unless it's love that has as its foundation, the Cross. Of course, the Cross was the greatest example of love which man has ever known and ever will know.

Keeping the Cross as the foundation of our love, due to the fact that Jesus there gave Himself for us, we are at the same time, to give ourselves to others. And how do we do that?

We do it by loving them through the Cross, which is the Biblical way of love. This type of love is not self-seeking, but rather the very opposite. In fact, considering that this is love anchored in the Cross, of necessity, it could not be anything else.

If we show concern for a Brother who is wavering, and do so in the shadow of the Cross, our concern will have a telling effect.

GOOD WORKS

The phrase, *"And to good works,"* presents that which will naturally follow true Faith in the Cross. As we previously stated, *"good works"* will not establish Faith in the Cross, but Faith in the Cross will definitely establish *"good works."*

(25) "NOT FORSAKING THE ASSEMBLING OF OURSELVES TOGETHER, AS THE MANNER OF SOME IS; BUT EXHORTING ONE ANOTHER: AND SO MUCH THE MORE, AS YE SEE THE DAY APPROACHING."

The structure is:

1. Christians are to be faithful to Church.

2. In Church, we encourage each other.

3. As the signs of the times point to the imminent return of Christ, we are to be even more diligent regarding our faithfulness to Christ, and in every manner.

CHURCH ATTENDANCE

The phrase, *"Not forsaking the assembling of ourselves together,"* carries with it a far greater meaning than merely a gathering of Christians on a regular basis. We must not forget, that it's the Holy Spirit Who is prodding Paul to write these words.

Whenever Christians gather together in like faith, there is a strength and an encouragement which comes from such an assembly. In other words, we obtain something from the Lord by going to Church and mixing with other Believers, that we cannot obtain anywhere else.

In an assembly of Believers, faith is greatly exercised and, thereby, greatly increased. Consequently, it becomes much easier to believe God for the things we need.

NOTES

As well, this is so important, that Jesus said, *"For where two or three are gathered together in My Name, there am I in the midst of them"* (Mat. 18:20).

WRONG DIRECTION

The phrase, *"As the manner of some is,"* tells us plainly, that some Christians during the time of the Early Church were not being faithful. The Holy Spirit here plainly says, that such direction is a flirtation with spiritual disaster. To fail to obey this injunction, is to fail to obey, and will bring upon such an individual serious consequences.

As the manner of some Christians during Paul's day was that of unfaithfulness regarding attendance at Church, what is your manner, and I speak of you the Reader?

Your *"manner"* should be to attend Church every single time the doors are open, if it's at all possible. That means Sunday Morning, Sunday Night, that is if Service is conducted on Sunday Nights, and it refers to midweek Bible Study, on whatever night such is held. It also includes special meetings such as Revival Services and Campmeetings, etc. This should be the manner of the Child of God!

EXHORTATION

The phrase, *"But exhorting one another,"* refers to encouraging one another to be faithful to Church.

It should be understood that the Christians in those days were for the most part under persecution. If they were Gentiles, which most were, they had been brought out of paganism, with all of its attendant idol worship. In fact, in every major city, there were scores of temples devoted to particular idol gods. In fact, the entire structure of society was built around these *"gods."* Whichever god was worshipped, many of the people wore clothing to symbolize that particular god, and even styled the furniture in their houses after a certain fashion in devotion to their god or gods. Therefore, when they gave their hearts and lives to Christ, their lives miraculously and gloriously changed, but to be sure, the change was not so very much appreciated by their relatives and their former friends. In many cases, these people, whomever they may have been, made life miserable for the Christians.

It was the same way with Jews, except in a little different manner. While the Jews didn't worship idols, still, for a fellow Jew to accept the hated Christ, was the worst abomination that most Jews could contemplate; consequently, they literally excommunicated anyone of their own who came to Christ. From then on, he was treated by his family as if he was dead.

Wherever it was that the Christians assembled together for Service, many times they were monitored, with the intention of causing problems for anyone who attended. Under these circumstances, one can see how that it would be somewhat easy to just simply not attend Service. And yet, under these circumstances, the Holy Spirit through the Apostle Paul, is telling the people that despite the difficulties involved, they must *"not forsake the assembling of themselves together."* Now let me ask this question:

If the Spirit of God insisted even in those troubled times that Christians not fail to attend Church, don't you think such insistence holds true now, especially considering that there is presently no persecution for attending Church!

THE LAST DAYS

The phrase, *"And so much the more, as ye see the day approaching,"* refers to the last days, and, therefore, the insistence by the Holy Spirit that Believers, especially now, be faithful to Church.

These are the last days, and in fact, the last of the last days, and we speak of end time events. By that, we are referring to the Rapture of the Church, the rise of the Antichrist, the Great Tribulation, and the Second Coming of Christ. To be frank, all of these things I've just mentioned are just ahead of us. So, the Holy Spirit is plainly telling us, that it is absolutely imperative that we be faithful to Church.

While there are many reasons that this should be done, in fact must be done, the principle of a group of Believers gathering together provides a spiritual strength that cannot be attained in any other way. In this of which we speak, a tremendous impact is made as well, on the spirit world. And I feel, that the Holy Spirit is referring to this above

NOTES

anything else, even though there are many other reasons that make it necessary that we be faithful in gathering together to worship the Lord.

One of the principle reasons that the Holy Spirit here mentions the last days is because of the great apostasy that will come upon the Church during this time. When one considers that we have actually already entered into this apostasy, then we begin to realize just how important all of this actually is.

Apostasy is a departure from Truth, and anyone who claims to know the Lord, and cannot sense that the Church is presently departing from Truth as never before, if that be the case, then that Christian sadly and regrettably has become a part of the apostasy. In fact, that is the case with a great number of modern Christians, and the situation is only going to get worse. In this climate, the Holy Spirit is telling us how so very important it is that we not forsake the assembling of ourselves together.

CHURCH

When we speak of attending Church, that needs qualification.

In fact, most Churches shouldn't be attended. The people actually should run from some Churches. I speak of those which aren't proclaiming the Truth, and in fact, are teaching *"another Jesus, another gospel, all by another spirit"* (II Cor. 11:4). Let me be a little clearer:

To whatever degree your Pastor is preaching the Cross, to that degree he is preaching the Gospel. Of course, that would go for an Evangelist as well! If the Preacher is not preaching the Cross at all, then he is not preaching the Gospel at all, and should be shunned. The following somewhat describes most Churches:

1. Many Churches proclaim a modernist gospel, which is no more than a social gospel. It is a gospel of ethics, i.e., *"The Golden Rule."* These Preachers do not believe the Word of God and certainly do not believe in the Cross. At the same time, there is a large group of Charismatic Preachers who claim to be Spirit-filled, but who denigrate the Cross, even referring to it as *"past miseries,"* and claiming that it was the greatest defeat

in human history. They encourage their followers to flee the Cross. Pure and simple, these Preachers are *"enemies of the Cross of Christ."* The Apostle then said:

"Whose end is destruction, whose God is their belly, and whose glory is in their shame, who mind earthly things" (Phil. 3:18-19).

The name of the game for these particular Churches is *"money."* And, Paul said, *"O man of God, flee these things; and follow after Righteousness, Godliness, Faith, Love, Patience, Meekness"* (I Tim. 6:10-11).

Once again please allow me to parrot the Apostle: Flee these Preachers and flee these Churches!

2. There are some Preachers who preach the Cross somewhat. By that I mean they preach the Cross as it regards sinners being saved, but not at all thereafter. Many if not most of these Preachers simply do not know the Message of the Cross as it refers to the everyday living of the Child of God. Probably one could say, that most Fundamentalist Churches fall into this category.

While what these Preachers proclaim is true and correct as far as it goes, the problem is, it just doesn't go far enough. Consequently, most of their people will not live in victory, but rather defeat, and no matter how hard they try to do otherwise. In fact, most Christians who truly love the Lord attend these type of Churches. As should be obvious, these Churches, even though not going far enough, still, are a thousand times better than the ones in the first category.

3. The Churches which proclaim the Cross of Christ as it regards the sinner being saved, and as well, as the Source of Victory for the Christian, is actually the type of Church which should be indicative of all Churches. Such Preaching, which is the *"preaching of the Cross"* (I Cor. 1:18, 21, 23), will develop strong Christians, actually that which true Christianity ought to be. Regrettably, there aren't very many of these type of Churches, and simply because the Message of the Cross has all but been lost in the last few decades. But thank the Lord, this is beginning to change! The Message of the Cross which is the true Bible Message, is beginning to be heard, practiced, and preached, by more and more people and Preachers of the Gospel.

As we previously stated, the Message of the Cross requires a complete rethinking of our Biblical positions. This is a total way of life, actually that for which Jesus died.

What gives this such impetus of course, is that this is the manner in which the Holy Spirit works. He works totally and completely within the parameters of the Finished Work of Christ (Rom. 8:2). And of course, when He works, great and mighty things begin to happen.

THE CROSS IS THE BAROMETER

I think the Reader can see by now exactly what we are teaching. The Cross is the barometer.

Martin Luther stated, *"According to the manner one views the Cross, according to that manner will one view the Reformation."* In other words, the Cross then was the dividing line, as the Cross has always been the dividing line, even beginning in Genesis Chapter 4.

Going back again to the words of Paul as it regards faithfulness to Church, *"And so much the more, as ye see the day approaching,"* I personally feel that the Cross of Christ is now the dividing line between the True Church and the Apostate Church. In fact, it's always been that way, but I believe that the Holy Spirit is going to make it that way now more than ever.

Parroting what Martin Luther said, please allow me to state the following:

"According to the manner in which one views the Cross, according to that manner will one view the Gospel." Or let us say it in another way, *"According to the way one views the Cross, according to that way will they view the Word of God."* What I'm saying is this:

Unless one properly understands the Cross, which is actually the meaning of the New Covenant, which refers to all that Jesus did in the Sacrificial Offering of Himself, then one cannot truly understand the Gospel. I realize that's blunt, but I intend for it to be that very way. The reason there is so much defeat today in the ranks of Christendom, and I speak of spiritual failures, is simply because of a lack of understanding of the Cross. It is impossible for any Christian to walk in perpetual victory, unless that Christian properly understands the Cross. It simply cannot be done otherwise!

That's the reason that I plead with you the Reader to give one of these Commentaries to a Pastor friend, or any Preacher of your acquaintance, or anyone for that matter. What we're speaking about here, as should be obvious, is of extreme importance.

The Church is facing the concentrated powers of darkness. These demon spirits and fallen Angels to be sure, have great power. While they do not at all have power as the Holy Spirit, still, they have far greater power than any human being. I'm trying to say this:

Paul said, *"For we wrestle not against flesh and blood, but against principalities, against powers, against the rulers of the darkness of this world, against spiritual wickedness in high places"* (Eph. 6:12). This is spiritual warfare!

It's going to take more than pious platitudes, or intellectual knowledge to overcome these type of things. It's going to take the Power of God. But the great question is, how is the power of God activated within our lives?

THE POWER OF GOD

If the Christian doesn't understand the Cross, there is no way that Christian, as stated, can walk in perpetual victory. They might have victory some of the time, or even part of the time, but they cannot walk in victory all of the time. Consequently, the lives of most Christians are not lives of joy and happiness as they ought to be, but in most cases, the very opposite. Why?

Most of the Pentecostal and Charismatic worlds erroneously believe, if they are Baptized with the Holy Spirit with the evidence of speaking with other Tongues, which incidentally is Scriptural, and desperately needed by all Believers, that this automatically guarantees victory. It should be obvious that it doesn't! And because it doesn't, many Pentecostal and Charismatic Preachers are no longer preaching the Holy Spirit as they should. In fact, I am told that only about a third of the people who attend Assemblies of God and Church of God Churches, the two largest Pentecostal Denominations, actually even claim to be Spirit-filled. When I was a child, and a part of one of these particular

NOTES

Denominations (back in the 1940's), I think I can say without fear of contradiction, that at least 90% of the people in these Churches at that time, were Spirit-filled.

While there are many reasons for the great decline, I personally feel that at least one of the reasons for the lack of emphasis presently on the Holy Spirit is because in many Spirit-filled lives, there is not a noticeable change. To be sure, even though this is true, it's not the fault of the Spirit, but rather the individual.

What is wrong?

The problem is misplaced faith on the part of the Spirit-filled Christian. Not being taught the veracity of the Cross, most modern Christians put their faith in other things. As we previously stated, the *"other things"* might very well be good things; however, even though they may be good, and even spiritual, the Holy Spirit will not function in that capacity. So that leaves the Believer functioning on his own ability and strength, which is a guarantee of failure. That's the reason that the failure rate among Spirit-filled Christians is not too much different than their nonspirit-filled counterparts. Now please don't misunderstand:

The Baptism with the Holy Spirit is the greatest thing that can ever happen to a Christian. I consider myself to be one of the strongest proponents in the world of the Spirit Baptism. To be frank, the Christian is not going to really amount to anything for God, nor realize much of anything in Christ, unless that Christian is Spirit-filled. And again, to be sure, we teach according to the Word of God, that every single Baptism with the Spirit, will always be accompanied by speaking with other Tongues as the Spirit of God gives the utterance (Acts 2:4; 10:44-46; 19:1-7). In fact, I think it would be impossible to overemphasize the mighty Baptism with the Holy Spirit. But at the same time, the following must be noted:

THE HOLY SPIRIT AND THE CROSS

Everything the Holy Spirit does for any Believer is done strictly by and through what Christ did at the Cross.

In the first place, the Holy Spirit couldn't even come into the hearts and lives of Believers to abide permanently before the Cross.

That's why Jesus told His Disciples shortly before His Crucifixion, and when He was teaching them about the Holy Spirit, *"And I will pray the Father, and He shall give you another Comforter* (the Holy Spirit), *that He may abide with you forever;*

"Even the Spirit of Truth; Whom the world cannot receive, because it seeth Him not, neither knoweth Him (one must be saved before they can be Baptized with the Holy Spirit)*: but ye know Him* (they were already saved)*; for He dwelleth with you, and shall be in you"* (Jn. 14:16-17).

If it is to be noticed, He said, *"For He* (the Holy Spirit) *dwelleth with you* (which He did before the Cross)*, and shall be in you* (which could take place only after the Cross)."

The Holy Spirit, even as we've already said several times in this Volume, couldn't come in to abide permanently in the hearts and lives of Believers before the Cross, simply because the blood of bulls and goats couldn't take away sins (Heb. 10:4). Due to this fact, the sin debt still hung over the heads of all Believers, even the great Patriarchs and Prophets of the Old Testament. They were saved, but only by looking forward to what the Sacrifices represented, which was Christ and Him Crucified (Gen. 15:6).

At any rate, and without going into a long discussion, the Cross made it possible for the Holy Spirit to come into our hearts and lives, and I speak of Believers, and to there abide permanently.

Now that He abides there permanently, as should be obvious, He has been sent to do a specific work (Rom. 8:26-27). He wants to develop His Fruit within our lives (Gal. 5:22-23). However, He does all of this, and in fact can only do all of this on the basis, of what Christ did at the Cross. In other words, the Holy Spirit works within the confines of the legal work of Calvary. Please notice, that I said that it is a *"legal work."* Without going into detail, He functions within those legal parameters. That's why Paul said:

"For the Law of the Spirit of Life in Christ Jesus hath made me free from the Law of Sin and Death" (Rom. 8:2).

Notice that he referred to all of this as a *"Law."* Now of course, this is not the Law of Moses, but rather another Law also developed

by God, as it regards the manner in which the Spirit works within our hearts and lives. This *"Law"* is *"in Christ Jesus,"* which refers to what Christ did at the Cross.

WHAT THE HOLY SPIRIT DEMANDS OF YOU

Now that we've established the fact as to how the Spirit functions and operates, we need to know what He requires of us.

In fact, not much! He doesn't require that we perform any works, give great sums of money, be very religious, pray so many hours a week, fast so many days a week, etc. He only requires one thing, and a very simple thing at that!

He requires that you as a Believer know and understand that everything you have from God comes to you solely and completely through what Christ did at the Cross. You must understand that! You must believe that! Now if you have doubts about that, you have just jeopardized the entirety of your Christian experience. Faith is the principle on which God works, but more particularly, He works on the principle of our Faith manifested in the Cross of Christ.

Now many Preachers will tell you that since you have come to Christ, you must leave the Cross and go on to other things. As I've already stated, many of these same Preachers refer to the Cross as the greatest defeat in human history. If you listen to these Preachers, and irrespective as to whom they might be, you will destroy yourself. Because what they're teaching and preaching is not only not the Gospel, it is pure heresy, and if followed, will bring about destructive results in one's life. In fact, those who would preach and teach such things were labeled by Paul as *"Satan's ministers"* (II Cor. 11:13-15).

To help you to understand the Cross a little better, please allow me to say it in this manner:

The Cross of Christ is an event which took place in history, but has continued results, and in fact, results which will never be discontinued. It's the *"results of the Cross"* of which we speak. We're not trying to put Christ back on a Cross, and neither are we trying to put Christians on crosses. In fact, the latter is one of the false doctrines perpetrated about the Cross, of which we will have more to say in a moment.

You as a Believer must anchor your Faith in the Cross of Christ, keep your Faith in the Cross of Christ, not allow your Faith to be removed from the Cross of Christ, and then the Holy Spirit will work mightily on your behalf, doing all the great things which He Alone can do. Then you will realize the full potential of the power of the Spirit. And to be sure, the Holy Spirit is God! This means there is nothing that He cannot do. But still, He does require of us and strongly so, that our Faith always be in the Finished Work of Christ. That's what Jesus was speaking of when He said of the Spirit, *"He shall glorify Me: for He shall receive of Mine, and shall show it unto you"* (Jn. 16:14).

When you embark upon this *"Life"* provided by what Jesus did at the Cross, referred to as *"the Spirit of Life"* (Rom. 8:2), you will then begin to know and understand what real Christianity actually is. It's the most wonderful life there could ever be, but only if we do it God's Way, and the Cross is God's Way.

ERRONEOUS TEACHING ABOUT THE CROSS

I mentioned several paragraphs back, about putting Christians on the Cross, etc. What I meant by that is this:

Many Christians read the Words of Christ when He said, *"If any man will come after Me, let him deny himself, and take up his cross daily, and follow Me,"* and from these words draw an entirely, erroneous conclusion.

They think that Jesus is saying that taking up the cross daily is referring to an existence of suffering. In other words, they always link the Cross with suffering. While that is correct as it refers to the Sufferings of Christ, it is definitely not correct as it refers to Christians.

The work that Christ carried out at the Cross is a Finished Work. This means, that we must not attempt to add anything to that Finished Work, because in fact, we cannot add anything to that Finished Work. And to insinuate that we as Christians have to suffer in order to be what God wants us to be, is at the same time saying, whether we realize it or not, that the Work of Christ is not a Finished Work.

NOTES

Most Preachers explain all of this by going back to the words *"let him deny himself,"* thinking this refers to some type of Spartan life that's devoid of all pleasure of any nature. In other words, the harder we make our way, this is supposed to be taking up the Cross daily, etc.

Now it should be obvious as to why most Christians don't want to hear about the Cross. They know that it's right, simply because Jesus said it; however, they somehow think if they can just ignore the Cross, that maybe they will not be pulled into this vortex of suffering. And if they do see another Christian undergo some type of difficult situation, they always label that as *"bearing the Cross"* and then add the following, *"I pray that the Lord doesn't ask me to do that!"*

I realize that I've already explained all of this from this very Passage of Scripture in this Volume; however, what we're speaking about is so important, of such consequence, that I want to make doubly certain that you the Reader hear, see, and understand, exactly what we are saying. I don't want you to miss it, because if you do miss it, you will miss one of the greatest statements ever made by Christ. It affects your life in a tremendous way.

When Jesus spoke of denying ourselves, He wasn't speaking of asceticism, but rather of denying ourselves as it regards our own efforts and ability to live this life by our own strength and machinations. One simply cannot do that. In fact, it is impossible! We must let the Spirit do this for us, which we've already addressed, which He does according to what Christ did for us at the Cross. That's what Jesus is talking about!

When he said, *"take up the Cross daily, and follow Me,"* He was speaking of you understanding that every single thing we receive from God comes strictly and totally through what He (Christ) did at the Cross. Our focus must ever be on the Cross! Our understanding must ever be in the Cross! The object of our Faith must ever be the Cross!

Were it not for the Cross, God couldn't even look at us. It is the Cross which opened up the way to God, which Paul is explaining over and over again even in this Epistle to the Hebrews.

Instead of suffering as many teach, Jesus is actually telling us that we are to enjoy the benefits of all that He did at the Cross. He suffered greatly that we might have these things, and to be sure, we could not have these things unless He had suffered greatly. But the Cross is a Finished Work, and we are to enjoy the results and the benefits of that Finished Work, which is what He was speaking about when He mentioned *"more abundant life"* (Jn. 10:10).

DAILY

In fact, all of this is so very, very important that we are to take up the Cross *"daily"* in our following of Christ.

This means that the Cross must ever be before us. We must not allow it to be something that merely happened in the historical past, with our only thoughts in that direction being a song that we sing sometimes, etc. We must understand the part the Cross plays in our everyday living. We must know that there is no victory outside of the Cross. This must be understood and thought out on a daily basis, which the Holy Spirit means for us to contemplate constantly.

Most Christians only think of the Cross in the past tense. And then they only think of it in a sentimental way. *"Jesus died for me, and His suffering was terrible,"* is about the extent of their understanding of the Cross.

As a Believer, you must understand the part the Cross plays in your living today. In fact, it has just as much to do with your daily existence in the Lord, as it did in your initial Salvation experience. To be sure, you couldn't have been saved unless you trusted Christ and what He did at the Cross. At that time, you would not have understood very much about that, but you definitely did have to believe (Jn. 3:16).

Now that you are a Believer, and growing in Grace and the knowledge of the Lord, the Holy Spirit expects you to know more. In fact, the Holy Spirit uses the words *"know," "knowing,"* or *"known,"* some thirteen times in Romans, Chapters 6, 7, and 8. The problem with most Christians is that they fall into the category mentioned by Paul when he used the words concerning this very thing, *"Know ye not"* (Rom. 6:3). The tragedy is, most

Christians simply don't know, simply because it hasn't been preached to them behind the pulpit. *"Faith cometh by hearing and hearing by the Word of God"* (Rom. 10:17).

Getting back to our original subject, Church must be measured by the barometer of the Cross. Paul said, *"We preach Christ Crucified"* (I Cor. 1:23).

What is your Preacher preaching?

(26) "FOR IF WE SIN WILFULLY AFTER THAT WE HAVE RECEIVED THE KNOWLEDGE OF THE TRUTH, THERE REMAINETH NO MORE SACRIFICE FOR SINS,"

The exegesis is:

1. The willful sin which is spoken of here, is the transferal of Faith from Christ and Him Crucified, to other things. Here, Paul would have been speaking of Christian Jews putting their Faith in the Levitical Sacrifices, instead of Christ. However, it is definitely not limited to that.

2. One cannot move their Faith from the Truth if they have not first heard and received the Truth, which these Christian Jews had. Their sin was a departure from Truth. The Truth is *"Christ and Him Crucified."*

3. When one rejects Christ as the only sacrifice for sin, there remains no other sacrifice. In other words, one has just closed the door to Salvation.

TO SIN WILLFULLY

The phrase, *"For if we sin willfully,"* refers to several things:

1. He is speaking here of Believers who are on the verge of no longer believing. Believing what?

2. Of no longer believing in Christ and His Great Sacrifice as the only manner of Salvation.

3. Such a sin is always a willful sin, because it can be no other. It has to do with the next phrase.

4. The Holy Spirit here through Paul is not speaking of other types of sin. Some people have misunderstood this as to think that if anyone sins willfully, they cannot be forgiven. The truth is, every single sin that anyone commits is in some way a *"willful sin."* No, Paul is speaking here of a certain type of sin, which is the type of sin that can damn one's soul. He is speaking of turning away

from Christ and His Sacrifice on the Cross, ceasing to believe in Him as the Savior, and thereby believing in something else. This *"willful sin"* is limited to this particular type of sin.

Even then, if the person at a point in time, renounces their unbelief, and desires to come back to Christ, every clue in the Bible is, that the Lord will gladly accept them. The idea is, if a Believer ceases to believe in Christ, and renounces Christ and the Cross, and remains in that condition, there is no way that person can be saved. The Sacrifice of Christ being the only way, and that being renounced, the door is closed.

THE KNOWLEDGE OF THE TRUTH

The phrase, *"After that we have received the knowledge of the Truth,"* speaks of the Bible way of Salvation, which is *"Jesus Christ and Him Crucified"* (I Cor. 2:2).

"Knowledge" in the Greek as here used, is *"epignosis."* It is not the simple word *"gnosis,"* which is commonly used, but something far greater. Delitzsch defines it by saying: *"When 'epignosis' is used, there is the assumption of an actual direction of the Spirit to a definite object and of a real grasping of the same."*

Paul, by the use of this word, gives us to understand that he means by it not merely a shallow historical notion about the Truth, but a living believing knowledge of it, which has laid hold of a man and fused him into union with itself.

So, we are not speaking here of sinners having merely heard the truth and then rejecting it, as many teach, but rather individuals who have heard the truth, received the truth, and made the truth a part of their lives. As well, when we say *"Truth"* we're speaking of *"Jesus Christ and Him Crucified,"* as the only answer for sin, which Paul again describes in Verse 29. The willful sin in this Passage as stated, is the definite rejection of His Atoning Sacrifice.

I want the Reader to fully understand here the meaning of the word *"Truth."* Of course, we know that Truth is the Word of God. In fact, the Word of God is the only revealed Truth in the world, and in fact ever has been. However, when we say *"The Word of God,"* we are at the same time saying *"The Sacrifice*

of Christ," for that's what the Bible exclusively teaches. That's why I keep talking about the Cross, because the Cross is Truth, even as Truth is the Cross, which is here so clearly borne out. And we must remember, it's the Holy Spirit Who referred to the Sacrifice of Christ as *"Truth"* (Jn. 1:14; 8:32; 14:6; 16:13).

The point is this: There is no other Truth! In fact, all Biblical Knowledge springs from the Truth of the Cross.

THE SACRIFICE FOR SIN

The phrase, *"There remaineth no more sacrifice for sins,"* refers to the Sacrifice of Christ as being the only Sacrifice which will cleanse from sin. This means when the Catholic Church claims that the Church itself is Salvation, and by that we refer to keeping the sacraments of the Church, they have at the same time denounced the Sacrifice of Christ. One cannot have it both ways! Salvation is either in Christ or it's in the Church. We know it's not in the Church, so that means that anyone who claims it is, and if they can get people to follow them, they have just damned that person's soul!

Unfortunately, many Protestant Churches fall into the same category. They claim that one must belong to their Church, or subscribe to their rules, or whatever! Let the following be carefully observed!

There is Salvation only in the Sacrifice of Christ. Of course, that refers to Jesus dying on the Cross, thereby paying for our sins. Salvation requires Faith in Him, and to be more particular, Faith in Him and His Sacrifice, in order to be saved. It's not a very difficult thing, but it is demanded (Jn. 3:16).

We must never separate Christ from His Sacrifice. If we do, we have just traded Jesus the Savior, for Jesus the intellectual, or Jesus the Healer, or Jesus the Miracle Worker, or Jesus the good man, or Jesus the whatever! Once again, all of this other than *"Jesus the Savior,"* is *"another Jesus"* (II Cor. 11:4).

What kind of Jesus are you serving? Or more particularly, who is this Jesus you are serving?

The problem with the human race is sin! And to be sure, the problem in the Church is as well, sin! The idea is this!

Every Christian knows and understands that the problem with the world is sin, but most Christians don't have the knowledge they should have as it regards Christians and sin.

Of course, Satan wants you to quit just exactly as he was successful in getting some of these Christian Jews to turn their backs on Christ. That's his ultimate goal. But if he cannot do that, he will surely try to get you into a mode to where that sin dominates you, and even though you are saved, your Christian experience is certainly not what it ought to be. And in fact, that's where most Christians are presently. Again I state, the problem is sin!

If it wasn't sin, why would the Holy Spirit through Paul say, after instructions were given regarding victory, *"For sin shall not have dominion over you: for ye are not under the Law, but under Grace"* (Rom. 6:14).

Sin is the problem with the Christian, and Satan does his very best to dominate you with sin in some way. With some it's sins of passion, such as one of the vices, and with others it's sins of pride, such as unforgiveness, apathy, lukewarmness, heresy, greed, etc.; nevertheless, in whatever capacity it is, sin is the most debilitating and destructive factor there could ever be in the heart and life of a Christian. It makes for a miserable existence.

It is only through Faith in the Cross of Christ, which gives the Holy Spirit the latitude to work within our hearts and lives, which can keep us free from sin, and in effect, walking in victory perpetually, i.e., *"walking after the Spirit"* (Rom. 8:1).

BACKSLIDERS

Many have misunderstood these Passages, thinking that it is saying that a backslider cannot come back to Christ. That's not what it's saying!

As long as a backslider, and anyone for that matter, retains his Faith in Christ and His Atonement, he can be renewed to repentance. However, that needs qualification:

There are millions of people, even many backsliders, who believe that Jesus Christ is the Son of God, and who believe that He died on the Cross for lost humanity, and as well, believe that one must express faith in that in order to be saved. Even though such Faith

is correct, if Faith stops there, the person is not saved. In fact, most of these people don't even claim Salvation.

Their Faith is merely a mental acceptance of Who Christ is and What He has done. That doesn't save anyone. That's what one might call *"vain or dead faith"* (I Cor. 15:17; James 2:17). That individual must accept what they have believed, thereby making Christ their Savior and their Lord, before their Faith is actually valid.

However, if a person, including a backslider, rejects Christ and His Gospel, which is the Cross of Christ, and remains in that condition, he becomes hopeless as far as Salvation is concerned.

(27) "BUT A CERTAIN FEARFUL LOOKING FOR OF JUDGMENT AND FIERY INDIGNATION, WHICH SHALL DEVOUR THE ADVERSARIES."

The structure is:

1. Judgment will ultimately come upon all Christ rejecters. This speaks of the Great White Throne Judgment (Rev. 20:11-15).

2. *"Fiery indignation"* refers to that which is on the part of God, and pertains to the zeal of God in punishing apostates. In other words, it angers God for individuals to spurn Christ, especially considering the great price He has paid for their Salvation.

3. This judgment will be so severe, that it will *"devour the adversaries,"* which actually refers to hellfire, and above all, hellfire which is eternal (Rev. 20:11-15).

JUDGMENT

The phrase, *"But a certain fearful looking for of judgment,"* refers to the fact that this is all that the Christ rejecter has in front of him. It makes no difference whether he believes it or not; ignoring it won't make it go away. Judgment is coming.

As we've already explained in previous Commentary, *"The Great White Throne Judgment"* looms ahead for all unbelievers. None will escape that judgment, all will be there. The end result of such is the Lake of Fire, which will last forever, and which will *"devour the adversaries,"* referring to the fact, that there will be no escape.

The Reader must understand, that man is an eternal soul. This means that the soul and the spirit will never die. At the conclusion of the coming Millennial Reign, which will last a thousand years, there will be a second resurrection of damnation, when bodies made of eternal material will be given to every lost soul. With these eternal bodies, all will be cast into the Lake of Fire (Rev. 20:4-6, 11-15).

Some may claim that God is cruel for doing such a thing. Let's look at the next phrase:

FIERY INDIGNATION

The phrase, *"And fiery indignation,"* refers to anger on the part of God, even great anger, because of men rejecting Jesus Christ.

When one comprehends the great price that Christ has paid in order that men might be saved, then one begins to understand the reason for this *"fiery indignation."*

Of course, the unredeemed do not even believe they need to be saved, that is in their natural state of depravity. What they don't realize, or else they refuse to realize, is that sin is the ruination of everything in the universe. It is the cause of all sorrow, heartache, pain, sickness, death, and dying. It is the cause of all of man's inhumanity to man. And to be sure, it is more than a mere act, but actually is empowered by the Evil One himself, Satan. All of this has its birth in Lucifer sometime in the dateless past, leading a rebellion against God. Approximately one-third of the Angels threw in their lot with him (Rev. 12:4). Consequently, this battle between light and darkness has raged from then until now, and will not have its conclusion, until Satan (Lucifer), along with all his cohorts, which refers to all of mankind as well who have rebelled against God, are cast into the Lake of Fire (Rev. 20:10-15).

For the universe to be filled with Righteousness and Holiness, this problem of Satan and all of his followers must be addressed first. It has been addressed in Christ and what He did at the Cross.

THE GREAT PRICE HE PAID

The Ordinance of *"the Lord's Supper"* was given to us by Christ for several reasons, but foremost that we may remember the price that He paid (I Cor. 11:24-25). That price was the Cross.

The Church has a tendency to place the Cross in a subsidiary position, thereby making other

things premier. Some make the Resurrection premier, while others make the Baptism with the Holy Spirit premier. And then some count the Cross as little or nothing as it regards this Plan of Salvation, rather attributing Salvation to a false conception of Christ, such as the *"Jesus died spiritually"* doctrine, etc.

While of course, the Resurrection is of supreme importance, it was not that great work that Jesus told us to not fail to remember, but rather the Cross. As well, while the Baptism with the Holy Spirit is of supreme significance in the heart and life of the Believer, still, it was the Cross which made this Baptism possible. So in effect, Christ plainly tells us to *"remember the Cross."*

The price that was paid there is actually beyond our comprehension. For God, the Creator to become man, i.e., the creature, is beyond the pale of human thinking. And then, that which He left in order to come here is also beyond our comprehension, not having anything to compare with what He had. Consequently, to attempt to try to explain the price He paid, considering our lack of knowledge, presents itself as a futile effort. We simply cannot do such!

The only way we can do justice to this all important act is to place the Cross in its proper place of preeminence. This more than anything else, will obey the command of Christ to *"remember Me"* (I Cor. 11:24-25).

THE ADVERSARIES

The phrase, *"Which shall devour the adversaries,"* refers to destruction, which is hellfire, which will ultimately come to all who reject Christ.

"Adversaries" in the Greek is *"hupenantios,"* and means *"those who are hostile, those who oppose."*

While it refers to those who oppose Christ, more than all, and that which the entirety of the Text proclaims, it refers to those who reject the Plan of Redemption, which was brought about by what Jesus did at the Cross. This is the thrust of the subject and as well, the thrust of the judgment.

While the subject matter definitely does refer to opposing Christ, more than all, it refers to opposing what He did in order to redeem mankind. The idea is this:

If one attempt to accept Christ without the Cross, or else place the Cross in an incidental position, according to what Paul said, one has not accepted Christ, but rather *"another Jesus"* (II Cor. 11:4). And that's where the Church makes its great mistake.

While the Lord doesn't expect much from believing sinners coming to Christ, He in fact, expects very much from Believers. You as a Believer must not divorce Christ from the Cross in your thinking. In fact, when you think of Christ, which should be constantly, it should always be in connection with His Cross. That's why He came to this world, and I speak of the Sacrificial Offering of Himself on the Cross, and that's why you are saved. It's not because of your great faith, or whatever; you are saved totally and completely because of what Jesus did at the Cross on your behalf, and your Faith in that Finished Work. That is the Gospel! As well, you continue to grow in Grace and the Knowledge of the Lord because of your continued Faith in that Finished Work.

Paul is telling these Christian Jews, if they repudiate Christ and what He did for them at the Cross, in favor of other things, in this case going back to the animal sacrifices, they would completely destroy themselves. As well, let the Reader understand, that whatever part of the Church does the same thing, and I speak of forsaking the Cross for other things, such as humanistic psychology or whatever, they can expect the same end. I cannot see how anyone who reads these Passages, wouldn't come to the same conclusion!

(28) "HE THAT DESPISED MOSES' LAW DIED WITHOUT MERCY UNDER TWO OR THREE WITNESSES:"

The structure is:

1. An argument from the greater, the Cross, to the lesser, the Law, brings out the seriousness of the situation.

2. To despise the Law of Moses was a very serious matter, but this is more serious still.

3. From these statements, one certainly should gather the tremendous significance of the Offering of Christ.

THE LAW

The phrase, *"He that despised Moses' Law,"* is meant to impress upon us the severity of

NOTES

all that God does. And yet, we must not take this as a general assertion, as true of whoever in any way broke the Mosaic Law: but as an alleging of a well-known fact, that in certain cases a breaker of the Law was subject to the penalty following.

"Despised" in the Greek is *"atheteo,"* and means, *"to set aside, to disesteem, to cast off, disannul, bring to naught, reject."*

DIED WITHOUT MERCY

The phrase, *"Died without mercy under two or three witnesses,"* is derived from Deuteronomy 17:2-7, the last words being a direct quotation from Verse 6 in that section.

There the subject is apostasy from Jehovah to the worship of idols. That sin, which by the acknowledgment of all, had in ancient time robbed Israel of the name of God's people, is tacitly placed by the side of the sin of those who forsake Christ.

Some may claim that since we are living in the day of Grace that these admonitions don't apply; however, I must remind the Reader that judgment unto Grace is much more severe than it was under Law. Paul said:

"And the times of this ignorance (Old Testament times) *God winked at; but now* (during this age of Grace) *commandeth all men everywhere to repent"* (Acts 17:30).

And then the Apostle said, *"For the Wrath of God is revealed from Heaven against all ungodliness and unrighteousness of men, who hold the Truth in unrighteousness"* (Rom. 1:18).

While God is long-suffering and merciful, if men continue to reject His way, the ultimate result can be nothing but judgment.

Many in the modern Church attribute all inclement situations such as adverse weather, or whatever, to Satan. However, to do such a thing, places God in a subservient position, in a sense answerable to Satan, which is preposterous!

No! While Satan may definitely be the one who carries out certain things, it is God Who gives him permission to do what he does, and in fact, God Who oversees all things. This means, that every single thing that happens on this Earth, God has either allowed it or directly caused it; either way, He is responsible! Jesus said as much in His statement:

"Are not two sparrows sold for a farthing? And one of them shall not fall on the ground without your Father.

"But the very hairs of your head are all numbered" (Mat. 10:29-30). So what am I saying?

God instituted the Law of *"sowing and reaping,"* and to be sure, this Law is in motion constantly (Gal. 6:7). In fact, the actual sin which takes people to Hell is the sin of rejecting Jesus Christ, and the price that He has paid for our Redemption (Jn. 16:8-9).

However, while the world is one thing, the Church is something else altogether. And we must remember that Paul, more than anything else, is speaking here to the Church. While his statements definitely include all, the greater thrust is toward Believers.

In fact, the Gentile world during the time of the Law was not held responsible for the Law; consequently, those who died without mercy for repudiating the Law were Jews.

While all presently without God, if they die in that state, will definitely be lost forever; still, the *"much sorer punishment"* as given in the next Verse, is reserved for those who know the way, namely the Church, but abandon the way.

SERIOUSNESS OF THE MATTER

When the Lord began to give me the Message of the Cross in 1996, which Revelation has continued unto this hour, and I trust will ever continue, at the same time, He placed a burning burden within my heart, to proclaim this Message to the entirety of the Church. He has instructed me to emphasize this Message as I've never emphasized any Message.

It's not because this is something new, because it definitely isn't. Actually, the Cross is the foundation of the Church, and actually the foundation of all that God has ever done as it regards the human race. The Message of the Cross actually began with the Fall of Adam and Eve in the Garden of Eden. God's Message to Satan through the serpent at that time was a brilliant prediction of the Cross (Gen. 3:15). The *"seed of the woman bruising the head of the serpent, and the serpent bruising His* (Jesus') *heel,"* is a prediction of the Cross. Genesis Chapter 4 outlines it perfectly as it regards the Sacrifice

NOTES

of Abel. And so it was thereafter, and so it is now!

In fact, the Message of the Cross is of such magnitude that John in his vision of the Throne of God, said, *"And in the midst of the Elders, stood a Lamb as it had been slain, having seven horns and seven eyes, which are the seven Spirits of God sent forth into all the Earth"* (Rev. 5:6).

If it is to be noticed, Christ is referred to here as *"a Lamb as it had been slain."* The Holy Spirit is then pictured so much a part of this, that in some ways the *"Lamb"* and the *"Spirit"* are pictured as one and the same. The idea is this:

In fact, Christ and the Holy Spirit are two separate and distinct Persons of the Godhead. But the Holy Spirit works so very much within the parameters of what Christ did at the Cross, that He is here pictured in this context. And yet for all of this, the Message of the Cross has all but been lost to the modern Church. Consequently, the Church has no moorings, and the people have no victory.

To proclaim this Message, the Lord has instructed me to use our Television Network and as well, the SonLife Radio Network. At the time of this writing in late August of 2000, we have some 30 stations on the air. Actually the Radio Network is only about five months old at this particular time. The Lord has instructed me to put these stations all over the nation, even several thousands of them, which we have set out to do. The entirety of this Radio effort, 24 hours a day, is geared to the Message of the Cross. And to be sure, I definitely believe this is the primary reason that the Lord has given us this Network. It is imperative that the Body of Christ hears this Message.

Beginning in the 1970's, the Pentecostal and Charismatic sections of the Church began to drift toward humanistic psychology. That drift now is a wholesale acceptance of this false way. Whether the Leaders of these Denominations understand it or not, this is a vote of no confidence as it regards the Cross of Christ. Either Jesus addressed every single problem of man at the Cross, or else He didn't! I happen to believe that He did. One cannot have it both ways. Regarding the sins, perversion, and aberrations of man, we either trust Christ, or we trust humanistic wisdom, which the Holy Spirit through James said is *"earthly, sensual, devilish"* (James 3:15).

For those who continue on this path, and I speak of the path which leads away from the Cross of Christ, judgment is inevitable. It cannot be any other way!

(29) "OF HOW MUCH SORER PUNISHMENT, SUPPOSE YE, SHALL HE BE THOUGHT WORTHY, WHO HATH TRODDEN UNDER FOOT THE SON OF GOD, AND HATH COUNTED THE BLOOD OF THE COVENANT, WHEREWITH HE WAS SANCTIFIED, AN UNHOLY THING, AND HATH DONE DESPITE UNTO THE SPIRIT OF GRACE?"

The structure is:

1. If judgment was demanded for those who trampled the Law, it is more demanded for those who reject the Cross.

2. Treading underfoot the Son of God, is a sin against God the Father Who gave the Son to become the Sin Offering.

3. Counting the Blood of the New Testament an unholy thing is a sin against God the Son Who shed His Blood.

4. The word *"counted"* refers to a conscious judgment resting on deliberate weighing of the facts. Here it implies a deliberate, contemptuous rejection of the Sacrifice of the Son of God.

5. The *"unholy thing"* refers to counting the Blood of Jesus as having no more sacred character or specific worth than the blood of any ordinary person.

6. Doing *"despite unto the Spirit of Grace,"* is a sin against God the Holy Spirit, Who convicts of sin, and we speak of the sin of rejecting Christ as Savior.

GREATER PUNISHMENT

The phrase, *"Of how much sorer punishment,"* refers to the fact that Jesus is greater than Moses; the New Covenant is better than the Old, founded on better promises and established by a better Sacrifice; consequently, to reject Christ, and more specifically, to reject the Sacrifice of Christ, is the worst sin of all.

The Cross of Christ stands at the intersection of the world, i.e., *"at the intersection of mankind."* Man must deal with Christ and

NOTES

the Cross. To ignore it, is to reject it. And at the same time, it is the responsibility of the Church to take this Message, and I speak of *"Jesus Christ and Him Crucified,"* to the entirety of the world. The entirety of the framework of the Word of God proclaims this glaring Truth. Whenever God gave the great Revelation to Abraham, one of the first things He told him was, *"In thee shall all families of the Earth be blessed"* (Gen. 12:3). The pivot Scripture of all Scriptures says, *"For God so loved the world..."* (Jn. 3:16). The last Message given by Christ, and given just before His Ascension was, *"Go ye into all the world, and preach the Gospel to every creature"* (Mk. 16:15).

This is the responsibility of every single Christian and not just a few. It is sad, when it is to be realized that Islam gives about 100 times the amount of money than Christians in the spread of its false message. Of course, we realize that this is not done as it regards the burden of Moslems as a whole, in fact, they have no burden, because they have no message. This money comes from Moslem governments; nevertheless, God has richly blessed Christianity, and in that blessing, He has blessed Christians. The money is there, but money is only a part of the problem.

The main problem is the Message. Most of the Church is preaching something that's not the Gospel. In fact, if it's not the Cross, then it's not the Gospel.

Even during the time when I did not know and understand the part the Cross plays in our Christian experience as it regards overcoming victory, I preached strongly the Cross as it regards the initial Salvation experience. God rewarded the Message with hundreds of thousands brought to a saving knowledge of Jesus Christ, and I exaggerate not!

But during those days, even though I did not understand the Cross as it regards our Sanctification, I did know that humanistic psychology was not the answer, or any other philosophy projected by man. I knew the answer was in the Word of God, but I did not know exactly how. Thank God, even though it took several years of seeking His Face, the Lord showed me the key to all victorious living. He plainly told me, as He took me to the Sixth Chapter of Romans, *"The solution *for which you seek is found in the Cross."* And so it was! And so it is!

If the Reader thinks I'm too strong on the subject, let the Reader understand that I have no choice. I see these words, *"Of how much sorer punishment,"* and knowing what they mean, referring to the fact that they are addressed to the Church, how can I do less than place total emphasis on the great Message of *"Jesus Christ and Him Crucified"*! (I Cor. 2:2).

THE REJECTION OF THE SON OF GOD

The phrase, *"Suppose ye, shall he be thought worthy, who hath trodden under foot the Son of God,"* proclaims the reason for the punishment, and even the *"sorer punishment."*

"To trample underfoot" is a strong expression for disdain. It implies not only rejecting Christ, but also despising Him — Him Who is no less than *"the Son of God."* But let the Reader understand the following:

The thrust of all of this is not so much the rejection of Christ per se, but rather, the rejection of what Christ has done to redeem humanity, and we speak of the Cross. This is the *"willful sin"* here addressed. It is the individual, either rejecting the Cross as the answer to man's dilemma, or ignoring the Cross. Either way, man has rejected the only way of Salvation.

In fact, untold millions in this world presently think of Christ as a *"good man"* or even a *"miracle worker,"* etc. But they place no value on His Atoning Sacrifice. Irrespective as to what they think of Him Personally, if they do not accept His Sacrifice for sin, they cannot be saved.

NEUTRALITY?

There is no neutrality as it regards the Cross. We either accept it or we reject it. And if we call ourselves accepting it, but instead turn to other things, such as humanistic psychology, we have in fact rejected the Cross. As I've said over and over again, one cannot have it both ways. Man's problem is sin, and Jesus went to the Cross to atone for sin. There is no other cure, no other panacea, no other remedy, other than the Cross.

This is why I feel the modern Church is in such danger. A great part of the Charismatic world is openly and even blatantly rejecting

the Cross, referring to it as *"past miseries."* Many in that genre refer to the Cross as the greatest defeat in human history. Consequently, their followers are admonished to forsake the Cross, which can be construed as none other than *"blasphemy!"* I speak of the so-called *"Word of Faith"* Churches!

Every single person in this world who is saved, is saved simply because of what Jesus did at the Cross. Every iota of victory possessed by any Believer, is because of the Cross of Christ. All overcoming strength is because of the Cross of Christ. Every blessing, all prosperity, all healing, all Spiritual Growth, all the Fruit of the Spirit, all the Gifts of the Spirit, anything and everything possessed by the Christian, and I speak of that given by the Lord, have come exclusively to the Believer by and through what Jesus did at the Cross, which makes it possible for the Holy Spirit to do all of these things for us. The Cross is the central focus, as the Cross is the centrality of the Gospel.

While you may grow weary with my repetition, you must not grow weary with the Truth which I present. There is no other Way! And any Preacher who would point to another way, you should run from that Preacher, because he's not preaching the Truth.

Let me say it again, one cannot remain neutral as it regards the Cross. Neutrality is the same as opposing the Cross.

To use an illustration, if a person has a fatal disease, and there is a medicine which will cure that disease, the individual must take the medicine for it to be effective. In fact, he can address the medicine in one of three ways:

He can reject the medicine, refusing to take it; he can not reject the medicine, but yet not take it; or he can take the medicine. The first two ways will amount to his death, with only the last way giving him life. It is the same with the Cross!

THE BLOOD OF THE COVENANT

The phrase, *"And hath counted the Blood of the Covenant, wherewith he was sanctified, an unholy thing,"* refers to a person who has found the Lord, i.e., *"has been saved,"* but is now expressing unbelief toward that which originally saved him.

The Scripture doesn't say *"could have been Sanctified,"* but rather *"was Sanctified."* This comes about only by Faith expressed in Christ and what Christ has done at the Cross (Eph. 2:13-18; I Cor. 6:11). This tells us that it is possible for Believers to turn their backs on Christ, and thereby become unbelievers, and, if remaining in that condition, be eternally lost.

"The Blood of the Covenant" is an expression used of the blood that established the Old Covenant (Ex. 24:8; Heb. 9:20) and also of the Blood of Jesus that established the New Covenant (Mat. 26:28; Mk. 14:24; Lk. 22:20; I Cor. 11:25).

While these admonitions were written by Paul for the entirety of mankind, they were more specifically directed toward the Christian Jews of his day. And yet let me emphasize, the Truth that was pointed at them, is as well, pointed toward all of mankind, as well as the modern Church.

As we've already stated, some Christian Jews of that particular time it seems had already apostatized and others were seriously considering doing so. What did this mean?

Of course, and as would be obvious, all Christian Jews had been saved out of Judaism. And now because of discouragement or whatever reason, some were going back into that way. And the following is what it entailed.

These Jews who had accepted Christ, who had been enlightened, had tasted of the Heavenly Gift, and had been made partakers of the Holy Spirit, had tasted of the good Word of God, and of the powers of the world to come (Heb. 6:4-5), which means they had been sanctified, which refers to being set apart unto God, if they went back into Judaism, would have to stand before a Jewish tribunal in a Synagogue, and publicly denounce Jesus Christ as an imposter, as a blasphemer, and Who should have been crucified. This is what is meant by *"trodding underfoot the Son of God, and counting the Blood of the Covenant, wherewith they had been sanctified, as an unholy thing."* As should be obvious, if they remained in this state they couldn't be saved.

And according to the last phrase of this Verse, it is almost certain, that some of these

Jews actually blasphemed the Holy Spirit, which we will address momentarily.

HOW COULD ANY BELIEVER REJECT CHRIST?

To be more particular, how could these Jews who had accepted Christ, who knew the joys of sins forgiven, who experienced the great Peace of God which floods the sanctified soul, then turn their backs upon Christ, and especially reject Him after this fashion?

Many modern Preachers claim that such is not possible; however, if it's not possible, why did the Holy Spirit have Paul to write the entirety of the Epistle to the Hebrews? To be frank, such thinking is silly! It is not only possible, it in fact happened, and actually, it has continued to happen from then until now.

The modern Church in its ignoring the Cross, is certainly not to be placed in the same category which we have just addressed; however, one must admit, that such position is definitely going in that direction. And that is a frightful thing!

Turning away from the Lord is not an easy thing, nor is it a quick thing. It is a process of spiritual declination, which takes place because of a lack of consecration on the part of the Believer. Most of all, it is an improper evaluation of the Cross, and our relationship to that Finished Work. Many Christians, not understanding the Cross, at least as it regards their overcoming experience, struggle mightily against sin, always without victory. There is a terrible, discouraging factor in such a lifestyle. Consequently, many grow discouraged and quit. They haven't really abandoned Christ and the Cross, they just simply have not properly understood the Finished Work of Christ, thereby attempting to live this life by their own strength, which is impossible. Of course, if they remain in the state of the forsaking of Christ, they will be just as eternally lost, as these whom Paul addresses in this Epistle.

But again I emphasize, that most modern Christians who lose their way, do so because they do not understand God's prescribed order of victory. The Christian Jews of Paul's day were different. In all likelihood, they definitely did understand the Cross, but purposely chose to reject the great Sacrifice of Christ. But at the same time, how similar is this with many modern religious leaders, who ought to know better than the course which they are presently taking!

God is merciful, gracious and true. He is longsuffering, not willing that any should perish. Thank God for that, or none of us would be saved. But the Reader must understand, that Light rejected, is Light withdrawn. And that's the state in which the present Church finds itself.

It's going to have to make a decision as to whether it accepts the Cross or rejects the Cross! There will be no middle ground.

If it rejects the Cross, the results are inevitable. It is judgment! If it accepts the Cross, it will be victory unparalleled!

THE SPIRIT OF GRACE

The conclusion of the question, *"And hath done despite unto the Spirit of Grace?"*, refers to the Holy Spirit. It is the Holy Spirit Who performs the Work of Grace in the believing sinner's heart and life upon conversion, which Jesus paid for at the Cross. It is the Holy Spirit Who thereafter carries out every Work of God in the Believer's life, again all paid for by Christ. Paul does not often refer to the Holy Spirit in these Passages, being occupied for the most part with the Person and the Work of the Son. As well, and as should be obvious, he sees the Spirit as a Person, not an influence or a thing, for it is only a Person who can be insulted.

"Despite" in the Greek is *"enybrizo,"* and means, *"insolent self-assertion which disregards what is due to others. It combines arrogance with wanton injury."*

In the New Testament there are a variety of ways of referring to the Spirit, but only here is He called *"The Spirit of Grace"* (Zech. 12:10). The expression means, *"the Spirit through Whom God's Grace is manifested."*

The idea is, and to which we have already alluded, it is the Holy Spirit Who performs every single work in the heart and life of the Believer, and again as stated, all paid for by the Work of Christ on the Cross. That's the reason that Jesus said:

"Wherefore I say unto you, all manner of sin and blasphemy shall be forgiven unto

men: but the blasphemy against the Holy Spirit shall not be forgiven unto men" (Mat. 12:31).

BLASPHEMING THE HOLY SPIRIT

The question here begs to be asked: If these Christian Jews in their turning their backs on Christ, at least those who did, if they in fact blasphemed the Holy Spirit which would insure their doom? or did they merely grieve Him?

It is most certain that they definitely grieved Him, and severely. And due to the particulars of the situation, and I speak of them having to publicly deny Christ, actually publicly stating that He was an imposter and a blasphemer and thereby deserved crucifixion, it is no doubt positive that at least some of them blasphemed the Holy Spirit. There are several particulars about blaspheming the Holy Spirit which we should address. They are:

1. Only a Believer can blaspheme the Holy Spirit, or else one who strongly professes to know God, such as the Pharisees of old, but who in fact doesn't, and who in fact never has. It has to do with light given, and light professed. Those who have never known the Lord, and who make no profession of Faith of any kind, cannot blaspheme the Holy Spirit. How can they blaspheme someone of Whom they know nothing!

2. The manner in which the Holy Spirit is blasphemed, and once again I speak of so-called Believers, is to attribute the Works of God to the devil. This is what the Pharisees did regarding Christ.

When Jesus was healing the sick and casting out demons, *"The Pharisees heard it, and said, this fellow doth not cast out Devils, but by Beelzebub the Prince of the Devils"* (Mat. 12:22-32). As stated, due to this accusation, Jesus pronounced that they had in fact blasphemed the Holy Spirit.

As we have stated over and over again, every single thing done in the Believer's life by God, is done through the Person, Work, Office, Power, and Agency of the Holy Spirit. This means, that it's a dangerous thing to refer to something as being of the Devil, when in fact, it is of God, in other words, a direct work of the Holy Spirit.

I have heard Preachers make fun of speaking in tongues, and do so in a most debilitating way. In doing this, did they blaspheme the Holy Spirit?

Only the Lord can determine when the line is crossed. Suffice to say, a person who would do such a thing, is treading on dangerous ground. Once again, I suspect that all of this has to do with the amount of Light that has been given to such an individual.

The Pharisees of old who made these statements about Christ, had been given Light as no human beings in history had ever been given Light; consequently, they were totally without excuse.

3. If a person has truly blasphemed the Holy Spirit, that person will never again turn to the right way, and in fact will have no desire to turn to the right way. So, the idea that there are people who cry, plead, and beg to be saved, but cannot, and because they think they've blasphemed the Holy Spirit, is blatantly incorrect. Such a thing has never happened, at least as far as God is concerned.

While it certainly is possible that some people might believe a lie, and no doubt have, that's their doings and not God. The very fact that a person would want to come to the Lord is proof that they have not blasphemed the Holy Spirit. It is the very Spirit of God Who has put the desire within the person's heart to want to be saved, and to be sure, He wouldn't do such a thing, if that person had in fact, blasphemed Him.

(30) "FOR WE KNOW HIM THAT HATH SAID, VENGEANCE BELONGETH UNTO ME, I WILL RECOMPENSE, SAITH THE LORD. AND AGAIN, THE LORD SHALL JUDGE HIS PEOPLE."

The composite is:

1. Paul first of all appeals to the understanding of his Readers.

2. "Vengeance" is an unfortunate translation, because the word conveys the idea of vindictiveness which does not reside in the original Greek word. The emphasis is not on that. It is rather on the certainty that the Lord will act. The wrongdoer cannot hope to go unpunished because avenging wrong is in the hands of none less than God.

3. Paul leaves no doubt about the Lord's intervention, for He is here named and so is His activity.

4. That a man claims to be a member of the people of God does not exempt him from judgment. God judges all. That being the case, let not the apostate think that he, of all people, can escape.

A CERTAINTY OF JUDGMENT

The phrase, *"For we know Him that hath said, 'Vengeance belongeth unto Me, I will recompense,' saith the Lord,"* is meant to imply, that every single thing is going to be judged by the Lord, Who Alone is the Righteous Judge. In fact, the very One Whom some of these Christian Jews was repudiating, namely the Lord Jesus Christ, they will ultimately face as Judge. The Scripture says of Him:

"And He shall not judge after the sight of His eyes, neither reprove after the hearing of His ears:

"But with Righteousness shall He judge ... and He shall smite the Earth with the rod of His mouth, and with the breath of His lips shall He slay the wicked" (Isa. 11:3-4).

Every single thing that man does, for that he will ultimately answer to God. I realize that's a solemn statement, but it happens to be true.

Of course, every believing sinner who comes to Christ at that particular time wipes the slate clean. In other words, his sins were judged at Calvary and will never again be brought against him. It is the same with Believers who sin, and dutifully take that sin to the Lord. He has promised to forgive, cleanse, and forget, and that He does (I Jn. 1:9). But for those who turn their backs on God, even as Paul is here addressing as it regards certain of these Christian Jews, if they remain in that state, they will lose their souls, and as well, they will suffer the wrath of God, even as Paul here proclaims.

But what about Christians who embark upon a wrong direction, and I speak of a direction that is unscriptural whatever it might be, even as untold millions have done and continue to do? This is answered in the next phrase.

THE LORD SHALL JUDGE HIS PEOPLE

The phrase, *"And again, the Lord shall judge His people,"* is taken from Deuteronomy

32:36, even as the previous quotation of this Verse was taken from Deuteronomy 32:35.

The idea here is, that the Lord will judge Believers when they deserve it, and chastise them when they ought to be chastised. The mere fact that we are His people will not save us from chastisement if we deserve it, anymore than the fact that one is a beloved child will save him from correction when he does wrong. This Truth was abundantly illustrated in the history of the Israelites; and the same great principle applies to Christians as well! In fact, Paul will address chastisement in the Twelfth Chapter of this Epistle.

If a Christian sins, and that refers to whatever type sin, we have the privilege of taking the problem to the Lord, where it will be correctly handled; however, the idea in this is that we are sorry for our failure, and we certainly do not desire that it continue. In fact, in that capacity, the Lord places no limitations. The truth is, most Christians not knowing the Way of the Cross, are dominated by sin in some manner, with them having to go to the Lord over and over again. While such is certainly regrettable, and will definitely cause grievous problems in the life of the Believer, still, the Lord will be faithful to forgive irrespective of the number of times requested (I Jn. 1:9). Such a person doesn't want the problem in their life, whatever it might be, but due to the fact that they do not know God's prescribed order of victory, are doomed to continue repeating the situation. However, even then, the Lord will ultimately bring on chastisement.

But yet, we are faced with myriads of Christians who do wrong, at times grossly wrong, but who do not think they are doing wrong; consequently, those individuals do not ask forgiveness and help from the Lord. They have embarked upon a course which is totally unscriptural, and in fact, which is sin, because any deviation from the true way of the Lord is in principle, rebellion against Him. But yet, that's where untold millions of Christians presently find themselves. In other words, they are deceived! What about these particular individuals?

First of all, the Holy Spirit will move upon them greatly, attempting to bring them back to the right way and place. With some He succeeds in doing so, and with others He has

no success. What happens to those particular individuals? And to be sure, they number into the untold millions.

The Lord cannot abide any wrongdoing or wrong direction in the hearts and lives of His people. With some of these individuals, they will go the way of these Christian Jews, which means they will ultimately lose their souls. With others, while they won't lose their souls, they will definitely lose the Blessings of God in many and most ways. And to be sure, they will lose great reward at the Judgment Seat of Christ (I Cor. 3:11-15). Let it ever be known, that no one gets by with God! And especially His people.

Jesus plainly told us, *"Judge not, that ye be not judged.*

"For with what judgment you judge, you shall be judged: and with what measure you mete, it shall be measured to you again" (Mat. 7:1-2).

This is speaking of making a negative judgment of one's motives, and then passing judgment upon the person, which no human being is qualified to do. Only God can do that.

In fact, everything must be judged Scripturally, in fact, it is demanded that everything be judged Scripturally. The Word says, *"To the Law and to the Testimony: if they speak not according to this Word, it is because there is no light in them"* (Isa. 8:20).

When it comes to accepting wrong doctrine, which again millions of Christians have done and continue to do, consequences will be suffered for that as well. The entire Epistle to the Galatians is written for that very purpose. These individuals were trading Grace for Law, and Paul said if they did this, they would be *"entangled again with the yoke of bondage"* (Gal. 5:1).

LEADERSHIP

Many Christians have the erroneous idea, that if their Pastor embarks upon a certain direction, or the Leaders of their Denomination, that irrespective as to whether that direction is right or wrong, they will be held blameless in their following if in fact, such direction is wrong. Nothing could be farther from the truth!

To be sure, this is the Spirit that is projected by many Preachers and so-called religious leaders, however, such thinking is definitely not of God. Every single Christian is going to have to answer for himself personally. He cannot pass the buck to others, so to speak. Every Believer must know the Word, be guided by the Word, and base all their decisions and actions on the Word. It doesn't matter what others do, and it doesn't matter what it costs you to do right, even if it means being put out of your Church. In fact, that has always been the cost of true Discipleship. Christ must come first in all things. In fact, He must be first, second, third, fourth, etc.

Let us ever take to heart this which the Spirit has said through Paul, *"The Lord shall judge His people."* To be sure, the Lord meant exactly what He said, and we should know, that He means exactly what He says.

(31) "IT IS A FEARFUL THING TO FALL INTO THE HANDS OF THE LIVING GOD."

The exposition is:

1. God says what He means and means what He says.

2. God is active and working, and doing so constantly, as proven by the words *"Living God."*

3. Paul is speaking here of falling into the hands of the Lord in a negative way. Such is a fearful thing!

Several things are here said in this Verse. They are:

A FEARFUL THING

This word is being spoken here to Believers. In fact, the unredeemed have very little knowledge of God, at least that which is correct. It is Believers to whom the Spirit is here speaking.

As a Christian, and as stated, I should understand that Grace does not cover willful wrong direction. Also, it does not cover incorrect doctrine. Unfortunately, many Christians think that because we're living in the day of Grace, that God winks at wrongdoing. In fact, the Scripture blatantly says otherwise:

"And the times of this ignorance (Old Testament times) *God winked at; but now* (this age of Grace) *commandeth all men everything to repent"* (Acts 17:30). Christians should fear going in wrong directions, because they will ultimately have to answer.

NOTES

TO FALL

The basic idea of all of this is, that Christians by accepting false doctrine, fall from Grace (Gal. 5:4). This refers to substituting something else in place of the Cross.

All Grace comes through the Cross, and in fact everything that comes from God to Believers. To guarantee an uninterrupted flow, the Believer must at all times keep his Faith in the Finished Work of Christ, i.e., *"the Cross."* If Faith is removed from the Cross to other things, and irrespective as to what those other things might be, a *"fall"* is the guaranteed result. With the Believer going in the wrong direction, if there is not a correction, chastisement will be the ultimate result (Gal. 2:20-21).

THE LIVING GOD

"The hands of the Living God," refers to that which is negative. By the word *"living"* we are given to understand, that God is active in all things. Every single thing done by one of His children is very important to Him. When we go in wrong directions, the Holy Spirit immediately begins to make the attempt to pull us back to the right way, and I speak of the Way of the Cross. Due to how much He loves us, He will take whatever steps necessary to accomplish this — but will stop short of forcing our wills.

If the Believer insists on continuing on the wrong course, the Lord will apply sterner measures, and if that is rejected as well, there can come a time that the Spirit of God will leave. Far better the individual being chastised by the Lord, even strongly, than the Lord letting the individual go. It was said of one of the tribes of Israel, *"Ephraim is joined to idols: let him alone"* (Hos. 4:17).

That is the worst thing that can happen to a Believer. In fact, what does happen to such a Believer?

If a Believer has reached such a place that the Lord has done everything within His power to bring the individual back, short of forcing the will, which He will not do, that person will be eternally lost, that is if the Lord continues to pull back from him.

I do believe for some, that even though the Lord may withdraw from them for a season, He ultimately comes back, with some then repenting. But if He doesn't come back at all, there is no way that person can maintain Salvation.

I've had people mention certain Preachers or individuals to me, who were obviously living in sin, whether of morals or doctrine, but who seemed to suffer no chastisement from the Lord whatsoever. What about these people?

The Holy Spirit through Paul answers this question: *"But if ye be without chastisement, whereof all are partakers, then are ye bastards, and not sons"* (Heb. 12:8).

Despite their profession, this means that such people are really not Christians.

(32) "BUT CALL TO REMEMBRANCE THE FORMER DAYS, IN WHICH, AFTER YE WERE ILLUMINATED, YE ENDURED A GREAT FIGHT OF AFFLICTIONS;"

The composite is:

1. Paul wants these Christian Jews to remember the former days, referring to the time of their Salvation.

2. As Believers, they were given light as it regards the Lord Jesus Christ.

3. Persecution immediately came from family and friends.

CALL TO REMEMBRANCE

The phrase, *"But call to remembrance the former days,"* recalls the earlier proofs that these Christian Jews had given of their faithfulness and love.

In the last six Verses, Paul has enforced his exhortation by an appeal to the danger of falling away and the fearful consequences of unfaithfulness. From warning he now turns to encouragement. These individuals were to call to mind and ever keep in remembrance what the Grace of God had already enabled them to endure. As Theophylact has said, he bids them imitate, not others, but themselves.

These *"former days"* and despite the persecutions, were days of victory. That's why Paul refers back to this time, even as every Christian should contemplate. In other words, he is telling them, at least as it regards a course of direction, to go back to where you got in.

Every single person who has come to Christ has done so by accepting Christ and what He did for them at the Cross. That's the first thing the Holy Spirit illuminates to

the sinful heart, *"Jesus died for me."* In this, the sinner sees himself as wicked and therefore lost, and as well, sees Christ and His Cross as the only hope.

Unfortunately, after coming to Christ, many, if not most, Believers then leave the Cross, and primarily, because their Churches direct them to other things. Perhaps it's done inadvertently; nevertheless, it is done in most cases!

What do I mean by these statements?

Most new Christians are not taught that the Cross of Christ, i.e., *"the Finished Work of Christ,"* i.e., *"the great Sacrifice of Christ,"* is not only the means of their Salvation, but also figures in everything they will be in Christ thereafter. In other words, the Christian must look to the Cross of Christ at all times, and not only as it regards the initial Salvation experience.

Not being taught this, Christians begin to look to themselves, and I speak here of all types of good works, or their Church, or something else. In other words, their Faith shifts from the Cross to other things. As stated, most of this is done inadvertently, but the results will be the same, and I speak of failure.

When they go to their Pastors about their problems, that is if they do so, they are generally told to *"get more involved,"* or that they *"need to increase their faith,"* or a hundred and one other such type things.

While these things no doubt are good within themselves, they really do not address the problem. The problem is, that Christian is no longer depending on the Finished Work of Christ, but rather something else. In fact, this is the great sin of the modern Church.

THE WAY SATAN WORKS

Immediately after the believing sinner comes to Christ, Satan sets about to hinder that Believer in any way and every way possible. The Evil One uses temptation in various ways.

There is only one way to meet that temptation, whatever course it might take, and that is by the Believer placing his trust and faith completely in Christ and what Christ did for him at the Cross, understanding that it is in the Cross that all victory was won. When he does this, the Holy Spirit will then grandly and gloriously help him, and the temptation is thrown over. However, most Christians at this stage don't look to the Cross, because they don't know to look to the Cross. Consequently, they attempt to face the situation in any number of ways.

Most of the time they face the issue with nothing but their *"willpower,"* which is always woefully insufficient (Rom. 7:18). Oftentimes, upon hearing other Christians talk about meeting the Devil with the Word of God, they will quote particular Scriptures in the face of temptation, thinking somehow this will turn aside the thrust of the Evil One. They are confused when it doesn't!

Others try stamping their feet so to speak, and rebuking the Devil. But then they find that doesn't work either.

In such a situation, which to be sure affects every single Christian, they are successful in holding off certain temptations. However, almost all the time, Satan will be successful in one or two particular efforts. In other words, the Christian will succumb in those capacities, whatever those capacities might be.

Upon such a thing, the Christian knowing he has done wrong, instantly comes under condemnation. At that point, he asks the Lord to forgive him, which the Lord has promised to do, and in fact, will always do (I Jn. 1:9).

With forgiveness, comes an instant restoration of fellowship. Many Christians mistake this for victory, when actually it isn't. While it is certainly true that their wrongdoing has been forgiven, to be sure, Satan will come back. In this situation, the individual now finds himself failing again and again. Each time he asks forgiveness from the Lord, and each time forgiveness is granted; however, this is not the Lord's way. In fact, this Believer is now being dominated by his sin nature (Rom. 6:12).

TRY HARDER?

In such a situation, the Believer becomes very frustrated. In fact, the same thing is now happening to him, that happened to the Apostle Paul. The Apostle said of his own experience, and this was before he was given the Revelation of the Cross, *"For that which*

NOTES

I do I allow not" (Rom. 7:15). Actually, the Greek word here for *"allow,"* should have been translated *"understand."* Then it would read: *"For that which I do I understand not."*

This is where most Christians are. They are struggling with all their strength not to do wrong, but in some way sin is dominating them, and they are left confused and without understanding.

Of course, the Lord told Paul what the answer was, with the Apostle then giving us that answer in Romans, Chapter 6.

He explains there how that the Believer is *"in Christ,"* and in Christ by virtue of the death, burial, and resurrection of our Redeemer. Christ was our Substitute, doing for us what we could not do for ourselves. Our simple Faith in Him, places us in His crucifixion (His death), His burial, and His Resurrection (Rom. 6:3-5). This means that all of our victory is without exception in Him, and more particularly, what He did for us at the Cross. That's the reason I continue to say that our Faith must remain in the Cross, for it was there, that all victory was won.

Until the Believer learns this, it doesn't really matter what he does, or how hard he tries, the end result is always going to be the same — failure. He can go to Preachers, have them lay hands on him, and even though the Preacher may be truly used of God, and even though the manifestation which follows may definitely be of the Spirit, even though at that time he will be blessed, he will find a short time later, that the same problem returns. That's why Jesus said:

"You shall know the Truth, and the Truth shall make you free" (Jn. 8:32).

The trouble with Christians, we're seeking a Touch, when in reality we need the Truth. Because it's so important, please allow me to say it again:

Until the Christian learns the Truth of the Cross, sin is going to continue to dominate that Christian in some way, and that despite all his efforts otherwise. God has only one way of Victory, and that is through what Jesus did at the Cross. When we place our Faith in the great, Finished Work of Christ, the Holy Spirit then helps us, which guarantees us victory. In other words, the Holy Spirit guarantees all that Christ did for us at the Cross, but for us to have all of these benefits, He at the same time, demands that we exhibit Faith in the great Sacrifice of Christ, and actually continue to do so, all the days of our lives (Rom. 8:2). That's why Jesus said, and to which we have already alluded, *"If any man will come after me, let him deny himself* (don't try to gain the Victory by his own actions), *and take up his cross daily, and follow Me"* (Lk. 9:23).

WALKING AFTER THE SPIRIT

Someone asked me once, as to the definition of victory. The answer is simple, it is *"walking after the Spirit"* (Rom. 8:1).

And how do we *"walk after the Spirit"*? First let's see what it's not.

Walking after the Spirit is not doing spiritual things. Many people confuse the two. They think if they do spiritual things, such as reading their Bibles, praying, witnessing to souls, faithful attendance to Church, etc., that this is *"walking after the Spirit."* It isn't! While those things are definitely good, and in fact that which all true Christians will do, that's not what Paul was talking about.

"Walking after the Spirit," in its most simplistic definition, means to simply place one's Faith in the great Sacrifice of Christ, understanding that it is in Christ that all Life, Salvation, and victory are found. In fact, Paul uses the phrase *"in Christ,"* or one of its derivatives such as *"in Whom,"* some 170 times in his Epistles. Our victory is found totally and completely in Christ, and that means what Christ did at the Cross on our behalf. That's the reason, and which we've already stated several times in this Volume, that Paul also said, *"For the Law of the Spirit of Life in Christ Jesus, has made me free from the Law of Sin and Death"* (Rom. 8:2).

Again, as I've said over and over again, the Holy Spirit doesn't demand much of us, but He does demand that we place our Faith in Christ, and that refers to what Christ did for us at the Cross, and keep our Faith in that Finished Work. When we do this, and continue to do this, the Holy Spirit, Who is the key to all of this, helps us grandly, and we then walk in all the overcoming victory afforded by Christ, but only in that manner. Then, *"Sin shall not have dominion over us:*

for we are not under the Law, but under Grace" (Rom. 6:14).

LAW

When most Christians hear about *"Law,"* they don't really know what you're talking about. And yet, if it is to be noticed, Paul talks about Law constantly, especially in Romans and Galatians. Why does he do this?

In effect, it is the Holy Spirit Who addresses this subject through him, and for good purpose and reason. The reason is, the problem has always been Law, and the problem now is Law. What do we mean by that?

When we say *"Law,"* we're not actually speaking of the Law of Moses, even though that was basically what Paul was addressing. So, how does that affect us now? To make it very simple, I will explain it in this fashion:

If we try to live for the Lord in any fashion, except total and complete Faith in the Cross of Christ, we have placed ourselves under *"Law"* whether we understand that or not. As such, we are guaranteed of failure.

Most of these things we do in attempting to live for the Lord, or to draw closer to Him, or to walk in victory, are very good things within themselves. In fact, and as stated, they are spiritual things; however, while the doing of the things, whatever they might be, is not wrong, our dependence on them is wrong. By putting dependence on all of these things, we have in effect turned them into a *"Law,"* which of course God can never honor.

I realize it sounds confusing, but if you'll understand it in the following fashion, most of the confusion will be taken away.

The Christian doesn't have to learn a long list of rules as to what to do and what not to do. All you have to understand is that your salvation, your life, and your victory are all found totally and completely in what Jesus did at the Cross on your behalf. As stated, you are *"in Christ."* Consequently, you are to have faith in that, and you are not to allow Preachers to pull your faith away from that to other things. If you maintain your Faith in the Cross of Christ as it regards your life and living, the Grace of God will then flow to you in an uninterrupted manner, and the Holy Spirit will guarantee that it does. That's why Paul said, *"You're not under Law, but under Grace"* (Rom. 6:14).

Now please understand, this is not one way of victory for the Child of God, it is the only way. God has provided only one Sacrifice, and that is the Sacrifice of His Son, the Lord Jesus Christ. Satan will do his best to draw you away from this Finished Work. Don't allow him to do such. And don't allow him to use Preachers or anyone else for that matter to entice you away. Put your faith in the Cross of Christ, and keep your faith in the Cross of Christ. That's where all life and victory are found (Rom. 6:3-14; 8:1-2, 11; I Cor. 1:18, 21, 23; 2:2).

ILLUMINATION

The phrase, *"In which, after ye were illuminated,"* refers to the enlightenment the Gospel brings to the mind of the Believer.

When the person comes to Christ, the Holy Spirit immediately takes up abode in the heart and life of the individual. And then immediately, the Believer should also ask the Lord for the Baptism with the Holy Spirit, which is promised to all Believers (Jn. 14:17; Acts 1:4-5).

At any rate, the Divine nature that is now in the Believer, opens up understanding as it regards spiritual things. For the first time in his life, the individual now begins to understand some things about the Lord, and about God's Word, which were impossible before conversion. In fact, if the Believer will place his faith in the Cross of Christ, trusting in the Spirit to do His Work, this illumination will continue to expand all the days of his life. In fact, it is the most glorious life there is.

A person really doesn't know how to live until they find Christ, Who in fact, is Life. The true purpose and meaning of life now becomes evident, which is to please God, and which is done through our Faith in Christ. In other words, Christ is everything!

AFFLICTIONS

The phrase, *"Ye endured a great fight of afflictions,"* refers to the persecutions that came their way after conversion. With Jews, that could have been quite extensive.

Their families and friends immediately, would have begun to use extensive pressure for them to renounce Christ and go back into Judaism. That failing, at a particular point in time, they would actually go through a type of ceremony, which one might even refer to as a funeral, and from then on would treat their Christian relatives, as if they were dead. Their names were no longer allowed to be mentioned, and they were accorded no recognition whatsoever. If close loved ones became ill, they were not allowed to visit. And if the Christian Jew became ill, to be sure, no one from his family would visit him. If a loved one died, they were not allowed to attend the funeral. If they passed each other on the street, on the part of the non-Christian relative, there would be no recognition.

Some could handle this, and some couldn't! However, and as stated, if they determined to go back into Judaism, they would have to go through a ceremony in the Synagogue, and would be expected to publicly denounce Christ, and in the most negative of terms. So as we see, these *"afflictions"* were quite severe.

In most of the countries of the world presently, it doesn't cost very much to live for Christ. Were that to change, I wonder how many Christians we would have left? There is one thing for sure:

The false prophets and the false apostles would thin out considerably.

(33) "PARTLY, WHILST YE WERE MADE A GAZINGSTOCK BOTH BY REPROACHES AND AFFLICTIONS; AND PARTLY, WHILST YE BECAME COMPANIONS OF THEM THAT WERE SO USED."

The exegesis is:

1. Some of the Christian Jews had been made a spectacle by being exposed to insult and injury.

2. The second group had suffered by being associates of the former group.

3. All must be given up for Christ, even our very lives if necessary!

A GAZINGSTOCK

The phrase, *"Partly, whilst ye were made a gazingstock both by reproaches and afflictions,"* refers not only to the things just listed, but as well, to public ridicule.

For many people, the latter, and we speak of public ridicule, is the hardest thing of all to take. Most people, even Christians, go with the flow. If they are in any way, made a *"gazingstock,"* i.e., *"laughingstock,"* for their convictions, most can't handle that! Consequently, most at this point, fold and buckle, as one might say.

These particular Believers were not merely reviled in words, they were also made to endure positive sufferings of various kinds. Oftentimes this fell out to financial loss, and to be sure, all who could be hurt in this manner definitely had such visited upon them.

Of course, the non-Christian Jews considered themselves to be of God. Even though they blasphemed Christ, they still considered themselves to be God's chosen people. So, whatever it is they did to their fellow Christian Jews, they were doing it all in the Name of the Lord. And in fact, that's the way with much of this nature. The following should be noted:

Despite claims to the contrary, those who are in actuality enemies of the Lord, are not content to merely disagree with others whom they claim to be wrong; they feel they must attack the individual as well, and even destroy him if necessary. In other words, in this persecution, they will go as far as the law will allow. Again, it's all done in the Name of the Lord. But yet, this is one way that is easy to tell if a person is actually of the Lord. Those who are truly of the Lord will not do such things. While they will definitely oppose false doctrine, they will not try to hinder or hurt the individual who is promoting the false doctrine. They will pray for him, and leave him to the Lord, thereby, taking no further steps.

COMPANIONS

The phrase, *"And partly, whilst ye became companions of them that were so used,"* refers to Christian Jews who tried to be of help to Jews newly converted, and coming under severe persecution. Consequently, the persecution would extend to those attempting to help, even though they were not relatives, etc. The idea is, *"Your friend is my enemy!"*

(34) "FOR YE HAD COMPASSION OF ME IN MY BONDS, AND TOOK JOYFULLY THE SPOILING OF YOUR GOODS, KNOWING IN YOURSELVES THAT YE HAVE IN HEAVEN A BETTER AND AN ENDURING SUBSTANCE."

The structure is:

1. Some of these Christian Jews had helped Paul, and they were hated for this.

2. They did this even though it cost some of them dearly!

3. They had at that time seen the big picture, which refers to eternity, and which is an example for all modern Believers.

MY BONDS

The phrase, *"For ye had compassion of me in my bonds,"* evidently refers to the time that Paul was in prison in Rome, as recorded in Acts Chapter 28.

Some have claimed that the words *"of me,"* and as they referred to Paul, are not in the original Greek texts. Those who claim that, knowing that the statement given in the King James is another strong proof that Paul is the author of Hebrews, are mainly those who do not believe he wrote the Epistle.

Paul was hated by the religious leaders of Israel, even to the point of murder. In fact, they did everything that was in their power to murder the Apostle, with him being spared only because of the protection of the Lord. Their hatred for him knew no bounds.

They blamed him for every single Jew who accepted Christ. In fact, they blamed him for the entirety of the Gospel of Christ, feeling that if it had not been for him, Christianity would have died. While that's not true, still, it definitely is true, that Paul was the principal player in the Early Church.

So if it wasn't bad enough for Jews to accept Christ, at least in the minds of non-Christian Jews, it was worse yet when they did all within their power to help the Apostle Paul, as evidently many of them did.

FINANCIAL LOSS

The phrase, *"And took joyfully the spoiling of your goods,"* presents the fact, that those who did help Paul, were persecuted severely, and that many of them in addition to what was already being done, great pains were taken, to hurt or even destroy them financially.

In fact, many modern Denominations follow the same principle. If they oppose a fellow Preacher, the leadership of these Denominations, is not satisfied to merely have a parting of ways. At the same time, they feel that they must destroy the Preacher in question, whomever he might be. Consequently, they seek to step outside of their own Denomination, and try to do all they can to hurt him in any way possible, and in any capacity. In fact, if such is carried on in the business world, the guilty parties can be prosecuted, because they are definitely breaking the law. Unfortunately, self-righteousness knows no law. It justifies its actions in many and varied ways. In fact, there is actually nothing these religious leaders won't do, and as previously stated, if the law of the land allowed it, they would actually murder the person in question. They justify their actions by claiming that what they're doing is for the good of the Work of God. In other words, they really consider themselves to be working for the Lord in these perfidious actions. It was the same with the non-Christian Jews of Paul's day.

The reason their modern counterparts do these things is because Christ is not really the Head of their Church. In fact, they serve as their own head; consequently, they make up their own rules. In fact, the Word of God is actually never consulted as it regards their course of action. They become a law unto themselves.

IN HEAVEN A BETTER SUBSTANCE

The phrase, *"Knowing in yourselves that ye have in Heaven a better and an enduring substance,"* proclaims these particular Christian Jews, as looking at the big picture. While some of them did suffer financial loss here, and because of serving Christ and especially because of helping Paul, they looked beyond that, realizing that by their actions they were laying up treasures in Heaven, which was the far more important.

What we are addressing here is consecration far beyond the norm. If something affects their pocketbooks in an adverse way, most Christians do not respond too favorably. In other words, if the scene was put into today's timeframe, I'm afraid that most Christians would be of little service to Paul, especially considering that he was in prison at the time.

In fact, if the Ministry of the Apostle Paul was set down into this present time, I wonder how many Christians would really support

Paul, even without these other problems such as prison, etc.? I don't think very many would!

I think that most would bridle at Paul's insistence upon Faith in the Cross of Christ, and considering that the Apostle was very hard on false doctrine, I think the support would have been scarce. Regrettably, the Christianity of most people extends only a certain distance. Most of it doesn't nearly extend to *"Heaven with its better and enduring substance."*

(35) "CAST NOT AWAY THEREFORE YOUR CONFIDENCE, WHICH HATH GREAT RECOMPENCE OF REWARD."

The composite is:

1. This first phrase shows that it's possible for a Believer to cast away their confidence, which means to lose faith.

2. That which we do here for Christ will bring forth great reward in Heaven — and in fact, great reward which will be eternal.

3. The faith of the Believer is the single most important thing he can have. Every attack by Satan is in one way or the other against our Faith; consequently, in all that he does against us, the main thrust is always to get us to quit believing.

THE CASTING AWAY OF CONFIDENCE

The phrase, *"Cast not away therefore your confidence,"* refers to the fact, that some of these Christian Jews had in fact done just that, and others were seriously considering abandoning Christ.

"Confidence" in the Greek is *"parrhesia,"* and means *"outspokenness, frankness, plainness of speech."* The idea as it is here used, refers to their confession of faith. They have confessed Christ, which means they had expressed faith in Christ as the Savior of humanity, by virtue of His Sacrificial Offering of Himself on the Cross, and above all, they must not throw this away.

"Cast away" in the Greek is *"apoballo,"* and means, *"to throw off, or throw away."* This is a strong statement as given by Paul, and conveys the thought of a reckless rejection of what is valuable. Because the earlier conduct of these Christian Jews showed that they knew the value of their possession in Christ, Paul can appeal to them not to discard it. As Christians, they had a confidence

that was based firmly on Christ's saving work and that would be the height of folly to lose. What they had already endured for Christ's sake entitled them to a reward. They must not lose sight of this! The New Testament does not reject the notion that Christians will receive rewards, though, of course, that is never to be the prime motive for service.

REWARD

The phrase, *"Which hath great recompence of reward,"* refers to the fact, that everything will be answered at the Judgment Seat of Christ.

"Reward" in the Greek is *"misthapodosia,"* and means *"requital, remuneration."* The idea is, that God will owe no man anything. Anything done for Him, will receive a just reward. As well, the reward here addressed, refers to this present life, and above all in the life that is to come.

(36) "FOR YE HAVE NEED OF PATIENCE, THAT, AFTER YE HAVE DONE THE WILL OF GOD, YE MIGHT RECEIVE THE PROMISE."

The exegesis is:

1. Proper faith demands proper patience.

2. It is our responsibility to do the Will of God, irrespective as to what that Will might be.

3. The Promise will come, but we aren't told exactly when. In fact, it may be at the Judgment Seat of Christ. The idea is that we be faithful to the end.

PATIENCE

The phrase, *"For ye have need of patience,"* proclaims to us a great lesson. Proper faith will always have proper patience.

This tells us that God may not send the great blessing right now, whatever that great blessing might be. Anyway, the blessing is not to be preeminent, but rather doing the Will of God.

In the last several decades, the Church has been led down a primrose path. In other words, due to improper teaching on faith, the attention of the Church has become riveted on the blessing, i.e., *"the Promise."* Consequently, there is not much love for God in all of this, simply because there cannot be much love for the Lord in all of this. If our

eye is on the reward, that's where our heart is. We must understand the following:

If we are to live right and to do right, we will leave everything in the hands of the Lord. To be sure, He will not overlook anything. He who notes the sparrow's fall, and numbers the very hairs of our heads, as should be obvious, knows all things. If we leave the reward up to Him, and not busy ourselves about these things, the Lord will handle the situation in His Way, which is 10,000 times better than our way.

THE WILL OF GOD

The phrase, *"That, after ye have done the Will of God,"* proclaims this to be the most important thing in our lives and experiences. If we properly do that, and I refer to carrying out the Will of God as it regards all things, or at least do our very best to do this, we can rest assured that God will handle everything else. That's where the attention should be! That's where the emphasis must be!

Many Christians are fearful of the Will of God. They have been led to believe that God may want them to do some horrendous thing, such as moving to Siberia, etc. Consequently, they have very little relationship with the Lord, thinking that He will now ask of them such things in such a case.

Such thinking is ludicrous! First of all, if God asks anything of anyone, He will automatically give that person a love for that particular thing or locality, which changes the complexion altogether. There is no such thing as a person toiling and laboring for the Lord in some fashion or some place, where they are grossly unhappy. That does not exist, being only a fabrication of the Devil, which causes many Christians to lose out on what they could have from the Lord.

Doing the Will of God is the most fulfilling, satisfying, completeness that a person could ever know. This is the secret of real life, of true living. In fact, anything else other than the perfect Will of God, always and without exception, falls out to hurt for the individual involved.

THE PROMISE

The phrase, *"Ye might receive the Promise,"* refers to that which will definitely come, whatever it might be. However, none of that is to be our concern.

We are to love the Lord enough, and to have enough faith in Him, to know that He will provide for us, will take care of us, and will always do for us what we need.

There are some Christians who seem to be blessed now more than others. If that is in fact the case, and I find myself seemingly not blessed as much, that is not to be my concern. The Lord knows what He is doing. He tailor-makes the experience of every Christian, and does so for our betterment, which we must understand.

As a Believer, I am to trust the Lord, understanding *"that He is a rewarder of them that diligently seek Him"* (Heb. 11:6); however, it is first of all, my business to *"believe that He is,"* and at the same time *"diligently seek Him,"* and then leave the rewarding up to Him. As previously stated, we must not get our eyes on the Promise, as important as the Promise is. We must remember, that this Promise comes from God, in effect, a Promise He has made, and to be sure, God keeps His Promises!

(37) "FOR YET A LITTLE WHILE, AND HE THAT SHALL COME WILL COME, AND WILL NOT TARRY."

The composite is:

1. This expression comes from Habakkuk 2:3.

2. The idea is, that whatever reward the Lord sees fit to give us here, will be nothing in comparison to that which will be given there.

3. The Rapture of the Church should be the crowning thought as it regards all Christians, and of course, we speak of the coming Resurrection. It is then, when every Promise will be fulfilled.

This particular Scripture says several things to us. Some of them are as follows:

A LITTLE WHILE

This of which the Holy Spirit speaks through Paul, may seem to be in the never, never; however, in the light of eternity, which is the manner in which it should be observed by all Believers, whatever the timeframe may be, is not long.

In fact, the expression is very much stronger in the Greek text. Expositors translate it:

"For yet a little — a very little — while and He that cometh will come and will not delay." Another translates it: *"For yet a little — ever so little — while."*

So, if the Holy Spirit deemed the timeframe but short some 2,000 years ago, which He definitely did, then how much closer are we presently?! The truth is, we're living in the very last of the last days, perhaps even the last months of the last days. The Church has already entered into the last great apostasy, which will only grow worse. This means that the Rapture of the Church cannot be very long off. In other words, it could happen at any moment (I Thess. 4:16-18).

HE WILL COME

The phrase, *"And He that shall come will come,"* refers to the Lord coming Personally Himself.

Once more the hope of His Coming is set before these Hebrew Believers, and all others as well, even unto this present hour, as an animating and certain expectation. He who cherishes that hope finds in it a moral power that makes real a life of victory. As we have stated, this Passage is derived from Habakkuk 2:3-4. Verse 4 pertains to Verse 38.

Christ is the subject of Habakkuk's vision. Not the beginning, but the perseverance of God's righteous man as opposed to declension and apostasy, is the force of the quotation here. As the righteous man receives life by faith, so by faith he continues to live; but if he draws back, God has no pleasure in him. In fact, the Holy Spirit in Habakkuk states the cause of his drawing back — pride.

WILL NOT TARRY

The phrase, *"And will not tarry,"* means that there is an appointed time for the Rapture of the Church, and at that appointed time, this great happening will come about.

Some claim that the Rapture of the Church is either pushed up or delayed because of actions of the Church, etc. That isn't so!

First of all, God is omniscient, meaning He knows all things. So in simple terms, that means that He knows exactly when He is coming for the Church, and to be sure, that particular date, whatever it is, and He Alone knows, will not be pushed up or delayed. While some things of the Lord are delayed by the lack of faith on the part of men, there are other things, such as the Rapture and the Second Coming, etc., which are not moved by man's faith or the lack thereof.

A PERSONAL EXPERIENCE

I never cease to marvel at the manner in which the Holy Spirit uses the Word of God in any and every capacity. The original point in Habakkuk, is that the faithful must await God's good time for the destruction of their enemies, the Chaldeans.

But as well, even as the Holy Spirit records in Hebrews 10:37, it refers to the Rapture of the Church and as well, to the Second Coming.

On a personal basis, the Holy Spirit gave me this Promise in Habakkuk in 1993, if I remember the year correctly. The exact quotation is:

"And the LORD answered me, and said, write the vision, and make it plain upon tables, that he may run that readeth it.

"For the vision is yet for an appointed time, but at the end it shall speak, and not lie: though it tarry, wait for it; because it will surely come, it will not tarry" (Hab. 2:2-3).

In seeking the Face of the Lord concerning a moving and operation of the Holy Spirit as it regards my own personal Ministry, the Lord, as stated, gave me this Promise. It is now beginning to happen, even though it has been some years in coming. And I believe what will happen, is going to usher many people into the Kingdom of God. Consequently, this Passage as used by Paul, is very dear to me personally.

(38) "NOW THE JUST SHALL LIVE BY FAITH: BUT IF ANY MAN DRAW BACK, MY SOUL SHALL HAVE NO PLEASURE IN HIM."

The composite is:

1. Faith is the principle by which God deals with man.

2. It is possible for a person to come to Salvation, and then to draw back to the place and position of being lost. Such is a denial of the Faith.

3. God has a soul.

4. God is saddened by the loss of Faith among Believers, thereby putting them in the category of unbelievers.

FAITH

The phrase, *"Now the just shall live by faith,"* is derived from Habakkuk 2:4. In essence, this is the Abrahamic Covenant (Gen. 15:6). As well, this was the Divine spark that lit the Reformation when Martin Luther, an Augustinian Monk, was led to this Text by the Holy Spirit, with it being illuminated to him. In simplistic form, it means that the justified person is justified by God upon the basis of, and in answer to, his faith in the Lord Jesus, and more particularly, what Jesus did for him at the Cross.

First of all we must understand, that it is on the basis of Faith and Faith alone, in which God deals with the human race. So what do we mean by that?

As just stated, it means that God gave His Son, the Lord Jesus Christ, to pay man's terrible sin debt, which He did by dying on the Cross. He died for all men, including those who had placed their faith in Him even before the Cross, which includes all the Old Testament Saints.

God then requires that all men simply exhibit Faith in Christ and what He did at the Cross, accepting Him as their Savior, thereby believing that the price He paid was and is sufficient. That's what the central Text of the Bible tells us:

"For God so loved the world, that He gave His Only Begotten Son, that whosoever believeth in Him should not perish, but have everlasting life" (Jn. 3:16). That's all that God requires of the human race.

That means that we cannot come to Salvation by the giving of money, by the doing of good deeds, by belonging to certain Churches, by *"being good,"* through or by education, or any other way. Those things are referred to as *"works,"* which God can never accept. In essence, these *"works"* attempt to *"buy"* Salvation, in which much if not most of the world constantly engages. In the first place, the terrible debt that man owes to God in the realm of sin which in effect, is a crime against God, is of such magnitude, that there is absolutely nothing that man can do to assuage this debt. It's like trying to pay the debt of a trillion dollars with a few pennies. So, man not able to accomplish his own Salvation, God had to do this thing for man, which He did, by becoming man, and going to the Cross, all on man's behalf.

Simple faith in Christ and what He did for us instantly brings about Salvation, which means that God instantly imputes to man a perfect righteousness, actually the perfect, pure, spotless Righteousness of Christ.

Inasmuch as *"Faith"* is required of all men, this angers some, because they consider themselves much better than others. In other words, the Jew grew very angry with Paul because he boldly proclaimed that they must accept Christ in the same manner as the Gentiles, which was and is by Faith. It is the same with many educated and rich people. Many of them don't want to admit that they have to come the same way as the poor and the uneducated. Also, those who subscribe to a code of ethics are loathe to admit, that they have to come the same way as the drunk or the drug addict, etc. Nevertheless, God's Way is the Way of Faith, and unless men come His Way, they cannot be saved, and that means the eternal loss of the soul into hellfire (Rev. 20:11-15).

EXACTLY WHAT DOES FAITH MEAN?

Whenever Paul or Peter mention Faith, or any of the other writers in the Bible for that matter, they are always, and without exception, speaking of Faith in Christ, which refers to what Christ did at the Cross. There are two things we must here remember:

1. Our faith must be exclusively in Christ. It must not be Christ plus something else, but always Christ Alone. And this is one of the major problems as it regards humanity.

Many attempt to believe in Christ plus the Church, plus good works, plus other things, etc. To add anything to our Faith in Christ, nullifies such Faith, which means that God will not honor it. And that's the reason that millions walk down Aisles of Churches, joining the Church, thereby thinking this affords Salvation for them. Their faith is in that Church, and more particularly, in the joining of that Church, than anything else. Christ is mentioned and thought of in a nebulous

way, but to their minds, their Salvation rests in them joining the Church. Pure and simple, these people aren't saved.

The Church, plus anything else, has absolutely nothing to do with Salvation, that being entirely in Christ. It's certainly not wrong to join a Church, but it is definitely wrong to think that doing such affords Salvation or anything of spirituality for that matter. Joining a Church simply means that we are joining in fellowship with other like Believers, in order to be more effective, hopefully, for the work of God.

2. When we say *"Faith in Christ,"* we must always remember, that it is Faith in what Christ did at the Cross. As we must never separate Faith from Christ, we must never separate Christ from the Cross.

Millions claim to have faith in Christ, but they really do not properly understand what they are actually saying. We must understand in our minds, that when we speak of Christ, when we think of Christ, it is always in connection with the Cross. While of course, the Resurrection, the Ascension, and the Exaltation of Christ are very, very important, as would be obvious, still, it was not these things which purchased our Redemption, but rather what Jesus did at the Cross. This must never be forgotten or misunderstood.

THE JUST SHALL LIVE BY FAITH

All we've previously said, primarily refers to the sinner coming to Christ; however, as Paul uses this Text, the greater thrust of the statement refers to those who have already come to Christ and are now ordering their life after Christ. Unfortunately, in many Church circles, we properly tell people how to get saved, just as I have already attempted to do so, but then we lead them wrongly after they come to Christ. As the believing sinner is saved by Grace through Faith (Eph. 2:8-9), the believing Christian is kept by Faith. And what do we mean by that?

"Live" in the Greek is *"zao,"* and means, *"to live life."* It refers to our everyday living, the manner and way we order our behavior.

Because we have exhibited Faith in Christ and what He did at the Cross, we are now saved, i.e., *"just."* As already stated, we can attain such, i.e., *"Justification,"* only by trusting in what Christ has done for us. We are *"just"* only on that basis. And we remain just only on that basis. But this is where the problem arises.

SALVATION BY FAITH, SANCTIFICATION BY SELF!

What do we mean by the statement, *"Salvation by faith, and Sanctification by self"*?

It means that millions of people come to Christ, are saved, and are saved by Faith, because that's the only way one can be saved, and then they attempt to bring about Sanctification in their lives by the machinations and efforts of self. In other words, they try to sanctify themselves.

The word *"Sanctification"* simply means to be *"set apart unto God."* Now that we belong to Christ, the Holy Spirit lives within our hearts and lives, and is there to perform an intended task, which is to make us more and more Christlike. This is done basically by the *"Fruit of the Spirit"* being developed within our lives (Gal. 5:22-23).

He can only do these things in one way, even as we've stated over and over again, and that is by us continuing to exhibit Faith in the great Sacrifice of Christ, which makes all of these things possible. The Believer must understand the following:

As the sinner can do absolutely nothing to save himself except have Faith in Christ, likewise, the Believer can do absolutely nothing to sanctify himself, except to continue to have Faith in Christ, which means to have Faith in what Christ did at the Cross on our behalf. The Believer cannot make himself holy, cannot make himself righteous, cannot draw himself closer to God by his own efforts and machinations, in effect, cannot really do anything by his own strength and ability which will affect anything with God. The Scripture continues to say, *"The Just shall live by Faith,"* which means that he will order his life by Faith, which refers to the fact of what Christ did at the Cross, and our Faith in that.

But yet, the great full-time effort of the Church falls into the realm of *"self-sanctification."* The only thing that such efforts succeed in doing is to make us self-righteous, which is the bane of the Church.

POSITION OR ACTIVITY?

Many Christians think that one draws closer to God by one engaging oneself in spiritual activity. While the activity is good, and will definitely bless the individual, and in fact, which every Christian should do, still, none of this activity will draw us closer to God, will help us be stronger in the Lord, will give us victory over the world, the flesh, and the Devil, etc. And that's where we make our mistake. We think by involvement or activity, that such does something for us in the spiritual sense. Again I say, it doesn't!

Everything that we presently are in Christ, and everything we hope to be in Christ, is all given to us freely according to our *"position in Christ."* Jesus died for us, and we in effect, died with Him, i.e., *"were baptized into His death"* (Rom. 6:3-5), were buried with Him, and raised with Him in newness of life. Consequently, we are *"in Christ."* That is our spiritual position, brought about totally and completely through what Jesus did at the Cross, and our faith in that. That's the way it is and the way it always will be. So, if I want to get closer to God, which every Christian should definitely desire, what do I do?

It can only be done in one way and one way alone. I am to understand that everything I am in Christ, and everything I hope to be in Christ, comes totally and completely by my position in Christ, which refers to what He did for me at the Cross. My Faith is to be anchored there, which will give the Holy Spirit the latitude to work within my heart and life, and do all the great things which He Alone can do. In this manner, I not only grow closer to the Lord, but I constantly grow closer to the Lord, which is the intended purpose of all of this (Rom. 8:1-2, 11; Gal. 5:5).

DOES THIS MEAN I'LL NEVER HAVE ANY MORE PROBLEM WITH THE DEVIL?

No, not at all! Just because your Faith is now right, meaning that it's in the right object which is the Cross, doesn't mean that Satan is going to back off. In fact, he is going to oppose you all the days of your life, and do so in every way possible. But you need have no fear, as long as you properly abide in Christ, and you do that by constantly exhibiting Faith in the Finished Work of Christ. Listen to what Paul said:

"For we through the Spirit wait for the hope of Righteousness by Faith" (Gal. 5:5).

This means as we consistently exhibit faith in the great Sacrifice of Christ, and not allow our Faith to be deterred to other things, that the *"hope of Righteousness"* will be developed in us. It's a process, which means that it takes some time. Just because you have your faith properly placed in the Cross, doesn't mean that you will be instantly mature in a spiritual sense. But notice what he said in this:

He said this *"hope of Righteousness"* comes by *"Faith,"* which refers to Faith in the Finished Work of Christ, which refers to position, and not activity. The phrase *"through the Spirit"* refers to the fact that this is the way the Spirit works. In fact, and as we've stated repeatedly, every single thing that the Lord does for us, is all done by and through the Office, Person, Power, and Agency of the Holy Spirit.

I keep saying these things, because sometimes it's hard for all of us to fully comprehend a particular Truth. We say we know it, but in reality we don't. And the sad truth is, most of the Church doesn't understand that everything that is done for us by God, is always and without exception, a Work of the Spirit. And at the same time, this Work of the Spirit is not automatic. It doesn't require much on our part, but it definitely does require something, and what is that?

The Holy Spirit simply demands that we understand that He can do all that He does for us, according to what Christ did at the Cross. The Work of Christ at the Cross was a legal work, within which confines the Spirit works. In other words, He will not go outside of those parameters. This is so iron clad in fact, that He refers to this as a *"Law"* (Rom. 8:2).

Now that doesn't mean we have to understand everything about the great Finished Work of Christ, which in effect is the New Covenant. In fact, no one understands everything about this, simply because it is inexhaustible. That's the reason that Paul referred to this Covenant as the *"Everlasting Covenant"* (Heb. 13:20).

But you as a Believer do have to understand that all that you have in the Lord has been made possible by what Jesus did at the

NOTES

Cross. You are to place your faith in that, and then the Holy Spirit will do great and mighty things for you (Rom. Chpt. 8).

CONSECRATION

We Christians use the word *"consecration,"* quite often, and of course, referring to consecration to the Lord. When we see individuals who are faithful to Church, etc., we refer to them as *"consecrated to the Lord."* In fact, that may definitely be; however, not necessarily so!

The correct Scriptural interpretation of Consecration to the Lord is that we are trusting totally and completely in the Cross of Christ, understanding that this is the Source of all Spiritual Blessings (Eph. 1:3). This is true consecration, which again, is *"position."* Let me make this statement:

Consecration is what we do, while Sanctification is what we are. However, that which we do as it regards Consecration, is found only in one aspect, and that refers to having Faith in the Cross of Christ. That is the total extent of our *"doing."* If we try to *"do"* anything else, thinking it makes us consecrated, we have then placed ourselves in the realm of works, which can never bring on true consecration.

But we in the Church have become accustomed to thinking that a person is consecrated to the Lord, if they don't do certain things, or if they do certain things such as prayer, faithfulness to Church, etc. Not so!

Now, when a person is properly consecrated to the Lord, which means that they are exhibiting Faith in the Cross of Christ, to be sure, that person will definitely do certain things; however, he will do these things as a result of consecration, and not in order to be consecrated.

For instance, if a person is truly trusting in Christ and what Christ has done for us at the Cross, which is His consecration, he at the same time will have a prayer life, will be faithful to Church, will be faithful in his giving to the Lord, will *"come out from among them and be separate,"* etc. (II Cor. 6:14-18; 7:1).

DRAWING BACK

The phrase, *"But if any man draw back,"* portrays the fact that such can be done, and of course, Paul is speaking here of Believers. In fact, this is what the major thrust of this Epistle to the Hebrews is all about. Some of the Christian Jews had already drawn back, with others seriously contemplating doing so. What does it mean to draw back?

It means to draw back from Faith in Christ, and more particularly, to draw back from Faith in what Christ did at the Cross on our behalf. This is what the Apostle is here talking about.

The Lord will never throw over any Believer because of sin. If He did, there wouldn't be any Believers left.

While sin will definitely cause the Believer all kinds of problems, and will definitely separate one from God, the Lord doesn't wash the Believer out because of sin. But let not the Reader think that sin is to be taken lightly. There is a terrible *"deceitfulness to sin"* which refers to deception. Sin also hardens the heart (Heb. 3:13). So, let not any Believer think he can look at sin with impunity, or use the Grace of God as a license for sin. The answer of the Holy Spirit to that through Paul is, *"God forbid!"* (Rom. 6:1-2).

But again I emphasize, if the Lord threw over every Christian who has sinned, there wouldn't be anyone left. Thank God we have a recourse for sin, and that is to take it to the Lord, where He cleanses us and washes us from the effects of sin (I Jn. 1:9). In fact, that is the intercessory Work of Christ, which He is carrying on at this very moment at the Throne of God before the Father (Heb. 7:25; 9:24).

The only thing that can permanently separate a Believer from the Lord is when the Believer quits believing, which means he no longer evidences Faith in Christ and what Christ did for him at the Cross. As stated, this is the *"drawing back"* of which Paul is here speaking. We get saved by trusting in what Christ did at the Cross, and if we lose our way, and God forbid that would happen, but if it did, it would be because of losing Faith in the great Sacrifice of Christ. Faith in that great work got us in, and faith no longer evidenced in that great work, will put us out.

Millions claim presently that if you're not in their Church, that you're not saved; consequently, for those who believe that, if one is in that particular Church, whatever it might

be, and they are put out of that Church, these same people equate such with that person then losing their soul. They have equated salvation with their Church, and so if a person is no longer in that Church, they equate them as being lost. Such is ridiculous! In fact, it is ridiculous beyond compare! It would be funny, if it wasn't so serious.

I'm ashamed to say such, but many in the Denomination with which I was formerly associated, actually believe such foolishness. Pure and simple, those who would believe such, at the same time means they are not exhibiting Faith in the great Sacrifice of Christ. That being the case, they aren't saved!

They may claim their Faith is in Christ; however, in reality it is in Christ plus their Church, which nullifies their Faith in Christ. The Holy Spirit will not accept such.

But to be frank, many Denominations believe this foolishness. While most of them did not begin this way, as little by little in their minds, they make their Church bigger and bigger, at the same time, Christ becomes less and less. That's what happened to the Denomination with which I was formerly associated. While there are still many Godly Preachers in that Denomination, and of course, Godly people as well, still, the trend sadly and regrettably is away from Christ toward other things. In other words, they are *"drawing back"* from Faith solely in Christ and Him Crucified. That is the great danger throughout the entirety of the Church, and we speak of all Denominations, and even independent groups, etc.

This means that if you, the Believer, have your Faith in anything other than the Finished Work of Christ, in some way, in some degree, you are *"drawing back,"* which if continued, even as the next Verse proclaims, can lead you *"to perdition."*

NO PLEASURE IN HIM

The phrase, *"My soul shall have no pleasure in him,"* is speaking of God. Even though this particular phrase is not a direct quotation from Habakkuk, still, that which is said in that particular Book makes it clear that God is not at all pleased with the one who draws back. Some have claimed that Paul is here speaking of himself, or else the writer, whomever he may have been. Such does not fit the Text.

The beginning of Verse 38 begins with a direct quotation from the Prophet Habakkuk, and the balance of the Verse falls into the same category.

It should go without saying, that God is grieved over such conduct on the part of any Believer. Considering the price that was paid for our Salvation, for one to come to Faith, and then draw back from Faith, presents a heartrending situation.

The Lord said through the Prophet Ezekiel, *"Have I any pleasure at all that the wicked should die? saith the Lord GOD: and not that he should return from his ways, and live?"* (Ezek. 18:23).

Through the same Prophet, the Lord also said, *"As I live, saith the Lord GOD, I have no pleasure in the death of the wicked; but that the wicked turn from his way and live"* (Ezek. 33:11).

(39) "BUT WE ARE NOT OF THEM WHO DRAW BACK UNTO PERDITION; BUT OF THEM THAT BELIEVE TO THE SAVING OF THE SOUL."

The structure is:

1. There must never be a thought in the mind of the Believer about drawing back.

2. However, we are plainly told here that it definitely is possible for a Believer to quit believing, and thereby be eternally lost.

3. Salvation of the soul is strictly by Faith, and that refers to Faith in what Christ did at the Cross, to which the Believer should ever look.

DRAWING BACK UNTO PERDITION

The phrase, *"But we are not of them who draw back unto perdition,"* refers to two things:

1. It is possible to lose Faith in Christ, and thereby lose one's soul.

2. There is no reason that any Believer should ever do such a thing. If faith is maintained in Christ and what He did for us at the Cross, there is no danger.

"Perdition" in the Greek is *"apoleia,"* and means *"spiritual ruin, destruction, eternal loss."* We are speaking here of the losing of one's soul, which Paul has already addressed in Verses 26-31.

In effect, Paul is saying, *"I'm a Jew, and I have suffered terrible persecution, but I'm not*

going to give up my faith in Christ because of that, and in fact, there has never even been a thought of doing such." But yet, some had definitely *"drawn back unto perdition."*

FAITH

The phrase, *"But of them that believe to the saving of the soul,"* refers to the fact that the key to all that we have in Christ is Faith, and more particularly, Faith in the Finished Work of Christ. This is the only thing that saves the soul, and the only thing that keeps the soul saved.

*"O Savior, as my eyes behold the
  wonders of Thy might untold,
"The heav'ns in glorious light arrayed,
  the vast creation Thou hast made,
"And yet to think Thou lovest me —
  my heart cries out, 'How can it be?'"*

*"As at the Cross I humbly bow and gaze
  upon Thy thorn-crowned brow,
"And view the precious bleeding form
  by cruel nails so bruised and torn,
"Knowing Thy suffering was for me,
  in grief I cry, 'How can it be?'"*

*"How can it be? How can it be? Was
  ever Grace so full and free!
"From heights of bliss to depths of woe
  in loving kindness Thou didst go,
"From sin and shame to rescue me —
  O Love Divine, how can it be?"*

CHAPTER 11

(1) "NOW FAITH IS THE SUBSTANCE OF THINGS HOPED FOR, THE EVIDENCE OF THINGS NOT SEEN."

The composite is:

1. Faith guarantees the substance.

2. The substance will ultimately materialize.

3. Even though we cannot see it now, except by Faith, our Faith guarantees the substance that will ultimately come.

FAITH IS THE SUBSTANCE

The phrase, *"Now faith is the substance,"* in essence says that Faith is the title deed.

"*Substance*" in the Greek is "*hypostasis,*" and refers to "*one's property or effects.*" The word was also used in the Roman world to refer to "*the whole body of documents bearing on the ownership of a person's property, deposited in the archives, and forming the evidence of ownership.*"

Moulton and Milligan in their "*Vocabulary of the Greek Testament*" say of these uses, "*These varied uses are at first sight somewhat perplexing, but in all the cases there is the same central idea of something that underlies visible conditions and guarantees a future possession.*" Thus, they translate "*Faith is the title deed of things hoped for.*"

The act of exercising true faith as one prays, or as one leans on the resources of God, is itself the title deed or evidence of the sure answer to our prayer or the unfailing source of the Divine supply. It is God's guarantee in advance that we already possess the things asked for.

They may still be in His Hands, awaiting the proper time for their delivery, but they are ours. In other words, they are "*substance.*"

If the answers to our prayers are not forthcoming at once, let us rest content with the title deed which God has given us, namely, a Holy Spirit energized act of faith. We may be absolutely certain that our God will honor this title deed at the right time (Wuest).

A DEFINITION OF FAITH

Even though Paul does not go into much detail here as it regards a definition of faith, still, what he in fact does say, sheds great light on this very important subject. The simple statement, "*Now faith is the substance,*" tells us volumes, even as we've already addressed.

And yet, everything that he has previously said in the preceding ten Chapters has actually been a definition of Faith within itself. He has held up the Cross in every way possible, directing our Faith to that Finished Work. In other words, true Faith, at least that which God will recognize, is always that which is Faith in "*Christ and Him Crucified.*"

Therefore, the true definition of Faith is that we simply believe. However, we are to have a proper object for our Faith, before God will recognize our "*believing.*" That proper object is "*Jesus Christ and Him Crucified.*"

NOTES

And now in the Eleventh Chapter, the Apostle proceeds to explain to the Christian Jews, and all others for that matter, what such faith will bring about. He has told us what faith is, what the object of our Faith must be, and now he tells us the results of our Faith.

THINGS HOPED FOR

The phrase, "*Of things hoped for,*" proclaims a declaration of the action of faith. It makes promises present and real and unseen things visible. This means, that these "*things hoped for*" are not mere figments of the imagination; their basis is "*the Word of God.*" If we keep this in mind, the words, still remaining general in their form, agree with all that has led up to them and with all that follows; in other words, every hope, at least that's generated by the Holy Spirit in the heart and life of the Believer, will be realized. If it pertains to this life, it will come in this life. And yet, some things which we now hope for, may not be realized in this life, and because they do not necessarily apply to this life. For instance, Abraham was promised the land of Canaan, but the Patriarch when he died, only owned the small burial plot where he and his family were laid to rest. But to be sure, it was possessed by his descendants, and in the coming Kingdom Age, Abraham will personally see the realization of this which God had promised.

We must always understand, that the Promises of God are always much larger than we at first think or realize. And to be sure, God always keeps His Promises.

It has been said that the phrase, "*Faith is the substance of things hoped for,*" refers to that which is without substance. But this difficulty is only apparent; for in regard to ourselves these objects of our hope do not yet exist, since they still belong to the future (Rom. 8:24-25). Nevertheless, if God has promised them, and whatever they might be, the Promises will come to pass.

The only true hope in the world is that of the Child of God. It is true because it is anchored in Faith, which is anchored in the Word, which is anchored in the great Sacrifice of Christ, which makes it all possible.

The hope that the world entertains, is an elusive hope based upon what men may do or may not do, or even on the wisp of chance, which in reality, is no hope at all. It is no more than a gamble, a throw of the dice so to speak! But the hope registered in the heart of the Child of God, is based upon the entirety of the Word of God, which gives it substance. Consequently, it is a hope which will definitely be realized, and without fail!

EVIDENCE

The phrase, *"The evidence of things not seen,"* refers to the fact, that our evidence is not based upon the senses, which yield uncertainty, but rather on the Word of God. There are realities for which we have no material evidence though they are not the less real for that. Faith enables us to know that they exist and, while we have no certainty apart from Faith, Faith does give us genuine certainty. To have Faith is to be sure of the things for which we hope. Faith is the basis, the substructure of all that the Christian life means, all for which the Christian hopes.

"Evidence" in the Greek is *"elegchos,"* which means *"a proof, that by which a thing is proved or tested."* Thayer in commenting on its use here defines it as follows: *"That by which invisible things are proved and we are convinced of their reality."* Actually, *"substance"* and *"evidence"* are very similar. But yet, *"evidence"* although included in *"substance,"* adds to the simple idea of assurance, a suggestion of influences operating to produce conviction which carry the force of demonstration. It goes back to what we have said about *"hope."* The hope of the Child of God, is not a mere wisp, as that of the world, but rather hope based on evidence, and that evidence is the Word of God, and our Faith in that Word.

(2) "FOR BY IT THE ELDERS OBTAINED A GOOD REPORT."

The structure is:

1. Faith is the foundation of everything which pertains to God.

2. The *"Elders"* refer to the Old Testament Patriarchs, Prophets, and Saints.

3. *"A good report"* refers to that which God says about them, and not man.

FAITH

The phrase, *"For by it,"* would have probably been better translated, *"For by Faith,"* because that's actually what it says.

To the Hebrew Christians reading this Epistle, and all others as well, the principles of Faith set forth in this Chapter would have a deep effect. They would be made to see that the great heroes of Faith, much honored by Jewish tradition, in reality had looked forward to the Coming of Christ, Whose Redemptive Work would make their Faith complete.

These Personalities of Faith had held fast their *"confidence, which has great recompense of reward"*; they fulfilled God's will, patiently waiting to receive the Promise. In fact, these renowned men and women of Faith were examples of cheerful courage in the face of adversity and examples of endurance that were strengthened by fierce trial. We would do well to consider their example.

THE ELDERS

The phrase, *"The elders,"* refers to a great list of faith-worthies, but by no means, includes all.

Incidentally, in this list given which we will study, no report is given of Adam and Eve — not a word of any repentance, faith, or holiness of life. Their spiritual and eternal fate are completely hidden, which lends much credence to the idea that they died lost.

Considering these great faith-worthies, we should contemplate the following:

Those who are growing faint and cowardly, and thinking of shrinking back, of returning to Judaism, let them consider all these heroes of Faith named in the Old Testament. If they desert, they do not desert *"to"* but *"from"* these men and these women and thereby place their names on that horrible list marked *"perdition"* (Heb. 10:39).

They, who maintain their faith, join this glorious list which the Holy Spirit gives us here in this Eleventh Chapter.

In this Book of Hebrews, the Holy Spirit desires to show us the power and potential there is in dynamic faith, and by that, we speak of Faith in Christ, and His great Sacrifice. To have Faith in God is to have Faith in Christ and His Finished Work. To have Faith in the Word is to have Faith in the Finished Work of Christ. They are all one and the same!

And yet, as we go through this dynamic Chapter, we will see various needs as it respected the individuals involved, and how

Faith met each and every need, irrespective as to what it was.

A LIFE WITHOUT FAITH

There is a great difference between a life that is empty and one that is full. It was toward the end of the law career of the atheist Clarence Darrow that he confessed: *"At the close of my life, I am not sure of how much or how little I have really accomplished, if anything, for the fellow beings of my day who live as my neighbors for a time and then are seen no more. I am reminded of what Simon is reported to have said when Jesus came to his boat in the early morning, 'Master, we have toiled all night, and taken nothing'."*

It is ironical, that Clarence Darrow would quote the Bible at this time in his life; the Bible which he professed not to believe!

One can only read this with a great sadness of heart. And yet, when we read the very opposite, and I speak of this Eleventh Chapter of Hebrews, we come away with a far different reaction.

A GOOD REPORT

The phrase, *"Obtained a good report,"* which refers to the only way that such can be obtained — we speak of Faith, and more particularly, Faith in God and His Word, which translates into *"Jesus Christ and Him Crucified."* As we go down through this long list, we will see that the Faith mentioned, is Faith in Christ.

If in fact, it is Faith and Faith alone which can guarantee a *"good report,"* then it also means at the same time, that nothing else before God will bring about these desired results. Good works will not do such, nor anything else one might contemplate. It is only Faith! And when we say *"Faith,"* let the Reader understand, that always and without exception, we are speaking of Faith in Christ and His great Sacrifice.

FAITH WHICH PRODUCES WORKS

While works will never produce Faith, Faith will definitely produce works.

In orthodox evangelical circles today, the popular conception of the nature of saving faith is tragically inadequate. *"By Grace, through Faith, plus nothing,"* has become the

watchword; however, that does not adequately state the case. Saving faith can never be *"plus nothing."* For saving faith cannot exist apart from repentance. Paul said:

"Testifying both to the Jews, and also to the Greeks, repentance toward God, and Faith toward our Lord Jesus Christ" (Acts 20:21).

Repentance is concerned, not only with the past, but even more with the present and the future. It involves not only sorrow for the sins of the past, but the submission of the soul and life to the Lordship of Christ for the present and the future. There is a sense in which we must believe in Christ, not only *"with all our heart,"* but with all our life as well.

James said, *"To be hearers of the Word, but not doers, is to deceive ourselves"* (James 1:22). He also said, *"Faith without works is as dead and worthless as the body without the spirit"* (James 2:14-16).

"Faith in Christ" which leaves the *"Believer"* free of any allegiance and devotion to Him is shear presumption. A *"plus nothing"* Faith avails nothing. Only obedient faith is saving faith — living, conquering faith that *"overcomes the world."*

GOD'S HONOR ROLL

Some have called this Eleventh Chapter *"God's Honor Roll."* It is indeed a wonderful record of the triumphs of faith on the part of imminent servants of God who lived in three different dispensations:

1. Abel, Enoch, and Noah, lived in the Dispensation of Conscience.

2. Abraham, Isaac, Jacob, and Joseph lived during the Dispensation of Promise.

3. Moses and all the others thereabout, lived during the Dispensation of Law.

All these were but preparatory periods leading on to the present glorious dispensation of the Grace of God. But in all these past ages we see that Faith was the controlling power that enabled men to walk with God and triumph over the corrupting influences of their times. It is important to remember that God has never had two ways of saving men. While the Revelation of His Grace has come gradually, and various rites and ceremonies have been linked with it at different times, these latter have had nothing to do with the regenerating or justifying of the individual. It has always been true that Faith in God's Word, whatever that Word may have been, which in some way has always pointed to Christ, has alone justified man before Him, and through that Word men have been saved in all ages, thus entering into His spiritual kingdom and recognizing His authority in a world at variance with that Divine Rule (Ironside).

(3) "THROUGH FAITH WE UNDERSTAND THAT THE WORLDS WERE FRAMED BY THE WORD OF GOD, SO THAT THINGS WHICH ARE SEEN WERE NOT MADE OF THINGS WHICH DO APPEAR."

The exegesis is:

1. We understand from this Verse that God functions from the principle of Faith.

2. It was through faith that God created the solar system. This is why Science cannot trace the creation back to its origin. There is an unseen force that does not submit itself to experimental science, and this is the object of faith.

3. As it regards God, His Faith created His Word; as it regards human beings, His Word creates Faith.

4. The visible worlds (the universe) were not created out of material in existence, for at the beginning there were no materials. Faith created it all, through the spoken Word of God.

THROUGH FAITH

The phrase, *"Through faith,"* proclaims this great principle as beginning with God. However, where the opposite of unbelief is prevalent in man, such is not possible with God, because unbelief is a product of disobedience to God. As best we can understand, God works from the principle of Faith which pronounces His Word, with the logical conclusion being the announcement of that Word. However, His Faith never produces idle words, but rather that which creates and constructs.

This Faith of which we speak, is so prevalent in God's creation, that the entirety of mankind, even fallen man, operates on this principle, whether he understands it or not. In fact, every Scientist has come by his discoveries strictly on the basis of faith. Every experiment has been entered into on the

basis of Faith. They may not understand that as such, but that's actually what it is. In fact, were there no faith, there would be no experimentation. The very nature of such demands Faith.

The societies of the world which function best, do so on the basis of faith. I speak of the so-called market economy, or the *"law of supply and demand,"* as it is called! In fact, there is enough Christianity in the United States, and certain other countries, which has imbued the very system with faith, which has made these countries the envy of the world.

To go to the other end of the spectrum, and we speak of Communism, we find a system which is completely unworkable, simply because it stifles all faith. And then there are many countries of the world that are controlled more or less by witchcraft, which of course nullifies faith.

Now let the Reader understand, that the faith which we here mention is not saving faith, but it is faith nevertheless. The only type of Faith that God will recognize as saving faith is that which is evidenced in Jesus Christ and His great Sacrifice.

CREATION

The phrase, *"We understand that the worlds were framed by the Word of God,"* refers to creation, along with everything that goes with creation.

"Understand" in the Greek is *"noeo,"* which means, *"to perceive with reflective intelligence."* It is distinguished from the mere physical act of seeing. It is the perception of the mind consequent upon seeing. It means that our knowledge of this fact is derived only from Faith, and not from our own reasoning. In the first place, how in the world can we properly reason worlds being brought into existence by the mere decree of God's Word? To understand such we would have to be God; consequently, we as creatures can only comprehend up to a certain level as it regards the Creator.

"Worlds" in the Greek is *"aion,"* and means *"the material universe, and the periods of time as administered by God."* In other words, we are speaking here of a well ordered creation.

The words *"were framed"* in the Greek are *"katartizo,"* which means *"to fit out or equip, so that person or thing thus equipped or fitted out, might carry out the purpose for which it was made."* It speaks of a wise adaptation of part to part and of the whole to its purpose, in this case, of the created universe and the periods of time, all brought into being by the Word of God (Wuest).

Expositors say: *"The Word of God is an invisible force which cannot be perceived merely by sense. The great power, and great it is, which lies at the source of all that is, does not itself come into observation; we perceive it only by faith which is 'the evidence of things not seen'."*

THE WORD OF GOD

"Word" as is used here in the Greek, is not the translation of *"logos"* as it usually is, and as is used in John 1:1, which is expressed there as a designation of the Son of God as the Word of God in the sense that He is in Himself all that Deity is — Deity expressing itself not in words as parts of speech, but in the Revelation of a Person. This Greek word that Paul here uses is *"hrema,"* which *"speaks of articulate utterance."* This word is never used as a designation of God the Son. It is the Word of God to which reference is made here, not the Son of God. God spoke the Word, and a universe sprang into existence (Wuest).

NOT MADE OF THINGS
WHICH DO APPEAR

The phrase, *"So that things which are seen were not made of things which do appear,"* takes us beyond comprehension. Once again, we come back to faith.

To which we have already alluded, when God began creation, He did not begin with the materials that we presently see. He began with nothing, thereby speaking into existence the things which do appear.

Men have speculated all through the centuries as to the origin of the universe, and have questioned whether matter is eternal, or whether it was directly created by God. By Revelation, we know that matter is not eternal, and in fact, was created by God. This means that faith alone gives apprehension of the Truth. By Faith we understand Genesis Chapter 1. It is only unbelief and willful rejection of the testimony of God that makes

men stumble at and pervert so wondrous an unfolding of the beginnings of the created heavens and Earth. Faith bows in subjection to the witness God has given and glorifies Him for such a marvelous unfolding of the Divine Wisdom.

The late F. W. Grant has aptly pointed out the incongruity of the position of a scientist like Charles Darwin, whose book, *The Origin of the Species*, was hailed by many as throwing a flood of light upon the method of creation; and yet in that very book, Darwin never touches the question of origins! The truth is, in the very nature of things, he could not do so, for no man who is not subject to the Holy Spirit knows anything whatever about the beginnings of the material universe, and creatures living in it. But to faith all is plain. The simplest Christian with his Bible before him would say, *"By faith we understand"* (Ironside).

The gist of all of this is, if this vast universe has been called into existence by the mere Word of God, and it definitely has, then that tells us there is nothing which we may not believe He has ample power to perform. In fact, this is the manner in which God answered Job.

JOB

When the Patriarch Job questioned God concerning the terrible plight in which he found himself, when God ultimately answered, He did so by pointing to His creation (Job, Chpts. 38-41).

In essence, the Lord was telling Job, that if He (God) could create the heavens and the Earth and all that therein is, then Job need not worry about his little problems. The Creator could handle that with ease!

Consequently, the Holy Spirit opens up the great portrayal of Faith, by pointing to the unlimited Power of God, which again tells us, that God Who can do such things as this, will have no difficulty honoring His Word to us. In other words, the Holy Spirit starts out from the highest possible standard. Thereafter, everything else as it regards His dealings with man, seem quite small by comparison. In fact, that within itself generates Faith, which it is meant to do!

(4) "BY FAITH ABEL OFFERED UNTO GOD A MORE EXCELLENT SACRIFICE

THAN CAIN, BY WHICH HE OBTAINED WITNESS THAT HE WAS RIGHTEOUS, GOD TESTIFYING OF HIS GIFTS: AND BY IT HE BEING DEAD YET SPEAKETH."

The composite is:

1. Understanding from the previous Verse that God operates by Faith, we now learn that man is to operate by faith as well.

2. The very beginning of the illustration of faith as it regards man, centers up on Faith in Christ and Him Crucified.

3. By this and this alone did Abel obtain witness that he was righteous.

4. God testified to the fact that He accepted the gift presented by Abel, which was the life of an innocent victim, a Lamb, expressed by the pouring out of its blood, which symbolized Christ Who was to come.

5. Abel himself testifies, and even though dead, continues to testify, that Salvation is through sacrificial blood, and is only through sacrificial blood.

BY FAITH

The phrase, *"By Faith,"* follows in the same train as the opening of Verse 3. That particular Verse proclaims Faith to be the manner of God, while Verse 4 proclaims faith to be the manner of man as well. In other words, God would deal with man on the principle of faith, and man would deal with God *"by Faith."* And this is where the great problem with humanity begins.

Man attempts to deal with God by works, by merit, by education, by the intellect, with money, and various other things; however, these other things always reach a deaf ear as it regards God. If man wants to deal with God, wants to address God, wants God to hear him, he must deal by and through Faith. However, there is a step two to the process.

Unfortunately, a great part of the Church attempts to deal with God by Faith without the correct object. In other words, people will claim that their Faith is in God, or in Christ, or in the Word of God, etc. While those things are certainly correct, they actually do not say very much within themselves. And as well, most Christians only have a vague idea of what it all means.

When it comes to the matter of believing, James said, *"Thou believest that there is*

NOTES

one God; thou doest well: the Devils also believe, and tremble" (James 2:19).

Therefore, such Faith as we have just mentioned, while correct as far as it goes, really doesn't go far enough. The Believer must understand and know the object in which he is to express faith. Actually, the next phrase gives us this information.

A MORE EXCELLENT SACRIFICE

The phrase, *"Abel offered unto God a more excellent sacrifice than Cain,"* immediately proclaims what the object of our Faith must be. It must be *"Jesus Christ and Him Crucified"* (I Cor. 2:2). In other words, to just say that one believes in God, or in God's Word, or even in Christ, within itself, as stated, doesn't say very much. Our Faith must be in Christ and His great Sacrifice. This is the manner in which God deals with man, and this is the manner in which man can approach God — by and through the Sacrifice of Christ, which Paul grandly highlights throughout the entirety of this Epistle to the Hebrews.

It is grandly significant that Paul chooses Abel as the first example of what Faith can do for the one who exercises it, and to be sure, Paul was told to use this example by the Holy Spirit. In the case of Abel, it was the matter of his personal Salvation which was in view, as was also the case with the recipients of the Letter to the Hebrews. If Abel's appropriation of Salvation was by means of Faith, and that the object of his faith was to be the Cross of Christ, for that's exactly what the Sacrifice represented, that would mean that all who follow must come in the same manner.

It also tells us, that the salvation of the soul, which of course is the spiritual condition of man, is that which is by far the most important. While all other things may carry a measure of significance, it is sin that has separated man from God, and it is only the Sacrifice of Christ which can address this situation.

Abel's sacrifice was more excellent than that of Cain's, his brother. And that which made it more excellent was not its quantity but its quality. Its quality inhered in the fact that it was the Offering which God had prescribed, a Blood Offering, which was to be symbolic of the coming Redeemer, Whom the Lord had already promised would come

(Gen. 3:15, 21). Incidentally, Abel *"brought of the firstlings of his flock and of the fat thereof."* Then the Scripture says, *"And the LORD had respect unto Abel and to his offering"* (Gen. 4:4).

WHY WAS ABEL'S SACRIFICE MORE EXCELLENT?

In Abel we have the basic truth that approach to God is on the ground of Sacrifice; and that the offering up of a living creature whose blood was designed of God to illustrate the sacrifice and death of His Own Blessed Son. That it was not any mere assumption on the part of Abel that led him to select a lamb of the flock for his offering, nor simply an arbitrary act of his will, is evident from the fact that we are told, *"By faith Abel offered to God a more excellent sacrifice than Cain."* Faith is taking God at His Word. Manifestly, therefore, we are to understand that God Himself had revealed the truth that approach to him must be by sacrifice. This revelation was impudently ignored by Cain, as has most of the world ever since.

In looking at the material of other writers as it regards why Abel's sacrifice was more excellent, most have ventured a number of reasons that really have no bearing on the subject.

The sacrifice which God had told the first family to offer was to be symbolic of His Son, the Lord Jesus Christ. That and that alone was why it was more excellent, and why God would accept only that, and up to this moment will accept only that.

Whatever else that Cain may have brought as an offering, which the Scripture says was *"the fruit of the ground,"* had no bearing on anything (Gen. 4:3). No doubt what he brought to God was beautiful, but it could not be accepted by God, and for two reasons:

1. First of all, this sacrifice was meant to address sin; therefore, a bloodless offering, and for many reasons, would not suffice. Man has been attempting to offer to God all type of offerings ever since, other than the correct one, as it pertains to sin. As God could not accept such then, God cannot accept such now!

2. The Offering which would be presented as it regards sin, had to be symbolic of the coming Redeemer, the Lord Jesus Christ. He

would give His Life on the Cross, pouring out His Life's Blood, all on our behalf, that all sin may be atoned. Consequently, the animal sacrifices which preceded Him, must be symbolic of Him, or else it could not be accepted by God. Due to the fact that Jesus has now come, and has died on the Cross on our behalf, no more animal sacrifices are necessary, His One Offering of Himself sufficing for all time. Irrespective, before the Cross or after the Cross, Faith always had to be in that great Sacrifice.

A SACRIFICE FOR SIN

In fact, the *"fruit of the ground"* which Cain brought as an offering, would later be accepted in Mosaic Law, but only as an Offering of Thanksgiving. In fact, it is perfectly proper to give any type of offering of this nature to God, which He will always accept; however, when it comes to an offering for sin, there is only one Sacrifice which God will accept, and that is the Sacrifice of His Son, the Lord Jesus Christ, of which the blood sacrifices before the Cross were symbolic. This is very important, and the Reader should properly understand what we are here saying:

This is the reason the Cross has always been so very, very important. It is there and there only that sin was addressed, atoned for, and done so by Christ giving Himself literally as an Offering for sin (Isa. 53:10). And why do I stress this so strongly?

Many in the modern Church, are attempting to address the problem of sin by other means. They are trying to do it with humanistic psychology, by particular works of penance, by punishment, etc. For instance:

In most of the Pentecostal Denominations, if one of their Preachers has a problem as it regards sin of some nature, he is required to do penance. The penance is two years without preaching, or some such period of time. He is required also to undergo several months, or even up to two years of psychological counseling. Plus he is required to move out of the town where he has lived and take up residence somewhere else, plus several other such like things.

To the carnal mind, all of these things would sound very good; in fact, the world would applaud this vigorously; however, all of this is *"the fruit of the ground,"* i.e., *"the efforts of one's own hands,"* which God cannot accept, and because these things do not at all address the problem. There is not a single thing in the Word of God as it regards such foolishness, and simply because such foolishness isn't Scriptural.

There is only one answer for sin, and that is the Sacrifice of Christ. Doing penance, or anything else that one could think of, will not address the problem, will not solve the problem, and in fact, will only tend to make the matter worse. As stated, God has only one solution for sin, and that is *"Jesus Christ and Him Crucified"* (I Cor. 2:2).

FAITH

The question is, do we have Faith in the Sacrifice of Christ? We do know that Abel had faith in that Sacrifice, and we do know that Cain did not have faith in that Sacrifice.

It's very easy to understand why the world will not express faith in the Sacrifice of Christ, but not so easy to understand why the Church, at least for the most part, follow suit. If the Church recommends anything else other than the Biblical manner of cleansing, which is faith in what Jesus did at the Cross, then we must come to the conclusion, that the Church simply lacks Faith in Christ and what He has done for us. I don't see how we can come to any other conclusion.

It is faith that is demanded, which we are clearly even blatantly told here in this Fourth Verse. However, and to look at the other side of the coin so-to-speak, it must be Faith registered in the Sacrifice of Christ, and that Sacrifice exclusively.

RIGHTEOUSNESS

The phrase, *"By which he obtained witness that he was righteous,"* proclaims the fact that Righteousness comes exclusively from Christ, and that it comes to us as Believers according to our Faith in this Finished Work of which we have been speaking.

Man has no righteousness, and man by his own machinations cannot get any righteousness. Righteousness can only come by and through Christ.

God has always had Righteousness, and in fact, God is Righteousness. However, this Righteousness could not be awarded to man,

by decree or fiat. In order for this Righteousness to be imparted to man, God would have to become man, would have to live a Perfect Life in obedience to the Law of God in every respect, and do so, not as God, but as a man filled with the Spirit. In so doing, He would then gain the Righteousness of the Law; however, this Righteousness of the Law could be obtained only by one keeping it perfectly, which Christ did! (Gal. 4:4-5).

However, there was another aspect of the Law, referred to as the *"curse of the Law"* (Gal. 3:13-14). This referred to its penalty which came upon all men who broke the Law, which all did! That curse had to be addressed, simply because it answered to the tremendous crime of man against God.

To answer this curse, in other words to take its penalty, Jesus Christ would have to go to the Cross and die — die for sins He didn't commit, which we in fact did commit, and which penalty we should have suffered. But on our behalf, He took the penalty which was death, thereby satisfying the curse, meaning that the Law no longer condemned us, at least for those of us who believe and trust Christ (Jn. 3:16; Eph. 2:8-9; Rev. 22:17).

When Christ atoned for all sin, which He did, whether it was past, present, or future, this destroyed the legal right of captivity that Satan held over man. Sin was that legal right, and with sin now atoned for, Satan had no more legal claim on man.

So, when Jesus died, He not only satisfied the claims of Heavenly Justice against man, but He also destroyed Satan's hold upon humanity, again, for those who believe (Jn. 3:16).

Jesus did all of this as our Substitute (Isa., Chpt. 53), and as our Representative Man (I Cor. 15:45-50). In other words, God allowed Him to take our place in order that He may do for us what we could not do for ourselves.

An exhibition on our part of simple Faith in Him and what He has done, imputes to us the Righteousness of Christ. In fact, this Righteousness can be obtained in no other manner. This is the way that Abel received His Righteousness, and every other human being since who has trusted Christ.

Of course, during the time of Abel, Christ had not yet come; however, God had instituted the Sacrificial system which would serve as a substitute until Christ could come, which it did. It was not Faith in that Sacrifice per se that brought righteousness to Abel, or anyone else for that matter, but rather Faith in Who the Sacrifice represented, which was Christ. And to be more particular, it was faith in What the Sacrifice represented, which was what Christ would do on the Cross.

Man's problem has ever been in trying to obtain righteousness in some other manner. Those other ways include everything from the proverbial *"A"* to *"Z."* But let it ever be known, that there is only one way that Righteousness can be obtained, and that is through Faith in Christ and what He did for us at the Cross. As we've stated over and over again, Jesus must never be thought of apart from the Cross.

THE TESTIMONY

The phrase, *"God testifying of his gifts,"* refers to the Sacrifice. If it is to be noticed, it is expressed in the plural, i.e., *"gifts."* It refers to the following:

Abel's Sacrifice was a lamb. Here was a lamb for one man; in Exodus Chapter 12, it was a lamb for a family; in Leviticus Chapter 16, it was a lamb for a nation — Israel; and in John 1:29, it was a lamb (Christ) for the whole world.

"Testifying" in the Greek is *"martureo,"* and means *"to be a witness, to give evidence, to bear record."*

There are some who believe from this statement, *"God testifying of his gifts,"* that God sent fire from Heaven and consumed the sacrifice, thereby testifying of His acceptance. Even though the Scripture is not clear on this particular subject regarding this instance, it is very probable that this is what happened. The Lord did do this on other occasions (Gen. 15:17; Lev. 9:24; Judg. 6:21; I Ki. 18:38; I Chron. 21:26; II Chron. 7:1).

HE THAT LIVES

The phrase, *"And by it he being dead yet speaketh,"* refers to the fact that even though his physical body died, Abel is now with the Lord. Jesus said so!

He said, *"I am the God of Abraham, and the God of Isaac, and the God of Jacob? God is not the God of the dead, but of the living"* (Mat. 22:32).

Jesus was saying that even though the physical bodies of these three Patriarchs had died, their souls and spirits were alive, and in fact alive unto God. If they are, then all who trusted the Lord before the Cross fall into the same category, including Abel.

Though Abel is dead, yet *"by it* (the Sacrifice)*"* he yet speaks, telling to all who live after, that Salvation is through Sacrificial Blood. In 12:24, the statement is made that Jesus' Blood speaks better things than the blood of the sacrifice offered by Abel. As well, it is not Abel's own blood which is in view here, but the blood of the offering Abel presented to God.

This is shown by the historical background and analysis of the Epistle, the argument of which is that *"The New Testament in Jesus' Blood is superior to and takes the place of the First Testament in animal blood."*

The blood of Abel's offering spoke symbolically of a Sacrifice for sin that God would one day offer. But Jesus' Blood is the actual sacrifice, and speaks of the Salvation which He procured for us on the Cross. It was the blood offering that Abel presented to God, which represented Christ, through which he was declared righteous. This is in accord with Pauline doctrine where the great Apostle speaks of *"being now justified by His Blood"* (Rom. 5:9).

CAIN

Cain followed his reason, as has most of the world, and ignored Revelation. He argued that his own good works as manifested by the produce which he had grown, would be sufficient. In other words, he was denying his need for a Savior. He didn't deny God, rather bringing Him an offering, which God wouldn't accept, and because the main problem was that he denied his own need. That was the problem, it's been the problem all the way through the many centuries, and it is the problem now.

Man argues that he doesn't need a Redeemer, or if he does need one, he can serve as his own Redeemer, which in effect, is what Cain was doing.

THREE PATTERN MEN

Abel, Enoch, and Noah were three pattern men selected by the Holy Spirit from the Dispensation of Conscience which extended from the expulsion of our first parents from Eden to the destruction of *"the world that then was,"* by the flood.

Eliphaz, in the Book of Job, directs attention to *"the way which wicked men of old have taken, whose foundation was overthrown with a flood: which said unto God, 'depart from us'."*

Here, on the other hand, we are asked to contemplate three men who found their delight in God, and glorified Him by faith in a day when corruption and violence were rapidly filling the Earth (Ironside).

(5) "BY FAITH ENOCH WAS TRANSLATED THAT HE SHOULD NOT SEE DEATH; AND WAS NOT FOUND, BECAUSE GOD HAD TRANSLATED HIM: FOR BEFORE HIS TRANSLATION HE HAD THIS TESTIMONY, THAT HE PLEASED GOD."

The composition is:

1. Enoch was transferred from Earth to Heaven without seeing death.

2. After he was translated, a thorough search was made for him, but of course, he was not to be found. As well, from the Text, we know that the population who lived near him knew that it was God Who had translated him.

3. He had a testimony that pleased God, and in the next Verse we are told what that testimony was.

ENOCH

The phrase, *"By faith Enoch was translated that he should not see death,"* refers to God transferring Enoch to Heaven in his physical body while he was yet alive. He departed this earthly scene without dying. In fact, he has lived in Heaven already for some 5,300 years. He will come back and die as one of the two witnesses (Rev. 11:3-11).

There is an indication in Genesis 5:21-24, that Enoch gave his heart to God at 65 years of age. After that he walked with the Lord for 300 years, and then was translated. This means that he was translated when he was 365 years old.

He was the Father of Methuselah who lived longer than any other human being. Methuselah was 969 years old when he died (Gen. 5:27).

In Jewish apocalyptic thought, Enoch was a very popular figure, and several books are ascribed to him. But in the New Testament he figures only in Luke 3:37 and Jude 14, along with this Eleventh Chapter of Hebrews. And yet, in Jude 14, we are told that the Lord spoke extensively through Enoch, with him even then prophesying of the Second Coming.

WAS NOT FOUND

The phrase, *"And was not found, because God had translated him,"* refers to his translation being well known. The idea is, his translation was evidently witnessed by others, but when revealed was met by unbelief. After a search was made, and in fact, an exhaustive search, without him of course being found, those in the area where he had lived, now agreed that in fact, he had been translated by God. In fact, before the flood, a period of about 1,600 years from the time of creation, only three men are recorded in the Word of God as in fact, living for God. Those three were Abel, Enoch, and Noah. To be sure, there may very well have been others, perhaps many others, but the indication is that there wasn't much faith in the Earth at that time. The Scripture plainly says of that period, *"And God saw that the wickedness of man was great in the Earth and that every imagination of the thoughts of his heart was only evil continually"* (Gen. 6:5). This makes the faith of these three particular individuals all the more remarkable!

HIS TESTIMONY

The phrase, *"For before his translation he had this testimony, that he pleased God,"* is akin to Genesis 5:22, where it says that he *"walked with God."* And I might quickly add, he did this for 300 years, which means that he kept faith all of this time, despite the wickedness all around him. It appears that he spent his life in publicly reproving a sinful generation, and in warning them of the approaching judgment (Jude vs. 14-15).

The wickedness that engulfed the Earth of that day and ultimately led to its universal deluge seems to have been ripe at the time of Enoch. Incidentally, he was the great-grandfather of Noah.

Whatever the reasons that God took him that he should not see death, one of those reasons most likely was that those around him would have ultimately murdered him, were it not for his translation. The only other occurrence of a translation was that of Elijah. However, their translations, which simply means to be moved from one place to another, in this case from Earth to Heaven, prefigures the coming Resurrection, when all Saints will be Resurrected, changed, and then translated (I Thess. 4:13-18).

Incidentally, there is no hint in the Text that Enoch knew this would happen, until the actual moment of its occurrence.

(6) "BUT WITHOUT FAITH IT IS IMPOSSIBLE TO PLEASE HIM: FOR HE THAT COMETH TO GOD MUST BELIEVE THAT HE IS, AND THAT HE IS A REWARDER OF THEM THAT DILIGENTLY SEEK HIM."

The structure is:

1. The only thing that pleases God is faith.

2. It must be Faith in Christ and His Sacrifice.

3. God is a rewarder of those who have faith, and who diligently seek Him.

PLEASING GOD

The phrase, *"But without faith it is impossible to please Him,"* tells us what Enoch's testimony actually was. It was faith in God, but it was more than just a generalized faith.

We know from Jude Verse 14, that the Lord had given Enoch a Revelation of coming events, all the way to the Second Coming of the Lord. This Revelation would have made no sense at all, if the Lord had not as well informed him of the First Coming of Christ, which of course would have included the Cross. The Lord had shown him the Second Coming *"with ten thousands of His Saints."* There could be no Saints without the Cross. So the Faith which Enoch had, had to have centered up on the Cross. Of course, when I use the word *"Cross,"* it is to be understood that Enoch, or no one for that matter before Christ, would have understood anything concerning the wooden beam we refer to as a *"Cross"*; consequently, when we use such a term as it refers to the time before Christ, we are always using it in a generic sense, referring to the Sacrifice of Christ.

INSTRUCTION

Surely we as Believers should understand that these examples are given for our instruction. We learn from God's dealings with Enoch, that the only thing that really pleases Him is Faith. We must not forget that. And of course, when we say Faith, as always, we're speaking of Faith in Christ, and more particularly, the Finished Work of Christ. If we want to please God, and surely as a Believer we do, then our concentration should be on this all important aspect of our relationship.

I've been asked several times as to what is the proper definition for *"victory"*? I have given the answer several times that the definition is *"walking after the Spirit"* with the understanding of course, that the Spirit of God will always lead us to the Cross; however, to be more specific, I think one could say that victory is simply keeping our Faith in the Cross of Christ, and not allowing it to be moved (Rom. 8:1-2).

Just this morning in prayer meeting I was asked the question as it relates to this, *"What status are we in, if during the course of our faith, there is a failure?"* I believe my answer is correct.

As a Believer, our victory doesn't move up and down, providing we keep our Faith in the Cross of Christ. The only way that one can lose victory is to shift one's faith from the Cross to something else. That is the loss of victory, and will lead to all type of problems.

While we're certainly not condoning failure of any nature, and to be sure, failing the Lord in any capacity hurts; however, we must remember that our victory is totally and completely in Christ, and not at all in ourselves. As long as our Faith remains in Him, and what He has done for us, our lives are constant victory.

This and this alone, faith in the sacrifice of Christ, is what pleases God!

BELIEVING GOD

The phrase, *"For he that cometh to God must believe that He is,"* places Faith as the foundation and principle of the manner in which God deals with the human race. The Truth is, *"believing"* is the definition of Faith. It is what Faith does!

Paul here lays down the gauntlet with the greatest of emphasis that faith is absolutely necessary. He does not say simply that without faith it is difficult to please God; he says that without faith it is *"impossible"* to please Him! There is no substitute for faith.

Though Christ has provided the means of access to God, which He did by the Sacrificial Offering of Himself on the Cross, still, the choice to enter is ours. Paul here places responsibility upon the Believer; if we want to please God, we must have faith.

This means that we will take God at His Word and act upon it. If He says we may draw near, and He definitely does, then we must believe and do it. Faith is believing what God says, simply and solely because He said it. In order to receive from God, several things are here said:

1. We must come to the Lord with our problems; we must come with our needs; above all we must come to Him in order to have fellowship with Him; we must come to Him in order to praise Him and to express our gratitude to Him, which should make up a great part of our audience in His Presence.

2. We must believe Him, that is, we must have faith in Him.

3. We must believe that He is, which is far more than just merely believing in His existence. I'll define it momentarily!

4. We must believe that He is a rewarder of them who come to Him.

5. We must diligently seek Him.

COME TO GOD

The privilege of being able to take our needs to the Lord, to obtain His leading and guidance, and above all to have fellowship and communion with Him, is the greatest blessing and privilege that any human being could ever have. To think of the possibility of being able to go to someone Who is *"all-powerful," "all-knowing,"* and *"all-present,"* opens up doors of possibilities beyond comprehension. So why is it, that many if not most Christians do not take advantage of this tremendous opportunity?

There are two reasons for that, *"unbelief,"* and *"sin."* We'll take the latter first.

The very moment we come into the Presence of God, which every Believer has the

privilege to do constantly, the Holy Spirit and without fail, if there is sin in our lives, will begin to deal with us about that sin. And to be frank, it's impossible to proceed any farther with God, until the sin is handled. To be sure, it can be handled very quickly and very easily (I Jn. 1:9), but the problem with many Christians is, they really don't want to cease and desist as it regards some particular pet sin within their lives. That's why the Holy Spirit through the Apostle said, *"I beseech you therefore, Brethren, by the mercies of God, that you present your bodies a living sacrifice, holy, acceptable unto God, which is your reasonable service.*

"And be not conformed to this world: but be ye transformed by the renewing of your mind, that ye may prove what is that good, and acceptable, and perfect Will of God" (Rom. 12:1-2).

And then many Christians simply do not believe that God hears and answers prayer. I think one of the reasons for that is because of the religious climate in which we presently find ourselves:

The Church as a whole in the last several decades has been greatly swayed, and in the wrong way I might quickly add, by the erroneous doctrine of *"Word of Faith,"* or whatever type of appellative one would like to apply. In other words, the Church has had more teaching on faith in the last half-century than possibly the balance of its existence all put together; however, almost all of this teaching has been wrong, i.e., *"unscriptural!"*

In the first place, faith itself has been the object instead of the Cross being the object, which makes it little different than the Eastern mind cult religions. As we've said over and over again, faith within itself is not really the problem, it's the object of Faith which is the problem. Everyone has faith, but only a few have it in the Cross, where all Faith must reside, or else it's faith that God will not recognize. The modern faith teaching excludes the Cross altogether, with many in this false doctrine, even repudiating the Cross, referring to it as the greatest defeat in human history, etc.

In this false teaching, and false it is, we have not been taught prayer, but rather a *"proper confession."* In other words, *"confession"* is, they say, the trigger that energizes Faith; consequently, adherents to this doctrine are taught to simply confess things over and over again, those things they want and desire. In fact, prayer is looked at somewhat askance in these circles, and because, according to this teaching, prayer is an admittance that something is amiss, and nothing can ever be amiss in these *"super people,"* who have this *"super faith."*

Of course, all of this teaching, while it might sound good to the carnal ear, has no Scriptural support whatsoever.

Paul said, *"When I am weak, then am I strong,"* which blows to pieces their hypothesis (II Cor. 12:10). What did the Apostle mean by this?

Our problem is, and it's just as acute with Believers as it is with unbelievers, is our own supposed strength. Irrespective of all the so-called super faith, within ourselves we are no match for the Devil, cannot bring about the needed things within our hearts and lives, in other words, we simply cannot live the life we ought to live within our own power and strength. It doesn't matter how strong we think we are, the end result of that effort is going to be the same — failure.

When we finally come to the place that we realize we actually are *"weak,"* which means that we have to trust God completely, allowing the Holy Spirit to do for us what Alone He can do, then we've found real strength. That's what the Apostle means! (II Cor. 12:7-10).

No! Prayer is not an admittance that something is wrong, but rather that something is needed, and it is only God Who can meet this need. So we must throw aside all of this foolish teaching we've heard in the last half-century, and avail ourselves of the glorious opportunity to be able to *"come to God."*

MUST BELIEVE

As I've already stated, but because it's so important I'll say it again, *"believing"* is the definition of Faith. It's what Faith does.

For Faith to be what it ought to be, and as we've already stated, and because it's so very, very important, we'll keep saying it, the Cross must always be the object of one's Faith. This simply means that we understand that all

NOTES

Salvation, all Blessings, all prosperity, all healing, all the work of the Holy Spirit, Who is really the One Who makes all of these things possible, are all done, and without exception, through what Jesus did at the Cross on our behalf. If we don't believe that, then we're not believing properly, and God cannot really help us (Rom. 6:3-5, 11, 14).

As we've already stated, for some ten Chapters in this Epistle to the Hebrews, Paul has opened up to us the object of our Faith, which is the Cross of Christ. He has addressed this great factor in every way possible. He took us into the Holy of Holies with the High Priest under the old Levitical order, and then took us again into the Holy of Holies with our Great High Priest, the Lord Jesus Christ, showing how superior the work of Christ is in His great Sacrifice, to the Levitical order of old. Therefore, as he deals now with Faith, which is the ingredient of the foundation of our walk with the Lord, He means for us to always have the Cross as the object of our Faith. He has shown us the object, now he shows us the way.

What I've just told you is one of the greatest things that you as a Christian can ever hear. But the great question looms large, *"Do you believe what I've just said?"*

Our Faith in God is never to be something nebulous. In fact, the world has that kind of faith. Even the Devil has that kind of faith (James 2:19).

The idea is, our Faith must be in Christ, and more particularly, must be in His Finished Work, i.e., *"the Cross."*

HE IS

Most have limited this short statement to the bare bones idea of simply believing that God exists. That's not what it says!

"He is" is active. In other words, it refers to God as doing things. In other words, He is the Creator; He is the answerer of prayer; He is the worker of miracles; He is the healer of the sick; He is the leader, teacher, and guide; He is our all in all!

This is the same thing that God answered Moses, when the great Law-Giver to be asked the question, *"When I come unto the Children of Israel, and shall say unto them, The God of your fathers hath sent me unto you;*

and they shall say to me, What is His name? what shall I say unto them?

"And God said unto Moses, I AM THAT I AM" (Ex. 3:13-14).

We must believe that God is whatever it is that we need Him to be, and what might that be?

First of all, front and center, we need a Savior. He is that! After that, if we need a financier, He is that! If we need a teacher, He is that! If we need an engineer, He is that! If we need a healer, He is that! I really doesn't matter what we need, He is that and more.

REWARDER

The phrase, *"And that He is a rewarder,"* proclaims the fact that He will do whatever it is that we need, providing that it's in His Will.

"Rewarder" in the Greek is *"misthapodoaia,"* and means *"a remunerator, to perform, recompense, render, requite, restore, yield."* In other words, God will definitely do good things for the Believer. Do you believe that?

Paul had already told the Hebrews, *"For God is not unrighteous to forget your work and labor of love, which you have showed toward His Name"* (Heb. 6:10).

What we are speaking of here is the entirety of a mindset which looks to God for everything. We want Him to lead us and guide us, to provide for us, and to ever draw us closer to Him, and all of this He will gladly do, for this is what He desires to do. In other words, when a person comes to Christ, they come into the economy of God (Lk. 12:21-31). And to be sure, this is the greatest life there is. To put it all together, He has promised us that if we would *"Seek first the Kingdom of God, and His Righteousness, that all of these things would be added unto us"* (Mat. 6:33; Lk. 12:31).

DILIGENTLY SEEK

The phrase, *"That diligently seek Him,"* is literally *"seek Him out."* Vincent says: *"God's beneficent will and attitude toward the seeker are not always apparent at the first approach. In such cases our faith must not flag, especially in the face of delay, believing that diligent seeking will ultimately find its reward."*

NOTES

This is very dear to me personally. At a crisis time in this Ministry, the Lord gave me a Promise that I've held onto, and which characterizes this of which Paul has said to the letter. It pertains to that which I refer to as the *"parable of the three loaves."* It's found in Luke 11:5-13.

Jesus told the story of a man who went to a friend at midnight asking him to *"lend me three loaves."*

He went on to explain that a friend (another friend) on his own journey had come to him, and he had no food to set before him; consequently, he was attempting to borrow something which he needed.

The answer was, *"Trouble me not: the door is now shut, and my children are with me in bed; I cannot rise and give thee."* Incidentally, Jesus said it was at midnight when all of this was taking place (Lk. 11:7).

Jesus then went on to say, that even though the man would not get out of bed and give him the loaves strictly on the basis of their friendship, because of the man's continued asking, in other words, continuing knocking on the door, he ultimately arose and *"gave him as many as he needed"* (Lk. 11:8).

Our Lord then went on to say, *"Ask, and it shall be given you; seek, and you shall find; knock, and it shall be opened unto you."*

He then went on to emphasize that if we *"ask for bread, He wouldn't give us a stone,"* etc.

And finally, *"If you then, being evil, know how to give good gifts unto your children: how much more shall your Heavenly Father give the Holy Spirit to them who ask Him?"* (Lk. 11:9-13). This rhema Word was given to me in January of 1992.

For four and one half years I held onto this Promise, which was a great strength to me. To be sure, at times I would grow very discouraged, but every time, the Holy Spirit would encourage me with this which the Lord had given unto me. I was to keep asking, keep seeking, and keep knocking.

At the end of that period of time, which was sometime in 1996, the Lord began to open that door. First of all, He gave me the Revelation of the Cross, or I should say, that He began to give me the Revelation of the Cross, because it continues unto this hour. He then began to enlarge the Telecast, plus give me a very unique Revelation as it regards Radio, which we immediately began to institute.

I have diligently sought Him, I do diligently seek Him, and I shall continue to diligently seek Him! To be sure, I am believing Him for the greatest harvest of souls that I've ever known, which will necessitate a Moving and Operation of the Holy Spirit that one might say is unparalleled. But I believe that God is going to do these great and mighty things, and because He has always done great and mighty things, and because He has done them for me as well.

(7) "BY FAITH NOAH, BEING WARNED OF GOD OF THINGS NOT SEEN AS YET, MOVED WITH FEAR, PREPARED AN ARK TO THE SAVING OF HIS HOUSE; BY THE WHICH HE CONDEMNED THE WORLD, AND BECAME HEIR OF THE RIGHTEOUS-NESS WHICH IS BY FAITH."

The diagram is:

1. God revealed to Noah that He was going to send a flood upon the Earth.

2. Upon receiving this Revelation, Noah was *"moved with fear,"* which in this case, means *"to reverence, to stand in awe of."*

3. He obeyed the Lord in preparing an Ark, which saved his house.

4. His faith served as a condemnation to an unbelieving world.

5. In his believing God, he obtained righteousness which is by faith, which is very similar to that done by Abraham.

THE REVELATION

The phrase, *"By faith Noah, being warned of God of things not seen as yet,"* means that God told Noah that He was going to send a flood upon the Earth, a flood incidentally of such proportions as the world had never seen before, and in fact would never see again, with the conclusion being that Noah believed God. He believed Him in the face of something that was so absolutely preposterous as to defy description. He believed it despite the fact, that no one else believed him, even though he preached to them and warned them.

The Bible says that God spoke to Noah. Whether it was in an audible voice or through a vision, we aren't told; nevertheless, ever how the manner that God addressed Himself to

NOTES

this man, it was so powerful that he had absolutely no doubt as to what was being said. And as stated, he believed God (Gen. 6:6-22).

FEAR

The phrase, *"Moved with fear,"* is not here the normal word for fear, which refers to acting under the influence of fright. The Greek word is *"eulabeomai,"* which means, *"to act cautiously, circumspectly, to reverence, to stand in awe of."* It means that Noah acted with *"pious care, a reverent circumspection,"* that he do exactly what the Lord had told him to do. In other words, he was careful to obey the Lord to the letter.

PREPARATION

The phrase, *"Prepared an Ark to the saving of his house,"* refers to him doing exactly what God told him to do. By acting thus upon the Word of the Lord, he condemned the world and became heir of the Righteousness which is according to faith. The very building of the Ark was in itself a sermon to the antediluvians. Every tap of Noah's hammer was a part of his preaching of Righteousness to that generation. It declared him to be a man of faith, and it manifested their utter unbelief.

It might be said that the human race owes its existence to the fact that one man was *"moved with fear."* It is sad but true, that fear as a factor in Salvation is decried at the present day, with the claim that only love is the True Gospel; however, this Passage tells us that fear can definitely be a factor in one's Salvation.

CONDEMNATION OF THE WORLD

The phrase, *"By the which he condemned the world,"* refers to that which always is the case when true Faith is registered in the Word of God; consequently, anger is generally the response.

This doesn't mean that Noah condemned the unredeemed personally, as many Preachers think, but rather, that the very fact of his ministry condemned the world, which such ministry always does.

The world holds its own self-righteousness in high regard; consequently, whenever the Righteousness of Christ is held up as the answer and the only answer, which automatically states that the self-righteous direction of the world is wrong, it arouses hostility. And to be sure, it is the same in the Church. Whenever the Preacher fully preaches Christ, and that the Righteousness of Christ is the only Righteousness which will be accepted by God, and that it is obtained only through Faith in what Christ did at the Cross, this Message is not accepted by most of the Church. It as well, arouses hostility. Again I state, it's not that the Preacher of Righteousness personally condemns individuals, but that the Righteousness of Christ clashes with self-righteousness.

When the hostility responds, it generally responds with animosity toward the Messenger, as well as the Message.

RIGHTEOUSNESS WHICH IS BY FAITH

The phrase, *"And became heir of the Righteousness which is by Faith,"* proclaims the only manner in which Righteousness can be obtained. Righteousness is always by Faith, and more specifically, it refers to Faith in the great Sacrifice of Christ. Of course, those before the Cross, more or less, would have had a dim view of this coming event, but according to the fact that God had instituted the sacrificial system, which He definitely did from the very beginning, they knew that it represented a coming Redeemer Who would give His life for humanity. Exactly how it was to be done, of that they would have had no knowledge. But that it would be done, this they knew!

There has never been any way for anyone to be saved, except by and through Faith in Christ, which pertains to Faith in His great Sacrifice.

(8) "BY FAITH ABRAHAM, WHEN HE WAS CALLED TO GO OUT INTO A PLACE WHICH HE SHOULD AFTER RECEIVE FOR AN INHERITANCE, OBEYED; AND HE WENT OUT, NOT KNOWING WHITHER HE WENT."

The structure is:

1. Abraham was called by God to do something which would have worldwide and eternal repercussions.

2. He obeyed, because he had Faith in what God had said.

3. He obeyed, even though he didn't really understand, at least at the time, what God was saying.

NOTES

ABRAHAM

The phrase, *"By Faith Abraham,"* proclaims the manner in which this great man began his adventure with the Lord. Too many and too often, begin their journey by *"sight"* instead of faith. They don't last long!

Faith as it is here given, proclaims a settled trust in the Lord, exhibited by Abraham. This is remarkable, especially when we understand that this man's history was that of idol worship. In other words, he had no history of God, as did Abel, Enoch, or Noah. Joshua says of Abraham, that he was an idolater when Grace found him (Josh. 24:2-3).

Of the manner in which God revealed Himself to Abraham, we aren't told. Josephus, the Jewish historian, says that after God had revealed Himself to the Patriarch, that Abraham was the first to declare boldly that God, the Creator of the universe, is One, and that the sun, moon, and stars had no inherent power of their own. Because of these statements, Josephus said, the Chaldeans rose against him, and so he then left to go to Canaan with God's help.

OBEDIENCE

The phrase, *"When he was called to go out into a place which he should after receive for an inheritance, obeyed,"* indicates Abraham's immediate obedience to God's Call. In line with this, Paul gives more space to Abraham than to any other individual on his list. He sees Abraham as an excellent example of what he has in mind, for Paul does not see Faith as making a good guess based on the best human estimate of the possibilities. Abraham's faith accepted God's Promises and acted on them even though there was nothing to indicate that they would be fulfilled.

Even though an *"inheritance"* is here mentioned, which of course includes the entirety of the land of Canaan, there is no record that the Lord had furnished this information to the Patriarch at the time of his call. *"He was called to go out,"* but regarding all the things that eventually happened, of that he then had no knowledge it seems; consequently, the more we learn of this man, the more we realize how great his Faith in God actually was.

NOT KNOWING

The phrase, *"And he went out, not knowing whither he went,"* refers to the fact that although he knew where God had told him to go, which was the land of Canaan, he knew absolutely nothing about the land, what type of people were there, or what awaited him in any capacity. In fact, this is the manner in which God usually works.

He generally just gives us enough information for the next step, with us having to trust Him for the rest. This builds faith and creates dependence; however, all of this is for our good, and for our good alone. Most of the time, we only have enough faith for the next step, and not at all for the entirety of this which the Lord is doing. To be frank, our faith even for the immediate step most of the time, falls short, with the Lord having to supply even that limited amount.

The Reader must understand, that God has far larger plans for us than we could ever dare begin to realize. That which the Lord had for Abraham was so staggering, so overwhelming, so absolutely phenomenal, that it literally beggars description. But of course, Abraham didn't know that then, and in fact, all the days of his life he only saw and knew in part.

While that which the Lord has for us, may not be nearly as far-reaching as that of Abraham, in one sense of the word it actually is. God has no small plans, only those which are outsized. And to be sure, He definitely has a distinct plan for every single Believer, irrespective as to whom that Believer might be. Of that we can be certain!

It's our business to make certain that the totality of God's Plan for our lives is realized. That, even as this great Eleventh Chapter of Hebrews proclaims, is all done by Faith. We must believe God.

GOD'S PLANS

God's plans may be delayed, but they are never stopped. Let the Reader understand that. And to be sure, the delays are never caused by Him, but always by us. And always, our problem is Faith, and more particularly, misplaced faith.

If the Believer can keep his eyes on *"Jesus Christ and Him Crucified,"* the Holy Spirit,

Who is the secret to all of this anyway, will then carry out in our lives what needs to be done. That's the combination:

The Cross, our Faith in the Cross, and the work of the Holy Spirit Who always works within the parameters of the Cross. That's why Paul said, *"But God forbid that I should glory, save in the Cross of our Lord Jesus Christ, by Whom the world is crucified unto me, and I unto the world"* (Gal. 6:14).

Concerning Abraham, Jesus said to the Jews, *"Your father Abraham rejoiced to see My day, and he saw it, and was glad"* (Jn. 8:56).

How did Abraham see Jesus' day? He saw it by faith. To be frank, the entirety of the Call of God upon Abraham's life, was in regard to the coming of the Lord Jesus Christ, Who would redeem fallen mankind. In fact, that was the purpose of every single Prophet and Priest of Old Testament times, to point to the coming Christ, as now the purpose of every Believer is to point to the Christ Who has already come. That and that alone is our mission!

(9) "BY FAITH HE SOJOURNED IN THE LAND OF PROMISE, AS IN A STRANGE COUNTRY, DWELLING IN TABERNACLES WITH ISAAC AND JACOB, THE HEIRS WITH HIM OF THE SAME PROMISE:"

The structure is:

1. Abraham went into the land where God told him to go and dwelt there.

2. It was *"the land of the Promise,"* speaking of a particular promise, the one in Genesis 12:7 and 13:15.

3. Abraham, Isaac, and Jacob are mentioned because they cover the entire period of the sojourn in Canaan.

THE LAND OF PROMISE

The phrase, *"By faith he sojourned in the Land of Promise,"* actually reads in the Greek text *"the land of the Promise,"* speaking of a particular Promise.

By the Holy Spirit using the words *"the Promise,"* while He was definitely speaking of the Land of Canaan per se, more than all, it had reference to what all of this meant. I speak of the coming Redeemer.

The nation of Israel would be raised up out of the loins of Abraham and the womb of Sarah, for the express purpose of doing three things:

1. To give the world the Word of God.

2. To serve as the womb of the Messiah, so to speak!

3. To evangelize the world.

They succeeded in the first two, but with great difficulty. Rejecting the very One Whom they were raised up to bring into the world, they failed miserably regarding the third purpose; however, in the coming Kingdom Age, when they finally accept the One Whom they have rejected, namely the Lord Jesus Christ, they will then carry out this third purpose of World Evangelism.

How so much the phrase *"the Land of the Promise,"* holds for the entirety of the human race. Thank God, this *"Promise"* extended all the way to my family. When God first gave the Promise to Abraham, He told him, *"In thee shall all families of the Earth be blessed"* (Gen. 12:3). Even though billions of families have rejected that Gospel call, thank God that my family got in.

We were nothing, the poorest of the poor, without God and without hope, but Oh happy day! Oh happy day! The day that God the Holy Spirit brought the Gospel to our little town, our world would never be the same again. Through Jesus Christ, the Spirit of God would bring us out of darkness into light.

At this very moment, we are laboring with all that is within us to install Radio Stations in every single city, town, and village in the United States. Even though it costs us just as much money to put a Station into a small town of one thousand people, as it does a major city, still, I believe the Lord has instructed us to not ignore the small places. He reminds me, that my family as well lived in a little tiny town in Northeast Louisiana, a place of no importance, except the Lord thought it important enough that this great and glorious Gospel would be brought to the confines of that small place. As stated, my entire family came to Christ and by the Grace of God, the Lord has helped us to bring untold thousands of souls to a saving knowledge of Jesus Christ.

So, even though it costs just as much money to install a Radio Station in a small town as it does a major city, still, the Lord has instructed me that these *"small places"* must not be forgotten. He has souls there, eternal souls, more precious than words could ever

begin to describe. Because you see, that *"Promise"* which God gave to Abraham so long, long ago, it reached out some 4,000 years into the future and touched my family, and to be sure, that *"Promise"* is still reaching out, and in fact, it will ever do so, and because it is *"The Promise of God,"* which in fact is Jesus Christ, and more particularly, *"Jesus Christ and Him Crucified"* (I Cor. 2:2).

A STRANGE COUNTRY

The phrase, *"As in a strange country,"* presents Abraham living in this land, not as its owner, but as a resident alien. One might say that he as a *"stranger"* dwelt in a *"strange land."* Consequently, the Patriarch had to live there as *"in a foreign country."* He had no rights.

To be frank, this phrase proclaims the *"sojourn"* of all Believers on this Earth, *"as in a strange country."* As the song says:

"This world is not my home,
"I'm just a traveling through.
"My treasures are laid up, somewhere beyond the blue.
"Jesus beckons me, to Heaven's open door,
"And I can't feel at home in this world anymore."

TABERNACLES

The phrase, *"Dwelling in tabernacles with Isaac and Jacob,"* proclaims the truth that all of these trod the pilgrim path, dwelling as strangers in the Land of Promise, their tent and altar witnessing to the double character of the pilgrim and worshipper.

Actually the word *"tabernacles"* should have been translated *"tents,"* because that's actually what the Greek says. This means that these Patriarchs acquired no fixed property, no title to the land, except the small portion purchased as a burial place. This to be sure, is indicative of the entirety of the human race. The only thing that we actually ever really occupy permanently, one might say, is the burial plot. We are meant to be pilgrims and strangers here, actually putting down no roots, because this is not our permanent dwelling, that being Heaven.

While this land would ultimately belong to their seed, and in totality, at this moment it was meant to be a type of the pilgrim journey of the Child of God. Let us take a lesson from this!

HEIRS

The phrase, *"The heirs with him of the same promise,"* proclaims the fact, that what God promised to Abraham, He promised as well to those who would follow him. In a sense, as they (the Jews) had the *"same Promise,"* you and I have the *"same Promise."* There is a difference, however, as it regards the Jews and the Gentiles, in that the former were promised the land of Canaan as their eternal possession. In fact, under David, they did possess the greater part, but then ultimately lost it due to rebellion against God.

At this very moment (2000), Israel is still contending with the Arabs for *"the Land."* This contention will increase until it is ultimately settled by the Antichrist, which will take place shortly. However, the false peace tendered by the man of sin, will soon come to an end, with the nation of Israel once again facing destruction. They will be saved by the Second Coming (Rev. Chpt. 19), when they will at that time accept Christ. They will then occupy all of that which was promised to Abraham, with the nation of Israel then becoming the greatest nation on the face of the Earth, with the Lord Jesus Christ ruling as their King, which in a sense He will do forever.

(10) "FOR HE LOOKED FOR A CITY WHICH HATH FOUNDATIONS, WHOSE BUILDER AND MAKER IS GOD."

The composite is:

1. *"City"* and *"foundations,"* actually read in the Greek text, *"the city"* and *"the foundations,"* specifying a particular city with particular foundations, which refer to the Heavenly Jerusalem.

2. All of this which the Lord was leading Abraham to do, would ultimately lead for all Believers the occupying of *"the city which has the foundations."*

3. God is totally the author of this of which we speak.

OBSERVATION

The phrase, *"For he looked,"* refers to his

Faith, and that its object was the Promises of God, which spoke of the great Plan of God for the entirety of the human race. Considering then that very little was known concerning this of which we speak, this Tenth Verse suggests that God had made wonderful revelations to Abraham, which are not necessarily recorded in the Old Testament. For instance, terminology which this Verse provides, concerning the New Jerusalem, is not described for us until we come to the closing Chapters of the Book of Revelation. It will be the home of all the Saints of God, and toward that Abraham looked and, because of its glory, counted things then present as of small moment. We should take a cue from these statements:

We know that for which Abraham looked, but what is it to which the modern Church looks?

The faith of much of the modern Charismatic community, and I speak of those who go under the guise of *"faith,"* are looking solely at material things concerning the here and now. In other words, money! In fact, the entirety of the Church world, with some few exceptions, has little interest in the there and then, but rather in the here and now. This we do know:

Abraham, Isaac, and Jacob, had such a Revelation from the Lord concerning that which is to come, that they were not overly concerned about the here and now. Their faith made them willing to live in tents, even to endure patiently their unsettled life, since whatever they presently endured was but temporary, in view of that which was to come. What a lesson for us presently!

THE NEW JERUSALEM

The phrase, *"For a city which hath foundations,"* as stated, should have been translated, *"the city which hath the foundations."* All of this portrays to us the fact that Abraham knew and understood, that everything God was doing, which included the possession of the land of Canaan, which those who followed him would not occupy until many years later (Gen. 15:13-16), were all leading to something Heavenly. The idea that the Holy Spirit would mention *"the foundations,"* is meant to note the permanency of all that God does, by contrast with the world which has no foundations to its empires, etc. Everything that man builds will rot and crumble, while everything that God builds will last forever. Abraham saw this, understood, and knew this, which seems to escape most of the modern Church.

BUILDER AND MAKER

The phrase, *"Whose Builder and Maker is God,"* actually refers to Christ, Who is the Creator of all things (Jn. 1:1-3).

One might say that God is the Owner, while Christ is the Architect, and the Holy Spirit is the Builder (Col. 1:15-18; Ps. 104:30).

The prevailing religion of Abraham's day was idolatry, and the claim which the Patriarch set up to a special call from the Most High, might have been deemed entirely fanatical. To start off on a journey through a pathless desert; to leave his country and home, and all that he held dear, when he himself knew not whither he went; to go with no means of conquest, but with the expectation that the distant and unknown land would be given him, but yet he would not actually then possess it, could not but have been regarded as a singular instance of visionary hope.

The whole transaction, therefore, was in the highest degree an act of simple confidence in God, where there was no human basis of calculation, and where all the principles on which man commonly act would have led him to pursue just the contrary course. It is, therefore, not without reason that the Faith of Abraham is so much commended.

(11) "THROUGH FAITH ALSO SARA HERSELF RECEIVED STRENGTH TO CONCEIVE SEED, AND WAS DELIVERED OF A CHILD WHEN SHE WAS PAST AGE, BECAUSE SHE JUDGED HIM FAITHFUL WHO HAD PROMISED."

The exegesis is:

1. Sarah's faith overcame her initial doubt.

2. Her faith brought forth a miracle in that she was able to conceive, even though she was past age.

3. Her Faith was in God Who had promised, which means that she hung onto the Promise.

SARAH

The phrase, *"Through faith also Sarah herself received strength to conceive seed,"* implies that there was something remarkable in the fact that she should manifest this faith. Perhaps there may be reference here to the incredulity with which she at first received the announcement that she should have a child (Gen. 18:11, 13). However, even though everything pointed to the impossible, she rose above her doubt and unbelief, and was able to claim the Divine Promise.

Even though Paul does not state the authority for his assertion that the strength of Sarah was derived from her faith, nor when particularly it was exercised, still, the Text implies this. Consequently, this should be an encouragement to all who have a struggle of faith.

THE GOOD FIGHT OF FAITH

Whether the Believer understands it or not, every single struggle within his life, is in one way or the other, a struggle of Faith. What do we mean by that?

Every attack by Satan, and irrespective of the manner in which he attacks, whether it be physical, material, financial, domestical, or spiritual, it is all but for one purpose, and that is to destroy our faith, or at least to seriously weaken our Faith.

Paul said to Timothy, *"Fight the good fight of faith, lay hold on Eternal Life, whereunto you are also called, and have professed a good profession before many witnesses"* (I Tim. 6:12).

Most of Satan's efforts against our Faith is to move it away from the Cross to something else. And when our Faith is placed in something else, for all practical purposes, the fight will cease. Many Christians take that for victory, when in reality, it's the very opposite.

Satan only opposes that which does him great harm. Naturally, he does not oppose that which is error or wrong, actually aiding and abetting such direction, as should be obvious. But most Christians have it backwards.

They think if they're suffering difficulties and problems, with Satan attacking on every hand, that this means that something is wrong in their life. Quite the contrary, it is because something is very right in your life, and Satan is trying his best to oppose you because of this very thing.

He knows that if your Faith is properly placed, and that refers to being placed in the Cross of Christ (Rom. 6:3-5, 11, 14; 8:1-2, 11), that the Lord is then going to be able to do great things within you and through you. So he opposes your Faith.

In fact, Satan little opposes most Christians simply because their faith is misplaced, therefore, no threat to him. I have watched Christians come into the Truth of the Message of the Cross, with Satan immediately then beginning to oppose them. This would be confusing to them, never having experienced such before, and for the simple reason that their faith previously had been misplaced and they were no threat to Satan, at least not in a spiritual sense, which is the only sense that counts.

In this struggle, some give up and quit, with the old hackneyed expression, *"I tried it and it didn't work!"* Please note the following:

THE CROSS, A TOTAL WAY OF LIFE

As I've said over and over again, the Cross is not merely a Doctrine. It is actually the foundation of all true, Biblical Doctrine. It is a total way of life. Most of the Church needs to rethink its position, actually bringing about a reformation. When one begins to properly understand the Cross, which is the Source of all Blessings, and of course, when we speak of the Cross, we are actually speaking of what Jesus there did, one will find that this affects how we interpret the Word of God, how we interpret Christ, in fact, and as stated, it becomes a total way of life. That's at least one of the reasons that it's hard for the Church to accept the Message of the Cross. Everything has to change! In fact, the entirety of our interpretation of the Word of God has to change! And for this reason:

Once the Believer properly sees and understands the Cross of Christ, the Believer's thinking actually changes. He then sees

everything in the Word of God, in the light of the Cross. In fact, the Word of God will then come alive as never before, and much more understandable than ever before. In fact, one cannot properly understand the Word, unless one properly understands the Cross. The two, *"the Word"* and *"the Cross"* are synonymous (Jn. 1:1, 14, 29).

While Satan will definitely oppose the Message of the Cross as he opposes nothing else (I Cor. 1:18, 21, 23; 2:2), irrespective, the Believer will enter into a dimension of spirituality led and controlled by the Holy Spirit which has not been previously experienced. In other words, the Blessing by far outweighs the opposition.

That's why Paul referred to this as the *"good fight of Faith."* While it is a *"fight,"* it is a *"good fight,"* simply because victory is guaranteed. And as well, you're fighting for something worthwhile. Sadly and tragically, the struggle and efforts of most Christians are wasted on pursuits that lead no place spiritually.

Sarah had a struggle with her Faith, as every true Believer will, but she persevered and God brought her out, and gave her one of the greatest miracles in the history of humanity.

Incidentally, many Scholars have problems with the word *"seed,"* as in *"to conceive seed,"* as it referred to Sarah. They refer to the fact that woman has no seed, which of course, is correct — at least with one exception.

In the first Promise given by God as it refers to Redemption, He said, *"And I will put enmity between thee* (Satan) *and the woman, and between thy seed* (all men who serve Satan) *and her Seed* (this refers to the coming of the Messiah, the Son of God and Mary)*"* (Gen. 3:15).

Knowing that the Seed to which He here referred to was Jesus Christ, the Holy Spirit through Paul, refers to the same thing.

Isaac was the promised child, a work of the Spirit, through whom would ultimately come the Messiah, God manifest in the flesh, in what we refer to as the Incarnation (Isa. 7:14). So, the *"Seed"* of which Paul here spoke, pertained to Christ, Who would come through the lineage of Abraham, and Isaac, etc. Therefore, Paul didn't make a mistake here as some claim.

THE MIRACLE OF FAITH

The phrase, *"And was delivered of a child when she was past age,"* refers to the struggle.

Her bringing forth this child, had to do with the coming Redeemer, the Lord Jesus Christ, Who would die on the Cross, in order to redeem lost humanity. So we're speaking here of the Cross!

For man to be redeemed, God would actually have to become man (Isa. 7:14), *"made of a woman, made under the Law"* (Gal. 4:4).

He would have to keep the Law of God perfectly, which no man had ever done, but which Christ did do, and then would have to address its terrible penalty of death, by dying on the Cross, which He did, thereby, *"redeeming us from the Curse of the Law"* (Gal. 3:13-14).

I think I can say without fear of contradiction, that the degree of opposition brought by Satan, is according to the degree of the Promise of God. In other words, if it's a mighty work that is to be done, there will be a mighty opposition. As someone has well said, *"Faith must be tested, and great faith must be tested greatly."*

Through the lineage which would come forth from Abraham, which was the reason for the great opposition by Satan, the Redeemer would ultimately be born. Consequently, despite the opposition, Faith ultimately prevailed. Now let's look closer at the miracle of faith:

THE MIRACLE PRODUCED BY FAITH

As we previously stated, God's plans are always much larger than our plans. That which God desires us to do, whatever it might be, is in fact, beyond us in every capacity. In other words, what is to be done within our lives, and which God wants us to do, can only be done by the Holy Spirit; however, the work of the Spirit is always predicated on our Faith (Gal. 5:5). As I keep saying, the Spirit doesn't require much of us, but He does definitely require Faith on our part, and Faith which must always have as its proper object, the Cross of Christ. Again, please allow me to emphasize the following:

This was the struggle of Faith in Sarah's heart and life. To go straight to the bottom

line, her Faith in God pertained to her bringing forth the child, through whose lineage, would come the Christ, Who would redeem mankind, by dying on a Cross. Of course, she would have had no knowledge of the Cross; however, she definitely did know that *"the Seed"* she would produce, would ultimately fall out to the Redemption of humanity. Let's say it another way:

All faith evidenced before the Cross, was evidenced in the principle of what the Cross *"would do"*; all faith evidenced since the Cross, is evidenced in the principle of what the Cross *"did do."* This means that the Cross of Christ has always in some way, been the object of true Faith. Listen to the following:

On the Mount of Transfiguration, the Bible said, *"And, behold there talked with Him* (with Christ) *two men, which were Moses and Elijah:*

"Who appeared in glory, and spake of His decease which He should accomplish at Jerusalem" (Lk. 9:30-31).

In this phenomenal happening, which Peter, James, and John were privileged to witness, the topic of conversation on that memorable day was, the Crucifixion of Christ, which would take place in a short time. This tells us two things:

1. The Redeemer and the manner of Redemption, which would be His decease, which refers to the Cross, was the general thrust of the Faith of both Moses and Elijah during their lifetimes of Ministry. In fact, it was to Moses that the Lord showed the manner of death, which would be the Cross. It referred to the brazen serpent on the pole, which was lifted up in the wilderness (Num. 21:9; Jn. 3:14-15).

God had shown Abraham that it had to be by *"death,"* through which Justification would be received (Gen. 22:1-2, 8-9, 14), but to Moses He showed the *"manner"* of that death, which was the Cross.

As well, Elijah knew exactly what God had shown Abraham and Moses, and which had been so dramatically portrayed to him on the day the fire fell and consumed the sacrifice (I Ki. 18:30-39).

2. Inasmuch as Moses had been dead, at least physically speaking, for some 1,600 years, thereby having been in Paradise for

that length of time, and that Elijah had been translated that he should not see death, and had been in Heaven for some 900 years, we know the topic of conversation in both places had been that of the coming Redemption, i.e., *"what Christ would do on the Cross."*

So, Faith must always be linked to the Cross, which of course is the great Sacrifice of Christ, or else it's not Faith, at least the kind that God will recognize (Eph. 2:8-9).

Faith properly placed, will always ultimately produce a miracle of tremendous proportions, even though there is a struggle at times, of getting our Faith properly placed, and keeping our Faith properly placed!

GOD IS FAITHFUL

The phrase, *"Because she judged Him faithful Who had promised,"* refers to God Who had made the Promise regarding her bringing a son into the world. On the merely human level, there was no hope for this miracle to be brought about. Sarah had been barren all her life, and on top of that, she was now 90 years old. As well, Abraham was 100, so the idea that he could father children at this age, was slim indeed!

Even though all of this placed Abraham and Sarah in the position of *"impossible"* as it regarded bringing forth the child, what is impossible with men, is possible with God (Mat. 19:26).

Everything done through us and by us as it pertains to the Lord is always done by and through the Person of the Holy Spirit. In fact, it has to be a Work of the Spirit, or else God cannot accept it.

Therefore, with Abraham and Sarah, all hope of the flesh had to die. In other words, they had to be brought to the place that they had exhausted all their physical, mental, intellectual, and material resources. In other words, there had to be absolutely nothing left but Faith in God. And that's exactly what happened!

Despite their own personal problems, which means that many times they were unfaithful, they judged God to definitely be faithful. And herein lies a great truth:

THE PROMISE STILL HOLDS

Getting from the *"Promise"* to the *"Possession,"* is never a simple, short, or

easy task. And that's where the test of Faith comes in.

The implication in this phrase is that they finally got their eyes on the Lord instead of themselves. As someone has well said, Abraham and Sarah had to deal with their sin, before Isaac could be born. And what does that mean?

Their sin was in looking to themselves, and by that I refer to their own efforts at trying to bring about the Promise of God, instead of looking solely to the Lord. That is the entire crux of the Christian experience. Let's look at it in another way:

That is our sin as well! The Holy Spirit cannot bring forth in our lives that which He desires, until we quit attempting to do it by our own machinations, whatever they might be, and instead, glue our eyes strictly and totally onto the Finished Work of Christ. In doing this, we are at the same time saying that we know we cannot carry this forth ourselves, and at the same time, we realize that Jesus has already done it for us at the Cross. In other words, in the Cross is the potential for all blessings. When we finally *"give up and let Jesus take over,"* which refers to looking to what He did on Mount Calvary on our behalf, then the Holy Spirit can take over in our lives, just exactly as He did with Abraham and Sarah so long ago, and a miracle will be born.

THEY JUDGED GOD AS FAITHFUL

How do you judge God? Whether you realize it or not, by your actions you are judging God every day.

If you are attempting to live this Christian experience in any other manner, other than by Faith in the Cross of Christ, you are in effect, judging God as not being faithful to His Promise. What is that Promise?

In fact, He gave the Promise to Abraham. He told the Patriarch, which Promise incidentally included you and me, and in fact the entirety of mankind, *"I am 'Jehovah-Jireh',"* meaning, *"the Lord will provide"* (Gen. 22:13-14).

Provide what?

He would provide a Redeemer for mankind, which He did!

To be sure, God kept His Promise, in providing a Savior Who would redeem mankind, and as well, would give us Eternal Life, and provide for us an overcoming victory. In other words, everything we need, is found in that which He provided, which all translates into *"Jesus Christ and Him Crucified"* (I Cor. 2:2).

Now how do you judge God? Do you judge Him as having done this great thing? And if you do, you will trust Him implicitly, which refers to looking exactly as to what He did, which is the Sacrifice of Christ. Otherwise, you will look to other things, which regrettably, most of the modern Church is presently doing!

God promised through Abraham that He would give to the world a Redeemer Who would save man from sin. He also promised that accompanying this Redemption, He would give us the Holy Spirit (Gal. 3:13-14). And then He promised us that we could live a victorious, overcoming, Christian life, meaning that sin in no way, shape, form, or fashion, would dominate us (Rom. 6:14). He promised us that if we would look to the Cross, which refers to what Jesus there did, with all of its continuing benefits, that we could have all of this for which He paid such a price (Rom. 6:3-5; 8:1-2, 11).

Now if you believe that, you will understand that it all comes through the Cross, and that this is where your Faith must be anchored. Accordingly, you will judge God as having kept His Promise!

If not, you will trust other things, but I warn you. All these other things are *"broken cisterns, that can hold no water"* (Jer. 2:13).

(12) "THEREFORE SPRANG THERE EVEN OF ONE, AND HIM AS GOOD AS DEAD, SO MANY AS THE STARS OF THE SKY IN MULTITUDE, AND AS THE SAND WHICH IS BY THE SEA SHORE INNUMERABLE."

The diagram is:

1. *"Therefore"* introduces the inevitable result of true Faith.

2. The smallness of the beginning is brought out, in that Abraham was only one man, and he was *"as good as dead."* But Faith in God worked a miracle.

3. That which Faith in God brought forth, is as the *"stars of the sky,"* and the *"sand by the seashore."* God's Blessing is beyond human calculation.

SPRING FORTH

The phrase, *"Therefore sprang there even of one, and him as good as dead,"* refers to the hopelessness, absolute hopelessness, of Abraham's situation, but yet which brought forth the multitude. God did exactly what He said He would do!

All of this is meant to teach us valuable lessons. It is meant by the Holy Spirit, that we transfer these lessons to ourselves and, therefore, apply them to ourselves. In other words, the Lord through what Paul here said, is prodding you to exercise the same faith as Abraham and Sarah.

We may draw back from that, thinking that we could not even begin to measure up to that of Abraham and Sarah; however, we must always remember, that we're not looking to Abraham and to Sarah, or even to ourselves for that matter, but rather to God. While God's work for us is not the same as that of Abraham and Sarah, nevertheless He definitely has a work for us to do, and their experience is related here in order that it might help us (I Cor. 10:11).

DO WE WALK BY SIGHT OR DO WE WALK BY FAITH?

Paul said to the Corinthians, *"For we walk by faith, not by sight"* (II Cor. 5:7). But our problem is, most of the time we do walk by *"sight,"* which refers to that which Abraham and Sarah were doing, before they began to walk by faith.

What does it mean to walk by sight?

In effect, this means that we are placing our faith in ourselves and circumstances, instead of in the Lord and what He did at the Cross on our behalf.

If we look at ourselves, we, exactly as Abraham and Sarah, will see many problems. If we look at circumstances, which Abraham and Sarah also did in the beginning, what we see won't be good. Consequently, we begin to doubt, with all of its attendant results, which means that we are *"walking by sight."*

When we *"walk by Faith,"* this means simply that we are not looking at ourselves, are not looking at circumstances whatever they might be, but rather looking to Jesus and what He did for us at the Cross. We know if we keep our Faith anchored in the Cross, that the Holy Spirit will then do great and mighty things for us and within us, which is the way it must work anyhow.

What must be done, we cannot do! In fact, it is literally impossible for us to do these things which God demands of us. And what things am I speaking of?

It really doesn't matter! Perhaps we could divide it up into two sections, thereby making it easier to understand:

1. The Holy Spirit wants to develop Righteousness and Holiness within our hearts and lives, in other words the *"Fruit of the Spirit"* (Gal. 5:22-23), therefore, Christlikeness. If this is done, it at the same time will give us victory over all sin (Rom. 6:14).

2. While that just stated is the Holy Spirit working *"in us,"* the Lord also has a work which He desires of us, which must be done *"through us."* In other words, He has a work for you to do, whatever it might be!

All of this can only be done in one manner:

Abraham and Sarah are a perfect example that all of this can never be done by human machinations, but only by Faith. They were meant to serve as our examples, and we are meant to learn from them. One cannot walk by sight, but rather one must walk by Faith! And then this great thing can be done within our hearts and lives, but only then!

THE MIRACLE PRODUCED

The phrase, *"So many as the stars of the sky in multitude, and as the sand which is by the sea shore innumerable,"* records what God did through this amazing couple. But it was all *"through faith!"*

Sarah's faith, though obscured at times, shines out brightly indeed when we remember how utterly impossible from a human standpoint it was that she should ever become the mother of the promised child. That there was a breakdown on the part of both herself and her husband — a breakdown which brought Hagar — a work of the flesh — into the home and led to unhappy circumstances later — is perfectly true, but all this was only temporary. That which God delights to remember of this great lady is that she *"counted Him faithful Who promised."* And so the Apostle reminds us:

"From this one, as good as dead, the Lord has brought forth such a multitude as the stars in Heaven, and the sands which are by the seashore." However, in their lifetimes, they did not see all of this, even as the next Verse brings out. But this only shows us that Faith is so powerful, that it will never die.

When Paul mentioned *"the stars of the sky in multitude,"* he was referring back to Genesis 15:5, when the Lord said to Abraham, when he was in a state of doubt, *"Look, look now toward Heaven, and tell the stars, if thou be able to number them: and He said unto him, 'So shall thy seed be'."* That's when the Scripture said, *"And he believed in the LORD; and He counted it to him for Righteousness"* (Gen. 15:6).

Later, the Lord again reinforced that promise by again mentioning the *"stars,"* but this time adding that about the *"sand"* (Gen. 22:17-18).

FAITH IS AS BIG AS GOD

When I was a kid coming up, and especially after Frances and I married, my Grandmother was a source of unparalleled strength to me. I was just beginning to preach the Gospel, and she was to me at that time, my Bible School, my Seminary. Her lessons were to the point, and they minced no words.

I can see that faraway look in her eyes even to this day, as she seemed to look past me, into the very heart of God. She would say to me:

"Jimmy, God is a big God, so ask big!"

I've never forgotten that, and by the Grace of God I will never forget it. It has helped me touch a great part of this world for the Lord Jesus Christ.

"Ask big," for this is the God of Abraham, of Isaac, and of Jacob! This is the God of Paul and of Silas! This is the God of Peter, James, and John!

Oh how I sense the Presence of God, even as I dictate these notes. Faith is as big as God, which means that Faith, that is if it's true Faith in Christ and what He has done at the Cross on our behalf, has no limitations. God is the God of the impossible!

The Lord said to me in October of 1991, at a time of great crisis for me and this Ministry, at a time when I didn't know of the Victory of the Cross, *"God is not a man, that*

He should lie; neither the son of man, that He should repent: hath He said, and shall He not do it? Or hath He spoken, and shall He not make it good?"

He then said to me, *"What I have blessed, nothing can curse!"* (Num. 23:19-20).

His Word then said, *"He hath not beheld iniquity in Jacob, neither hath He seen perverseness in Israel: the LORD his God is with him, and the shout of a king is among them"* (Num. 23:21).

This prophecy is actually a portrayal of *"Justification by Faith."* Was there iniquity in Jacob? Was their perverseness in Israel?

God was looking at them through Christ; consequently, He beheld no iniquity or perverseness. He looks at you the same identical way. So what am I saying?

I'm saying, that on that memorable day in 1991, because of Christ and what He did for me at the Cross, the Lord saw no iniquity or perverseness. What did He see?

He saw and heard *"the shout of a King."* That King is Christ, and the *"shout"* is the *"shout of victory!"*

Therefore, if Christ shouts *"victory,"* then I shout *"victory!"*

(13) "THESE ALL DIED IN FAITH, NOT HAVING RECEIVED THE PROMISES, BUT HAVING SEEN THEM AFAR OFF, AND WERE PERSUADED OF THEM, AND EMBRACED THEM, AND CONFESSED THAT THEY WERE STRANGERS AND PILGRIMS ON THE EARTH."

The structure is:

1. These things which God had promised, were far larger than the ones to whom they were promised. The Promises incorporated eternity.

2. However, by Faith they saw them, and knew they were real.

3. The Promises of God are not of this present world.

ACCORDING TO FAITH

The phrase, *"These all died in faith,"* in the Greek text actually says, *"According to Faith."* They died, one might say, under the regime of faith, and not of sight (Vincent). That is, all died with the exception of Enoch.

Seven Verses up to this point have begun with the emphatic words *"By faith."*

Consequently, we must not change the order of the original. In fact, there is a change here, but not in the emphasis of this thought.

We should not expect to read *"By faith these died"*; what is said is, *"In accordance with faith all these died"*; faith had been the support and guide of their lives, and their deaths were in accordance with the same principle. That is, they did not die in possession of what had been promised, but saw at a distance the Blessings of which God had spoken.

There is nothing in the world greater than to *"die in faith."* In fact, that was not only the lot of the Patriarchs as here described, but also every single Believer who has lived from the very beginning until now. While it is certainly true, due to the First Advent of Christ and what He did at the Cross, that we have more now than they had then, at least as it regards the Promises of God; still, most is yet to come. But the Truth is, as the year 2000 rolled around, signifying a new century and a new millennium, we are closer today than ever. Actually, all of these things of which we speak are now even at the door.

One must *"live in the Faith,"* and above all, one must *"die in the Faith."*

THE PROMISES

The phrase, *"Not having received the Promises,"* tells us in no uncertain terms, that the Promises of God are not of this present world. What are these Promises?

In fact, the Promises of God are of such magnitude as to defy all description. They include Eternal Life, which points to the coming Resurrection when we shall all be changed (I Cor. 15:51-57), which as stated, is even at the door. It is called *"the Rapture of the Church"* (I Thess. 4:13-18), and will include every Saint of God who has ever lived from the time of Abel through the coming great Tribulation.

Then every Saint of God just mentioned, will come back with Christ to this Earth, in what is referred to as the Second Coming (Rev. Chpt. 19). Then Israel will be brought back to God, and done so by accepting the One Whom they rejected so long, long ago, namely, the Lord Jesus Christ (Zech., Chpts. 12-14). At that time, Israel will not only accept Christ, but will also accept the Cross. The Scripture says:

"In that day there shall be a fountain opened to the House of David and to the inhabitants of Jerusalem for sin and for uncleanness" (Zech. 13:1).

There is only one fountain, and that is the one that is filled with blood, and as the songwriter said, *"Drawn from Immanuel's veins."* That is the Cross!

AFAR OFF

The phrase, *"But having seen them afar off,"* proclaims the fact, that the Promises of God do not include only this mortal coil, this present life. In fact, Paul also said, *"If in this life only we have hope in Christ, we are of all men most miserable"* (I Cor. 15:19).

Cannot the Reader now see the abominable error of the present *"money gospel"* which in reality is no gospel at all! Whatever the Lord seeks to give us in this present world is well and good; however, to trade the *"there and then"* for the *"here and now,"* is the most foolish of all trades. But of course, the great claim is that one can have both! Is that correct?

It doesn't take a Biblical Scholar to see what is here being said. Our hope, our blessing, in fact, for all that Jesus died, are not found on this side of the Resurrection. We must never forget that. This means that if we put too much emphasis on the things of this present world, we are of all men most foolish.

Some of these people mentioned here in the Text, were blessed abundantly in the financial sense, but they placed no stock whatsoever in those things. In fact, their home was a *"tent,"* and because they ever looked at themselves as the last phrase tells us, as *"strangers and pilgrims on the Earth."*

PERSUADED?

The phrase, *"And were persuaded of them,"* refers to the fact, that the Revelation of God to them, had been so poignant, so powerful, so real, and given with such impact, that they gladly traded that which they could see, for that which they could not see.

To which we have already alluded, one of the greatest problems of the modern Church, is the *"here and now."* In fact, the far greater majority of the Church, that is if we include all who claim to be *"Christian,"* don't even

believe in a coming Rapture. The reason is not difficult to locate.

They have no clear understanding of the True Promises of God. They do not know what they really are, and because they have no true Revelation. This means they do not really know Christ, and they do not know Christ because they do not place any confidence in the Cross. I think the perilous state of the modern Church can be traced to that one problem — not understanding the Cross of Christ. If one understands the Cross, then one understands the story of the Bible, in fact, the great Plan of God as a whole. The Cross is what makes all the Promises valid. Without the great Sacrifice of Christ, there would be no *"Promises."* The Cross *"made"* it all possible, and the Cross *"makes"* it all possible!

A vote of no confidence in the Cross, is a vote of no confidence in the Promises of God. As we keep saying, one cannot have it both ways. One is either *"persuaded"* of this which the Lord has promised, or else one is not persuaded. And irrespective as to what one might say, one's direction proclaims how one is persuaded. Let me be clearer:

According to one's interpretation of the Cross, accordingly is there *"persuasion."* For one to have a part understanding of the Cross means they have a part understanding of the Promises. And that is the position of much of the modern Church!

EMBRACED THEM

The phrase, *"And embraced them,"* refers to the fact, that the Promises of God, although not presently seen except from a distance, were nevertheless accepted in all faith. In other words, this is where they placed their hope, their dreams, their past, their present, and their future. It must be the same presently, for in fact, nothing has changed.

We as Christians have either embraced this present world, which will lead to nothing but trouble and even destruction, or else we have embraced the Promises of God, which are afar off. One cannot have a middle ground, it is either one or the other! And to be sure, it is very easy to look and see as to what is being *"embraced!"*

The part of Christianity which has sold out to the world, has all the earmarks of the world, while those who have embraced the Promises, have those earmarks as well.

STRANGERS AND PILGRIMS

The phrase, *"And confessed that they were strangers and pilgrims on the Earth,"* holds true unto this present hour. The Christian, that is the true Christian, must never forget that. We do not march to the world's beat, and neither do we sing its song. That which is of interest to the world, is not of interest to us, and that which is of interest to us, is definitely not of interest to the world. And never forget, if the two become intermingled, something is badly wrong with the Church. In the anonymous Epistle to Diagnetus, probably of the Second Century, there occur these words concerning Christians: *"They inhabit their own country, but as sojourners: they take part in all things as citizens, and endure all things as aliens: every foreign country is theirs, and every country is foreign."*

(14) "FOR THEY THAT SAY SUCH THINGS DECLARE PLAINLY THAT THEY SEEK A COUNTRY."

The composite is:

1. The terminology of the Believer points to their emphasis.

2. Our emphasis *"declares plainly"* which way we are headed.

3. The emphasis of the Believer if it is correct, automatically declares that this present world is insufficient, and thereby, we seek something else.

WHAT DO YOU SAY?

The phrase, *"For they that say such things,"* refers to the conversation and terminology of faith.

The Church is divided into two parts: the True Church and the Apostate Church. Some of the time, they are intermingled. Even though much of the terminology at times is the same, still, if one listens closely, one can hear the difference.

For instance, the True Church is looking for the Rapture, says so, and orders its behavior to that end. The Apostate Church has no regard for the Rapture, and in fact, doesn't even believe there will be a Rapture, and says so!

The True Church follows after the Spirit, while the Apostate Church ignores the Spirit.

The True Church looks exclusively to the Cross as the Source of all things from God, while the Apostate Church ignores the Cross and even at times, repudiates the Cross. Consequently, Jesus said:

"For by thy words thou shalt be justified, and by thy words thou shalt be condemned" (Mat. 12:37).

DECLARE PLAINLY

The short phrase, *"Declare plainly,"* refers to the fact, that the true Believer leaves no room for doubt. He declares plainly what he believes, why he believes it, and in Whom he believes. If he doesn't declare it plainly, then he really doesn't believe what he timidly suggests. The Scripture plainly says:

"Let the redeemed of the LORD say so, whom He hath redeemed from the hand of the enemy" (Ps. 107:2).

I have made the statement many times, that the Cross of Christ is the dividing line between the True Church and the Apostate Church. As also stated, that has always been the case, but the Holy Spirit is going to make it more pronounced now than ever. So what am I saying?

The die is being cast. Do we believe that the Cross of Christ is the foundation of the Faith, or do we believe in something else? If we do believe in the Cross, we are going to have to boldly say so. And when we do, many will be asked to leave their respective Church. That's the price that one may have to pay, but in fact, that's the price that God has always demanded. The opposition has little come from the world, but most always from the professing Church. That is going to be more pronounced now than ever.

THE MORALIST

I think I am just now beginning to understand the manner of the prime thrust of Satan within the Church. I observe Churches which claim to be Spirit-filled, but are yet extremely legalistic, while at the same time embracing the things of the world. The two at first do not seem to match, but after a little observation it becomes very clear that they perfectly match.

While these Churches, and they are in the far greater majority, claim the Spirit, they at the same time embrace the ways of the world, and oppose the Cross. They are moralists! And what do we mean by that?

While mouthing Christ, and while claiming the Holy Spirit, they in effect, have fabricated their own Salvation. They have set up their rules and regulations, and their Salvation is in abiding by these particular rules and regulations, which of course, excludes the Cross. They do not really see themselves as they really are, and if they did, they would understand the need for the Cross.

They consider themselves to be very moral, simply because they have abided by their particular, formulated integrity. It fools many people, because they talk about the Lord constantly just as the Pharisees of old, in fact whom they emulate, and yet they claim the Spirit.

Irrespective of their claims, and irrespective of their profession, that which denies the Cross has denied Christ. Now here is the second clincher to all of this:

While some of these openly repudiate the Cross, and I primarily speak of the Word of Faith people, many do not consider themselves as opposing the Cross. In fact, they pay lip service to the Cross by mentioning the death of Christ, etc. However, their trust and confidence are not in that Finished Work, which they prove by their emphasis. Their salvation, whether they realize it or not, is a salvation of law and works, which in reality, is no salvation at all (Gal. 2:16).

These Churches are primarily accepted by the world, which should be a tip-off. And as well, they deceive many people because of their religion of ethics and morality. While all true Christians will definitely have ethics, and will definitely uphold true morality, the difference is that theirs comes from Christ, while the other supposed morality, and supposed it is, comes from rules and regulations, i.e., *"law."*

Before God, and before the Scriptures, all of this is *"declared plainly,"* but sometimes, it is not understood plainly by many Christians.

SEEK A COUNTRY

The phrase, *"That they seek a country,"* refers to that which is not here, and has no reference to that which is here.

Even though words such as *"city"* and *"country,"* are here used, and to be sure, Heaven is definitely a real place; however, more than anything else these words symbolize the entirety of the Plan of God for the human race, at least for those who will believe (Jn. 3:16).

The word *"seek"* implies Faith. It also implies a way of life, a particular direction, a particular lifestyle. In other words, what the true Believer is seeking is not at all that which the world seeks.

(15) "AND TRULY, IF THEY HAD BEEN MINDFUL OF THAT COUNTRY FROM WHENCE THEY CAME OUT, THEY MIGHT HAVE HAD OPPORTUNITY TO HAVE RETURNED."

The structure is:

1. Of what country are you *"mindful,"* the *"here and now"* or the *"there and then"*?

2. God does not make slaves of people. Had these mentioned so desired, they could have returned to that which they had left. They had free wills, but they *"willed"* to go God's way.

3. Regrettably, some, even many, have returned to the former ways.

MINDFUL

The phrase, *"And truly, if they had been mindful of that country from whence they came out,"* in the Greek text, means *"habitually remembered."*

The old song says, *"This world is not my home, I'm just traveling through. My treasures are laid up somewhere beyond the blue. The Angels beckon me to Heaven's open door, and I can't feel at home in this world any more."*

Those of which Paul speaks had come to the place that they knew that this world was not their home, and conducted themselves accordingly.

Paul also said of this time, *"And the Scripture, foreseeing that God would justify the heathen through faith, preached before the Gospel unto Abraham, saying, in thee shall all nations be blessed"* (Gal. 3:8).

This shows that they of whom Paul here speaks, was *"mindful"* not of the country they had left, but rather of that which they sought. It is proven by their actions:

When Abraham wanted a wife for Isaac, he wanted her to be from his homeland. There was a reason for that, even though I will not now address that reason. But he did not go back there himself. Instead, he sent a servant to get the bride and said to him, *"Make sure that you do not take my son back there"* (Gen. 24:6).

After Jacob had spent 20 years in Mesopotamia, he still regarded Canaan as *"my own homeland"* (Gen. 30:25); and he heard God say, *"Go back to the land of your fathers"* (Gen. 31:3).

Abraham buried Sarah in Canaan, not Mesopotamia, and in due course he was buried there himself (Gen. 23:19; 25:9-10), as were Isaac (Gen. 35:27-29) and Jacob (Gen. 49:29-33; 50:13), Jacob being brought up from Egypt for this purpose.

Joseph commanded that the same be done for him (Gen. 50:24-26; Ex. 13:19; Josh. 24:32).

All these men wholeheartedly accepted God's Word. Had they been earthly minded, they could have gone back to Mesopotamia. But their hearts were set on their Heavenly Home, and they did not go back. Single mindedly they walked the path of faith.

The Reader shouldn't misunderstand! All of these particular places we have here named, including Canaan, were but symbolic of the Way of God. At that particular time, Canaan represented the true Way of God, while the balance of the world represented other things. It really hasn't changed presently.

Today it is no longer the land of *"Canaan,"* but rather, the *"Church."* And yet, the earthly institution referred to as *"the Church,"* must never be confused with *"the General Assembly and Church of the Firstborn, which are written in Heaven"* (Heb. 12:23). In other words, the true Church has no bearing on our names being written on some earthly church roles, but rather written in the Lamb's Book of Life, which is in Heaven.

The Believer must ever understand, that you have been *"brought out"* of darkness into Light. You have *"come out"* from the world, and are no longer a part of its system. In other words, you are *"in the world,"* but definitely not *"of the world!"*

OPPORTUNITY?

The phrase, *"They might have had opportunity to have returned,"* proclaims the

NOTES

fact, that if they had been *"mindful of that country from whence they came out,"* they definitely could have, and in fact, would have gone back. This graphically portrays the free moral agency of man. It is *"free will"* which got you in, and if someone so foolishly desires, *"free will,"* God forbid, can get you out. What if they had returned?

In fact, the entirety of the Epistle to the Hebrews was written for this very reason. Some of the Christian Jews were in fact, returning to the former ways. And regrettably, millions since, and I think I exaggerate not, have returned to those ways. Concerning this, Jesus said:

"No man, having put his hand to the plough and looking back, is fit for the Kingdom of God" (Lk. 9:62).

All of this shows that the Patriarchs remaining in God's Way as strangers and sojourners was voluntary. They preferred it, with all its inconveniences and hardships. The same thing is true of all the people of God now.

If they choose to return to the world, and to engage again in all its vain pursuits, there is nothing to hinder them. There are *"opportunities"* enough. In fact, there are abundant inducements held out, even as Paul will later say concerning Moses. But go back? Go back to what?

Having been enlightened and having tasted of the Heavenly Gift, and having been made a partaker of the Holy Spirit, and having tasted of the good Word of God, and the powers of the world to come, how could one forsake all of this, to go back to the *"beggarly elements, whereunto ye desire again to be in bondage"*? (Gal. 4:9; Heb. 6:4-5).

(16) "BUT NOW THEY DESIRE A BETTER COUNTRY, THAT IS, AN HEAVENLY: WHEREFORE GOD IS NOT ASHAMED TO BE CALLED THEIR GOD: FOR HE HATH PREPARED FOR THEM A CITY."

The exegesis is:

1. They have made their choice *"now."*

2. They desire something better, because they have seen it *"afar off."*

3. That which they desire, is not of this world, but rather has its origination in Heaven.

4. Because of their Faith, God is not ashamed to be called their God.

5. And to show that He is not ashamed, He has prepared for them a city, where they will be with Him forever.

NOW

The short phrase, *"But now,"* proclaims the fact, that if one is to have this *"better country,"* they must forsake at the same time, this present country, i.e., *"the ways of the world."*

Paul said, quoting Isaiah, *"Now is the accepted time; behold, now is the Day of Salvation"* (II Cor. 6:2; Isa. 49:8).

While deathbed repentance is definitely valid, as true repentance is valid at any time, the truth is, most don't have a deathbed opportunity. That's the reason the Prophet and the Apostle said that *"now is the accepted time."*

A BETTER COUNTRY

The phrase, *"They desire a better country,"* presents the fact that through faith the Patriarchs were willing to connect their whole life and that of their children with waiting at God's bidding for the fulfillment of the Promise — wandering and sojourning until God's Own time should come when He would grant a home and a country of their own. The idea is, the sojourning in the land was a symbol of their Faith in God, that the *"better country"* was ultimately coming.

Every single Believer who has gone before us is now with the Lord. In a sense, they have gained that better country, but in another sense, a great deal is yet future.

That which is future awaits the Second Coming, when all Saints will come back with Christ to rule and reign on this Earth for a thousand years, after which time, the heavens and the Earth will be cleansed by fire (II Pet. 3:12), with the New Jerusalem then coming down from God out of Heaven, to take up a permanent abode on this planet, which means that God will literally change His Headquarters from Heaven to Earth (Rev., Chpts. 21-22). Consequently, in view of this, Peter said:

"Nevertheless we, according to His Promise, look for new heavens and a new Earth, wherein dwelleth righteousness" (II Pet. 3:13).

Then *"the Promise"* will be totally, completely, and fully realized.

NOTES

Paul said, *"Then cometh the end* (the end of all rebellion against God), *when He* (Jesus) *shall have delivered up the Kingdom to God, even the Father; when He* (Jesus) *shall have put down all rule and all authority and power"* (I Cor. 15:24).

AN HEAVENLY COUNTRY

The phrase, *"An heavenly,"* presents the adjective *"heavenly"* as connecting *"country"* with God and with all it means to belong to God. In other words, this of which the Apostle speaks is not of this world in any shape, form, or fashion. It is all *"heavenly,"* i.e., *"all of God!"*

Let it ever be understood, that all of this of which we speak, all of this which the Holy Spirit has revealed unto us, this *"better country,"* this *"heavenly,"* is attainable only through and by what Jesus did at the Cross, and our Faith in that Finished Work. As the Cross made it all possible, then it is absolutely necessary that we have Faith, and maintain Faith, in that which makes it all possible.

Paul said, *"But now in Christ Jesus ye who sometimes were far off are made nigh by the Blood of Christ . . . for through Him we both* (Jews and Gentiles) *have access by One Spirit* (the Holy Spirit) *unto the Father"* (Eph. 2:13, 18).

GOD IS NOT ASHAMED

The phrase, *"Wherefore God is not ashamed to be called their God,"* is because they have commended themselves to God by their Faith.

Wuest says, *"The expression 'to be called their God' is most interesting in the Greek. The word 'called' is 'epikaleisthai,' the simple verb meaning 'to be called,' the preposition meaning 'upon.' Thus the compound word means 'to be called upon.' The idea is, therefore, that of adding an additional name to the one which one already has, namely, a surname. God was not ashamed to be surnamed their God. He is called the God of Abraham, Isaac, and Jacob. And this is shown by the fact that He has prepared for them a city, introducing them into the perfection of social life, fellowship with Him."*

However, it must be ever remembered, that poor, sinful human beings are not brought to this state of acceptance by God, except through what Jesus did at the Cross. That and that alone made everything possible.

While it is certainly true that the Cross was still a futuristic event during the time of the Patriarchs, still, it was their Faith in that coming event, as shadowy as it might have been at that particular time, which gave them their standing with God.

Let us never forget, that it is the Cross and the Cross alone, which makes all of this possible.

PREPARATION

The phrase, *"For He hath prepared for them a city,"* refers to the past tense. It is not that God will one day prepare their city, but that He has already done so.

Out of all of this, we must understand that the life of the Patriarchs was, in all essential respects, such as we should lead. They looked forward to Heaven; they sought no permanent possessions here; they regarded themselves as strangers and pilgrims on the Earth. So should we be.

In our more fixed and settled habits of life; in our homes; in our residence in the land in which we were born, and in the society of friends, we should yet regard ourselves as *"strangers and sojourners."* We have here no fixed abode. In fact, the houses in which we dwell will soon be occupied by others; the paths on which we go will soon be trod by the feet of others; the fields which we cultivate will soon be ploughed and sown and reaped by others.

Others will read the books which we read; sit down at the tables where we sit; lie on the beds where we repose; occupy the chambers where we shall die, and from whence we shall be removed to our graves.

If we have any permanent home, it is in Heaven; and that which we have, the faithful lives of the Patriarchs who went before us serve to teach us, and the unerring Word of God everywhere assures us (Barnes).

THEIR FAITH

When the Patriarchs died, and we speak of all who lived before Christ, in fact, at that time they didn't go to Heaven, but rather down into Paradise, which was in the heart

of the Earth. The only thing that separated Paradise from the burning side of Hell itself, was a great gulf, even as related by Christ (Lk. 16:26). So, they didn't realize that *"City"* even at that time. But their Faith would ultimately take them there.

The reason they could not then be admitted into Heaven, with the possible exception of Enoch and Elijah, was because the sin debt was still attached to them. Even as Paul said, *"it is not possible that the blood of bulls and of goats should take away sins"* (Heb. 10:4). To be sure, they were saved, but they did not have the benefits which we have since the Cross.

When Jesus died on the Cross, thereby paying the sin debt for all of humanity, at least for all who will believe, even before His Resurrection, He went down into Paradise, and liberated those souls from that particular place, where they had actually been held captive by Satan, thereby making them his captives, and taking them to Heaven with Him (Eph. 4:8-10).

Now when Believers die, their souls and spirits immediately go to Heaven to be with Christ, there to await the coming Resurrection of the Righteous, which we refer to as the Rapture of the Church, when a Glorified Body will then be joined to the soul and the spirit (Phil. 1:21-23; I Thess. 4:13-18).

(17) "BY FAITH ABRAHAM, WHEN HE WAS TRIED, OFFERED UP ISAAC: AND HE THAT HAD RECEIVED THE PROMISES OFFERED UP HIS ONLY BEGOTTEN SON,"

The diagram is:

1. All faith must be tested, and great faith must be tested greatly.

2. This test of Faith would include the manner in which God would redeem humanity, which would be by the death of His Son.

3. Isaac was looked at by God alone as the son of promise, and heir to all things of Abraham, and not Ishmael, showing us that it is only that which is birthed by the Spirit which God can accept.

THE TESTING OF FAITH

The phrase, *"By faith Abraham, when he was tried,"* presents Paul returning from the Patriarchs in general to Abraham in particular. This was a test of Faith, perhaps one of, if not the greatest test ever, put upon a human being.

In fact, the faith of all Believers is tested constantly, although certainly not to this degree; nevertheless, the testing continues on an ongoing basis.

The Greek word used here for *"tried,"* is rendered *"tempted"* in Matthew 4:1, 3; 16:1; 19:3; 22:18, 35, and in 22 other places in the New Testament. The same word is translated *"prove"* in John 6:6.

It does not mean here, as it often does, to place inducements before one to lead him to do wrong, but to subject his faith to a trial in order to test its genuineness and strength. The meaning here is, that Abraham was placed in circumstances which showed what was the real strength in his confidence in God.

Satan *"tempts"* us, while God *"tries"* us. The meaning is according to the following:

Even though the same Greek word is used for both *"tempt"* and *"tried,"* it has a different meaning according to whom we are referring, whether God or Satan. Although there is no evidence that Satan was involved whatsoever in this particular incident, in fact, Satan is definitely involved many times, with Job as the perfect example.

Satan, of course, *"tempts"* us, in order that our faith may fail; God *"tries"* us, in order to strengthen our Faith. God cannot tempt men to do wrong, hence James saying, *"Let no man say when he is tempted, I am tempted of God: for God cannot be tempted with evil* (cannot tempt men to commit evil), *neither tempteth he any man"* (James 1:13).

As well, it is God Who sets the parameters as it regards how strong that Satan can tempt a particular individual (Job, Chpts. 1-2). Let no Believer think that Satan can do anything he so desires. In fact, he can only do what the Lord allows him to do, being held on a leash so to speak, at all times. To believe otherwise, would make God subservient to the Devil, which of course, is preposterous! Satan has latitude in any and all things, only up to the point in which God allows him such latitude. In fact, he has to go hat in hand asking permission, even to do what he does do, and then as stated, God sets the parameters and not the Evil One.

NOTES

Consequently, James also said, *"Blessed is the man that endureth temptation* (that which Satan is allowed to bring against him)*: for when he is tried* (God allows the trial and test of Faith), *he shall receive the crown of life, which the Lord hath promised to them that love Him"* (James 1:12).

Genesis Chapter 22 records this great test of Abraham.

The Scripture says, *"That God did tempt Abraham"* (Gen. 22:1). The Hebrew word for *"tempt"* is *"nacah,"* and means, *"to test, prove."* No inducement to sin is implied. In fact, it should have been translated *"test."*

The Reader is not to think that God allows testing in order that He might see, for He already knows. He allows such, in order that we might see. Probably one could say without fear of contradiction, that one's Faith is never quite as strong as one thinks it is, even when, as Abraham, we pass the test.

THE OBJECT OF OUR FAITH

The testing of our faith is allowed by the Lord, even induced by the Lord, not so much to test the quantity, but rather the quality. By that, I refer to the proper object of Faith. Every Christian has Faith (Rom. 12:3), but most Christians do not know what the proper object of their Faith ought to be. If asked, most would reiterate that they have *"Faith in God,"* or *"Faith in Christ,"* or *"Faith in the Word of God."* All of that is correct, but at the same time, doesn't really say very much.

In this Volume, I have already addressed this subject, and I do so again only because it is so very, very important. In fact, nothing could be more important as it regards the Child of God. If the Believer doesn't have the proper object to which his Faith must be attached, the end result, and without exception, will be failure and defeat.

For the last 50 or so years, most teachers of Faith have claimed that one must increase their Faith, and they have proposed all type of methods by which this could be done. That is incorrect!

At a particular time, *"the Apostles said unto the Lord, increase our Faith."*

Jesus answered by saying, *"If ye had faith as a grain of mustard seed, you might say unto this sycamine tree, be thou plucked up by the root, and be thou planted in the sea; and it should obey you"* (Lk. 17:5-6).

He was telling them in this statement, even as we've already stated, that it was not the quantity of their faith that was important, but rather the quality. And by quality, we are referring to the proper object of Faith. He didn't explain that to them at the time, because it would have been pointless to have done so. In fact, He said to them as it regards such teaching:

"I have yet many things to say unto you, but ye cannot bear them now.

"Howbeit when He, the Spirit of Truth is come (the Holy Spirit), *He will guide you into all Truth: for He shall not speak of Himself; but whatsoever He shall hear, that shall He speak: and He will show you things to come.*

"He shall glorify Me: for He shall receive of Mine, and shall show it unto you" (Jn. 16:12-14).

THE CROSS AND THE HOLY SPIRIT

The Holy Spirit couldn't come into the hearts and lives of Believers to abide permanently, until the Cross was a fact. At the Cross, Jesus paid the terrible sin debt owed by man to God, which meant that man could be totally and fully justified upon Faith, thereby totally and perfectly cleansing the temple, making it possible for the Holy Spirit to now abide permanently. Hence Paul would say:

"Know ye not that ye are the temple of God, and that the Spirit of God dwelleth in you?" (I Cor. 3:16).

It is the Holy Spirit Who guarantees the results of our Faith, that is if our Faith is properly placed (Gal. 5:5). That proper place is the Cross, which refers to what Jesus there did on our behalf, which has continued results, and in fact, results which will never be discontinued (Eph. 2:12-19).

There is no power in the Cross per se; however, it is what took place at the Cross, which gives the Holy Spirit, in Whom resides the power, the latitude to work in our lives. Hence Paul said:

"For the preaching (Word) *of the Cross is to them that perish foolishness; but unto us which are saved it is the Power of God"* (I Cor. 1:18). In other words, the Cross is what makes the power possible, simply because the

legal work of Christ carried out at the Cross, gives the Holy Spirit the legal right to exert His power on our behalf, hence Paul also referring to this as *"the Law of the Spirit of Life in Christ Jesus"* (Rom. 8:2).

As I've already stated, I'm addressing this in every way possible, simply because there is nothing more important in the Believer's life than the proper object of his Faith.

THE GROWTH OF FAITH

The Holy Spirit through Paul also said, *"So then Faith cometh by hearing, and hearing by the Word of God"* (Rom. 10:17).

This means simply, that we hear the Word of God being properly taught and preached, and if we properly hear it, our Faith will definitely increase. Now notice that I said *"properly!"*

If we hear the Word of God improperly taught and preached, it will fall out to our harm, as should be obvious. What do we mean by the Word of God being properly taught and preached?

To properly teach and preach the Word of God, the Preacher must have a proper knowledge of the Cross. In fact, even as we've said many times in this Volume, the Word and the Cross, or the Cross and the Gospel, or the Cross and Faith, are all synonymous. In other words, when you've said one, you've said the other.

The story of the Bible is the story of the Creation, Fall, and Redemption of man. The Creation takes up the first two Chapters of the Bible (Gen., Chpts. 1-2), the Fall takes up the Third Chapter, and man's Redemption covers the entirety of the balance of the Bible. It begins in Genesis Chapter 4 with an example of the manner in which man would be redeemed, which would be by the Cross, symbolized by the slain lamb and its shed blood. That theme is then carried throughout the entirety of the Word of God. Every Prophecy in the Old Testament, in one way or the other, whether directly or indirectly, points to the coming Redeemer, and His manner of Redemption, i.e., *"the Cross."* In fact, the great Sacrificial System of the Mosaic Law, all typified, and without exception, the Cross of Christ. Every vessel in the Tabernacle and Temple, in some way personified the Life, Ministry, and Death of Christ on behalf of lost humanity.

Likewise, all instruction given in the New Testament, points back toward that Finished Work. In other words, everything, and without exception, is based on the Sacrifice of Christ.

So, if the Preacher is to properly teach and preach the Word, he must do so with the understanding that the Word of God is in fact the Cross, one might say, and the Cross is in fact, the Word of God.

If the Believer hears it in that fashion, which means that his Faith is properly placed, growth will automatically come about within his heart and life. This is the manner in which the Holy Spirit works and, I might quickly add, the only manner. If we attempt to make other things the object of our Faith, and irrespective as to how good in their own right those other things might be, the Holy Spirit simply will not work for us. To be sure, He will always do all that He can on our behalf; however, He will not break *"the Law of the Spirit of Life which is in Christ Jesus."* Faith ever placed in the Cross, and ever maintained in the Cross, every guarantees His leading, guidance, empowerment and help. Faith otherwise placed, closes off His help to us. That's a sobering thought, considering that we must have His help, but it happens to be the truth.

THE OFFERING OF ISAAC

The phrase, *"Offered up Isaac,"* refers to the fact, that even though God stopped Abraham's hand at the last moment, still, in the mind of Abraham, the Patriarch had already offered up Isaac.

The construction in the Greek makes it clear that while the testing of Abraham was still in progress, he had already offered up his son, that is, before the trial had come to an issue, by the act of his obedient will, through Faith in God, he had committed himself to the completion of the act. This means that Abraham met the test through faith before there was any visible evidence of God's intervening Hand. The Patriarch fully expected to offer his son as a Sacrifice, and as fully expected God to raise his body from the dead out of the ashes of the burnt Sacrifice

(Wuest). As stated, there has probably never been a test of faith exactly like this!

WHAT DID THIS TEST OF FAITH INCLUDE?

The phrase, *"And he that had received the Promises offered up his only begotten son,"* proclaims by this action, as well as the terminology, that this test of Faith, was far more than merely a conflict between Abraham's love for his son and his duty to God. It may well have included that, but the major thrust of the test was in two parts:

1. In this test of the Patriarch's Faith, he had difficulty in reconciling the different Revelations made to him. God had promised him innumerous posterity through Isaac; yet now He called on him to offer Isaac as a sacrifice. How then could the promise be fulfilled?

Though he did not understand, Abraham knew how to obey. His faith told him that God would work out His purpose, even if He had to raise the boy from the dead.

2. The greater action of all of this, was that God would show the Patriarch as to how the great work of Justification by Faith, which He had shown the Patriarch some years earlier, would be worked out (Gen. 15:6). It would be through the death of God's only Son. As God called upon Abraham to offer up his son, through whom the Messiah would ultimately come, God would give His Son, of Whom the former was but a type. So, from this graphic illustration, in other words, so graphic that it beggars description, God would show Abraham the manner in which all of this would be done.

But it would remain until the time of Moses, over 400 years later, that God would portray the *"means"* by which this death would be carried out, which would be by the Cross (Num. 21:9). The manner in which both of these types were carried out is worthy of consideration.

The manner of the offering of Isaac was not precipitated by sin and failure. It rather only spoke to obedience. This typified God Who would give His Only Son, Who would acquiesce perfectly to this Sacrifice, even as Isaac had obeyed and acquiesced perfectly.

To the contrary, the manner in which this Revelation came to Moses as it regards the *"means"* of this Sacrifice, which would be the Cross, came out of sin and failure, as it could only come out of sin and failure.

To which we've already alluded, Israel, due to the difficulty of the way, *"spoke against God, and against Moses"* (Num. 21:5).

They complained bitterly about the way, and then said *"our soul loatheth this light bread,"* speaking of the Manna, which was in essence, a complaint against Christ, of Whom the Manna was a type.

The Scripture says that *"the LORD sent fiery serpents among the people, and they bit the people and much people of Israel died"* (Num. 21:6).

At that point, the Lord told Moses to *"make thee a fiery serpent, and set it upon a pole: and it shall come to pass, that everyone that is bitten, when he looketh upon it, shall live"* (Num. 21:8).

Jesus alluded to this in His statement to Nicodemus, by saying, *"And as Moses lifted up the serpent in the wilderness, even so must the Son of Man be lifted up"* (Jn. 3:14). Of course, Christ was speaking of His being lifted up on a Cross.

Inasmuch as Jesus died for sinners, this Revelation which came to Moses concerning the *"means"* of the Sacrifice which was demanded, that is if man was to be saved, had to come out of sin and failure, which it did.

So in these two Revelations, we have the manner in which Justification by Faith would be brought about, which would be by the death of God's Only Son, which was shown to Abraham, and the means by which this death would be carried out, which would be by the Cross, which was shown to Moses.

(18) "OF WHOM IT WAS SAID, THAT IN ISAAC SHALL THY SEED BE CALLED:"

The structure is:

1. *"Of whom it was said,"* refers to Genesis 21:12.

2. Abraham had other sons, Ishmael by Hagar, and six others by Keturah, whom he would marry after the death of Sarah (Gen. 25:1-2). But it was Isaac whom the Lord had designated to be the chosen one, through whom the Messiah would ultimately come.

3. Isaac was the promised son, and thereby, was totally and completely a work of the Spirit. This refers to the fact, that

had not God performed a miracle, Isaac could not be born. In fact, I think it could be said that every single thing God does, could be labeled in one sense as a miracle.

THE PROMISED ONE

The phrase, *"Of whom it was said,"* refers to this one being predetermined by God (Gen. 21:12). The statement was originally made to Abraham to assure him that the promise was not to be fulfilled through Ishmael by the bondwoman Hagar, but through Isaac. Of course, it was implied that Isaac was to reach manhood; and yet, not withstanding this, and notwithstanding the fact that Abraham fully believed this, he prepared deliberately, in obedience to the Divine command, to put him to death.

ISAAC

The phrase, *"That in Isaac shall thy seed be called,"* refers to the fact that the posterity of Abraham was to be named after Isaac, which meant that it was to descend only from him, and not Ishmael, etc.

The word *"called"* in the Scriptures, is often equivalent to the verb *"to be."* To name or call a thing was the same as to say that it was or that it existed.

It does not mean here that his *"spiritual"* children were to be called or selected from among the posterity of Isaac, for that being the case, it would have only referred to Jews, but that the posterity promised to Abraham would descend neither from Ishmael nor the sons of Keturah, but in the line of Isaac.

This is a strong circumstance insisted on by the Apostle, to show the strength of Abraham's Faith. It was shown not only by his willingness to offer up the child of his old age — his only son by his beloved wife — but by his readiness, at the command of God, to sacrifice even him on whom the fulfillment of the Promises depended (Barnes).

(19) "ACCOUNTING THAT GOD WAS ABLE TO RAISE HIM UP, EVEN FROM THE DEAD; FROM WHENCE ALSO HE RECEIVED HIM IN A FIGURE."

The composite is:

1. The word *"accounting"* refers to the fact that Abraham came to a conclusion, meaning that he would obey God whatever!

2. He knew the Promise could not fail, so he reasoned (accounted) that God would have to raise Isaac from the dead.

3. Isaac's death took place symbolically, in the sacrifice of the ram: correspondingly, the restoration was only a symbolic restoration from the dead, *"in a figure."*

ACCOUNTING

The word *"accounting"* in the Greek is *"logisamenos,"* and means, *"reckoning, supposing, concluding."*

This one word tells us that Abraham had been extremely perplexed at the demand of God for him to offer up Isaac in sacrifice. While the struggle of doing this to his own son was paramount to say the least, the indication is, that it was a struggle of faith more than anything else. Abraham knew and understood his purpose and mission in life. He lived totally and completely that the great Promises of God would be carried out through him. He understood, what it all meant, at least as far as a poor human being could understand.

He knew that through him the Messiah would ultimately come into the world, which would be the greatest event in human history, and by far we might quickly add, and that Isaac was the promised son who would establish the lineage. So, realizing what was at stake, he struggled in his own mind and spirit, to know for certain that it was God telling him this. He reasoned that it was, and then set out to obey, irrespective of the cost.

GOD IS ABLE

The phrase, *"That God was able to raise him up, even from the dead,"* proclaims the fact, that the Patriarch reasoned that it took a miracle from God to bring Isaac into the world, and that God could perform another miracle in raising him from the dead. Abraham reasons in his mind and spirit that it was God Who gave life to his aged body to begin with in order that he could father Isaac, and life to Sarah's womb who incidentally had been barren all her life, in order that she could conceive; therefore, God, the Patriarch reasoned, would have to give life once again to Isaac out of the ashes of his burned body. He knew that the Promise of God could not fail as it regarded the seed that would be raised

up through Isaac, so he reasoned that God would have to raise the boy from the dead.

This fits in perfectly with the Genesis narrative, for as Abraham went off with the boy to sacrifice him — and as we have seen he was fully determined to go through with the command — he said to the servants, *"Stay here with the donkey while I and the boy go over there. We will worship and then we will come back to you"* (Gen. 22:5).

We pass over these words lightly, I think little realizing the vast struggle of faith which took place here. But Abraham reasoned in his mind and spirit that *"God is able!"* That is the crux of it all: *"God is able!"* This is the lesson, I think, that the spirit desires that we here learn. Whatever else it says, whatever direction it takes, *"God is able!"*

A PERSONAL EXPERIENCE

In one way or the other, every single Believer has to prove to himself that *"God is able!"* And that refers to anything that must be done. While of course our own personal circumstances are of far less degree than that of Abraham, still, there has to be a time in our Christian experiences, that we come to the conclusion, and beyond the shadow of a doubt, that *"God is able!"*

When the Lord first called Frances and me into Evangelistic Work, which was in 1956, our situation looked anything but promising. We lived in a little tiny town in Northeast Louisiana, by the name of Wisner. My Dad had built a church in this community several years earlier, and it was there that I met Frances, and we were married. Other than the day that the Lord saved me, that was the greatest thing that ever happened to me. The Call of God was on my life, and Frances was definitely made a part of that Call, in which she has proved so efficient and faithful through these many years.

The Lord has helped us to touch a great part of this world with the Gospel of Jesus Christ, but the beginnings of this Ministry didn't look very promising, to say the least.

At this particular time in 1956, we were preparing to go into full time Evangelistic Work. While that particular time would not completely come until 1958, still, it actually began at that earlier year.

Without going into detail, knowing what the Lord had called me to do, and yet not knowing how in the world it could be done, even as insignificant as it seemed to be at the time, I remember one particular afternoon in question. It was to be a moment in which the Lord would move upon me greatly, letting me know that *"He is able!"*

We were living at the time in a little tiny 32' long house trailer. Frances had gone somewhere for an hour or so, and I remember taking this time while being alone, to go to the Lord in prayer. The scene is freeze-framed in my mind, and will be there forever.

As I went to prayer that afternoon, all of these things were weighing heavily on my mind. How could I go into full-time Evangelistic Work, considering that almost no Preachers or Churches even knew that I was alive? How would I get started? How could we make a living? Donnie was then 4 years old, and how could I be an Evangelist, and at the same time give him proper schooling?

And then the Spirit of God began to come upon me that memorable afternoon. We had learned a little chorus a few weeks earlier. The words are:

*"My Lord is able, He's able, I know
    that He is able,
"I know my Lord is able to carry me
    through.
"My Lord is able, I know that He's
    able,
"I know my Lord is able to carry me
    through."*

*"For He has healed the brokenhearted,
    and set the captive free,
"He's healed the sick and raised the
    dead and walked upon the sea,
"My Lord is able, He's able, I know
    that He is able,
"I know my Lord is able to carry me
    through."*

THE SPIRIT OF GOD BEGAN
TO MOVE UPON MY HEART

The Holy Spirit took the words from that song, *"My Lord is Able,"* and began to impress them mightily upon my mind. He just kept saying that over and over to me, *"I am able!" "I am able!" "I am able!"*

Without going all into detail, the Lord let me know that memorable afternoon, that all that He had called me to do, that He was able to bring it all to pass. I must trust Him, and do so explicitly, but never fear, He was able.

And so He was, and so He is, and so He ever shall be.

This doesn't mean that there were not difficult days. In fact, there have been many of those, but every single time, He has proven and beyond the shadow of a doubt, that He is able.

A FIGURE

The phrase, *"From whence also he received him in a figure,"* actually says, *"And figuratively speaking, he did receive Isaac back from death."*

The idea is, at the last moment, God stayed the hand of the Patriarch even as he was ready to plunge the knife into his son's breast. Abraham had passed the test. He did not bind the Power of God to the life of Isaac but was persuaded that it would be effective in his ashes when he was dead no less than when he was alive and breathing.

Instead, God chose *"a ram caught in a thicket by his horns,"* and told the Patriarch to offer up this animal as a *"burnt offering in the stead of his son."* So, figuratively, Isaac died in the ram, and figuratively, at least in the mind of Abraham, his son was raised from the dead. The latter is due to the fact, that in the mind of Abraham, he had already offered up Isaac, i.e., *"committed himself to the death of his son."*

As well, all of this was a *"figure,"* of the manner in which God would redeem humanity, which would be by death, and furthermore, the death of His only Son, the Lord Jesus Christ.

(20) "BY FAITH ISAAC BLESSED JACOB AND ESAU CONCERNING THINGS TO COME."

The diagram is:

1. The Patriarch's had a faith that looked beyond death.

2. Their faith was so great, that they held a firm conviction that death could not frustrate God's purposes.

3. Consequently, they could speak with confidence of what would happen after they

died. Their faith, being stronger than death, in a way overcame death, for their words were fulfilled.

BY FAITH

The phrase, *"By faith Isaac blessed Jacob and Esau,"* does not concern itself with the spiritual condition of the two men, one being righteous and the other unrighteous, but rather what their seed would bring forth. As well, let us state, that true Faith, which Isaac definitely possessed, always brings a *"Blessing"* — even to the members of the family who aren't righteous.

However, the greater blessing will always be to those who exhibit Faith, even as Jacob did. Esau had no faith in God and no regard for the coming Promise. He was concerned only with the things of this present world. Nevertheless, the Faith of Isaac blessed him anyway, although not at all like the blessing of Jacob. The seed of Esau would be concerned only with the things of this world, while the seed of Jacob, which pertained to the Jews, would look up to God.

If it is to be noticed, Paul says nothing about Jacob's deception of his old father. Actually, at this stage he is not interested in the struggle of faith, as it was on the part of Jacob, but rather the Faith of Isaac. He doesn't even mention Isaac attempting to give the blessing to Esau, with that once again concerning the struggle of faith. In fact, the struggle in one way or the other, is a given in the hearts and lives of all Believers.

This perhaps would have been a great lesson to the Christian Jews of Paul's day. Some of them as well, were having a great struggle with their Faith, which is what the Epistle to the Hebrews is all about. The Apostle is telling them, that these Patriarchs rose above their struggles, and were able to pronounce great blessings of faith that reached out even until Paul's day, and continues unto this hour, and in fact, will never die.

All of this is meant to be an encouragement to us as well.

THINGS TO COME

The phrase, *"Concerning things to come,"* concerns the Revelation of God given to these men, which reached out in Faith to

the future. On each occasion, Isaac spoke out of a firm conviction that Blessing given in accordance with God's purposes could not possibly fail. Though as stated there were marked differences in the two Blessings, concerning Jacob and Esau, but these are passed over. They are at this time not relevant. The important thing is Isaac's faith. Fittingly, the sons are listed in the order in which they received the Blessings, not that of their birth.

(21) "BY FAITH JACOB, WHEN HE WAS A DYING, BLESSED BOTH THE SONS OF JOSEPH; AND WORSHIPPED, LEANING UPON THE TOP OF HIS STAFF."

The structure is:

1. The words *"By faith Jacob,"* proclaim the fact, that the vision had come down to this Patriarch.

2. His faith was as strong or stronger when he was dying, than at any other time.

3. The blessing he pronounced on the two sons of Joseph, proclaimed his faith, and above all, proclaimed his faith for the future.

4. As he blessed, he worshipped, showing that the Spirit of God was in the Blessing.

5. His staff intimates the Word of God, of which we will have more to say momentarily.

FAITH

The phrase, *"By faith Jacob,"* proclaims the Faith of the Patriarch shining as brightly as his father Isaac, and his grandfather Abraham. And so with that particular word, even though Paul doesn't mention it here, we have the last Patriarch mentioned, who made up the great phrase, *"The God of Abraham, of Isaac, and of Jacob."* These three would be used by the Lord to bring the entirety of the nation of Israel into the world, raised up for the specific purpose of giving the world the Word of God, which they did, and as well, serving as the womb of the Messiah, Who was the fulfillment of all the prophecies. Sadly and regrettably, they didn't recognize Him when he came; nevertheless, He came! He, the Lord Jesus Christ, fulfilled the Promise, and in fact, was the Promise! God brought it all about by the *"Faith"* of these three men.

DEATH

The phrase, *"When he was a dying,"* proclaims the fact, that even though the Patriarch would die, his faith would not die, actually coming down to this very hour. In fact, faith cannot die, and that is what makes it so great. And of course, when we speak of Faith, we are speaking of Faith in Christ, and what Christ would do, and in fact did do at the Cross, all on our behalf. That was ever the object of the Faith of these individuals.

We know from the Text that his Faith burned brighter at the time of his death than at any other time. This means, that despite the problems throughout his life, despite the horrific struggle with the flesh, despite the ups and downs, despite the many failures, there is nothing left now but victory, and all because of his Faith in God, and more particularly, What and Whom God had promised. God had promised a Redeemer, and Jacob knew this Redeemer would come through these sons that God had given unto him.

The only thing that anyone can take with him when he dies is his faith. And of course, the only ones who have faith, and we're speaking of the Faith which God will recognize, are those who have placed their trust in the Lord Jesus Christ. He Alone must ever be the object of our Faith.

THE BLESSING

The phrase, *"Blessed both the sons of Joseph,"* pertains to Manasseh and Ephraim, both born to Joseph in Egypt.

Isaac's action in blessing Jacob, and Jacob's in blessing Ephraim, illustrate Romans 9:16. Isaac willed to bless Esau, and Joseph ran to set Jacob's hands aright, but neither could defeat the purpose of God. As with Isaac, the Blessing went against the natural order of birth.

At the time of the Blessing, Joseph tried to have the major blessing given to Manasseh, the firstborn. But Jacob crossed his hands to pick out Ephraim as the greater. God is not bound by human rules like those that give pride and benefit of place to the firstborn. He fulfills His purposes and He chooses. This incident, like the blessing of Jacob by Isaac, again illustrates the theme of the Patriarchal blessing with its fulfillment far distant. At the time the words were spoken, fulfillment could be known only by faith.

NOTES

While each son received a Blessing, the greater Blessing was given to Ephraim, the younger.

Though Jacob's natural eyesight was dim, his spiritual discernment was not. Deliberately, Jacob crossed his hands *"guiding his hands wittingly"* (Gen. 48:14), or as the Hebrew reads, literally *"he made his hands to understand."*

Note it is expressly said in the Genesis account, that *"Israel"* did this: it was the new man that was acting, not the old man, *"Jacob."* And *"by faith"* he blessed both the sons of Joseph. Truly, it was not by sight or reason.

What was more unlikely than that the children of these two young Egyptian princes, for this is virtually what they were, should ever forsake Egypt, the land of their birth, and migrate to Canaan! How unlikely, too, that each of these boys should become a separate tribe in Israel. And how improbable that the younger should be exalted above the elder, both in importance and number, and should become *"a multitude of peoples"* (Gen. 48:19). How impossible for Jacob to foresee (by any human deduction) that long centuries afterwards, Ephraim should become representative of the kingdom of *"Israel,"* as distinct from *"Judah."*

But Jacob had heard God, had rested on His Word, and had believed in the sure fulfillment of His Promise. What a grand display of faith! Nature's eyes might be dim, but faith's vision was sharp: in his bodily weakness the strength of faith was perfected (Pink).

JACOB

When the Patriarch was dying, he blessed; when he was dying he became a blessing. This is the way we ought to die — letting our lives become a blessing. If we live the transformed life and we walk in the pathway of Righteousness, Holiness, and Duty, then the day of our death will be a blessed day; it will be a blessing to others as well.

It is Faith that does all of this, and Faith alone! But let it ever be remembered, that when we say *"Faith,"* the ultimate object must always be *"Christ and Him Crucified"* (I Cor. 2:2).

WORSHIP

The short phrase, *"And worshipped,"* portrays to us the fact, that the Spirit of God was involved in all that Jacob did in these final hours. This portrays the fact as to how God honors Faith.

Worship is what we are, while praise is what we do.

All of these individuals did what they did, whether of Blessing or of obedience, or both, all through Faith, which means they had their Faith fixed on the proper object, which was Christ. Anything else, and I'm speaking of any other object of our Faith, is not actually true faith, or true obedience, or true blessing. In fact, that's where much of the Church is presently:

There are tens of thousands of Churches across the land and around the world, who are in effect *"blessing Churches!"* There is nothing wrong with that, in fact it is very right, if the blessing is based on the right foundation; however, most of the time it isn't.

True worship comes out of the Spirit of God, Who Alone guarantees the Blessing. Everything He does, is done on the basis of Christ and Him Crucified. The Scripture refers to this as *"The Law of the Spirit of Life in Christ Jesus"* (Rom. 8:2). So what am I saying?

I'm saying there can be no true blessing without true worship, and all of this comes through what Jesus did at the Cross. If our Faith is properly placed in the Cross of Christ, and that alone, then we can bless people with the assurance that the blessing is from God and not the sound of mere words. As stated, Jacob's worshipping, showed that the Spirit of God was present, Who instigated the worship, and guaranteed the Blessing.

THE WORD OF GOD

The phrase, *"Leaning upon the top of his staff,"* is not recorded in the Genesis account of Chapter 48 in that Book; however, that in no way means just because it wasn't recorded, that it didn't happen. More than likely, Paul derived this information from the Jewish Targums, which in effect was a Commentary on the Old Testament. The Holy Spirit told him the information was correct,

irrespective of where he derived it. Let's look at it a little closer:

The *"staff"* of the ancients was far more than a mere walking stick, etc. While it definitely was a stick, and while it definitely was used for walking, it had far greater significance than that. On the staffs were carved all the history of whatever was desired. In the case of Jacob, there would have been carved on his staff, at least in abbreviated form, all the happenings from Adam to his day, as it pertained to God dealing with men. As stated, it would be in very abbreviated form; however, it was all there in chronological order. In fact, one could in essence say, that this was the *"Bible"* of that particular time.

So, when he *"leaned upon his staff,"* he was in effect leaning on *"the Word of God."* He was in effect saying that everything which had been done was real, and every Promise that was made by God, would definitely come to pass. Understanding it in this light, the entirety of the Text now becomes more understandable.

The Patriarch blessed the two boys, and then leaning heavily upon his staff, begins to worship God, recalling all the great Promises carved upon this piece of wood.

(22) "BY FAITH JOSEPH, WHEN HE DIED, MADE MENTION OF THE DEPARTING OF THE CHILDREN OF ISRAEL; AND GAVE COMMANDMENT CONCERNING HIS BONES."

The composite is:

1. The faith held by Joseph, was the same identical faith as those who had gone before him.

2. His faith looked beyond death.

3. That faith said that in due course, God would send the people back to the land of Canaan.

4. When the children of Israel did go back, they were given commandment to take his bones with them. While he lived most of his life in Egypt, his heart was in Canaan, the land of the Promise.

JOSEPH

The phrase, *"By Faith Joseph,"* portrays one of the most striking personalities in the entirety of the Word of God. He is the only man in the Bible of whom no faults or sins are recorded. This doesn't mean that he never sinned, because the Bible says that *"All have sinned"*; however, regarding Joseph, whatever those faults and failures were, they were not recorded, and because he was a type of Christ in a very unusual way. He is also the first to be spoken of as having the Spirit in him (Gen. 41:38). Others before him had the Holy Spirit, but he is the first one to be spoken of in this capacity.

DEATH

The phrase, *"When he died,"* once again brings faith up to the last moments. This portrays the fact, as with the others, that he looked beyond his lifespan, believing what God had said about the future.

As we read these simple statements written here by Paul, but yet with such a wealth of meaning, what will it be like when we have the opportunity in the portals of glory, to converse with them personally, and discuss these glorious things. In a sense, their journey is ours, because as stated, the same faith we possess is that which they possessed. In a sense, their faith has come down to us, which is what God intended.

What a privilege to be a part of such nobility, such giants of the Faith, such men and women of honor.

Looking at all of this in a secular sense, every single freedom we presently possess, all prosperity we now have, in this which we refer to as *"western civilization,"* are all made possible, and without exception, by the faith of these here mentioned, and others not mentioned. Of course, the world knows this not at all; nevertheless, it is the Truth!

THE DEPARTURE OF ISRAEL

The phrase, *"Made mention of the departing of the children of Israel,"* proclaims the possibility that Joseph had been given added revelation concerning this coming time. While he very well knew what God had spoken to his great grandfather Abraham, his grandfather Isaac, and his father Jacob, about this coming time, every indication is, that the Lord had given him more light on the subject. On his dying bed he said:

"And God will surely visit you, and bring you out of this land into the land which he

NOTES

sware to Abraham, to Isaac, and to Jacob" (Gen. 50:24).

THE COMMANDMENT

The phrase, *"And gave commandment concerning his bones,"* proclaims the certitude of this coming event, and that his home was not Egypt, but rather the Promised Land of Canaan (Gen. 50:25).

As well, the experience of Joseph is meant to be a portrayal to us of the Truth, that this world is not our home. Our heart is with Christ, and Christ is in Heaven. Before the Cross, the Promised Land consisted of a little part of this present world; since the Cross, it consists of the portals of glory, which Paul referred to as a *"better country."*

THE OLD TESTAMENT

The Reader must understand that the Old Testament is much more than mere history. While it definitely is that, at the same time, it is the story of our Redemption. Every experience of these Patriarchs and Prophets of Faith, presents another step toward our Salvation. If we read the Old Testament in that light, it will take on a brand-new meaning.

For the fulfillment of Joseph's dying request (Ex. 13:19), *"Moses took the bones of Joseph with him"* out of Egypt; and the Scripture further says, *"And the bones of Joseph buried they in Shechem."*

(23) "BY FAITH MOSES, WHEN HE WAS BORN, WAS HID THREE MONTHS OF HIS PARENTS, BECAUSE THEY SAW HE WAS A PROPER CHILD; AND THEY WERE NOT AFRAID OF THE KING'S COMMANDMENT."

The exegesis is:

1. With Moses, and what God would reveal to him, faith is about to be enlarged.

2. Him being a *"proper child,"* means more than him merely being a pretty baby. By Revelation they knew that he was favored by God.

3. Knowing this, which means they believed that God would protect them and him, they were not fearful of the king's commandment.

MOSES

The phrase, *"By Faith Moses,"* proclaims the beginning of the manner in which God will deal with the human race in an entirely different way. He would give His Law to Moses, which would in effect be God's Standard of Righteousness. It has served as the Standard ever since for all nations, at least for all those who have even a modicum of intelligence.

The Revelation of God which pertains to His dealings with man has always been a progressive Revelation. In other words, the Lord always adds to what He has already given.

From the time of the Fall, God had ordained that man would approach Him, at least to the degree that they then could, by sacrifice — and we speak of the sacrifice of an innocent victim, namely a clean animal, which involved the shedding of blood. This is portrayed in Genesis Chapter 4, and continued up unto the time that the Law was given to Moses, a little over 2,400 years later.

A PROPER CHILD

The phrase, *"When he was born, was hid three months of his parents, because they saw he was a proper child,"* means that in the sight or estimation of God, Moses was comely. The *"Faith"* here spoken of, concerned his parents, with the next Verse pertaining to his faith.

"Proper" in the Greek is *"asteios,"* and means *"comely."* The construction in the Greek text is a dative of respect, which means, *"he was comely with respect to God."*

As we've stated, the parents of Moses did not take the risk they did, simply because he was a handsome baby. By Revelation from the Lord, they knew that God had His Hand on this child, and were thereby given instructions to protect him at all costs. I doubt very seriously that the Lord gave them very much information; however, what He did give them, gave them a firm grasp of the situation and that God's Hand was in the entirety of the matter.

The parents of Moses were Amram and Jochebed (Ex. 6:20). Jochebed was the daughter of Levi, the son of Jacob (Num. 26:59).

We aren't told how old that Amram or Jochebed were when Moses was born. We do know that Amram lived to be 137 years old.

Moses was born to Amram 80 years before the exodus (Acts 7:22-30), which means it was definitely possible that the father and

mother of Moses were alive at the time of the Exodus; however, it is not likely that they were, meaning that Moses had been born to them late in life.

AN EVIL COMMANDMENT

The phrase, *"And they were not afraid of the king's commandment,"* refers to the fact as stated, that they had a Revelation from God on which to base their faith, for Faith comes by God's Word (Rom. 10:17).

Pharaoh had given the mandate that all male children of the Israelites were to be killed at birth.

We might say in passing that the children of God are by God obligated to obey the laws of the country in which we reside, and disobedience to these laws is sin against God. But we are obligated to obey these laws only up to the point where obedience to such laws would mean disobedience to God. Consequently, the parents of Moses were entirely within their rights in this case, for the reigning Pharaoh was violating the Law of God which forbids murder. This law was given to Noah long before Moses (Gen. 9:1-7).

(24) "BY FAITH MOSES, WHEN HE WAS COME TO YEARS, REFUSED TO BE CALLED THE SON OF PHARAOH'S DAUGHTER;"

The diagram is:

1. Now we come to the faith of Moses.

2. Moses refused the crown of Egypt.

3. This is not indicative at all of the modern gospel.

THE FAITH OF MOSES

The phrase, *"By Faith Moses, when he was come to years,"* refers to him coming to the age of 40 (Acts 7:23). Up till this time, he had been raised in the palace of the Pharaoh. He had been adopted by Pharaoh's daughter, whose name Josephus said was Thermuthis. It is said that she adopted him in order to make him her father's successor as ruler of Egypt.

It is believed that Moses was adopted at possibly about five years old, and at that time began his education as the son of Pharaoh's daughter. The Scripture says that he was *"learned in all the wisdom of the Egyptians, and was mighty in words and in deeds"* (Acts 7:22).

Josephus also said that he was put in command of the Egyptian war against the Ethiopians and conquered them completely.

THE REVELATION OF GOD TO AMRAM

After the death of Joseph and his brothers, the Israelites, as their descendants were now called, flourished in Egypt. Meanwhile, the Egyptians, forgetful of the benefits they had received from Joseph, began to envy the prosperity and happiness of the Children of Israel. The kingdom, meanwhile, had passed to another dynasty, and they became very cruel to the Israelites, forcing them to cut numerous canals from the river, build walls around their cities, and erect pyramid after pyramid.

They spent about 100 years enduring these afflictions. Eventually, they suffered a still greater cruelty. One of the Egyptian wise men, who was able to somewhat foretell the future, told Pharaoh that a very special child would be born to the Israelites. If he were allowed to live, he would diminish the Egyptian dominion and free the Israelites. He would excel all men in virtue, and would obtain everlasting fame.

Alarmed, the King commanded that every male child born to the Israelites be thrown into the Nile River, and that if any parents should try to save their offspring, they and their families would be killed.

Amram, a Hebrew of noble birth, was greatly troubled because of this law, and he prayed to God. Appearing to him in his sleep, God reminded him of what He had done for the Israelites in the past, and told him He would continue His favor in the future. *"And, therefore,"* He continued, *"that I will provide for your common welfare, and particularly for your own fame. For that child, whose birth has caused such dread that the Egyptians have doomed the Israelite children to destruction, shall be your child. He will be concealed from those who seek to destroy him. He will deliver the Hebrew nation from their bondage in Egypt, and his memory will live as long as the universe, not only among the Hebrews, but among other nations also"* (Josephus).

REFUSED

The phrase, *"Refused to be called the son of Pharaoh's daughter,"* refers to a settled

disposition on the part of Moses. As stated, he was now 40 years old.

The indication is that God had begun dealing with him about this very matter. He could have been the Pharaoh of Egypt, the mightiest man on the face of the Earth, but of this he would refuse.

I think this doesn't match much modern gospel. Moses, according to the present message, would have been urged to remain in the Palace of Pharaoh, thereby ultimately becoming Pharaoh. It would be claimed that he could do much more for the Lord as Pharaoh of Egypt than otherwise. And how do I know that this modern gospel would propose such a scenario?

I know this because of what is presently being done. Bartenders are told they can keep tending bar after coming to Christ, country western singers can keep singing that particular type of music, gamblers can keep gambling, night club performers can continue their performances, etc.

Let the Reader understand, that if one is to truly follow Christ, that one must at the same time refuse the system of this world. And that means everything about the world. We as Christians do not march to its drums, do not respond to its invitations, and do not sing its songs.

The idea that the youth can be won to the Lord or kept for the Lord, by using the rock-'n'-roll spirit, is preposterous indeed! No one will be won to the Lord and no one will be kept for the Lord.

The Child of God must *"refuse"* all that Pharaoh offers. There could have been no greater position in the day of Moses than this position as the most powerful man in the world; however, that was not what God told him to do. While he did tell Daniel to stay in the palace, he told Moses to leave. And yet, Daniel's life was totally set apart from that of the heathen who were all around him. As well, the situation regarding Moses and Daniel was totally different!

(25) "CHOOSING RATHER TO SUFFER AFFLICTION WITH THE PEOPLE OF GOD, THAN TO ENJOY THE PLEASURES OF SIN FOR A SEASON;"

The structure is:

1. Moses made a choice; every Believer must do the same.

2. To oppose the spirit of the world, one will incur upon himself affliction. This is inevitable!

3. There is pleasure in sin, but it's only for a short time.

THE CHOICE

The phrase, *"Choosing rather to suffer affliction with the people of God,"* proclaims the choice which Moses made. He traded the temporal for the eternal, which is the opposite of what many modern Christians do. Someone said, *"Moses chose the slave-driver's lash rather than Egypt's crown."* His act was an expression of his deliberate choice. He joined his people because they were *"the people of God."* To stand aloof for the sake of ease and pleasure would for him have been apostasy from God, and it is apostasy for anyone else as well!

The Faith of Moses had brought *"conviction of the things not seen,"* which *"are eternal"*; hence he looked not at *"the things seen"* which are *"for a season"* (II Cor. 4:18).

THE PLEASURES OF SIN

The phrase, *"Than to enjoy the pleasures of sin for a season,"* presents the choice that must be made, *"affliction with the people of God,"* or *"the pleasures of sin for a season."*

The significance and source of this refusal lay in his preferring to suffer ill-usage with God's people rather than to have a short-lived enjoyment of sin ... It was because they were God's people, not solely because they were of his blood, that Moses threw in his lot with them. It was this which illustrated his faith.

He believed that God would fulfill His Promise to His people, little likelihood as at present there seemed to be of any great future for his race. On the other hand there was the pleasure of sin, the enjoyment which was within his reach if only he committed the sin of denying his people and renouncing their future as promised by God.

That which is said here, which concerns the enjoyment to be reaped from sin, does not refer to the pleasure of gratifying sensual appetite and so forth, but to the satisfaction of a high ambition and the gratification of finer tastes which he might have had by remaining in the Egyptian court.

NOTES

To be sure, the denial of the type of sin here mentioned, is far harder than the denial of sensual gratification. To be frank, almost none presently, as stated, would refer to the former as that of *"sin."* They would refer to it as *"opportunity,"* or a way to serve God in a greater dimension, etc.

(26) "ESTEEMING THE REPROACH OF CHRIST GREATER RICHES THAN THE TREASURES IN EGYPT: FOR HE HAD RESPECT UNTO THE RECOMPENCE OF THE REWARD."

The diagram is:

1. The value of Christ up beside the world.

2. The reproach of Christ is greater than the riches of Egypt.

3. The reward of Christ is so much greater than the highest reward of the world, that there is no comparison.

ESTIMATION

The phrase, *"Esteeming the reproach of Christ greater riches than the treasures in Egypt,"* carries a wealth of meaning:

1. *"Esteeming"* in the Greek is *"hegeomai,"* and means, *"to consider, to give account, to judge."* Moses looked at the Promises of God, although not yet realized, and in fact wouldn't be realized during his lifetime, believed those Promises, and judged them to be greater than the throne of Egypt.

2. The reproach of Christ, as hard as that is on the flesh, is deemed as far greater than the riches of Egypt. The reason is the reward to which that reproach will lead.

As well, we are told here that there definitely will be a reproach, that is if one truly lives for God.

3. By Paul using the Name of *"Christ"* which means *"the anointed,"* tells us, that Moses reckoned and understood that Christ was the fulfillment of all the Promises, and we speak of the Promises given to Abraham, Isaac, Jacob, etc. While these great Promises in fact included other things, those other things ultimately, and without exception, led to Christ. In fact, the entirety of the theme of the Word of God is Christ, and more particularly, *"Christ and Him Crucified"* (I Cor. 2:2).

4. Even though none of this would be realized in Moses' lifetime, he knew there was

a Resurrection coming, which was all centered up in Christ, which presented the true picture of eternity, and not the foolish thinking of the Egyptians and their pyramids as it regarded the afterlife.

5. This tells us that Moses saw the big picture, and that what was coming, which would be eternal, was of far greater value than the *"treasures in Egypt."*

6. All these treasures were temporal, while the true riches of Christ are eternal.

7. Every single person in the world has to make the same decision. Do you esteem *"the reproach of Christ greater riches than the treasures in this present world"*?

ISRAEL

The words that Paul used here, concerning the reproach of Christ, are almost exactly a quotation from Psalms 89:50-51. The Psalmist said: *"Remember, Lord, the reproach of thy servants; how I do bear in my bosom the reproach of all the mighty people;*

"Wherewith thine enemies have reproached, O LORD; wherewith they have reproached the footsteps of thine Anointed (Christ)."

Here the writer of this Psalm in effect speaks of himself as bearing *"the reproach of the Anointed"* of the Lord; pleading in His Name and identifying himself with his cause. *"The Anointed"* of course, is Christ, for that's what the word *"Anointed"* means.

Throughout the whole of their history the people of Israel were the people of the Christ. Their national existence originated in the Promise to Abraham, which was a Promise of the Christ; until the fullness of time should come their mission was to prepare the way for Him. The reproach which Moses accepted by joining the people of the Promise was, therefore, *"the reproach of the Christ."* In fact, He Who was to ultimately appear as the Messiah was already in the midst of Israel (Ps. 69:9; Col. 1:24; I Pet. 1:11).

(Incidentally, the literal Greek says, *"The reproach of the Christ."*)

CHRIST

The reproach has always centered up in Christ. The reason for that is clear and simple. Jesus is the only way to God. He plainly said

of Himself, *"I am the Way, the Truth, and the Life: no man cometh unto the Father, but by Me"* (Jn. 14:6).

That statement is blunt and to the point, and leaves no room for side issues. If one doesn't accept Christ, one cannot be saved! There is no way to the Father except by and through Christ, and in effect, such terminology means not only that He must be accepted as it regards His Person, but as well, one must accept the Price that He paid that man might be saved. That Price was the Cross, which speaks of His poured out Blood, all which was demanded, in order that the Righteousness of God might be satisfied.

So, when we speak of accepting Christ, we speak as well of accepting all that He has done, which of course is the Cross.

Man doesn't like that. In fact, he doesn't like that at all. The Moslems say that the way to God is through Mohammad. The Jews, having rejected their Own Messiah, claim that the way to God is through Moses. Catholicism says that the way to God is through Mary. The Mormons say that the way to God is through Joseph Smith, whomever in the world that is! Hinduism says there are millions of gods and you can be one yourself. Buddhism, Shintoism, and Confucianism, in essence claim, that man is god. Humanistic psychology in essence claims the same thing! Irrespective, man bridles at the idea that Jesus Christ is the only Way to God.

Untold millions in the world claim their good works as the way to God, or the fact that they haven't done bad things, etc. At any rate, this is the reason that Jesus Christ is the center of all controversy. But it happens to be true, He is the Way and in fact, the only Way.

THE REWARD

The phrase, *"For He had respect unto the recompence of the reward,"* means that Moses habitually *"looked away"* from the treasures in Egypt, and fixed his eye on the Heavenly Reward. History, of course, has vindicated him. We do not so much as know the name of the Pharaoh of his time; and even if we did, he would be of interest to us only because of his link with Moses. But the choice

Moses made resulted in his influence still being felt. It is faith that always emerges triumphant, not worldliness.

If one wants to look at tangible results, as it regards *"reward,"* one should look at the last two Chapters of the Book of Revelation, which are the last two Chapters in the Bible. This is a tangible reward that is absolutely breathtaking in scope, eternal in consequence, and rich in greatness, grandeur, and beauty. But yet, the greatest reward of all is being an *"heir of God, and joint heir with Christ"* (Rom. 8:17). The culminating meaning of all of this is absolutely beyond comprehension. And if such could be summed, it would be summed up in the two words *"with Christ."* He is in fact, the reward, the great reward, the eternal reward.

These statements as given here by Paul were meant for the entirety of the Church, and for all time; however, they were especially directed at the Christian Jews who in fact, were suffering reproach for Christ, with some of them having turned back to Judaism, hence the writing of this Epistle. This no doubt carried great weight with them to realize that they were being called to participate in the same kind of experiences and attitudes the great Moses had.

(27) "BY FAITH HE FORSOOK EGYPT, NOT FEARING THE WRATH OF THE KING: FOR HE ENDURED, AS SEEING HIM WHO IS INVISIBLE."

The structure is:

1. The forsaking of Egypt here has to do with him leaving Egypt personally, and not the Exodus of all the Israelites which took place some 40 years later.

2. Paul here speaking of their being no fear of Pharaoh, doesn't contradict Exodus 2:15, which states that fear was the motive of his flight. What is in Paul's mind is not Pharaoh's wrath as the cause of Moses leaving, but rather the consequence of his leaving.

3. This he was strengthened to do because he saw an invisible Monarch greater than Pharaoh. That Monarch was Christ.

THE FORSAKING OF EGYPT

The phrase, *"By faith he forsook Egypt,"* does not refer as stated, to his forsaking Egypt concerning the Exodus, which would take

place about 40 years later, but rather his flight consequent upon his killing the Egyptian.

From a child, Moses had been brought up in the Palace of the Pharaoh. He had lived in the lap of luxury, been surrounded by servants, with his every wish being someone's command. To which we have previously alluded, he was being groomed to be the Pharaoh of Egypt himself. Consequently, he had received the finest education regarding the arts and science of the Egyptians, which means that he had received the best education in the world of that time, at least in a secular sense; however, even as the Bible relates, even though Paul doesn't mention it here, his education in the things of the Lord, which is actually the only real education, is now about to begin (Ex. 2:15-4:18). As he was educated some 40 years in the Palace of Pharaoh, he was also educated some 40 years by God in the wilderness. As someone has well said, it took about 40 hours to get Moses out of Egypt, but 40 years to get Egypt out of Moses. Of all this education in Egypt, the Holy Spirit alludes to it only in the sense of saying, *"By Faith he forsook Egypt."*

It should be here understood, that God cannot use anything of this world. Many Christians are fond of speaking as to how God could use the great talent or ability of some particular individual, if they would only give their heart to Christ. Not so!

God only uses what He Himself has birthed, and the reason for that is simple: everything that man is, has, or touches, is polluted and because man himself is totally depraved as a result of the Fall in the Garden of Eden. Consequently, we make a grand mistake when we think in any measure that the Lord uses anything that man was born with, or anything of this world's system. In fact, even after a person comes to Christ, it is generally quite some time, even as it was with Moses, before the person is ready to be used of the Lord. It must ever be all of the Spirit and none of the flesh. And to be sure, that is the most difficult place to reach in the life of the Believer, and I speak of the place of total Spirit control! Thankfully, before the Lord begins to use us, He doesn't demand that the Spirit have total control. If He did, no one would be used. In fact, He begins to use us, the moment the Spirit has even some control. So, let the Reader understand, if he is being used by the Lord, and that means to any degree, it only refers to the fact that the Spirit has some control. In other words, all of us yet have a long way to go!

GRACE

If it is to be noticed, the Holy Spirit here through Paul, doesn't mention Moses killing the Egyptian (Ex. 2:11-12), and why? There are two reasons:

1. There is some indication that Moses at this particular time was casting about for a way to help his fellow Israelites. I doubt seriously that a wholesale Exodus was in his mind, which would later come to pass, but it seems that some thoughts were beginning to form concerning freedom for his people. So he undertakes to help them by means of the flesh, which God can never honor. So, the Holy Spirit doesn't here mention this particular act, and because *"the flesh"* in the life of a Believer is just as hateful to God, as it is in the life of Pharaoh, etc.

2. Beginning one's ministry by committing manslaughter is not exactly the best way to start out; however, that's exactly what happened to Moses! But God forgave this man this particular sin, as evil as it was, and such a thing being washed, cleansed, and forgiven, Grace will not again allude to this situation. Isn't God good?

THE WRATH OF MAN

The phrase, *"Not fearing the wrath of the king,"* is not, as we have stated, a contradiction of Exodus 2:15, which does state that fear was the motive of the flight of Moses from Pharaoh. In addressing this, R. Milligan wrote in his New Testament Commentary:

"When Moses fled into Midian, he certainly did fear the wrath of Pharaoh, as we learn from Exodus 2:14-15. But surely he did not fear him any more than did his parents, Amram and Jochebed, when they concealed their child three months, and then committed him to the care and providence of God by exposing him on the bank of the river in an ark of bulrushes. And yet Paul says of them, 'they were not afraid of the king's commandment' (Heb. 11:23).

"Manifestly then, Paul uses the word 'fear' in both these instances in a relative sense. Moses and his parents both feared the tyrant, so far that they thought it necessary to use all lawful means for their personal safety, but they did not fear him so far as to disobey God on his account, nor had they any fear that he would be able to nullify or set aside the decrees and purposes of God concerning Israel.

"In this sense, it may be truly said of both Moses and his parents that they did not fear 'the wrath of the king.' And this being so, it is certainly more natural to understand the Apostle as having this type of reference to the flight of Moses into Midian."

The animosity of the world, and regrettably, the animosity of most of the Church, is going to be tendered against the one who seeks to live *"by faith."*

WHAT DOES IT MEAN TO LIVE BY FAITH?

Whatever it means, it has been the same from the very beginning, even as these illustrations provide as given to us by Paul in this Eleventh Chapter.

As well, and which I certainly hope by now is very obvious, Faith in God is the only way. It's the only Way that God will recognize, the only Way that He will condone, and the only Way He will bless. In fact, any other type of effort meets with His severe disapproval, as also by now should be very obvious. So what exactly does it mean to live by Faith?

Even though terms may be used such as *"Faith in God,"* or *"Faith in the Word,"* or *"Faith in Christ,"* and which are all correct; still, if the definition stops there, it leaves something to be desired.

Whenever *"Faith"* or *"believing"* are mentioned in the Bible, at least as it speaks of the Lord, always and without exception, if traced down to its roots, it refers to *"Christ and Him Crucified"* (I Cor. 2:2). As we've already stated, Redemption is the story of the Bible, which means that its entire thrust is *"Redemption,"* and of course, we know that Redemption is brought about by Christ and Christ Alone, and more specifically, is brought about by what He did at the Cross, all on our behalf. So, when one mentions Faith, one must at the same time be saying Christ and the Cross.

This means that the Cross of Christ must ever be the object of our Faith.

A TOTAL WAY OF LIFE

When one begins to understand this, it will become a total way of life. He will begin to read the Bible in the light of the Cross. He will understand that every Blessing that he receives from the Lord, comes exclusively from the Cross. He will begin to understand the tremendous Doctrines of the Faith, such as Grace, Reconciliation, Justification, Sanctification, etc., and that all and without exception, come through and by the Cross of Christ.

In this capacity, he will place not faith or trust in himself, but place all faith and trust totally and completely in Christ, and His great Sacrifice. Such an attitude refers to a mindset as well as a lifestyle. This is God's Way, and I speak of the Way of the Cross, and it is the Way which Satan opposes more than he opposes anything else. That's why Paul referred to this by saying, that we must *"fight the good fight of faith"* (I Tim. 6:12). To be sure, it is a fight, but it is a good fight, because this particular fight, will always, and without exception, lead to total and complete victory (Rom. 6:14).

FRUIT OF THE SPIRIT AND WORKS OF THE FLESH

We read of the account of both of these in the Fifth Chapter of Galatians. Either one is possible in the life of the Christian; however, one can have the Fruit of the Spirit only by one means, and if that means is not attained, the *"works of the flesh"* will definitely show themselves in the life of such a Believer. And to be sure, those particular *"works"* are ugly indeed!

Now let the Reader understand the following:

Whenever the person comes to Christ, that person now has to live for God. If it's done right, it is the most beautiful, wonderful, and fulfilling life that there could ever be. If not done correctly, it can be devastating. Please note carefully:

If the Believer doesn't know and understand the Message of the Cross, which is God's Way, or if the Believer doesn't subscribe to

the Message of the Cross because of unbelief, irrespective as to whom that individual might be, the *"works of the flesh"* are going to manifest themselves in that person's life (Gal. 5:19-21).

Now please understand, it's not that maybe these things will happen, it is a guarantee that they will happen. While it is true that all listed here, and others not listed, may not manifest themselves, however, to be certain, there will be a manifestation of the *"works of the flesh"* in some way. The only way this can be avoided is by the Believer exhibiting Faith in the Sacrifice of Christ and doing so at all times. When the Believer does this, the Holy Spirit then exerts His almighty power on the Believer's behalf, and the Believer can then walk in victory — but only then (Rom. 8:1-2, 11).

Understanding this, we certainly should realize how important this teaching is. We are dealing here with the issues of life and death, and to be sure, if we go God's Way, victory will be ours; otherwise, no victory at all will be ours, with these terrible *"works"* manifesting themselves, which will definitely lead to untold problems and difficulties, and can lead to the loss of one's soul (Gal. 5:21).

While most Christians are fond of claiming that they have no problem with *"adultery, fornication, uncleanness, lasciviousness,"* etc., while that may be true in the outward sense, it's definitely not true in the spiritual sense. Please let me explain:

A MATTER OF THE HEART

While it is definitely true, that most Christians have not actually committed acts of adultery, fornication, uncleanness, lasciviousness, etc., and I speak of since becoming Christians, still, if that Christian doesn't know and understand the Message of the Cross, they have definitely committed these sins in their heart (Gal. 5:19).

For instance, and to give an example of this of which I speak, Jesus spoke of committing adultery in the heart, by a man looking at a woman to lust after her (Mat. 5:28). The point I make is this:

The only way a Believer can defeat evil thoughts in his mind and heart, is by looking to the Cross, where Jesus defeated all of these powers of darkness (Col. 2:14-15).

Paul also said that we must *"bring into captivity every thought to the obedience of Christ"* (II Cor. 10:5). How can we do this?

Even though this statement given by the Apostle covers a far wider scope than the obscene thoughts to which we are momentarily addressing ourselves, it definitely includes this of which I speak.

By one's own efforts, it is impossible for the Believer to obey this command. I don't care how much willpower he uses, how strong he may think he is, he simply does not have it within himself to do this of which we speak — bring every thought into captivity to the obedience of Christ. However, it definitely can be done, if we do it God's Way.

The beautiful thing about this of which I speak, is that it includes every single facet of our lives. When we give you the answer to the question as it regards *"evil thoughts,"* it also includes everything else from the worse to the worst. Therefore, when you learn this secret, you've learned it all.

It's a shame that it's a secret, but sadly that's the category in which the Cross presently falls. The Church has had so little preaching and teaching on this great subject, which is actually the foundation of the Church, that it hardly anymore knows where it is or where it's going.

The only way the Believer can live this life, which means that works of the flesh will not manifest themselves in his life, is that he understands that everything comes to him through the Cross of Christ. That is to ever be the object of his Faith. When this is done, and continues to be done, the Holy Spirit, Who is God, and Who can do all things, will carry out the necessary work within the heart and life of the Believer. This is God's Way, and it is the only way (Rom. 6:3-5, 11).

Understanding what Paul was saying in the first few Verses of Romans 6, and accepting this which the Holy Spirit gave us through the Apostle, we can now say with certitude, *"sin shall not have dominion over you"* (Rom. 6:14).

TO SAY *"NO"* OR *"YES!"*

Since I've been a child, I have heard Preachers say that sin is a matter of *"choice!"* While that is correct, it definitely isn't correct in the way in which they said it.

They were claiming that anytime a Christian does something wrong, that it's simply because he chose to do that thing which was wrong, meaning that he could either say *"yes"* or *"no"* to whatever it is that has proved his undoing.

In fact, that's one of the biggest mistakes of the modern Church.

What these Preachers were advocating, whether they realized it or not, was *"willpower."* They dress it up by saying that once a person becomes a Believer, that person now has the capacity to say *"yes"* or *"no"* as he so desires. That being the case, if one does wrong, well then it means they have willfully chosen to do wrong and, therefore, they need to be punished. As stated, none of that is correct.

Every person has the capacity to make the choice, but only in one direction. A person's choice is limited to whether he chooses to go God's Way, or another way. Let's look first at the unsaved:

Let's address ourselves first of all to the worst alcoholic of which one could think. There is no way that individual can say *"no"* to alcohol. He is hopelessly bound. However, he still has the capacity to say *"yes"* to Jesus Christ, if he will only do this (Jn. 3:16). His free moral agency in that capacity is always free to act, but only in that capacity.

When it comes to the Believer, it is actually the same identical thing. The Believer has the free moral agency to say *"yes"* to Christ as it regards all things concerning his daily living, or he can say *"no"*! That's where his free moral agency begins, and that's where his free moral agency ends.

In fact, there are untold millions of Christians who have said *"yes"* to Christ as it regards their initial Salvation, but in effect, said *"no"* to Him, as it regards their personal, daily living. Now the sadness is, many of these Christians do not really know or understand that they have said *"no"* to Christ, actually thinking they have totally and completely said *"yes"* to Him. Let me explain it this way:

When we speak of saying *"yes"* to Christ, we are actually speaking of saying *"yes"* to Christ and what He did at the Cross, understanding that this is the source of all victory, power, and blessing. If we do not know or understand the part the Cross plays in our ongoing Christian experiences, then because of lack of knowledge in this area, which in effect characterizes almost all of modern Christianity, we have in effect put our faith in something else, which means, whether we realize it or not, that we have just said *"no"* to the Grace of God (Gal. 2:20-21). That being the case, that which follows will not be pretty.

Having his faith and trust in something else other than the Cross, the Believer in some capacity, will begin to find himself unable to overcome sin. Having his faith in something other than the Cross of Christ, he has just frustrated the Grace of God, which means he has stopped the help of the Holy Spirit (Rom. 8:2, 11; Gal. 2:21). In this situation, which again most Christians presently find themselves, and because they do not know the Victory of the Cross, such a Christian will quickly find that his willpower is simply not strong enough. Paul addressed this very thing in Romans 7:18. At that time, the great Apostle didn't know the Victory of the Cross, even though he definitely was saved and baptized with the Holy Spirit. Consequently, not knowing that Victory, he was depending on his willpower, and he found that he didn't have the power and strength to say *"no,"* which means, that he was being forced into an action he did not want to engage (Rom. 7:15). I'll say it again: that's the state of most modern Christians.

Now is that person culpable? Most definitely, yes! Whether they realize it or not, they are guilty of not trusting Christ. The sad part of all of this is, most of these individuals think they are trusting Christ, when in reality they aren't. Most of the modern Faith is really in ourselves instead of in Christ and what He did at the Cross. Such faith is that which God will never recognize.

Until such a Christian learns the Victory of the Cross, despite him exerting his willpower trying to say *"no,"* he will find that his situation will get worse and worse. In other words, the *"works of the flesh"* will manifest themselves more and more in his life. This is why Paul also said, *"A little leaven leaveneth the whole lump"* (Gal. 5:9). Despite all of his efforts otherwise, such a Christian will find the situation steadily

NOTES

growing worse, and because these things we have stated, actually fall into the category of *"laws"* (Rom. 7:23-25; 8:2).

THE FRUIT OF THE SPIRIT

Of course, and as is obvious, the *"Fruit of the Spirit"* is the total opposite of the *"works of the flesh"* (Gal. 5:22-23).

But notice, it is the *"Fruit of the Spirit,"* and not the individual. In other words, it is only the Holy Spirit Who can develop such fruit within our lives. Again, if one is to notice, this is labeled as *"fruit"* meaning that it takes time to grow and develop.

All of this means that it's not possible for a human being, even the most consecrated Christian in the world, to develop this fruit himself. When he attempts to do so, as possibly all of us have tried at one time or the other, it will not be Fruit of the Spirit which is developed, but rather *"works of the flesh."* So what is the Believer to do?

Once again, we go back to the Cross. When Jesus died there, He atoned for all sin, making it possible for the Holy Spirit to come in to the heart and life of the Believer and to there abide, and to do so permanently (Jn. 14:16).

Inasmuch as the Spirit works exclusively within the parameters of the Finished Work of Christ, we are simply to exhibit Faith in that Finished Work, realizing that it included us, and then the Spirit will definitely plant, cultivate, and develop His Fruit within our hearts and lives. This is the only way it can be done.

However, when we put our Faith in something other than the Cross of Christ, we frustrate the Grace of God, which means that the work of the Spirit stops, which as would be obvious, stops the development of the *"Fruit."*

The Cross is where Jesus paid it all, and that not only refers to our initial Salvation experience, but as well to our everyday living (Lk. 9:23). Faith in what Jesus there did, gives us all the benefits for which He paid such a price. It is all centered up in three things:

1. The Cross (Rom. 6:3-5, 11, 14; Gal. 6:14).
2. Our Faith in the Cross (Rom. Chpt. 4).
3. Our Faith in the Cross gives the Holy Spirit the latitude to work (Rom. 8:1-2, 11; Gal. 5:5).

ENDURED

The phrase, *"For he endured, as seeing Him Who is invisible,"* speaks of Christ.

"Endured" in the Greek is *"kartereo,"* and means, *"to be strong, steadfast, patient."* It actually speaks of the 40 year sojourn of Moses at the back side of the desert. This gathers the 40 years in Midian into one exhibition of wonderful perseverance in Faith. It was during those 40 years in Midian that Moses kept before himself his great destiny, that of leading God's people out of Egypt, and kept trusting God despite his flight from Egypt and his enforced absence from that land, that God would yet bring him back there and effect the deliverance of the Chosen People. He had no idea as to how this could be done, and more than likely, when God finally appeared to him in this capacity, it probably was different than he had thought, as it usually is.

All of these years, his Faith had been in Christ, *"Who is invisible."* This is in effect where faith actually is, *"the invisible vs. the visible."* To be sure, the invisible will little by little become visible, but in the meantime, we have to work our way around the unholy visible. That is where the test of Faith comes in.

(28) "THROUGH FAITH HE KEPT THE PASSOVER, AND THE SPRINKLING OF BLOOD, LEST HE THAT DESTROYED THE FIRSTBORN SHOULD TOUCH THEM."

The structure is:

1. The final example of Faith given here by Paul in connection with Moses concerns the Passover.

2. The protection of the Children of Israel resided in the Blood.

3. As the Blood was the protection then, the Blood of the Lamb, i.e., *"the Lord Jesus Christ,"* He is the protection now.

THE PASSOVER

The phrase, *"Through Faith he kept the Passover,"* refers to the fact, that by the commandment of the Lord, he *"instituted the Passover."* *"Kept"* is the translation of the Greek *"poieo,"* which means, *"to institute."*

The Greek Scholars say that the verb here is in the perfect tense which speaks of the continuing significance of the service of the Passover to the time of its conclusion, not that the Passover is looked at here as a permanent institution, for it was not, being only typical and, therefore, transitory in its nature, in operation only until the Reality, Which and Who was Christ, to Whom it pointed, appeared. But its significance, namely, that as a type of the Sacrifice of the Lord Jesus, is of permanent value (Wuest).

Linking *"Faith"* with the *"Passover,"* refers to an enlargement on that which had been instituted from the very beginning, as it regards the sacrifices of the lambs (Gen. 4:4). Salvation, and in fact, every single thing that man receives from God, and with no exceptions, has always come through the Sacrifice of Christ, of which the animal sacrifices were types. While the Passover would definitely take this a step further in its symbolism, still, the principle was the same — the shedding of the blood of an innocent victim, i.e., *"Christ."* In fact, the Ordinance which we know as *"The Lord's Supper,"* actually came out of the *"Passover."* It was during the eating of the Passover, that the Lord instituted this sacred Ordinance (Mat. 26:26-29). As is obvious, the Lord's Supper portrays the Death of Christ on the Cross, in the giving of His Body, which was broken, and the shedding of His Blood, which purchased our Redemption.

THE SPRINKLING OF BLOOD

The phrase, *"And the sprinkling of blood,"* referred to the blood of the Paschal Lamb on the lintels and doorposts of the houses (Ex. 12:22).

"Sprinkling" in the Greek is *"proschusis,"* and means, *"to pour on, an affusion."* While the Blood was in the case of the first Passover, sprinkled on the doorposts and lintels, in the case of the post-Exodus legislation, it was poured upon the Altar (Wuest).

There was nothing in the previous experience of either Moses or the Israelites to justify this action, but their faith in God, thereby believing what He said, was vindicated when *"the destroyer of the firstborn"* passed over them. Moses had nothing to go on but the conviction that God had directed him. Clearly, faith was his mainspring.

THE IMPOSSIBLE MADE POSSIBLE

Moses entered on an undertaking wholly beyond the power of man to accomplish, and against every human probability of success. It was no less than that of restoring to freedom several millions of downtrodden, oppressed, and dispirited *"slaves,"* and conducting aged men, tender females, helpless children, with numerous flocks and herds, across barren wastes to a distant land. He undertook this against the power of probably the most mighty monarch of his time; from the midst of a warlike nation; and when the whole nation would be kindled into rage at the loss of so many slaves, and when he might expect that all the power of their wrath would descend on him and his undisciplined and feeble hosts.

He did this when he had no wealth that he could employ to furnish provisions or a means of defense; no armies at his command to encircle his people on their march; and even no influence among the people himself, and with every probability that they would disregard him (Ex. 3:11; 4:1).

He did this when the whole Hebrew people were to be aroused to willingness to enter on the great undertaking; when there was every probability that they would meet with formidable enemies on the way, and when there was nothing human whatever on which the mind could fix as a basis of calculation of success. In fact, if there ever was any undertaking commenced opposed to every human probability of success, it was that of delivering the Hebrew people, and conducting them to the Promised Land. To human view it was quite as hopeless and impractical as it would be now for a stranger from Africa, claiming to be a native prince there, and to have a commission from God, to liberate the two and a half million of slaves in this country some 200 years ago, and conduct them to the land of their fathers. In all the difficulties and discouragements of the undertaking of Moses, therefore, his only hope of success must have arisen from his confidence in God.

FAITH IN GOD

All of this was an undertaking where there were many certain trials before him. The people whom he sought to deliver were poor and oppressed. An attempt to rescue them would bring down the wrath of the mighty

monarch under whom they were. They were a people unaccustomed to self-government, and as the result proved, prone to ingratitude and rebellion. The journey before him lay through a dreary waste, where there was every prospect that there would be a want of food and water, and where he might expect to meet, as stated, with formidable enemies. In all these things his only hope must have been in God. It was He only Who could deliver them from the grasp of the tyrant; Who could conduct them through the wilderness; Who could provide for their wants in the desert; and Who could defend a vast multitude of women and children from the enemies which they would be likely to encounter.

There was nothing in this to gratify ambition, or to promise an earthly reward. All these prospects Moses gave up when he left the court of Pharaoh. To be the leader of a company of emancipated slaves through a pathless desert to a distant land, had nothing in itself that could gratify the ambition of one who had been bred at the most magnificent court on Earth, and who had enjoyed every advantage which the age afforded to qualify him to fill any exalted office.

The results of this man's action, demeanor, and character showed that he never designed to be himself the king of the people whom he led forth, and that he had no intention of aggrandizing his own family in any case (Barnes).

THE POWER OF GOD

The phrase, *"Lest he that destroyed the firstborn should touch them,"* proclaims by the sprinkling of the blood that Moses acknowledged that he was as much the object of the just judgment of God as was Pharaoh himself. In fact, there was no moral difference between them. Both were sinners. Neither of them was innocent. Both stood under the sentence of death; and, being guilty, both merited it.

This is where self-righteousness has a problem. I remember some time back, a man wrote me, somewhat incensed, because I had stated that Cain and Abel were both under the Judgment of God. It was the blood sacrifice alone which spared Abel, and the lack of blood sacrifice which doomed Cain. It was the same with Moses and Pharaoh, and in fact, the same with every individual who has ever lived.

For anyone who doesn't see that, it shows that they don't believe that all men need a Redeemer. I suppose they think in their minds that they are above such need.

The Truth is, all are justly doomed, and thereby, all can be saved, that is, if they will trust in the solution provided by God, which is His Only Begotten Son, the Lord Jesus Christ, and the Sacrifice which He afforded at the Cross of Calvary. Let all understand, that any Israelite who would have refused to have placed the blood on the doorposts of their houses, as commanded by God, would have witnessed the death of their firstborn. Thankfully, all obeyed! But let it ever be understood, that it was the blood that protected them, and nothing else! Let it also be understood, that it's the blood that protects you now, and more particularly, the Blood of Jesus Christ.

The Holy Spirit states in I Corinthians 5:7, that the Passover pictures Christ's Sacrifice of Himself in order to save sinners sentenced to die.

Two great facts appear in the Passover, the certain doom of the firstborn and as well, his certain Salvation. He was doomed to death by God, not because of his conduct, but because of his birth. Of course we speak of being born in original sin. This latter fact he could not alter; and he was, therefore, hopelessly lost. He was, however, absolutely saved, and because of the value of the life sacrificed for him. He knew he was saved because God had pledged Himself to most certainly save all who sprinkled the shed blood upon their doorposts. There is some indication that some of the Egyptians, as well, may have availed themselves of the protection of the blood (Ex. 12:38).

All sinners are justly doomed by God to death. But He loves them as He loved the firstborn and, therefore, the Lamb of God has suffered that death. His Precious Blood, that is, His priceless life, poured out, attests the fact.

The Word of God promises eternal safety to whomever will seek salvation in that atoning Savior. The Believer in Christ knows,

therefore, that he shall never perish; and this knowledge is based on two facts outside of himself: these are, the preciousness of Christ's Blood to God; and the faithfulness of God to His Own Promise.

(29) "BY FAITH THEY PASSED THROUGH THE RED SEA AS BY DRY LAND: WHICH THE EGYPTIANS ASSAYING TO DO WERE DROWNED."

The composite is:

1. The crossing of the Red Sea is attributed to God (Ex. 14:14).

2. The pronoun *"they"* refers to all the Israelites who evidenced faith in following Moses across the dry bed where the Sea had been.

3. The Egyptians lacked faith, and the result was disaster. Their fate shows that the faith of Moses and the Children of Israel was real and not just a formality.

THE MIRACLE OF THE RED SEA CROSSING

The phrase, *"By Faith they passed through the Red Sea as by dry land,"* presents that body of water becoming a temple to Israel, but a tomb to Egypt. The faith that sprinkled the blood, and the unbelief that refused its shelter, fixed this great gulf between them.

Some of these Israelites who went out of Egypt with Moses were anything but shining examples of faith. But the facts seem to be, that all of them had at least some faith, which they had to have, in order to follow Moses through the Sea, and it is on this that attention is focused.

The crossing of the Red Sea is definitely attributed to God (Ex. 14:14) and to the east wind that God sent (Ex. 14:21); but Paul prefers to concentrate on the faith that enabled the people to respond to what God had done. That their faith and not merely their courage was important is shown by the fate of the Egyptians.

Some may claim that it took no Faith whatsoever to follow Moses across the dry Sea bed; however, I remind all who would think such a thing, that the Scripture says, *"And the water was a wall unto them on their right hand, and on their left"* (Ex. 14:22).

It took faith to trust the Lord that this wall of water, which perhaps stood 100 or more feet high on either side, which defied all laws of gravity, wouldn't come crashing down upon them while they were in the middle of the Sea bed. In fact, that's exactly what happened with the Egyptians when they pursued after the Israelites (Ex. 14:26-31).

Incidentally, those who claim that the Red Sea at this particular location was only a foot or so deep, have no proof at all for their statement. Irrespective as to how deep it was, the Scripture says they passed through *"by dry land."*

THE EGYPTIANS

The phrase, *"Which the Egyptians assaying to do were drowned,"* proclaims the fact that God orchestrated the entirety of this miraculous event. The same God Who opened the Red Sea for the Israelites, and did so by His miraculous powers, at the same time, closed the Red Sea on the Egyptians, thereby destroying their army. God did it all! It just remained for Moses and the Children of Israel to evidence Faith in this which God did, and which they did!

It is amazing how that unbelief in the hearts of many refuse to believe in the miracle-working power of God. It is more amazing still, when many of this number include those who profess to be Christians. With these individuals, the days of miracles are always over, and in fact, they try to explain away the miracles of the Bible, by natural means.

The Truth is, the Lord of Glory is a miracle-working God. In fact, one might say, and without fear of contradiction, that in some way, everything He does is a miracle. While it's not always to the degree of the opening of the Red Sea, still in some way, when God answers prayer, every time He has to do certain things which defy the laws of nature, and as well, the passions of men. While He does not tamper with anyone's free moral agency, He definitely does maneuver individuals into certain positions which are of their own choosing, but which falls out to the purposes of God. In fact, He is doing this constantly!

All of this shows us that Moses balanced the best of the world with the shame of Christ and deliberately chose the latter. He saw its future wealth.

(30) "BY FAITH THE WALLS OF JERICHO FELL DOWN, AFTER THEY WERE COMPASSED ABOUT SEVEN DAYS."

The exegesis is:

1. We are here told, that the falling of the walls of Jericho should be ascribed to Faith.

2. The taking of Jericho is a striking example of the power of faith.

3. Faith requires obedience, even in that which we do not understand.

THE WALLS OF JERICHO

The phrase, *"By faith the walls of Jericho fell down,"* proclaims another miracle of unprecedented proportions. While it was God of course, Who performed the miracle, we are here told, exactly as in the previous Verses, that the Faith of Joshua and the Children of Israel played a tremendous part in this, even as faith always does. The idea is, God operates totally on the principle of faith on the part of His followers. He demands that we believe Him, have Faith in His Promises, etc.

Much of that today which is referred to as *"Faith,"* is actually presumption. In other words, God has not promised many things which are claimed and, therefore, will not respond to human commands.

Many have attempted to teach that if enough faith can be mustered, anything can be done; however, that is blatantly false! Anytime anything which claims to be faith, seeks to circumvent the Will of God, in reality it's not faith, but as stated, is presumption. God will never honor such! As we've stated, it's not the quantity of faith that makes the difference, but the correct object of Faith, which must always be the great Sacrifice of Christ.

Let not the Reader forget, that the Faith which opened the Red Sea, and thereby saw the deliverance of the Children of Israel, plus destroying their enemies, was all predicated on the Passover, which of course symbolized the Crucifixion of Christ. As well, the walls of Jericho falling down were likewise predicated on the same thing (Josh. 5:10).

OBEDIENCE

The phrase, *"After they were compassed about seven days,"* proclaims obedience, which did not make sense at all to the natural mind. We cannot doubt, the unmeasured contempt and ridicule of their foes during this time.

Apart from the conviction that God would act, nothing could have been more pointless than the behavior of God's people. They did not attack. Instead, they simply walked around the city once a day for six days and then seven times on the seventh. But once more, faith was vindicated, for *"the walls of Jericho fell down."*

These walls fell not by any natural causes, or by any means that were in themselves adapted to secure such a result. It was not because they fell of themselves; nor because they were assailed by the hosts of the Israelites; nor was it because there was any natural tendency in the blowing of horns to cause them to fall. None of these things were true; it was only by confidence in God in obeying what He had said to do, that such a little effort adapted to such a purpose could have been employed at all; and it was only by continued faith in Him, that they could have been persevered in day by day, when no impression whatever was made. But yet, God had told them, that if they obeyed, that *"the wall of the city shall fall down flat"* (Josh. 6:5).

Exactly as God told them this would happen, exactly it did happen!

THE JERICHO'S IN OUR LIVES

As deliverance from Egypt was a type of our Salvation, likewise, the Promised Land was a type of the Baptism with the Holy Spirit. But there are Jericho's which seek to hinder our progress into this inheritance. How do we get them down?

We do so in the same identical manner that Joshua did so long ago, that is, by obeying the Lord. And what obedience does He now demand?

Jericho didn't fall before Joshua, in the strict sense of the word, but rather it fell before Christ. The Scripture says:

"When Joshua was by Jericho, that he lifted up his eyes and looked, and, behold, there stood a Man over against him with his sword drawn in his hand."

He introduced Himself, *"As Captain of the Hosts of the Lord"* (Josh. 5:13-14). This was an appearance of the Lord of Glory, and before Whom Jericho would fall!

It is the same Lord of Glory to Whom you are to look. He, through the Spirit, will exert His mighty power on your behalf, the same as He did on behalf of Israel so long, long ago. Jericho will fall, but it will not be by the machinations of man or the brilliance of brainpower. It will only be by the Power of God.

The obedience demanded of you is very similar to the obedience demanded of Israel. Their marching around the walls of the city, in essence, was a claim of victory over its inhabitants. You, as well, are to understand, that God has already given you the victory, just as surely as He had already given Israel the victory. While that city had not yet crumbled, it was as good as destroyed, and because the Word of the Lord had said so! It is the same with the Jericho in your life.

Quit listening to the Devil, as he attempts to tell you that he is too strong for you. He is a liar! Beside that, you, even as the Children of Israel so long ago, are not depending on yourself, but altogether on *"the Captain!"* And please be certain, the Lord Jesus Christ is definitely the Captain. He has conquered every power of darkness, and did so at the Cross. As they look to the Captain, you are to look to the Captain!

The Spirit of God had already told them to eat the Passover, which they did. Once again, a lamb for each house was slaughtered, symbolizing the Crucifixion of Christ. Its flesh was roasted with fire, symbolizing the judgment which would come upon Christ instead of upon us. They would *"eat the flesh"* which spoke of what Christ would do on the Cross by the giving of Himself, and one's faith in that Sacrifice. They would eat the flesh with *"unleavened bread,"* which symbolized His Perfect humanity, and Perfect body. They would eat it with *"bitter herbs,"* also symbolizing the slavery of Egypt from which they had been delivered (Ex. 12:3-11).

As they looked forward to the coming Sacrifice, symbolized by the Passover, we look back to the finished Sacrifice, and celebrate it symbolically by taking the Lord's Supper. The idea is, the victory is in the Sacrifice of Christ, and our obedience in placing our Faith and Trust in this which Christ has done.

Just as surely as Jericho fell so long, long ago, your Jericho's will fall also. They must!

They have no choice! But always remember, it is only your Faith in the Finished Work of Christ which batters down these strongholds that Satan seeks to erect in your life. No Jericho need stand; no Jericho must stand; all must give way before Christ, because all have given way before Christ.

SEVEN

Incidentally, "seven" is God's perfect number, which denotes completion, totality, and perfection. Man's number is "six" which always denotes imperfection and incompleteness.

God has a perfect Salvation and a perfect victory. He will settle for nothing less, and we must settle for nothing less. This means that we must not attempt to come to a compromise with the Jericho's, but rather insist upon, and in fact demand, total victory within our hearts and lives. Of course, the demand is not made of God, but of ourselves. We must not settle for "six" when we can have "seven."

Even as I dictate these notes, I sense the Presence of God. There is faith which rises in my heart, faith which demands that I tell you that victory can be yours, and in every capacity. If Jericho fell before Joshua, it will fall before you. You're serving the same God that Joshua served, and you have the same faith which Joshua had.

Christians are too easy to say, "If I only had the faith of Joshua," or some such Bible Character. The truth is, there isn't but one kind of faith, at least that God will recognize, and that's Faith in Christ and His Finished Work. If you believe that, then you have the same Faith that Joshua had, and in fact every one of these Patriarchs and Prophets. As I've said over and over again, it's not the quantity of faith, it's the quality of faith. And to be sure, the correct object of faith, which is always the Cross of Christ, gives one the quality that is needed.

(31) "BY FAITH THE HARLOT RAHAB PERISHED NOT WITH THEM THAT BELIEVED NOT, WHEN SHE HAD RECEIVED THE SPIES WITH PEACE."

The diagram is:

1. The list of the champions of Faith whose victories are especially noticed is closed by a woman who was a Gentile, and as well, an outcast.

NOTES

2. She "perished not" because she placed her faith in the red cord of Redemption.

3. She received the spies with peace, which in essence, means that she received the Word and the Holy Spirit, of whom the spies were types.

THE HARLOT RAHAB

The phrase, "By Faith the harlot Rahab perished not with them that believed not," proclaims no doubt, one of the most astounding miracles of all. As we have stated, this woman was a Gentile, and as well an outcast, and an outcast of the worst type. She was a harlot!

Some have tried to soften the description of Rahab and have tried to make her out to be a hostess or an innkeeper, or at the worst, forced into temple prostitution; however, the Holy Spirit here designates her as "the harlot." Both the Greek and Hebrew words signify a secular prostitute, and not a temple prostitute. This is beautiful and significant that a woman from such a background could become such an example of faith. But she did!

She is mentioned favorably in James 2:25, and she is listed in the genealogy of the Lord as the wife of Salmon (Mat. 1:5), which would have made her the grandmother of David, several times removed, and of course, the grandmother of the Lord of Glory, the Son of David.

There were only four women mentioned in the genealogy of Christ, Tamar, Rahab, Ruth, and Bathsheba; however, the latter was not mentioned by name, only that this lady who was the wife of David, "had been the wife of Urias" (Mat. 1:3, 5-6).

Rahab and Ruth were Gentiles. Tamar and Bathsheba were Jews. Thus, Christ descended from both Jews and Gentiles. As stated, Rahab was a harlot. Both Tamar and Bathsheba committed adultery (Gen. 38; II Sam. 11:1-5). Ruth was of the cursed Moabites (Ruth 1:22).

All were products of Grace, which is by Faith (Eph. 2:8-9). By this we are given to understand, that this which these women had been, they no longer were. The Grace of God changed them, as the Grace of God will change anyone who places Faith in Christ. The Lord doesn't save us in our sin, but from our sin.

BELIEVED NOT

The word translated *"believed not"* is not the simple word for *"faith,"* but rather the Greek word that means, *"to be disobedient."* It speaks of disbelief manifesting itself in disobedience.

The word here speaks of the failure on the part of the inhabitants of Jericho, to be persuaded that God had given the land to the Israelites, and the consequent refusal to surrender Jericho.

Any time the unsaved cooperate with God, they are always blessed; however, it is seldom that they do such a thing.

The natural inclination of the depraved mind and spirit, which characterizes all unredeemed, is to oppose God. Actually, there is a built in animosity in the hearts of all unredeemed against God, whether they realize it or not. This being the case, if they are put to the test, most of the time they will oppose God's Way, and God's people.

However, the greatest opposition of all always comes from those who claim to be God's people. We see that in Cain killing Abel, Joseph's brothers opposing him, and Saul attempting to kill David, etc. As well, the greatest hindrance to Paul in the spread of the Gospel was not Rome, but rather those inside the Church, Who were trying to proclaim another gospel (II Cor. 11:4). It is the same presently:

The True Church is opposed by the Apostate Church more so than anything else. Many times, those in the Apostate Church claim by and large, the same Doctrines as those in the True Church. And yet, you can recognize the false by their fruit (Mat. 7:15-20). The Apostate Church will always oppose the True Church. While at times they will attack the Message, more than all, they will attack the Messenger.

RECEPTION

The phrase, *"When she had received the spies with peace,"* proclaims Rahab's faith.

"Received" in the Greek is *"dechomai,"* and means *"friendly reception."*

"With peace" speaks of the act of Rahab in receiving the spies without enmity, and in not allowing them to suffer harm from others.

To help the Reader understand the happenings of that time, perhaps the following would provide some information:

When the Children of Israel crossed the Jordan River, which incidentally is in a valley, they were camped on the slopes of Mount Pisgah, on the shank of Moab. From this position, the elevation slopes down to the Jordan River and then rises back up to the city of Jericho. Consequently, those in Jericho could easily see the several millions of Israelites camped on the other shore, and of course, the Israelites could easily see Jericho, even though it was approximately five miles on the other side of the River Jordan.

It can well be imagined that the inhabitants of Jericho in observing this vast horde, and knowing who they were, would have talked of nothing else. Of course, all knew of the great miracles which had taken place in Egypt and the Red Sea, some 40 years earlier. They also knew how Israel had recently defeated the two kings of the Amorites (Josh. 2:9-11). They also knew that they worshipped Jehovah, the unseen God. And of course, they attributed the miracles and victories, and rightly so, to Jehovah; however, most of them would have claimed that their gods contained greater power.

But in the midst of all of this was Rahab, who heard all of the stories of the miracles as the others, but it struck her heart differently. Even though her information was the same as the other Jerichoites, something stirred within her when she heard these accounts, and that something made her heart receptive. Of course, it was the Holy Spirit!

It is obvious, that this lady was sick of her present lifestyle, sick of the worship of these pagan gods, sick of the emptiness of her heart, sick of the lack of peace. And if a heart is hungry, God will bring bread. Consequently, He directed the two spies to her abode or inn, or whatever it was. To these men she said, *"For the LORD your God, He is God in Heaven above, and in Earth beneath"* (Josh. 2:11). This means that she accepted Jehovah as her God, thereby renouncing the pagan gods she had formerly worshipped.

She asked if they would spare her when Israel took the city, and they promised that she would be protected, and in fact, all who would be in her house. The sign would be *"a scarlet thread in the window"* (Josh. 2:18).

And so it was! Her entire family was spared when Jericho was taken, and as we've already stated, she became one of the great women in Israel, actually in the lineage of the Messiah, and all because of her Faith in God.

(32) "AND WHAT SHALL I MORE SAY? FOR THE TIME WOULD FAIL ME TO TELL OF GEDEON, AND OF BARAK, AND OF SAMSON, AND OF JEPHTHAE: OF DAVID ALSO, AND SAMUEL, AND OF THE PROPHETS:"

The composite is:

1. With a neat, rhetorical flourish, Paul shows that his subject is far from exhausted, even though he does not propose to continue his list.

2. We will find, if we search the record, that each of these individuals battled against overwhelming odds, but triumphed, and all because of their Faith.

3. As well, some of these people had moral problems in their lives. The truth is, in every Saint there is always to be found something reprehensible. Nevertheless, although faith may be imperfect and incomplete, it does not cease to be approved by God (Calvin).

IS IT NECESSARY TO SAY MORE?

The question, *"And what shall I more say?"*, refers to the fact that enough has now been said to guide all who are willing to search the Scriptures for themselves.

With a brief mention of names which would call up before the minds of his readers achievements almost as wonderful as those on which he has been dwelling, Paul passes from the Elders who received witness from God by their Faith, and speaks in general terms, but all the more distinctly of the triumphs which faith has won in these as well!

The idea of all of this, which is overly obvious, is *"Faith."* That's the principle by which God works, and that is the principle by which He deals with men. And when we say *"Faith,"* even as we've said many times, even though it has many nuances and side issues, the bottom line always is *"Jesus Christ and Him Crucified."* In fact, all the Faith these individuals evidenced in Old Testament times had as its proper object Christ, and the manner

in which He would redeem humanity. Of course, their knowledge of this event would have been somewhat different than ours, for the simple reason that it was before the fact; nevertheless, the Sacrifice of Christ was always the object of their Faith, even as it must always be the object of our Faith. That's what it's all about!

FAITH WORTHIES

The phrase, *"For the time would fail me to tell of Gideon, and of Barak, and of Samson, and of Jephthae: of David also, and Samuel, and of the Prophets,"* proclaims four of these as being Judges, one a King, and the other the first Prophet, at least the first one who stood in that Office.

The first four of these are mentioned only here in the New Testament. Samuel is mentioned only twice elsewhere in the New Testament. David, of course, is mentioned frequently. There seems to be no reason for the order in which they are named.

Paul does not go into detail about what these men did. But if we examine the Old Testament record, we find that each man battled against overwhelming odds so that, humanly speaking, there was little chance of his coming out on top. For men in such positions, Faith in God was not a formality. It meant real trust when the odds seemed stacked against them. The idea is they set worthy examples in their difficult circumstances.

There seem to have been defects in the faith of four of them. Gideon was slow to take up arms; Barak hesitated and went forward only when Deborah encouraged him; Samson was enticed by Delilah; and Jephthah made a foolish vow and stubbornly kept it.

Often the men whom the Holy Spirit chooses to become leaders seem to be the most unlikely choices. Yet, God sovereignly selects and anoints, because He sees something in the heart that is not obvious to others.

Whatever the problems there might be in an individual's life, the Lord can handle those things, that is if a man or woman will have Faith in God. This is a tremendous Truth, and in a sense applies to every single human being. The idea of this list is as follows, and probably would apply to all listed in this Eleventh Chapter:

If one looks closely enough, one will find difficulties and problems in all, even the greatest. But that is not the criteria by which God uses individuals. Don't misunderstand, God can never condone sin or spiritual failure of any nature; however, if that person has Faith in God, in other words, if they truly believe, God can take their Faith and straighten out their problems, and then mightily use them. It's the lack of Faith which shuts the door to God helping the individual. And sadly and regrettably, that's one of the great sins of the modern Church.

FAITH

God can help anybody out of anything, except a quitter. Now that's so important, that I must say it again:

The difficulties and problems along the way as it regards this Christian life, are indicative of every single Believer. It is a growth process, and sometimes the growing is not easy; however, there is nothing that the Lord cannot handle, cannot cleanse, cannot forgive, and cannot rectify, unless that person is a quitter. If they quit, which shows a lack of faith, then there is nothing that even God can do. And to be sure, the shores of Christianity are littered with the wrecks of spiritual cripples who quit. They refuse to finish the race; they refuse to get up out of the dust; therefore, they tie God's hands.

Faith is never an uneventful exercise. To say it another way, the faith journey is never uneventful. Actually, the one with Faith hits the dirt just about as often as the individual without faith. The difference is, the one without faith stays in the dirt and refuses to get up. The one with Faith, gets up, and when he does, which is an exhibition of faith within itself, to be sure, and without exception, the Holy Spirit will always brush the Believer off, start him back out on the road to victory, and give him all the help he needs to get there. God doesn't like quitters! (Lk. 9:62).

One of the great troubles as it regards this great Faith walk, for that's what it is, is fellow Christians who try to hinder faith. In other words, instead of trying to help pick the individual up, they instead kick him back down. There could be no greater sin than that! The reasons should be obvious, they

are hindering what the Holy Spirit is endeavoring to help.

God help me to be a Preacher of the Gospel who will render aid to the faith of any individual. I don't care who that person is, I don't care what they've done, I don't how sordid that it's been, if they're trying to get up, God help me to lend them all the support that I have, in order to get them back on their feet. That God's way! That's the reason for the death of Christ on Mount Calvary.

Humanity was down for the count! And there was no way that we could rise once again, and no matter how hard we tried. To be sure, the scene was not pretty, as such scenes never are. But God didn't leave the situation as it was. In fact, He became a Man, and came down here to this cesspool, and lifted man up above the shadows and planted his feet on higher ground. It took the Cross to accomplish this task, but the Lord paid the price irrespective as to its cost.

As a Believer how can I do less? Especially considering that this is God's way. You as a Believer should ask yourself this question: *"Am I helping the Faith of others, or am I hindering their Faith?"*

THE MODERN CHURCH

The Word of God must be the criteria for all things. When we make rules and regulations that have no Scriptural foundation, and when asked as to why these rules have been made, only being able to give the lame excuse, *"That's our tradition,"* then we're in serious spiritual trouble! It is a terrible sin to hinder the faith of others, and that's what unscriptural rules always do. The following we believe, is the Bible way:

First of all, there are no perfect people, and that includes Christians. Even the Godliest have character flaws, which are indicative, sadly and regrettably, of humanity. In fact, all of these character flaws will not be handled until the Resurrection.

No, this in no way is meant to condone sin of any nature. Sin is awful! It's a terrible affront against God. And to be sure, God doesn't save us in sin, but rather from sin. Nevertheless, sin is a problem the Church has to deal with, and sometimes very severe situations, and we must ever understand, that these situations must always be dealt with in a Scriptural manner.

Sometime back, we had a situation in our organization which involved one of our Ministers, and which constituted a morals problem. Without going into detail which is not necessary, we had to deal with this problem. What did we do?

First of all, it must be handled Scripturally. We must ever realize, that we're dealing with someone whom God has called, in whom dwells the Holy Spirit, and for whom Jesus died. Consequently, we must deal with that person in that particular manner.

The usual, unscriptural route for most Church Denominations in such a situation, is to tell the individual he can no longer preach for two years, or some such length of time. In the first place, there's absolutely nothing in the Word of God to substantiate such foolishness.

God called this man to preach, and who am I to tell him that he can't preach. That's ridiculous! In fact, it's a gross sin to even remotely think of engaging in such a thing. To do such, is to tamper with that which is the domain of God alone. Actually, if you're going to throw out every Preacher who has sinned, you wouldn't have any left. You must remember, that for every one who is found out about something, there are hundreds who aren't found out, but in the eyes of God, it's all the same. Exposure is not the sin, but in reality exposure is what most Churches address. They do so, because of self-righteousness, which of course is embarrassed by exposure.

RESTORATION

In fact, the entirety of the Bible is the story of restoration. And then to be more detailed, Paul tells us the following:

"Brethren, if a man be overtaken in a fault, ye which are spiritual, restore such an one in the spirit of meekness; considering thyself, lest thou also be tempted" (Gal. 6:1).

Incidentally, the word *"fault"* in the Greek is *"paraptoma,"* and means *"a moral failure."* We are told to *"restore such an one in the spirit of meekness."*

How is that to be done?

Paul is speaking here to the Galatians, who had been brought in right, actually brought

in under his Ministry; however, false teachers had come in, attempting to pull them away from Grace to Law; consequently, for those who allowed such to happen, the results and without exception, were going to be failure of some nature. In other words, the *"works of the flesh"* were definitely going to manifest themselves, even as it always will in such cases (Gal. 5:19-21).

These individuals had moved their Faith from the Cross to something else, mostly themselves, which always guarantees failure. So here's what Paul says must be done:

We are to tell the individual why they have failed: it is because, as just stated, that their Faith is in something else other than the Cross of Christ. This being the case, there is always going to be failure in some manner. Again, as previously stated, it may not be known by others, but to be sure, it's there in some way.

So, the one who is *"spiritual,"* which means he understands that all Victory is in the Cross of Christ, which means that our Faith must always be in the Cross, which guarantees the help of the Holy Spirit, must explain this to the one who has failed.

While it is certainly true that there are some people who just want to go in a wrong direction, and if that is the case, and they refuse to come back to the Cross, which will guarantee continued failure, then ultimately that person has to be disfellowshiped (I Cor. Chpt. 5); however, most Christians fail, simply because they do not know and understand God's prescribed order of victory, which is the Cross of Christ. So they must be told why they have failed, and how they can get their faith right, and maintain victory in Christ. That is the restoration process outlined by the Holy Spirit.

That's exactly what we did with the individual in question, which to date, has worked out beautifully. His Ministry is stronger than ever, and his life is right with God, and because his Faith is right with God.

Now what good would it have done, for us to stop this man from preaching for two years, and as well, to level other foolish demands on him?

It would not have done any good, it could have completely destroyed him, which is generally the case in all of these efforts.

We do not have any Scriptural right to punish other Believers. In the first place, the Lord Jesus Christ has already been punished for us. And for us to claim that more punishment is needed, is in essence saying that what He suffered at the Cross is not enough and needs something added, which is a gross sin!

As well, even as James plainly said, *"There is one Lawgiver, Who is able to save and to destroy: who art thou that judgest another?"* (James 4:12).

In other words, he is saying, *"Who do you think you are, thinking you are qualified to judge or punish another Christian?"* In fact, only self-righteousness would even think of doing such a thing.

(33) "WHO THROUGH FAITH SUBDUED KINGDOMS, WROUGHT RIGHTEOUSNESS, OBTAINED PROMISES, STOPPED THE MOUTHS OF LIONS,"

The exegesis is:

1. Only through Faith in Christ can the powers of darkness be subdued.

2. We see from these Verses, that the solution for all things is the same, Faith in Christ and Him Crucified.

3. The problem with much of the Church is, that it makes works the criteria instead of Faith, which God will never honor.

THROUGH FAITH

The phrase, *"Who through Faith,"* is meant to proclaim, and by giving all of these different examples, that it doesn't matter what the problem is, what the need is, that Faith is always the ingredient. That's at least one of the reasons that the Church makes a grievous mistake when it proclaims different solutions for different problems.

For instance, some years ago, the Church was big on marriage seminars, which have pretty well fallen by the wayside. At the moment, all the rage is *"prosperity seminars,"* etc.

The Truth is there is nothing in the Word of God which substantiates such efforts. In other words, we're being unscriptural when we go in those directions.

If the Christian will understand that everything we receive from the Lord comes through the Sacrifice of Christ, and that we are to always have Faith in that Finished Work, and in fact, maintain Faith in that Finished

Work, this is all that God requires. To be sure, the Holy Spirit will then work out in our lives all the things which are needed, and whatever those things might be. In other words, this will handle the marriage problems and the prosperity problems, and in fact, any other type of problem we might have.

VICTORIES

The phrase, *"Subdued kingdoms, wrought righteousness, obtained promises, stopped the mouths of lions,"* proclaims the fact, that Faith in God was all that was required for each of these situations, whatever they might have been, even as the next few Verses proclaim.

I'm trying to say that there wasn't one type of Faith for *"subduing kingdoms,"* and another kind for *"stopping the mouths of lions,"* etc., simple Faith in God sufficed for all.

Paul is proclaiming these things to Christian Jews who were very seriously considering defecting from Christ. And the reason for their proposed defection was a lack of Faith. In other words, they were losing Faith in Christ and what He had done at the Cross. In fact, that's where the problem always is, irrespective of the timeframe.

It is my personal feeling, that the situation presently as it regards the Church, is more dangerous than it's ever been before, or at least since the Reformation. The reason is this:

If Faith is the criteria, and it definitely is, then the Church is in serious trouble. For Faith to be that which God will recognize, it must have, and without exception, as its proper object, the Cross of Christ. While the Church has had more teaching on Faith in the last 50 years than ever before in its history, despite all of that, the Church pretty well finds itself at this present time, faithless! How can that be?

The teaching that the Church has received has not centered Faith up on the Cross, but rather something else. And it really doesn't matter what else is proposed, if it's not Faith in the Cross, then it's not true Faith.

So, we have multiple thousands of Churches that go under the name *"Word of Faith,"* and the truth is, as it regards the majority of these Churches, they have no Faith at all. In fact, most of them don't even believe in the Cross, at least as it regards the Sacrifice of Christ, referring to it as the greatest defeat in human history. Such is rank blasphemy!

It is Faith alone in the Cross which God will recognize (Rom. 8:1-2; Eph. 1:3-7). In fact, every time Paul uses the phrase, *"in Christ,"* or *"in Him,"* etc., he is speaking of what Christ did at the Cross on our behalf, to which our Faith must always be directed.

(34) "QUENCHED THE VIOLENCE OF FIRE, ESCAPED THE EDGE OF THE SWORD, OUT OF WEAKNESS WERE MADE STRONG, WAXED VALIANT IN FIGHT, TURNED TO FLIGHT THE ARMIES OF THE ALIENS."

The diagram is:

1. These mighty feats were performed by ordinary men and women, who had Faith in an Almighty God.

2. If God deems something should be done, and He can find a man or a woman who will exercise faith, irrespective as to what that situation is, faith will overcome it.

3. The Holy Spirit keeps telling us that whatever is the need, faith in God is sufficient to meet the test.

MIRACLES OF FAITH

As I study these examples given here by Paul, my Faith is encouraged, which is exactly what the Holy Spirit intends. That which God has called me to do, and in fact, what He has called you to do as well, can be done. Please understand the following thought:

The Holy Spirit is telling us here, that Faith can overcome any obstacle, and irrespective as to what that obstacle may be. To be sure, there will always be hindrances, problems, difficulties, and in fact, difficulties at times so severe, as to make the situation seem to be impossible. In fact, as far as we are concerned, it is impossible. But we're not the ones who are going to have to do this thing. It is God Who will do whatever needs to be done.

All He requires from us is that we believe Him. Just last night in prayer (Sept. 8, 2000), the Lord spoke this to my heart:

In essence, He said to me, *"I have given you a vision, and to be sure, I will also bring about the provision."* Let's say it another way:

1. God gives a vision.

2. He is the provision, or in other words, He will provide for the vision.

3. Satan comes in with division. Notice how this word is pronounced: *"di-vision."* Satan wants your vision to die! And how can he do that?

If he can get us to looking at circumstances and situations, he can cause the vision to die. In fact, he did exactly this with Israel when the spies came back with an evil report. The people looked at the walled cities and the giants, etc. Despite the protests of Caleb and Joshua, who proclaimed the fact that, *"We are able to possess the land,"* the unbelief of the ten spies affected the entirety of Israel, which destroyed an entire generation, and delayed the entrance into the Promised Land by nearly 40 years.

While you and I may be susceptible to circumstances and situations, God isn't! So that's what our Faith is all about. We are to believe that God, Who is not susceptible to circumstances and situations, and Who is not moved by these things whatsoever, can bring about whatever is needed, irrespective as to what it might be. He only demands that we have Faith in Him. In other words, don't look at the problems, look at the Lord, Who is able to do all things, and believe Him. That's Faith!

VICTORY IN JESUS

As the Lord moved upon my heart last night, His Spirit impressed upon me that despite the problems, despite the difficulties and circumstances, that He would provide. Whatever was necessary, He would provide! And I believe it, and to be sure, I believe it with all of my heart.

God has called me for World Evangelism. He has called me to carry out this Vision by the means of Television, Radio, Crusades, print materials, and Videos. It takes two things to get this done. I will address the lesser first:

1. It takes money! While the media reaches a staggering number of people, which is the only way that Evangelism can really be carried out as it regards the masses, it takes a sizeable amount of money to do this. And for that money to come in, we have to cross all types of hurdles. Tragically, instead

of the Church trying to help us, the far greater majority seeks to hinder, by discouraging anyone from giving to this effort. Nevertheless, God is able! He has given the *"Vision,"* and He will make the *"Provision."* The only thing that can bring in *"di-vision"* is my lack of Faith. And God help me, that I believe Him and that despite the obstacles.

2. That which is the most important of all, is the moving and operation of the Holy Spirit, for which I pray constantly. I cannot do anything without the Holy Spirit, and I can do anything with the Holy Spirit, at least that which He directs me to do. This is the greatest need of all, the Anointing, the leading, and the Power of the Spirit. I pray about this more than I pray about anything else.

If the Spirit has His Way in my life, then the money will come in. But above all, people will be saved; lives will be changed; Believers will be Baptized with the Holy Spirit; the sick will be healed, and people will be delivered. But it is only through the Spirit that these things can be done. And He works exclusively according to my Faith in the Finished Work of Christ (Rom. 8:2).

(35) "WOMEN RECEIVED THEIR DEAD RAISED TO LIFE AGAIN: AND OTHERS WERE TORTURED, NOT ACCEPTING DELIVERANCE; THAT THEY MIGHT OBTAIN A BETTER RESURRECTION:"

The structure is:

1. We learn from these Verses that Faith produces different types of miracles.

2. Some were not delivered from torture, with their victory being that they didn't lose their Faith.

3. The great goal of Faith must always be the *"better Resurrection,"* and not anything else. This means that whatever happens here, whether we are delivered or not, whether we are healed or not, whether we get the money or not, such is only a chapter in the book. The end result must always be the *"better Resurrection."*

A MIRACLE

The phrase, *"Women received their dead raised to life again,"* presents as would be obvious a tremendous miracle of faith. In fact, there could be very little that would be greater than one being raised from the dead.

And the God Whom we serve is able to do these things, providing it fits His purpose.

As well, He can do such now, just as He did such in Bible times. We make a great mistake, when we limit God to particular time frames. God is limited only by our Faith and His Wisdom. Our lack of faith limits Him, and at times He limits Himself, because it's wisdom to do so.

ANOTHER MIRACLE

The phrase, *"And others were tortured, not accepting deliverance; that they might obtain a better Resurrection,"* proclaims the Apostle dealing with another side of Faith, which is just as powerful as that which he has been addressing.

The word *"tortured"* in the Greek is *"tumpanizo,"* and is an extremely strong word, meaning *"to torture with the tumpanum."* This was a wheel-shaped instrument of torture, over which people were stretched as though they were skins, and then horribly beaten with clubs or thongs.

The word *"deliverance"* is preceded by the Greek article, in effect saying, *"the deliverance."* It was the deliverance offered at the price of denying their faith, that was refused. They did this in order that they might attain to a better Resurrection than the one mentioned in the previous phrase of this Scripture, namely, a mere continuation of life on Earth. They were looking forward to the Resurrection that would be unto glory, which they would not obtain, if they denied their Faith.

The idea is, God didn't deliver them as far as the cruel torture was concerned, even letting them die.

Now many in the modern Church would claim that these individuals simply didn't have faith; however, the words *"Who through faith,"* includes these as well as all the others. Yes, they had Faith, and great Faith at that! They had so much Faith in fact, that despite the torture, despite the horrible pain, despite death, they would not renounce Christ, but continued to proclaim His Name even unto the end. In fact, untold thousands have died in this manner, and possibly down through the centuries, even millions.

To be stronger with my statement, how dare anyone claim that these were faithless!

The Holy Spirit says otherwise. The problem is this:

Those who would claim such foolishness, and I speak of those who claim that these didn't have Faith, are basing all of their results on material things. These types of individuals judge the faith of Christians, by the cost of the suit of clothes they wear, or the make and model of the car they drive. Nothing could be more foolish, even downright stupid! In fact, such people don't really have any faith themselves, only hot air.

All of this life is a dress rehearsal for eternity. We must never forget that. As we have stated, the goal of all true Faith is the *"better Resurrection,"* which will take place when the trump sounds (I Thess. 4:13-18).

(36) "AND OTHERS HAD TRIAL OF CRUEL MOCKINGS AND SCOURGINGS, YEA, MOREOVER OF BONDS AND IMPRISONMENT:"

The exegesis is:

1. The word *"others"* introduces a different class of victories achieved by Faith.

2. The criteria for Faith is not necessarily deliverance from difficulties, but rather that we do not lose our Faith.

3. The modern Church for the most part, has a false definition of Faith, and because they have an improper faith, i.e., *"an improper object of Faith."*

OTHERS

The phrase, *"And others had trial of cruel mockings and scourgings,"* refers to *"another of a different kind."* This word *"others,"* as stated, introduces a different class of victories achieved by faith. Mockings and scourgings were endured by the martyrs just mentioned, and they were not delivered, at least in the way we normally think of such. All of this is an attempt by Satan, to get the person to renounce their Faith. In fact, during the times of the Early Church, when thousands of Christians were tortured to death, and in fact, died in every conceivable way possible in the Roman arenas, many times, they were offered freedom if they would only say *"Caesar is Lord."* This of course, was an attempt to get them to change the object of their Faith from Christ to Caesar. Rather than do that, untold thousands died, and in fact, died horrible deaths.

NOTES

In late May of 2000, we were in Rome, Italy, with a tour. We visited the Coliseum, where it is known that many Christians died. We saw the places where they kept the lions and other wild animals, starving them, so they would be ravenous with hunger, when they were unleashed on the victims.

We saw the tunnels through which the Christians had to walk as they were ushered into the arena. One can only imagine the horror that took place those many centuries ago. Now tourists look and gaze where Christians once wept!

But where today is mighty Rome of old? Her Caesar's are peanut vendors and her great military generals are organ grinders. And where is Christianity? It spans the globe, with untold millions who profess that glorious Name of Jesus Christ. It is only Faith that has done this.

MOREOVER

The phrase, *"Yea, moreover of bonds and imprisonment,"* was that which experience the Apostle personally knew. In fact, he also knew the *"trial of cruel mockings and scourgings."*

The words *"yea, moreover"* are used commonly to express a climax. One might say, that some imprisonments were even to be more dreaded than scourging (Jer. 38:9).

When we all stand at the Judgment Seat of Christ to give account, which every Believer shall, even from the very beginning, I wonder how will the Faith of many modern Christians stand up beside those of which we here speak? And to be sure *"Faith"* and *"Faithfulness"* will be the criteria of that judgment.

Thankfully, our sins have been judged at the Cross, and will never be brought up again. But to be sure, our faithfulness as it regards this life given to us by the Lord, will definitely be judged, with rewards meted out accordingly.

(37) "THEY WERE STONED, THEY WERE SAWN ASUNDER, WERE TEMPTED, WERE SLAIN WITH THE SWORD: THEY WANDERED ABOUT IN SHEEPSKINS AND GOATSKINS; BEING DESTITUTE, AFFLICTED, TORMENTED;"

The diagram is:

1. In all of this, we see the purposes of God brought forth, and done so by the Faith of the individual.

2. While God could deliver from any situation, His purpose might be for some Believers to suffer in this manner.

3. The Believer should want and desire above everything else, the Will of God, and at all costs.

WHAT PRICE, FAITH?

We could easily dissect this Scripture as to its several parts, giving occasion and examples of this which the Apostle speaks; however, each statement is fairly self-explanatory. The idea is, that we learn the lessons here taught. Some of them are:

1. The idea of all of this is, that these individuals cried to God for deliverance from these excruciating situations, even which took their lives. But God did not answer them, at least in the manner in which they requested. He did answer, but by giving them even more Faith, that they may stand the test, even unto death. One would have to say, that this is the greater faith of all.

2. By the word *"tempted"* being included, we know that in many of these cases, the individuals were given opportunity to recant, which means to renounce their Faith in Christ. If they would do so, the torture would stop, and their lives would be spared. Needless to say, such a temptation would be great; however, many of them, and no doubt one could say, most of them did not succumb to that temptation. They were stoned; they were cut asunder with saws; they were mass slaughtered with the sword; they were destitute, afflicted, and tormented, but they didn't lose Faith! And that's all that really matters.

The sufferings lasted but for a short time. The *"better Resurrection"* lasts forever!

(38) "(OF WHOM THE WORLD WAS NOT WORTHY:) THEY WANDERED IN DESERTS, AND IN MOUNTAINS, AND IN DENS AND CAVES OF THE EARTH."

The structure is:

1. The world is not worthy of the Child of God.

2. The word *"world"* does not refer here to the corrupt world system, but the world considered as an economy, or a particular way of life, which is unworthy of these, because it is an economy ruled by sense, whereas the world of the Child of God is an economy ruled by faith.

3. The world drove them out, thinking them unworthy to live in it, while in truth it was unworthy to have them living in it.

THE WORLD

The phrase, *"Of whom the world was not worthy,"* refers to the fact that the few true Christians in this world are of far greater worth, and in every sense, than all the balance of the world put together. As well, these are the words of the Holy Spirit, and not mere hype. But of course the world being spiritually depraved, doesn't know this.

Every freedom in this world, all prosperity, whatever it is that men might refer to as *"good,"* and of course I refer to that which truly is good, it is because of the Believers in this world. This in a sense, can be divided in two ways:

First of all, the world owes a debt of gratitude to the Jew. Of course, they do not recognize that at all, even with many parts of the world harboring a deep resentment against the Jewish people.

For some 1,600 years, the only people in the world who knew God were the Jews. Admittedly, they didn't do a very good job, and neither do we as the Church, but still, under God they were the only light in the world of that day. As a consequence, they gave to the world the Word of God, which is a worth and value all out of proportion to our ability to comprehend. As well, they brought the Messiah into the world, which was the greatest happening in the history of mankind, even though they did not recognize Him.

According to Romans Chapter 11, the Church has been grafted in to take the place of the Jewish people, who will ultimately be brought back after the Second Coming. Under Christ, the Church is now the light of the world.

As one looks at the nations of the world, regarding those who have at least a modicum of Biblical Christianity, these nations enjoy the greatest freedoms and the greatest prosperity. As well, and because of the Presence of the Holy Spirit more or less in these particular countries, and especially the United States and England, almost all the technological advancement has come from these areas.

Now as should be obvious, this doesn't mean that the scientists in question are

Spirit-filled, but rather, it speaks merely of the Presence of God in an overall way.

I do not mean to be unkind, but I do not consider Catholicism as true Biblical Christianity. In many senses of the word, I consider it to be as pagan as Islam, etc. And if anyone takes the Bible seriously, I think, they would as well have to come to that conclusion. And regrettably, there are many parts of that which we refer to as *"true Christianity,"* which are also spiritually corrupt. By now I'm sure the Reader understands, that if it's not *"Jesus Christ and Him Crucified,"* then it's not truly the Gospel.

MALTREATMENT

The phrase, *"They wandered in deserts, and in mountains, and in dens and caves of the Earth,"* refers to the lot of some Believers, not all of the time, but some of the time.

The world oftentimes maltreats Believers, and especially in countries which do not recognize Jesus Christ, simply because they do not know the worth and value of these ones in their midst.

As we have seen in these examples, the Lord doesn't always pave the road with gold, or even deliver the blessed one from negative circumstances, but that doesn't at all mean that they are lacking in Faith. The Lord does what He does, in His Own way, and for His Own purposes. To be sure, He loves every Believer with a love that is far greater than you and I could ever realize. But yet, the Lord knows all things from beginning to end. To be sure, He Who notes every sparrows fall, and even numbers the very hairs of our heads, if in fact, He allows us to suffer, even as untold millions down through the several millennia have suffered, He does so for good purpose and reason. We know that He can change any situation which He so desires, and in any way He so desires. So if our lot is less than we would like, we should do the following:

1. We should look at ourselves very closely, even asking the Holy Spirit to reveal to us any wrong direction which we might be engaging, which can definitely hold back the Blessings of God. The Holy Spirit cannot sanction wrong doctrine, wrong direction, self-will, or sin.

2. If we know in our heart that all is right, and to be sure, that's not difficult to determine, and our lot in life is less than we might think it ought to be, we should acquiesce to the Will of God, thanking Him for what in fact He has seen fit to give us. We must always remember that God is good! And as the song says, He's not good just some of the time, but He is good all of the time.

If our lot in life, be it physical, financial, domestic, or otherwise, is less than it seems it could be, and if despite our importunity the Lord hasn't seen fit to change it, we must remember that whatever our lot is now, it's only for a short time. By comparison with eternity, in ages to come, it won't even be remembered. Remember this, your hope and my hope, and in fact the hope of every true Believer, is focused on *"a better Resurrection"* (Heb. 11:35).

(39) "AND THESE ALL, HAVING OBTAINED A GOOD REPORT THROUGH FAITH, RECEIVED NOT THE PROMISE:"

The composite is:

1. The word *"all"* claims every single Believer before the Cross.

2. They passed the test, and did it through faith.

3. None of these received the Promise, which refers to the coming Messiah, the sum and substance of all the Old Testament Promises (Lk. 1:67-79; Rom. 1:2-5). The next Verse which we will momentarily address, explains this.

THESE ALL

The short phrase, *"And these all,"* is meant to claim by the Holy Spirit, those who saw great miracles and those who didn't. They're all put in the same category. This means that the miracles were not the yardstick of measurement, but rather *"Faith."* Unfortunately, the modern Church has a tendency to judge one's faith by yardsticks which present a wrong measurement. Tragically, the modern judgment too often centers up on monetary things, which is about as far removed from the True Gospel as anything could be.

True Faith, while at times bringing about the miracles, signs, and wonders mentioned, rather develops Christ in one's life. The Fruit of the Spirit is the criteria of this Faith, i.e., *"Christlikeness!"* If we fail to see that, then we fail in our understanding of Faith.

A GOOD REPORT

The phrase, *"Having obtained a good report,"* refers to that soul judged accordingly by the Holy Spirit. Unfortunately, much of the modern Church ignores that of the Spirit, having devised its own scheme. The *"good report"* is all based on Faith in Christ, and Faith in Christ alone. Unfortunately, much of the Church seeks to add to that. In other words, it's Christ plus, which God cannot accept. And more unfortunate still, many if not most Preachers, and even the people, opt for the good report given by man, rather than that given by God.

I'm concerned that most of the Readers, not being Preachers, would have some difficulty in understanding this of which I speak. Let me be a little clearer:

THE APOSTATE CHURCH

Satan is very subtle in his approach. Actually, he is a religious figure, and as such, he is well versed in religious ways. In other words, as an angel of light (II Cor. 11:13-15), he deceives many. And how does he do that?

In the first place, he generally always has some *"Truth"* mixed in with his *"lie."* The truth serves as the bait, and the Believer is pulled in, and not realizing what is happening, oftentimes takes the bait and thereby the *"lie."* And what type of lie are we speaking about?

Anything that is not strictly and purely Faith in the Cross of Christ and that alone, is a *"lie."*

For instance, there is nothing spiritually or Scripturally wrong with Denominations, whether forming one or belonging to one. Ideally, they can serve as a tool to help further the Cause of Christ; however, oftentimes, and in fact almost all the time, the leaders in these Denominations gradually attempt to turn them into something spiritual, which they aren't, and can never be.

By that I mean, they project the idea that belonging to their Denomination equals Salvation. While some will not go that far, many project the idea that if one belongs to their

particular Denomination they are spiritually superior, and if they do not belong to that certain group, while they might be a Christian, they are something less.

In fact, this is not an isolated thing, incorporating itself in almost all Denominations, and even local Churches. In fact, the great criteria for spirituality presently, is simply to belong to a certain Church, etc. This goes under the idea of *"covering."*

In other words, it is taught that if you belong to a certain Church, that you enter into its *"covering,"* which means that you are protected, blessed, etc., which also at the same time means that if you belong to other Churches, that you do not enjoy this protection, etc.

As stated, it's all very subtle, and is all ladled out with great religiosity. But the truth is, *"Jesus Christ and Him Crucified"* is no longer the criteria for all things with God. They have gradually substituted something else to take its place. In other words, they have taken the faith of the individual from Christ, and moved their Faith over to the Denomination or that particular local Church. The object of faith has now changed, and has done so very subtly, so subtle in fact, that most Christians hardly know what has happened. They have come to believe the *"lie."*

These Christians, and they number into the millions, who follow such directions, are now given a *"good report"*; however, what they don't realize, is that their *"good report"* is that given by man and not God.

In all of these scenarios, the people actually get the very opposite of what they are told. In other words, instead of getting protection and blessing, the end result, and without exception, will always be *"works of the flesh"* (Gal. 5:19-21). If one's Faith is not totally and completely in *"Jesus Christ and Him Crucified"* there is no way that the results can be anything else than *"works of the flesh."*

THE PRICE THAT MUST BE PAID

I do not think it is possible for a Believer to stay in such an environment, and at the same time, continue to have proper Faith in Christ. Such Churches, and to be sure, they make up the far greater majority, are not preaching Christ, but rather *"another Jesus, by another spirit, which is presenting another gospel"* (II Cor. 11:4). It is virtually impossible for a Believer to stay in such a spiritual climate, without the *"leaven ultimately leavening the whole lump"* (Gal. 5:9). Under such circumstances, the Holy Spirit through Paul plainly taught that under such circumstances, *"Christ is become of no effect unto you"* (Gal. 5:4). If that course is maintained, he also stated that such a person would *"be entangled again with the yoke of bondage"* (Gal. 5:1).

You as a Believer, and because it's so very, very important, should carefully inspect what your Pastor is preaching. Is he preaching the Cross, or other things? If he's preaching more *"other things"* than he is the Cross, you might give him this Commentary on Hebrews. If he ignores it, you would be best finding another place to attend Church.

Of course, there will always be a price to pay to follow the Lord. Many times we have to go against family and friends. But what is more important, the *"good report"* given to you by the Lord, or the *"good report"* given to you by men?

Please remember this: the price that you are called on to pay, whatever it might be, is far less than the price paid by many of these mentioned in the latter portion of the Eleventh Chapter of Hebrews.

THROUGH FAITH

The short phrase, *"Through Faith,"* proclaims the only manner, in which this *"good report"* can be obtained.

Always and without exception, even as we have repeatedly stated, when the words *"believing"* or *"Faith"* are used in the Bible, at least as it pertains to the Lord, traces back to *"Jesus Christ and Him Crucified"* (I Cor. 1:18, 21, 23; 2:2).

The word *"faith"* is bandied about in the modern Church in all types of ways; however, if it's faith in anything, and no matter how religious it might sound, except the Cross of Christ, then it's not faith that God will recognize. In fact, when most Christians exclaim that they have *"Faith in Christ,"* the truth is, most hardly know what they mean by that statement. They think they understand it, but regrettably, most don't!

NOTES

When asked what thy mean by that, most would answer, *"I believe Him,"* or words to that effect. While of course, all of this is true and correct as far as it goes, the truth is, it doesn't go far enough. If that's as much as the Christian knows, it is just about certain, whether the Christian will admit it or not, that such a one is living in spiritual defeat.

Faith must always have as its object the *"Sacrifice of Christ."* This means, even as we have just portrayed, such faith must not be divided with the Church, Preachers, good works, manifestations of the Spirit, or anything else for that matter. While all of these things we have mentioned, may or may not be good in their own respective right, those things didn't die on the Cross for you. The problem with the Church is by and large according to the following:

Many if not most in the modern Church look to the wrong thing as it regards their *"Source."* While they always speak of the Lord as their Source, most of the time, whether they realize it or not, they are looking toward a Church, or a Preacher, or their good works, or something else.

The Believer must know and understand, that every single thing he receives from the Lord, and irrespective as to what it is, is given to him in one way only, and that's through the Sacrifice of Christ at the Cross, and our Faith in that. That's the way the Holy Spirit works, and the only way He works. Jesus plainly said of the Spirit, *"He shall glorify Me"* (Jn. 16:14). That means that He will not glorify the Church, will not glorify Preachers, will not glorify good works, will not glorify anything for that matter, except Christ. How does He glorify Christ?

THE HOLY SPIRIT AND CHRIST

He glorifies Christ in two ways:

1. *"He guides into all Truth"* (Jn. 16:13). Of course, Truth is the Word of God. But the story of the Word of God is the story of man's Redemption, which was all brought about at the Cross of Christ. Therefore, in all the things that He teaches us about the Word of God, in some way, everything streams toward the Cross. This is the Truth of which He speaks.

The entirety of the Old Testament points toward the coming Christ, Who would redeem man by His Sacrificial Offering of Himself. This was all typified by the Sacrifices of the Levitical Offerings.

Now that this is done, all instruction in the New Testament points back to that celebrated event. Everything is based on the Cross of Christ.

2. The Holy Spirit glorifies Christ by receiving of all that Christ did for us at the Cross, and showing it unto us (Jn. 16:14-15).

After He taught this to His Disciples, He then proceeded to tell them how He was going to be offered up, which would cause rejoicing in the world, but would cause them great sorrow, but then their sorrow would be *"turned into joy"* (Jn. 16:20). All of this, the Cross, the Resurrection, and the Exaltation of Christ, would make it possible for the Holy Spirit to come into this world in a way heretofore unknown. Now He would abide in the hearts and lives of Believers forever (Jn. 14:16).

The Holy Spirit glorifies Christ by taking all the things that Christ purchased for us at the Cross and making them available to us. Considering the great price paid for all of this, it stands to reason, that the Lord would want us to have everything which He there purchased, and purchased I might quickly add, with His Own Precious Blood (I Pet. 1:18-20).

REVELATION

These things which I reveal to you now, have come to me by Revelation. To be sure, it is not something new, actually being the foundation of the faith from the very beginning. But Satan has been very successful in pushing the Church away from its true foundation, which is the Cross. As a result, most Christians, and even most Preachers, hardly know the Source of their victory; consequently, there is little victory in the hearts and lives of most Believers. To be sure, they desire the victory, with many of them even laboring diligently trying to obtain such, but without much success. Let me give a personal testimony.

In the 1980's, the Lord gave me many, many souls. Through Television aired all over the world, we saw literally hundreds of thousands brought to a saving knowledge of Jesus Christ. Regarding Salvation for the

NOTES

lost, I preached the Cross, and preached it strongly. God rewarded the Message, as He always shall!

At the same time, I tried to correct the Church regarding areas which I knew to be wrong. In fact, the Lord plainly told me to call attention to these wrong directions. During this time, He also told me, that in all of this *"my own would turn against me."* I'm so very glad at that particular time, that I didn't know the extent of that which the Lord said to me. I'm not sure I could have stood it!

In those days, and by the Spirit, I knew what was wrong, but I didn't know how to correct it, which means that I did not understand the Cross as it pertains to our everyday experience with the Lord. As stated, I understood the Cross and preached it strongly, as it regards our initial Salvation experience, but beyond that, I had no knowledge of the Cross, and in fact, didn't know anyone who did. And in that context, the following must be noted:

Before one can properly turn the Sword of the Spirit on others, one must properly turn the Sword of the Spirit on himself. That I didn't do, and because I didn't understand how it was to be done, in which Satan took advantage.

Turning the Sword of the Spirit on one's self, refers to dying to self. And what does that mean?

DYING TO SELF

It is most bitter to a man to learn that all his goodness must be slain with the Sword of the Lord just as much as all his badness. God cannot give victories to *"the flesh,"* i.e., to *"self."* Hence, *"the flesh"* must be *"put to death"* — the *"old man"* must die and the *"new man"* brought forth in a life of victory in Christ and with Christ.

This is all done by the Believer understanding that at Salvation he died with Christ, which means that he was baptized into the death of Christ, was buried with Christ, and was raised with Christ in newness of life (Rom. 6:3-5).

This means that the *"old man"* has died, and the *"new man"* now lives (Rom. 6:6). However, our problem is this:

If we do not understand how the *"new man"* lives, which is by continued Faith in the Cross of Christ, we will find that the *"old man"* is quickly resurrected. And that's our problem!

By the *"old man"* we refer to trust placed in *"self"* which translates into *"flesh,"* which refers to the effort to live this Christian life without the help of the Holy spirit. Even though the Holy Spirit is definitely present within our lives, He demands that we exhibit Faith in the Cross at all times, in order for Him to work. But the problem of most Christians is, that they do not understand this.

If most Christians will think back, after they were saved, as far as the greater majority are concerned, the Church which they then began to attend, little directed them to the Cross, if at all! In fact, most Christians, despite living for the Lord many, many years, have little been directed toward the Cross at all. The Pastor not understanding the Cross, directs them to other things, and even though he may be very sincere, he is at the same time, very wrong. Consequently, the *"old man"* is resurrected, which means that the Christian is trying to live the Christian life by his own efforts, which is extremely frustrating.

That's exactly the trap that I fell into, and it is the trap that almost all of the modern Church is in presently. While it is certainly true that the Preachers to whom we listen, at least for the most part, do not blatantly tell us to ignore and forsake the Cross, however, due to lack of knowledge in this area, they direct the Christian to *"works."* Such a course is always the road to spiritual disaster. But, as stated, most Preachers, I think, do this simply because they don't know any better.

And because I didn't know any better, as stated, Satan took full advantage of that, as he always will, which almost destroyed me.

In the late fall of 1991, at a time of serious crisis for this Ministry, with me not even knowing if it could continue, I laid my Bible on the table and said, *"I don't know the answer, but I know the answer's in this Book, and by the Grace of God I'm going to find the answer."*

It took nearly six years of crying and praying before the Lord, even day and night, and I exaggerate not, but the Lord did see my tears, did hear my cry, and did answer my prayer.

In late 1996, the Holy Spirit began to show me the road to victory. First of all, He showed

NOTES

me the Sixth Chapter of Romans. In effect, He showed me the Cross. He plainly and clearly told me from the Word of God, that the answer for which I sought was found in the Cross, and the Cross alone! And as I've already stated several times in this Volume, He told me as well, that my Faith must always be in the Cross, for this was the manner in which the Holy Spirit worked.

Since that day, this Revelation has continued to expand, with it becoming a total way of life, which is actually what the Word of God teaches. It is Christ living in us, and doing so by and through the Power and Person of the Holy Spirit (Gal. 2:20). Consequently, and by the Grace of God I might quickly add, I now experience a victory for which I had so long sought. The Sword of the Spirit has been applied to my own life, and to be sure, it is producing the most glorious life that one could ever have. This is the *"more abundant life"* of which Jesus spoke (Jn. 10:10). This is the *"rest"* which He promised (Mat. 11:28-30).

Now there is no longer any trust or dependence on *"self,"* or *"good works,"* or anything else for that matter, with the exception of Christ and what He did for me at the Cross. My Faith is totally and completely in Him and in His great Sacrifice. This and this alone is the Christlike life!

THE PROMISE

The phrase, *"Received not the Promise,"* refers to the coming Messiah, as stated, the sum and substance of all the Old Testament Promises.

As I've repeatedly stated, all the prophecies and predictions of the Old Testament point toward this *"Promise."* And what is the end result of that *"Promise"*?

Jesus Christ came into this world to save sinners. He did that by dying on the Cross. His Sacrifice is what purchased our Redemption, and His Sacrifice Alone is what purchased our Redemption. We must never forget that.

Irrespective that the Old Testament Saints received not the Promise, in other words Jesus didn't come before their deaths, still, they died in Faith, and Faith I might quickly add that He would come, in which He definitely did. Now let's look at the next Verse which sheds more light on *"the Promise."*

(40) "GOD HAVING PROVIDED SOME BETTER THING FOR US, THAT THEY WITHOUT US SHOULD NOT BE MADE PERFECT."

The structure is:

1. From the very time of the Fall, God began the process of providing a perfect Salvation.

2. This *"better thing"* is the Sacrifice of God's Son, which would provide this perfect Salvation.

3. All the Old Testament Saints were made perfect (a perfect Salvation) by that Sacrifice, exactly as we are presently.

THE PROVISION OF GOD

The phrase, *"God having provided some better thing for us,"* presents that which God had promised to Abraham (Gen. 22:14).

Of course, we do not have an account of all that went on between the Lord and Abraham that particular day when the Patriarch was to offer up Isaac, but we do know, that more than likely, a lot more was said than the information we are given, because Abraham *"called the name of that place Jehovah-Jireh."* The name actually means, *"the Lord will provide."* That of course is a confirmation of what God said in the Garden of Eden immediately after the Fall, concerning the seed of the woman, which would bruise the head of Satan (Gen. 3:15).

Of course, that which the Lord was to provide, was a Redeemer Who would bring forth Redemption for lost humanity. That Redeemer was and is the Lord Jesus Christ.

As we have stated concerning the Old Testament Saints, they *"did not receive the Promise,"* they only foresaw that it would be fulfilled and died in that Faith. But this failure to obtain the fulfillment of the Promise was not due to any slackness on the part of God, nor to any defect in their Faith; there was a good reason for it, and that reason was that *"God had in view some better thing for us."* The *"better thing"* is that which this Epistle has made it its business to expound, the perfecting of God's people by full communion with Him mediated by the perfect Revelation of His Son and His perfect

Covenant (Heb. 8:7-13), and His better Sacrifice (Heb. 9:23).

BETTER

"Better" in the Greek is *"kreisson,"* and means *"greater, strength, stronger, best."* It is used here repeatedly by Paul in this Epistle to the Hebrews with a definite theological significance.

Paul penned this letter to the Hebrews to encourage and to strengthen wavering Hebrew Christians. His argument to those converts who were deeply rooted in Old Testament traditions is that the Gospel of Christ is far superior and that Jesus in fact fulfilled what the Old Testament merely promises. In this argument, the Apostle often uses the word *"better"* to show ways in which Faith in Jesus and what He did at the Cross are superior to the Faith of the Old Testament that it supplants.

Jesus' Gospel is superior, for Jesus is superior to the Angels, who are considered mediators in a sense of the Old Testament Message to man (Heb. 1:4). However, Jesus brings a superior hope, which enables us to approach God Himself and does not leave us standing outside a drawn veil (Heb. 7:19).

The Son of God provides a superior Covenant relationship (Heb. 7:22; 8:6), anchored in better Promises (Heb. 8:6). All this is guaranteed by a better Sacrifice than that of the animals offered on Old Testament Altars (Heb. 9:23).

All the Old Testament Saints were commended for their faith, but we have more, we are recipients of what they hoped for, as God in Jesus has planned something better for us (Heb. 11:40).

How wonderful it is to realize that in Jesus, and His great Sacrifice on the Cross, that God has provided the very best for you and me!

COMPLETE

The phrase, *"That they without us should not be made perfect,"* lays the stress not necessarily on the Church to which this phrase points, but rather on Christ Who would make it all possible for both the Old Testament and the New Testament Saints.

Alford says: *"The Advent and Work of Christ has changed the estate of the Old*

Testament Fathers and Saints into greater and perfect bliss; an inference which is clear in many other places in Scripture. So that their perfection was dependent on our perfection: their and our perfection was all brought in at the same time, when Christ 'by one Offering perfected forever those who are sanctified' so that the result with regard to them is, that their spirits, from the time when Christ first descended into Paradise and then ascended up into Heaven, enjoy heavenly blessedness, and are waiting with all who have followed their glorified High Priest within the Veil, for the resurrection of their bodies, the Regeneration, the renovation of all things."

The idea of all of this is, at least as it regards the Old Testament Saints, that the blood of bulls and goats could not take away their sin, so even though they were saved, the sin debt still remained. The sin debt was removed when Christ did on Calvary, and because the sin debt was removed, Satan could no longer hold the Old Testament Saints in captivity down in Paradise, which Jesus spoke of in Luke Chapter 16. When He died on the Cross, thereby satisfying the demands of Heavenly Justice, which means that all sin was then atoned, past, present, and future, at least for those who have believed, who do believe, and who would believe, Satan then had no more legal claim on the Old Testament Saints, or anyone for that matter who places their Faith and Trust in Christ and what He did at the Cross. Regarding these Old Testament Saints, Jesus literally went down into Paradise immediately upon His Death at Calvary, and liberated them from that pit, and took them to Heaven (Eph. 4:8-10).

The whole thing as Paul gives it here, actually presents itself in two parts. The fathers had one part *"in the Promises,"* and we the other *"in the fulfillment,"* and neither would have been complete without the other.

Christ was predicted in the Old Testament, even from the very beginning, and of course those predictions were fulfilled in His First Advent.

The *"better things"* referred to here as possessed by Christians, are the privilege of seeing those promises fulfilled in the Messiah; the blessings resulting from the Atonement;

the more expanded views which we have under the Gospel; the brighter hopes of Heaven itself, and the clearer apprehension of what Heaven is which we are permitted to enjoy.

The argument of all of this is, that if the Hebrew Christians went back into Judaism, thereby forsaking Christ, they would be forfeiting all of this, which would be a tragedy of unparalleled proportions.

Considering that all the Old Testament Saints died in the Faith, thereby looking forward to that which was to come, and now that it had come, for these present Hebrew Christians to apostatize, would be tragic indeed! If the Old Testament Saints, under the influence of the mere *"Promise"* of future blessings, were enabled thus to persevere, how much more reason is there for us to persevere, who have been permitted, by the coming of the Messiah, to witness the perfection of the system!

THE GREAT SIGNIFICANCE

There is no part of the New Testament of more value than this Chapter; none which deserves to be more patiently studied, or which may be more frequently applied to the circumstances of Christians. These invaluable records are adapted to sustain us in times of trial, temptation, and persecution; to show us what Faith has done in days that are past, and what it may do still in similar circumstances. Nothing can better show the value and the power of Faith, or of a true experience with Christ, than the records in this Chapter. It has done what nothing else could do. It has enabled men to endure what nothing else would enable them to bear; and it has shown its power in inducing them to give up, at the command of God, what the human heart holds most dear.

Among all of these lessons which we may derive from the study of this portion of Divine Truth, let us learn from the example of Abel to continue to offer to God the sacrifice of true Faith which He requires, though we may be taunted or opposed by our nearest kindred; from that of Enoch to walk with God, though surrounded by a wicked world, and to look to the blessed translation to Heaven which awaits all the righteous; from that of Noah to comply with all the directions of God, and to make all needful preparations for the future events which He has predicted in which we are to be most interested; from that of Abraham to leave country, and home, and kindred if God calls us to, and to go just where He commands, through deserts and wilds, and among strange men; and like him, also, to be ready to give up the dearest objects of our earthly affection, even when attended with all that can try or torture our feelings of affection — feeling that God, Who gave, has a right to require their removal in His Own way — and that, however much we may fix our hopes on a dear child, He can fulfill all His purposes and promises to us though such a child should be removed by death; from that of Abraham, Isaac, and Jacob, to regard ourselves as strangers and pilgrims on Earth, having here no permanent home, and seeking a better country; from that of Moses to be willing to leave all the pomp and splendor of the world, all our brilliant prospects and hopes, and to welcome poverty, reproach, and suffering, if need be, that we may identify ourselves with the people of God; by the remembrance of the host of worthies who met danger, and encountered mighty foes, and vanquished them, let us learn to go forth in our spiritual conflicts against the enemies of our souls and of the Church, assured of victory; and from the example of those who were driven from the abodes of men, and exposed to the storms of persecution, let us learn to bear every trial, and to be ready, at any moment, to lay down our lives if necessary, in the cause of Truth and of God.

Of all those holy men and women who made these sacrifices, which of them ever regretted it, when they came calmly to look over their lives, and to review them on the borders of the eternal world? None! Not one of them every expressed regret that he had given up the world; or that he had obeyed the Lord too early, too faithfully, or too long.

Not Abraham, who left his country and kindred; not Moses, who abandoned his brilliant prospects in Egypt; not Noah, who subjected himself to ridicule and scorn for many years; and not one of those who were exposed to lions, to fire, to the edge of the sword, or who were driven away from society

as outcasts, to wander in pathless deserts, or to take up their abodes in caverns and caves, none ever regretted the course which they had chosen (Barnes).

OUR PRESENT CIRCUMSTANCES

When we reach Heaven, we shall see that we have not endured one pain too much, and that through whatever trials we may have passed, the result is worth all which it has cost.

We must ever understand, that whatever be our present lot, the journey will soon be ended, and soon what are now objects of faith will become objects of fulfillment; and in their enjoyment, how trifling and brief will seem all the difficulties and problems of our present pilgrimage.

In all of this, we must remember that it is Christ Who has made it all possible. And we must also remember, that He gave us this great Salvation, this perfect guarantee of an eternal future, this eternal life, this escape from the bondages of darkness, this transference from darkness to light, at a fearful price. But it was the price that He paid by the giving of Himself on the Cross. Considering that, what complaint do we have as it regards these minor annoyances.

There are very few people who suffered more for Christ than the Apostle Paul; however, he refers to all of this as but *"our light affliction, which is but for a moment"* (II Cor. 4:17).

At whatever price, what a privilege it is to live for God!

*"He, Who safely keepeth, slumbers
   not, nor sleepeth;
"Tho' by all the world forsaken,
   wherefore should I fear?
"That which He hath spoken never
   can be broken,
"Who shall harm the trusting heart
   when He is near?"*

*"He will keep me ever, where no
   power can sever,
"From my heart, the love that hides
   me, in His secret places.
"There in faith abiding, all to Him
   confiding,
"Thro' His Spirit I am sealed, an heir
   of grace."*

"He will keep me ever; like a gentle
   river,
"Peace from Him, my Lord and
   Savior, comes with joy to me;
"In its quiet flowing, life and health
   bestowing,
"Til within the gates of pearl the King
   I see!"

━■━

CHAPTER 12

(1) "WHEREFORE SEEING WE ALSO ARE COMPASSED ABOUT WITH SO GREAT A CLOUD OF WITNESSES, LET US LAY ASIDE EVERY WEIGHT, AND THE SIN WHICH DOTH SO EASILY BESET US, AND LET US RUN WITH PATIENCE THE RACE THAT IS SET BEFORE US,"

The composite is:

1. The *"cloud of witnesses"* here mentioned, refers to all the Old Testament Saints.

2. The *"witnesses"* does not refer here to the Saints looking down on Earth and observing the present situation, but rather that their faith was a witness or example to us who are presently running this race.

3. The Christian runner must rid himself even of innocent things which might retard him, and most certainly of sins which greatly hinder.

4. So long as he stands still, he does not feel these *"weights"* and *"sins"* as being burdensome and hampering; however, once he begins to run, these encumbrances are instantly felt. To be sure, the Christian is *"running this Christian race."*

A CLOUD OF WITNESSES

The phrase, *"Wherefore seeing we also are compassed about with so great a cloud of witnesses,"* refers as stated to all the Old Testament Saints who looked forward to the coming Promise, Who is the Lord Jesus Christ, but who did not see the bringing about of that event in their lifetimes, but yet died in Faith believing that He would ultimately come. The word *"witnesses"* here doesn't carry the idea of the Saints who are now in Heaven, watching and observing us as we run this race, as some teach.

"Witnesses" as here used in the Greek is *"martus,"* which means *"one who testifies, or can testify, to what he has seen or heard or knows by any other means."* It is used in a legal way in the sense of witnesses to a contract or legal document. In an ethical sense it was used in the early Church to designate those who have proved the strength and genuineness of their Faith in the Lord Jesus by undergoing a violent death. The word does not include in its meaning, the idea of a person looking at something. Peter uses it of himself (I Pet. 5:1) as a witness of the sufferings of Christ, that is, one who has been retained and commissioned to testify to the sufferings of Christ which he has seen.

The heroes of faith of the previous Chapter are the cloud of witnesses, testifying to the efficacy of the Faith way of salvation and victory. Paul calls them, so to speak, to the witness stand to bear testimony to what they have seen and heard and felt as to what Faith could and did do for them, so that the Jews of his day, and all other people for that matter, might become convinced that the Salvation which Christ wrought out on the Cross, must be appropriated by faith, not works (Wuest).

The whole idea of Paul's statement, consequently, is not that of these witnesses as spectators looking at this early scene from Heaven, but rather, that their testimonies serve as examples urging us on to Faith in Christ as our Great High Priest.

THE VERACITY OF THE CROSS

In this entire scenario, we see something of utmost importance, which undergirds everything that Paul says in the entirety of this Epistle to the Hebrews.

The nation of Israel, as is obvious, and because they have rejected Christ and even crucified Him, were continuing on in their Temple worship. But worse than that, many if not most Christian Jews were continuing to do the same thing. They were attempting to meld the Law with Christ, with in fact, the Church in Jerusalem leading the way. In fact, I think one could say without fear of exaggeration, that this of which I have just said was an abomination in the Eyes of God.

For the Jews who had confessed the Name of the Lord, the Holy Spirit through this

Epistle is calling them to flee the camp of Judaism, with which they have been identified all too long after acknowledging the Messiahship and Saviorhood of the Lord Jesus. Judgment was soon to fall upon Jerusalem and those who were linked with the temple service. The time had come to separate completely from a system which God no longer recognized because His Own Son had been rejected and crucified. All of these things, and we continue to speak of temple worship, were now but empty forms which once had been divinely appointed to typify the Person and Work of Christ. To attempt to reform that system or to restore it to a place in the Divine favor was vain. The only path for those who would be faithful to God was that of separation from it all, but separation to the rejected One.

As is known, the Lord used Titus the Roman general as His instrument, to destroy every vestige of that old way. As stated it had once been right, actually called into being by God; however, in its entirety it was meant to portray the Coming Redeemer Who with the Offering of Himself, would redeem humanity, which the blood of these bulls and goats in their sacrifices could never do. But yet, they perfectly typified Him Who was to come.

Now that He had come, and had paid the price on Calvary's Cross, to attempt to carry on this old way, which Christ had now fulfilled, was a mockery to God. It in effect stated, and loudly so, that what Jesus did at the Cross was of no consequence.

PAUL

In fact, this was Paul's greatest problem in the Early Church. Christian Jews came from the Church in Jerusalem (Gal. 2:11-15), attempting to infiltrate the Churches established by Paul, and thereby to insert their gospel of legalism. In fact, much of the writing in Paul's fourteen Epistles deals with this issue. And if the Truth be known, had it not been for Paul, it is doubtful that the Early Church could have weathered that storm.

While there is every evidence that the original Twelve (Matthias taking the place of Judas), stood with Paul; still, there is no record that they lifted their weight as they should in order to oppose this scourge. In other words,

at least as it regards this issue, it seems they little opposed the wrong direction of legalism, while at the same time accepting Paul's Message of Grace. Every record is, when put to the test, they came through with flying colors (Acts 15:7-12), and I continue to speak of the Twelve, but as it regards raising a strong voice against the continued practice of the Law by many Christian Jews, it seems they were somewhat silent. However, concerning this issue, I do not want to read more into the Text than should be read, but this I do know:

I think the Scriptures bear out in stark reality that which I have stated concerning this issue, and above all, we know how much that God disdained the continued practice of the Law, by what He did to Jerusalem and the Temple in A.D. 70, making it literally impossible to continue this type of worship.

THE PRESENT APPLICATION OF THE CROSS

If there was ever a glaring lesson portrayed, it is portrayed here. The entirety of the Epistle to the Hebrews could not be more explicit. As stated, it should be a stern warning to the Church.

If the Lord detested in those days, the Church, at least the Jewish section, attempting to downplay the Cross, is He no less angered presently? In fact, it can be no other way. Peter said:

"But there were false prophets also among the people (in Old Testament times), *even as there shall be false teachers among you, who privily shall bring in damnable heresies, even denying the Lord that bought them, and bring upon themselves swift destruction."*

He then said, *"And many shall follow their pernicious ways, by reason of whom the way of truth shall be evil spoken of"* (II Pet. 2:1-2).

When the Apostle spoke of the Lord *"buying us"* he of course, was speaking of what Jesus did at the Cross. The *"heresies"* here of which he speaks, pertain totally and completely to any so-called gospel which is outside of the Cross, or makes less of the Cross than it should.

These false teachers of Paul's day, did not deny the Cross, they merely ignored it as having no bearing on one's relationship with Christ, rather projecting Law, etc. It is the same presently. For instance:

Most of the modern Church, and I speak of those who claim to be fundamental in belief, opt for humanistic psychology as the answer to man's problems. Most of these Preachers, and they number in the tens of thousands, do not deny the Cross of Christ, they merely ignore it. In other words, while they do not disavow the Cross as the answer for the human condition, at the same time, they do not hold it up as the answer, rather promoting, as stated, humanistic psychology. However, any way it is approached, such action is a vote of no confidence, as it regards the great Sacrifice of Christ, irrespective as to the claims of these religious leaders, etc.

Although I'm not sure about the year (I think it was 1997), someone sent me a copy of the Pentecostal Evangel, which is the weekly voice of the Assemblies of God, the largest Pentecostal Denomination in the world. In that particular issue, as it regards individuals with problems, whatever those problems might be, the editor was advocating the psychological 12-step programs, stating that if the Church being attended did not have such a program, they were to search out one which did.

In fact, the overseer of the Church of God of Cleveland, Tennessee, the second largest Pentecostal Denomination in the world, is a practicing Psychologist (the year 2000).

There is no way these two systems of humanistic psychology and the Sacrifice of Christ can be joined together. They are total opposites, which means that whichever one is accepted, the other must be blatantly rejected.

I want to go on record loud and clear, as saying, that such a position is rank heresy, exactly as Peter stated! Now I think you understand why they detest this Evangelist.

I can say no less as it regards the modern *"faith movement."* Pure and simple, it is heresy. And please understand, these things, plus much and many we have not named, are heresy simply because of their denial of the Cross, whether by word or action. It is the same identical thing as the Christian Jews of Paul's day were doing, which was ultimately answered by the Wrath of God.

NOTES

Let the Reader understand, that all Believers who sit under such ministries, i.e., *"such spiritual leadership,"* will be greatly hindered in their walk with God, and as some of the Christian Jews of Paul's day, could even lose their souls. We're speaking here of the issues of life and death, actually, the single most important thing in the world. As someone has well said, *"We do what we do because we believe what we believe."* So my point is this:

It is absolutely impossible, for any Believer to sit under false teaching, and not come away unaffected. The *"leaven"* will always affect its work, and if not ultimately rooted out, will ultimately corrupt the whole (Gal. 5:9).

CORRECT DOCTRINE

Unless one properly understands the Cross of Christ, which of course refers to His great Sacrifice, which is really the story of the Bible, one cannot properly understand the Word. It's just that simple! To the degree one understands the Cross, accordingly one understands the Word.

That's the reason that Paul said, *"But we preach Christ Crucified"* (I Cor. 1:23).

That's the reason he also said, *"For I determined not to know anything among you, save Jesus Christ and Him Crucified"* (I Cor. 2:2).

He also said, *"But God forbid that I should glory, save in the Cross of our Lord Jesus Christ, by Whom the world is crucified unto me, and I unto the world"* (Gal. 6:14).

And then in Romans Chapter 6, which someone has rightly labeled *"the mechanics of the Spirit,"* the Apostle showed us exactly what the Cross means to us, not only in our initial Salvation experience, but as well, in our ongoing living for God. And then when the Cross is properly understood, even as Romans Chapter 6 teaches, then the Apostle shows us in Romans Chapter 8, which has been called *"the dynamics of the Holy Spirit,"* as to what the Spirit of God will do within our hearts and lives, when we properly understand the Cross, and put our Faith therein.

As well, in Romans Chapter 7, the Apostle shows us the fruitless life of the Believer who attempts to live this Christian experience by his own strength and efforts, which means he is attempting to do so without the help of the Holy Spirit. In fact, this was the personal experience of Paul after he was saved and baptized with the Holy Spirit. He did not at that time understand the Cross and what it all meant; therefore, he tried to live this life by the means of the flesh, which refers to our own efforts other and apart from the Holy Spirit. Of course, such a direction is impossible!

The Apostle concluded that terrible scenario by saying, *"O wretched man that I am! Who shall deliver me from the body of this death?"* (Rom. 7:24). Regrettably, the Seventh Chapter of Romans is where most modern Christians find themselves. They do not know the way of the Cross as outlined in Romans 6; therefore, they do not have the help of the Holy Spirit, at least as they should have, as given to us in Romans Chapter 8.

I'm trying to say, if the Preacher is not preaching the Cross, he is not preaching the Gospel. Consequently, those who sit under such ministries are going to be deeply affected, but all in the wrong way. Regrettably, that is the state of most of the modern Church.

THE WORKS OF THE FLESH

The phrase, *"Let us lay aside every weight, and the sin which doth so easily beset us,"* says several things to us:

First of all, there are millions of Christians who are attempting to obey this Verse, as it regards the *"laying aside"* of particular weights and sins in our hearts and lives; however, they are simply unable to do so. Why?

If one properly understands the Cross, which refers to what Jesus there did for him, and puts his faith totally in that, which guarantees the help of the Holy Spirit (Rom. 8:2), then he will be free to *"lay aside"* these particular things. Otherwise, it will be impossible!

Within one's own strength and ability, it is impossible to obey this which the Holy Spirit tells us through Paul that we must do. Most Christians who are struggling with something of this nature, do not think of themselves as attempting to lay aside these weights and sins by their own efforts and ability, but rather think they are attempting to do so by the power of the Holy Spirit. They think because they are engaging themselves in spiritual things, such as speaking in tongues, memorizing Scriptures and quoting them,

having hands laid on them, praying and fasting, etc., that such is the Biblical way.

While all of these things named, and many such like not named, are definitely Scriptural, and definitely right in their own way and place, that's not the answer to victory. And that comes as a shock to most Christians.

Even though these things mentioned are spiritual things, in the manner in which they are carried out in the hearts and lives of most Christians, God looks at them as *"works"* or else *"walking after the flesh"* (Rom. 8:1). Our problem is, we've turned these perfectly Scriptural disciplines into *"works."*

The secret to all Christian victory is simple Faith in the Cross of Christ, which refers to what He there did on our behalf. When you as a Believer make the Cross of Christ the object of your Faith, and you continue to do so all the days of your life (Rom. 6:3-5, 11, 14), then the Holy Spirit will begin to work with you, doing within you and for you, that which only He can do. I'm trying to say, that you cannot lay aside these weights and sins without the power of the Holy Spirit. And considering that He works exclusively within the parameters of the great Sacrifice of Christ, you must ever place your Faith in that Finished Work. When you do this, and continue to do this, then it's very easy to lay aside these things mentioned. Otherwise, you will fight and struggle, and the harder you fight and struggle, the worse these problems become in your heart and life (Rom. 8:1-2, 11).

WORKS OF THE FLESH IN THE HEARTS AND LIVES OF CHRISTIANS

If the Believer doesn't understand the Cross, the works of the flesh will definitely show themselves in the heart and life of that Believer. I realize that's a strong statement, but it happens to be true. And it doesn't really matter who the Christian is, if the Cross is not properly understood, which refers to our dependence totally and completely on the great Sacrifice of Christ, without exception, works of the flesh are going to begin to show themselves in one's life. It is inevitable!

That's a chilling thought, but it happens to be true. Paul said:

"Now the works of the flesh are manifest, which are these; adultery, fornication,

uncleanness, lasciviousness, idolatry, witch-craft, hatred, variance, emulations, wrath, strife, seditions, heresies, envyings, murders, drunkenness, revellings, and such like" (Gal. 5:19-21). What was happening was this:

Paul had established the Galatian Churches. Of course, they had been established on the right foundation, which means that the Galatians had the proper teaching. They had been saved by trusting in the shed Blood of Christ, and they were kept by continuing faith in the Cross.

However, false teachers came in from Jerusalem, attempting to add Law to Grace, which of course, is impossible. That's the reason that Paul wrote this Epistle to the Galatians, and the reason he was so harsh in many of his statements.

What was being taught these Galatians by these false teachers was heresy. And Paul knew that if they accepted this false teaching, it would fall out to great spiritual harm on their part, and possibly even the loss of their souls. He plainly tells them here, that attempting to travel a course of any direction other than the Cross is going to lead to works of the flesh being manifested.

Now many Christians may look at this list, beginning with *"adultery, fornication, un-cleanness, and lasciviousness,"* and auto-matically think, *"I'm not guilty of these,"* etc. However, the truth is, that these terrible vices begin in the heart, before they're carried out in the act. My statement is this:

It is impossible for any Christian to not harbor the thoughts of these terrible sins in his heart, unless his faith and trust are com-pletely in the great Sacrifice of Christ, which then gives him the help of the Holy Spirit. Not performing the act is not enough. There must not even be any desire within our hearts. In fact, these first four sins mentioned in Verse 19, are far more widespread in Christendom than one would think.

For instance, most Christians would not even remotely think of themselves as com-mitting the sin of *"idolatry"*; however, if we're looking to anything else for life and victory outside of the Cross of Christ, we have made an idol of that thing, and most of the time, it centers up in *"self."* In other words, we're try-ing to live this life by our own machinations,

whether we understand it or not, and we have made an idol out of *"self."* And yet, many Christians make idols out of their religious Denominations, their particular Church, or even particular Preachers. In other words, their trust is in those things and those people, whomever they might be, instead of the Sac-rifice of Christ.

At this very moment, millions of Chris-tians think that by belonging to a certain Denomination, that such insures Salvation or at least some type of spiritual superiority. Pure and simple they have made an idol out of that Denomination or Church.

And then look at *"heresy."* Any belief sys-tem other than the Cross of Christ is heresy. That's a strong statement, but it is true!

Because of its seriousness, let me say it again:

If you as a Believer do not properly under-stand the Cross of Christ, and thereby make that the object of your Faith, which guaran-tees the help of the Holy Spirit, the *"works of the flesh"* are going to manifest themselves in your life. And unless they're rooted out, you could lose your soul (Gal. 5:21). The idea is we must go God's Way. Any other way leads to death. The Holy Spirit through Solomon plainly said, *"There is a way which seemeth right unto a man, but the end thereof are the ways of death"* (Prov. 14:12).

FALSE DIRECTION

There are some Christians who think they understand the Cross and Grace, but in fact, understand it erroneously, thereby turning the liberty of grace into license. In other words, inasmuch as the Grace of God is greater than all sin, in which it definitely is, then, so they think, sin is not so very serious. The idea is, sin doesn't matter so much, they say, be-cause Grace abounds (Rom. 5:20).

Nothing could be farther from the Truth! Paul's answer to that was, *"What shall we say then? Shall we continue in sin, that grace may abound?"*

He then said, *"God forbid. How shall we, that are dead to sin, live any longer therein?"* (Rom. 6:1-2).

The Lord doesn't save us in sin, but rather from sin. And once we're saved, the Holy Spirit comes within our hearts and lives, and it is His business to rid us of all sin. Now please understand that statement, because it's very, very important.

The Holy Spirit works tirelessly, to help us *"lay aside every weight and sin which doth so easily beset us."* Sin is a terrible affront to God. It is the cause of all the sorrow, heartache and problems in the world today, and in fact ever has been. The Cross of Christ is God's answer to sin. In fact, that should tell us exactly how awful that sin is. To address this problem, God had to become man, and had to go to the Cross in order that the terrible guilt and power of sin might be broken. So, as a Christian, sin is abhorrent to us, even as it must be abhorrent to us.

THE LAW OF THE SPIRIT OF LIFE IN CHRIST JESUS

In fact, this problem is so horrible that the Lord referred to it as the *"law of sin and death"* (Rom. 8:2). This means, as should be understood, that sin will bring death and will bring it in every capacity. There is only one power that can overcome that particular law, and that is another Law. It is called, *"the Law of the Spirit of Life in Christ Jesus"* (Rom. 8:2). This Law and this Law alone, can overcome the law of sin and death. But how does it do this?

In fact, most Christians don't have the slightest idea as to how the *"Law of the Spirit of Life in Christ Jesus,"* performs this task. If most think about it at all, they just sort of think it's automatic, or something which just happens.

Others think because they speak with other tongues occasionally, that this is the answer. While tongues definitely are Scriptural and real, and are definitely a blessing to any Saint of God, that's not what this Passage is speaking about.

First, and as we've already explained in this Volume, this of which we speak is a *"Law,"* which means, that it was devised by God, and to be sure, it is going to be kept. And when I say *"kept,"* I'm meaning that the Holy Spirit is going to keep this Law, and of that one can be sure.

It is called *"The Law of the Spirit of Life,"* because it generates life in the heart and life of the Believer. Where does this life come from?

NOTES

The total phrase is, *"The Law of the Spirit of Life in Christ Jesus,"* which means, that this Life comes exclusively from Christ.

To be sure, Christ has always had Life. He is God, so Life flows from Him; however, it took the Cross for that Life to be imparted unto us.

That's what Jesus was talking about when He said, *"If any man thirsts, let him come unto Me, and drink. He that believeth on Me, as the Scripture hath said, out of his innermost being shall flow rivers of living water"* (Jn. 7:37-38).

And then John said, *"But this spake He of the Spirit, which they that believe on Him should receive: for the Holy Spirit was not yet given; because that Jesus was not yet glorified"* (Jn. 7:39).

Thank the Lord, Jesus has now been glorified, which means, that He died on the Cross on our behalf, was raised from the dead, with His Sacrifice being accepted by God. He was glorified the moment He was raised from the dead, which means that His appearance on our behalf in the Presence of God is guaranteed (Heb. 9:24).

All of this *"Life"* comes from Christ, but more particularly, is made possible by what He did at the Cross. As we've already stated, Christ is God, and as such, has always had life. The problem was He could not impart this life to Believers, except through the Person of the Holy Spirit. And the Holy Spirit could not carry out this work, until Christ had affected His great Sacrifice at the Cross. At the Cross, Christ removed the sin debt of man, by atoning for all sin, past, present, and future, at least for those who will believe (Jn. 3:16). When this was done, the Holy Spirit could then impart the Life of Christ to seeking souls. That alone gives victory over the law of sin and death.

FAITH

To have this great impartation of life which Paul speaks about in Romans 8:2, one simply has to exhibit Faith in the Finished Work of Christ. Perhaps I can say it better in this manner:

One does not have to worry about the Holy Spirit doing His Office work within our hearts and lives, which is to rid us of all sin, and thereby to perfect the Fruit of the Spirit within our lives, providing our Faith is in the Cross of Christ. That's what Paul was speaking about incessantly in Romans 4, where he spoke of the Faith of Abraham, when he said, *"Abraham believed God, and it was counted unto him for Righteousness"* (Rom. 4:3).

To sum it all up, Abraham was believing in what God was going to do as it regarded sending a Redeemer into this world. That's why Jesus addressed Himself to this by saying to the Jews, *"Your Father Abraham rejoiced to see My day: and he saw it, and was glad"* (Jn. 8:56).

Faith exclusively is the ingredient by which God works. And by that statement, it is always meant *"Faith in the great Sacrifice of Christ."* As I've said over and over again, if we think of Jesus outside of the Cross, we are not properly understanding Him. That's why Paul said, *"Jesus Christ and Him Crucified"* (I Cor. 2:2).

When we place our Faith in what Christ did for us at the Cross, this shows that we understand that we could not do this thing ourselves, and that He had to do it for us, which He did. This denotes humility along with Faith and Trust in Christ, and Christ exclusively. Then we won't try to live this life by our own strength and ability, but will do so by Faith in Christ, which always refers to Faith in what He did at the Cross. This gives the Holy Spirit the latitude which He must have, in order to perform His work within our hearts and lives.

THE RESURRECTION

Many Christians are fond of referring to themselves as *"Resurrection Saints,"* etc. Most of the time, those who say this, are belittling the Cross.

Of course, the Resurrection as should be overly obvious, is of extreme importance; however, let the Reader understand, that the Resurrection was a foregone conclusion once Jesus died. The fact that He atoned for all sin, which opened up the way to God for all men, at least all who will believe, guaranteed His Resurrection.

The wages of sin is death, and there being no sin in Christ, and due to the fact that He had atoned for all sin, Satan could not keep

Him in the death world. To be sure, the Evil One could definitely keep every other person who had ever lived in that death world, even the great Patriarchs and Prophets of the Old Testament, and because, the sin debt still hung over their heads. So he had a right to make them his captives, which he did, even though he could only go so far with that captivity (Eph. 4:8-10).

But Jesus had no sin. The Scripture says of Him, *"For such an High Priest became us, Who is holy, harmless, undefiled, separate from sinners, and made higher than the heavens"* (Heb. 7:26). Therefore, death could not hold Him.

Furthermore, Paul also said, *"For if we have been planted together in the likeness of His death, we shall be also in the likeness of His Resurrection"* (Rom. 6:5).

This means, that we definitely cannot enjoy the fruits of His Resurrection, unless we properly understand the *"likeness of His death,"* which means that we were actually *"planted into His death"* (Rom. 6:3).

As important as the Resurrection was and is, it was not the Resurrection which affected your Salvation, but rather the Cross. That's why Paul said, *"I will glory in the Cross"* (Gal. 6:14). He didn't say, *"I will glory in the Resurrection,"* etc.

In fact, the moment that Jesus died on the Cross, the Scripture says, *"when He had cried again with a loud voice, yielded up the Ghost."* It then said:

"And, behold, the Veil of the Temple was rent in twain from the top to the bottom" (Mat. 27:50-51).

This signified that the way to God, even into His very Presence of the Holy of Holies, was now open, and open to all, who would avail themselves of what Christ did at the Cross on their behalf. This didn't await the Resurrection, and for all the obvious reasons.

That way was opened at the Cross, and with it then opened, the Resurrection of Christ was a foregone conclusion.

Therefore, while it is definitely true that we are *"Resurrection people"* we are that only because of what Jesus did at the Cross on our behalf. In fact, in spirit, we are actually seated at this very moment with Christ in Heavenly Places (Eph. 2:6); however, we are there solely and completely because of the Cross, and nothing else we might quickly add!

THE RACE

The phrase, *"And let us run with patience the race that is set before us,"* refers to the fact, that we don't run too very well, if we are encumbered by *"weights"* which greatly slow us down, and *"sin"* which can get us off the track completely. Let's say it again:

"Weights" drastically slow us down, while *"sin"* can *"easily beset us,"* which refers to getting us off the track completely.

The specific word for a race (dromos) is not used here, the general term for an athletic contest (agon) being chosen instead. This gives the idea of a certain type of race which is placed before the Christian. It is like a road that stretches out before one's gaze (Wuest).

The idea of this *"race"* is finishing the course. It is not the idea of all running, and only the one who crosses the finish line first is the winner. The idea is, that the Believer not quit this race, not stop running, but run completely until the finish line is crossed. It doesn't really matter how many times the person falls down on this particular course, just as long as he gets up and keeps running. Of course, any distraction is a severe hindrance as would be obvious. So we're not taking lightly any distractions along the way; however, the emphasis is on finishing the course, hence Paul saying of himself, *"I have fought a good fight, I have finished my course"* (II Tim. 4:7).

PATIENCE

"Patience" in the Greek is *"hupomone,"* and *"includes both passive endurance and active persistence."* It implies that there will be hindrances along the way, all placed there by Satan, with the intention of causing the Believer to quit running altogether, or else to run in a wrong direction. Both, as would be obvious, are extremely destructive.

We not only have to run this race, but we have to run it in the right direction, and it is sin, which can get us off course. And what is that sin?

Whatever it might be, whatever course it takes, whatever direction is takes, it can be

traced back to *"unbelief."* And what do we mean by that?

If it is to be noticed, Paul used the definite article when he said, *"the sin."* He is actually referring to trusting in something else other than the Cross. That is *"the sin!"*

The words *"easily beset"* are the translation of the Greek *"euperistatos,"* meaning *"readily, deftly, cleverly."* It also means, *"to place itself around."* It speaks of the sin that readily and easily encircles the Christian runner, like a long, loose robe clinging to his limbs, which will have a tendency to throw him off course. In fact, because of unbelief in the Cross of Christ, whether through ignorance or otherwise, millions of Christians are running a race, but it's in the wrong direction. Consequently, it will not come out to a correct conclusion, but rather to the loss of their souls. That's how critical this thing actually is.

In simple terms, *"patience"* refers to the following:

These things I'm teaching you are not learned easily. It may seem simple enough to put our Faith in the Cross of Christ and to leave it there; however, Satan fights this more than he fights anything else. And to be sure, he fights it moreso from inside the Church than from anywhere else.

The idea is, this *"Cross Life,"* this *"Law of the Spirit of Life which is in Christ Jesus,"* is not an uneventful course. It is somewhat like running a gauntlet. There are enemies on either side of the course who are attempting to drag us down, and doing so by any means at their disposal. The only way we can win, which means to run straight and true, is to keep our eyes on Christ Who in fact, has run this race before us, and has already won the victory on our behalf. If we trust in what He has done for us, which again refers to the Cross, we are guaranteed to cross the finish line. But only if we keep our eyes on Him!

We must never forget, that our Faith is never quite as strong as we think it is. That's the reason we have to *"grow in grace and the knowledge of the Lord."* That's the reason it's referred to as the *"Fruit of the Spirit,"* which refers to the fact, that fruit has to be cultivated and has to grow. In other words, none of this comes easily or quickly.

Unfortunately, in the last several decades, we have been taught that all we have to do is to confess the right thing, and it instantly comes to us. None of that is Scripturally correct. While a right confession is definitely important, it is only the confession that one has in the Cross of Christ which stands the test. That's the confession we must have. In fact, that's why Paul said:

"Likewise reckon ye also yourselves to be dead indeed unto sin, but alive unto God through Jesus Christ our Lord" (Rom. 6:11).

The word *"reckon"* refers to a conclusion or bottom line. The idea is, I will confess what Jesus has done for me at the Cross, and thereby reckon myself to be dead indeed unto sin, but alive unto God through Jesus Christ my Lord.

Paul also said, *"For we through the Spirit wait for the Hope of Righteousness by Faith"* (Gal. 5:5).

The word *"wait"* here refers to patience, and could be translated *"wait patiently."*

Wait patiently for what?

We want Righteousness totally and completely to be affected within our hearts and lives. Only the Spirit of God can do this. When we look at ourselves, too often we see failure instead of victory. That's why it's referred to as *"the hope of Righteousness."*

In Christ I have a position of Righteousness, which refers to imputed Righteousness, which refers to Righteousness that was given to me without merit or price, upon my Faith in Christ when I was saved. However, the development of Righteousness in my heart and life is a Work of the Spirit, which requires time and patience. In other words, the Holy Spirit is busy bringing my *"condition of Righteousness,"* up to my *"position of Righteousness."* As stated, this is not done easily or quickly.

But we are to continue to have Faith that the Spirit is going to work this out within our hearts and lives, which He definitely will, if we will maintain our Faith in what Christ did for us at the Cross.

QUITTERS

As I've stated elsewhere in this Volume, the Lord can deal with failures. In fact, there has never been a Believer who hasn't failed at one time or the other, and in fact, many times. And when I speak of *"failure,"* I'm speaking

actually of being overcome by sin, and thereby sinning in some way. But God can deal with failures, and in fact, He has already done so at the Cross. But God cannot deal with quitters.

That's what Satan wants you to do — quit. He wants you to get discouraged and stop. He wants you to say, *"I've tried the Cross and it doesn't work for me,"* or words to that effect. But I have good news for you.

The very next Verse in this Twelfth Chapter of Hebrews, tells us what we are to do:

(2) "LOOKING UNTO JESUS THE AUTHOR AND FINISHER OF OUR FAITH; WHO FOR THE JOY THAT WAS SET BEFORE HIM ENDURED THE CROSS, DESPISING THE SHAME, AND IS SET DOWN AT THE RIGHT HAND OF THE THRONE OF GOD."

The composite is:

1. It is to Jesus we must look.

2. It is Him and what He did for us at the Cross, in which our Faith must be placed.

3. The Cross must ever be the object of our Faith, which is the price that He paid.

4. By the mere fact of Christ being presently seated at the right hand of the Throne of God, refers to the fact, that what He did for us at the Cross will see us through, if we maintain our Faith in His Finished Work.

LOOKING UNTO JESUS

The short phrase, *"Looking unto Jesus,"* means we are to run this race *"with no eyes for anyone or anything except Jesus."* It is He toward Whom we run. There must be no divided attention.

"Looking" in the Greek is *"apharao,"* and means *"to turn the eyes away from other things and fix them on something."* The word also means, *"to turn one's mind to a certain thing."* Both meanings are applicable here, the spiritual vision turned away from all else and together with the mind, concentrated on Jesus.

Paul is continuing to speak of the *"race."* The minute the Greek runner in the stadium takes his attention away from the race course and the goal to which he is speeding, and turns it upon the onlooking crowds, his speed is slackened. It is so with the Christian. The minute he takes his eyes off of the Lord Jesus, and turns them upon others, his pace in the Christian life is slackened, and his onward progress in grace hindered (Wuest).

However, the word *"looking,"* as stated, also carries the idea of not only fixing our gaze on something, in this case Christ, but as well, to turn our mind to a certain thing. What is that certain thing?

Most of the Christian world looks at Jesus in all the wrong ways. In fact, it is so wrong most of the time, that Paul referred to the situation as *"another Jesus"* (II Cor. 11:4).

We must not only fix our eyes on Him as a Person, but we must turn our mind to a certain thing as it regards Him, and that refers to the price that He paid, which Paul will refer to in this Verse. In other words, when we look at Christ, we are to look at Him as the crucified Lord, Who has been raised from the dead, and is now seated with God in Heavenly Places (Eph. 2:6), and as well, has been highly exalted, and given a name which is above every name (Phil. 2:9).

But all of this is because of what He did at the Cross.

So, we must always look to Him as the Sacrifice, which paid the terrible debt of my sin, thereby making it possible for me to be justified by Faith, and thereby for the Holy Spirit to come in and abide (Gal. 3:13-14).

Many Christians are looking exclusively to a healing Jesus. To be sure, He definitely is the Healer, but if we attempt to understand that apart from the Cross, then we are not properly looking at Him. The same can be said for the miracle Jesus, the Church Jesus, the Blessing Jesus, etc. To be sure, Jesus is everything to us, however, He is everything to us strictly on the merit of what He did for us at the Cross.

GRACE

God has always had an abundance of Grace. In fact, I think one could say without any fear of contradiction, that God is Grace. So, the fact of Grace has never been the question. The great question was, as to how this Grace could be imparted to sinful man.

The Cross of Christ was and is the answer to that. Through the Cross as a medium, or an instrument if you please, God was able to impart Grace to undeserving sinners.

NOTES

How did the Cross make all of this possible?

It made it possible, because there Jesus dealt with the sin question, by atoning for all sin. He did so by His Death. Man's simple faith in this great Finished Work of Christ, then makes it possible for God to pour Grace upon the undeserving individual.

In fact, it is not possible to deserve Grace. The very moment we think we do, that's when we nullify Grace. That's why Paul said, *"I do not frustrate the Grace of God: for if Righteousness come by the Law, then Christ is dead in vain"* (Gal. 2:21).

Christians frustrate the Grace of God, which spells total defeat for that particular Christian, by trying to live the Christian life, without the help of the Spirit. That is done by us trying to do the work ourselves, which means we're not looking to the Cross of Christ. Looking to the Cross, allows the Spirit to work, which then gives us an uninterrupted flow of the Grace of God.

So, the Reader must ask himself as to what type of Jesus to whom he is looking? There is nothing more important!

THE AUTHOR AND FINISHER OF OUR FAITH

The phrase, *"The Author and Finisher of our Faith,"* proclaims Who He is, and What He did! Actually the Text in the Greek reads: *"The Author and Finisher of the Faith."*

"Author" in the Greek is *"archegos."* Here it means not so much that Christ perfected Faith, but rather that He as our leader, Who by His death has opened up a new way — a way that has bridged the gap between Earth and Heaven itself. Jesus is the pioneer Who has created the path that we now follow by Faith into the very Presence of God. He did this by and through the Cross.

"Finisher" in the Greek is *"teleioo,"* and means *"to carry through completely, to finish, to make perfect or complete."* While the idea definitely directs itself to the development of our Faith, it moreso directs itself to the manner in which this is done. Once again it is the Cross.

That's the reason we keep saying that one's Faith must ever be anchored in the Cross of Christ. The Cross must ever be the object of our Faith. This is the manner in which we begin Faith, the manner in which we develop Faith, and the manner in which we finish our Faith, i.e., *"bring it out to full development."* This is all done by what He did at the Cross on our behalf.

So, the only way we can rightly run this race that is set before us, is by looking unto Jesus, understanding that it is Faith in what He did at the Cross, which will guarantee us the finishing of this course.

This is the reason that I keep saying that Faith placed in anything else, is in reality no Faith at all. In fact, the Church has had more teaching on Faith in the last half of the 20th Century, than possibly all the other centuries put together; however, for the most part, it has been Faith in something else other than the Cross. Consequently, it is Faith that God will not recognize, which the Holy Spirit cannot bless, and which will fall out to no good for the Believer.

As Paul referred to *"another Jesus,"* and *"another spirit,"* and *"another gospel,"* we might as well refer to *"another faith."* In essence, this is what Paul did say when he made the statement:

"I marvel that ye (the Galatians) *are so soon removed from Him that called you into the Grace of Christ unto another gospel: which is not another"* (Gal. 1:6-7).

He could just as easily have said there *"another faith,"* because that's what the word *"gospel,"* actually means.

As Hebrews 12:2 so graphically illustrates, it is only Faith in the Cross of Christ which God will recognize as true Faith. Jesus is the Author and Finisher only of *"the Faith,"* which refers to His great Sacrificial, Atoning Work.

ENDURED THE CROSS

The phrase, *"Who for the joy that was set before Him endured the Cross, despising the shame,"* refers to what He was before the Incarnation, and that He gave it all up in order to redeem humanity, even though it would have to be done through and by the horrible agony and shame of the Cross. It carries the same connotation as, *"Who, being in the form of God, thought it not robbery to be equal with God: but made Himself of no reputation,*

NOTES

and took upon Him the form of a servant, and was made in the likeness of men."

Paul then said, *"And being found in fashion as a man, He humbled Himself and became obedient unto death, even the death of the Cross"* (Phil. 2:6-8).

If mankind was to have a way to God, which would be through Faith and Faith alone, it could only be brought about by Christ going to the Cross, despite the fact of its awful, ignominious shame. What He gave up on our behalf, cannot be comprehended by mere mortals. We can only go so far into that unknown, and then we have to withdraw. Being mere creatures, we cannot comprehend the Creator becoming a creature, which in fact, He had to do, in order to redeem mankind.

God couldn't die; therefore, inasmuch as the price of death was demanded, God would have to become man, in order for this terrible thing to be carried out. The terrible fact of sin had to be addressed, and it would have to be addressed full throttle so to speak!

To be sure, even as the phrase *"endured the Cross"* proclaims, this particular death was an awful thing. It was so awful in fact, that it beggars description.

It was not so much Him dying, but rather what He had to do in His dying. He would have to bear the sin guilt of the entirety of mankind and for all time. The penalty of every single sin, and no matter how vile it may have been or might be, must be laid upon Him. Actually, this is what the great Prophet Isaiah said:

"All we like sheep have gone astray; we have turned every one to his own way; and the Lord hath laid on Him the iniquity of us all" (Isa. 53:6).

Oh how I sense the Presence of God even as I dictate these words. The idea is that the iniquities of men fell all at once upon Him and He bore them away. Jehovah caused the sins of the whole world to meet upon Him. He suffered the judgment for them all, which judgment was death.

"Shame" in the Greek is *"aischune,"* and means *"disgrace, disfigurement."* The idea is, that He despised the shame attendant upon a death by crucifixion, namely, the fact that this kind of a death was meted out upon malefactors.

No citizen of the Roman Empire was crucified, no matter his or her crime. Crucifixion was only for slaves, and even the worst criminals among slaves, etc.

Actually, this is the reason that the religious leaders of Israel demanded His crucifixion. Execution according to Jewish Law was by stoning, but they wanted Him crucified.

They were well acquainted with Deuteronomy 21:22-23, which stated, *"And if a man have committed a sin worthy of death, and he be to be put to death, and thou hang him on a tree: His body shall not remain all night upon the tree, but thou shalt in any wise bury him that day; (for he that is hanged is accursed of God;) that thy land be not defiled, which the Lord thy God giveth thee for an inheritance."*

In the evil minds of these religious leaders, if they could persuade Pilate to crucify Him, their thinking was that His claims regarding Messiahship would be blasted. The people would think that if He was really the Messiah, God surely wouldn't allow Him to be crucified, which meant that He was cursed of God.

What they didn't understand was, this was the very purpose and reason for His coming. The Cross was ever His destination, even having been predicted through Moses by the *"serpent on the pole,"* which was a graphic object lesson, and to which Jesus referred in His conversation with Nicodemus (Num. 21:9; Jn. 3:14).

Nevertheless, the shame and disgrace were awful. Beside the ignominious horror of being crucified, He hung on the Cross, literally stripped of all clothing. The artists in attempting to portray this scene, picture Him with a loincloth over His privates; however, He was not afforded even that on this horrible day. He died in shame and disgrace, in fact, all that evil men could heap upon Him.

RELIGION

As well, it must be remembered that it was not so much the world which did this, even though Rome definitely was a complicitor, but rather the Church of that day. It was the religious leaders of Israel who perpetrated this foul, dastardly, hideous scheme. They murdered their own Messiah.

The tragedy is, that Satan always works more grandly inside the Church than he does otherwise. The irony is, they crucified the Lord in the Name of the Lord! Hence Jesus crying on the Cross, *"Father, forgive them; for they know not what they do"* (Lk. 23:34).

Whenever any part of the modern Church opposes the Cross, holds up another means as a proposed way of Salvation, and more specifically opposes the Messenger of the Cross, they are in effect, *"trodding underfoot the Son of God, and counting the Blood of the Covenant . . . an unholy thing."* They are *"doing despite unto the Spirit of Grace"* (Heb. 10:29). In other words, they are of the same crowd that crucified Christ some 2,000 years ago, and because they are of the same spirit.

The tragic thing about this is, this crowd as then, is in the far, far greater majority. As there were few who stood up for Christ on that dark day of so long ago, there are few who truly stand up for Him at present.

Oh to be sure, they claim to stand up for Him, but the Truth is, the Jesus they promote, is not the Crucified One, but rather *"another Jesus, which is another gospel, all promoted by another spirit"* (II Cor. 11:4).

So the Reader must ask himself the question, as it regards the Church where he attends, and the Preacher to whom he follows, is Christ being preached, the Christ of the Cross, even as Paul outlines in 12:2, or is it another Christ?

AN ETHICAL GOSPEL

The ethical gospel is primarily the gospel presently being preached in most of the modern Church world. And what do we mean by that?

This gospel touts the *"golden rule,"* proclaims the necessity of *"doing good,"* and *"not doing bad things,"* etc. It all sounds good to the carnal ear; regrettably, it is believed by most.

The Lord Jesus Christ is held up as a good man, even as an example, but if inspected closely, He is only window dressing for this ethical gospel.

None of that will save anyone, will deliver anyone, will set any captive free, and in fact, will address the sin question at all. Pure and simple, it is a gospel of *"works."*

In the first place, man is incapable within himself of *"doing good."* While he may keep some part of the so-called golden rule some of the time, the truth is, he woefully falls down regarding that which God demands, which is a spotless, pure Righteousness.

Man's problem is sin, and that means that man's condition is terminal. As well, sin is so awful, so vile, so destructive, so powerful, and has such a force to its application, that it takes more than mere rules to address the horror of this situation. In fact, even as we are now studying, it took the Cross.

The only answer for a hurting, dying, Hell-bound world, is Jesus Christ and Him Crucified. There is no other answer! Jesus as the *"good man,"* or even as the *"miracle worker,"* will not suffice. It is only what He did at the Cross which addresses this horrible problem and sets the captive free.

And to accept Him, one must do much more than portray a vapid, mental acceptance of the Cross. Jesus addressed this very succinctly when He said, *"Verily, verily I say unto you, except ye eat the flesh of the Son of Man, and drink His Blood, you have no life in you"* (Jn. 6:53).

What did He mean by that?

First of all, He wasn't speaking of literally eating His flesh and drinking His Blood, because He then said, *"It is the Spirit that quickeneth; the flesh profiteth nothing: the words that I speak unto you, they are spirit, and they are life"* (Jn. 6:63).

He was speaking of the death that He would die on the Cross, which of course, would necessitate the shedding of His Precious Blood, which would atone for all sin.

And for one to reap the benefits of what He there did, one must place such Faith in that Finished Work, that the Holy Spirit through Paul would explain it by saying that we are literally *"baptized into His death"* (Rom. 6:3).

This definitely means to accept Christ, but more than all, it means accepting what He did at the Cross on our behalf, understanding that this was the only way that man could be saved, and that we must believe in His death totally and completely as the only solution that answers this terrible need.

If we treat the Cross lightly, we are not eating His flesh and drinking His Blood. If

we ignore the Cross, certainly we should understand that we aren't eating His flesh and drinking His Blood. If we suggest something in addition to the Cross, that means we aren't properly eating His flesh or drinking His Blood.

We must understand, that our Salvation, our Victory, our eternal life, our relationship with the Lord, literally everything we have, and ever hope to have, are all found in the Cross of Christ, and exclusively the Cross.

THE PASSOVER

The ancient, Jewish Passover, is an excellent case in point. They literally *"ate the Passover,"* which refers to the lamb that was roasted, etc.

The eating of this little animal, and by all means eating it all, refers to the entire family, which they were commanded to do (Ex. 12:10). All of this typified Christ, and more particularly, the Sacrifice that He would make of Himself on the Cross.

Unless you as a Believer fully understand that every single thing you have from God comes exclusively through the Cross of Christ and in no other way, which means that your Church, or certain Preachers, or your good works, will never suffice — until you come to that place and position, you aren't actually *"eating His flesh, and drinking His Blood."* Once again, it is the matter of the correct object of your Faith. It must be the Cross and the Cross exclusively.

Now if you read these words, and have doubts about what I'm saying, then your Faith is not exclusively in the Cross, but is divided, or is totally in something else. That means that you either aren't saved, or else you are fastly going in a wrong direction, which will only lead to spiritual destruction somewhere down the road. There is no alternative to this thing, it is the Cross or it is nothing!

In fact, that shouldn't be hard to understand. The entirety of the Old Testament points to the Cross of Christ, as it regards all the prophecies, and as it regards the Law of Moses. Of all the hundreds of millions of Sacrifices offered over the some 1,600 years of Mosaic Law, every single one of those Sacrifices pointed to the Cross, and did so in such a graphic manner that the object lesson is unmistakable. And now that the Cross is a fact, the entirety of the Message of the Apostle Paul, who in fact was given the meaning of the New Covenant, points directly and squarely to the Cross. In fact, the meaning of the New Covenant is actually the meaning of the Cross (Rom. 6:3-14). But yet, Satan fights the Cross as he fights nothing else, and for all the obvious reasons!

As I've already said several times in this Volume, the Church has already entered into the last great apostasy. And by that I speak of the events which are soon to come upon this world, the rise of the Antichrist, the coming great Tribulation, the Second Coming, all which will be preceded by the Rapture of the Church.

THE LAST APOSTASY

One writer said some time ago, and he was completely correct, that while much of the Church is claiming that conditions are getting better and better, the Bible teaches the very opposite. The reason the Church thinks this, is because they're not looking at the situation spiritually, but rather carnally.

The apostasy of which the Word of God describes (I Tim. 4:1-2; II Tim. 3:1-7), is as should be obvious, a spiritual apostasy, which refers to a departure from Truth.

The modern Church has never been richer and has never been bigger. But it's like a 500 pound man: while he may be big, he is certainly not healthy.

At this particular time, the majority of the modern Church can be labeled as *"having itching ears."* Consequently, they are heaping to themselves teachers who will cater to *"their own lusts,"* and because they *"will not endure sound doctrine"* (II Tim. 4:3-4). Consequently, they have *"turned away their ears from the Truth, and are turned unto fables."* That is the condition of the modern Church presently, more so, I think, than it's been in the entirety of its history.

The Church has departed from the Cross, which means they have departed from the Truth, which means they are seeking *"fables."* So, the Bible teaches this:

The spiritual situation must deteriorate before the Rapture of the Church can take place, instead of otherwise. I realize that's

not commonly taught, and in fact, is taught almost not at all. But it just happens to be the truth (II Tim. 3:1-7).

This will serve to separate the true from the false. And the dividing line will be, and in fact is, the Cross of Christ. In fact, it has always been the Cross, but it's going to be the Cross presently more than ever!

WHY WAS THE CROSS NECESSARY?

Paul said that Jesus had to *"endure the Cross."* Why did He have to do that?

As we've already stated, the Cross was the most shameful death that could be devised by evil men. Jesus had to go to the Cross, even though this was the most shameful spectacle, and in fact, because it was the most shameful spectacle.

Even though He wasn't cursed by God, and because He had never done anything to warrant such a curse; still, He had to be made a curse for us, which means that He took the curse which we should have taken (Gal. 3:13-14).

And the curse which He took, had to include every sin that had ever been committed, and would ever be committed, even the vilest. That curse was death, but it was death in the most shameful, ignominious, horrifying, humiliating way. In other words, Jesus literally died as a spectacle of shame. He died between two thieves, and was mocked by the religious leaders of Israel while He was dying (Lk. 23:35-36).

The Cross was necessary, and in all of its ignoble horror, simply because the sin of man was so bad. That's the problem with mankind, and more specifically, that's the problem with the Church.

It doesn't want to admit how bad the situation is, thinking it can be addressed by their own pitiful efforts.

It is understandable that the unredeemed would think such things, but not so understandable at all as it regards the Church. For any Preacher or any Christian for that matter, to demean the Cross in any way, to belittle the Cross in any way, to place it in a subservient position, and God forbid, to deny the Cross, is at the same time saying, *"I can save myself."* Coming from Christians, and I might say Christians so called, can be concluded as none other than *"blasphemy!"*

The horror of the Cross was absolutely necessary because man's condition was so absolutely bad. As stated, it was terminal, meaning there was no way he could save himself.

The Reader must never forget that sin is more than a mere abstraction. It is more than a slight maladjustment. It is rather a total pollution. Isaiah described it when he said:

"The whole head is sick, and the whole heart faint. From the sole of the foot even unto the head there is no soundness in it; but wounds, and bruises, and putrifying sores: they have not been closed, neither bound up, neither mollified with ointment" (Isa. 1:5-6).

As is obvious, the Prophet was using physical descriptions to describe spiritual conditions.

This is what makes the drivel of humanistic psychology so absolutely preposterous. And even more than that, that Preachers could hold up this facade as an answer to the ills of man, is beyond belief. And then to go even farther, for Preachers who claim to be Spirit-filled, to tout this nonsense, is as stated, outright blasphemy! In fact, I think I can say without fear of scriptural exaggeration, that the acceptance by the modern Church of humanistic psychology, is the greatest sign of all of departure from Truth. To accept that drivel, is to reject the Cross, and to reject the Cross, is to reject Salvation.

THE RIGHT HAND OF THE THRONE OF GOD

The phrase, *"And is set down at the right hand of the Throne of God,"* refers to the fact, that His work of providing Salvation is finished. He is sat down, and remains seated. He need never arise and repeat His work on the Cross for sinners. It is a Finished Work. He is not only seated, but He occupies the position of preeminence, at the Right Hand of God.

How so much I sense His Presence! How so much this great Truth drives home to my heart! How so much is this a Finished Work! How so much is this the Grace of God! How so much did Jesus open up the way, and as the song says, *"The way to Heaven's Gate."* If the Cross was awful, and it definitely was, then the Victory is wonderful. So, we can say, that the victory is just as wonderful as the Cross was awful.

NOTES

The idea of all of this is, that His Victory is ours as we recognize our union with Him. He did it all for us, which means He did none of this for Himself. He then is to be the Object before the souls of His people.

Because of Him, I am free! Because of Him and more particularly, and more specifically, what He did at the Cross, I am forever free. And as well, my freedom is complete. It's not a partial freedom, but a total freedom.

This means that I'm free from the guilt and the power of sin. Because of what Jesus did at the Cross and my Faith in that Finished Work, the God of all the ages, has declared me as *"not guilty."* And due to my continued Faith in that eternal Sacrifice, the power of sin is broken within my life. No wonder Peter said:

"Whom having not seen, we love; in Whom, though now ye see Him not, yet believing, ye rejoice with joy unspeakable and full of glory" (I Pet. 1:8).

In all of this, when we are commanded to *"look unto Jesus,"* it refers to looking at Him in two capacities — that of the Cross, concerning the great price He paid for us, and as well, looking at Him now *"at the right hand of the Throne of God."* The idea is, that our attention is to be directed unto the Prince and Perfecter of Faith — not of *"our faith"* — that would be a poor thing — but of Faith itself.

The Elders witnessed to Faith in one or other of its activities, but Jesus ran the entire course of Faith from the beginning to the end and furnished a perfect testimony. The Elders, as exampled in Chapter 11, had traveled a part of the path and triumphed over some difficulties, but He had been subjected to every trial. He was sheltered from none.

The Elders trusted in God and were delivered; He was a worm and no man, and was forsaken. But as Prince and Perfecter of Faith, He won the victory by submission, and we speak of submission to the Cross, and is now sat down in a glory magnified in proportion to the depth of His abasement and obedience. Reward is never the motive of faith, but ever its encouragement (Williams).

When looking at Him, nothing is easier than to lay aside a weight; when not looking at Him, nothing is harder.

He has Himself reached the goal, and His Presence marks the point at which the race will close.

It is Jesus Who begins and brings to perfection our faith, and this means, that we must run the race with our eye ever fixed upon Him; in Him is the beginning, in Him the completion of the Promises (II Cor. 1:20); and in the steady and trustful dependence upon Him, and what He did at the Cross, consists our faith.

(3) "FOR CONSIDER HIM THAT ENDURED SUCH CONTRADICTION OF SINNERS AGAINST HIMSELF, LEST YE BE WEARIED AND FAINT IN YOUR MINDS."

The exegesis is:

1. Christ is ever the example, and in fact, the only example.

2. Christ suffered terrible opposition from the human race, and especially the religious leaders of Israel, and so will we, that is if we properly follow Him.

3. We must not faint and collapse on this journey, and will not do so, if we ever "consider Him."

CONSIDER HIM

The phrase, "For consider Him," means to consider by way of comparison. Jesus had to endure far more than we will ever be called upon to endure; consequently, our difficulties and even sufferings, whatever they might be, are but insignificant by comparison to His.

All that He endured, was that the way might be opened to God for all men, at least those who will believe. That which we endure, is that we might arrive at this place He has opened for us, and at great price we might add, which is the very throne of God. That is the ultimate goal!

We are to "look to Him" in order to run the race and finish the race. We are to "consider Him," as it regards the difficulties along the way. Whatever the difficulties were, they didn't stop Him, and if we always "look to Him," and "consider Him," they will not stop us as well.

The things which hinder us are "weights" and "besetting sins." As one great Preacher said:

"If we think of besetting sin as a savage beast, and the man of faith running his appointed race with this beast ever following hard after him, we can see at once the striking picture presented here. We who would out-run sin must not be loaded down with needless weights. It is when these things are cast aside that we are able to leave the fierce pursuer behind.

"But we must have an Object before us as well, in order to keep up our courage unto the end; and so we are bidden to look steadfastly upon Jesus, Who Himself is the Leader and Completer of faith. His was the life of faith in all its perfection. He then is to be the Object before the souls of His people.

"In the hour of discouragement when one feels inclined to cry with Jacob, 'All these things are against me,' lift up your eyes, tempted one, and look upon Him Who knew such grief as you shall never know, and yet Who sits as Victor now in highest glory. Let Him be your heart's Object. Let Him be your soul's delight and lifted above the cares and griefs of the present moment, you will be enabled to run unweariedly and without fainting, your appointed race" (Ironside).

THE OPPOSITION OF SINNERS

The phrase, "That endured such contradiction of sinners against Himself," refers to opposition. However, when the Holy Spirit through Paul uses the word "sinners," He is of course speaking of all who do not know God, but more specifically, of the religious leaders of Israel. The way of these religious leaders was a contradiction against Himself. In other words, they contradicted His way of Faith, by proposing another way. As well, this "contradiction" did not stop with mere verbal opposition, but went to the extent of murder, even as the next Verse proclaims.

John said of Him, "He was in the world, and the world was made by Him, and the world knew Him not."

He then said, and which was the most stinging of all, "He came unto His Own, and His Own received Him not" (Jn. 1:10-11).

As should be obvious, by Paul here using the word "sinners," any direction that is proposed as it regards Salvation, other than Christ and Him Crucified is a "sin!" Those who do such are lost and are thereby, labeled as "sinners!"

The sin here referred to is not so much acts of sin, but rather the sin of *"unbelief,"* as it regards Christ and His Sacrifice.

He said, *"I am the Way, the Truth, and the Life: no man cometh unto the Father, but by Me"* (Jn. 14:6).

The Jews disavowed His claims, rather proposing another way, a way of their own devising.

Presently, many in the modern Church mouth these same words that Jesus uttered, but then subtly, and sometimes not so subtly, propose another way. They cry *"Savior"* and at the same time point to *"self."* They talk about *"Faith"* but then propose *"fables."* They talk about *"Christ"* but recommend *"psychological counseling."* Need I say more!

AGAINST CHRIST

Anything that proposes any other way except Christ and Him Crucified, is *"against Christ!"* One cannot have it two ways: it is either one or the other.

Even though the following is said with sadness, still it must be said.

Most of the Churches are against Christ! Of course, they do not claim to be and would strongly disavow that they are; however, if the Message is other than the Cross, then pure and simple, it is *"against Christ."*

I realize that the Reader may think that I press the point too much. But when we consider that we're speaking here of the issues of life and death, in fact, the very weight of one's Salvation, then all of this takes on a significance of outsized proportions. In other words, there is absolutely nothing more important than this of which I speak.

As someone has well said, *"There is nothing worse than a false way of Salvation."* How true that is.

So, if I err, I would rather err on the side of preaching *"Christ and Him Crucified,"* in other words, preaching it too much, than not enough. The truth is, it's impossible to err in proclaiming this truth too much, this veritable way of Salvation, this only way of Salvation. Our problem is, we don't preach it enough.

TO WEARY AND FAINT

The phrase, *"Lest ye be wearied and faint in your minds,"* present the fact that there

definitely is opposition to the Child of God in his efforts to live for God, and to carry out the work that the Lord has called one to do.

In the last several decades, the Church has been greatly influenced by that which I refer to as the *"faith message."* Actually, despite all the talk about faith, there is really no faith at all, and because this particular type of faith has as its object other than the Finished Work of Christ. At any rate, in this teaching, which as stated has greatly influenced the Church, and to its detriment I might quickly add, the Church has been taught that if one has the right confession, that one will never have difficulties and problems, etc. Consequently, these particular false teachers, would conclude Paul's statement about being *"wearied"* and *"fainting in one's mind,"* as to be a *"bad confession"*; however, if whatever is being taught doesn't match up perfectly with the Word of God, then something is wrong with what is being taught.

While every Christian should always have a good confession, and while we always must dwell on the positive irrespective that the negative is present, a proper confession never denies reality and neither does it lie. Confessing that you don't have a headache, when obviously you do, is not faith but rather fabrication.

MINDS

If one is to notice, Paul spoke here of the attack by Satan being in the *"minds"* of Christians. What did he mean by that?

In fact, it is always the mind which constitutes the thought processes of the Believer, which Satan attacks first. He attempts to place doubts in our minds, causing us to go into unbelief, which first of all robs us of our peace. He mostly does this by directing our attention to circumstances. He wants to get our thinking out of the region of *"faith"* into the region of *"sight."* If he can do this, get you to looking at circumstances and situations, instead of looking to the Lord, he will drive you into a *"laboring and heavy laden"* posture (Mat. 11:28-30). In this posture, we become *"weary"* with the struggle, and we *"faint in our minds,"* which means that we *"give up."*

In such a scenario, which incidentally affects all Believers, the following should be noted:

1. As stated, no Believer is immune from these attacks. The Evil One strikes the strongest Christians as well as he does the weakest, all in this fashion (I Pet. 4:12).

2. There is nothing we can do to stop the attacks; however, there is definitely something we can do that will lessen their frequency. The more that we give in to such a situation, the more that Satan pushes in this direction. This should be obvious! (I Pet. 5:7).

3. In such a scenario, it is not the quantity of faith that is deficient, but rather the quality. Unfortunately, in the past several decades, most all the teaching has centered up on increasing one's faith. That is not your need. Your need and my need, is the correct Object of Faith which must always be the Cross of Christ (Gal. 6:14).

4. When our Faith is properly placed in the Finished Work of Christ, and it remains in that Finished Work, the Holy Spirit can then help us. And to be sure, the help of the Spirit, is what we must have. Satan holds no fear of us, at least fear of our own immediate strength; however, he wants no part of the Holy Spirit! (Rom. 8:11).

5. When the Holy Spirit begins to work, the first thing He will do, is to redirect your faith toward the Cross. The idea is this:

If Jesus paid such a price for you at the Cross, which He definitely did, then to be sure, He is definitely going to protect His investment, so to speak. In other words, He's not going to let you go down (Heb. 13:5).

6. We must always remember, that every attack leveled at us by Satan, while it definitely is of Satan, is allowed by the Lord. And we must always remember, that Satan can only press so hard as the Lord allows. In other words, it's the Lord who sets the parameters and not Satan (Job, Chpts. 1-2).

7. The Lord allows Satan certain latitude, in order to strengthen our Faith. It is all a *"test."* Of course, with Satan it is temptation, but with the Lord it is a test. Satan means to steal, kill, and destroy, while the Lord allows this in order for us to be strengthened. To be sure, the Lord doesn't allow the *"test"* in order that He might know our situation. He already knows that. He allows it, that we might know and see. And the idea is, our Faith is never quite as strong as we think

it is, in which the test always brings out (Heb. 11:17).

8. If the Believer will look at these situations as the Believer should, which means that we understand that it is a test, and which is allowed by the Lord in order to strengthen our Faith, and that if we will believe Him, He definitely is going to see us through, the situation will then take on a positive aspect.

Our problem is, in the middle of all of these situations, the oppression at times tendered by the Evil One becomes so severe, that it's hard for us to see the true picture (II Cor. 12:7).

9. As a Believer, you must always remember, that always and without exception, you can steer your thought processes (our minds) toward Christ and what He has done for us at the Cross. When we dwell on that, understanding that He there defeated every power of darkness, then Faith will begin to build within our hearts, and the Evil One will be dispelled. The entire effort by Satan is to try to get us to become so discouraged that we will simply quit. Unfortunately, he has succeeded with some (Rom. 12:1-2).

WHAT JESUS DID AT THE CROSS

As I've stated in previous Commentary, the Christian must understand that the way of the Cross is a way of life. In other words, this is not just a particular doctrine, but actually the foundation of all Doctrine.

The Believer must ever understand, that what Jesus did at the Cross, while definitely making a way for us to be saved, also addressed every other single problem that besets the human race. Now please read those words carefully. In other words, His Work being a Finished Work, left out nothing. Whatever we can think of, and whatever it is we cannot think of, all and without exception were included in the Atonement. But most Christians don't realize this. They've never gone that far in their thinking. Regarding the Cross, if they think of it much at all, they think of it only in the sense of the initial Salvation experience (Rom. 6:3-5, 11, 14).

We must come away from such thinking, understanding that the Cross was far more than that. In fact, the Cross and the Cross alone, made it possible for the Holy Spirit to come into the hearts and lives of Believers and to abide permanently (Jn. 14:16-17). That within itself opens up possibilities beyond comprehension.

However, before I address that, please allow me to state the following:

Most Christians never think of the Cross as the answer to our dilemma, as it regards discouragement, confusion, disillusionment, stress, oppression, or disturbances of any kind. But to be sure, and as stated, what Jesus there did, addresses everything, which means that He left nothing unaddressed. The idea is this:

Everything that man lost in the Fall, Jesus addressed in the Atonement. While it is true that we do not yet have all of these things for which He paid such a price, and in fact will not have all of them until the coming Resurrection; still, what we do have, is enough to walk in victory, and I mean total victory, 24 hours a day, 7 days a week. No, I'm not teaching that if we have our Faith properly placed, that Satan will stop all attacks. As I've already stated, Satan is going to continue to try to hinder us in every possible way that he can, until the day we die, or else the Trump sounds. That's a foregone conclusion; however, and as well which we've already stated, the Lord is the One Who actually allows all of this, but always for our good.

Our thinking should not be, *"This is going to destroy me,"* but rather, *"This is going to make me stronger!"* Hallelujah! Hallelujah! Hallelujah!

This great Work of Christ is not compartmentalized. In other words, He doesn't have one type of faith for one type of problem, and another type of faith for another type of problem. The Cross answers it all, and our Faith in the Cross guarantees all that the Cross affords.

I suppose that most Christian Bookstores are filled with books on how to overcome certain weaknesses within our hearts and lives. *"How to Have a Better Marriage!"* *"How to Better Oneself!"* *"How to Overcome Your Fears!"* In fact, the list is endless.

For the most part, and I think I can say without fear of contradiction, virtually all the time, these books are worthless. In fact, they are worse than worthless, because they not only do not help, they lead one away from the true help afforded by Christ.

NOTES

The Cross answers it all! If you as a Believer will understand that every single need that you have, every single question that you have, every single weakness that you have, were all answered at the Cross, you will be well on your way to total victory.

Understanding that, you must put your Faith exclusively in this which Jesus did, understanding, that He did it all on your behalf. He didn't do it for Himself, but rather for us. And to be sure, He paid a terrible price; consequently, it stands to reason, if someone has paid a staggering price for something, and did it all for us, it stands to reason that He definitely wants us to take advantage of that which He has done. It must grieve greatly the Heart of God to see Christians staggering and stumbling, trying to find solutions in a thousand different ways, and all those ways wrong, while the Cross is available to each and all!

THE HOLY SPIRIT

Ever since I've been a child, I have realized the value of the Holy Spirit. Actually, I was baptized with the Spirit when I was 8 years old. Consequently, I have made every effort to be led by the Spirit, to be guided by the Spirit, and to be empowered by the Spirit. However, when the Lord began to give me the Revelation of the Cross, at the same time, He began to show me the manner and way in which the Spirit works within our hearts and lives.

To be sure, the Holy Spirit, Who resides in the heart and life of every Believer, will always do all that He can on our behalf. That's why He's there. But our problem is, we do not know, or one might say, *"properly know,"* the manner and way in which He works. When the Lord showed me this, it completely revolutionized my life, my thinking, my Ministry, and in fact, everything.

He took me to Romans 8:2, *"For the Law of the Spirit of Life in Christ Jesus has made me free from the law of sin and death."*

Once I understood this particular Passage of Scripture, then everything else about the Holy Spirit began to fall into place. I began to see how that He works, when He works, and the method by which He works.

By the use of the word *"Law,"* which we've already addressed in previous Commentary in this Volume, the Lord let me know that this was more than just a supposition. In other words, the way and manner in which the Spirit works, is according to a Law, which has been devised by the Godhead; consequently, the Holy Spirit most definitely will not break this Law.

He then showed me that it's all *"in Christ Jesus,"* which refers to what Christ did at the Cross. In other words, this *"Law"* states, that the Holy Spirit works entirely within the parameters of the Finished Work of Christ. Now do you the Reader understand what that means?

It means that every single thing that the Spirit does for us and with us, that He does according to the legal work carried out by Christ at Calvary. And yes, what Jesus did at the Cross is definitely a legal work, even as Romans 8:2 proclaims.

As I've already said, probably some 50 times in this Volume, with the Believer understanding that everything he has from the Lord comes exclusively through the Cross of Christ, and by no other means or ways, then he must place his Faith in that which Christ has done. This is the *"Law!"* And of course, I would certainly hope that the Believer would understand, that we are not speaking here of the Law of the Moses, but rather the *"Law of the Spirit of Life in Christ Jesus."*

Once you learn this Law, and to be sure, it's not hard at all to understand and to learn, then you have learned the secret to all victory in Christ. And as stated, that refers to victory in any and every capacity.

THE GUARANTEE OF VICTORY

Please notice the following:

1. Proper Faith in the Cross of Christ, means that sin will not have dominion over me (Rom. 6:14).

2. Proper Faith in the Cross of Christ, which means I am *"walking after the Spirit,"* will stop all condemnation in my life (Rom. 8:1).

3. Proper Faith in the Cross of Christ, guarantees me victory over every demon power of darkness (Col. 2:14-15).

4. Proper Faith in the Cross of Christ, gives me *"rest"* from all self effort in trying to attain victory by my own machinations. Jesus has already done it all for me (Mat. 11:28-30).

5. Proper Faith in the Cross of Christ, guarantees me *"more abundant life"* (Jn. 10:10).

6. Proper Faith in the Cross of Christ, assures healing for me in every capacity (I Pet. 2:24).

7. Proper Faith in the Cross of Christ, guarantees my financial prosperity (Phil. 4:18-19).

8. Proper Faith in the Cross of Christ, guarantees that I am complete in Him (Col. 2:10).

9. Proper Faith in the Cross of Christ, takes away all fear (II Tim. 1:7).

10. Proper Faith in the Cross of Christ, guarantees me victory in all things (I Jn. 5:4).

11. Proper Faith in the Cross of Christ, guarantees me the help of the Holy Spirit (Rom. 8:11).

(4) "YE HAVE NOT YET RESISTED UNTO BLOOD, STRIVING AGAINST SIN."

The diagram is:

1. Paul is here pointing to the fact that Jesus resisted to the extent, that He shed His Blood on the Cross, all on our behalf.

2. As should be obvious, the Lord doesn't require us to do that, especially considering that it's already been done, and will never need to be repeated.

3. *"Striving against sin"* and thereby, bringing about the victory, is never brought about by physical means, but always through our Faith in what Jesus did for us at the Cross.

RESISTING

The phrase, *"Ye have not yet resisted unto blood,"* contains a twofold meaning:

1. Paul was addressing himself to Christian Jews, instructing them to resist the sin of unbelief. They were being tempted to go back into Judaism, which would have spelled their spiritual ruin. He reminds them, that whatever temptations they are facing pushing toward that erroneous course, had not yet required the *"shedding of blood,"* i.e., *"the giving up of their lives"*; however, by the use of the word *"yet"* he is telling them that it might actually come to that. In fact, in a very short period of time, it definitely did. Untold thousands had to give up their lives for the Cause of Christ.

When Rome was gutted by fire, Nero attempted to place the blame on the Christians, simply because he was being accused of starting the inferno which took many lives. At that time the persecutions began, quickly spreading across the Roman Empire, which saw many Christians killed and slaughtered in every conceivable way possible.

2. True victory over sin can never be achieved by any efforts of the flesh, which refers to any and all things we might do outside of the help of the Holy Spirit. Victory over sin can only be attained, by the Believer understanding that he is *"dead indeed unto sin,"* which means that he actually died with Christ in His Crucifixion, which is all done by faith on our part, *"but at the same time, alive unto God through Jesus Christ our Lord"* (Rom. 6:11). In other words, Christ dealt with sin and all its ramifications at the Cross; consequently, it's our Faith in that Finished Work, which guarantees us victory.

Understanding that, the Holy Spirit through Paul then said, *"For sin shall not have dominion over you"* (Rom. 6:14).

If we attempt to address sin in any other way than through Faith in the Cross of Christ, which guarantees the help of the Holy Spirit, we are doomed to failure. Regrettably, most Christians not knowing or understanding the Truth of the Cross, are dominated by sin, i.e., *"works of the flesh,"* and which will not improve, no matter how hard they try otherwise. Until they understand the Cross, and what Jesus there did for them, there will be no victory over sin, as there can be no victory over sin. The Cross is not one of several ways, but in fact, the only way. Now we should begin to understand the tragic state of the modern Church, and because it has almost no knowledge of the Cross as it regards these things of which I speak.

The truth is, millions of Christians are striving against sin, but in the wrong way, which guarantees their defeat, and not only guarantees defeat, but also guarantees that the situation will steadily get worse.

STRIVING AGAINST SIN

The phrase, *"Striving against sin,"* presents that which we should carefully note.

First of all, was Paul speaking about a particular sin as it regards these Christian Jews? Yes, he was!

It was the sin of unbelief, which in fact, is the foundation sin of all sin. In other words,

in some way, all sin springs from unbelief. And what do we mean by unbelief?

Some of these Christian Jews, which necessitated the writing of this Epistle to the Hebrews, were registering unbelief in Christ and the Cross, thereby tempted to go back into Judaism, which in fact, it seems that some of them had already done.

Now the modern Christian may look at that statement and automatically come to the conclusion that it has no effect on him personally. But yet it does!

While the modern Christian is certainly not tempted to go into Judaism, that was not the real problem anyway, only the result of the problem. The real problem was a lack of Faith in Christ and His vicarious Offering of Himself on the Cross. And that problem is the problem, and in fact, has always been the problem.

Do you as a Believer look to the Cross exclusively, or do you look to other things? (Gal. 6:14).

THE PLIGHT OF MOST MODERN CHRISTIANS

The problem with some Christians is an outright denial of the Cross. I speak of many in the Charismatic community, and more specifically, of those who consider themselves to be *"faith people,"* etc. They are outright denying the Cross, claiming that it was the greatest defeat in human history, etc.

At least, this shows a total lack of knowledge of the Word of God, and at worst, it is rank blasphemy.

But most Christians don't fall into that category. It is not so much that they reject the Cross, as it is that they simply do not know and understand anything about the Cross. But there's another problem with that:

Most Christians think they do understand everything about the Cross. As a typical illustration, we received an e-mail (or maybe it was a letter) a short time ago, with the individual exclaiming, *"Why are you talking so much about the Cross? I'm a Christian, so I understand everything about the Cross,"* or words to that effect.

The truth is, that particular individual, whomever he may have been, didn't understand anything about the Cross. And how do I know that?

I know that simply because had he truly known about the Cross, he would not have made such a ridiculous statement. Notice the following:

Paul said, *"As ye have therefore received Christ Jesus the Lord, so walk ye in Him"* (Col. 2:6).

The Apostle is here saying two things:

1. We received Christ (were saved) by trusting in Him and what He did at the Cross on our behalf.

2. The words *"so walk ye in Him,"* refer to the fact, that we are to *"live"* for the Lord, in the same manner in which we were saved by the Lord, which refers to Faith in the Cross of Christ. In other words, the same faith we exhibited for Salvation is to continue to be exhibited for our ongoing *"walk."* Most Christians don't know that.

Most Believers part with the Cross at their initial Salvation experience. They come into the Church, and hearing almost nothing about the Cross from behind most pulpits, they set out to live this Christian life, by various different ways and means — all of them wrong!

This confuses them, and if they go to their Pastor, more than likely, he will tell them that they need to *"try harder,"* or *"be more faithful,"* or *"be sure that they get all sin out of their lives,"* etc.

If it is to be noticed, all of this advice, plus much we haven't named, centers up on *"self"* instead of Christ. In other words, the Believer is told that he must *"do something."* In fact, such sounds good to most ears, simply because there is something in us which tends to think that we can get this job done ourselves. To be sure, the problem doesn't leave just because we become a Christian. Christian pride is just as devilish as sinner pride; however, it's very difficult for us to think of it in those terms. Let's say it in another way:

God had given the covenant of circumcision to Abraham (Gen. 17:10-14). All who followed Abraham were to keep this Covenant. But the Scripture says that Moses had failed to circumcise his little boy. The Scripture further says, *"that the Lord met him, and sought to kill him"* (Ex. 4:24-26).

Why Moses did this, we aren't told; however, the situation was serious enough, that

Moses found himself in deep trouble with the Lord, even at the beginning of the carrying out of the great Call upon his life.

In a short time, Moses would be commanded to announce to Pharaoh that Jehovah, the God of Israel, was about to slay his (Pharaoh's) son. But Moses had to learn that disobedience regarding rebellion in him was just as hateful as in Pharaoh; and that God, because of His nature, must judge with death a sin wherever found.

Therefore, on approaching Egypt this Holy God sought to judge this little boy, Eliezer, because of Moses' disobedience in not having had him circumcised, as God had commanded. The Passage throws a great light upon the inner life of Moses.

It may be assumed, from what is related, that he yielded to the wishes of his wife in this matter, meaning that she did not want to circumcise the child, though he knew he was disobeying God. The particulars are not fully given because the Holy Spirit did not think this necessary, but evidently, in order to save the child's life, and urged to it by Moses, she circumcised him herself, and then with anger and passion declared that her husband's religion was a religion of blood, i.e., of blood-stained rites.

Thus, Moses had to learn that God would judge him before He judged Pharaoh, and that rebellion in the one was the same as rebellion in the other; and this lesson must have enabled Moses to proclaim this dreadful truth with the force of a personal experience.

THE WORD OF GOD

This is a moral principle which Romans Chapter 6 and Colossians Chapter 2, and many other Passages, teach. Christians, under the New Covenant, are circumcised, spiritually speaking, in the Death of Jesus Christ; that is, we *"die"* as to our old nature. We then go forth with a message of death and of life; but we must have a personal experience of the bitterness, to the natural will, of that spiritual circumcision. We must consent to *"die,"* if we would be effective messengers of the Cross. And how do we do that?

Death to sin can only come about by complete trust in what Christ did at the Cross. At Salvation we died with Him, and as well, we were raised with Him in *"newness of life"* (Rom. 6:3-5).

Now the Reader may wonder as to what all of this has to do with one living a victorious, Christian life? The answer is simple:

God hated disobedience in Moses, just as much as He hated it in Pharaoh. Circumcision, and I continue to speak of that ancient rite given by God to Abraham, was a symbol of the Cross of Christ, and our involvement in that great Work. The cutting of the skin on the male member, was a sign of separation from the world unto God, and that separation brought about by what Christ did at the Cross, which symbol was the shedding of blood. Of course, and as would be obvious, blood was shed whenever the circumcision process was engaged.

The whole point of this is, that God would not tolerate Moses ignoring the Cross, of which Circumcision was a symbol, any more than He will tolerate modern Christians ignoring the Cross. If after we come to Christ, we attempt to live this life by means other than total trust in what Christ did on our behalf, such a direction angers God, to say the least. In fact, as Moses was about to suffer a physical death, the Believer will suffer a spiritual death. The analogy is the same!

Perhaps I have used a rather laborious illustration to explain my point, but I did so, because I want the Believer to understand how serious all of this is. *"Striving against sin,"* can only come out to a successful conclusion, if it is done God's Way, which is the Way of the Cross. Nothing else will work.

"Striving" in the Greek is *"antagonizomia,"* which means *"to fight agonizingly against."* It speaks of a terrific fight. And as repeatedly stated, it's a fight we cannot win unless we *"fight the good fight of faith,"* which means to constantly place our Faith in what Christ has already done for us, i.e., *"the Cross."*

(5) "AND YE HAVE FORGOTTEN THE EXHORTATION WHICH SPEAKETH UNTO YOU AS UNTO CHILDREN, MY SON, DESPISE NOT THOU THE CHASTENING OF THE LORD, NOR FAINT WHEN THOU ART REBUKED OF HIM:"

The structure is:

1. The exhortation here is derived from Proverbs 3:11.

NOTES

2. As we are supposed to correct our children, the Lord also corrects us, and because we are His children. It is called *"chastening."*

3. *"Chastening"* does not have in it the idea of punishment, but of corrective measures that will eliminate evil in the life and encourage that which is Righteous.

THE EXHORTATION

The phrase, *"And ye have forgotten the exhortation which speaketh unto you as unto children,"* refers, as stated, to Proverbs 3:11-12. The object of the Apostle in introducing this here, is to show that afflictions are designed, on the part of God, to produce positive effects in the lives of His people, and that we ought, therefore, to bear them patiently.

In the previous Verses, he directs us to the example of the Savior. In this Verse and the following, for the same object, he directs our attention to the design of trials, showing that they are necessary to our welfare, and that they are in fact, proof of the paternal care of God. In fact, this Verse might be rendered as a question, *"And have you forgotten?"* etc.

When he used the term, *"which speaketh unto you,"* he is meaning, that this applies to all, with no exceptions.

By the phrase, *"As unto children,"* he is using language such as a father uses.

EVERY WORD WHICH PROCEEDETH OUT OF THE MOUTH OF GOD

As well, we should understand from this as used by Paul, that every single Passage in the Word of God, no matter how obscure they may seem to be, is in fact, valid and applicable. Everything in the Bible from Genesis 1:1 through Revelation 22:21 is the Word of God. If it is general instruction, it applies to all, and for all time, unless it is dispensational. In other words, there were many instructions given concerning the Law of Moses and such like, which are no longer applicable, and because Jesus has fulfilled all of those particular Statutes and Commandments, etc. But otherwise, and as here given from Proverbs, let not the Reader think that it doesn't apply. It does!

That's why Jesus said to Satan, *"Man shall not live by bread alone, but by <u>every word</u> that proceedeth out of the Mouth of God"* (Mat. 4:4).

CHASTISEMENT

The phrase, *"My son, despise not thou the chastening of the Lord,"* speaks of correcting mistakes and curbing the passions. It speaks also of instruction which aims at the increase of virtue. However, and as stated, the word *"chastening"* does not have in it the idea of punishment, but of corrective measures which will eliminate evil in the life and encourage that which is good.

Some may argue that *"punishment"* and *"correction"* are the same, and if we say otherwise, it is merely a play on words; however, that is not correct.

If an individual breaks the laws of the land and is confined to prison, that is punishment. The State means to punish the individual, and this is the method by which it is done. No correction is involved, only punishment.

With the Lord, and as it concerns His children, He does not punish, but rather corrects. In other words, by whatever it is that He allows to happen, it is meant for our instruction, our reproof, and as stated, our correction. He designs the entire situation, whatever the situation might be, and we are meant to learn from the experience. If we think of it as punishment, then we're judging God wrongly, and will fail to learn what He is attempting to teach us. That's why the Holy Spirit through Paul told us to not *"despise the chastening of the Lord."* We are to understand that it is for a reason, and is meant for our good. In fact, God never does anything with us or for us, but that it is meant for our good.

Every sorrow the child of God is permitted to endure is designed by God for blessing. It is instruction by discipline. It is the Divine method used for our education.

As well, we should remember, when God speaks of discipline and rebuke, it is *"sons"* whom He addresses. It s interesting that this warning is called *"that word of encouragement,"* because that's what the word *"exhortation"* means. The certainty of the situation encourages the Believer rather than dismays him because he knows that it is God's discipline for him.

REBUKE

The phrase, *"Nor faint when thou art rebuked of Him,"* proclaims the second of two negative responses the Believer can have toward this. They are:

1. First of all, as the previous phrase says, we can despise the chastening of the Lord. He who does so but hardens himself against God and thereby, refuses to learn the lessons which the chastening is designed to teach him. Who has hardened himself against God and prospered?

Unfortunately, many Christians have grown perturbed or even angry with God as it regards their particular situation. They feel they don't deserve what is happening, or else the Lord is not moving fast enough they think, to alleviate the situation.

Such an attitude only tends to question God, which is the road to disaster. As a Believer, we must understand that God knows best about all things. Consequently, we should seek to learn what He is attempting to teach us. And we must never forget, that if we do harden ourselves against God, we only lengthen the process longer than God originally intended; therefore, we have only ourselves to blame. There is no profit in that course.

2. On the other hand, one may faint under the chastening. There are some souls who lose all courage when trouble comes. Like *"Little-Faith"* in *"Pilgrim's Progress,"* they are constantly cast down by the trials of the way. This too is to miss the Blessing.

Such individuals succumb to a position of *"whining,"* which God must deplore!

For instance, how many of you like to be around a whining kid? But that's what the fainting soul actually does! So what am I saying?

I'm saying that we should hold our head high, square our shoulders, put a smile on our face, and believe God for two things:

First of all, that we may quickly learn the lesson which He is teaching us; and second, that we may allow this thing, whatever it might be, to draw us ever closer to the Lord. That is the intention of the Divine Spirit, and it should be our intention as well.

(6) "FOR WHOM THE LORD LOVETH HE CHASTENETH, AND SCOURGETH EVERY SON WHOM HE RECEIVETH."

The composite is:

1. Chastening from the Lord is one of the greatest signs that He loves us, and loves us dearly.

2. Every Christian needs chastening. None are excluded!

3. If one claims to be a Christian, and there is never any chastening, the Truth is, they actually aren't a Christian.

THE LOVE OF GOD

The phrase, *"For whom the Lord loveth He chasteneth,"* proclaims, as should be obvious, a tremendous truth.

"Those He loves" comes first in the Greek, which gives it a certain emphasis. God disciplines people He loves, not those to whom He is indifferent. It is the *"son"* who is corrected and *"every son"* at that. It does not, of course, mean that He sends chastisement which is not deserved; or that He sends it for the mere purpose of inflicting pain, etc. That cannot be. But it means that, by His chastisements, He shows that He has a paternal care for us. He does not treat us with neglect and unconcern. The very fact that He corrects us shows that He has towards us a father's feelings, and exercises toward us a paternal care. If He did not, He would let us go on without any attention, in which we would pursue a course of sin that would involve us in ruin. To restrain and govern a child, to correct him when he errs, shows that there is a paternal solicitude for him, and that he is not an outcast. And to be sure, one must ever understand, that there is in the life of every Child of God *"something"* that deserves correction, and because the Lord loves us, He will definitely correct us.

EVERY SON

The phrase, *"And scourgeth every son whom He receiveth,"* refers to all who truly belong to Him.

In the ancient world it was universally accepted that the bringing up of sons involved disciplining them. Therefore, we should not read back modern permissive attitudes into our understanding of this Passage.

"Scourgeth" in the Greek is *"mastigoo,"* and means *"to whip, flog, beat."* As should be obvious, some of the training can be described as none other than strong. And as we've already stated, irrespective as to whom the Christian might be, and irrespective as to how holy he might think he is, there is

NOTES

always something in us, which needs correcting, and sometimes severely so!

The idea of all of this is, that many of these Christian Jews, if not all of them, were undergoing persecution from fellow Jews who did not believe in Christ. At times the persecution was very severe. The Apostle is here telling them that in effect, God was allowing the persecution, and doing it for their good. Consequently, instead of chaffing under the rod of correction, they were to accept it as from the Lord, understanding that He was doing or allowing such, because of His great love for them.

Evidently, they were voicing objections to their treatment, claiming that if Christianity was what it ought to be, why were they undergoing such opposition and persecution? The Apostle tells them that all of this is a part of the training process.

All of us would like to think, that we have it all together. In other words, we are so mature in the Word, so advanced in the Lord, in fact so close to God, that while others may need correction, such wouldn't apply to us.

The truth is, there is a good chance that those who think such thoughts, are actually in need of correction more than anyone else. The first step toward learning the lesson, is to realize our need for the lesson, whatever it might be.

And once again we emphasize, the Holy Spirit through Paul said, *"Every son,"* which means that none are excluded.

(7) "IF YE ENDURE CHASTENING, GOD DEALETH WITH YOU AS WITH SONS; FOR WHAT SON IS HE WHOM THE FATHER CHASTENETH NOT?"

The exegesis is:

1. We are to endure the chastening with aplomb and dignity, seeking to learn the lesson which desires to be taught.

2. The reason that God deals with us in this fashion, is because we definitely are Believers, i.e., *"His Children."*

3. If we are truly Believers, which means we are a *"son,"* without question, we will experience chastisement.

THE ENDURING OF CHASTENING

The phrase, *"If ye endure chastening,"* refers to three things:

1. The word *"endure"* means that the chastening will not go on forever.

2. During the chastening, we are to learn the lesson which the Holy Spirit desires that we learn.

3. The implication is, that if we properly endure the chastening, which means to do so without complaint or fault finding, even as the Tenth Verse says, it will turn out to our *"profit."*

GOD DEALS WITH US

The phrase, *"God dealeth with you as with sons,"* refers as well, to several things:

1. God deals only with those who belong to Him, at least in this fashion.

2. Due to the fact that He has paid such a price for us, He has the right to correct us.

3. Whatever part that Satan plays in all of this, we are to understand, that it is God Who is dealing with us. While He may use Satan, and many other things or people for that matter, He is the One Who draws the parameters.

ALL TRUE CHILDREN OF GOD SUFFER CHASTISEMENT

The conclusion of the question, *"For what son is he whom the father chasteneth not?"*, has reference here to an earthly father. The idea is, if a father truly cares for his son, he will use whatever measures necessary, to whip the boy into shape. If an earthly father will do this, how much more will our Heavenly Father do the same?

We were not saved merely in order to miss Hell. The Lord has much more in store for us, than merely a different location in eternity, as important as that might be.

The moment we come to Christ, the Holy Spirit Who has superintended everything as it regards our conversion, now comes into the heart and life of the Believer to abide, and to abide permanently. To be sure, He is there for a particular purpose, and that is to carry out the Will of God in our hearts and lives (Rom. 8:27).

That means that He isn't there to do our will, but rather God's Will. And to be sure, this is where the rub comes in. The biggest problem the Holy Spirit has with us, is the problem of *"self-will."* That's the reason that Jesus said, *"If any man will come after Me, let him deny himself* (deny his self-will), *and take up his Cross daily, and follow Me.*

"For whosoever will save his life shall lose it (insist upon self-will)*: but whosoever will

lose his life for My sake* (turn one's life totally over to Christ), *the same shall save it"* (Lk. 9:23-24).

The idea is, that our *"wills"* become the same as the *"Will of God."* Regrettably, that's easier said than done. The Holy Spirit has to perform major surgery on some of us, spiritually speaking, in order for this to be brought about.

BLESSINGS AND AFFLICTIONS

Unfortunately, most of the modern Church has no delight at all in these particular Passages. We want nothing but blessings; however, let us address that for just a moment:

First of all, God is definitely a Blesser. He blesses grandly and gloriously His Children, and does so continuously. However, we must understand this:

While we learn much about God from blessings, how good He is, how beneficent He is, the Truth is, however, we don't learn anything about ourselves. We can only learn about ourselves through afflictions.

Anyone can rejoice in the midst of Blessings; however, it's not so easy to rejoice in the midst of afflictions.

Afflictions tell us what we are, whether we like it or not. And that's the reason they are so necessary. If we had our way, we would opt for nothing but Blessings; however, God is not Santa Claus. He is our Parent, and as such, He is going to conduct Himself toward us accordingly.

There have probably been 100,000 books printed in the last few decades on how to skip *"boot camp."* But if we truly belong to the Lord, such to be sure, is not to be.

(8) "BUT IF YE BE WITHOUT CHASTISEMENT, WHEREOF ALL ARE PARTAKERS, THEN ARE YE BASTARDS, AND NOT SONS."

The diagram is:

1. Every true Believer is a partaker of chastisement.

2. Freedom from discipline is not evidence of a privileged position. Rather the reverse is true. Such individuals are bastards — *"not sons."*

3. Sadly, the far greater majority of professed Christendom falls into this latter category.

WITHOUT CHASTISEMENT?

The phrase, *"But if ye be without chastisement,"* presents a fearsome prospect.

Some may ask the question as to how we are to recognize chastisement, which is always from the Lord, from normal negative consequences which sooner or later come to all unbelievers?

First of all, if the person is truly a Christian, to be sure, they will truly know. As a Believer, we have a relationship with our Heavenly Father. And to be sure, that relationship is strong. It is so strong in fact, that the Holy Spirit will constantly warn us as it regards wrong direction or improper conduct. And when the correction comes, as sooner or later it will with all, it will be very recognizable by the Saint of God. In fact, it will be just as recognizable as it was when we were children and were corrected by our earthly fathers, even as the next Verse proclaims.

PARTAKERS

The phrase, *"Whereof all are partakers,"* pertains to all who are Believers.

Some have asked the question if sickness is a part of chastisement?

Not necessarily so, but it definitely can be. The human body ages and ultimately wears out, that is if the Lord allows us to live that long. That's not chastisement, as should be obvious. And as well, there are millions of Christians who suffer some type of physical disability, and it's not chastisement, but then again, sickness can definitely fall into the category of chastisement. If such be the case, I definitely think that the Believer would understand the origin.

The Church has been so messed up in the last few decades from the *"faith teaching,"* which in reality is no faith at all, that any more, it hardly knows where it's been, where it is, or where it's going. And as with all false doctrine, the situation if not corrected, will only get worse (Gal. 5:9). And how can it be corrected?

The Church must come back to the Cross. This is its true foundation, and as such, if the foundation isn't right, nothing else is right.

BASTARDS?

The phrase, *"Then are ye bastards, and not sons,"* proclaims a very strong statement, as should be obvious.

"Bastards" in the Greek are *"nothos,"* and refers to *"one born of a slave or a concubine, or of the illegitimate in general."* The point is they are not heirs, not members of the family. For them the father feels no responsibility. As we've already stated, their freedom from discipline, and I speak of professing Christians, is not evidence of a privileged position, but rather the very opposite.

Some time back, particular individuals were mentioned to me who were living in obvious sin, but yet seemed to suffer no ill effect, despite the fact that such had been going for many years.

Of course, I'm not the judge; however, I answered the Brother in this vein: *"Despite their profession of Christianity, quite possibly they're not actually sons, but bastards!"* The reason they suffer no chastisement despite their lifestyles, is simply because they don't belong to the Lord. To be sure, if they belonged to Him, even as this Text plainly says, they would be partakers of chastisement in some form.

It is said that approximately 100 million people in the United States profess Christianity. The true number of those who are actually saved, is far, far less. While God Alone knows that number, the lack of fruit in most lives gives a pretty good indication of what they really are, despite their claims.

(9) "FURTHERMORE WE HAVE HAD FATHERS OF OUR FLESH WHICH CORRECTED US, AND WE GAVE THEM REVERENCE: SHALL WE NOT MUCH RATHER BE IN SUBJECTION UNTO THE FATHER OF SPIRITS, AND LIVE?"

The structure is:

1. Earthly parents are used here as an example.

2. If we understood we were to be subject to our earthly parents, surely we understand that we should be subject to our Heavenly Father.

3. The implication is, if we aren't subject to Him, we could lose our souls.

EARTHLY PARENTS

The phrase, *"Furthermore we have had fathers of our flesh which corrected us, and we gave them reverence,"* refers as stated, to earthly parents; however, there is something here which should be addressed:

Paul is only using this as an example. In no way does this give credence to the idea that it's proper for one Christian to chastise another Christian. All chastisement is carried out by God. James addressed this by saying: *"There is one Lawgiver, Who is able to save and to destroy: who art thou that judgest another?"* (James 4:12).

In essence, James is saying, *"Who do you think you are, thinking you are qualified, to punish a fellow Christian?"*

It is only self-righteousness which would think that it could do such a thing. Let me give you an example:

Frances was mentioning to me the other day about listening to a particular Christian singer over Television, and how beautiful and how well that he sang. She was commenting on his voice, and as well, the excellent spirit that he seemed to have.

She went on to say how that he made mention of the fact that he had a problem a short time back. In fact, even though I do not know the man personally, I am acquainted with the type of problem he had.

Now of course, the only answer for that particular problem, or any problem of sin for that matter, is to take it to the Lord, which I'm assuming that he did.

Now what good would it have done, for some foolish Preachers in some particular Denomination to have told him that because of his problem, he couldn't sing any more for two years, or some such period of time? Thank the Lord that he wasn't a member of such a Denomination.

God gave the man the talent to sing, and despite the problem he had, he was using it for God's Glory. Who am I, or any other man for that matter, to tell him that he cannot use this talent that God has given him?

Individuals who do such, are attempting to play God, and I might quickly add, they're doing it very poorly.

Chastisement must be left solely in the domain of the Lord, and must never be thought to be the prerogative of any human being. While it is certainly true that we are subject to our earthly parents when we are children, even as this Text brings out, and as Christians we are also subject to the laws of the land, however, that's where the subjec-

tion ends. The only thing that I owe any other Christian, and that goes for all Preachers as well, is *"love"* (Rom. 13:8). While as a Christian I owe obedience to civil authorities, that is if they do not require something that defiles my conscience, I do not owe such obedience to any other Christian, simply because they are a Christian, or even some type of supposed leader. That's the case if we desire to be Biblical; however, if we desire to make up our own rules as we go along, which much of the Church regrettably does, then that's another matter altogether.

SUBJECTION

The conclusion of the question, *"Shall we not much rather be in subjection unto the Father of spirits, and live?"*, refers to our Heavenly Father. The phrase, *"Father of spirits"* is contrasted to *"fathers of the flesh,"* which concern our earthly parents. Their relation to us is limited, His is universal. They are related to us on the fleshly side: He is the Creator of our essential life. Our relation to Him is on the side of our eternal being.

The words *"and live"* while including the future life, are not limited to that sphere, but also refer to this present existence. The idea is, *"have true life"* (Wuest). The idea is, when Believers subject themselves to God, accepting life's sufferings as discipline from His Fatherly hand, we enter the life that is alone worthy of the name.

An earthly father chastens his son as seems fit to his imperfect judgment; but the Heavenly Father disciplines with infallible judgment and perfect love.

God chastens us because we are His children, and because He loves us supremely. The fruitful branch is purged that it may bring forth more fruit; the self-willed child is chastened in order to the production of the peaceable fruit of righteousness. Love chastens, but not without a motive; and so we must not be discouraged.

(10) "FOR THEY VERILY FOR A FEW DAYS CHASTENED US AFTER THEIR OWN PLEASURE; BUT HE FOR OUR PROFIT, THAT WE MIGHT BE PARTAKERS OF HIS HOLINESS."

The structure is:

1. The chastening of our earthly parents may or may not have been for our good.

2. All chastening of the Lord, and because His knowledge is perfect, is *"for our profit."*

3. The object of His chastening, is to rid us of anything and everything that would hinder our Christlikeness.

THEIR OWN PLEASURE

The phrase, *"For they verily for a few days chastened us after their own pleasure,"* presents by the use of the word *"pleasure,"* that the chastening may or may not have been proper.

"Pleasure" in the Greek is *"dokeo,"* and means *"to be of opinion, to think, suppose."* Thus, the word indicates that the judgment of the parents on matters of discipline is based on opinion at best, conjecture, and supposition. It is, therefore, not infallible as should be obvious, as is the case of the judgment of our Heavenly Father.

All of this points to the difference in the quality of the discipline which we receive from our earthly fathers and that which we receive from God. They disciplined us *"for a little while,"* which refers to the brief days of childhood, and they did it according to the best of their knowledge. They did their best, and of course, we're speaking here of earthly parents trying to do the right thing, but the phrase seems to imply that earthly parents often make mistakes. God makes no mistakes!

PROFIT

The phrase, *"But He for our profit,"* presents the difference between human liability to mistake and the perfect knowledge of our Heavenly Father, Who seeks our profit, and cannot err in the means which He employs.

If we properly understand this, then whatever is happening to us at the moment, which we know has been designed by the Lord, and designed for our good, makes the situation more tolerable. The main thing that all Believers should understand is this:

1. We must understand that everything from the Lord comes to us through the Sacrifice of Christ; consequently, our Faith must ever be in that Finished Work.

2. We must be consecrated totally and completely to the end that the Holy Spirit

will work successfully within our lives, which He always will, if our Faith is properly placed in the Cross of Christ.

3. We must always realize that every single thing that happens to us as Believers, is allowed or designed by the Holy Spirit. He Who notes the sparrow's fall, and numbers the very hairs of our heads, presents Himself as being totally occupied in every facet of our lives. We must understand this. While chastening is needed by every Believer, even if our Faith and Consecration are exactly as they ought to be, to be sure, chastening can be lessened by us conducting ourselves as we should. As would be obvious, some need more correction than others.

HOLINESS

The phrase, *"That we might be partakers of His Holiness,"* proclaims a work of the Holy Spirit.

The only way that an individual can be Holy before God, and we speak of the Holiness alone which God will recognize, is for the Holy Spirit to carry out this work in one's heart and life. It is impossible for any human being to make himself holy, irrespective as to what he might do.

Holiness is attained by the Believer evidencing Faith exclusively in Christ and the Cross, which then gives the Holy Spirit latitude to work in our lives.

"Holiness" in the Greek is *"hagiotes,"* and means *"sacred, pure, blameless, sanctity."* It points to God's holy character. The aim of God's chastisement of His people is to produce in us a character like His Own.

However, let us emphasize again, that this is not a contrived holiness which is perpetrated by many Churches, but rather the Holiness of God. It refers to an absence of all sin, spiritual pollution, and spiritual failure of any nature. There is only one way this can be obtained in the Believer's life, and that way comes in two parts:

1. The Believer must ever look to the Cross of Christ, understanding that it was there that Christ met every need. Our Faith in that Finished Work, brings about the help of the Holy Spirit, Who Alone can perfect holiness within our hearts and lives.

2. Even with us properly doing this of

which I have spoken, chastening is still needed. In fact, this tells us how bad the problems of *"self"* and *"sin"* actually are.

Pride presents itself as a terrible factor in the life of all Christians. Only the *"Cross"* and *"chastening"* can eliminate this scourge. There must be total dependence on Christ, and chastening is needed in order to bring this about.

It is ironical, many in the modern Charismatic community, and I speak of Preachers, are attempting to make men rich, at least that's what they claim, while the Holy Spirit is trying to make us holy. The terrible Truth is, that those who follow such teaching, will gain neither — earthly riches or Heavenly Holiness.

(11) "NOW NO CHASTENING FOR THE PRESENT SEEMETH TO BE JOYOUS, BUT GRIEVOUS: NEVERTHELESS AFTERWARD IT YIELDETH THE PEACEABLE FRUIT OF RIGHTEOUSNESS UNTO THEM WHICH ARE EXERCISED THEREBY."

The diagram is:

1. Even though chastening is *"profitable,"* it is not enjoyable, as should be obvious.

2. If it is properly entertained, it will without fail, yield the *"peaceable Fruit of Righteousness,"* which is the intention of the Spirit.

3. This is not a matter of accepting a minor chastisement or two with good grace; it is the habit of life that is meant.

GRIEVOUS

The phrase, *"Now no chastening for the present seemeth to be joyous, but grievous,"* presents the fact that the trials to which we are exposed at times, do not for the moment give joy, but are often hard indeed to bear. This tells us that some chastening can be very severe indeed!

I think the Holy Spirit is as well, speaking here of the degree of chastening. The degree that one has to undergo, not only pertains to the development of Holiness without our lives, but also I think, pertains to the work which God has for us to do. For instance, one might say, and I think be correct, that Moses endured chastening for some 40 years, as it regards his stay at the back side of the desert. God was preparing Moses for a formidable task, as would be obvious. This task required every vestige of Egypt to be erased from the heart and life of the great Lawgiver. It didn't take

long to get Moses out of Egypt, but it took a long time to get Egypt out of Moses.

This tells us, that while chastening may definitely be employed by the Lord because of sin within our lives, it can also be employed as it regards preparation. And that preparation can be *"grievous."*

As well, all of this tells us that chastening is not meant to impart pleasure, nor is this its design. All chastisement is intended to produce pain in some way, and the Christian is as sensitive to pain as others. In fact, our Faith in Christ does not blunt our sensibilities, or make us a stoic. If anything, it increases our susceptibility to suffering. In other words, we feel it even more keenly.

I think one can say, and without fear of contradiction, that our Lord Jesus probably felt pain, reproach, and contempt more keenly than any other human being ever did. While our experience with Christ does not render us insensible to suffering, etc., it does bring about two things within our hearts and lives:

1. It enables us to bear the difficulty without murmuring and complaining, or at least it should!

2. It turns the affliction into a blessing on the soul, which leads to Righteousness.

To be Christlike no price is too high to pay! To be Christlike, no path should be avoided that will bring about this result.

While as Christians we certainly do not seek chastisement, and in fact, do not desire it at all. But at the same time, we do know that chastisement is unavoidable, and it always is for our good.

THE PEACEABLE FRUIT OF RIGHTEOUSNESS

The phrase, *"Nevertheless afterward it yieldeth the peaceable fruit of Righteousness,"* proclaims what chastening is all about.

"Yieldeth" in the Greek is *"apodidomi,"* and means *"to give back."* In other words, all of this is carried out by the Holy Spirit for a specific purpose. That purpose is to bring forth the *"peaceable Fruit of Righteousness,"* i.e., *"Holiness."* We go back again to John Chapter 15:

Jesus said, *"Every branch in Me that beareth not fruit He taketh away* (that which chastisement does): *and every branch that beareth fruit, He purgeth it* (the process of chastisement), *that it may bring forth more fruit"* (Jn. 15:2).

The *"peaceable"* fruit stands in contrast with the unrest and trouble which have preceded during the time of *"chastening."* But there is more than rest after conflict, for the object of the conflict is attained; the Fruit consists in Righteousness (Prov. 11:30; Isa. 32:17; Phil. 1:11; James 3:17).

EXERCISE

The phrase, *"Unto them which are exercised thereby,"* refers to those who have been trained by chastisement. As we have stated, it is not a matter of accepting a minor chastisement or two with good grace; it is the habit of life that is meant. When that is present, the *"peaceable fruit"* follows.

In all of this, Paul might be throwing out a hint to his readers, that suffering at times, was apt to render people irritable, even impatient with one another's faults. The latter record even of the martyrs, for example, shows that the very prospect of death did not always prevent Christians from quarreling in prison. This all tells us, that chastisement must be accepted in the right spirit; otherwise it does not produce the right result.

Our earthly fathers chastened us as it seems fit to their imperfect judgment; but the Heavenly Father disciplines with infallible judgment and perfect love.

Most all of the chastisement, even as we've already stated, centers up on the *"will,"* i.e., *"self-will."* Whatever direction it may take, this is generally where the Holy Spirit is working. And until the will is won, there is warfare, but when won there is peace; and the fruit of that peace is upright conduct. But this only results for them who are exercised by the chastisement.

(12) "WHEREFORE LIFT UP THE HANDS WHICH HANG DOWN, AND THE FEEBLE KNEES;"

The structure is:

1. In view of the fact that chastisement is from the Lord, and understanding this, we are to do certain things.

2. The *"hands hanging down"* stipulate discouragement and defeatism. The Holy Spirit through the Apostle is telling us that during the times of chastisement, we should lift our hands and praise the Lord, and as well, go to work for Him.

3. *"Feeble knees"* speak of wrong direction, and the idea is, *"get out of that slough of despondency, and get moving for the Lord."*

HANDS WHICH HANG DOWN

The phrase, *"Wherefore lift up the hands which hang down,"* refers to discouragement that can come about, and in fact does come about in the hearts and lives of many Christians who are enduring chastisement. The Holy Spirit has given extremely valuable teaching here through Paul. He has told us that all of this is profitable for us, and is going to produce a Work of Righteousness within our lives; consequently, in view of that, and I speak of that which is coming, which refers to great blessings, we should not be discouraged.

Even though the metaphor of the hands hanging down covers a wide territory, for a moment I'll just look at one of its many sides.

Knowing that this speaks of discouragement, and knowing how hard it is to praise the Lord during such times, the admonition is, *"Praise the Lord anyhow!"* Praising the Lord is some way generally includes the raising of the hands.

As well, it speaks of surrender to God, which in effect says, *"I may not know exactly why You are doing this, but I know it is for my profit, and I'm going to praise the Lord in view of that."* In fact, surrendering to the Lord is a great part of the Christian experience. We may think it's simple, and almost all Christians may claim they have surrendered to the Lord. But the truth is, despite what most think, most haven't!

FEEBLE KNEES

The phrase, *"And the feeble knees,"* refers to one who is totally discouraged, and in fact, has become immobile, or else going in the wrong direction.

More than likely, the entire Twelfth Verse is derived from Isaiah 35:3. It says: *"Strengthen ye the weak hands, and confirm the feeble knees."*

However, even though the Holy Spirit through Paul didn't bring it out here, except maybe in a very limited way in the next Verse,

NOTES

I do not think it would be improper to include the balance of this which was given to Isaiah. The Prophet said:

"Say to them that are of a fearful heart, be strong, fear not: behold, your God will come with vengeance, even God with a recompence; He will come and save you.

"Then the eyes of the blind shall be opened, and the ears of the deaf shall be unstopped.

"Then shall the lame man leap as an hart, and the tongue of the dumb sing: for in the wilderness shall waters break out, and streams in the desert" (Isa. 35:4-6).

Of course this is speaking of the coming Millennium, when Christ will set up His eternal Kingdom; however, if the Holy Spirit saw fit through Paul to use a part of this statement, which He definitely did, then I do not think we do violence to Scripture to be able to tell anyone and everyone undergoing chastisement, that victory is on the way. Great and wonderful things are about to happen. So we can *"lift up our hands which hang down,"* and to be sure, our *"feeble knees"* will then be strengthened.

(13) "AND MAKE STRAIGHT PATHS FOR YOUR FEET, LEST THAT WHICH IS LAME BE TURNED OUT OF THE WAY; BUT LET IT RATHER BE HEALED."

The composite is:

1. The chastisement is intended to make the paths straight, which refers to our daily walk before God.

2. Healing is intended, and healing will definitely come.

3. All of this has to do with the Cross, which we will address momentarily.

STRAIGHT PATHS FOR YOUR FEET

The phrase, *"And make straight paths for your feet,"* concerns itself with out *"walk"* before the Lord. In fact, Paul uses the word *"walk"* quite a few times as it regards our Christian experience (Rom. 4:12; 6:4; 8:1, 4; 13:13; I Cor. 3:3; 7:17; II Cor. 5:7; 6:16; 10:3; Gal. 5:16, 25; 6:16; Eph. 2:10; 4:1, 17; 5:2, 8, 15; Phil. 3:16-18; Col. 1:10; 2:6; 4:5; I Thess. 2:12; 4:1, 12; II Thess. 3:11).

"Straight paths" in the Greek doesn't necessarily refer to paths which have been crooked, but more generally in the sense of it being the *"right path."* The idea is, that

NOTES

chastisement is tendered by the Lord, to bring us to the *"straight paths,"* or *"right paths,"* of the Cross. Any other path is wrong, out of the way, and will result in terrible, spiritual lameness, which we will address directly.

Understanding the Gospel as it was given to Paul, which in essence was and is, *"Jesus Christ and Him Crucified,"* and understanding how strongly he preached the Cross, I do not think we are doing violence to Scripture to conclude his statements in this manner.

The idea is, any path other than the Cross, is a wrong path, and will always, and without exception, lead to dire circumstances. Chastisement is meant to pull us to this right path, and I think one can say without fear of exaggeration, that this is the reason for most, if not all, chastisement.

LAME FEET

The phrase, *"Lest that which is lame be turned out of the way,"* refers to the condition of most Christians, spiritually speaking. Most are spiritually lame, which means they don't walk right, simply because they are on the wrong path. Spiritual lameness results from trying to live this life by our own efforts and ability, which means we're doing so without the help of the Holy Spirit. Most Christians are confused by that statement, and because most have been taught wrong.

Most Christians either believe that the work of the Holy Spirit is all automatic, or else they believe that by them doing spiritual things, that this constitutes *"walking after the Spirit"* (Rom. 8:1). Both directions are wrong, i.e., *"wrong paths."*

As stated, the way of the Cross constitutes the only *"straight paths"* there actually are. The manner in which we find these paths and walk on them, is not by activity, but rather by understanding our position in Christ. If the Reader can bear our repetitiveness, we will say it again.

The following constitutes *"straight paths"*:

1. Everything the Believer receives from the Lord comes exclusively through the Finished Work of Christ, i.e., *"the Cross"* (Rom. 6:3-5, 11, 14).

2. Our Faith is to ever be in that Finished Work. This is the critical part of our living for God. The object of our faith is the single

most important thing there is. The problem with most of Christianity is that the object of its faith is something else other than the Cross. And to be sure, it doesn't really matter what it is, or how good it might be in its own right, if it's not Faith in the great Sacrifice of Christ, then it's not Faith which the Holy Spirit will honor (Rom. Chpt. 4).

3. Once our faith is properly placed, and our faith remains in that proper place, the Holy Spirit will then function greatly on our behalf (Rom. 8:1-2, 11). This is what constitutes *"walking after the Spirit"* (Rom. 8:2). The Spirit will only walk on *"straight paths,"* i.e., *"right paths,"* and one might even say, this is the *"Law,"* as derived from Romans 8:2.

HEALED

The phrase, *"But let it rather be healed,"* refers to what the chastisement is intended to bring forth, which can only be done, by the Believer being brought to the Cross, and understanding this, the great Sacrifice of Christ, as being the answer, and in fact, the only answer to all things. When this path, the path of the Cross is followed, only then can the lame feet be healed.

As should be obvious, this speaks of our daily walk before God, which means that now we are *"walking"* as we should.

"Healed" in the Greek is *"iaomai,"* and means *"to make whole."* And as well, it speaks of being made *"whole"* in every way, spiritually, financially, physically, mentally, domestically, etc.

A few hours ago (Sept. 19, 2000) we were taping Television programs for *"A Study in the Word."*

I asked the question on the Telecast, *"Is it possible for a Believer to be brought to an understanding of the Cross of Christ, without somehow a crisis being affected in his life?"*

If *"chastisement"* can be construed as a *"crisis,"* and which I definitely think it can, then I think the Scripture is all too clear, that such has to be before the Believer can begin to think right, and believe right. And of course, by this statement I am speaking of the Believer coming to the place to where he surrenders himself totally to Christ, which translates into complete Faith in the Cross of

Christ, which then gives the Holy Spirit the latitude to work within our hearts and lives.

It would seem that all of this should be very simple and easy, would it not? However, that is not the case. Most Christians do not like to admit that they are wrong about something, and Preachers most of all do not like to admit they are wrong about something. But as I've said repeatedly, there's been so little teaching on the Cross in the last several decades, that the modern Church is all but Cross illiterate. Consequently, most Christians are living less than victorious lives, actually with works of the flesh being manifested in their daily experiences. This is a terrible situation to be in, but yet, to solve the problem, most of the time we just simply try to increase what we're already doing, which makes a bad matter worse. In other words, what we're doing now to live this Christian life is mostly wrong, and then when we add to that, we only exacerbate the situation.

To bring the Christian out of that situation, most of the time, if not all the time, chastisement is required. In fact, I think these Passages as given by Paul do proclaim the fact, that such cannot be done without chastisement. That's the reason that it is plainly stated, *"For whom the Lord loveth He chasteneth, and scourgeth every son whom He receiveth"* (Heb. 12:6).

Almost the entirety of the modern Church needs *"healing,"* and that healing can only come about by the Church going back to the Cross. If it takes chastisement to bring the Church to this particular place, then chastisement will be a cheap price to pay.

(14) "FOLLOW PEACE WITH ALL MEN, AND HOLINESS, WITHOUT WHICH NO MAN SHALL SEE THE LORD:"

The structure is:

1. Every Christian should eagerly seek peace with all men, but not at the expense of compromising the Gospel.

2. A holiness that is continuously more perfected should ever be the goal of the Believer. This speaks of Christlikeness!

3. Our holiness is obtained by faith and trust in Christ and what He did at the Cross. Without such Faith, there is no holiness, and there is no Salvation.

PEACE

The phrase, *"Follow peace with all men,"* must be the continuous effort of every true Christian.

"Follow" in the Greek is *"dioko,"* and means *"to run swiftly in order to catch some person or thing, to run after, to press on."* It is used of one who in a race runs swiftly to reach the goal (Phil. 3:12). The word is seen, therefore, to have a sense of urgency about it, of intensity of purpose.

Every effort must be made to live peacefully with all men, but not at the expense of Holiness, i.e., *"the compromising of the Word of God."*

We as Believers are to ever make war with sin, but not with men. People are often selfish and abrasive, but this is not the way Christians should be. For us, peace is imperative, and we must *"make every effort"* to attain it.

However, after every effort is made, there are some people with whom one simply cannot live at peace. After having done our best in this respect, then the Words of Christ must apply. He said:

"Moreover if thy brother shall trespass against thee, go and tell him his fault between thee and him alone: if he will hear thee, thou hast gained thy brother.

"But if he will not hear thee, then take with thee one or two more, that in the mouth of two or three witnesses every word may be established.

"And if he shall neglect to hear them, tell it unto the Church: but if he neglect to hear the Church, let him be unto thee as an heathen man and a publican" (Mat. 18:15-17).

HOLINESS

The short phrase, *"And Holiness,"* refers to being set apart unto God. Such must be characteristic of the Believer. Although the Believer lives in the world, we must always in one sense be different from the world and separate from the world. Our standards are not the world's standards. Holiness and Sanctification are actually the same thing.

THE REQUIREMENT

The phrase, *"Without which no man shall see the Lord,"* is extremely important, and must be correctly understood.

This statement has been often quoted, *"without Holiness no man shall see the Lord,"* but which is a misquote.

Most of the time such thinking proceeds from the idea that a certain set of rules made up by men, must be obeyed, with such obedience construed as holiness, and disobedience construed as a lack of holiness, with the person then condemned.

Much of this teaching has been based upon the idea that holiness is an experience called by some the *"second blessing,"* or the *"second work of grace,"* and that those who do not obtain this experience, although regenerate, will eventually lose their souls and will never see the Lord. But this is incorrect, and finds no countenance whatever in the Text itself, or anywhere else in the Bible. In fact, the very opposite is true.

TWO THINGS TO FOLLOW

We are exhorted in this Text to follow two things, one manward and the other Godward. First, we are to follow peace with all men. That is, we are to make that our object in our dealings with our fellow men.

Manifestly we shall never attain to this in the full sense. Even our Blessed Lord Himself, though He came preaching Peace, did not find all men ready to be at peace with Him. And the Believer, however earnestly he pursues the ideal, even as we've already stated, will still find men who refuse to live peaceably.

Godward, we are to follow Holiness. This is to be the trend of our lives. We are ever to seek to become more and more like Him, the Holy One. Apart from this, no man, whatever his profession, shall see the Lord.

THE PROBLEM WHICH HAS ALWAYS PLAGUED THE CHURCH

The moment we see the words *"Holy,"* or *"Holiness,"* or *"Sanctification"* in the Bible, most of the time our thoughts go in wrong directions.

First of all, there is no way that any human being, even the Godliest of Believers, can effect these great Works of Grace within our lives. All of this is a Work of the Spirit. He Alone can make us what we ought to be, and without Him we cannot be what we ought to be (Rom. 8:1-2, 11).

First of all we must understand, that every single Believer has a position of Holiness before the Lord, and was granted this at the moment of Salvation (I Cor. 6:11). This automatically comes with imputed Righteousness. In other words, the moment that the believing sinner expresses and evidences Faith in Christ and what He did at the Cross, at that moment a perfect Holiness is ascribed to that individual. It is not earned, and in fact it cannot be earned. It comes simply by Faith.

As stated, that is the Believer's position, which in fact, never changes; however, the actual condition does change constantly, and is what Paul is here discussing.

It is the business of the Holy Spirit to bring the *"condition of holiness"* so to speak, of the Believer up to the *"position of holiness."* It is the business as well of the Believer to yield and consecrate to the Spirit in order that this be done. And how is that done?

It is done by the Believer constantly evidencing Faith in the Cross of Christ, in other words, ever making the Cross the object of one's Faith. When this is done, the Holy Spirit can perfect the condition of Holiness in one's life.

The major problem, however, is man-devised holiness, and which has always been the problem. Of course, such constitutes holiness which God will not accept, and which only succeeds in breeding self-righteousness. But regrettably, that' where most Christians actually are, that is if they think of holiness at all. Such succeeds only in gendering strife, wrath, discord, and as stated, self-righteousness. In fact, it is the bane of the Church!

To be sure, those who follow that type of holiness, will not *"see the Lord."* It's only those who follow God's prescribed order, which is the Cross of Christ, which gives the Holy Spirit the latitude in which to work, who *"shall see the Lord."*

(15) "LOOKING DILIGENTLY LEST ANY MAN FAIL OF THE GRACE OF GOD; LEST ANY ROOT OF BITTERNESS SPRINGING UP TROUBLE YOU, AND THEREBY MANY BE DEFILED;"

The exegesis is:

1. It is only by the Grace of God that Holiness can be perfected in our lives.

2. *"Roots of bitterness"* spring up in hearts and lives when Believers seek to attain to Holiness other than by the Grace of God.

3. *"Defilement"* refers to *"works of the flesh,"* which will definitely come about, if our course is anything but God's prescribed order, which is the Cross.

THE GRACE OF GOD

The phrase, *"Looking diligently lest any man fail of the Grace of God,"* presents several great truths:

1. We are to be diligent in our pursuing the Grace of God.

2. It is only by *"the Grace of God"* in which Holiness, or any other Blessing from the Lord, can be attained.

3. It is quite possible to *"fail of the Grace of God,"* which refers to stopping the flow (Gal. 2:21).

The Grace of God simply refers to the goodness of God that is extended to undeserving Believers. It is intended to come in an uninterrupted flow, and definitely will do so, upon the proper provision of Faith. The Grace of God comes to all individuals strictly by and through the great Sacrifice of Christ. God has always had Grace, but until the Cross, it could not be extended quite so readily. Since the Cross, which makes the application of Grace possible, Grace is extended to the Believer like a Niagara so to speak.

In view of the fact that it is the Cross of Christ which makes Grace possible (Rom. 3:24; 4:16; 5:2, 20; 6:14; Gal. 6:14; Eph. 2:8-9), then we should know how important the Cross actually is.

HOW TO KEEP THE GRACE OF GOD COMING TO YOU

We know from this Passage, as well as Galatians 2:20-21, and others similar, that the Grace of God can be frustrated and even stopped. Of course, such a thing is tantamount to total defeat, but which regrettably characterizes the lives of many if not most Believers, I think.

First of all, and as should by now be obvious, the Grace of God is not an automatic thing. Were that so, then it wouldn't be possible to fail of the Grace of God or to frustrate the Grace of God. So, what is it that frustrates the Grace of God and what is it that keeps the Grace of God coming to the Believer in an uninterrupted flow?

I suppose if most Christians had to answer that question, they would go back to the word *"Holiness,"* surmising in their minds that Grace is stopped if we aren't holy enough! Whatever it is they would think, most would probably conclude in their minds that our *"works,"* have something to do with this, etc. None of that is correct.

First let's see why Grace is stopped or at least hindered.

Whenever the Believer attempts to live this Christian life by faith in his spiritual activity, such as faithful Church attendance, the paying of our tithes, daily Bible study, witnessing to souls on a regular basis, etc., all things incidentally which are very, very good; still, because these things are good, they deceive us. Let me explain it this way:

It's certainly not the doing of these things which are wrong. In fact, these are things that every Christian surely will do, and because they are a part and parcel of the Christian experience, and will definitely bring blessings to the Believer. The problem is the object of our Faith. It's the thinking that these things merit us something with God, or provide some type of Holiness or Righteousness which steers us wrong. And yet that's where most of Christendom is.

Most Christians would vehemently deny that the object of their Faith is their works, but that's exactly where it is with most, irrespective as to what they say or think. And how do I know that?

If the Believer doesn't understand the Message of the Cross, and regrettably, most don't, the only other place for the object of our Faith is our works.

When we say things of this nature, many Christians claim that we're demeaning prayer, or faithfulness to Church, or witnessing to souls, etc. To be frank, that's ridiculous! I suppose at least one of the reasons that some Christians grow somewhat testy when we broach this subject, is because we've hit a nerve. There is something about the *"doing of religion,"* that makes us feel holy, etc. And when someone takes those props away, we get a little angry. Nevertheless, that's where

most Christians presently are. And the hurtful thing about all of this is, instead of these things bringing about the intended result, they bring about the very opposite. Our situation doesn't get better but worse; the sin which doth so easily beset us is not eradicated, but gets worse; and we're left somewhat confused!

The truth is, by depending on these things which I have mentioned and many I haven't mentioned, which means to make them the object of our Faith, all we succeed in doing, is to stop the Grace of God. Holiness, Righteousness, purity, victory, etc., are never provided by anything that we can do in the realm of works, irrespective as to how good and noble those works might be. All of these things, and without exception, are provided by the Holy Spirit, and He does so on one basis, and that is on the basis of the great Sacrifice of Christ.

In other words, you as a Believer must put your Faith in the Cross of Christ and do so exclusively, if you want the Grace of God to come to you, and to come to you in an uninterrupted flow. You must understand that it is the Cross that makes Grace possible; it is the Cross where Jesus paid the price; it is the Cross that defeated every power of darkness.

WEAK CHRISTIANS AND STRONG CHRISTIANS

We have a tendency to judge Christians by their works. Now don't misunderstand, works definitely are very important, and the truth is, every good Christian will definitely have good works. In other words, proper faith will always produce proper works; however, proper works will never produce proper Faith. You must ever remember that. But that's what most of the modern Church is attempting to do.

They are attempting to produce faith by works, and to use a pun, it simply won't work.

Strong Christians, at least in the eyes of God, are those who totally and completely look to the Finished Work of Christ. In other words, the Cross is ever the object of their Faith. They understand that this is where all Blessings are derived; they understand that the Cross is the means by which the Grace of God, i.e., *"the goodness of God,"* can keep

NOTES

coming to the Saint of God. Their faith is not in themselves, not in their religious Denomination, not in their particular Church, not in Preachers per se, but in Jesus Christ exclusively, and more particularly, what Christ did at the Cross.

A weak Christian is judged by God, as one who has his faith in his works, and irrespective as to how many works there might be. As one I think can surely see, this is the very opposite of the thinking of most of the modern Church.

Once again, please allow me to emphasize, that we're not demeaning works. Instead of less works we should have more. In other words, Christians should definitely do more for the Lord, certainly not less! The idea is, and that which I'm trying to get you to see, is that these things do not constitute strength with God, do not earn us anything from God, and do not really perfect any Righteousness or Holiness within our hearts and lives. And if a Christian is engaged in such, and that's where their Faith is, they are looked at by the Lord as a *"weak Christian,"* and for all the Biblical reasons.

Some years ago, in reading after an English Preacher, who has long since gone on to be with the Lord, he made a statement which at first shocked me, but yet I knew it was true.

He said, *"The Church must repent not only of its bad, but as well of its good!"* At that moment I knew what he said was right, but at that particular time I didn't really understand why it was right. Only when the Lord began to open up to me the Cross did I understand what he was saying.

We can all understand repenting of the bad things we do, but repenting of the good? What the man meant was this:

He wasn't meaning that we should cease and desist as it regards good works. He was meaning that our Faith must never be in these things, but always in Christ and Him Crucified. And by the way, he was right when he said we ought to repent before the Lord of depending upon those things.

MY FAITH IS IN CHRIST

The heading we've just given, is that which almost every single Christian will say. But despite saying it all the time, most Christians really don't know what they are saying. They think they do, but most actually don't! No, what I'm saying is not a mere play on words, but rather the very core of the problem.

While it is definitely correct that all true Christians definitely do have their faith in Christ; still, not really knowing what that actually means, I'm afraid that most Christians instead, are more trusting in their own religious works than anything else. I'm not questioning their love for Christ or their devotion to Christ. And to be sure, every single true Christian knows that Jesus died for them; however, that's about the extent that they know as it regards the Cross. That's where their faith starts and stops.

To properly understand the statement, we must properly understand the word *"faith."* To make it very simple, the word just simply means *"to believe."* However, it carries far more than a mere mental assent, or an acknowledgement of the truthfulness of something.

As the word is used in the Bible, Faith refers to a total and complete giving of oneself to Christ, and in every capacity — to be sure, to a far greater capacity than most realize.

And how do we do that?

We do that simply by evidencing Faith in the Finished Work of Christ. That's what Faith in Christ actually means. That's the reason I keep saying, that when we speak of Christ, when we think of Christ, it must always be in connection with the Cross, for that's where the price was paid. So, when one speaks of having Faith in Christ, one should at the same time understand that it actually refers to what He did for us as it regards His giving of Himself on the Cross of Calvary. That is proper faith, which means it's that to which the Holy Spirit will always respond favorably (Rom. 6:3-5, 11, 14; 8:1-2, 11; Gal. 6:14).

ROOT OF BITTERNESS

The phrase, *"Lest any root of bitterness springing up trouble you,"* presents that which bears bitter fruit. The metaphor is taken from the growth of plants. Such growth is slow, but what is in the plant will surely come out in time.

What I'm going to say is I think, very, very important. And if the Holy Spirit helps you to understand this of which we say, and I know He will, if you will look to Him for His leading, these truths could be a lifesaver to you.

"Roots of bitterness" spring up in the hearts of Believers, and we are speaking here of Believer, whenever they *"fail of the Grace of God."* The reason is this:

When Believers attempt to live this life for Christ by the means of the *"flesh,"* which we are condemned to do if we do not understand the Message of the Cross, as we've already stated, this stops the flow of Grace, with the situation then becoming intolerable. This is what causes *"burnout,"* emotional problems, stress, etc. and it's because we're trying to do this thing in our own strength, which in fact, only the Holy Spirit can do.

In all of this, it's so easy to become bitter, which is exactly what millions have done. At this stage, many quit trying to live for God, and if they don't quit, their lives are totally unproductive as far as the Cause of Christ is concerned.

It's somewhat like going back to the *"burning bush"* in the desert, as it regarded Moses, but which was not consumed (Ex. 3:1-5).

If we are looking to the Finished Work of Christ, which then gives us the help of the Holy Spirit, the bush can burn forever and not be consumed; however, if we're trying to do this thing, as stated, *"in the flesh,"* which refers to our own strength and efforts, which means we're not looking to the Cross, to be sure, the bush will be consumed, which translates into the fact, that we will be consumed.

As I dictate these notes, on September 21, 2000, I have been preaching the Gospel not much short of 50 years.

In the early years of my Ministry, preaching Revivals and Campmeetings all over the nation, I would often hear of particular Preachers suffering what was referred to as *"burnout."* As well, I heard Preachers talk constantly about all Preachers needing some type of *"hobby,"* which was supposed to address this problem, etc.

I don't mean to be cold or calloused; however, *"burnout"* is a result of the flesh, while *"hobbies"* are an effort of the flesh. I'm not denying the fact of *"burnout,"* but I am denying that such is the result of overwork, etc.

Burnout is always caused by trying to do the Work of God by our own strength and efforts, i.e., *"by the efforts of the flesh,"* i.e., *"efforts which are totally of man and not of the Spirit."* And to be sure, no *"hobby"* is going to address that problem.

THE HOLY SPIRIT

If the Spirit of God is doing the work within us, there will be no problem with burnout, or emotional disturbance or stress, etc. Listen to what Paul said:

"For if you live after the flesh, you shall die (be destroyed spiritually, mentally, and emotionally)*: but if you through the Spirit do mortify the deeds of the body, you shall live"* (Rom. 8:13). So the great question is asked, as to how that one succeeds in functioning according to the Holy Spirit? We are here plainly told, that all of this must be done, and in fact can only be done, *"through the Spirit."*

We know that every single Believer in the world, and I speak of those who truly are Believers, have the Holy Spirit.

We also know, that the Holy Spirit is God, and as such, He can do anything.

We also know that something is wrong, when so many Christians are experiencing all types of problems. This means, that the Holy Spirit is not doing all that He can do. To be sure, if He is functioning properly within our hearts and lives, we will have victory on every front and in every situation. This doesn't mean an absence of problems, but it does mean victory in the spiritual sense, which to be sure, will flow over into every other aspect of our life and living.

HOW DO WE BRING ABOUT THE FULL WORK OF THE HOLY SPIRIT WITHIN OUR LIVES?

To have this brought about, which guarantees the greatest life and living that one could ever experience, there are only two things which must be done. They are:

1. Even as we've said over and over again in this very Volume, the Believer must understand that every single thing we need from the Lord in order to live this life and be what we ought to be, comes exclusively through the Finished Work of Christ. Jesus addressed

every single problem in the Atonement. Nothing was excluded, and everything was included. So, whatever it is that's troubling you, to be sure it was addressed at the Cross. That means the Cross is your answer!

2. Understanding that, you must place your faith unequivocally in the Finished Work of Christ. You must understand that this is the Source of your help, and place your Faith accordingly.

This means, that you full well understand that what is required of you, you literally cannot do. In fact, there's not a single human being in the world who can do what the Lord requires of us, not even the strongest Christian in the world. But at the same time, you must realize that Christ has already done everything for you, and did it at a fearful price. Of course, we're speaking of what He did at the Cross.

Actually, when your Faith is placed in the great Sacrifice of Christ, this is what constitutes *"walking after the Spirit"* (Rom. 8:1). The Holy Spirit will always lead the Believer to the Cross (Jn. 16:14). He always glorifies Christ, and what Christ has done in order to liberate fallen humanity. And when you put your Faith in the Sacrifice of Christ, which incidentally, the Holy Spirit demands, you then have His full help. And as we've already stated, there is nothing He cannot do.

MORE ABUNDANT LIFE

Jesus said:

"The thief cometh not, but for to steal, and to kill, and to destroy: I am come that they might have life, and that they might have it more abundantly" (Jn. 10:10). The *"more abundant life"* of which He here spoke, concerns the *"Spiritual Life"* produced by the Spirit, which is derived from Christ and what He did at the Cross (Rom. 8:2). This pertains to victorious, Christian living, which is the greatest life that one could ever have. As stated, it is furnished solely by the Spirit, and on the basis of the Finished Work of Christ.

However, many in the modern Church have turned this around, to where it pertains only to *"things."* I speak of money, and the things that money can buy. Consequently, these so-called Christians are not looking to the Cross, but rather to foolish Preachers who can tell them how to get rich, etc. This

is rank heresy, and the Holy Spirit through Paul said, *"They which do such things shall not inherit the Kingdom of God"* (Gal. 5:21).

To be frank, these particular Preachers, and they number into the multitudes, are preaching and teaching *"another Jesus, by another spirit, which is another gospel"* (II Cor. 11:4).

Such a gospel will not change anyone's life, will not bring about any type of spiritual victory, and will not throw aside the forces of darkness. In other words, individuals who follow such teaching, thinking they're going to get money or whatever, are instead going to be destroyed. All of this is *"of the flesh,"* and the Scripture plainly says in respect to this, *"For if you live after the flesh, you shall die"* (Rom. 8:13).

The Cross of Christ is the only answer for hurting humanity, and in fact, for humanity in general, and not some fake pot of gold at the end of some fake rainbow.

DEFILEMENT

The phrase, *"And thereby many be defiled,"* speaks of *"works of the flesh"* which most certainly will attach themselves to those plagued by a *"root of bitterness."*

The Christian should understand, that he has only two ways to go. He can go the way of the *"Cross,"* or he can go the way of *"self."* The Cross has only one way, while self has untold numbers of ways.

The reason that Paul gave so much teaching on the problem of *"self,"* i.e., *"the flesh,"* is simply because there is already a propensity in the heart of all Believers to go in that direction. So it's a road that's not only well trod, but easily trod; however, it leads to nothing but sorrow, heartache, pain, and disappointment. And in fact, it can lead to the loss of one's soul.

The problem with self is, that it's always very religious. It's also very subtle and very deceitful. We invoke the Name of Jesus, and quote a few Scriptures, and think we are *"walking after the Spirit."* We aren't! And then we wonder why the defilement, i.e., *"failure"*?

Satan never fights self, but rather aids and abets efforts in this direction. But to be sure, he relentlessly fights the Cross of Christ, and for all the obvious reasons!

(16) "LEST THERE BE ANY FORNICATOR, OR PROFANE PERSON, AS ESAU, WHO FOR ONE MORSEL OF MEAT SOLD HIS BIRTHRIGHT."

The structure is:

1. It is only through the Cross that victory over the flesh can be obtained.

2. Esau, although of the family of God, did not know God, and because he rejected God's way which is Christ and the Cross.

3. He sold his birthright, which pertained to the Blessing of Abraham, because he had no concern or regard for spiritual things.

ESAU

The phrase, *"Lest there be any fornicator, or profane person, as Esau,"* proclaims to us several things:

1. The Holy Spirit here says with terrible severity that Esau was a *"profane person."*

2. He was *"profane"* because he rejected God's Way, which is the Cross, and which results are inevitable. Being *"profane"* was not the cause, but rather the result.

3. The Holy Spirit through Paul is here saying, that any Believer, exactly as Esau of old, who rejects God's Way of the Cross, will conclude exactly as Esau. Such is a chilling prospect! But such is true.

HIS BIRTHRIGHT

The phrase, *"Who for one morsel of meat sold his birthright,"* pertains to spiritual things.

The birthright implied the first place or rank in the family; the privilege of offering sacrifice and conducting worship in the absence or death of the father; a double share of the inheritance; and in this instance the honor of being in the line of the Patriarchs, and the transmitting of the Promises made to Abraham and Isaac. What Esau parted with we can easily understand, by reflecting on the honors which have clustered around the name of Jacob, i.e., *"the God of Abraham, Isaac, and Jacob."*

Most read this Passage and conclude that Esau did this, rejected his birthright, because he was a fornicator and profane person; however, the idea lends toward the following:

The entirety of the subject of Hebrews is Faith in Christ and what He did for humanity

at the Cross. This great Promise of a coming Redeemer was given to the Patriarchs, even as Paul has addressed repeatedly in the Eleventh Chapter. Esau rejected this Promise. In other words, he had no regard or concern for that of which we speak. He wanted his own way, and in a sense his own religion, with the result being that he became a fornicator and profane person.

In essence, Esau did the same identical thing as Cain, and untold billions of others ever since. He was in the Family of God, but he was not of the Family of God, exactly as the majority in the modern Church presently.

The birthright of this man was, *"the God of Abraham, Isaac, and Esau."* But he didn't want that, and because it meant placing his faith and trust in One Who was to come, Who would redeem fallen humanity. In essence, Esau was saying that he didn't need a Savior, exactly as so many who follow in his train.

THE MODERN CHURCH

Most miss the intent of this Passage as given by Paul, automatically dismissing it as a man who chose the gratification of fleshly desires. However, as stated, that is not the idea of the Text. Fleshly gratification and immorality of many and varied stripes, always follow the rejection of the Cross, for that's what all of his comes down to. We must remember that we are speaking here of Believers, or at least those who claim to be Believers. As stated, Esau was in the family but not of the family. There is a vast difference in being *"in the Family of God"* than being *"of the Family of God."* Every single Christian is in the world, but we are definitely not supposed to be of the world.

(17) "FOR YE KNOW HOW THAT AFTERWARD, WHEN HE WOULD HAVE INHERITED THE BLESSING, HE WAS REJECTED: FOR HE FOUND NO PLACE OF REPENTANCE, THOUGH HE SOUGHT IT CAREFULLY WITH TEARS."

The composite is:

1. Esau wanted the Blessing, but he didn't want the Christ of the Blessing, one might say.

2. He was rejected by the Holy Spirit, even as all are rejected who reject *"Christ and Him Crucified."*

3. He did not seek repentance with tears, but rather the Blessing. In other words, he would not repent of his erroneous direction.

THE BLESSING

The phrase, *"For ye know how that afterward, when he would have inherited the Blessing,"* proclaims Esau, as millions, desiring the Blessing without the Blesser. Everyone wants the Blessing, whatever that might be, but let it ever be known, that the only way that the Blessing can be received, is by Faith in the Redeemer and what He did at the Cross on our behalf. There is Salvation or Blessing in no other (Acts 4:12).

Of Esau God says, *"As it is written, Jacob have I loved, but Esau have I hated"* (Mal. 1:1-3; Rom. 9:13).

The Psalmist said, *"Through Thy precepts I get understanding: therefore I hate every false way"* (Ps. 119:104).

Esau was projecting a *"false way,"* which means that he placed no faith or confidence in the coming Redeemer, which means that he really did not look at himself as needing a Redeemer, which is the condition of most of the world.

REJECTED

The phrase, *"He was rejected,"* proclaims the fact that even though it was Isaac who tendered the rejection, it was actually God Who rejected him. God will reject a person only on one condition, and that condition is that they do not believe in Christ and Him Crucified as the answer to fallen humanity. The Scripture says of God, *"Wherefore I was grieved with that generation, and said, they do always err in their heart; and they have not known My ways.*

"So I sware in My wrath, they shall not enter into My rest."

Paul then said, *"Take heed, Brethren, lest there be in any of you an evil heart of unbelief, in departing from the Living God"* (Heb. 3:10-12).

God can only accept the Sacrifice of Christ; consequently, He can accept only those who put their faith and trust in that Sacrifice.

This was the Faith of the Patriarchs. They were men who made mistakes, and at times, took wrong directions, but not as it regards

their ultimate Faith in the Coming Redeemer. They believed what God said about this coming great Sacrifice, even though their understanding at the time was only partial. It has not changed from then until now.

The whole of the Plan of God is the salvation of the human race. That was and is done solely and completely by the Sacrifice of Christ. That's what the Bible is all about, in fact, that is the story of the Bible.

The addendum to that is, that fallen man must express Faith in that Sacrifice, whether they lived before Christ or after Christ (Eph. 2:8-9). Without question, God must reject any faith that is in anything else other than the Sacrifice of Christ. Esau, pure and simple, did not have that Faith, did not want that Faith, and would not accept that Faith, but yet he wanted the Blessing. Such is not to be!

REPENTANCE

The phrase, *"For he found no place of repentance, though he sought it carefully with tears,"* proclaims the end result of such a direction. The pronoun *"it"* doesn't refer to the repentance, but rather to the Blessing. He wanted the Blessing, as is obvious, but he did not want to repent of his foul ways of faith in things other than Christ. Primarily, it was faith in himself, as it generally always is with most.

Some have tried to claim from these two Verses, that God will not forgive *"fornicators"* or those who are *"profane."* Were that the case, there wouldn't be many people saved. No, and as stated, Esau more and more became these things after his rejection of the *"Blessing."* This is not to insinuate that the seed was not already in his heart, for it definitely was.

God will forgive any sin except blaspheming the Holy Spirit, which does not enter into this situation, and the sin of unbelief. As it regards the sin of unbelief, there is no ground on which God can bring about forgiveness, simply because the ground of forgiveness, which is the Sacrifice of Christ, has been rejected. That — unbelief — was the problem with Esau, and it is the problem with the majority of the world. In fact, it's even the problem with the majority of the Church.

(18) "FOR YE ARE NOT COME UNTO THE MOUNT THAT MIGHT BE TOUCHED, AND THAT BURNED WITH FIRE, NOR UNTO BLACKNESS, AND DARKNESS, AND TEMPEST,"

The exegesis is:

1. Paul is referring here to Mt. Sinai.

2. He is more specifically mentioning the Law.

3. The Law was given with great overtones of judgment, symbolized by the *"fire, blackness, darkness, and tempest."*

MT. SINAI

The phrase, *"For ye are not come unto the mount that might be touched,"* is in effect saying to these Christian Jews, *"you had better carefully consider the Law with which you are proposing to once again embrace."*

The Apostle gave the warning as it concerned Esau, because what some of them were proposing, was exactly what Esau had done. He wanted them to see the road they were proposing to travel.

Esau wanted the Blessing, but he denied that which gave the Blessing, which was Christ. These Christian Jews were contemplating doing the very same thing. They must know, that if they did this thing, as God rejected Esau, He would also reject them. To reject Christ and His Cross, is to be rejected by God.

JUDGMENT

The phrase, *"And that burned with fire, nor unto blackness, and darkness, and tempest,"* refers to the august Power of God represented by these symbols. All of this took place when the Law was given on Mt. Sinai (Ex. 19:16-20).

The idea is, we can face God respecting His Law according to the symbols here given, or we can face Him through the Blood of His Son and our Savior, the Lord Jesus Christ. Paul is trying to convey to these Christian Jews, at least to those who were contemplating going back to the Law, exactly what they were facing. What is being said is according to the following:

Man must answer to God. Whether he denies the existence of God, or whether he claims some fabricated deity as God; still, he will answer to his Creator at the Judgment. If he attempts to answer in any way except through the Sacrifice of Christ, he is going to face *"the fire, the blackness, the darkness, and the tempest."* The latter is a chilling prospect. But this is what the Holy Spirit is saying through the Apostle.

(19) "AND THE SOUND OF A TRUMPET, AND THE VOICE OF WORDS; WHICH VOICE THEY THAT HEARD INTREATED THAT THE WORD SHOULD NOT BE SPOKEN TO THEM ANY MORE:"

The exegesis is:

1. The Trumpet announced God and His Holiness.

2. The Trumpet was following by the *"voice of words,"* which was so powerful, that the people could not stand the sound.

3. They begged that it would stop!

THE TRUMPET AND THE VOICE

The phrase, *"And the sound of a trumpet, and the voice of words,"* presents that as stated, which accompanied the giving of the Law.

Some may look at the giving of the Law as exampled here and recorded in Exodus Chapter 20, and the advent of Grace one might say, as given on the Day of Pentecost, and wonder as to why the great difference? As it regards Grace, while the advent of the Holy Spirit was accompanied by the sound of a *"rushing mighty wind"* (Acts 2:2), still, there was no comparison between the two. In fact, the record will show that some 3,000 men died at the time the Law was given as a result of judgment because of sin (Ex. 32:25-28), whereas 3,000 men were saved on the Day of Pentecost (Acts 2:41).

The difference in these two days or times lies within the difference of Law and Grace. That's the reason that no one, at least if they're in their right mind spiritually speaking, would want to try to function spiritually according to Law. A thrice-Holy God can accept nothing less than perfection, which man is incapable of rendering. Man's only hope is Grace, but yet, it seems that many Christians insist upon trying to live by *"Law."* While it's not the Law of Moses of which we speak, but rather law which they have fabricated themselves or else by someone else, it is still law, which God cannot bless. When we take this route, we *"fail of the Grace of God,"* exactly as Paul mentioned in Verse 15. The conclusion to that is always defilement.

A WORD WHICH THEY COULD NOT BEAR

The phrase, *"Which voice they that heard intreated that the word should not be spoken to them any more,"* relates the Voice of God as being of such power, that it could not be stood by the people (Ex. 20:19; Deut. 5:22-27). So terrible was His Voice to them, so awful the penalties which fenced round their approach to Him, that they shrank back from hearing His Words.

(20) "FOR THEY COULD NOT ENDURE THAT WHICH WAS COMMANDED, AND IF SO MUCH AS A BEAST TOUCH THE MOUNTAIN, IT SHALL BE STONED, OR THRUST THROUGH WITH A DART:"

The diagram is:

1. The people could not stand the Holiness of God.

2. God coming this close, meant that death was very close, and because of the sinfulness of the people.

3. Once again we state the fact, that if any person attempts to please God through the keeping of Law, he must render a perfect obedience, and he must understand, that not one single soul, except Christ, has ever succeeded in doing such.

THE COMMANDS

The phrase, *"For they could not endure that which was commanded,"* presents the fearfulness of the giving of the Law on Mt. Sinai, and one of the commands laid on the people, namely, that neither man nor beast should even touch the mountain under penalty of death. Paul uses the phrase, *"which was commanded,"* which makes it all terrifyingly present. The command that nothing touch it indicates the Holiness and separateness of the mountain, and because God had now come down on this particular place. The quotation is from Exodus 19:13.

The meaning is not that the commands themselves were intolerable, but that the *"manner"* in which they were communicated inspired a terror which they could not

bear. In other words, they feared that they would die.

JUDGMENT

The phrase, *"And if so much as a beast touch the mountain, it shall be stoned, or thrust through with a dart,"* proclaims the absolute poignancy of the moment.

"Touch" in the Greek here is *"thiggano,"* and means *"to touch, handle."* It implies a touching or a grasping which affects the object. In classical Greek it is often used of touching or handling some sacred object which may be desecrated by the one who lays hands on it. Here, to touch the mountain, was to profane it. The reason, as stated, pertains to the absolute Holiness of God, which is beyond the comprehension of mere mortals.

During all of this time, the only way that man could approach God was by means of the Sacrifices. We have the first record of such in Genesis 4, and which continued up unto the time of Moses. During the giving of the Law, the very heart of the Levitical system was the sacrificial order, which pertained to five separate Sacrifices (Lev. Chpts. 1-5). Of course, the Sacrifices from the very beginning all and without exception, represented Christ and the price that He would pay in order to redeem lost humanity. The Law never did present a way to reach God, and simply because man was incapable of fulfilling its demands. But Christ did meet all of its demands, and as well, suffered its penalty on the Cross, which atoned for all sin, and made it possible for man to come directly to God, but in the Name of the Lord Jesus Christ.

(21) "AND SO TERRIBLE WAS THE SIGHT, THAT MOSES SAID, I EXCEEDINGLY FEAR AND QUAKE:"

The structure is:

1. If this sight was terrible to Moses, and it definitely was, who in fact was one of the godliest men who ever lived, then how more terrible it must have appeared unto the people.

2. The word *"fear"* is intensified as to its meaning by the prefixed preposition which literally says, *"I am frightened out or away."*

3. Men constantly blaspheme God, never once realizing His awesome power, which in fact, is so awesome as to defy all human comprehension.

THE TERRIBLE SIGHT

The phrase, *"And so terrible was the sight,"* proclaims in the strongest language possible, that no lasting blessing can come to fallen man through the Law. The very circumstances under which that fiery Law was given should have impressed upon him his utter inability to meet its requirements, and thus have led him to cast himself upon the matchless Grace of God, which alone can undertake for a sinner whose fallen nature is in opposition to the Divine Will. But Israel, even though they shrank in terror from the manifestations of Divine Power, self-confidently declared, *"All that the Lord hath spoken will we do, and be obedient,"* thus making themselves responsible to keep every Commandment in order to enter into Blessing (Ex. 19:8). They should have asked for Mercy and Grace realizing their total inadequacy. But there seems to be something in man, even we modern Christians, which makes us think that we can in fact meet the requirements of the Law. The idea is this:

If even the lower creation, made subject to vanity because of man's sin, would not be permitted to so much as touch the Mount, and if Moses who might be considered the very best in all Israel, trembled at the thought of drawing nigh to God under such circumstances, what possible hope could there be of any ordinary man standing before Jehovah on the ground of legal righteousness?

Oh Reader can you not see the absolute need for the glorious Grace of God? Can you not see the hopelessness of legal righteousness?

EXCEEDING FEAR

The phrase, *"That Moses said, I exceedingly fear and quake,"* is not found in the Sinai narrative, but did occur at the time of the golden calf (Deut. 9:19). Quite possibly the Jewish Targums records these words of Moses, which were not included in the Holy Scripture. No doubt, there was much that happened at that memorable time which is not recorded here.

At any rate, Paul is picturing an awe-inspiring occasion, one that affected all the people and terrified even Moses, the man of God.

Once more the two Covenants are contrasted (vss. 18-29); and for the fourth time (vs. 25) a warning of mingled goodness and sternness is addressed to the readers of the Epistle.

The seven outward and visible signs of the Old Covenant (vss. 18-19) are contrasted with the seven inward and spiritual realities of the New (vss. 22-24). The first are: the mountain, the fire, the blackness, the darkness, the tempest, the sound of the trumpet, and *"the words,"* i.e., the Ten Commandments — the Law. It doomed to death.

The second are: the City, the Angels, the Firstborn, the Judge, the Righteous, the Mediator, and the Blood that speaks peace and life, all which we will momentarily address.

(22) "BUT YE ARE COME UNTO MOUNT SION, AND UNTO THE CITY OF THE LIVING GOD, THE HEAVENLY JERUSALEM, AND TO AN INNUMERABLE COMPANY OF ANGELS."

The structure is:

1. Instead of returning to Mt. Sinai and the Law, the Readers are urged to continue their approach to Mt. Sion, the spiritual mountain and city where God dwells and reigns.

2. The Angels are introduced here because they are the usual accompaniment of God's Glory and ministers of His Will.

3. The previous Passages have portrayed Law, while these Passages portray Grace. There is quite a difference!

THE HEAVENLY JERUSALEM

The phrase, *"But ye are come unto Mount Sion, and unto the city of the Living God, the Heavenly Jerusalem,"* refers to the eternal abode of the Saints of God, with its description given in Revelation, Chapters 21 and 22. No one has ever reached this City by Law, but only by Grace. In fact, all the Old Testament Saints who now grace this *"Heavenly Jerusalem,"* were taken there only after Jesus died on the Cross. Before then, they went down into the heart of the Earth, referred to as *"Paradise,"* or *"Abraham's bosom"* (Lk. 16:22).

This was the case because the blood of bulls and goats could not take away sin; therefore, the sin debt remained, which means that Satan still had a claim on those Righteous Saints

(Eph. 4:8). Now due to the Cross, whenever a Christian dies, they instantly go to the *"Heavenly Jerusalem."*

Paul's mention of *"the Living God"* emphasizes the thought that this City is no static affair; it is the city of a vital, dynamic, Living Being, One Who is doing things. This is where God dwells and reigns.

Paul also in Galatians 4:19-31 contrasts the Old Testament with the New Testament by speaking of Sinai and the Jerusalem which is above. The idea is, that the Law could not get anyone to that Heavenly Jerusalem; that could only be done by what Christ did at the Cross.

The Apostle is here showing the excellent advantages which Believers have under the New Covenant vs. the Old Covenant. The very words *"ye are come,"* proclaim the fact that due to the Grace of God, they were already citizens of the Heavenly Jerusalem, and were entitled to its privileges (Phil. 3:20).

JERUSALEM

The name of this city recurs again and again in both the Old Testament and the New Testament.

In the time of David, the city of Jerusalem was occupied by the Canaanites. It lay secure on mountainous heights in a wedge of land between the southern and northern sections of the land then occupied by the Twelve Tribes of Israel. David took the city by force. His action was politically motivated as well as spiritual: there was historic jealousy between the two sections of Israel. By establishing his Capital in the captured city of Jerusalem, David was able to avoid the jealousy that might have occurred if he had chosen a site in either the north or the south.

It was during the reign of David and Solomon that this city was developed not only as the Capital of a united Israel but also as its center of worship. Throughout subsequent sacred history, Jerusalem was viewed as the place where God has established His Name, and succeeding Temples were always built on the original site.

Most of the events of Bible history have their focus in Jerusalem, which became the central location that represents for all time Israel's occupation of the Promised Land.

NOTES

JERUSALEM'S SPIRITUAL SIGNIFICANCE

Jerusalem became the political and spiritual center of the life of Israel. Israel's kings ruled here, and it was here that the Temple, which symbolized the unity of the people and its faith, was constructed. Most of the events of Old Testament history after the monarchy was established, focus on Jerusalem, and it is in part from these events that Jerusalem derives her theological significance.

Historic revivals were initiated in Jerusalem by Godly kings, and here too apostasy was spread by evil rulers. In a real sense, the spiritual condition of Jerusalem at any time in history was a barometer of the spiritual condition of the nation. The Ministry of the great Old Testament Prophets, such as Isaiah and Jeremiah, took place in Jerusalem — as did the murder of so many of the messengers God sent to warn His people.

JESUS

Some of Jesus' Ministry took place in Jerusalem. It was the home of the leaders who so fiercely resented Him and who plotted to achieve His execution. It was outside the walls of the Holy City that Jesus died, was buried, and rose again. And it was in Jerusalem that the Gospel was first preached and the first Church formed.

Both the magnificent and the dreadful events of sacred history combine to give Jerusalem a unique place in Scripture, and they gave it its distinctive theological associations. Paul saw the historic Jerusalem and the Jerusalem of his day in a sense, as representative of slavery, even as we are here addressing. Again and again the freeing Power of God was rejected by Israel, and her experience demonstrates the destructive power of Law when Law is confused with Faith as a way of Salvation (Gal. 4:21-31).

JERUSALEM'S PROPHETIC DESTINY

The Old Testament portrays a distinctive future for God's people. The Children of Israel will be restored to nationhood, to be exalted over the other nations of the world. Jerusalem will then be the center of worship of the world when the promised time of renewal comes. The Messiah will take His waiting Throne, and that Messiah will be the Lord

Jesus Christ, and the nation will then be finally secure. This future is affirmed by most of the Prophets (Zech., Chpts. 12-14).

The New Testament introduces the concept of a Heavenly Jerusalem, to which we have briefly alluded. All that Jerusalem has been in sacred history as a political and spiritual center has foreshadowed what God intends to do on Earth. That perfect future world center of political and religious life is spoken of as the new or Heavenly Jerusalem (Heb. 12:22; Rev. 3:12; 21:2, 10).

All of this is the main reason for the present tension over Jerusalem between the Palestinians and the Israelis. In fact, this tension will only increase until the advent of the Antichrist, whose appearance is shortly to come to pass. There is much more behind all of this than a mere political problem, or a demand for land. The contention goes back all the way to the time of David, and will find its climax in the Second Coming, which will be the greatest event in human history (Rev. Chpt. 19).

ANGELS

The phrase, *"And to an innumerable company of Angels,"* represents untold thousands. In fact, in the vision of John the Beloved of the New Jerusalem, he said, *"And I heard the voice of many Angels round about the Throne . . . and the number of them was 10,000 times 10,000, and thousands of thousands"* (Rev. 5:11).

The word in the Greek is *"myriads of myriads"* and in the Hebrew is *"chiliads of chiliads."*

It refers to *"countless numbers,"* and if taken literally, the number is 100 trillion.

MOUNT SION

When Paul used the term, *"Ye are come unto Mt. Sion,"* he was speaking of God's free electing Grace. We read in Psalms 78:68, *"He chose Mt. Zion which He loved."* When there had been a complete breakdown under the former order, God exalted David, the man after His Own heart, to the position of King in Israel, and confirmed the Promises to him and to his seed after him, and established his throne upon Mt. Zion, which cannot be removed forever (Ps. 125:1). *"Out of Zion, the perfection of beauty, God hath shined."*

From that sacred Mount blessing goes forth to mankind, and eventually in the day of Jehovah's power, *"the Lord shall roar out of Zion,"* *"the Law shall go forth from Mt. Zion,"* when *"the Deliverer shall come to Zion"* and all God's glorious Promises be fulfilled, when *"the Lord shall reign in Mt. Zion."*

It will be the center of New Covenant Blessing in that wondrous day, and of course, we're speaking of the coming Kingdom Age. And for us at the present time, it speaks of pure grace superceding the legal Covenant. It is not to Mt. Sinai then, the Mount of Law, but to Sion, the Mount of Grace, we have come.

This of course, which we have addressed, is the Jerusalem that shall be in the coming Kingdom Age, with Jesus Christ reigning as its King and President. Israel, as stated, will once again be the leading nation in the world, that which God originally intended, but which they tried to obtain in all the wrong ways. Now it will come to pass, but only after they have accepted Christ not only as their Messiah, but as well, as their Savior. In other words, Israel must come to the Cross. That's what the Prophet Zechariah was addressing when he said, *"In that day* (the Second Coming) *there shall be a fountain opened to the House of David and to the inhabitants of Jerusalem for sin and for uncleanness"* (Zech. 13:1).

That *"fountain"* is the Cross where the Precious Blood of our glorious Savior was shed for lost humanity.

> *"There is a fountain filled with blood,*
> *"Drawn from Immanuel's veins,*
> *"And sinners plunged beneath that flood,*
> *"Lose all their guilty stain."*

THE CITY OF THE LIVING GOD

Even though Paul couples the two together, *"Mt. Sion"* and *"the Heavenly Jerusalem,"* the latter is not to be confounded with the earthly city of the great King, which will yet be the joy of the whole Earth. Our portion, and I speak of the Church, and in fact, all who will be in the First Resurrection, is not to be in this world even when Christ Himself reigns, but we are to reign with Him from the Heavenly Jerusalem above. This of course, is the New Jerusalem, the Bride, the

Lamb's wife of Revelation Chapters 19 and 21. It embraces all the Heavenly Saints, that is, all those who have died in faith throughout the centuries, all who in every dispensation believed God, and that of course includes all the Old Testament Saints as well, all who were quickened by His Spirit.

The Heavenly Jerusalem is preeminently the Home of the Church and, therefore, is designated as the bridal city; but Saints, as stated, of all other dispensations who have passed through death and entered into Resurrection Life will, as one has expressed it, be upon its *"Heavenly Roll."* This Heavenly Jerusalem will be the Throne Seat of the entire universe of God, and actually will be transferred from Heaven to Earth (Rev. Chpt. 21).

(23) "TO THE GENERAL ASSEMBLY AND CHURCH OF THE FIRSTBORN, WHICH ARE WRITTEN IN HEAVEN, AND TO GOD THE JUDGE OF ALL, AND TO THE SPIRITS OF JUST MEN MADE PERFECT,"

The diagram is:

1. Those who are Born-Again will occupy the Heavenly Jerusalem.

2. God is the Judge as to who will occupy this City.

3. *"The spirits of just men made perfect,"* can only come about, and in fact has come about, by Faith in Christ and what He did at the Cross on our behalf.

CHURCH OF THE FIRSTBORN ONES

The phrase, *"To the General Assembly and Church of the firstborn, which are written in Heaven,"* pertains to every Born-Again Believer from the time of Abel up to the Second Coming.

"Firstborn" here is in the plural in the original. The reference is not to Christ personally, but the entire Church, both those on Earth and in Heaven. The statement literally is, *"Church of the firstborn ones, whose names are written in Heaven."*

The title *"Church of the Firstborn"* emphasizes the dignity of the Church. By using this title, the Holy Spirit points out not only the priority of the Church, but also its honored position. We who believe the Gospel are exalted to be Children of God; we are made *"heirs of God, and joint-heirs with Christ"* (Rom. 8:17).

BECAUSE OF THE CROSS

This unique position pertains only to the members of Christ's Church rather than to Angels, and is granted to those alone who believe because of our union with Jesus Christ.

Someone asked me the question once, *"Are we saved because of Who He is or What He did?"*

While it must quickly be said that He, and of course we refer to the Lord Jesus Christ, is the only One Who could have paid the price for man's Redemption; still, it is What He did which brought us our Redemption, which refers to the Cross.

Jesus Christ is God, and in fact, has always been God. As God He had no beginning, is uncreated, unformed, and unmade and has always been. Of course, it's impossible for mere mortals to comprehend such terminology; however, God the Creator, and Jesus is God, cannot be described in mere human terms; my point is this:

Man is not saved just because Jesus is God. As stated, He has always been God, but that didn't save anyone. The problem is this:

While God in his omnipotence could have regenerated fallen man without going to the Cross, and simply because He has the power to do that; nevertheless, regeneration without the sin question being addressed would not have really solved the problem. God's nature demanded and rightly so, that the terrible crime of sin be addressed and paid in full. There was no way that man could do this and at the same time be salvaged. While all of mankind going to eternal Hell, and burning there forever and forever, would have satisfied that sin debt, such a payment would have destroyed the entirety of the human race. So if man was to be salvaged, God would have to pay the terrible price Himself, which He did by becoming Man and going to the Cross. So it was What He did, which ransomed the souls of men, and saved them from eternal doom. And to be sure, it was a price of such unparalleled proportions, that it literally defies all description.

THE PRICE WAS THE CROSS

To comprehend the horror of the Cross, man simply cannot do. And when I speak of *"horror"* I do not speak of the physical pain, but of the spiritual suffering instead.

Isaiah Chapter 53 proclaims the terrible, spiritual agony of the Cross, as nothing else in the Word of God. It was on the Cross that Christ bore the sin penalty of the world. That penalty was death, but a death of unimagined proportions. God would literally smite His Only Begotten Son with judgment, judgment incidentally, which should have come upon us (Isa. 53:4).

Some claim that He was cursed by God, but that's not correct. The Holy Spirit through Paul said that Christ was *"made a curse for us,"* and that is different than being cursed (Gal. 3:13).

The reason He had to be *"made a curse,"* is because He had no sin.

"Curse" in the Greek is *"ginomai,"* and means *"to become, come into being, partake."* Consequently, having no sin, the only way He could be made a curse, was to be made to suffer the penalty of sin which was death, which He did! And let it be quickly said, that while on the Cross, as some claim, He definitely did not take upon Himself the nature of Satan and thereby die a lost sinner, and be Born-Again in Hell as they continue to claim. Such teaching is blasphemous!

First of all, Christ had to be a Perfect Sacrifice, which He was, which means there was no sin about Him of any capacity, whether personal or contrived. He was made to be a curse, which meant that He took the penalty that all of us should have taken; however, there was a great difference in Him taking the penalty and us, and that difference is this:

Had we taken the penalty, which would have been eternal death, there would have been no reprieve, and because in fact, we were sinners. But due to the fact that He had no sin, and that His Death atoned for all sin, past, present, and future, then death could not hold Him. The wages of sin is death, and if there had been one sin in Christ, or one sin unatoned, Jesus could not have been raised from the dead. Legally, He would have had to have remained in the death world; however, due to the fact of Him being absolutely sinless, and that His Death atoned for all sin, for all time, and for all human beings, at least for all who would believe, the wages had been

paid, and Satan had no legal right to hold Him in death.

That's why the Veil in the Temple was rent from the top to the bottom at His Death. His Death opened up the way, which meant that the Resurrection was a foregone conclusion (Mat. 27:51).

Due to this great, Finished Work, the moment that a sinner says *"Yes,"* to Christ, he is instantly placed *"in Christ,"* which means that he is now *"a new creature: old things are passed away; behold, all things are become new"* (II Cor. 5:17). At that moment, he becomes a member of the *"Church of the Firstborn,"* and his name is *"written in Heaven."*

GOD THE JUDGE OF ALL

The phrase, *"And to God the Judge of all,"* refers to the fact that God has judged all who are in the *"Church of the Firstborn,"* as perfectly justified in His sight.

There is now no separating Veil, that having been taken away by the Cross of Christ, no cloud of darkness hiding His Face; but in the blessed consciousness of justification from all things, we stand unabashed in His Holy Presence, knowing that for us the sin question has been forever settled, and His Perfect Love has cast out all fear.

Israel saw God as remote. When they came to Sinai they found a Righteous God Who was both a Lawgiver and a Judge. Before His Law and Judgment they stood sinful and guilty; they dared not touch the mountain made holy by His Presence. The same Law which bound them to God in a Holy Covenant, also forbad them complete access into His Presence. But under the New Covenant, a Covenant incidentally ratified in the Blood of Jesus, the Believer is given perfect access into God's Presence.

In Christ, we are brought near to God. We find a God Who is not cold or passive, but Who is kind and gracious. God, our Judge, Who incidentally, and as stated, has judged us as justified, is a God of love and longsuffering; He invites us to share our innermost feelings with Him. In confidence and assurance we lay our lives before Him, and we also have a personal relationship with Him as the Judge of all men. But again I state, we aren't fearful of Him as Judge, because He has already judged our sins in Jesus Christ, and they will never again be brought up before us. We are justified!

When Jesus died on the Cross, the guilt of sin was taken away, which means that the guilty verdict in Heaven was changed to *"not guilty!"* And as well, the power of sin was broken, which in effect, amounts to a *"double cure."*

Oh dear Reader, can you now sense His Presence, even as you read these words. The price He paid for us was not only sufficient, but will ever be sufficient, and there will never be anyone in time or eternity, who will ever dare claim that it's not sufficient. Paul said:

"But now in Christ Jesus ye who sometimes were far off are made nigh by the Blood of Christ" (Eph. 2:13).

JUSTIFICATION

The phrase, *"And to the spirits of just men made perfect,"* tells us several things:

1. All of the purification processes of the Law of Moses, could only address themselves to the outward. But the Blood of Jesus cleanses not only the outward, but even the spirits of men. At the Fall in the Garden of Eden, the spirit of man was cut off from God. But through Christ, the spirit of man has been reunited with the Spirit of God, and because it has been perfectly cleansed.

2. The words *"just men"* refer to *"Justification by Faith."* This is what God promised Abraham would happen (Gen. 15:6), and it's exactly what did happen, when Jesus died on the Cross. Simple Faith in Him, cleanses from all sin.

3. The word *"perfect"* adequately describes *"Justification by Faith."* A Perfect God can only accept a perfect Salvation, which means that He can only accept a perfect Justification. That's exactly what Christ afforded by His Death at the Cross, and that's exactly what we presently have, a perfect Justification.

In the true sense of the word, it is not possible for *"Justification"* to be anything but perfect. Anything less, automatically destroys the meaning of the act. Justification is a legal work, which means that God has legally declared man *"not guilty,"* based upon a legal faith, which is placed in a legal work, and thereby guarantees a legal Righteousness, the *"imputed Righteousness of Christ."*

However, let it be known, that this is the only type of *"legal Righteousness,"* that God will accept. While the Law definitely had a legal righteousness, for it to be legally obtained, it had to be perfectly kept, which was impossible for man to do. So, anyone who tries to obtain a legal righteousness through the Law, is automatically condemned, for that's all the Law can do. But when one accepts Christ, one is given the Righteousness of Christ, which He affords us as the *"Second Man"* (I Cor. 15:47).

(24) "AND TO JESUS THE MEDIATOR OF THE NEW COVENANT, AND TO THE BLOOD OF SPRINKLING, THAT SPEAKETH BETTER THINGS THAN THAT OF ABEL."

The structure is:

1. It is Jesus Christ to Whom we must look.

2. He Alone is the Mediator (the go-between) between God and man.

3. By His Death on the Cross, He has established a *"New Covenant."*

4. His shed Blood is the basis of this New Covenant, which paid the terrible sin debt.

5. His Blood speaks to all men, and for all time of the veracity of this New Covenant.

6. The New Covenant, established on His shed Blood, is much better than that of the animal sacrifices of Abel, and all others of the Old Testament.

JESUS

The phrase, *"And to Jesus,"* proclaims the Son of God as the center point, the foundation, the establishment, one might say, of the entirety of the Word of God. And more particular, everything, even as here, always centers up on what He did at the Cross in order for man to be saved. No fallible man this Christ such as Moses himself was, who because of his failure was debarred from entering the Land of Promise! Christ Jesus the Eternal Son of God, Who became Man in order to take upon Himself our sin and blame, has met every claim of that violated Law and now mediates the New Covenant of free Grace, into the Blessing of which we have been brought.

Never must this be minimized in the heart and thinking of the Believer! Never must we make less of Who Christ is, and more particularly, What He did, and as an aside, it is impossible to make more of this than we should. The crowning sin of the Church is, in not preaching as the foundation Gospel of all that we preach, *"Jesus Christ and Him Crucified"* (I Cor. 2:2). This must ever be the center of our thinking, the power of our preaching, the thrust of our argument, the very sinew and muscle of our Gospel. It is Jesus and Jesus Alone Who has redeemed us.

Preacher, preach Jesus, and when we say such a thing, we're always saying, and without exception, preach Jesus and Him Crucified. Saint of God, worship Jesus, and in your worship of Him, always understand that you are worshiping Him not only because He is God, which He definitely is, but above all, because of the great Price that He has paid for our Redemption. Dear Saint, feel free, and even come boldly into the very Presence of God, the very Holy of Holies, but always remember, that you have this privilege, because of the great Price that He has paid.

THE MEDIATOR

The short phrase, *"The Mediator,"* presents the crowning excellence of the New Dispensation, in contradistinction from the Old.

The function of a Mediator is to intervene between two parties in order to promote relations between them which the parties themselves are not able to effect. The situation requiring the offices of a Mediator is often one of estrangement and alienation, and the Mediator effects reconciliation.

In the Old Testament, the Prophet and the Priest fulfilled most characteristically the office of Mediator in the institution which God established in terms of Covenant relations with His people. The Prophet was God's spokesman; he acted for God in the presence of men (Deut. 18:18-22). The Priest acted on behalf of men in the Presence of God (Ex. 28:1; Lev. 9:7; 16:6; Num. 16:40; II Chron. 26:18; Heb. 5:1-4).

In the Old Testament, however, Moses, of all human instruments, was the Mediator par excellence (Ex. 32:30-32; Num. 12:6-8; Gal. 3:19; Heb. 3:2-5). He was the Mediator of the Old Covenant, because it was through his instrumentality that the Covenant at Sinai was dispensed and ratified (Ex. 19:3-8; 24:3-8; Acts 7:37-39). It is with Moses that Jesus

NOTES

as Mediator of the New Covenant is compared and contrasted.

CHRIST AS MEDIATOR

However, whatever might be said of the Prophets and Priests, or even Moses of the Old Testament, the designation *"Mediator"* belongs preeminently to Christ, and even those men who executed mediatory offices in the Old Testament institution were thus appointed only because the institution in which they performed these functions was the shadow of the archetypical realities fulfilled in Christ (Jn. 1:17; Heb. 7:27-28; 9:23-24; 10:1). Jesus, even as we are here studying, is the Mediator of the New Covenant (Heb. 9:15; 12:24). And it is a Better Covenant (Heb. 8:6) because it brings to consummate fruition the Grace which Covenant administration actually embodies. Christ is the *"One Mediator between God and men"* (I Tim. 2:5). To invest any other with this prerogative is to assail the unique honor that belongs to Him, as well as to deny the express assertion of the Text.

Though the title *"Mediator"* is not often used, the Scripture abounds in references to the Mediatory Work of Christ.

PREINCARNATE MEDIATION

As the eternal and pre-existent Son, He was Mediator in the creation of the Heavens and the Earth (Jn. 1:3, 10; Col. 1:16; Heb. 1:2). This activity in the economy of creation is correlative with His Mediatorship in the economy of Redemption. The omnipotence evidenced in the former and the prerogatives that belong to Him as Creator are indispensable to the execution of Redemption. It is in Redemption, however, that the extensiveness of His mediation appears. All along the line of the redemptive process, from its inception to the consummation, His mediacy enters.

Election as one might say, which refers to the fact that God elected that humanity would be saved by the Sacrifice of Christ, is the ultimate fount of Salvation, and of course, could not take place apart from Christ. All were chosen in Him before the foundation of the world, which means, that the great plan of Salvation was formulated in the Mind of God, before man was ever created (Eph. 1:4; I Pet.

1:18-20). As well, all who will receive Him, are predestinated to be conformed to His Image (Rom. 8:29).

However, it must be ever understood, that Predestination is never centered up on the individual per se, but rather as to how one is saved, and then what is to happen to that person after they are saved. It is always the *"Plan"* which is predestinated, and not actually the person. The person, whether in Salvation or in Sanctification, must cooperate with the *"Plan,"* or else what is predestined cannot be brought to pass.

MEDIATION IN SALVATION AND REDEMPTION

It is particularly in the once-for-all accomplishment of Salvation and Redemption however, that the mediation of Christ comes to the fore (Jn. 3:17; Acts 15:11; 20:28; Rom. 3:24-25; 5:10-11; 7:4; II Cor. 5:18; Eph. 1:7; Col. 1:20; I Jn. 4:9).

The accent falls upon the Death, Blood, and Cross of Christ as the action through which Redemption has been wrought. In the Scriptures the Death of Christ is always conceived of as an event in which Jesus is intensely active in obedience to the Father's Commandment and in fulfillment of His Commission (Jn. 10:17-18; Phil. 2:8).

It is Jesus' activity as Mediator in the shedding of His Blood that accords to His Death its saving efficacy (effectiveness). When Salvation wrought is viewed as Reconciliation and Propitiation, it is here that the mediatory function is most clearly illustrated. Reconciliation presupposes alienation between God and men and consists in the removal of that alienation. The result is Peace with God (Rom. 5:1; Eph. 2:12-17).

Propitiation is directed to the wrath of God, and Jesus, as the Propitiation, makes God propitious or rather reconciled to us (I Jn. 2:2).

CONTINUED MEDIATION

Christ's Mediation is not confined to His Finished Work of Redemption. His Mediatory activity is never suspended. In our participation of the fruits of Redemption, we are dependent upon His continued intervention as Mediator.

Our access to God and our introduction into the Grace of God are through Him; He conveys us into the Father's Presence (Jn. 14:6; Rom. 5:2; Eph. 2:18). It is through him that Grace reigns through Righteousness to eternal life, and Grace and Peace are multiplied to the enjoyment of the fullness of Christ (Rom. 1:5; 5:21; II Cor. 1:5; Phil. 1:11).

The most characteristic exercises of devotion on the part of the Believer are offered through Christ. Thanksgiving and prayer are not only exercised in the Grace which Christ imparts, but also presented to God through Christ, which is a part of His Mediatorial Work (Jn. 14:14; Rom. 1:8; 7:25; Col. 3:17; Heb. 13:15).

The acceptableness of the Believer's worship and service springs from the virtue and efficacy of Christ's Mediation, and nothing is a spiritual sacrifice except as rendered through Him (I Pet. 2:5).

Even the pleas presented to others for the discharge of their obligations derive their most solemn sanction from the fact that they are urged through Christ and in His Name (Rom. 12:1; 15:30; II Cor. 10:1).

CHRIST AS OUR HIGH PRIEST

The continued Mediation of Christ is specially exemplified in His Heavenly Ministry at the right hand of God. This Ministry concerns particularly His Priestly and Kingly offices. He is a Priest forever (Heb. 7:21, 24).

An important aspect of this Priestly Ministry in the Heavens is intercession directed to the Father and drawing within its scope every need of the people of God. Jesus is exalted in His human nature, and it is out of the reservoir of fellow feeling forged in the trials and temptations of His humiliation (Heb. 2:17-18; 4:15) that He meets every need of the Believer's warfare. Every Grace bestowed flows through the channel of Christ's intercession on our behalf (Rom. 8:34; Heb. 7:25; I Jn. 2:1) until the Salvation which He has secured will reach its fruition in conformity to His Image.

The Priestly Ministry of Christ, however, must not be restricted to intercession. He is High Priest over the House of God (Heb. 3:1-6), and this administration involves many other functions as well. In His Kingly office

He is exalted above all principality and power (Eph. 1:20-23), and He will reign to the end of bringing all enemies into subjection (I Cor. 15:25). This is Christ's Mediatorial dominion, and it embraces all authority in Heaven and in Earth (Mat. 28:18; Jn. 3:35; 5:26-27; Acts 2:36; Phil. 2:9-11).

It is Endtime events that will finally manifest and vindicate Christ's Mediatorship; the Resurrection and Judgment will be wrought by Him. All the dead, just and unjust, will be raised by His summons (Jn. 5:28-29). It is in Him that the just will be raised to immortality and incorruption (I Cor. 15:22, 52-54; I Thess. 4:16), and with Him we will be glorified (Jn. 11:25; Rom. 8:17; 14:9).

The final Judgment referred to as *"The Great White Throne Judgment"* will be executed by Him as well (Mat. 25:31-46; Jn. 5:27; Acts 17:31; Rev. 20:11-15).

IN CONCLUSION

Christ's Mediatorship is thus exercised in all the phases of Redemption, from the election of the Plan in God's eternal counsel to the consummation of the Plan as it regards Salvation. He is Mediator in humiliation and as well in exaltation. There is, therefore, multiformity attaching to His Mediatorial activity, and it cannot be defined in terms of one idea or function.

His Mediatorship has as many facets as His Person, Office, and Work. And as there is diversity in the Offices and tasks discharged and in the relations He sustains to men as Mediator, so there is also diversity in the relations He sustains to the Father and the Holy Spirit in the economy of Redemption.

The faith and worship of Him require that we recognize this diversity. And the unique glory that is His as Mediator demands that we accord to no other even the semblance of that prerogative that belongs to Him Alone as the One Mediator between God and man.

GROSS SINS

That's the reason that to place something ahead of the Cross of Christ or to add something to the Cross of Christ, which impugns the Mediatorship of Christ, is at least one of the most awful sins that can be committed. In fact, this is one of Satan's greatest efforts in the field of deception.

NOTES

The Catholic Church is a great case in point, but by no means, the only one. This spirit pervades all of man's proposed relationship with God.

As the Catholic Church makes Mary or even the Church itself the Mediator along with Christ, many Protestants do the same thing as it regards their own particular Churches or Denominations. The moment that anyone thinks that belonging to a particular Church or Denomination, affords one some type of spirituality, one has just sinned against the Mediatorship of Christ.

When one adds anything to the Blood of Christ, or to be more particular, Faith in that Shed Blood, as necessary in order for restoration and forgiveness to be enjoined, one has grossly sinned.

The Blood of Jesus Christ is the only answer for sin, and when penance is added to that Finished Work, we sin against the Mediatorship of Christ, and I would hope that the Reader can understand how gross such a sin actually is!

THE NEW COVENANT

The phrase, *"Of the New Covenant,"* presents the first time the word *"New"* is applied to the Covenant in this fashion. In all other places in which we read of the New Covenant (Lk. 22:20; I Cor. 11:25; II Cor. 3:6; Heb. 8:8, 13; 9:15) a word is used which implies newness of kind and quality; here it is a Covenant which is newly made — literally *"young,"* having all the freshness of youth in comparison with that which long since was waxing old.

The next phrase presents that on which this Covenant, this *"New Covenant"* is based.

THE BLOOD OF SPRINKLING

The phrase, *"And to the Blood of sprinkling,"* presents Christ as the Mediator of a New Covenant through the shedding of His Blood. This is *"blood of sprinkling,"* blood which cleanseth the conscience from dead works to serve a Living God. It was typified by the blood of the Covenant with which Moses sprinkled all the people (Ex. 24:4-8; Heb. 9:19).

"Sprinkling" in the Greek is *"rhantismos,"* and means *"aspersion,"* which refers to the act of scattering. The idea is this:

When the believing sinner accepts Christ, which means to accept what He did at the Cross on our behalf, this refers to the Sacrifice of Himself in the shedding of His Blood. The giving of His spotless, pure, unpolluted, perfect Blood, which contains and is the life of the human being, sufficed in the eyes of God as payment for all sin. The life of Christ was poured out in the shedding of His Blood, a sacrifice to God, which paid the total debt of mankind which was owed by man to God, and Faith in that by man, absolves him of all indebtedness. In other words, God declares the person at that moment and thereafter as *"not guilty."* That's the actual meaning of *"Justification by Faith."*

Let us emphasize again, that all of this is done by Faith on the part of the individual, which means that the person believes in Christ and what He did at the Cross. That being done, all sin is cleansed, which in effect, says that the Blood has been sprinkled over and within the entirety of the individual, leaving nothing untouched (I Jn. 1:7). One might say that the Blood is scattered over the entirety of man's being, thoroughly and completely cleansing him from all sin.

THE BLOOD OF JESUS CHRIST, THE ONLY PAYMENT FOR SIN

This and this alone, the shed Blood of Christ, and one's Faith in that shed Blood is the only payment for sin that God will accept. Let the Reader survey those words very carefully, for they are extremely important.

To which we have already alluded, the great sin of the Church, is attempting to add something to that payment. In fact, this is the problem which attaches itself to all Christians. And what do we mean by that?

It is not only the Cross which brings about our Salvation, but as well, it is the Cross alone which brings about our Sanctification.

That's the reason that we keep saying that the Believer should ever have the Cross of Christ as the object of his faith. There is nothing more important than this! And if the Reader doesn't realize the seriousness of this statement, then the Reader doesn't really understand what is being said.

The only way the Believer can walk free from sin, in other words, with sin not having

dominion over him in some way, which refers to the *"works of the flesh,"* is for the Believer to exhibit constant Faith in what Christ did at the Cross, which then insures the help of the Holy Spirit (Rom. 8:1-2, 11). However, it is so very easy for the Believer to inadvertently fall into the syndrome of *"works."* We do it, not even really realizing that it is *"works."* Perhaps it would be better said in the following manner:

It is impossible for the Believer not to fall into *"works,"* if the Believer doesn't fully understand these things of which we say concerning a perpetual Faith in the Cross of Christ, which means that the Cross is the answer and solution for all problems. The Believer must know and understand as to how the Holy Spirit works within our lives, which is graphically portrayed to us in Romans Chapter 8. As someone has well said, Romans, Chapter 6 portrays to us the *"mechanics of the Spirit,"* which portrays *"how"* He works, as Romans, Chapter 8 portrays the *"dynamics of the Spirit,"* which portrays *"what"* He actually does within our hearts and lives. The tragedy is, most Christians know next to nothing about these things of which we have just stated; therefore, there is no place else to go but *"works,"* which guarantee spiritual defeat (Eph. 2:8-9).

IS THE BLOOD OF CHRIST THE OBJECT OF FAITH FOR THE MODERN CHURCH?

I do not think I'm exaggerating when I say that the modern Church exhibits less Faith in the Cross of Christ than possibly at any time since the Reformation. And I say that with a broken heart, knowing the terrible results that always accrue from such direction.

When I began in the Ministry in the 1950's, the blight of the Church in those days was *"modernism."* This was the new theology, which pretty well denied about everything about the Word of God. To be sure, that problem still prevails in the Church, but has been surpassed of late by a bigger and more horrendous problem.

The Church World which makes up the part which doesn't believe in the Baptism with the Holy Spirit with the evidence of speaking with other tongues, having rejected this light, there is very little left but an empty shell.

Regarding the other half of the Church World which proposes to believe in the Baptism with the Holy Spirit, regrettably, such belief is little more than in name only. Almost the entirety of the Church World, and we speak of both sides which we have just addressed, have for all practical purposes, adopted humanistic psychology as the answer to the ills and aberrations of man. This is a vote of *"no confidence"* as it regards the Cross of Christ, which the Bible claims as the only answer for this dilemma.

And then there are parts of the Charismatic Church World, mostly in the *"Word of Faith"* camp, which are openly repudiating the Cross, referring to it as *"past miseries,"* and *"the greatest defeat in human history."* The greater tragedy is, millions of people who claim to be Spirit-filled are following this erroneous direction, which is little short of blasphemy, if not actually being blasphemy! As Paul said to the Church at Corinth concerning false teachers, *"Ye suffer fools gladly"* (II Cor. 11:19).

In that camp, faith is held up as the answer to man's dilemma; however, the faith of which they speak, is not Faith in the great, Finished Work of Christ, but rather faith in other things. Actually in *"self."* While it's claimed to be *"faith in the Word,"* it is rather faith in a perverted Word. In other words, any faith which is claimed, and claimed to be in the Word of God, must be understood as being in the Cross of Christ, or else one is not properly interpreting the Word (Jn. 1:1, 14, 29).

The Message of the Cross is the only Message which God will recognize. God give us Preachers who will proclaim this Message and Christians who will believe this Message.

THE BLOOD THAT SPEAKS

The phrase, *"That speaketh better things than that of Abel,"* refers to Abel's animal sacrifice as recorded in Genesis Chapter 4.

In the original there is no reference to the blood of Abel shed by Cain, as some have supposed; but the allusion is to the Faith of Abel, or to the testimony which he bore to the great and vital truth of what his animal sacrifice represented, namely Christ. As should be obvious, the Shed Blood of Christ speaks much better things than the blood of the animal sacrifice offered by Abel. One might say it this way: The Blood of Jesus is the *"reality"* of which the offering of Abel was only a *"type."*

Abel proclaimed by the sacrifice which he offered, the great truth, that Salvation could be only by a bloody offering — but he did this only in a typical and obscure manner; Jesus proclaimed it in a more distinct and better manner by the reality.

The object here is to compare the Redeemer with Abel, not in the sense that the blood shed in either case calls for vengeance, but that Salvation by blood is more clearly revealed in the Christian Plan than in the ancient history; and hence illustrating, in accordance with the design of this Epistle, the superior excellency of that of Christ over all which has preceded it.

In fact, there were other points of resemblance between Abel and the Redeemer, but on them the Apostle does not insist. For instance, Abel was a martyr, and so was Christ; Abel was cruelly murdered, and so was Christ; there was aggravated guilt by the murder of Abel by his brother; and so there was in that of Jesus by His brethren — His Own countrymen; the blood of Abel called for vengeance, and was followed by a fearful penalty on Cain, and so was the death of the Redeemer on His murderers — for they said, *"His Blood be on us and on our children,"* and they are yet suffering under the fearful malediction then invoked; but the point of contrast here is, that the Blood of Jesus makes a more full, distinct, and clear proclamation of the Truth, that Salvation is by Blood, and more particularly, the Blood of Christ, than the offering made by Abel ever did.

Such is the contrast between the former and the latter Dispensation; and such the motives to perseverance presented by both.

In the former, and we refer to the Law, all was imperfect and alarming. In the latter, and we refer to Grace as made possible by the Cross, all is alluring and animating, with Heaven opened to the eye of faith.

Having stated and urged this argument, the Apostle, in the remainder of the Chapter, warns those whom he addresses in a most solemn manner against a renunciation of their Faith in Christ.

NOTES

(25) "SEE THAT YE REFUSE NOT HIM THAT SPEAKETH. FOR IF THEY ESCAPED NOT WHO REFUSED HIM THAT SPAKE ON EARTH, MUCH MORE SHALL NOT WE ESCAPE, IF WE TURN AWAY FROM HIM THAT SPEAKETH FROM HEAVEN:"

The exegesis is:

1. Beware that you refuse not Christ Who speaks from Heaven.

2. If the Jews of old did not escape who refused the Law, how can one now escape who refuses the One to Whom the Law pointed, namely Christ?

3. If a Believer ceases to believe in Christ, he then becomes an unbeliever, and will be eternally lost, that is, if remaining in that condition.

IT IS CHRIST WHO SPEAKS

The phrase, *"See that ye refuse not Him that speaketh,"* refers implicitly to Christ.

The glory, the wonders, and the splendor of the Heaven from whence Christ speaks, add to the majesty of His Voice and makes certain the doom of all who turn away from it. To refuse Moses who spake on Earth was to perish; how much surer, therefore, the judgment of those who refuse Christ Who speaks from Heaven (Williams).

The idea is, do not turn away from Him Who has addressed you in the New Dispensation, and called you to obey and serve Him. The meaning is, that God had addressed them in the Gospel as really as He had done the Hebrews on Mt. Sinai, and that there was as much to be dreaded in disregarding His Voice now as there was then.

He does not now speak, indeed, amidst lightnings, and thunders, and clouds, so to speak, but He speaks by every message of Mercy; by every invitation; by every tender appeal. He speaks by His Son (Heb. 1:2); He speaks by the Holy Spirit, and by all His calls and warnings in the Gospel.

In a sense, Paul once again goes back to his words in Hebrews 3:7-8, where he said, *"Wherefore, as the Holy Spirit saith, 'today if you will hear His Voice, harden not your hearts. . .'."*

THE WAY GOD SPEAKS

Several times in this Epistle Judaism and Christianity have been contrasted, and here

the contrast concerns the way God speaks. Some feel there is a contrast between Moses and Christ. This may be so, but the basic contrast is between the way God spoke of old and the way He now speaks. The idea is this:

Some Christian Jews may have even had the thought then, as even some Christians have presently, that inasmuch as this is the day of Grace, the Mercy of God will graciously cover whatever it is they might do. In other words, if they go back into Judaism, trusting in the old Levitical way, instead of the Way of the Cross, that the Mercy and Grace of God would make allowances; however, nothing could be further from the truth. Over and over again in this Epistle, the Apostle warns against such thinking, if in fact, such thinking existed.

There are millions presently who think the same thing. Inasmuch as Grace abounds to a much greater degree than sin, they, therefore, take sin lightly (Rom. 5:20).

Paul's answer to that is cryptic and to the point:

"What shall we say then? Shall we continue in sin, that grace may abound?

"God forbid. How shall we, who are dead to sin, live any longer therein?" (Rom. 6:1-2).

"See" in the Greek is *"blepo,"* and means *"see to it."* It speaks of a continuous action. The idea is *"ever keep a watchful eye open,"* thus, *"ever be seeing to it that you refuse not Him that speaketh."*

"Refuse" in the Greek is *"paraiteomai,"* and means *"to deprecate, to prevent the consequences of an act by protesting against and disavowing it, to decline, refuse, avoid."*

"Him that speaketh" refers back to Jesus, the Mediator of the New Testament Whose Blood speaks of better things than the sacrificial blood which Abel shed regarding the sacrifice of his animal offering.

The Apostle is addressing himself here to the very heart of the Gospel, which speaks of the great Sacrifice of Christ, and the absolute necessity of Faith in that Sacrifice. We must not miss his point, or more particularly, the point of the Holy Spirit.

THE TIME OF THE LAW

The phrase, *"For if they escaped not who refused Him that spake on Earth,"* refers to

God giving the Law on Mt. Sinai. The actual reading of the Text is:

"For if they escaped not when they refused on Earth Him Who warned."

The terrors which accompanied the giving of the Law were designed to impress all hearts with the fearful peril of disobedience. In shrinking from the Voice of Him that warned them on that memorable day, the Hebrews were made to know that they could not escape the declaration of the Law or the terrible penalties which awaited all transgressors.

In fact, Israel of old *"refused Him,"* which means that in their manner of life they rejected what God said and failed to live up to what He commanded (Deut. 5:29), which brought about their destruction in the wilderness. It seems they forgot the terrible warning of Mt. Sinai, even as millions of Christians are forgetting the constant warnings given by the Holy Spirit presently!

NO ESCAPE

The phrase, *"Much more shall we not escape, if we turn away from Him that speaketh from Heaven,"* speaks to both Believers and unbelievers.

The argument is similar to that of Hebrews 2:2-3, where the same word *"escape"* is found. He from Whom they turned aside on Earth is He Who now speaks to us; but then His Voice was heard amidst earthly terrors, now His Revelation comes through His Son Who is exalted in Heaven.

If we do not hearken to the word of life and promise that is ever coming to us from God through His Son, and more particularly, through the great Sacrifice of Himself, it will be because we deliberately *"turn away,"* for the excuse of the panic-stricken Israelites on that day at Sinai, cannot be ours.

The Voice that spoke that day on Earth fell on the outward ear, but He Who speaks from Heaven makes His Voice heard in the inner conscience; the first Voice may well claim not to be understood; however, the Voice which now speaks, will definitely find us out, and is neglected only through stubbornness or will. Much less, then, shall we escape if we turn away from Him Who presently warns from Heaven.

As we have previously stated, under the Old Covenant God spoke through Moses;

under the New Covenant, God speaks through His Son, which pertains to the Sacrificial Offering of Himself on the Cross, all on our behalf. In other words, the Holy Spirit speaks to us, by constantly pointing us to the Cross.

(26) "WHOSE VOICE THEN SHOOK THE EARTH: BUT NOW HE HATH PROMISED, SAYING, YET ONCE MORE I SHAKE NOT THE EARTH ONLY, BUT ALSO HEAVEN."

The diagram is:

1. When God spoke at Sinai, the mountain literally shook.

2. What God now says through His Son, is of far greater import than the old Law. It shakes both Heaven and Earth.

3. What Christ did at the Cross and in His Resurrection, shook both Heaven and Earth.

THE SHAKING OF THE EARTH

The phrase, *"Whose Voice then shook the Earth,"* as stated, refers to the Voice of God which spoke the Law on Sinai. His Voice then was of such magnitude, such power and authority, that the mountain literally trembled when He spoke. It was meant to impress upon Israel the solemnity of the moment, which it most definitely did.

THE PROMISE

The phrase, *"But now He hath promised,"* refers to what Paul will say as it regards the prophecy of Haggai, but as well, the entirety of the Promise from the very beginning, as it regards the Lord Jesus Christ. This Promise had the beginning of its fulfillment at the First Advent of Christ, and will have its total fulfillment at the Second Advent. But irrespective as to how it is approached, it is all in Christ, for He and exclusively, is the *"Promise."*

And to take it a step farther, it is what He did, which refers to the Cross, which literally shook both Heaven and Earth. We must never allow our attention to be drawn away from the Sacrifice of Christ, which has made all things possible, and which fulfills all things.

THE SHAKING

The phrase, *"Saying, yet once more I shake not the Earth only, but also Heaven,"* is taken from Haggai 2:6. As stated, it refers to the First Advent of Christ, Whose Death on the Cross, shook both Heaven and Earth. His Death, and because it atoned for all sin, broke the legal claim of Satan on humanity; therefore, every principality and power in the spirit world of evil, were totally and completely defeated. The Scripture says concerning these things, *"He made a show of them openly, triumphing over them in it"* (Col. 2:14-15).

Consequently, the Voice which now speaks, of course retains its same power as it did on Mt. Sinai, but because of the Cross, now speaks Grace, which brings Salvation, Healing, Reconciliation, Eternal Life, prosperity, and Blessing of every description. In a sense, the *"Voice"* is the same; however, due to what Christ did in His Sacrificial Offering of Himself, all the righteous demands of the Law given that day at Sinai have now been satisfied. *"The handwriting of ordinances that was against us, which was contrary to us, have been taken out of the way, and nailed to His Cross"* (Col. 2:14). One can only shout *"Hallelujah!"*

As well, that which Jesus did at the Cross, will ultimately bring forth *"new Heavens and a new Earth, wherein dwelleth Righteousness"* (II Pet. 3:13).

One can say, and without fear of contradiction I think, that it is the Cross which shook both Heaven and Earth, and in such a way, that the entirety of the world of evil has been totally and completely defeated, which will ultimately see the prevailing of total Righteousness. The deed has been done, and the work is even now being completed.

(27) "AND THIS WORD, YET ONCE MORE, SIGNIFIETH THE REMOVING OF THOSE THINGS THAT ARE SHAKEN, AS OF THINGS THAT ARE MADE, THAT THOSE THINGS WHICH CANNOT BE SHAKEN MAY REMAIN."

The structure is:

1. This *"Word,"* is the Word of the Cross.

2. That which Jesus did at Calvary will ultimately remove all things of the curse and those that are man made which need to be taken away.

3. Only that which is of God, and completely of God, will remain.

THIS WORD

The phrase, *"And this Word,"* refers to the *"Word of the Cross,"* where Jesus atoned for all sin, and opened up the way for believing man, to the very Throne of God.

I Corinthians 1:18 says, *"For the preaching of the Cross is to them that perish foolishness; but unto us which are saved it is the Power of God."*

The word *"preaching"* as here used by Paul, in the Greek is *"logos"*; consequently, it should not have been translated *"preaching,"* but rather, *"Word"* or *"Message."* It would then read, *"For the Word of the Cross. . . ."*

The Cross is the dividing line, the intersection, the foundation, of all that God has done through Jesus Christ to redeem lost humanity. In fact, the Cross is the story of the Bible. It is the foundation of the Faith. From this foundation all doctrine must spring, or else it's not correct Biblical Doctrine. This is *"the Word"* (Jn. 1:1, 14, 29).

YET ONCE MORE

The phrase, *"Yet once more,"* refers to what is going to be done with the Heavens and the Earth, all made possible by the Cross.

Paul said, *"That in the dispensation of the fullness of times* (that which is yet to come) *He might gather together in one all things in Christ* (made possible by what Christ did at the Cross), *both which are in Heaven, and which are on Earth, even in Him"* (Eph. 1:10).

This Passage tells us, that the Cross is of far great magnitude than most could ever begin to think. It addressed not only the terrible problem which faces man, the problem of sin, but it also addressed itself to the revolution of Satan against God, which took place long before man was ever created (Isa. 14; Ezek. Chpt. 28).

Whenever Paul uses the phrase *"in Christ,"* or one of its derivatives such as *"in Him,"* etc., without exception, he's always speaking of what Christ did at the Cross. So, what Jesus there did, answered the entire problem of sin and rebellion, going all the way to its root, which is Satan himself, and his rebellion against God, which started the entirety of the process of evil to begin with.

All that Jesus did at the Cross, has not yet been brought to fruition; however, but to be sure, everything for which He there paid, and He paid it all, will be realized. That realization is portrayed in Revelation, Chapters 21 and 22.

THE REMOVAL

The phrase, *"Signifieth the removing of those things that are shaken, as of things that are made,"* refers to the act of God transferring to a new basis, this present universe which is under the curse of Adam's sin, that new basis being a new and perfect universe.

This universe has been soiled by man's sin and Satan's rebellion against God. Every mark of that sin, which has brought about the curse, must be removed and in totality.

John speaks of this in the words *"I saw a new Heaven and a new Earth: for the first Heaven and the first Earth were passed away"* (Rev. 21:1). The universe was created by God, but it will be made to pass away, and to be substituted by a new universe which will exist forever. Thus, transitory, perishable things must pass away, in order that the eternal things may appear in their abiding value.

To be sure, this shaking has already begun, and actually began when Jesus was crucified. It will continue until all that man has gloried in will be broken to pieces, and he shall learn as Nebuchadnezzar of old that the Most High ruleth in the kingdom of men.

WHICH CANNOT BE SHAKEN

The phrase, *"That those things which cannot be shaken may remain,"* refers to all for which Jesus paid at the Cross. Even as the next Verse says, *"It is a kingdom which cannot be moved."* Consequently, this phrase tells us the following:

It is only Faith in the Cross of Christ which will not be moved, because it cannot be moved. It is that *"which cannot be shaken,"* and in fact, the only thing that *"will remain."* What Jesus did at the Cross is eternal; consequently, it is only the faith evidenced in the Cross which is also eternal.

(28) "WHEREFORE WE RECEIVING A KINGDOM WHICH CANNOT BE MOVED, LET US HAVE GRACE, WHEREBY WE MAY SERVE GOD ACCEPTABLY WITH REVERENCE AND GODLY FEAR:"

The composite is:

1. Due to what Jesus did at the Cross, our Faith in that Finished Work, has placed us into the Kingdom of God.

2. It is a Kingdom which cannot be moved.

3. We receive admittance into this Kingdom by the Grace of God, which was made possible at the Cross.

4. Understanding what God has done to save us, which again refers to the Cross, we should serve Him with reverence and Godly fear.

A KINGDOM

The phrase, *"Wherefore we receiving a Kingdom,"* refers to our entrance into this Kingdom, which was done by the Born-Again experience, and all made possible by the Cross of Christ.

The *"Kingdom"* is not a frequent subject in this Epistle (the word occurs in a quotation in Heb. 1:8 and in the plural in Heb. 11:33). This is in contrast to the synoptic Gospels, where the *"Kingdom"* is the most frequent subject in the teaching of Christ. However, the *"Kingdom"* which we presently have, is only in the spiritual sense. That which He refers to in these Verses pertain not only to that sense, but also to the material sense which is yet to come.

CANNOT BE MOVED

The phrase, *"Which cannot be moved,"* is in contrast to the earthly kingdoms created by man, which can be shaken and in due course will be shaken. Not so God's Kingdom! Paul does not simply say that it will not be shaken, but that it cannot be shaken. It has a quality found in nothing earthly. This *"kingdom"* is founded on the *"Everlasting Covenant,"* which of course refers to what Christ did at the Cross (Heb. 13:20).

I have repeatedly stated in this Volume, that the Cross of Christ which has always been the dividing line between the True Church and the Apostate Church (Gen. Chpt. 4), is now going to be made such by the Holy Spirit in an unmistakable fashion. In other words, the Cross of Christ and its great Message, is going to be so prominently proclaimed, that one will have to either accept it or reject it. According to that statement, it should be obvious as to what remains is the True Church or the Apostate Church. Faith in what Jesus did at the Cross on our behalf, will alone provide a foundation *"which cannot be moved."* Everything else will be shaken and thereby moved.

GRACE

The phrase, *"Let us have grace,"* refers to the product of the Cross.

It should be noticed, that Kingdom is something we *"receive."* It is not earned or created by Believers; it is God's gift.

Grace is simply the goodness of God extended to undeserving Believers. It is made possible, as stated, by the Cross of Christ, and man's Faith in that Finished Work.

The idea of this phrase as Paul uses it, is that these Christian Jews must not go back to the Levitical offerings of *"works,"* but rather must trust in the Grace of God.

GODLY FEAR

The phrase, *"Whereby we may serve God acceptably with reverence and Godly fear,"* in essence, exhorts all to appropriate the enabling Grace of God (Heb. 4:16; 12:15) so that they may serve God so as to be well-pleasing (acceptable) in His sight (Wuest).

"Reverence" in the Greek is *"eulabeia,"* which means *"caution, circumspection, discretion."*

"Godly fear" is from the Greek *"deos,"* which means *"the apprehension of danger."* It is not the word *"phobos"* normally used for fear, which speaks of the terror which seizes one when danger appears. Consequently, *"deos"* speaks, not of a slavish, cringing apprehension, but of a wholesome regard for a Holy God and His standards and requirements, which if a person violates, he must suffer the consequences.

Let not the Reader think, that just because we live in the day of Grace, that God has suspended all judgment. In fact, the very opposite is true:

The Grace of God makes the Lord much more available to all of humanity; therefore, He requires much more of humanity. The Scripture plainly says, *"And the times of this ignorance* (Old Testament Times) *God winked* at (due to the fact that there was little knowledge of God); *but now* (this Day of Grace) *commandeth all men everywhere to repent"* (Acts 17:30). The idea is, *"for unto whomsoever much is given, of him shall be much required"* (Lk. 12:48).

(29) "FOR OUR GOD IS A CONSUMING FIRE."

This Passage is not merely, as people often say, that God out of Christ is a consuming fire, or that He is a consuming fire to the unsaved alone, but it is His very nature that is here in view.

Consuming fire is holiness manifested in Judgment, and God, Who is Light and Love, must consume everything that is contrary to His Holy Will. For the Believer, of course, this will mean eventually absolute conformity to Christ, when the last vestige of the flesh has been destroyed. This is the work of the Spirit, and is meant to be taking place constantly in the heart and life of each Believer. Consequently, we are to walk in Grace, seeking to serve in newness of spirit (by the Power of the Holy Spirit) and not in the oldness of the letter (Law and works).

This is an expression apparently taken from Deuteronomy 4:24. To put it bluntly, Paul emphasizes that God is not to be trifled with. It is easy to be so taken up with the love and compassion of God that we overlook His implacable opposition to all evil.

Admittedly, the Wrath of God is not a popular subject today, but it looms large in Biblical teaching. Paul is stressing the fact that his Readers overlook this wrath at their peril.

The idea is, God has gone to extraordinary lengths to save lost humanity, which refers to the Cross of Christ. If we ignore that terrible price paid, a price incidentally paid by God, and paid not with such corruptible things as silver and gold, but by the Precious Blood of Jesus (I Pet. 1:18-20), the judgment will be commiserate with the quality of the price that was paid. This must not be forgotten!

In fact, Jesus plainly said that the *"Holy Spirit will reprove* (convict) *the world of sin, and of Righteousness, and of judgment:*

"Of sin, because they believe not on Me;

"Of Righteousness, because I go to My Father and you see Me no more;

"Of Judgment, because the prince of this world is judged" (Jn. 16:8-11).

The word *"judgment"* as it is here used by Christ, plainly tells us that Satan has already been judged, and all who follow him will be judged likewise. That judgment will be on the basis of men *"not believing in Christ,"* which means that they did not believe Him as it regards Who He was and is, and What

He did as it regards the Salvation of lost humanity by going to the Cross. The Cross rejected, is judgment deserved!

"If you from sin are longing to be free,
look to the Lamb of God;
"He, to redeem you, died on Calvary,
look to the Lamb of God."

"When Satan tempts, and doubts and
fears assail, look to the Lamb of God;
"You in His strength shall over all
prevail, look to the Lamb of God."

"Are you weary, does the way seem
long? Look to the Lamb of God;
"His love will cheer and fill your heart
with song, look to the Lamb of God."

"Fear not when shadows on your
pathway fall, look to the Lamb of God;
"In joy or sorrow Christ is all in all,
look to the Lamb of God."

━━■━━

CHAPTER 13

(1) "LET BROTHERLY LOVE CONTINUE."

It is said that *"brotherly love"* is the most important virtue in the New Testament. Those who are linked in the common bond having been saved through Faith in the Death of Christ, cannot but have warm feelings toward one another (Rom. 12:10; I Thess. 4:9; I Pet. 1:22; II Pet. 1:7). Calvin said, *"We can only be Christians if we are Brethren."*

Furthermore, brotherly love cannot continue, unless the Cross continues to be the object of our Faith.

"Brotherly love" as used here by Paul is from the Greek word *"philadelphia."* It is not *"agape"* normally used of God's love (Jn. 3:16), which is produced in the heart of the yielded Believer by the Holy Spirit (Rom. 5:5). As well, it is not the type of love defined by Paul in I Corinthians Chapter 13.

The particular Greek word for love here used is *"phileo,"* which speaks of *"human affection, fondness, a nonethical, though perfectly legitimate, form of love."* It refers to our social actions one might say, toward our brothers and sisters in the Lord.

NOTES

In the general decay of their faith, and we continue to speak of Christian Jews, tendencies to disown Christian fellowship had obviously become apparent (Heb. 10:24-25).

The word *"brother"* in the Greek is *"adelphos,"* and means *"from the same womb."* Thus, the basis of their Christian fondness and affection for each other, the Source of their Christian fellowship, was the fact that they all came from the same Source, having one Father God, and Him being their Heavenly Father, due to the fact that Jesus had died for them on the Cross. The idea seems to be:

Due to some of the Christian Jews seriously considering going back into Judaism, it seems there had been an estrangement between them and the Jews who were remaining loyal to the Lord. Hence Paul is telling the faithful Jews that they should continue to show brotherly love toward the defectors, at least where possible.

BROTHERLY LOVE

The admonition given here by the Apostle, is quite different from that practiced by most modern Denominations.

First of all, it certainly would be obvious that the situation among these Jews in Paul's day was of far greater severity than most anything at present. Some of these Christian Jews were turning their backs on Christ, actually repudiating Him, even denying Him, which they had to do in order to go back into Judaism. Paul is telling the Jews who had continued to be faithful, as stated, that they were to continue to be kind and gracious to these individuals, whatever they had done, and whomever they may have been.

At the present time, many if not most religious Denominations, if a Preacher doesn't obey whatever it is they say to do, and irrespective as to how unscriptural it might be, two things are then set in motion:

First of all, they practice *"shunning,"* on the individual in question. Friends are parted and even members of an immediate family. It is somewhat like the Jewish practices of old as it regarded excommunication, when all type of curses were pronounced upon the individual who was out of favor.

The second thing carried out pertains to every effort being made, to utterly destroy the Ministry of the one in question. They will go to any lengths to do this, not only in their own Denomination, but will seek to reach outside of their Denomination to carry out their perfidious work. They take the position that inasmuch as the individual has refused to obey them, he is now *"fair game."* In other words, anything they desire to do to him, and I mean anything, they legitimize, claiming they have the spiritual right to do so.

I realize that most of the laity would have absolutely no knowledge of these things of which I say. In fact, most would think that such attitudes and actions went out in the Dark Ages, never dreaming that such continues to be carried out in practice, in many if not most religious Denominations.

As I've stated, such actions are quite different than the admonition of the Holy Spirit through Paul, to *"let brotherly love continue."* In other words, the Apostle is saying, that just because these Jews have turned their backs on Christ, as terrible as that might be, love for the person is not to be discontinued. While of course, fellowship in such a case would be disrupted and even completely severed; still, the practice of love towards such an individual must continue, wherever possible. In fact, this is the very heart of Christianity.

(2) "BE NOT FORGETFUL TO ENTERTAIN STRANGERS: FOR THEREBY SOME HAVE ENTERTAINED ANGELS UNAWARES."

The exegesis is:

1. As love has been made the foundation, duty is now expressed as it regards Christians.

2. Sometimes angels, we are here told, are disguised as men.

3. The idea is great blessing will always follow Christian hospitality.

STRANGERS

The phrase, *"Be not forgetful to entertain strangers,"* presents the Apostle under the guidance of the Holy Spirit, broadening his original statement.

In those days, accommodation at inns was expensive, and in any case inns generally had a bad reputation. But as Christian Preachers traveled around, Believers gave them lodging and so facilitated their mission. In fact, without hospitality in Christian homes,

the spread of the Faith would have been much more difficult (Morris).

Whereas it would be a pleasure to show hospitality to some Preachers, unfortunately, the same could not be said for all. It seems that some Preachers possibly during that particular time, had made a nuisance of themselves, actually imposing on their hosts. After several rounds of this, one can see that many Christian families just simply would not want to get involved again. However, if too many took this position, the work of God could be seriously hindered; consequently, the Apostle, as guided by the Holy Spirit, in effect, tells Christian families everywhere, to not withdraw from this very necessary work, to make the best of the situations, and who knows, in their entertaining of *"strangers,"* they may even entertain an angel at times without knowing it, until later.

It is very unfortunate that Preachers at times are lacking in tact, thoughtfulness, and even kindness. Far too many take the position that just because they are a Preacher, the Church owes them something, etc. As well, sometimes the supposed calling seems to be a cover for *"laziness."*

While there are definitely true men and women of God who do not conduct themselves in this fashion; still, there are far too many who do!

ANGELS

The phrase, *"For thereby some have entertained angels unawares,"* definitely would have had a tendency to provide a positive incentive.

Inasmuch as the word *"Angels,"* means *"Messengers,"* some have attempted to abbreviate this statement as referring to certain Preachers as special messengers of God, etc. While that definitely could have a bearing here, and no doubt does, we must not rule out the principal direction of the statement, which actually refers to literal Angels.

The doctrinal part of Paul's Epistle to the Hebrews is now finished, and this last Chapter gives us, as is usual in the Apostle's writing, exhortations regarding the behavior of those who have laid hold in faith upon the truth heretofore declared. Brotherly love, as stated, is emphasized. Those who have been drawn to Christ out of a world that rejects Him should be characterized by love for each other. Regrettably, it has often been otherwise.

If our Christianity doesn't address itself to practical living, which refers to our conduct toward our fellow Brother and Sisters in the Lord, then our Christianity is very weak. Proper profession will always translate into proper practical application.

(3) "REMEMBER THEM THAT ARE IN BONDS, AS BOUND WITH THEM; AND THEM WHICH SUFFER ADVERSITY, AS BEING YOURSELVES ALSO IN THE BODY."

The diagram is:

1. With the persecutions now beginning, some Christians were imprisoned for their Faith. Fellow Christians were exhorted not to forget these.

2. Despite the potential of persecution because of association, still, Christians were to look at those imprisoned for their faith, as being a part of their family, in which they actually were, their Christian family.

3. All Believers are a part of the Body of Christ, which means that all Believers are members of the same Family of God.

BONDS

The phrase, *"Remember them that are in bonds,"* refers to Christians who were beginning to be imprisoned for their faith. So this means, that the Epistle to the Hebrews was probably written by Paul after he had been released from his first imprisonment, which imprisonment is recorded in the Book of Acts (Acts, Chpts. 23-28).

In A.D. 64 much of the city of Rome was destroyed by fire. To divert the suspicion that he had started it for his own entertainment, Nero accused the Christians of having done this thing, about whom the public were also prepared to believe the worst.

Having forced a conviction for arson against certain Christians, he conducted mass arrests, and among other tortures, burned his victims alive in public.

What was disastrous for the Christians was that Nero's action had left a legal precedent for translating this popular position into official action.

It is believed that Paul may have been released from prison in Rome in about A.D. 62;

although, this date varies with different Scholars. At any rate, the persecution of Christians would have begun in A.D. 64.

At this particular time, prisoners were not well treated, and they depended — often even for necessities like food — on sympathizers. Sometimes people withheld help for fear of identifying themselves with the prisoners and thereby suffering similar punishment. But Christians are told here by Paul to have compassion on those in prison *"as if you were their fellow prisoners."*

FELLOW PRISONERS

The phrase, *"As bound with them,"* refers to the statement just made, *"fellow prisoners."* The idea was according to the following:

"If one part suffers, every part suffers with it" (I Cor. 12:26). Believers should feel so much for their friends in prison and for *"those who are mistreated"* that they become one with them. Compassion must be an essential part of Christian Living.

In back of all of this, the idea is, the very ones who were supplying help for those imprisoned, may very shortly be dependent on others for the same type of help.

THE BODY OF CHRIST

The phrase, *"And them which suffer adversity, as being yourselves also in the body,"* refers to the Body of Christ, and that if one suffers, as stated, in a sense, all suffer.

While oftentimes, the head of the house was imprisoned, their families were left with little way to care for themselves, with many losing what few possessions they actually had, and all because they would not acknowledge the lordship of Caesar. *"Remember them,"* Paul is saying.

Many families had lost their fathers or mothers because of martyrdom; some were left orphaned and alone. How so much these needed the love and compassion of other Christians!

(4) "MARRIAGE IS HONOURABLE IN ALL, AND THE BED UNDEFILED: BUT WHOREMONGERS AND ADULTERERS GOD WILL JUDGE."

The structure is:

1. Marriage is sanctioned and encouraged by the Holy Spirit.

2. Lawful sex between a husband and wife holds no defilement.

3. To satisfy the sex drive outside of marriage, will find the one doing such, ultimately judged by God.

MARRIAGE

The phrase, "Marriage is honourable," presents the Apostle addressing here a position in the Early Church which wasn't Sound Doctrine.

There seemingly was an effort being made to show that celibacy was a more holy state; that there was something in marriage that rendered it dishonourable for those who were in the Ministry, or for those of either sex who would be imminently pure. In fact, this same question keeps popping up even until this present time.

Celibacy is one of the supports on which the Papal system rests, and has been one of the principal upholders of all the corruptions among Priests and Nuns. This is certainly not to say this group alone has these problems of immorality; however, I think we can say without any fear of contradiction, that immorality is far more prevalent in the Catholic Priesthood than in any other similar rank of society.

The Apostle here asserts, without any restriction or qualification, that marriage is honourable in all; and this proves that it is lawful for Ministers of the Gospel to marry, and that the whole doctrine of the superior purity of a state of celibacy is false.

NO IMPURITY IN MARRIAGE

The phrase, *"And the bed undefiled,"* pertains to the fact that sexual intercourse between a husband and wife present no defilement, whether spiritually or physically. The Holy Spirit through the Apostle proclaims the physical side of marriage as important and *"pure."* Contrary to the views of some thinkers in the ancient world, there was nothing defiling about it.

IMMORALITY

The phrase, *"But whoremongers and adulterers God will judge,"* proclaims all sexual conduct outside of marriage as being absolutely defiled. This means that all forms

of sexual sin come under the Judgment of God, at least if not repented of and forsaken. In fact, this was a novel view to many in the First Century. For them chastity was an unreasonable demand to make; consequently, the Gospel of Christ charted a new course in its day in a heathen world that was filled with immorality of every stripe.

The New Testament speaks just as strongly as the Old Testament against immorality of every nature. However, there is an important shift of rationale. There is a powerful new reason why sex outside of marriage is repugnant to the Lord. But some New Testament statements on immorality have often been misunderstood.

For instance, the New Testament never suggests that immorality is acceptable. But it makes clear how we should deal with individuals who fall short.

DEALING WITH THE WORLD

We must not avoid such persons who are outside the Christian fellowship. Paul told the Corinthians not to associate with *"sexually immoral people."* Later he had to write and explain.

He did *"not at all mean"* to suggest withdrawal from *"the people of this world"* (I Cor. 5:10). That would mean isolation from the very people Christians are called to lead to Jesus! Certainly Jesus did not avoid such persons; and as the story of the woman caught in the act of adultery illustrates, Jesus' first concern was to bring forgiveness, and then, with it, release from the power of every kind of sin (Jn. 8:1-11).

CHRISTIANS

There must be discipline for those within. Thus, sexual immorality in the fellowship is to be dealt with decisively by the Christian community, especially if the individual refuses to repent (I Cor. 5:1-12).

The rationale is explained in I Corinthians 6:12-20. In a Christian's relationship with Christ, the Believer is actually an organic part of the Lord's Body. It is unthinkable that Christ would be involved in immorality. Thus, our bodies, linked with Jesus and being the temples of the Holy Spirit, must be kept holy. We are to treat ourselves as holy instruments, to be used in God's service and not involved in sexual sins.

Finally, Paul reminds us, *"You are not your own: you were bought with a price. Therefore honor God with your body"* (I Cor. 6:19-20).

The Scripture plainly tells us that judgment is coming for those who fail to heed the warning as it regards sexual immorality. Those who practice such and refuse to repent will ultimately be judged and excluded from the Eternal Kingdom (I Tim. 1:10; Heb. 13:4; Rev. 21:8; 22:15).

THE WAYS OF THE LORD

As we've already stated, sexual intercourse outside of marriage is sin for both the married and the unmarried. God forbids it, for our good. The Commandments against adultery and sexual immorality are rooted deep in the character of God as a faithful and loyal person. We are to mirror His faithfulness and show the same kind of loyalty in our relationships.

The serious nature of adultery or immorality of any nature, are seen in references to it in the Old Testament and in the Book of Revelation as an illustration of the ultimate unfaithfulness, apostasy, and spiritual idolatry. The New Testament reinforces the serious nature of sex sins for Believers by reminding us that we are linked forever with Christ and indwelt by the Holy Spirit. Jesus has paid the ultimate price for us, and, as His Own people now, we are to commit our bodies to the Lord's service, thereby not to serve sinful passions.

Every human being, having a sex drive, will experience the pull of temptation toward immorality of some nature. To surrender is not only wrong but also foolish. Like other sins, immorality erodes our character and brings guilt and suffering. As the Biblical proverbs remind us, we need to be guided by the traditions of the Godly and the commands of the Scripture, for they are *"the way to life, keeping you from the immoral woman, from the smooth tongue of the wayward wife. Do not lust in your heart after her beauty or let her captivate you with her eyes, for the prostitute reduces you to a loaf of bread, and the adulteress preys upon your very life"* (Prov. 6:23-26).

Even though this Passage in Proverbs deals more so with idolatry and spiritual adultery

NOTES

than anything else, it definitely also includes physical immorality.

(5) "LET YOUR CONVERSATION BE WITHOUT COVETOUSNESS; AND BE CONTENT WITH SUCH THINGS AS YE HAVE: FOR HE HATH SAID, I WILL NEVER LEAVE THEE, NOR FORSAKE THEE."

The structure is:

1. *"Conversation"* should have been translated *"manner of life."*

2. The exhortation is against covetousness in the form of love of money.

3. *"Content"* refers here to the ability of the Christian who is dependent upon the Holy Spirit, to be independent of outward circumstances.

4. Dependent upon the Holy Spirit, we should be happy with what He provides.

5. The Lord will always come to our rescue.

MANNER OF LIFE

The phrase, *"Let your conversation,"* as stated, should have been translated, *"manner of life."* The word *"conversation"* today is limited in its meaning to converse between two or more persons; however, in A.D. 1611, when the King James Version was translated, it then meant what the Greek word means, *"manner of life, behavior."*

COVETOUSNESS

The phrase, *"Be without covetousness,"* in effect says, *"let your manner of life be without covetousness."*

Covetousness is a very grave sin; indeed, so heinous is it that the Scriptures class it among the very gravest and grossest crimes against man and God (Eph. 5:3). In Colossians 3:5, the Holy Spirit through Paul classifies it as *"idolatry,"* while in I Corinthians 6:10, it is set forth as excluding a man from Heaven.

Its heinousness, doubtless, is accounted for by its being in a very real sense the root of so many other forms of sin:

1. Departure from the faith (I Tim. 6:9-10).

2. Lying (II Ki. 5:22-25).

3. Thievery (Josh. 7:21).

4. Domestic trouble (Prov. 15:27).

5. Murder (Ezek. 22:12).

6. Many foolish and hurtful lusts (I Tim. 6:9).

Covetousness has always been a very serious menace to mankind, whether in the Old Testament or New Testament period. It was one of the first sins that broke out after Israel had entered into the Promised Land (Josh. Chpt. 7); and also in the early Christian Church immediately after its founding (Ananias and Sapphira, Acts Chpt. 5); hence so many warnings against it.

A careful reading of the Old Testament will reveal the fact that a very great part of the Jewish Law — such as its enactments and regulations regarding duties toward the poor, toward servants; concerning gleaning, usury, pledges, gold and silver taken during war — was introduced and intended to counteract the spirit of covetousness.

THE MODERN GREED GOSPEL

Never before in the history of the Church has covetousness been given such a place of honor as it has presently. It has been disguised under the heading of *"faith,"* when it reality, it is pure greed. I speak of the modern greed gospel.

Unfortunately, the far greater majority of the modern so-called *"faith ministry"*, has sunk to the abominable level of none other than pure greed. Seminars abound on *"how to be successful,"* with the emphasis totally and completely resting on *"money"* and the things that money can buy. Righteousness and Holiness are *"out,"* while money is *"in!"*

One religious con artist, who goes under the pretension of being a Preacher, says over Television, *"God wants you to be rich!"* And then he adds, *"If He doesn't want you to be rich, then God lied!"*

"Get rich quick" schemes abound over what is referred to as *"Christian Television,"* by gullible Christians being told, *"if you'll give so much money, you will get ten times as much in return,"* or some such like figure. If these religious scams were practiced over the secular media, the perpetrators could expect to go to jail.

So, why do Christians send millions of dollars to such scams, when it is so obviously unscriptural?

Quite possibly, the correct answer is, *"covetousness appeals to covetousness!"*

CONTENTMENT

The phrase, *"And be content with such things as ye have,"* presents the underlying thought that one should be satisfied with that which meets our need, and that we not desire more than meets our need.

"Content" in the Greek is *"arkeo,"* and means *"to be possessed of unfailing strength, to be strong, to suffice, to be enough, to be satisfied, contented."* Taking the word on out to the totality of its Greek meaning, we find the word *"self,"* which actually means, *"to be self-sufficient."*

This latter word was used by the Stoics to express the favorite doctrine of the sect, that man should be sufficient to himself for all things, able by the power of his will to resist the shock of circumstance.

In a sense, this is correct in a Scriptural way, but in an entirely different manner.

For instance, Paul was self-sufficient because he was Christ-dependent; therefore, the word *"content"* refers here to the ability of the Christian dependent upon the Holy Spirit and, therefore, independent of outward circumstances. As should be obvious, there is a tremendous lesson here.

THE CHRISTIAN AND CIRCUMSTANCES

The Child of God upon coming to Christ enters into God's economy. This is outlined in Luke 12:15-34.

As should be understood, every Believer should be zealous and industrious, for God hates laziness. At the same time, we are to look to the Lord for our sustenance regarding everything, and that means taking everything to Him in prayer. We are to seek His Will as it regards all things, thereby, trusting Him completely.

Consequently, such a Believer is not dependent on circumstances as it regards the system of this present world. Our Source is God and God Alone! He, who feeds the ravens, will definitely feed us!

THE PROMISE OF GOD

The phrase, *"For He hath said, I will never leave thee, nor forsake thee,"* was probably taken by Paul from Joshua 1:5 and I Chronicles 28:20.

In the Greek the phrase *"He hath said,"* actually states, *"He Himself hath said."* That is, the Lord Jesus Himself Personally made this Promise.

The word *"leave"* is not from the usual Greek word which means, *"to leave,"* but from a word which means, *"to uphold"* or *"sustain."* In the Greek there are two negatives before the word *"leave,"* presenting a very strong statement. The Promise is *"I will not, I will not cease to uphold or sustain thee."* We are assured, therefore, of the sustaining Grace of God as we go through trials and testing times.

The word *"forsake"* is a composite of three words, *"to leave," "down,"* and *"in."* The first has the idea of forsaking one. The second suggests rejection, defeat, helplessness. The third refers to some place or circumstance in which a person may find himself helpless, forsaken.

The meaning of the word is that of forsaking someone in a state of defeat or helplessness in the midst of hostile circumstances. The word means in its totality, *"to abandon, to desert, to leave in straits, to leave helpless, to leave destitute, to leave in the lurch, to let one down."*

There are three negatives before this word, making the Promise one of triple assurance. It is, *"I will not, I will not, I will not forsake thee."*

This means, that not only do we have the assurance of God's all-sufficient sustaining Power to hold us true to Him and in perfect peace as we go through testing times, but we have His Promise that He will never abandon us, never desert, us, never leave us in straits but will come to our help, never leave us destitute but will supply all our need, never leave us in the lurch but will see to it that we are rescued from the difficulties in which we sometimes find ourselves. He will never let us down (Wuest).

(6) "SO THAT WE MAY BOLDLY SAY, THE LORD IS MY HELPER, AND I WILL NOT FEAR WHAT MAN SHALL DO UNTO ME."

The diagram is:

1. On the authority of the Word of God, we can boldly exclaim our confidence in the Lord, that He will help us.

2. To have the Lord has one's helper, is to have the highest authority and power there is.

3. If the Lord is our helper, we need not fear man.

BOLDNESS

The phrase, *"So that we may boldly say,"* proclaims not only what we ought to say, but also the manner in which it should be said.

"Boldly" in the Greek is *"tharrheo,"* and means, *"to exercise courage, to have confidence, to be of good cheer."* Consequently, when we declare the sure Promises of God, we are not being reckless. We are simply taking God at His Word and acting confidently in full assurance of His love.

All of this means that despondency should be foreign to the true Christian.

However, the weight of such boldness must never be within ourselves, in other words of our strength and ability or even our faith, but rather in Christ and Christ Alone! There is such a thing as a bold bravado which goes under the guise of faith, but rather is centered up in self. This mostly comes from those who do not understand the Cross.

If our faith is proper, that is according to the Word of God, it will always and without exception be anchored in the Cross of Christ. This is where God made everything possible for us, through the Sacrifice of His Son and our Savior, the Lord Jesus Christ. Faith in that completely destroys false self-confidence. It puts the emphasis where it belongs, which is completely in Christ. In fact, proper boldness or proper faith can only be had by the Believer, if the Believer properly understands the Cross. Otherwise, our acclamations are little more than arrogance.

HELPER

The phrase, *"The Lord is my helper,"* is derived from Psalms 118:6. As stated, there could be no higher authority and power.

"Lord" in the Greek is *"kurios,"* and is actually the Greek derivative of the Hebrew word *"Jehovah."* It speaks of *"covenant."*

In the Old Testament when *"Lord"* was used, it as well referred to *"Covenant,"* but it referred to that which was to come, namely the Lord Jesus Christ. Now it refers to that which has come, meaning we now have a fulfilled Covenant, i.e., *"the New Covenant"* (Heb. 12:24). And of course, and as should be obvious, this Covenant is what Jesus did at the Cross on our behalf.

So, *"The Lord is my helper,"* or rather is able to help me, according to His great Sacrifice at Calvary. While the Covenant was definitely valid before the Cross, it is even more valid presently, because it is now based on an accomplished fact, and not merely a Promise to come.

The idea is, due to the Finished Work of the Cross, the Lord has much more latitude in order to help us. The idea also is, He wants to help us, and in every capacity.

HELPER IN WHAT?

He wants to help us in everything!

The first thing the Believer should do is to set out to learn the Word of God. Of course, this is a lifelong project, but it is amazing how the Holy Spirit will open up the Word, if the Believer with diligence, sets himself to learn the Word. And to give you a head start, if the Believer will understand that the Bible is the story of Redemption, which is centered up in the Cross and will, therefore, place his faith totally and completely in that Finished Work, he will find the Word of God much easier to understand.

In this capacity, prayer becomes very important as well. We should talk everything over with the Lord, seeking His leading and guidance in all things. Nothing is too small for His attention (Mat. 10:29-30), and nothing is too big for Him. We must understand, that He wants to lead us, wants to guide us, wants to give direction, wants to give wisdom, and wants to help and in every capacity. We will find that such help is forthcoming, if we have a proper relationship with Him, which demands a knowledge of the Word, and a diligent prayer life. Prayer establishes communication and relationship.

And then of course, one of, if not the most powerful ingredient of all, is Faith. But yet, we cannot properly have Faith if we do not know the Word of God and its Author as we should.

And let the Reader understand, as we've been saying over and over again in this Volume, the great, Finished Work of Christ, must ever be the object of our Faith. That is the same as saying that the Word is the object

of our Faith, that is if we properly understand the Word (Rom. 10:17). As we've already stated, the Word and the Cross are in one sense of the word, synonymous. The Word being the story of man's Redemption means that if we are to properly understand the Word, we must as well understand the reason for the Word, which is the great Sacrifice of Christ.

To have the Lord as one's helper is the guarantee of success; however, we should understand that *"success"* with the Lord, might not be our idea of success. He has a will for us, and we should seek that will constantly. The problem with many Christians is, they're trying to force the Lord into helping them to carry out their own personal will, instead of His Will, which He of course, will never do. He has a will for our life, and He will definitely help us achieve that will, which is a million times better for us than anything else of which we might think.

MAN-FEAR

The phrase, *"And I will not fear what man shall do unto me,"* tells us several things:

1. If our Faith is properly placed in Christ, the Lord is guiding our lives. As should be obvious, He has all power.

2. Consequently, man can do no more to me than the Lord permits, and whatever the Lord does permit, will be for our own good.

3. Consequently, there should be no man-fear in our hearts whatsoever. Men may rule, but God is constantly in the business of overruling.

4. As stated, the Believer is in the economy of God, which is totally different than the economy of this world. Those who do not know the Lord, in some way, definitely do have man-fear.

Richard Nixon, the former President of the United States, was once asked the following question: *"Mr. President, how many friends did you have left after Watergate?"*

The President's answer was rather revealing. He said: *"Most people are your friend because of what you can do for them or to them."*

Regrettably that's true, but at the same time, and to which the President was alluding, such individuals really aren't friends.

Nevertheless, at least part of that scenario refers to the fear factor. But what a pleasure it is, to be able to live this life and not have to fear what man can do to you. We know, even as the previous Chapter proclaims, that at times, the Lord did not choose to deliver individuals from particular evil men. In other words, He allowed some Believers to be tortured, and even to be killed; however, irrespective as to what it looked like on the surface, and irrespective as to the instruments used, it was God Who was in control all along. We as Believers have to understand that. We belong to Him, and whatever happens to us, whether it be positive or that which looks to be negative, it is always either caused by the Lord or allowed by the Lord. Either way, He does it for our good, and either way, and as stated, He is always in control.

(7) "REMEMBER THEM WHICH HAVE THE RULE OVER YOU, WHO HAVE SPOKEN UNTO YOU THE WORD OF GOD: WHOSE FAITH FOLLOW, CONSIDERING THE END OF THEIR CONVERSATION."

The structure is:

1. These Christian Jews were reminded to respect Preachers of the Gospel who were attempting to teach them the Word of God.

2. The idea is, that these Ministers were faithfully delivering the Word.

3. The Faith of these Preachers was in the Finished Work of Christ, which these Christian Jews were encouraged to follow.

4. Their Faith was a proven Faith, because it resulted in a Christlike manner of life.

PREACHERS OF THE GOSPEL

The phrase, *"Remember them which have the rule over you,"* should have been translated, *"Remember them which are your leaders,"* or *"Remember them who have been chosen by the Lord to serve as your guides."*

"Rule" in the Greek is *"hegeomai,"* and means, *"to lead, to guide."*

If we are correct in believing, despite what many have alleged to the contrary, that the Apostle Paul was the author of this Epistle, we can well understand how earnestly he would now plead for complete separation from the ancient system as it regarded these Christian Jews, the glory of which had departed since the rejection of God's Son.

The dark clouds of judgment were hanging low over the land of Palestine. In a little while the city would be a ruined heap. No more would the smoke of sacrifice ascend from Jewish Altars. Moreover, most of the apostolic company had either been called Home or were laboring in distant lands. Paul himself was very shortly to be martyred by the executioner's ax.

With all these things pressing upon his soul, he urges the Hebrew Believers to make a complete break with that system which had rejected the Lord of Glory (Ironside).

At any rate, Christ had fulfilled all of the Levitical Law, and for it to be continued was an insult. As well, I think the Lord was greatly displeased with Christian Jews attempting to maintain the Levitical order along with belief in Christ. One or the other had to go, which is what this Epistle is all about.

There are some who claim that Paul is here addressing Ministers who have already gone on to be with the Lord, encouraging these Believers to remember what these Preachers had taught them as it regards the Word of God; however, it doesn't really matter whether he was speaking of those since gone or those presently ministering, the admonition is the same.

THE WORD OF GOD

The phrase, *"Who have spoken unto you the Word of God,"* refers to preaching and teaching. *"The Word of God"* is the totality of the Christian Message, and the expression reminds the Readers that this is no human invention, but rather of Divine origin.

Ministers of the Gospel who rightly divide the Word of Truth, and then faithfully deliver that Word without compromise, are the greatest asset to any nation or people. The Word of God is the only revealed Truth in the world, and in fact, ever has been. There is nothing more important, and there is nothing more important than faithfully delivering that Word.

It alone holds the answer to the ills of man; it alone can bring about changed hearts and lives; it alone as the song says, *"can take what's wrong and make it right."*

And then again, there is nothing worse than Preachers who compromise the Word of God, or rather pervert it to their own gain and end.

Any people who are unfortunate enough to sit under such Ministers, are unfortunate indeed! And regrettably, for every one Preacher who truthfully and faithfully proclaims the Word of God, there are scores of others who purposely misinterpret it for personal gain, or ignorantly misinterpret it. Either way, such preaching and teaching destroys lives, or at the very least, deprives the people of the benefits they can have in Christ.

FAITH

The phrase, *"Whose faith follow,"* presents that which the proper interpretation of the Word brings about. The object of the Word is *"Faith!"* The object of Faith must be the Finished Work of Christ.

It is my belief, that every Believer in their initial understanding of the Word must without fail understand the Sacrifice of Christ. If that is properly understood, proper Faith will then be generated, and the entirety of the Word of God will begin to come into focus. Considering, that the story of the Bible is the story of man's Redemption, which is the story of the Cross, makes it imperative to understand the Bible in this fashion.

WHAT TYPE OF FAITH ARE YOU FOLLOWING?

If it is to be noticed, the Apostle here proclaims the necessity of these Christian Jews following the faith of those who had correctly preached the Word. This is a very interesting statement. And from this statement we must ask the question, *"Whose faith are you following?"* Or *"What type of faith are you following?"* There is nothing more important than that as it regards your spiritual welfare.

Every Believer in the world, at least in some fashion, follows a particular Preacher. That's not wrong, for the simple reason that the Lord has set in the Church, *"Apostles, Prophets, Evangelists, Pastors, and Teachers."* This is *"for the perfecting of the Saints, for the work of the ministry, for the edifying of the Body of Christ"* (Eph. 4:11-12).

But in reality, what the people are following is the *"faith"* of this particular Preacher. For the Preacher who is into humanistic psychology, the people are following faith in that particular humanistic method. For the

Preachers who espouse the *"greed gospel,"* that is the type of faith being followed. If people are attending a Church pastored by a modernist, they are following the faith of an individual who doesn't believe the Bible, but rather other things.

Believers who follow Pastors who do not believe in the Baptism with the Holy Spirit with the evidence of speaking with other tongues, to be sure, that's the type of faith they will have, which means they will not have the leading and guidance of the Spirit. In fact, the list in this regard is almost endless. That's the reason that I've stated, that those who have the privilege to sit under Preachers who truly and rightly divide the Word of Truth, and faithfully deliver the Word, and who earnestly seek the Lord, that they will be anointed by the Holy Spirit to deliver the Word, such people are blessed indeed! Regrettably, there aren't many of those Preachers around.

MANNER OF LIFE

The phrase, *"Considering the end of their conversation,"* is the same as the word *"conversation"* in Verse 5. It could be translated, *"considering the manner of their lifestyle."* The idea is, whatever type of Faith they have, such Faith will produce a particular type of lifestyle. Nothing could be more important than this, so we should heed these words very carefully.

If our faith is produced by the rightly divided Word, it will at the same time, produce a quality manner of life. Conversely, a perverted Word will produce a perverted lifestyle.

(8) "JESUS CHRIST THE SAME YESTERDAY, AND TODAY, AND FOR EVER."

The composite is:

1. Jesus Christ is the Author and the Finisher of our Faith.

2. Faith anchored in Christ and what Christ has done at the Cross, will never change.

3. This Verse is meant to point to correct doctrine, which is anchored in the Cross of Christ, which the next several Verses proclaim.

JESUS CHRIST

The phrase, *"Jesus Christ the same,"* is meant to portray to the Christian Jews, and everyone else for that matter, that Jesus of

Nazareth of the New Covenant, is the same as the Jehovah of the Old Covenant. And that Person is the Messiah, the unchangeable One. In other words, Christ is the One to Whom the entirety of the Old Covenant pointed; consequently, He is the fulfillment of all the predictions of the Old Testament. This is at least one of the things that made the sin of these people so horrifying! Going back into Judaism meant that they not only were losing Christ, but they were going back into something that actually, at least in the Mind of God, no longer existed.

YESTERDAY, TODAY, AND FOREVER

The phrase, "Yesterday, and today, and forever," covers the entire range of time.

"Yesterday" refers to all the great Faith Worthies of Chapter 12, and that the Lord was very real to them then.

"Today" refers to Paul's time, with the Holy Spirit through the Apostle saying that as the Lord was to the Patriarchs and Prophets of old, He will be to those in the Early Church.

"Forever," refers to our present time and all of the future, guaranteeing that Christ is the same now as then, and will be forever.

Christ doesn't change, which means that the Word of God doesn't change, which means that correct doctrine doesn't change, and which means that Faith doesn't change. While progressive revelation may take men further into the Word of God, the basic foundation will not change. In a sense, everything stays the same.

Admittedly, under the Old Covenant, the Revelation of God was somewhat limited; nevertheless, one will find in the Old Covenant the seed bed of everything we presently have in the New. After the Cross, the Lord is able to reveal Himself in a much greater degree to humanity, and especially to Believers. This is done through the Person of the Holy Spirit, Who functions according to the Finished Work of Christ.

The idea doesn't present itself that Christ changed, but that the Cross made it possible for Him to reveal Himself in a greater way.

(9) "BE NOT CARRIED ABOUT WITH DIVERS AND STRANGE DOCTRINES. FOR IT IS A GOOD THING THAT THE HEART BE ESTABLISHED WITH GRACE;

NOTES

NOT WITH MEATS, WHICH HAVE NOT PROFITED THEM THAT HAVE BEEN OCCUPIED THEREIN."

The exegesis is:

1. Every doctrine that's not based squarely on the Cross of Christ, can be concluded to be "strange," i.e., "perverse."

2. The heart can only be established with the Grace of God, which always comes through the Cross.

3. "Meats" stand for external ceremonies, which can never change the heart.

DIVERS AND STRANGE DOCTRINES

The phrase, "Be not carried about with divers and strange doctrines," refers to anything that changes the object of Faith from the Cross to something else.

Paul has put strong emphasis on the centrality of Christ's Sacrifice and keeps this steadily in view as he approaches the end of his Letter. In his statement here, he does not specify particular erroneous doctrines, for there is no need to do that. The idea is, that irrespective as to what type of doctrine it is, and the Greek word "divers" actually means "many-colored," if it's not based squarely on the Cross of Christ, then it is wrong. The unchangeability of Christ guarantees this.

"Strange" in the Greek is "xcnais," and means "foreign to the Gospel," or that which is not based on the Sacrifice of Christ.

GRACE

The phrase, "For it is a good thing that the heart be established with Grace," actually means that this is the only right way that the heart can be established. The heart, as often, stands for the whole of the inner life; and this is sustained, not by anything material, such as food, ceremonies, etc., but by Grace. God is the Source of the Believer's strength as we live out this Christian life, and He is the Source through what Christ has done for us at the Cross, all made available by the Holy Spirit, according to our Faith in that Finished Work.

As previously stated, the Grace of God, always and without exception, comes to us through what Christ did for us at the Cross, in other words, the Cross was and is the instrument through which Grace is made available. Also, as we have repeatedly stated, the Grace of God is simply the goodness of God extended to undeserving Believers.

MEATS

The phrase, *"Not with meats,"* is meant to refer to all types of religious ceremonies. The idea is the heart of man cannot be changed with outward ceremonies, or rules and regulations for that matter, but only by the Grace of God.

All human systems of teaching will but lead one to another; consequently, the whole scheme becomes more and more elaborate, and, regrettably, the more elaborate it becomes, the more appealing it is to most people. As someone has well said, *"The doing of religion is the most powerful narcotic there is."*

PROFIT

The phrase, *"Which have not profited them that have been occupied therein,"* proclaims everything other than simple faith in Christ and His Finished Work, as of no value.

Many say that religious ceremonies and exercises appeal to them and help them. If that is so, then the Holy Spirit is in error saying that they are profitless. Religious emotion is a very different thing from spiritual endowment. The latter enriches the Spiritual Life; the former impoverishes it.

True Spiritual Life exists only in the realm of Grace. In that realm Christ is all, and self — even religious self — is made dead and kept dead.

The idea of all of this is, it is impossible to live the life we ought to live, in other words to be what we ought to be in Christ, unless we do it the way that it is laid out by the Holy Spirit. The enemy of our souls, and I speak of the Devil, constantly seeks to insert doctrine which is not Biblical. He is very subtle in his approach, and most of the time dresses up his fare in extreme religious garb, which fools most people.

As we have said in every way we know how it should be said, the Cross of Christ is the only answer for humanity. What Jesus there did, even as the next Verses will proclaim, makes it possible not only for us to be saved, but also to live a righteous and a holy life.

NOTES

The Holy Spirit works exclusively according to what Jesus did at the Cross, and our Faith in that Finished Work (Rom. 8:1-2, 11). There is no profit otherwise!

(10) "WE HAVE AN ALTAR, WHEREOF THEY HAVE NO RIGHT TO EAT WHICH SERVE THE TABERNACLE."

The diagram is:

1. The *"Altar"* is used here by Paul as a symbol for the entirety of the Plan of God as it regards the New Covenant.

2. But more specifically, it speaks of the Cross of Christ, and what Jesus there accomplished on our behalf.

3. Paul makes it crystal clear that those Christian Jews who persisted in adhering to the First Testament Sacrifices can have no part in the blessings of the New Testament. One cannot have both. The two Testaments are mutually exclusive.

THE ALTAR

The phrase, *"We have an Altar,"* is used in this sense by Paul, as stated, to describe all that Christ has done at the Cross on behalf of lost humanity. In fact, what He did, replaced in totality all of the Old Covenant, which it was always intended to do. Paul is actually saying that the Cross is distinctive to the Christian way. It was on a Cross that the Christian Sacrifice was offered. Thus, it may not improperly be spoken of as an *"Altar."*

This means, that the Sacrifice, Who is Christ, and which took place on the Cross, is the only Sacrifice that can be accepted by God. At the same time, this means that the old Levitical Sacrifices any more can no longer be accepted by the Lord, as should be obvious, Christ having replaced all of that.

At the same time, the Believer should understand that this *"Altar"* of which Paul here speaks, directs attention only to the Cross of Christ and nothing else, and we speak of modern efforts to replace the Cross. It is Faith in this Altar alone, which God will recognize.

This means, if we try to make our particular *"Church,"* a part of this Altar, or our Denomination, or our good works, or anything else for that matter, we have placed ourselves outside of God's Order. Consequently, I would surely think that the Reader would understand how so very serious this is.

The pronoun *"we,"* includes the entirety of the true Body of Christ, both Jews and Gentiles. In fact, the pronoun *"we"* completely erases all distinctions, meaning that with the Lord it is no more *"Jew or Gentile,"* or even *"male or female,"* for that matter (Gal. 3:28). All are equal at the Cross.

NO RIGHT TO EAT

The phrase, *"Whereof they have no right to eat which serve the Tabernacle,"* bluntly and plainly says, that one cannot serve Christ and the Levitical Order at the same time. In effect, and even bluntly so, the Apostle is saying that the Christian Jews are going to have to cease their activities as it regards Temple worship. By continuing this, they are making a mockery of the Sacrifice of Christ.

At the moment the Apostle was writing these words, the Temple was still standing in Jerusalem, with its Altar in front, on which sacrifices were continually offered. However, in a very short time, all of this was totally destroyed by the Romans, God using the Roman General Titus as His instrument to put a stop to this continued process.

In effect, and even as we have already stated, the modern Church falls into the same category. We cannot serve Christ and the Church at the same time; we cannot serve Christ and our own good works at the same time; we cannot serve Christ and anything else at the same time.

When we speak of *"serving Christ,"* we're speaking of our Faith and Trust being in what Jesus did at the Cross.

The word *"right"* is the translation of the Greek *"exousia"* which has the idea of delegated right or authority. It was a technical term used in the law courts of that day, of a legal right.

The figure of eating at this Altar, and we speak of what Jesus did at the Cross, pertains to the Blessings of the New Testament among which is fellowship with God made possible by the Blood Sacrifice that Christ offered at Calvary. When we place our faith in that Finished Work, that is the same as *"eating His flesh and drinking His Blood,"* which means that we have trusted completely in what He did at the Cross in the offering up of Himself in Sacrifice (Jn. 6:53-56, 63).

THE PROBLEM WITH THE MODERN CHURCH

The problem with the modern Church, is having no faith at all in the Cross of Christ as it concerns our daily living for God, whether either through ignorance or unbelief, or else a divided faith. In other words, many Christians somewhat believe in the Cross, and at the same time somewhat believe in other things as it regards their daily walk before God, i.e., *"their victory."* Either way is disastrous!

The Holy Spirit through the Apostle here plainly tells us, that if we are going to *"serve the Tabernacle,"* which refers to placing our Faith in something that's not the Cross, at the same time, we cannot have the blessings of the Cross. As stated, the two ways are mutually exclusive. Whichever one is accepted, cancels out the other.

(11) "FOR THE BODIES OF THOSE BEASTS, WHOSE BLOOD IS BROUGHT INTO THE SANCTUARY BY THE HIGH PRIEST FOR SIN, ARE BURNED WITHOUT THE CAMP."

The structure is:

1. Paul uses an Old Testament example of the Sacrifices offered on the Great Day of Atonement.

2. This is done to show the superiority of the Sacrifice of Christ over the Levitical Offerings.

3. He portrays in all of this, how that this particular Sacrifice, and in fact all the Sacrifices, were types of Christ, and which were fulfilled in Christ. Consequently, they are no longer needed.

THE ANIMAL SACRIFICES

The phrase, *"For the bodies of those beasts,"* refers to the animal sacrifices of various different types, such as lambs, goats, Bullocks, Rams, etc. All of these were types of Christ, which were meant to portray Christ, as it regarded the Sacrifice of Himself, which He would carry out when He came, and which He did!

FOR SIN

The phrase, *"Whose blood is brought into the sanctuary by the High Priest for sin,"* refers to this particular man, on the Great Day of Atonement, bringing the blood of these sacrificed animals into the Holy of Holies, with it being applied to the Mercy Seat, and as well to the horns of the Altar of Incense.

All of this was carried out because of *"sin."* While the blood of bulls and goats couldn't take away sin, it could in a sense cover sin, until Christ would come.

Man's problem is sin; that means our problem is not economic, but rather sin; our problem is not physical, but rather sin; and sin is a problem for which man has no cure. There is only one cure for this terrible problem, and it is the great Sacrifice of Christ, which refers to the offering up of Himself on the Cross. That and that alone is the remedy!

BURNED

The phrase, *"Are burned without the camp,"* presents here a tremendous truth.

The victim personating sin was wholly burned without the camp, and thus was symbolized God's wrath against sin.

We must understand, that sin is the ruination of everything good on the face of this Earth. It is the cause of all heartache, suffering, pain, sorrow, death, dying, and sickness. It is the cause of all loneliness, all depression, all hurt, all poverty, all hunger, etc. Sin is the destruction of everything that is righteous, holy, and true. That's the reason that God's wrath burns against sin.

When we think of this wrath being poured out upon His only Son, Who took our place, wrath in which we rightly deserved, then we should understand how great the love of God actually is.

In these Verses we have the direct Commandment to come outside the camp of Judaism in holy separation to the Lord Jesus Himself. We have an Altar, He tells us, of which they who serve the Tabernacle have no right to eat; that is, our Altar and our service are all of a Heavenly character.

Since Christ has died, there is no Altar on Earth; but in Heaven, that of which the Golden Altar was a type, where Christ makes intercession for us. To talk of any other Altar, as is done in Romanism for instance, and some sects of Protestantism, is to deny the truth of the Finished Work of Christ.

"No blood, no Altar now,
"The Sacrifice is o'er;

"No flame nor smoke ascends on high,
"The Lamb is slain no more."

(12) "WHEREFORE JESUS ALSO, THAT HE MIGHT SANCTIFY THE PEOPLE WITH HIS OWN BLOOD, SUFFERED WITHOUT THE GATE."

The exegesis is:

1. It was to Jesus that all the Levitical Order pointed, and it is Jesus Alone Who fulfilled and satisfied the Levitical Order.

2. Only what Christ did at the Cross can sanctify a person, which means that person is *"set apart for God."*

3. He made this possible by the shedding of His Own Blood, which refers to His Sacrifice of Himself for sin — sin incidentally which we had committed.

4. As the bodies of the slain animals were taken outside the camp and burned, as it referred to those sacrificed on the Great Day of Atonement, likewise, Jesus suffered outside the city walls of Jerusalem, thereby fulfilling the type.

JESUS

The phrase, *"Wherefore Jesus also,"* presents the human name of Christ, which brings before us the picture of the Man suffering for us.

Paul uses the symbolism of the Great Day of Atonement, in fact, the entirety of the Tabernacle, along with all the Sacrifices, actually every single part of the Levitical Order, all pointing directly to Christ. All of it was meant to typify Him in some manner, as it regards His Life, His Death, His Resurrection, actually His very Exaltation in the Presence of God there to appear on our behalf (Heb. 9:24).

SANCTIFICATION

The phrase, *"That He might sanctify the people,"* refers to being *"set aside for God."* Sanctification regarding its full meaning refers to total victory over sin. It doesn't speak of sinless perfection, because the Bible doesn't teach such; however, it does refer to the fact that one who is sanctified, is not dominated in any way by sin (Rom. 6:14).

The moment the believing sinner comes to Christ, he is instantly washed, sanctified, and justified (I Cor. 6:11). This is because the individual is now in Christ, and all in Christ is perfection; consequently, all Believers at Salvation have the *"position"* of Sanctification. It was not obtained by earning it or meriting it, but by simple Faith in Christ.

However, the actual *"condition"* of the Believer falls far short of his *"position"*; therefore, it is the business of the Holy Spirit, Who now resides in the heart and life of the Believer, which is the case with all who are saved, to bring our *"condition"* up to our *"position."* This can only be done in one manner:

If the Believer attempts to live this life outside of simple Faith in the Cross of Christ, which will forfeit the help of the Holy Spirit, the Sanctification process, which is actually a progressive work, will be halted. That's what Paul was talking about when he referred to *"frustrating the Grace of God"* (Gal. 2:20-21). As the Believer exhibits Faith in the Cross of Christ, and continues to do so, in effect *"taking up the Cross Daily"* (Lk. 9:23), which Jesus said we must do, this will give the Holy Spirit latitude to work, and the Believer will find the Fruit of the Spirit being developed in his heart and life, which of course is the Sanctification process (Gal. 5:22-23). Otherwise, it will be *"works of the flesh"* (Gal. 5:19-21).

THE BLOOD OF JESUS

The phrase, *"With His Own Blood,"* presents the price that was paid, in order that man might be *"sanctified,"* i.e., *"set free from sin."* The expression puts emphasis on the fact that Christ did not need an external victim (as did the High Priests) but brought about the Sanctification in question by the Sacrifice of Himself. *"Blood"* clearly signifies *"death,"* as is commonly the case in the New Testament — and, for that matter, in the Old Testament as well.

We should understand from this, that the situation of man was and is so bad, that it took such a price in order to address the situation; therefore, if such a price was demanded as the Blood of God's Own Son, how in the world do we think we can bring about the needed results in our hearts and lives, outside of the Cross?

WITHOUT THE GATE

The phrase, *"Suffered without the gate,"* presents Christ fulfilling the type, in that He

took the outside place, there to bear the judgment that our sins deserved.

The Sin-Offering was burned *"without the camp."* Jesus Who in all other points fulfilled the Law of Atonement fulfilled it in this point also, in that He suffered *"without the gate"* (Mat. 27:32; Jn. 19:20).

The two expressions answer to one another, each denoting that which lay beyond the sacred precincts, outside the special dwelling place of God's people.

The place where He was put to death was called *"Golgotha,"* the Place of the Skull, and hence the Latin word which we commonly use in speaking of it, *"Calvary"* (Lk. 23:33).

Calvary, as it is now shown, is within the walls of Jerusalem; but when Jesus was crucified, it was outside the walls of the city.

Snell argues from Leviticus 10:1-5; 24:14, 23 that *"people were taken outside the camp"* when they were accursed under the Law and rejected, as much as the ritually useless bodies were after the sacrifice was finished. He goes on to argue that *"our Lord's Offering has been first compared with that on the Day of Atonement"* . . . and it is next said to have involved formal rejection by the authorities of Judaism. In fact, that does seem to be the point of reference.

Jesus was rejected by Jewish authorities, and His Death outside Jerusalem symbolized this (Morris).

(13) "LET US GO FORTH THEREFORE UNTO HIM WITHOUT THE CAMP, BEARING HIS REPROACH."

The diagram is:

1. Paul now exhorts the Christian Jews to leave apostate Judaism and the Temple sacrifices, and serve Christ only.

2. The words *"without the camp,"* proclaim Christ as fulfilling all of the Levitical Order, which should have been understandable by these Jews.

3. Even though the Jews in general claim that Christ was accursed, and because He was Crucified, *"this reproach,"* Paul says, *"must be borne by them."*

UNTO CHRIST

The phrase, *"Let us go forth therefore unto Him,"* presents Christ as the only bearer of Salvation.

Paul is now urging these Christian Jews to leave apostate Judaism once and for all, along with the Temple sacrifices, placing their faith exclusively in Christ as their High Priest. In other words, the Apostle is drawing a line in the sand, so to speak. The Holy Spirit through him is telling the Christian Jews, that it is Christ Alone Who can save, which means that all other ways must be abandoned, even that which was once of God, as Judaism. The idea is this:

If something which was truly of God, as the old Levitical Order, had to be abandoned, simply because Christ had fulfilled all its precepts, then how much more must everything else be abandoned which is man-made in favor of the Cross!

The words *"Let us go forth,"* refers not only to going someplace, but at the same time, it also refers to leaving something. When we go to Christ, we must leave everything else, which means all type of man-made religions.

At first glance, that may seem to be very simple; however, Satan has been so successful at disguising his efforts, that millions think they're trusting Christ, when in reality, they trust something else entirely.

As we've often said in this Volume, millions presently belong to a certain Church, or Denomination, and they think by such association, that such has something to do with their Salvation. In other words, they link belonging to that particular organization with Salvation. Pure and simple, they trust in that particular *"Church,"* and not Christ. They have somehow intermingled the two.

Others do the same with their own good works. For instance, when the Catholic Nun, Mother Teresa died, many Protestants, who should know better, equated her good works with Salvation. Not so!

I do not judge the dear lady, but pure and simple, if she was trusting in her good works to save her, she died eternally lost. That's blunt, but I don't know of any other way to express the statement. That goes not only for her, but also for any other individual who falls into the same category, which in fact, includes most!

Once again, we go back to Cain and Abel (Gen. Chpt. 4). Abel trusted in the death of

the innocent victim, the clean animal, which typified Christ, while Cain trusted in the labor of his own hands, which God could not accept. The situation hasn't changed from then until now. The criteria is still *"Christ and Him Crucified."* If Faith is placed in anything else, it is Faith that God will not recognize.

WITHOUT THE CAMP

The phrase, *"Without the camp,"* represents Christ, as stated, fulfilling the Levitical Order.

The suffering *"without the gate"* was a symbol of His rejection by the Jews. All who would be His must share the reproach which came upon Him, Who was cast out by His people and crucified: they also must go forth *"without the camp,"* forsaking the company of His foes. Each one must for himself make the choice between the Synagogue or Christ; between the two, there can be no fellowship.

This tells us that Christ is outside the camp of Judaism, and the Readers are encouraged to go to Him where He is. To remain within the camp of Judaism would be to be separated from Him.

REPROACH

The phrase, *"Bearing His reproach,"* refers to sharing in the rejection He had undergone. In other words, we as well must *"bear the disgrace He bore."*

To align one's self with Christ is to subject one's self to scorn, reproach, and perhaps more. But consistently throughout the Epistle Paul has argued, as he does here, that it is well worth it.

The Jews held that the way Christ died, which refers to crucifixion, proved him to be accursed (Deut. 21:23; Gal. 3:13). Paul is saying that the Christian Jews must be ready to stand outside Judaism with the Christ Who bore the curse for them *"outside the camp."*

The idea is, that our devotion to Him must be, as if we were going forth with Him when He was led away to be crucified. He was put to death as a malefactor. He was the object of contempt and scorn. He was held up to derision, and was taunted and reviled on His way to the place of death, and even on the Cross.

To be identified with Him there, to follow Him, to sympathize with Him, to be regarded as His friend, would have been subjecting one to similar shame and reproach. The meaning here is, that we should be willing to regard ourselves as identified with the Lord Jesus, and to bear the same shame and reproaches which He did.

When He was led away, amidst scoffing and reviling, to be put to death, would we, if we had been there, have been willing to be regarded as His followers, and to have gone out with Him as His avowed Disciples and friends?

It is easy to profess to love Him when such profession subjects us to no reproach. However, I think the following must be noted:

THE CROSS IS A REPROACH

I think one of the reasons that there is little reproach today in following Christ, is because the Christ being served, is *"another Christ"* (II Cor. 11:4). In fact, the entirety of the *"reproach"* as it regards Christ, is the Cross. It was the Cross then, and it is the Cross now!

I believe the Holy Spirit is about to make the Cross so prominent, so unavoidable, that either it must be accepted or rejected. In other words, there will be no neutral ground!

Now the Reader must consider, that most of the Denominations presently, do not hold up the Cross as the answer to man's dilemma, but rather something else altogether. In fact, their *"gospel,"* which is pure and simple, *"another gospel,"* at least for the most part, is an admixture of several things. Most Denominational leaders, and I think I exaggerate not, hold up their own particular *"Denomination,"* and *"humanistic psychology,"* as the answer to the ills of man. Most of them aren't going to change.

In refusing to change, even as the Pharisees and Sadducees of old who crucified Christ, they will as well, do their best to destroy the messenger of the Cross. In fact, they will not be able to repudiate the Doctrine of the Cross, so they will little take that direction. While there may be some small effort in that direction, for the most part, they will zero their attack on the one who brings the message of the Cross. That's what Cain did, and that's what his followers have done ever since!

(14) "FOR HERE HAVE WE NO CONTINUING CITY, BUT WE SEEK ONE TO COME."

The structure is:

1. *"Here"* represents the fact that the earthly Jerusalem has served its purpose, at least as far as the old economy is concerned.

2. Our *"continuing city"* is the New Jerusalem, which is not the same as the earthly Jerusalem.

3. What we now have is only a down payment on that which is to come.

HERE

The short phrase, *"For here,"* concerns this present world, which holds nothing for the Child of God, and which most definitely will ultimately perish. That's why Jesus said:

"Lay not up for yourselves treasures upon Earth, where moth and rust doth corrupt, and where thieves break through and steal:

"But lay up for yourselves treasures in Heaven . . . for where your treasure is, there will your heart be also" (Mat. 6:19-21).

Everything the Christian does, every thought we think, every action we take, must be always with an eye on the eternal reward, and not at all on what is here in this present world. The very fact that one is temporal while the other is eternal, presents itself as enough to portray the difference — and what a difference it is!

NO CONTINUING CITY

The phrase, *"Have we no continuing city,"* portrays earthly Jerusalem, at least for that particular time, as having finished its course. Was this a warning by the Holy Spirit as to what was soon to come? A short time from now, Titus, the Roman General, would completely destroy Jerusalem.

The object of Paul seems to be to comfort the Hebrew Christians on the supposition that they would be driven by persecution from the city of Jerusalem, and doomed to wander as exiles. He in effect is telling them, that their Lord was led from that city to be put to death, and they should be willing to go forth also; and anyway, their permanent home was not Jerusalem, but Heaven; and they should be willing, in view of that blessed abode, to be exiled from the city where they dwelt, if in fact, it became necessary.

ONE TO COME

The phrase, *"But we seek one to come,"* presents the union of two thoughts:

1. We are free to go forth from the city so long held sacred, for our hopes are bound up with no abiding earthly sanctuary.

2. We must not shrink from the reproach of Christ, even though it may sever us from kindred and friends; for by the very profession of our faith we are *"strangers and sojourners,"* seeking after the Heavenly Jerusalem.

How impressive are these words of Paul, when read in the light of the events then unlooked for, yet so near at hand, issuing on the eve of the destruction of both Temple and City!

People love to look for earthly security. But the best earthly security is but insecure. We are admonished here to pursue that which is really lasting. We should strive for the abiding city, not in maintaining our grip on any fleeting earthly one.

(15) "BY HIM THEREFORE LET US OFFER THE SACRIFICE OF PRAISE TO GOD CONTINUALLY, THAT IS, THE FRUIT OF OUR LIPS GIVING THANKS TO HIS NAME."

The composite is:

1. *"By Him"* refers to what He did at the Cross on our behalf.

2. The *"Sacrifice of Praise"* refers to praising Him for what He did.

3. This is to be done continually.

4. *"The fruit of our lips"* is to be thanksgiving to His Name.

BY HIM

The short phrase, *"By Him,"* should have been translated *"Through Him."* Through His Sacrifice, which has made Atonement, we are hallowed, and fitted for our priestly service (I Pet. 2:5) (Ellicott).

The Jews approached God by the blood of the sacrifice and by the ministry of their High Priest; however, that which we have just stated, was a Type of the One Who was to come, namely the Lord Jesus Christ. We approach God today, and do so through Christ, but more particularly, what Christ did at the Cross in the shedding of His Blood. In other words, the Cross makes it possible for us to approach God. And let it be clearly understood, that this is the only way for man to approach God. If any other way is attempted, and to be sure, such ways are constantly being brought forth, they are automatically rejected. It is the Blood of Jesus Christ that makes everything possible.

THE SACRIFICE OF PRAISE

The phrase, *"Therefore let us offer the Sacrifice of Praise to God continually,"* refers to constantly thanking Him for the Cross, which opened up the way.

We as Christians no longer have to offer up an animal sacrifice, but rather trust in the Sacrifice already offered by Christ, in the offering of Himself. Whenever we praise Him and thank Him for what He did for us, we literally enter into His Sacrifice, and do so by the acclamation of our lips.

In systems like Judaism sacrifices were offered at set times, but for Christians, praise goes up all the time. Since a loving God is working out His purposes all the time, there are no circumstances in which praise should not be offered (I Thess. 5:18).

Quite possibly, Paul derived this Verse from the words of David, *"I will bless the LORD at all times: His praise shall continually be in my mouth"* (Ps. 34:1).

Let the Reader understand, that three things are here said:

1. We are to praise the Lord.

2. We are to do so, continually.

3. Our Praise should center up on the great Sacrifice of Christ, in other words, thanking Him continually for what He has done for us.

While of course, we should thank the Lord for everything; still, the greater part of our Praises should always be for the Cross, i.e., *"the Sacrifice of Christ."*

THE FRUIT OF OUR LIPS

The phrase, *"That is, the fruit of our lips giving thanks to His Name,"* in effect says *"the Sacrifices now acceptable to God are those of praise addressed to God, in the Name of the Lord, which refers to the price that He paid."*

His Name is *"Jesus,"* which means *"Savior,"* which speaks of His Sacrificial Offering of Himself on the Cross.

The *"fruit of our lips"* must ever be praise to His Name, and not expressions of doubt and unbelief. He has paid a great price for what we have, and the truth is, eternity will not be long enough to properly praise Him for this great Redemption.

(16) "BUT TO DO GOOD AND TO COMMUNICATE FORGET NOT: FOR WITH SUCH SACRIFICES GOD IS WELL PLEASED."

The diagram is:

1. Those who are truly looking to Jesus and what He did at the Cross, will in fact, also *"do good."*

2. *"To communicate"* carries the idea of sharing worldly goods with those who have had theirs confiscated by their persecutors.

3. The Lord expects us to sacrifice in order to do these things, if we have to.

4. Doing such *"is well pleasing"* to Him. And to be sure, anything that pleases Him will be blessed.

DO GOOD

The phrase, *"But to do good,"* presents that which must be done by Christians, and in fact, will be done, that is if the person is truly following the Lord; however, the Reader must understand, that such *"good"* will never be recognized by the world, but will actually be impugned, and because it stems from Christ. No goodness as it represents Christ will actually ever be fully recognized.

Our Ministry (Jimmy Swaggart Ministries) has built 157 school in Third World countries, that is if I correctly remember the exact number. These schools are not elaborate affairs, but actually small buildings that house classes up through the 6th grade. Some few of them went through high school, but most stopped at the grade mentioned.

These schools would accommodate from 200 to 300 children, and sometimes they would have two sessions a day, thereby doubling the number who could attend. In most if not all these schools, we also furnished a hot meal at noon.

Not one single time did the News Media ever recognize this which was being done. In fact, in their constant efforts to hurt us, some reporters would even claim that the schools did not exist. Actually, Television programs were done, denying the existence of these schools. We would furnish proof, and to their

credit, almost without exception, most of the Television Stations would air a retraction of their erroneous reports. Why did they and why do they conduct themselves in this manner?

It is because all of this was being done in the Name of the Lord, Which and Whom they would not recognize.

However, if the Believer is doing anything that is good for worldly recognition, then he's doing it for all the wrong reasons. Everything done of this nature, must be done and without fail, as unto the Lord, and as unto the Lord Alone.

I only bring up the subject as I did concerning the schools, because the News Media were claiming that we were taking up money from the people for these particular projects, and they were not being done, etc. That was our only purpose, in those days, for even bringing up the subject.

At times in those days, we would go to one of the sites where one or more schools were in the process of being constructed, and would invite reporters to go along; however, we never were able to get one to do so. The only conclusion I can arrive at, is that they had no interest in the Truth.

COMMUNICATION

The phrase, *"And to communicate forget not,"* refers to sharing with those in need.

Paul is saying here, that our obligations to the Lord are not exhausted with praise. Good deeds must also be included.

"Communicate" in the Greek is *"koinoneo,"* and means *"to make one's self a sharer or partner"* with someone else in his poverty or need. The idea is this as it regards these particular circumstances:

The Saints were exhorted to share what they had of earthly goods with their fellow Saints who, undergoing persecution, had been brought to a state of poverty by reason of the fact that their persecutors have confiscated their goods (Heb. 10:34).

The Jews normally lived as a close-knit group. In foreign cities in the Roman Empire, they pretty much kept to themselves, somewhat making their way as a group. Naturally, due to the fact that the religious leadership of Israel had crucified Christ, there was tremendous dissention among Jews as it regarded the Lord. In fact, there wasn't much middle ground if any.

Consequently, whenever a Jew gave his heart and life to Christ, he was excommunicated from the Synagogue, which carried with it severe penalties. If he was employed by a fellow Jew who didn't believe in Christ, which of course most didn't, he was instantly terminated from his job. Furthermore, no other Jew was allowed to give him any type of employment. If he was living in an apartment owned by another Jew, he was summarily evicted, and would not be able to find housing except among Gentiles. If money was owed in these circumstances, and we refer to money being owed to other Jews, it was instantly demanded, and if the person wasn't able to pay, their goods were confiscated, etc., at least as far as possible under Roman Law. And Rome for all practical purposes, allowed particular groups to have their own religion without interference, as long as it did not impact Rome in a negative way. Any hurt or harm that Jews could do to a fellow Jew who had given his heart and life to Christ, would be instantly done, and would continue to be done. As a result of this, some had been reduced to poverty, with all of this playing into the fact that some were recanting their Faith in Christ, which is the very reason for this Epistle.

So Paul is telling Christian Jews who have not been so severely impacted as others, to share with them, and in fact, the Holy Spirit is prodding this through Paul.

I would trust that the Reader would understand, that this doesn't apply to loafers and shirkers, but only to those who were truly in need. Unfortunately, the Church seems to have always had a ready supply of those who won't work, and rather attempt to sponge off others. The Holy Spirit through Paul had a word for these also. He said, *"That if any would not work, neither should he eat"* (II Thess. 3:10).

SUCH SACRIFICES

The phrase, *"For with such Sacrifices,"* presents the only type of sacrifices which God will accept other than the Sacrifice of Christ.

The idea of this is, which is very, very important, is that good works are brought about

NOTES

by one's Faith in the great Sacrifice of Christ, instead of good works being performed in order to generate Faith. To say it another way, good works will never generate proper faith, while proper faith will always generate good works. And by *"proper faith,"* we are speaking of Faith in the great Sacrifice of Christ, which the Believer should maintain at all times, understanding that the Cross of Christ is responsible for every single thing we have from the Lord (Rom. 6:3-5, 11, 14; 8:17).

Unfortunately, the far greater majority of the modern Church seeks to generate proper faith by their works. Because the works are generally good, and possibly always good in the eye of the beholder, the individuals are easily deceived into believing that this is the way. I suppose that every Christian at one time or the other has fallen into this trap. And considering, that there is almost no preaching or teaching on the Cross, at least at this present time, the position of *"works"* characterizes most Christians. All of this is very subtle, and not very easily understood, which makes it so deceptive. Nevertheless, this is what is happening.

If the Christian doesn't understand what proper faith actually is, which means he doesn't understand the Cross, there is no place else to go but *"works."* Most Christians when they first get saved, hearing almost nothing about the Cross of Christ, they begin to emulate older Christians in the Church where they attend. So almost exclusively, they start out on the road of *"works,"* simply because they don't know anywhere else to go. This is tragic, especially considering the consequences, but Satan has been very successful at maneuvering the Church away from its true foundation; consequently, the sacrifices being offered, are the works of our own hands, really not that much different than those of Cain recorded in Genesis Chapter 4, which are an insult to Christ.

THAT WHICH PLEASES GOD

The phrase, *"God is well pleased,"* speaks of the sacrifices of good works that follow true faith. And why does this please the Lord?

It pleases Him, because such an individual has their faith anchored totally and completely in the Finished Work of Christ. In fact, this is the only Faith that will please the Lord, and is the Faith that will produce such sacrifices.

There are actually 12 things recorded in the Word of God that please the Lord. They are:

1. Blessing Israel (Num. 24:1). It pleased God to bless Israel, because Israel was to be the vehicle through which the Word of God would be given to the world, and as well, which would serve as the womb of the Messiah, so to speak, Who would deliver mankind through and by His Death on the Cross.

2. It pleased God that Israel was His people (I Sam. 12:22). The reason for this pleasing Him is basically the same as the previous. I think one could say that it was the mission for which they were assigned, which caused Him to be pleased with them, which again pertains to Christ and His great Sacrifice. The Lord is pleased with no one outside of Christ.

3. The Lord is pleased with unselfish praying (I Ki. 3:10). This was the prayer of Solomon which pertained to governing Israel. Considering their mission, this pleased the Lord.

4. Christ's suffering for men (Isa. 53:10). This speaks directly of the Cross.

5. Christ as His Servant (Mat. 3:17; 12:18). The mission of Christ was to redeem humanity, which He did by the offering of Himself on the Cross.

6. It pleased the Lord to save men by the foolishness of preaching the Cross (I Cor. 1:18-24).

7. It pleased the Lord to set members in the Body of Christ, which pertains to their functions, and who were brought into the Body of Christ by Faith in the Cross (I Cor. 12:18).

8. The coming Resurrection pleases the Lord (I Cor. 15:38). Of course, this was all made possible by the Cross.

9. It pleased the Lord that Christ is the fullness of the Godhead Bodily (Col. 1:19). God became Man, i.e., *"Christ,"* in order to go to the Cross.

10. It pleases the Lord to call Preachers to preach the Gospel of Christ (Gal. 1:15). The Gospel of Christ is the Gospel of the Cross.

11. It pleases the Lord for men to have Faith (Heb. 11:5-6). This speaks of *"the Faith,"* as it regards Faith in what Christ did at Calvary on our behalf.

NOTES

12. It pleases the Lord for sacrifices of praise to come from our lips continually (Heb. 13:15-16). This pertains to Faith in the Cross of Christ, which will produce praises in the heart and life of such recipients, which will translate into good works.

I think one can see from these examples, that this which pleases God, always points to Christ, and more particularly, what Christ has done in order to redeem lost humanity.

(17) "OBEY THEM THAT HAVE THE RULE OVER YOU, AND SUBMIT YOURSELVES: FOR THEY WATCH FOR YOUR SOULS, AS THEY THAT MUST GIVE ACCOUNT, THAT THEY MAY DO IT WITH JOY, AND NOT WITH GRIEF: FOR THAT IS UNPROFITABLE FOR YOU."

The composite is:

1. The Pastors of whom Paul speaks here evidently were preaching the same Gospel that he was preaching; consequently, he tells the people to obey this Gospel which they are hearing.

2. They are to submit themselves to the true Word of God which is being taught.

3. These Pastors, whomever they may have been, had the spiritual welfare of these people at heart, as is obvious.

4. Every Preacher will one day give account for his Ministry, and the souls who sat under his Ministry.

5. It is the consuming desire of every true Preacher of the Gospel, that all who sit under his Ministry would heed the True Gospel he preaches. At the Judgment Seat of Christ, such will bring joy. For those who would not listen, there will be grief.

6. Even if a Preacher is preaching the True Gospel, if the people will not listen, as would be obvious, they cannot be profited.

OBEDIENCE

The phrase, *"Obey them that have the rule over you,"* has reference to Pastors; however, the emphasis is not on the Pastor but rather on the Gospel he preaches. Paul evidently knew these particular individuals, whomever they may have been, were preaching the Truth.

It must be remembered, that some of these Christian Jews were seriously contemplating recanting their Faith in Christ. These Pastors, naturally, were pleading with them not to do such a thing, knowing it would result in the loss of their souls.

These statements made by Paul, do not carry any idea at all of blanket obedience or submission, which some have attempted to claim. Such has caused many people to be lost. It is actually obedience to the Gospel which is being preached, which is here enjoined.

SUBMISSION

The phrase, *"And submit yourselves,"* refers to submitting to the True Gospel which is being preached by these true Pastors.

It does *not* pertain to submitting one's conscience or control of one's life. Once again, many souls have been lost by individuals blindly following, and then find out too late that they've been following the wrong thing.

No person who truly loves the Lord can obey Preachers preaching false doctrine, and neither can they submit themselves to such. To do such, is the sure road to spiritual destruction. To be sure, such a person when they stand before the Lord will not be able to shift the blame to these individuals whom they were following. Every individual is going to have to personally answer to the Lord, which means that we must personally answer for the Gospel we hear and receive.

RESPONSIBILITY

The phrase, *"For they watch for your souls,"* refers to those Preachers who truly have the spiritual welfare of the people at heart.

Several things are here being said:

1. There is nothing more important than the soul of man.

2. Understanding that, then the task of watching over the souls of men, is the most important task in the world.

3. This is first of all to be done, by the true Word of God being preached and taught.

4. As well, the Preacher of the Gospel must seek the Lord constantly, in order that he be anointed to preach the Gospel, which alone will give it power.

TO GIVE ACCOUNT

The phrase, *"As they that must give account, that they may do it with joy, and*

not with grief," presents the fact, that every single Preacher in the world, will give account to God for his Ministry, and in effect, the Gospel that he has preached. Then we should realize how imperative it is that we as Preachers strive to preach the True Gospel of Christ, and to do so without fear or compromise.

The *"joy"* and the *"grief"* can be taken two ways:

1. If the Preacher has been faithful to his calling, and has not compromised the Gospel, he will be able to stand before the Lord with *"joy."* If not, there will be great *"grief,"* as should be obvious!

2. Assuming that the True Gospel is preached, it can be taken to mean that the joy refers to those who heeded, while the grief refers to those who would not heed.

Quite possibly both points are correct.

UNPROFITABLE

The phrase, *"For that is unprofitable for you,"* refers to the fact, that even though the Preacher of the Gospel is preaching the Truth, if certain people will not heed what he is preaching, then the Gospel, as true as it may be, will be of no profit to these particular individuals.

The idea is, that at least some of these Christian Jews who were contemplating going back into Judaism, had excellent Pastors, men who had truly preached to them the Gospel. However, they had not heeded; therefore, the fault could not be laid at the feet of these particular Preachers.

Even though the True Gospel is preached, if it is not mixed with faith by the hearer, then it will be to no avail. The Scripture is emphatic on this (Heb. 4:2).

It is bad enough to not have an opportunity to hear the True Gospel, but worse yet, when the True Gospel is heard, and then it is rejected because of a lack of faith. In other words, the individual simply doesn't believe what he is hearing.

(18) "PRAY FOR US: FOR WE TRUST WE HAVE A GOOD CONSCIENCE, IN ALL THINGS WILLING TO LIVE HONESTLY."

The diagram is:

1. Request for prayer was common with Paul.

2. The Apostle had a good conscience, in that he was doing all that he knew to do to walk as close to God as was possible.

3. No doubt, honesty in all things as it regards a Child of God, is one of the greatest attributes that one could ever have.

PRAYER

The phrase, *"Pray for us,"* presents by Paul, as stated, a common request (Rom. 15:30; Eph. 6:18; Col. 4:3; I Thess. 5:25; II Thess. 3:1).

"Pray" in the Greek is *"proseuchesthe,"* and in essence means, *"keep praying for us."*

Paul has rebuked his Readers from time to time; he has warned them of dangers in their conduct and exhorted them. But he depends on them, too, and looks to them now to support him with their prayers.

I think it is obvious throughout Paul's Epistles, the tremendous value that he places on prayer. I would understand from his statements, that he was a man of constant prayer. In other words, he prayed about everything, and because everything needed to be prayed about.

Prayer is fellowship with the Lord, and it is fellowship that every Believer, as should be obvious, desperately needs. As well, it is communion, which speaks of the very reason for fellowship. The Holy Spirit through the Apostle has already stated that we should offer *"the sacrifice of praise to God continually."* In other words, this should be ever *"the fruit of our lips giving thanks to His Name"* (vs. 15).

When we understand that every good thing we have comes from the Lord, we should without fail, continue to thank Him for His many and varied Blessings. Also, we should take everything to Him in prayer, seeking His leading, guidance, and direction. Such an attitude and position, guarantees success.

For things we need, we should make these petitions to Him. He is able to do all things; however, at the same time, we must ardently seek His Will in all things. The longer we live for the Lord, and the closer we get to God, the more we realize how faulty our personal wills actually are, and how absolutely valuable that His Will actually is. Consequently, if we have any spiritual sense at all, we very quickly come to the place that we not at

all want our wills in anything, but always His Will.

WHY PRAYER, IF GOD ALREADY KNOWS ALL THINGS, AND CAN DO ALL THINGS?

While it is certainly true that the Lord knows all things and can do all things, which means that He doesn't need any help whatsoever; still, in His Grace, He has given the Church the privilege of having a great part in His Work. In other words, if we do not carry out our end of the load, then the Work of God will simply fall down.

The Church doing its part, which of course speaks to every Believer, which the Lord has given us the privilege to do, will get the job done, simply because it is certain that the Lord is going to do His part. This means, that each Believer has a function, and should seek the Lord as to what that function is, and then seek His daily guidance in carrying out that function.

All of this builds faith, confidence, trust, maturity, and strength in the heart and life of each Believer. In fact, that's what it's intended to do.

The Lord doesn't need us; in fact, He doesn't need anything that we have. There is absolutely nothing within our possession as it regards our own personal beings, which can benefit Him in any way; consequently, His allowing us to have a part in this great work, is strictly for our benefit and not His, and as well, is done because of His Love and Grace.

Therefore, it is absolutely necessary that we pray constantly that we might have His Will and leading in all things.

Also, it is especially imperative, that the Church pray for its leaders, even as Paul requested prayer constantly for himself. On a personal note, even as Paul, I constantly ask you the Reader, and those who know us and are benefited in some way by this Ministry, to constantly pray for us. I need your prayers, in that I might do exactly what the Lord wants me to do, and do it in the way that He wants it done. So I too say with Paul, *"Pray for us!"*

A GOOD CONSCIENCE

The phrase, *"For we trust we have a good conscience,"* concerns any and all things; however, I personally think that he is here speaking of the way he has handled the Law of Moses as it regards this Epistle to the Hebrews. When Paul stood before the High Priest in Jerusalem, he had as well stated that he had a good conscience (Acts 23:1).

Having a good conscience is a most unusual reason for requesting prayer. We could understand it if Paul spoke of his difficulties or the like, lacking knowledge of the circumstances, however, we cannot be sure. Yet it seems that the possibility at least existed, that some of the Readers may have been accusing him of some fault. Consequently, he protests that he has a clear conscience, as it regards whatever it is that is at hand, and that this is the reason for asking for their fellowship in prayer.

Addressing himself to matters as he has in this Epistle to the Hebrews, and making some of the strong statements he made, one can well understand how that some would have grown angry at his position; however, it must be understood, that even though this was Paul's position and rightly so, in reality it was that of the Holy Spirit.

One never had any doubt as to where Paul stood. What he believed was crystal clear, and as well, it was crystal clear in the manner in which he pointed out error. Such a position, and above all, such a clarity of purpose and position, rankles some extremely so, and as well, even arouses hatred in the hearts of those who are guilty of the error. However, the good conscience I think mostly centers up in the following:

In this Epistle, he had delivered his soul. He had not pulled any punches, had not compromised the Gospel in any way. These Christian Jews would now know exactly as to what they were doing. Whether they would believe it or not is something else; however, none of them would now have an excuse, because the Holy Spirit through the Apostle had been crystal clear. His conscience was clear, in that he had faithfully delivered the Word.

How so much, the modern Church desperately needs the clear, concise, *"certain sound"* of the Gospel Trumpet. How so much it is plagued with compromise, the shading of the truth, and downright unbelief. How so refreshing it is to hear, *"Thus saith the Lord!"* And as well, how many Preachers

NOTES

can say presently with Paul, *"I have a good conscience"?*

HONESTY

The phrase, *"In all things willing to live honestly,"* refers to his daily living for the Lord, in other words his conduct, and as well to his handling of the Gospel. His life was honest, and his presentation of the Gospel was honest as well!

In a sense, he is here denying that he had in any way acted dishonestly in respect to his handling of the Law of Moses, in the writing of this Epistle. He had properly interpreted that great Law, and as well, he had properly interpreted the Gospel as it relates to the Law.

(19) "BUT I BESEECH YOU THE RATHER TO DO THIS, THAT I MAY BE RESTORED TO YOU THE SOONER."

The structure is:

1. *"I beseech you"* is also a common expression of the Apostle.

2. The phrase *"restored to you the sooner"* lends credence to the thought, that Paul may have been in prison when this was written.

3. I personally think this particular Scripture is another proof that Paul wrote Hebrews.

I BESEECH YOU

The phrase, *"But I beseech you the rather to do this,"* refers back to his request that they pray for him.

At the most, he realized that in all probability it would not be very long until he sealed his testimony with his blood, and yet if in answer to prayer he might be restored to service for a little time, he would value this, while being in all things subject to the Will of God (Ironside).

Once again let us touch on prayer.

Who can tell how much each servant of Christ is indebted to the prayers of God's hidden ones? To bear such up before Him is a wondrous Ministry, the full fruit of which will only be manifested in that day when every secret thing will be revealed and each one will be rewarded according to his own service. We speak of the Judgment Seat of Christ.

Let none think that it is a little thing to pray. There is no higher Ministry, no more important office, than that of the Intercessor.

RESTORED

The phrase, *"That I may be restored to you the sooner,"* lends credence by its terminology that Paul may have been in prison when this was written. Of course, this is not certain, as the statement could have meant several things; however, coupled with Verse 23, it is not improbable that the Apostle was in prison at this time.

If in fact that was the case, and it pertains to the incarceration portrayed in the Book of Acts, then the Apostle was released it is believed, with him ministering for a few more short years, before being imprisoned the second time and paying with his life, as recorded in II Timothy 4:6-8.

And yet, if this Epistle was written in A.D. 67 or even the early part of '68, as some believe, then it would have pertained to his second and last imprisonment, from which he was not delivered, at least as it regards being restored to the Church.

(20) "NOW THE GOD OF PEACE, THAT BROUGHT AGAIN FROM THE DEAD OUR LORD JESUS, THAT GREAT SHEPHERD OF THE SHEEP, THROUGH THE BLOOD OF THE EVERLASTING COVENANT,"

The exegesis is:

1. Peace with God is obtained by faith and trust in Christ and what He did at the Cross on our behalf.

2. Jesus Christ rose from the dead. This is the only reference in this Epistle to the Resurrection of our Lord.

3. Christ is the great Shepherd of the sheep, meaning that He is the Head of the Church.

4. He is all of this through what He did at the Cross, which necessitated the shedding of His Blood.

5. The New Covenant is *"the Everlasting Covenant,"* meaning that it will never have to be replaced, in that it is perfect.

THE GOD OF PEACE

The phrase, *"Now the God of Peace,"* proclaims the fact that peace has been made between God and fallen man, and done so through what Jesus did at the Cross on behalf of man. The context here speaks of the Substitutionary Atonement of Christ on the Cross, and is in effect, very similar to Paul's

words in Colossians 1:20, *"Having made Peace through the Blood of His Cross."*

That which separated a Holy God from sinful man, namely, sin, was put away at the Cross. The death of Christ paid for sin, satisfied the righteous demands of the broken Law, and made it possible for God to bestow mercy on the basis of justice satisfied.

We have an echo of all this in Ephesians 2:17, *"And came and preached peace to you who are far off (the Gentiles) and to them that are nigh (the Jews)."* In fact, God is called *"the God of Peace"* a number of times in Paul's writings (Rom. 15:33; 16:20; II Cor. 13:11; Phil. 4:9; I Thess. 5:23).

PEACE

"Peace" connotes the fullest prosperity of the whole man, taking up as it does the Old Testament concept of the Hebrew *"Shalom."* Here it reminds us that it is God in Whom all our prosperity is centered. There is no well-rounded life that does not depend on Him.

The expression is especially suitable in view of what the Epistle discloses of the condition of the Readers. They have had to cope with some form of persecution and were still not free from opposition. Some were tempted to go back from Christianity and have had to be warned of the dangers of apostasy. They may have even had doubts about who their true leaders were. It is well for them to be reminded that real peace is in God and in God Alone, and is obtained solely through Jesus Christ, and our faith in Him and what He did for us at the Cross.

However, it must be made crystal clear, that the *"peace"* here mentioned, was and is, brought about solely by what Jesus did at the Cross. That and that alone, made it possible for fallen man to have Peace with God, and because that and that alone, satisfied the righteous demands of a thrice-Holy God.

Man had sinned grievously against God, and had done so repeatedly and in fact, constantly. Consequently, it is God Who has been offended and offended greatly! As well, the sin which so greatly offended Him, carries with it the total threat of absolute destruction of all things which are holy, good, pure, and true, thereby bringing about sorrow, hurt, pain, and waste of every description.

There was no way that man could address this terrible problem; consequently, man's condition was terminal. If it was to be assuaged, in other words settled, God would have to do it Himself, which He did, by becoming Man, serving as the Last Adam and the Second Man (I Cor. 15:45-50), which was culminated by Him giving up His Life on the Cross, which satisfied the righteous demands of God, and as stated, made it possible for God to bestow mercy on the basis of justice satisfied.

THE RESURRECTION OF CHRIST

The phrase, *"That brought again from the dead our Lord Jesus,"* presents the only mention of the Resurrection of Christ in this Epistle to the Hebrews.

If it is to be noticed, Paul in this Epistle never mentioned the great healing power of Christ, or His miracle working power, or any of the great things He did in His earthly Ministry. While these things, of course, were very, very important, as anything about Christ was and is very important; still, the entirety of this Epistle to the Hebrews, is directed toward the Crucifixion of Christ, and what that great Sacrificial Offering actually meant.

Again we will emphasize the fact, that all of these other things, and most certainly the Resurrection of Christ were and are extremely important; still, it was the Crucifixion of Christ, i.e., *"the Cross,"* which made possible the entirety of the great Salvation Plan. It was the Cross and the Cross alone, which did this. I emphasize that for the following reasons:

The great Plan of God for the human race, and more particularly the Church, is as follows:

1. Every sinner that's ever been saved has been saved by trusting in Christ and what Christ did at the Cross. As well, every single Blessing and all Victory which comes to the Saint of God, all and without exception are made possible by what Jesus did at the Cross. This means that every solution is found in the Cross; every answer to every question is found in the Cross (Gal. 6:14).

2. Considering that, our Faith must ever have as its object, the Cross of Christ. This

NOTES

is very, very important! Every effort by Satan is to move our Faith from the Cross to other things. This is where he places all his energy. He really doesn't care where these other things are, or what these other things are, just as long as our Faith is not in the Cross.

Consequently, every Believer must *"fight this good fight of faith"* which refers to keeping our Faith in the Cross of Christ, and there alone.

The correct object of your Faith, which must be the Cross of Christ, is the single most important thing in your life (Rom. Chpt. 4).

3. With your Faith properly placed in the Cross of Christ, and remaining in the Cross of Christ, the Holy Spirit will then do His great and mighty office work within your heart and life (Rom. 8:1-2, 11, 13).

Whatever it is that we are to have from the Lord, or to be in the Lord, must and without fail, be done by the Holy Spirit. He Alone can carry out the needed work; however, everything He does is predicated on the Finished Work of Christ, which means that we must have our Faith exclusively in that Finished Work.

UNDERSTANDING THE CROSS

When one begins to understand the Cross of Christ, at that moment one begins to understand the New Covenant. For this is what the New Covenant is all about. In fact, it is beautifully typified in that which we refer to as the *"Lord's Supper"* (I Cor. 11:23-30).

When one begins to understand the Cross, one begins to understand the Bible, because the very story of the Word of God is the story of man's Redemption, which is the story of the Cross. As well, to properly understand the Cross of Christ is to properly understand the Resurrection of Christ. Paul said:

"For if we have been planted together in the likeness of His Death (understanding of the Cross), we shall be also in the likeness of His Resurrection" (Rom. 6:5).

THE SHEPHERD

The phrase, *"That great Shepherd of the sheep,"* presents the One Who died for us, and Who God raised from the dead. The language seems to be derived from Isaiah

63:11. *"Where is He Who brought them through the sea, with the Shepherd of His flock?"* — though the thought here is, of course, quite different. Christ is called a *"Shepherd"* and the great treatment of the shepherd theme is in John Chapter 10 and again in I Peter 2:25 (Mat. 26:31; Mk. 14:27).

It is a piece of imagery that stresses the care of our Lord for His Own, for sheep are helpless without their shepherd. But an aspect we in modern times sometimes miss is that the shepherd has absolute sovereignty over his flock (Rev. 2:27; 12:5; 19:15).

The adjective *"great"* is used because Christ is not to be ranked with other shepherds. He stands out (Morris).

THE BLOOD OF THE EVERLASTING COVENANT

The phrase, *"Through the Blood of the Everlasting Covenant,"* once again points to the Cross.

The New Testament or New Covenant is called the eternal one, in contrast to the First Testament which was of a transitory nature. It was within the sphere of the eternal covenant that Christ, having did for sinful man, was raised up from among those who are dead. In fact, He could not be a High Priest after the order of Melchizedek if He were not raised from the dead.

Sinful man needs a Living Priest to give life to the believing sinner, not a dead Priest merely to pay for his sins. Thus, it was provided within the New Testament (New Covenant) that the Priest Who offered Himself for sacrifice, would be raised from the dead. We have a prophetic type of this in Aaron's rod that budded (Wuest).

COVENANT

It is interesting to see how the thought of *"Covenant"* persists to the end. In fact, it has been one of the major themes of this Epistle. The Greek Text brings out the point that this Covenant will never be replaced by another as it replaced the Old Covenant. It is perpetual in its validity. And it was established by Blood. Paul never forgets that. For him the Death of Jesus is central.

At the same time, his linking it with the Resurrection shows that he did not have in

mind a dead Christ but One Who though He shed His Blood to establish the Covenant, lives forever.

Last in this Verse in the Greek (and with some emphasis) come the words *"our Lord Jesus."* The expression is unusual outside of Acts, where it occurs a number of times. It combines the Lordship of Christ and His real humanity, two themes of continuing importance (Morris).

By virtue of His Atoning Sacrifice as the Good Shepherd, He is the Great Shepherd of the sheep. He could not be such had He not, as the Good Shepherd, shed His Blood for the sheep and so established the Everlasting Covenant. Once again, we emphasize the fact, that it is the Cross of Christ which made all of this possible. In fact, even as this Passage tells us, His Sacrifice was so perfect, so total, so complete, that it will never have to be repeated, or added to in any way; consequently, it can be called *"The Everlasting Covenant,"* simply because, it is eternal.

While we do not yet have all the results or the benefits of this Everlasting Covenant, to be sure all will ultimately come about, and I speak of the coming Resurrection. Whereas every Saint is now washed, Sanctified, and Justified, then we will all be *"Glorified."*

But still, there will be more enemies to be put down, the last which will be death (I Cor. 15:26). At this time, Satan along with all fallen angels and demon spirits, along with all human beings who have rejected Christ, will be *"cast into the lake of fire and brimstone,"* where they will be *"for ever and ever"* (Rev. 20:10-15).

Then Paul said, *"Then cometh the end, when He (Christ) shall have delivered up the Kingdom to God, even the Father; when He (Christ) shall have put down all rule and all authority and power"* (I Cor. 15:24).

The last two Chapters of Revelation portray what the Everlasting Covenant, i.e., *"The New Covenant,"* will bring about, which is perfection. In other words, a perfect covenant, for that's what this Covenant is, will ultimately bring about a perfect environment. I speak of the New Jerusalem outlined in these last two Chapters of Revelation.

However, the Everlasting Covenant will not end there, but will portray its results that will be obvious to all of God's creation, forever and forever (Rev. 22:5).

However, we must ever remember, that this Covenant, this New Covenant, this Everlasting Covenant, has all been made possible *"through the Blood!"* This is so important, even as we've already mentioned elsewhere in this Volume, that some seven times in the last two Chapters of Revelation, the Holy Spirit refers to Christ as the *"Lamb"* (Rev. 21:9, 14, 22-23, 27; 22:1, 3). It is done in this manner, in order that we may never forget what has made it all possible.

(21) "MAKE YOU PERFECT IN EVERY GOOD WORK TO DO HIS WILL, WORKING IN YOU THAT WHICH IS WELLPLEASING IN HIS SIGHT, THROUGH JESUS CHRIST; TO WHOM BE GLORY FOR EVER AND EVER. AMEN."

The diagram is:

1. Christ through the Holy Spirit can equip the Believer with everything good for doing His Will. It is all done through the Cross.

2. The Holy Spirit works in us to do that which is wellpleasing in the sight of God.

3. It is all *"through Jesus Christ,"* which refers to what Christ did at the Cross.

4. Because it is Christ Who made possible all that we have from the Lord, and did so by and through His Death on the Cross, it is to Him that all the glory belongs.

TO DO HIS WILL

The phrase, *"Make you perfect in every good work to do His Will,"* refers to that which the Holy Spirit has been sent to do, and Who will do such through Christ, all made possible by what Christ did at the Cross. If it is to be noticed, He is in our hearts and lives to carry out the *"Will of God"* and not our particular wills (Rom. 8:27).

To *"make perfect"* is the translation of two different words in this Epistle. In the one, which is of frequent occurrence (Heb. 2:10; 10:1; 12:23), *"perfect"* stands contrasted with that which is immature, which has not attained its end and aim.

The other, which is used here (and in a somewhat different sense in Heb. 10:5 and Heb. 11:3), rather conveys the thought of completeness, complete equipment, or preparation.

WELLPLEASING IN HIS SIGHT

The phrase, *"Working in you that which is wellpleasing in His sight,"* should have been translated, *"Working in us. . . ."*

We should not overlook the significance of the word *"us."* As he has done so often, Paul links himself with his Readers. He looks for God to do His perfect work in them and in him alike. He is not aloof and a special case; he needs the Grace of God as much as they do. He wants God to do in us *"what is pleasing to Him,"* where *"pleasing"* renders a word *"euarestos"* used only here in Hebrews, but eight times elsewhere in the New Testament. In Titus 2:9 it refers to slaves being pleasing to their master; elsewhere it always refers to people being acceptable to God.

THROUGH JESUS CHRIST

The phrase, *"Through Jesus Christ,"* proclaims the fact that men can do what is acceptable to God only through Jesus Christ.

The sufficiency of Christ as a Savior appears in the Offices which He fills in this Epistle. These, one might say, are the holy garments of His Heavenly Priesthood:

Chapter 1: The Sin Purger.

Chapter 2: The Captain of Salvation.

Chapter 3: The Son over His Own House.

Chapter 5: The Great High Priest.

Chapter 6: The Forerunner.

Chapter 8: The Mediator.

Chapter 12: The Prince and Perfecter of Faith.

Chapter 13: The Great Shepherd.

In these several Ministries He meets His people's need as:

Sinful, feeble, children needing food and love, infirm worshipers, apprehensive pilgrims, incompetent covenanters, defective Believers, and defenseless and foolish followers.

I realize that the previous description does not present that which is very pleasing; however, it happens to be true.

By contrast, all in Him is perfection — perfection of cleansing and victory and the supply of love and food for His children; perfection in worship, and as a forerunner in making sure the road and certain the entrance for His people; perfection as the Negotiator of the Everlasting Covenant, so making its permanence absolute; perfection in the provision of the Faith in which and by which the righteous live; and perfection in the care and guardianship of His foolish and defenseless flock.

Pending His return, fellowship with Christ can only be enjoyed outside the camp and inside the Veil. Corrupt Christianity is the present-day *"camp"* (Williams).

THE GLORY

The phrase, *"To Whom be glory forever and ever. Amen,"* presents the One Whom God the Father has made both Lord and Christ. Exalted to the Father's right hand, He is now the Great Shepherd guiding His chosen flock through the wilderness of this world.

Soon, as the Apostle Peter tells us, He will return in Glory as the Chief Shepherd (I Pet. 5:4), to Whom all the undershepherds must render their account.

Meantime, by His Spirit, He is working in those for whom He once wrought so effectively on Calvary's Cross. By this inward work He is sanctifying His people to Himself, daily making us more like our blessed Master, to Whom all the glory of our Salvation belongs both now and for eternity. And so the *"Amen"* closes the doctrinal and practical parts of the Letter (Ironside).

(22) "AND I BESEECH YOU, BRETHREN, SUFFER THE WORD OF EXHORTATION: FOR I HAVE WRITTEN A LETTER UNTO YOU IN FEW WORDS."

The structure is:

1. Paul once again uses one of his favorite sayings, *"I beseech you, Brethren."*

2. He pleads with these Jewish Christians to receive his Word of Exhortation.

3. Considering the subject matter, the Letter is short.

BRETHREN

The phrase, *"And I beseech you, Brethren,"* closes with an affectionate appeal.

The Letter has had its share of rebukes and stern warnings, without a doubt, the strongest that Paul has written, with the exception possibly of Galatians. In fact, the statements are stronger in Hebrews, but more general; the Letter to the Galatians is more personal, perhaps making it seem stronger. Paul now

softens the impact a little with this appeal and with the affectionate address *"Brothers."*

EXHORTATION

The phrase, *"Suffer the Word of Exhortation,"* in effect, points to the fact, that Paul has actually written a sermon. It refers to the arguments and counsels in this whole Epistle — which is, in fact, a practical exhortation to perseverance in adhering to the Christian Faith amidst all the temptations which existed to apostasy.

This Letter is in some ways, the most important, I think, written by Paul. He explains in graphic detail the tremendous work accomplished by the Atonement, portraying to all, that which Christ actually did regarding His Death on the Cross. Nothing in the entirety of the Bible comes even close as it regards this which is the foundation of the Christian Faith.

Even though the Epistle was written to Jewish Christians, it is in fact for the entirety of the Church, both Jewish and Gentile. In fact, because it was written to the Jews, the Apostle opens up the Old Testament, portraying to us the Types and Shadows which graphically pointed to Christ, as found nowhere else in the New Testament.

It is sad that most of Paul's Epistles were written because of error that had sprung up in the Church. But yet, even though we are saddened by the error, the Holy Spirit used the occasion to perfect and bring out great Truths, which may have not been addressed otherwise.

"Suffer" in the Greek is *"anecho,"* and means, *"to bear with or endure."* Paul pleads with the recipients not to become impatient at his counsels in this Letter. As stated, he has been forced to say some very strong, even very hard things; however, he wants his Readers to know, that what he has said has been for their good. It is not meant to be personal on his part, therefore, he now pleads.

IN FEW WORDS

The phrase, *"For I have written a Letter unto you in few words,"* have been misunderstood by many. The idea is this:

Considering the subject matter, the Letter is short. In fact, some of the subjects could have been dealt with at much greater length.

The Apostle has addressed himself to the most complicated subjects in the entirety of the Word of God. Actually, ample illustration of these subjects would fill up a library; so, it was only by the power and help of the Holy Spirit that he was able to break down very complicated subject matter into brief discussions, but yet which enabled the Reader to perfectly understand what was being said.

To explain Christ in His role as Mediator, as High Priest, as Intercessor, to explain the great Work of the Cross, that in fact which had been in the planning stages from before the foundation of the world (I Pet. 1:18-20), and to do all of this in some 13 short Chapters, necessitated the inspiration of the Holy Spirit not only in subject matter, but as well in the almost impossible art of brevity. Therefore, the Apostle says, *"I have written a Letter unto you in few words."*

But Oh, what a Letter! How thankful we are that it was written! How grateful we are, that even though the Apostle probably wrote it from prison, that the Holy Spirit deemed it necessary. So much closer we are to the Lord, because of this *"Letter."*

If in fact, Paul wrote this Letter during his first imprisonment, it would have been written from the *"hired house"* where he was incarcerated (Acts 28:30-31).

If it was written during his last imprisonment, which concluded in his execution, it would have been written in the Mammertine Prison.

In early summer of 2000, I had the privilege, along with Frances, Donnie, Debbie, Gabriel, and Matthew (Jennifer was in school), along with others, to be in Rome, and to visit this Prison. It is a cell or cave one might say, chiseled out of solid rock, underground. Of course, there are stairs now leading down into the cell, but during Paul's time, there was only a trap door in the ceiling, which led to another cell immediately above this place where Paul spent the last few months of his life.

From this place he wrote II Timothy and as stated, possibly this Epistle to the Hebrews.

As we stood there that afternoon in late May, there is no way that I have words to properly express the feelings of my heart.

I tried to quote to the small crowd gathered in that room some of the last words of the great Apostle which were written, *"For I am now ready to be offered, and the time of my departure is at hand.*

"I have fought a good fight, I have finished my course...." I got no further! The Presence of God filled the room.

Rome little noticed when the great Apostle died. In fact, Rome was his executioner. Little did they realize, and in fact not at all, that this man under Christ, would do more for civilization than any human being who has ever lived.

The Apostle Paul!

(23) "KNOW YE THAT OUR BROTHER TIMOTHY IS SET AT LIBERTY; WITH WHOM, IF HE COME SHORTLY, I WILL SEE YOU."

The composite is:

1. Timothy was a close companion of Paul, beginning with his Second Missionary journey (Acts 16:1-5).

2. *"Is set at liberty,"* probably refers to the younger Apostle being sent on a special mission. There is actually no evidence that Paul is speaking of him being released from prison.

3. The last phrase of this Verse lends credence to the idea, that Paul may have written this Letter during the conclusion of his first imprisonment. Or he could have written it after his first imprisonment. At any rate, it seems that he was hoping to visit certain Churches with Timothy.

4. This Verse, I feel, proves beyond a shadow of a doubt, that Paul wrote the Epistle to the Hebrews.

TIMOTHY

The phrase, *"Know ye that our Brother Timothy is set at liberty,"* presents a strong circumstance showing that Paul, as stated, was the author of this Epistle. From the first acquaintance of Timothy with Paul he is represented as his constant companion, and spoken of as a brother (II Cor. 1:1; Phil. 1:1; Col. 1:1; Phile. vs. 1).

There is no other one of the Apostles who would so naturally have used this term respecting Timothy; and this kind mention is made of him here because he was so dear to the heart of the writer, and because he felt that they to whom he wrote would also feel an interest in his circumstances.

As well, the phrase *"set at liberty,"* in no way demands the meaning of Timothy being released from prison. This is language which would be used rather of one who had been sent on some mission, than of one who was just released from prison.

But on the supposition that the expression relates to release from imprisonment, there would be an entire incongruity in the language. It is not, as we should then suppose, *"our brother Timothy is now released from prison, and therefore I will come soon with him and see you"*; but, *"our brother Timothy is now sent away, and if he returns soon, I will come with him to you."*

In Philippians 2:19, 23, Paul then a prisoner at Rome, speaks of the hope which he entertained that he would be able to send Timothy to them, as soon as he should know how it would go with him. He designed to retain him until that point was settled, as his presence with him would be important until then, and then to send him to give consolation to the Philippians, and to look into the condition of the Church.

Now the Passages before us agrees well with the supposition that this event had occurred: that Paul had ascertained with sufficient clearness that he would be released, so that he might be permitted yet to visit the Hebrew Christians; that he had sent Timothy to Philippi, and was waiting for his return; that as soon as he should return he would be prepared to visit them; and that in the meantime, while Timothy was absent, he wrote to them this Epistle.

And at the same time, this may very well not have been the scenario, but this is as close as we can come to that which possibly may have happened.

I WILL SEE YOU

The phrase, *"With whom, if he come shortly, I will see you,"* leaves no clue whatsoever, if this actually happened.

Many situations such as this are mentioned casually in Paul's Epistles, and thereby, offering no further explanation. The truth is, these particular events, are not the interest of the Holy Spirit. Geographical locations

and particular time frames are not the thrust of these Letters, but rather, instructions from the Lord as to how we ought to live, which pertains to our manner of Trust in Christ. As the entire thrust of the Old Testament is toward Christ, the entirety of the instruction given in the New Testament pertains to Christ. What He did for us at the Cross is the thrust of the Epistles, with the Holy Spirit giving us instructions as it regards our Faith in that Finished Work, all in order that Christlikeness might be developed within our hearts and lives.

(24) "SALUTE ALL THEM THAT HAVE THE RULE OVER YOU, AND ALL THE SAINTS. THEY OF ITALY SALUTE YOU."

The exegesis is:

1. As to exactly what Church, or group of Churches, Paul here intends, we aren't told.

2. This Epistle was written, not the Pastors of Churches, but to the Jewish members of these Churches, hence addressed to them.

3. The recipients of this Letter are told to greet the Pastor on behalf of Paul, and in fact, all the Saints in that particular Church or Churches.

4. It is almost certain from the statement, *"They of Italy salute you,"* that the Epistle was written from Italy. Consequently, it seems very likely it was during the time that Paul was in prison, probably during the first imprisonment.

GREETINGS

The phrase, *"Salute all them that have the rule over you, and all the Saints,"* more than likely refers to their Pastors and other Saints in that particular Church, or Churches.

There are some who feel that Paul was actually speaking of the original Twelve Apostles, when he spoke of those *"who have the rule over you."* Such certainly is possible, but there is no evidence either way.

As well, we have no way of knowing exactly as to whom this Epistle was actually sent. As of course is obvious, it was written for the very purpose of addressing the Jewish issue, and so it definitely would have been sent to a prominent person, whomever that individual may have been. And no doubt, copies were made of it very quickly, with it then being passed around, even as it was intended.

It is almost certain, that the Epistle would have caused much discussion, and probably even some furor. The Law/Grace issue was very big then, and when it is to be considered that some Jews were defecting from Christ and going back into Judaism, even going so far as to publicly renounce Christ, the Epistle could not have helped but hit some nerves.

ITALY

The phrase, *"They of Italy salute you,"* without a doubt I think, proves the case that this Epistle was written from Italy and more than likely, Rome. As well, the manner of this benediction is Paul's style. He would greet those in the respective Churches, and as well would send greetings from wherever he was writing a particular Epistle.

Considering these things, I really do not see how anyone could doubt that Paul wrote this Epistle. It is highly unlikely that the Holy Spirit would have inspired someone else to copy Paul's style word for word. As well, to have written this Epistle, one would have had to have been an expert in the Old Testament, which certainly fit the case of Paul. In my estimation, there was no one in the world of that day who knew the Old Testament as this particular Apostle.

(25) "GRACE BE WITH YOU ALL. AMEN."

In all of Paul's Epistles, he closes with a statement concerning Grace. In fact, he is referred to by most Bible Scholars as *"the Apostle of Grace."* What does this mean?

First of all, Grace is simply the goodness of God extended to undeserving Believers. While God has always had Grace, it took the Cross to open up the way, that Grace might be abundantly bestowed upon those who evidenced Faith. In fact, Faith is the only requirement for Grace. And when we say Faith, we're speaking of Faith exclusively in the Cross of Christ, i.e., *"what Jesus there did on behalf of a lost and dying world."*

In fact, Grace is irrevocably tied to the Cross. If one understands the meaning of the Cross, one understands the meaning of the New Covenant, and because the meaning of the Cross is the meaning of the New Covenant. It's what Jesus did there, in atoning for all sin, which opened up the way to the very Presence of God,

NOTES

hence the Veil which hid the Holy of Holies being rent asunder at the time of the Death of Christ (Mat. 27:51). By God doing this at the Death of Christ, He was in effect telling all of mankind, that what Jesus had done, had now opened up the way. In other words, through the Substitutionary Offering of Himself on the Cross, Christ had now become the Mediator. No other man, woman, or institution would ever be needed. And he became the Mediator by what he did at the Cross.

With the sin debt completely removed, which the Cross did, this sin barrier was broken down between God and man, for sin had always been the barrier. Faith in Christ places the individual automatically in the Presence of God, which of course, was and is vastly superior to the old Levitical way, which could not do such a thing.

THE SIGNIFICANCE OF THIS EPISTLE TO THE HEBREWS

There is no book in the New Testament more important than this Epistle, and of course none which would be more perceptible in the Canon of Scriptures. Every Reader of the Old Testament needs such a guide as this Epistle, written by someone who had an intimate acquaintance from childhood with the Jewish System; who had all the advantages of the most able and faithful instruction, and who was under the influence of inspiration, to make us acquainted with the true nature of those institutions. Nothing was more important than to settle the principles in regard to the nature of the Jewish economy; to show what was typical, and how those institutions were the means of introducing a far more perfect system — the system of Faith in Christ.

If we have the right feelings, we shall have sincere gratitude to God that He caused our Faith to be prefigured by a system in itself so magnificent and grand as that of the Jewish, and higher gratitude for that sublime system of Faith in Christ, of which the Jewish, with all its splendor was only the shadow.

There was much that was beautiful, cheering, and sublime in the Jewish system. There was much that was grand and awful in the giving of the Law, and much that was imposing in its Ceremonies. In its pure days, it was incomparably the purest and most noble system of faith on Earth, and because it was given directly by God.

THE LAW

It taught the nature of the one true God; inculcated a pure system of morals; preserved the record of the Truth on the Earth, and held up constantly before man the hope of a better system still in days to come.

But at the same time, it was expensive, burdensome, precise in its prescriptions, and wearisome in its ceremonies (Acts 15:10).

As well, it was adapted to one people — a people who occupied a small territory, and who could conveniently assemble at the central place of their worship some three times in a year. It was not a system adapted to the whole world; nor was it designed for the whole world. When the time came, therefore, to introduce Who had always been the design of the Jewish economy, it ceased as a matter of course. The Jewish Altars were soon thrown down; the Temple was razed to the ground, and the city of their solemnities was destroyed. Consequently, the religion of the Hebrews, one might say, passed away to be revived no more in its splendor and power, and it has never lived since, except as an empty form.

CHRIST, THE FULFILLMENT

This Epistle teaches us why the old economy passed away, and why it can never be restored. This Book of Hebrews is the true key with which to unlock the Old Testament; and with these views we may remark, in conclusion, that he who would understand the Bible thoroughly should make himself familiar with this Epistle; that the Canon of Scripture would be incomplete without it; and that to one who wishes to understand the Revelation which God has given, there is no portion of the Volume whose loss would be a more irreparable calamity than that of the Epistle to the Hebrews.

(Regarding the closing remarks, the author owes a debt of gratitude to Albert Barnes regarding his notes on the New Testament.)

IN CONCLUSION

It is Saturday morning, September 30, 2000, as I conclude the notes on this Commentary

NOTES

on Paul's Epistle to the Hebrews. To differentiate between various Books of the Bible isn't wise; however, considering the fact that some particular Books or Epistles serve as intersections, which Hebrews certainly does, makes this Epistle, at least in my opinion, one of the single most important works in the entirety of the Bible. As nothing else, and as stated, it explains the Old Testament, and above all, it explains Who Christ is, and What Christ did; consequently, it is a treatment on Christ and the Cross as nothing else in the entirety of the Word of God.

In 1996, the Lord in answer to soul-searching prayer, intercession incidentally which had lasted for over five years, began to give me the Revelation of the Cross. To be sure, this was not something new, actually being the very foundation of all that God has ever done on this Earth as it regards the Salvation of man.

What He told me and showed me, which actually continues unto this hour, has completely revolutionized my life and ministry. I think I can say without any fear of exaggeration, that for the first time in my Christian life, and I speak of such a life which has now spanned well over half a century, for the first time I know what Jesus meant when He spoke of *"more abundant life"* (Jn. 10:10).

The Cross has opened it up, and I speak of the entirety of the Word of God, as I have not previously known.

I might quickly add, that all I have been given, and as stated, continue to be given, has been derived from the Apostle Paul. It was to him that the meaning of the Cross was given, which is actually the meaning of the New Covenant. So I guess I can say, that I have an affinity for Paul that is beyond the normal. Few men in history have equaled this man, and possibly no one has ever equaled this man. Because of him, we know what Christ did at the Cross, why He did what He did, and how that it was all done for us.

THE EPISTLE TO THE HEBREWS

In the writing of this Commentary on this grand Epistle, and walking through its pages with the Apostle, as the Holy Spirit through him opened up this great Truth of the Cross, not one word contradicted that which I believed the Lord had given unto me, but rather enlarged its meaning and to an extent that is beyond comprehension. I know, and beyond the shadow of a doubt, that I now have a greater understanding of what Jesus did for me and in fact, the entirety of the human race, on that memorable day when He bore the sin of the world (Jn. 1:29). It fills my heart with such gratitude, that at times, even going about my daily duties, I will break down and begin to weep. I find myself awakening in the night, and doing so night after night, with wellsprings of joy springing up within my soul, thanking Him for what He has shown me.

I do not know why we as human beings seemingly, have to find out these great Truths the hard way? I don't know why, as Paul, we have to come to the place of *"Oh wretched man that I am . . ."* before we are pliable enough in the hands of the Holy Spirit, that He can properly show us Christ. For Christ is the mainspring of it all! It is Jesus, as it always will be Jesus, but more particularly, it is, *"Christ and Him Crucified"* (I Cor. 2:2).

If you have taken your time to read the literary efforts of this Evangelist, I would pray that the study of this material has affected you, as the writing of this material has affected me. If so, or even partially so, then it has been well worth the labor we have expended as it regards the privilege of this effort. If you've seen only me, then I have failed in my efforts; however, if you now see Christ in a greater way, then in some small way, I have succeeded in what we are attempting to do.

Jimmy Swaggart

"Earthly pleasures vainly call me,
"I would be like Jesus;
"Nothing worldly shall enthrall me,
"I would be like Jesus."

"He has broken every fetter,
"I would be like Jesus;
"That my soul may serve Him better,
"I would be like Jesus."

"All the way from Earth to glory,
"I would be like Jesus;
"Telling o'er and o'er the story,
"I would be like Jesus."

NOTES

"That in Heaven He may meet me,
"I would be like Jesus;
"That His words 'well done' may
greet me,
"I would be like Jesus."

BIBLIOGRAPHY

The Expositor's Bible Commentary

Barnes' Notes on the New Testament

The Student's Commentary on the Holy Scriptures

Ellicott's Commentary on the Whole Bible

Fjordbak's Exposition and Commentary on Hebrews

The Expositor's Bible

The Pulpit Commentary

Hebrews — Ironside

Wuest, Word Studies in the Greek New Testament

The International Standard Bible Encyclopaedia

The Zondervan Pictorial Encyclopedia of the Bible

Richards Expository Dictionary of Bible Words

The Zondervan Topical Bible

Interlinear Greek-English New Testament

Atlas of the Bible

The Bible Self-Explained

Zodhiates — The Complete Word Study New Testament

Young's Literal Translation of the Holy Bible.

NOTES

NOTES

NOTES

NOTES

NOTES

NOTES

INDEX

━■━

The index is listed according to subjects. The treatment may include a complete dissertation or no more than a paragraph. But hopefully it will provide some help.

As well, even though extended treatment of a subject may not be carried in this Commentary, one of the other Commentaries may well include the desired material.

For all information concerning the *Jimmy Swaggart Bible Commentary,* please request a Gift Catalog.

You may inquire by using Books of the Bible.

- Genesis (639 pages) (11-201)
- Exodus (639 pages) (11-202)
- Leviticus (435 pages) (11-203)
- Numbers
  Deuteronomy (493 pages) (11-204)
- Joshua
  Judges
  Ruth (329 pages) (11-205)
- I Samuel
  II Samuel (528 pages) (11-206)
- I Kings
  II Kings (560 pages) (11-207)
- I Chronicles
  II Chronicles (528 pages) (11-226)
- Ezra
  Nehemiah
  Esther (288 pages) (11-208)
- Job (320 pages) (11-225)
- Psalms (688 pages) (11-216)
- Proverbs (320 pages) (11-227)
- Ecclesiastes
  Song Of Solomon (245 pages) (11-228)
- Isaiah (688 pages) (11-220)
- Jeremiah
  Lamentations (688 pages) (11-070)
- Ezekiel (508 pages) (11-223)
- Daniel (403 pages) (11-224)
- Hosea
  Joel
  Amos (496 pages) (11-229)
- Obadiah
  Jonah
  Micah
  Nahum
  Habakkuk
  Zephaniah *(will be ready Spring 2013)* (11-230)

- Matthew (625 pages) (11-073)
- Mark (606 pages) (11-074)
- Luke (626 pages) (11-075)
- John (532 pages) (11-076)
- Acts (697 pages) (11-077)
- Romans (536 pages) (11-078)
- I Corinthians (632 pages) (11-079)
- II Corinthians (589 pages) (11-080)
- Galatians (478 pages) (11-081)
- Ephesians (550 pages) (11-082)
- Philippians (476 pages) (11-083)
- Colossians (374 pages) (11-084)
- I Thessalonians
  II Thessalonians (498 pages) (11-085)
- I Timothy
  II Timothy
  Titus
  Philemon (687 pages) (11-086)
- Hebrews (831 pages) (11-087)
- James
  I Peter
  II Peter (730 pages) (11-088)
- I John
  II John
  III John
  Jude (377 pages) (11-089)
- Revelation (602 pages) (11-090)

For telephone orders you may call 1-800-288-8350 with bankcard information. All Baton Rouge residents please use (225) 768-7000. For mail orders send to:

Jimmy Swaggart Ministries
P.O. Box 262550 • Baton Rouge, LA 70826-2550
Visit our website: www.jsm.org